D0532294

S M C
BOOKSTORE
SEP 20 2000
USED BOOK

Psychology

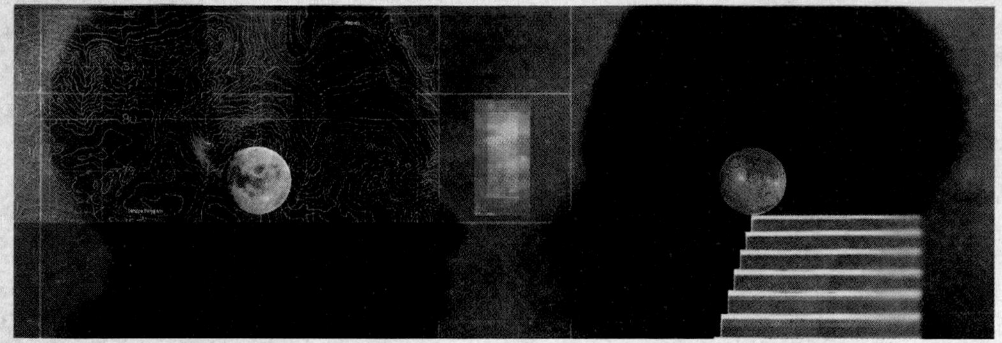

Psychology

BEHAVIOR IN CONTEXT

LYLE E. BOURNE, JR.
UNIVERSITY OF COLORADO, BOULDER

NANCY FELIPE RUSSO
ARIZONA STATE UNIVERSITY

W • W NORTON

NEW YORK • LONDON

Printed in the United States of America
First Edition

The text of this book is composed in Palatino
with the display set in Futura and Bodega.
Composition by UG.
Manufacturing by World Color Book Services.
Book design by Mspace.
Cover and chapter-opening illustrations: Stuart Bradford.

Library of Congress Cataloging-in-Publication Data

Bourne, Lyle Eugene, 1932–
Psychology: Behavior in context / Lyle E. Bourne, Jr., Nancy Felipe Russo.
p. cm.
Includes bibliographical references and index.
ISBN 0-393-97209-7
1. Psychology. I. Russo, Nancy Felipe, 1943– . II. Title
BF121.B619 1998
150—dc21 97-43774

ISBN 0-393-97209-7

W. W. Norton & Company, Inc., 500 Fifth Avenue, New York, N.Y. 10110
http://www.wwnorton.com

W. W. Norton & Company Ltd., 10 Coptic Street, London WC1A 1PU

1 2 3 4 5 6 7 8 9 0

This book is dedicated to:

The memory of Bruce Rowland Ekstrand, esteemed colleague, tireless collaborator, true friend, who helped me through many critical decisions in my life and in the process taught me a lot about psychology.

LEB JR.

And to Allen Meyer, friend, partner, soulmate, and critic who challenges me to think more deeply and in doing so enriches my life.

NFR

Contents in Brief

Contents

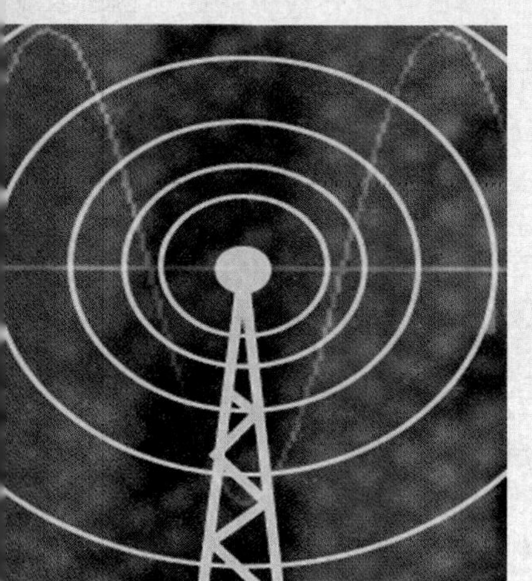

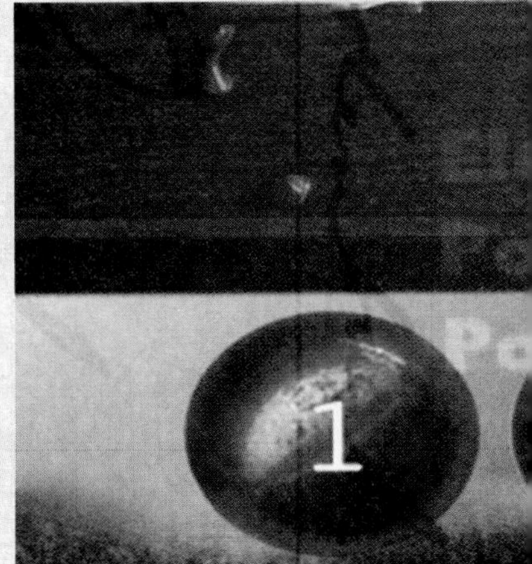

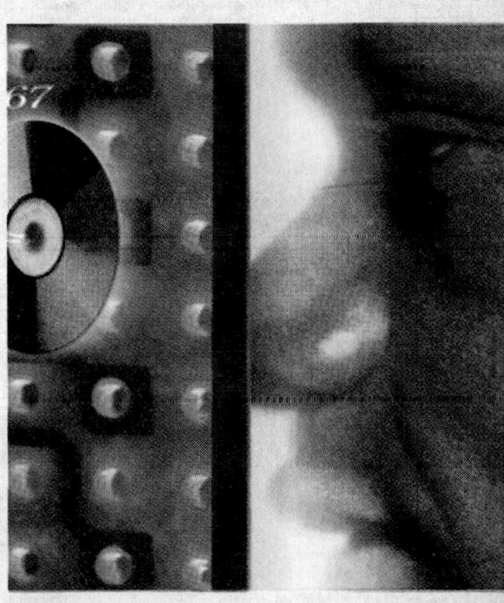

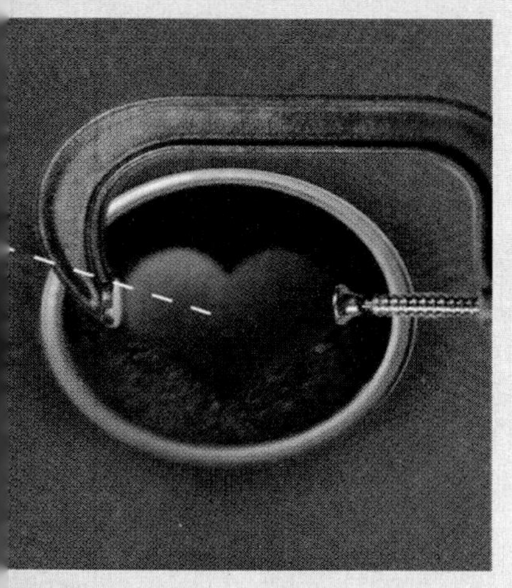

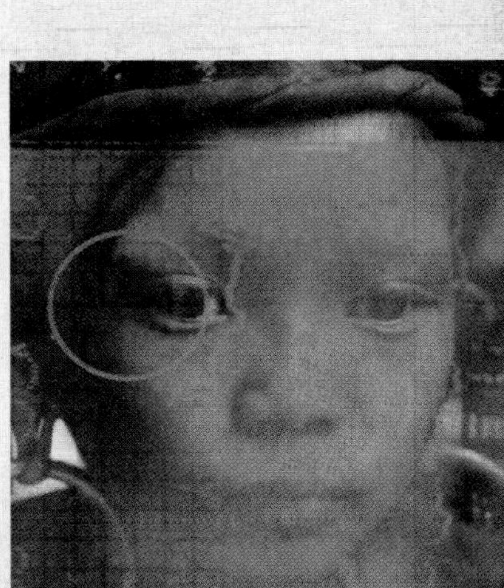

CHAPTER 14 PERSONALITY 506

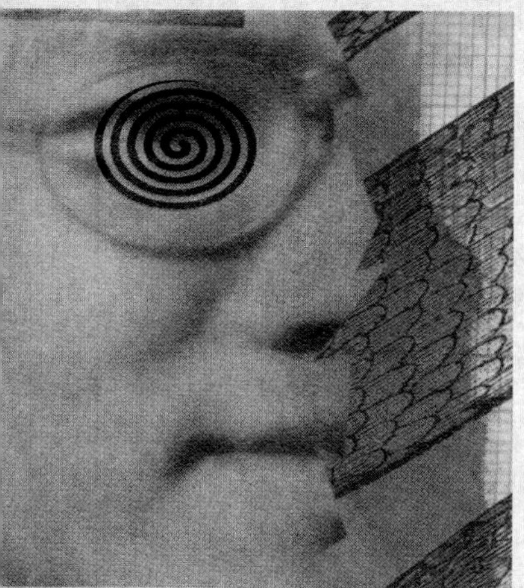

CHAPTER 15 PSYCHOPATHOLOGY 540

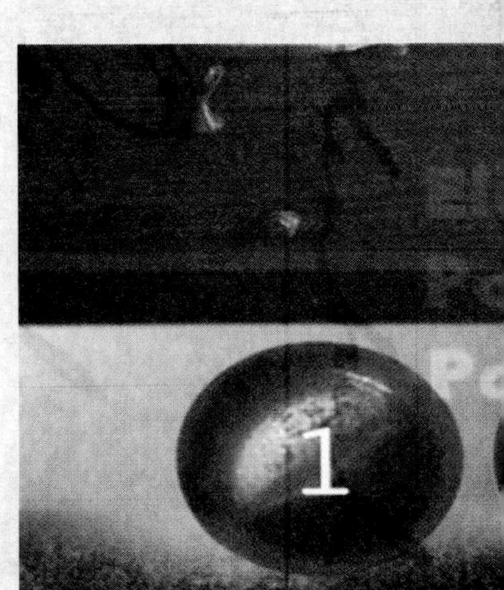

Preface

Being literate is more than just being able to use words. According to Webster's *New World Dictionary*, literacy also means having or showing extensive knowledge, experience, or culture. Similarly, becoming literate in psychology—the scientific study of behavior and mental processes—means more than just memorizing psychological terms and findings. Psychological literacy involves learning about psychology's origins, its methods, its foundations, its content, and how its various components relate to one another. It involves acquiring skills to use and to apply psychological concepts and methods. It involves learning the values and ethics that are unique to psychology and developing an understanding of the diversity and complexity of the discipline. And it involves knowing that human behavior always occurs in a context, most importantly a social context.

Our goal in this book is to set you on the path toward psychological literacy. To this end, we attempt to tell the story of psychology, giving you a sense of what psychologists know and do, how psychology has evolved as a scientific discipline, and how to evaluate evidence related to psychological questions.

We also want you to learn what difference psychology can make in your life. We believe that changes taking place in our society and in the world pose immense immediate and future challenges. These challenges demand an appreciation of the complexity of human behavior and mental processes, as well as of the diversity of human experience. Although psychology will never have all the answers and solutions to personal and societal problems, it is a valuable tool for understanding many of the causes and consequences of human actions. So, we have tried to craft an introduction to psychology that focuses on concepts, methods, and applications that we believe will be particularly helpful in preparing for the future. We have also tried to create the conditions that will enable you to "learn to learn," and to acquire the concepts, skills, and perspectives that will equip you to deal with worldly issues from the standpoint of a psychologist.

In this text, we cover major contemporary topics in psychology in sufficient depth to give you the background needed for advanced undergraduate courses. We have not attempted to be exhaustive—there's more to psychology's story than we are able to tell! Psychology is a huge field, ranging from the study of neural networks to social networks. To cover it all requires volumes. Thus, the introductory psychology course needs to provide an adequate sampling of current issues and methods so that you can generalize to other topics as the situation requires and so that your teachers have some choice about topics to emphasize in lectures. Our goal has been to provide you with the knowledge and skills that you need to explore the rich variety of the field in an informed way.

Basic Themes of the Book

The framework for our story about psychology begins with the familiar but fundamental observation that human beings differ from one another in multiple and complex ways. Psychology is the one discipline among the social and biological sciences that focuses on the individual person as an intact organism. Psychologists seek to understand individual differences among people, exploring how those differences reflect experiences associated with different environments and with gender, ethnicity, and other aspects of culture. If all people were genetically identical and developed in

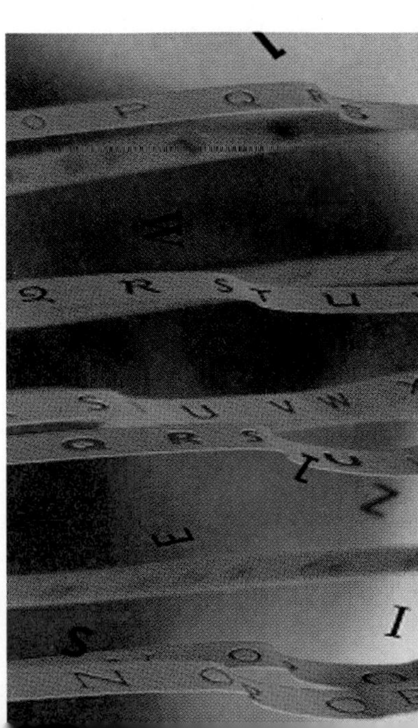

identical contexts, general psychological principles, by definition, would be true of all people. But, in fact, people are neither the same genetically nor do they experience the same environments. Psychology's great challenge is to identify the similarities and differences among people in an effort to predict and understand each individual's behavior in context.

To develop a full understanding of human uniqueness and diversity, we need to appreciate both the biological and sociocultural foundations of behavior. Although human beings have developed biological mechanisms that play an important role in behavior, people live in a variety of sociocultural contexts that affect their behaviors to an even greater degree than can be accounted for on the basis of biological or genetic factors alone. Human similarity and diversity are affected by both biology and experience, including the experiences associated with a variety of social categories such as gender, race, ethnicity, and sexual orientation. Thus, we examine *both* the biological and sociocultural foundations of behavior early in the book and build on them throughout subsequent chapters.

Psychology is a living, open-ended science that is constantly evolving in light of new evidence and contributing in new ways to human welfare. What psychology is and what it means are continuously expanding, and this knowledge often has new meanings or applications to problems of everyday living. We strive to stimulate an active, open-minded stance and critical perspective in our readers, asking them to think about particular issues, to identify the yet unanswered questions, and to project future possibilities. Throughout the book, we identify how psychology can be applied to seek solutions to problems facing us now and in the twenty-first century. We do this both in the text as well as in "Seeking Solutions" boxes that describe applications of basic psychological principles to real problems.

Psychology is everywhere, not just in textbooks. It is in newspapers, on radio and TV, and in everyday conversations with friends and family. You need to be able to think critically to evaluate all the information about psychology that you will encounter in the text, in the media, in conversation. Keep an open mind when you read or hear statements about psychological findings. Try to evaluate, logically and scientifically, what you read and hear, both in this book and elsewhere. Throughout the text as well as in special "Thinking Critically" boxes, we encourage you to question assumptions and we demonstrate how to evaluate findings. To help you develop the skills that will enable you to think critically, in Chapter 2 we discuss some techniques that will help you to evaluate knowledge.

Like any body of knowledge, psychology can be used well or misused. Knowing the facts is not always enough; you often have to examine how those facts fit together and can be applied. We have tried to write an accurate account of psychology as it is known today. We challenge you to think actively and critically about our presentation, evaluate our logic, scrutinize our assumptions, and reason beyond the material that we have chosen to include. If you accept this challenge, you are likely to find this excursion into the field of psychology a highly rewarding one, both intellectually and personally.

For the Student: Supplements Package

Psychology: Behavior in Context is supplemented by specially developed materials to help you master the concepts of the course. Henry Cross of Colorado State University has written a study guide for students that should be especially helpful in reinforcing the concepts covered in the textbook. Each chapter of the study guide includes discussion questions that encourage active review of the text chapter, as well as completion, matching, and multiple-choice self-tests that will help you to review for exams. There is also an interactive study guide called PsychWeb, which is available on the World Wide Web. This Web page consists of interactive tutorials on such topics as Interacting with Correlation, Testing the Validity of Astrology, Transmission of Nervous Impulses, Solving Problems, Drugs and Behavior, Emotional Response, In the Mind of the Child, and Diagnosing Psychopathology. It also includes drag-and-drop matching exercises for key figures, interactive quizzes, a glossary, and links to relevant outside sources.

For the Instructor: Supplements Package

We know that teaching introductory psychology is a difficult and demanding task, and we have taken special steps to ease your burden. In addition to writing an accessible text that can provide a foundation for lectures on a variety of topics, we offer a detailed instructor's resource manual, written by Amy Dabul Marin of Phoenix College. This manual has a host of teaching tips, including ideas for active learning approaches in the classroom, which are coordinated with the text. Besides including chapter outlines and descriptions of key concepts and theories, each chapter of the instructor's resource manual offers specific suggestions for lecture openers, sample lecture outlines, ticket-in and ticket-out assignments, activities and demonstrations, critical thinking exercises, sociocultural connections, applications to everyday living, computer exploration, and lists of additional resources. Besides the instructor's resource manual, we also have available a test-item file, prepared by Lisa Farwell of UCLA and Mark Rittman of Cuyahoga Community College. This is a set of 1,600 multiple-choice, completion, and short essay items. Both the questions from the test-item file and from the study guide are available in a computerized version for Macintosh and Windows. This will provide you with a total bank of 3,200 questions. In addition, we also have available an Introduction to Psychology Transparency Set, which consists of selected figures from the text, as well as classroom demonstrations.

To help you introduce topics, illustrate particularly difficult topics, and emphasize important points, you may also want to make use of W. W. Norton's Introduction to Psychology Video. This features thirteen four-minute sequences of high-quality original footage, including interviews, animated diagrams, and experiments in progress.

In addition to the above-mentioned ancillaries, you may also want to use Norton Presentation Maker. This is a CD-rom that contains all figures that are in the text, selected out-takes from the Introduction to Psychology Video, and the interactive animated tutorials that are part of the Web study guide.

With Special Thanks

We would like to start by thanking our colleagues who took the time to critique the manuscript, offering us suggestions that helped us to clarify, reorganize, and polish the manuscript so that it emerged in its present form. We would also like to thank those who participated in focus groups. We are grateful to the following people:

Joel Alexander, *Western Oregon University*
Ronald Baenninger, *Temple University*
Phillip G. Batten, *Wake Forest University*
Jill Booker, *University of Indianapolis*
K. Robert Bridges, *Pennsylvania State University, New Kensington*
Victor Broderick, *Ferris State University*
Shelley B. Calisher, *University of Colorado*
Lisa Curtin, *Appalachian State University*
Amy Dabul Marin, *Phoenix College*
Donald Devers, *Northern Virginia Community College*
Wendy Eisner, *Nassau Community College*
Peter Foltz, *New Mexico State University*
Jules Harrell, *Howard University*
Sid Hochman, *Nassau Community College*
Matthew Hogben, *State University of New York, Brooklyn*
D. Brett King, *University of Colorado*
Cindy J. Lahar, *University of Vermont*
Richard Lambe, *Providence College*
Catherine Craver Lemley, *Elizabethtown College*
Richard Lippa, *California State University, Fullerton*
Richard Marrocco, *University of Oregon*
Donald H. McBurney, *University of Pittsburgh*
Susan E. Mickler, *Seton Hall University*
Teri Nicoll-Johnson, *Modesto Junior College*
Darlene Palmer, *Blinn College*
Judy Primavera, *Fairfield University*
Kat Quina, *University of Rhode Island*
Mark P. Rittman, *Cuyahoga Community College*
Joel Rosenberg, *University of Alabama*
Nancy Sauerman, *Kirkwood Community College*
Catherine Seta, *Wake Forest University*
Lawrence C. Shaffer, *State University of New York, Plattsburgh*
Linda J. Skinner, *Middle Tennessee State University*
Donna J. Tyler Thompson, *Midland College*
Judith Tomhave, *Moorhead State University*
David Trafimow, *New Mexico State University*
Toviah Vitiello, *Kirkwood Community College*
William Wallace, *University of Montevallo*
Robin Lea West, *University of Florida, Gainesville*
Susan Kraus Whitbourne, *University of Massachusetts, Amherst*

Preparing the manuscript has been a team effort, involving the contributions of numerous colleagues, friends, and family members along the way. At home, Rita Yaroush and Allen Meyer played essential roles in the process—

proofreading, criticizing all chapters, creating new art ideas, and suggesting lively examples for the text. Ria Hermann-Currie and Amy Dabul Marin provided invaluable technical assistance, particularly in developing the art manuscript. Angela DuMont and Vonda Wall spent long hours typing and retyping drafts, running down references, and preparing the glossary. For additional help in preparing the glossary, we would also like to thank Jean Denious, Stefanie Hader, and Leslie Mansen. We would like to express a special thanks to students Melissa Covarrubias and Jean Denious for participating in the video that accompanies the book. We also would like to thank Thomas A. Russo and Marlisa Vinciguerra for their legal assistance, and our colleagues in the Psychology Departments at the University of Colorado and Arizona State University for lending us their books, supplying references, and serving as sounding boards for how best to deal with technical concepts in their respective fields. In particular, Leona Aiken, Jay Braun, Eddie Casteñeda, Dave Chiszar, Bob Cialdini, Linda Craighead, Henry Cross, Mary Davis, Bill Fabricious, Sara Gutierres, Reid Hastie, Paul Karoly, Doug Kenrick, George Knight, Steve Maier, Gary McClelland, Dave Miklowitz, Bill Oliver, Steve Neuberg, John Reich, Jerry Rudy, Delia Saenz, Kurt Schlesinger, Linda Watkins, Jack Werner, and Mike Wertheimer deserve special mention for their generosity in sharing their personal thoughts and libraries. We also would like to thank our colleagues who were involved in the writing and production of the supplements that accompany the book: Henry Cross, Bill Oliver, Amy Dabul Marin, Lisa Farwell, Mark Rittman, and Art Kohn and Kwamba Productions.

At Norton, Cathy Wick, who got us started in all this, and Sandy Lifland played essential roles in shaping and fine-tuning the manuscript. In addition to her insightful feedback, Cathy provided important encouragement during the rough spots. We are grateful for her inspiration and support. Sandy added much of substance to our text and played a critical role in transforming some technical concepts into accessible prose. The wonderful insights, competence, encouragement, and tireless efforts of Cathy and Sandy were essential to our success. Other individuals at Norton who played key roles include Ruth Mandel, who steadfastly tracked down just the right photos to illustrate our concepts; April Lange, who found excellent people to write the ancillaries for the book and coordinated the writing, editing, and production of all of the supplements; Kathy Talalay, who coordinated the production of the textbook, made sure that all the pieces were there when they needed to be, copy edited and checked references when needed, and whose calming presence has been much appreciated; Elana Passman, who ably assisted Ruth Mandel in tracking down cartoons and photographs; Frank Forney, who produced the art program; Roberta Flechner, who did the layouts and pulled together all of the pieces of the book into a beautiful whole; and Roy Tedoff, who expertly managed the manufacturing of the book.

We hope that you enjoy and learn from our book, and we'd like to learn from you too. We welcome your feedback. Please e-mail us (Lyle Bourne at lbourne@clipr.colorado.edu or Nancy Felipe Russo at nancy.russo@asu.edu) with your comments and suggestions for how to make the story of psychology more useful and relevant from the student's point of view.

LEB Jr.
NFR
November 1997

Psychology

82
81
80
Tundra Polygons

CHAPTER 1

What Is Psychology?

OBJECTIVES

After reading this chapter, you should be able to:

1. Define psychology and give examples of where it can be useful.
2. Identify the goals of psychology.
3. Outline some fundamental issues, questions, and controversies in psychology.
4. Present an overview of the history of psychology.
5. Describe the major contemporary trends in psychology.
6. Describe employment possibilities for psychologists.

You turn on the television and a news flash lights the screen: 230 people have been killed in an explosion in the air over Long Island Sound. Is it a bomb or a missile or a malfunction on TWA Flight 800 that caused the tragedy? Was it an act of terrorism against the United States or an unavoidable accident? What did the passengers feel just before the plane plunged into the Atlantic Ocean? How did the families of the victims react when they were told the news? What did you think when you heard that the plane had gone down and that all aboard were killed? How could you evaluate the conflicting information that you were hearing?

Psychologists have a role to play in helping the public to deal with the shock of disasters like these. They attempt to ease the public's fears about technology and terrorism, helping people to live with uncertainties and conflicting information and to realize that most plane trips do not end in disasters. Moreover, psychologists conduct research to find ways to lower crash rates, investigating how pilot error or maintenance error may be avoided. Psychologists also investigate such processes as memory, thinking, and reactions to normal and extraordinary events, to learn more about what goes through a person's mind both in normal, everyday interactions, and at times of unusual stress. Indeed, perhaps the most fundamental goal of psychology is to understand, through research, all aspects of human behavior and mental processes. Psychologists also are instrumental in helping the victims of disasters like this one. Where there are survivors of plane crashes, psychologists talk to the survivors and try to help them to overcome their fears and their survivors' guilt and to find the strength to get on with their lives. Psychologists also talk to victims' relatives, trying to help them to come to terms with the deaths of their loved ones. Thus, psychologists have important roles to play both in research and in practice, to help individuals and society to confront personal and world tragedies and challenges.

Every new generation confronts previously unmet challenges, and your generation is no exception. Dramatic changes are taking place: at work, at home, in the schools, and on the streets. You will need to be well trained and more flex-

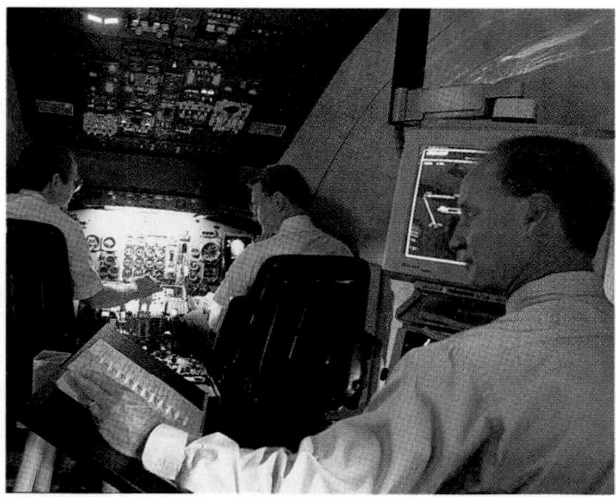

► *Psychologists play many important roles in today's society, such as (left) counseling victims in times of crisis, and (right) studying human performance in environments like this flight simulator.*

ible to cope with ongoing technological change at school and at work. In all walks of life, you will encounter increased cultural diversity among people, and you will be more successful in relating to all people if you are able to understand how different backgrounds may affect behavior. The closing of factories, crowding in the cities, economic disparity, the changed makeup of families, and changes in the availability of health care will lead to other changes in society. More than ever, you will need to look beyond learning specific facts and details and instead *learn to learn,* acquiring concepts, general skills, and perspectives that will enable you to turn life challenges into opportunities for accomplishment, personal growth, and service to others. The study of psychology can help you to face these challenges rather than be overwhelmed by them.

Although psychology doesn't have all the answers to the problems of the future, it does have an important part to play in solving many of them. One key to meeting the challenges of the twenty-first century is understanding the causes and consequences of human actions, including your own. Psychology deals with what and how we learn, think, feel, want, and do. Psychological knowledge has an enormous scope, from dealing with important biological issues, such as how the brain preserves our memories, to life-relevant social problems, such as how to reduce crime, to serious personal questions, such as why it is you like some people but love others. For more than one hundred years, psychologists have observed, researched, and pondered how an organism's physical state, mental state, and environment affect its behavior. This book introduces you to psychology's diverse perspectives, paying special attention to concepts, methods and applications that can help you prepare for the future.

The Study of Psychology

Next time you are at a party, tell someone that you are studying psychology and watch what happens. Standard responses include: "Uh oh, are you analyzing me?" or "Let me tell you about a problem I have. . . . " But interest in abnormal behavior and solving personal problems is just one aspect of psychology. Psychologists are also interested in normal behavior—the thoughts, memories, feelings, desires, attitudes, and actions of daily life.

Psychology has a part to play in seeking solutions to the problems of the twenty-first century.

So what exactly is psychology? ***Psychology*** is the scientific study of behavior and mental processes—and behind that definition is a rich and diverse reality. ***Behavior*** encompasses a wide range of observable actions, from such simple movements as blinking, pointing, nodding, pushing a lever, through very complex activities such as eating, writing, driving a car, talking, kissing, dancing, cooking, playing basketball, answering questions on a test. ***Mental processes***, including perceptions, thoughts, memories, expectations, desires, and feelings, are unobservable and known only to the individual, but they are revealed in observable behavior. Although primarily interested in human experience, psychologists can be found studying all animals, not just the human animal. Some of our most important scientific psychological knowledge comes from animal research (Domjan & Purdy, 1995). But some psychologists don't study animals of any kind—they can be found instead behind computer terminals, studying artificial intelligence.

The object of psychology is to give us a totally different idea of the things we know best.
—Paul Valéry (1943)

Designing a Psychological Study

Suppose you decide that you want to study what makes people angry. Anger is an internal state or feeling, one of those unobservable mental processes. Scientific methods are ***empirical***, which means that they are based on systematic observation of real things that are happening. So how can unobservable anger be studied scientifically? First, you need to conceptualize, or define anger, by identifying behaviors or ac-

The goals of psychological research are to describe, predict, understand, and control behavior and mental processes.

"Well, you don't look like an experimental psychologist to me."

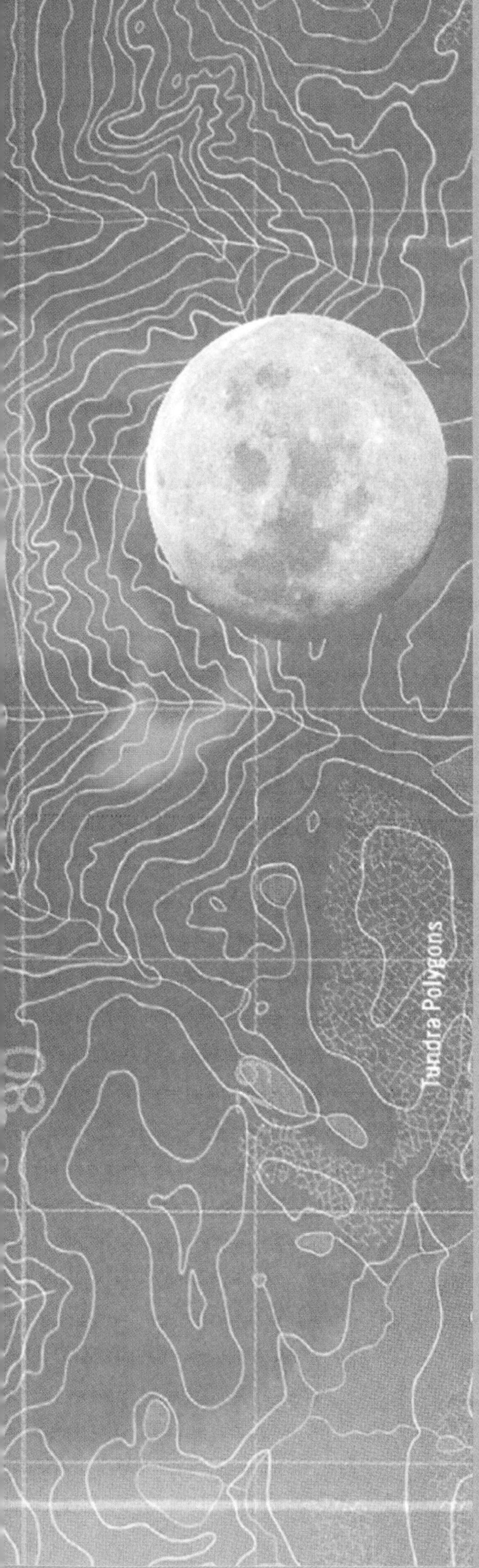

SEEKING SOLUTIONS

The Role of Psychology in Addressing Social Problems

The world is changing rapidly, and people will have to adapt to these changes to be successful. How can psychology help you to address the personal and social problems that will accompany these changes? Here are some of the possibilities to consider.

• *Changes in the Workplace.* Dramatic shifts are taking place in the workplace, requiring workers to be flexible and able to cope with change. Advances in technology will require high-level skills and continual retraining. As one executive observed, the economy is moving from needing a lot of hard-working people to needing fewer, smarter-working people (Cascio, 1995). Psychology can address these changes in the workplace by teaching creative thinking and cognitive and coping skills that will help people to be flexible in the face of change.

• *Increased Cultural Diversity.* A projected shortage of skilled workers in the United States will necessitate developing and utilizing the efforts of all members of society. More than 90 percent of the new entrants to the U.S. workforce in the 1990s will be women, minorities, and immigrants. Regardless of your gender, ethnic origins, sexual orientation, or able-bodiedness, whether you are young, middle-aged, or elderly, newly arrived in the United States or native born, you will work with a diverse group of co-workers, subordinates, and supervisors, and thus will need to understand and relate to people with different personal attributes, backgrounds, and experiences. Psychology can help you to understand group dynamics and the origins of stereotypes and prejudice, so that you can overcome them and judge people based on their own merit rather than on gender or ethnic origins.

• *Deteriorating Social Conditions.* The world continues to experience population pressures and environmental destruction, as well as an ever-widening gap between rich and poor, entrenched prejudice and discrimination, functional illiteracy, an aging population, and the scourge of AIDS. Psychology can help you to deal with these economic and social problems by teaching you to understand issues from diverse points of view and to come up with complex and creative approaches that may not have been tried before.

• *Urban Strife.* High rates of unemployment, poverty, substance abuse, crime, teenage pregnancy, and disease, particularly AIDS, hypertension, cancer, and diabetes, are found everywhere but are concentrated in and particularly undermine urban ethnic minority communities. Psychology can help to build on the many strengths of ethnic minority communities and to find creative solutions to the problems of urban life.

• *Changing Family Structures.* Work and family life are intertwined, and changes in society have profound effects on both. Families' circumstances have changed, but many of soci-

▼ *Traditional assembly lines are still a part of the production of bicycles, as in the photo at left. Other factory workers, as in the photo on the right, have been retrained for high-technology tasks.*

ety's institutions were designed during an era when every family was expected to consist of a husband, a wife, and children, and when men were expected to be the breadwinners, and women the homemakers. Yet, although the rate of change has declined in the 1990s, according to projections by the Census Bureau, only an estimated 55 percent of families in the year 2000 will consist of a husband, wife, and children. Psychology can help your generation to redesign social systems that will better serve all kinds of families.

- *New Genetic Knowledge.* The Human Genome Project, a scientific project to map the characteristics of all human genes, may have a personal and social impact as it makes traditional assumptions about the relationship of heredity and environment obsolete and creates ethical dilemmas about what, if any, actions to take based on our knowledge. Psychology can help people gain a sophisticated comprehension of the interrelationships among genes, biology, and behavior. It can also help people to develop new ways of thinking about our biology and our human identity.
- *Evolving Gender Roles.* Advances in reproductive technologies, including *in vitro* and *in vivo* fertilization, pose significant challenges to basic assumptions about motherhood and fatherhood, and rights and responsibilities of family members. Psychology can help people understand changes in the meaning of gender and in the nature of gender roles and thereby develop increased intimacy and meaning in human relationships, while helping people to avoid the miscommunication and conflict that may also arise out of evolving gender roles.

The challenges ahead will require complex and comprehensive solutions, solutions that involve critical thinking, confronting one's own values, looking beyond immediate self-interest, and interacting effectively with people who hold diverse perspectives. Will you be ready?

▼ *Technology is changing our everyday and leisure activities as well as our working lives.*

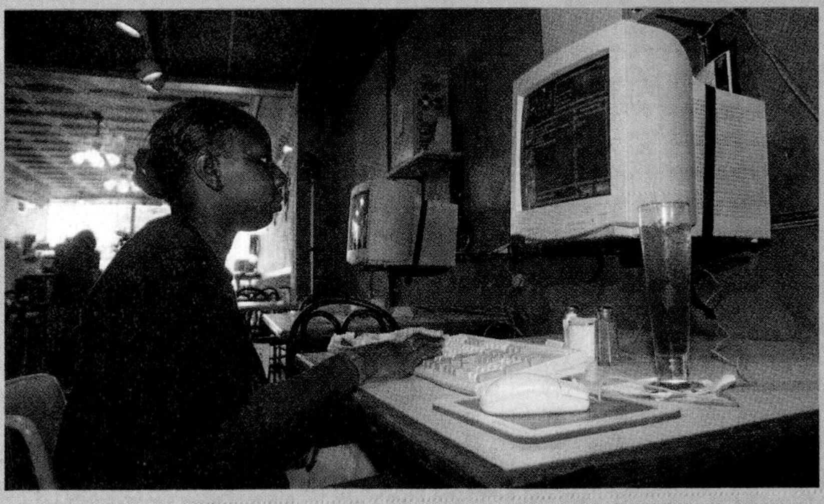

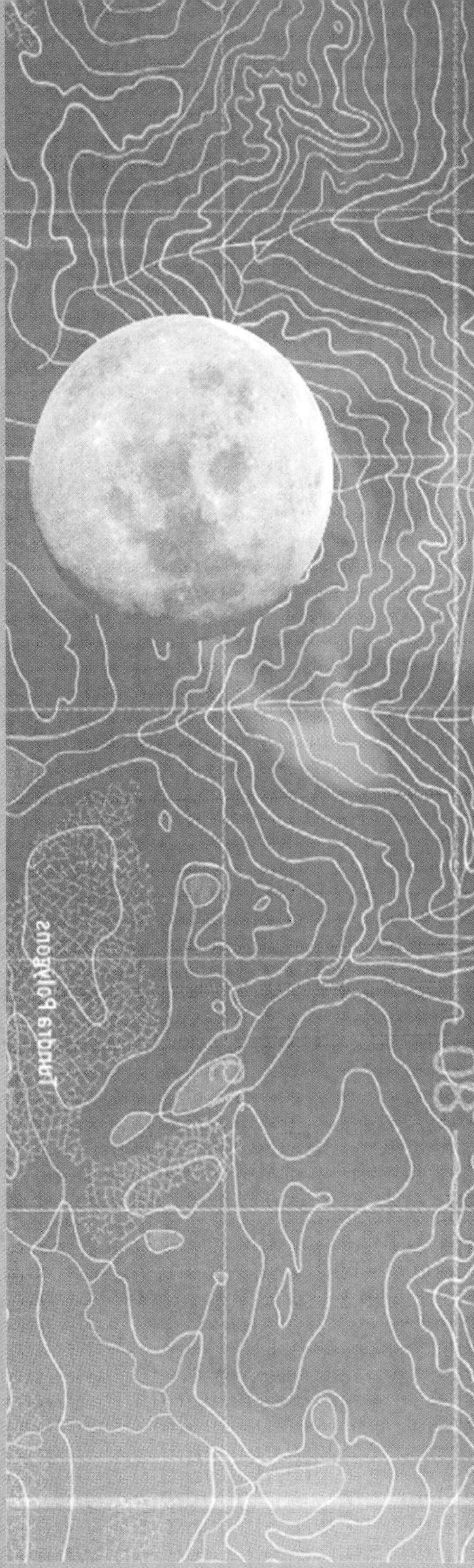

tions that *can* be observed and objectively measured and that are associated with anger. You might decide to investigate people's anger by observing whether they breathe more rapidly, tense up, and grit their teeth in reaction to certain stimuli thought to be anger-producing. Alternatively, you might ask them to rate how angry they feel or to fill out a rating scale especially designed to measure angry feelings. Or you might use devices to measure muscle tension or heart rate in reaction to "angry" stimuli. Psychologists commonly make inferences about internal mental processes by observing an external response of some sort. Indeed, some people suggest that psychology should be defined as the "science of behavior" and let it go at that, because internal processes can rarely if ever be measured directly. We define psychology as the "scientific study of behavior and mental processes," because the goal of much of psychological research, even though it always involves observable behavior, is indeed to understand the mental processes that are not so easily observed.

Psychology is an empirical science. It relies on data that come from objective, systematic observations of its primary subject matter, behavior.

Once you are able to describe behavior in measurable ways, then what? Psychologists wish to do more than merely describe behavior (novelists do that better anyway). Like other scientists, psychologists seek to predict, understand, and control, modify, or manipulate the phenomena they study. Thus, once you have a good measure of anger, you can study questions like "Are some people more likely to get angry than others? Why do people get angry? What can be done to prevent people from getting angry?"

In designing a study, however, investigators must deal with real people who bring their own values, expectations, and biases with them. These aspects of the individual can affect the data collected. A classic study of children's imitation by Albert Bandura, Dorothea Ross, and Sheila Ross, provides an exquisite example of just how downright tricky the business of psychological research can be. Bandura, Ross, and Ross wanted to test a theory about the way people imitate one another. They demonstrated that both nursery school boys and girls were more likely to imitate a role model of the opposite gender if that model was seen as controlling rewards, that is, in charge of the toys, candy, or other desirable items. When rewards were at issue, subjects were observed to repeat and follow the lead of the model. It was *easier*, however, to get the girls to identify with the male models than the boys to identify with the female models. It turned out that, despite the experimenters' efforts to make the female model more powerful than the male model (by giving her control of rewards), some children simply did not buy that view of reality. Some of the children held persistently to their belief

THINKING CRITICALLY

Domestic violence is a major problem in the United States today. An estimated 2 million women a year in the United States are severely assaulted by their male partners (Koss et al., 1994). Suppose you wanted to study this kind of violence. How would you conceptualize it so that it could be studied?

Most people agree that knocking another person across the room with a fist is violent. What about hitting someone to defend yourself or in order to keep a child from being hurt? Would you put an open-handed slap to the face into the same category as shooting, stabbing, or kicking someone? What about killing someone's dog? Researchers who have conceptualized domestic violence as *any* slapping, hitting, kicking, and so forth (no matter how forceful or for what purpose) have reported married women to be as violent as their mates (Strauss, Gelles, & Steinmetz, 1980). Researchers who do not consider behaviors used in self-defense as violent, or who focus on the severity of damage caused by the behavior (such as bruises, broken bones, head injury), find that generally men are the overwhelming perpetrators of family violence, and women and children the victims. How one conceptualizes and consequently measures domestic violence results in a very different picture of the nature, extent, and impact of such violence (Brush, 1990).

that only a male *could* control resources. In the words of one subject: "He's the man and it's all his because he's a daddy. Mommy never really has things that belong to her . . . " (Bandura, Ross, & Ross, 1963).

This study was reported more than thirty years ago, but it illustrates an enduring and basic fact: research participants may interpret experimental events very differently from the way the experimenter intended. Human beings are not only biological and social organisms; they are organisms with a consciousness and a sense of self. Human beings *act on* as well as *react to* their environments, and they perceive and are aware of meaning in the events of their lives. They hold cherished values and beliefs that may conflict with one another. They are organized into groups, where they take on roles and social statuses, all of which may affect how they interpret events and act in specific situations—including the situations constructed in psychological experiments. In Chapter 2, you will learn about some of the techniques psychologists have developed in response to the challenge of the human factor in psychological research.

▲ *Strategies for stress reduction differ around the world. Chika Minakuchi, a Japanese postal worker, paid 50,000 yen (US $435) to drink beer, sing to canned music, and smash valuable antiques at a karaoke lounge.*

Interpreting Psychological Research

The data of any scientific study, once collected, need to be interpreted and explained. The same data might mean different things to different investigators because of their different theoretical points of view, their different assumptions, or perhaps because of their different values. For example, there is a variety of data on the heavy use of alcohol on college campuses. How can this be explained? Is it just that "boys will be boys" (or "girls will be girls")? Or are college campuses just too liberal about social norms these days? Or are intelligence and social drinking highly correlated? Or is there a gene for intelligence that is linked to the gene for alcoholism? Some of these possibilities are obviously facetious or extreme. But they illustrate how scientific data can be subject to wide interpretation.

Throughout your reading, in this book and elsewhere, be prepared to find psychologists disagreeing on the meanings of their objective measures, on the interpretations of their data, and on the conclusions to be drawn. One of your tasks in reading this book is to learn to think critically about the concepts, methods, results, interpretations, and conclusions of the studies you encounter—whether they are in your text, in the newspapers, or elsewhere.

"Doing psychology" requires a high level of critical thinking and self-awareness. It also requires concerted efforts to monitor how the values and biases of the researcher can influence both how we conceptualize a phenomenon and how we interpret the results of a study. It is difficult for anyone to understand conditions that are unlike any of those he or she has experienced. Psychologists with a wide range of ethnic backgrounds, values, cultural experiences, and points of view thus provide a source of rich debate, creativity, and intellectual breadth to the field.

Human beings pose the greatest challenge to psychological research because they have a consciousness and sense of self.

Fundamental Questions about Human Behavior

Throughout the history of psychology—and throughout this book—certain basic questions about human nature and human behavior occur over and over again. Great debates have raged over the "right" answers to these basic questions. The answers given depend on the assumptions you make about people. Yet, each side typically has something worthwhile and convincing to say about the issue. Keep these controversies in mind as you read through the book, and remember that each side has a window onto some of the truth.

Nature versus Nurture

Clint Eastwood as a child.

Think about the great diversity of people you know. Some may be terrific musicians, others may write poetry. Some may be mathematical whizzes, others may be mechanically inclined. What accounts for these differences? Is your intelligence a result of ***nature*** (is it inherited from your parents) or is it a function of ***nurture*** (is it what you have learned and experienced since birth)? Or do you think that both kinds of factors influence your behavior? Your view on this question can make a difference in many aspects of your life, perhaps even on how well you do in college.

For example, would you interpret failure on a psychology exam as an indication of being innately incapable of understanding psychology, or as a sign that you need to study harder? Carol Dweck and her colleagues have found that children who believe people are "born smart" see passing and failing as signals of lack of ability and give up on school if they don't get good grades (they call them "entity theorists"; Dweck, Hong, & Chiu, 1993). In contrast, children who believe that people have to work to become smart focus on what they need to do to learn, and they view their failures as part of a learning process that expands their intelligence (they call them "incremental theorists"). During elementary school, when successes are easy, these beliefs don't seem to make much difference in school performance. When children enter junior high or middle school and begin to be challenged in their work, however, the "fall from smarts" begins for entity theorists. In contrast, incremental theorists earn better grades than predicted—even the low-achievers who had poor grades and low confidence in elementary school show big increases in their grades in junior high or middle school—some earning the highest grades in the class (Murray, 1995)! Thus, beliefs about nature versus nurture can have profound effects on attitudes and behavior. They can affect how hard people try based on whether they believe that human nature and abilities are fixed or are capable of change. They can also affect whether society makes efforts to

▼ Free will or determinism? These teenagers participate in a pregnancy prevention program using "Baby Think It Over." A crying doll teaches students one of the realities of parenting. The program is designed to prevent early motherhood.

THINKING CRITICALLY

The Justice Department reports that the murder rate among fourteen- to seventeen-year-olds increased 165 percent from 1985 to 1995. In 1993, a survey found that one out of ten students attending inner-city high schools agreed that it was "OK to shoot a person if that is what it takes to get something you really want." According to criminal justice expert J.A. Fox, "This generation has more deadly weapons in their hands, more dangerous drugs in their bodies, and a much more casual attitude about violence. In addition, too many kids are undersocialized and undersupervised" (Associated Press, 1995). Where does Fox's explanation fall with regard to the fundamental controversies in psychology?

Fox mentions both biological (drugs in the body) and environmental (guns, lack of supervision) factors as determinants of youth behavior. Still, he tends to emphasize the environment (nurture) and not the role of heredity (nature). When he talks about attitudes toward violence he seems to suggest that the conscious mind plays the major role. His focus is primarily on "present causes," although undersocialization suggests "past causes." His referral to "this generation" suggests that he sees what's going on as tied to time and place and therefore not applicable across cultures. When he says ". . . too many kids . . . ," he implicitly makes allowance for individual differences. Thus, Fox assumes deterministic causes for behavior, considers both mind and body, emphasizes nurture over nature, recognizes conscious processes primarily, allows for both past and present causes, and admits to both general laws and individual differences in explaining youth behavior.

improve education or living conditions for all individuals.

Rarely a week goes by without a newspaper report about gang violence, random killings, guns in the schools. Recently, in southern California, a gang member pulled out a gun and shot a woman in the stomach when she attempted to stop the gang from spray-painting a wall. Suppose you decide that environmental influences, not heredity, caused his behavior. Next you need to ask how much the behavior was determined by the past (did he grow up in poverty or come from a bad family?) and how much was due to the present (did he feel peer pressure to prove how tough he was?). Some psychologists emphasize the past, particularly experiences at critical points in childhood and the way children are treated by their parents. Other psychologists focus on the here and now, on current circumstances, and how the gang member fits into his gang. If you believe that past events are the more important determiners of behavior, you probably also believe that behavior can be changed by proper education and training. If you believe that present circumstances are the most important factor, then you are likely to want to focus on changing those circumstances rather than on re-educating the individual.

Free Will versus Determinism

Consider the causes of alcohol abuse. In the view of some people, alcoholism is a disease. An alcoholic person drinks because he or she has a chemical imbalance. In the view of others, all of us, even the so-called alcoholics among us, drink because we choose to drink and we could stop drinking if we chose to do so. To what extent is any aspect of our behavior a result of ***free will*** (personal choice) or ***determining causes*** (forces like heredity that are independent of personal choice)? Is behavior caused by genetic and/or environmental forces over which we have no control, or are we always free to choose how we will behave regardless of who we are or what our circumstances might be. People have differing opinions on this issue, and their differing assumptions can affect their attitudes and behaviors toward others. Most psychologists take a deterministic approach, and seek to discover which particular causes lead to particular behaviors.

Mind versus Body

Does the mind exist independently of the body, or are mind and body inextricably linked? When the body ceases to function, does the mind also shut down? Wilder Penfield triggered memories in people undergoing surgery when he electrically stimulated part of their exposed brain. Because they were under local rather than general anesthesia, patients were conscious and able to report that they experienced the sensation of certain colors or heard the sound of certain clicks, depending on what regions of their brain had been stimulated (Penfield and Roberts, 1959; Penfield, 1975). This would seem to indicate a link between mind and body. But loss of bodily sensations does not mean that a person ceases to function. People who have been paralyzed may lose the ability to feel bodily sensation but can retain the ability to remember and think and dream. Thus, Jean-Dominique Bauby, who was a victim of a stroke that left him completely paralyzed except for one eye, retained his mental faculties and communicated through blinking this one eye. Using a special code in which he communicated letters through blinking his eye, he wrote a book about how he experienced a life where the connection between brain and body had been lost (Bauby, 1997).

Do we need a concept called the "mind" in order to understand behavior, or can our behavior be explained solely in terms of how our biological systems (particularly the brain and nervous system) act and react to the external world? Once we explain behavior in terms of biology, physiology, biochemistry, and other basic sciences, do we need, in addition, concepts that describe the contents and processes of consciousness (that is, the "mind")?

Determinism asserts that all behavior is perfectly predictable on the basis of external causes, while free will implies that each of us decides how to behave.

Let's assume that the mind is a useful concept. If so, are events and processes of the mind always conscious? G.B. is a college student who gets anxious during quizzes. What accounts for G.B.'s anxiety? Is his anxiety determined by conscious thoughts, say, about the consequences of failure, or is it controlled unconsciously, by processes that happen automatically and lie entirely outside of his awareness? The steps psychologists would take to help G.B. with his test anxiety are very different, depending on whether or not they believe that it is determined by conscious or unconscious processes. If the thoughts are conscious, a psychologist could help G.B. to change or replace those thoughts with other conscious thoughts (such as "I am well-prepared for the quiz"). If anxiety arises from unconscious sources, a psychologist might teach G.B. how to relax, perhaps by using deep breathing exercises. Psychologists are not agreed on how much of our behavior can be explained by conscious and unconscious processes, but it is clear, as we will see later, that both kinds of processes affect how we behave.

Universality versus Cultural Specificity

To what extent are there scientific laws of behavior that are truly universal across cultures or groups? Most of the major journals in psychology are published in the United States, and most of the published research on human behavior is based on U.S. samples. The extent to which principles derived from this research are applicable across cultures can be and is widely debated. For example, many years ago, research in the United States found that the more often we are exposed to a stimulus (such as Chinese characters or made-up "nonsense" words), the better we like it (Zajonc, 1968). This "law" has been found in more than twenty published American studies (Smith & Bond, 1994). A series of studies in Belgium, however, found different results. Exposure to objects initially led to *less* liking rather than more liking before the effect turned around and liking increased over time as found in the American studies (Vanbeselaere, 1983). One explanation for the difference is that it reflects a cultural difference in focus of attention, with the Belgian students spending more time paying attention to the context of the experiment and the American students focusing immediately on the stimuli presented. Whatever the reason, the effect of mere exposure has been shown to depend on the context, so that a simple "law" that says that exposure increases liking will not universally apply across cultures.

Can you think of any "laws" or "principles" of behavior that are likely to apply to all persons? You might answer that emotional expressions seem to be universal, that you can recognize anger across all cultures, although *why* anger is felt may differ in various cultures. Can you think of examples of psychological principles that you believe apply in the United States but not in other cultures, or that may differ in the United States, depending on what ethnic group a person belongs to? Child-rearing practices may vary in different cultures and lead to differences in whether individuals blame themselves or the situation for their failures or successes. Thus, there are certain principles of behavior that apply universally, but there are many others that are culture bound.

Fundamental Questions Reconsidered

We have phrased each of these issues as an *either/or* question, as in the format of a debate. This is the way psychologists typically present them for discussion. But both choices for each question are partially true. Think about whether your culture implies or assumes one or the other choice or allows both. Exposure to new knowl-

► *Most of us enjoy (or at least don't mind) having our pictures taken. But some native Americans not only object to being the subject of a photograph, but also feel the photographer is trying to steal a part of them. What we want to preserve on film also varies from culture to culture. The little girl in the photo will probably never seem as fascinating in her hometown as she is to these residents of South Korea.*

edge will require you to think carefully about your positions. Throughout this book, we will encourage you to analyze the assumptions on which the major psychological theories are based and challenge you to find your own answers to these fundamental questions.

Approaches to Psychology

The ideas, concepts, and methods of today's psychology have roots in the past. The World Champion professional boxer Muhammad Ali eloquently expressed the importance of this connection between past and present when he said, "When you fight me, you are fighting Jack Johnson, Sugar Ray Robinson, Joe Louis and Ezzard Charles all at once." Just as Ali recognized the influence of those giants who went before him, you can learn to recognize the influence of early contributors to psychology. As the story unfolds, think about how the answers to the questions above have changed throughout history and how even today, different psychologists still do not agree completely on the best way to answer them. Who knows, maybe you will be the person to come up with new answers (or better ways to ask the questions!). Figure 1-1 on pp. 14–15 presents a timeline of some major events and individuals in psychology's history that you will learn about in this book.

Early Approaches to Mind and Behavior

In the distant past, most of what people knew about human behavior and mental life was based on anecdotes, casual observation, intuition, logic, and plain old wishful thinking. In some parts of the world, unusual behavior was sometimes thought to be caused by "evil spirits," which needed to be let out, sometimes by opening the skull and sometimes by exorcism (driving out evil through prayer and ritual). As societies became more modern and as knowledge accumulated, however, philosophical discussions about the nature and workings of the mind became common among moralists, religious thinkers, medical doctors, and even novelists. But these discussions were largely inconclusive because there were no accepted methods for defining psychological "facts" and resolving differences of opinion on philosophical and psychological questions.

Late in the sixteenth century ***empiricism***, a school of thought based on systematic or scientific observations in the real world, emerged to provide a new method of discovering real psychological facts. Empiricists believed that knowledge was gathered through the senses. John Locke (1632–1704), for example, advanced the idea that the mind begins as a blank slate, or ***tabula rasa***, which is written on by experience. He believed that there is nothing in our minds to begin with, that heredity provides us with absolutely no knowledge of the world. He proposed that everything that comes into the mind is a product of experience. Thus, Locke believed that if a person who had been born blind had sight restored as an adult, he or she would not see in the same way as someone who had always had sight, because of not having had the experiences of seeing over a lifetime. This emphasis on the nurture end of the nature-nurture debate would be a starting point for resolving questions about the way the mind and the body are involved in behavior.

Psychophysics, Introspection, and Structuralism

Early psychologists, like Ernst Heinrich Weber (1795–1878) and Gustav Fechner (1801–1887), began with the assumption that "mind" is a valid concept, something different from "body" and necessary to account for human experience and behavior. They set out to study the relationship between our conscious mental experience ("psycho") and physical reality ("physics"). Not surprisingly, this area of study became known as ***psychophysics*** (see Chapter 5). In trying to predict psychological experiences from knowledge of the physical world, these researchers asked questions such as, "how is the physical intensity of a light related to how bright that light is judged to be?" Their work uncovered lawful relationships between physical stimulus intensity (e.g., loudness of sound) and magnitude of psychological experience (e.g., how loud the sound is perceived to be). The finding that psychological and physical worlds were different, but related in *predictable*, lawful ways gave hope that a science of the mind was indeed possible. Because this work is

[W]e should recognize that people have been "psychologizing" since they first began to wonder about themselves.

—James F. Brennan (1986).

1-1 Some Important Figures in the History of Psychology

Here are a few of the scientists and practitioners who made major contributions to the evolution and development of psychology.

1861: American Civil War
1881: B.T. Washington named head of Tuskegee Institute

1898: Gold rush to Klondike

1834: Ernst Weber proposes a law to relate stimulus intensity to sensory magnitude.

(1795–1878)

1860: Gustav Fechner publishes *Elements of Psychophysics.*

(1801–1887)

1879: Wilhelm Wundt establishes the first formal psychological research laboratory in Germany.

(1832–1920)

1890: William James publishes *Principles of Psychology,* establishing the functional approach in psychology.

(1842–1910)

1892: Christine Ladd-Franklin formulates color sensation theory.

(1847–1930)

1900: Sigmund Freud publishes *The Interpretation of Dreams* and presents his psychoanalytic theory.

(1856–1939)

1905: Alfred Binet (with Theodore Simon) develops the first standardized intelligence test.

(1857–1911)

1906: Ivan Pavlov publishes the results of his studies on classical conditioning in animals.

(1849–1936)

1908: Margaret Floy Washburn publishes *The Animal Mind,* stimulating the field of comparative psychology.

(1871–1939)

1910: Max Wertheimer studies perception of movement, which becomes the basis of Gestalt psychology.

(1880–1943)

1913: John Watson publishes *Psychology As a Behaviorist Sees It.*

(1878–1958)

1920: Francis Sumner is the first black to receive a Ph.D. in psychology and challenges psychology to be more sensitive to issues of race and ethnicity.

(1895–1954)

1922: Charlotte M. Bühler publishes *Psychology of Adolescence* and develops early ideas about humanistic psychology and the study of adolescence.

(1893–1974)

1938: B.F. Skinner publishes *The Behavior of Organisms* on operant conditioning.

(1904–1990)

1941: Neal Miller (with John Dollard) publishes *Social Learning and Imitation* about psychosocial or learned drives.

(1909–)

1950: Erik Erikson publishes *Childhood and Society* and discusses development over the life cycle.

(1902–1994)

1958: Herbert Simon presents an information-processing view of human thought.

(1916–)

1961: Eleanor Gibson (with Richard Walk) studies infant depth perception.

(1910–)

1975: E.O. Wilson publishes *Sociobiology* about the evolutionary basis of behavior.

(1929–)

1927: Anna Freud extends psychoanalysis to children with her book, *Introduction to the Technique of Child Analysis.*

(1895–1982)

1939: Kenneth Clark with his wife Mamie study self-conception and identity in African-American children; their research is cited in 1964 by the Supreme Court in *Brown* v. *Board of Education.*

(1914–)

1945: Karen Horney presents her sociocultural approach to psychoanalysis.

(1885–1952)

1954: Abraham Maslow develops a positive humanistic view about human motivation.

(1908–1970)

1961: Albert Bandura develops social learning theory.

(1925–)

1970: Mary Ainsworth and her colleagues study infant-mother attachment.

(1913–)

1987: Anne Anastasi, a prominent contributor to psychological testing and assessment, receives the National Medal of Science Award.

(1908–)

1914: Start of World War I

1929: The Great Depression

1941: U.S. enters World War II

1957: U.S.S.R. launches Sputnik

so enduring and significant, some argue that 1860, the year in which Fechner's classic *Elements of Psychophysics* was published, marks the beginning of scientific psychology.

Most people designate the "official" birth of psychology as occurring in 1879. At the time, Wilhelm Wundt (1832–1920) proclaimed psychology to be an independent experimental science and established the first formal psychology research laboratory in Leipzig, Germany. Wundt sought to create a "chemistry of consciousness," patterned after successful scientific analyses in the physical sciences. Wundt believed that just as a molecule of table salt (NaCl) consists of separate elements of sodium (Na^+) and chlorine (Cl^-) but has different properties than those elements, so ***consciousness***, or subjective experience, consists of psychical structures or compounds (defined as ideas, emotions, and actions) that can be separated into basic psychical elements. He viewed psychical compounds as resulting from freely and actively choosing where to direct one's attention. In his theory, the mind was a structure, and the goal of psychological science was to analyze the mind into its elementary structural parts. This view of psychology is sometimes called ***structuralism***.

▲ *Wilhelm Wundt in his laboratory.*

Wilhelm Wundt established the first formal laboratory for the scientific study of psychology, focusing on the analysis of the immediate conscious content of the mind.

Wundt believed that a psychologist should use what he called ***introspection*** to study the contents and structure of consciousness. As a trained introspectionist, you focus your attention on what is going on in your own mind at the instant a stimulus is presented to you. You report carefully only what you directly observe in your mind's eye, but you avoid reporting the meaning of the stimulus observed. For example, upon being presented with a golf ball, you might say "I am aware of roundness, hardness, and whiteness" (the elements in the mind's eye) rather than an interpretation of the image as a golf ball.

Functionalism and Behaviorism

E.B. Titchener brought Wundt's ideas to America and developed them into a school of psychology called structuralism

A British-born student of Wundt, Edward Bradford Titchener (1867–1927), brought Wundt's thinking to America and insisted that American psychology focus exclusively on discovering the elements that formed the structure of consciousness. Titchener had a dogmatic personality, tolerating little disagreement about the principles of psychology as he saw them. He always lectured to classes in academic robes, symbolizing his absolute authority as master teacher. But Titchener's purist version of Wundt's ideas did not go unchallenged in the United States. First, even as Wundt admitted, introspection was not a totally reliable scientific method. Even trained introspectionists who were asked about the same stimulus sometimes disagreed about what they experienced, and there was no independent way to verify the accuracy of one report over another. Moreover, to pragmatically minded American psychologists, structuralism also didn't seem to lead anywhere—it made no connection between the elements of the mind and what people actually did. In the view of many, structuralism was not asking the right question—it focused on what was in consciousness rather than how or why it got there in the first place or what it meant for behavior.

Early American psychologists believed that the structuralist approach was incomplete and sought an alternative to structuralism. As a result, ***functional psychology***, or ***functionalism***, began to emerge in the late nineteenth and early twentieth century. It focused not on the mind itself but rather on how the mind influenced behavior. Like the structuralists, the functionalists were interested in understanding consciousness, but they added an emphasis on how consciousness affected our actions.

American functionalists were influenced by the writings of the English naturalist, Charles Darwin (1809–1882). Darwin had developed a theory of evolution based on species survival and natural selection. According to this theory, certain individual members of a species are more likely than others to survive and reproduce because they have characteristics that fit better or are more adaptable to a hostile environment. Functionalists picked up on Darwin's idea that the characteristics of a species evolve because they have survival value. They believed that, because consciousness is a characteristic of our species, it should serve some survival function and that the purpose of psychology should be to examine the *function* of consciousness. Functionalists argued that the primary role of consciousness was to *mediate* (i.e., to intervene, or to "act in-between") the needs of the organism and the demands of its environment. From the functionalist viewpoint, the best way for anyone to adapt to a complex environment is to come into that environment equipped with a set of highly functional "mental tools." Preeminent among these tools is the ability to learn. This ability, in large measure, is what sets human beings apart from other animals, and allows us, despite our relatively limited physiology, to adapt to diverse environments and to create diverse cultures.

One of the most prominent functionalists was William James (1842–1910), who argued that feelings, desires, thoughts, cognitions, reasonings, and decisions are all fundamental phenomena of mental life. James conceived of the human mind as a master control structure, whose general function was to enable a person to make good choices that maximized survival. To James, psychologists should be concerned not only with *what* the mind is made of, i.e., the contents of consciousness, but also with *how* it controls behavior. James founded the first teaching laboratory in psychology in the United States at Harvard University, and wrote the first psychology textbook, *Principles of Psychology*, a work so significant that it is still assigned reading in many of our colleges and universities.

Another distinguishing feature of functionalism was the concern of its proponents with *practical*, useful applications of psychology in settings like the classroom and the workplace. This overt concern with practical applications was a distinguishing feature of the North American approach to all science. The work of Edward Thorndike (1874–1949) on learning and problem solving provides a prime example of applied psychological work in the functionalist tradition. Thorndike found that responses producing rewards would be repeated, while responses leading to punishments would result in change to another response. This "law of effect" had influential theoretical and educational implications for strengthening some behaviors and weakening others in the classroom (see Chapter 6). Thorndike also examined the effectiveness of different instructional methods and developed a variety of scholastic aptitude tests (see Chapter 8), introducing lasting changes in American educational practice.

The trend begun by the functionalists, to move away from the study of the content and structure of thought and toward research on behavior, reached its pinnacle in the writings of John B. Watson (1878–1958). To Watson, using introspection to study mental processes was not a legitimate scientific enterprise. He believed that only publicly verifiable responses, responses that could be observed and measured by other independent observers, could fulfill the requirements of a truly rigorous scientific discipline. Watson called such responses "behaviors," and the school of thought associated with Watson became known as ***behaviorism***. Nearly as dogmatic in his approach as Titchener, Watson called for a shift in the focus of psychological science, arguing that behavior or systematic relationships between environmental stimuli and responses must be studied in their own right, rather than as a means for inferring unverifiable (hence unknowable) mental processes. Watson believed that behaviors (responses of the organism) are affected directly by specific stimuli in an organism's environment and that the goal of the psychologist is to identify orderly, lawful, and predictable stimulus-response relationships.

The law of effect states that responses are strengthened or weakened as a consequence of their effects.

Although behaviorist thinking borrowed many concepts and methods from functionalism, it also owed a great intellectual debt to nonfunctionalist influences in psychology. In particular, Watson was strongly affected by the research of the renowned Russian physiologist, Ivan Pavlov (1849–1936). Pavlov provided several impressive experimental demonstrations of classical conditioning (rudimentary learning) that Watson interpreted in stimulus-response terms (see discussion in Chapter 6). Watson took Pavlov's research as the confirmation that behavior was governed by general laws, and envisioned the possibility that all behavior, no matter how complex, could be reduced to simple units, in this case, learned or conditioned stimulus-response units.

Watson's position was that a true science of psychology, a behaviorism, could be based only on public data that could be measured and replicated.

Adopting the concept of *tabula rasa* from John Locke, Watson believed that, if he could control the environment (the stimuli), he could control behavior (the responses). There would be no need to invoke the concept of mind or to intro-

Give me a dozen healthy infants, well-formed, and my own specific world to bring them up in and I'll guarantee to take any one at random and train him to be any type of specialist I might select—doctor, lawyer, artist, merchant-chief and yes, even beggar-man and thief, regardless of his talents, penchants, tendencies, abilities, vocations, and race of his ancestors.
—Watson (1924/1930 p. 104)

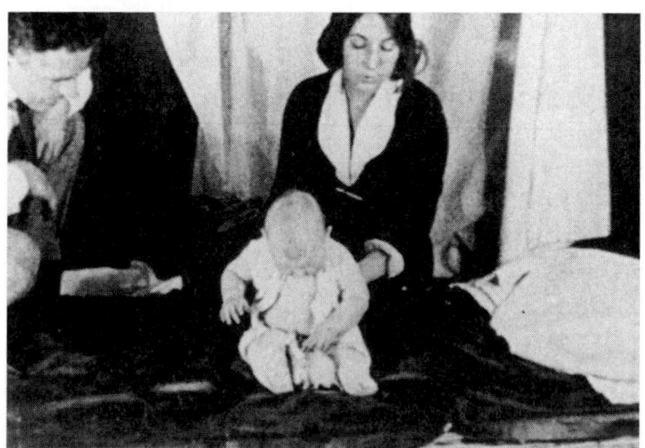

◄ *John B. Watson and Rosalie Rayner with Little Albert, in whom they conditioned a phobia of rats.*

▲ *B. F. Skinner with one of his subjects.*

duce the principles of heredity to explain behavior. Watson's emphasis on the prediction and control of behavior became the dominant force in American psychology from 1930 through the late 1950s.

Perhaps the most prominent of all behaviorists was B.F. Skinner (1904–1990). Rather than seeing behavior as a response to some stimulus, however, Skinner emphasized behaviors that are spontaneously produced by an organism to affect its environment. These spontaneous responses are subsequently either strengthened or weakened according to their consequences (rewards and punishments) in particular contexts. This is the principle of reinforcement, perhaps the most fundamental principle underlying all learning (see Chapter 6 for further discussion).

Gestalt Psychology

Gestalt psychology rejected the ideas of analysis into elements, arguing that the whole is more than the sum of its parts.

Around 1910, at about the same time that John Watson was formulating a behaviorist objection to structuralism, ***Gestalt psychology*** surfaced in Germany as another reaction to structuralism. The German word *Gestalt* has no exact English translation. Roughly, it means "organized whole." Gestaltists argued that the processes of perception, experience, and consciousness are organized into unified patterns or Gestalts. For Gestalt psychologists, the structuralist approach to consciousness is wrong-headed. You don't understand consciousness by asking a person to think about the elements of a stimulus. Taking our earlier example, upon being presented with a golf ball, the natural response is not to see the elements, "white" or "round," in the mind's eye, but rather to see the meaningful whole, the "golf ball" itself. Gestaltists, such as Max Wertheimer (1880–1943), claimed that we experience the world not as a matrix of unrelated elements, as structuralism claimed, but as a collection of *meaningful* objects. Moreover, they believed that the whole is more and different from the sum of its parts (see Figure 1-2). Some of these Gestalts are learned, but many of them are built into the brain and thus are there from birth to organize and give meaning to our experience of the world around us. Like other psychologists, Gestaltists aimed to develop a complete *science* of psychology. But they differed from others by emphasizing behavior at a global or wholistic level.

Behaviorism remained widely influential through the 1930s, 1940s, and 1950s, while Gestalt psychology lost its identity as a separate school of psychology. Its contributions to psychological knowledge are enduring, however. In the 1960s, when psychology underwent what has been called a "cognitive revolution," mental processes as well as Gestalt psychology were rediscovered. Gestalt ideas can be found in a variety of places today, especially in the modern study of higher mental processes, such as thinking, language, problem solving, and information processing.

1-2 The Concept of Emergent Properties

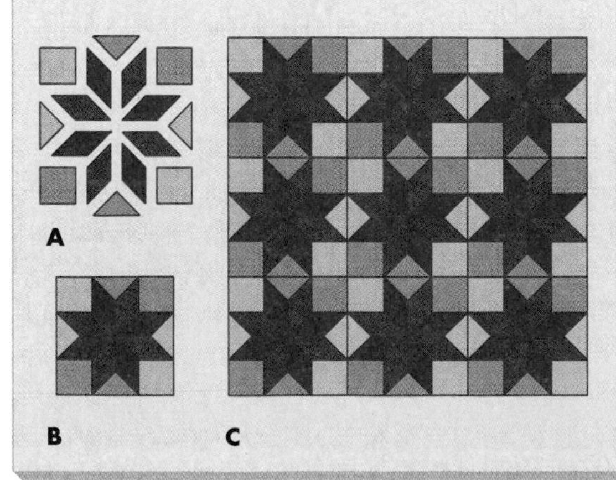

Gestalt psychologists emphasized emergent properties of psychological processes, that is, "the whole is more than the sum of its parts." This concept can be demonstrated by analyzing the pattern of a quilt. Small geometric elements (A) can be organized into a block to form a pattern (B). Sets of these blocks can in turn be arranged to form a higher-order pattern (C). Similarly, the properties or characteristics of psychological processes emerge from the organization of smaller elements. To understand the properties of the whole, the whole must be studied, not just the parts.

Psychoanalysis

With the exception of Wundt, most early psychologists neglected the concept of motivation in their theories. But clearly, no one reacts or learns if there is no reason to do so. Sigmund Freud (1856–1939) attempted to set the record straight. Freud's approach, called ***psychoanalysis***, promoted the idea that the emotional and motivational aspects of behavior are fundamental and are far more complicated than simple biological models can explain. It also emphasized the importance of early childhood events and experience as major determiners of later adult behavior.

Psychoanalysis is said to have begun with the famous case of "Anna O." Anna O., a patient of Freud's colleague, Joseph Breuer, was relieved of her symptoms when she was able to describe a previously unconscious traumatic memory that came to light while she was under hypnosis. Sigmund Freud was fascinated by this "talking cure" and began to explore it clinically. He aimed to produce psychic relief from symptoms through ***catharsis***, a venting of pent-up emotional energy. As he progressed, Freud aban-

Table 1-1 A Comparison of Five Early Schools of Psychology

Perspective	Leaders	Primary Method	Subject Matter	Principle
Structuralism (1875–1930s)	W. Wundt E. Titchener	Introspection and naturalistic observation	Elements of conscious experience	Conscious experience is composed of primary mental elements.
Functionalism (1890–1930s)	W. James E. Thorndike	Introspection and experiment	Functions of the mind	Psychological adaptation by the mind is just as important as the mind's structure.
Psychoanalysis (1900–1940s)	S. Freud	Introspection and case history	Unconscious motivation and conflicts	The content of the unconscious mind, much of which is acquired early in life, is a major determiner of adult behavior.
Gestalt Psychology (1912–1940s)	M. Wertheimer K. Koffka W. Köhler	Experiment and naturalistic observation	Organization in perception and conscious experience	Perceptions, experiences, and mental events are different from the sum of their parts.
Behaviorism (1913–1950s)	J. Watson B.F. Skinner	Experiment	Behavior specifically defined as observable performance or action	All behavior can be explained by stimulus-response connections and changed by conditioning new stimulus-response connections.

doned the use of hypnosis, developing a substitute method called ***free association*** (allowing the patient to talk about anything that came to mind) as a tool to retrieve unconscious memories. Freud's primary scientific tool was the case study method (see Chapter 2), which he used to revolutionize the theory and treatment of abnormal behavior and later to develop an explanation for human motivation and personality in general. Freud's theory stressed innate and early childhood forces in the determination of adult behavior and personality. His work was expanded over the years by the neo-Freudians, such as Karen Horney, Erik Erikson, and Anna Freud (Freud's daughter), all of whom placed equal or greater emphasis on family, social, and cultural forces. A comparison of the five early theoretical perspectives in psychology can be found in Table 1-1.

Contemporary Approaches to Mind and Behavior

The original forms of structuralism, functionalism, behaviorism, Gestalt psychology, and psychoanalysis are no longer central to modern psychology. Nonetheless, certain principles and outgrowths of these perspectives do appear in contemporary psychology. There is renewed interest in the original question of how to explain the contents of consciousness (the focal question of structuralism) and how to apply psychology to improve social institutions such as education and the criminal justice system (a major mandate of functionalism). Most behaviorists are no longer radical anti-mentalists, though their fo-

Freud emphasized the motivational and emotional aspects of behavior.

▼ *Sigmund Freud in his office in Vienna.*

Humanistic psychology adopts a principle of free will and focuses on how and why individuals perceive the world in their own unique ways.

cus is still on the endpoint, that is, on responses. Gestalt principles are still applied to the analysis of perception. Although it would be hard to find a pure Freudian psychoanalyst among clinicians today, there are currently a host of modern psychodynamic therapists (Freedheim, 1992).

The psychodynamic, behavioral, and sociocultural perspectives have roots in historical schools of psychology but are different in their modern forms. The psychodynamic perspective reflects a Freudian psychoanalytic legacy, relying heavily on unconscious causes and motivational conflicts in the control of behavior. The behavioral perspective is the modern version of behaviorism, emphasizing the importance of stimuli, contingencies, and environmental contexts in controlling behavior. The sociocultural perspective reflects a recent and growing awareness that individuals function within, and cannot be fully separated from, their social environments. It emphasizes how individual behavior is a product of the social and cultural context, and reflects past and present experiences in one's particular family, neighborhood, society, and culture. Other contemporary perspectives that have emerged include the humanistic approach, the cognitive approach, and the biological approach, which we will discuss in more detail below. Table 1-2 summarizes the major emphases of various perspectives, along with some illustrative areas of interest for each.

The Humanistic Approach

Behaviorism and psychoanalysis were the two major schools in U.S. psychology during the early part of the twentieth century. In the 1940s, a "third force" movement emerged to provide an alternative orientation toward understanding behavior. This movement found greatest expression in what today is called ***humanistic psychology***. Focusing on the creative nature of human behavior and thought, psychologists such as Charlotte Bühler (1893–1974), Abraham Maslow (1908–1970), and Carl Rogers (1902–1987) founded and promoted a humanistic approach based on the fundamental assumption that each person is unique and valuable in his or her own right. Humanistic psychologists are convinced that people make life choices and thereby determine their own fate by the conscious exercise of free will. They hold that purpose, reason, and intuition are more important than are environment or biology in determining the course of personal development. Each of us is motivated primarily to "actualize" all of our potential for behavior. While behaviorists and psychoanalysts think deterministically and see behavior as a closed system, humanists believe in an open system in which every human being strives to achieve his or her potential (see Table 1-3).

Today, elements of a humanistic perspective can still be found in the work of some feminist

Table 1-2 Seven Contemporary Perspectives in Psychology

Perspective	Focus	Areas Studied
Biological	Physiological bases of behavior	Transmission of messages within the body; relation of blood chemistry to moods and motives; genetic and environmental influences on behavior
Behavioral	Observable responses	Acquisition and changing of responses through learning, such as learning to fear particular objects or situation or learning to stop smoking or overeating
Cognitive	Mental processes	Information processing, memory, reasoning, and problem solving
Humanistic	Human experience and potential	Achieving our potential; seeking maturity and fulfillment; taking responsibility for our decisions and our own lives
Psychodynamic	Unconscious drives and conflicts	Personality traits and disorders studied in terms of sexual and aggressive drives or unresolved childhood conflicts
Sociocultural	Cultural variations in behavior and thought	Behavioral and cognitive similarities and differences among people of varied ethnic origins, societies, and cultures
Evolutionary	Genetic basis of behavior	Shaping of behaviors by genes, evolutionary processes, and natural selection

Table 1-3 Sides Taken by Various Perspectives on Fundamental Psychological Issues

Issue	Perspective					
	Biological	Evolutionary	Psychodynamic	Behavioral	Cognitive	Humanistic
Nature vs. nurture	Nature	Nature (through inheritance)	Nature (plus childhood experience)	Nurture	Primarily nurture	Nurture
Universality vs. specificity	Universality	Universality	Universality	Both	Both	Specificity
Mind vs. body	Body	Body	Both	Body	Mind	Mind
Free will vs. determinism	Determinism	Determinism	Determinism	Determinism	Determinism	Free will

psychologists, particularly women of color, cross-cultural psychologists, and social psychologists. These contemporary humanistic psychologists are well aware of the need to be rigorous, quantitative, and scientific in their approach to the study of human behavior. But they differ from their more deterministic colleagues in insisting on the uniqueness of each individual and on the need to understand behavior from each person's unique perspective (e.g., Landrine, Klonoff & Brown-Collins, 1992).

The Cognitive Approach

Another popular theoretical framework in modern psychology is one that emphasizes cognition and the mental processes going on inside the mind. This ***cognitive approach*** views human beings as active information processors, constantly interacting with their environments and using their mental capacities as they do so. A major influence on this approach has been the analogy between the way human beings think and act and the way computers process information. Cognitive psychologists often create computer models of the human mind in order to understand or to make better guesses about how the mind works and the role it plays in behavior.

According to the cognitive approach, information is processed at several locations in the brain. This processed information can either affect behavior immediately, or it can be stored in memory and influence behavior at a later time. In either case, behavior is conceived as more than a response to a stimulus. Cognitive psychologists believe that many internal events or processes almost always occur between stimulus and outcome.

The Biological Approach

The mind is inextricably linked to the brain. Some psychologists believe that the mind can only be fully understood through studying the brain and the nervous system. This idea represents another important contemporary approach in psychology called the biological approach, and within it, the subfield of behavioral neuroscience. This approach emphasizes the importance of biological factors in shaping behavior and seeks to understand the relationship of the body to the mind.

Weber, Fechner, Wundt, and James all speculated about the relationship between the speed of nerve impulses and how long it took various body parts to react to a stimulus, and about which areas of the brain were responsible for various mental powers or abilities. But the techniques needed to study these relationships were not developed until quite recently. Today, we have the technology to identify and to measure physiological processes. There have been rapid advances in ***neuroscience***, which is the study of how the nervous system works, right down to the functioning of individual nerve cells (neurons). With these developments has come a strong resurgence of interest and excitement in the biological, and especially the neurological, bases of behavior. This interest was one of the factors leading to the passage of federal legislation signed into law by President Bush that declared the 1990s to be "the decade of the brain." Discoveries in behavioral neuroscience are coming so rapidly that some people would describe the field as *the* major wave in psychology's future (see Chapter 3).

The Evolutionary Approach

Some behaviors seem natural, in the sense that they occur with no special training, motivation, or thought. Everyone has heard about the "natural" athlete who excels at a sport while making little apparent effort. People seem to have natural predispositions to particular traits or social behaviors. For example, "he's just an ornery person" or "she's so outgoing and personable." There is a contemporary point of view about behavior that claims that much of what we do in life is inherently pre-programmed. This assumption appears most prominently in ***evolutionary psychology***, the study of how the evolutionary principle of natural selection shapes social behavior in human beings and animals. The genes we inherit from our parents predispose us to act in ways that are adaptive, enhancing our chances of surviving and multiplying. Theoretically, these genes have been selected by evolution over the generations to include those that successfully perpetuate our species and exclude those that do not. Thus, when individuals with these genes survive, they are able to reproduce and pass on the genes to new generations, ensuring the survival of the genes.

The influence of natural selection can be seen most prominently in what is called ***altruism***, or self-sacrifice in the service of others. E.O. Wilson (1929–), one of the founders of the field, sees altruism as one of the behavioral themes that is grounded in genetic heritage. We tend to be most altruistic with our closest relatives (Wilson, 1978). For example, we are more likely to share our food, money, and other resources with members of our family than we are with nonrelatives. Someone who risks death or injury does so to enhance the survival of the group he or she represents. In cases like this, we are said to be acting to preserve our genes by protecting kin who have the same genes that we do. (Chapter 12 has a more complete discussion of influences on helping behavior.) Evolutionary psychologists note that kinship is of great importance in all human societies, and the likelihood of altruistic behavior is directly related to the genetic relatedness of the people involved

THINKING CRITICALLY

Alcohol abuse is a major psychological problem for individuals and for our society. There is clear evidence that alcohol abuse leads to accidents, acts of violence, irrational behavior, and illness. What do you think the different modern perspectives on psychology have to contribute to an understanding of alcohol abuse?

For psychologists with a biological perspective, alcohol abuse is considered to be a disease called alcoholism. A biological psychologist is likely to search for a genetic basis for the disease and to search for physiological changes underlying the erratic behavior of alcoholic individuals. One question might be: Do alcoholic individuals inherit any biological condition, such as a nervous system that is especially susceptible to addiction, that predisposes them to alcoholism? A cognitive psychologist might or might not think of alcohol abuse as a disease. The focus of this approach is likely to be on whether the principles of learning, memory, and thought can help to understand the satisfaction an abuser derives from alcohol use. Retraining programs might be created to modify behavior or to substitute some other form of behavior for alcohol use. A humanistic psychologist would accept the individual with all of his or her bad behavior and would work to help him or her to see the elements of choice in life, the fact that alcohol use is a matter of choice, and that alcohol abuse generally interferes with attaining the goal of self-fulfillment. Other perspectives would ask different questions about alcohol abuse. What do you think an evolutionary psychologist would say about the problem?

(Essock-Vitale & McGuire, 1985). Evolutionary psychology lies at the nature end of the nature-nurture question and underlies the important study of behavioral genetics (see Chapter 3).

Psychology as a Profession

Besides coming to an understanding of some history and general themes of psychology, it is also valuable to know what psychologists do and where they practice their profession to arrive at a complete picture of the breadth of the field today. Psychology in the twentieth century has evolved into a vast empirical science. Today, psychologists make hypotheses and conduct studies in diverse areas, including how we develop, perceive, learn, and think, what kind of personality we have, and how we interact socially with other people. Within a particular area of study, specific issues or problems dictate the approach rather than adherence to one theoretical framework. Most psychologists are eclectic. They focus on one perspective, but they also use what works from other approaches based on what the problem or issue is.

According to the International Union of Psychological Science, in 1991 there were more than 500,000 psychologists in the world. About half of them were in the United States. Because the state of psychology in the United States has the most direct bearing on the experiences of students studying in U.S. institutions, we focus here on the experiences of North American psychologists. Keep in mind, however, that there are differences in both the number and specialties of psychologists across nations, particularly between industrialized and nonindustrialized nations.

It is common for psychologists to have multiple roles: researcher, teacher, health service provider, administrator, and consultant, among others. Psychologists in the United States can be found working in educational settings (including schools, colleges, and universities), human service settings (including hospitals, clinics, and independent practice), profit and nonprofit organizations (as personnel consultants or human factors experts at corporations or foundations), and government (psychologists can even be found working for members of Congress). Figure 1-3A shows where recent doctoral recipients were employed full-time in 1995.

Psychologists play multiple roles, including researcher, teacher, health service provider, administrator, and consultant.

Psychologists can use their expertise in a variety of areas including sports psychology, where they help athletes to develop their full potential; rehabilitation psychology, where they help injured people to regain their physical and mental functions; and industrial/organizational psychology, where they help corporations to select and train their workers more effectively. To help you appreciate the diversity of psychology's applications fully, we will discuss how and where psychologists use their knowledge, abilities, and skills. Note that the education,

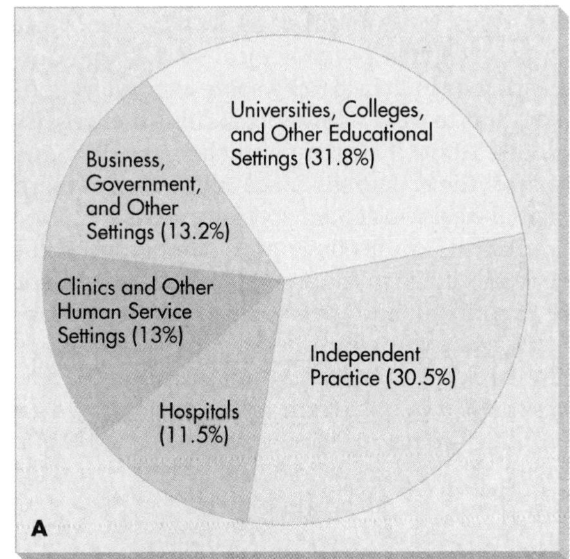

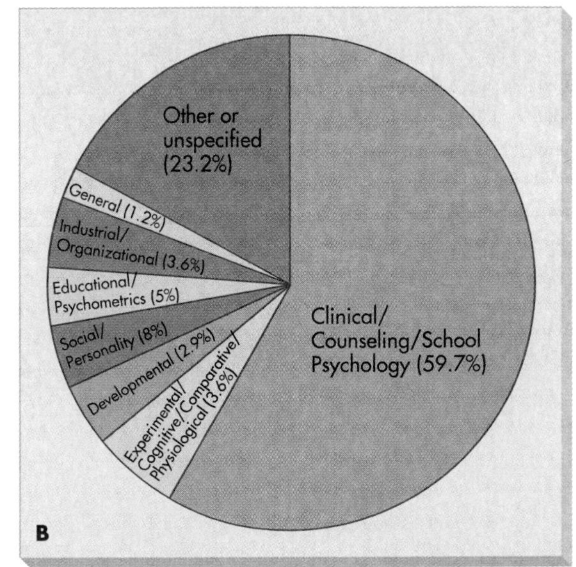

1-3 What Psychologists Do

(A) In 1995, almost one-third of all psychologists had independent practices. Psychologists were also working in business, universities, clinics, and hospitals. But fewer psychologists were working in clinics or in hospitals than in 1993, possibly because of cutbacks in money for health care. (B) Although more than half of psychologists were clinicians or counselors or school or community psychologists, psychologists can also be found in many other subfields of psychology. (Source: Profiles of APA Members, 1995. Prepared by the APA Research Office.)

▲ *A broad range of careers is available to psychologists. Here, sports psychologist Lisa Francine, left, consoles an athlete after a loss at the Centennial Olympic Games.*

training, and certification requirements for psychologists depend on their area of specialization, and vary by state and country. Typically in the United States, at least a Master's degree is needed to provide psychological services. Most psychologists have doctoral degrees, generally doctorates in philosophy (Ph.D.), in education (Ed.D.), or in psychology (Psy.D). Figure 1-3B shows the breakdown into areas of specialization for psychologists who obtained their doctorates between 1960 and 1992.

Psychologists as Health Service Providers

When people in general talk or think about psychologists they typically picture clinical psychologists or counselors. These are therapists who work in counseling, clinical, or school settings, applying psychological knowledge and techniques to help people solve everyday problems and to deal with more serious mental disorders. About half the psychologists who have earned their degrees since 1960 are in these mental-health-oriented specialty areas.

Clinical, counseling, and school psychologists specialize in the assessment and treatment of emotional and personal adjustment problems. They are concerned with psychopathology and are trained to diagnose and treat problems ranging from the normal crises of growing up to extreme psychotic conditions. Many of these psychologists work in mental hospitals, mental health clinics, schools, or in private practice. They are trained in both research and clinical skills, and consequently adopt a flexible approach to psychopathology. They should be distinguished from psychiatrists, who hold a doctor of medicine (M.D.) degree, are trained primarily as professional practitioners, and are likely to adopt a less flexible, biologically based orientation toward diagnosis and therapy.

► *A clinical psychologist administers a diagnostic test.*

Psychologists as Scientists and Educators

Academic/research psychologists fall into a variety of research-oriented subfields. They are most often employed in colleges and universities. Success in these subfields typically requires a research-oriented doctoral degree for career advancement, particularly for jobs in major university settings. Many in the academic/research subfield are experimental psychologists. Historically, experimental psychology refers to a way of studying behavior, namely, using the experimental method (see Chapter 2). In recent years, the label has come to refer to psychologists who study the fundamental behavioral processes, including learning, sensation and perception, skilled performance, motivation and emotion, language, cognition, and communication. Although they primarily conduct basic research—that is, research into the most basic principles of behavior without regard to their real-world applications—experimental psychologists are sometimes asked to apply their laboratory training to relevant practical problems. Thus, governmental or industrial research laboratories, nonprofit research organizations, hospitals, and businesses might also provide employment opportunities for experimental psychologists.

Physiological and biological psychologists, behavioral neuroscientists, neuropsychologists and behavioral geneticists are closely associated with experimental psychologists, and together they are sometimes considered the basic scientists of psychology. They share many common research methods with experimentalists, but they are particularly interested in the biological foundations of behavior. They apply techniques of biological science and experimental procedures to determine how the nervous system, hormones, genes, and other biological systems interact with behavior. Biological psychologists typically work in universities, although many of them are found in medical schools or biology departments, where they collaborate with researchers in other disciplines who are interested in the prediction and control of behavior.

Social psychologists study the behavior of individuals in situations involving other people.

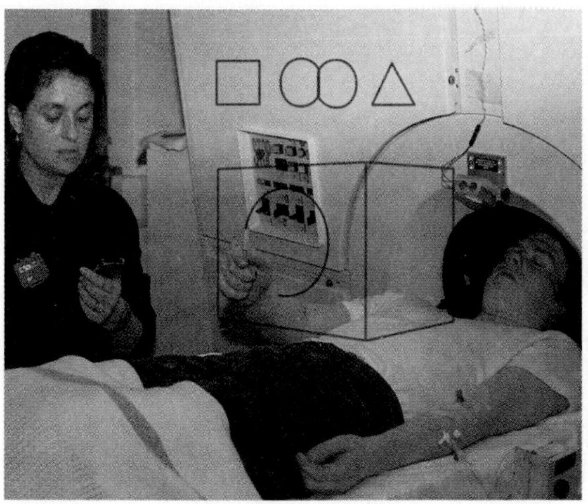

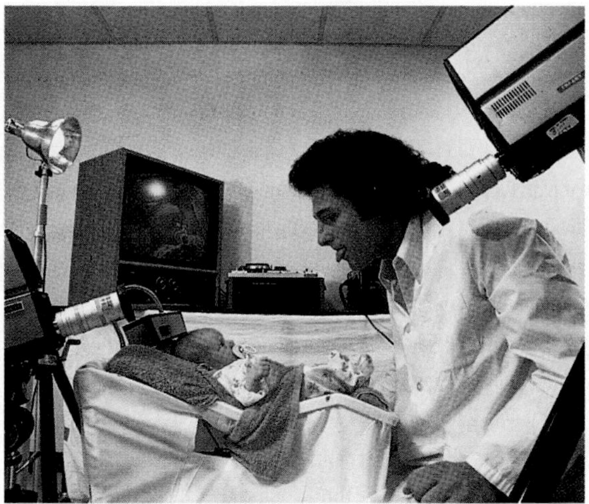

◀ (Left) Neuroscientist Gabriella Bottini studies what occurs in the brain when a volunteer executes a drawing task.

◀ (Right) A researcher studies an infant at the University of Washington's Child Development and Mental Retardation Center, Seattle.

Their aim is to determine how social factors influence the behavior and thoughts of people. Their concerns include: (a) how we perceive and think about other people; (b) the manner in which we form beliefs, attitudes, and values; (c) the behavior of people in groups; (d) how social roles and categories are learned; (e) conformity and obedience; and (f) the effects of mass social communication, such as television or advertising campaigns. The majority of social psychologists work in universities and colleges, although some can be found in advertising agencies, management consulting firms, and other applied settings. Social psychologists use diverse methods to find answers, including conducting experiments in laboratories, making naturalistic observations in settings such as shopping centers and airports, and asking people to fill out surveys in their homes or on the street.

Developmental psychologists study the manner in which behavior and related psychological processes change over the lifespan. Most developmental psychologists specialize in the study of some subpart of the field, such as cognitive development or socialization, or in a particular age group, such as infants, adolescents, or the elderly. While some developmental psychologists are rigorous experimentalists, many also use nonexperimental methods.

The focus of industrial/organizational (sometimes called I/O) psychology is on work-related behaviors in industrial settings, emphasizing employee job satisfaction, efficiency, and morale. Such psychologists might also study how a work schedule is planned and how to raise the satisfaction of consumers of an organization's services or products. Sometimes industrial psychologists consult with management on such matters as the development of better employee-management relations, the design and implementation of training or retirement programs, or the optimal design of an incentive system to motivate management and employees to work effectively for company goals.

Reflections and Observations

Psychology began as a scientific discipline, formed by pioneering scholars interested in the human mind. These early psychologists were trained in philosophy, medicine, and the natural sciences, but they had a strong desire to understand, through the methods of science, what makes people "tick." As they learned about the mind and behavior, applications of their findings began to emerge, leading to the professional practice of psychology, especially in health-related fields.

Yet, the field of psychology reflects the larger social and cultural context. Thus, social context has influenced everything from the questions that psychologists ask to the kinds of people who have access to training in psychological skills and knowledge. For the first seventy-five

UNDERSTANDING HUMAN DIVERSITY

Pioneering Women in Psychology

Christine Ladd-Franklin (1847–1930)

Mary Whiton Calkins (1863–1930)

Margaret Floy Washburn (1871–1939)

Katharine May Banham (1897–)

Although today we often take higher education for granted, at one time only individuals with social status and access to money were able to obtain a higher education. Not surprisingly, this meant that most psychologists in psychology's early years were white, upper-class males. Nonetheless, the establishment of women's colleges in the 1830s and the push for co-education in public institutions meant that women could be involved in the field from its beginnings. Despite barriers, many became prominent in the field. Their stories (as well as those of the men who aided them) are a rich source of insights and inspiration (see Guthrie, 1976; O'Connell & Russo, 1980, 1983, 1988, 1980; Russo & O'Connell, 1992).

Yet, before gender discrimination in education was legally banned, even the most talented women were prohibited from receiving advanced degrees—even though they had earned them with distinction. Christine Ladd-Franklin produced an original theory of color vision which is still influential today. Ladd-Franklin met all requirements for the Ph.D. degree from Johns Hopkins University in 1882 except one—she wasn't male. The degree was finally awarded to her more than four decades later, in 1926, after she had established an international reputation and had been identified as one of the fifty most distinguished psychologists of the time (Cadwallader & Cadwallader, 1990).

Similarly, Mary Whiton Calkins earned but was denied a Ph.D. from Harvard University, despite the unanimous support of her department. The founder of one of the first dozen psychological laboratories in the United States, Calkins invented the paired associate technique for studying memory and developed a theory of self psychology. Although William James judged her his brightest student, the Harvard trustees were not ready for co-education. Later, Calkins declined to accept a substitute degree from Radcliffe, Harvard's "sister" women's college, observing that such an action would serve to perpetuate a discriminatory system. Although Calkins never was officially awarded a Ph.D., she too was recognized as one of the fifty most distinguished psychologists and became the first woman to be elected president of the American Psychological Association (Furumoto, 1990).

Even women who were permitted to earn degrees had to overcome other barriers. Margaret Floy Washburn, who became the first woman to actually be awarded a Ph.D. in psychology and the second woman to be elected president of the American Psychological Association, had to interrupt her studies and change institutions because Columbia University

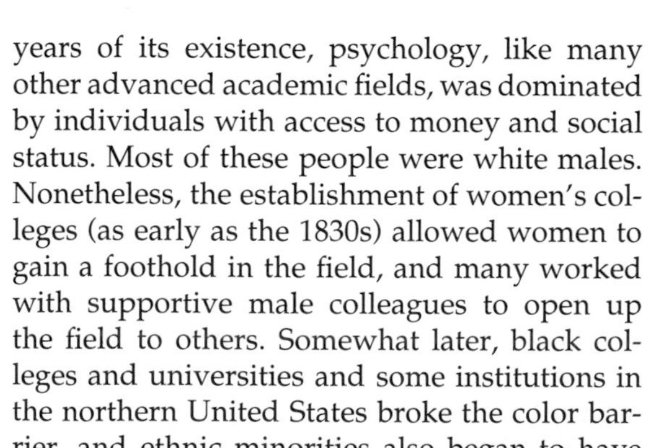

years of its existence, psychology, like many other advanced academic fields, was dominated by individuals with access to money and social status. Most of these people were white males. Nonetheless, the establishment of women's colleges (as early as the 1830s) allowed women to gain a foothold in the field, and many worked with supportive male colleagues to open up the field to others. Somewhat later, black colleges and universities and some institutions in the northern United States broke the color barrier, and ethnic minorities also began to have access to advanced psychological training. They too challenged psychology to broaden its vision and open its doors. Their stories are a source of inspiration for all psychologists (Guthrie, 1976; O'Connell & Russo, 1990).

Higher education is still working hard to overcome its restrictive legacy. Although discrimination persists in employment and advancement, the number of women in the field of psychology has increased, such that more than half of the full-time doctoral students in psychology are now women. Recruiting ethnic minorities to the field continues, and the proportion is slowly growing—nearly one out of five full-time doctoral students in psychology is from an ethnic minority group. The American Psychological Association has a variety of special programs to address issues related to discrimination in psychology, whether it be based on gender, ethnicity, able-bodiedness, or sexual orientation. Psychology, like the larger society, will continue to evolve and change as the field responds to the demands of the twenty-first century.

had no fellowships for women, no matter how brilliant (Goodman, 1980). Sometimes the barriers for women in psychology were concrete—as part of her doctoral requirements at the University of Montreal, a Catholic institution, Katharine Banham took a tutorial course with Père Forêt, a Dominican priest who was dean of the faculty. Where do you think the tutorial took place? In the confessional, the only place they were allowed to be alone together in the monastery! Nonetheless, Banham persevered. In 1934, she became the first woman to obtain a doctorate from that institution, earning it "avec distinction" (Banham, 1980, p. 35).

Inez Beverly Prosser (1897–1934)

Psychology reflects the larger social context, which means that ethnic minority women did not earn advanced degrees until well into the twentieth century. Although African-American Gilbert Haven Jones received his Ph.D. in psychology in Germany in 1901 and Francis Sumner his Ph.D. from Clark University in 1920, it was not until 1933 that a black woman, Inez Prosser, received a doctorate in educational psychology (Ed.D.). A year later, Ruth Howard became the first black woman to receive a Ph.D. in psychology (Guthrie, 1976; Howard, 1980). And it was not until 1962 that Martha Bernal became the first Chicana to obtain a Ph.D. in psychology.

Ruth Howard (1900–)

Early women psychologists especially sought to use their training and skills to subject stereotypes about the so-called "inferior abilities" of women to scientific scrutiny. Two pioneers deserve special mention: Helen Thompson Woolley and Leta Stetter Hollingworth.

Martha E. Bernal (1931–)

Helen Thompson Woolley, who received her Ph.D. in 1900, became a major figure in the field of child development. She subjected beliefs about women's mental inferiority to experimental examination, demonstrating that males and females were more similar than different. A strong advocate for women's sufferage, Woolley often spoke at sufferage rallies, scheduled last to provide a voice of reason to counter the passionate speeches of others. She also led a walk-out during a professional meeting when a black member's attendance was questioned (Rosenberg, 1982).

Helen Thompson Woolley (1874–1947)

Leta Stetter Hollingworth, who was the first to use the term "gifted," is known for her distinguished contributions to child psychology and education. Barred from teaching in the New York public schools because she was married, she became a staunch advocate for women's rights, and was known as the "scientific pillar" of the women's movement. Her research challenged myths and stereotypes about women, including the idea that women have decrements in performance due to the phase of their menstrual cycle (Benjamin & Shields, 1990).

These are just a few highlights of some of the lives and circumstances of women contributors to psychology. Today, when women are found in equal numbers in the field, it is sometimes easy to forget the struggles that made such opportunity possible. However, all students can draw inspiration from the talent, determination, and accomplishments of psychology's remarkable women.

Leta Stetter Hollingworth (1886–1939)

Objectives Revisited

The themes of this book emerge out of psychology's quest to understand the behavior of individuals in diverse contexts and from multiple points of view. The field's rich intellectual history, with dual roots in philosophy and physiology, encompasses a wide variety of perspectives, from biological to sociocultural. From its early beginnings in the United States, applications of psychological knowledge to improve society have been an integral part of the psychological enterprise. Let's review the questions and objectives considered in this chapter.

Objective 1. Define psychology and give examples of where it can be useful.

Psychology is the scientific study of behavior and mental processes. Behavior encompasses all the activities and performances of an organism, from simple movements, like stepping on the brake, to complex performances, like playing the violin. Mental processes include perceptions, thoughts, memories, expectations, and emotions. The scientific study of these phenomena has a great deal to offer in helping you meet

KEY TERMS

behavior

mental processes

nature

nurture

free will

determinism

empiricism

tabula rasa

psychophysics

consciousness

structuralism

introspection

functionalism

behaviorism

Gestalt

psychoanalysis

free association

humanistic psychology

cognitive approach

neuroscience

evolutionary psychology

altruism

sociocultural perspective

the challenges of the twenty-first century: changes in the workplace, increased cultural diversity, changing family structures, and evolving gender roles.

Objective 2. Identify the goals of psychology.

Psychologists seek to understand human nature and the differences among individuals through research, and to improve the general public welfare by the development and application of scientific psychological principles and knowledge. To these ends, psychologists develop concepts to represent behavior and mental processes so that they can be measured by verifiable empirical methods. The fact that human beings have a consciousness and a sense of self makes the study of *human* behavior particularly difficult. Because both research and the application of psychological principles involve controlling or modifying human behavior, and because people often disagree about the meanings and implications of psychological concepts, methods, and findings, doing psychological research requires being guided by high ethical standards, integrity, concern for other people, and recognition of diversity in values and perspectives.

Objective 3. Outline some fundamental issues, questions, and controversies in psychology.

Is heredity or environment more important to behavior? Is behavior determined by genetic or environmental influences, or does it arise out of free will? Do we need a concept of the mind to explain behavior, or is understanding the body sufficient? Does the conscious or the unconscious mind exert a stronger influence on behavior? What about the influence of culture and society—are some principles universal or are they culture-specific? These are some of the major issues that have occupied psychologists for over one hundred years. You should understand that phrasing these questions in an either/or manner is not sufficient, because the answer to each of them probably lies between the extremes. But these are issues that you should keep in mind as you read the remainder of this textbook. We encourage you to think creatively about ways to address them.

Objective 4. Present an overview of the history of psychology.

Highlights of the history of psychology include the formation of various schools of thought and theories during the later 1800s and early 1900s, beginning with psychophysical and introspective experiments, leading to points of view about the mind and behavior such as structuralism, functionalism, behaviorism, Gestalt psychology, and psychoanalysis, which eventually yielded to a broad but integrated approach that encompasses the best of these various and diverse early theories.

Objective 5. Describe the major contemporary trends in psychology.

The major contemporary trends in psychology include psychodynamic, behavioral, sociocultural, humanistic, cognitive, biological, and evolutionary approaches. The psychodynamic perspective emphasizes unconscious causes for and motivational conflicts underlying behavior. The behavioral perspective highlights the relationship of stimuli to responses in various environmental contexts in the control of behavior. The sociocultural perspective focuses on the influence of the social and cultural factors on behavior. The humanistic approach focuses on the creative, purposeful nature of individuals and on internal controls rather than external forces as the major determiners of behavior. The cognitive approach seeks to understand the principles by which the mind, as a processor of information, mediates between the environment and behavior. The biological approach (and especially its subfield, behavioral neuroscience) looks for the answer to behavioral questions in the functions of the nervous system, especially higher centers in the brain. The evolutionary approach tries to find traits and social behavior that are common across members of a species, stressing the importance of the survival of genes that have been passed along through the generations.

Objective 6. Describe employment possibilities for psychologists.

As in many other fields, there is a trend in psychology toward expansion, specialization, and application. Although psychologists are typically trained in a particular subspecialty, they can and often do study the same problems from somewhat different theoretical and methodological perspectives. Professional practice or the application of psychology, especially in the mental health field, has been a major area of growth within psychology since World War II. Psychologists have worked hard to address issues related to a wide variety of types of discrimination, and to support diversity in the values and perspectives of psychologists.

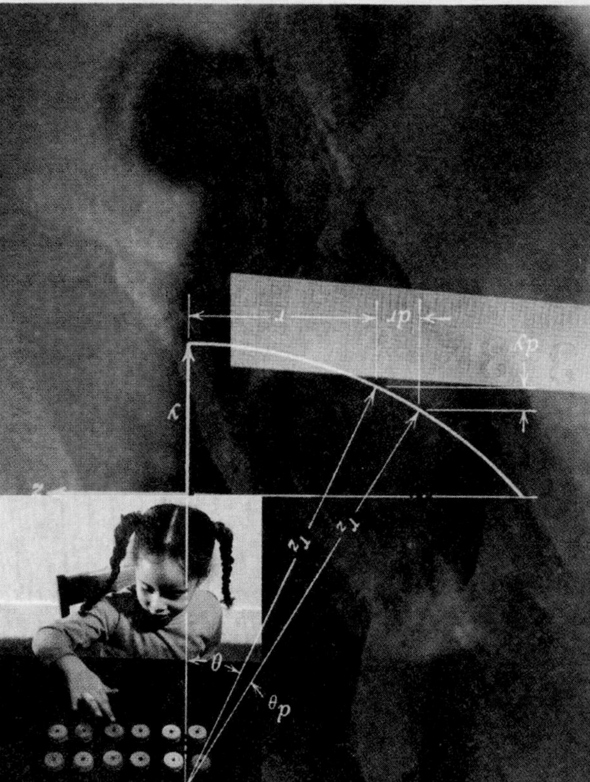

CHAPTER 2

The Methods of Psychology

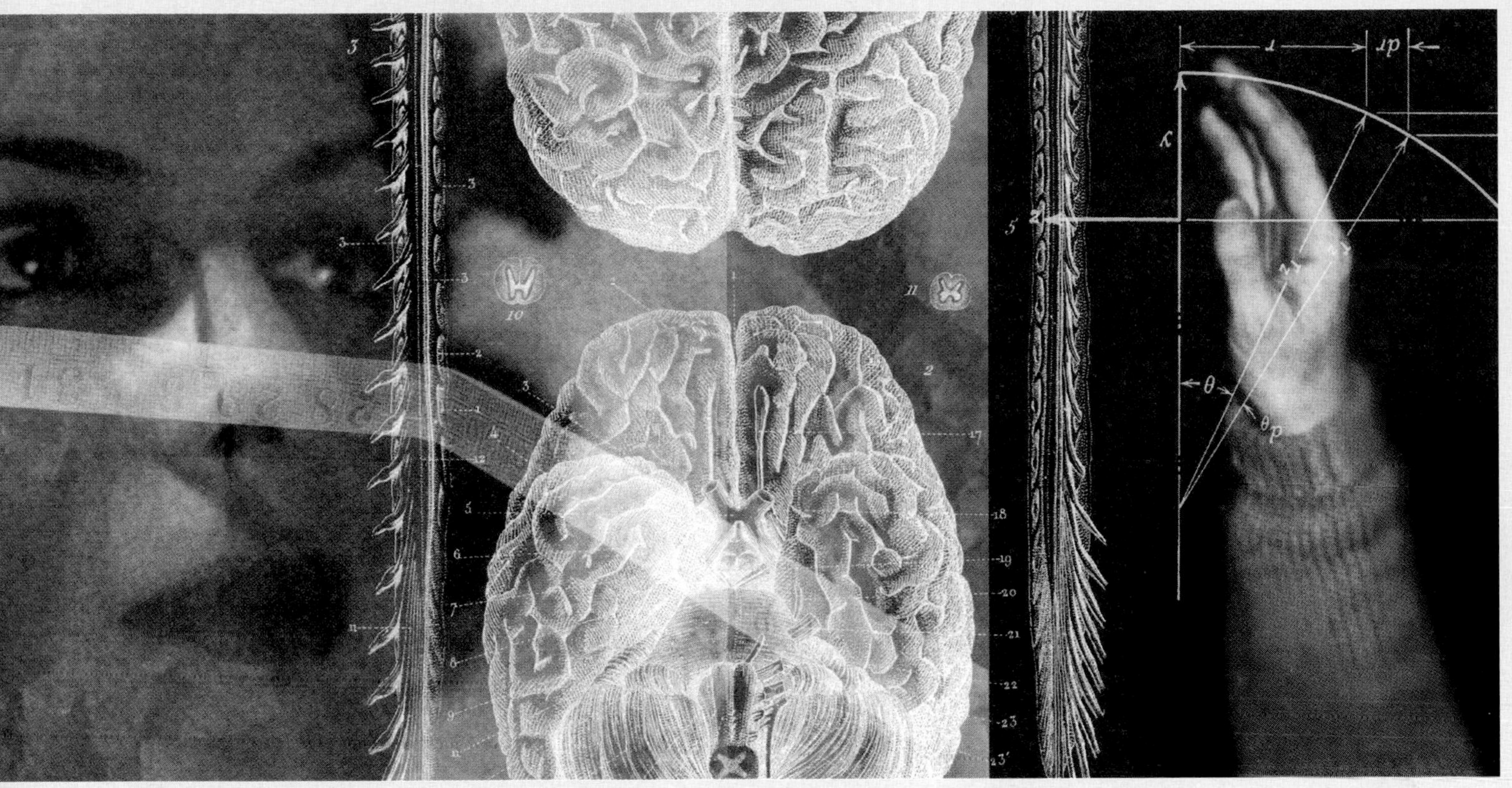

OBJECTIVES

After reading this chapter, you should be able to:

1. Explain the role of theory in psychological research, including how it relates to hypotheses, variables, operational definitions, and methods.
2. Describe psychological research based on case study, observational, correlational, and experimental methods.
3. Describe and discuss some benefits and problems of cross-cultural research.
4. Describe what validity of a psychological study is and identify various types of bias that can undermine it.
5. Identify ways to avoid unethical treatment of human beings and animals in research and practice.

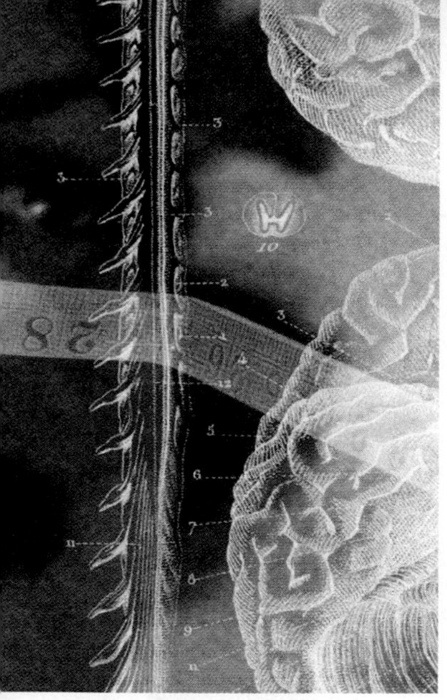

The creative aspect of psychological inquiry, the getting of ideas, does not distinguish it from other creative activities such as literature, art, and invention. What does set psychological and scientific inquiry apart is the manner of gathering, analyzing, and reporting facts.

—Ray Hyman (1965)

You wake up one morning feeling groggy and achy all over. Your nose is running, your throat feels like you've swallowed an elephant, your head is splitting. You drag yourself over to your medicine cabinet to look for some miracle drug to cure yourself, but alas, all you have is toothpaste. Then you remember your grandmother's oft-repeated advice, "Have some chicken soup if you want to cure a cold!" You prepare some chicken soup, eat as much as you can, and feel much better by mid-morning.

Chicken soup to cure the common cold is a common-sense remedy. Similarly, you might think that psychology is just common sense. But just as researchers have used scientific methods to find that there actually is something in chicken soup that does work on cold symptoms, so psychologists can take common-sense statements and beliefs (including such contradictory common-sense statements as "Absence makes the heart grow fonder" and "Out of sight, out of mind") and decide which of two or more conflicting statements is true, and under what conditions. Psychology is more and different from mere common sense because it uses scientific methods to establish truth.

To a psychologist, common-sense statements, even though they seem to have a "kernel of truth," cannot be accepted at face value. They must be tested. Psychologists have an extensive collection of sometimes ingenious scientific methods for investigating common-sense examples and other psychological questions. We use these methods to tell the difference between fact and fiction and to avoid being misled by theories that intuitively appeal, but nonetheless are false. In this age when "pop psychology" is a multimillion dollar business, when the public is barraged with claims of effectiveness for such things as astrology and psychic surgery, and when psychics offer 900 numbers (which people actually call), we cannot overstate the importance of learning to apply scientific methods to evaluate claims.

In short, B.S. (here B.S. stands for bad science) detectors are a requirement for living in the modern world. In this chapter, we take you "behind the scenes," introducing you to the way psychologists ask and answer the questions that generate the findings appearing in your newspapers and textbooks, including this one. Learning about psychological theories and methods will equip you with the critical thinking skills to begin to evaluate the merits of psychological knowledge as presented in the media.

Theories and Psychological Research

Psychologists develop theories and conduct research to understand and explain behavior. A *theory* attempts to make sense out of many disparate observations (or facts) by stating a general principle that connects, integrates, and explains them. To use the analogy of Jules-Henri Poincaré (1854–1912), "Science is built up of facts, as a house is with stones, but a collection of facts is no more a science than a heap of stones is a house." A coherent overriding structure is needed in both cases. In science, the theory provides this structure.

Anyone who has a pet knows that you can teach it new tricks by giving it rewards. But did you know that your animal's behavior will be more persistent and vigorous if you reward it only every so often, not every time? This procedure is well-known to animal trainers and

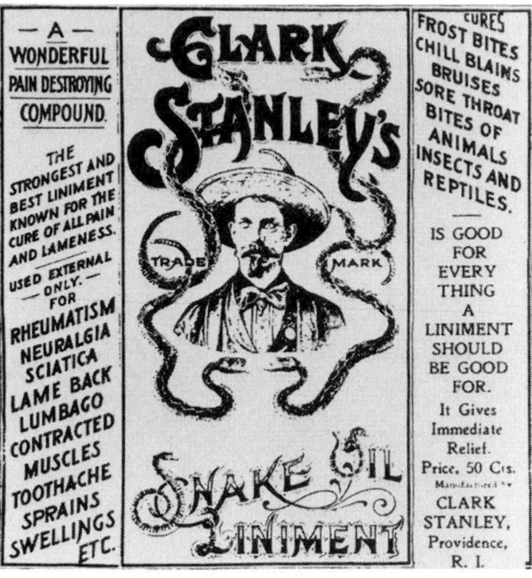

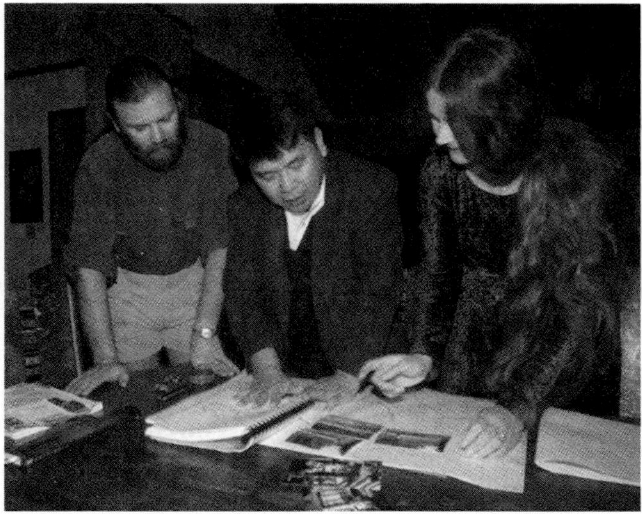

◀ *Real cures or placebos? Stanley's snake oil was advertised as a miracle cure for all ailments; in the ancient Chinese practice of* feng shui, *living spaces are aligned with nature and energy fields in order to ensure harmony and good fortune.*

works regardless of the animal—dog, cat, ferret—or the trick—sitting up, retrieving, licking your hand. How can you explain this phenomenon? Can you use your explanation to make predictions about training people? The principle in this example is called partial reinforcement, and there is a theory about how it works that you will learn about in Chapter 6. This theory explains a variety of observations about the use of rewards and gives them a special meaning. The theory gives you a basis for predicting what will happen if you try training other animals to do different things, as well as a starting point for designing experiments to test those predictions. Thus, theories organize individual observations and facts and put them in a context that gives them special meaning and relationship to one another.

The Role of Theories

A good theory is extremely valuable because it extends our knowledge beyond the facts in front of us (the raw data), enabling us to predict how *others* might behave, at another time and in another place. Theories may arise from many sources, including an investigator's personal observations or hunches, empirical findings from prior studies, or even as extensions of a previous theory. But there is no one grand theory in psychology that will explain all we know of human behavior and mental processes. To date, we have only limited theories that can be roughly classified into different perspectives, which we will call the biological, behavioral, cognitive, humanistic, and sociocultural perspectives.

The fact that psychology is a science means psychological theories are required to make *testable* predictions about *observable* behavior. That is, they must make predictions that can be objectively tested. Just because a theory is popularly accepted doesn't mean it is right. For example, people once incorrectly theorized that evil spirits caused mental disorders and would drill holes in a patient's skull to release them. Psychology requires that such theories be tested, rather than accepted based on hearsay. Researchers must even test psychological theories that deal with mental processes that can only be indirectly observed—for example, they might test theories about how people privately think by measuring how they publicly behave.

◀ *Psychologist John Chambers theorized that African Americans enjoy better health if they possess a strong sense of heritage. Here, Chambers is shown taking a blood-pressure reading as part of his research.*

Moreover, theories that deal with mental processes outside our conscious awareness must also make testable predictions.

Theories are the explanatory glue that puts psychological facts into a meaningful form. The basic task of psychological research is to *test* systematically whether the predictions of a particular psychological theory actually do occur.

Testing theories requires making observations of behavior in ways that can be reproduced and verified. For example, the observation that some battered women stay with husbands who beat them was once explained by a psychodynamic theory that said women were by nature masochistic; *ergo* (therefore) women liked to be abused, and were attracted to men who battered them. In fact, a notorious Russian politician and outspoken critic of President Boris Yeltsin, Vladimir Zhirinovsky, recently explained his own battering of a female colleague in the Russian Parliament by arguing that ". . . she enjoyed the experience." Although we can't observe masochism directly, we can determine whether women really do seek out relationships with batterers. In their efforts to test this theory, researchers have found that battered women typically start their relationships with "nice," loving partners. Battering emerges *after* a woman has fallen in love and made a commitment. Why do some women stay with an abusive partner? Many factors appear to play a role. In particular, battered women may have low self-esteem, or they may be afraid of being injured or killed if they try to leave their partner. Mothers often have children to think of, and they lack the education, job skills, and other resources that would permit them to support themselves and their children on their own. Contemporary theories about why battered women stay with their partners dismiss masochism and focus on gender roles and norms and on women's economic opportunities (Koss et al., 1994).

Theories provide explanations that link observations, suggest other factors to be studied, and provide predictions (hypotheses) about how such factors will be related to each other.

Theories give meaning to research findings. They shape the way we see the world and generate new questions that go beyond our previous observations. Ideas for generating theories can come from anywhere—there are no rules for the creative process of theory generation. Testing a theory is another matter entirely. There are procedures and rules that must be followed if a theory is to be verified by scientific methods.

THINKING CRITICALLY

Try your hand at an operational definition. How would you operationally define "learning"?

This is a hard one. Learning is the acquisition of new knowledge or new skill. Many operational definitions of learning have been attempted by psychologists. A behavioral approach might be to record the strength of a learned response over several trials. For example, you might conduct several brief study trials in which you would give your research participant a list of words to learn—apple, lettuce, bread, chicken, etc. You would record how many words the learner correctly remembers on a test after each trial. If learning occurs, recall performance should increase after each successive trial. Improvement in measured performance would be the operational definition of learning.

Some researchers think that learning is really an electrical or chemical change in the brain. Does this suggest another kind of operational definition of learning to you?

Testing Hypotheses

In order to test theories or hypotheses, we need to identify the variables that are being examined. A ***variable*** is a characteristic of anything that can take on two or more values. Variables are characteristics that differ among people, objects, or events over time or in quantity. The specific predictions about how one variable is related to another are called ***hypotheses***. Smoking, the probability of cancer, viewing television, and aggressive behavior are variables. "Smoking causes cancer" and "viewing violence on television increases aggressive behavior" are examples of hypotheses. Variables are the "things" that the hypotheses are trying to relate. Psychologists test the hypothesized relationship between variables through doing research.

Suppose you want to study the causes of fear. How might you go about it? You can use operational definitions for variables that can be measured and manipulated. ***Operational definitions*** define variables in terms of the procedures ("operations") used to produce or measure them. To study fear, for example, you need to define it in a way that permits measurement by you or anyone else who wants to repeat your study. You might define fear physiologically in terms of a rapidly beating heart and sweaty palms. You would then measure people's heart rate and how much their palms sweat to determine their level of fear. Alternatively, you could develop a behavioral assessment "a fear scale," on which you would ask participants to rate their level of fear under specified circumstances. Or you might try observing and recording the speed with which a person escapes from an aversive situation as a fear index. Can you think of other possible measures? The possibilities for operational definitions are bounded largely by the researcher's imagination. Given the wide variety of operational definitions possible for any particular concept, you will find it important to ask how the variables have been operationally defined when discussing the results of a particular study.

Psychologists thus use research methods to operationally define or produce and measure variables and test their relationships. They use these procedures and techniques to test a hypothesis. They can produce results consistent or inconsistent with that hypothesis. Either way, the results might suggest new theoretical ideas to be tested in a subsequent study. Figure 2-1 presents the flow of events involved in theory development, from theory to hypothesis to methods to hypothesis tests, leading either to confirmation or revision of the theory.

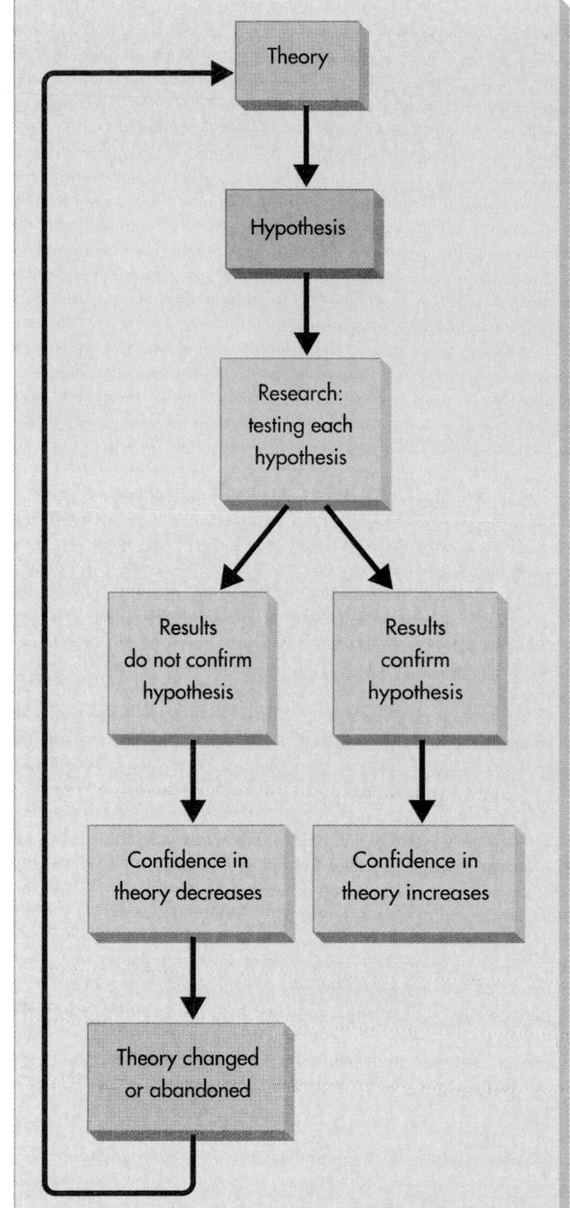

2-1 Steps in Developing a Theory

The steps in theory development are: (1) formulating a hypothesis or statement of a relationship between two (or more) variables that is predicted by the theory; (2) applying one or more methods to test that hypothesis; (3) evaluating the results, usually by statistical analysis; and (4) interpreting the results and deciding whether they confirm or contradict the hypothesis. Confidence in the theory increases or decreases in light of new results.

Types of Psychological Methods

Psychologists use a wide variety of methods to collect data and to test hypotheses derived from theories. They can be grouped into three different kinds of research: descriptive, correlational, and experimental. Each serves a different purpose. Descriptive research is aimed at portraying what has occurred under a given set of conditions. Thus, researchers might study how people react when they lose everything in a natural disaster to determine whether depression is a common consequence. Correlational research is designed to determine how strongly one variable relates to another. For example, researchers might study the strength of the relationship between fighting in the first year of a marriage and the likelihood of eventual divorce. For reasons we will discuss in a moment, neither of these methods can establish a clear cause-and-effect relationship. Experimental research is ideally suited to that purpose; in an experiment, one variable is manipulated to observe how it affects another variable. Other variables are held constant. So, researchers might manipulate the size of a reward to a learner to determine whether size changes the speed of learning, other things being equal.

► *An example of correlational research in action: the amount of alcohol in this driver's bloodstream is correlated with his ability to perform tasks, such as touching his nose and walking a straight line.*

These three types of methods—descriptive, correlational, and experimental—are not mutually exclusive. In fact, sometimes two or more types are applied in combination to the same problem. We might try to apply all three types, for example, to a question about how alcohol consumption affects behavior. When this can be done, the convergence of methods provides an especially strong foundation for claims about the effects of one variable on another.

Descriptive Research

Descriptive research portrays what occurs, for example, how people react to natural disasters like floods or tornadoes, or earthquakes. Two types of methods used to collect data in descriptive research are individual case studies and observational methods. The goal of descriptive research using these methods is to observe and record behavior, without intervention by the researcher. Descriptive research can be a treasure trove for generating theories about a wide variety of types of behavior.

Individual Case Studies

The ***case study*** method (or case history) provides descriptive data through intensive in-depth scrutiny of a single individual or a small group of individuals to find out as much as possible about what is going on with each. Often a combination of measures is used, including biographical data on the individual, scores on psychological tests, and information obtained by extensive interviews.

A case study is a descriptive research method that involves intensive in-depth examination of some aspect of the behavior of a single individual.

Case study procedures are most often used to investigate abnormal or unusual behavior. One familiar example of these procedures, based on a case study of a woman with multiple personality states, was used in the classic 1957 movie *The Three Faces of Eve.* The film portrayed the woman's three identities, each distinct in style and interests from the others. One of them was bland and nonsocial (Eve White); another was outgoing and sometimes abrasive (Eve Black); a third (Jane), which emerged during therapy, was relatively more balanced and seemed to be aware of both Eve White and Eve Black. As in the real case of Chris Sizemore (who later was found to have even more identities), Eve shifted from one personality state to another, even within a single conversation, often without awareness. By examining the case histories of patients like "Eve," psychologists have developed theories of the causes of dissociative identity disorder (once known as multiple personality disorder), the most important of which appears to be child abuse (see Chapter 15).

Case studies are particularly useful when a researcher ventures into new areas where the relevant variables are unknown. Early case studies of alcoholic individuals, for example, stimulated interest in alcohol's effect on the nervous system and behavior (Pinel, 1990). Thus, case studies of alcoholic individuals revealed memory loss that seemed to increase with age. This observation led to the discovery that alcohol use could lead to vitamin deficiencies that could affect nerve cells crucial to memory. But case studies have limitations. While they are valuable in the early stages of formulating theories and hypotheses, they cannot be used to establish causation. They also don't necessarily generalize to the larger population, because the case may be exceptional and unusual and hence not representative of the general population. Finally, there is a danger of researcher bias if, for example, the researcher, through extensive contact, becomes so personally involved with the case that it undermines his or her ability to consider multiple interpretations of the data.

Naturalistic Observation

Naturalistic observation is a research method for systematically measuring and recording events as they occur naturally in the real world, without interfering in any way with these events. The use of naturalistic observation has

SEEKING SOLUTIONS

Understanding Behavior Through a Case Study

How are our brains organized? How are our brains involved in perceptions? Could you have serious brain damage and not even realize it? Important insights into these questions can be found in neurologist Oliver Sacks's "The Man Who Mistook His Wife for a Hat," which provides a case study of a man with damage to the right side of his brain. The classic story of Dr. P. demonstrates the usefulness of the case study method.

> Dr. P. was a musician of distinction, well-known for many years as a singer, and then, at the local School of Music, as a teacher. Sometimes a student would present himself, and Dr. P. would not recognize him; or, specifically, would not recognize his face. The moment the student spoke, he would be recognized by his voice. Such incidents multiplied, causing embarrassment, perplexity, fear—and, sometimes, comedy. For not only did Dr. P. increasingly fail to see faces, but he saw faces when there were no faces to see: when in the street he might be found genially, Magoo-like, patting the heads of water hydrants and parking meters, taking these to be the heads of children; he would amiably address carved knobs on the furniture and be astounded when they did not reply. At first these odd mistakes were laughed off as jokes, not least by Dr. P. himself. Had he not always had a quirky sense of humour and been given to Zen-like paradoxes and jests? His musical powers were as dazzling as ever; he did not feel ill—he had never felt better; and the mistakes were so ludicrous—and so ingenious—that they could hardly be serious or betoken anything serious. . . . How could he, on the one hand, mistake his wife for a hat (as he did on one occasion) and, on the other, function, as apparently he still did, as a teacher at the Music School? . . .
>
> He saw nothing as familiar. Visually, he was lost in a world of lifeless abstractions. He construed the world as a computer construes it, by means of key features and schematic relationships. The scheme might be identified—in an "identi-kit" way—without the reality being grasped at all.
>
> The testing I had done so far told me nothing about Dr. P.'s inner world. Was it possible that his visual memory and imagination were still intact? I asked him to imagine entering one of our local squares from the north side, to walk through it, in imagination or in memory, and tell me the buildings he might pass as he walked. He listed the buildings on his right side, but none of those on his left. I then asked him to imagine entering the square from the south. Again he mentioned only those buildings that were on the right side, although these were the very buildings he omitted before.

The fact that Dr. P. could do some things quite well (he was good at identifying physical features), but not others (he couldn't tell his shoe from his foot), suggests that the brain is specialized in certain ways. Dr. P.'s brain was able to detect features of stimuli normally, but it could not put the features together into meaningful wholes. Specific perceptual problems like this result from damage to particular parts of the brain. This provides support for a theory that views the brain as a collection of independent functioning parts or modules. Moreover, it also demonstrates that more than one part of the brain is usually involved in a particular behavior or perception. Sacks' study of Dr. P. uses the case study method. It capitalizes on the existence and discovery of this unique individual. In science, we normally want more than one example of a phenomenon, but people like Dr. P. are rare. Psychologists might try to follow up this case study by conducting an experiment using brain-damaged animals as subjects. They could try to determine whether any behavioral changes, similar to those exhibited by Dr. P., could be produced. Thus, the findings from case study observation could be further refined through controlled experimentation to determine causes of particular behaviors that have been observed.

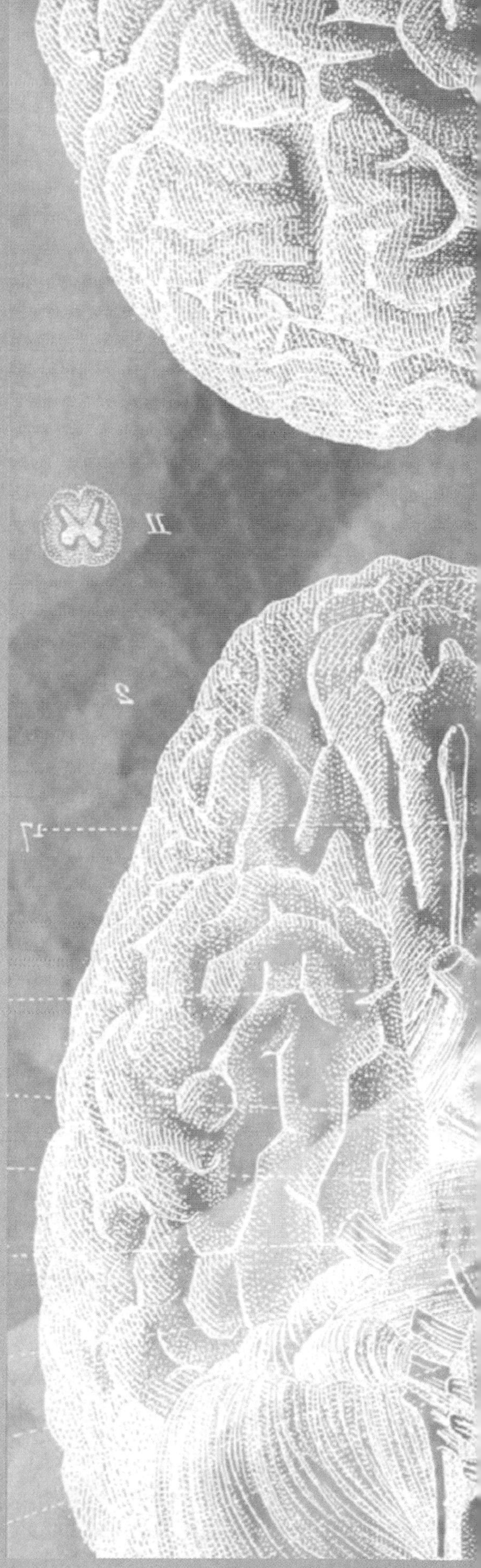

Source: Excerpted from Oliver Sacks, *The Man Who Mistook His Wife for a Hat and Other Clinical Tales* (NY: Harper & Row, 1987, pp. 8–22).

provided important knowledge about the conditions under which human beings and other animals develop, learn, and live. Airports, shopping centers, museums, playgrounds, classrooms, homes, supermarkets, libraries, subways, assembly lines, parks, wards in mental hospitals—these are just a few of the settings for naturalistic observation of human behavior.

Naturalistic observations in psychology are usually taken on individuals behaving or interacting in a normal or typical environment

Naturalistic observation usually entails numerous measures of several individuals, taken without manipulating or controlling anything in the situation. The methods used for this purpose are sometimes called unobtrusive measures because the researcher acts merely as a bystander, the proverbial "fly on the wall." The researcher might observe from behind a one-way mirror, from a distance, or using electronic surveillance equipment, while the subjects are unaware that they are being observed. In studies of animal behavior in natural settings, the investigators usually conceal themselves in the background, where the animals will not notice them.

THE FAR SIDE By GARY LARSON

"For crying out loud, that's us! Someone's installed the one way mirror in backward!"

Naturalistic observation is particularly important when artificial manipulations of a phenomenon might interfere with or destroy it. For example, if a researcher wants to know about how competence and self-esteem relate to behavior in the classroom, bringing a child into a controlled laboratory setting is unlikely to answer the question. The researcher would be better off going to the classroom and observing how children behave in the natural setting. Behavioral coding schemes can be pre-established to allow observers to record systematically all behaviors reflecting competence, evidence of high and low self-esteem, and depression. Analysis of these recordings can tell the researcher if low self-esteem and the tendency to act depressed occur together in the natural setting.

Participant observation is a form of observational research in which the investigator joins a group. This approach was used in a famous study called "When Prophecy Fails" by Leon Festinger and his colleagues (Festinger, Riecken, & Schachter, 1956). In the early 1950s, a charismatic leader named Marion Keech claimed to have received messages from outer space predicting that on December 21, 1950, a flood would destroy the world. Keech and followers were to be rescued by a flying saucer, however. Keech attracted a group of loyal followers who believed the prophecy to the point of selling their homes, quitting their jobs, and giving away their possessions. The researchers were interested in how the group members would react when their prophecy didn't come true—how would they handle such a blow to their belief system? How could the researchers observe the reaction? They couldn't just hang over a fence and unobtrusively observe the group members' behavior as they waited for the flying saucer to pick them up. So they pretended to believe the prophecy, joined the group, and observed what happened as the deadline for the cataclysm came and went without incident. This study provided a demonstration and test of the theory of cognitive dissonance (see Chapter 12), in the sense that followers sought to justify their actions and to reconcile the fact that the flood had not come. The leader of the group solved the dissonance problem by announcing that the flood had been stopped and the world saved as a reward to those who had believed in the prophecy and given up everything. Now, with dissonance eliminated, the faithful could go home with their beliefs intact. The "Heaven's Gate" incident in which a large number of cult members committed suicide together in 1997 provides a recent opportunity to observe cult members' reaction to prophecy's failure, but in this case, there seem to be few survivors to follow.

▶ Because verbal skills in young children are limited, the observational method is often used in studying them.

Advantages and Limitations of Descriptive Research

The observational method allows research to be conducted on important natural phenomena that should be examined scientifically and that would be impossible or unethical to reproduce in the laboratory. For example, it is important to understand how people react under conditions of extreme stress or bereavement, but it is impossible to create these situations artificially. However, we can learn quite a bit about how people cope with these stressors by observing the behavioral aftermath of a flood, a tornado, or other natural catastrophes. Such research has produced important benefits to people who live through such natural disasters, as psychologists learn how to counsel people who have lost friends, family, and cherished possessions in a disaster.

Unlike case studies, where the researcher relies on the subject's own memory of what happened, naturalistic observations are made by an objective observer while the behavior is taking place. This is clearly an advantage. But there are possible disadvantages if the behavior of the subject is altered by the presence of an observer, or if the observer is not completely objective or unbiased. Another limitation of this method is that causation cannot be established because no variables are either manipulated or controlled.

Naturalistic observation can raise certain ethical questions. Is it ethically acceptable for a scientist to observe and record people's behavior without their knowledge and consent? How would you feel if you found out, after the fact, that a psychologist had videotaped you at a party without your knowledge? In a real case, government researchers wanted to observe the effects of LSD on people. They conducted an experiment in which people were given LSD without their knowledge. One subject who was given LSD leapt to his death while under the effects of the drug. The family subsequently sued the government for the wrongful death of the man. A tough question for every study is: Do the benefits gained from observing people under these conditions outweigh the ethical cost of taking the observation without their consent?

Correlational Approaches

Correlational approaches seek to discover the strength and direction of the (co-)relationship, or the ***correlation***, between two variables. As you know, a variable is any characteristic of an object, event, or person that can take two or more values. Some examples are self-esteem, depression, competence, or assertiveness. Thus researchers might measure pleasant events and depression to see how they relate to each other. Unlike naturalistic observation, where the goal of observing is to describe some behavior in detail, the goal of correlational approaches is to determine the nature of the relationship between variables.

To determine the correlation between variables, researchers compute a statistic called a ***correlation coefficient***, which is a number that can range in value from +1.0 to −1.0 (see Appendix for an explanation of how to compute a correlation coefficient). The correlation coefficient represents both the strength and the direction of a relationship. The strength is indicated by the *absolute size* of the number. Thus, if a change in one variable is matched perfectly by a change in a second variable, that relationship would have a correlation coefficient of 1.0. For example, if we measured the distance between several pairs of U.S. cities first in miles and then in meters, we would expect the two sets of measurements to have a correlation of 1.0. Because there is rarely a perfect relationship between one variable and another in studies of human behavior, however, we can expect to find correlations in psychological research that are greater than 0 but less than 1.0. For example, the correlation between intelligence and grade

THINKING CRITICALLY

Which represents the stronger relationship, a correlation of +.45 or one of −.45?

Did you say neither? That's right—the sign (plus or minus) only represents the direction of the relationship. The absolute size of the number—.45—represents the strength of the relationship. In this example, the number is the same size in both cases. What's the difference between the two relationships being described? In the former, +.45, both scores vary in the same direction (as one goes up, so does the other). For the latter, −.45, the scores vary in opposite directions (as one goes up, the other goes down).

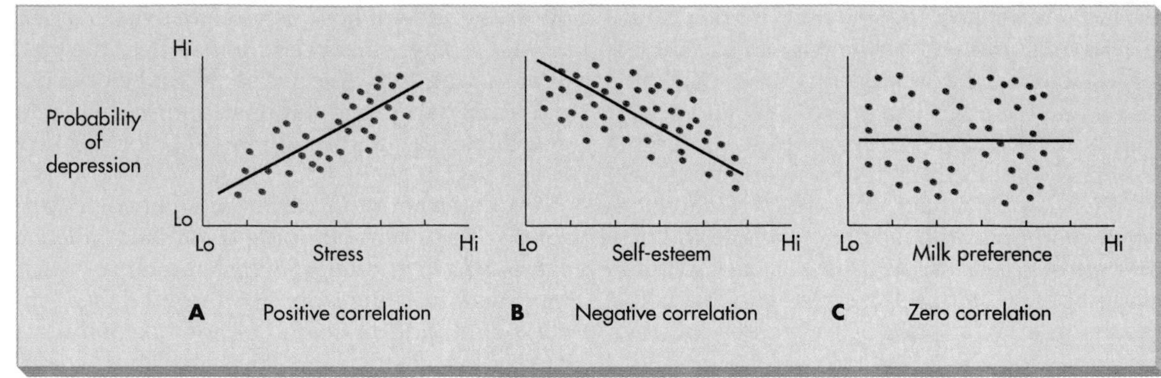

2-2 The Concept of Correlation

When two variables are correlated, one can be used to predict the other. If the relationship is positive (A), when one variable increases the other one does as well. As stress increases, so does the probability of depression. If the relationship is negative (B), when one variable increases, the other one decreases. As self-esteem increases, the probability of depression decreases. When there is no relationship between the two variables, they vary at random and one cannot be used to predict the other (C). There is no relationship between liking milk and the probability of depression.

point average in grade school is around .50, which is considered to be reasonably strong for many purposes. A correlation of 0 would mean, of course, that there was no relationship between the two variables—a change in one would not predict a change in the other. You might expect a 0 correlation between the probability of sunshine in New York and the price of eggs in China.

Correlation coefficients also indicate the direction of a relationship—whether the relationship is positive or negative (see Figure 2-2). If a correlation is positive (indicated by a plus sign in front of the number), it means that as one variable increases, so does the other. So, study time and test scores have a positive correlation because, as you study more, you are likely to do better on an exam. If the correlation coefficient is negative (shown by a minus sign), it means that as the value of one variable increases, the value of the other will go down. Thus, as your hours of sleep increase, your feeling of tiredness will decrease.

We can use the correlational approach to test theories that have been derived from case studies and naturalistic observations. For example, we can test whether self-esteem is related to depression. Because it is obviously unethical to damage anyone's self-esteem to see if that will cause severe depression, the correlational approach is probably the best way to try to examine this relationship. To test the theory, we need to develop some precise self-report or survey measures of depression and self-esteem. We can conduct surveys of a sample of people from the general population. For each person in the study, there would be two scores, one for self-esteem and one for depression. The object would be to determine whether self-esteem scores and depression scores vary, or change, together. Researchers have indeed found such a relationship—the higher the depression score, the lower the self-esteem score (Turner & Roszell, 1994). Note that the direction of the relationship is inverse, and therefore the correlation coefficient is negative.

While it is extremely useful to know the relationship between variables, a correlation does not mean that one variable causes the other to change. Thus, for example, although we know that feelings of self-esteem are negatively correlated with depression, lack of such feelings does not necessarily *cause* depression. Maybe it's the other way around. Maybe depression lowers feelings of self-esteem. Maybe they mutually affect each other. Or maybe there's a third variable that causes both. You know that self-esteem is correlated with depression. Perhaps higher self-esteem leads both to greater feelings of competence and to lower levels of depression. In fact, self-esteem, feelings of competence, and depression are all correlated with each other (Turner & Roszell, 1994). But simply knowing they are correlated cannot tell us which causes which—or whether there is yet another variable, for example, something genetic, affecting them all.

Specific data collection techniques are often used in correlational research, including psychological tests, interviews, and surveys. In each of these techniques, participants respond to questions selected and designed to measure well-defined variables. Their responses are then analyzed to determine if, on the average, measures of one variable change significantly with changes in others.

◀ Psychologists in South Africa give workers at a platinum mine a problem to solve, hoping to identify which ones will emerge as leaders.

Psychological Tests

Most of us have had experiences with psychological tests at school or at work. Psychologists have developed and standardized psychological tests to measure just about any kind of behavior you can imagine, from religiosity to sexuality. These tests generally consist of some number of objective, multiple-choice type questions, administered according to a rigorous procedure. ***Diagnostic tests*** are tests that are used for both clinical and research purposes. They include intelligence tests, which are tests of general ability, and tests of specific personality traits; both kinds of tests are commonly administered in the United States as part of educational or job application processes.

To be useful, a test must have ***validity***; that is, it must measure what it is supposed to measure. A test that is supposed to measure intelligence but that actually measures how hard you try on the test is not valid. And a test must also have ***reliability***; it must give the same score if it is given to the same individual a second time. An intelligence test that says that you are mentally retarded on one day and a genius on the next is not a reliable test of intelligence.

Interviews

Both psychological tests and interviews are often used in conjunction with the case study method. An ***unstructured interview*** does not have specific questions; rather it allows for free, wide-ranging probing, such as, "Tell me more about your relationship with your family." The subject of the questions may change based on the interviewer's hypotheses about what is behind the interviewee's responses. ***Structured interviews***, on the other hand, typically consist of a series of prearranged questions. Structured interviews are often employed to collect data from a sample of people selected from a larger population. The data are then used to draw conclusions about how people in the larger population behave. Corporations often hire psychologists and marketing experts to conduct this type of interview to determine the public's reaction to their products. Sometimes the research is descriptive in purpose (for example, how many people like "Brand X"), and sometimes the research is designed to identify relationships among variables (for example, are women more likely to buy "Brand X" than men?).

Surveys

Surveys fall somewhere between interviews and psychological tests. They consist of a series of pre-set questions, with little flexibility to probe in other directions. The purpose of a survey (sometimes conducted as an opinion poll) is typically to determine general opinions, attitudes, feelings, or behaviors related to a specific issue. For example, the National Opinion Research Center of the University of Chicago periodically conducts a survey of adult sexual

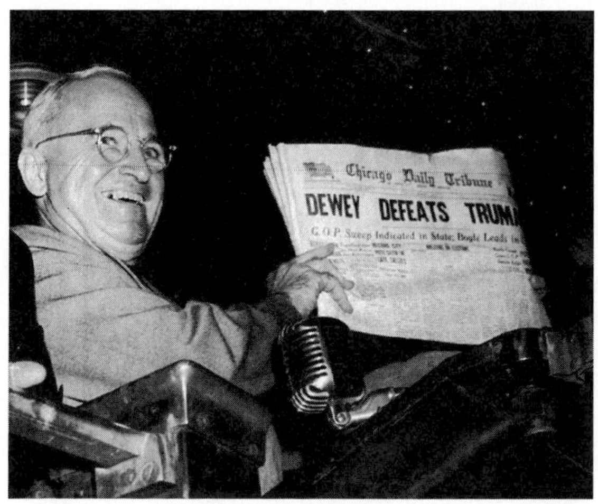

◀ When surveys fail: the editor of the Chicago Daily Tribune put too much confidence in a Gallop Poll predicting Thomas Dewey's victory over Harry Truman in the 1948 Presidential election. Truman was delighted to point out the error.

Correlational research seeks to discover relationships among variables and to use that information to predict one variable from another. Data collection techniques used by psychologists in correlational research include psychological tests, surveys, and interviews. Correlational research is particularly useful when it is neither possible nor ethical to manipulate the variables of interest.

behavior in the United States, the data from which are used by the National Institutes of Health to formulate national health policy (Smith, 1990).

Biases in Correlational Research

The positive side of survey research is that peoples' true opinions can be expressed painlessly through this medium. When conducted as opinion polls, these results can directly influence important political and social decisions. But biases can creep into research in many ways. Opinion polls can be manipulated (for example, by using questions designed to elicit certain answers) to make them appear to favor policies that the pollsters want supported (Tversky & Kahneman, 1971). Moreover, participants may not give their true opinions, either because they don't understand the questions or because they say what they think is socially desirable or will please the interviewer. One of the essential research skills for the development of test and questionnaire items is the ability to select and word questions to minimize biases.

Sampling bias is another potential problem for correlational research. For example, if a sample of research participants is not representative of the larger population, the research will have limited generality. By "representative," we mean that all individuals in the population have an equal chance of being included in the study, even though only a few will be selected. A representative sample does not differ in any systematic way from the larger population. When evaluating correlational research, carefully scrutinize the nature of the sample of people who were studied. How were they recruited to participate? If the sample is not representative of the larger population from which it is supposed to come, watch out! The results may be so misleading as to be potentially harmful.

THINKING CRITICALLY

Does a large correlation between two variables mean that changes in one variable *cause* changes in the other?

The answer is no. Consider the following example. Stanovich (1986) was interested in predicting use of birth control methods. So he collected data in Taiwan on a large number of behavioral and environmental variables. Can you guess which variable was most strongly correlated with use of birth control procedures? Answer: The number of electric appliances (fans, toasters, etc.) in the household. The larger the number of appliances, the more likely contraception was being used. Are you now prepared to argue for passing out toasters to combat teenage pregnancy? Not likely. Two variables, like number of home appliances and birth control use, can be related (correlated) without one being a cause of the other. They are probably both related to one or more other variables, like income or educational level, which underlie or are the real cause of the correlation. If you understand that, you've got the basic concept of correlation and its distinction from cause and effect.

Experimental Methods

Case studies, observational techniques, and correlational methods provide important information about human behavior, but they suffer from a common limitation. Because these methods do not involve manipulating and controlling variables, they do not allow firm conclusions to be drawn about ***cause-effect relationships.*** For most psychologists, it is not enough to know that one thing changes as another one changes (i.e., co-varies with another); we want to know *why* things vary together. That is, we want to understand the *causes* of behavior. The experimental method provides the tool for identifying cause-effect relationships.

The basic logic of the experimental method is illustrated any time we wonder about "What causes what?" For example, you might wonder if garlic causes a difference in the flavor of spaghetti sauce; to find out, you'd vary the amount of garlic on different occasions to see whether and how the flavor changes. Or you might wonder if changing your training routine would improve your time in a ten-kilometer race. What makes the scientific experimental method different from these everyday examples is the systematic rigor and care taken in manipulating conditions and using precise, accurate, and sensitive measures of the variables of interest.

Independent and Dependent Variables

How do you run an experiment to determine a causal relationship between two variables? First you need an ***independent variable***, the variable hypothesized to cause or influence the behavior or process you are studying. Then you need to define a ***dependent variable***, the variable that is hypothetically caused by the independent variable. Figure 2-3 presents an example of a simple experimental design to determine whether watching violence on television, an independent variable, increases the likelihood of violent behavior, a dependent variable (i.e., to see if it is *dependent* on the manipulation of the *independent* variable). To do the experiment, you need: (1) two or more equivalent groups of research participants; (2) an independent variable controlled and manipulated by the experimenter (for example, hours exposed to TV violence), and (3) a dependent variable that you can accurately measure (number of violent actions). Your goal is to determine whether the number of violent actions by participants changes when you manipulate the number of hours spent watching TV violence. If you increase the number of hours spent watching TV violence and there is an increase in violent actions (for example, more hitting, kicking, or biting), you can assume that the independent variable has caused the dependent variable to change.

After you have hypothesized a relationship between two variables, you select a sample of research participants and divide them, in the

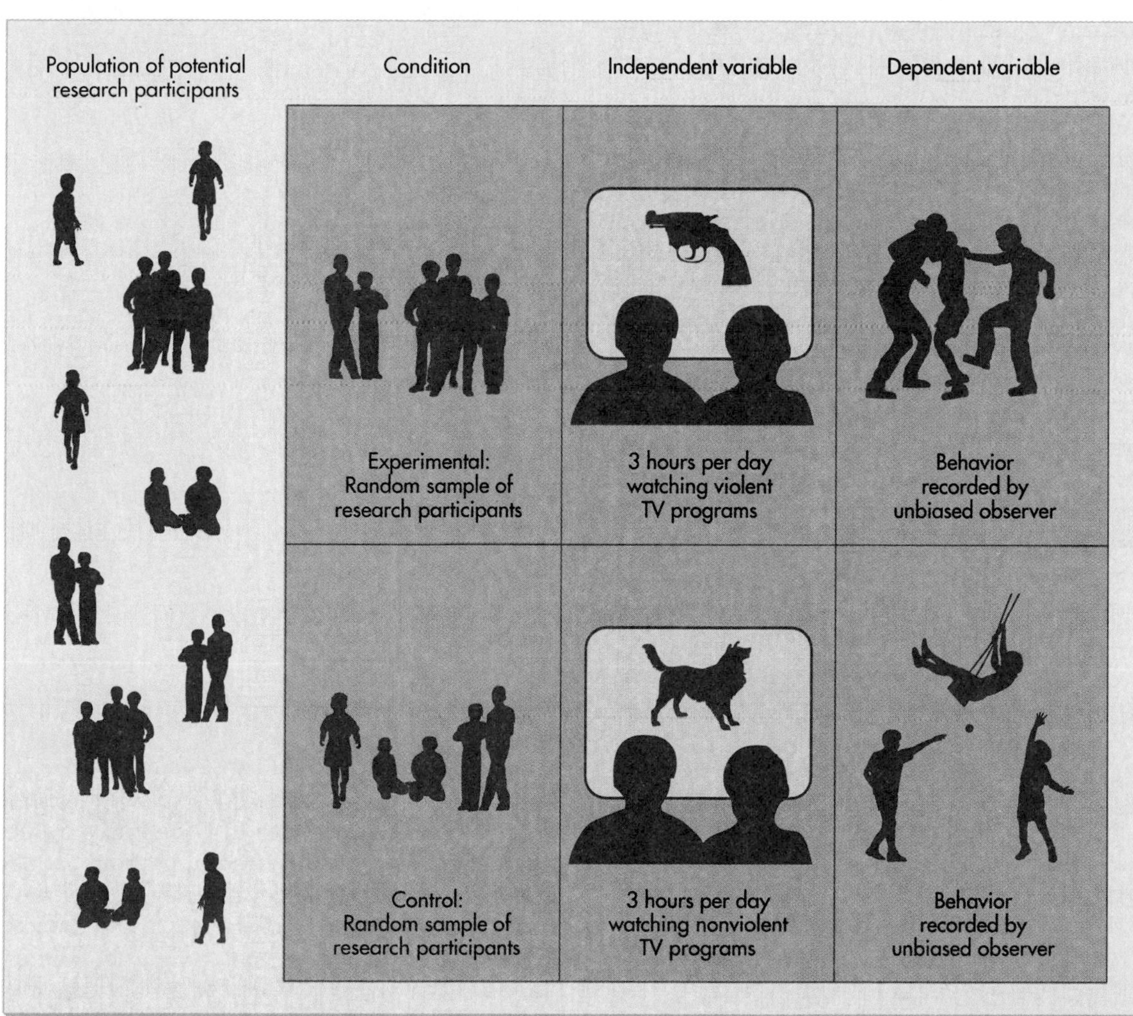

2-3 The Design of an Experiment

Here is a schematic example of an experimental design. After stating the hypothesis that watching violence on TV increases aggression, the experimenter must define conditions and randomly assign research participants to them. The experiment thus begins with two equivalent groups of participants. Manipulation of the independent variable (in this case, watching a violent or nonviolent TV program) must be the only difference between the two conditions of the experiment. Whenever possible, the person who measures the dependent variable (in this case, aggressive behavior) should be unbiased, that is, the experimenter should not know the hypothesis being tested. (Source: Based on Josephson, 1987).

The independent variable is manipulated, and the dependent variable is measured by the experimenter. If there is a relationship, the independent variable is considered to be the cause and the dependent variable the effect.

simplest case, into two groups: an ***experimental group***, which experiences the condition of interest (for example, viewing TV violence for X hours), and a ***control group***, which does not (for example, no TV viewing). The independent variable is number of hours spent watching TV violence—in the experimental group, X hours and in the control group O hours. You treat the groups identically except for the manipulated independent variable, which your hypothesis says will affect the dependent variable. If you find out that, after these experiences, the groups are no longer equal with regard to the dependent variable, then you can conclude that the independent variable *caused* the difference.

If we design the experiment so that the two groups experience everything in the same way except that one group is exposed to more of the independent variable, then any observable difference in the dependent variable is logically caused by the independent variable. It could not be caused by anything else, because nothing else was allowed to vary. But, if we don't control our experiment properly, variables other than the independent variable might influence the dependent variable. If a variable is unintentionally allowed to co-vary with the independent variable, it is called a ***confounding variable***. For example, suppose you selected the participants for the experimental group from School A in an urban neighborhood and the participants for the control group from School B in a more rural area. Let's suppose that the results of the experiment support your hypothesis—the experimental group commits more violent acts after exposure to TV violence. Great! But if urban kids are, for some reason, more violent than rural kids, there might be a problem with that interpretation. We can't be sure that the difference in TV viewing conditions produced our results when subject population is confounded with it. Differences in the inherent violence of the two populations rather than differences in TV viewing might have produced the results. Interpretation of the data is simply not clear. For the outcome to be unambiguous, you would have to test both urban and rural research participants in both viewing con-

Random assignment of subjects in an experiment means that each subject has the same probability of being assigned to a particular group or condition.

THINKING CRITICALLY

In a study to discover if having psychotherapy is effective in curing addictive behaviors such as cigarette smoking, researchers created two groups: (1) people who had had psychotherapy, and (2) people who had not. The researchers found the cure rate was *lower* for the group of people who had had psychotherapy (that is, people in the group who hadn't had psychotherapy were more likely to be cured). Would that lead you to conclude that psychotherapy is ineffective for curing smoking? If not, why not?

The answer lies in the importance of random assignment for interpreting research results. Cigarette smokers were not randomly assigned to two equal groups. Rather, groups were formed by self-selection. People themselves decided whether or not to try psychotherapy. As it happens, people who turn to psychotherapy for help are likely to have more difficult problems than those who do not. Further, they seek psychotherapy only after they have found self-cures to be ineffective (Schachter, 1982). Because people with the most serious problems turn to psychotherapy, it is their choice (self-selection) that determines whether they end up in the experiment's psychotherapy group. Because self-selection rather than random assignment determines the composition of the experimental and control groups, the findings give an erroneous picture of psychotherapy's effectiveness. This study did not produce valid results because it did not use random assignment to create comparison groups.

Gahan Wilson Sunday Comics reprinted courtesy of the Register and Tribune Syndicate, Inc.

► *The techniques that psychologists employ sometimes affect the behavior they are trying to measure.*

ditions. Part of being a successful researcher is to take the discovery of confounding variables in stride—and to respond by designing more carefully controlled experiments!

Random Assignment and Control Groups

Psychologists select and assign research participants to two or more equivalent groups through a process of ***random assignment***, whereby each participant is as likely to be assigned to one group as to another. This procedure distinguishes the experimental method from other research methods and is crucial for achieving valid experimental results. Experimenters hope to create groups in which the differences between group members occur at random. Thus, random assignment equalizes groups on all factors except the independent variable. If an experimental difference occurs, experimenters can then conclude that it was caused by the independent variable.

Researchers can make random or unbiased assignments in various ways. For example, as people arrive at the laboratory, the experimenter can toss a coin and assign the "heads" participants to one group and the "tails" participants to the other. The experimenter needs to use enough participants in each group so that, on average, the groups are about equal on basic background variables such as natural anxiety, intelligence, gender, or any other factor that might affect the dependent variable in the experiment.

If we wanted to assess the effects of a newly created drug on behavior, we would need an experimental group that takes the drug and a control group that does not. In our study of the effects of television violence, the experimental group is the group that watched violent television shows and the control group is the group that watched nonviolent television shows. We might set up the experiment so that the participants in the experimental group would watch three hours of violent TV shows and the participants in the control group would watch three hours of nonviolent TV shows (see Figure 2-3). At the end of the three hours, we would observe the participants in both groups to see if violent behavior (such as kicks, punches, yells) increased in the experimental group but not in the control group.

Why do you need a control group? For one reason, just knowing that you are in a research

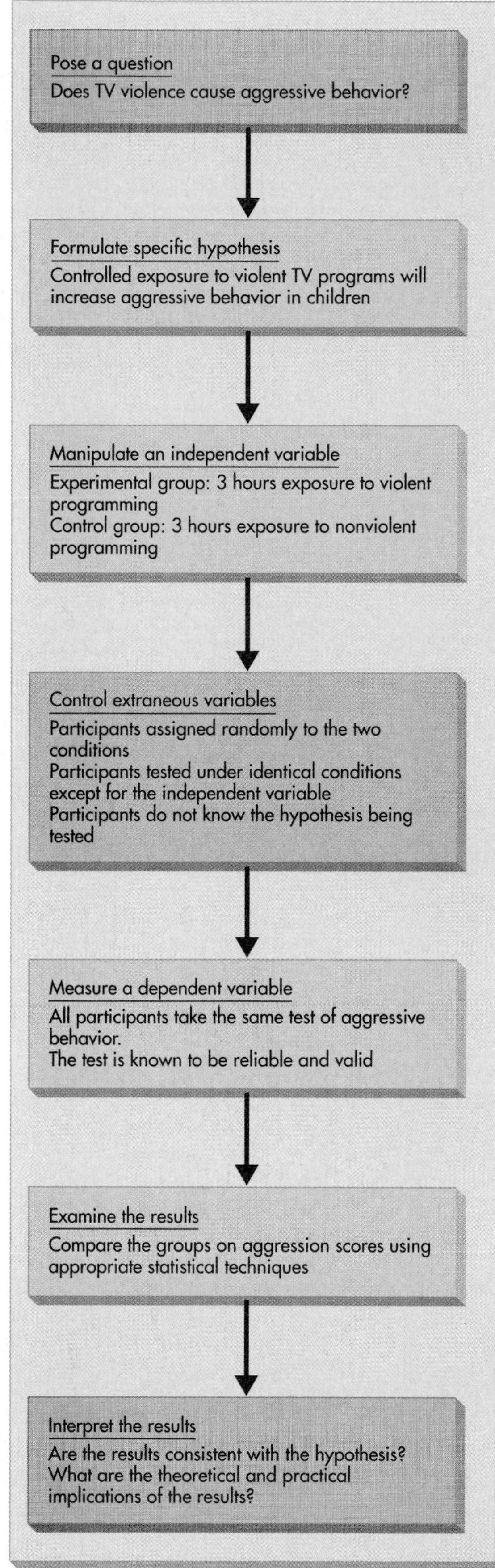

Pose a question
Does TV violence cause aggressive behavior?
Formulate specific hypothesis
Controlled exposure to violent TV programs will increase aggressive behavior in children
Manipulate an independent variable
Experimental group: 3 hours exposure to violent programming
Control group: 3 hours exposure to nonviolent programming
Control extraneous variables
Participants assigned randomly to the two conditions
Participants tested under identical conditions except for the independent variable
Participants do not know the hypothesis being tested
Measure a dependent variable
All participants take the same test of aggressive behavior.
The test is known to be reliable and valid
Examine the results
Compare the groups on aggression scores using appropriate statistical techniques
Interpret the results
Are the results consistent with the hypothesis?
What are the theoretical and practical implications of the results?

2-4 Schematics of an Experiment

An experimenter poses a question, formulates a hypothesis, randomly assigns participants to an experimental or control group, manipulates the independent variable and sees whether the dependent variable has changed. The experimenter then examines and interprets the results to see if they are consistent with the hypothesis and to explain their implications for theory and practice.

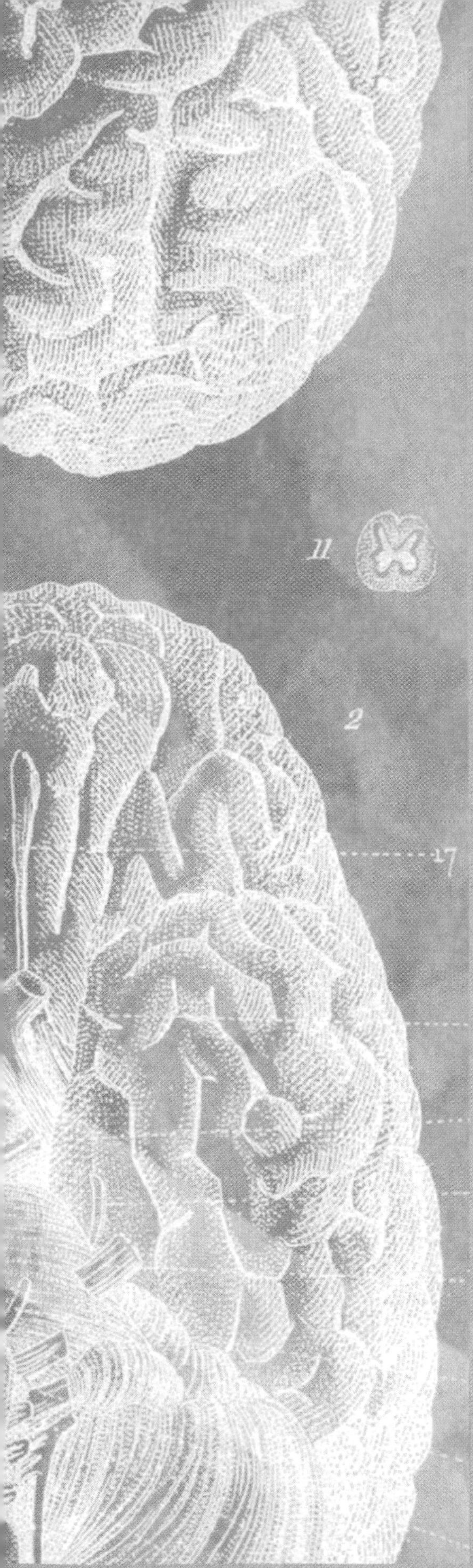

SEEKING SOLUTIONS

Do We Need Our Dreams?

Everyone dreams. But what happens if your dreaming is interrupted? The mysteries of dreaming—the reasons we dream and the relationship of dreaming to health and well-being—are of great interest to psychologists, especially those who study human consciousness and its altered states. Correlational and experimental methods can be applied to examine psychoanalytic theory's hypothesis that the function of dreams is to release pent-up psychic energy; that is, to get rid of tensions from anxiety-producing events that have occurred when we're awake (Antrobus, 1990). Using this theory, we can further hypothesize that exposure to anxiety-producing information increases one's need to dream and that if someone is not permitted to dream, he or she will become abnormally anxious. To study the relationship of dreaming to anxiety, we first have to develop objective measures of dreaming and anxiety. But how can we tell whether a sleeping person is actually having a dream? And how can we measure anxiety?

There is a fairly reliable sign of dreaming during sleep, called rapid eye movements (REMs). If you wake a sleeper whose eyes are moving about rapidly, the person usually reports having been interrupted during a dream (Dement, 1974). Using sophisticated equipment that can record the electrical activity in muscles that control the movement of the eyeball, researchers have found that people do not dream continuously throughout sleep, but only during relatively brief time periods. We can measure anxiety in many ways, including paper and pencil tests, activity sensors (how much a person fidgets in his or her chair), and physiological indices, such as heart rate, the amount of electrical activity on the skin, and the presence of certain (anxiety-related) hormones in the bloodstream.

We can use the experimental approach to test our hypothesis about tension release during dreams. We reason that waking a person when a dream begins results in dream deprivation, which is our independent variable. We are trying to determine whether anxiety (the dependent variable) is affected by the independent variable (dream deprivation) by awakening participants an equal number of times but under different conditions: (1) the participant would be awakened at the onset of rapid eye movements (dream deprivation), or (2) the participant would be awakened during non-rapid eye movement periods (non-dream deprivation). Half of the participants in the experiment would sleep under conditions of dream deprivation (experimental group) and the other half under conditions of non-dream deprivation (control group). To find out whether our dependent variable (anxiety) is affected by the difference in conditions (i.e., difference in the independent variable), we measure it as well after the participant awakens the next day.

To create two equal groups, we randomly assign research participants to experimental and

► *What are the effects of sleep deprivation? In 1959, disc jockey Peter Tripp stayed awake for over 200 hours to raise money for the March of Dimes; he was studied by psychologists after his stunt. He experienced hallucinations and paranoia during his stunt.*

control conditions. In both conditions, the participants sleep in a laboratory while their sleep patterns and eye movements are monitored. The experimental condition is the dream deprivation condition. Every time rapid eye movements are detected, the members of this group are immediately awakened, given a simple task to do, and then allowed to return to sleep. Members of the control condition are awakened equally often but at times unrelated to rapid eye movement activity, given the same simple task to do as those in the experimental group, and then allowed to go back to sleep. In other words, the experimental and control groups are treated identically, except for the independent variable (dream deprivation). The experimenter manipulates the independent variable (in this case, prevents dreaming) to see if this produces the predicted difference between the two equal groups (control and experimental) on the dependent variable (anxiety).

Is a control group really needed? What if we ran only the condition where participants were dream deprived? If we did that and then discovered that participants were moderately anxious on the day following dream deprivation, what could we conclude? Virtually nothing, because we would not know whether the typical participant with or without dream deprivation would be at a moderate level of anxiety no matter what (just being wakened could make the subject anxious) or might be anxious about something unrelated to the experiment, such as final exams!

What if we run the two groups, but we don't use random assignment of research participants to experimental and control conditions? Could we be sure that participants in the dream-deprived condition were not, in general, more anxious than the non-dream-deprived participants in the first place? Perhaps we assigned to the experimental group the first students to sign up, filling that group before assigning students to the control group. What about the possibility that anxious students might book their appointments early and be more likely to show up first? The experimental group might turn out to be more anxious, but could we be sure it was because of dream deprivation? We might believe our experimental treatment had an effect when in fact the participants who had been assigned to the experimental condition were more anxious in the first place.

Our research example is hypothetical, but you may now be curious about what the research evidence actually says about the effects of dream deprivation on anxiety. It turns out that the relationship is very complex. REM sleep may indeed be related to dealing with emotional stress, but the mechanisms are far from clear. Greenberg, Pillard, and Pearlman (1972) performed an experiment very similar to our hypothetical example. They showed an anxiety-producing film to a group of research participants and then randomly assigned them to two groups, one of which was deprived of REM sleep. Research participants deprived of REM sleep exhibited more anxiety in response to a second showing of the film than those allowed to engage in REM sleep. Perhaps dreaming reduces anxiety by helping people deal with newly experienced anxiety-producing information.

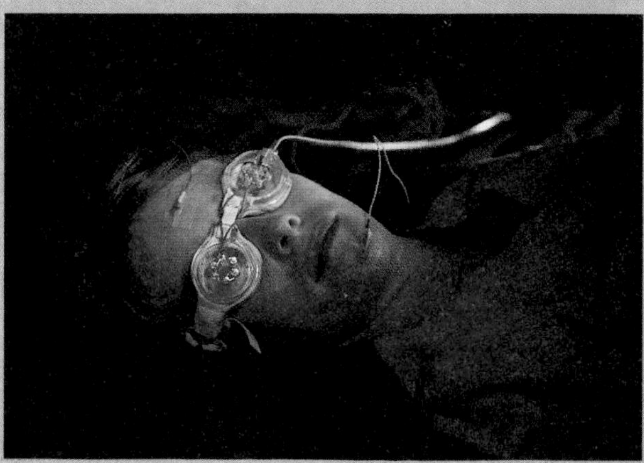

◀ *This apparatus is used in psychophysiologist Stephen Laberge's sleep laboratory at Stanford University. According to Laberge, 1% of people are capable of "lucid dreams," that is, aware they are in the real world while at the same time aware of their dream-state surroundings.*

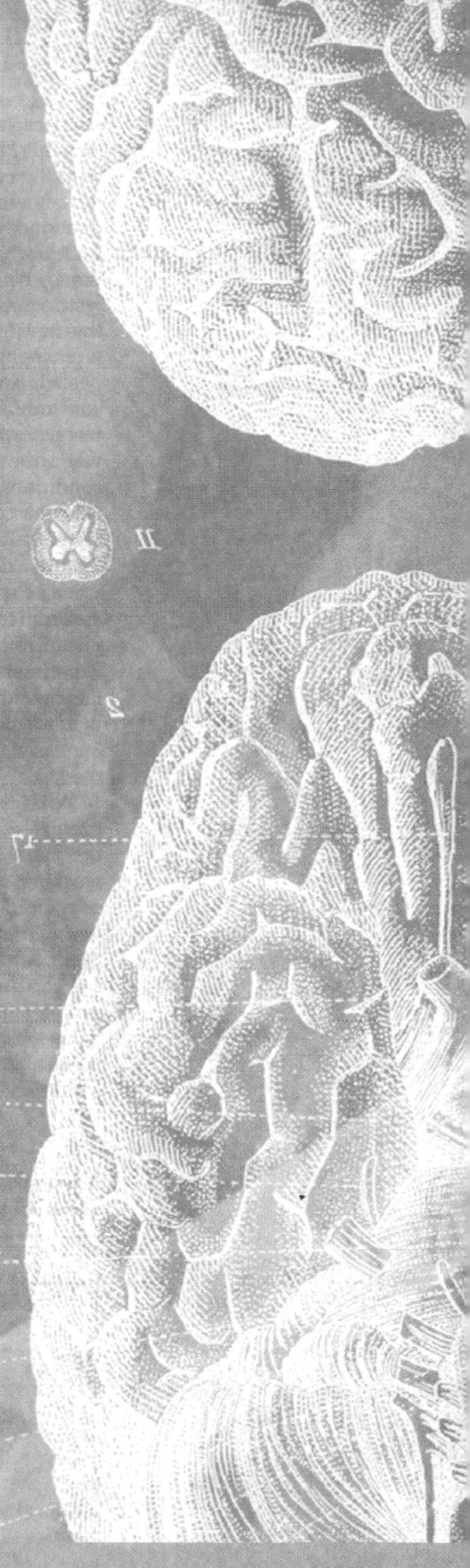

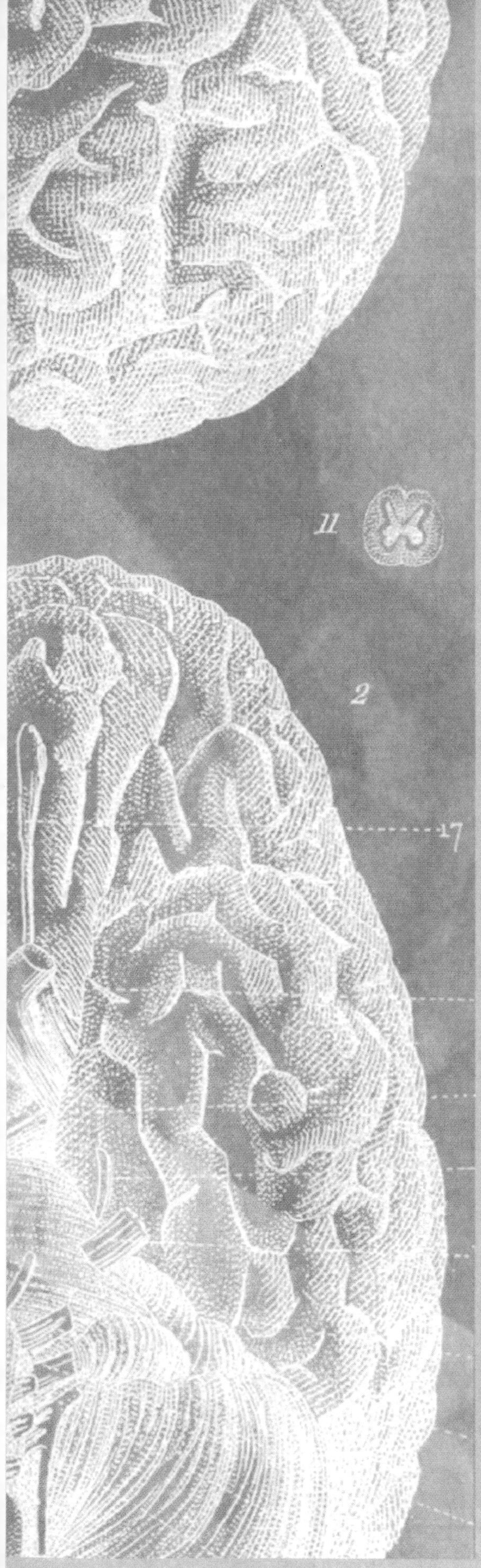

UNDERSTANDING HUMAN DIVERSITY

Some Sources of Bias in Research

Values and expectations related to gender, race, ethnicity, and sexual orientation have been found to affect the research process in a variety of subtle and not-so-subtle ways. In response, the American Psychological Association (APA) has published guidelines for researchers to sensitize them to various forms of bias that can occur at the various steps in the research process, from deciding on what question to study, to publishing the results, to what language is used to communicate findings (Denmark et al., 1988; Herek et al., 1991).

Bias can occur right in the very beginning of the process, in the way researchers explain how the world works: that is, in their theories. Psychological theories reflect the ideology of the larger culture, and if the larger culture is biased, this can lead researchers, regardless of gender or ethnic background, to accept biased theories (O'Connell & Russo, 1991). For example, some theories have incorporated role expectations for middle-class white males as ideals of maturity and adjustment. A highly influential example of this bias is found in Freudian theory (see Chapter 14). Because the theory begins with the assumption that male development is the norm and one's conscience develops out of a fear of castration, Freud considered female development to be "deviant" since females don't have to worry about castration. Going a step further, Freud also viewed females as destined to have penis envy and immature consciences, among other disadvantages (a view totally unsupported by actual research).

The way researchers ask their research questions and formulate hypotheses to test their theories can determine the kinds of answers they will obtain. For example, one consequence of stereotyped gender role conceptions is the assumption that deviation from traditional gender roles is abnormal and will have harmful effects. This has led to asking how children might be "harmed" if their mother works, which leads to a very different picture of the effect of maternal employment on children compared to asking how children benefit if their mother works.

Research can be biased in sampling—who gets included in the study. In some areas of research, such as achievement and moral development, major theories have been based on initial research findings obtained solely from males (Kohlberg, 1966; McClelland et al., 1953). A male bias has also been found in animal research. A recent review of leading animal research journals found that male animals continue to be much more likely to be research subjects than female animals. One study that examined issues of three leading journals appearing in 1991, found that of the 7,499 animals that had their sex identified, 75 percent were males. Further, 58 percent of the studies that had included only one sex had generalized the results to both sexes; 92 percent of the time this happened, the researchers were inappropriately generalizing from males to females (Sechzer et al., 1994).

The ways that variables are defined and measured can create differences in performance between groups not related to the aim of the study. For example, length of time before responding to a stimulus (reaction time) has been used to measure ability. But it can be affected by such things as motivation, test anxiety, and willingness to take risks. Low anxious boys perform best under time pressure conditions, and their response time is faster when they are being evaluated. Anxious girls, however, strive for accuracy, and their response time is therefore slower when they are under time pressure (Plas & Hill, 1986).

Gender and ethnic stereotyping can also create both experimenter and observer expectancy effects. The power of these effects is the reason the "double-blind" procedure was developed. Researchers assume that if the experimenters/observers do not know which group the research participants are in, their expectations won't bias their observations. But it is difficult to hide the gender and ethnicity of research participants. In studies where it has been done, stereotypes are found to produce observer effects. In an early study, researchers presented adults with a videotape of an infant and asked them to rate the infant's behavior on several dimensions. Researchers told half the research participants that the infant was female; they told the other half that the infant was male. When they thought the infant was male, participants perceived "him" as expressing anger; when they thought the infant was female, they perceived "her" as expressing fear (Condry & Condry, 1976).

These are just a few of the ways that cultural values and expectations can affect the research process. As you read about various studies—in your coursework or elsewhere, see if you can identify if such biases are affecting their results.

The Ethical Treatment of Human Research Participants

The basic underlying motivation of these principles is to ensure that, on balance, psychological research and treatment contribute to the benefit of humankind. More specifically, the welfare of research participants must be carefully considered before any procedure is undertaken. In a study that manipulates self-esteem and measures depression, for example, the beneficial results of conducting the study must outweigh any risks to self-esteem that the study creates for participants. These principles assert that the psychologist will (1) protect the confidentiality of research participants' records, (2) not knowingly use any procedures that result in harm or injury to a person, (3) fully disclose the purpose, procedures, and results of any study in which the individual participates, (4) obtain voluntary and informed consent from individuals before they participate in research. Psychologists in professional practice must follow much the same rules, but in addition, they must ensure that any testing performed on a client is appropriate for that individual and that any therapeutic treatments are designed to enhance the individual's welfare.

Where the rules cannot be followed to the letter, special care must be taken to adhere to the spirit of the rules. Thus, consent to use children or impaired adults who might not understand the procedures must be obtained from a parent or legal guardian. When information about the experiment might establish expectations that could influence the outcome of an experiment, full disclosure can be withheld until after the data have been collected.

There have been studies, conducted before these principles were in place, that might not be possible today. For example, one researcher, Philip Zimbardo of Stanford University, ran a study in which students were randomly assigned to be guards or prisoners in an experiment on prison life. "Prisoners" were arrested at their homes, frisked, and handcuffed. They were stripped and given prison uniforms and numbers, were addressed by number rather than name, and subjected to various other dehumanizing conditions. "Guards" wore uniforms and reflector sunglasses, were addressed as "Mr. Corrections Officer, Sir," and proceeded to further degrade the prisoners, making them clean toilets with their hands, disrupting their sleep, and using physical punishment and solitary confinement for minor infractions. The experiment was terminated after only six days because of the guards' brutality (see Chapter 12). Zimbardo acknowledged at the 1996 Convention of the American Psychological Association that his study probably did not meet contemporary ethical guidelines and could not have been conducted today.

"He fabricated evidence in his report on fraudulent science research."

The Use of Animals in Psychological Research

If you've even had a tetanus shot, taken medicine for a cold or infection, or given medicine to

► Ethical standards for the use of animals in research have changed in recent years. What to do with "unemployed" animals like Chandra and Shasta, who are no longer used in experiments, is now a new dilemma.

a pet to prevent distemper or rabies, you have benefited from research on animals. The fact that some animals are biologically quite similar to human beings means that researchers can use these animals to collect results that will be generalizable to human behavior and mental processes. At one time, the white rat was so widely used in psychological studies that it became a symbol of psychological research. In particular, many of the principles of learning and motivation that you will read about in this book are based on research with animals (Domjan & Purdy, 1995). But the trend in psychology today has been to focus increasingly on human behavior. Thus, only about 8 percent of current psychological studies involve animals. A small fraction of those involve pain or the termination of the animal's life.

Some people believe it is immoral and never justified (Nicholl & Russell, 1990) to use animals in scientific research. But psychologists point to major contributions to human welfare in the treatment of mental disorders, vision and hearing defects, brain injury, and chronic pain that have resulted from psychological research using animals. While most people would agree that human life has a higher priority than the well-being of animals, most of us also want animals to be treated humanely and spared unnecessary pain and suffering (Plous, 1996). Thus, the APA has issued special ethical guidelines backed by federal regulations for research with animals. These require humane treatment of all experimental animals and high standards of animal care, and they warn researchers against inflicting pain or harm unless there is no alternative and the means are justified by the potential scientific, educational or human welfare value of the goal.

Objectives Revisited

Psychology's quest for understanding behavior and mental processes has involved the development and application of a host of theories and methods, each with its own particular strengths and limitations. As a whole, psychologists have created a diverse body of knowledge about how individuals behave in different contexts. The remainder of this book is devoted to introducing you to that knowledge and equipping you to use it to evaluate claims about research findings that you will encounter in books, magazines, and newspapers. Having read this chapter, you should understand the role of theory in psychological research, the strengths and limitations of different types of psychological methods, the biases that can influence the process, and the ethics that guide its conduct. Let's review the chapter objectives.

Objective 1. Explain the role of theory in psychological research, including how it relates to hypotheses, variables, operational definitions, and methods.

Psychological research starts with a *theory*, which is a set of self-consistent principles that organize and explain individual "facts" or observations. *Hypotheses* are predictions derived from a theory that predict how variables relate to each other. *Variables*, which are characteristics of people, objects, or events that can take two or more values, are operationally defined so that methods can be used to test the relationship of the variables to see if the theory is correct.

Objective 2. Describe psychological research based on case study, observational, correlational, and experimental methods.

The *case history* method is an intensive examination of one individual, usually based on background data and the results of psychological tests and in-depth interviews. The *observational method* is an investigation of spontaneous behavior in either a naturalistic or a controlled setting. It usually involves observing numerous individuals, as opposed to a case study, which is based on one person. The *correlational method* examines the strength and direction of relationships among different variables that are measured but not manipulated, using procedures like psychological tests, interviews, and surveys. Correlational approaches cannot specify whether one variable directly causes changes in the other, however. The *experimental method* is a way of determining cause and effect by examining behavior under circumstances in which everything is controlled or held constant except for the independent variable, which is manipulated by the experimenter to see how it affects the dependent variable. A combination of these methods is often the most revealing approach to research questions.

Objective 3. Describe and discuss some benefits and problems of cross-cultural research.

Cross-cultural research is distinguished by its inclusion of culture as a variable of analysis. Cross-cultural research focuses on how culture shapes and affects behavior. It also can test the generality of theories and can reveal cultural biases in research that is limited to one culture.

Objective 4. Describe what validity of a psychological study is and identify various types of bias that can undermine it.

To be *valid*, the relationships measured in psychological research must also apply to real-world behavior. Researchers must be able to generalize their findings in a particular study to behavior that occurs at another time and place. Validity also refers to the fit between what is supposed to happen in a research study and what actually does happen. A variety of problems can bias research findings, including confounding variables and inappropriate control groups, unrepresentative samples, and experimenter and participant expectancies.

Objective 5. Identify ways to avoid unethical treatment of human beings and animals in research and practice.

Research and applications must follow ethical guidelines and requirements established by the APA to avoid inflicting unnecessary pain and stress on human and animal research participants. In research with human participants, psychologists should protect confidentiality, not knowingly use harmful procedures, fully disclose the purpose, procedures, and results of a study, and obtain voluntary and informed consent of all participants. Ethical guidelines backed by federal regulations also mandate humane treatment for all experimental animals and require researchers to justify any procedures that might cause pain or harm.

KEY TERMS

theory

hypothesis

operational definition

case study

naturalistic observation

correlation

validity

reliability

unstructured interview

structured interview

independent variable

dependent variable

confounding variable

random assignment

experimental group

control group

expectancy effect

double-blind experiment

placebo

placebo effect

ethics

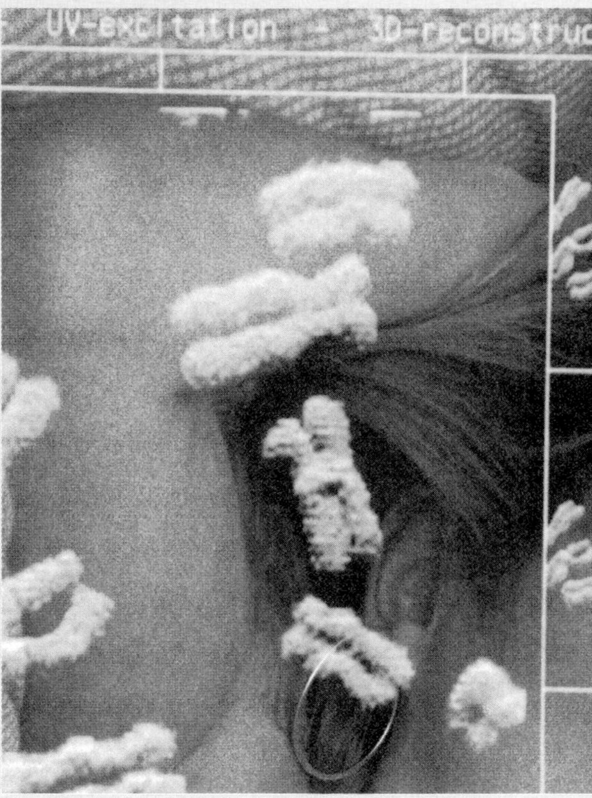
UV-excitation - 3D-reconstruct

C H A P T E R 3

Biological Foundations of Behavior

O B J E C T I V E S

After reading this chapter, you should be able to:

1. Describe the neuron and discuss its role in the transmission of information throughout the body. Explain what it means to say that neurons are the building blocks of the nervous system.
2. Describe the major parts, the organization, and the primary functions of the human nervous system.
3. Give a general description of the endocrine system and identify some major endocrine glands.
4. Present an overview of behavioral genetics. What is it? How do we study it? What do we know about it?

In 1848, twenty-five-year-old Phineas Gage had an accident. He was dynamiting rock in his job on a railroad construction crew. An explosion sent a three-foot-long iron rod, about an inch in diameter, hurtling through the air. It struck him in the face, entering under his left cheek and exiting through the top of his skull. It tore away a substantial portion of the front part of his brain, along with pieces of his skull and flesh. Although he immediately had convulsions, he was able to talk with others just a few minutes later. He even walked up a flight of stairs before receiving medical treatment two hours later. He healed and became his old self again—his old physical self, that is—in just a few weeks.

But a personality transformation had occurred. Gage changed from being polite, conscientious, and hard-working to being profane, flighty, and irresponsible. His physician, Dr. J.M. Harlow, reported: "Previous to his injury, though untrained in the schools, he possessed a well-balanced mind, and was looked upon by those who know him as a shrewd, smart businessman, very energetic and persistent in executing all his plans. In this regard his mind was radically changed, so decidedly that his friends and acquaintances said he was 'no longer Gage' " (Harlow, 1869). No longer a motivated and industrious worker, Gage lost his job with the railroad and became a sideshow exhibit in P.T. Barnum's museum in New York. He survived for twelve more years, with little further change in personality or behavior.

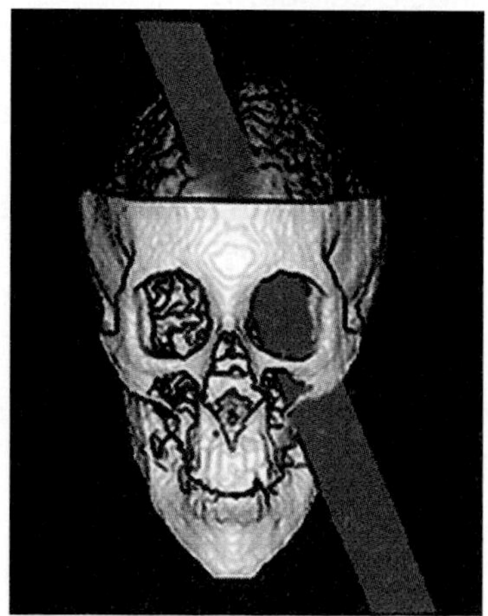

▼ *The skull of Phineas Gage, after the bizarre accident that didn't affect his speech, intelligence, or ability to move, but dramatically changed his personality.*

What accounts for the transformation in Gage's behavior? The angle of the wound suggests that Gage suffered massive damage to the front part of the brain, which is involved in the expression of emotions, in motivation, and in cognitive activities. J.M. Harlow's careful recording of Gage's experience provides a classic case study of the effects of damage to the brain on behavior. But there are others that also focus on personality changes resulting from brain injury (Kupfermann, 1991). The case of Phineas Gage and these other cases demonstrate the importance of understanding relationships between the brain and behavior. Biological factors are involved in some way in all types of behavior, including higher mental processes. Knowing behavior's biological roots can suggest what may be wrong when someone acts abnormally, or "different" from what is considered "normal."

We will organize our discussion of the biological processes that underlie behavior around fundamental concepts in these three areas: (1) the structure and function of the nervous system, whose basic units are ***nerve cells*** (also called ***neurons***), (2) the endocrine system, which is composed of glands that manufacture and secrete chemical substances called ***hormones*** into the bloodstream, and (3) behavioral genetics, which is concerned with ***genes*** and heredity. These areas make up the basic subject matter of behavioral neuroscience. Although the name suggests a focus on the nervous system, behavioral neuroscientists study how the biological building blocks of neurons, hormones, and genes work together to enable us to behave as we do.

To understand the biological underpinnings of behavior, we will need to address questions like the following: How is our experience stored in the brain? How does information travel through the nervous system? How does the structural organization of the brain affect what we perceive, learn, and remember? How do hormones affect anxiety, aggression, or sexual behavior? Do genes, which we know influence our height and hair color, also place limits on how well we learn and remember or think and feel?

. . . the slightest reflection shows that phenomena have absolutely no power to influence our ideas until they have first impressed our senses and our brain. . . . The experiences of the body are thus one of the conditions of the faculty of memory being what it is.

—William James (1890)

The Human Nervous System

Every moment of every day, even when you are sleeping, your nervous system is active, exchanging millions of signals that correlate with thoughts, feelings, and actions. Take a simple behavior like recognizing a friend coming toward you. How are you able to tell a friend from a stranger, who is of similar height and build? Visual (and perhaps auditory) information about the person is sensed and sent to your brain (for example, female, medium height, brown hair, glasses). There, the information is interpreted ("Hey! That's Betsy.") and translated into a signal for action. Finally, the brain sends a command to the voice and other action systems ("I guess I'll go over and find out what Betsy's up to."). All this occurs in a fraction of a second and often without full conscious awareness. Your nervous system makes this rapid and automatic recognition possible.

Single-celled creatures don't have nervous systems. They are in immediate contact with their environment and don't need to communicate between cells, since there is just one cell. Multi-celled creatures, on the other hand, need some mechanism for intercellular communication. In human beings, this communication by means of the nervous system enables the inside of the body to "know" what is happening to the outside of the body, the left side to "know" what the right side is doing, and thoughts and feelings to be coordinated with actions. In human beings, the nervous system is the primary information-processing and communication system, creating and carrying messages from one location to others over a network of interconnected neurons. Neurons are the key biological elements for information transmission in the nervous system. They are organized into neural circuits, also called pathways, which control the direction, speed, and destination of a message traveling through the nervous system. The nervous system is by far the most complex biological system of the human body. The human brain alone consists of at least 10 billion and possibly as many as 100 billion neurons, each of which is directly connected to some 100 to 10,000 other neurons.

There are three general functions of the nervous system in human beings and other animals: (1) sensing specific information about external and internal conditions (input), (2) integrating (or processing) that information, and (3) issuing commands for a response from the body's muscles or glands (output). Thus, the nervous system is the foundation for our ability to perceive, understand, and react to our environment.

Knowing biology, especially the nervous system, hormones and genetics, is fundamental to understanding behavior.

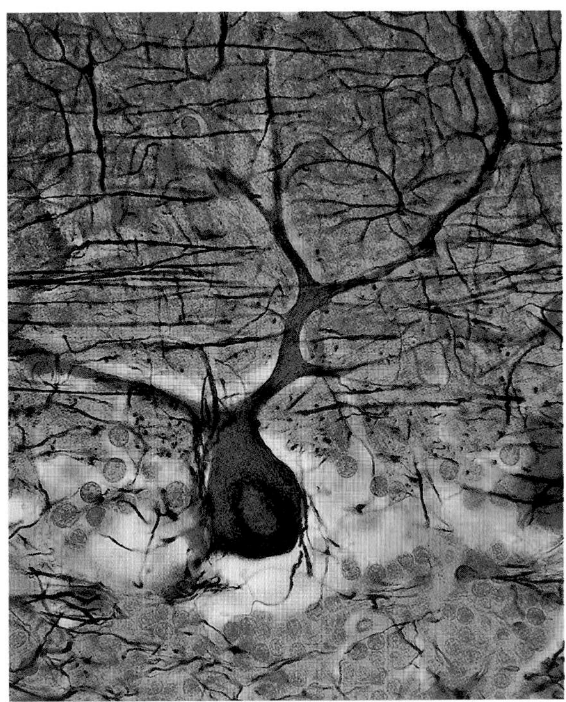

◀ *A neuron in the cerebellum, magnified 1,400 times.*

Neurons

The typical neuron consists of three basic parts—the ***cell body*** (which includes the cell nucleus), ***dendrites***, and ***axon*** (see Figure 3-1). Each neuron has both input and output zones for receiving and sending signals. The dendrites (from a Greek word meaning tree), which are short branch-like fibers extending from the cell body, are the input zones, where information is first received. The role of the dendrites is to pick up signals from other neurons. A neuron can have from just a few to several hundred dendrites. The axon, which is a single fiber that extends from the cell body, provides the exit, or output, pathway for the neural signal. Some axons are quite long and measure a meter or more; others are very short and are measured in micrometers. Axons conduct signals away from the cell body and end in branching axon terminals that are usually located near (but not in contact with) the dendrites and cell bodies of other neurons. The terminals of one neuron, the gap between the neurons, and the dendrites of the next neuron are collectively known as the ***synapse***. Signals are transmitted away from one neuron across a tiny space, called the ***synaptic cleft***, and then to the dendrites of the next neuron in the chain, as shown in Figure 3-2.

Any neuron can have from 100 to 10,000 syn-

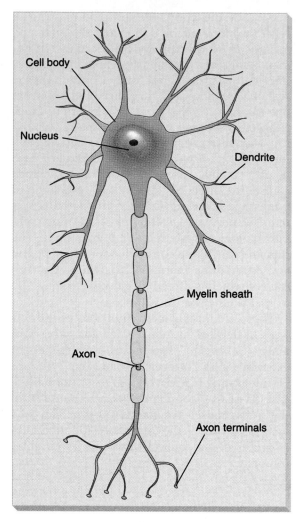

3-1 The Basic Parts of a Neuron

Most vertebrate nerve cells consist of three basic parts—the dendrites, the cell body, and the axon. The axon ends in the axon terminals. A myelin sheath often covers the axon of a cell, increasing the cell's rate of conduction and its action potential.

3-2 A Chain of Neurons

The basic parts of a neuron—dendrites, cell body, and axon—are illustrated for a chain of neurons. Many axons are encased in a myelin sheath, which increases the cell's rate of conduction and its action potential. The axon of the motor neuron ends in the axon terminals, which make contact with another cell—another neuron—as the signal is passed along the nervous system, or in a muscle or gland. The arrows show the direction of the flow of information. The green arrows represent the signal carried by sensory neurons *into* the nervous system (to the interneurons in the brain or spinal cord); yellow arrows represent the signals processed by the interneurons, which in turn relay the signal to motor neurons; blue represents the signals carried away by the motor neurons to their ultimate destinations (muscles or glands). (Source:Adapted from Starr and Taggart, 1995, p. 571)

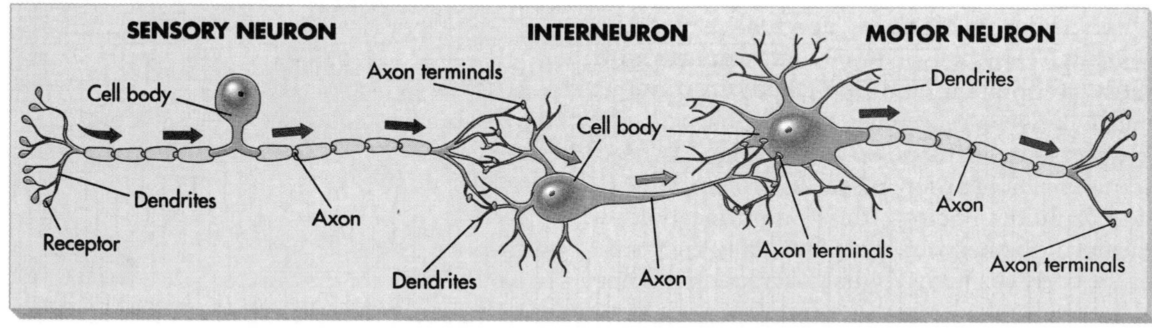

aptic connections with other neurons. The interconnectedness of neurons, especially in the brain, increases during early development and decreases after maturity. Researchers believe that these interconnections support mental capacities and that the slight losses in memory and other cognitive abilities that come with aging might be associated, in part, with the dying off of neurons and the consequent loss of interconnections (Miller, 1995).

The nervous system is made up of three kinds of neurons that specialize in three general functions. ***Sensory neurons*** respond to incoming stimuli (input) such as sounds, sights and touches, and transmit information from sense organs (ears, eyes, skin) toward the brain and spinal cord. ***Interneurons*** in the spinal cord and the brain integrate (process) the information coming in on sensory pathways. ***Motor neurons*** relay information (output) away from the brain and spinal cord to the body's action systems, the muscles and glands, which in turn respond as directed.

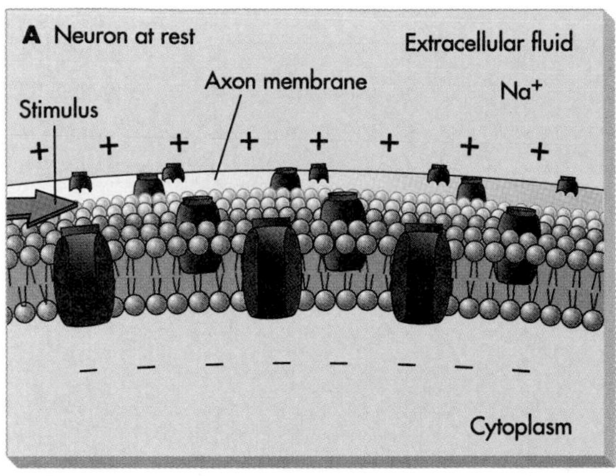

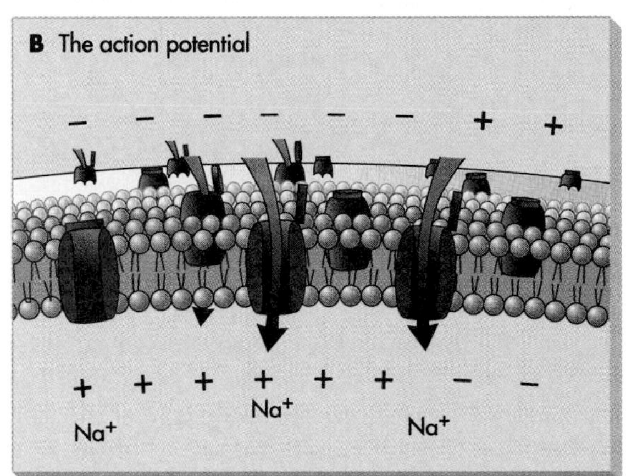

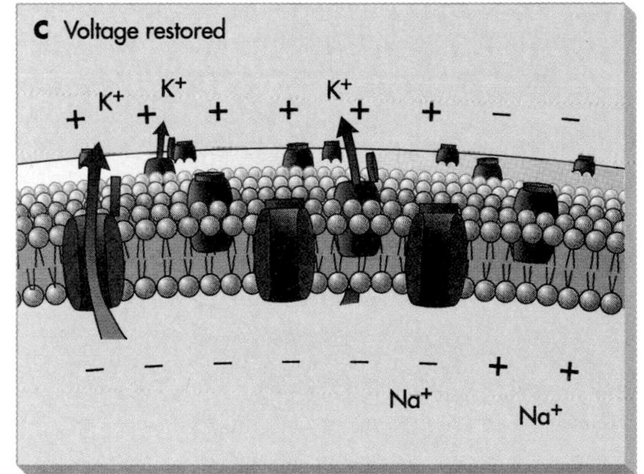

3-3 The Electrochemistry of the Nerve Impulse

The figure shows three panels: during a resting state, during an action potential, and during a restored resting state. (A) When the neuron is at rest, the inside of the cell is negative with respect to the outside. The sodium gates remain closed, so that sodium (Na^+) ions remain on the outside of the cell, while potassium (K^+) and chloride (Cl^-) ions are inside the cell. (B) When a stimulus to the neuron occurs, it initiates an action potential, which causes the sodium gates to open, and the sodium ions to move into the cell, temporarily changing the cell's electrical polarity. (C) When enough sodium ions move across the membrane, the sodium gates close, and the potassium gates open, allowing the potassium ions (K^+) to flow out of the cell and returning the electrical balance of the cell to a resting state. (Source: Starr and Taggart, 1995, pp. 564–65).

Transmission of Nerve Impulses

When a neuron is stimulated, the nerve impulse that is generated travels down the axon and into the axon terminals, where it causes the release of specialized chemicals. These chemicals travel the small distance across the synapse to the next neuron. Thus, information is conveyed both (1) within neurons (***axonal conduction***) and (2) from one neuron to the next (***synaptic transmission***).

Axonal Conduction

Axonal conduction is based on changes in electrical charge inside and outside the neuron. Neurons, like most other cells in the human body, exist in a fluid that contains several kinds of ***ions***—electrically charged atoms or groups of atoms. Certain of these ions are positively charged, while others are negatively charged. Ions with the same charge repel each other; those with different charges attract each other. Without the separation created by the cell membrane, the ions would all mix together, and the positive and negative charges on the various ions would neutralize each other. "Gates" in the cell membrane regulate which ions can enter or leave the cell. The opening and closing of the gates allows the inflow and outflow of ions, which determines the relative concentrations of certain ions both inside and outside the cell and can lead to a change in electrical charge within the cell from negative to positive and back again.

When a neuron is at rest, its cell membrane maintains an unequal distribution of ions that lets potassium (K^+) and chloride (Cl^-) ions pass into the cell but keeps most sodium (Na^+) ions outside (see Figure 3-3). This creates a voltage

A neuron is a biological cell, consisting of a cell body, an axon, and dendrites, specialized to carry "information" from one place to another.

3-4 The Action Potential

The graph shows the change in electrical charge across the membrane of the cell before and after it is stimulated. The voltage difference between the inside and the outside of the cell is −70 millivolts when it is at rest, with the inside of the cell negative with respect to the outside. When the cell is electrically stimulated, an action potential is triggered, appearing as a spike on a graph, wherein the voltage difference goes to +40 millivolts, with the inside of the cell now positive with respect to the outside. When the action potential is spent, the cell experiences a refractory period, during which it begins to return to the resting state of −70 millivolts.

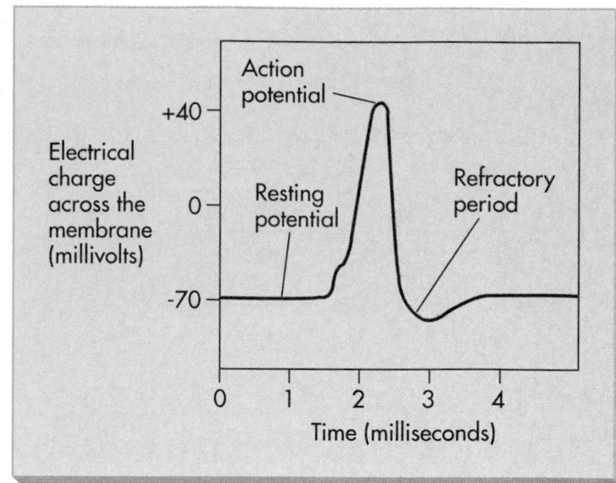

An action potential is an electrical signal that travels the length of a neural axon.

difference (a difference in electrical charge), with the inside of the cell negatively charged (at about −70 millivolts) compared to the outside. The difference in relative electrical charge between the inside and the outside of the cell means that the cell is in a ***polarized state***, that is, it has potential energy (the ***resting potential***), which can be released by a stimulus to the cell membrane. Think of the neuron as a flashlight battery, charged and ready to be turned on.

The potential energy of a cell is released by a stimulus that is of sufficient intensity or duration that it changes the flow of positive and negative ions across the cell membrane. This is like the pressure of your fingers increasing enough to move the switch on a flashlight to turn it on. When the stimulus becomes strong enough or lasts long enough that it goes above a critical point called the ***threshold***, it triggers an ***action potential***, which is a brief reversal in the electrical charge on the inside and outside of a cell (appearing as a "spike" on recording devices; see Figure 3-4). The stimulus does this by disrupting the cell's membrane, causing its sodium (Na^+) gates to open and positively charged sodium ions to rush into the cell. This temporarily changes the cell's electrical polarity so that it becomes positively charged inside and negatively charged outside. When enough sodium ions move across the cell membrane so that the inside of the cell changes from negative to positive, the cell's sodium gates shut. Its potassium gates then open to let potassium (K^+) ions flow out of the neuron, and the electrical balance moves back toward the resting state. (Actually, there is a short period of time before it returns completely to normal, called the ***refractory period***, when a cell is *less* sensitive to stimulation because of inertia in the gating.)

The disturbance created by the movement of ions causes the sodium gates at the next region of the membrane to open. The action potential thus continues down the length of the axon, much as a wave moves in water (see Figure 3-5). Unlike a wave, however, the action potential maintains its original intensity for the entire length of the axon. Once the stimulus is above a certain threshold, the action potential initiated along the axon is the same strength no matter how strong the stimulus, just as a gun fires at the same strength no matter how hard you pull the trigger. This is called the ***all-or-none principle.***

3-5 The Movement of the Action Potential

A neuron has a charge of about −70 millivolts when at rest; that is, there are more negative ions on the inside than on the outside. Stimulation of the neuron changes the cell membrane so that it becomes permeable to the positive sodium ions that move inside the cell. If enough positive ions move in, a positively charged action potential is triggered, which ripples down the nerve, somewhat like a wave. Unlike a wave, however, the strength of the action potential does not diminish, but is constant over the length of the nerve.

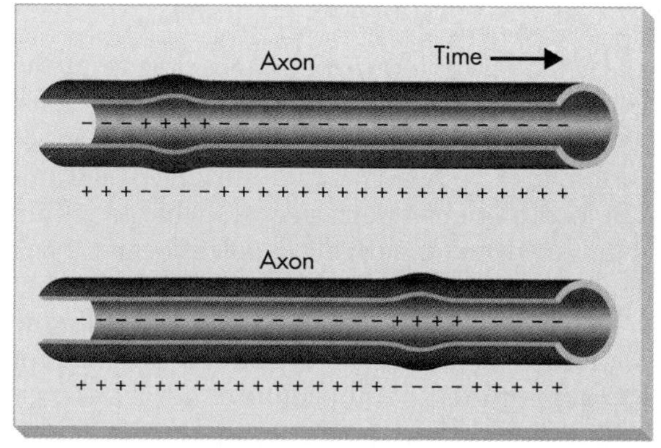

Myelin is a fatty substance deposited around the axons of many sensory and motor neurons. Functionally, this myelin sheath greatly enhances the speed of axonal conduction. In the largest myelinated axon, action potentials travel approximately 270 miles per hour, compared to about half that speed in small, unmyelinated neurons. Some diseases reflect degradation of the myelin in the nervous system. Multiple sclerosis, for example, is the result of the degeneration of myelin, which leaves areas of scarring (sclerosis) that are nonconductive to action potentials. The symptoms of this progressive, and as yet incurable, disease include visual problems (when it attacks the optic nerve) and jerky and uncoordinated movements of body limbs when it attacks the neurons that control muscles.

Synaptic Transmission

At the synapse, the axon of one neuron (now known as the presynaptic cell) does not touch the dendrites on the next neuron (now known as the postsynaptic cell). How, then, does a neural signal bridge the synaptic cleft? The answer is by chemical action. Specialized chemicals called ***neurotransmitters*** are stored at the presynaptic cell's axon terminal buttons in ***synaptic vesicles*** (little pockets or sacs). When a nerve impulse reaches the end of an axon, like the flame of a fuse setting off a firecracker, it causes the terminal button to release neurotransmitters into the synaptic cleft between two neurons (or between a neuron and a muscle or gland cell). The neurotransmitters then float across the synaptic cleft and travel to specialized receptor molecules located in the dendrites of the postsynaptic cell (see Figure 3-6).

There are many different kinds of molecules that function as neurotransmitters, and each kind works only at certain receptor sites. In general, a neurotransmitter can be thought of as working like a key, needing to find the right lock on the postsynaptic cell where it fits and can "get in" to activate the neuron and trigger an impulse. Each receptor site (lock) accepts neurotransmitters (keys) of only particular shapes. "Shape," of course, refers to the chemical or molecular shape or structure of the trans-

▲ *The comedian Richard Pryor, who suffers from multiple sclerosis.*

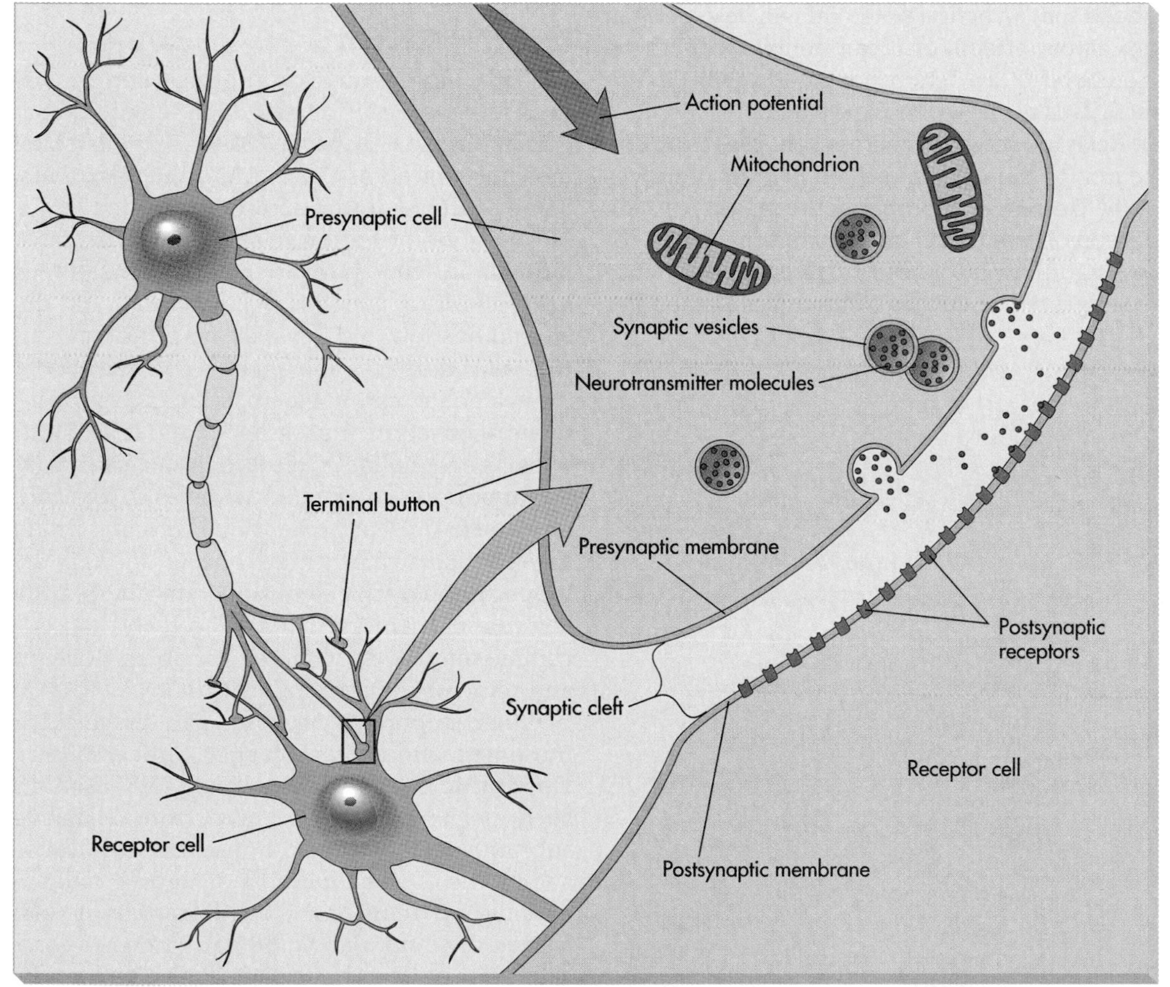

3-6 Synaptic Transmission

Nerve impulses are transmitted from one neuron to another through synaptic transmission, wherein neurotransmitters from the presynaptic cell are released into the synaptic cleft between the two neurons, float across the synaptic cleft, and then bind with receptors on the postsynaptic cell.

3-7 Lock-and-Key Theory of Synaptic Transmission

For synaptic transmission to occur, transmitter molecules released from the presynaptic membrane must bind to receptor molecules on the postsynaptic membrane. Each receptor molecule will only bind with certain neurotransmitters of particular chemical or molecular shape or structure just as a lock will only accept particular keys.

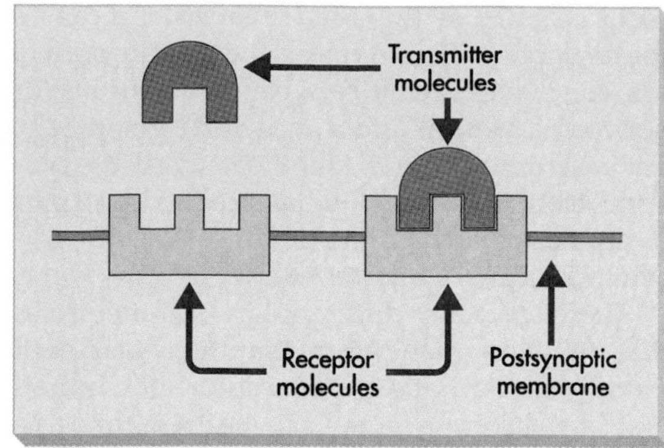

mitter molecule, which must match up with the chemical or molecular structure of the lock on the receptor site of the postsynaptic cell (see Figure 3-7).

The same transmitter substance can act in at least two ways, depending on the type of "lock" it opens up in the postsynaptic cell: it can either excite the postsynaptic cell, increasing the likelihood that an action potential will be generated (excitatory effect), or it can inhibit (reduce) the likelihood of an action potential (inhibitory effect). This is shown in Figure 3-8.

Relaying messages across synapses from one neuron to the next in a chain or tract of nerves is the clearest and probably the fastest way the nervous system has of transmitting and processing information. But there is new evidence to suggest that neurons communicate in another way that is broader and more diffuse. Such communication in the brain looks like radio broadcasting, with neurotransmitters traveling widely like the ripples in a pond through the fluid-filled space surrounding the cells. These transmitters can be picked up almost anywhere in the brain by any properly tuned receiver (by binding to receptors in other neurons). This mode of communication is called ***volume transmission***. Because it covers greater distances, volume transmission takes place over a much longer time scale than ordinary synaptic transmission and involves slower, more diffuse changes in the brain, such as changes in the brain's general receptivity to synaptic signals (Agnati, Bjelke, & Fuxe, 1992). The full significance of volume transmission is as yet not clearly known, but there is some reason to think that it is involved in massive brain changes such as those that occur in epileptic seizures and in the effects of mind-altering drugs.

3-8 Excitation and Inhibition

If the binding of the neurotransmitter from the presynaptic cell to receptors on the postsynaptic cell causes positively charged sodium ions to enter the cell, the action potentials in the postsynaptic cell will increase. This has an excitatory effect. If binding of the neurotransmitter from the presynaptic cell to receptors on the postsynaptic cell causes positively charged sodium ions to leave the cell and/or negatively charged chloride ions to enter the postsynaptic cell, the action potentials will decrease. This has an inhibitory effect.

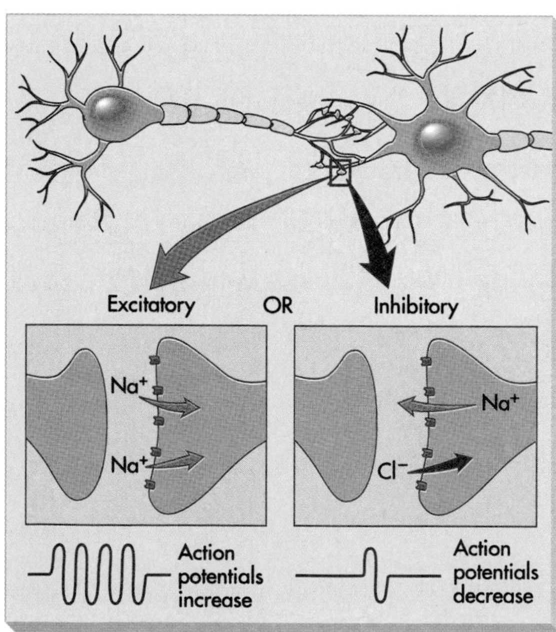

Neurotransmitters

To date, more than sixty different neurotransmitters have been identified, each with a specific molecular shape or "key" that fits some molecular receptors, or "locks," but not others. Some of the neurotransmitters are listed in Table 3-1. One of the most common neurotransmitters in the human nervous system is ***acetylcholine***, which is manufactured and delivered by motor neurons, the neurons that control the muscles and glands of the body. Acetylcholine can have either excitatory or inhibitory effects on muscle and gland cells. Thus, when acetylcholine is released, it can either trigger or suppress action mechanisms. Acetylcholine is also present in the spinal cord and brain. There are particularly high concentrations in the hippocampus, an area of the brain that plays a key role in memory. Thus, conceivably, acetylcholine may be essential for our ability to learn and remember (McGaugh, 1989).

Other important neurotransmitters include those with effects on perceptions and emotions. ***Dopamine*** is involved in a variety of sensations such as the high experienced from addictive substances. Too much dopamine can cause symptoms of schizophrenia, including hallucinations and delusions. Too little dopamine will lead to the muscular rigidity and tremors characteristic of Parkinson's disease. ***Noradrenaline*** (norepinephrine) affects brain areas

Table 3-1 Selected Neurotransmitters and Some of Their Effects

Neurotransmitter	Biochemical Classification	Effect on Synapses	Examples of Behavioral Effects
Norephinephrine (Noradrenaline) (NE)	Catecholamine	Inhibitory and excitatory	Role in learning, memory, alertness, emotions, autonomic nervous system arousal; excess produces wakefulness, behavioral arousal, emotional arousal; deficit produces memory impairment and possibly depression
Dopamine (DA)	Catecholamine	Inhibitory	Role in emotional arousal (in "pleasure circuits"), voluntary movement, thought, learning, memory, and possibly depression; excess produces involuntary movements; deficit produces memory and motor impairment
Serotonin (5-HT)	Indoleamine	Inhibitory and excitatory	Role in sleep, appetite, temperature regulation, emotion, behavioral activity; excess produces dreaming, hallucinations; deficit produces sleeplessness, increased aggressiveness, and possibly depression
Acetylcholine (ACh)	Amine	Excitatory and inhibitory	Released at neuromuscular junction; excess produces motor impairment; deficit produces memory impairment
GABA (gamma-aminobutyric acid)	Amino acid	Inhibitory	Role in motor behavior and sleep and eating disorders; excess produces unconsciousness, coma, death; deficit produces anxiety, seizures, epilepsy
Glycine	Amino acid	Inhibitory	Role in spinal reflexes and other motor behaviors
Glutamate	Amino acid	Excitatory	Role is not fully understood; excess produces excitation, dizziness, numbness
Neuropeptide Y (NPY)	Peptide	Excitatory	Role in hunger and eating or appetite
Substance P	Peptide	Excitatory and inhibitory	Affects sensory neurons; role in pain regulation; deficit increases pain sensitivity
Endorphins	Peptide	Inhibitory	Role in learning, memory, pleasure, mood, appetite; inhibits pain by interfering with Substance P

concerned with emotional states, dreaming, and awaking. Too little noradrenaline can lead to sleep disorders and depression. ***Serotonin*** acts on brain cells that control sensory perception, temperature regulation, sleeping, and emotions. Eating disorders and depression may result from too little serotonin. Measuring levels of this chemical may enable doctors to identify early those people who are prone to depression or suicide and to take therapeutic steps to intervene. In a more common case, taking a glass of warm milk may help you to sleep at night because the warm milk contains an amino acid that the brain uses to make serotonin.

Exogenous (meaning "originating outside the body") psychoactive drugs can cause neurotransmitters to be released or not deactivated or to mimic the effects of neurotransmitters by binding to their receptors. Drugs that act in this way are called ***agonists***. Thus, cocaine (a dopaminergic agonist) causes dopamine to remain at the synapse longer than it would naturally, leading to such pleasurable effects as euphoria, increased energy, and heightened self-confidence. Nicotine mimics acetylcholine (a cholinergic agonist). Like the short-term effects of excessive acetylcholine, excessive nicotine exposure may cause irritability, water retention in

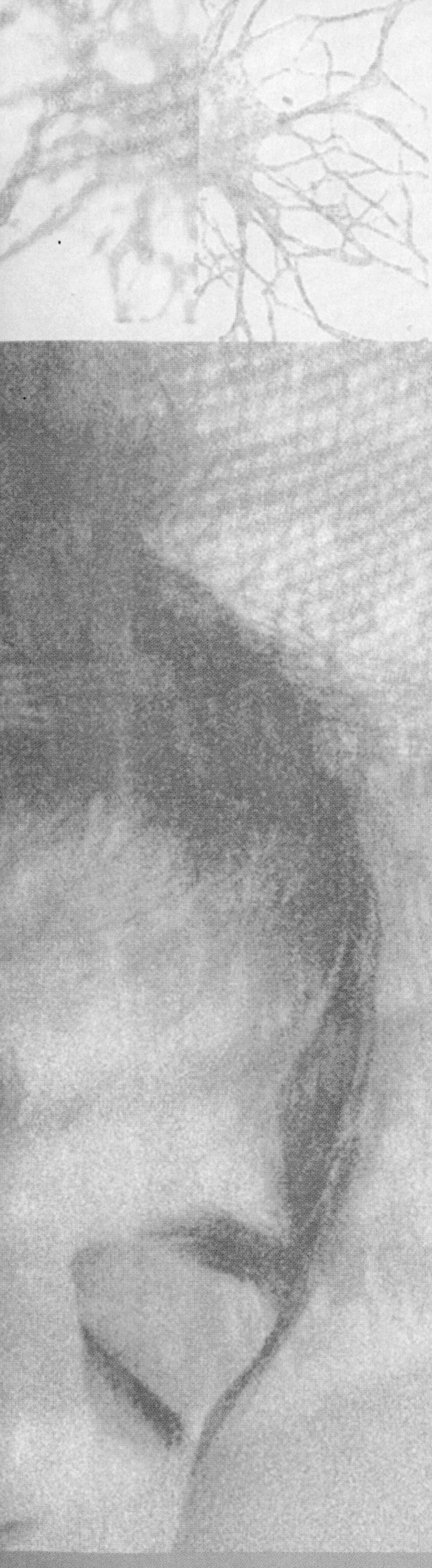

SEEKING SOLUTIONS

Disruptions to Transmission of Information in the Nervous System

Here are three examples of disorders of the nervous system. Using what you have learned about the transmission of information in the nervous system, how would you describe each of the following problems?

Case 1 Henry M.

Henry M. cannot retain new information unless he repeats it over and over to himself or writes it down. When he stops repeating or loses the note, his memory is gone. He remembers things that he learned long ago, but not anything new. Henry's problem developed after he had brain surgery to cure his epilepsy. After surgery, his seizures were reduced, but he was left with a serious memory deficit. He can see, hear, walk, and talk normally. His above normal IQ was unaffected by the operation. And yet, he seems unable to store any new facts in memory, or, if he stores them, he cannot retrieve them on later occasions.

Case 2 Robert W.

An automobile accident left Robert W. paralyzed from the neck down and confined to a wheelchair. Nonetheless, Robert has become an accomplished artist, who learned to paint by holding the brush in his mouth. He is creative, intelligent and articulate. How might the PNS or CNS be implicated? Can you give other, less extreme, examples of behavior that also illustrate this kind of problem?

Case 3 Maria F.

Maria F. is blind. Like many babies who are born with a low birth weight, she was given oxygen at birth to keep her alive. Unfortunately, medical science learned later that giving babies too much oxygen before their eyes are fully developed can destroy the visual system. What parts of the nervous system might be involved in Maria's problem? Does this mean that Maria is doomed to a life of little accomplishment?

Henry M.'s input and output functions are intact. What he suffers from is a deficit in central processing, brought about by the brain surgery in which the hippocampus was destroyed.

Robert W.'s central processing system is normal (perhaps even above normal with respect to creative abilities). But his input and output systems are blocked at the neck. The descending spinal nerves—the input and output lines in the spinal cord—have been severed, leaving him without sensation and paralyzed from the neck down. Messages cannot be received by or sent from the brain to the lower part of his body.

Maria F. has damage to the input side of her nervous system. This is the side that receives stimuli from the environment and transmits that information to the central nervous system. Maria is blind, which means she is missing only one type of input—visual. (Deafness can represent damage to another type of input—auditory.) One remarkable characteristic of the various sensory systems that provide input is the extent to which one system can compensate for deficits in another. Stevie Wonder is blind; Ludwig van Beethoven became deaf in later life; Helen Keller was both blind and deaf. Impairments in sensory function did not incapacitate these individuals. They learned to process whatever information they could receive from their environments in other ways, thereby demonstrating how the highest levels of human accomplishment are possible without full sensory functioning when environments provide opportunities for such individuals to learn and use their skills.

Ludwig van Beethoven

Helen Keller

Stevie Wonder

the body, increased heart rate and blood pressure, and gastric upset. Other exogenous chemicals can prevent, block, or inhibit the action of a natural neurotransmitter; these are called ***antagonists***. Curare, first discovered by South American Indians who used it to paralyze their prey or enemies, blocks the action of acetylcholine by occupying its receptors on postsynaptic neurons (in other words, it is a cholinergic antagonist).

◀ *A South American hunter uses a blowgun to shoot an arrow at his prey. The arrow's tip is coated with curare, which blocks the action of acetylcholine at the junction of motor neurons and muscles, causing paralysis and, ultimately, death from suffocation.*

Endorphins

Another influence on nerve transmission is illustrated by the action of neurochemicals called ***endorphins*** (a contraction of *endo*genous and m*orphine*), a widely publicized neurochemical belonging to a class called opioid peptides. Endorphins are manufactured and secreted in the body to reduce pain. Endorphins spread throughout the nervous system and fill up some, perhaps many, of the neurotransmitter receptors for pain signals. Thus, if pain stimulation persists, the release of the neurotransmitter for pain can be blocked by endorphins. The behavioral end result is that you feel less pain, just as if you took a small dose of morphine or opium. This phenomenon has long been known and employed by physicians using acupuncture in China without full awareness of its biological basis. We now know that acupuncture works, in part, because when an inserted acupuncture needle is rotated, pain-blocking endorphins are released (see Chapter 13). Endorphins probably also account for the ability of athletes to "play with pain" and might be the reason behind "runner's high," which is the exhilaration a long-distance runner feels after the race when the pain is over but the chemical effect lingers. This effect is similar to that produced by heroin and morphine, which also block pain by binding to receptors for pain.

THINKING CRITICALLY

Long-distance runners often speak about the "high" that comes with finishing a marathon. This good feeling can only partly be attributed to how well the runner did in the race, because slow running finishers also report the experience. Put together what you know about pain, morphine, and endorphins to come up with a reasonable explanation for the "runner's high."

Running a marathon is a painful experience. The longer you run, the closer you get to the finish line, the more intense your pain becomes. But the body manufactures and secretes endorphins to reduce pain. The body might secrete endorphins during long-distance running as a defense against pain. Pain diminishes after the race as the body relaxes and the muscles begin the process of recovery. But endorphins linger on in the body for some time. When there is no pain to oppose, endorphins might have the "feel good" property associated with morphine. Thus, it is possible that the lingering endorphins create the "runner's high."

▲ *Runner's high: extremely stressful exercise may produce a buildup of the brain's natural painkillers, endorphins, which counteract pain and produce a kind of euphoria.*

Organization of the Human Nervous System

The nervous system is able to create order out of the trillions of signals it processes because neurons are linked together into tracts and bundles organized by structure and function. Or-

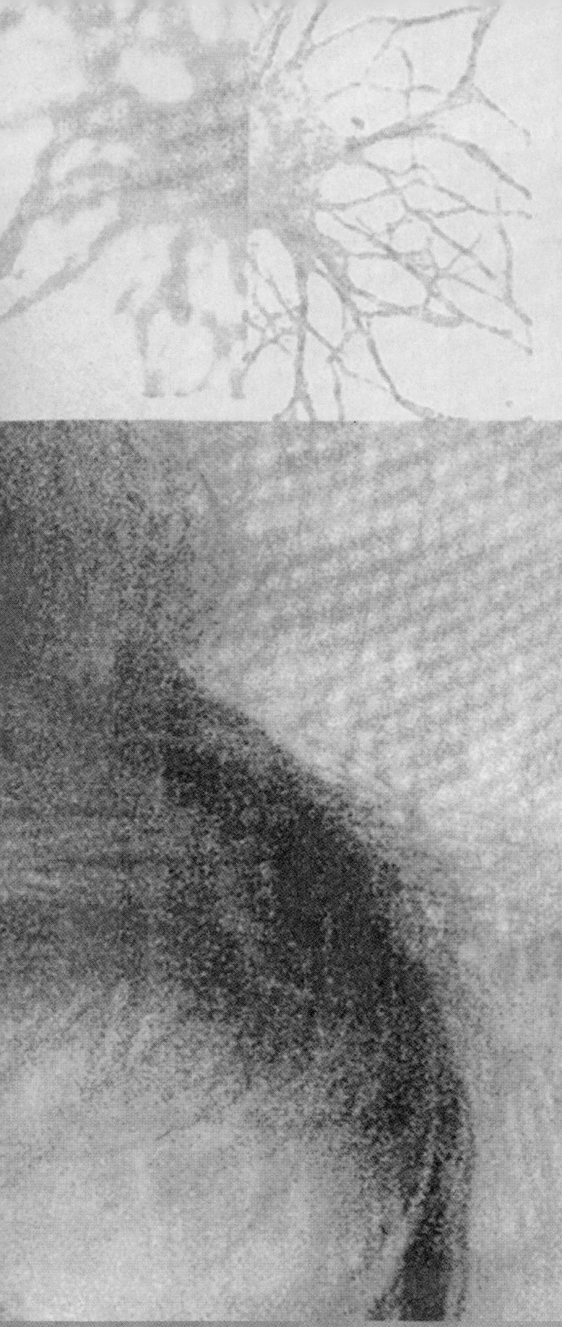

SEEKING SOLUTIONS

How Do Drugs Produce Their Effects?

People have used mind-altering drugs since the beginning of recorded history. Beer making and consumption have been known for 4,000 years. American Indians smoked or drank plant extracts that cause hallucinations to induce healing through trance states. Western writers, musicians, and artists have used drugs as a means to enhance sensitivity and creativity in their work. Not only are many of the drugs addicting, many also have psychoactive effects that work over the short term to change mood and over the long term to change the drug taker's personality.

Through psychological and pharmacological research, we are beginning to understand the mechanisms for these changes. We now know that drugs can alter brain function either by excessively exciting or inhibiting synapses. In some cases, a drug causes rapid, uncontrolled firing of postsynaptic neurons. In other cases, the drug blocks the normal flow of impulses from one neuron to the next. Synapses can be overstimulated by drugs that mimic the action of neurotransmitters, causing neurotransmitters to be released excessively in the absence of normal signals or interfering with inactivation of neurotransmitters in the synapse. Amphetamine (speed), for example, is a psychological stimulant; it produces its effect by provoking the release of noradrenaline at synapses in the brain. Nicotine produces a stimulating effect by mimicking the effects of acetylcholine. But synapses can also be inhibited or shut down by substances that block receptor sites on the postsynaptic neuron, block the synthesis or storage of neurotransmitters in the presynaptic cell, or prevent the release of neurotransmitters. Valium, a well-known muscle relaxant, antidepressant, and anti-anxiety drug, increases the normal effects of GABA, an inhibitory neurotransmitter at brain synapses. The tranquilizer chlorpromazine attaches to the postsynaptic cell to block the normal effects of acetylcholine and noradrenaline.

Although many psychoactive or mind-altering drugs can produce both psychological and physiological dependence, certain compounds, for example, opium, morphine, and crack cocaine, are particularly addictive. The short-term effect of taking any one of these drugs, which is generally described as "feeling good," results in long-term changes in the way brain synapses function. Cocaine, for example, causes a sudden increase in the release of dopamine in brain areas that serve our emotions and sensations of pleasure and pain. Massive release of dopamine results in a depletion of dopamine in presynaptic cells, making less available for later release. After a few experiences of this sort, stimuli that would normally evoke pleasure no longer do so. The depletion of dopamine in these brain areas leads to feelings of depression. Consequently, the only way the drug taker can feel normal again is to rely more or less continually on the drug. This vicious circle leads to serious problems for the user. But, as we are all well aware, they also create major social problems that burden even the nonuser.

ganized components of the nervous system function to communicate, store, and generate information.

The two major divisions of the human nervous system are the ***central nervous system (CNS)*** and the ***peripheral nervous system (PNS)***. The CNS consists of the brain and spinal cord and is primarily responsible for storing and processing information coming to it. The PNS consists of nerve tracts scattered throughout the body, carrying information from the sensory systems to the CNS and from the CNS to the muscles and glands of the body.

Take a look at the overview of the human nervous system provided in Figure 3-9. Follow the path of information in this real case of a person encountering an unexpected event: A former firefighter is driving home on the highway when he notices a smashed car flipped over on the side of the road. His eyes are stimulated first, triggering recognition of the damaged car, a driver trapped inside the vehicle, and smoke

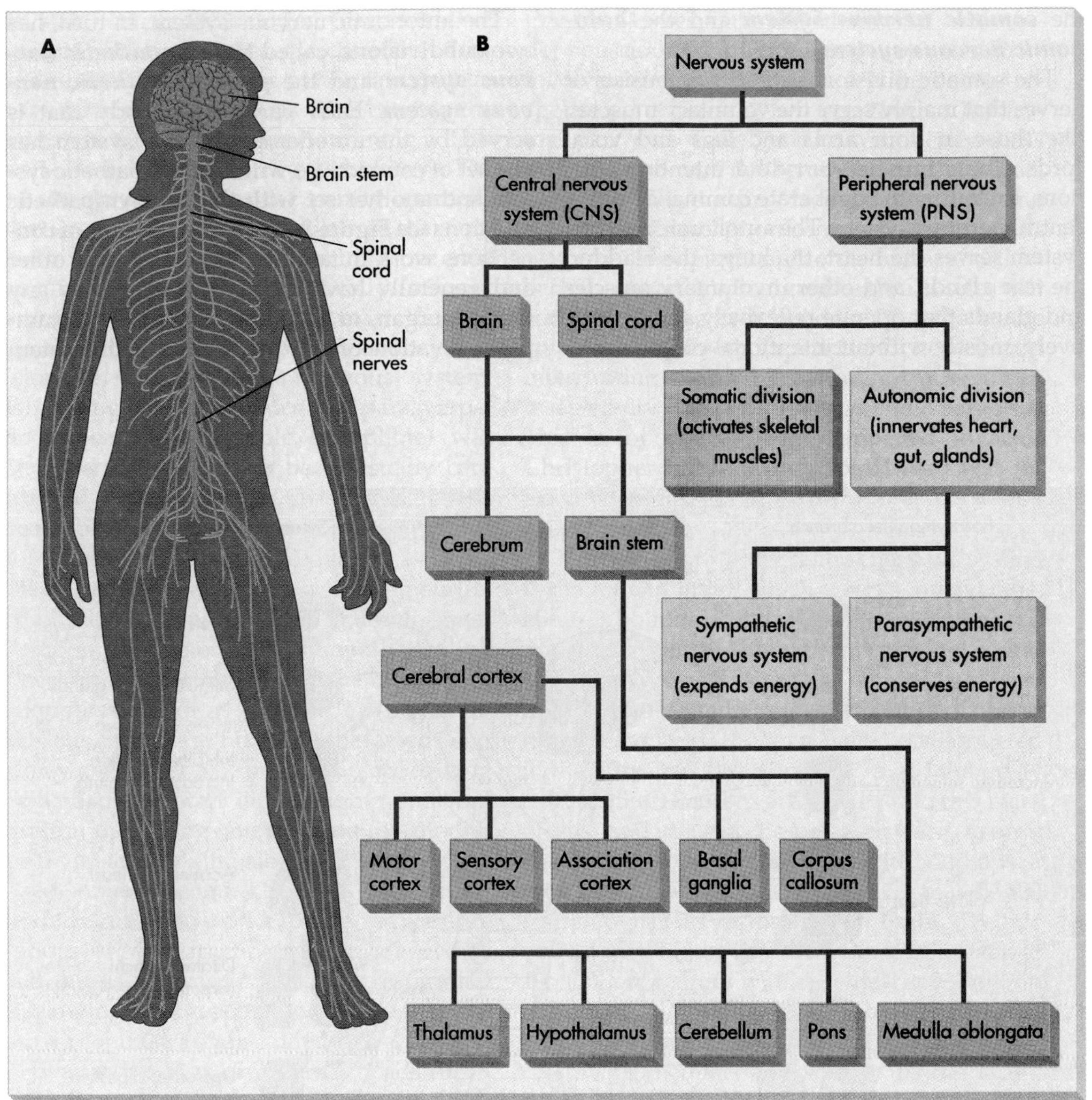

3-9 Organization of the Nervous System

The nervous system is divided into the central nervous system (CNS)—which consists of the brain and spinal cord—and the peripheral nervous system (PNS)—which consists of the somatic and autonomic divisions. The CNS is shown in red and the PNS in blue.

coming out of the engine. He formulates a plan, which is translated into neural signals enabling him to take action—to stop, run to the smoking car, and pull the dazed driver out of the car before it explodes in a burst of flames. All of this takes place over the course of a few seconds, probably without conscious awareness. Now, think of situations that you encounter every day. Think about all the lights, sounds, and other sources of information in your environment, and the great variety of possible ways you have of responding to them. Any and all stimuli automatically initiate an informational process within the PNS; that information finds its way into the CNS, which supports conscious cognitive processing, leading ultimately to deliberate responses to these stimuli.

The Peripheral Nervous System

The PNS has sensory neurons that carry information about the body and the environment to the CNS and motor neurons that convert the decisions of the CNS into action. The motor component of the PNS is subdivided further, into

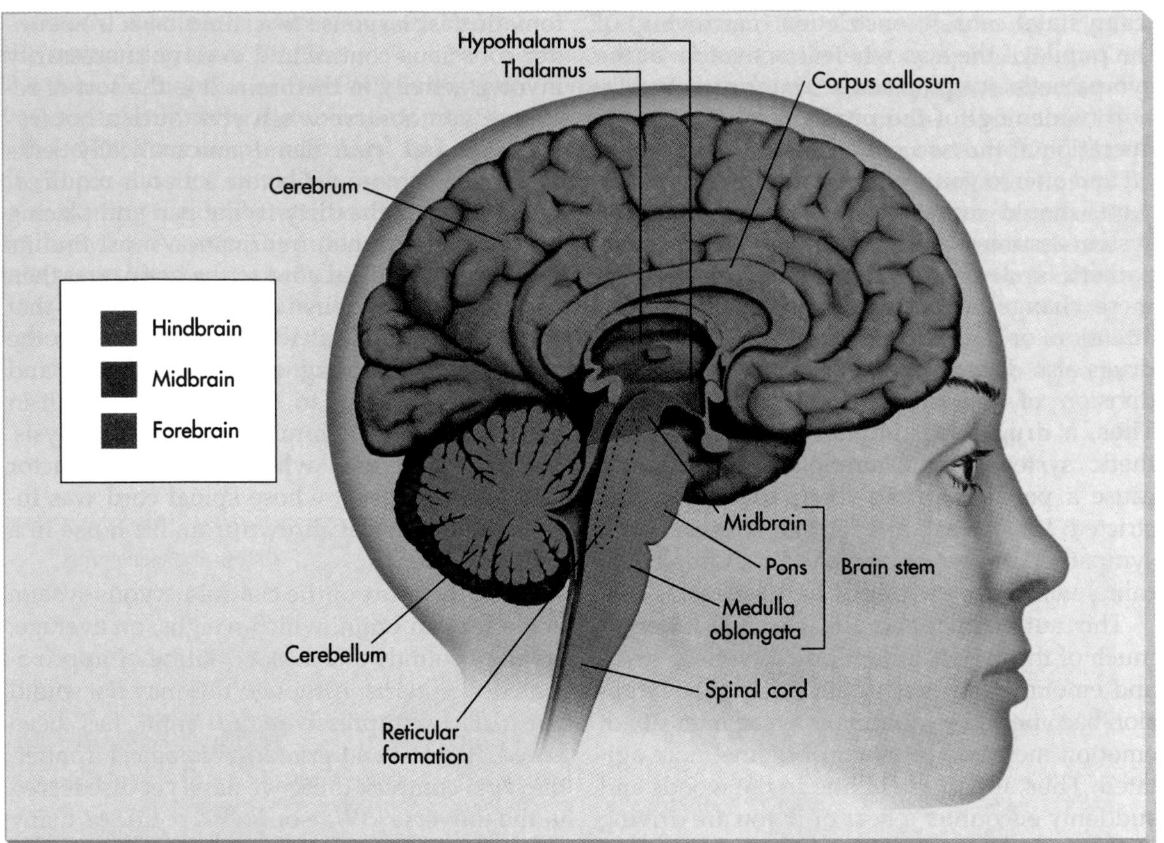

3-11 The Human Brain

This is a midsagittal, or side, view of the brain, which results when the body is divided along the midline into two equal halves. You are looking at the inside surface of the right half of the brain. The forebrain (in blue) is the largest and most recently evolved division of the brain. The midbrain (in green) is the smallest division. The second largest division is the hindbrain (in red), which is the oldest part of the brain and similar in structure for all vertebrates.

events. As we will learn in detail, the brain is the center for complex human information processing.

Although it is a simplification, we can think of the brain as being divided into three major parts that are further subdivided on the basis of structure and function. From the top of the spinal cord on up, in order of evolution, these parts are the (1) hindbrain, (2) midbrain, and (3) forebrain (see Figure 3-11).

The ***hindbrain***, the oldest part of the brain, has changed little in millions of years of evolution. Whether you examine the primitive brain of an alligator or the newly evolved brain of the human species, the structure and function of the hindbrain are similar. Its functions are primarily to serve complex but automatic activity, such as breathing. It includes the reticular formation, pons, medulla, and cerebellum. The ***midbrain***, which is the smallest division of the three in human beings, makes connections with the hindbrain and the forebrain and also has important functions in emotional feelings and reactions. It lies deep within the brain, covered by the forebrain. The ***forebrain***, which is largest in human beings and contains the most recently evolved parts of the brain, is involved both in initiating movements and in conducting higher mental processes such as thinking and language.

Some components of the brain that are of special interest to psychologists are also highlighted in Figure 3-11. The spinal cord connects to the brain at the ***brain stem***. From the bottom up, the brain stem consists of the medulla oblongata, the pons, the reticular formation, the cerebellum, and terminates in the thalamus and hypothalamus. Capping these structures are two cerebral hemispheres that are covered by an outer layer of neural tissue ("gray matter") called the ***cerebral cortex*** ("bark" in Latin for its similarity to the bark, or outer layer, of a tree limb). These cerebral hemispheres are connected by a bundle of fibers (about 200 million axons) called the ***corpus callosum***, by which the two hemispheres communicate with each other. Figure 3-12A provides a top view of the brain, which shows how the two cerebral hemispheres are divided by a deep groove that runs down the middle of the brain. Figure 3-12B depicts the hemispheres as they would appear if

▼ *An inside view of an actual brain.*

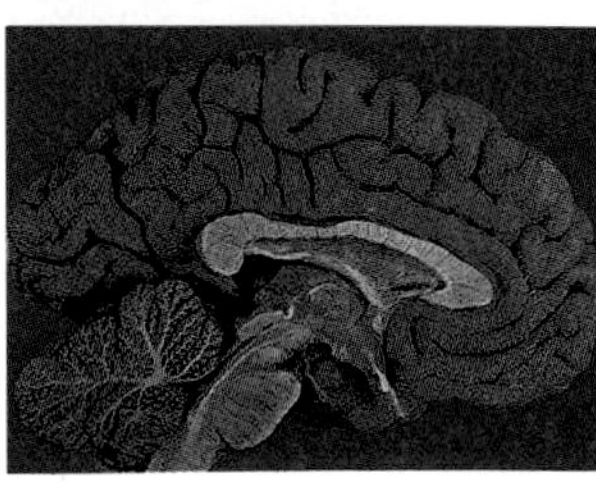

they were pulled apart to reveal the corpus callosum.

To visualize the arrangement of the major structures of the brain, imagine making a fist, plunging it deep into a large mass of pizza dough, and then holding your arm up with the dough completely covering your fist. Your wrist and fist (with a few small attachments) constitute the brain stem. The lower portion of your arm represents the spinal cord, which is connected to the brain at the brain stem. The mass of dough hiding your fist and surrounding the upper part of the brain stem is the cerebrum, which coordinates cognitive and emotional functions. If you baked the dough and then divided it down the middle, the two halves would represent the cerebral hemispheres. Buried in the dough, beneath the cerebrum, but above your fist might be a sausage standing in for the corpus callosum, a structure that connects the two cerebral hemispheres and allows them to communicate. If you then covered this mess with a thin sheet of mozzarella cheese, the cheese layer would be the cerebral cortex (approximately 4.5 mm thick in a real brain); the cortex is responsible for higher mental processes in human beings.

The Brain Stem

The brain stem is the part of the hindbrain that is involved in automatic but vital functions of the body, such as breathing, blood circulation, and sleep. Spread throughout the lower to middle brain stem is a network of fibers called the ***reticular formation***, which plays a key role in arousal. The reticular formation alerts the forebrain to receive and process incoming sensory information and is critically involved in sleep and emotion. Without it, we are not aware of sensory information. Damage to the reticular formation results in coma because the forebrain cannot be aroused. Have you even wondered why general anesthesia makes you unconscious? It depresses the activation of the reticular formation.

Other brain stem structures control relatively complex but automatic physiological and performance functions. The ***medulla oblongata***, an elongated bundle of fibers, is closest to and looks like an extension of the spinal cord. It controls heartbeat, circulation, and breathing. Have you read about college students who die from too much alcohol in drinking contests? The cause of death is typically respiratory or heart

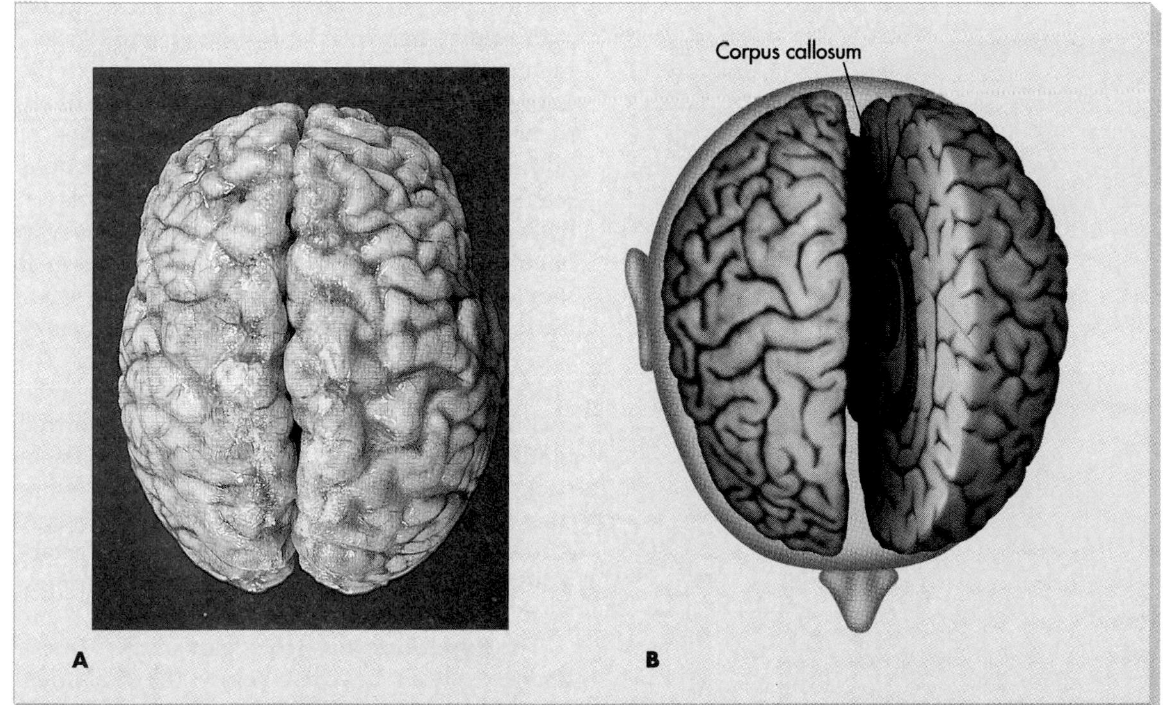

3-12 The Corpus Callosum

(A) The photo is a top view of the brain, showing the fissure that divides the two cerebral hemispheres. (B) This drawing separates the two cerebral hemispheres to reveal the underlying corpus callosum.

failure due to alcohol's depressive effect on the medulla.

Also in the brain stem is the ***pons*** (from "bridge" in Latin), a roundish neural structure just above the medulla that connects ("bridges") parts of the brain stem to one another and to the spinal cord. It plays a role in sleep and respiration. Another brain stem structure is the ***cerebellum*** ("little brain" in Latin), lying just behind the pons and medulla and looking a bit like a small version of the cerebrum, mainly because of its wrinkled or convoluted surface. The cerebellum is important for some types of learning and memory and coordinates voluntary movements necessary for balance and smooth and graceful motion, from basketball to ballet. Birds, which must have precise muscle coordination to fly through trees and scoop up insects, have large cerebellums compared to other parts of their brains. Damage to the cerebellum leads to uncoordinated movements, which can be seen in Parkinson's disease patients and some long-term alcoholics, even when they are sober.

At the top of the brain stem are the neural centers that relay information between various sense organs and the cerebral cortex. The functions of these centers are not entirely known, although they are believed to process or transform some of the incoming information rather than just pass it on. The major sensory relay center is the ***thalamus*** (from the Greek *thalamos* for "inner chamber"). Information from all sensory systems, except smell, passes through the thalamus, where it is redirected to higher brain centers. Thus, the thalamus coordinates information coming from two or more different input systems (Ungerleider & Haxby, 1994).

3-13 The Limbic System

The limbic system lies between the cerebral hemispheres and the brain stem, and is particularly involved in arousal, motivation, emotion, and memory. Major structures include: the thalamus, which receives sensory information from various sensory systems, does some initial processing, and relays the information to the cerebral cortex; the amygdala, which is involved in emotional responses; the hippocampus, which is involved in storing memories; and the hypothalamus, which is involved in emotional and motivational behaviors, including fighting, fleeing, eating, drinking, and mating. The hypothalamus links the nervous and endrocrine system by producing pituitary gland hormones, which stimulate the pituitary gland to release its hormones into the bloodstream. (Based on Bloom, Lazerson, and Hofstadter, 1985).

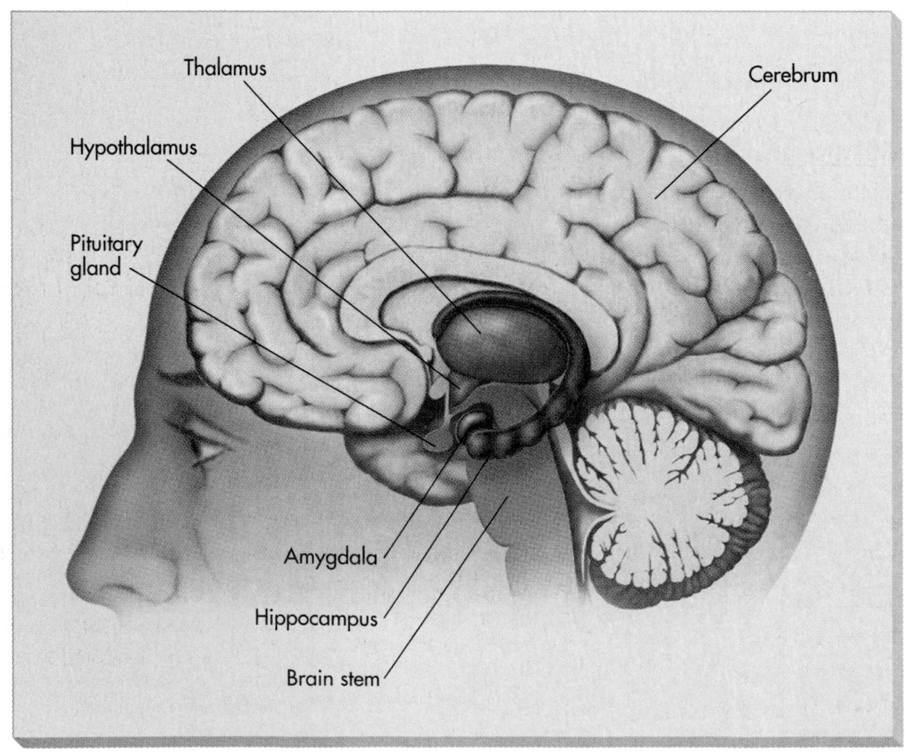

The Limbic System

Between the brain stem and the cerebral hemispheres, there is a donut-shaped group of structures involved in emotion and memory (see Figure 3-13). This neural group is called the ***limbic system***, and includes the hypothalamus, along with the amygdala, the hippocampus, and a number of other centers and pathways.

The ***amygdala*** (Greek for "almond," so named because of its almond shape) plays a role in eating, drinking, sexual behavior, and in the aggressive aspects of emotions. Electrical stimulation to the amygdala in animals, and presumably in human beings as well, can trigger extreme aggression and intense rage. Removing parts of the amygdala can reduce the intensity of those emotional reactions (Miller, 1995).

The ***hippocampus*** (for "sea horse," because of its "S" shape) appears to be important to the encoding and retrieval of long-term memories (Squire, 1987). It enables you to "smell" a rose over again when you think about it, and retrieve memories of events that are associated with the odor. Most of these sensory memories are likely to be pleasant, as in childhood memories of home cooking aromas. But these connections may also play a role in the flashbacks reported by rape victims, combat troops, and others who have experienced violence first hand, even if they do not have conscious awareness of associating a particular odor with their experiences (see the discussion of posttraumatic stress disorder in Chapter 15). One of our students who had been raped behind a garbage can reported that for several years after the experience flashbacks of the rape experience would occur every time she encountered the smell of garbage. Knowing that such connections can be established is a first step toward altering or stopping them.

The ***hypothalamus*** (the "gatekeeper" of the limbic system) lies just below the thalamus, where it serves as a link between the brain and

THINKING CRITICALLY

Stimulation of certain areas of the limbic system and some areas connected to the limbic system appears to produce extremely pleasurable sensations in some animals. What do you think are the implications of this finding? There may be powerful implications for shaping human behavior.

James Olds and Peter Milner (1954) were the first to report that animals learned to press a lever or to make other unusual responses when rewarded only with electrical stimulation to these "pleasure centers" of the brain. In some cases, rats quite literally starved when given a choice between pressing one lever for food and another for electrical brain stimulation. Animals rewarded in such a way crossed electrified grids, swam through water (which they usually avoid), and underwent extreme exertion to have their pleasure centers stimulated. Some of the animals whose pleasure centers were stimulated pushed a pedal up to 5,000 times an hour until they dropped from exhaustion.

In follow-up studies with human volunteer participants, investigators found that electrical stimulation in these brain areas produced reports of extremely pleasurable experiences, equivalent to the sensations of sexual orgasm (Wise & Rompre, 1989; Blum, Cull, Braverman & Comings, 1996).

The data suggest that these areas of the brain generate the sensation of pleasure; other brain areas might function in creating sensations of pain or other nonpleasureable experiences. Some people have suggested that brain stimulation might be the route to mind control. Nonetheless, it pays to be skeptical of these broad overgeneralizations since other factors may also be involved.

the endocrine system (a system that produces chemical messengers known as hormones). Not only does the hypothalamus control behavior through its neural connections, it also manufactures, secretes, and controls hormones and neurotransmitters that enter the bloodstream and have widespread behavioral effects. The hypothalamus is involved in a variety of behaviors vital to the survival of the species, including eating, temperature regulation, sexual arousal, and fighting. It monitors the state of many vital internal organs—keeping your heart throbbing and stomach churning when you are in the throes of passion (or indigestion, as the case may be). Because the hypothalamus connects the brain and internal organs, the "higher mental processes" of the cortex can often dampen the so-called "gut" emotional reactions of anger, rage, and hatred (Maier, Watkins, & Fleshner, 1994).

The hypothalamus also plays a role in sleeping and biorhythms. The hormone melatonin, although produced elsewhere, acts on the hypothalamus and aids its control of biorhythms. Manufacturers of synthetic melatonin have advertised that, through its action on the hypothalamus, small doses can counteract insomnia and jet lag (Haimov & Lavie, 1996). Somewhat more outrageous claims promote melatonin as a means of slowing down aging, fighting disease, and enhancing libido. You should understand that there are few neuroscientific facts about melatonin at this time and that most of these claims have insufficient evidence to be taken seriously.

Recently, some researchers have suggested that the hypothalamus may also be related to homosexuality among men. The anterior hypothalamus of homosexual men, obtained after death at autopsy, has been found to be about half the size of the anterior hypothalamus in heterosexual men, and closer to the size found in women (LeVay, 1991). This difference is interesting in that it suggests a possible structural basis for homosexual behavior. But the results need to be interpreted cautiously. Only nineteen homosexual men were examined in this study. Furthermore, given that the observations were made at autopsy, we cannot conclude with certainty that a small hypothalamus causes or even predisposes toward homosexual behavior. The alternative—that homosexual behavior or AIDS (since most of the subjects died of that disease) causes the hypothalamus to shrink—is an equally reasonable hypothesis. In other words,

The human cerebral cortex is the largest structure in the nervous system and provides the biological material underlying complex behavior and higher mental processes.

this is a correlational study, and we cannot distinguish which is the cause and which is the effect.

The Cerebral Cortex

The human brain stem is not very different from those of most other mammalian species. In contrast, the human cerebral cortex, the outer layer of the cerebrum, is much more elaborated than in any other species of animal (see Figure 3-14). Because of this elaboration, the human brain is two-thirds of the weight of the entire human nervous system, weighing approximately three times more than would be expected for such a size mammal (Ackerman, 1992). Its surface is wrinkled, or convoluted, much of it hidden in grooves that greatly enlarge its surface area (to about 2.5 square feet, or about the size of a small desktop, if it were flattened out). The cerebral cortex, or cortical tissue, that human beings have in such abundance, provides the basis for our higher mental processes. As we have mentioned, the cerebral cortex covers the two cerebral hemispheres, which roughly look like mirror images of each other and are connected by the corpus callosum. The cerebral hemispheres receive and transmit specific information that allows us to learn, reason, and plan.

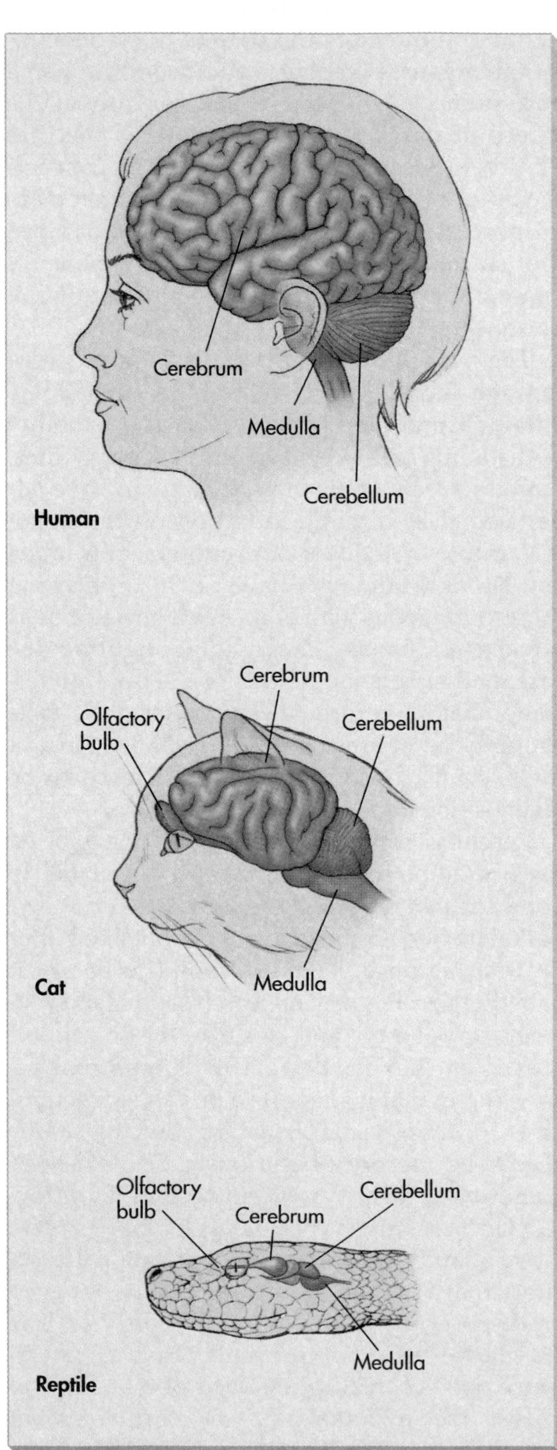

3-14 Increasing Cerebral Development

The forebrain comes to dominate the other structures of the brain in vertebrates that are higher on the evolutionary scale. This allows for more advanced cerebral development, including a larger cerebrum in human beings than in reptiles. The cerebrum of the reptile is about equal in size to its cerebellum. The cerebrum in the cat is much larger than its cerebellum. The cerebrum in the human being is many times the size of the cerebellum.

Deep fissures (folds) like the central fissure and the lateral fissure divide the cerebral cortex. These fissures roughly separate each of the cerebral hemispheres into four lobes: (1) the ***frontal lobe,*** which is responsible for associating different kinds of information, as well as for motor behavior; (2) the ***occipital lobe,*** which serves the visual system; (3) the ***temporal lobe,*** which is involved in hearing and verbal behavior; and (4) the ***parietal lobe,*** which serves other sensory systems. These cortical lobes work together to receive and interpret sensory information, integrate it with existing memories, process the result to develop a plan of action and execute that plan through the motor systems of the body. The locations of these four lobes is outlined in Figure 3-15.

The cerebral cortex is divided not only structurally but also according to the particular functions it controls (see Figure 3-16). Various sensory systems and action mechanisms of the body map onto five different functional areas of the cortex: (1) the ***motor cortex*** controls the voluntary movement of particular parts of the body and is in the frontal lobe; (2) the ***somatosensory cortex*** receives information from sensory receptors (about pain, touch, and temperature) beneath the skin and in various muscles and joints of the body and lies in the parietal lobe; (3) the ***visual cortex*** receives and integrates visual sensations and is in the occipital lobe; (4) the ***auditory and speech centers*** receive auditory information and produce speech and are in the temporal lobe; and (5) the

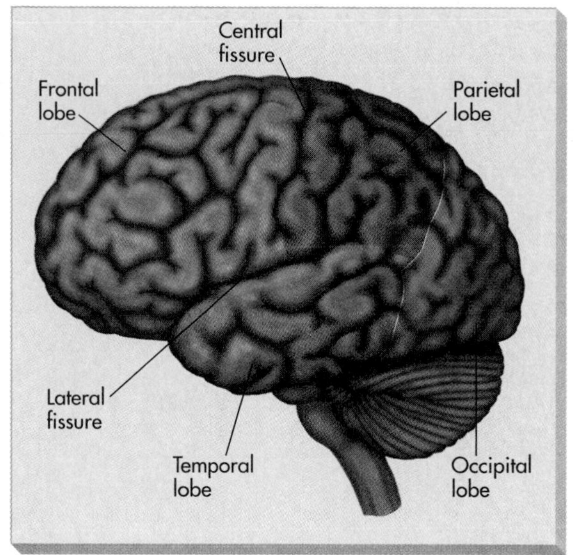

3-15 The Four Lobes of the Cortex

The frontal lobe is largely the association and motor cortex and is responsible for planning movements, inhibiting inappropriate behaviors, and some aspects of memory. The occipital lobe is part of the somatosensory cortex and is largely responsible for vision. The temporal lobe is part of the somatosensory cortex and the association cortex and is largely responsible for hearing, advanced visual processing, and verbal behavior. The parietal lobe is part of the somatosensory cortex and the association cortex and is responsible for body sensations.

relatively large and diffuse ***association cortex***, which is primarily in the frontal lobe, is not specialized for specific tasks, although it controls a wide range of behavioral functions and appears to be highly flexible or programmable (see Figure 3-17; each muscle group has a control center in the motor cortex). Most high-level cognitive skills such as memory, intelligence, and problem solving are supported primarily in the association areas of the brain. Moreover, electrical or mechanical stimulation of the association cortex has resulted in patient reports of vivid memories, often from long ago. This observation led investigators to suggest that perhaps everything an individual ever experienced is stored in the association cortex, just waiting to be stimulated for recall (Cohen & Eichenbaum, 1993).

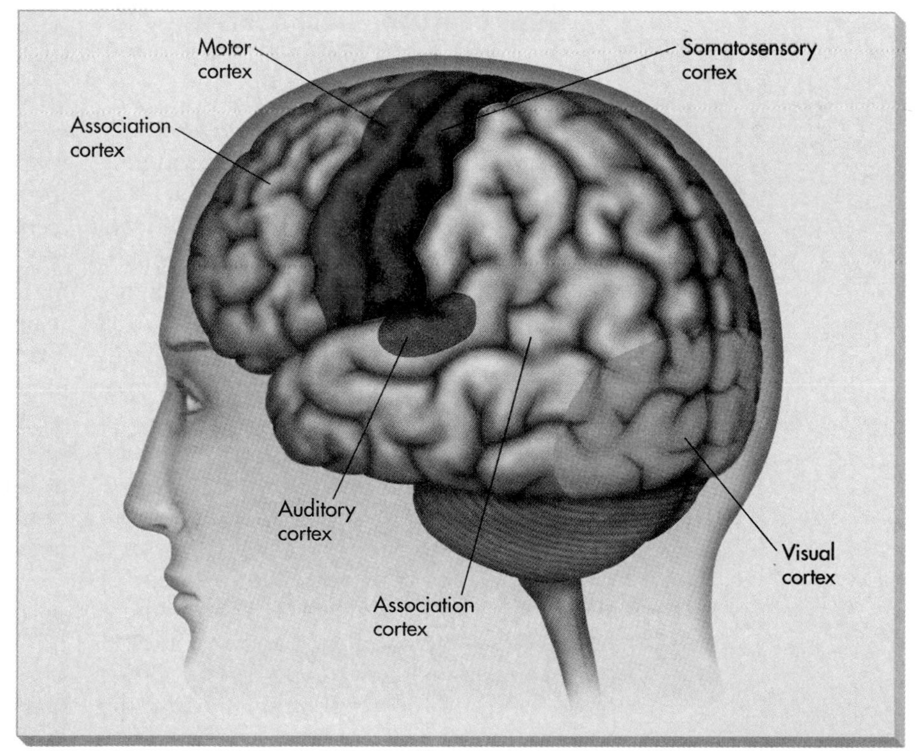

3-16 Functional Areas of the Cortex

The cortex is divided into sections based on function. The motor cortex receives information from and controls voluntary movement of particular body parts and muscles. The somatosensory cortex receives information coming from the skin and muscles. The visual cortex receives and integrates visual information. The auditory and speech centers receive auditory information and produce language. The association cortex is not specialized for specific tasks but integrates and controls information related to high-level cognitive skills. A larger percentage of the area of the human brain is devoted to the association cortex than is the rat brain or the cat brain.

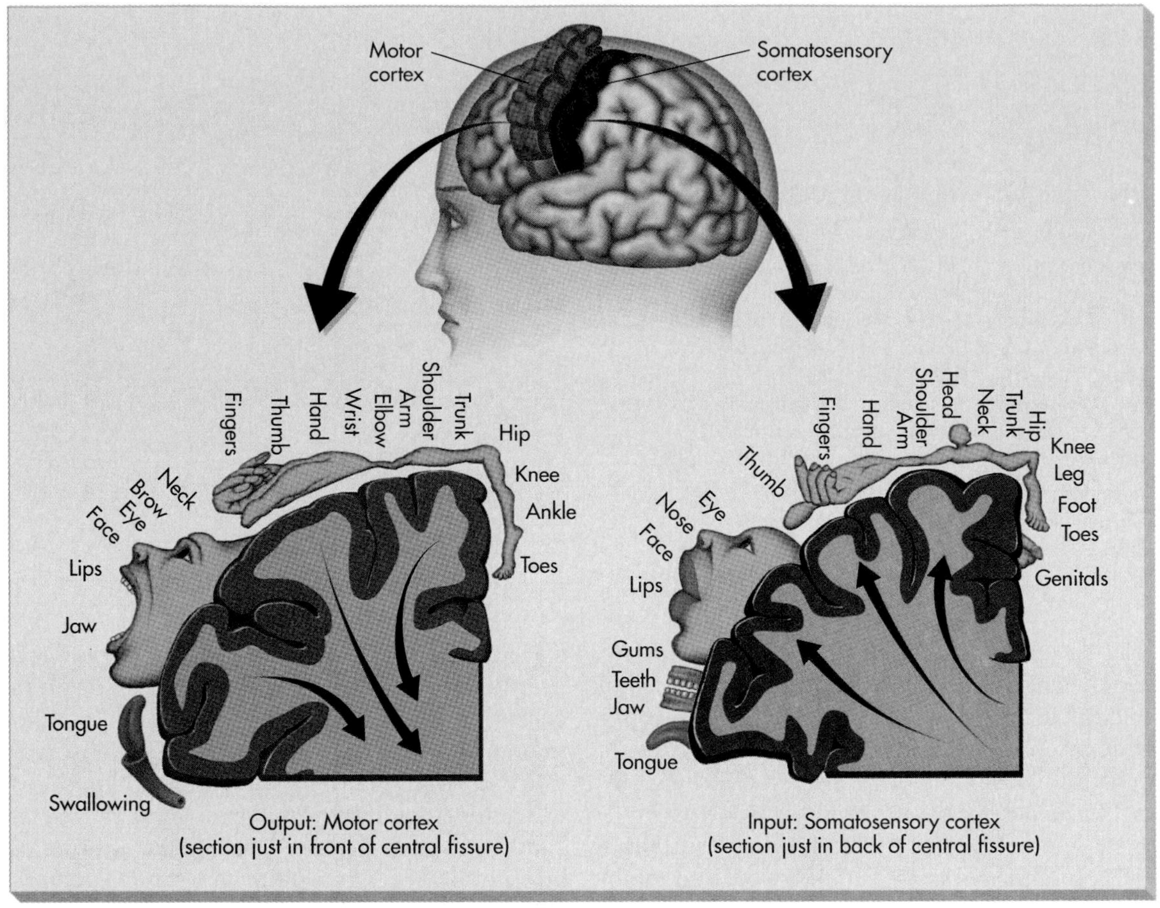

3-17 Motor and Somatosensory Projection Areas of the Cortex

A homunculus for the motor cortex shows the proportion of the cortex devoted to each body part in the motor cortex and another homunculus shows the proportion of the cortex devoted to each body part in the somatosensory cortex. The amount of cortical tissue is not proportional to the body part's size but rather to the amount of control needed from the cortex. Thus, more cortical tissue is devoted to the tongue, thumb, and fingers than to the upper arm. (Source: Penfield and Rasmussen, 1950)

Brain Function, Brain Damage and Brain Recovery

A nervous system that could simultaneously perform multiple tasks might have separate specialized subsystems, or modules, for each job. There could be one neural module for breathing, another for talking, a third for smelling, and so on. Each module could be "hard-wired" to do one and only one job. In fact, this may be how certain primitive parts of our brain function. Some parts of the brain are highly specialized.

Hard-wired modules do not afford much flexibility, however. Consider the frog, whose nervous system is quite primitive. Frogs have a very accurate, automatic bug detector wired into their visual systems that allows them to flick out their tongues at just the right moment to catch a passing fly. But this ability comes at a cost. In a classic study, Roger Sperry (1982) reported the results of an operation in which the frog's optic nerve was severed, inverted, and then reconnected and allowed to regenerate. In the regenerated optic nerve, then, the signals in the frog's bug detection system were "upside down." The behavioral consequence was that, when the frog spotted a fly overhead, its tongue immediately snapped out—but 180 degrees in the wrong direction. Because the frog's bug detection system is hard-wired, it is unable to adjust to an upside-down visual world. Frog brains are "non-plastic," in this and many other ways, so they never learn to correct for the interference created by this operation. Fortunately, only some parts of the human brain are so hard-wired. Other parts are less differentiated, more programmable, and highly flexible in function so that the human nervous system can and does perform many functions simultaneously.

Plasticity

The adaptability of the human brain was dramatically illustrated in a series of classic experiments (Carr, 1935). Research participants wore

SEEKING SOLUTIONS

Biological Clocks

There is a rhythm to most biological systems and to at least some behaviors, and the biological and psychological rhythms might be linked. The most common rhythm is one that repeats itself approximately every 24 hours and is called a *circadian rhythm* (circa: "approximately"; dies: "day"). Rhythms might be "driven" by external stimulation, such as the light-dark cycle from the earth's turning on its axis. Indeed, there is recent evidence of a light-sensitive hormone, called melatonin, in human beings and other animals that helps to synchronize bodily functions with day-night cycles (Holden 1992). But we also know that many rhythms, though influenced by environmental factors such as light or heat, are basically endogenous or internal, that is, genetically inherent in the system's structure and functioning. We can see this by studying the system's cyclic activity in the laboratory where the influence of the environment can be factored out (for example, the organism can be kept in constant darkness or constant light). Even under these conditions, circadian rhythms still turn out to be typically about a day in length. In human beings, the rhythms actually seem to be slightly longer than 24 hours. Thus, it is possible that night/day cycles train us into a 24-hour rhythm, a rhythm that normally would be 24.5 to 25 hours long (Minors & Waterhouse, 1981).

Almost all physiological processes show a variation in time and a rhythm of some sort, including the levels of many blood constituents and the levels of various chemicals in the urine. Examples are the twenty-eight-day menstrual cycle in women, the twenty to twenty-two day testosterone cycle in men (yes, men have cycles too), and the ninety-minute dream cycle during sleep. Even body temperature varies cyclically during the day—from a low of 97 degrees to highs over 99 degrees (98.6 is just an average). Evidence suggests that the nervous system is the master controller of all the other body rhythms. Variation in nervous system functioning is especially interesting to psychologists because it means there could be rhythms in behavior as well as in physiological activity. Indeed, there appear to be daily variations in such things as mood, eye-hand coordination, and memory.

If circadian rhythm is not exactly dependent on light and dark illumination, there might be some internal "biological clock" that does the regulating. All organisms, from algae to human beings, seem to have such a built-in clock, which incidentally might still require synchronization by light-sensitive hormones. Recently, a master clock candidate has been located in the human brain. This is a structure in the hypothalamus called the *supra-chiasmatic nucleus*. The supra-chiasmatic nucleus appears to be essentially identical in all mammals. If the nucleus is destroyed, then rhythmic behavioral patterns are eliminated. Sleeping, eating, body temperature, and many other normally rhythmic activities are fragmented and occur randomly in time.

Recent evidence shows that illness and various drugs can disrupt body rhythms. The effect of a drug (and hence how big a dose to give) may depend on the circadian levels of numerous other chemicals in the body. Depending on the time of day, the proper dosage of drug to obtain the desired effect could be either twice as much as the standard or only half as much (Holden, 1992). In a similar vein, it has been shown that toxic drugs have different effects at different times of the day—a dose that will kill an animal at one time will have a much less drastic effect at another time. These results are important to the drug treatment of disease, including the ability to use otherwise toxic drugs (say to cure cancer) if they are administered at the proper time of day.

◀ *These Japanese students snatch a few moments of sleep at the Detroit Metro Airport as they wait for their continuing flight. Traveling through numerous time zones disrupts the body's circadian rhythm.*

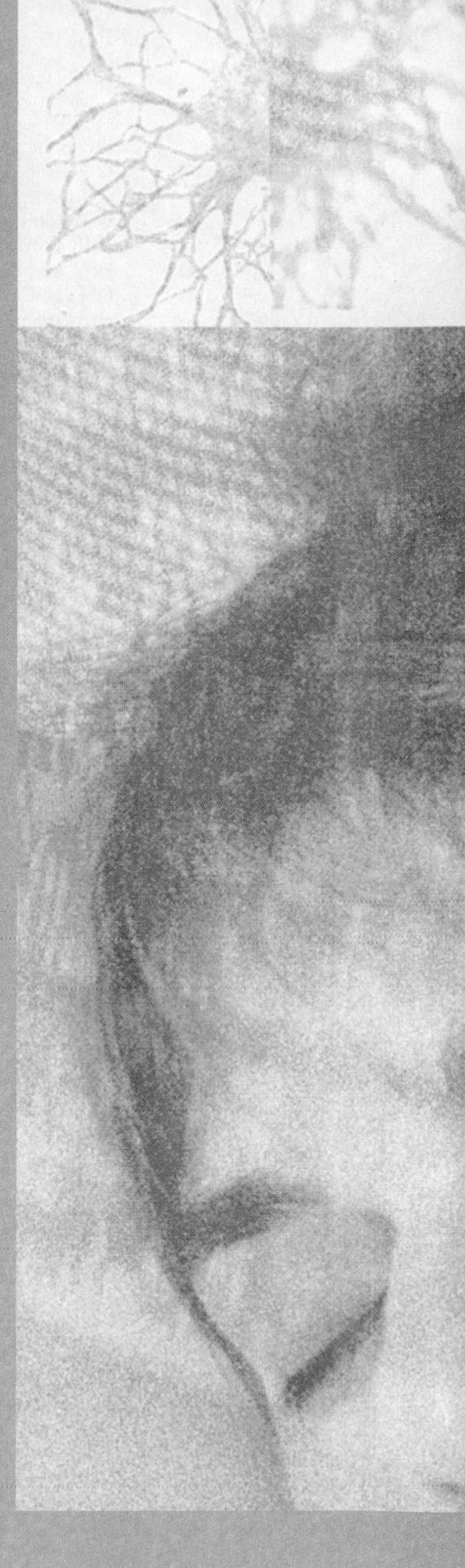

optical lenses that turned the world upside down and backward (right-left reversal). When the lenses were first worn, participants saw a confusing environment and their movements were totally uncoordinated (much like the frog with an inverted optic nerve). Sounds from objects "seen" on the right were heard on the left. Objects seen as above were in fact below. The participants' behavior was reduced to trial and error.

After three days of wearing the lenses, however, the research participants' helplessness gave way gradually to skilled movements within a new visual frame of reference. In other words, the participants adapted to the distortions created initially by the lenses, so that they were no longer perceived as distortions. The brain had been fully retrained. Incidentally, what do you think happened when subjects removed their glasses? Right! When the glasses came off, participants reported new and opposite distortions in the "normal" environment. They needed to readapt to the norm. Fortunately and in contrast to the frog's inflexibility, people could adjust to new visual worlds rather quickly.

Plasticity is a term commonly used to refer to the capacity of the brain to adapt and change. In some sense, we can "program" and "reprogram" parts of the brain through interactions with the world. Experience can literally modify biology, including the biology of the brain.

Some parts of the brain change continuously throughout a lifetime, programmed and reprogrammed by interactions with the environment. How can this happen? Can we grow more neurons? Apparently not. The number of neurons in the human brain reaches its maximum in early infancy. But existing neurons frequently grow larger, and develop new branches of axons and dendrites (Purves & Hadley, 1985). Studies have shown that an enriched environment can lead to larger neurons, with more branching of dendrites, an increased number of supporting or nutrient cells, and greater density of blood vessels. The increased dendritic branching is particularly significant, as it means each dendrite can integrate information from a greater number of sources, facilitating performance on a variety of learning and memory tasks. These structural changes in the neurons, brought on by environmental influences, may be at the heart of the brain's adaptability, plasticity, and programmability.

Dendritic branching becomes even more important as we grow older. Nearly all people lose some neurons with age. Increased dendritic branching compensates for this loss, enabling us to stay alert, because the total number of connections in the brain is preserved. There is some reason to think that practice or activity can help to maintain or even increase these connections. Researchers have recently reported that estrogen (a female sex hormone) treatment might enhance dendritic growth in women, reducing the memory loss that usually accompanies Alzheimer's disease (Matthews et al., 1997; Honjo et al., 1995). In contrast, for people who become senile, surviving neurons fail to maintain or increase their branching. Consequently, the number of connections in the brain falls, eroding the capacity to process information (Buell & Coleman, 1981). Dendritic branching is also *decreased* by certain experiential factors. For example, exposure to alcohol over a period of time has been found to produce shrinkage in the human brain.

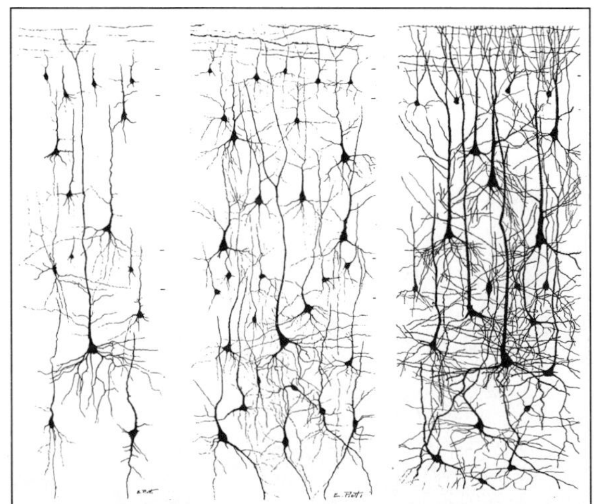

► *Neural connections grow rapidly at the beginning of life. Shown here are sections of the human cortex in a) a newborn, b) a three-month-old, and c) a fifteen-month-old.*

Lateralization

Like most of the human body, the cerebrum is bilaterally symmetrical—there are both right and left cerebral hemispheres, and one appears to be nearly the mirror image of the other. To a certain extent, each hemisphere of your brain receives information from and controls the action of one-half of your body. Functional control by the cerebral cortex tends to be contralateral, this is, the right cortex controls the left side of the body, and the left cortex controls the right side. For example, if you lay your left hand on a hot stove, the pain message is carried via your sensory nerves and spinal cord to the right hemisphere of your brain. One exception to this rule is your visual system: half of the information coming into each eye goes to one side of the brain and half to the other, as you can see in Figure 3-18. Normally, we are not aware that the two halves of our brains are receiving different information because the two hemispheres communicate with each other across the corpus callosum.

Occasionally, and usually as a last resort, the corpus callosum is severed surgically in epileptic patients in an attempt to prevent seizures from spreading from one cerebral hemisphere to another. This procedure is called the split-brain operation. To illustrate the effects of a split-brain operation, consider the following test. A split-brain subject sits facing a divided visual display. On the left side of the display, the image of a spoon is flashed, and on the right the image of a knife appears (see Figure 3-19). The subject, who has been instructed to focus on the midline of the screen, is asked to report verbally what he or she sees. The split-brain subject answers, "a knife," as both the image of the knife and the language center of the brain are in the left hemisphere.

Next the experimenter places a number of table utensils in front of the patient, but behind a cloth screen, and asks the patient to pick out with the left hand the item he or she has seen. The patient will choose a spoon, as the left hand is controlled by the right motor cortex, and that hemisphere saw the image of the spoon. But when asked what he or she has chosen to match the visual stimulus, the patient will respond again by answering "a knife." Nonetheless, that verbal response is typically hesitant and often accompanied by expressions of doubt, suggesting that he or she knows that something unusual is occurring. The image of the knife, flashed on the right side of the screen, is perceived in the left cerebral hemisphere, which is responsible for verbal behavior, among other activities. The nonverbal right hemisphere, specialized for spatial activities, sees the spoon that was projected onto the left side of the screen. Lacking the interconnections of the corpus callosum that would permit resolution of discrepancies and integration of sensory information, the two cerebral hemispheres register different images and respond differently (Sperry, 1974, 1982).

This condition does not manifest itself normally outside of these laboratory circumstances, because there are ways for the split-brain pa-

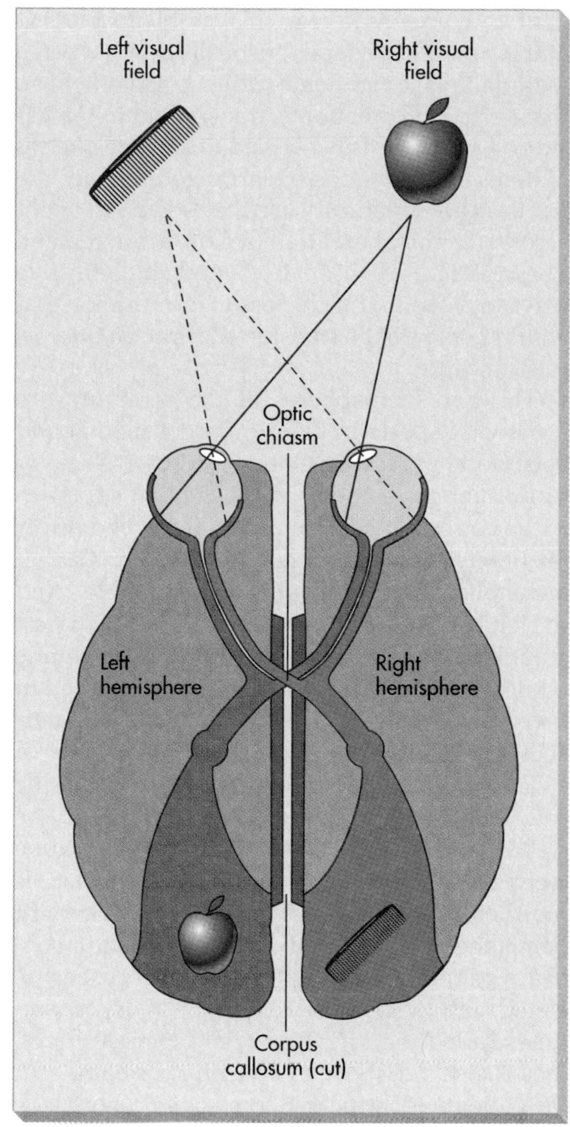

3-18 The Visual Pathway

Schematic representation of what the two eyes see when fixated on a single point in the environment. Information from the left visual field is focused on the inside of the retina of the left eye and the outside of the retina of the right eye. These two parts of the two retinas both project to the right cerebral hemisphere. This means that an object in the left visual field is registered only by the right hemisphere as long as the eyes remain fixated on the center spot. Similarly, information from the right visual field is registered only by the left cerebral hemisphere. Normally, information is shared between the hemispheres via the corpus collosum, but if this band of fibers has been severed, no sharing of information will be possible.

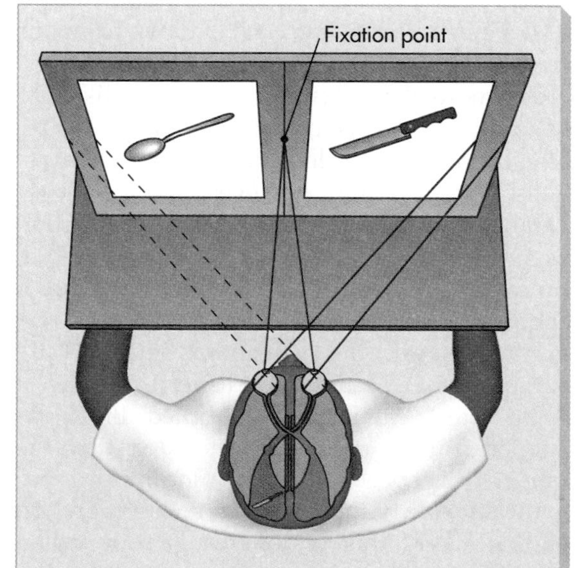

3-19 The Set-up for the Split-Brain Experiment

Visual information on the right side of the screen is projected to the split-brain patient's left hemisphere, which controls language. When asked what he sees, the patient will reply that he sees a knife.

tient to compensate for this problem. For example, patients characteristically hold written material to the right side of their visual field so that verbal information is transmitted to the left side of the brain. When asked to arrange a series of items according to a prearranged pattern, patients characteristically use their left hand (right cerebral hemisphere) to make the arrangement. These patients devise fairly simple but effective ways to make up for the loss of information that would generally be transferred through the corpus callosum.

The two hemispheres of the cerebrum are somewhat specialized for different mental and behavioral processes. One or the other is said to be dominant, resulting in the general superiority in performance of one side of the body over the other, as in right or left handedness. The left hemisphere is dominant in most people. And the left hemisphere appears to control analytical abilities such as language and problem solving, while the right hemisphere is more involved in holistic activities such as form and space perception and music (Sperry, 1982).

Each hemisphere also plays its own unique role in emotions. Evidence suggests that the right hemisphere is more involved in negative feelings and their expression, and the left is more involved in positive feelings. If the right hemisphere is damaged, leaving the left in control, a patient will appear continuously cheerful, elated, and even indifferent to the injury (sometimes called the "indifference" reaction). If, on the other hand, the left hemisphere is damaged, the patient will appear gloomy, angry, hopeless, guilty, and full of despair (sometimes called the "catastrophic reaction") (Springer & Deutsch, 1985).

If a general principle can be drawn from our current knowledge of the brain, it is that higher-order, more plastic functions are not as likely to be localized (that is, contained in a specific region of the brain) as lower, "hard-wired" functions. Interestingly, however, the relatively "high" brain function of language production was one of the first to be localized. In 1861, Paul Broca (1824–1880), a French surgeon, wrote about a patient who had lost virtually all capacity to speak (the patient was called "Tan" because this was the only distinct syllable he could utter). After the patient died, Broca examined Tan's brain and concluded that the cause of his speech loss was a localized injury to the left side of the frontal lobe. In recognition of this work, this brain area is now called ***Broca's area***. Research has consistently shown that it is intimately involved in the production of speech. Shortly after Broca reported his discovery, Carl Wernicke (1848–1905), a German neurologist, found that damage to the left hemisphere's temporal lobe created problems for speech comprehension. This area is now called ***Wernicke's area***. These early studies of localization of language functions in the left cerebral hemisphere led to the hypothesis that, in most people, the left hemisphere is specialized for language.

Recovery of Function

Is it possible to reprogram or rewire the brain after brain damage? This is a complex question, to which the answer must be "partly yes, partly no." We have much to learn about the damaged brain's ability to recapture its functions. New studies suggest that the brain's ability to heal itself after injury is greater than previously believed. For example, researcher Timothy Pons and his colleagues found that substantial reorganization in the brain occurred over twelve years after mature macaque monkeys had the nerves of the arm severed where they leave the spinal cord. The part of the brain normally localized to receive sensory stimuli from the arms had rewired itself to receive sensory stimuli from the face (Pons, Garraghty, & Ommaya, 1991). Experiments of this sort are, of course, impossible with human beings, but the clinical data suggest that human brains are even more adaptable than those of monkeys. Patients who have lost some abilities due to closed head injuries (for example, from a blow to the head that does not penetrate the skull), can benefit from cognitive retraining techniques, if they are young enough, if they are willing to persist in the effort, and if the retraining begins soon enough after the injury. Some researchers believe cognitive retraining results in inducing undamaged parts of the brain to take over functions previously carried out by damaged parts (Levine, Eisenberg, & Benton, 1991).

Methods for Observing the Brain in Action

Until recently, the bony skull and thick layers of tough, plastic-like membrane that encase the human brain made it virtually inaccessible for study. Researchers were dependent on two

UNDERSTANDING HUMAN DIVERSITY

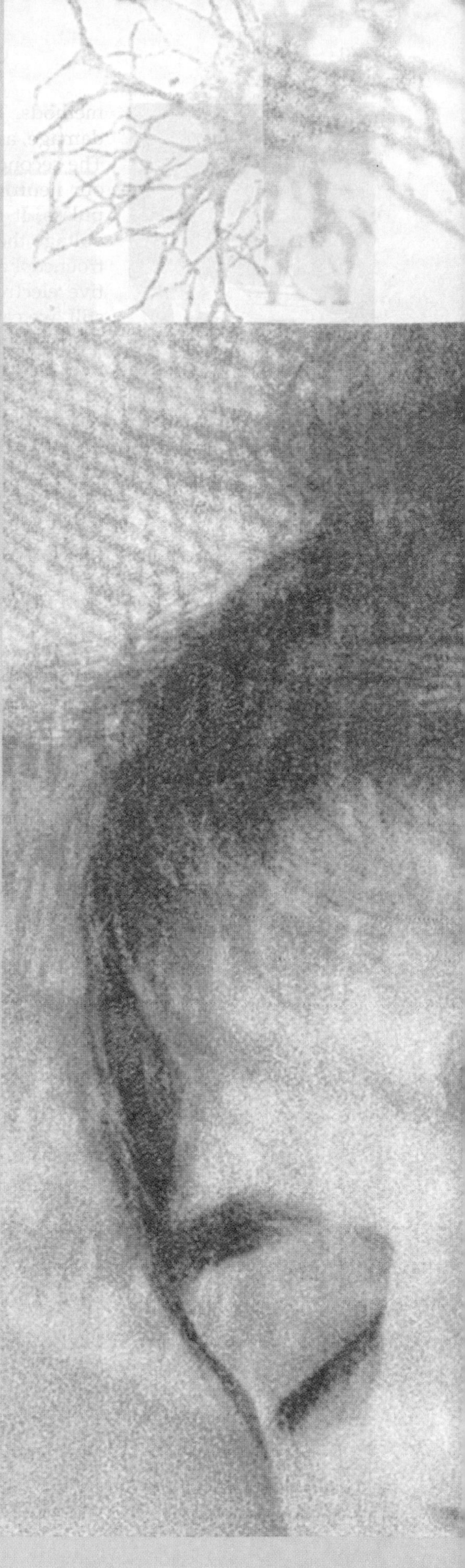

Brain Size, Intelligence, and Gender

What is the relationship between brain size and intelligence? Are people with bigger brains smarter? The answers to these questions have been argued about for more than a century.

As the average man's body is larger than the average woman's body, so is the average man's brain bigger than the average woman's brain. The argument that "bigger is better" has been used over the years to justify gender discrimination (Shields, 1975a). But many "lower animals" have larger brains than any human being, man or woman. The size of the human brain ranges from about 1,000 to 2,000 grams—relatively puny compared to the elephant brain, which ranges from 5,000 to 8,000 grams (Harvey & Krebs, 1990). Elephants are obviously much larger than humans and need a bigger brain to manage their greater body mass. So we should compare brain sizes *relative* to body size. With that correction, human beings take the lead over elephants—our brains are 2.33 percent of our body compared to an elephant's mere .20 percent. But the lowly shrew puts human beings to shame with a brain/body size ratio of a whopping 3.33 percent! So it seems unlikely that a relationship between brain size and what we call intelligence exists when comparing species.

Does such a relationship exist within a single species? The best recent studies, using magnetic resonance imaging (MRI) to measure the size of living human brains, estimate a correlation of about .35 between brain size and intelligence after controlling for body size (Willerman, Schultz, Rutledge, & Bigler, 1991). Women have a smaller average brain than men, even when correcting for body mass (Ho, Roessmann, Straumfjord, & Monroe, 1980). Yet, women are not simply smaller versions of men; they have different proportions of fat and muscles. This may also translate into differences within the brain itself, which may relate to differences in brain size. Thus, many researchers suggest that the relation between brain size and IQ should apply only when comparing men to other men or women to other women, but should not apply when comparing women to men. Further research will try to identify relationships between the size of specific brain structures and different kinds of intelligence in both men and women (Andreasen et al., 1993).

Although women have, on average, smaller brains than men, there is no difference in overall intelligence between males and females. Some researchers have explained this paradox by focusing on specific intellectual abilities where gender differences are sometimes found. For example, men's ability to visualize objects in space exceeds women's on the average (Ankney, 1992; Rushton and Ankney, 1995), particularly performance on tasks requiring mental rotation of images. Other researchers report no relationship between brain size and mental rotation performance in an all-female sample (Wickett, Vernon, & Lee, 1994). Further, women's performance on mental rotation tasks has been found to improve by 30 to 50 percent from just one exposure to the test. This finding makes attributing gender differences in mental rotation performance to inherited brain characteristics questionable at best (Peters, Chishold, & Laeng, 1995).

Even if there is a correlation between brain size and intelligence, how should it be interpreted? Two key principles apply. First, correlation is not causation. Just because brain size and intelligence are correlated does not mean that big brains cause big intelligence. It might be the other way around; intelligence based on knowledge and skill acquired through experience causes the brain to get bigger. Or alternatively, both big brains and big intelligence are caused by still another, as yet unknown factor. Second, heredity is not biology. Brain size reflects heredity but it also reflects environmental influences. Certain environmental conditions can promote or diminish brain growth and intelligence (Jacobsen, 1991). For example, poor nutrition at early ages can reduce brain size by as much as 20 percent. Moreover, average brain weights of mature newborns do not differ for males and females, leading some researchers to conclude that differences that are found in later life reflect environmental rather than genetic factors (Ho, Roessmann, Hause, & Monroe, 1981).

The relationship between brain size and structure, gender, and intelligence is complex and continues to be controversial. While new brain-imaging methods are enabling researchers to correlate intelligence scores with a variety of brain characteristics, we suspect that real understanding of the relationship between the brain and intelligence will not occur simply by applying better technology and obtaining more refined images. We look forward to the day when the research is able to identify how brain mechanisms determine types of intelligence.

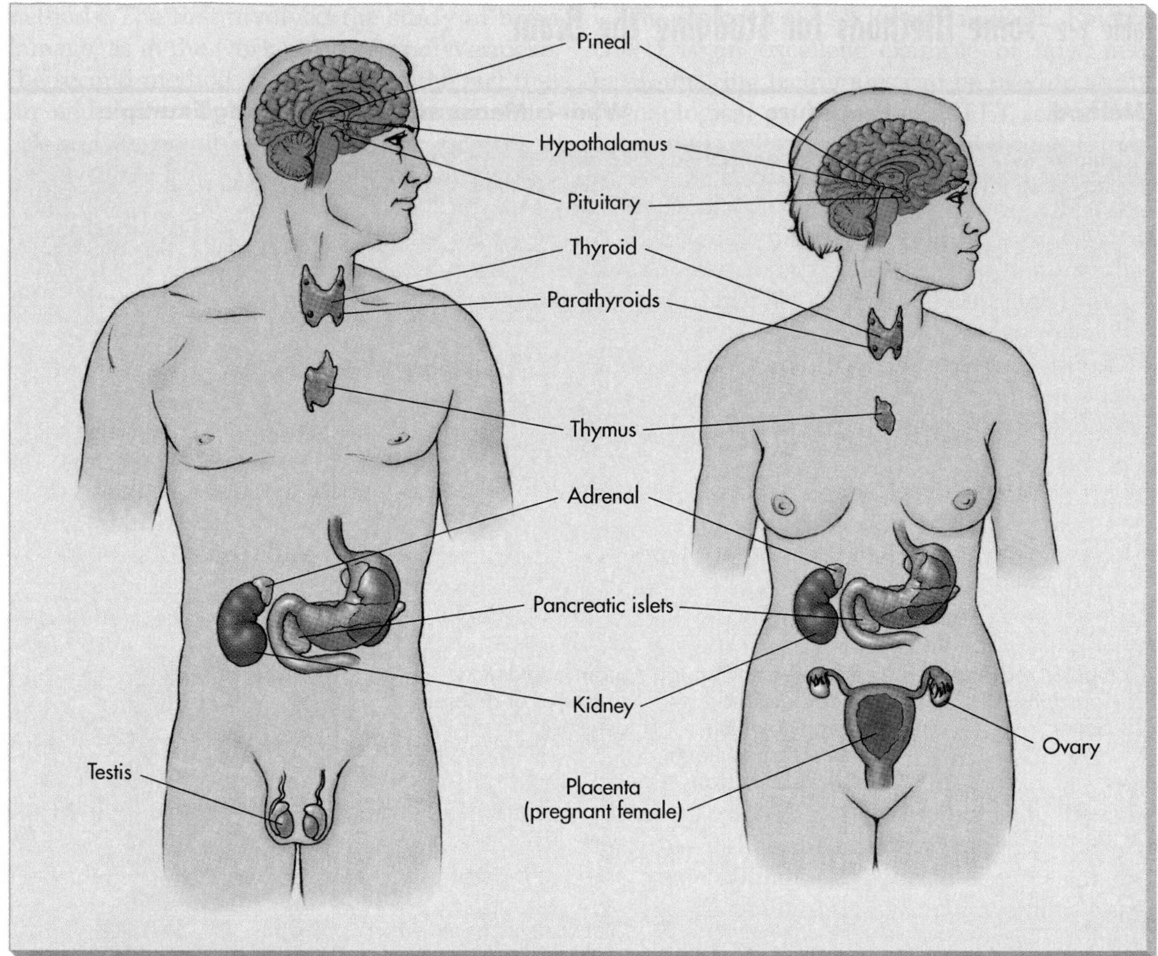

3-20 Endocrine Glands and Hormones

The endocrine glands produce hormones and release them into the bloodstream. Various hormones affect cell and body metabolism; others affect mood and emotion.

▼ *Robert Wadlow (1918–1940), at 8′11″, is considered the tallest person in history according to the Guinness Book of World Records. Here he poses with his family, who were all normal height.*

the endocrine system are slower and longer lasting than those of the nervous system. To understand how these systems work together to influence how you think, act, and feel, you need to know some of the major glands, their hormones, and their behavioral effects (see Figure 3-20).

The Pituitary Gland

Often referred to as the "master gland," the ***pituitary gland*** secretes hormones that regulate the activity of many other endocrine glands. The pituitary gland's growth hormone serves a number of metabolic functions involved in the growth and maintenance of the body. Overproduction of the growth hormone in childhood causes the child to become a giant, sometimes almost reaching a height of 9 feet. Too little growth hormone causes the child's growth to be stunted. Either effect can be produced by damage to or a tumor on the pituitary gland. Manufactured (synthetic) drugs designed to control the growth hormone can counteract these adverse effects if taken at an early age.

The pituitary gland also produces other essential hormones that affect the autonomic nervous system. Among other things, these hormones regulate cell metabolism (thyroid-stimulating hormone), energize the body to react to stress or emergency (adrenocorticotrophic hormone, ACTH), direct the concentration of urine (antidiuretic hormone, ADH), and regulate the contraction of the uterus during childbirth (oxytocin). The secondary effects of many of these substances appear as behavior we usually label "emotional" or "anxious."

The Thyroid Gland

The ***thyroid gland***, located in the neck, consists of two lobes shaped like the capital letter H. Its

THINKING CRITICALLY

The anatomical and functional bilateral symmetry of the human cerebral cortex has tempted many people to conclude that personality differences might be explained by individual differences in cortical function. For example, we occasionally hear that right brain and left brain dominance lead to different kinds of personalities, with left-brain people being careful, logical, and verbal, and right-brain people being visual, illogical, and holistic. Does this make sense to you?

You need to be cautious. It has become popular to use cortical lateralization as an oversimplified way to account for a variety of behavioral or psychological phenomena. But remember that there is really just one brain, with many complex, interconnected parts, including the two hemispheres, and that those parts work together in a highly coordinated way. Both hemispheres are probably capable of storing all types of information, even though one hemisphere, depending on the task to be done, will dominate. Personality can hardly be localized in or determined by one hemisphere. Furthermore, much of personality is a learned phenomenon, highly dependent on experience. Differences in brain organization between men and women and across cultures show that the process by which our brains are organized (programmed) strongly depends on experience.

major function is to secrete thyroxin. Thyroxin's biological functions include regulating body metabolism. These functions in turn influence psychological processes such as mood and motivation. Sometimes symptoms of depression can be traced to a malfunctioning thyroid gland. Too little thyroxin (a condition called hypothyroidism) in infancy can have particularly devastating effects. If untreated, it can lead to cretinism, a condition characterized by severely retarded mental and physical development. In adults, low thyroxin can be accompanied by mental confusion and poor motor coordination. Fortunately, this condition can be counteracted by medication.

The Adrenal Glands

The ***adrenal glands***, located just above the kidneys, produce, among other substances, adrenaline (epinephrine) and noradrenaline (norepinephrine). Noradrenaline also functions as a neurotransmitter in interneuronal exchanges. These two hormones regulate bodily functions that affect mood and emotion, blood pressure, blood sugar level, and redistribution of blood between internal organs and voluntary muscles. They act antagonistically, with one reversing the effect of the other (for example, adrenaline increases blood pressure while noradrenaline decreases blood pressure).

The adrenal glands are under the indirect control of the central nervous system. Suppose something threatening happens to you. The CNS is activated, and you become consciously aware of at least some aspects of this event. At the same time, the CNS stimulates neurons in the hypothalamus to secrete a hormone that flows to the pituitary gland. That hormone in turn stimulates the pituitary gland to secrete adrenocorticotrophic hormone, which is carried through the blood to the adrenal glands. At the adrenals, ACTH triggers the release of adrenaline.

The bodily effects of the release of adrenaline and noradrenaline into the bloodstream are almost exactly the same as those brought on by activating the sympathetic and parasympathetic nervous systems. Thus, we have a clear case of two systems performing basically the same work. Hormonal effects can last long after the nervous system has settled down, however. The subjective awareness of this phenomenon is revealed by our continuing to feel anxious for several minutes after the cause of our anxiety has passed. Have you ever come close to having an automobile accident? If you felt anxiety long after the danger passed, it was probably because of the prolonged effect of hormones from the adrenal glands in the bloodstream.

The Sex Glands

Sex hormones include the gonadotrophins, secreted by the pituitary, and the hormones secreted by the ovaries in women and by the testes in men. Upon stimulation by certain gonadotrophins, the ovaries produce the hormones estrogen and progesterone, and the testes secrete the androgens, including testosterone. In a sense, "male" and "female" sex hormones are misnamed; both types are found in *both* sexes.

Sex hormones work together in most species of animals to regulate such functions as (1) development and release of the female's eggs and the growth of the male's sperm, (2) mating behavior, (3) control over some aspects of the birth process, (4) control over the milk supply in the mother's mammary glands, and (5) control over parenting behaviors such as building nests, sitting on eggs, and tending the newborn. As we mentioned earlier, recent research suggests that treatment with estrogen might actually combat memory loss in women with Alzheimer's disease, although the reasons are not entirely clear and there is additional evidence to be collected (Matthews et al., 1997). Reproductive or sexual behavior is tightly regulated by hormones in virtually all species, although learning and socialization override hormones in human beings. We will discuss the relationship of sex hormones and social behaviors in more detail in Chapter 10.

Behavioral Genetics

The nervous system and the endocrine system are two-thirds of the biological story about behavior. It remains for us to discuss how genes interact with neurons and hormones in the complex processes involved in the biology of behavior.

Behavioral genetics is a field of research in psychology that aims to determine ***heritability***, or how much of the variation in traits or abilities is due to genetic and how much to environmental influences. Behavioral genetics began in England with Sir Francis Galton (1822–1911) and his study of the inheritance of genius in the families of eminent persons. Galton discovered that genius "runs in families" and concluded that it is, to a significant degree, a heritable behavioral trait. Since Galton's time, an extensive research literature has accumulated to suggest that genetics plays an important role in many behaviors. Researchers have found that complex behaviors related to personality, psychopathology, and cognition are all influenced to some degree by genetics (Plomin, Corley, DeFries, & Fulker, 1990a). They have also found, however, that genetics alone is never sufficient to explain variations in behavior among individuals. Rather, it is a contributing cause along with environmental and possibly other factors.

Understanding the relationship of biology to behavior is at the heart of the nature-nurture controversy discussed in Chapter 1. Why do some people within a given population or group perform better on math tests than others, and why are some people more likely to get into a fight than others? Is variation in the behavior of individuals within a population determined by differences in genes (nature) or experiences (nurture)? Today, most psychologists believe such variation has both genetic and environmental aspects. They try to explain variability in a trait like intelligence or height or musicality in terms of the genetic and environmental differences among people within that population.

Phenotype versus Genotype

Technically, a ***phenotype*** is the overt or outward biological or psychological characteristic of an organism; its ***genotype*** is the gene structure known or thought to underlie the phenotype. Now, consider the sex of an organism, whether it is male or female. Typically, an individual's sex is determined by what might be called a "glance in the pants" method—that is, assignment is based on the phenotype (visible genitalia). But problems with this method make clear why genotypes and phenotypes are not the same thing. The fact is that 1 out of 20,000 people have a phenotypic sex conflicting with his or her genes (see LeVay, 1991). María José Martinez Patiño found this out in 1985 when, to her surprise, she was identified as male in a genetic sex-determination test. She was competing as a hurdler in the World University Games in Kobe, Japan, and although she was unquestionably anatomically female (phenotype), at the genetic level she was male (genotype). This discovery was psychologically, financially, and socially devastating to her. In addition to being disqualified from competing in the games, she lost her athletic scholarship *and* her boyfriends. The International Amateur Athletic Federation subsequently recognized that chromosomes do not determine gender (the behavioral, social, and psychological aspects of being a man or woman) and eliminated genetic testing for this purpose (sex is now noted during the course of the routine physical examination given athletes in such contests). Patiño had to battle for three years before her female sex was recognized and certified. But she won her fight and qualified to compete in the 1992 summer Olympics (Lemonick, 1992).

Understanding the distinction between genotype and phenotype can help you appreciate the genetic basis of traits and behaviors that are subtle, complex, and likely to be determined by many interacting factors. One such trait of great interest is intelligence. History provides numerous examples where unfounded assertions about the biological roots of intelligence have been used to justify discrimination based on social characteristics such as gender and ancestral origin. An early contributor of social psychology, Gustav LeBon, used invalid assumptions to argue against women's access to higher education:

> In the most intelligent races, as among the Parisians, there are a large number of women whose brains are closer in size to those of gorillas than to the most developed male brains. This inferiority is so obvious that no one can contest it for a moment, only its degree is worth discussion. All psychologists who have studied the intelligence of women, as well as poets and novelists, recognize today that they represent the most inferior forms of human evolution and that they are closer to children and savages than to an adult, civilized man . . . (LeBon, 1879, pp. 60–61).

LeBon's thinking was distorted by his prejudices, and his conclusions were wrong. Similar incorrect statements about the biological inferiority of Jews, Italians, Irish, African Americans, or just about every minority group, have been made by others. Although there might be significant relationships between genetics and some aspects of intelligent behavior (Bouchard & McGue, 1981), no studies have demonstrated that general intelligence is linked exclusively to the genetics of sex or ethnicity (Peters, 1991).

The Transmission of Heredity: Genes

The biological inheritance transmitted from parents to offspring is contained in ***genes***, which are large molecules of deoxyribonucleic acid (DNA). Genes are carried on ***chromosomes,*** which are structures found in the nuclei of all cells. Each chromosome carries as many as 100,000 genes. According to recent estimates, if all of the DNA in all the genes of a human body were laid out in a line, that line would reach the moon and return—20,000 times! As shown in Figure 3-21 the nucleus of each human cell contains forty-six chromosomes; forty-four are in twenty-two *matched* pairs. The twenty-third pair consists of the sex chromosomes, which are XX if you are a genetic female or XY if you are a genetic male.

Through a process of cell division called ***meiosis***, each normal human sperm and egg (ovum) is equipped with twenty-three chromosomes. The combination of the egg and sperm, called ***fertilization***, results in a cell, called a ***zygote***, with forty-six chromosomes—the number needed to form a new individual—arrayed in twenty-three pairs. The genes carried on these initial forty-six chromosomes direct the development and growth of all other cells in the body. Taken as a whole, the genes make up a unique genetic script, or ***genome***, for every individual organism. Your particular genome is created by the combination of chromosomes you receive from your biological father and mother.

▲ *Phenotype and genotype. These identical twin girls have exactly the same genotype, but significantly different outward appearance (phenotype). They were raised in different environments, the girl on the left in Puerto Rico and her sister in the United States.*

Genes are biochemical structures that account for heritable biological traits like hair color and height and for some aspects of psychological characteristics like intelligence and personality.

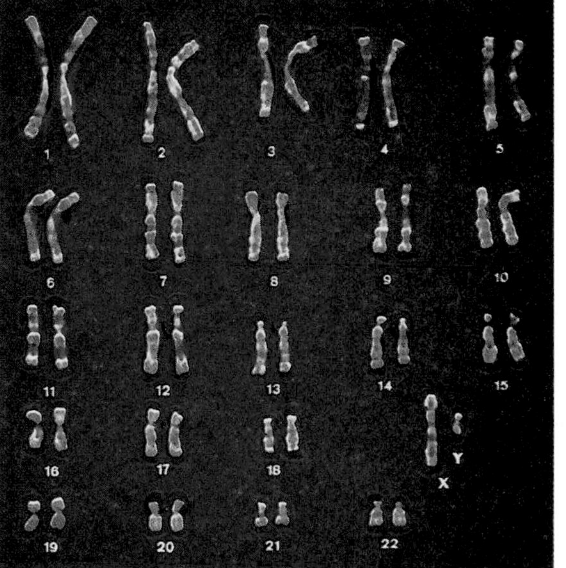

3-21 Paired Human Chromosomes

Males and females cannot be distinguished by the first 22 pairs of chromosomes, but in pair 23, males and females differ. Females possess two similar chromosomes for pair 23, both called X chromosomes: thus the female genotype is XX. Males have two types of chromosomes in the twenty-third pair, one X and one Y chromosome, and thus have an XY genotype.

Genes and Intelligence

Perhaps the most publicized behavioral genetic studies have focused on intelligence. A comprehensive summary of the world literature on intelligence (typically measured as an intelligence quotient or IQ) correlations among relatives was published in 1981 (Bouchard & McGue, 1981). In all, researchers examined 111 studies that analyzed almost 250,000 cases. The pattern of correlations they found shows that the higher the proportion of genes that two individuals have in common, the higher the correlation in their IQs. The average IQ correlation is .85 for identical twins, which suggests a large role for heredity but also a substantial contribution on the part of environment.

There are also other ways to look at the environmental contribution to IQ. Researchers at the University of Minnesota reported a compelling study of identical twins who were brought up in different families (Bouchard, Lykken, McGue, Segal, & Tellegen, 1990). Fifty such pairs, who lived apart during childhood and adolescence, were compared as young adults on several tests of mental abilities. The resulting correlation between pair members on these measures averaged .75, about the same as the correlation for twins reared together. This is striking evidence for a genetic basis of intelligence (although, of course, it doesn't tell us exactly what that genetic basis is). Nonetheless, critics have pointed out that twins reared apart in this study still lived together during their early, formative years. Further, they were fostered in quite similar households, which might have provided environments that were almost the same as those they would have had if they had grown up in the same family. Despite the mounds of data that have been collected, the debate over the genetics of intelligence is still unsettled (APA 1995 report).

Genes and Homosexuality

Behavioral genetic studies have also examined whether sexual preference might have a genetic basis. Bailey and Pillard (1991) advertised in homosexual publications in U.S. Midwestern and Southwestern cities to recruit male homosexual research participants. They found that 52 percent of identical twin brothers of gay men were also gay, while only 22 percent of fraternal twin brothers and 11 percent of adoptive brothers

THINKING CRITICALLY

What do you think about the strength of the evidence for the genetic basis of homosexuality provided by the Bailey and Pillard study?

Take a few moments to consider what problems, methodological or otherwise, might be involved in this kind of research, which involves behavior that is heavily socially stigmatized. What is the likelihood that, if one member of a pair of twins admits to being gay, the other will as well? It is conceivable that, among identical twins, such an admission is more probable than among fraternal twins or nontwin brothers, simply because identical twins reared together generally experience the same environmental influences. Consider also the fact that the samples are not random, but are self-selected. The researchers advertised in homosexual publications, which are more likely to be read by homosexual than by heterosexual men, whether they are twins or not. If the researchers had advertised in publications that were read by both homosexual and heterosexual men, however, it is possible that more homosexual men would volunteer for a study of sexual preferences than would heterosexual men. So, there are problems with this study. It does not establish a genetic basis for sexual preferences with any certainty. To study the question of a genetic basis for homosexuality, researchers might instead use national records on all twins born in the country. They could then try to contact these twins and ask them whether they were homosexual or heterosexual. The results in such a study, however, would be only as good as the truthfulness of the twins about their homosexuality or heterosexuality.

were gay. From these results, the researchers concluded that homosexuality may have a genetic or biological basis—the more closely related two people are, if one is homosexual the other is more likely to be homosexual as well. This research offers yet another opportunity to think critically about how behavior genetic research is conducted and about the validity of conclusions drawn from this research.

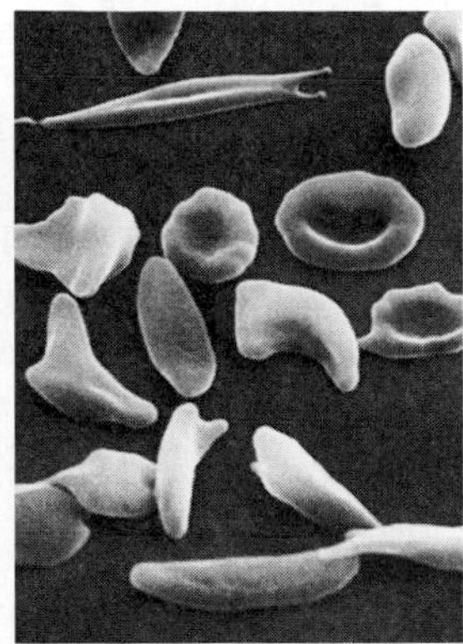

◀ *At left are normal red blood cells; at right, sickle cells. Sickle cell anemia, characterized by red blood cells that become misshapen and resemble a sickle, is a genetically transmitted disease. Most common among African Americans (affecting about 1 in 600), sickle cell anemia is considered a positive adaptation to conditions in Africa, where children born with the trait coped better with malaria than those born without it. Symptoms include chronic fatigue and pain, and increased vulnerability to infection.*

Human Genetic Disorders

More than nine out of ten babies born in the United States and Canada are biologically normal and healthy (Wegman, 1990). Most birth defects (also called congenital abnormalities) are due to environmental factors, such as mother's smoking or drug use, viruses, and exposure to radiation. Sometimes, however, the processes of fertilization and meiosis produce an individual with an abnormal set of genes. Of babies born with such problems, about 30 percent appear to have behavioral and/or biological abnormalities of genetic origin. To date, over 5,000 types of genetic defects have been identified (McKusick, 1994), including Down syndrome, cystic fibrosis, Tay Sachs disease, phenyketonuria (PKU), and sickle cell anemia.

Risk of having a particular problem of genetic origin can vary with age of mother, sex, race, and ethnic origins. For example, Down syndrome is a common genetic disorder more likely to be found in children of older mothers. Although overall the risk is 1 out of every 800 births, it increases to 1 in every 25 births for women over forty-five. Down syndrome results from the presence of an extra chromosome on the twenty-first chromosomal pair. Like most other genetic diseases, Down syndrome cannot be prevented, nor can its symptoms be eliminated through drug treatment.

Other disorders, like hemophilia (the "bleeders' disease") and color blindness, occur mostly in males, because they involve genes that are sex-linked, that is, genes found on the sex chromosomes. Moreover, there are genetic disorders associated with ethnic origins. For example, the most common fatal genetic disease of Caucasian children is cystic fibrosis. An estimated one of twenty-five Caucasians in Central Europe and North America carries the gene for this metabolic disorder that diminishes the capacity of their digestive and respiratory systems, and kills about half of its victims before they reach age twenty-six. Approximately one out of thirty Jews from Eastern Europe carries the Tay-Sachs gene, which results in a genetic disorder that interferes with the neuron's ability to transmit impulses. Because of a defect in body metabolism, the neurons of an afflicted individual become swollen with fatty deposits. Although an infant with this disease may appear normal at birth, brain damage often can be detected after six months. Vision and hearing are impaired, and muscles weaken. Death usually occurs before the child is five years old.

Along with approximately 200 other chromosomal and congenital abnormalities, these conditions can be detected in prenatal testing. One technique, called ***amniocentesis***, can be used by about the sixteenth week of pregnancy. A doctor uses a needle to withdraw a sample of the mother's amniotic fluid from the amniotic sac surrounding the fetus. This fluid contains cells that have been sloughed off by the fetus. Technicians make these cells reproduce in the laboratory and then examine them for defects. Although cures for these disorders are unlikely, frank discussions with the parents of the options available can follow if defects are observed in fetal cells.

Developments in medical and behavioral genetics are viewed differently by people of different religious and ethical viewpoints. The implications for individuals, families, and society are complex. Emotions are likely to run high. It will, therefore, be important to think critically about these issues. Understanding the facts about genetics and prenatal development is the first step in understanding the full implications of new reproductive technologies in general, and genetic screening in particular.

KEY TERMS

neuron

cell

dendrite

axon

axonal conduction

resting potential

action potential

refractory period

all-or-none principle

myelin

synapse

synaptic transmission

neurotransmitter

volume transmission

endorphin

central nervous system

peripheral nervous system

somatic nervous system

autonomic nervous sysem

Interaction of Genes and Environment

The contributing causes of behavior lie partly in the environment and partly in genetics. We tend to react aggressively in certain situations because we encounter provocative threats or frustrations. But how we react—whether we freeze, flee or fight—might in fact be based on built-in predispositions, acquired throughout our evolutionary history. Some social patterns, especially among animals lower than human beings, appear so abruptly in their behavior and are so common across members of a given species that they are unlikely to have been learned. They seem to be based on something biological, such as the unique genetic structure inherited by all members of the species. Thus, in the case of some fairly complex behaviors, an organism's response to environmental stimuli seems to be controlled by natural processes built up through natural selection and other evolutionary principles. There is evidence, for example, that human mating patterns are determined in part by dispositions in men and women that have been shaped in evolutionary time by adaptation to constraints imposed by both biological and environmental differences between the sexes (Buss, Larsen, & Westen, 1996). The new field of evolutionary psychology has grown up around attempts to explain social behavior by applying the principles of evolutionary theory. Thus, for example, it explains altruism—helping behavior in animals and human beings—by referring to the relatedness of the individual being helped to the helping individual. It maintains that animals or people are more likely to help someone who shares some of their genes because this will lead to the survival of the shared genes, which can then be passed on to new generations.

The effect of genes on behavior is, in all cases, indirect, whereas the impact of the environment is immediate and easier to observe. No organism is purely and simply a product of its heredity or of its environment. The truth of the matter is captured in a characterization by Herbert Simon (1992): unlike jello, organisms do not totally conform to the shape of their environmental "mold"; but neither are they "rocks" that maintain their shape regardless of the mold they are placed in. For all but the simplest animals, environment plays a vital role in shaping behavior. Further, the environment's importance seems to increase with the complexity of the animal. In every case, behavior is the product of interacting genetic and environmental forces, and our task is to find out how those forces work together.

Objectives Revisited

Psychologists study the behavior of biological organisms, primarily human beings. Behavior has its roots in the nervous system, in the endocrine system, and in genetics, each of which is a subarea of biology. Biological knowledge, then, is one of the major cornerstones or foundations for the study of psychology.

Objective 1. Describe the neuron and discuss its role in the transmission of information throughout the body. Explain what it means to say that neurons are the building blocks of the nervous system.

Neurons are biological cells specialized to conduct and transform information in the form of electrical and chemical impulses. The typical neuron has three basic components—the cell body, the dendrites, and the axon. Information transmission within a neuron, called *axonal conduction,* is accomplished by an *all-or-none action potential* that results from the movement of ions across the nerve cell membrane and traverses the length of the axon. Transmission from one neuron to another involves the release of chemical transmitters across a *synapse.*

Neurons combine to form circuits or pathways that help to detect different types of stimulation in the environment and to respond appropriately. Neural pathways combine to form neural structures, and neural structures combine to form divisions of the nervous system.

Objective 2. Describe the major parts, the organization, and the primary functions of the human nervous system.

There are two major divisions of the human nervous system, the *peripheral* and the *central nervous system*. The peripheral nervous system (PNS) includes the sensory and motor neurons outside of the brain and spinal cord. The PNS can be subdivided into the *somatic* and *autonomic systems*. The somatic nervous system is involved in skeletal movement and body sensations. The autonomic nervous system controls the body's involuntary muscles and glands, regulates involuntary physiological functions, and is involved in emotional reactions. The autonomic nervous system is further subdivided into *parasympathetic* (calm state) and *sympathetic* (active state) branches.

The *central nervous system* (CNS) consists of the brain and the spinal cord. The brain has three major divisions: the hindbrain, the midbrain, and the forebrain. The hindbrain and the midbrain are, collectively, sometimes referred to as the brain stem, which contains such structures as the medulla oblongata, the pons and the reticular formation, hard-wired structures that control vital body functions, such as breathing and heartbeat. The forebrain contains the thalamus (a major relay center in and out of the brain) and the hypothalamus (a major behavioral control center), and the cerebrum. The cerebral cortex is the most flexible of all parts of the nervous system, and controls most higher mental functions. It consists of two hemispheres that work in a coordinated way, sharing information by means of a connection called the corpus callosum.

Objective 3. Give a general description of the endocrine system and identify some major endocrine glands.

The endocrine system is composed of the various glands, located throughout the body, that manufacture and secrete chemical messengers called *hormones* into the bloodstream. Endocrine hormones are involved in numerous physiological processes, such as growth, regulation of metabolism, response to stress, and regulation of behaviors associated with sexual activity and fight or flight. Hormones can either inhibit or activate the transmission of nerve impulses.

Objective 4. Present an overview of behavioral genetics. What is it? How do we study it? What do we know about it?

Behavioral genetics is concerned with the relative contributions of heredity and environment to behavior. Genetic research techniques used with human beings include twin comparisons, family studies, and adoption studies. These studies have demonstrated some genetic involvement in intelligence and in various personality characteristics. Yet, in all known cases, genetics and environment work interactively to determine variations in a behavioral trait.

sympathetic nervous system

parasympathetic nervous system

reflex

brain

hindbrain

midbrain

forebrain

limbic system

cerebral cortex

corpus callosum

plasticity

lateralization

endocrine system

hormones

heritability

genotype

phenotype

genes

chromosomes

meiosis

fertilization

zygote

genome

amniocentesis

UNIVERSAL FOUNDATIONS OF HUMAN BEHAVIOR

CULTURAL FOUNDATIONS OF HUMAN BEHAVIOR

- Subjective Culture
  - Symbols
  - Language
  - Beliefs
  - Norms
  - Values
- Material Culture
- Promoting Understanding within and across Cultures
  - Ethnocentrism
  - Cultural Relativism

SOCIAL FOUNDATIONS OF HUMAN BEHAVIOR

- Membership in Groups
- How the Social Structure Can Affect Intergroup Relations
  - Promoting Group Conflict
  - Reducing Group Conflict
- Social Status and Social Roles

SOCIAL CATEGORIES

- Gender
- Ethnicity
- Race
- Minority Groups

SOCIOCULTURAL ISSUES IN PERSPECTIVE

C H A P T E R 4

Cultural and Social Foundations of Behavior

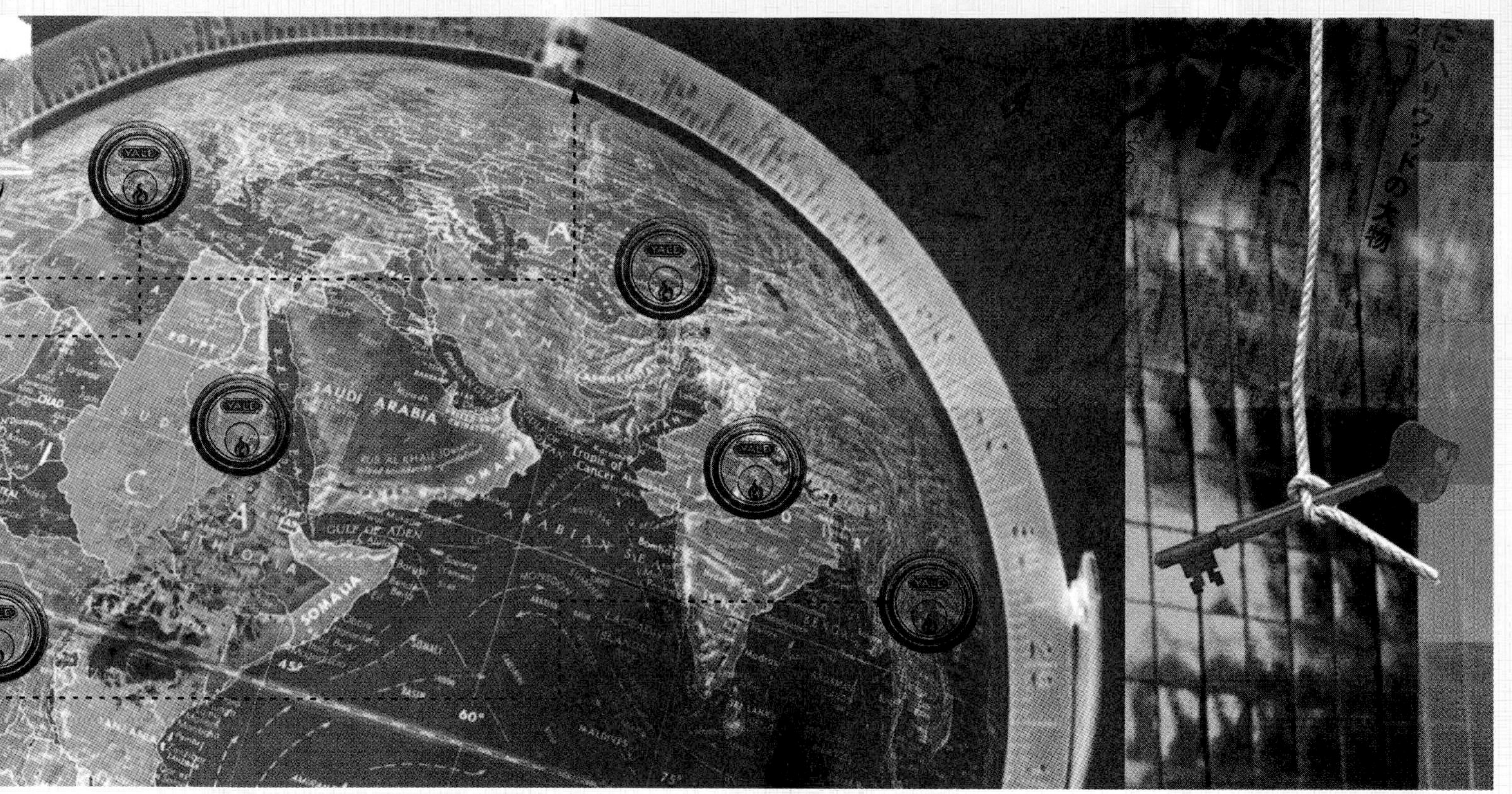

O B J E C T I V E S

After reading this chapter, you should be able to:

1. Distinguish among biological, social, and psychological universals.
2. Define culture, and discuss how cultures can vary across and within societies.
3. Distinguish between subjective and material culture, and discuss how they can influence behavior.
4. Compare the concepts of ethnocentrism and cultural relativism, and identify some of their possible negative consequences.
5. Explain the concepts of group, in-group, and out-group, and discuss the relationship of the social structure to behavior in groups, particularly with regard to intergroup cooperation and conflict.
6. Discuss social status, roles, and stratification.
7. Explain the concept of social category and discuss the categories of gender, race, ethnicity, and minority group.

SEEKING SOLUTIONS

Meeting Our Biological Needs in Diverse Cultural Contexts

We tend to think that basic biological and bodily functions are straightforward and invariant. After all, everyone has to eat, drink, breathe, sleep. Nonetheless, all these functions and others—even defecation—are subject to modification in style and substance as a result of people's cultural differences.

Everyday activities, such as eating with a knife and fork, separate many Americans from Europeans by a gulf nearly as wide as the Atlantic Ocean itself. While both cut up their food with the knife in the right hand and the fork in the left, etiquette books have instructed Americans to set down their knife and transfer their fork to their right hand to bring the morsel to their mouth. Europeans bring food to their mouth with the fork still in the left hand. (Note: the European approach ensures that the knife will not slip off the plate and soil the tablecloth.) While Americans will use their fork to scoop up mashed potatoes and peas, some Europeans will invert their fork and mound the potatoes and peas on the back of it with their knife, for a more perilous if adventuresome trip to the mouth.

Of course, knives and forks are not standard for dining around the world. In India and Bangladesh, the basic utensil is humankind's original one, the hand—and only the *right* hand—which scoops up rice and other food, often using a piece of flat bread for the purpose (in South Asia, as well as in much of the Middle East, to eat with the *left* hand would be unthinkable, and unspeakably rude with company, because that hand is involved in certain cleansing activities of the backside). In Ethiopia, the primary utensil is the entire tablecloth, which is made of *injera*, a large round sheet of thin, limp, spongy bread. Several kinds of food are piled on the *injera*, which covers the tabletop, and diners tear off pieces of this bread to clutch bites of food.

The West has long been aware of chopsticks—they first appeared in Chinese restaurants and now come with every kind of East Asian fast food. Although they serve people well from Vietnam and Cambodia to Korea and Japan, recent news reports indicate that skill with chopsticks is declining among Japanese youth as North American standbys such as hamburgers and french fries invade their culture. Could it be that some day the last stronghold of chopsticks will be among North Americans who dine out?

What is eaten or drunk varies around the globe. Human infants will eat almost anything up until about age two, when they become reluctant to try new foods. Foods of one's culture become liked because they are familiar and associated with happy situations (Rozin, 1991). But foods that some cultures find repulsive are delicacies for others. *Haggis*, the national dish of Scotland, features oats cooked in a sheep's stomach. Some tribes in East Africa puncture a cow's jugular vein with a sharp arrow to "milk" it of blood (the cow does not suffer ill effects from this procedure). Sometimes the blood is drunk straight, and sometimes it is mixed with milk to create a drink that is a good source of protein and iron. As a guest of honor of Bedou-

cific behaviors. For example, all cultures have families, but who exactly is included in "family" varies widely. Even social universals for the most basic biological functions—such as eating and elimination of body wastes—differ, depending on cultural context.

Psychological universals are psychological processes that operate in all individuals, regardless of culture. A central goal of the science of psychology is to identify basic processes, especially those involved in perception, learning, memory, cognition, motivation, and emotion, that are similar across time and place. In addition to understanding how these processes work to shape behavior in a particular cultural context, psychologists also want to know how these processes might differ, depending on cultural context.

What is an example of a psychological universal? All humans tend to categorize objects ins in the Arabian peninsula, you might be served sheep's eyes at a feast. In the Australian outback, Aborigines might offer you *witchety grubs* (they're exactly what they sound like). In fact, many cultures have consumed insects, from nectar-laden ants in the American Southwest to locusts in Africa. The American aversion to eating insects has led to strict food standards to eliminate insect particles that would in fact add substantial nutrient value to food.

Another unusual food preference is dirt eating, a time-honored practice in the American South, whereby individuals, typically African-American women, obtain nutrients missing in their diet by eating certain kinds of dirt. Although the Japanese have a fondness for raw fish, the Masai of East Africa consider eating fish, cooked or otherwise, obscene. On the other hand, the Masai drink cow's blood. In Hong Kong, you might have to be nimble with your chopsticks as certain crustaceans are served alive and attempt to return to the sea by walking off the plate and out the door. Certain New Guinea tribes like to eat the brains of their dead relatives to absorb their spirits, but authorities have banned the practice in recent years because it could transmit a fatal neurological disease, *Kuru*.

Talking about the elimination of bodily waste, especially for those from households affected by Victorian sensitivities, can be difficult, even though this activity is something everyone must do. But there is great diversity in various cultures' practices and attitudes toward this subject. Most Americans can readily accept that the same bathroom is used by both sexes in a home, but feel embarrassed if they walk into the wrong public restroom by mistake. In contrast, in France, it is common to have female attendants for male restrooms. In Western countries, we sit atop a "throne" for defecation; in many Middle Eastern countries, it is common simply to have a hole in the floor with areas marked for where to place your feet. And, of course, the French have invented the bidet for cleansing the backside after defecation.

▼ *Some people eat foods that most others would consider disgusting.*

and events, lumping different objects and events together in one category and responding to them all in the same way. This tendency is extremely adaptive. If we didn't categorize, we would often find ourselves hopelessly mired in the extraordinary variations the environment presents us. For example, by some estimates, we can distinguish between over 7 million color sensations alone. What would happen to traffic if we couldn't group some of these sensations under the category "red"? It would be difficult, if not impossible to ensure that all red traffic lights produced exactly the same color sensation.

Categorization is a basic psychological process, but the categories created for classifying stimuli in the environment may vary across cultures. Take the following items: pencils, sticks, trees, hair, hits in baseball, shots in basketball, telephone calls, and medical injections. Would

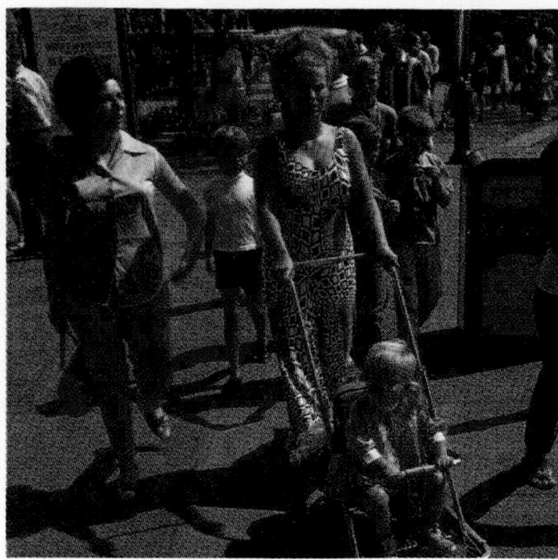

▲ *Appropriate public dress for women differs according to culture. Here, Afghan women wear the traditional* burqu *covering as compared to women at an American Disney World.*

you group them into one category? English speakers typically would not. But the Japanese have a word, *hon*, that means something like "long, thin things," and includes them all. Our categories should definitely not be taken for granted.

Another psychological universal is our sense of self—our understanding that we are physically distinct and separate from others. We all have a sense that "I am the person, here in this place, engaged in this particular activity." But though we may have a universal awareness that we are separate "selves," how we think of ourselves varies across culture (Shweder & LeVine, 1984; Triandis, 1995). In the United States, for example, the self is more likely to be seen as independent and striving for self-fulfillment. In East Asian societies, the self is more likely to be viewed as interdependent and working for the good of the larger group or society. These differences in how we view our selves are powerful influences on our thoughts, feelings, motives, and actions (Markus & Kitayama, 1991).

Biological, social, and psychological universals operate in all human beings, but how such universals are expressed in behavior may vary depending on culture.

▼ *Although everyone in the United States shares the same national culture, differences in beliefs and customary behaviors abound.*

Cultural Foundations of Human Behavior

Think about where you live, the books you read, the sports you play. Think about the groups you and members of your family belong to—from Little League to Scouts, to the P.T.A. Think about your environment—from the public schools to the shopping malls to the sports stadiums and the fast food outlets. All of these are part of your culture, and all play a part in shaping how you think, feel, and relate to the world. What exactly is this thing called culture that has such a powerful impact on how you present and think of yourself?

Most broadly, ***culture*** has been defined as an "all-encompassing" network of experiences that includes concepts, habits, skills, instruments, arts, sports, morals, laws, customs, institutions, and any other learned capabilities acquired by human beings as members of a society (Kottak, 1991, p. 37). In short, culture is the whole way of life of a collection of people. It includes how you view the world, what you think is important, and how you solve your problems—the "collective programming of the mind" (Hofstede, 1980).

Cultures are not fixed and rigid entities. Because culture is constantly changing, research findings of even a few years ago may no longer apply to the current situation. Think about the example of women working in the United States. In 1940, 24 percent of workers were female. In 1994, 46 percent of workers were female (Herz & Wooton, 1996). The culture has changed as women have entered the workforce in larger numbers. This affects the women themselves, their spouses, and their children. It can affect what and when they eat, how much they can spend, and their views about their self-esteem and their independence. Thus, as culture changes so do findings about the people within that culture.

There is great variation within cultures. Even in relatively homogeneous cultures, families or kinship systems often evolve their own traditions. Members of neighborhoods, villages, states, and regions may share experiences and traditions that differ from the larger culture. In complex societies, individuals often grow up in and interact with more than one culture. American culture was once described as a great "melting pot," the idea being that people of all cultures would merge together to become "Americans." Actually, what really happens seems more like a "tossed salad," rather than a melting pot, with some people retaining cultural distinctiveness while contributing to society as a whole.

Subcultures are groups with different cultural traditions that exist together in a larger society. Cultural variation in large, complex nations such as the United States, Canada, Mexico, China, and India is a result of multiple geographical regions, religions, ethnic groups, occupations, and lifestyles that coexist in the larger culture. The subculture that exists in the U.S. South has a tradition of "Southern hospitality," which emphasizes generosity and warmth toward friend and stranger alike. The Amish subculture is a tightly knit religious farming community in Pennsylvania that resists use of modern technology, adheres to modest standards of dress, and holds to a strict code of nonviolence. Ethnic communities in the United States that preserve cultural traditions and create shared experiences also constitute subcultures. Gay subcultures form the basis for another subculture that is especially prevalent in cities where large numbers of gay men and women live and work.

What happens when individuals raised in one culture interact over an extended period of time with those of another? ***Acculturation*** refers to cultural change occurring on both group and individual levels when two distinct cultural groups come into direct, continuous contact. For immigrants, acculturation at the individual level involves taking on behaviors, beliefs, values, and symbols, including language, of the dominant cultural group. When immigrant children in the United States learn to speak English, read English-language books and newspapers, eat fast food, and listen to American music, they are being acculturated. ***Assimilation*** refers to when the immigrants shed or lose the customs of their country of origin in the process of learning their new culture.

Researchers have found that increasing identification with one culture does not typically result in losing identification with another. When people strongly identify with more than one culture, they are called ***multicultural***—or ***bicultural*** when two cultures are involved (Oetting & Beauvais, 1991). Multiculturalism can be a source of strength, creativity, and flexibility, as multicultural individuals have the option of adopting the best of what each culture has to offer. Yet, when cultures have incompatible components, as when the individualistic, youth-oriented American culture collides with a collectivist Asian culture in which obedience to and respect for others, particularly elders, is emphasized, lowered self-esteem, confusion, and inner turmoil may be the result (Sue & Sue, 1990). A discussion of the health consequences of stress associated with acculturation is found in Chapter 13.

Culture can be divided into two components (Ogburn, 1922). ***Subjective culture*** refers to intangible human creations, such as ideas, beliefs, values, and language. ***Material culture*** refers to tangible products of human activity, ranging from audiocassettes to computer chips to salsa to zinc oxide. Psychology studies how both aspects of culture influence human behavior and mental processes, with emphasis on subjective culture (Triandis, 1972).

▲ *The United States has a particularly rich tapestry of subcultures. Shown are a Chinese New Year parade and a Gay Pride March.*

▼ *Modern technology meets traditional culture.*

◄ *Cultural differences have been the topic of many Hollywood films. In* The Air Up There, *Kevin Bacon plays a basketball coach who travels to Africa looking for the next superstar player and finds himself in the midst of many humorous cultural misunderstandings.*

SEEKING SOLUTIONS

Examining the Material Culture We Take For Granted

With the passing of time, cultural changes resulting from intercultural contact become taken for granted, and we fail to appreciate how much "our" culture came from somewhere else. What aspects of our culture owe a debt to culture from around the world? In 1937, Ralph Linton showed how much the then-modern Americans of the 1930s owed their technological and cultural well-being to sources from all over the globe. Here's an update, with a salute to Linton's "One Hundred Percent American" (Linton, 1937).

A look at the origins of just a few of the things that American college students may use in their daily lives illustrates the diverse origins of the "good old American way."

Consider the average day of James, and see how many objects he uses owe their origins to other cultures. Upon awakening, he rises from his bed, which is in a shape that originated in either *Persia* (now Iran) or *Asia Minor*, and looks at the clock (a medieval *European* invention, no doubt manufactured somewhere in the *Pacific Rim*, e.g., Korea, Taiwan, the Philippines, Singapore, China, Malaysia). He takes off his pajamas, a garment of *East Indian* origin and name, and hangs them on a teakwood rack, from *Thailand*.

He goes into the bathroom, where the room's glazed tiles for floors and walls had their origins in the *Near East*, with the art of enameling on metal having been developed by *Mediterranean* artisans of the Bronze Age. His bathtub and toilet are but slightly modified copies of *Roman* originals, the flush toilet a product of the Minoan civilization (*Crete*).

Gloria, James' friend down the hall of their apartment building (imperial *Rome* also had its apartment buildings, called *insulae*), has arisen earlier for more complicated rituals, such as applying eye liner and makeup, that would have been familiar to *Sumerian* and *Egyptian* women 5,000 years ago. She dons her dress (a garment hardly distinguishable from those worn in ancient *Mesopotamia*), woven by methods initially developed in *Southwestern Asia* and substantially improved in eighteenth-century *England*. The rayon in the dress's blend also owes its origin to England, but from twentieth-century England. Gloria drapes about her neck a bright scarf made of silk, of ancient *Chinese* lineage, and slips on a linen jacket, made from flax, which was originally domesticated in the *Near East*.

For breakfast, Gloria has a slice of cantaloupe, first domesticated in *Persia*, and a bowl of corn flakes, from a grain originally domesticated by *Native Americans*, followed by a cup of tea, the beverage of *China* from time immemorial. A capsule of vitamin C, discovered by *Norwegian* scientists, is washed down by water. The glass holding the water was an invention of the ancient *Egyptians*.

James, meanwhile, is hurriedly putting on his trousers, a garment familiar both to ancient *Persians* and ancient *northern Europeans* and made of wool, a fiber from an animal native to *Asia Minor*. He pulls on a shirt of cotton, a fabric first domesticated in *India*, secured with buttons whose prototypes appeared in Stone Age *Europe*. He pulls on his most comfortable shoes, moccasins designed by *Native Americans*, and makes sure he has his favorite ballpoint pen, an *Argentinian* invention. His parting effort for his appearance is a quick spray of his hair with an aerosol can, which owes its propellant capability to a *Norwegian* inventor.

This morning, his complete breakfast is a cup of java which, in spite of its name, comes from a bean originally grown in the *Ethiopian* Highlands, its sugar sweetener having been created in ancient *India* and dispersed by *Arab* traders. Had he more time, he might have used a couple of eggs from a fowl domesticated in *Southeast Asia* to make *huevos rancheros* spiced with chiles domesticated in *Mexico*, accompanied by strips of bacon cured in a process invented in *northern Europe*, all of which he would have eaten off a plate of *china*, which needs no further comment.

Because one of the inflatable tires, an *Irish* invention, of his bicycle, an *English* invention, is flat, James picks up the receiver of his telecommunications device, invented by a *Scot*, and calls Gloria to see if they can carpool together. Gloria meets James at her car, a device first invented in nineteenth-century *Germany*. She speeds off, thanks to high-octane gasoline invented by a *Russian*, and drops James off at the university. They decide to meet later for a cup of hot chocolate, a substance originally from *Mexico*.

Just an ordinary, all-American day.

Table 4-1 Components of Culture

Component	Definition	Example
Symbol	An image, sound, object, or action that stands for something else	A dove symbolizes peace; a red heart symbolizes love
Language	A system of symbolic communication using words	English, Spanish, Chinese, and Swahili
Beliefs	A statement about reality accepted as true	The earth revolves around the sun
Norms	Standards of desirable behavior, sometimes codified into laws	Can range from norms governing dress and tone of voice in an elevator to laws against murder and rape.
Values	A general conviction about what is good or bad, right or wrong, appropriate or inappropriate	Competence and excellence are good; lying is bad
Material culture	The tangible products of human activity	Bluejeans, computers, books, motorcycles, sewing machines, video games, polio vaccines, guns

Subjective Culture

Subjective culture can be divided into five components: symbols, language, beliefs, norms, and values (described and summarized in Table 4-1). Human beings are born with a unique capacity to create culture and to transmit that culture from generation to generation through psychological processes. Developing higher mental processes that involve attention, cognition, memory, and reasoning is facilitated by learning such subjective cultural inventions as mathematics, language, and memory tools from other members of the culture who are already proficient in them (Vygotsky, 1978).

Symbols

A symbol is something that stands for something else but may have no intrinsic meaning in itself. A symbol can be an image, sound, or action that *represents* a particular event, or state of affairs within a particular culture. Symbols are usually linguistic, but can be nonverbal, such as a country's flag. The great public outrage that arose over disrespect to the U.S. flag demonstrates people's powerful emotional attachment to symbols.

Subjective culture is the collection of all intangible human creations, such as symbols, languages, beliefs, norms, and values. Material culture, in contrast, refers to artifacts of human activity, ranging from audiocassettes to zinc oxide.

Language

All human cultures organize symbols into ***language***, a system of symbols with meanings shared by a society's members. A lovely insect flying outside your window might be called a butterfly, or, just as readily, a choocho. You call it a butterfly because members of your culture told you that was its name, but in Japan, people call it a choocho. Another important aspect of language is the rules for how linguistic symbols, such as letters and words, can be meaningfully combined. Thus, every English speaker knows that *yrje* is not likely to be an English word; even if you can't identify the norms this combination of letters violates, it just doesn't "look right" (but it means foggy, windy weather in Norwegian). Likewise, English speakers judge the sentence, *All human cultures have symbols into language organized* to be ungrammatical, because it doesn't "sound right" (although in German, this would be the correct word order).

Language allows members of a culture to share beliefs, thoughts, and feelings, and is the primary means for transmitting culture from

▼ *The flag is a powerful symbol. At right, immigrants become U.S. citizens, taking their oath and reciting the Pledge of Allegiance; on the left, a protester burns a flag.*

▲ *A class in American Sign Language (ASL).*

one generation to the next. Without language, each generation of human beings would have to start over.

Although all cultures have spoken language, written language is a relatively recent development (emerging about 5000 years ago). In recent times, visual languages have been developed that enable people who cannot hear and/or speak to communicate complex concepts and relationships without having to resort to writing. American Sign Language (ASL) is a formal visual language with its own unique vocabulary and grammatical structure (Bellugi & Klima, 1972). It is not based on English, but like English (and other languages) ASL has its own dialects depending on the part of the country in which it is used (Wilbur, 1979).

Language provides ready-made categories for classifying our experiences and draws our attention to particular features in our environment. It thus provides cultural symbols to represent meaning and to organize how we think about and remember the world. In consequence, cultural variations in language can influence our cognitive processes, particularly memory (Hunt & Agnoli, 1991). The extreme version of this theory is the Sapir-Whorf hypothesis, which contended that because language is used to categorize and manipulate reality, it determines the individual's actual experience of reality by shaping perception and thought. This extreme version has not been supported by research, as language is not the only determiner of perception and thought. Thus, having different words for several kinds of snow or grazing or camels or corn will draw your attention to the differences and give you a means to represent them mentally and remember them, but it is not necessary for you to have different words for you to see the differences between them (see Chapter 8).

THINKING CRITICALLY

Suppose Chinese is your native language, but you also speak English. A researcher asks you to read descriptions of people written in Chinese and in English. One person is described as having strong family ties and lots of worldly experience—a type of person called "shi gu" in Chinese, but not so easily labeled in English. The other person has creative abilities and is temperamental—called an "artistic" type of person in English, but not so easily labeled in Chinese. If you were asked to write about your impressions of the person, do you think that you would have a different impression of the person if you were writing in Chinese than you would if you were writing about the person in English?

Indeed, researchers have found that language used under such conditions makes a difference. When reading and writing in Chinese, the research participants developed a more distinct impression of the "shi gu" person. But when reading and writing in English, their impression of the "artistic" person was more distinct (Hoffman, Lau, & Johnson, 1986).

Language affects what we pay attention to, how we organize information, and what we remember. Thus, the language labels probably affected how information about the person was processed and therefore led to different impressions of the same person.

▼ *These two women, on opposing sides of the abortion debate, have very different beliefs.*

Beliefs

What do bear gallbladders, rhino horns, and tiger bones have in common? Two things. First, millions of Asians *believe* in their medicinal effects. Second, the major reason for their effectiveness appears to be the power of that belief. That is, these cures work because people believe they will work (placebo effect), not because of any real curative power. Rhino horn (which is basically compacted hair) is used to increase sexual desire and stamina and to cure a range of ailments from headaches to typhoid fever. Tiger bones are used to treat malaria, dysentery, typhoid, and ulcers, increase longevity, and cast out devils. Bear gallbladders are used to treat a variety of ailments. None has any proven medicinal effects, yet desire for them continues to foster poaching and illegal trade in these animal parts. This is just one example of how beliefs can have a powerful effect on people's thoughts, feelings, and actions.

Beliefs are views of reality that people consider to be true. They can be based on faith, other people's opinions, tradition, logic, or observation. When a belief is "scientific," it is verifiable through a method of systematic observation, that is, we can use scientific methods to test if it is true.

Beliefs are the basis for expectations, which in turn affect our perceptions (what we observe), cognitions (what we think), motivations (what we want), and emotions (how we feel). To take one example, ***stereotypes*** are beliefs about the attributes of members of groups. They lead to expectations that all members of the group will have the same attributes and behave in the same way. These expectations in turn will influence our perceptions, attitudes, and feelings toward members of the group.

The controversy over abortion illustrates how beliefs can vary widely, even within a culture, and how differences in beliefs can have tangible effects when people act on them. This controversy reflects a fundamental difference in the belief about when the developing organism should be defined as an individual person, with all the legal rights and protections given to people in society. According to the U.S. legal system, personhood begins at birth. But some people believe that personhood begins at conception, while others believe it begins sometime later in pregnancy (the exact point varies). In some countries, personhood is defined as sometime after birth during the first year of life. The point here is not that a particular definition of personhood is right or wrong, but rather how differences in beliefs can raise passions, create controversy, and generate discord within and between societies.

▲ *Beliefs vary tremendously in different cultures. Here, Tamu shamans in Nepal attempt to placate a restless spirit. On seeing this photo, one of the shamans exclaimed, "This is exactly what the gods, the witches, and the ancestors look like. It must be a very good camera."*

Norms

Norms are the learned rules and expectations by which a society guides members' behavior. Norms, which sometimes become codified into laws, specify how people who hold different positions in the social order will interact. For example, lower-status people (children, students, workers) are expected to listen to and not interrupt higher-status people (parents, teachers, employers).

Norms help society control the behavior of individuals. Individuals are rewarded for conformity and punished for deviance. Guilt and shame, which occur when we violate norms, are among the most effective means a culture has to control behavior so that people can live harmoniously. All cultures have norms, but they vary widely in how they develop, elaborate, and enforce them. One example of the power of norms to control behavior can be seen through differences in rates of alcoholism across cultures. The rates of alcoholism shown in Figure 4-1 range from .45 percent in Taiwan to 22 percent in Korea. In Taiwan and China, there are strong norms against drinking or being drunk in public. In the United States, norms against drinking vary for different groups, but the dominant culture does not provide strong sanctions against public use of alcohol or drunkenness (with the exception of drunk driving, and that development is relatively recent). In Korea, where there are strong norms for males to drink in certain social situations—such as drinking contests after work—alcoholism occurs almost entirely in males (Helzer & Canino, 1992).

◀ *Norms can be a source of miscommunication. Here, different ideas about norms governing polite conversation collide.*

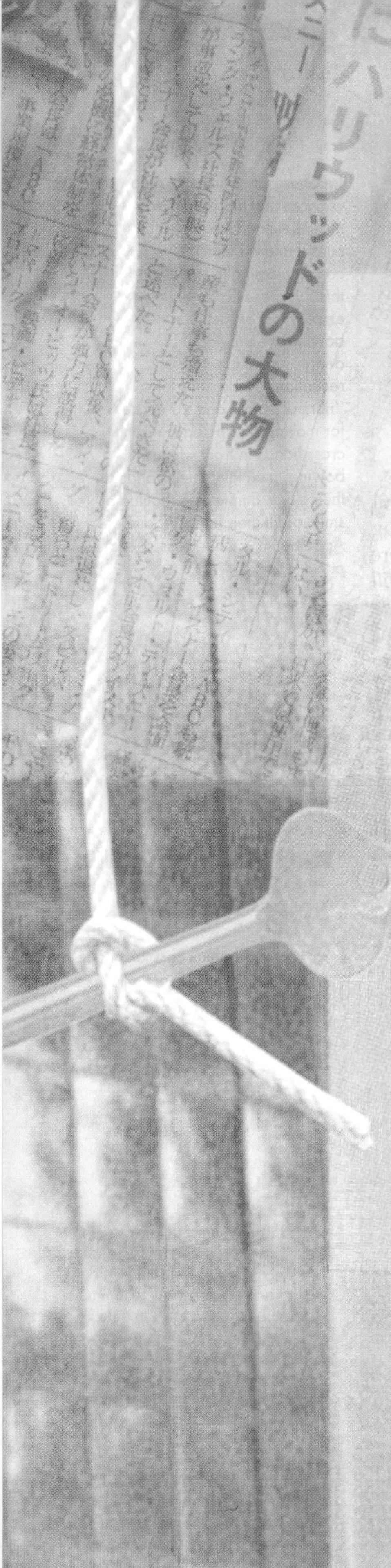

SEEKING SOLUTIONS

Breaking Down Cultural Barriers to Communication

Norms vary across cultures, subcultures, and time periods, sometimes becoming a source of conflict and miscommunication. How do they lead to such miscommunication? Eye contact is an important social cue across cultures, but its meaning varies. In American culture, eye contact regulates interaction and communicates rapport. It signals whose turn it is to speak, and people look at the other person more when listening than when speaking. Eye contact is a sign of attention and therefore respect. Teachers tell students "look at me when I am talking to you," and in U.S. courtrooms, juries typically expect defendants to look people in the eye if they are innocent and have nothing to hide. Avoiding eye contact is considered to reflect inattention, dishonesty, and evasiveness (Henley, 1977).

In some subcultures, however, looking someone directly in the eye is rude, an insult, or an aggressive challenge, while looking down is a sign of respect and recognizing the authority-subordinate relationship. In Navajo culture, for example, averting one's eyes is a sign of respect, and looking strangers directly in the eye is considered rude. In fact, African Americans, Mexican Americans, Puerto Ricans, and Native Americans have all been found to use eye contact differently than do whites during social interaction.

In an early naturalistic study of the conversations of sixty-three black and sixty-three white pairs, Marianne LaFrance and Clara Mayo (1976) found that black listeners gazed less at the person speaking than did white listeners. LaFrance and Mayo also found that blacks and whites exhibited differences in turn-taking cues. These differences could interfere with communication between blacks and whites. For example, among white speakers, ending a sentence or phrase with a pause and a sustained gaze is a turn-taking cue that the floor is yielded. Thus, when black speakers exhibited this behavior, the white person would begin to speak—not realizing that the black speaker had not finished—and both would talk at once. Conversely, when white speakers signaled in this way that they had finished their statements, the black speaker would not perceive the cue, leaving the white speaker waiting expectantly for the black speaker to take the floor.

Norms also affect interaction distances, that is, the distance people maintain when talking with others. They differ, depending on gender and ethnicity, and can be another source of miscommunication between people of different cultures. Researchers have found that, on average, interaction distances are somewhat larger for African Americans than for Euro-Americans. Distances for Hispanics, on the other hand, are smaller than those for the other two groups (Aiello & Thompson, 1980; Pagan & Aiello, 1982). Psychologists have used this knowledge to foster better interracial communication. They have studied how African Americans' judgments of police competence are affected by interaction distances, that is, by how far the police stand from community members when they speak to them. In one study, groups of white police officers were either trained to use the larger interaction distances more typical of African Americans or the smaller interaction distances more typical of Euro-Americans. The officers then conducted a series of interviews with black citizens. Black citizens preferred the officers who used the larger distances and judged them as more competent—personally, socially, and professionally (Garrett, Baxter, & Rozelle, 1981).

The study demonstrates how violation of an implicit norm (interaction distance) can lead to negative consequences. In this case, police officers who used closer interaction distances than the norm were judged as less competent. The study is a useful illustration of the point that implicit norms have power and can be a source of misunderstanding across ethnic groups. In particular, it has practical application in the case of white officers interacting with blacks in black communities. However, whether violating an interpersonal distance norm leads to lowered judgments of competence in other ethnic groups or even with regard to other black-white relationships requires further study. It may be that a poor history of police-community relationships gives violation of interpersonal distance norms special meaning for African-American community members interacting with the police.

One important value dimension that varies across cultures is that of individualism versus collectivism—the extent to which the culture emphasizes the interests of individuals (individualist) versus the interests of the group as a whole (collectivist). Individualistic and collectivist values affect how we think about ourselves, how we relate to other people, and how we bring up our children (Stigler, Shweder, & Herdt, 1990; Triandis, 1995). In keeping with the individualist values of the United States, a popular saying is, "The squeaky wheel gets the grease." In Japan, where family and group interdependence and interpersonal harmony are emphasized, they say, "The nail that stands out gets pounded down."

Cultures not only differ in how much they emphasize individual development over social solidarity and connection to others, they also link those values to specific behaviors in different ways. In keeping with the individualistic values of American culture, Americans typically begin speeches on a note that calls attention to themselves, establishing their credibility and worth as independent, self-motivated individuals. In contrast, Japanese speakers reflect the collectivist values of their culture by apologizing for their shortcomings, thus demonstrating their interdependence on others and arousing sympathetic understanding and feelings of connection between the audience and the speaker (Markus, 1992). In the United States, education and achievement are viewed as individual accomplishments, sometimes attained by sacrificing ties to others. In contrast, in East Asian cultures such as Japan, achievement and education are viewed as contributions to the group. The idea of the Walkman is also a reflection of Japanese collectivist values. Mr. Morita, head of the Sony corporation, loved classical music, and wanted to be able to listen to it while traveling to work without bothering other commuters. With the Walkman, he could listen to music without imposing on the outside world (Trompenaars, 1994).

In individualist societies, social experiences at work or school are structured around the individual. Competitive motivation, individual ambition, and personal accumulation of wealth are emphasized. Thus, businesses recognize and promote people for their individual achievements. In contrast, in collectivist societies, social relationships are structured around groups (e.g., the family, tribe, religious community, country). Group harmony, cooperation, and responsibility are emphasized and rewarded. Values also influence both the content of norms and which norms become codified into law. Compared to cultures in the West (British and Italian samples) that value individualism, Eastern cultures (Japanese and Hong Kong samples) that value collectivism have more norms dealing with obedience, loss of face, restraining emotional expression, and maintaining harmonious relationships in groups (Argyle, Henderson, Bond, Iizuka, & Contarello, 1986).

Values are abstract evaluations expressing broad preferences, while norms are evaluations that apply to specific situations.

When social structures, such as educational systems, emphasize individualism, they can create psychological conflicts for individuals whose cultural values stress cooperative effort for mutual gain within the group. For example, Native Hawaiians have higher drop-out rates from school than other groups living in Hawaii, because speaking out and competing in school settings conflict with traditional values of cooperation and mutual support found in Native Hawaiian culture (Miike, 1996).

When we talk about cultural differences between groups, we minimize differences among

◀ *The collectivist values of Japan are reflected in the structure of its workplace. At left, workers participate with managers in quality circles, where the group discusses ideas to improve productivity and working conditions. Companies also become involved in the lives of their workers. On the right, group calisthenics are provided to foster group solidarity while improving physical and mental performance.*

▲ *Many new occupations are made possible by material culture: pictured is Mae Jemison, the first black female astronaut in the United States.*

individuals within each group, and exaggerate differences between the groups. But, people are never just members of one unified, homogeneous culture. In fact, the beliefs, norms, and values of individuals vary widely within cultures. In fact, some researchers have argued that a person can be both individualistic and collectivistic, depending on the context (Schwartz, 1990; Ho & Chiu, 1994). For example, a person may be individualistic when competing with others for a job, but collectivistic when it comes to activities involving family relationships (Rhee, Uleman, & Lee, 1996).

Portraying American culture as individualistic glosses over the fact that individualism is more represented in behavior typically expected of males than females in the United States. Behavior traditionally expected of American females represents more collectivist values such as nurturance, promoting group harmony, and helping others save face (Tannen, 1990). Similar gender differences are found in many cultures. Beatrice and John Whiting (1975) report that among 110 nonliterate societies studied, girls were more likely than boys to be taught to be nurturing, obedient, and responsible, while boys were socialized to be self-reliant and achievement-oriented. Thus, a culture may be "individualist" when compared to others, but within a particular culture, there is diversity in how norms of individualism are applied. Further, any specific individual may or may not hold the values or adhere to the norms of the larger culture.

Material Culture

Not only are our behavior and thought influenced by the components of our subjective culture, they are also affected by the tools and technology of material culture. The invention of objects and systems of modern technology has been encouraged by values of progress, science, and material comfort, and has deeply affected everyday life. Consider what life would be like without television (invented in 1927, popularized in the 1950s), the telephone (invented in 1876) or the automobile (invented in 1885). Today, 98 percent of U.S. households own at least one TV set, and more than 90 percent of Americans sixteen and older are licensed to drive. Can you name five new occupations that appeared in the past century because of new technology? Countless new careers have appeared—pilot, telemarketer, computer programmer, cable TV installer, truck driver, astronaut, fast-food vendor, X-ray technician, and TV anchorperson are a few examples.

We often take our material culture as a given, and fail to consider how it affects (and sometimes limits) our behavior. Yet, material culture provides us with tools such as calculators and books that help us develop our higher mental processes. Environmental and engineering psychologists, in particular, study how the design of environments and objects can encourage or interfere with particular forms of behavior or social interaction (McAndrew, 1993). Stop for a moment and think about the factors that go into your typing speed on a computer. What did you come up with? Hand-eye coordination? Finger dexterity? Amount of practice? These are all person-related variables. But what about environmental variables, such as amount of noise in the room or level of illumination? These are obvious influences. But situational effects can also be subtle—for example, did you think about the keyboard's design?

Take a look at a computer keyboard (see Figure 4-3). Notice how the order of the top row of keys is Q-W-E-R-T-Y and so on. This design is called a "QWERTY keyboard" for that reason. In the QWERTY design, the letter "J" is hit by your right index finger—the finger most people can most easily control. Did you ever wonder why "J" rather than a more commonly used letter such as "S" was chosen for that spot on the keyboard? The QWERTY design reflects the cul-

4-3 Material Culture and Behavior

We don't always recognize how the design of environments and objects in our material culture can encourage or interfere with particular forms of behavior or social interaction. The QWERTY design (A), which was so effective in prompting optimal typing speed on early typewriters, now limits human performance on the computer keyboard where key jamming is no longer an issue. The redesigned keyboard (B) has the most commonly used keys in the "home" rows and the less frequently used keys in the upper and lower rows. This design may lead to faster typing speeds.

tural evolution of the keyboard, which began with the mechanical typewriter (Norman, 1988). Allowing typewriter keys representing the most frequently used letters to be struck by our most nimble fingers resulted in jammed keys on the old machines. People could type so fast that one key couldn't get out of the way of the one to follow. So the QWERTY design was specifically selected because *it slowed down typing speed.*

Today, computers respond more rapidly than any individual can type, but we still use the QWERTY keyboard. Attempts to change the keyboard layout to increase typing speed have met with intense resistance. We don't know what the upper limit on typing speed might be if the keyboard was redesigned for optimal performance. The limits the QWERTY keyboard sets on human performance demonstrate how aspects of our environment subtly determine our behavior. But what was once a subtle limitation sometimes becomes obvious once it is pointed out to us.

We continually make and remake both our material and nonmaterial culture when we become aware that old forms no longer meet current needs. For example, the entry of women into the workforce required redesigned work clothes and tools to fit a wider variety of physiques. The large number of adult Americans of working age with some sort of work disability (nearly one in eleven in 1990) led U.S. lawmakers to make laws leading to an overhaul of our material culture (U.S. Bureau of the Census, 1992). Thus, laws governing architectural design standards and public transportation have made our physical environment more accessible to people with disabilities, reflecting efforts to remake a material culture developed on the assumption that all individuals are able-bodied.

Technology can transform our material culture with both positive and negative results. Technology has increased our life expectancy and creature comforts, while at the same time amplifying the destructiveness of weapons and endangering the planet through environmental pollution. Technology has contributed to a world full of both environmental pleasures and pressures. And the pressures—such as noise, air pollution, traffic congestion, crowding, and threat of violence—all contribute to the stress many Americans experience on a fairly constant, day-to-day basis.

These stressful conditions are more prevalent in crowded cities than in sparsely populated rural areas. Several social problems increase with population density, including mortality rates, inadequate care for children, delinquency, and rate of admission to mental hospitals (Gove, Hughes, & Galle, 1979). Research on population density demonstrates the important role psychological factors play in whether or not our material culture (density being just one example) creates physical and psychological distress.

▲ *The stimulation of being in a crowd can have positive effects, as these teenagers experienced at a Lollapalooza concert (left), or negative effects, as in this crowded Japanese subway (right).*

Work by Jonathan Freedman (1975) suggests that increasing density has an arousing effect, intensifying feelings people have, whether positive or negative. If a person considers the context pleasant, such as at a party, then pleasant feelings are intensified. In unpleasant contexts, such as at a crowded store during last-minute holiday shopping, negative feelings are intensified. People may actually report crowding as less stressful if they can attribute their arousal from crowding to another source, such as a film they are watching (Worchel & Brown, 1984).

Material culture can thus have profound effects on behavior that sometimes go unnoticed or are attributed to other sources. Understanding the behaviors of individuals, both within and across cultures, requires examining the roles material culture plays in shaping those behaviors—from "micro" elements of the material culture such as design of a computer keyboard, to "macro" elements such as population density.

Promoting Understanding within and across Cultures

As a result of advances in the material culture—telephones and television, the Internet and jet planes—individuals find themselves in

▼ *Sensitivity to people with disabilities has also changed our material culture. The label on this wine bottle is written in Braille.*

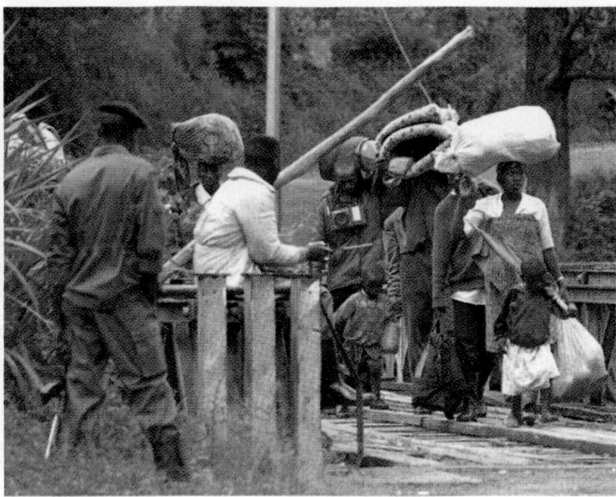

► *Rwandan refugees: some recent victims of ethnocentrism.*

greater contact with others. Whether individuals with different cultural backgrounds live in the same society or in different societies, they must learn to understand each other's point of view to prevent miscommunication and even violence. Such understanding requires avoiding ethnocentrism and recognizing the importance of cultural relativism.

Ethnocentrism

Ethnocentrism is the act of judging other individuals and cultures by the standards of your culture. In contrast, cultural relativism is the idea that each culture should be evaluated by its own standards, with no custom being right or wrong in and of itself.

Ethnocentrism refers to judging other cultures by the standards of your own. People often view their own cultural traditions as right and proper, while considering other traditions inferior, strange, or even savage. While this attitude can promote group cohesion, solidarity, and pride, taken to an extreme it can also result in unjustified rejection and condemnation of other people and lay a foundation for hostilities. The conflict between Protestants and Catholics in Northern Ireland which has been ongoing since the 1600s, the Holocaust perpetrated by the Nazis against the Jews in the 1930s and 1940s, the "ethnic cleansing" in Bosnia and that between the Tutsis and Hutus in Rwanda in the 1990s are but four of many examples of ethnocentrism's destructive consequences.

Cultural Relativism

Cultural relativism is the idea that each culture should be evaluated by its own standards, with no custom being universally right or wrong in and of itself. Cultural relativism requires both understanding the values and norms of another culture while suspending our own values and norms. For example, when the United States military was based in Saudi Arabia during Desert Storm, liquor was not allowed on the American bases out of respect for the Saudi's cultural ban on drinking alcohol.

Although understanding and relating to people of diverse backgrounds has become a necessity for both individual and societal survival, cultural relativism also has its dangers. Taken to an extreme, it can be used to defend against outside interference in programs of persecution, violence, and murder against men, women, and children. Amnesty International reports that state-sponsored torture still occurs in more than fifty countries. Genital mutilation of African women has been defended on the basis of cultural relativism. In the United States, a Muslim father murdered his daughter because she dishonored his family by having relations with an American man. He used cultural relativism to defend his behavior. So the basic question becomes, how far should we take the concept of cultural relativism?

One way to avoid the dangers of cultural relativism is to identify overarching worldwide values and norms. Nations have signed international treaties written under the auspices of the United Nations—for example, those identifying illegal weapons of war and specifying appropriate treatment of prisoners—in an attenpt to establish an international legal culture. Celebrating and respecting cultural differences while seeking unifying ideals and common goals is one of the most complex challenges we must meet in the twenty-first century.

Social Foundations of Behavior

Across and within cultures, people live in organized groups called societies. A ***society*** is a structured group of individuals within a geographical or political boundary who share a culture. ***Social structure*** refers to how society is organized into groups, including family, peer, educational, occupational, military, political, and religious groups. When people talk about needing to learn "the System," they are often talking about learning how the society is structured, including who has power to get things done. Health care, educational, transportation, social service, and justice systems are all part of our social structure.

Membership in Groups

A ***group*** is defined as two or more *interacting* individuals who share particular expectations and goals. For example, two people getting together to study are a group. Sororities, fraternities, and athletic teams are also groups. Boards of directors for corporations are groups. The Beatles were a group. The gangs, "Crips" and "Bloods," are groups. Basically, groups are made up of people who feel united and believe they share rights and obligations. Groups with a particularly strong sense of identification and loyalty among members to the exclusion of nonmembers are called ***in-groups***. People who are not in one's in-group form the ***out-group***. Out-group members are viewed more negatively than in-group members, sometimes even with hostility and contempt (Crocker & Luhtanen, 1990).

Social psychologists have studied the influence of groups on individuals, particularly in terms of how children are brought up and how groups affect task performance, decision-making, and leadership (Baron & Byrne, 1991). They have also been particularly interested in the processes that people use when they select and compare themselves to other group members. These topics will be discussed in Chapter 12.

Socialization refers to how individuals learn to become members of groups, beginning with the family. In the United States, people enter and leave group affiliations many times during their life cycle: socialization is a lifelong process. Consider the occupational socialization that goes on in college. Do students in business school, for example, dress differently than students in liberal arts colleges? Probably so. These distinctions reflect the process of socialization in action.

Cultures vary in the way they socialize children, and these variations can lead to average differences in personality among people from different cultures. For example, parents who are warm and supportive to their children, frequently hugging and praising them, are more likely to have children who develop positive, optimistic world views. In contrast, physically or emotionally abusive or indifferent parents are more likely to have children who have negative, pessimistic world views. Around the world, in cultures where parents are more rejecting and neglectful, children are more likely to be emotionally unstable, hostile, aggressive, and have lowered self-esteem. Although there is a large amount of individual variation, these general findings appear to hold, whether comparing across cultures or within cultures (Rohner, 1986).

▲ *Socialization takes many forms. Here, etiquette instructor Anne Oliver teaches manners to a young girl in Atlanta.*

Groups are defined as two or more interacting individuals who share particular expectations and goals, as well as sharing feelings of unity and holding the same beliefs about common rights and obligations.

Socialization is a process by which individuals learn how to behave as members of a group, beginning with the family.

How the Social Structure Can Affect Intergroup Relations

Suppose you decided to observe a boys' camp, and found the campers involved in a tournament of competitive games. The boys in one cabin are competing for prizes against those in another. You find that the boys are friends with the peers they live with, but they are hostile toward and hold stereotypes about the boys from the other cabin. You are asked to explain these attitudes and behaviors. What would you want to know? Would you want to give them psychological tests and find out about their personalities? Would you hypothesize that "like follows like" or that differences in other characteristics between the two groups are the source of the attitudinal differences? Would you say "boys will be boys and boys are naturally territorial and competitive," so there's nothing to explain? Or would you recognize that the social structure might be the source of the atti-

◀ *The ultimate in-group, as portrayed in the movie* Clueless.

▲ *In the Robbers Cave experiment, one group of boys raids the cabin of the other group.*

tudes and the key to understanding the intergroup relations?

Promoting Group Conflict

Antagonism and conflict between groups can be promoted or discouraged by cooperative or competitive social structures. A social structure that requires cooperation between groups to achieve common goals will lead the groups to develop mutually positive images of each other. Competitive social structures that pit groups against each other for mutually exclusive goals will promote intergroup hostility. Muzafer Sherif and his colleagues demonstrated this principle in a creative field experiment similar to the one described above (Sherif, Harvey, White, Hood, & Sherif, 1961). This classic research, which is known as the Robbers Cave study, clearly illustrates several key concepts in social psychology.

Sherif and his colleagues conducted a series of experiments over a period of three weeks at a boys' camp established specifically for research purposes. The boys were not previously acquainted and had been screened for good health and psychological adjustment. The researchers unobtrusively observed interactions among the boys by playing the roles of camp counselor and sports director.

During the first week, the camp was structured so that spontaneous friendships could develop. The boys were allowed a free choice of buddies and time was spent in camp-wide activities. The boys were then housed separately in two cabins. They were divided so that about two-thirds of a boy's best friends were housed in the other cabin. After only a few days in this new social structure, new in-group friendship patterns and shared norms about group activities began to emerge.

During the second week, the researchers organized a tournament of competitive sports between the two cabins, with prizes for the winners. This competitive structure rapidly led to greater solidarity for the in-group (members of the same cabin) and hostility toward and stereotyping of the out-group (members of the other cabin). The conflict began with name-calling and escalated to food fights, flag burning, cabin raids, and even fistfights. At this point, an observer entering the scene would have concluded the boys were "wicked, disturbed, and vicious" (Sherif, 1966, p. 85).

Reducing Group Conflict

The competition became so fierce that, during the last week of the experiment, the researchers had to find ways to reduce intergroup conflict. Their technique was based on subtly induced cooperation. They created several ***superordinate goals***—goals requiring both groups to act cooperatively to solve a common problem. The groups had to find and eliminate a stoppage in the water supply, and they had to pull together to start a truck that had broken down. The cumulative impact of such cooperative activities reduced hostility and stereotyping and made new cooperative activities possible. At the end of the three weeks, the two groups generally had favorable attitudes toward each other and friendships with members of the out-group reemerged.

If you looked to personal characteristics to explain the boys' behavior, you would overlook the impact that social structure had on the intergroup relationships. This research demonstrates the importance of recognizing how people's beliefs, attitudes, and actions reflect the social structure in which they live and work.

As you read about research that seeks to understand intergroup attitudes (between men and women, ethnic groups, people of different ages, occupations, sexual orientations, and so on), think about how the social context as well as personal attributes could influence what is happening. Look at both the situation *and* the person when you try to explain behavior. Can you think of other applications of this principle? For example, you might want to ask what it is about the social structure that contributes to the elevated homicide, suicide, and illness rates associated with our cities.

Social Status and Social Roles

Social status refers to where a person fits into a social structure, that is, to one's recognized position within that society or group. Think about the first questions asked when two adult Americans meet for the first time: "What do you do?" "Where do you live?" "Are you married?" "Do you have kids?" These are all questions about status. Holding a status involves rights and obligations, which means that individuals of a certain status can be expected to behave in particular ways. A parent is expected to be responsible in raising his or her child. A supervisor is expected to be fair while making sure the job gets done. A person may hold a variety of positions in society, each with its own status and social roles (see Figure 4-4).

Your ***social role*** represents the expectations and behaviors corresponding to your particular status or position in a social structure. In the classroom, for example, the two statuses, professor and student, have their own social role expectations. Families contain members with a variety of statuses: mother, father, daughter, son, uncle, aunt, and grandparent. Your family status (for example, daughter) defines your role relationships with other family members. Because societies may be organized differently, role relationships may have varying meanings across societies. One study reports that traditionally in China, the most important relationship has been father-son, while in India, it is mother-son, and in the West, spouse-spouse (Hsu, 1971).

Although a person may simultaneously hold many statuses, sometimes one status may have far greater significance than the others. A status that has exceptionally great significance for shaping a person's life is described as a ***master status***. Within American society, occupation is typically significant enough to be considered a master status. Thus, when Americans are introduced to others, one of the items of information typically mentioned is occupation. Marriage and parenthood also are important statuses.

Highly visible characteristics such as gender, ethnicity, and physical appearance can also function as master statuses. Because gender role norms and values often supersede those of other roles and operate in a wide variety of situations, gender functions as a master status. People who diverge from norms of physical appearance, whether they are exceptionally bad- or good-looking, fat or skinny, tall or short, are sometimes defined in physical terms, to the exclusion of other personal qualities. Physical disability sometimes also becomes a master status, which is why persons with disabilities often ask that people not refer to them as "the disabled." This request can be seen as an effort to remove their disability from the master status category.

Sometimes a status may involve more than one role. For example, the status of college student may have a variety of roles associated with it. A student may take the roles of a student government officer, a student athlete, a fraternity brother, a cafeteria worker, a professor's aide, or a student newspaper reporter. ***Role conflict*** is the term used when roles associated with different statuses are incompatible, as when a man who is both a father and a worker is asked to work long hours on his child's birthday. In some urban high schools today, African American students report that they will be socially ostracized as "trying to be white" if they attain good grades (Steele, 1992). This is an example of an attempt to *create* role conflict between the student role and the role of minority group member—a great irony, as slaves were forbidden to learn to read or write and once risked death to become secretly educated. As a youth, the great nineteenth-century black leader Frederick Douglass even traded bread to poor white boys for them to teach him how to read (Douglass, 1845).

Social status may also reflect one's wealth and power. ***Social stratification*** refers to how scarce resources, power, prestige, and social rewards are distributed in a society. In other words, it represents how social and economic

▲ *The master status of actor Christopher Reeve has changed, from Superman to advocate for research on spinal cord injuries.*

Master status is a status of exceptionally great significance for shaping a person's life.

Status is an individual's recognized social position within society, whereas social role includes the expectations and behaviors corresponding to a particular status.

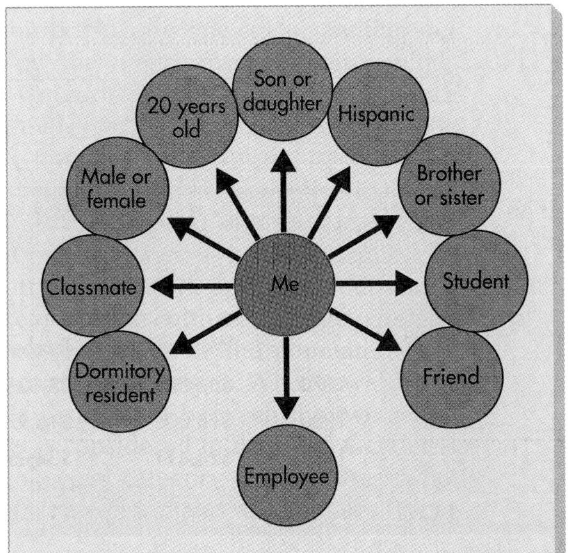

4-4 Social Status

The person in this figure—"me"—occupies many positions in society, each of which involves distinct statuses.

cathy® by Cathy Guisewite

► *Once our gender is known, we acquire gender related expectations that influence how people perceive and interact with us.*

goes in the cultural package varies across cultures, however (Lips, 1993).

Take something as widespread as the mock fighting and chasing activities known as rough-and-tumble play. Such activities are found in children around the world. In the United States, such play occurs mostly in groups of the same gender. In fact, some psychologists believe that boys' rough-and-tumble play is a factor that leads girls to withdraw from playing with them, creating gender segregation in activities early in childhood that, in turn, create differences in interaction styles that widen over time (Maccoby, 1990). But is rough-and-tumble play a necessary characteristic of the male gender? No, it depends on the culture. In some cultures, such as the !Kung of Botswana and the Pilaga Indians, girls often engage in rough-and-tumble play, by themselves as well as with boys (Etaugh & Rathus, 1995).

Learning about gender includes coming to think of ourselves as being either male or female (***gender identity***) and acquiring a multitude of expectations for how we, as males or females, should interact with others in various settings (***gender roles***). Suppose you were given a picture of a male and a female and asked the following question: "One of these people is a very affectionate person. When the person likes other people, they hug or kiss them a lot. Which person likes to hug and kiss a lot?" Would your answer be affected by whether the person was male or female? Researchers described thirty-two stories of this kind to middle-class children in twenty-four countries, asking them to indicate whether the person in the story was more like a woman or a man. By five years of age, 57 percent of the children made stereotyped responses, associating aggressive, dominant, and strong characteristics with males, and affection and gentleness with females. Stereotypes increased over time, and by the time the children were eleven years of age, 90 percent had acquired the idea that women were appreciative, complaining, emotional, excitable, gentle, meek, submissive, soft-hearted, talkative, and weak. Men, on the other hand, were considered ambitious, adventurous, boastful, coarse, confident, cruel, disorderly, independent, jolly, loud, and steady. But the cultural package varied as well. For example, Japanese children saw women as dominant and steady, and German children saw women as more adventurous, confident, jolly, and steady—characteristics associated with males in other countries. The children in the countries studied thus developed gender role expectations at a similar time and in a similar way, but exactly what characteristics were associated with women and men varied substantially with cultural context. In

► *Female bullfighter Cristina Sanchez has defied gender expectations.*

UNDERSTANDING HUMAN DIVERSITY

How Many Genders Are There?

Although all cultures have the concept of gender, in some cultures gender is not based on sexual characteristics, and there may be more than two genders. How is this possible?

Some northwestern Native American tribes have a category called *berdache*, that appears most usefully described as a third gender. *Berdache* category members are biologically male but have a separate status and gender role than most males and females of the tribe. The behavior of these individuals does not meet the definitions of social categories used in the United States, such as transvestite, transsexual, or homosexual: *Berdache* do not always cross-dress; they do not appear to question their biological maleness, and homosexuality is not always related to being a member of this social category. They are frequently known for spiritual and artistic accomplishments, and they have used their special powers to bless ceremonies and assume other spiritual responsibilities. Since they typically do women's work, in some tribes they marry men (Williams, 1986).

In India, *hijras* are a kind of third sex. *Hijras* are males who worship Bahuchara Mata, an Indian mother goddess. They wear female dress and behave in many ways as females. By having their penis and testicles surgically removed, they gain the power to bless or curse male infants. Some of them describe themselves as "Neither man or woman," while others say, "We *hijras* are like women" (Nanda, 1990).

Another approach to constructing gender can be traced to the mountains of North Albania. There a tribal society existed well into the twentieth century that was characterized by blood feuds and a strict gender hierarchy in which women were little more than the property of their fathers or husbands within their clan. However, a woman could change her gender role and avoid an arranged marriage by becoming a "sworn virgin" and living a chaste life. Families without male heirs could declare a female infant a son and consequently rear her as a boy. An older girl could also swear an oath to take the place of a deceased father or brother as head of the family. These women shared the same status as men, dressed in men's clothing, and even carried weapons, the most esteemed male privilege. According to tradition, some sworn virgins even entered into marriage with other women (Dekker & van de Pol, 1989). Similarly, many Native American tribes also had an alternative gender category for women (Ward, 1996). Clearly, concepts of rigid gender roles do not accurately reflect the great diversity in gender-related behavior found cross-culturally and over time. As you learn about how gender reflects and affects psychological processes such as learning, cognition, motivation, and emotion, always keep in mind that the particular values, motives, and behaviors associated with a specific gender vary across cultures, and across time within a culture. Even the number of genders is subject to debate.

▼ *Hijras of India, often self-described as "neither woman nor man," are an example of a third gender.*

particular, countries that were technologically developed and urban had more egalitarian views toward gender roles. In less economically developed countries, male's self-concepts were more active and stronger than women's (Williams & Best, 1990).

Throughout history, gender has been a major organizing principle for human culture (Lerner, 1986). Not only people, but subjective and material culture are also engendered in many ways. Most languages make some sort of gender distinction. Physical objects (such as dolls and guns) as well as psychological traits (nurturance and mathematical ability) can have gender-related meaning. Think about gender role assumptions in the design of material culture, as when work clothes and equipment are designed to fit male bodies (creating gender differences in accident rates on the job). Think about what happens when city planners assume a gendered division of labor in the family and build home and work environments miles apart. Role conflicts are created for all workers trying to be successful on the job and effective, caring parents when their children are sick. In short, our cultural concept of gender shapes the design of our physical and social environments. And like the QWERTY typewriter keyboard, sometimes our gendered environments can undermine performance in unrecognized ways.

Sex is primarily a biological concept based in large measure on differences in reproductive anatomy between males and females, whereas gender is primarily a psychological concept based on differences in behavior or expectations about the behavior of males and females.

THINKING CRITICALLY

There's a popular belief that women are more oriented toward marriage and parenthood than men. Given what you have learned about gender and culture, would you expect this to be true?

If you said that it probably depends on the culture, you are right. A study of college students from four cultures, the United States, France, Tunisia, and Mexico, demonstrated that the emphasis on core gender-related life goals—marriage and parenthood—varied with culture. In Tunisia and the United States, women gave more importance to marriage than men; in France and Mexico, men emphasized marriage more than women. In the United States and France, women wanted more children compared to men; in Tunisia and Mexico, the reverse was true (Almeida Acosta & Sanchez de Almejda, 1983). The moral of the story? Keep in mind that the particular values, motives, and behaviors associated with a specific gender vary across cultures, and across time within a culture.

Ethnicity

The word "ethnic" comes from the word *eth'nos*, which means "people" or "nation." Today, ***ethnicity*** is a social category that distinguishes people based on their common social and cultural characteristics, such as nationality, religion, and language (Betancourt & López, 1993). Individuals may have more than one ethnic affiliation, and the salience of a particular ethnic identity, that is, the ethnic identity a person is consciously aware of having at any particular moment, may depend on the social situation. For example, someone with an Irish American father and a Mexican American mother may emphasize Irish ancestry at a Saint Patrick's Day party and Mexican ancestry at a Cinco de Mayo celebration. African Americans and Polish Americans have different ethnic identities in New York City, but if they are in China, their ethnic identity as Americans becomes salient. Some multiethnic individuals resist being asked to choose among ethnic identities when describing themselves. Champion golfer Tiger Woods, for example, describes himself as "cablinasian," a word coined to reflect his multiethnic heritage (Caucasian, Black, Indian, and Asian). (See Figure 4-6 for a look at some of the major ethnic groups in the United States and how they have grown.)

Ethnicity is a social category that distinguishes people based on their common social and cultural characteristics, such as nationality, religion, and language.

Characteristics that define a particular ethnic group vary. Typically a *combination* of characteristics expresses a particular ethnicity. Physical characteristics sometimes indicate ethnic group membership, but often they do not: northern European ethnic groups (for example, Germans, Dutch, Danes, English) are not distinguishable by their physical characteristics, and

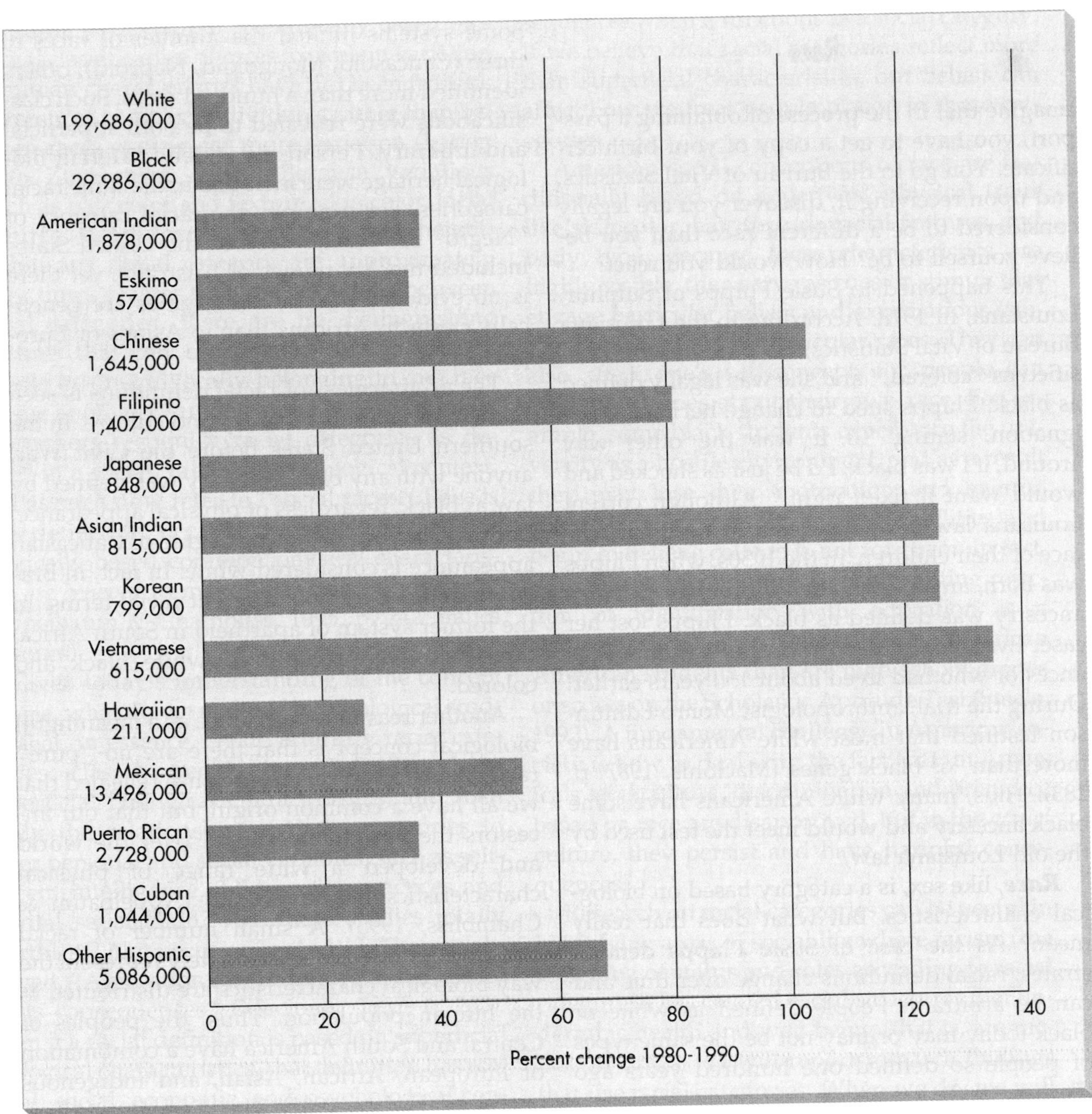

4-6 Race and Ethnicity

The figure shows some major U.S. ethnic groups and how their numbers have changed between 1980 and 1990. The numbers beneath the racial or ethnic group indicate the total number of each group in 1990. The bars in the graph show the percent change from the numbers in 1980 and those in 1990. (Source: U.S. Bureau of the Census, 1992)

neither are African or Native American ethnic groups (Zulus look like Swazis, and Choctaws like Chickasaws).

Although language is frequently an indicator of ethnic identity, Serbs, Croats, and Bosnian Muslims all speak the same language. They differ in religion, however, which in this case is the dominant characteristic in defining ethnicity. The single Chinese ethnic identity, on the other hand, encompasses a great variety of religions, including Buddhist, Taoist, Christian, and Muslim. In contrast, one religion can encompass many ethnic groups. Consider the more than 2.6 million Muslims living in North America. They are sometimes stereotyped as having a Middle Eastern heritage, but they could also be from Africa, South Asia, or the former Soviet Union, among other places, and they speak many different languages. What should be clear from all of this is that it is not easy to define boundaries between ethnic groups.

Clearly, the concept of ethnicity is complex, difficult to understand and still evolving. Research on this subject is an important task for contemporary psychologists because being part of an ethnic group determines many aspects of one's subjective and material culture (Betancourt & López, 1993).

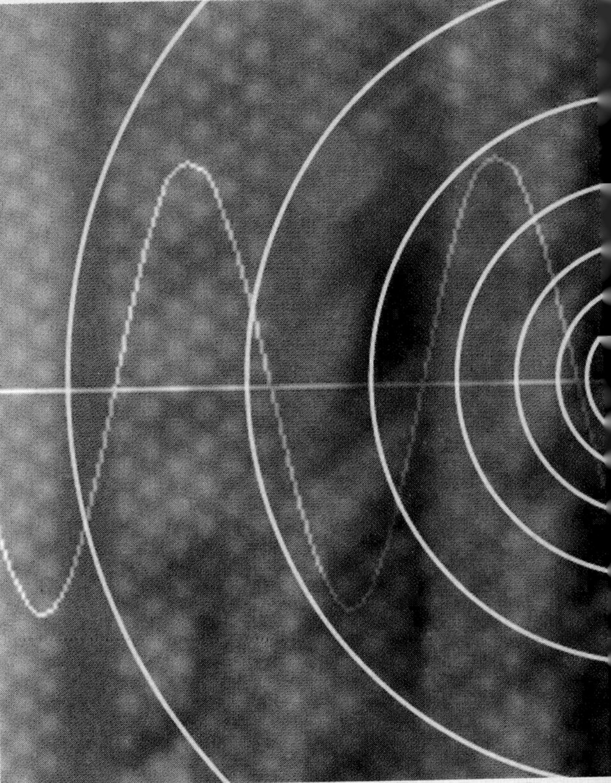

C H A P T E R 5

Sensation and Perception

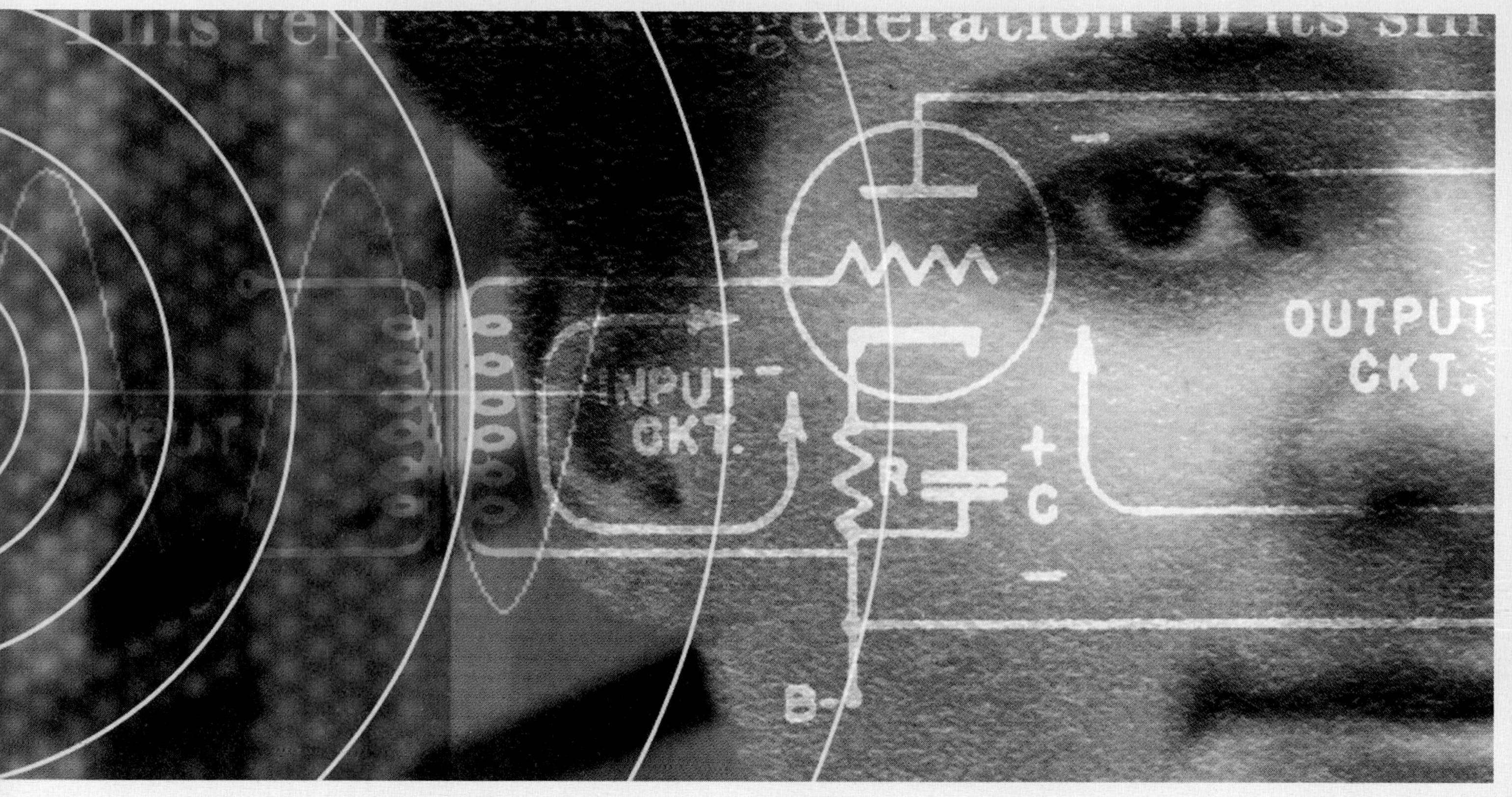

O B J E C T I V E S

After reading this chapter, you should be able to:

1. Describe sensory systems and the chain of events from stimulus input to conscious perception.
2. Discuss the physical and sensory processes involved in seeing.
3. Explain what is meant by bottom-up and top-down processes, and discuss how these processes are illustrated in visual object and depth perception.
4. Discuss the physical, physiological, and perceptual processes involved in hearing.
5. Discuss the physiological and perceptual processes involved in the other human senses: sensing body position and movement, touch, smell, and taste.

Riding high above Agrabah, the town in the movie *Aladdin*, you can control your magic carpet by pulling up or pushing down on its edges. At least this is possible at the Epcot Center in Florida, where the illusion of reality is created by miniature, head-mounted television sets that provide compelling input to your visual system. Perhaps a high-speed chase between pyramids in ancient Egypt is more to your liking. If so, the Luxor Hotel in Las Vegas has flight-simulator technology that produces on-screen action synchronized with seats that can move up to three feet in all directions. Or maybe you'd just like to see the good old U.S.A. without worrying about the wear and tear on your tires. The arcade video game, "Cruisin' U.S.A.," lets you drive a 2,650-mile race through 3-D footage that takes you from the redwoods of California to Washington, D.C. Virtual reality is no longer confined to science fiction—theme parks, video arcades, museums, and psychological laboratories are just some of the places where individuals can become "virtual tourists" (Fryxell, 1995). The role of computer technology in creating such experiences is widely heralded. But without basic research in the psychology of sensation and perception, such advances simply could not have taken place.

► *Wearing fiber-optic gloves and a computerized visual display, a NASA researcher experiences the electronic world of "virtual reality."*

We generally don't think about sensing, perceiving, and experiencing the world because these psychological processes are more or less automatic. But when a virtual reality contraption can enable us to perceive objects or places as if we were really there, instead of sitting in a chair hooked up to a machine, we may start to wonder about how we sense, perceive, and experience the world. How do we convert distant stimuli (energies) into meaningful forms that we can easily recognize, understand, and interact with? The answer to this seemingly simple question is in fact quite complex, and requires knowing something about physics, about biology, and about culture, as well as about psychology. You need to know how our eyes, ears, and other senses convert information contained in physical stimuli (such as light and sound waves) into neural messages. Further, you need to know how memory (our knowledge and skills) and context (especially the sociocultural context) can shape the meaning we attach to these neural messages that come from our senses. This chapter provides you with the basic facts about sensation and perception. Before delving into the individual senses, we will first discuss some general concepts that apply to all of them.

Sensation and Perception: An Overview

When you listen to a conversation between two friends, the vibration of their vocal chords creates waves in the air that strike your ears, setting in motion a chain of events that ends in your hearing recognizable words. Sensation and perception are the processes that make this possible. The chain of events begins with some form of physical energy impinging on your sense organs and ends with a conscious experience. Psychologists typically distinguish between sensation and perception in this chain of events. ***Sensation*** refers to converting the stimulus—a sound or sight or taste—as it arrives at receptors in the ears, eyes, or mouth, into neural impulses; ***perception*** involves processing and comparing and interpreting sensory stimuli to give them meaning.

Sensory and perceptual processes actively work together to accept, transform, organize, and interpret the environment around us. They provide answers to three essential questions about living: "What is out there?" "Where is it located?" "What is it doing?" Take a look at Figure 5-1. What do you see? Now turn the page, and look at Figure 5-3. Look at Figure 5-1 once again. Your eyes are presented with the same patterns of light both times, but your perception of Figure 5-1 has changed. After seeing Figure 5-3, you are able to process the information in Figure 5-1 differently, so that you perceive a meaningful object. You have just experienced how perception translates a visual sensation into an object you can recognize.

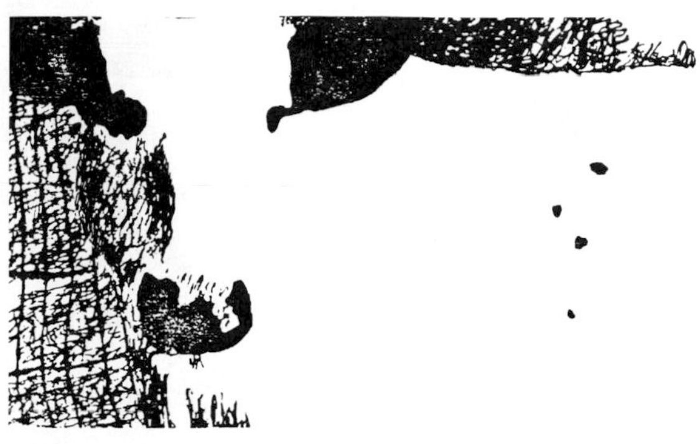

5-1 The Difference between Sensation and Perception

What do you sense and what do you perceive in this drawing? Examine the drawing for fifteen seconds and see if you can identify what it is. If you are having trouble figuring out what this picture is, you are experiencing the difference between sensation and perception. Turn to page 136 to see more clearly what it is. (Source: Sekuler & Blake, 1990, p. 18).

Proximal and Distal Stimuli

What do we sense? Psychologists distinguish between proximal and distal stimuli. ***Proximal stimuli*** are physical energies, such as light and sound, that impinge directly on our senses. ***Distal stimuli***, on the other hand, are the objects themselves in the "real" world. There are huge differences between the objects in the real world and the stimulus energies that transmit information about them. Consider just one example. You perceive a distant tree as being three-dimensional, having height, width, and depth. But in fact the pattern of light falling on your eye is only two-dimensional, since the sensitive part of the eye is basically a flat surface (see Figure 5-2). Nonetheless, as we will explain below,

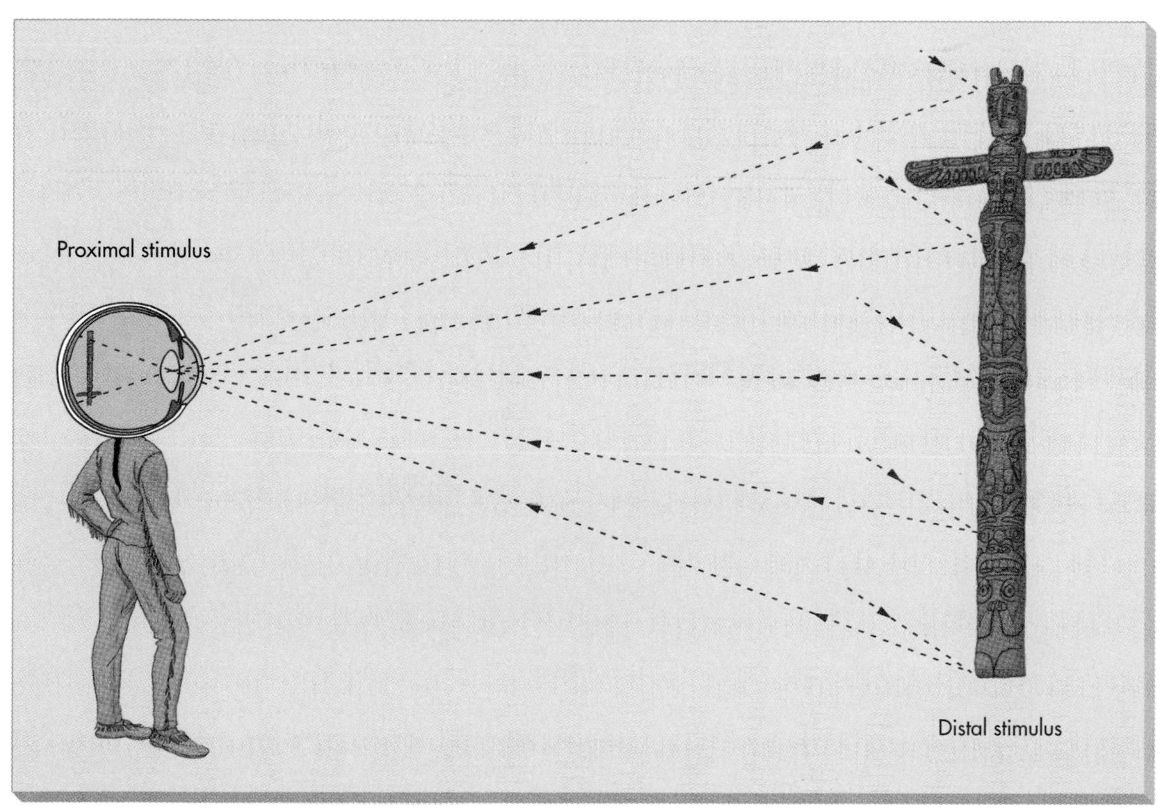

5-2 Proximal versus Distal Stimuli

Consider a person looking at a totem pole or a tree or a building or a statue. The person sees the object only because light is reflected from it into the person's eye. We can describe the stimulus (here, the totem pole) in two ways: (1) as a distal stimulus, in which we specify the dimensions of the totem pole and its location in the environment; (2) as a proximal stimulus, in which we specify the size and location of the totem pole on the person's retina.

5-3 Perceptual Learning

In this figure, you can easily see that the drawing is a cow. If you now go back to Figure 5-1, what do you see? If you now easily perceive that Figure 5-1 is a cow, even though before you could not identify what the drawing was, you have experienced perceptual learning. (Source: Sekuler & Blake, 1990, p. 20)

you are able to translate a two-dimensional proximal stimulus into a three-dimensional distal stimulus. Virtual reality is possible because we can stimulate the senses (manipulate the proximal stimuli) to produce neural messages as if they were actually coming from a nonexistent three-dimensional distal stimulus. Similar techniques are used in producing 3-D movies.

From Sensory Systems to Sensations

The line between sensation and perception is arbitrary, but in general, sensation happens first, when a sensory system is stimulated by some physical event; perception follows, as the sensation is translated into meaning.

How much do you know about your senses? Most people know there are at least five senses used to perceive the external world: vision, hearing, smell, taste, and touch. Some characteristics of these systems are shown in Table 5-1. But there are other senses that help you perceive your internal world. What can you sense about your muscles, your heart rate, your breathing, and other body functions? Sensory systems located in the muscles, joints, and glands of the body enable you to feel your current internal state. Biological organisms have many sensors located throughout the body. Indeed, the human body might be described as a mass of sensors—wall-to-wall sensory systems, as it were—some picking up external stimulation and some detecting your internal world.

Each sensory system includes three basic components: specialized cells called receptors, which transform physical energy into neural impulses; specific nerve pathways, which carry these neural impulses from the receptors to the brain; and particular brain regions, where the impulses are received and interpreted.

Our receptors are constantly bombarded with both external and internal physical stimuli. But as Diana Ackerman (1990) has so eloquently described, "the brain is silent, the brain is dark, the brain tastes nothing, the brain hears nothing. All it receives are electrical impulses—not the sumptuous chocolate melting sweetly, not the oboe solo like the flight of a bird, not the tingling caress, not the pastels of peach and lavender at sunset over a coral reef—just impulses" (p. 307). Our conscious perceptions are constructed from neural impulses that the brain receives via the peripheral nervous system. Where do these neural impulses come from?

Neural impulses normally begin at your sensory receptors. Receptors in your sense organs are specialized for converting physical energies

Table 5-1 Characteristics of Our Sensory Systems

Sense	Stimulus	Receptors	Stimulus Equivalent to Absolute Threshold
Vision	Electromagnetic energy, photons	Rods and cones in the retina	Candle flame viewed from a distance of 48 km (30 miles)
Hearing	Sound pressure waves	Hair cells on basilar membrane of the inner ear	Ticking of a watch in a quiet room 6 m (20 ft.) away
Taste	Chemical substances dissolved in saliva	Taste buds on the tongue	1 tsp. of sugar dissolved in 2 gal. of distilled water (1 part in 2,000)
Smell	Chemical substances in the air	Receptor cells in the upper nasal cavity	1 drop of perfume in a three-room house (1 part in 500,000,000)
Touch	Mechanical displacement of the skin	Nerve endings in the skin*	The wing of a bee falling on your cheek from a distance of 1 cm (0.39 in.)

*Yield sensations of warmth, cold, touch, pain.

that strike them into neural messages. These neural impulses that now represent the objects in our environment then travel from our receptors over the peripheral nervous system's network of sensory neurons to the brain. By studying the relationship between physical stimuli and what is perceived, psychologists attempt to understand the intervening mental processes—how we are able to experience the taste of chocolate, to hear the nightingale's song, to feel the sun's radiance, and to smell the scent of the rose.

Sensation primarily reflects the built-in biological apparatus that an organism is born with or that develops during its lifetime. While there is some variation in sensory systems from individual to individual, members of a given species are all pretty much alike with respect to what they can sense in the environment. Moreover, most species, including human beings, have some brain cells that are "hard-wired" to detect certain patterns of stimulation. These hard-wired cells are largely predetermined by genetic makeup. We know that rabbits have built-in "hawk detectors" that enable them to recognize and then escape from these predators, and frogs have built-in "bug detectors" that help them capture the insects that are their food. Similarly, the ability to detect simple patterns (for example, lines and edges) may be hard-wired in the human brain, thus enabling us to make distinctions that are important to our survival.

Perception, on the other hand, is deeply influenced by memory and by culture, because the interpretation of any stimulus implies a reference to and comparison with something that we already know. Thus, something as fundamental as a brain's perceptual pattern detectors can be influenced by experience. Research on the visual system has established that experience early in life is required for normal development. In a classic study (Blakemore & Cooper, 1970), kittens were raised for the first five months of their lives in an environment that restricted their visual experience either to horizontal or to vertical lines. When later allowed to explore in a nonrestricted environment, kittens showed strong and permanent effects of their early limited experience. Those who had seen only vertical lines responded to a black stick when it was presented in an upright position but not when it appeared horizontally. Those kittens who had experienced only horizontal lines responded to the stick only when it was presented horizontally, because they were unable to interpret vertical lines. The first five months of life are critical for kittens.

▲ *The universal activity of eating involves nearly all the senses. Here, in a scene from the film* Eat Drink Man Woman *the characters see the beautifully prepared Chinese meal, smell its aromas, feel the utensils and the texture of the food on their tongues, hear the sizzling of hot dishes, the sounds of chewing, and the clinking of tableware, and, of course, taste the food itself.*

Although experiments like this have never been done on human beings, for obvious ethical reasons, this research suggests that raising a human infant in a restricted environment (analogous to raising a kitten in an environment with only vertical lines) would lead to limited development of its perceptual and cognitive capacities (Haith, 1986). Indeed, studies of adult human beings who were born blind but later had their vision restored show that adaptation to their new sensory capability is difficult and that they might never achieve the level of adaptation found in normal people (see Von Senden, 1932). People who have had their sight restored as adults have difficulty identifying even the simplest objects, like pencils or faces, on the basis of sight alone. Thus, if a person does not have the necessary visual experience early in life, so that meaning can be attached to visual images independent of other sensory input, the ability to interpret these images, which in all respects are no different from the images seen by normally sighted individuals, never develops. A case of a fifty-year-old man living in Oklahoma who regained his sight confirms Von Senden's earlier findings (Sacks, 1995). When the bandages were removed after surgery to restore his vision, the man initially reported that he had no idea what he was seeing, "There was light, there was movement, there was color, all mixed up, all meaningless, a blur. Then out of the blur came a voice that said, 'Well?' Then, and only then, he said, did he finally realize that this chaos of light and shadow was a face—and, indeed, the face of his surgeon" (Sacks, 1995, p. 114).

The room fell silent. Someone thought she heard a pin drop.

Sensitivity and Its Measurement

When his plane was hit and disabled by enemy fire, U.S. pilot Scott O'Grady parachuted to earth in the middle of hostile Bosnian territory. He hid and survived by eating bugs and bark and grass. He had to let his rescuers know that he was still alive without alerting the enemy. He had to send a signal that would be strong enough for his would-be rescuers to detect but that would not give away his position to the enemy. Somehow he succeeded in getting off a weak signal detected by U.N. forces but missed by the enemy. Stimuli vary in strength. Sometimes they are detected and sometimes not, even when we're trying to detect them. Often, stimuli are so weak that our sensory systems are just not able to detect them clearly. In many cases, it might not matter. We can get closer to see better, or we can wait until the sound gets louder. But what if the stimulus poses some danger? Was the sound that awakened you an intruder? Did I see something move off to the left of the path? Is the gas from the stove leaking? How much stimulation is needed before we can detect and recognize it? How much does a stimulus have to change before the change is noticed? The science of psychophysics, which began roughly in the mid-nineteenth century, sought to answer these questions by measuring the relationships between the external world and the perceptual experiences it triggers (see Chapter 1).

An absolute threshold is the level of energy at which a stimulus can just barely be detected; a difference threshold is the level of energy at which a difference between two stimuli can be detected.

Although these questions are simple enough, they have life-or-death implications in some circumstances. Health-care professionals scrutinize X-rays for signs of cancerous growths. If these are noticed early enough, the cancer can be removed to save a patient's life. Air traffic controllers must be able to detect small changes in flight paths to warn pilots of conditions that could lead to mid-air collisions. Thus, if two planes are about to fly into the same air space, controllers must notice and alert the pilots to alter their courses. Everyday tasks, like driving a car, require minute-to-minute detection of the presence and change of unanticipated stimuli. Thus, if we suddenly see a pedestrian in the crosswalk, we can step on our brakes to stop the car before it hits him. Early psychophysicists developed the concepts of absolute threshold and difference threshold to describe sensitivity to environmental stimuli.

▶ *Workers in air traffic control rooms such as this one must be acutely sensitive to changes in stimuli.*

Absolute Threshold

The ***absolute threshold*** is the minimal amount of energy needed to detect the presence of a stimulus. How do we measure absolute threshold? The first thing to realize is that sensory thresholds are not constant. Sometimes we seem to be able to detect a particular stimulus, while at other times, we cannot detect the same stimulus. If the stimulus is detected a certain proportion of the times that it is presented, researchers consider that detecting the stimulus is not a matter of chance. The choice of the number of times that the stimulus is detected is arbitrary, but the usual convention is that the absolute threshold has been reached if the stimulus is detected on half of its presentations. The absolute threshold for the human senses under nondistracting conditions is remarkably low. To give you an idea of how sensitive the various senses are, in Table 5-1, we provide some real-life examples of stimuli that are equivalent to absolute threshold values. Thus, for example, in a quiet place you can hear a watch ticking twenty feet away, and under ideal viewing conditions you can just barely see a candle flame that is thirty miles away.

Difference Threshold

The ***difference threshold*** (also known as the ***just noticeable difference*** or ***j.n.d***) represents a person's ability to detect a difference between two stimuli. The assumption is that it takes a certain minimal amount of physical difference before detection is possible. For example, a warning sign for skin cancer is a change in a wart or mole. Was that mole there before? This is a question concerning the absolute threshold. Has it changed in size or color? This question concerns the difference threshold.

Suppose we supply you with earphones for a hearing test, and then present you with two tones. Your task is to determine whether you hear two different tones or the same tone twice. The difference threshold is defined as the point where you correctly identify the two tones as different about half the time.

Ernst Weber and Gustav Fechner studied the relationships between the lights and sounds of the physical world and our psychological experience of them (see Chapter 1). From this work came ***Weber's law***, the first law of psychophysics. It states that the difference threshold is a constant proportion (percentage) of stimulus size or intensity. Thus, to detect a difference in the loudness of sounds, there must be about a 9 percent difference between the two stimuli. If you raised the volume on the TV, you would not detect a difference until the sound was physically 9 percent greater than before. Although a 9 percent increase in a loud sound is, in absolute physical terms, a greater increase than a 9 percent increase in a soft sound, the two increases appear perceptually to be equal. Difference threshold values have been established for all of our sensory systems. Table 5-2 lists some of these values.

Signal Detection Theory

Imagine that you're a police officer on duty in a dangerous neighborhood. You have to be alert

Table 5-2 Difference Threshold for Selected Sensations

	Difference Threshold	
Sensory Dimension	**In Percent**	**As a Ratio**
Brightness	1.6	1/62
Loudness	8.8	1/11
Pitch	0.3	1/333
Pressure (on forearm)	13.6	1/7
Lifted weight	1.9	1/53
Smell (rubbery)	10.4	1/10
Taste (salty)	20.0	1/5

THINKING CRITICALLY

If the difference threshold for visual brightness is 2 percent, how much brighter than a 20-unit light must a second stimulus be in order to be detected as different? What is the brightness of the light that is just detectably different from an 80-unit stimulus?

In the first case, the answer is .4 units (2 percent of 20 is .4). In the second case, the answer is 81.6 (2 percent of 80 is 1.6, plus 80 equals 81.6).

to any signs of conflict or violence. You study the people walking down the street. Are they carrying weapons? Are they about to attack someone? Is that a gun or just a hand in a pocket? If you're mistaken, the consequences could be deadly. When a threshold is measured in the laboratory or in the doctor's office, the consequences are usually not so serious. Moreover, in the laboratory or the doctor's office, there are no distracting stimuli. In real life, on the other hand, consequences often do matter, and you usually have to make discriminations among stimuli in "noisy" environments. Have you ever missed the ringing of your telephone because the TV was blaring and your roommate was talking at the same time? What about the possibility of missing a traffic signal because you were distracted by a glut of road signs, or the signs of a major storm because you thought the clouds were the kind that would pass over quickly? ***Signal detection theory*** explains the detection of a target or a "signal" in the midst of distracting, irrelevant stimulation (termed "noise"). Detection is based on comparing the neural activity generated by the signal to the neural activity generated by the noise alone. The greater the average difference between the signal and noise activity, the greater the probability of detecting the signal.

In addition to the comparison of signal- and noise-generated neural activity, signal detection theory further assumes that detection involves

5-4 Responses in Signal Detection

On a signal detection trial, a hit occurs when a signal is present and the individual says yes. A miss occurs when a signal is present and the individual says no. A false alarm is defined as a yes response when a signal does not occur, and a correct rejection is defined as a no response when a signal does not occur. Over a series of trials, an individual's pattern of responses depends on his or her decision criterion. For example, if there is a high cost to missing an occurrence, the decision criterion will be low. Lowering the decision criterion will produce more hits and fewer misses, but also more false alarms and fewer correct rejections.

Signal occurs	Individual responds: Yes	Individual responds: No
Yes	Hit	Miss
No	False alarm	Correct rejection

making a decision (see Figure 5-4). There will always be some uncertainty about the existence of a signal because of the competing background noise. Yet, you must decide whether the signal is present or not. How important is it to detect the signal (or difference between two stimuli) when you are really not sure? Signal detection theory says that when you are deciding whether a signal is present, you always have a decision criterion in mind. Thus, if it is more important that you not miss a target stimulus than it is that you avoid false alarms (saying a stimulus has occurred when it has not), your decision criterion is likely to be set low. Consider the difference between detecting noises in hostile territory if you are on military patrol and you know that there might be snipers around, compared with detecting noises if you are on a Sunday afternoon stroll in a Vermont forest. The criterion you set for what constitutes an unusual sound is likely to be much lower in the former case than in the latter. You can't afford to "miss" a sniper, so you "hear" more sniper sounds, which could save your life at the cost of producing more false alarms.

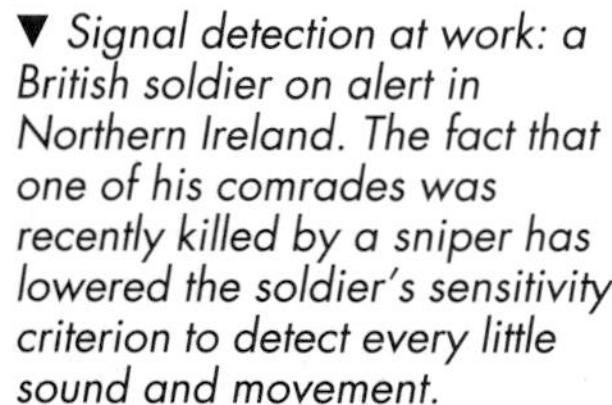

▼ *Signal detection at work: a British soldier on alert in Northern Ireland. The fact that one of his comrades was recently killed by a sniper has lowered the soldier's sensitivity criterion to detect every little sound and movement.*

Signal detection theory is applied today in a variety of diagnostic situations. One study showed that your psychological state—expectations, training and skill, motivation, fatigue and the like—can influence your decision criterion—whether you are biased toward being lenient or conservative about guessing—in circumstances where you are not really sure about a potential stimulus (Swets, 1992). For example, lines on an X-ray photograph look like fuzzy shadows or noise to an untrained eye. The same lines can be clear signals of bone fractures to the trained radiologist who knows what to expect. The soldier on sentry duty has a very different criterion for signal detection of potential danger at a military facility in peaceful Missouri versus one in war-torn Bosnia. After a terrorist threat, airport personnel lower their decision criterion and become more likely to scrutinize the contents of each piece of luggage carefully. The probability that a stimulus will occur combined with the costs and benefits of detecting or not detecting the stimulus both influence the decision criterion.

Today's research in signal detection provides a good illustration of several basic themes of this book. It points to the importance of considering both biology (the nervous system and sensory capacities) and context (the place and circumstances in which detection takes place) in seeking to understand the psychological processes involved in perception. It has provided methodological tools to understand differences in sensory capabilities among individuals and to diagnose sensory impairments. Finally, it has a wide variety of uses, including the development of training programs for professionals whose job effectiveness depends on their ability to monitor diagnostic systems and detect information early and accurately.

So far, we've been talking about the senses in a general way. Let's examine specific systems in more detail, with special attention to the visual system, which has been the most thoroughly studied of the sensory systems.

Seeing: The Essentials of Vision

Stop reading for a moment and look around you. Notice all the objects you see. Consider their color, shape, and texture, and how they appear from one angle and then from another. Next, consider that your perception of these objects results from electrochemical activity that occurs first in your eye's receptors and quickly thereafter in your brain, which leads to a conscious, meaningful experience. Contrast this with Dr. P.'s experience (described in Chapter 2). When presented with an object, Dr. P. could eloquently describe his sensations. Thus, when he was handed a red rose, he took it and described it as a botanist would describe a specimen, saying, "about six inches in length . . . a convoluted red form with a linear green attachment." He was unable, however, to construct these sensations into a perception of the object as a rose—something most people do automatically and effortlessly. In this section, we examine the complex physical, physiological, sensory, and perceptual processes that enable us to perform these constructions and to see meaning in our environment.

Light: Its Physical Nature

What do we see? We see a spectrum, or range, of electromagnetic energy radiating from diverse sources in the environment. The human eye is sensitive only to a certain kind of radiation, called ***light***, which is the visible range of wavelengths of the electromagnetic spectrum.

Light is the proximal stimulus for vision. It may travel directly to the eye from a light source, such as a light bulb, or it may reflect into the eye from objects in the environment. The light stimulus is then converted in the eye into neural signals; this conversion begins with the breaking down and reforming of chemicals in the eye as the "waves" of light strike the eye. Two properties of light are particularly important for vision: (1) light intensity, the amount of energy making up the light, which is perceived as ***brightness***; and (2) ***wavelength***, the distance between successive peaks of light waves, which is important to perception of color.

The human eye detects wavelengths of electromagnetic energy that are so small they are measured in nanometers (nm). One nanometer is equal to one thousandth of one millionth of a meter. The visible spectrum for human beings is usually described as ranging from 400 nm to 760 nm. Invisible wavelengths shorter than 400 nm are called ultraviolet; wavelengths longer than 760 nm are known as infrared (see Figure 5-5). Although we can't see these wavelengths, some animals can. For example, honeybees can see ultraviolet light and make distinctions among flowers that simply look colorless to us, if we can see them at all. Rattlesnakes have infrared detectors and can track prey even in the dark. But not all animals see color as well as we do. For a long time, it was thought that dogs were totally colorblind. Researchers have demonstrated recently, however, that dogs can

A

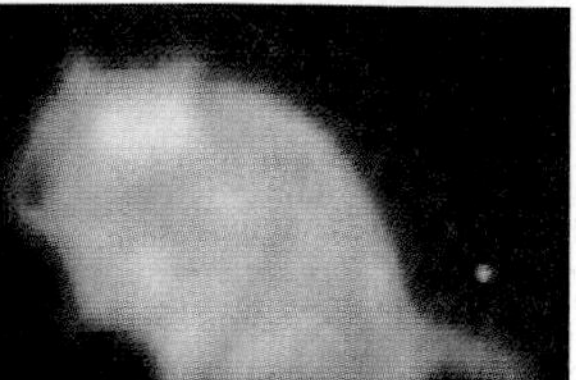

B

C

▲ *Infrared vision of pit vipers. (A) Pit vipers, like the rattlesnake shown here, are known for their ability to see in daylight and to detect warm-blooded prey in the dark by means of a pit organ. (B) The organ is sensitive to the infrared radiation of warm-blooded animals, forming crude images resembling this one of a gerbil. (C) The same animal in visible light.*

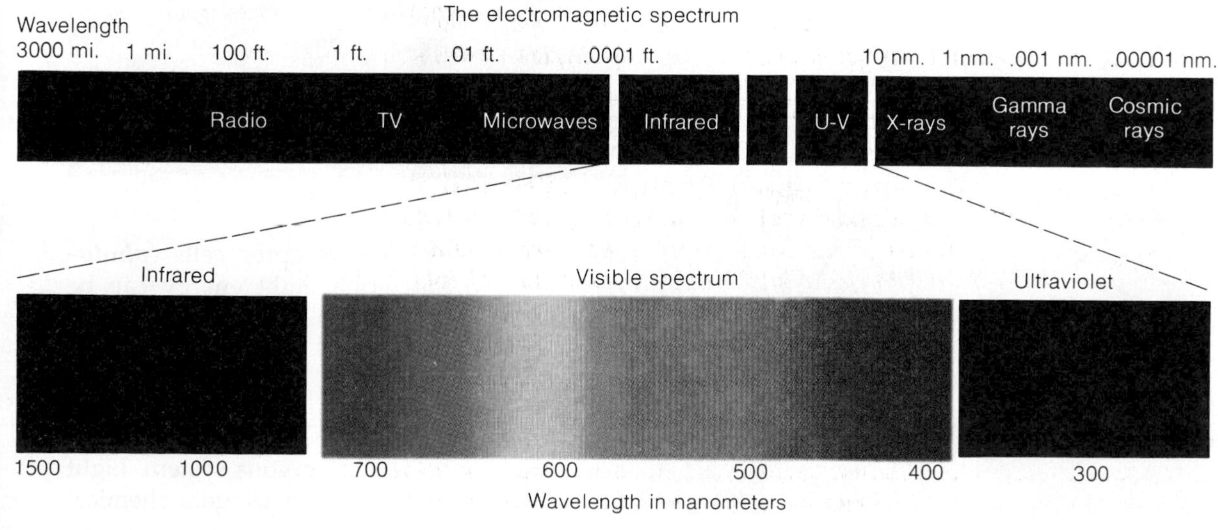

5-5 The Electromagnetic Spectrum

This is the full spectrum of electromagnetic radiation, with wavelengths shown in nanometers. A nanometer is about 1/1,000,000,000 meter (a meter is 39.37 inches). The visible spectrum (which is the area that the human eye can see) extends only from wavelengths of 400 nanometers to wavelengths of 760 nanometers.

Light is the visible range of wavelengths of electromagnetic energy.

make wavelength discriminations, though only in the short end of the visible spectrum (Neitz, Geist, & Jacobs, 1989).

The Eye and How It Works

The eyeball is an optical instrument that can be compared to a camera. Its various parts are exquisitely designed to focus an inverted image of the distal stimulus on the ***retina***, which is a layer of photosensitive receptor cells, thereby creating a proximal stimulus out of the light entering the eye from the outside (see Figure 5-6). Take a close look at a friend's eye. The curved transparent surface on the front is the ***cornea***, which bends the light rays entering the eye, partially focusing them. Behind the cornea you can see the ***iris***, the colored part of the eye, and the ***pupil***, the opening in the middle of the iris. Muscles in the iris constrict (narrow) the pupil to keep out light or enlarge (dilate) the pupil to let more light into the eyeball. Behind the iris is an elastic ***lens***, a translucent membrane that helps focus the proximal visual stimulus on the visual receptors. Small muscles pull on the lens to change its shape, making it thinner or thicker, which enables it to bend and focus the light rays further and to project a sharp inverted image on the retina. This changing of the shape of the lens is called ***accommodation*** and occurs automatically, without conscious control. Once the structures of the eye have produced the focused image of light (proximal stimulus) on the specialized light-sensitive receptor cells (***photoreceptors***) in the retina, light energy can be converted into neural impulses.

The retina is a layer of photosensitive receptor cells at the back of the eyeball. The lens is a translucent membrane, situated between the cornea and the retina of the eye, which helps focus the proximal visual stimulus clearly on the visual receptors.

THINKING CRITICALLY

Why is it that many people's eyes cannot create or maintain a sharply focused image on the retina, even under ideal circumstances?

Sometimes this is due to irregularity in the eye's shape. If the distance between lens and retina is too large or too small, the lens cannot adjust sufficiently to focus an object's image. This accounts for most common vision problems, such as nearsightedness (myopia) and farsightedness (hyperopia). Fortunately, most people can wear glasses or contact lenses to compensate for the eyes' inability to focus.

Your eyesight will change with age, even if it is normal to begin with. The lens loses its elasticity, and eye muscles weaken with age. Eventually, the lens will not be able to adjust to bring objects into focus, and you will need to hold books farther and farther away to maintain a focused image. This condition is called presbyopia.

Because eye muscles play such an important part in vision, you should rest your eyes, particularly with work involving small print and detailed attention. Close-up, detailed work requires a sustained pull on the eye muscles; looking far away lets the eye muscles relax. You can reduce strain on your eye muscles during studying by occasionally looking away from your book and looking at objects in the room that are at different distances from you (Owens & Wolf-Kelly, 1987).

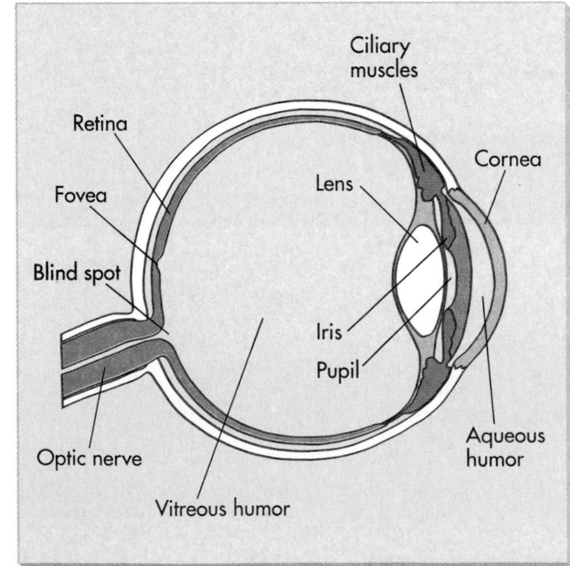

5-6 The Human Eye

The eye is a complicated structure with many parts. Its purpose is to present an optical image of the world to the retina, where the image is transformed (transduced) into nerve impulses that go to the visual cortex of the brain.

Rods and Cones

The retina is made up of neural tissue and is an actual outgrowth of the nervous system. Light falling on the human retina triggers chemical reactions in two major types of photoreceptors: ***rods*** and three kinds of ***cones***, named for their distinctive shapes. This photochemical reaction converts light energy into electrical activity in nerves; the breakdown of the photochemicals generates neural impulses.

Each type of photoreceptor contains a different photopigment that reacts chemically to a different range of wavelengths of light. Rods peak in sensitivity in the short wavelength region of the visual spectrum, at about 510 nm and are 1,000 times more sensitive to middle wavelength light than are cones. Cones peak in sensitivity at the longer wavelength region, at about 560 nm (see Figure 5-7 for a comparison of sensitivities of rods and cones).

The retina contains about 75 to 150 million rods and about 7 million cones. Cones are concentrated in the retina's central region, called the ***fovea*** (the most sensitive part of the retina), with the number of cones decreasing with distance from the fovea. Rods are completely absent from the fovea, with the number of rods increasing with distance from the fovea; they are more prevalent than are the cones in the periphery of the retina. Vision is sharpest in the fovea. To focus on an object, you need to move your eyes so that the object's image centers on the fovea. Look at the B in the string of letters below and notice how you cannot read many other letters without first moving your eyes. Focusing on the B centers its image on the fovea, which enables you to recognize and read the B. But it is difficult to see letters outside the fovea. Moving your eyes allows the image of another letter into the fovea so that it now can be recognized and read.

D N A R T S K C E & O S U R **B** N R U O E

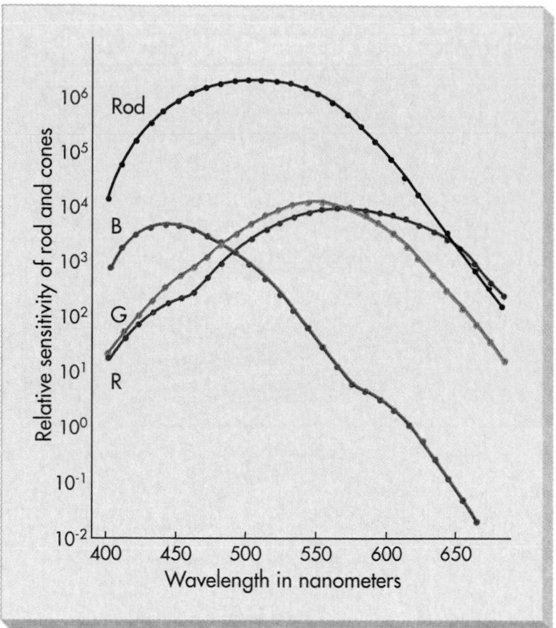

5-7 Sensitivity of Cones and Rods in the Retina

The retina contains three types of cone receptors (B, G, and R) and one kind of rod receptor. The graph shows the sensitivity of each type of receptor to different wavelengths of light. Notice that each receptor is sensitive to all wavelengths but in differing degrees. Each receptor can be characterized by the wavelength to which it is the *most* sensitive.

Receptive Fields

How does the eye translate the stimulation of millions of individual retinal cells into the perception of a meaningful object? Considerable condensation of visual information occurs, more so for the more-plentiful rods than for the cones, during this translation. Condensation is accomplished through a hierarchical pattern of converging cells, which is repeated all the way from the retina to the visual cortex of the brain. The first step in this process is accomplished by specialized nerve cells (***bipolar cells***) connecting the approximately 7 million cones and 75 to 150 million rods to another layer of cells in the eye—the approximately 1 million ***ganglion cells***. A single ganglion cell receives input from cones or rods located in a roughly circular region on the retina; this region of receptors on the retina connected to a single ganglion cell is called the ***receptive field*** of the ganglion cell. Given the large difference in the number of cones, rods, and ganglion cells, clearly many rods and cones become connected to the same

THINKING CRITICALLY

Your night vision is better if you look to the side of an object (say, a faint star) rather than directly at it. Can you figure out why?

Looking to the side of an object means that its reflected light passes through your lens at an angle, making the object's image fall on the periphery of the retina, where rods outnumber cones. Because rods are more sensitive to light intensity than cones, you can see an object, like a star, better at night when you focus its image on the rods.

The rods and cones are photoreceptor cells that lie in the retina, with the cones in the center and rods in the periphery. Rods are more sensitive to dim illumination than cones, and hence the rods are responsible for night vision. Cones are more sensitive to wavelength or color, for daytime vision, and detail.

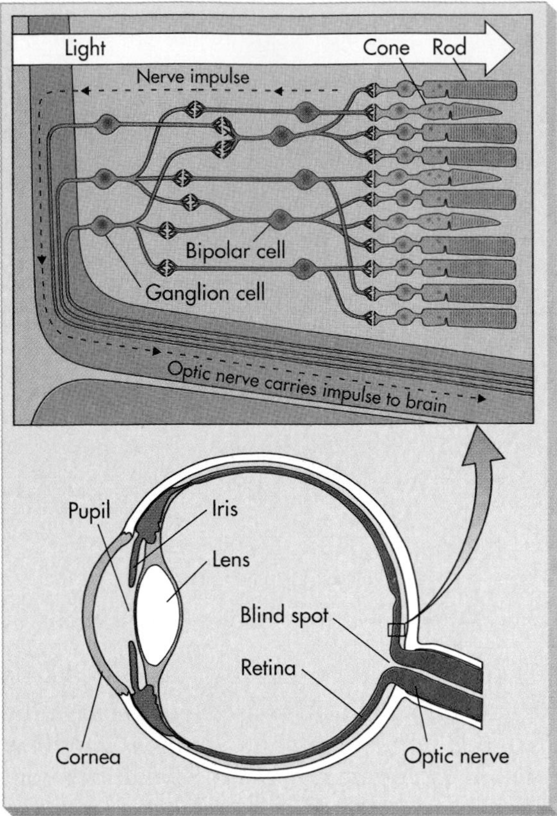

5-8 The Human Retina

This cross-section of the human retina shows the relationship of cones and rods to ganglion cells. Light passes through the eye and falls on the rods and cones, both of which are the light-sensitive cells at the back of the retina. Specialized nerve cells, called bipolar cells, connect the 7 million cones and the 75 to 150 million rods to 1 million ganglion cells at the front of the retina. Note how a ganglion cell can receive information from more than one bipolar cell, creating the possibility of complex patterns of messages. The axons of ganglion cells come together into the optic nerve, which leaves the eye and transmits neural impulses to the visual cortex of the brain. Because the place where the optic nerve leaves the eye has no rods or cones, we have a blind spot in our visual field. (Source: Adapted from Coren & Ward, 1989)

ganglion cell (see Figure 5-8). In this way, the eye reduces and organizes the massive influx of information in the proximal stimulus into something meaningful.

The axons of ganglion cells come together to form the ***optic nerve***, just as telephone wires come together to form a telephone cable. The optic nerve is the pathway from the eyeball to the visual cortex of the brain. Information about the visual stimuli passes along the optic nerve just as information from the person making a telephone call passes along the telephone wires. Along the way to the brain, the ganglion axons within the optic nerve continue to converge onto higher-level cells, which are the equivalent of relay centers in a telephone network. Information about the stimulus is passed from the ganglions onto the higher-level cells, which further condense the information until it reaches the brain.

A receptive field is a region on the retina from which receptor cells are connected to a single ganglion cell.

Incidentally, where the optic nerve exits the eyeball on the way to the brain, there are no receptors at all. Light focused on this spot, called the visual ***blind spot***, is not sensed. Normally, however, rather than seeing nothing, you actually experience a continuous field through the blind spot, as if the eye or the brain were filling in for the missing receptors (Ramachandran, 1992). In fact, you have to go to some lengths to "see" the blind spot (see Figure 5-9).

David Hubel and Thorsten Wiesel implanted microelectrodes in the visual cortex of a cat to study how single cortical cells respond to simple visual stimuli. The Nobel prize-winning researchers revolutionized our thinking about how stimulation of a receptive field produces meaningful experiences in the brain (Hubel & Wiesel, 1959, 1977, 1979). Hubel and Wiesel found that neurons in the visual cortex act as ***feature detectors***, which respond selectively to visual information (see Figure 5-10). They found that some cells in the brain are sensitive only to specific visual features, such as line orientation. When you look at a vertical line or edge, only cells in the visual part of your brain sensitive to vertical orientation are active; cells sensitive to other orientations are relatively inactive. But if the line is rotated from the vertical, a different set of cells, sensitive to the new orientation of the line will become active.

Hubel and Wiesel discovered three different types of feature detectors in the visual cortex, which they labeled simple, complex, and hypercomplex, based on the degree of abstraction the cells were sensitive to. A simple cell might, for example, respond to a vertical line, but only if the line was in a specific section of the field of vision. A complex cell responds to a vertical line regardless of its location—it acts as a general vertical-line detector. A hypercomplex cell seems to require a particular pattern; for example, it might act like a right-angle detector, responding only when two lines with different orientation intersect anywhere in the visual field. With cells acting as detectors, we begin to understand how the brain can respond uniquely to particular shapes, squares, triangles, and the like, giving us a physiological basis for perception of the external world (see p. 150 for a further discussion of feature detection in the context of bottom-up processing of information).

Pathways to the Brain

The neural pathways from the retina through ganglion cells and the optic nerve eventually reach the rear of the brain, where the visual cor-

5-9 Demonstration of the Blind Spot

Think of this as a big wheel with many spokes. To find your blind spot, hold this figure at arm's length, cover your left eye and stare at the black "x" on the left with your right eye. Move the figure slowly toward you until the disk within the spokes of the wheel disappears. The spokes of the wheel become connected when the disk falls within the blind spot, demonstrating top-down processing of visual information. (Source: Adapted from Ramachandran, 1992)

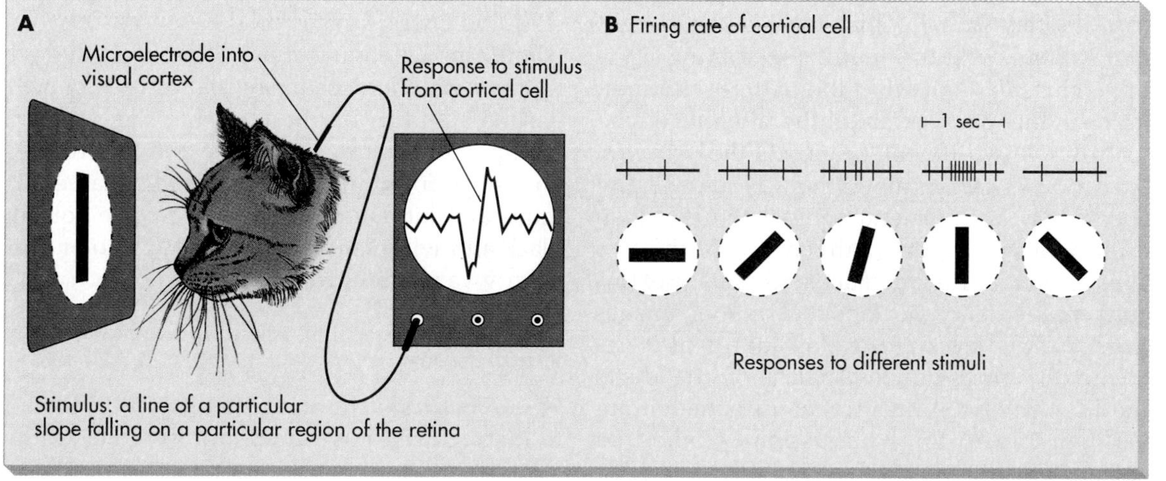

5-10 Mapping the Receptive Field of a Cell in the Visual Cortex

The figure shows how the receptive field of a cell is mapped. (A) To measure responsiveness to various stimuli, a cat has a microelectrode implanted in its visual cortex. A single cortical cell will be sensitive only to stimuli of a particular type and from a particular area of the retina; in this case, the cell is only responsive to a vertical bar. (B) Note that the cell responds (by firing) primarily to the vertical bar, although it will respond somewhat to a slanted bar that is less vertical and hardly at all to the horizontal bars or to the bar slanted in the other direction. (Source: Adapted from Hochberg, 1964; Hubel & Torstenn, 1963)

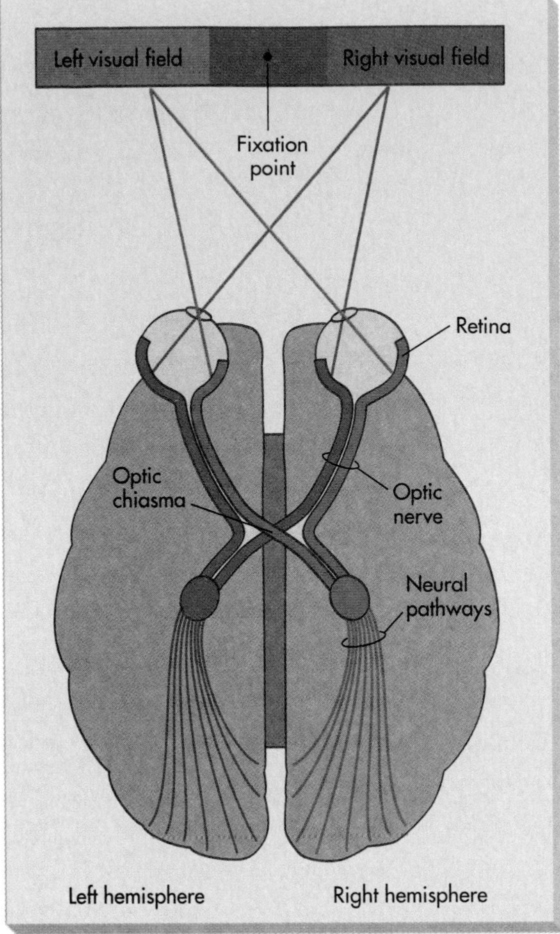

5-11 Neural Pathways for Visual Information

Because the optic nerve coming from each eye splits at the optic chiasma, the image to a person's right is sent to the left side of the brain, and the image to the person's left is sent to the right side of the brain. The neural signals are carried to the optic chiasma, and then to the visual cortex. Notice that the information from the right visual field goes to the left hemisphere and the information from the left visual field goes to the right hemisphere. There is some overlap of the two visual fields, however.

tex is located. Figure 5-11 depicts these pathways. Light falling on the right side of the visual field of both eyes is converted to signals going to the brain's left hemisphere, and information from the left visual fields ends up in the right hemisphere, with the neurons separating at the optic chiasma. Note that the pattern of stimulation in the two eyes is slightly different, owing to the slightly different location of the two eyes. At various locations along the way to the brain, specifically at the lateral geniculate nucleus in each hemisphere, the pathways from the two eyes converge. The brain takes advantage of this convergence and the fact that retinal images from the two eyes are slightly different to recreate the three-dimensionality of the distal world from two-dimensional proximal input (see pp. 155–56 for a discussion of binocular cues to depth).

Primary Functions of Vision

The eye senses and responds to light stimuli, to stimulus changes, and to differences between stimuli in the environment. Moreover, the eye is an adaptable mechanism that can see in near darkness and in bright sunlight. The eyes can see up-close writing on a page and tiny figures on a stage from high up in the back of an enormous amphitheater. They can perceive both in black and white and in color, though color sensitivity varies a lot from person to person.

Visual Acuity

Visual acuity is the ability to see fine detail and to distinguish between stimuli. In general, the better your acuity, the better your vision. A person with poor visual acuity has difficulty seeing objects clearly at a distance, reading, and doing other tasks requiring perception of fine detail.

If you are nearsighted, perhaps you have noticed that you see better when you turn up the lights. Visual acuity is poor under low lighting conditions, but it steadily improves with increases in illumination (see Figure 5-12). This phenomenon can be understood on the basis of how the rods and cones work. Acuity is better for cones than for rods because (1) cones are more tightly packed together on the retina than are rods, and (2) cones are more centrally located in the retina. In addition, because there are many more rods than cones, there must be more convergence from rods to ganglion cells than from cones to ganglion cells. Because information from many rods converges on a single ganglion cell, it is impossible to tell which of the rods within a field were actually stimulated. Because the information from fewer and more closely packed cones goes to a single ganglion cell, the brain can more precisely tell which cones were activated. Cones, of course, work only under relatively high levels of illumination, while rods work when the light is dim. Therefore, our visual acuity is much better in bright than in dim light.

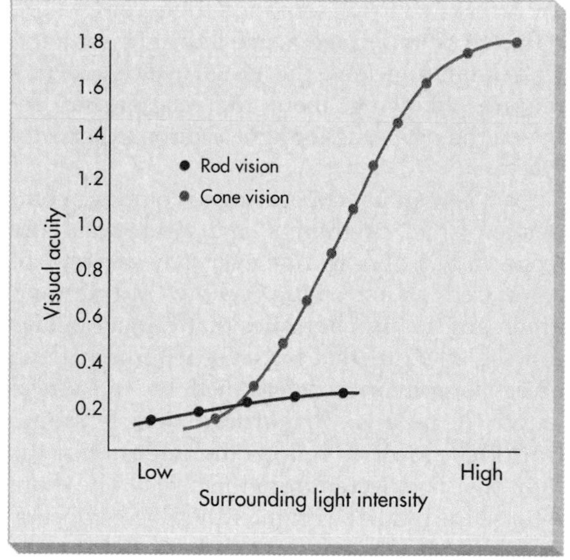

5-12 Visual Acuity as a Function of Light Intensity

Visual acuity depends on the intensity of the surrounding illumination. Our acuity is much better in daylight when our cones are functioning than at night when only our rods are functioning. (Source: Adapted from Hecht, 1934)

Dark Adaptation

When you first enter a darkened room from bright sunlight, you can hardly see at all. Everything around you is, at best, in fuzzy contour and has no color. But there is an initial rapid recovery of vision in the first five to ten minutes. Cones are capable of a rapid but limited amount of enhanced sensitivity when illumination drops, which produces the initial spurt of improvement in vision when you enter a dark room. Beyond this initial spurt, slower improvement continues for a total of about thirty minutes, due to changes in the rods, before your vision reaches maximal sensitivity. Rods function best at low levels of illumination (nighttime conditions) and only become fully efficient after complete dark adaptation. Overall, the increased ability to see as you remain in the dark is called ***dark adaptation*** (see Figure 5-13).

Dark adaptation is the increase in visual sensitivity you experience as you spend time in a poorly lit environment.

Color Perception

Consider the plight of Mr. and Mrs. X, who decided to paint their house in a subtle dusty rose color that they chose carefully from a set of paint chips. To their shock, when the paint was applied it appeared to be bright pink, causing great consternation on the part of the neighbors and the need for another paint job. How could Mr. and Mrs. X have made such a costly mistake? How could the paint look so drastically different when put on the house? The answer lies in the fact that color is not an inherent property of an object; it's the product of our brains. Color is a psychological experience that occurs as neural mechanisms respond to the stimulation of light rays reflected from an external object. The experience you have from a small color chip in an artificially lit paint store is unlikely

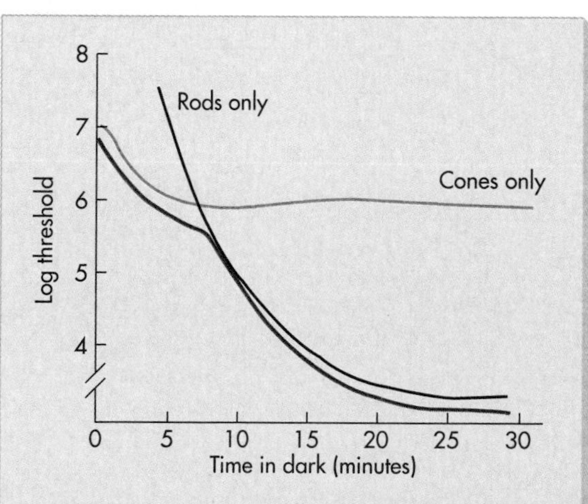

5-13 The Dark Adaptation Curve

As time in the dark increases, the lowest level of light (absolute threshold) that can be perceived decreases, and the eye becomes more sensitive to light. The purple line traces the overall sensitivity of the eye to light after various lengths of time in complete darkness. You will notice that this is not a smooth function. The overall sensitivity to light is a joint product of two separate underlying processes operating at different rates and reaching different final levels: (1) adaptation of the cones (orange line) and (2) adaptation of the rods (black line). Cone adaptation is rapid and virtually complete within the first ten minutes in the dark. Rod adaptation is slower but reaches a more sensitive final level. (Source: Adapted from Cornsweet, 1970) to correspond to the sensation triggered by light reflected from a large house in bright sunlight. Understanding how the visual process works requires knowing about the relationship between the properties of light and the experience of color.

Our perceptual experience of color is a composite of hue, brightness, and saturation. ***Hue*** technically refers to our everyday concept of color: red, orange, blue, yellow, purple, and green are the primary hues that human beings can see. The hue that we sense from any given object is primarily determined by the wavelength it reflects. ***Brightness***, which ranges from light to dark, reflects the intensity of the light that is reflected from the object. The more intense the light, the brighter the object appears.

Saturation refers to the hue's relative purity. If the light that is reflected is all one wavelength, the color is fully saturated. White light, which is a mixture of all wavelengths in the visible spectrum at roughly equal levels of intensity, is totally unsaturated; pink is a partially saturated red because it contains energy at many wavelengths; blood red, which has a narrower range of wavelengths, is deeply saturated. Figure 5-14 presents a color solid that shows how the same hue can vary in brightness and saturation.

How are color experiences produced from the physical energy contained in light? There are three types of cones, which have peak sensitivity to different wavelengths. We have one type for long, red wavelengths; one for middle, green wavelengths; and one for short, blue

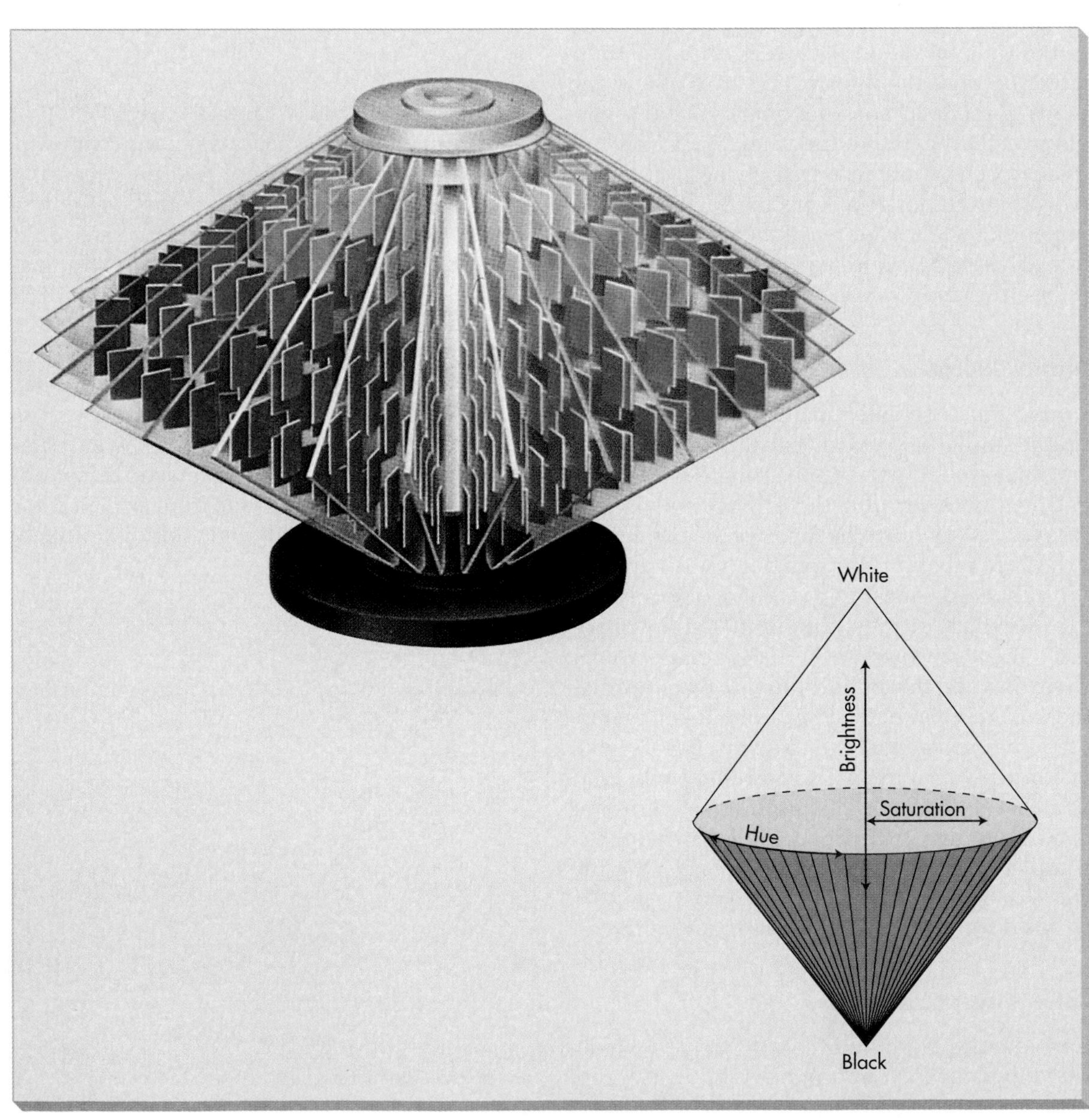

5-14 The Color Solid

Three dimensions of color sensitivity—hue, brightness, saturation—can be seen in this color solid. Gradual changes in brightness from black to white along the central axis, in saturation along the radius, and in hue around the circumference, are illustrated by the diagram in the lower right corner.

wavelengths. How do we see so many different colors if we only have red-sensitive (R), green-sensitive (G), and blue-sensitive (B) cones? First, recognize that if a light contains mostly long wavelengths, then R-cones will give a signal larger than either G-cones or B-cones. Light containing mostly short wavelengths, on the other hand, causes B-cones to be most active. Light containing equal amounts of all the visible wavelengths causes equal activity in all three cone types.

After cones have converted light into electrical impulses, mechanisms in the nervous system, beginning at the level of the bipolar and ganglion cells behind the retina, compare the cones' activity (see Figure 5-15). These mechanisms are called ***opponent-process channels*** because they increase or decrease their response, depending on their assessment of input from the three types of cones, R, G, and B. One of these channels, called the W/B (for white/black) or the L (for luminance) channel, sums up the amount of light falling on the cones and delivers a stronger (brighter) signal for more light. The R/G (for red/green) opponent-process channel increases its signal when red cones are more active than green cones and decreases its signal when green cones are more active. The Y/B (for yellow/blue) opponent-process channel increases its response when the sum of activity in red and green cones (the mixture producing a yellow sensation) is more active than blue cones and decreases its response in the opposite case. Thus, the combination of activity in the R/G and Y/B channels yields the color sensation we experience from any visible stimulus.

Take a long look (about thirty seconds) at the picture of the flag in Figure 5-16. Then look at a white wall or a blank sheet of white paper. What you will see is a ***negative afterimage***, where the colors of the afterimage are complementary to those in the original figure. This experience demonstrates opponent-process channels in color perception. By looking at the yellow-green image, you have temporarily exhausted the yellow and green channels, so the effects of the opponent channels (red and blue) become apparent.

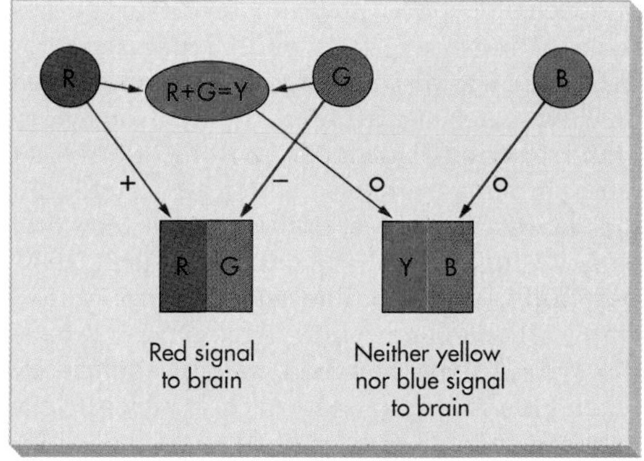

5-15 Opponent-Process Channels

How do we see red? Messages from three types of cones in the retina, R (red), G (green), and B (blue) cones, feed into three opponent-process channels in the nervous system, called R/G, Y/B, and L. The R/G channel decides whether the R or G cones are more active. The Y/B channel decides whether B cones or the sum of R and G cones are more active. High activity in the R/G channel coupled with moderate activity in the Y/B channel, as shown in this diagram, creates the perception of red. The L channel is not shown here.

5-16 The Negative Afterimage

Stare at the center of this flag for thirty seconds. Then look at a white wall or a blank sheet of white paper. You will see complementary colors—blue instead of yellow; red instead of green. This is a negative afterimage—evidence for opponent-process channels in color perception.

Color Deficiency

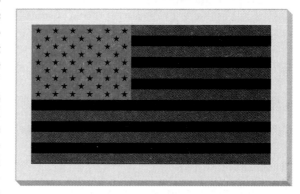

Most of us see the world in a variety of colors. Some people, however, do not have normal color vision owing to a defect in one or more of the three types of cones. This results in ***color blindness***, or more accurately, ***color deficiency***. Red-green deficiency is most common and caused by lack of appropriate photopigment in either R-cones or G-cones. Even when the red-green opponent process does not work properly, the yellow-blue opponent process is typically quite normal (Paramei, 1996).

People with this condition are unable to distinguish between red and green. They see a world of blue and yellow hues (see Figure 5-17). Yet, they might not realize that other people ex-

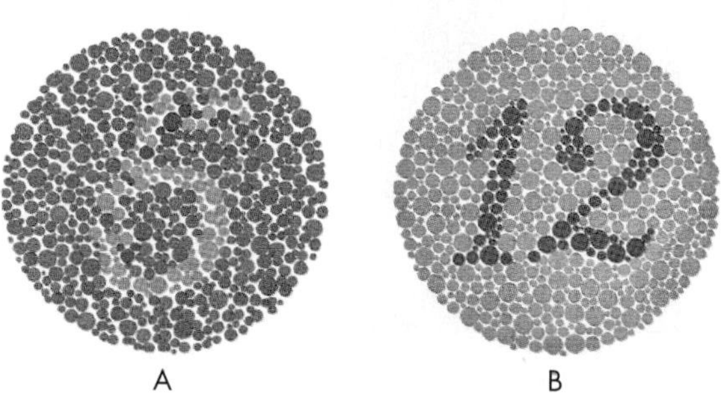

5-17 Tests for Color Deficiency

(A) People with normal vision see a number 6 in the circle, while those with red-green color deficiency do not. (B) Those with normal vision see the number 12 in the circle, while those with red-green color deficiency may see one number or none. (Source: AO Pseudo-Isochromatic Color Tests, American Optical Corporation) perience the world differently. Coren and Ward report the story of a man whose red-green color deficiency was discovered when he commented on how much he admired the skill of cherry pickers, because, after all "the only thing that tells 'em it's a cherry is . . . that it's round and the leaves aren't. I just don't see how they find 'em in those trees!" (Coren & Ward, 1989, p. 262). Tests of color deficiency are straightforward, reliable, and valid. Some students have discovered that they had a color deficiency when they saw such a test in their introductory psychology book!

Rates of color deficiency vary by sex and ethnic background. Among individuals of northern European ancestry, about 8 percent of males have a color deficiency. Among men of Japanese or Chinese ancestry, 4.9 percent have a color deficiency. For African Americans, Native Americans, Mexicans, and Inuit (Eskimos), the rate is 3.1 percent. Among females, the rate is less than 1 percent for all groups (Hurvich, 1981). Nonetheless, there does not appear to be any systematic variation in color deficiency across cultures.

Brightness Contrast

The color perception system also has a third channel, the L channel (for "luminance"), which is also known as the brightness channel or the white-black opponent process. This channel signals the total amount of light absorbed by the cones, and its activity primarily determines the experience of brightness. The L channel is sensitive to light ***reflectance***—the percentage of light that falls on an object that it reflects to the retina. But context, too, has an effect on brightness perception. Figure 5-18 contains two small squares that reflect equal amounts of light to your eye. (You can check the accuracy of that claim by covering up the surrounding backgrounds.) Yet, the squares do not appear to be equally bright. The square on the right, surrounded by a white field, appears darker than does the one on the left, surrounded by a black field. This phenomenon, ***brightness contrast***, results because the retinal regions perceiving the areas next to each square are not equally stimulated.

5-18 Brightness Contrast

Even though the two center squares reflect exactly the same amount of light to your eye, the one on the right appears darker because of its contrast with the white surrounding area.

Complex Visual Functions

Normally, we don't "see" pure wavelengths or intensities of light in isolation. Visual experience is much more complex than that. But complex visual experiences, like seeing a friend on the street, or seeing the words on a printed page, or seeing the threat of an oncoming car are all made up of these simpler individual parts. As visual experiences become more complex, extending beyond detection and the simple dimensions of hue, saturation, and brightness, the nervous system, memory, culture, and other factors come to play a more significant role in what we see. Experiences become more perceptual and less sensory.

Processing from Bottom Up and Top Down

Is the process of perceiving a "bottom-up" process, in which neurons in the visual cortex respond selectively to aspects of a visual stimulus—such as its edge orientation or movement or color—to recognize it? Hubel and Wiesel's research on feature detectors in the brain might suggest this conclusion. Or is perceiving a "top-down" process, in which the brain selects, organizes, and interprets incoming neural messages based on prior experiences and current expectations? Actually, the evidence is that both processes operate during perception. Which process is more important for a particular perception depends on the stimulus, its context, and the past experience of the perceiver.

Consider Figure 5-19. Which do you see, the letter B or the number 13? If all the information needed to answer were contained in the features of the stimulus itself, you could respond with certainty. If the stimulus were unambiguous—if the stimulus were clearly a B—the decision could be based on "bottom-up processing" of the available stimulus information. But what happens when the stimulus is ambiguous and the answer is not clear, as in this example? Not enough information is contained in the stimulus itself to enable you to distinguish between the two alternatives. You need additional information from the context to decide what the stimulus is. Suppose you are reading. You'll likely see an ambiguous stimulus like the one above as "another letter," the letter B. Alternatively, if you are adding up a column of numbers, then you'll probably see the ambiguous stimulus as the number 13. If you are a native speaker of Chinese and haven't been exposed to the English alphabet, the stimulus will probably stand out as a 13 (the Chinese use the same Arabic numerals that Westerners do). In such cases, the perception of the stimulus is controlled from the top down, that is, cognitively.

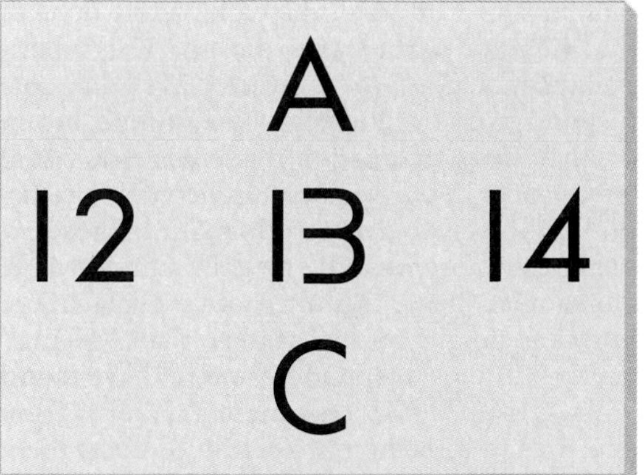

5-19 Top-down versus Bottom-up Processing

What you see initially in the middle position is either a B or a 13, depending on whether you are looking at the column of letters or row of numbers. Top-down information influences bottom-up interpretation of the same stimulus.

Because top-down processing plays such an important role in our ordinary, everyday perceptions, there is room for disagreement about the meaning of a stimulus, and how this is resolved can depend on sociocultural context. One study provided an interesting illustration of context effects on perception (Bagby, 1957). Participants saw two stimuli in a stereoscopic device, which presents different images to the two eyes. Participants from the United States and Mexico looked briefly at ten pairs of slides. One slide in each pair had typical U.S. content, showing such things such as a baseball game or a Wall Street executive; the other slide in each pair had Mexican content, showing a bullfight or a Mexican farmer (see Figure 5-20). When the physical images presented by a stereoscopic device are different, the retinal images on the two eyes compete with each other. Which of the photographs—the one with Mexican or U.S. content—did participants perceive more readily? All U.S. participants reported U.S. con-

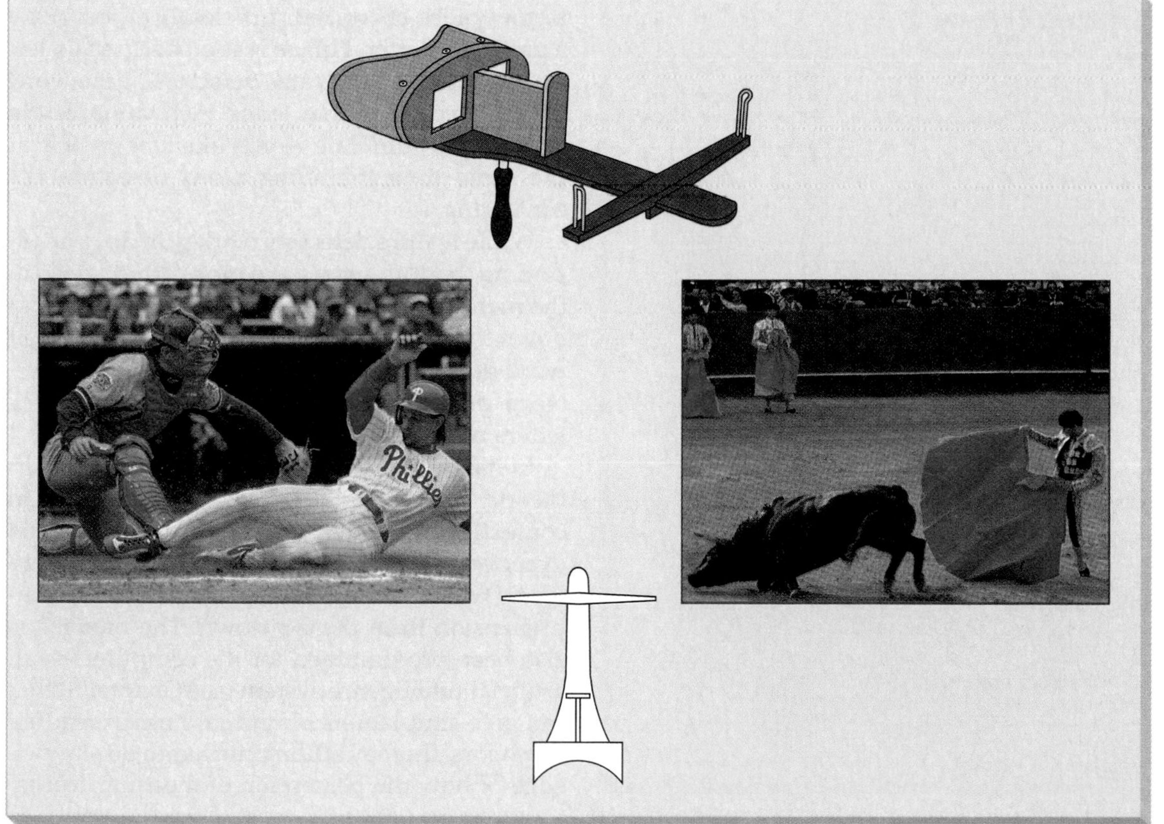

5-20 The Influence of Culture on Visual Perception

The stereoscopic device, invented by Oliver Wendell Holmes in 1861, presents separate images to each eye. When the two images are basically the same but portrayed from slightly different angles, the overall impression is one of depth. When the two images are different, it has been found that the person is more likely to perceive the image from his or her own culture; hence, an American would be more likely to perceive the picture of the ball game; a Spaniard would be more likely to perceive the picture of the bullfight.

▲ *The whole is different from the sum of its parts.*

tent on five or more of the pairs, while none of the Mexican participants did so. The experimenter concluded that culture plays a key role in perceptual dominance when stimuli are in conflict. One explanation for this is that visual experiences in our sociocultural context predispose us to perceive material similar to those experiences more readily (Segall, Campbell, & Herskovits, 1966). An alternative explanation, however, might be that, rather than "seeing" different things, respondents might have found it easier to *verbalize* scenes more familiar to them and thus have been more ready to report them to the experimenter.

Perception is almost always a combination of top-down and bottom-up processing. What we sense in the environment is in part a product of what exists physically and in part a matter of what we know about the environment. Literally, what we sense about the world at any given moment is a *construction*, based on what is sent to the brain from sensory systems and what already exists or is active in the brain (Kinchla & Wolfe, 1979).

James McClelland and David Rumelhart (1981) have developed what they call an interactive activation (neural network) model to describe the interplay of sensory and cognitive factors in the perception of meaning. To explain how we read, they assume that cortical detectors are activated and influenced both by information coming through the visual system (for example, light-dark patterns, line orientations) and by cognitive processes (for example, your knowledge of the English language) to recognize the meaning of each word. What you see on a page activates a hierarchy of detectors: feature detectors, letter detectors, and word detectors (see Figure 5-21). Feature detectors (simple and complex cortical cells) pick up the basic elements (for example, curved and straight lines). When a feature detector is activated, it in turn activates other detectors at the letter level. The vertical line detector activates the letter detector for *T*, *N*, and other letters containing a vertical straight line. Simultaneously, activated feature detectors inhibit detectors for letters that do not contain that feature (for example, they inhibit the letter detector for *S*). When enough feature detectors are activated, one particular letter detector will be energized sufficiently to recognize a particular letter. Full activation of a certain letter detector also activates detectors at the word level that contain that letter. Activation of the letter *T* will stimulate words like *time* or *trim*, at the same time inhibiting word detectors not containing *T*.

While feature detectors work primarily on incoming, bottom-up information, other levels in the hierarchy can pass information both up and down the line. Just as letter detectors can inhibit word detectors that do not contain those letters, word detectors can inhibit letter detectors for letters not contained in the word.

In its full version, the McClelland-Rumelhart theory also describes detectors sensitive to context, which allows the reader to form expectations about upcoming words in a sentence, further facilitating reading and text comprehension from the top down. The model has also been programmed for the computer, as an artificial intelligence system (see Chapter 8) that can give simulations of normal human reading behaviors, thereby adding further to our knowledge of how the perception of meaning works.

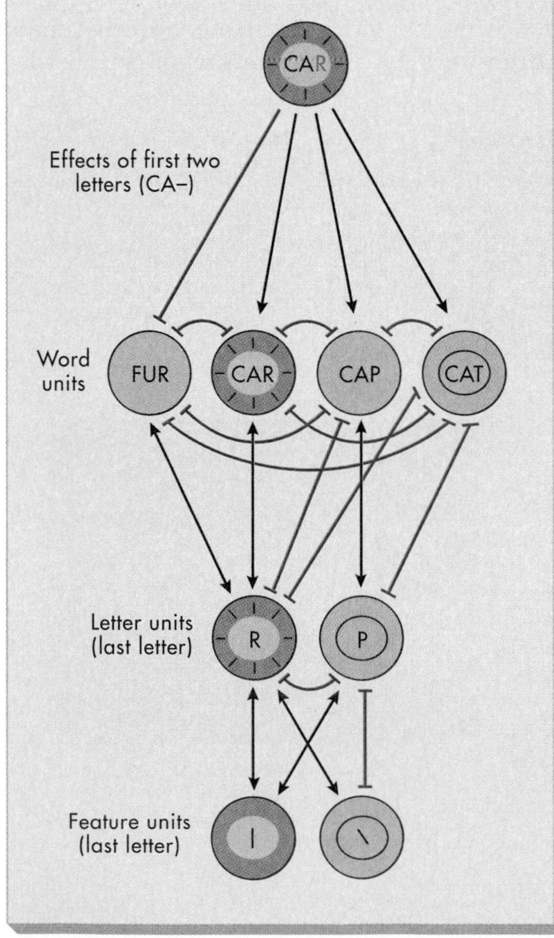

5-21 Neural Network Model

This is a simplified version of the McClelland-Rumelhart neural network model, in which neurons first identify the visual features of a letter, then identify the letter, and eventually recognize the word by identifying each of its letters in turn. In this example, the perceiver needs to identify the word "CAR" but sees clearly only the C and the A. Green lines with arrows signify activation, and red lines with cross bars signify inhibition. Features of the last letter, R, activate R and P letter units, but R more strongly (darker green) than P (lighter green) because the slanted line inhibits the P letter unit. Letter unit R in turn activates word units "FUR" and "CAR" and inhibits "CAP" and "CAT." Top-down input from the first two letters activates "CAR" but inhibits "FUR." Thus, "CAR" is the best response, even though its last letter is unclear. (Source: Personal communication from David Rumelhart)

Organizational (Gestalt) Principles

McClelland and Rumelhart tried to explain how meaningful words are perceived when the only input to the visual system is a collection of lines and curves. But most of the objects and scenes that we see, though meaningful, are not words. It is probably true that we perceive objects in much the same way that we perceive words, that is, through feature detection and organization. Well before McClelland and Rumelhart, Gestalt psychologists were concerned with this problem and discovered a set of perceptual organizational principles for objects (Koffka, 1935). Figure 5-22 illustrates four of the major Gestalt principles of object perception: ***proximity, similarity, closure***, and ***Prägnanz***.

Briefly, the first three of these principles state that adjacent stimuli (proximity) and identical stimuli (similarity) are perceived as belonging together, and incomplete objects tend to be filled in and perceived as wholes (closure). The most fundamental principle is Prägnanz, a German word which translates into English as "goodness of figure." This principle states that perceptual processes form objects by grouping together visual features in the simplest manner possible (Chater, 1996). The principle of Prägnanz predicts that two of the three images in the bottom row of Figure 5-22 will be seen as three-dimensional while the third image, which could be produced by the same stimulus is seen more simply as two-dimensional. The principle of Prägnanz predicts this perception because it is simpler to perceive a two-dimensional than a three-dimensional image.

The principle of Prägnanz is found across cultures. But cultural experience makes a difference in terms of how features are used to organize perception of a "whole." This was demonstrated in a classic study conducted in the former Soviet Union by A.R. Luria (1976). Luria asked research participants to name and classify the shapes in Figure 5-23. The research participants included educated women students in a teacher's school, semi-literate farm activists, and illiterate women from remote villages. Take a look at the items in Figure 5-23.

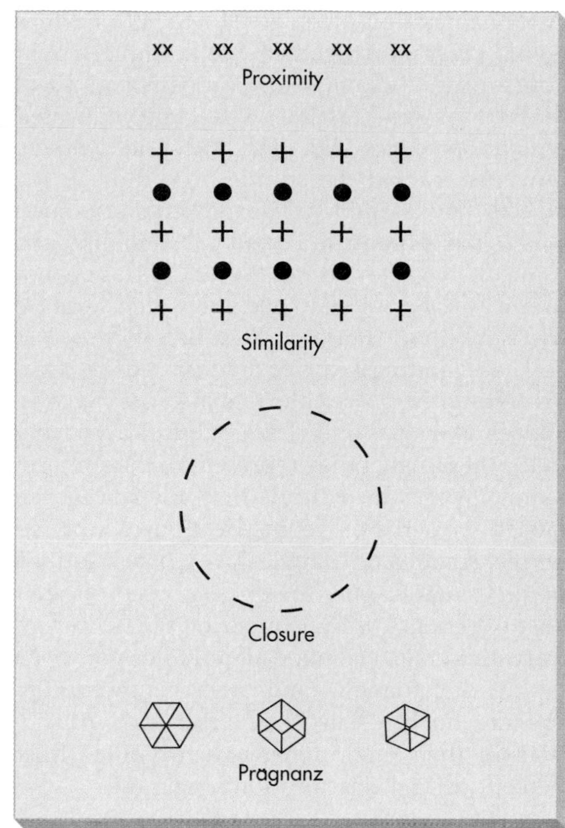

5-22 Gestalt Principles

Here are four examples of Gestalt principles of perceptual organization. Proximity: Elements that are close together tend to be perceived as a unit (you see five pairs of X's, not ten X's). Similarity: Identical or similar items tend to be perceived as a group (you see rows of X's and dots, not columns with mixed X's and dots). Closure: Incomplete figures tend to be filled in (to be perceived as wholes). Prägnanz: Given a choice among possible perceptions, the simplest one is preferred (all three figures can be perceived as three-dimensional, but the first is more simply seen as two-dimensional). (Source: Adapted from Weintraub & Walker, 1966)

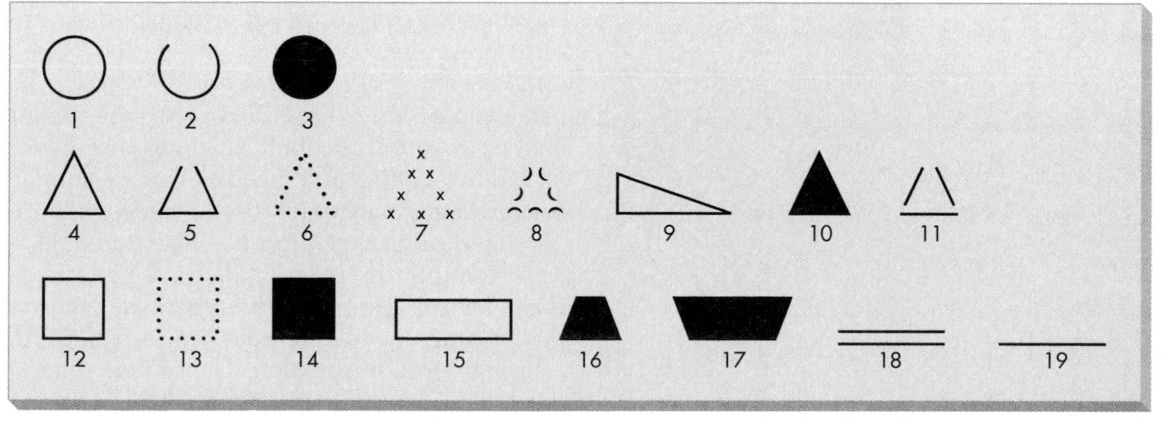

5-23 The Influence of Culture on Prägnanz

What names would you give these stimuli? Which ones would you group together? When Luria presented these stimuli to educated women, they perceived geometric shapes (triangles, squares), and grouped them accordingly. When the stimuli were presented to illiterate women, they perceived the stimuli in terms of common objects (bowls, plates) that they resembled. These findings can be interpreted as demonstrating the power of Prägnanz—we perceive shapes as wholes and classify shapes according to the wholes they represent in the simplest manner possible. Educated people who are trained to perceive geometric shapes as "wholes" respond to these stimuli accordingly. (Source: Luria, 1976)

▲ *Linear perspective is the apparent convergence of parallel lines. Think of standing on railroad tracks and seeing the lines converge in the distance. This view, down the platform of the Channel Tunnel at London's Waterloo station, gives a powerful impression of depth.*

What names would you give them? Which ones would you group together? For example, would you group numbers 4 to 11 together and call them triangles? That's what the educated women students did. The illiterate women, however, named the stimuli according to the objects they resembled. Thus, when one woman was asked if numbers 12 and 13 were alike, she replied "No, they're not alike. This one's not like a watch, but that one's a watch because there are dots" (Luria, 1976, p. 37).

These findings can be interpreted as demonstrating the power of Prägnanz: we perceive shapes as wholes and classify shapes according to the wholes that they represent in the simplest manner possible. Educated people have been taught to perceive geometric figures (for example, squares or triangles) as wholes, so they perceive and classify the objects based on their past experience with geometric figures. In contrast, illiterate people (who have not been taught that triangles and other geometric figures are "wholes") use their experience with objects in their environments to organize their perception and classification of stimuli.

THINKING CRITICALLY

Peter has no vision in one eye. Will he be able to perceive the location of objects in a three-dimensional world?

Your answer clearly must be yes. The cues from having two eyes at different locations on the head, that is, binocular cues, are the most powerful sources of depth information. But there are also monocular cues, such as object overlap (interposition), size, shading, texture gradients, and linear perspective, that in no way depend on having two eyes. These monocular cues are sufficient for depth perception in most circumstances. It is true, however, that Peter's depth perception will be poorer than that of people with two eyes.

Cues to Depth

While many of the things that we see in everyday life are two-dimensional, the real world is three-dimensional, and we have to interact with objects in a three-dimensional space. Success in this endeavor depends on ***depth perception***, that is, on your ability to judge the distance of objects and the relationship of objects to one another and to you. Two sources of incoming data are used to perceive depth and to construct its representation: (1) information extracted from the retinal image of either eye alone (***monocular cues*** for depth), and (2) information that requires both eyes simultaneously (***binocular cues*** for depth).

▼ *The distorted gravity at the Columbus (Ohio) Center for Science and Industry's Mindzone exhibit. The room, built on a 25-degree angle, produces a conflict in the brain's sense of equilibrium. Some visitors to the science center report losing their balance or feeling queasy.*

Several important monocular cues for depth are illustrated in Figure 5-24. These include: (1) ***interposition***, or object overlap—the complete object lies in front of the partial object; (2) ***size***—the larger of two objects tends to be perceived as closer, especially if they are similar objects; (3) ***shading***—both shadows that are attached to an object and those that are cast on the background contribute to the impression of depth; (4) ***texture gradients***—fine gradients in texture imply distance, while coarse gradients imply nearness; (5) ***linear perspective***—the apparent convergence of parallel lines gives rise to a strong depth impression. The combination of these cues gives rise to a three-dimensional im-

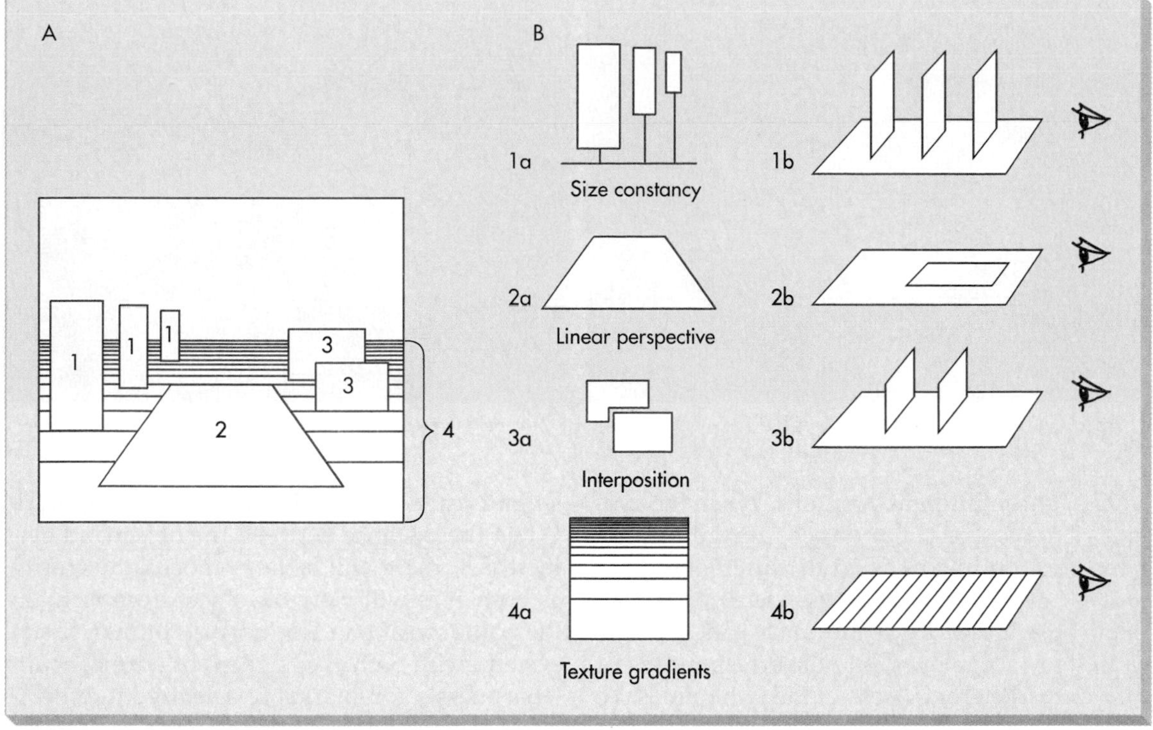

5-24 Monocular Cues, Prägnanz, and Depth Perception

The Prägnanz principle of organization can be applied to the perception of depth. (A) This is a drawing of a surface that can be seen either as stretching away from the eye or as a flat, two-dimensional surface. (B) Here are two explanations to account for the four parts of the drawing, with the right version illustrating how size, linear perspective, interposition, and texture gradients can give the perception of depth to a two-dimensional surface. In A1, the three posts could have been caused by B1a or B1b. Which seems simpler? In A2, the shape could be a trapezoid as shown in A2a, or a square as shown in A2b. Which seems simpler? In A3, one rectangle could be missing a corner as in B3a or be behind the nearer one as in B3b. Which seems simpler? In A4, the lines could be progressively closer together near the top of the picture as in B4a or they could be seen as equally close but stretching away into the distance as in B4b. Which seems simpler? In each case, organizing the scene in depth permits the objects to be simpler in form: the posts are all the same size; the shape on the floor is regular; the two rectangles are the same; and the textured floor is uniform. For these reasons, the flat scene is perceived as three-dimensional, because that is the simplest perception. This simpler perception is consistent with the principle of Prägnanz. (Source: Adapted from Hochberg, 1964)

pression that, consistent with the principle of Prägnanz, is the simplest way to perceive the collection of objects in Figure 5-24.

Another monocular cue to depth depends on motion rather than on the characteristics of stationary objects. When you look out the side window of a moving train or car, distant objects seem to move slowly, and closer objects seem to move faster (see Figure 5-25). The relative motion of these external objects, caused by their being at different distances, is called ***motion parallax***. Our visual system is very sensitive to this phenomenon. Only a slight difference in movement provides information about objects' relative distance (Rogers & Graham, 1979).

Binocular cues for depth are based on the fact that our two eyes are separated horizontally in the head, which means that they view objects

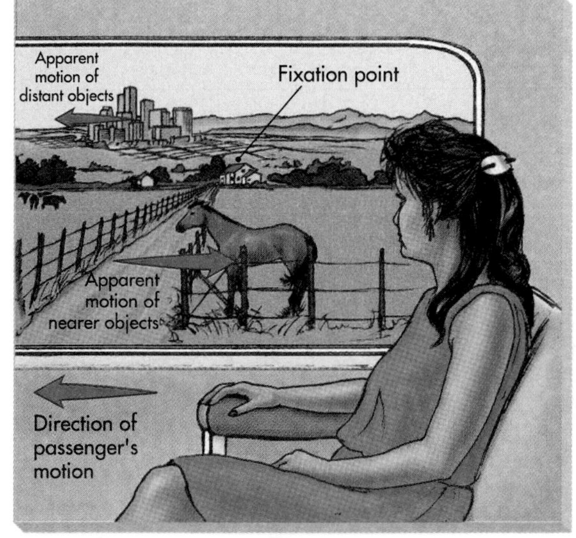

5-25 Motion Parallax

You have surely noticed that when you are moving in a car or train and are fixating on an object in the distance, nearer objects seem to move in the opposite direction and faraway objects seem to move with you. Of course, you are moving, not the stationary objects. This experience, called motion parallax, serves as a cue to the relative distance of objects.

▶ *These pictures illustrate how binocular disparity (sensitivity to the difference in retinal position of an object's image in the left and right eyes) can be used to create a perception of depth although none is present. Place a piece of paper between the two flowers such that only your left eye sees the left flower and only your right eye sees the right flower. Defocus your eyes so that the images merge.*

Binocular disparity causes us to see slight differences between the two-dimensional images focused on the two retinas, leading to the impression of three dimensions or depth.

from slightly different positions. When the eyes focus on an object, the object's image falls on the corresponding but slightly different regions of each eye's retina. Objects nearer or farther than the point of focus are unclear in part because they are imaged on noncorresponding or disparate (different) areas of the two retinas. To see this, hold your two forefingers in front of your nose and fix your gaze on the nearer one while you move the farther one away. As the distance between the moving finger and the stationary finger increases, the image of the moving finger will fall on an increasingly disparate retinal position from that of the stationary finger. If both of your eyes are able to focus on one identical image, however, the difference in the retinal position of the object's image in the left and right eyes will enable you to tell the distance of the object. This difference in retinal position is called ***binocular*** (or retinal) ***disparity***. When the distance between the object and eyes increases, there will be less binocular disparity, as both eyes will view the object from virtually the same position. The normal human visual system, with both eyes sighted at normal acuity (sharpness), is remarkably sensitive to binocular disparity and uses it as the most powerful of all cues to depth and object distance. Figure 5-26 demonstrates how this sensitivity can be used to create a perception of depth.

Perceptual Constancy and Visual Illusions

At different distances the same object, say, a friend of yours, casts different size images on your retinas. Retinal image size is the proximal stimulus corresponding to your friend. When your friend walks away from you, her image on

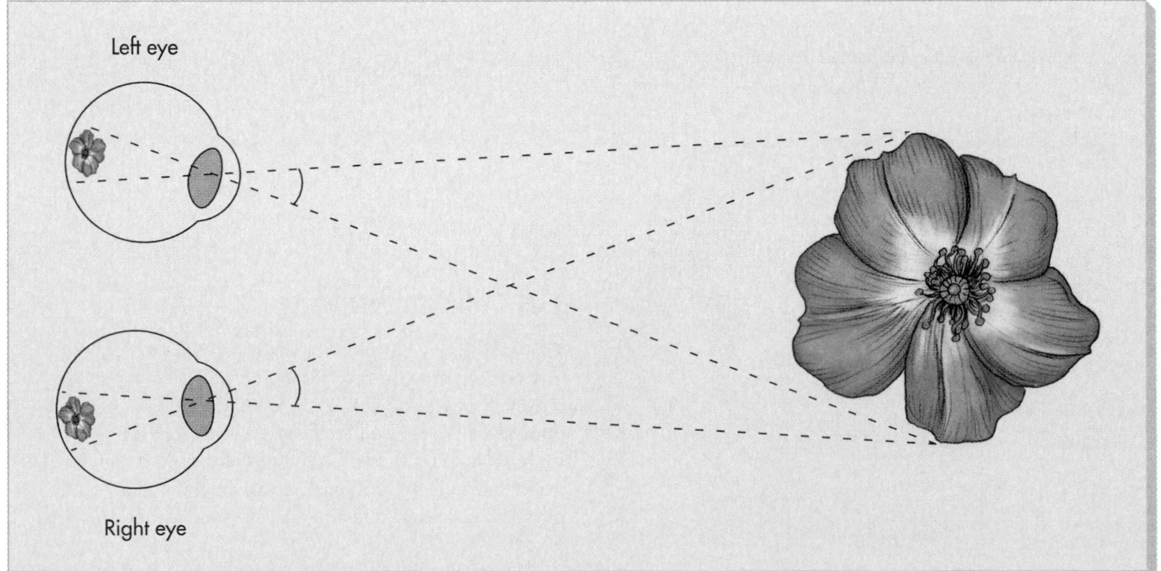

5-26 Binocular Disparity

Sensitivity to the difference in the retinal position of an object's image in the left and right eyes (binocular disparity) provides the most powerful of all cues to depth and object perception. This sensitivity can be used to create a perception of depth although what is viewed is actually two-dimensional.

SEEKING SOLUTIONS

Driving Safety and the Visual Perception of Motion

You are following another car on a dark, narrow country road and are having some difficulty seeing passing objects clearly and judging distances. Do you know why you should be particularly careful about not following that car too closely? What you are looking at directly is centered on and around the fovea and makes up only about 5 percent of visual input at any moment; the rest of the field is in the periphery. The center and the periphery of your visual field respond differently to motion, with things on the periphery of the field appearing to move more slowly. Think about what this might mean for driving safety.

When you drive, the center (where there are cones) and the periphery (where there are rods) of your eyes both provide information about how fast you're going. When visibility is reduced at night or in foggy conditions, central vision is also reduced, so that the judgment of speed is based disproportionately on information from peripheral vision. Because of this, speed is underestimated and you are moving faster than you think.

Another factor affecting perception of speed is an object's size. Have you ever watched planes take off and land at an airport? Little planes seem to zip right down; jumbo jets appear to float slowly to earth. The fact is, however, all planes land at about the same speed. Size of an object and its apparent speed are inversely related. Larger objects have to move much faster than smaller ones if they are to be perceived as moving at the same rate. With judgments about distance, size, and speed all interdependent, it is not surprising that errors in perception (illusions) occur. Such errors can be a matter of life and death for automobile drivers—and in ways you might not suspect. For example, there are approximately 8,000 collisions at railroad crossings each year. Why do drivers think they can beat the train? The fact is that the locomotive's huge size, which theoretically makes it easier to see, causes its speed to be seriously underestimated. Motorists thus overestimate the time for the train to reach the crossing, with deadly results (Leibowitz, 1983).

Perceptual illusions can be used to advantage, however. In any highway system, intersections called traffic circles or rotaries (roundabouts in the United Kingdom) are particularly dangerous. Many accidents occur because motorists won't slow down sufficiently to navigate through a rotary. Gordon Denton convinced motorists to slow down by applying the psychological principles you have just learned (Denton, 1980). Imagine a road with stripes painted across it from one side to the other. These stripes provide perceptual cues as to how fast a car is traveling by the rate at which the stripes are passed (that is, how many stripes are passed per second). When the stripes are close together, cars pass over more of them at a given rate of speed, causing drivers to overestimate how fast they are traveling. By changing the spacing of white stripes near the entrance to a rotary, Denton produced the illusion of change in speed. The stripes near the rotary were more closely spaced than those farther away, and as a result, motorists approaching the rotary thought they were speeding up so they slowed down! The result: accidents declined at over two-thirds of the rotaries with stripes (Sekuler & Blake, 1990).

▲ *Size constancy: it takes a moment to figure out what is happening in this picture. Which figures are normal human size?*

your retina shrinks. But, you don't perceive your friend as shrinking, even though her image on your retina has shrunk. If the proximal stimulus is the information we have about the distal stimulus, why doesn't perception of size change with changes in the size of the retinal image? One of the most remarkable capacities of our perceptual processes is their ability to maintain a stable or constant internal representation of the world, even when proximal stimuli are continually changing. How this happens depends on the fact that proximal stimuli, just like distal stimuli, occur in a context, that is, in a fabric of perceptual cues. Let's look at some examples.

The brightness of an object depends on how much light it reflects to the eye. This white page of paper reflects about 80 percent of the light falling on it, whereas the print reflects only about 5 percent (a 16 to 1 ratio for the paper over the print). This ratio remains constant even when the absolute amount of light changes. Thus, objects are perceived as having the same relative brightness both in intense sunlight and in a darkened room. A blank piece of paper will look white both in a dark cellar and in daylight because in both cases it reflects relatively more light to the eye than do the other objects around it. This is called ***brightness constancy***.

Perceptual processes represent an enduring object as constant in size, even though its retinal image may change drastically; this is called ***size constancy***. Figure 5-27 illustrates how you can

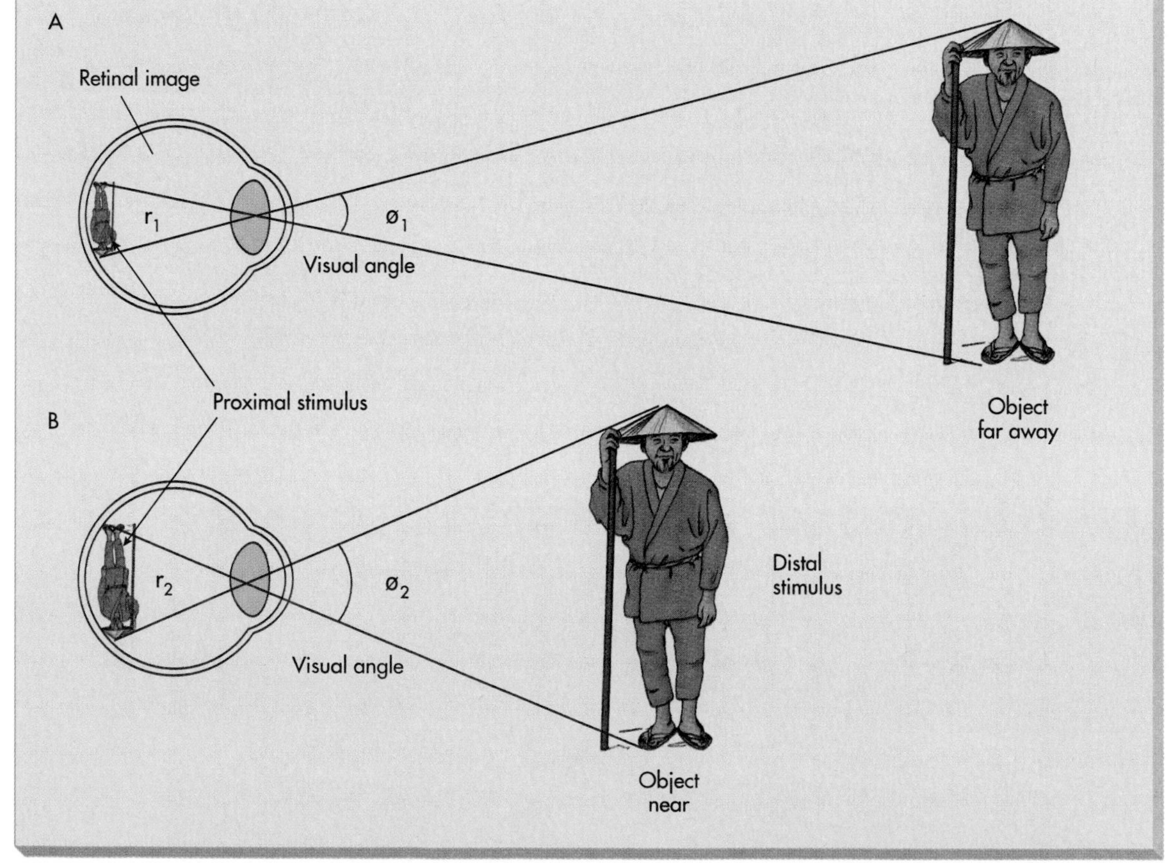

5-27 Size Constancy

This figure illustrates several factors involved in the perception of the same object at different distances. First, the size of the image that the object casts on the retina varies with the object's distance from the eye. The same is true of the visual angle. Close-up objects cast a larger visual angle ($\varnothing_2$) than distant objects ($\varnothing_1$) of the same physical size. Despite changing angles and changing retinal images, the object is perceived to be the same size, regardless of distance—this is size constancy.

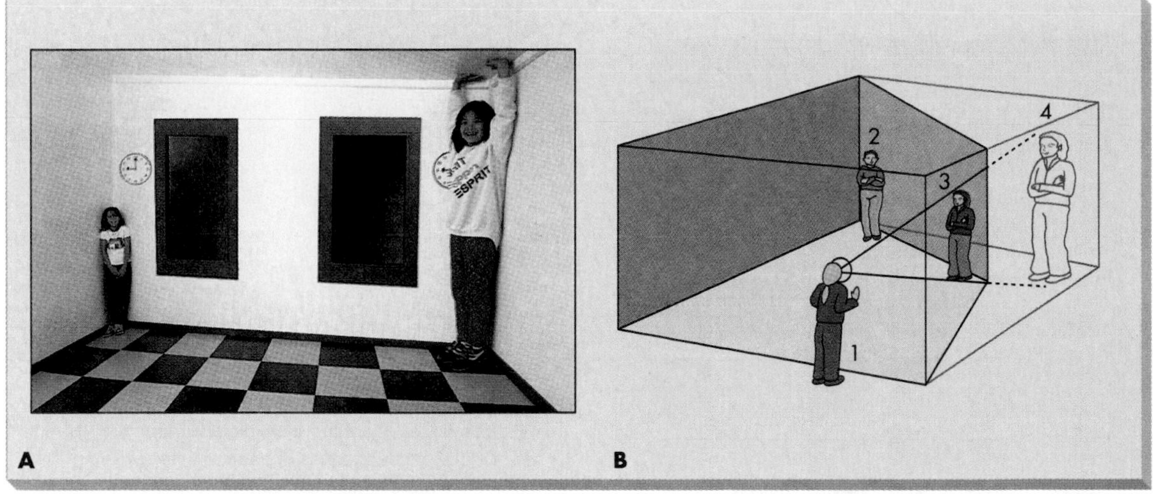

5-28 The Ames Distorted Room

(A) The person on the right looks much larger than the person on the left, even though they seem to be standing next to the same back wall. Actually, the person on the left is farther away as shown in the diagram. (B) The diagram shows the actual shape of the room. Note how the back wall actually slopes away from the viewer on the left. But the walls are arranged to provide the same retinal image as would a normal rectangular room when viewed from a certain position. Thus, the viewer (1) is misled into accepting the incorrect perceptual hypothesis that the room is rectangular and that the person on the right (3) is larger (having the apparent image of figure 4) than the person on the left (2).

accurately perceive people as being approximately the same size, even though they are at different distances from the viewing point.

What accounts for size constancy? For one thing, top-down processing is involved. Our stored knowledge of an object's properties, shape, brightness, or size, is part of the explanation, at least for familiar objects. But prior experience with an object is not absolutely necessary for its perceived features to remain constant. Experiments using unfamiliar objects as test stimuli have shown that our perceptual processes can produce stable and reasonably accurate internal representations of the true object size over a wide range of distances. So, something else is involved in maintaining perceptual stability.

Size constancy depends on relationships among three variables: (1) the size of the retinal image, (2) the actual size of the object, and (3) the distance of the object from the eye. For any particular object, you will always see it as constant in size as long as you can estimate accurately its distance and its retinal image size. Retinal image size is always accurately registered because it is present directly on the retina. Distance can usually be fairly well judged on the basis of monocular and binocular cues for depth. So size is seen as fixed or constant.

Many visual illusions are thought to be a consequence of inaccurate distance information combined with size constancy processes. Thus, you can "trick" the visual system into giving an inaccurate estimate of object distance, which leads to inaccurate perception of object size. This is the principle behind the perception of the size of people in the Ames distorted room, shown in Figure 5-28.

Visual illusions have fascinated psychologists and laypersons alike for ages. Psychologists have studied the bases of illusions on the assumption that if we can understand how they occur, we might get some important insight into normal visual processes. Figure 5-29 shows two visual illusions that may be created through the misuse of distance cues. In the Ponzo illusion, the two horizontal lines are physically equal in length, although the upper one appears longer. A size constancy explanation suggests that our perceptual processes estimate that the upper line is farther away than the lower line (largely because of the perspective cues) and that because the two lines have the same retinal size, the upper one seems larger. A related explanation applies to the Müller-Lyer illusion. In seeking to understand illusions, keep in mind that perceptions are based on all kinds of cues, and it is likely there is no single explanation for any given illusion (Coren & Girgus, 1973).

Constancy is the perception of regularities in visual objects when in fact the retinal images of those objects are changing.

Some illusions are physiologically based in that they arise automatically within the visual receptors and are seen in the same way by everyone. One such illusion is the brightness dis-

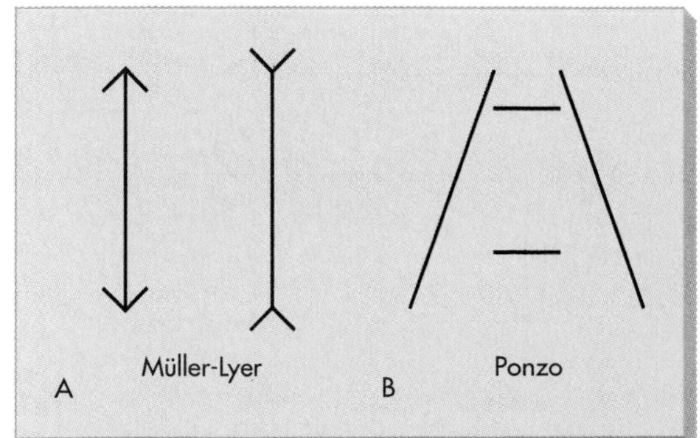

5-29 Visual Illusions

The Müller-Lyer illusion and the Ponzo illusion are two types of visual illusions that are thought to be caused by a "misapplication" of distance cues. (A) The arrows of the Müller-Lyer illusion create the impression of angles sloping toward (left) or away (right) from the viewer (see also Figure 5-32). (B) The Ponzo illusion is based on linear perspective, with the converging lines seen as receding into the distance.

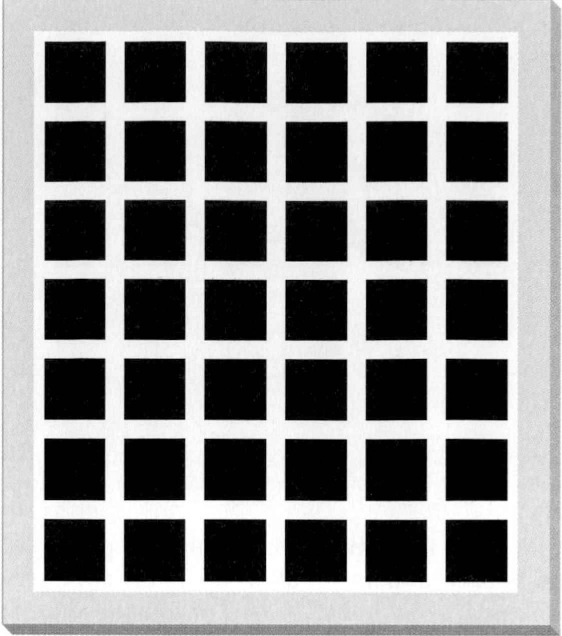

5-30 The Hermann Grid

Gray spots appear at the intersection of the white stripes, even though the physical illumination is constant throughout the Hermann grid and the white lines are actually equally white throughout the grid. This illusion arises out of the physiological structure of the visual system. Because of contrast, the eye perceives the white stripes as brighter when they are next to the black squares but as duller, and hence as gray spots, at the intersections of the vertical and horizontal white lines, where they are only next to the corners of the black squares. (Source: Adapted from Hering, 1920)

tortion produced by the Hermann grid shown in Figure 5-30. Here dark spots automatically seem to appear to everyone at the intersections of the horizontal and vertical white lines, even though these lines are actually uniformly white and do not have spots.

Some cognitive illusions, such as size and brightness constancies, can be influenced by experience and culture. For example, Pygmies from the Congo's dense tropical forest do not perceive size constancy when first introduced to unfamiliar great distances that are observable in grasslands (see Figure 5-31). These cultural or experiential effects are quite common. Thus, one study demonstrated that Polynesian students at the University of Guam were less influenced by the Ponzo illusion and were more accurate in their judgments of line size than were U.S. college students (Leibowitz, 1971). The greater experience of Western students with geometric forms seems to be the major contributing factor to this difference. The ability to identify three-dimensional objects by two-dimensional pictures is also affected by experience and may differ between people from Western and non-Western cultures, depending on what is focused on, the parts or the whole (Deregowski, 1989).

The Müller-Lyer illusion is one of several geometric illusions more likely to fool Westerners than members of African tribes. Some researchers believe that this is because Westerners live in an artificially "carpentered" or angled world, while the Africans who were studied lived in more rounded, less angular environments (Segal, Campbell, & Herskovits, 1966). Figure 5-32 shows how the illusion is enhanced when placed in the context of the "built" environment, with corners and corridors that indicate distance, and demonstrates the power of experience with our rectilinear environment in

5-31 The Grasslands Illusion

When shown both of these diagrams and asked which animal the hunter is attacking, most Western subjects will say that he is attacking the antelope. Researchers found that African subjects without experience with photographs and drawings will say that the hunter is attacking the baby elephant. This indicates that the tendency to use monocular cues to distance depends on experience with photographs and drawings. (Source: Adapted from Hudson, 1960)

5-32 Real-World Example of the Müller-Lyer Illusion

Our experience in our "carpentered" world teaches us that arrowheads (pointing inward or outward) at the end of a line are a cue to the line's distance from us and thus affect our judgment of its length, as shown in (A), which demonstrates the basic Müller-Lyer illusion. The other two diagrams demonstrate the Müller-Lyer illusion in our "carpentered world." (B) In this diagram, the line indicating the corner appears shorter than the line indicating the corner in (C). They are both the same length, however.

shaping our perceptions. We predict that no matter how hard you try, you will perceive the lines in the figure as different lengths, even after you measure them.

From Stimulus to Vision

The process of human vision is complex. Vision originates in the light that falls on a distal stimulus and ends with an interaction between bottom-up and top-down sources of information in the nervous system. The visual receptors, the neural pathways between eye and brain, and the visual cortex all play a role in communicating and interpreting the distal stimulus. Experience, prior knowledge, and cultural factors influence how bottom-up information is understood. Sometimes the distal object is seen pretty much as it is. But often we "see" in a way that cannot be accounted for by the physics of light energy. Vision is arguably our most important sense. It accounts in large measure for how we acquire knowledge about the world, from birth onward. Next, we will consider the other human senses. In future chapters, you will learn how information coming from all the sensory systems becomes a part of your memory and knowledge of the world.

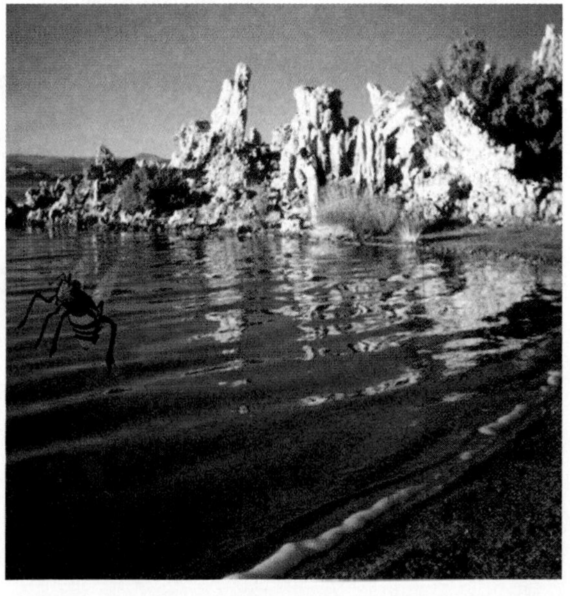

◄ *When you see these two images, you convert the light energy that arrives at the receptors of your eyes and then process the images into meaningful objects. You can stare at the two images and defocus your eyes so that the two images, which are taken from slightly different angles, are interpreted by your brain as one image that shows depth. When you do this, a giant bee will appear ready to fly off the page.*

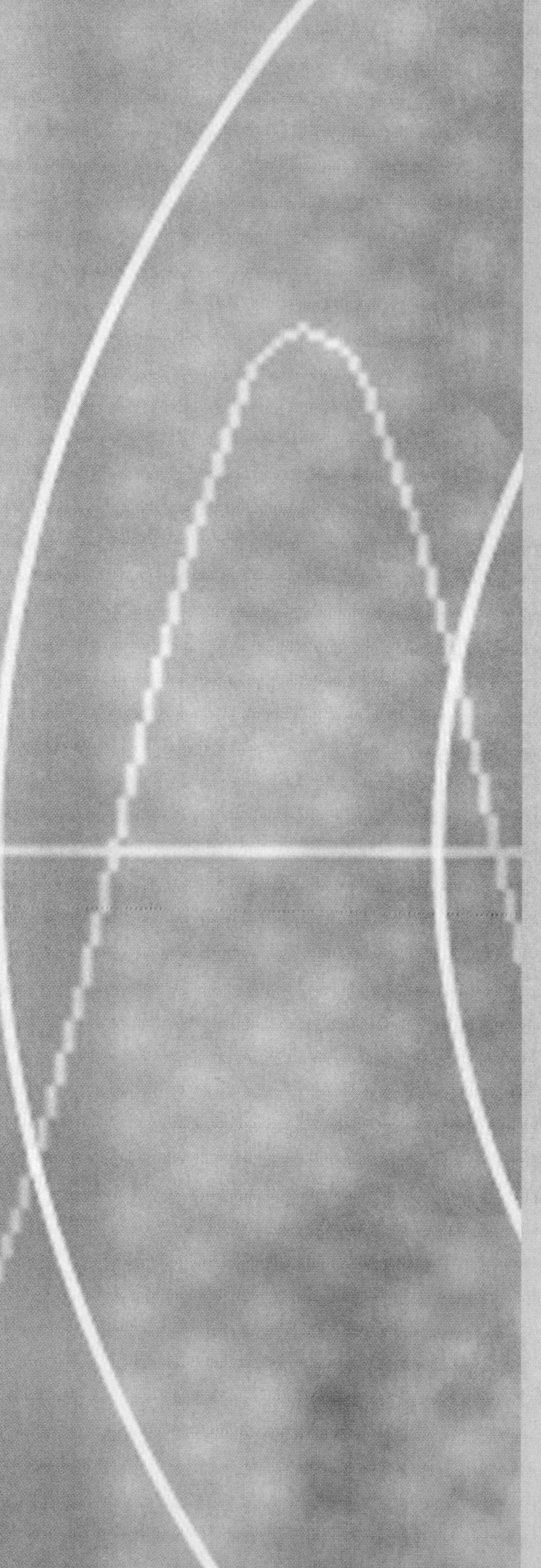

UNDERSTANDING HUMAN DIVERSITY

Perceptual Processes in Cultural Context

When we compare people of one culture to another, we find little variation in such sensory abilities as being able to discriminate between degrees of loudness of sound or brightness of light. But we do find tremendous individual variation in how sensory input is perceived, even among individuals in the same culture (Berry, Poortinga, Segall, & Dasen, 1992). Developmental and cross-cultural studies suggest that, as we interact with objects in our environment, we learn to interpret our sensory input based on our experience. Experiencing different cultural environments thus may lead to cross-cultural differences in perception. Such differences can help us to understand human diversity in perception, while at the same time recognizing human similarity in basic perceptual processes.

Studies of infants show that the ability to use different kinds of information from the environment changes over time. Consider what happens when five-month-old infants from the United States are exposed to a photograph of a window that is viewed at a 45-degree angle (which makes the window look like one edge is closer to the infants than another). They reach for it, but they do not consistently reach for the edge that would be closest to them. At seven months of age, however, they exhibit a reliable reaching preference for the closest edge (Yonas, Cleaves, & Pettersen, 1978).

Think about the information that is being processed when these infants view the picture and then reach for what would be the closest edge of the window. What does this reaching preference require? The infants must be able to perceive the window to be the same shape, whether or not it is viewed from different angles (shape constancy), and use that information to judge how far away they are from the window's various parts. This requires being able to make certain assumptions about size and shape that will serve as cues to both depth and object

◀ The infant is looking at a large photograph depicting a bank of windows turned at an angle of 45 degrees. The two edges of the stimulus are actually at an equal distance from the infant. When infants begin to use the information in the picture to judge depth (by 7 months of age), they reach out to touch the edge of the picture that they perceive to be closest to them. Before that (at 5 months of age), they show no preference in reaching for the picture (Source: Adapted from Yonas, Cleaves, & Pettersen, 1978).

perception. As infants gain experience of the world with age, they acquire size and shape constancy, both of which are cues to depth and object perception. But in the United States and other modern cultural contexts, such experience can also lead to vulnerability to certain visual illusions that can occur when such constancies are violated. This vulnerability is not as likely to occur for individuals raised in cultures with different sorts of environments.

Cross-cultural differences in susceptibility to illusions also provide evidence for the view that perception involves making inferences about our environment. The reasoning is that our interactions with objects and situations in our environment affect the inferences we make about depth or size and hence determine the outcomes of our perceptual processes (Segall, 1994). Thus, people from modern cultures have extensive experience with buildings and other right-angled objects and should therefore be more susceptible to visual illusions involving right angles than people from rural cultures without such experience. Indeed, this "carpentered world hypothesis" has been confirmed by research involving a number of illusions, including the Müller-Lyer illusion. One such study compared the responses of adults and children living in the United States with the responses of adults and children in several African countries. The researchers found that U.S. children were more likely to experience the Müller-Lyer illusion than were African children (Segall, Campbell, & Herskovits, 1966). Another study examined the susceptibility to visual illusions among people from different areas within Zambia, an African country with environments that have a wide range in "carpenteredness"—from the modern capital city of Lusaka (highly carpentered) to the open Zambezi Valley region (non-carpentered). Susceptibility to the Müller-Lyer illusion increased with the degree of carpenteredness (Stewart, 1973).

These studies support the idea that the processes that shape the translation of our sensations into perception begin early in life, and that perception is based on the ways we learn to interpret information about our environments, ways that are appropriate for our particular cultural contexts. They demonstrate how understanding basic psychological processes common to all people can also help us to understand and appreciate human diversity.

▼ People who live in African villages are less likely to succumb to visual illusions involving straight lines and angles than people who live in "carpentered worlds" such as Houston, Texas.

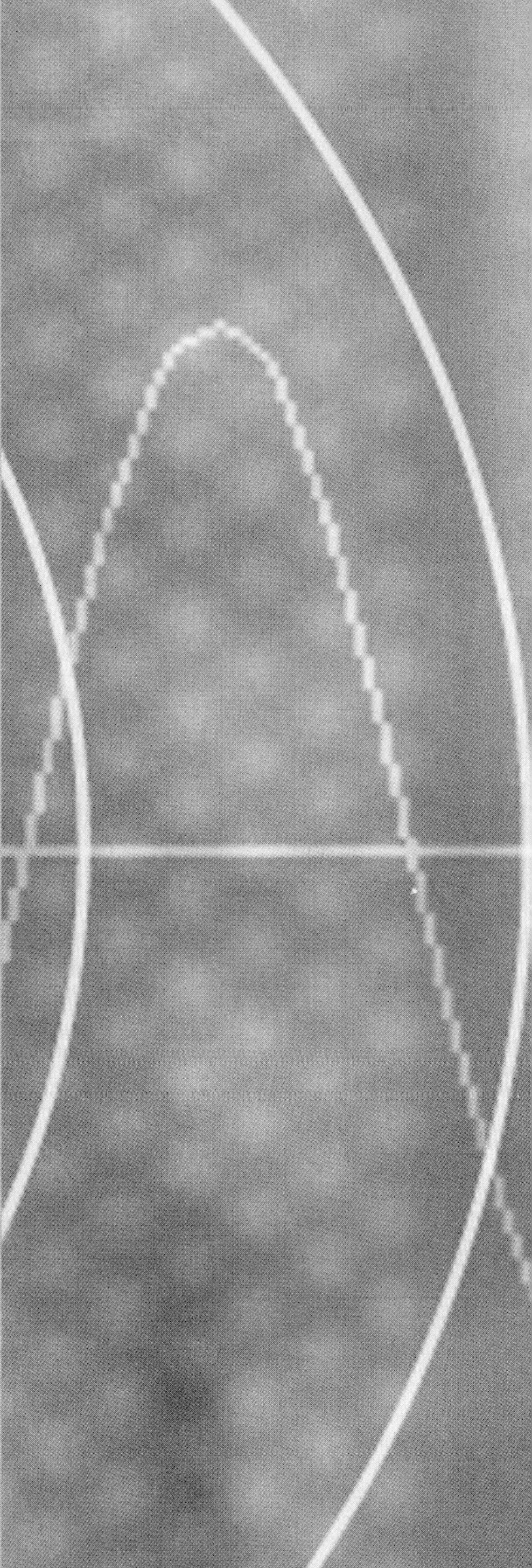

Hearing: Auditory Sensory Processes

Sound is the physical stimulus for hearing. Sound waves consist of rapid variations in pressure in a medium, usually air, and carry vibrations from a distal source to the eardrum.

It is difficult for those of us with normal hearing to appreciate what is missed when a person can't hear. Hearing has been called the "Cinderella of the senses" because of its "stepsister" status compared to vision (Gutin, 1993). Yet, hearing plays a critical role in communication, in the arts, and in the comprehension of what's going on around us when vision is unavailable. These facts were not lost on Helen Keller (1910), who became deaf and blind as a result of illness in infancy, but who, with great perseverance, overcame her impairments to become an accomplished writer and commentator on worldly events. She wrote that she felt "the impediment of deafness far more keenly than that of blindness" (Keller, 1968, p. 248).

JoAnn Gutin (1993) warns that hearing in the modern world is threatened; we're under "constant siege from age, drugs, and a world that includes snowmobiles and jet planes as well as Megadeth" (p. 46). What stands between us and complete silence? Our 32,000 hearing receptors. To appreciate how these receptors produce the experience of hearing, we need to understand the nature of sound, its impact on hearing receptors, and how proximal stimulation is converted into meaning.

Sound: Its Physical Nature

The air around us is composed of molecules. Vibrating objects—a vocal cord, a hummingbird's wing, a jackhammer—disturb the normally uniform pressure of these molecules, causing them to move back and forth. The resulting pressure variations create sound waves that spread outward through the air at about 331 meters per second (760 miles per hour), the speed of sound.

Sound waves are represented by waveforms that rise and fall at a certain rate. These waveforms have three fundamental attributes called amplitude, wavelength or frequency, and complexity. Waveforms are typically graphed as pressure changes over time. ***Amplitude*** refers to the strength of the sound wave and is graphically represented as the height of the wave crest. ***Wavelength*** is the distance between successive crests, and ***frequency*** measures the number of crests (or cycles or vibrations) the wave goes through in a second of time. (A cycle is one complete movement in pressure: from a baseline through a positive peak, to a negative peak, and then back to the baseline.) ***Complexity*** is determined by the number of different waves occurring at the same time. Figure 5-33 portrays one cycle of the waves created by two different sound sources, one simple or pure, the other more complex.

The simplest kind of sound is a pure tone, created by vibration at a single frequency. Pure tones can be produced electronically by audio-oscillators or mechanically by a tuning fork. But most tones that we hear—for example those produced by musical instruments or the human voice—are complex, consisting of combinations of a base or fundamental frequency (the lowest frequency of a sound) and several multiples (harmonics or overtones) of that frequency at different amplitudes. The specific combination of harmonics allows us to distinguish among a piano, a violin, and the human voice when they are all producing the same fundamental fre-

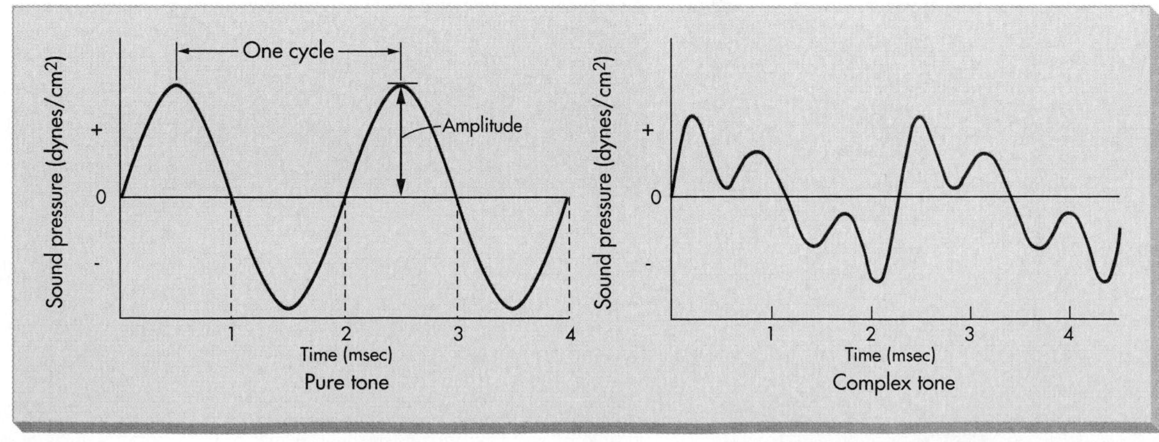

5-33 The Physical Properties of Sound

Pure tones are produced by a sound with a single frequency (for example, so many cycles of sound pressure change per unit of time). (A) The pure tone shown in the graph is produced by a frequency of 1 cycle every 2 milliseconds or 500 cycles per second. (B) The complex tone in this graph is made up of several pure tones, each with a different frequency. Sometimes complex tones have no obvious cyclic character, in which case they are likely to be heard as noise. When there is a cyclic or periodic repetition to the waves, as shown here, it will be heard as a musical tone.

quency, say, a middle C. Figure 5-34 presents some sound waves for complex tones produced by a variety of musical instruments. Noise is also a complex mixture of frequencies, but in the case of noise, the frequencies do not relate to each other in any regular way, and the sound is consequently atonal.

Sound frequency is measured in Hertz (Hz), which represents the number of waves or cycles that occur in 1 second. The normal human ear can detect sounds ranging in frequency from a low of about 20 Hz to a high of about 20,000 Hz. Sound amplitude is measured in decibels (dB), and the lowest amplitude that human beings can hear is defined arbitrarily as 0 dB. The highest amplitude that human beings can hear, before pain and damage set in, is about 120 dB. Figure 5-35 includes the amplitude (decibels) of some common sounds.

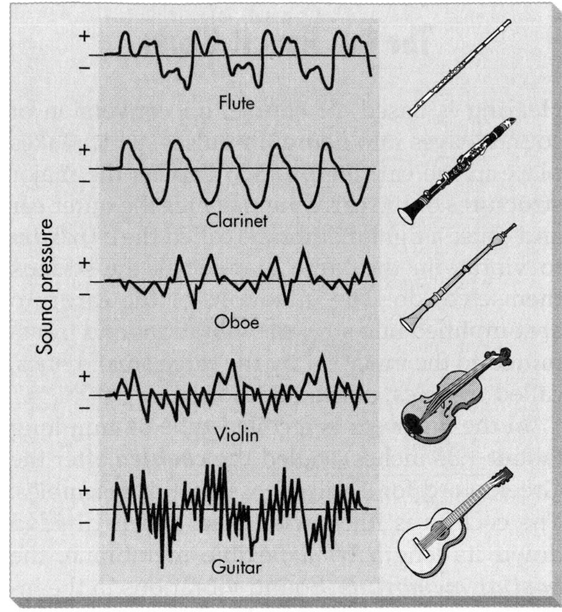

5-34 Sound Waves for Complex Tones

These are sound waves produced by a variety of musical instruments. These musical instruments can all play the same note. If you listen carefully as the instruments are played, you can hear the same note, but the sounds are somehow different. The sound pressure changes for each instrument are complex and not identical, but these sound waves all have the same fundamental frequency. They differ in other frequencies represented in the sound wave, which gives the sound produced by each instrument its characteristic timbre. (Source: Matlin, 1983)

Decibel level (Db)	
180	Rocket launch
170	
160	
150	Jet airplane taking off
140	
130	Threshold of pain
120	Thunder; rock band
110	Riveter
100	Subway
90	Lawn mower
80	Noisy automobile
70	Quiet automobile
60	Normal conversation
50	Business office
40	Rainfall
30	Quiet room
20	Whisper
10	
0	Absolute hearing threshold

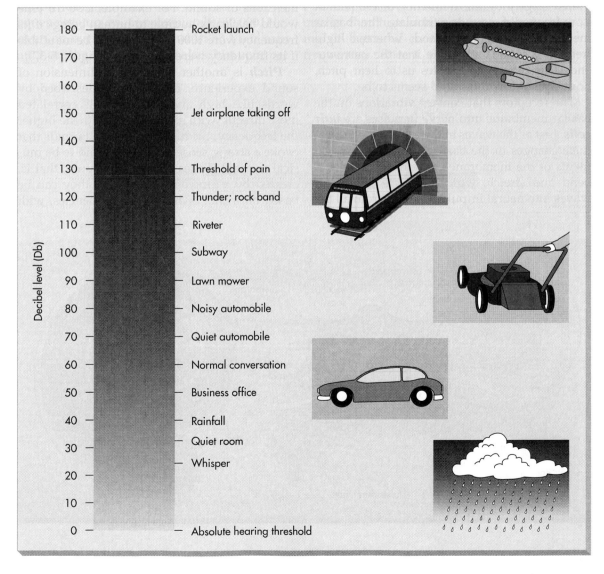

5-35 Loudness of Everyday Sounds

The intensities of various common sounds as measured in decibels (dB). The takeoff blast of the Saturn V moon rocket, measured at the launching pad is approximately 180 dB. For laboratory rats, prolonged exposure to 150 dB causes death. (Source: Adapted from Chapanis, 1965; Chapanis, Garner, & Morgan, 1949)

THINKING CRITICALLY

Knowing what you do about the sensitivity of human hearing to the proximal stimulus created by the same distal stimulus at the two ears, what can you say about the way your home stereo works?

Stereophonic high-fidelity recordings employ two or more microphones to record the sound from voices or musical instruments in the same way that the ears, if they were present, would receive it. Each channel of recorded sound is then reproduced through a separate speaker, and under ideal conditions, the ears of the listeners in the living room will receive sound that is similar to the sound they would have received if they had been present when the recording was made.

Amplitude, frequency, and complexity are the three primary physical dimensions of sound, corresponding to loudness, pitch, and timbre, which are the three primary psychological dimensions of sound.

1990) indicates that insects like the praying mantis have a relatively impoverished auditory system (only one ear), which picks up only quite high frequencies, above 25,000 Hertz. But this too has evolutionary significance. Mantises are preyed on by bats. Bats have difficulty seeing, especially in the daytime, but they have a sense of echolocation that allows them to "see" objects in their environments by bouncing sound waves off of them. They use high frequencies for echolocation, so sensitivity to such frequencies allows the mantis to anticipate and avoid bat attacks.

Spatial Localization of Sounds

The auditory system locates objects in space. While you can localize sounds with only one ear, the most sensitive cues are "binaural," analogous to "binocular" cues in vision. Because the ears are separated on the head, a sound source that is not directly in front or in back of a person will arrive at slightly different times and stimulate the ears in slightly different ways. For example, if a sound is located to the left, the left ear will receive, at a slightly earlier time, a slightly more intense stimulation than the right ear, which is in the "shadow" of the head. Normal hearing is so sensitive that we can reliably detect a time delay difference of only 5 microseconds (5 *millionths* of a second) between the two ears!

The Other Human Senses

For human beings, vision and hearing are the primary senses. But there is no way that we could carry on our normal interactions with the world if our senses were limited to these two. We couldn't smell flowers, we couldn't taste food, we couldn't feel our way in the dark. Remember, the human body is filled wall-to-wall with sensors. Almost anywhere a proximal stimulus comes in contact with the body, a sensation of some sort is likely to arise.

Sensing Body Position

Even blindfolded and wearing earplugs, we normally have no trouble sensing our body's orientation in space. We have internal sensory systems to detect the relative position of various body parts as well as the movement of both our body as a whole and its parts. Without seeing or hearing, we still know whether we are lying down, standing up, or sitting in a chair, whether our arms are raised or lowered, whether we are walking or standing still. Two sensory systems are instrumental for this bodily awareness: the kinesthetic and vestibular senses.

The Kinesthetic Sense

Close your eyes. Reach out your arms and touch the tip of your nose. You have just experienced your kinesthetic sense in action. The receptors for our kinesthetic sense are spread diffusely through the entire body, located in the body's muscles, tendons, and joints. They detect skeletal movements, or changes in the orientation of bones with respect to one another. These receptors are specialized nerve endings that sense whether bodily tissues, such as muscles and ten-

SEEKING SOLUTIONS

Perceptual Conflicts

Our momentary internal representation of the world is built from information provided simultaneously by all our sensory systems, and we human beings have a lot of them. Usually, the systems work harmoniously and without conflict. But if the brain receives conflicting information from two or more sensory systems, one of two things happens: either processing continues normally by ignoring all but one of the sources of conflicting information, or the processing is greatly slowed down.

In the first case, some incoming information is ignored. A familiar example is visual capture, when visual information overrides all other sources. The success of a ventriloquist depends on visual capture. On the one hand, an observer's auditory localization mechanism signals that the source of the dummy's voice is the ventriloquist's mouth, but on the other hand, the observer's visual system correlates the movement of the dummy's mouth with the speech sounds. Because the visual system indicates that the ventriloquist's mouth is not moving and the dummy's is, you experience a talking dummy. Ventriloquists do not "throw" their voices; they depend on visual capture. If you close your eyes when attending a ventriloquist's act, you will hear both the dummy's voice and the ventriloquist's voice coming from the same location.

Motion sickness provides another dramatic example of conflict between two types of perceptual information. The brain has two major sources of information about body motion: the visual system and the vestibular system. Normally, the two systems signal the same information about body movement. But if the entire room you are now in were tilted 30 degrees to one side, how would you know it? From the visual point of view you could not tell because visually everything in the room would be the same as usual. Your vestibular system, however, would signal that everything is tilted. When you're on a ship rocking in the waves, your vestibular system signals the motion to your brain. But below deck, as your body moves, so does the whole cabin. The visual system has no information about your movement and therefore signals the brain that your body is stationary. A common outcome of this conflict of sensations is nausea and vomiting.

To prevent seasickness or to eliminate it, you must restore agreement between visual and vestibular information. If you focus your view on something stationary, like the horizon or a large object on land, the visual system has a landmark against which it senses and interprets the rocking motion. It then signals the brain—in agreement with the vestibular system—that the body is rocking. The symptoms of nausea should disappear. Seasoned sailors adapt to the disagreement between the two systems, and so for them nausea is not a problem. But when they go ashore, they often report a short period of time when stable ground feels as though it were rocking!

◄ Ventriloquist Shari Lewis and "Lambchop."

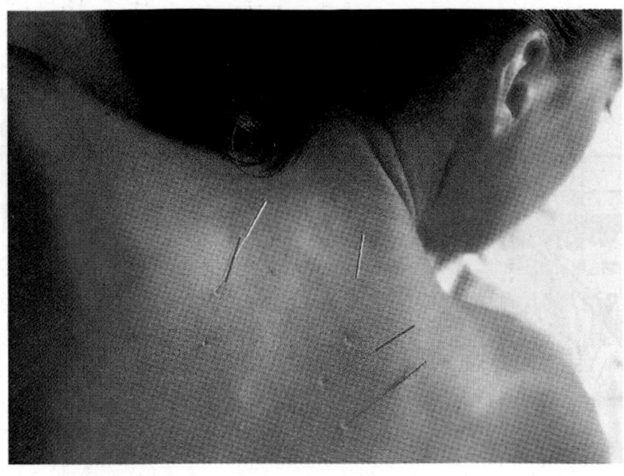

▲ *Acupuncture is an ancient Chinese medical practice that is still used today. In the photo at right, a patient receives an acupuncture treatment to help manage chronic pain.*

they respond to such a broad range of stimulation, pain receptors are a primary protection system for the body, alerting us quickly and automatically to stimuli that may damage tissue.

How do pain killers work? The body produces certain neurotransmitters, such as beta-endorphins, which have analgesic (pain-killing) properties because they inhibit the release of substance P from presynaptic nerve endings. Manufactured pain killers such as morphine may work in a similar fashion.

Most pain sensations respond to pain-reducing drugs. Sometimes, however, drugs are inadequate or ineffective. Are there other ways to interrupt transmission of pain signals over neural pathways, short of severing the pathways by surgery? Although its mechanism is not fully understood, ***acupuncture*** is one possibility. In acupuncture, sharp needles are inserted into selected areas of the skin and then twirled rapidly. This technique has been used as an effective method for inhibiting pain by Chinese physicians and other practitioners of Asian medicine. The general finding is that after twenty to thirty minutes of acupuncture, pain sensations are deadened for six to eight hours (Pool, 1973). Where the needles are inserted determines which part of the body will be anesthetized. For example, to inhibit pain when a tooth is being pulled, a needle is inserted into the web between the thumb and the index finger. To inhibit pain during a tonsillectomy, a needle is inserted just above the wrist. The mechanism by which acupuncture works to control pain is not known, although there is plenty of speculation. One promising theory asserts that the needles trigger impulses that close off or gate the normal pathways for pain, as we will discuss in more detail in Chapter 9.

Pain—like color—is not a quality of the physical, external world, but rather a psychological event that arises from the brain's interpretation of incoming stimulation. Both the experience and expression of pain are affected by beliefs and expectations, and vary widely among individuals and across cultures. Intense fear and concentration can inhibit pain, while depression and anxiety can enhance it (Dworkin et al., 1992). Not even the stimulation of pain receptors is necessary for the experience of pain. After amputations, people may still feel the missing limb, and sense pain in it. This experience is called phantom-limb pain. Such pain may persist even if the nerves in the limb's stump are surgically removed and pain pathways between the brain and spinal cord are eliminated. The pain can be severe. Arm amputees have reported feeling as if their fingernails were being pulled off (Melzack, 1992). Feeling pain in phantom limbs might result from the very lack of impulses from the missing limb to the somatosensory cortex. The brain may interpret the *lack* of receiving a normal limb signal as a sign of tissue damage (Knecht et al., 1995).

Active and Passive Touch

We can identify the shape of an object not only by vision but also by touch. To see how this works, we need to distinguish between two types of touch perception: active (or dynamic) touch and passive (or static) touch (Turvey, 1996). ***Passive touch*** produces the awareness of a simple experience such as pressure, warmth, coolness, roughness. ***Active touch***, which involves the manipulation of an object, produces information about the shape, weight, length, and possibly other characteristics of the object. Thus, even if you couldn't see, you'd be able to identify or tell the difference between a baseball and a pencil, just by holding and hefting these objects. Louis Braille, who was blind, made use of this ability to identify objects with active touch when he developed his system of using raised dots on paper to represent letters of the alphabet. This system, which was named after Braille, enabled blind people to "read" written material with their fingertips. A person skilled in Braille can read at a rate of about 105 words a minute, a decent rate but less than sighted reading, which proceeds at about 200 to 600 words per minute. With the advent of computer technology, a variety of devices have been developed to transform visual stimulation (as seen by a television camera) into patterns of vibration on the skin. These devices have had some limited success in allowing blind people to "see" physical objects, including printed material, by means of their tactile sensitivity.

The Chemical Senses

Two kinds of sensations are triggered by the absorption of molecules (the proximal stimulus) by chemoreceptor cells, that is, specialized neurons that respond to chemical stimuli. These sensations are mediated by the chemical senses: taste and smell.

Taste

The tongue has small bumps known as papillae that are visible on its surface. Inside these bumps are the onion-shaped taste buds, which contain clusters of about 50 to 150 individual receptor cells for taste. In all, there are about 10,000 taste buds on the tongue (McLaughlin & Margolskee, 1944; see Figure 5-42). Individual receptor cells are sensitive to chemicals dissolved in saliva. Taste receptor cells have a relatively short life, each living between four and ten days before wearing out and being replaced by a new one.

Traditionally, taste experiences have been categorized into four discrete types—salty, sweet, bitter, and sour. Schiffman and Erickson (1980) remind us that these sensations are merely points on a taste continuum—the taste of any particular substance is a complex combination of two or more basic components, analogous to the complexity of sounds or colors. We use the traditional four labels, but you should remember that there are many more than four distinguishable taste sensations.

Not all areas of the tongue are equally sensitive to all tastes. The sides of the tongue are most sensitive to sour substances. Salty tastes are present throughout, with a slight increase in sensitivity on the front sides of the tongue. The tip is most sensitive to sweet tastes, and the back of the tongue detects bitter tastes. Place a bit of salt at the tip of your tongue and then along the side. Repeat this experiment with some sugar. You will notice that the salty taste is much stronger along the side of the tongue, and the sugar taste is stronger at the tip. Different taste locations result from different concentrations of receptors in various regions of the tongue.

Biological, psychological, and cultural variables all influence the sense of taste. For example, the ability to taste the bitter substance phenylthiocarbamide (PTC) is inherited. Only about two-thirds of the American population are PTC tasters, experiencing a bitter taste from such substances as potassium chloride, which is

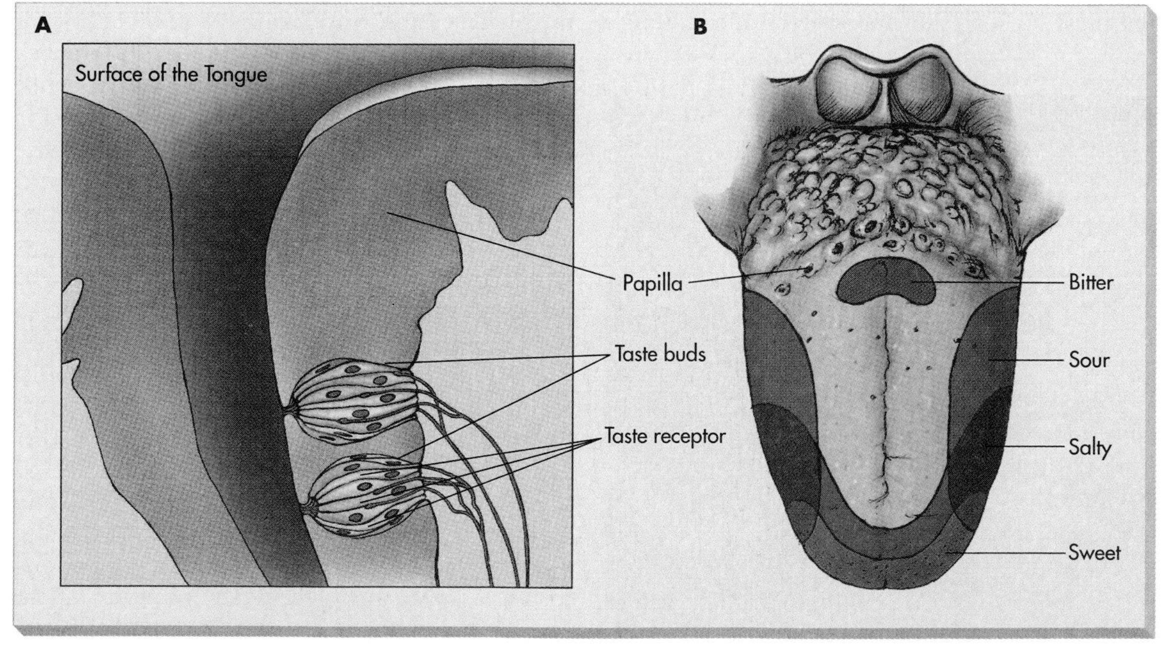

5-42 Taste Buds

(A) Taste buds are collectors of cells sensitive to soluble substances. They are located inside small bumps called papillae, which are on the surface of the tongue.
(B) Different areas of the tongue are most sensitive to the basic sensations of salt, sour, sweet, and bitter.

used as a salt substitute in low-sodium diets, or from coffee or saccharine (once used to sweeten diet sodas). Moreover, taste sensitivity changes with age, with sensitivity tending to decrease as people grow older.

Various substances can distort or suppress one or more of the four tastes. Artichoke hearts, for example, contain a chemical that reduces the sensitivity of all receptors except those sensitive to sweet substances. After you eat an artichoke heart, most substances will taste sweet to you. Try this experiment. Take a sip of water and swirl it around in your mouth. Most people experience water as neutral or slightly bitter in taste. Now eat a piece of artichoke heart (unmarinated!), chewing it thoroughly. Then sip some water and concentrate on your taste experience. The water should taste considerably sweeter than before.

Culture and learning also play an important part in what is considered to taste "good" (Douglas, 1979; Rozin, 1996). In some parts of the globe, grubs, grasshoppers, larks, blackbirds, and dogs are considered tasty delicacies. Exposure to a taste, even if it is initially disliked, leads to increased liking. Asking children to eat just one bite of a vegetable really can lead them to like vegetables eventually. Clearly, these differences in taste sensitivity have profound implications for the food and diet industries (Bartoshuk, 1978, 1993).

Smell

There is a close interaction between the two chemical senses, taste and smell. Indeed, much of what we call taste is at least in part attributable to the sense of smell, which is almost always stimulated in parallel with taste.

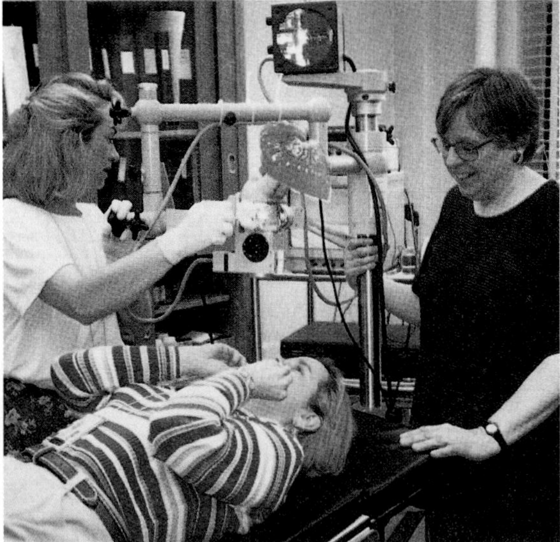

▶ *Drs. Linda Bartoshuk (right) and Laurie Lucchina (left) make a videotape of Dr. Valerie Duffy's tongue in a laboratory at Yale University. They are studying the connection between nutrition and the sensory properties of foods.*

Receptors for smell lie in the upper part of the nasal cavity (see Figure 5-43). Each nostril has about 30 million receptors, in a layer of cells called the ***olfactory epithelium***, giving us an extraordinary sensitivity to odors. To be sensed, an olfactory stimulus (odorant) must be in gaseous form. Nerve impulses are triggered in these olfactory cells by the absorption of the chemical molecules that make up an odor gas. Neural information from olfactory receptors has direct access to a part of the cortex called the olfactory bulb, without first passing through any neural way stations like the thalamus. This might signify the evolutionary importance and primacy of the sense of smell for many vertebrate species, enabling them to communicate with others and to detect food or danger.

The human sense of smell has a reputation for being weak relative to that of animals and to other human senses. But, in fact, human beings can distinguish up to 10,000 different odors. Moreover, human olfactory receptors can be excited by exposure to just one molecule of an olfactory stimulus (de Vries & Stuiver, 1961). Our individual smell receptors are not less sensitive than those of, say, dogs, which are considered to be highly sensitive to smells. So why are dogs rather than human beings used to sniff out hidden drugs in airport luggage? The difference is that dogs have about 100 times more receptors than people do. Finally, our ability to detect differences (difference thresholds) in concentration of odorants is comparable in sensitivity to our ability to detect differences with other senses (Goldstein, 1989). As a result, the human sense of smell has a reputation for insensitivity that it probably does not deserve.

Smell is not a purely automatic physiological system. It can be trained rather easily. Practice at attaching distinct labels to different odor experiences improves our ability to make discriminations. This fact has been well known to perfume, wine, and beer makers for centuries. We used to think that the average person could identify by name no more than fifteen or so different odors. It is now known that, with practice, we can increase our odor repertoire to seventy-five or more distinctive smells. No one yet knows what the limits are.

Smell seems to serve two primary functions for most species: to test what is edible and to communicate. As noted above, much of what

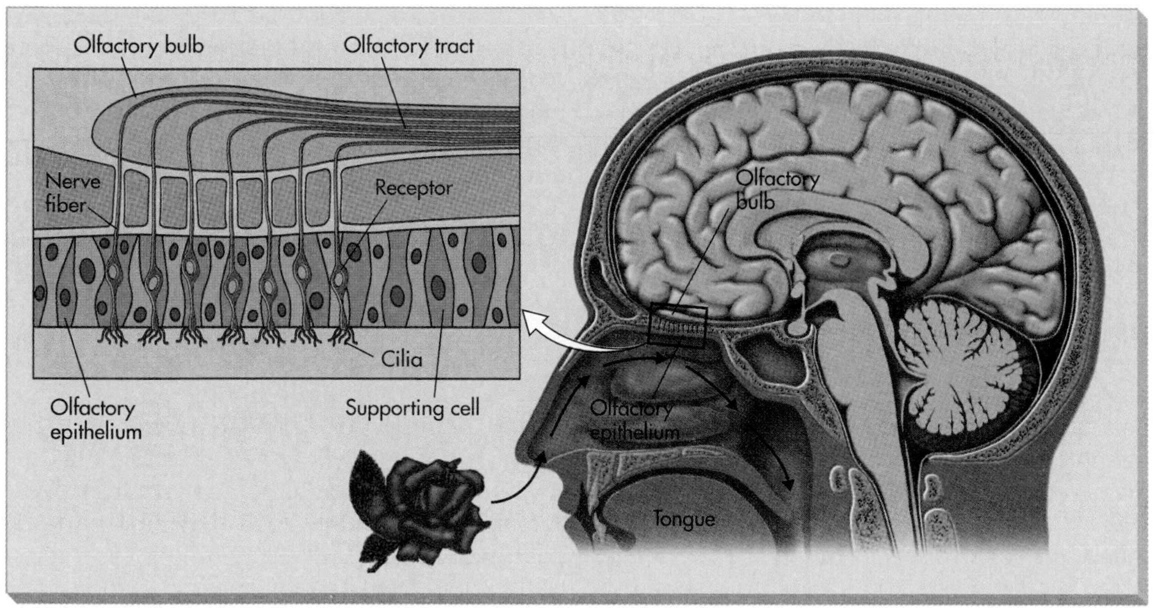

5-43 The Olfactory System

The receptor cells in the nose react to molecules in the area sending neural impulses to the brain through the olfactory bulb. (Source: Adapted from Amoore, Johnson, & Rubin, 1964, and Karapelou, 1993)

we experience as taste is derived from smell. When we suffer from a cold and our nasal passages are blocked, food seems dull and tasteless. Cut yourself some small pieces of apple and onion (say, half-inch cubes). Holding your nose with one hand, put one piece in your mouth and chew it for a moment; then put the other piece in your mouth. Can you tell the difference? As long as none of the gaseous odor reaches your olfactory cells, the apple and onion taste the same. Smell, not taste, is probably our primary sense for identifying and differentiating among foods.

The communication function of smell is more important to other species than to human beings. Chemicals produced for communication by smell are called ***pheromones***. Many animals have special glands to produce territorial pheromones, and some animals secrete these chemicals in their urine. You may have noticed that a dog often urinates at the corners of its yard. This behavior is the dog's way of marking its territory by its scent. Other dogs coming into the yard will immediately recognize the smell and leave if challenged. When an intruder enters a beehive, honeybees release an alarm pheromone. This pheromone signals the hive's other honeybees to gather for a concerted attack on the intruder.

Pheromones are also involved in courtship and mating behavior. If a male mouse is doused with a female pheromone, other males will eagerly try to mount it. Whether or not human beings are sensitive to pheromones is still controversial, and evidence supporting pheromone effects is indirect. Women differ in their sensitivity to certain musky smells at different times during their menstrual cycle. Their sensitivity to these smells is highest just before ovulation and is lowest during menstruation. Since these musky smells are related to male sex hormones, this cyclical variation may indicate a pheromone-like function, possibly a now vestigial carryover from an earlier period of human evolution (Russell, Switz, & Thompson, 1980).

Pheromones are chemical substances produced in the body and released into the air that provide a means of communication between animals, based on the sense of smell.

By holding your nose, you can produce ***anosmia***, an inability to smell normally. But anosmia is a condition that can be caused permanently by head injury or asthma or temporarily by the flu or a heavy cold. People who have permanent anosmia often report a corre-

◀ *Professor Ann C. Noble of the University of California, Davis, has developed this Wine Aroma Wheel to distinguish among the many different smells detectable by a highly trained nose.*

sponding loss of interest in food and in sex. You might have had similar feelings during your last prolonged cold. Observations like these are clearly consistent with the important role that smell plays in sensing the world around us.

What we see or hear tends to be remembered well on an immediate test but often fades soon after. In contrast, accumulating evidence shows that we can remember associations to odors for very long periods, without much decay in memory. "Smell is a potent wizard that transports us across thousands of miles and all the years we have lived. . . . Even as I think of smells, my nose is full of scents that start awake sweet memories of summers gone and ripening fields far away" (Helen Keller, cited in Ackerman, 1992). One experimenter asked subjects to remember a series of odors any way they could. Later, these subjects were asked to distinguish between pairs of odors, only one of which they had experienced earlier. Initial recognition of previously experienced odors was about 70 percent. That is, after initial exposure, an individual correctly picked the experienced odor from the pair about 70 percent of the time. But the interesting thing is that this figure showed little sign of dropping over time. After one year, subjects could still identify the correct odor 65 percent of the time. So it seems that olfactory memories typically last a year or more without serious forgetting. This is considerably more durable memory than is typical of visual, auditory, or other forms of sensory memory (Engen, 1987; Herz & Engen, 1996).

THINKING CRITICALLY

Can you speculate about how it is that the olfactory system has such a good memory?

One possibility is that olfactory signals travel a shorter and more direct route to the cerebral cortex than do messages from any other sensory system. They also travel to lower-lying areas of the brain, such as the limbic system, which are concerned with feelings and emotions. Overall, olfactory impulses are registered in more different areas of the brain, more quickly, and with less opportunity for interference or inhibition than those from any other system. Thus, odor memories may last longer because the brain can create a quicker and richer set of associations for an odor experience than for any other sensation.

Attention

Imagine that you are in your psychology class, listening to a lecture. You might find yourself nodding off, not able to stay fully awake, especially if you were up late the night before. Your level of alertness could drop so low that practically nothing gets through to you, and you pay little or no attention to the lecture. But even if you stay awake, there is no guarantee that you will be able to attend to all the important points of the lecture. Maybe your eyes wander to the window, or you keep thinking about an earlier conversation you had with someone. If so, you are not focusing on the lecture and will miss important points. Being awake and "listening" is no guarantee either that you will understand what is being said. Maybe you cannot track the meaning of the speaker, maybe he or she is not clear, maybe you just can't make much sense of what's being said. You are awake, you are looking in the right direction, you are hearing the words, but you miss the point.

As marvelous as our sensory and perceptual processes are in producing rich and complex representations of the world, they are subject to serious attentional constraints. Only a small portion of all the information available to our perceptual systems is registered and further processed in a meaningful way. Human beings have to be selective among sources of stimulation because attentional resources are limited (Hirst & Kalmar, 1987); this is known as ***selective attention***. Selection of information begins at the very point it is first registered by the senses.

Attention to incoming stimuli requires alertness, orientation, and awareness on your part. First, you must be alert enough to support proper focusing and understanding of an event. Blanking out guarantees that you'll miss some information. Second, you must be oriented to the message and the messenger to maximize perception of selected sensory information. For example, you can intentionally move and focus your eyes to make a particular location in space the clear center of your attention; you can position your ears so that they are oriented to receive sounds coming from a particular source; you can move your body so that you can most easily touch objects with your hands or other body parts. Finally, attention involves awareness; you must be able to concentrate, perhaps to the exclusion of everything else, to comprehend fully the meaning of the incoming sensory information.

Attentional resources are limited, however. You might have sufficient resources to perform two or more easy perceptual tasks at once, especially if each involves a different sensory system. For example, you can simultaneously attend to the movements of dancers and the sounds of a band without missing either. But a very difficult task might require all of your attentional resources, making it impossible to do other tasks—especially those that employ the same sensory system—at the same time.

◄ *The cocktail-party effect.*

Suppose you're at a party and everyone is talking in small groups all at once. Sounds from many different voices enter your ears at the same time. If you were to put a microphone where your head is and record the pattern of sounds reaching your ears on a sound spectrograph, you would see a very complex acoustical pattern. There would be many voice prints—each with a characteristic timbre, pitch, and loudness, and each located at a particular point in the room. In these difficult circumstances, it would not be possible to hear and understand fully all the conversations impinging on your ears. But your attentional resources do allow you to focus on a particular voice, even one that was soft relative to the others. And your attending ability lets you pick out a particular voice you want to hear. This selective attention effect is often called the cocktail party phenomenon, because as at a cocktail party, there are many conversations going on simultaneously, and you must choose where to direct your attention. Because of limitations on the capacity of attention, however, only one voice at a time can be processed for meaning. When you try to listen to two voices at once, you miss much of both (Moray, 1959; Posner, 1980). Whatever you get out of two simultaneous conversations is not accomplished by processing the information in a parallel, simultaneous fashion, but rather by rapidly switching attention from one voice to another, and filling in by guessing what you missed.

Nonetheless, the information contained in unattended voices or other sources of stimulation is not entirely neglected. Even when you concentrate on a single source, some unattended stimuli can get through. For example, if you are listening to one speaker, your attention can sometimes be diverted by a second voice mentioning some particularly significant word. People often tune in when they catch their name being mentioned in another conversation. Another example is that of a sleeping parent who will awaken at a baby's soft cry but who will be totally oblivious to other, louder noises. The practical result of this is that you can usually feel comfortable concentrating your attention on a single, primary task, knowing that important background information will not be entirely missed.

Despite their limitations and the difficulty of attending to all the stimuli that impinge on us, our senses are our access to the world, our peepholes into the environment. Relative to even the most sophisticated technological artifacts, such as the Mars Rover, human beings are rich in senses; we have wall-to-wall sensory systems. And when we are deprived of any of our senses, the others often become more acute, to make up for the loss of information from the damaged or nonworking sense. Research on perception has a wide variety of applications. Perception researchers use their methodological tools to assess sensory capabilities and to diagnose sensory impairments. Applications of research on perceptual processes range from the development of automobile dashboards and street signs, to training air traffic controllers and pilots, to enabling people who are blind to use computers, to enabling those who are deaf to hear, to designing virtual reality experiences.

Sensation and perception enable human beings to get information from the outside world as well as from inside the body. For human beings, vision is arguably the most important sense, but the other senses (especially hearing) are also vital sources of input from the environment. It might be useful to pause at this point and ponder the kinds of stimuli we can detect, the kinds of sensations they create, and the kinds of information we can extract from them. It's a mind-boggling array. And it is the reason we can learn and know the things that we do. In the next chapter, we will examine the ways in which we can change our behavior and knowledge through learning.

KEY TERMS

proximal stimulus

distal stimulus

absolute threshold

difference threshold

signal detection theory

retina

accommodation

rods

cones

fovea

receptive field

feature detectors

visual acuity

dark adaptation

color deficiency

brightness contrast

bottom-up processing

top-down processing

Prägnanz

monocular cue

binocular cue

Objectives Revisited

Behavior begins with receiving and interpreting the things that are happening around us. We could not respond, interact, or understand without stimulation. Information about our internal and external environments is received and interpreted by sensory and perceptual systems. These are psychological processes that reflect a combination of "bottom up" and "top down" processing, such that what we perceive reflects incoming sensory data as well as our previous experience. There is a lot more to behavior, of course, than just sensing and perceiving, but this is where it all begins.

Objective 1. Describe sensory systems and the chain of events from stimulus input to conscious perception.

Sensation and *perception* are the processes by which we receive and interpret information about the outside world. A proximal stimulus is sensed when it activates sense organs, which convert this sensation into neural impulses. Each sensory system includes three basic components: specialized cells called receptors, specific nerve pathways from the receptors to the brain, and particular brain regions where sensory information is processed. Sensory receptors convert physical energy such as light, sound, chemical, thermal, and pressure stimuli into electrical impulses that the nervous system can understand. Perception is the processing that follows receptor activity, that involves some higher-level cognitive functions of the organism, and that results in the meaning we attach to the stimulus. These two types of processes actively work together to produce a conscious experience of both the external physical world and the internal biological world.

Objective 2. Discuss the physical and sensory processes involved in seeing.

The human eye is sensitive to electromagnetic energy, called *light*, ranging in wavelength from about 400 to 760 nm. The eye is constructed much like a camera, forming an (inverted) image of the world on its rear surface, the *retina*. The retina contains four kinds of photoreceptors: the *rods*, which are very sensitive and function at low levels of light, and the three types of *cones*, which function at daylight levels of light and form the basis for color experiences.

Cones are located primarily in the center of the retina, in an area called the *fovea*. Rods are not found in the fovea and are more plentiful in the periphery of the retina. Rods and cones are connected to *bipolar cells*, which in turn connect to *ganglion cells* by means of a complex neural network. Each ganglion cell receives input from many rods and relatively fewer cones. The area of the retina (the collection of rods and/or cones) that influences a given ganglion cell is the *receptive field* of that ganglion cell.

The neural activity of the three types of cones is combined in the retina to form three neural channels of color information: a red-green opponent channel, a yellow-blue opponent channel, and a luminance (brightness) channel. All our color experiences result from various combinations of these three channels of information. The experience of color is based on three dimensions: hue, saturation, and brightness. *Hue* is the qualitative nature of the color; *saturation* is the purity of the color; and *brightness* is the dimension that ranges from black to white.

Cells of the visual cortex (called *feature detectors*) provide the first stages of pattern or object perception. These cortical cells tend to be sensitized to particular types of stimuli, such as horizontal lines, edges, and curves. These cortical cells are stimulated by incoming features sensed at the receptor. The combination of several kinds of cortical cells aroused by the incoming stimulation provides the basis for pattern recognition.

Objective 3. Explain what is meant by bottom-up and top-down processes, and discuss how these processes are illustrated in visual object and depth perception.

Perception is a combination of top-down and bottom-up processing. *Bottom-up processing* operates on the incoming sensory data received by the various sensory receptors. *Top-down processing* reflects one's experience and expectations, and is influenced by one's sociocultural history and environment. Neural network models are an attempt to explain how top-down and bottom-up processes might influence each other and result in a particular perception.

Gestalt principles describe how stimulus features are organized into whole and meaningful object perceptions. The basic principle is called *Prägnanz*, or "goodness of figure." Other Gestalt principles are *proximity*, *similarity*, and *closure*.

Two classes of cues are important to perceiving depth, those requiring both eyes (*binocular cues*) and those requiring one eye (*monocular cues*). Skilled artists can use certain monocular cues to give the viewer a realistic, three-dimensional perception of a two-dimensional canvas.

Perceptual constancies allow us to create and maintain a stable internal representation of an object even as the context, the orientation, and the physical characteristics of that object change. *Size constancy*, for example, refers to the process that allows us to see the same object as stable in size, despite our moving around and viewing it from different distances and angles. The tendency to maintain certain kinds of constancies varies cross-culturally, and members of different cultures may differ in their susceptibility to illusions.

Objective 4. Discuss the physical, physiological, and perceptual processes involved in hearing.

The physical stimulus for hearing is vibration or *sound waves* that travel through some medium, usually the air. Physical sound is described by its intensity, frequency, and complexity. The inner ear converts sound waves into neural impulses that vary on three psychological dimensions: loudness (amplitude), pitch (frequency), and timbre (complexity).

Objective 5. Discuss the physiological and perceptual processes involved in the other human senses: sensing bodily position and movement, touch, smell, and taste.

We are capable of sensing the position and movement of our bodies and various bodily parts in space, even without vision or hearing. Two sensory systems are instrumental in accomplishing this awareness: the *kinesthetic sense*, which is mediated by receptors spread throughout the body, and the *vestibular sense*, which has receptors in the semicircular canals next to the cochlea in the inner ear.

Four experiences based on contact between the skin and an object constitute the sense of touch: *pressure*, *pain*, *warmth*, and *cold*. These four experiences are mediated by specialized nerve endings (receptors) under the surface of the skin.

Taste and *smell* are interrelated senses that depend on the absorption of chemical molecules in solution or in gaseous form by receptors on the tongue and in the nose. Taste experiences vary along the dimensions of *salty*, *sweet*, *bitter*, and *sour*. Smell experiences are more widely variable and contribute to communication in some species and to the detection of food, danger, and mates.

interposition

texture gradients

linear perspective

motion parallax

binocular disparity

perceptual constancy

perceptual illusion

brightness constancy

size constancy

cochlea

basilar membrane

semicircular canals

loudness

pitch

timbre

kinesthetic sense

vestibular sense

free nerve endings

passive touch

active touch

taste buds

olfactory epithelium

pheromones

C H A P T E R 6

Learning

O B J E C T I V E S

After reading this chapter, you should be able to:

1. Distinguish among major forms of learning.
2. Describe the processes of acquisition, extinction, and spontaneous recovery in conditioning.
3. Define the law of contiguity, and describe how it relates to prepared learning.
4. Explain the law of effect and how it is elaborated in principles of reinforcement. Then describe positive and negative reinforcement, positive and negative punishment, and schedules of reinforcement.
5. Distinguish between discrimination and generalization, and explain how conditioning processes might result in superstitious behavior and learned helplessness.
6. Define cognitive learning, and explain why psychologists believe cognitive processes play an important role in classical and operant conditioning.

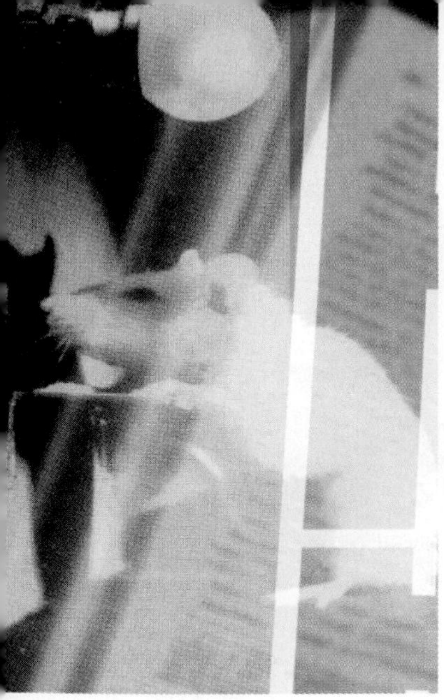

What is a kiss? Do you think kissing between lovers is "natural," that is, biologically determined? In Western society, the "deep kiss" (also known as the French kiss, soul kiss, and tongue kiss) seems "natural" enough. In the words of sexologist Leonore Tiefer, "To a European who associates deep kisses with erotic response, the idea of one without the other seems like the summer without the sun" (Tiefer, 1995, p. 77).

But the "natural" act of kissing is not found in all cultures. Erotica in China and Japan has graphically and creatively portrayed sexual positions, partners, and settings in all their variety, but kissing isn't a part of the picture. Indeed, only in the twentieth century did the Japanese create a word for kissing—*kissu*—which is clearly based on its English equivalent. The meaning of a kiss across cultures and over time varies widely: from a passionate act to a simple sign of respect, from an expression of friendship to a threat to health. The Thonga, of Africa, when they first saw Europeans kissing, found the act disgusting, something akin to "eating each other's saliva and dirt" (Tiefer, 1995, p. 78).

Within a culture, not every individual expresses affection in the same way. In our society, kissing is considered a sign of affection, but individuals differ as to who, how, and what they will kiss. For example, some people kiss relatives and friends on the lips, while others confine such kisses to cheeks. Some people hug their family members, while kissing the air, reserving actual lip contact for lovers. Some kisses involve only the pressing of lips; others engage tongues. These individual differences come about to some degree because of the different ways we have been raised and have been taught to respond to others. The great diversity in the meaning and practice of kissing across and within cultures is just one example of the profound influence of learning on behavior.

Learning principles seem to be at the heart of much of the cultural and individual diversity in the meaning and expression of affection. Learning is the mechanism by which we form attachments, are socialized, and acquire the values, norms, and knowledge of a culture—whether they are related to interpersonal interaction (such as kissing norms), intellectual develop-

► *What is the meaning of a kiss? In some cases (left) it is an obvious expression of affection. But the kiss between Mikhail Gorbachev and Erich Honecker (right) has a vastly different meaning.*

▲ *Learning, a fundamental psychological process, underlies a wide variety of human behavior.*

ment (such as language and mathematics), work, or other forms of behavior.

The survival of all living creatures depends on their ability to adapt to changes in their environments. Evolution is one mechanism of change that enables organisms to adapt to and survive in new environments. But evolutionary changes occur slowly over many thousands of years. These are the kinds of changes that permit an entire class or species of animals to adjust to an environmental niche. Evolution accounts for why some animals live on land and others live in the sea, for why some animals can fly and others are earthbound, for why human beings walk on two feet, while other creatures walk on four. If we had to rely on evolution, however, there would be no modern world as we know it. There would be no computers or internet; no automobiles or airplanes. The modern world requires a kind of knowledge and skills that evolution simply cannot produce. To create and survive in the shifting, day-to-day environment of the modern world, we need to be able to make quick changes. We need a way to interact rapidly and flexibly with the technology that surrounds us. The mechanism that serves this purpose is called ***learning***, a fundamental psychological process that permits quick adaptation to new or changing situations. While the ability to learn exists in varying degrees in all animal species, it reaches its peak in human beings and is reflected in the intellectual and artistic aspects of the cultures human beings have created. Learning is so fundamental to understanding human behavior that all branches of psychology, from behavioral neuroscience to psychotherapeutic practice, rely heavily on its principles. This chapter concentrates on the simplest and most basic learning processes that can be found in nearly all organisms. Chapters 7 and 8 will discuss more complex learning principles, including those that entail long-term memory and employ language, thinking, and other cognitive processes.

Learning and Behavior: Basic Concepts

What qualifies as learning? First, all learning involves a *change in mental state or behavior*—either in what we know or in what we are able to do. But the change is of a special kind. It is stable and long-lasting, resulting from experience and/or practice, not a temporary change resulting from fatigue, injury, illness, or any other transitory state, nor from natural biological processes such as growth or maturation.

Learning is a relatively permanent change in an organism's mental representation of and potential to behave in its environment, resulting from experience and/or practice.

What do we learn? Some learning is primar-

▲ *A complex activity such as driving involves all three types of learning: perceptual (learning to judge distances), response-based (learning to coordinate hand and foot movement to shift gears), and cognitive (learning the rules of the road).*

ily *perceptual* and is based on sensory discriminations, like learning to identify figures in photographs or differences among tastes of wine or types of music. Some learning is *response-based*, like learning to raise a hand before answering a question or acquiring the new motor skills to dance or play a video game or drive a car. Still other learning is essentially *cognitive* and might not rely on direct experience or practice, like learning the fact that the phrase "the real McCoy" originally referred to the excellent quality of the products of the black inventor, Elijah McCoy. We need to keep in mind that learning takes a variety of forms and that some kinds of learning are more complex than others.

Psychologists distinguish among the various kinds of learning. They study relatively reflex-like learning processes, for example, how an infant learns to control the startle response that is initially triggered by a loud bell. They study how animals and people can learn to connect stimuli and responses in new ways. This may be through associating a neutral stimulus with a particular response, such as when your pet dog associates the sound of a can opener with feeding time. Or it may involve a person or animal acquiring a new behavior in order to be rewarded; for example, a child learning to share toys and treats with a friend in order to be praised for doing so. Psychologists also study learning that is more complex and that involves learning skills or facts or ideas. This may be based on observing as much as on responding. It is the kind of learning that occurs when you listen to a lecture, study a textbook, or watch your piano teacher demonstrate the fingering of a complicated passage.

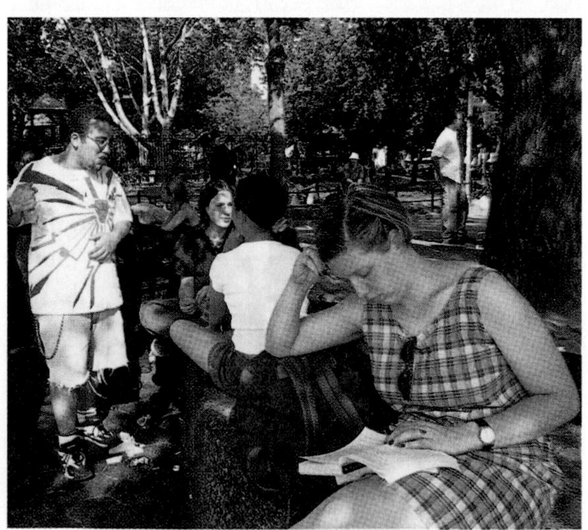

► *This woman, absorbed in her book, has habituated to the activity and noise going on around her.*

THINKING CRITICALLY

We introduced the concept of sensory adaptation in Chapter 5. The eyes, for example, adapt to the level of illumination that surrounds them. The sense of smell can adapt in time to foul odors. But is sensory adaptation the same thing as habituation?

Although some sensory adaptation might be involved in habituation, these two psychological processes are different. For one thing, sensory adaptation depends on the continuous presence of a stimulus. Once the stimulus is removed or changed, the sensory system returns to its original state. Habituation persists long after the stimulus ceases. For another, sensory adaptation takes place largely in the receptors of the system, while habituation involves the whole organism, including the nervous system. Can you think of other possible differences?

Habituation and Imprinting

The simplest form of learning, ***habituation***, is exhibited by just about all organisms, including the newborn human infant (Rovee-Collier, 1987). Habituation occurs when repeated stimulation causes decreased responsiveness to that stimulus. The organism learns essentially that nothing significant hinges on the occurrence of the stimulus and ceases gradually to respond to the stimulus. Suppose you moved to a new apartment near an airport or next to a railroad. At first, the loud noises would draw your attention, especially at night, and possibly interrupt your sleep. You have built-in mechanisms that cause you to become alert to unexpected or unfamiliar sounds or sights, just in case they signal danger. Over time, however, you will cease to notice these noises; you will learn that these sounds are not danger signals and that no avoidance or any other kind of response is necessary. The sounds are filtered out of your conscious awareness as you habituate to them. You can, however, hear them if they are brought to your attention. Can you identify stimuli in your own life to which you have habituated? Habituation has survival value because it isn't productive to respond to everything going on in your environment. A learning mechanism that sorts out stimuli having no consequences for you leaves you freer to pay attention and respond to things in the world that do have consequences. Of course, what is important, potentially useful, or potentially dangerous, and what can be ignored depend on your circumstances. City dwellers habituate to the ever-present machine-produced noises around them. Bedouins in the desert habituate to camel-beying.

Another rudimentary type of learning is ***imprinting***. Imprinting refers to the attachment that young animals form with other larger organisms in their surroundings. Konrad Lorenz (1952) demonstrated that, shortly after hatching, Greylag geese form an attachment to any moving object if they have been separated from their mother. Some Greylag geese even became imprinted on Lorenz himself! The learning that is represented by imprinting is quite specific to attachment relationships and occurs only during a critical early period of development. Such an attachment is important to the young animal's survival because the infant is very likely to need a larger animal to protect it from predators. Because imprinting occurs nearly universally within a species under the right circumstances, it appears to be a kind of learning that organisms are biologically prepared for. Further, once an attachment is made, it is difficult to break. Nonetheless, all early attachments do eventually change in time, as the individual matures, and so an inappropriate attachment to Lorenz does not condemn the young geese to a disturbed adulthood! Do human beings show imprinting during critical periods of development? This is a controversial issue.

◀ *Imprinting is a form of learning that depends on a critical period of development in which an animal forms a strong association between a response and a particular stimulus. Here greylag geese—who typically react to their mother goose with a following response—have learned instead to follow ethologist Konrad Lorenz.*

Associative Learning

The processes of ***associative learning*** are more flexible or less mechanical than the first two types of learning. Associative learning underlies the formation of relationships between environmental stimuli and responses to those stimuli. Almost any stimulus and response can be associated in this way, and the relationships that are formed between them are somewhat arbitrary. For example, a former high school basketball player described how before the beginning of a game while the band played the school's fight song, the players would wait behind the stands—hearts pounding, muscles tense—primed to run onto the court to the roar of the crowd at the song's end. Even as a college student, three years later, he couldn't hear the song without "getting a rush" that included a vivid memory of the experience combined with pounding heart and tense muscles. He had formed a strong association (relationship or connection) with the song and the sights and sounds of the basketball court; this was a clear case of associative learning. Stimulus and response can be connected through experience in a variety of ways, such that when the stimulus (or the thought or anticipation of the stimulus)

◀ *Because the fans have worn cheeseheads during emotion-filled Green Bay Packers games, does that mean these Green Bay Packers (pictured here on* The Tonight Show *after their 1997 Super Bowl win) will have a conditioned emotional response when they themselves don cheeseheads?*

occurs, the response follows, and this connection is relatively permanent. The two types of associative learning are classical conditioning and operant conditioning, which we will discuss in detail shortly.

Cognitive Learning

Before we begin a more detailed discussion of associative learning and conditioning, we need to make note of an even more complex form of learning, called ***cognitive learning***. Cognitive learning is probably the most common way human beings learn. Unlike associative learning, which can take place without your even knowing it, cognitive learning requires attention, focus, and consciousness. Cognitive learning is the learning of new skills, facts, and ideas. Learning to drive an automobile, learning a language, native or foreign, learning about psychology, and learning your way around the Internet are all good examples of cognitive learning. Cognitive learning is based on observing, remembering, and imitating. It is the kind of learning that takes place when you receive instruction, read a book, or watch a skilled mechanic repair some complicated equipment.

Classical Conditioning

In classical conditioning, a subject learns to respond to a formerly neutral stimulus as a result of repeated pairing of that stimulus with an unconditioned stimulus that elicits a reflexive, unconditioned response.

Infants of all cultures cry in response to pain. The association of pain with crying does not have to be learned. Consider Manny, an infant on his first visit to a doctor for a vaccination. A happy baby, he doesn't cry when he sees the doctor pick up the hypodermic needle. This soon changes, however, for the injection hurts and makes him cry. After that, he immediately cries at the sight of the doctor or any needle. Manny's crying demonstrates classical conditioning, a process that in this example builds on the unlearned association of crying in response to pain.

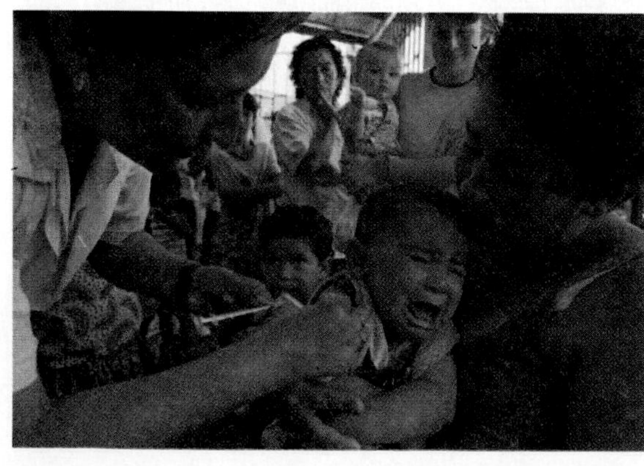

▶ *Regardless of culture, as long as doctors, nurses, and injection needles (conditioned stimulus) occur in conjunction with pain (unconditioned stimulus), children will learn to fear them.*

Stimuli and Responses

In ***classical conditioning***, a new, formerly neutral, stimulus (for example, sight of a doctor or a needle) acquires the ability to produce a response (for example, crying) that was originally produced in an automatic way by some other stimulus (for example, pain from the injection). Note that the response is not really "new"—the organism is already able to perform it. What's new is the association between the response and the new stimulus. Does the sight of a barbecue grill cause you to salivate? Does a picture of spoiled meat make you feel nauseous? If so, you have experienced classical conditioning.

Classical conditioning builds on the innate reflexes that you learned about in Chapter 3—these are unlearned associations between stimuli and responses. Because these initial associations are natural or inborn, they are called unconditioned. Unlearned responses are thus called ***unconditioned responses (UR)***, and the stimuli that produce them are called ***unconditioned stimuli (US)***. Their relationship, which is called an ***unconditioned reflex***, is typically represented as US-UR. In addition to crying and withdrawal behavior in response to pain, unconditioned responses include salivation in response to food, nausea in response to poisons, fear in response to perceived threats, shivering in response to cold, and coughing in response to a throat tickle, among many others.

Learning to respond to a formerly neutral stimulus is the essence of classical conditioning. It comes about as the result of repeatedly pairing the neutral stimulus with a stimulus that naturally produces a reflexive response. The choice of the neutral stimulus can vary, particularly when conditioning human beings, who are quite flexible in the associations they can learn. In fact, in the example above, Manny may not only cry at the sight of the needle or the doctor, he may cry at the sight of the doctor's office!

The Russian physiologist Ivan Petrovich Pavlov (1849–1936) discovered the principles of classical conditioning when he observed that his experimental subjects—dogs—unexpectedly learned to salivate to various laboratory sights and sounds in anticipation of being fed (see Figure 6-1). His original experiment on this process illustrates the three steps in classical conditioning. First, before conditioning occurred, the dog salivated only when food was placed in its mouth (dogs, like most mammals, salivate reflexively to the taste of food). The food was an unconditioned stimulus (US) that elicited an unconditioned response (UR), salivation. The sound of a bell was a neutral stimulus that initially didn't affect salivation. To condition the dog so that it would salivate at the sound of a neutral stimulus, Pavlov sounded a bell and presented the unconditioned stimulus (US) ***contiguously*** (close together in space and time) and repeatedly (although one presentation can be sufficient for learning under some circumstances). The repeated pairings of the neutral stimulus and the unconditioned stimulus are called ***conditioning trials***. On each classical conditioning trial, the neutral stimulus is typically presented first, and the US follows close behind. Typically, the learned response of salivation to the sound of the bell emerges gradually over many trials.

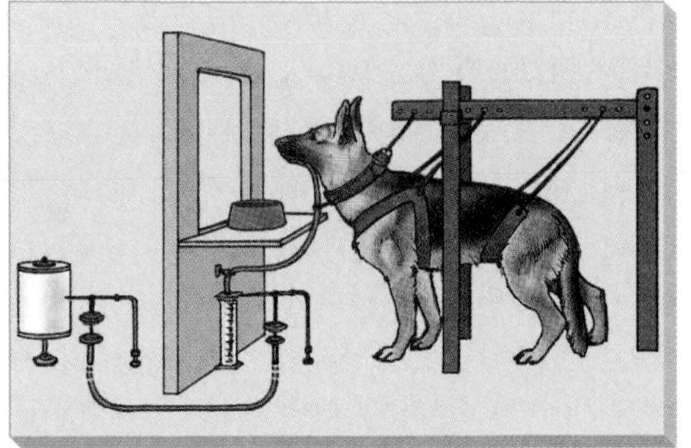

6-1 Pavlov's Apparatus

Pavlov placed a dog in a harness, with a tube in its mouth so that saliva could be collected. The amount of saliva secreted was recorded by a pen on a revolving drum.

Pavlov found that, after conditioning, the dog salivated in response to the neutral stimulus alone. The bell had become a ***conditioned stimulus (CS)*** that elicited salivation on its own. Pavlov called this salivary response, which mimicked the unconditioned response, the ***conditioned response (CR)***. He called the new relationship or association between a previously neutral stimulus and a learned response a ***conditioned reflex***, and he represented it as CS-CR. The new CR and the old UR were similar in Pavlov's experiment but not identical. The amount of salivation was greater for the UR than for the CR, and the CR occurred in antici-

In the conditioning framework, an unconditioned stimulus (US) is a stimulus that automatically and reliably elicits the same unconditioned response (UR) each time it is presented. A conditioned stimulus (CS) is a formerly neutral stimulus that comes to elicit a conditioned response (CR) after it has been repeatedly paired with the US.

THINKING CRITICALLY

Now that you know about classical conditioning, can you explain why some diet books tell dieters to confine eating to a particular place, such as a table in a particular room, and not in front of the television?

If you answered that eating in front of the television might result in the television becoming a conditioned stimulus that will elicit the conditioned response of eating, you have mastered the essential concept of classical conditioning. What starts out as a harmless indulgence—a little snack while watching the game—can become a near compulsion—"Every time I think of watching TV I get hungry." Dieters are often advised to confine their eating to a particular place to prevent high frequency neutral cues in their environment (such as the TV, their desk, their psychology textbook) from becoming associated with eating.

◀ Ivan Pavlov is credited with discovering classical conditioning, a process by which a dog in his laboratory learned to salivate at the sound of a bell as a result of experiencing repeated pairings of the bell with the presentation of food. Here Dr. Pavlov is shown observing his assistant and one of his research subjects at work.

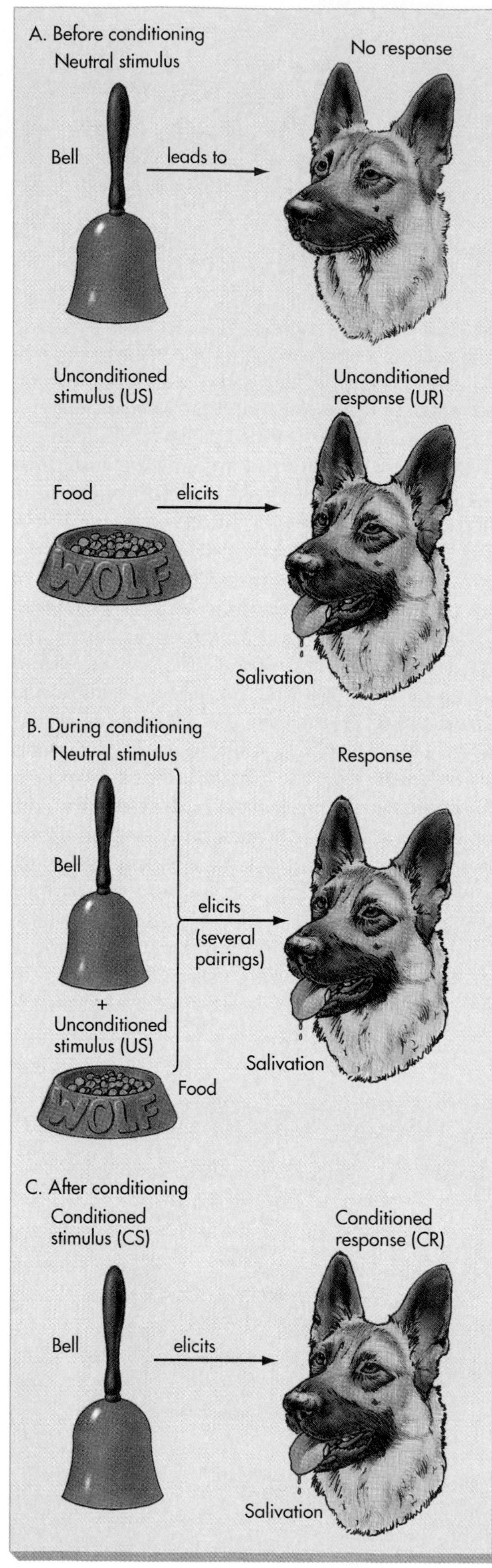

6-2 The Steps of Classical Conditioning

Before conditioning, food (US) elicits salivation but the bell (neutral stimulus) does not. During conditioning, the bell and food are presented contiguously over many trials. Eventually, the dog comes to salivate (CR) to the bell (which has now become a CS).

pation of the US. A CR is always adaptive and serves the organism's needs in some way (here, the CR of anticipatory salivation prepared the dog for food in its mouth). Figure 6-2 presents a summary of the steps of classical conditioning.

The eye blink is an unconditioned response commonly used in experimental studies of human classical conditioning. With the cooperation of a willing friend, use the eye blink response to try out these new concepts. The US is a light puff of air (blown *gently* through a straw at the eye of your friend). The puff will regularly and forcefully elicit an eye blink (the UR). The eye blink response can readily be conditioned to a neutral stimulus, for example, a tap on the table. Begin the conditioning process by pairing the CS (table tap) with the US (air puff). The CS should occur slightly in advance of the US. Periodically test for the occurrence of a CR by presenting the CS alone without the air puff. If and when your friend blinks to the formerly neutral stimulus (table tap) alone, he or she has acquired (learned to make) a CR.

Acquisition, Extinction, and Spontaneous Recovery

A conditioned reflex (CS-CR) is a learned association between a conditioned stimulus (CS) and a conditioned response (CR). ***Acquisition*** is the term psychologists use to refer to this learning process. Acquisition usually requires repeatedly pairing an unconditioned stimulus (US) with a conditioned stimulus (CS) to strengthen the conditioned reflex. It generally takes place gradually over a series of experiences or trials. Thus, acquisition is reflected in changes in the strength of the CR, which moves from zero (or close to zero) strength to some maximal level over several trials. CR strength can be measured in a number of ways, including response amplitude (for example, the amount of saliva produced) and response latency (the time it takes to make the CR after the CS has been presented). Usually, response strength will increase rapidly on the early conditioning trials, but improvement will slow down later and finally will level off (reach a plateau), at which point conditioning is said to be complete. These changes in response strength can be represented graphically as a ***learning curve*** (see Figure 6-3, panel A).

THINKING CRITICALLY

Have you ever experienced the resurgence of a fear or anxiety that you long ago thought you had conquered? If you have ever smoked cigarettes, you may have felt the craving for nicotine reappear, even after an extended period of abstinence. Can you explain these phenomena in terms of classical conditioning?

Conceivably, these and other examples of the reappearance of old habits or feelings are attributable to the process of spontaneous recovery. Old habits might never completely die. Cigarette smoking can be extinguished, but the underlying conditioned reflex might still survive. Understanding the phenomenon of spontaneous recovery can help you deal with learned emotions and behaviors that reappear just when you think you are rid of them. In therapy, patients need to understand that unwanted behavior or former feelings of anger or anxiety are very likely to return. They should not be discouraged by what appear to be setbacks. Such recurrence is temporary and to be expected on the basis of what we know about spontaneous recovery. But, if you believe you have conquered a fear and it returns, remember that extinction should be even easier the next time.

Once Pavlov's dog has acquired a conditioned reflex [bell (CS)–salivate (CR)] food (the original US) can be omitted, at least for a while, and the dog will continue to salivate at the sound of the bell. But if food is never again given to the animal in conjunction with the bell, the conditioned reflex (CS-CR association) will eventually weaken. Repeated ringing of the bell will eventually cease to elicit saliva flow if it is never again paired with food. This weakening of the association between CS and CR in the absence of the US is called ***extinction***. Eventually, the CS will no longer elicit the CR, and extinction will appear to be complete. After extinction, repeated presentation of the CS, whatever it may be (in this case, the bell), will have no impact—it will now be a neutral stimulus once again.

Acquisition refers to the rise in CR strength during conditioning.

Extinction is the weakening of a conditioned reflex by presenting the CS repeatedly and unaccompanied by the US.

But wait a minute! Have you ever had a resurgence of feelings for an "old flame" you thought you had long since forgotten (extinguished)? The person or the thought of that person (stimulus) still has the power to produce an emotional reaction (response) in you, even if years have passed since your last contact. Or have you had a resurgence of anxiety (response) at the thought or appearance of an old enemy (stimulus) after returning to the scene of your encounters? This reappearance of a conditioned response to a conditioned stimulus after extinction and the passage of time is called ***spontaneous recovery***. You can demonstrate it yourself. Start by conditioning a person to blink his or her eyes (CR) when you tap the table (CS), as described above. To extinguish the CR (eye blink to the tap) all you have to do is to tap the table repeatedly without delivering the puff of air. Soon, the tap no longer elicits an eye blink. Now wait a day and try again. Tap the table

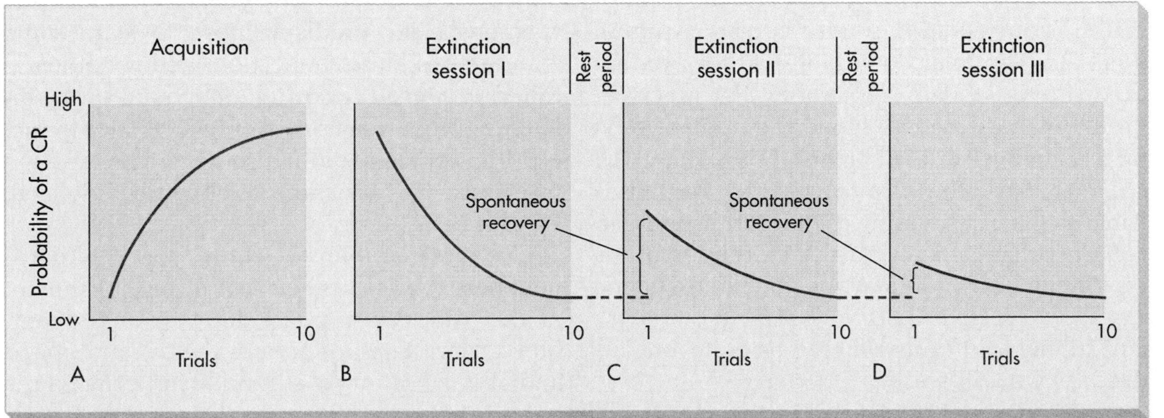

6-3 The Acquisition-Extinction-Spontaneous Recovery Sequence

An illustration of three fundamental aspects of classical conditioning: acquisition, extinction, and spontaneous recovery. (A) During acquisition trials, when the conditioned stimulus (CS) and unconditioned stimulus (US) are paired, the conditioned response (CR) is strengthened, represented by a rising curve. (B) When the CS is presented alone during extinction, the response weakens, represented by a falling curve. (C) After a rest period, without any additional exposure to either the US or the CS, there is a rebound effect, known as spontaneous recovery. The response spontaneously recovers, although at a lower level than at its strongest point during acquisition. With continued presentation of the CS, however, the response again weakens, and the curve falls once again. (D) The amount of spontaneous recovery decreases with each succeeding extinction session.

Spontaneous recovery is the reappearance of a previously extinguished CR resulting from the passage of time after extinction.

and observe what happens. Typically, the person will blink, demonstrating that the CS-CR connection was not completely eliminated by extinction. The person shows spontaneous recovery of the previously "extinguished" CR.

After spontaneous recovery, you can extinguish the CR once again by repeatedly tapping the table without the puff of air. Wait another few days; try it again; and again the CR may spontaneously reappear, although with somewhat reduced strength (it may take a bit longer to elicit it, for example). To get rid of a conditioned response altogether, you often have to repeat the extinction process several times, allowing for spontaneous recovery between each session. In time, the CR will stop, but it typically takes much longer to extinguish a response than it does to acquire it in the first place. Also, the conditioned reflex can be reestablished, that is, reconditioned quite rapidly. Only a few "refresher" trials, pairing the CS and the US once again, are needed to bring the conditioned reflex back to its original strength. What does this tell you about how hard it is to break habits? Long-term extinction of habits is extremely difficult to accomplish.

In general, classical conditioning occurs most readily when the CS and the US are close together, both in space and in time, with the CS preceding the US.

Law of Contiguity

In general, for classical conditioning to take place, the CS and the US must occur reasonably close together, both in space and in time, with the CS preceding the US. This is the ***law of contiguity***. Pavlov argued that stimuli activate brain areas (different areas for different stimuli) and that closeness in time permits some sort of interaction between activated areas, providing a basis for the connection that occurs during conditioning. There is growing evidence that Pavlov was on the right track (Krupa, Thompson, & Thompson, 1993). For any pair of stimuli, there is an optimal CS-US interval for producing learning, usually quite brief. For quick reflexes, such as the eye blink, the optimal time interval between the CS and the US is about 0.5 seconds. For other, more complex responses (such as the conditioning of the fear response in a car accident), the optimal CS-US interval for producing learning may be longer. In some cases, where the gastrointestinal tract is involved, the CS-US interval can be quite long indeed, as we will see.

Drawing by John Chase.

Prepared Learning

Taste aversions are a common experience. Consider, for example, a taste aversion to shrimp. Perhaps you initially loved to eat shrimp, but one day you got sick after eating some. As a result, you came to dislike the taste of shrimp, even though chances are that the shrimp had nothing to do with your getting sick. Why is food so easily associated with intestinal ills? In one experiment, rats were irradiated with X-rays (US) while they drank a sweet solution (CS). Rats normally prefer a sweet solution over unflavored water, but the X-rays made them sick (UR). After several pairings of CS and US, the animals became sick (CR) at the taste and smell of the sweet solution alone, even when no X-rays were given. Thus, the rats developed a conditioned aversion (strong learned dislike) to sweet water (Revusky, 1968). In a follow-up experiment, the experimenter repeated the same conditioning procedure but added a time interval of up to seven hours between the CS and the US so that the two stimuli were no longer contiguous. In other words, the rats drank the sweet water and were irradiated up to seven hours later. Even with such a long interval between the CS and the US, the rats still showed evidence of developing a dislike for the solution. This is highly unusual in classical conditioning which, in most cases, requires close temporal contiguity between the CS and US. Thus, there is something about powerful, illness-producing stimuli, about taste-related responses, or about the way the gastrointestinal system works that can extend the law of contiguity to very long intervals.

The fact that taste aversions are so readily conditioned suggests that some stimuli and responses might be more likely to be conditioned than others. The idea that there are species-specific predispositions to learn some stimulus-response connections and not others is called ***prepared learning*** (Seligman, 1971). Biological preparedness not only facilitates the acquisition process, but it also heightens the CR's resistance to extinction (Lovibond, Siddle, & Bond, 1993).

The work of John Garcia is especially pertinent here. Garcia argued that the establishment of a conditioned response depends on the combined characteristics of both the unconditioned and the conditioned stimuli. This principle is nicely illustrated in experiments by Garcia and Koelling (1966). In one experiment, they presented rats with a conditioned stimulus that consisted of a sweet-tasting solution, plus a light and a noise. The light and the noise were presented whenever a rat licked a tube containing a sweet solution. For some rats, the exposure to the "sweet-bright-noisy-water" was followed by X-ray that induced nausea. For other rats, the exposure to the "sweet-bright-noisy-water" was followed by an electric shock delivered to the paws. Both the shock and the nausea are USs that the rats would normally avoid. After a number of CS-US pairings, the rats were tested to determine what they had learned. In particular, did they associate the shock or their illness to the sweet taste, to the light, to the noise, or to the whole package? The design of this experiment is portrayed in Figure 6-4.

What the animal learned depended on what happened to the rat after drinking. The rats who were made nauseous after drinking the sweet-bright-noisy-water formed a conditioned aversion to the sweet taste, but not to the light or the noise. They resisted drinking a sweet solution. But they readily drank unsweetened water, even when the light and noise were present. Thus, their conditioned response was associated with the sweet taste, but not with the visual or auditory stimuli that were presented with it during conditioning. In contrast, the rats that received an electric shock to the paws following the CS formed a conditioned aversion to the light and noise, but not to the sweet taste. They drank the sweet solution when it was available alone, but would not drink anything in the presence of the light and noise. This suggests that the rats associated nasty gastrointestinal consequences (nausea) with taste stimuli while they associated the pain from electric shock to the paws with external stimuli such as lights and sounds. The rats, and by extension, perhaps all animals, seem to be prepared to associate certain classes of stimuli with certain outcomes. Stimuli involving seeing and hearing are more readily conditioned to "save your skin" responses, while stimuli involving taste and smell are more readily conditioned to "protect your gut" responses.

Studies of human infants also suggest preparedness for learning some types of behaviors more easily than others. Babies easily smile back when an adult smiles at them. Babies also seem prepared to detect ***contingencies*** (relationships) between their actions and changes in the environment (Watson & Ramey, 1972). Thus, a baby might learn that whether a caregiver will smile is contingent on (dependent on) whether or not the baby smiles.

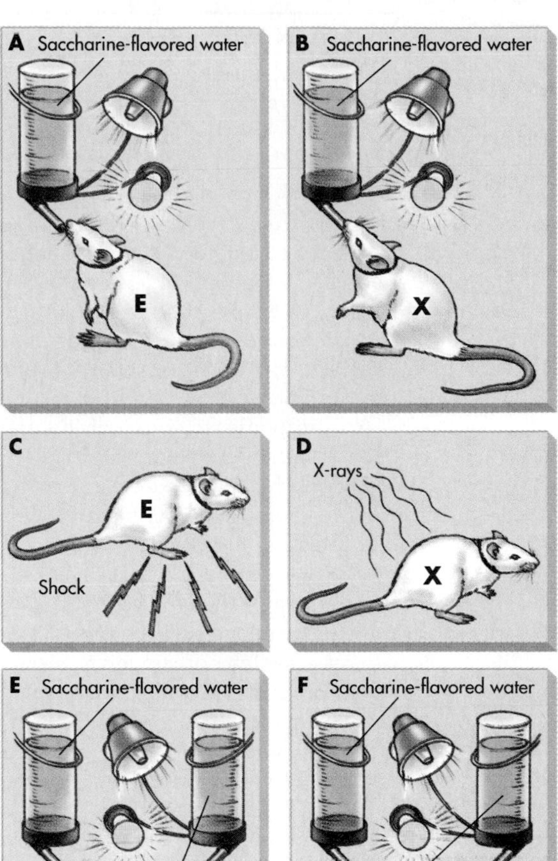

6-4 Prepared Learning

Establishing a conditioned response depends on the combined characteristics of both unconditioned and conditioned stimuli. Rats more easily learn the connection between (1) gastrointestinal illness and taste, and (2) pain to their paws and lights or sound (Source: Adapted from Garcia & Koelling, 1966)

Biological preparedness for learning is clearly an adaptive mechanism. Potentially harmful events are best avoided or quickly escaped. In nature, illness is usually caused by something that has been eaten, and injury is often caused by an external event (for example, a predator, a fall). Learning which foods or other animals or situations are threats to skin or gut is of considerable advantage to any creature. Built-in biological mechanisms that help rapid learning about these dangerous stimuli have major survival value.

We must be careful about generalizing about prepared learning from one species to another, however. For example, although human infants

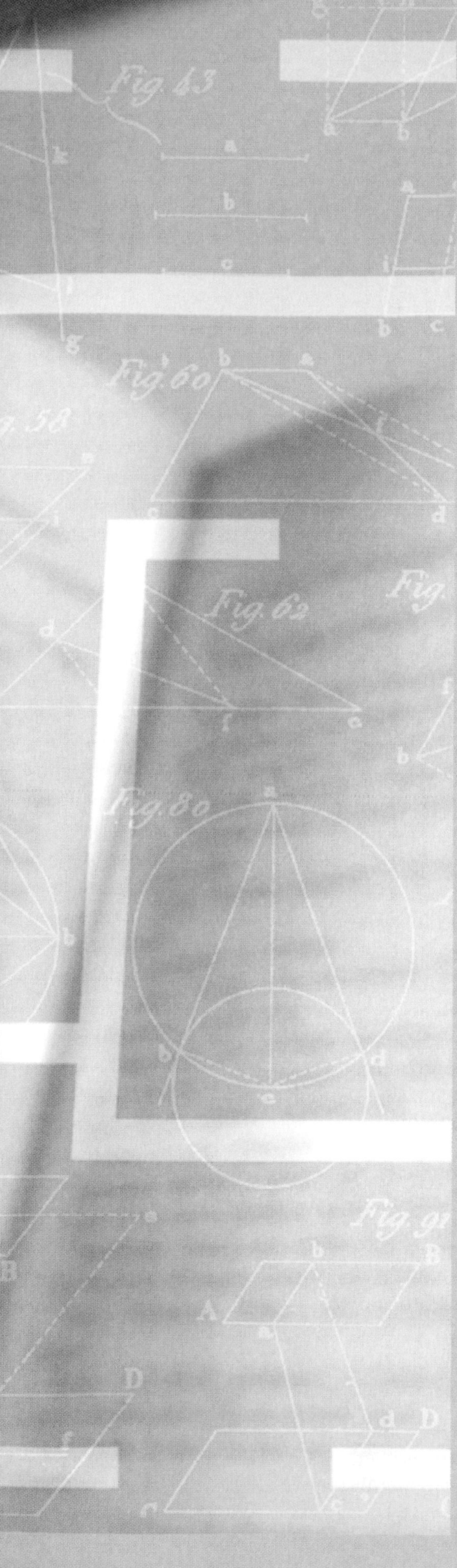

UNDERSTANDING HUMAN DIVERSITY

How Classical Conditioning Can Affect Your Attitudes Toward Others

Have you ever held a negative attitude toward someone, but when asked why you felt so negative, you couldn't really explain the source of your attitude? It may be that you have been classically conditioned to have a negative emotional reaction toward something about that person. Think about what is involved in classical conditioning: two events appear in rapid succession, with the second event eliciting some sort of response or reaction. Through the processes involved in classical conditioning, you can acquire negative responses toward individuals of varying ethnicity if they are paired with stimuli that already elicit those responses from you.

Your responses toward individuals of different ethnicities may even be physiological. Suppose you are shown slides of Chinese people just before you plunge your hand into ice cold water, which in turn causes your blood vessels to constrict. After several of these pairings, what will happen to your blood vessels when you see a picture of a Chinese person? Your blood vessels will constrict—no ice water will be necessary (Roessler & Brogden, 1943).

Not only can human beings make connections among concrete stimulus events—in the above example, among ice water, a picture, and a physiological response—they can also make associations between abstract ideas and emotional responses. For example, suppose you ask research participants to memorize and recall lists of words containing adjectives and names of various nationalities. Nothing is said about any connections between the words. One group reads lists in which "Swedish" is always followed by a negative word, such as "failure," "nasty," or "ugly," and "Dutch" is always followed by a positive word, such as "healthy," "pretty," or "nice." Another group reads similar lists, but with "Swedish" now followed by positive words and "Dutch" now followed by negative words. You then ask the students to tell you their feelings toward various nationalities. Arnold and Carolyn Staats (1958) used such a procedure to demonstrate that classical conditioning is at work in such a situation. In their study, the students liked the group that had been associated with the positive words better than the group that had been associated with the negative words.

Classical conditioning of attitudes can result even when stimuli involved are beyond our awareness. One study presented nine pictures of a woman going about her daily tasks, such as washing dishes, grocery shopping, and studying. Just before each of those pictures, another picture was presented so quickly that the student was not even aware of having seen it. In some cases, the picture was one associated with positive emotions, such as a group of smiling friends, a bridal couple, or a picture of a child with a Mickey Mouse doll. In other cases, the picture was associated with negative emotions, such as snakes or a dead body. The students were then asked about their attitudes toward the woman. Again, classical conditioning was found to be at work. Attitudes toward the women were positive or negative, depending on the type of picture that preceded the pictures of her—even though those pictures were presented so rapidly that they did not enter conscious awareness (Krosnick, Betz, Jussim, & Lynn, 1992).

These findings suggest how classical conditioning can play a role in shaping our attitudes toward members of various ethnic groups. As the authors of this study point out: "An entire childhood spent hearing a certain group of people referred to with negative affect or seeing them, either in the media or in reality, associated with situations that arouse negative affect may generate a fairly strong negative attitude" (Krosnick, Betz, Jussim, & Lynn, 1992, p. 159).

How might we counter classical conditioning effects on attitudes toward ethnic groups? Efforts to reduce bias in the media and promote balanced portrayals of members of ethnic groups (counterconditioning) are one approach. Being sensitive to when stimulus pairings occur that could create unwanted attitude associations and countering them by exposure to alternative pairings also might help. Increasing our knowledge and positive interactions with members of diverse ethnic groups should be helpful as well, since classical conditioning of attitudes is most effective when people have little information or direct experience with the attitude target (Cacioppo, Marshall-Goodell, Tassinary, & Petty, 1992).

Classical conditioning is not the only basic learning process that affects our attitudes toward members of different ethnic groups, but it can have powerful effects, and these effects can undermine our ability to function in a diverse society. Understanding this basic psychological process is the first step toward countering its unwanted effects.

can quickly learn relationships and behaviors related to locating and ingesting food, they don't have the motor capacity to escape aversive or unpleasant events, and they have difficulty in learning relationships associated with them. Because human infants have parents to protect them, this ability may not be as necessary for survival at birth as for other animals. Indeed, some neurological evidence suggests that mechanisms for forming associations between aversive events and their consequences may develop later in human infants than mechanisms for associating positive events with their consequences (Rovee-Collier, 1987, 1993).

THINKING CRITICALLY

Sheep ranchers want to prevent their sheep from being killed by coyotes or wolves but are limited in their rights to exterminate these animals by ecological and environmental pressure to preserve the indigenous species. Can you think of a way to use psychological research on taste aversions to help ranchers solve this problem?

Ranchers were advised by John Garcia and his colleagues (Gustavson, Garcia, Hankins, and Rusiniak, 1974; Garcia, 1990) to sacrifice a few sheep, poison their carcasses with lithium chloride (a drug that makes coyotes very ill but does not kill them) and to leave the poisoned meat out on the range for the coyotes to eat. Coyotes who consumed this "free lunch" quickly acquired a learned taste aversion to sheep meat. Therefore, they no longer preyed on sheep, turning instead to killing and eating a less-valued species such as rabbit. Sheep predation was significantly reduced.

▲ *In a practical application of classical conditioning, sheep ranchers put out sheep meat laced with a non-lethal, illness-producing lithium for the coyotes, who quickly developed an aversion to sheep and stopped preying on the flock.*

Applications of Classical Conditioning

Simple as they might appear, the importance of Pavlov's early observations should not be underestimated. Shortly after Pavlov's results became known in the United States, some psychologists, notably John B. Watson, began to argue that all behavior, human or otherwise, derives from classical conditioning (Watson, 1925). That is, Watson believed that everything that human beings and other animals do in their lifetime, above and beyond unlearned reflexes, is a matter of conditioning. Although this extreme view is no longer popular, most psychologists would agree that a significant portion of our behavior as parents, lovers, students, or shoppers includes our emotional responses and reflects classical conditioning.

Classical conditioning principles are widely applied in advertising. The old billboard ads that showed a handsome, rugged cowboy, the Marlboro man, with a cigarette hanging out of the side of his mouth were meant to condition a positive response to cigarettes. Joe Camel ads (USs) were designed to elicit a positive emotional response (UR) from the viewer. The US is presented along with a cigarette (CS). A sufficient number of pairings of US and CS causes the cigarette to produce a positive response (CR) on its own. As another example, jeans ads on television show how someone can attract one of the beautiful people as a mate through wearing a particular brand of jeans. Can you see how the positive emotional reaction (UR) to the people (US) involved in the ad becomes attached to the jeans (CS)? One of the important aspects of the classical conditioning process is that you don't have to be aware that it's happening (Squire, Knowlton, & Musen, 1993). You can be conditioned without even knowing it. Next time you watch television, see if you can identify when principles of classical conditioning are being used.

An early application of human classical conditioning is found in the work of O. Hobart Mowrer and Molly Mowrer on treating childhood bed-wetting (enuresis). The Mowrers de-

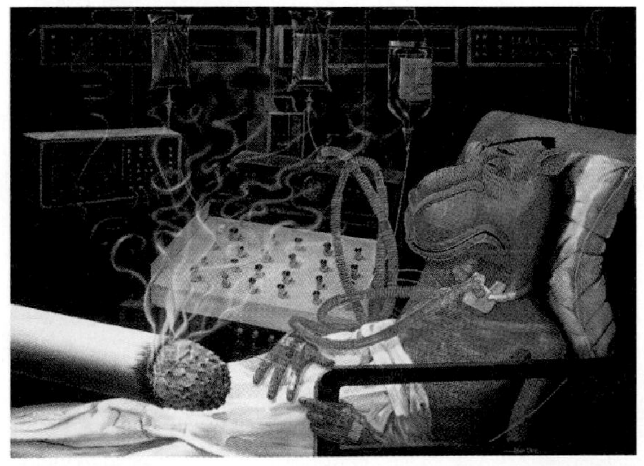

◀ *In an effort to reverse the conditioning effects of cigarette advertising, artist Alberto Ortiz developed some counterconditioning images of his own.*

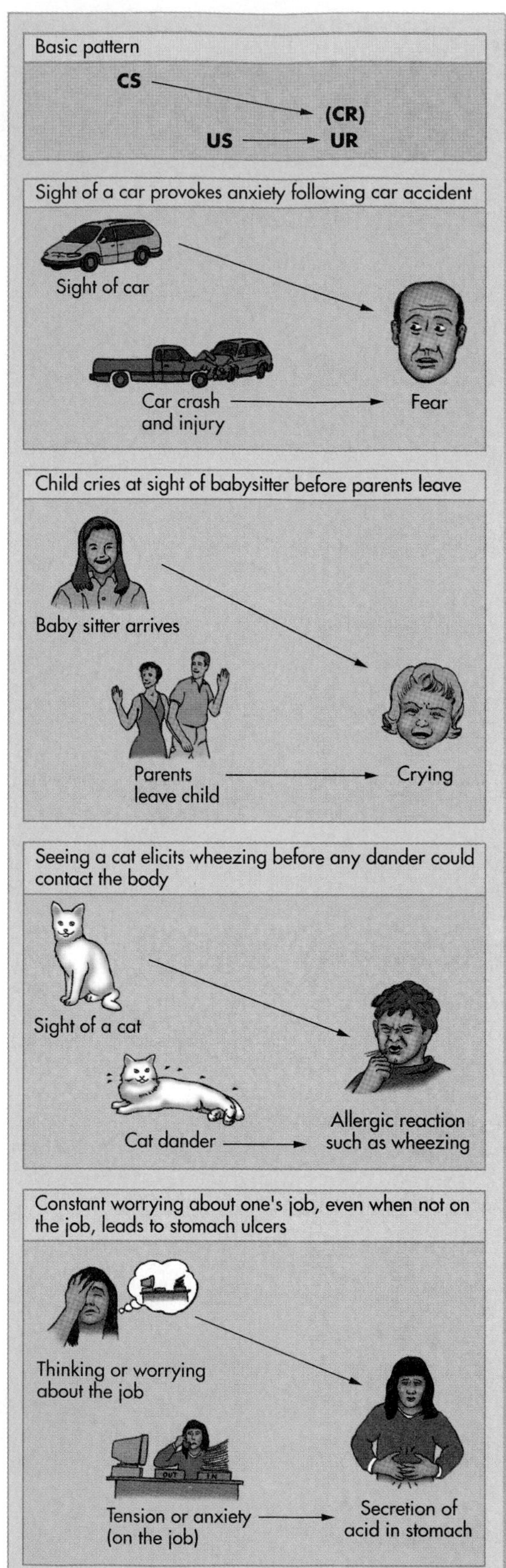

6-5 Everyday Examples of Classical Conditioning

Examples of classical conditioning abound in the everyday life of animals and human beings. One important example is in the conditioning of emotional responses such as fear. Suppose a person experiences terror from a wild car ride that ends in a crash and painful injury. The unconditioned responses of fear and pain occur in the context of "car" stimuli. The mere sight of a car may now cause the person to experience fear even after recovery from the accident. This and other everyday examples of classical conditioning are shown in the figure.

veloped a bed pad that caused a loud bell to ring the moment it was moistened with urine. The bell (US) thus elicited the UR of the child waking up whenever he or she wet the bed. In time, after pairing the sensation of having a full bladder (CS) repeatedly with the sound of the bell, the bladder cues alone became sufficient to wake up (CR) the child (Mowrer & Mowrer, 1930). Similar methods are still in use today to treat bed-wetting.

Health applications of classical conditioning are also beginning to be explored. In one case, researchers paired a distinctive odor (CS) with injection of a drug that reduced blood pressure (US). After a sufficient number of pairings, researchers were able to reduce blood pressure using the odor alone (Spencer, Yaden, & Lal, 1988). Some other everyday examples of classical conditioning are described in Figure 6-5.

Operant Conditioning

In classical conditioning, the organism is not really learning new responses; it is merely forming new associations between previous responses and new stimuli. In ***operant conditioning*** (also known as ***instrumental conditioning***), an organism learns new responses by *operating*, or acting on its environment, and being *instrumental* in producing desired outcomes in the environment. Thus, operant conditioning is learning to make the responses on which certain consequences are contingent, that is, learning that if a particular response is made, it will be followed by either rewarding (desired or sought-after) or aversive (undesirable or avoided) consequences (see Figure 6-6). A dog might learn that raising a paw will result in a treat. Once the dog has learned this relationship (contingency) between raising a paw (the response) and getting a treat (the consequence), it will be more likely to raise its paw in the future when it wants a treat.

Responses and Consequences

Operant conditioning is commonly associated with the American psychologists Edward L.

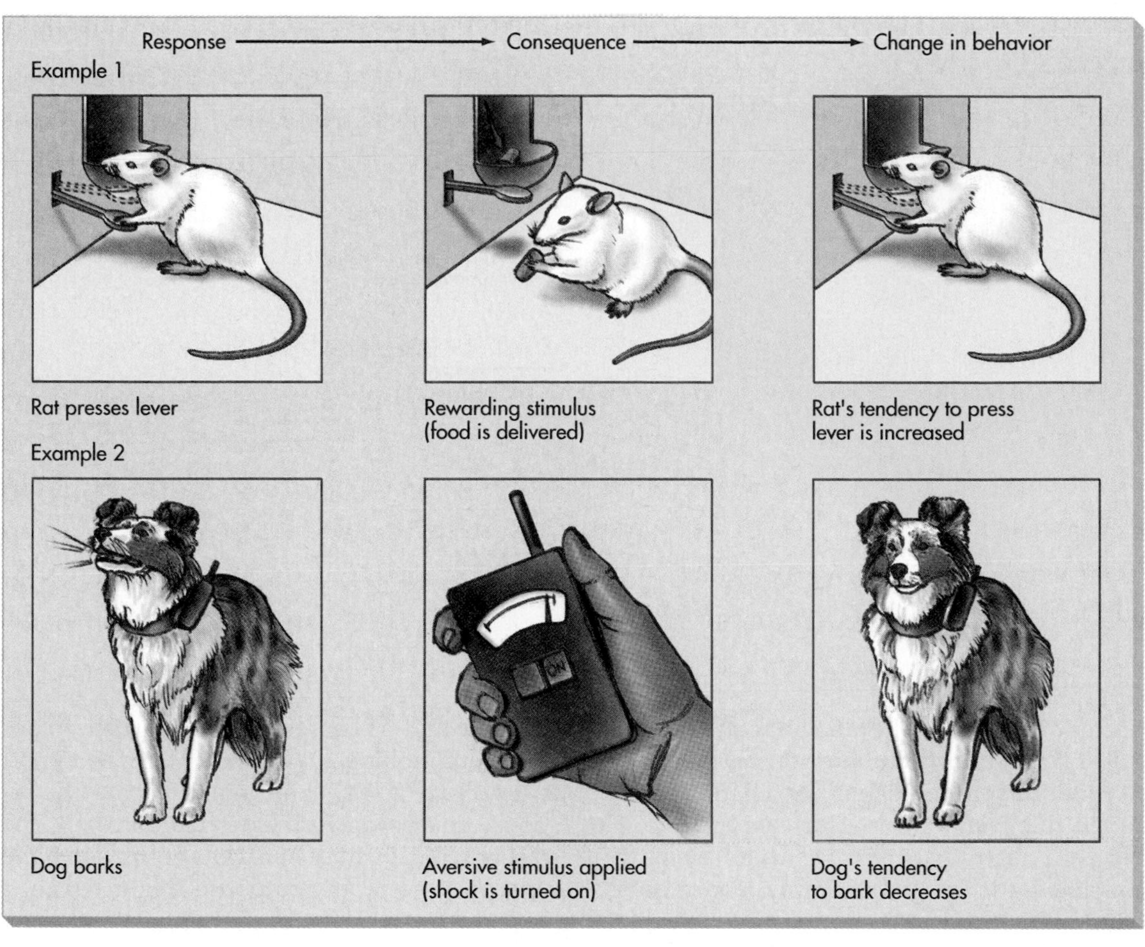

6-6 The Operant Conditioning Process

In operant conditioning, a response emitted by a person or animal produces a consequence or outcome, which changes the likelihood or probability that the response will be repeated.

Thorndike (1874–1949) and B.F. Skinner (1904–1990). Thorndike observed that hungry cats, placed in what he called a "puzzle box" (a confining cage), made a variety of responses until, through trial-and-error, one particular response produced escape and food. The cats made the response leading to escape more and more quickly each time they were placed in the box. To account for this change in behavior, Thorndike proposed a ***law of effect***: those responses followed by satisfying consequences are more likely to be repeated under similar circumstances. A corollary is: those responses that are followed by unpleasant (or annoying) consequences are less likely to be repeated. Thus, Thorndike concluded that the animal had learned to select a response when the correct response increased in strength and the incorrect responses decreased in strength.

Building on Thorndike's work, B.F. Skinner elaborated and popularized the principles of

In operant conditioning, the learner makes new responses to gain desired consequences.

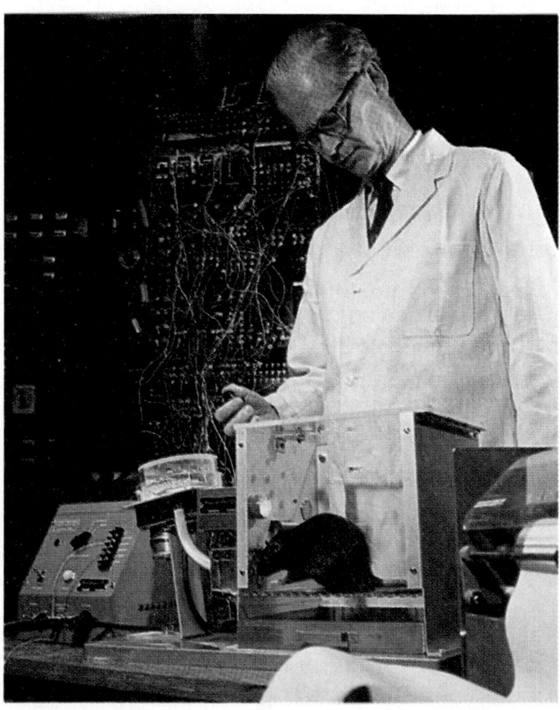

◀ *B.F. Skinner checking the operant chamber in his laboratory. When the light in the box illuminates, the rat presses the bar. The rat is then rewarded with a pellet of food, which rolls down the tube into the cage.*

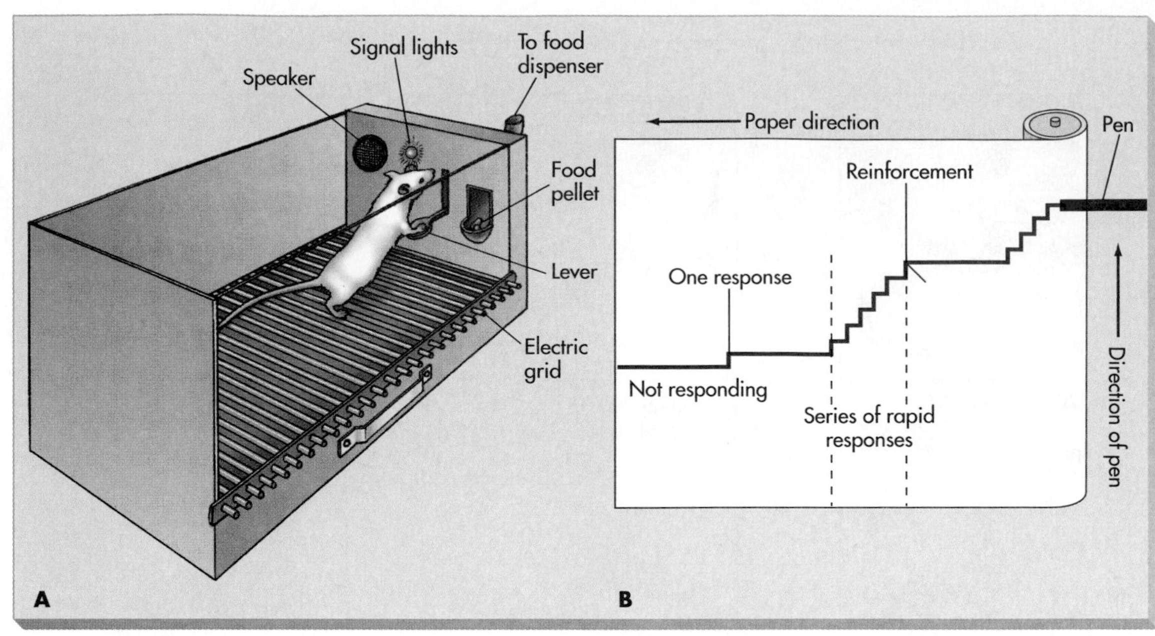

6-7 Operant Conditioning Apparatus

(A) B.F. Skinner designed the famous "Skinner box" to study principles of operant learning. This diagram presents the basic features of the Skinner box and Skinner's first subject, the lever-pressing rat. A speaker, signal lights, and electric grid provide auditory, visual, and pain stimuli. Food pellets (reinforcers) are delivered via a food dispenser. The rat makes operant responses by pressing a lever attached to one of the walls of the box. Skinner boxes have also been designed to study behaviors of other animals, such as the pecking responses of pigeons. (B) The Skinner box is hooked up to a cumulative recorder, which keeps a continuous record of responses and reinforcements made by the animal in the Skinner box. A drum continually unrolls paper under a pen at a constant speed. Every time the rat presses the lever, the pen is moved up a step. The faster the response, the shorter the "steps" made by the pen. Each reinforcement is marked with a slash.

operant conditioning. Skinner created a device called an ***operant chamber*** (also known as a ***Skinner box***) to investigate the relationship between the events of operant conditioning. He placed a slightly hungry rat inside a box that contained a lever and an empty food tray (see Figure 6-7). The animal was allowed to explore the box freely. In the process of exploration, if the rat happened to press down on the lever, a pellet of food would automatically drop into the tray. Pressing the lever, an unlikely response at the outset, was the response to be learned (the ***operant response***), and the food pellet was the stimulus consequence (called a ***reinforcer*** because it increases the probability that the response will be made again). Each lever press made by the rat while it was in the box was recorded. Skinner discovered that if the rat was rewarded with food each time it pressed the lever, the rate of presses increased systematically. The rat learned to *operate* on its environment in a way that provided a valued outcome or reward. Its operant response was systematically reinforced by the outcome or consequence of the response.

Acquisition, Extinction, and Spontaneous Recovery

The ***acquisition*** of an operant response occurs as the contingency (or association) between a response and its consequence is learned. In operant conditioning, the learner is free to respond in a variety of ways and must find the one response that produces the desired outcome. The learner typically does not know at first what the consequences of any response might be. So it might take a while before he makes the correct response. But if the desired consequence occurs right away and on every occasion when the correct response is made, the interval between one correct response and the next will decrease and the strength of the correct response will increase. The probability of (likelihood of making) an operant response rises rapidly at first, then increases more gradually, until it reaches an upper limit (similar to acquisition during classical conditioning).

If, after acquisition, a consequence (generally, a reward) no longer occurs, ***extinction*** will take place. The trained rat in Skinner's experiment will gradually decrease its lever pressing. In operant conditioning, extinction results when a response is no longer followed by a consequence. If the animal is removed from the training cage after extinction but then returned sometime later, ***spontaneous recovery*** will occur, as in classical conditioning. That pattern will repeat itself over several extinction periods, again as in classical conditioning. Total extinction can take a very long time. One way to minimize spontaneous recovery is to overextinguish the habit by carrying the extinction sessions on long after the original conditioned

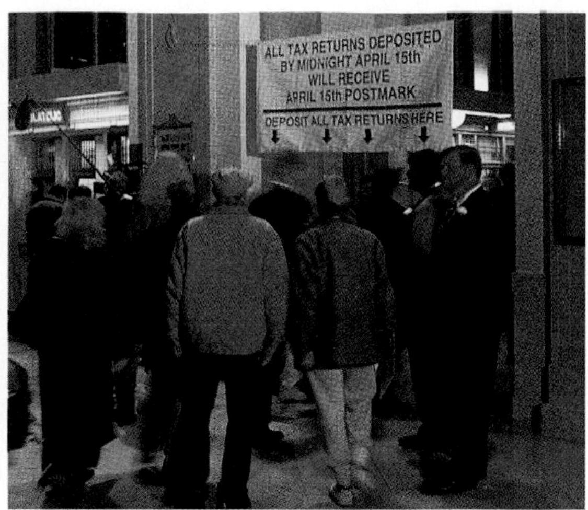

◀ *Winning the lottery is certainly an example of positive reinforcement—the purchase of a lottery ticket leads to a prize for a lucky winner. The line at the Post Office on April 15th illustrates negative reinforcement—people seek to avoid the penalty of a late tax return, so they go to the Post Office just before midnight.*

response has ceased to occur. Rather than removing the animal from the training cage after it has ceased to respond, it would be left there for a while, without response or reward. Response tendencies would continue to weaken under these circumstances, which would lessen spontaneous recovery the next time around.

Reinforcement

Reinforcement is the technical name for the consequences of a response that *increase the frequency* of or strengthen the response they follow. (Indeed, the word "reinforce" literally means "to strengthen.") Anything that occurs after a response that increases the probability of that response is called a "reinforcer." A particular stimulus might not always be reinforcing. For example, in the bar-pressing example, remember that we first deprived the rat of food to ensure that access to the food would be reinforcing. Food pellets would not be reinforcing for an animal that wasn't hungry! Some kind of motivation for the reinforcer must also exist.

There are both positive and negative reinforcers. ***Positive reinforcement*** occurs when a pleasant, rewarding, desirable, or sought-after stimulus increases the probability, or strength, of the response it follows. Thus, if giving a hungry rat a food pellet after it sits up on its haunches increases the likelihood that it will sit up, the process is called positive reinforcement. ***Negative reinforcement*** refers to the case in which the termination or removal of an unpleasant or aversive stimulus after a response increases the probability, or strength, of that response. For example, no longer getting soaked by the rain as a result of opening an umbrella would increase the likelihood of carrying and using an umbrella the next time rain is in the forecast. There is a contrast to be made between punishment and negative reinforcement. ***Punishment*** is an aversive stimulus that decreases the probability of a response. Thus, spanking or withdrawing a privilege from a child who fights with a sibling is aversive and punishing and likely to reduce the child's tendency to fight in the future.

Primary and Secondary Reinforcers

What makes a particular event something that will reinforce behavior? For some events the answer lies in the learner's biology. Thus, ***primary reinforcers***, such as food for a hungry organism, can modify behavior because of their innate reinforcing properties. Primary reinforcers affect behavior whether or not the subject has previously experienced them. A subject doesn't have to learn to eat; food is a primary reinforcer because it is naturally rewarding to a hungry animal or person.

For other stimuli, the answer lies in experience or prior learning, which, of course, depends in part on one's sociocultural context. Stimuli are capable of becoming learned reinforcers if the organism associates them with primary reinforcers. Once the subject learns about them, they become ***secondary reinforcers***. A potent example of a secondary reinforcer for human beings in most modern cultures is money. Why is it that most of us will perform the most

A positive reinforcer is any stimulus that when given as a consequence of some response will increase the frequency of that response. A negative reinforcer is any stimulus that when removed as a consequence of some response will increase the likelihood of that response.

▲ *Stimuli such as poker chips or tokens can become learned (conditioned) reinforcers if the organism associates them with primary reinforcers. Here a chimpanzee who has worked to earn tokens uses them to obtain food. This principle has been employed to establish economic systems based on the use of tokens ("token economies") to shape the behavior of prison inmates and patients in psychiatric hospitals.*

extraordinary tasks to get something that doesn't directly satisfy any biological need? You can't eat or drink money, you can't breathe it or have sex with it. Yet, some people can't seem to get enough money, even when they have more than they can possibly spend. Money becomes a reinforcer because we have learned that money will buy food, drink, and many other things; that is, money will buy primary reinforcement, and thus it can indirectly satisfy many kinds of needs, biological and otherwise. But its reinforcing value goes well beyond that, at least for some of us. In other cultures, where wealth is a less important concern, other objects or events, such as acknowledgment by a clan or tribal leader, might be secondary reinforcers more important than money.

Identifying Reinforcers

When you use operant conditioning to promote a behavior, you first need to identify what is reinforcing to the learner—those objects, events, or opportunities that the learner values. This can be tricky, for what is valued in some cultures by some individuals might not be valued in other cultures or by others in the same culture. For example, for most people in Western culture, playing a video game will function well as a reinforcer in a wide variety of circumstances. Yet, to a person who doesn't even know what a video game is, the opportunity to play a video game might not strengthen a desired response. Moreover, video games might not be available every time we need a reinforcer. In a different culture, shells or tokens of some sort might function well as reinforcers, although they have little value in Western cultures. Identifying effective reinforcers will be difficult unless you know something about the learner's preferences, habits, and sociocultural context.

Imagine yourself as a parent with a child, Susie, who loves to play Nintendo but doesn't much care for reading. If Susie has some free time, she will probably choose to spend it playing Nintendo, so it must be a source of reinforcement for her. If you wanted to reward Susie for brushing her teeth before going to bed, you would be better off offering her the chance to play Nintendo rather than extra time for reading. You might even decide to tell Susie that if she reads for a certain amount of time, you will let her play Nintendo. Identifying reinforcers to promote desired behaviors in diverse contexts is known as the ***Premack principle***, named after David Premack, who first suggested it (Premack, 1965). The assumption is that under conditions of free choice, the behavior that is most *probable* is the behavior that is most preferred and therefore most reinforcing. Allowing a learner to engage in preferred behaviors (playing Nintendo) can be used to reinforce other, less probable (less preferred) behaviors (reading).

Given two behaviors that differ in their likelihood of occurrence (assuming conditions of free choice), the less probable behavior can be reinforced with the opportunity to engage in the more probable behavior, according to the Premack principle.

THINKING CRITICALLY

Suppose that researchers establish that among a particular group of students (not psychology students, of course) watching TV is preferred over studying. That is, in a free choice situation, the students are more likely to choose to watch TV than to study. Applying the Premack principle, how would you increase the amount of time students spend studying?

If you said by making TV time contingent on studying (for example, for every hour you study, you can watch a half-hour of television), you have applied the Premack principle! Alternatively, suppose it is established that a group of convicts would prefer to spend their time playing softball rather than participating in a job training program. How could the prison administration increase participation in the program? Would using access to the softball field as a reinforcer for participating in the program work?

Positive and Negative Reinforcers

Both positive and negative reinforcement are used to increase the occurrence of particular behaviors. Suppose you have a little brother, David, who keeps forgetting to use his seat belt. You want to increase the probability that David will buckle up. How would you reinforce that behavior? Would rewarding him with praise or a hug after he buckles up work? If a hug increases his seat belt use, you have applied positive reinforcement. If David uses the seat belt to avoid the loud unpleasant sound that continues until he is buckled up, you have an example of successful negative reinforcement. Terminating a stimulus when the learner gives the desired response is called ***escape training***. Escaping from an aversive noise by buckling your seat belt reflects escape training. Other examples would include joining a gang to stop its members from hassling you, sitting in the back of the room to stop being called on in class, studying harder to stop getting low grades, and working cooperatively to reduce a prison sentence (time off for good behavior).

If you are confused by the reinforcement terminology, think of positive and negative reinforcement as "adding" and "subtracting" rather than as "good" and "bad." Thus, for positive reinforcement, you add something (a hug); for negative reinforcement, you take something away (an unpleasant noise). The result is the same in both cases: the frequency of the response increases (for example, seat belt usage).

Punishment

Both positive and negative reinforcement increase the frequency of a response. In contrast, punishment decreases the frequency of a response. Just as there are two kinds of punishment, positive and negative, there are two kinds of reinforcement, positive and negative. ***Positive punishment*** involves using an aversive stimulus (either physical or psychological) to eliminate or weaken a behavior. For example, if a child does something wrong, he or she can be corrected firmly. The aversive stimulus, whatever it might be, is made contingent on the behavior, with the goal of eliminating that behavior. In ***negative punishment***, an undesired behavior is weakened by removing a rewarding or pleasurable stimulus when the undesired behavior is exhibited. For example, parents might take away their teenager's driving privileges if he or she violates the household curfew, gets poor grades in school, or keeps bad company. In effect, negative punishment is a "fine" for undesirable behavior (Klein, 1991). Taking away some of a person's money as a fine for unlawful behavior is based on the principle of negative punishment. Removing aggressive children from their play groups and putting them in a room by themselves for a specified

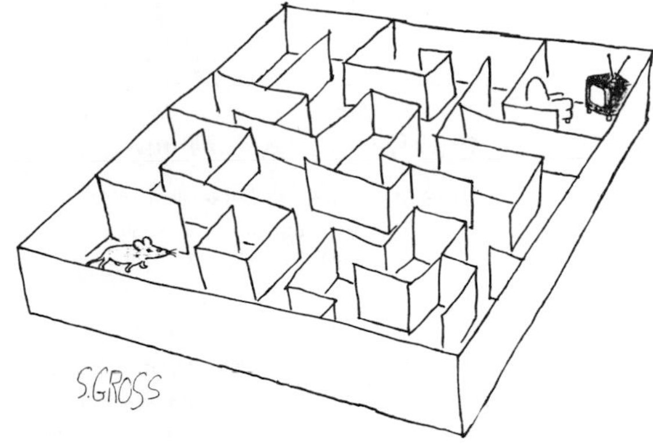

period of time, which is called "time out," is an example of negative punishment.

In deciding to use punishment to influence behavior, it is important to make sure that the stimulus used is actually punishing. A fine of $5,000 levied for pollution may seem like a lot of money to most people, but it means little to a multimillion dollar corporation that would have to invest 200 times that much in pollution control equipment to avoid the fine. Using time out from a play group to control a child's inappropriate behavior assumes that the child finds it rewarding to be in the group. This is usually true, but not always. If the time-out area is rewarding in itself, being there can actually increase disruptive behavior (as when a disruptive child is sent to his or her room where favorite toys are located).

For a time, psychologists believed that punishment suppressed performance but that it did not actually weaken the underlying associations between a response and its expected consequences. That is, they believed that punishment had at best a temporary effect on behavior and that the original response would eventually reappear, full blown. Recent research, however, shows that punishment can effectively elimi-

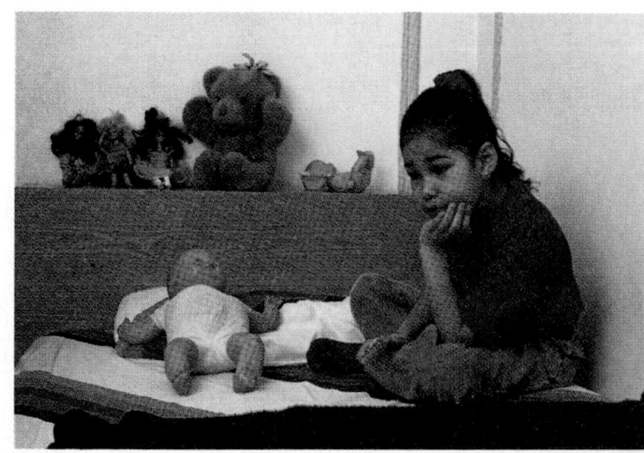

◄ *Negative punishment: five-year old Rachel sits unhappily on her bed during a "time-out."*

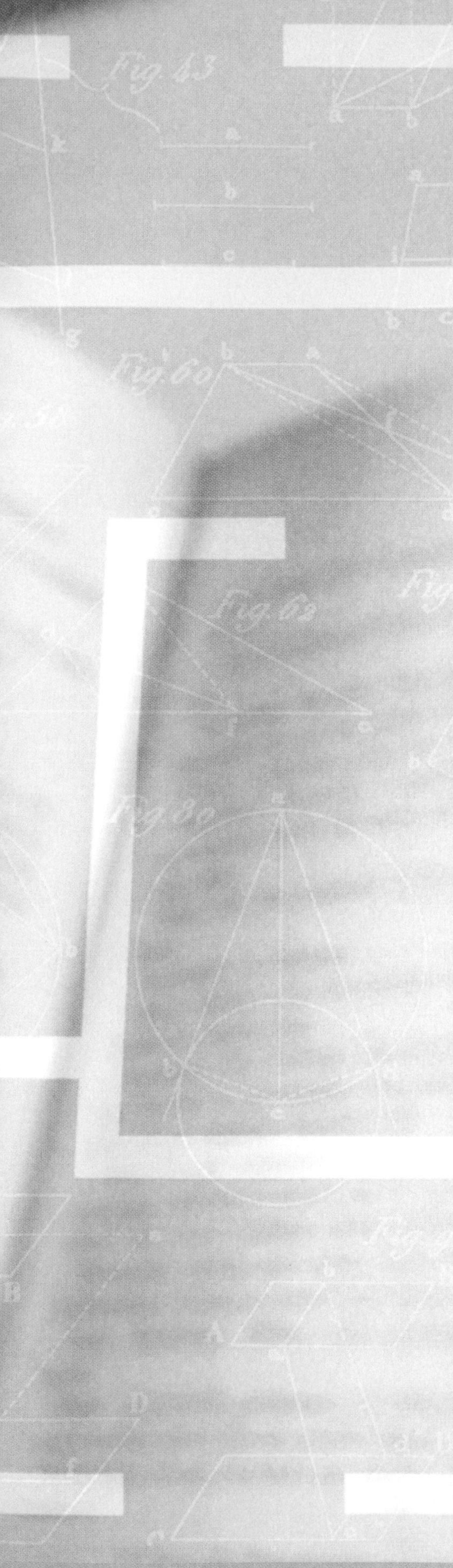

SEEKING SOLUTIONS

The Effective Use of Punishment

The answer to "What's the better motivation: The carrot or the stick?" depends on the situation. Although usually the answer is the carrot, there are times when immediate suppression of behavior is necessary (like when you have to teach your children not to touch a hot stove or not to run out in the street without watching for traffic). In these cases, the correct answer is likely to be the stick (metaphorically speaking!). When it is difficult to develop and reinforce incompatible behaviors—for example, when a person's undesirable behavior is so persistent and frequent that there are essentially no opportunities to reinforce alternative responses—punishment might be the only possibility.

If punishment is used to modify behavior, the following considerations are important (Schwartz & Robbins, 1995):

Severity. The more severe the punishment, the greater the suppression of the behavior. Behavior that is severely punished is more quickly suppressed and stays suppressed longer. For example, in one study, subjects used a specially designed cigarette case that delivered an electric shock when opened. The stronger the shock, the lower the rate of smoking (Powell & Azrin, 1968).

It is important to remember that undesirable behaviors are repeated because they are elicited or reinforced in some way. If punishment is to be used, it is important that the punishment be severe enough to suppress the response because, every time the behavior occurs, it is likely to be strengthened again by reinforcement. Starting with a weak and ineffective punishment will ultimately require a more severe punishment to suppress the behavior than if you began with a stronger punishment in the first place (Azrin, Holz & Hake, 1963). This is a tricky issue. Care must be taken, of course, to avoid punishment-induced aggression and/or injury.

Availability of alternative, reinforced responses. Punishment is sometimes ineffective because there is no obvious alternative or substitute behavior. Thus, scolding a child who cries when "she doesn't get her way" might not change the child's behavior, unless alternative ways of behaving, such as making a polite request, are pointed out and reinforced. Similarly, putting a person in jail for stealing is not likely to deter his behavior if stealing is perceived as being the only way to obtain money for food.

Timing. The shorter the time between the undesirable response and punishment, the more effective the punishment. When children are punished as they initiate an undesirable act (such as approaching a forbidden object), they will be less likely to initiate that behavior in the future. Although applying punishment before misbehavior is typically not feasible, it is possible to intervene early and to act immediately rather than postponing punishment (as in "wait until we get home—will you ever be in trouble").

Delay in punishment is thought to be one reason that suppressing violent behavior in dating and marital relationships is so difficult. Aggressive behavior is self-reinforcing. If a woman believes a batterer's promise that "he won't do it again" and therefore doesn't respond to the first violent act immediately by having him put in jail, or at least separating from him for a period ("time-out" strategy), the violent behavior will be strengthened.

Feedback. Punishment is more effective when accompanied by feedback or an explanation designed to link the undesired behavior to the punishment. Thus, feedback can be used to counter the effects of delayed punishment by verbally reinstating the circumstances requiring punishment (some circumstances can be physically reinstated as well, by returning the offender to "the scene of the crime").

The possibility that the person will not realize what he or she is being punished for is reduced by clearly specifying the reason for the punishment. Suppose a friend constantly interrupts you in an annoying fashion. If you respond by giving that friend a "dirty look" but do not explain what specifically annoys you, the friend may think you are angry at *what* was said rather than *how* it was said. As a consequence the friend may avoid talking to you about the subject in the future (but continue to interrupt you when talking about other topics). Using feedback to avoid inappropriate generalization is also seen in parents' behavior when they tell their child that "I'm punishing you because you did ____________ (a bad thing, clearly specified!), not because you are a bad child."

THINKING CRITICALLY

Describe the differences between punishment and negative reinforcement by using the example of a little boy who comes home after school and throws his coat on the floor and whose parent yells at him until he picks up the coat and hangs it in the closet. Does yelling act as negative reinforcement or as punishment in this case?

First, consider the definitions. Punishment is an unpleasant stimulus which is delivered contingent upon the occurrence of a particular undesirable behavior. Negative reinforcement is an unpleasant stimulus which is terminated upon the occurrence of a particular desirable behavior. In many everyday situations, punishment and negative reinforcement occur together and so are easily confused. The same unpleasant stimulus event is sometimes used to punish one response and negatively reinforce another. That is the case in our example. The parent's yelling serves both as a punishment and a negative reinforcer. It is punishment to the boy for throwing his coat on the floor, because it is an unpleasant stimulus that is delivered contingent on an undesirable response. It is a negative reinforcer because it is delivered continuously until the child picks up the coat and hangs it in the closet, at which point the yelling ends. The parent has punished coat throwing and negatively reinforced coat hanging.

nate many undesirable behaviors, from nail-biting and chronic coughing to hallucinations and obsessive thoughts (Klein, 1991). It has been successfully used to reduce self-mutilating and tantrum behavior of autistic and mentally handicapped children (Lovaas, Koegel, & Schreibman, 1979). In particular, time-out punishment has been successfully used to suppress disruptive mealtime behavior in retarded children, disruptive lunchroom activity in elementary school children, and tantrums in both normal and autistic children (Klein, 1991).

◄ *Aggressive behavior by a child may actually increase rather than decrease when the parent uses physical punishment to try to eliminate hitting or kicking. James kicks his younger sister. He is then spanked by his mother. But his mother, who was abused as a child, worries that she isn't doing the right thing, saying, "If I don't teach him different, is he going to grow up to be a rapist, a murderer?"*

Adverse Effects of Punishment

Although punishment can eliminate undesirable behaviors, using punishment to promote learning has been criticized by psychologists because of its potential side effects. Four of these are particularly important.

First, punishment may affect more behaviors than intended. For example, a parent might punish a child for hitting a playmate or for cutting in front of another child in line. This could weaken or eliminate not only aggressive behavior (for example, hitting another person), but also assertiveness, that is, standing up for one's rights and defending one's point of view in appropriate ways. As a result, the child might fail to be assertive when it is appropriate.

Second, a person might learn to suppress punished behaviors, but only when he or she is likely to be punished. The person might just learn to be more careful about when he or she engaged in the undesirable behavior. A child punished for fighting might play cooperatively with other children as long as parents are present but be as aggressive as ever when the parents aren't around.

Third, a person who is repeatedly punished by others might conclude that the most successful way to get others to do something is by threat or use of punishment. The most poignant example of this may be child abuse: while identified cases of child abuse represent only a small percentage of the population at large, about a third of the people who were abused as children grow up to be abusers themselves (Widom, 1989). Abuse is a learned way of dealing with

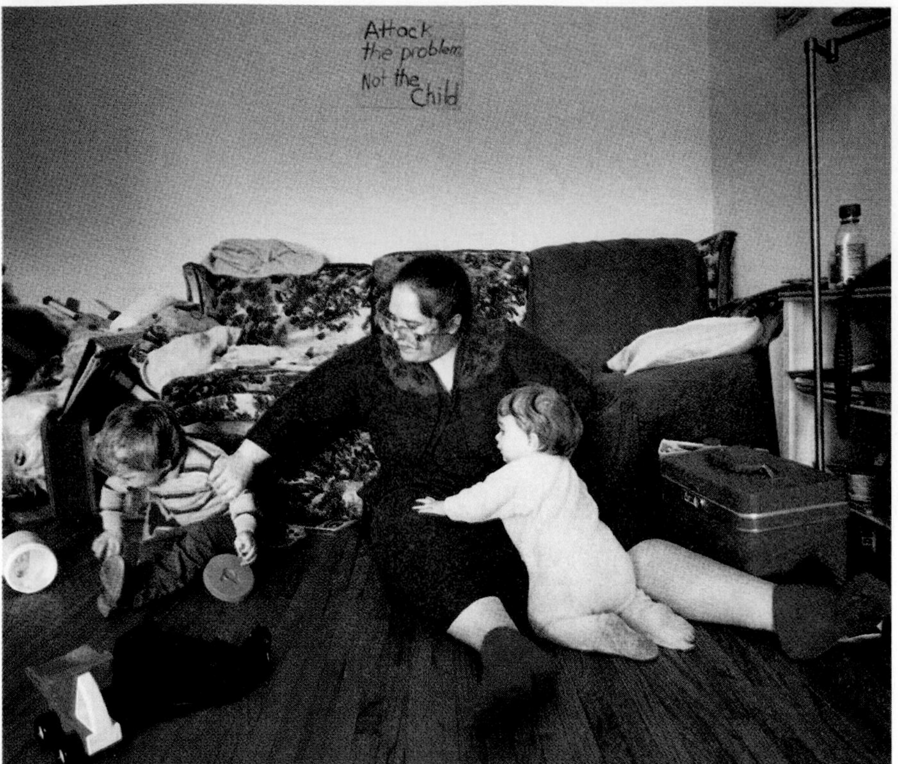

▲ *James' mother is trying to modify her own aggressive behavior toward her son, so that he won't respond with aggression when he gets frustrated or angry.*

others, particularly other family members. Alternative, more desirable behaviors such as reasoning or depriving children of privileges are weaker or not learned at all.

Finally, punishment brings the risk of pain-induced aggression. If punishment creates physical pain, anger and aggression may follow. It is known that aggression reduces feelings of anger, which makes it self-reinforcing. The opportunity to be aggressive is sufficient to reinforce learning in angry animals. When primates are exposed to the pain of electric shock, they attack other animals or things (such as the toys) in their environment (Azrin, Hutchinson, & McLaughlin, 1965; Plotnick, Mir, & Delgado, 1971). Irritated people report that they feel "good" after being aggressive (Bramel, Taub, & Blum, 1968). Although physiological mechanisms for such "good feelings" have not been fully defined, researchers have found that being verbally or physically aggressive toward a source of anger can reduce blood pressure in angry subjects (Hokanson, Burgess, & Cohen, 1963). Techniques based on negative punishment, such as time-out punishment mentioned above, might be better alternatives to pain-inducing positive punishment in the sense that they have fewer side effects.

Aggression in response to pain and adversity is *not* inevitable, however. People differ in the amount of anger they feel in response to these conditions. Further, reinforcing people to take positive, nonaggressive actions in response to adversity, while at the same time punishing aggressive responses quickly and effectively can lower the likelihood of aggression based on anger. Teaching people to deal with feelings of anger is an essential component of programs to modify aggressive behavior.

Ethical issues arise whenever punishment is used to control behavior. U.S. society has strong norms against "cruel and unusual punishment," no matter how well-intended. Ethical codes, institutional review boards, human rights committees, and laws all govern the use of punishment by psychologists in research and therapeutic settings (Klein, 1991). We will have more to say about this matter when we discuss some of the therapeutic uses of punishment in Chapter 16.

Variations in the Use of Reinforcement

Reinforcement is a powerful tool for forming new behaviors and changing old ones. It can be applied in a variety of ways. Research has identified some of the unique effects of these variations and some optimal ways in which reinforcement can be used to promote learning and memory of learned responses.

Schedules of Reinforcement

Suppose you set up a situation so that a pigeon will receive food if it learns to peck at a lighted key in its cage. In real-life learning situations, no animal or human being is given ***continuous reinforcement***, that is, reinforced for every correct response. Rather, ***partial reinforcement***, where the learner is reinforced for the correct response only some of the time, is much more common.

Continuous reinforcement occurs in training when every correct response is reinforced, whereas partial reinforcement occurs when only some correct responses are reinforced.

The pattern of reinforcement determines the rate at which the behavior will be learned as well as how resistant it will be to extinction. Continuous reinforcement produces the fastest initial learning, but the resulting responses are weak; they are easy to extinguish. No treats, no tricks! So you might begin training with continuous reinforcement, just to get the learner go-

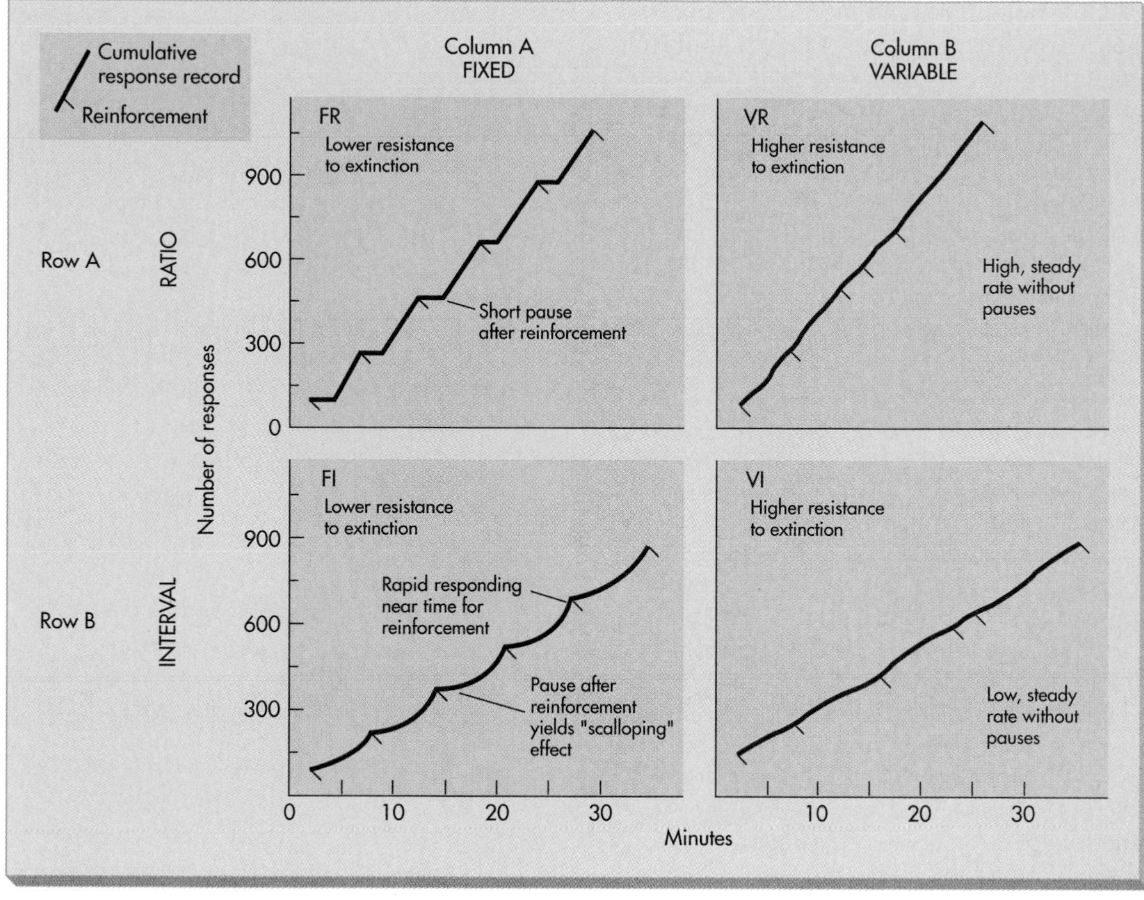

6-8 Schedules of Reinforcement

Operant response patterns vary with type of reinforcement schedule. In general, ratio schedules (Row A) produce higher response rates than interval schedules (Row B). Fixed schedules (Column A) produce higher response rates than variable schedules (Column B). These data come from animals who have learned to peck a key to obtain food and who are now being reinforced on one of the four standard schedules. Slash marks on the response functions indicate the occurrence of reinforcement. Under a fixed ratio (FR) schedule, there are brief pauses in responding after the occurrence of reinforcement. There are similar, longer pauses after reinforcement in the fixed interval (FI) schedule, producing a characteristic scalloped effect. Variable ratio (VR) and variable interval (VI) schedules produce steadier response rates than fixed ratio and fixed interval schedules. Although fixed schedules generallly have higher response rates during acquisition, variable schedules result in more resistance to extinction. (Source: Adapted from Ferster & Skinner, 1957)

ing. But if you want durable behavior that will stand up over time and will resist extinction, you should switch to partial reinforcement as soon as possible. The result is called the ***partial reinforcement effect***: Behavior controlled by partial reinforcement is much more resistant to forgetting and persists through longer periods of extinction than behavior controlled by continuous reinforcement.

When behavior is conditioned under partial reinforcement, several different patterns or schedules are possible. One way is to require the pigeon to make five pecks on a light in its cage before it gets a food delivery. This is called a ***ratio schedule*** of partial reinforcement (a ratio of 5 to 1). Alternatively, you could require the pigeon to wait for an interval of, say, ten seconds before food is made available, regardless of how many pecks it makes. This is called an ***interval schedule*** of partial reinforcement (a ten-second interval). Both of these types of schedules can vary across a training session, rather than remaining fixed throughout. Thus, the ratio might vary from time to time between 2 to 1 and 10 to 1 (pecks to pellets), or the interval might vary between five seconds and twenty seconds in an irregular fashion.

There are four basic types of partial reinforcement schedules found in real life and in the laboratory: ***fixed ratio, variable ratio, fixed interval***, or ***variable interval***. These possibilities can be viewed as a 2 × 2 combination of two variables as shown in Figure 6-8. First, the

◀ *Casinos depend on variable ratio schedules to make a profit.*

schedule might depend upon how many responses the learner makes (ratio schedule) or it can depend on how much time has passed since the last reinforcement (interval schedule). Second, the number of responses in the case of a ratio schedule and the amount of time in the case of an interval schedule can be fixed and invariant or random and highly variable. In a fixed ratio schedule, you reinforce after a fixed number of responses from the learner. For example, you might reinforce your pet ferret every fourth time it comes when called by name. In a fixed interval schedule, you reinforce the first response that occurs after a fixed amount of time. You might reward a rat in an operant conditioning chamber for its first lever press after one minute has passed. Pressing during the one-minute delay would do the rat no good. Note that getting a paycheck every Friday at 5 P.M. is a fixed interval schedule. In a variable ratio schedule, you reinforce every *n*-th response, say, every fourth response. Sometimes reinforcement is given after the first, sometimes after the sixth, sometimes after the tenth response in a random fashion, with the average being some specified value (*n*). The payoff schedule of a casino slot machine is a good example of a variable ratio schedule of reinforcement. Finally, in a variable interval schedule, you reinforce the first response after a certain average time interval, say, one minute. But sometimes only ten seconds has to elapse, sometimes two minutes, sometimes seventy seconds between responses, with the average time interval being set at a specific value. Hitchhiking is an example of a variable interval schedule.

Each schedule of reinforcement has its own unique effects on responding. Variable schedules (interval or ratio) lead to higher rates of responding than fixed schedules. They also pro-

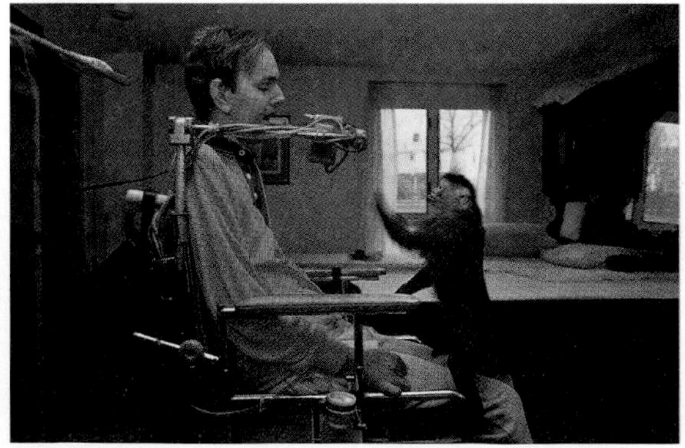

▶ *The technique of shaping behavior through successive approximations is used in training monkeys to serve as aides to disabled individuals. Here, a quadriplegic man is helped by a monkey.*

THINKING CRITICALLY

Consider job hunting in a tight market. Based on the principles of partial reinforcement, which job hunters should become less discouraged after several unsuccessful job applications: (1) people who have a history of being able to find work on the first application, or (2) people who have a history of receiving a number of rejections before finding their jobs?

The latter group of people should be less discouraged because their job-hunting behavior has a history of partial reinforcement. Let's consider this point further.

Jack Nation has applied operant conditioning principles to psychotherapy, noting that newly learned desirable behaviors, such as greater assertiveness, acquired under continuous reinforcement, will extinguish rapidly once the patient goes out into the "real world," where the therapist is not available to see that every response is reinforced (Nation & Woods, 1980). If psychotherapists want their patients to continue to engage in new and healthier behaviors long after formal therapy is over, they should take advantage of the partial reinforcement effect and replace continuous reinforcement with partial reinforcement during the therapy, a procedure Nation calls persistence training. Instead of reinforcing the patient every time he or she succeeds in making a new, desired response, such as being assertive and asking for what he or she has coming, Nation recommends that the therapist reinforce (usually with verbal praise) the patient for these responses only periodically. Continuous praise might be required at the outset as the individual is starting to learn, but the shift to partial reinforcement should be made just as soon as the patient begins to make the new response.

◀ *Through shaping, animals can be trained to behave in ways that are atypical. Johnny Peers and his "Muttville Comix Troupe of Dogs" seem to have mastered the technique.*

duce greater resistance to extinction. For example, ratio schedules tend to produce a steady rate of responding while interval schedules yield periods of slow and then more rapid responding. Your choice of reinforcement schedule should depend on what you are trying to teach the learner to do. Pigeons and rats have been trained to perform very routine or tedious tasks over prolonged periods of time for very little in the way of reward, provided the rewards are scheduled properly. They will also continue to perform for a long while after you stop giving rewards altogether.

Shaping

In some learning situations, the behavior desired is displayed only rarely. You could follow your psychology professor around for years waiting for him or her to turn a cartwheel so that you could reinforce this unusual behavior. But you can speed up learning by using a technique called ***shaping***. Shaping involves learning in graduated steps, whereby each successive step requires a response that is closer than the previous response to the desired performance. This is also known as the method of ***successive approximations***.

Suppose Gunther Gebel-Williams, the famous wild animal trainer, wanted to train a lion to roll over on command. Because lions very seldom do this in nature, Gebel-Williams might start by reinforcing the lion just for bending its head toward the floor. After the lion began consistently to orient toward the floor, Gebel-Williams might not administer reinforcement until after the lion had dropped to the floor. When the lion regularly dropped to the floor on command, Gebel-Williams might withhold reinforcement until the animal made slight rocking movements. In the next stage, he might reinforce the lion only if it actually dropped down and rolled onto its side. Eventually, he would reinforce the animal only when it rolled completely over. At this point, response shaping would be complete. Shaping begins by reinforcing virtually any response that is compatible with the final product and, at each successive stage, demands a closer and closer approximation to the final, desired result. This technique is very effective and has numerous applications, including training animals as aides to disabled individuals.

Does shaping work on people? At first blush, you might think not, because you can tell a person what to do ("get down on all fours and roll over on your back") and he or she will do it if the right motivation is there. But there are some behaviors or responses that don't lend themselves easily or completely to instruction and where shaping is a useful learning technique. Consider your tennis backhand stroke. You can be told how to do it, but thereafter will you do it properly? For most people, the answer is a resounding "no." You need to practice and to make successive approximations to a proper backhand. Each stroke that you try has a contingency, that is, a result, that is only sometimes reinforcing. The stroke has several component movements, and you don't learn them all in a single trial. You get better and better as the components fall into place with repetition.

Shaping is a learning technique in which an animal (or person) is trained to perform a difficult behavior through graduated steps or successive approximations.

Generalization and Discrimination

After either classical or operant conditioning, learners show a tendency to generalize what they have learned to new and different situations as well as an ability to discriminate among situations (see Table 6-1). ***Stimulus generalization*** occurs when the learner ignores distinctions among stimuli. For example, in Pavlov's experiment, if the sound used as the CS were replaced by a slightly lower- or higher-pitched sound, the dog would most likely continue to salivate (make the CR) whenever the sound occurred, demonstrating generalization from one sound to another. Or suppose pigeons were trained to peck a button illuminated with a 550-nanometer light (this is a greenish-yellow color for human beings). Other things being equal, the pigeons would tend to respond in the same way if tested with lights of higher or lower wavelengths. We can construct a ***gradient of stimulus generalization*** to indicate the degree to which a learned response generalizes to other stimuli (see Figure 6-9). The more similar a test stimulus is to the original training stimulus, the greater the likelihood the organism will respond to it in the way it has been trained. Thus, it is no surprise that the graph in Figure 6-9 shows the greatest number of responses by the pigeons to lights of illumination that are close to 550 nm.

Generalization occurs when a learner tends to make a learned response to stimuli other than the original training stimulus or to make responses other than the originally learned response in the presence of the training stimulus. Discrimination is the ability to tell the difference between stimuli or between responses and to act accordingly.

A person who has been trained to make a particular response sometimes will make a different response, especially if the originally learned behavior is somehow blocked or interfered with. Consider training a hungry rat in a Skinner box to press a lever for food pellets. The first successful lever press might be quite accidental. Let's say the animal strikes the lever with its left paw while exploring the cage. The immediate delivery of a food pellet reinforces the left paw response. The animal will have an increased tendency to make that same response again. With successive responses and reinforcements, the response will gain strength. But usually response strength will not be limited to left paw presses just because the animal began that way. Rather, response strength will generalize to other similar responses. For example, the rat may press the bar with its right paw, with both paws, with its nose, and possibly with other parts of its body. Thus, if you've learned to push open a swinging door with your right hand and if your arms are now full of books, you might now push the door open in some other way, say, with your hip. This is a case of ***response generalization***, which is the use of an alternative response, usually similar to the original response, when the original response is somehow blocked or impossible to use.

To discriminate you need to be able to tell the difference between two entities. In the context of both classical and operant conditioning, there are two important kinds of discrimination, ***stimulus discrimination*** and ***response discrimination***. Stimulus discrimination reflects the knowledge that two stimuli are different and might require different responses. Consider

Table 6-1 Generalization and Discrimination

	Generalization	Discrimination
Stimulus	Learner ignores distinctions between stimuli, responding to all of them in the same way.	Learner distinguishes between stimuli by responding to one and not responding to others.
Response	Learner responds in a variety of ways to the same stimulus.	Learner makes only one specific, unique response to a stimulus and withholds all other possible responses.

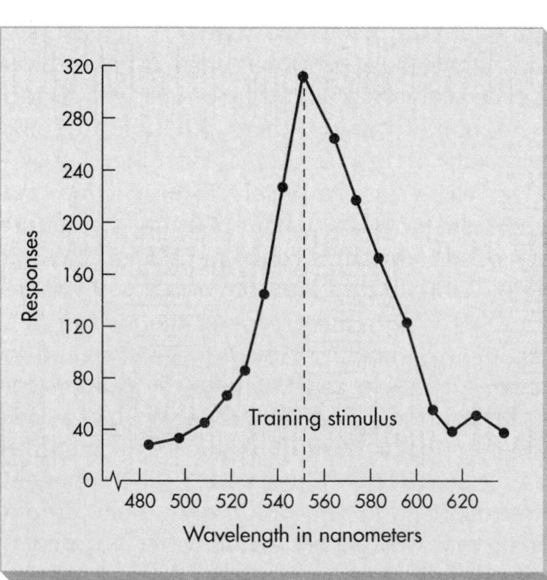

6-9 Gradient of Stimulus Generalization

The gradient of stimulus generalization is shown for a group of pigeons trained to peck a button illuminated with a light of 550 nm and then presented with test stimuli of several other colors, ranging from 480 to 620 nm. The graph shows that the closer the test stimulus was to the training stimulus of 550 nm, the more the birds pecked. (Source: Buttman, 1956)

◀ *Ronnie has problems with response discrimination.*

a classical conditioning example. Suppose a child is licked gently on the hand by a purring black cat during play (a pleasant sensation), but on another occasion is scratched by a calico cat (a painful sensation). If the child henceforth claps happily at the sight of the black cat and cries at the sight of the calico cat, he or she is exhibiting stimulus discrimination between the two cats.

In operant conditioning, learners can be taught to discriminate the conditions under which particular consequences happen. Suppose parents punish a young child for saying "dirty words." Is it reasonable to expect that, after a number of experiences, the child will never again utter such words? Probably not, given the laughter and status (positive reinforcement) such language can elicit from a childish peer group in Western culture. Thus, whether or not the child uses vulgar language depends on whether or not his parents are around. The child can discriminate between the presence and the absence of parents, and he learns to make his vulgar language contingent upon this discrimination. Responses are said to be under ***stimulus control*** when a stimulus is a signal or cue that a particular consequence (reward or punishment) will be delivered contingent upon the learner's behavior. Thus, the child's behavior would be said to be under the stimulus control of the parent's presence.

Discrimination and generalization can be thought of as learning processes that yield opposite results or types of behavior. In discrimination, the organism's responses become more narrowly controlled and defined. In generalization, responses occur with more variety or over a greater range of situations. Table 6-1 summarizes these processes.

Applications of Operant Conditioning

Operant conditioning principles apply to human beings of all ages and all cultures as fully as they apply to other animals. Effective reinforcers for people can include smiles and praise as well as food or money. For example, several studies have established that newborn human infants can discriminate and have a distinct preference for their mothers' voice over other female voices (DeCasper & Fifer, 1980). Moreover, the voice can be used to reinforce infant behavior almost immediately after birth. One commonly used procedure takes advantage of the infant's natural sucking response. If hearing the mother's voice depends on making a certain number of sucks on a pacifier, the infant quickly learns to suck at the required level (Cooper & Aslin, 1990). Infants are clearly capable of learning to make a response that is reinforced by the sound of the mother's voice. The fact that human babies are so responsive to operant conditioning provides evidence that we are born prepared to detect and respond to contingencies between our actions and their consequences.

Operant procedures can also be used to manage certain human behavior problems, including stuttering, temper tantrums, alcohol abuse, smoking, and excessive eating. These applied

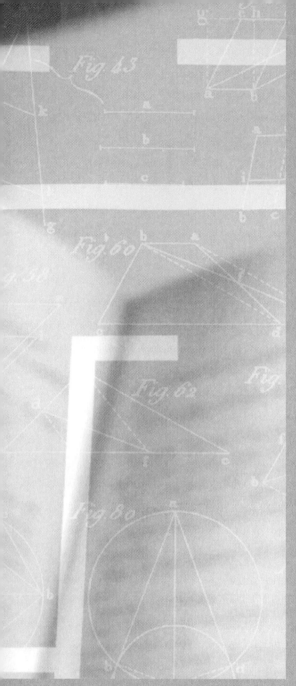

SEEKING SOLUTIONS

Behavior Modification

Behavior modification techniques can be used with good success by teachers to control inappropriate classroom behavior. For example, teachers often pay attention to withdrawn children in an effort to interest them in group activities. But this may serve to reinforce the child for playing alone. Teachers should pay attention, and thus reinforce, withdrawn children, not for playing alone, but for showing signs of participating in group activities. This is good operant conditioning, good application of reinforcement principles, and a good behavior modification technique. The teacher who does not know or fails to apply these principles will often encourage misbehavior, with its consequent class disruption. Ignoring inappropriate activities in their initial stages will help to ensure that they do not increase in frequency or strength over time.

A dramatic example of the use of behavior modification techniques is the case of Laura, a nine-year-old mentally retarded child. Almost immediately after she enrolled in a special school for retarded children, she began to vomit in the classroom. In fact, vomiting became an everyday occurrence. Whenever this happened, the teacher sent Laura back to her residence hall. No medical cause for the vomiting could be found, and no medication seemed to help. A psychologist suggested that her vomiting was not an uncontrollable reflex, but a response that Laura emitted (operant behavior) because of its positive consequences for her (she could get out of class).

In order to test this hypothesis, the psychologist decided to measure Laura's vomiting under three conditions: (1) extinction—the consequent event (reinforcement) is withheld; Laura had to stay in class, regardless of her vomiting; (2) reinstatement—the original reinforcement is reinstated; Laura would be returned to her residence hall if she vomited; and (3) a second extinction session—vomiting was not rewarded, and Laura was kept in the classroom.

The results were clear-cut. During the first extinction period, Laura vomited a lot. But gradually vomiting declined in frequency until it reached zero. Then reinstatement began (she could leave if she vomited). It was quite some time before she finally vomited again (spontaneous recovery), but when she did, she was allowed to leave. In no time, her vomiting reappeared; she vomited once a day and left class. Finally, during reextinction, she was again forced to stay in class despite her vomiting. Again, at first she vomited a great deal, but the vomiting gradually decreased to zero.

This classic case (Wolf, Birnbrauer, Lawler, and Williams, 1970) illustrates the application of several operant conditioning principles to a behavior problem: once the reinforcing event is discovered, its elimination can be used to terminate the undesired behavior (although the process will take time). The ability to reverse the behavior (bring back the vomiting and then make it go away a second time) is a control condition that eliminates an alternative interpretation, namely, that Laura might have quit vomiting without any change in the reinforcement contingencies.

techniques, commonly called ***behavior modification***, have successfully changed or eliminated such undesirable behaviors (see Chapter 16).

One particular application of behavior modification uses operant conditioning principles to modify the behavior of patients in mental hospitals. In order to teach patients to behave in a more socially acceptable manner, hospital staff and patients set up a token economy in which tokens (in this case, poker chips) are used as secondary reinforcers (Ayllon & Azrin, 1968). The patients can earn tokens by performing agreed-upon behaviors and can exchange these tokens later for special privileges. Tokens can be earned, for example, by the following behaviors: getting up quickly and at a regular time every morning; showing good personal hygiene habits, such as bathing and wearing clean clothes; performing clean-up chores around the ward; and working at off-the-ward jobs, such as gardening or doing the laundry. Tokens can then be used to make purchases: a bed with an inner-spring mattress to replace a cot, an opportunity to watch TV, or entrance to a fancy dining room rather than the customary undecorated hall.

Token economy programs have been extremely successful in managing patient behavior. Many long-term, difficult patients have adopted model ward behavior under a token system, and sometimes as a result the entire ward completely changes character. Techniques of this sort also can speed up the patients' re-education process, which leads to their more rapid discharge from hospitals. Token economies have also been used to treat other behavioral problems, including successfully treating children with attention deficit hyperactivity disorder. Although some lay people and experts feel that these programs dehumanize patients—training them like lower animals—the fact that the programs help the patients to learn new skills that they can then use in everyday life is certainly beneficial both to the patients and to society.

Table 6-2 Similarities and Differences between Classical and Operant Conditioning

	Classical Conditioning	Operant Conditioning
Processes	Acquisition Extinction Spontaneous recovery Generalization Discrimination	Acquisition Extinction Spontaneous recovery Generalization Discrimination
Association	Association between conditioned stimulus and unconditioned stimulus.	Association between response and reinforcing consequence.
Subject's response	Unconditioned response does not depend on subject's response. Involuntary. Conditioned response often resembles unconditioned response.	Consequence occurs only when subject makes a critical response. Voluntary. Response is often arbitrary.

The Interplay of Classical and Operant Conditioning

Although there are important differences, classical and operant conditioning are based on many of the same processes (see Table 6-2). In fact, many (possibly most) learning situations involve both classical and operant conditioning. Reinforcers used in operant conditioning can at the same time serve as effective unconditioned stimuli (eliciting a reflexive unconditioned response) that might simultaneously produce classical conditioning. For example, if food is used as a reinforcer in an operant conditioning situation, it will reflexively elicit salivation. Stimuli paired with the delivery of food (an unconditioned stimulus), such as the sound of a pellet dropping into the food tray or even the stimuli of the conditioning chamber itself, are likely to become associated with the US as conditioned stimuli and therefore provoke a conditioned response (salivating) even when food is withheld.

Superstitious Behavior and Autoshaping

An example of the interplay of classical and operant conditioning helps us to understand superstitious behavior. Consider the fact that the occurrence of chance or accidental reinforcers sometimes strengthens behaviors in unexpected or unintended ways. For example, a student buys a new pen before taking a big exam. She scores unusually well on the test and attributes her performance to her new "lucky pen," even though there is no relationship between the pen and her grade. Our tendency to form causal explanations for events that occur together but are not causally related is called superstition.

A closely related phenomenon that has been observed in the laboratory is called ***autoshaping***. A food-deprived pigeon is placed in a Skinner box that has a pecking disc or key and a food box mounted on a wall. Every so often the key is lighted, and shortly thereafter, food is delivered into the box automatically, regard-

▼ *Classical and operant conditioning work together. Ruff has made a connection between the sound of the can opener (CS) and food (US). But he is doing more than salivating in response to the sound of the can opener. Ruff has been reinforced for running to the kitchen, since every time he runs to the kitchen he is given food.*

DENNIS THE MENACE

"I think mom's using the can opener."

KEY TERMS

habituation

imprinting

classical conditioning

unconditioned response (UR)

unconditioned stimulus (US)

conditioned stimulus (CS)

conditioned response (CR)

acquisition

extinction

spontaneous recovery

contiguity

prepared learning

contingencies

operant conditioning

law of effect

reinforcement

positive reinforcement

ronment. *Associative learning* is somewhat more complex than the first two types and involves the acquisition of relationships between arbitrary stimuli and responses. *Classical conditioning* and *operant conditioning* occur primarily (though not exclusively) when organisms acquire learned relationships between overt stimuli and responses. *Cognitive learning* is acquiring knowledge and skill through observing and imitating or being instructed (orally or through reading) to form new mental representations that can be remembered over time.

Objective 2. Describe the processes of acquisition, extinction, and spontaneous recovery in conditioning.

Acquisition, extinction, and spontaneous recovery occur in both classical and operant conditioning. *Acquisition* is the gradual strengthening of a response over time or over repeated conditioning trials. *Extinction* is the reduction or elimination of a learned response when, in classical conditioning, the CS is repeatedly presented without the US or, in operant conditioning, the CR occurs without a consequent reinforcer. *Spontaneous recovery* is the reemergence of an extinguished CR or operant response, after an interval of time with no exposure to the CS in classical conditioning or to the conditioning context in operant conditioning.

Objective 3. Define the law of contiguity and describe how it relates to prepared learning.

Classical conditioning is thought to be mainly a function of the contiguous occurrence of the CS and the US during the learning trials. Through conditioning, the CS comes to substitute for or signal the onset of the US. Classical conditioning is most effective when the CS and the US occur close together in time and space (the *principle of contiguity*). But under some circumstances, conditioning can be accomplished even if the CS and US are separated by a long interval, as, for example, in taste aversion conditioning. In such cases, organisms seem innately prepared to associate a certain kind of response with certain kinds of stimuli. This phenomenon is known as *prepared learning*.

Objective 4. Explain the law of effect and how it is elaborated in principles of reinforcement. Then describe positive and negative reinforcement, positive and negative punishment, and schedules of reinforcement.

In *operant conditioning*, the frequency of a particular response is modified through the delivery of rewards or punishments made contingent on those responses. Thorndike was the first to propose the basic principle, called the *law of effect*, which states that responses followed by satisfying consequences become more likely in the future and, conversely, responses followed by annoying or aversive consequences become less likely. B.F. Skinner expanded and popularized the study of operant conditioning, classifying the effects of responses in terms of whether they increase or decrease response probability. A *reinforcer* is any consequence of a response that increases the likelihood of (or strengthens) that response.

Reinforcement can be either *positive* (a reward follows the response) or *negative* (an unpleasant stimulus is removed following the response). *Punishment*, which is any consequence that decreases the likelihood of a response, can also be positive or negative. *Positive punishment* consists of the occurrence of an unpleasant consequence after a response. *Negative punishment* involves removing a pleasant stimulus in order to weaken a response. Although effective under certain conditions, the use of punishment can have unwanted side effects.

Reinforcers can be presented after every CR (*continuous reinforcement*) or only after certain CRs (*partial reinforcement*). Partial reinforcement schedules can be made to depend either on the number of responses made per reinforcement (*ratio*) or on the elapsed time since reinforcement (*interval*), and they may be fixed or variable. Continuous reinforcement schedules lead to quicker acquisition but also to quicker extinction. Partial reinforcement schedules produce responses that are highly resistant to extinction (the partial reinforcement effect).

Objective 5. Distinguish between discrimination and generalization, and explain how conditioning processes might result in superstitious behavior and learned helplessness.

Discrimination and generalization are processes that yield opposite forms of behavior. *Discrimination* requires responses to be narrowly defined (response discrimination) and to occur only in specific situations (stimulus discrimination). *Generalization* yields more variable responses (response generalization) in a wide range of situations (stimulus generalization).

The technique known as *shaping* (reinforcing successively closer approximations to the desired behavior) is frequently used in operant conditioning to strengthen new responses that learners do not regularly make. Animals have sometimes been observed to engage in self-taught behaviors in laboratory studies, based on chance reinforcement contingencies (*superstitious behavior*). One particular kind of self-taught behavior, called *autoshaping*, can be explained as the interaction of operant and classical conditioning processes.

Learned helplessness occurs when the subject cannot control unpleasant events in the environment. Under these circumstances, the organism becomes conditioned to helplessness.

Objective 6. Define cognitive learning, and explain why psychologists believe cognitive processes play an important role in classical and operant conditioning.

Contemporary theories of conditioning place increasing emphasis on cognitive-mediating processes in learning and less on the idea that environmental stimuli and responses made by a learner are directly connected.

Cognitive learning, based on observation and imitation, is the primary learning mechanism for human beings. Cognitive learning is the acquisition, organization, and retention of knowledge and skills. Learning by reading, by instruction, and by observation of demonstrations are all common examples of cognitive learning.

negative reinforcement

punishment

primary reinforcer

secondary reinforcer

Premack principle

escape training

continuous reinforcement

partial reinforcement

ratio schedule

interval schedule

shaping

behavior modification

generalization

discrimination

autoshaping

learned helplessness

latent learning

cognitive learning

C H A P T E R 7

Memory

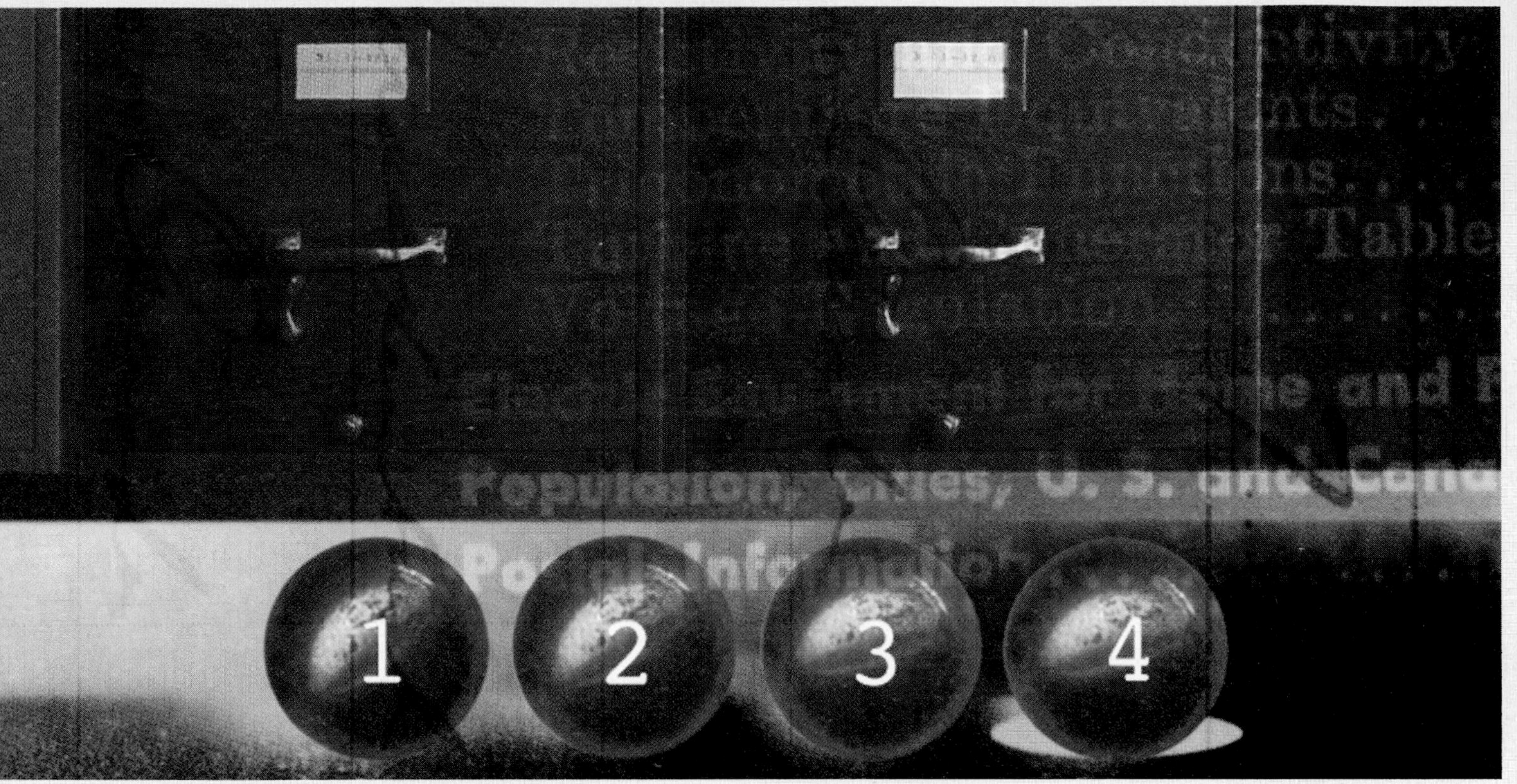

O B J E C T I V E S

After reading this chapter, you should be able to:

1. Describe and discuss some of the attributes of human memory.
2. Explain encoding, and relate it to rehearsal effects on learning and memory.
3. Distinguish among various types of long-term memory.
4. Describe the three methods used to measure memory retrieval.
5. Explain the factors that affect retrieval of or the failure to retrieve (forgetting) information from memory, and the three methods used to measure it.

Let's see how good your memory is. The following story, called "The War of the Ghosts" is a legend from a nineteenth-century Indian tribe living on the northwest coast of Canada. Read it at your normal rate, and then put it aside. After thinking about the story for a few minutes, write down all you can remember about it. When you are finished, compare your words with those of the original legend.

> One night two young men from Egulac went down to the river to hunt seals, and while they were there it became foggy and calm. Then they heard war-cries, and they thought "Maybe this is a war-party." They escaped to the shore and hid behind a log. Now canoes came up, and they heard the noise of paddles, and saw one canoe coming up to them. There were five men in the canoe, and they said:
>
> "What do you think? We wish to take you along. We are going up the river to make war on the people."
>
> One of the young men said, "I have no arrows."
>
> "Arrows are in the canoe," they said.
>
> "I will not go along. I might be killed. My relatives do not know where I have gone. But you," he said, turning to the other, "may go with them."
>
> So one of the young men went, but the other returned home.
>
> And the warriors went up the river to a town on the other side of Kalama. The people came down to the water and then began to fight, and many were killed. But presently the young man heard one of the warriors say: "Quick, let us go home; that Indian has been hit." Now he thought: "Oh, they are ghosts." He did not feel sick, but they said he had been shot.
>
> So the canoes went back to Egulac, and the young man went ashore to his house, and made a fire. And he told everybody and said: "Behold I accompanied the ghosts, and we went to fight. Many of our fellows were killed, and many of those who attacked us were killed. They said I was hit, and I did not feel sick."
>
> He told it all, and then he became quiet. When the sun rose he fell down. Something black came out of his mouth. His face became contorted. The people jumped up and cried.
>
> He was dead.

This legend was first used for the study of memory by the eminent British psychologist Sir Frederic Bartlett (1932). Bartlett asked his English research participants to read the legend, then reproduce it from memory, just as we asked you. While the participants found the words familiar, the gist of the story, its supernatural theme, and its style, structure, and organization were unusual by British (indeed European) standards of the time, and they were not entirely clear to the research participants. What they reproduced differed in systematic ways from what they had heard. Here's a typical example of how one individual reproduced the story:

> Two youths were standing by a river about to start seal catching when a boat appeared with five men in it. They were all armed for war.
>
> The youths were at first frightened, but they were asked by the men to come and help them fight some enemies on the other bank. One youth said that he could not come as his relations would be anxious about him; the other said he would go, and entered the boat.
>
> In the evening he returned to his hut, and told his friends that he had been in a battle. A great many had been slain, and he had been wounded by an arrow; he had not felt any pain, he said. They told him he must have been fighting in a battle of ghosts. Then he remembered that it had been queer and he became very excited.
>
> In the morning, however, he became ill, and his friends gathered round; he fell down and his face became very pale. Then he writhed and shrieked and his friends were filled with terror.

At last he became calm. Something hard and black came out of his mouth and he lay contorted and dead.

How did your version of the story compare with the original legend? How much was your re-creation influenced by your own previous experience or by your culture (which, of course, is likely to be quite different from the culture that produced the legend)? How did your version of the story compare with that of Bartlett's research participants? If you have been exposed to supernatural tales and other forms of myth, your memory may be very different from that of Bartlett's participants, who had not been exposed to such things. If not, your memory of the story may be very much like theirs.

When Bartlett analyzed the reproduced stories, he found that the research participants typically remembered only selective parts of the legend and that they forgot many of the story details. Further, they tended to change the information to make it more "normal" or less unusual *to them*. Specifically, the story was made to fit into what Bartlett called the cultural "schema" (an organized pattern of ideas) of typical British citizens. Indian canoes were recalled as "boats," the mysterious spiritual essence that issued from the main character's mouth was recalled as "vomit," and the abrupt ending of the story was expanded by many participants to resolve some or all of the loose ends. Their memory changed over time in the direction of what was familiar, demonstrating the strong influence of prior knowledge (much of which comes from our culture) on what we "remember."

Bartlett's study demonstrates two key points to keep in mind as you read this chapter. First, memory is not simply a passive recording of information in true and faithful form. Memory is an active, *constructive* process, involving coding and recoding information, linking new information to past memories, and making inferences about meaning. Second, language and culture play fundamental roles in memory. Our culture sensitizes us to particular events and objects, affecting what we pay attention to and remember (Harris, Schoen, & Hensley, 1992).

This chapter goes beyond the basic learning principles presented in Chapter 6. Here, we will talk more about cognitive learning, and we will focus on memory for what we have learned, asking such questions as: How are new facts and skills acquired? How are they represented in memory? Are there different kinds of memories? Are memories for facts ("knowing that such-and-such is the case") different from memories for skills ("knowing *how* to do something")? Why do we forget some things and remember others? How accurate are our memories, anyway? Can we improve our memory?

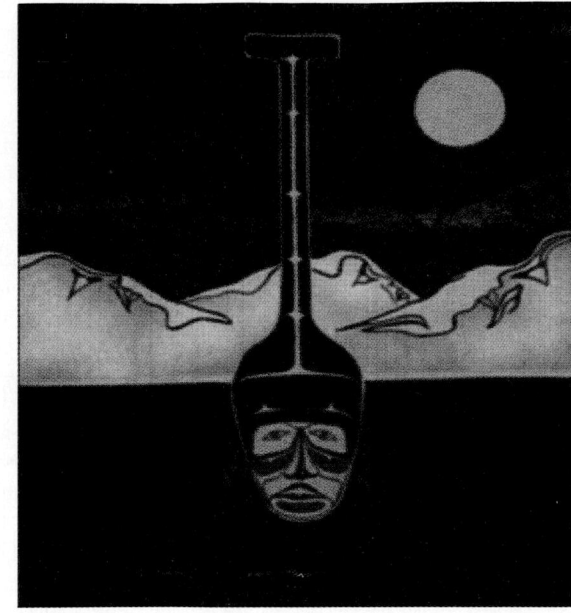

◀ *Canadian Native Art:* The War Paddle.

What Is Memory?

Memory is a psychological concept, a mental record of past experiences that we carry around in our heads. It is the ability to reproduce at some later time what we have experienced earlier. The memory record is cumulative, that is, each new experience adds to the existing record. Memory is always a part of what we do, and our actions are always affected by what we remember, whether we are conscious of these memories or not. Memory contains a variety of experiences: some of them unique and personal to each of us and some of them memories of world events that are likely to be shared by many of us; some of them are memories of facts or beliefs about our experiences and some of them are skills that permit us to perform in particular ways.

UNDERSTANDING HUMAN DIVERSITY

Gender and Memory

Suppose you showed a group of research participants eighty pictures of various kinds of cars; forty-eight hours later, you showed them eighty pictures again and asked them to tell you whether or not they recognized each one. Who do you believe would do better on this task, males or females? Suppose you followed the same procedure, but this time the pictures were faces of children. Now who would be more accurate in recognizing the pictures?

If you said males are better at recognizing cars, while females are better at recognizing children's faces, you have indeed predicted what happens when research participants are given the task described above (McKelvie et al., 1993). How can this be explained?

Given that memory is an active, constructive process that involves linking new information to our schemas of past experiences, we would expect gender to have an influence on memory. One way this happens is through the creation of *gender schemas*, which are the mental structures that we develop to organize and represent our knowledge related to gender. Gender schemas can affect what we pay attention to, how we encode information about our environment, and what we remember—and forget! (Martin, 1993).

Why do you think automobiles might be more related to the male gender and children more related to the female gender? Don't both men and women drive cars? There are several reasons. Historically, automobiles were primarily marketed to and driven by males. Automobiles have been used to signify status for males, and as a means for males to attract the opposite sex. Cars signify independence and freedom, central values of the Western white male gender role. In some places, such as Saudi Arabia, women are not even allowed to drive cars. Can you think of other ways that cars have been linked to male roles and status?

What about children and female gender roles? Given that traditional female socialization has emphasized childbearing and child rearing, it is not surprising to find that females are more likely than males to pay attention to, encode, and remember things related to children.

How does the development of gender schemas affect memory? Gender schemas develop early and play an important role in childhood socialization—by eighteen to twenty months of age, children (particularly boys) prefer toys and activities typically associated with their own gender. This increases opportunities to rehearse and remember gender-related behavior. By age two, children begin to develop gender stereotypes about various traits and activities (for example, "girls like dolls" and "boys are rough") and future roles (for example, "girls become nurses" and "boys become doctors") (Bauer, 1993; Martin & Halverson, 1981; Weinraub et al., 1984).

These stereotypes provide ready-made categories to direct attention to and encode gender-related information. Children vary, however, in the extent to which they embrace stereotyped gender-role preferences. When asked to relate information about a story they have been told, children with highly stereotyped preferences have different memories for gender-related information than those with less stereotyped preferences (Welch-Ross & Schmidt, 1996). In general, information that goes along with gender schemas is more easily remembered. Attention appears to be part of the reason. When researchers had fifth-graders read stories about characters and pointed out their non-stereotypical gender traits and activities, the children's memory for items that did not follow the stereotypes improved, suggesting that drawing attention to the elements led to better memory of them. But more is going on, since the non-stereotypical gender elements were still not as easily remembered as the gender-typical items (Koblinsky & Cruse, 1981).

Researchers are trying to explain how gender influences memory. They are asking: Does gender have an impact on memory because of exposure to experiences that develop gender schemas or because it influences initial attention or because of interest and motivation? Does gender affect encoding strategy or rehearsal or retrieval strategy? They are also looking into how we might reduce stereotyping while still maximizing memory potential.

The research linking gender to everyday memory performance reminds us that the outcomes of our cognitive processes are a reflection of our interactions with our environments and the expectations of our culture. Insofar as a culture is gendered—that is, insofar as it systematically provides males and females with different experiences and holds different expectations for their behavior in similar contexts—it is not surprising that gender schemas are available to influence our cognitive processes.

The importance of memory to our personal identity cannot be overemphasized. As film director Luis Buñuel so eloquently stated, "You have to begin to lose your memory if only in bits and pieces, to realize memory is what makes our lives. Life without memory is no life at all. Our memory is our coherence, our reason, our feeling, even our action. Without it we are nothing" (Buñuel, 1984, pp. 4–5).

The Processes of Memory

The existence of memories implies three processes, called encoding, storage, and retrieval.

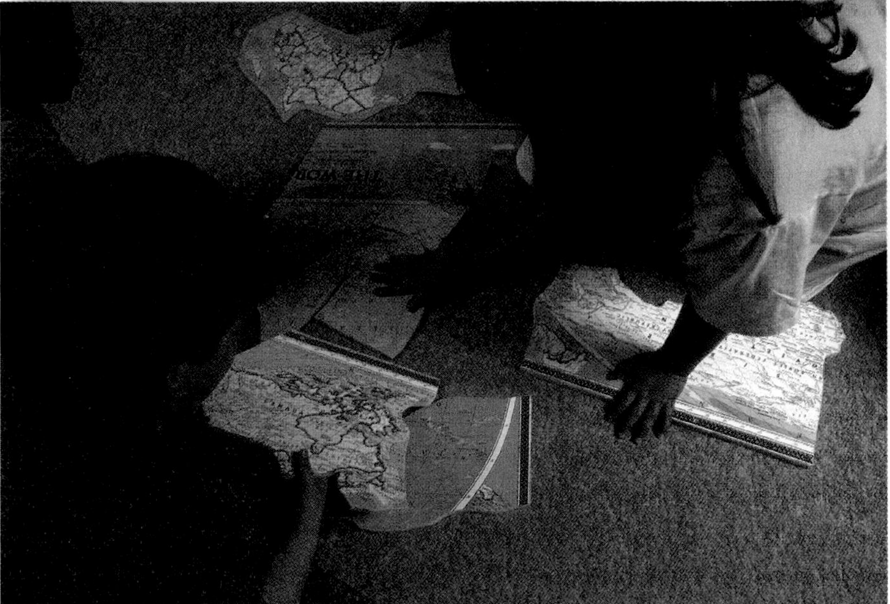

▲ *Children assembling a map puzzle. The mental representation of what a world map should look like has been encoded and stored in their memories.*

THINKING CRITICALLY

One of the most common experiences that each of us has is using coins to make purchases.

Quickly, whose likeness is on a penny? Whose likeness is on a dime? That's easy enough. Now for something harder. Which way is Lincoln facing, right or left, on the face of a penny? What else appears on the face of a penny? What appears on the reverse side?

Check out a real penny if you are not sure. Why is this simple memory test so hard? The test demonstrates a number of important features of memory that we will talk about in detail in this chapter. First, most people do not have a photographic memory. Memories even for the most familiar of events or objects are sketchy. Second, repetition, frequency, or familiarity do not guarantee accurate memory. Otherwise, we would be able to remember what is on a penny without any problems! Third, memory is economical in the sense that we do perfectly all right without the details of prior experiences. While memory for the penny is weak, we have absolutely no difficulty using coins correctly in everyday transactions (Nickerson & Adams, 1979)!

Events in the physical world enter memory, although they enter in a different form from either the proximal or the distal stimuli corresponding to the event. For an event to change from something physical to something mental, an *encoding* process is required to create mental representations of actual events. But encoding isn't enough. For a memory to endure, mental representations must be *stored* over time so that they can be available for use on later occasions. But even encoding and storing memories aren't enough. What good is a stored memory if you can't access it? For a memory to have impact later, it must be *retrievable* from storage. The complete story about how memory works, then, involves all three of these psychological processes.

Learning and memory depend on each other; you can't learn if you can't remember (whether or not you're aware of remembering or learning), and vice versa. Without the ability to encode, store, and retrieve information from memory, you can't learn or build on that information in subsequent experiences. And, without acquiring new information (learning), there is nothing to store in memory.

What we store as memories is not reality itself but rather internal models, or mental representations, of external reality. These ***mental representations*** may include people, objects, or events. Memories depend in part on the biological functioning of our nervous system, particularly the brain, and we assume that creating a memory involves changes (sometimes called

Mental representations of experiences—including representations of people, objects, and events—are, in current cognitive theory, the fundamental elements of memory.

memory traces) in the brain. Behavioral neuroscientists are currently conducting extensive research to identify the brain's counterparts of mental representations. There are some revealing recent studies of the neurological underpinnings of learning and memory, and we will discuss that research at relevant points in the chapter (Squire, 1992). But we currently know much more about the *behaviors* that reflect learning and memory than we do about the underlying biology. Most of this chapter, then, is concerned with the role of learning and memory in human behavior.

The Levels of Memory

You can point to many examples of nonpsychological memory systems in the external world—a grocery list is a kind of memory, so are an appointment calendar, a videotape, a compact disk, and a computer. These artificial memory systems have been a fertile source of ideas about human memory. The computer, in particular, has provided psychologists with a wealth of information-processing analogies for human memory and cognitive processes.

The classical theory of Richard C. Atkinson and Richard M. Shiffrin (1968, 1971) illustrates the information-processing approach. Here is how the analogy works. First, the environment—the distal stimuli—triggers one or more sensory systems. This environmental information then passes through three stages (levels) of memory called sensory memory, short-term memory, and long-term memory. These levels are shown schematically in Figure 7-1. At each level, cognitive processes operate on the information—giving it meaning, refreshing it, integrating it with other information and preparing to pass it along to the next level. Processing information in sensory memory so that it can be transferred to short-term memory, for example, requires extracting features, recognizing stimulus elements, recognizing feature patterns, and naming the stimulus. Processing information in short-term memory so that it can be transferred to long-term memory involves putting elements together into larger units, making associations, and organizing the information. Processing information in long-term memory involves making further connections to what you know—an event from your own past (episodic memory) or an abstract concept or rule (semantic memory).

Second, the amount of information that can be processed is *limited*. Conscious awareness or attention is the primary bottleneck. Look around. Many stimuli are clamoring for your attention. But your attentional resources typically allow you to be conscious of only one thing at a time. If you are distracted by a TV program while trying to study, what you will take away in memory from either your book or the TV program will be reduced from what it would have been if you did either one alone. So, you need a way to control and allocate your attention. Conscious, cognitive control processes determine which of the available information gets used and which gets ignored.

Finally, the flow of information in this system is *interactive*. The system receives information from two sources, one from inside the system (existing memory representations) and one from outside the system (environmental stimulation). Processes operating on information coming from the outside are called ***bottom-up***

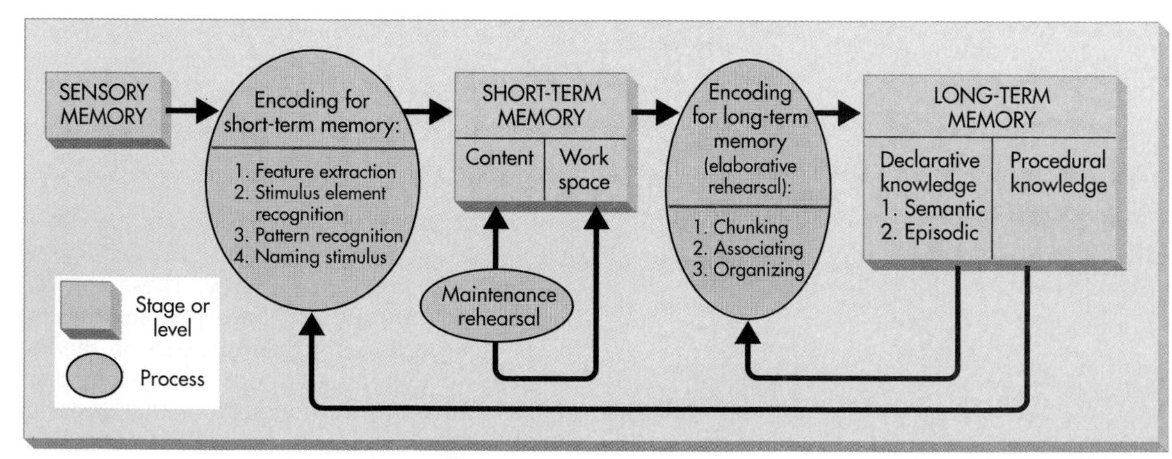

7-1 Memory as an Information-Processing System

A schematic diagram showing the stages or levels and processes involved in the Atkinson and Shiffrin memory theory.

processes (those that are stimulus- or data-driven), while processes using internal sources (those that are memory or knowledge driven) are called ***top-down processes*** (see discussion in Chapter 5). But remember that both sources of information and both types of processes are always involved and mutually influence each other at all times.

Sensory memory is the initial representation of proximal stimuli within a sensory system and lasts only for a moment (0.5 to 2 seconds). A brief glance at a string of symbols will be retained only momentarily unless it can be encoded into something meaningful, like a telephone number. Either the information is used during that sensory memory interval, or it is lost from the system. ***Short-term memory*** is more long-lasting, but still temporary. The contents of short-term memory typically are available to consciousness for only 15 to 20 seconds after initial input, unless they are repeatedly refreshed or rehearsed. For example, it will be necessary to repeat an unfamiliar phone number over and over to yourself to keep it in short-term memory long enough for you to dial it. ***Long-term memory*** lasts indefinitely. It consists of all of a person's stored knowledge and past experiences. This, of course, includes all familiar telephone numbers, such as your own or your best friend's, as well as all the other things you know about your world.

Information undergoes continuous transformation and processing as it flows through this memory system. Information processing begins with sensory memory. To remember the information from sensory memory, it must be encoded into a meaningful format and passed along to short-term memory. In short-term memory, that information must be processed in deeper, more elaborate ways so that it goes into long-term memory. The levels of memory differ from one another in three primary ways: the *duration*, *capacity*, and *type of coding* they employ. Table 7-1 summarizes these differences.

Before discussing this description of memory in detail, we should make note of the fact that all the empirical facts about memory are not yet in, and there is room for disagreement about the best theory. The information-processing theory that we have presented here was first proposed in the 1970s. Other theories have been suggested in the meantime, including one that conceptualizes memory as a single unitary system with no component parts (Craik, 1983; Craik & Jacoby, 1975; McClelland & Rumelhart, 1981).

◀ *Pablo Picasso produces a particularly artful sensory memory by using light to draw a centaur.*

Sensory, short-term, and long-term memory are three basic levels of memory. Sensory memory is the raw image of a distal stimulus. If a sensory memory is encoded, it can move to a more persistent form called short-term memory. Long-term memory is a relatively permanent memory, consisting of all that we know about the world.

Table 7-1 Fundamental Differences in Memory Modules

Type of Memory	Duration	Capacity	Coding	Forgetting
Sensory memory	Less than a second	Very high	"As is" according to the properties of the stimulus (for example, visual stimuli in iconic memory)	Decay
Short-term memory	20 to 30 seconds, if unrehearsed	Limited to 7 ± 2 items	Usually verbal	Decay, interference
Long-term memory	May be unlimited	Probably unlimited	Deeply processed and encoded semantically	Decay, interference, cue dependence

But the memory stages theory has stood the test of time and has recently been labeled the "modal" theory to signify the fact that it is the theoretical framework that most memory researchers adopt even today (Healy & McNamara, 1996).

Sensory Memory

Sensory memory retains the brief lingering impression of a stimulus on a sensory system after the stimulus itself has ended. For example, if you touch your hand with a pencil, you will continue to "feel" it for a second or two even after you take the pencil away.

Most research has focused on the visual and auditory systems, although there are presumably sensory registers for all of our senses. For visual stimuli, the effect is as though we have an extremely brief (approximately 500 milliseconds) "photographic memory," technically called an ***iconic memory***, which gives us a persistent mental image of the stimulus (*icon* is from the Greek word for image, or likeness). Iconic memory is like, but not quite the same thing as, an afterimage. You get afterimages when a flashbulb goes off in your face or when you draw circles of light with a sparkler on the Fourth of July. These effects require relatively intense stimulation to occur. Short-lived iconic memories of any visual stimulus occur, no matter what the intensity of the stimulus is. Moreover, sensory memories are produced in all of our sensory systems for stimuli that are adequate to trigger them. In hearing, for example, we have ***echoic memories***, which are mental echoes of a stimulus.

There are several key points to remember about sensory memory. First, this is a high-capacity form of memory, registering virtually all incoming data available at the receptor. Second, data collected in sensory memory are in raw form, uninterpreted, and at that point uninfluenced by top-down processes. Third, this memory is short-lived, fading in less than 1 second for visual information. In fact, sensory memory is so brief that we are typically unaware of its existence.

George Sperling devised the first accurate method for studying visual sensory memory (Sperling, 1960). Research participants were shown three rows of four symbols (numbers and letters):

7 H T 9
P D 3 1
2 K 8 G

The matrix of symbols was briefly flashed (for less than one-tenth of a second), and then the participants were asked to recall the whole matrix. Typically they would start reading off what they saw, reading from left to right and top to bottom. One person might say, "7, H, T, 9, ah . . . " and fail on the remaining symbols because the sensory image had disappeared. But if the participant really had an image of the whole matrix, he or she should be able to report any row, as long as it was reported before the image disappeared. Sperling demonstrated that if at the time of the flash he inserted an arrow pointing to the row to be reported first, the participant could report any row he asked for. Reporting would be best if the arrow came on before the participant saw the array, because the person could then focus on the crucial row. But the participants could report any row, even when the arrow came on *after* the array, provided it was immediately afterward. If presentation of the arrow was delayed until the image had faded, the participants could not report very well. As the delay interval between the array and the arrow widened, from no delay up to a one-second delay, report accuracy decreased. With a one-second delay, the accuracy of report was no better than when there was no arrow (see Figure 7-2).

If we want to use the information in sensory memory, we must quickly encode it into a more durable form. Processing begins with *attention*, which selectively determines what, out of the massive amount of information in sensory memory, will "get through" for further examination. Attention allows us to focus on parts of the stimulus and thereby recognize some of its

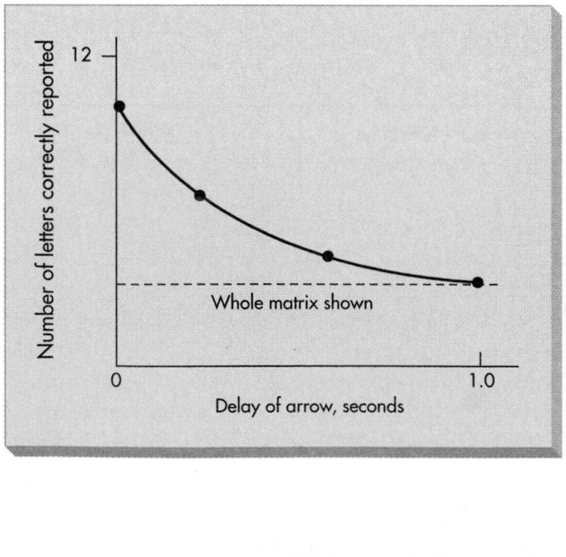

7-2 Decay of Visual Sensory Memory

Sensory memory begins at a near-perfect level but decays rapidly. Information in sensory memory must be quickly processed to a meaningful level rapidly if it is to be transferred into short-term memory.

features and feature patterns. But any weaknesses in sensory memory may create substantial problems for further processing of sensory information. For example, some psychologists have suggested that people of normal intelligence who have difficulty in reading may suffer from a deficit in iconic memory. Researchers in one study followed Sperling's method for studying visual sensory memory and briefly presented sixth graders with letters or shapes arrayed in circles on a screen. When each circle disappeared from the screen, it was replaced by a marker that pointed to the position that one of the previous letters or shapes had occupied. The sixth grader's task was to report the letter or shape that had appeared in that position. Poor readers performed as well as good readers as long as the marker appeared not more than one- or two-tenths of a second after the figures were removed. For longer delays, however, the performance of poor readers declined, as if they had lost the information in their iconic memory more quickly than the good readers (Morrison, Giordani, & Nagy, 1977).

Sensory memory can be thought of as a kind of "snapshot" of the world, storing raw sensory information for a short period. Only information transferred to some other type of memory will be preserved beyond a second or two.

Short-Term or Working Memory

Short-term memory is traditionally thought of as the intermediate stage between sensory memory and long-term memory. It is the "workbench" of your consciousness, and includes your awareness of the sensations, feelings, and thoughts you are experiencing at a given moment. But it differs from sensory memory in several ways. First, while the capacity of sensory memory is extremely large, the capacity of short-term memory is severely limited. It can hold only a limited amount of information at any one time. Second, whereas the contents of sensory memory are unprocessed, information in short-term memory has been encoded, matched with existing memories, and subjected to top-down influences. The resulting mental representation is no longer a point-by-point replica of the original stimulus. Finally, although information in short-term memory fades less rapidly than that in sensory memory, it does fade and will be completely lost in about twenty to thirty seconds, unless it is processed further.

7-3 Short-Term Memory as a Workbench

This diagram shows the workbench analogy to human short-term memory. There are two parts, one devoted to the storage of items (content) and the other used for processing those items (work space). (Source: Adapted from Klatzky, 1980)

Short-term memory consists of both content and work space. The content is information we can immediately recall or directly "read out" (for example, recalling verbatim five words on a list), which is in current awareness or consciousness and is primarily (although not exclusively) verbal and auditory in nature. The contents of short-term memory can be worked on or processed (organizing the five recalled words into a phrase or short sentence).

Roberta Klatzky (1980) introduced the analogy of a workbench in a carpentry shop to conceptualize how the content and the work space operate together in short-term memory (see Figure 7-3). The carpenter's materials are piled up on part of the bench (content area). The rest of the bench is where the carpenter works on materials with tools (processing area) to create something that wasn't there to begin with. How much space the carpenter devotes to each aspect is variable and changes from job to job. Some jobs require large amounts of work space, leaving little room for keeping materials handy. Other jobs require little work space, allowing more space for the materials. Just as the carpenter must contend with a workbench of a limited size, all of us must do our mental work with limited short-term memory capacity.

Short-term memory normally can handle about seven items of information when little or no work must be done on the information. For example, in the memory-span task, research participants are read a series of digits (try "4-3-9-8-7-5-6") and are simply asked to repeat them (no work on them is required). Memory-span experiments show that people typically have a normal, untrained capacity of seven, plus or minus two (that is, between five and nine) items. However, when research partici-

▲ *Rajan Mahadevan, who memorized the first 50,000 digits of Pi, probably used some sort of chunking system to commit to memory such a large string of numbers.*

pants are required to work on this information in short-term memory (for example, adding successive numbers), the maximum number of items that can be kept immediately available drops, because resources must be shifted to working memory to process the information already in the system (Baddeley, 1990).

Short-term memory is not limited to individual digits or letters. Individual items of information can be grouped into ***chunks***, the units of short-term memory, which combine, integrate, or unite separate items. For example, t-a-b-l-e contains five separate letters. But the word *table*, which contains those letters, constitutes a single chunk. A chunk can contain many individual bits or pieces of information, just as long as those pieces are somehow integrated or cohesive. Short-term memory can hold seven, plus or minus two, chunks of information, so the word *table* is merely one of the seven that you can retain. Try remembering table, spoon, lamp, wagon, tree, bench, moon. That's a total of thirty-two letters, but seven words. You probably can remember all seven of these short words, at least for a while, even though it means remembering thirty to fifty individual letters. But if you were tested on a string of letters that you could not easily chunk into words (try, "b-r-h-s-k-q-m-e-x-p"), you would probably remember seven or fewer different letters. Because you can normally handle only about seven chunks, you should try to squeeze as much information as possible into each chunk to maximize your short-term memory.

Can you think of examples in your daily activities where chunking has been used to facilitate recall? What about telephone numbers? How much more difficult would it be to learn 6-0-3-5-5-5-2-7-5-8 than (603) 555-2758. Or the new zip codes? Consider trying to learn 8-7-0-2-9-1-8-0-1 vs. 87029-1801.

Meaningfulness enhances the effectiveness of chunking. Consider the following sequence of letters: T-V-F-B-I-J-F-K-Y-M-C-A. It has twelve letters and is thus beyond the span of short-term memory for letters. It may help to chunk the sequence into four groups of three letters, TVF-BIJ-FKY-MCA, but these chunks don't form words or anything meaningful. Consider the same letter sequence, however, chunked in a different way: TV-FBI-JFK-YMCA. Now it becomes easy to remember the twelve letters because they are chunked (recoded) into a smaller number (four) of meaningful units. Each unit contains more than one letter, making the overall capacity larger than seven letters. Chunking information into larger meaningful units is one of the most important processes of working memory. It is also one key to expanding your own memory capacity.

Long-Term Memory

Long-term memory differs from sensory and short-term memory in three ways: First, its capacity is so large that, for all intents and purposes, it can be considered unlimited. That is, according to some theorists going back to Sigmund Freud (1917), everything you ever learned or experienced might be stored and available for retrieval from long-term memory if you could just find a way to access it. Have you ever been reminded about an old experience that you hadn't thought about in years? Clearly the memory was there, but simply not retrieved over the years. Second, once information is stored in long-term memory, it is much more resistant to forgetting than is information either in sensory or short-term memory. Nonetheless, you probably don't remember all the details of an old experience because some of what happened never got past sensory and short-term memory and so is not available to be retrieved.

Third, items of information in long-term memory are richly interconnected. When new information is added to long-term memory, it is associated with all existing information that bears any relationship to it. Thus, when you learn a new fact, you understand that fact partly in terms of your existing knowledge and beliefs. In addition, new information can change the meaning and memory of information that has previously been stored. The effect of our previous knowledge and beliefs on what we remember was demonstrated in a study that showed that beliefs about occupations (occupational stereotypes) can influence our long-term memory of events (Cohen, 1981).

Think about your expectations for a woman who is a waitress compared to one who is a librarian. Which woman is more likely to drink beer? Wear glasses? Listen to classical music? Drink wine? After identifying activities associated with each of these occupations, the researchers developed videotapes of a woman celebrating a birthday that combined those activities in various ways. For example, the woman on the tape might wear glasses (librarian stereotype) and drink beer (waitress stereotype). The researchers then showed the videotapes to research participants. Some participants were told the woman was a waitress, others that she was a librarian. Later, the researchers asked the participants what they remembered having seen ("What did the woman drink?" "What kind of music did she listen to?"). How well an acitivity was remembered depended on how closely it fit occupational stereotypes. When research participants thought they were watching a waitress drink beer, for example, they were more likely to remember the activity than when they saw her drink wine. The reverse was true when the librarian was seen to drink beer versus wine. This difference remained stable over time and was found when participants were tested seven days later (Cohen, 1981). Thus, long-term memory, while immense in capacity, can still be inaccurate (it may not be the same as what actually happened) and is subject to considerable bias and distortion from the inter-association of new information with old memories.

Sometimes, rather than exhibiting bias or distortion in retrieval from long-term memory, we just fail to remember anything at all about a previous experience. If long-term memory is unlimited and if the information it contains is resistant to forgetting, why should we have such memory failures? The answer often lies not in the storage of facts but in the retrieval process (Brown, 1991). We will have more to say about "forgetting" later in this chapter.

Encoding

To make future use of a current experience, you must somehow form or encode representations that can be retrieved at a later date. Representations can take a variety of forms, psychologically, from new associations, as we saw in the case of conditioning, to sensory images and verbal descriptions. There are events and processes going on neurologically as well as psychologically during the encoding and consolidation of new memories. Recent work in behavioral neuroscience has focused on a protein called CREB found in the nucleus of nerve cells in the brain (Abel et al., 1995; Carew, 1996; Silva & Giese, 1997). When a signal is passed from one nerve cell to another in certain areas of the brain, an electrochemical process is set up in the cell, which spreads to the cell's nucleus. There the signal activates the CREB protein. In turn, the activated CREB targets a site on the cell's DNA, turning on a specific set of genes. This sequence is depicted in Figure 7-4. Proteins manufactured by the turned-on genes induce growth in the cell's dendrites, strengthening the connection between the activated neurons. It is now believed that this strengthened connection is the structural underpinning of a newly encoded association or memory.

The level of activity in the neurons is a long way from the practical behavioral task of encoding new information, however. To encode psychologically, sensory memory must hold onto stimuli long enough for some of that information to be captured in short-term memory. The information that gets to short-term memory is already encoded by top-down processes that recognize these stimuli as meaningful. Mc-

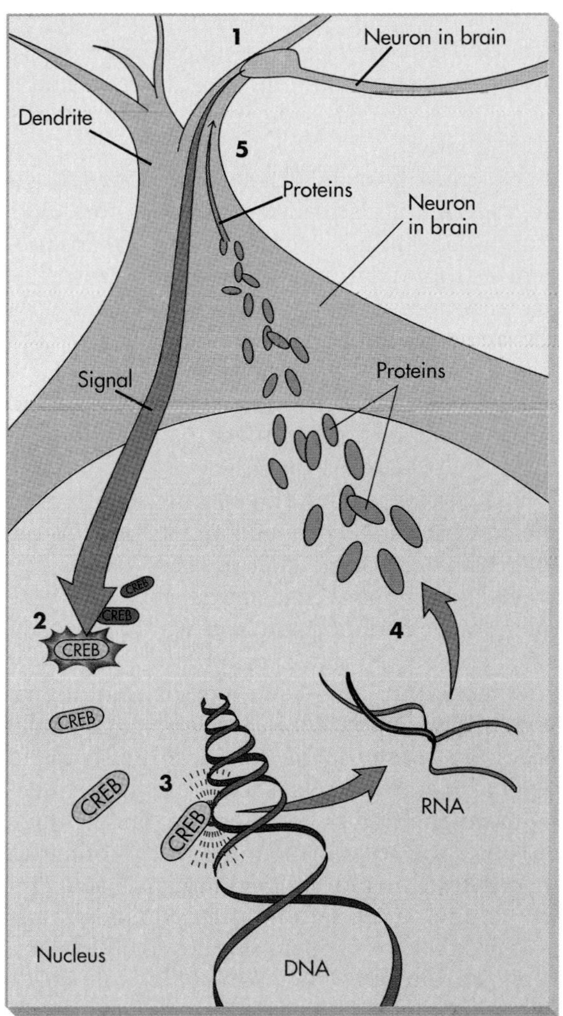

7-4 How Nerve Cells Create Lasting Memories

When a protein called CREB, which is found in the nucleus of nerve cells, is activated by incoming signals or nerve impulses from other nerve cells, it creates a memory record of that information. Researchers believe that this occurs as follows: (1) an incoming signal arrives at the dendrites of a neuron; (2) the signal travels to the nucleus of the cell, where it activates CREB; (3) CREB turns on certain genes in the cell's DNA; and (4) proteins made by these genes induce growth of the dendrites, thus strengthening its connections with other neurons. CREB creates a physical basis for memory of the event that first triggered the nerve impulse. (Adapted from Silva & Giese, 1997)

Clelland and Rumelhart (1981) have given us one description of how top-down processes work in the identification of meaningful stimuli (see Chapter 5). Encoding at the level of short-term memory, however, might not be complete enough to ensure transfer to long-term memory. To remember the items on something even as simple as a grocery list, for example, takes conscious effort. New meaningful information does not automatically stick in memory. Reading for new knowledge or studying class notes for an exam entails an intentional attempt to put new information into long-term memory. Thus, encoding usually requires conscious use of learning processes and strategies.

Maintenance and Elaborative Rehearsal

Maintenance rehearsal is the overt or mental repetition of an item or set of items to keep those items in consciousness until they can be acted upon. Elaborative rehearsal is the enhancement of the meaning of items so they can be stored more permanently in long-term memory.

What are learning or encoding strategies, how do they work, and what kinds are most useful in forming lasting memories? One simple and obvious encoding strategy is repetition or rehearsal. There are two types of rehearsal: one to maintain information in short-term memory and one for transferring information to long-term memory.

The first type is called ***maintenance rehearsal*** (this is also called ***shallow processing***). Simply repeating an item to yourself helps prevent it from dropping out of short-term memory. The item is not transformed but simply repeated, usually verbally, to keep it "alive and fresh" in memory. If someone gave you a phone number to call, you might repeat it over and over to yourself until you get to the phone and dial it.

But, having dialed and reached your party, the number is likely to fade and be unavailable for retrieval on some later occasion unless you do something more than just repeat it. Suppose the number is important. You want to remember it so you can dial it again later. To encode new items into long-term memory, additional processing beyond simple rehearsal is generally necessary. ***Elaborative rehearsal*** (also called ***deep processing***) creates a more complex mental representation of new items by linking them in some way to information already contained in long-term memory. Try chunking. You might try to find a pattern in the phone number (444-3232) or look for similarities to other numbers you already know (492-*1492*, "oh, that's when Columbus arrived in America"). Any-

THINKING CRITICALLY

Deep processing has been shown to lead to better learning and memory than shallow processing. How can we test the difference in the two kinds of processing?

You could present the following list of twenty words to two groups of your friends:

fast	shoe	rug	ticket
cold	cook	play	car
book	steal	walk	toy
chair	right	mad	stamp
lost	drink	kick	house

For one group of friends, present each word and ask them to think of another word that rhymes with it (a shallow-processing task). For the other group, ask them to think of a word that means the same thing as the word does (a deep task requiring subjects to process meaning). Don't tell either group that you are going to test their memories for the twenty words. You should find that recall is better for the group asked to think of synonyms than for the group asked to think of rhymes.

Note that neither of these two groups was warned about the memory test, and thus neither presumably had any intention of learning the words. Nonetheless, they did learn many words and were able to recall them later, especially in the deep-processing condition. This means that the type of processing that you apply to materials to be learned is a critical variable. What if you had had a third group who was told merely to memorize the words? Thomas Hyde and James Jenkins (1973) demonstrated that telling subjects to memorize the words does not give a better recall performance than does deep processing without instructions to memorize. Hyde and Jenkins concluded that instructions to learn may improve recall by inducing deeper processing.

thing you can do while rehearsing to form a more elaborate mental representation of the material will enhance the likelihood of its being encoded into long-term memory.

According to Fergus Craik and Robert Lockhart (1972), there are many different levels or types of memory processing. Some involve only superficial or shallow treatment of an item, and others involve deeper processing. Shallow processing leads to poor learning and recall compared with deep processing. Deep processing forces individuals to attend to the information's semantic (meaning) aspects. Shallow processing involves non-semantic aspects, such as the sound of words. The amount and type of rehearsal that is performed determine how much and what kind of information is transferred from short-term to long-term memory. The deeper (more effortful) the processing, the stronger and more elaborate the encoding in memory. Deep processing appears to increase the number of connections or associations between new and already known information. Those associations then serve as cues for recalling the new information on a later occasion. Social and cultural influences are represented in linguistic structures and semantic concepts and can affect storage and retrieval of information in long-term memory. Thus, a person who lives in a city may remember how to get somewhere based on such cues as street signs, store names, or buildings, while a person who lives in a remote area may remember a certain tree or cluster of bushes or a stream as cues to how to find their way. Or, as we saw in our opening example, college students in England or in the United States might remember "The War of the Ghosts" quite differently from the Native Americans who created it. Regardless of what the cues are, however, a person's ability to remember an item increases with the number and complexity of representations it produces.

Other Encoding Procedures

There are two variations of elaborative rehearsal that are particularly useful for encoding new material. One is to arrange the material to be encoded and stored according to some already familiar organization. If what you want to remember is a grocery list, maybe you could categorize the items—*dairy products*: milk, butter, yogurt; *vegetables*: celery, carrots, spinach, lettuce; *fruits*: apples, pears, grapes—to make the long list shorter and easier to remember. The other involves the formation of mental images. You might try making up a vivid mental image of the items, picturing the vegetables, for example, as combined in a salad.

Organization

The importance of organization can be demonstrated in a number of ways. Suppose you were asked to remember the following list of words: *coherent, to, easy, well, messages, are, and, remember, organized*. Because there is no apparent relationship among the words, the list is likely to be difficult to remember in its entirety. But suppose now you were given a list of the same words arranged in an orderly, logical way: *well, organized, and, more, coherent, messages, are, easy, to, remember*. You will do far better on the memory task with the organized list than with the random one. A single coherent image or message is easier to remember and retrieve than several unrelated items (see Figure 7-5). A sentence will always be easier to remember than

A Random

B Organized

7-5 How Organization Affects Memory

Even though the same items appear in Panels A and B, recall will be greater for the items in Panel B. Presentation as an organized scene facilitates memory.

Organizing material is a powerful way to enhance encoding and improve memory. Chunking is a way of organizing a large amount of material into meaningful groupings that combine separate items.

the same words in scrambled order (Kintsch, 1974).

Possibly the most important organizational encoding technique is chunking, which we introduced earlier in this chapter. An especially impressive demonstration of this technique was provided by Anders Ericsson (Ericsson, 1985; Ericsson & Charness, 1994; Ericsson, Chase, & Faloon, 1980). Ericsson and his colleagues studied a memory-span task in which an individual was asked to recall a randomly ordered list of digits, immediately after the digits were read aloud by the experimenter. When relatively fast presentation rates are used (one digit every one or two seconds), people typically can remember only seven plus or minus 2 digits, relying primarily on short-term memory and maintenance rehearsal techniques. To a typical person, each digit in the list represents one chunk. Ericsson's research participant was limited in this way on his initial memory-span attempts. But at a certain point, he discovered a useful chunking strategy. His experience as a long-distance runner led him to adopt the strategy of encoding groups of three or four digits as running times. Thus, the sequence 4-1-3 would be chunked as a slow one-mile time; 9-2-7 as a good two-mile time; 6-5-8 as an awful one-mile time; and so on. Short sequences that couldn't be interpreted as running times were coded as ages of people he knew or imagined. Other sequences were encoded as familiar dates, such as 1776 or 1941. This chunking method depends on associating digit sequences with information already in long-term memory. If it can be done, then the person is freed from having to maintain the individual digits in a limited short-term memory. Ericsson's research participant was not a genius; yet after 190 hours of practice (spread out over five days) he achieved a digit span of over *eighty* items, as shown in Figure 7-6.

Even though he did not claim that everyone can develop an eighty-digit memory span, Ericsson was able to replicate these findings with several other highly motivated research participants. With intensive, long-term, deliberate practice, each person developed his or her own chunking system. The common feature of all of these systems was the connection of chunks of digits with information already in long-term memory. Everyone developed an incredible skill for rapidly encoding digit sequences and retrieving them from their highly organized memories. Moreover, these skills were not limited simply to digit span; Ericsson and Polson (1988) found a similar level of skill in a restaurant waiter who could handle the complete dinner orders of sixteen people without writing anything down (Ericsson & Charness, 1994).

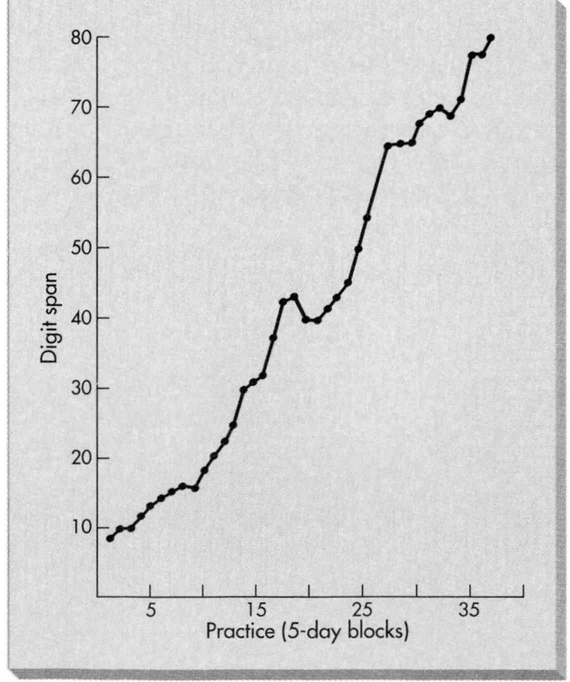

7-6 Chunking to Expand Memory

This figure shows a research participant's memory for randomly ordered digits. Across 190 hours of practice (38 five-day blocks), his memory span increased tenfold as he developed a strategy to organize the digits into chunks that were meaningful to him. (Source: Adapted from Ericsson, Chase, & Faloon, 1980)

Imagery

The ease with which imagery can be used depends on the nature of the materials to be learned. If you are learning from pictures, diagrams, movies, or other audiovisual media, the use of imagery is straightforward because the information is already in "imageable" form. But verbal material, especially abstract verbal material, may not be imaged so readily, and will require effort to convert it from verbal to visual form. The ease with which this conversion can be made is correlated with how abstract the material is. Words that refer to objects, such as *table, door, grass, telephone, dress* are relatively easy to image. Words that refer to ideas or abstractions, such as *freedom, envy, nation, fate, thought,* on the other hand, typically fail to evoke images unless they have been specifically linked to them in the culture.

Words that are easy to image are typically learned faster by everyone than are words that are hard to image. It is the encoding of words as images that somehow enhances their storage

SEEKING SOLUTIONS

Mnemonics: Memory Tricks

We know that imagery and organization can help us remember, but what are some practical suggestions for using imagery and organization?

Mnemonic tricks, which are based on imagery and organization, can be used to help you in remembering specific information. Each of them can be used to assist your memory for specific information. One such mnemonic aid, called the peg-word system, requires you to memorize a set of "memory pegs" in advance. A convenient system of pegs consists of the first x numbers and words that rhyme with those numbers. The rhyme helps retrieve the word when given the number. For example:

One is a bun.	Six is sticks.
Two is a shoe.	Seven is heaven.
Three is a tree.	Eight is a gate.
Four is a door.	Nine is wine.
Five is a hive.	Ten is a hen.

Once you know the peg-word system, you can use it for a variety of memory tasks. Suppose, for example, your task is to memorize a shopping list in its proper order. Use your imagery skill to "hook" each item to be purchased to one of the number-word pegs. This can be done by using an image that entails an interaction between a peg word and a list item. If coffee is the first item, imagine a steaming hot cup of coffee with a bun lying on the saucer. If milk is second on the list, think of a shoe filled to overflowing with milk. Continue hooking each item on the shopping list onto the next number-word peg. When you get to the store, reciting the numbers in order, 1 through x, will bring to mind each peg word, which will, in turn, activate an image of the desired item with which it has been paired. Try it. Even though the system seems to require some excess or superfluous baggage, it works!

Another common mnemonic method is the method of loci (locations). Again, memory pegs are required, but this time the pegs are a familiar sequence of locations that can easily be recalled in order. Locations might be based on things you would see on a long walk from your home, for example, a mailbox, a church, a big oak tree, etc. Each item to be learned is associated with a different location, possibly through imagery again. If milk is on your list, you could think of milk spilling out of the mailbox, drenching the ground. Coffee might be visualized at a church social. And so on. To recall the list, just take a mental walk, imaging each location to recall the desired item. Bizarre images are more likely to be remembered (Paivio, 1986).

A somewhat different, but proven mnemonic method is natural language mediation, which can be used to remember unfamiliar items. The basic idea is to transform the unfamiliar term into a word or words that are already a part of your natural language. For example, if you are trying to learn the new terms *olfaction* (for smell) and *gustation* (for taste), you might think of "oil factory" (a smelly place) and "gusto" (a great taste).

A method that uses both imagery and natural language mediation is called the key-word method, which is readily applicable to learning the vocabulary of a second language. Suppose you want to use this method to learn the Spanish word *carta*, meaning "(postal) letter." You first transform the unfamiliar Spanish word into an English word that sounds similar, such as "cart." Then construct a visual image of a letter inside a shopping cart. You can use that image to help you remember the meaning of *carta* when you encounter it in the future—*carta*—cart—letter.

One final mnemonic device is the use of the acronym. Recall that an acronym is a string of letters, usually pronounceable, standing for a series of words and typically made up of the first letter of each word in the series. For example, HOMES is an acronym used to remember the names of the Great Lakes: Huron, Ontario, Michigan, Erie, and Superior. If you are creative, you can make up your own acronyms for new material you have to learn. Suppose you want an easy way to remember the five mnemonic devices we have just discussed—*p*eg word, method of *l*oci, *n*atural language mediation, *k*ey word, and *a*cronym. Can you make up an acronym to remember them? If so, you will have condensed a lot of information into one chunk. Sometimes it helps to reorganize the information. How about the word PLANK? P for peg; L for loci; A for acronym; N for natural; K for key. Test yourself later to see if it works.

▶ *Mnemonic strategies should not be more difficult to recall than the facts they are intended to help you remember.*

in long-term memory, perhaps by giving the learner two kinds of representations, one verbal, the other visual, that can be retrieved later (Paivio, 1986). For hundreds of years, memory experts have relied heavily on ***mnemonics***, or tricks for remembering, which use images to enhance memory. Individuals who make up visual images of the material to be learned perform at a much higher level than do individuals who do not use images. Incidentally, the more bizarre the image you create, the better your memory will be (Bower, 1972; McDaniel, Einstein, DeLosh, May, & Brady, 1995).

Even abstract items can be imaged, though perhaps only with great effort. For example, justice might be represented by a blindfolded woman holding balanced scales, envy by a green-eyed monster, and a nation by its flag. If you want to remember a list that contains abstract items, try to imagine the items in a stack, one on top of another. Visualize what the stack would be like (for example, blindfolded justice holding up a green-eyed monster waving a flag). Try another example. Do you remember the lobes of the cerebral cortex (from Chapter 3)? They are the frontal, occipital, temporal, and parietal lobes. Try to come up with a distinctive image for each one, based on its name. A clock might do for the temporal (time) lobe, a pear for the parietal. If you can find a memorable image for each lobe and somehow visualize a composite picture of them, you might never again forget the names of these parts of the brain.

Trying to image a list or a story for purposes of remembering may be more important in some cultures than in others. Educational practice in industrialized societies like the United States, for example, emphasizes the language skills of reading and writing. Less industrialized cultures have stronger oral traditions that require remembering what has been seen or heard, rather than writing it down. How might this difference affect the encoding of oral information? Two groups of students—one in Ghana and one in New York—were asked to read and remember "The War of the Ghosts" story that you learned about at the beginning of this chapter. Students listened to the story without taking notes and without being told they would be tested. Two weeks later, all students were asked to write down as much as they could remember. Their stories were scored for number of words and number of themes recalled. Which group of students would you predict had a greater amount and accuracy of recall as measured by number of words and themes of their stories? As depicted in Figure 7-7, Ghanaian students used both more words and included more themes in their stories than did New York students. Their superior performance was attributed to their culture's long oral tradition, which requires developing skill in encoding oral information (Ross & Millsom, 1970).

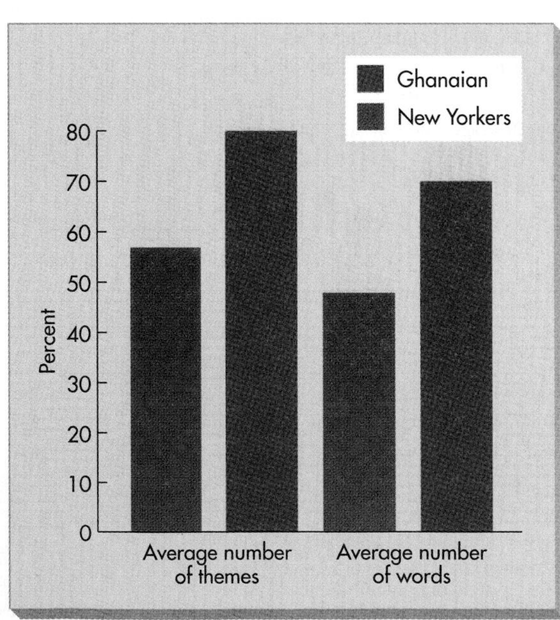

7-7 Culture Influences Encoding

There is cross-cultural variation in the ability to encode information in sounds, that is, in the ability to remember material presented orally rather than visually. When students from Ghana and students from New York were asked to listen to and then recall "The War of the Ghosts" story, the Ghanaian students used more words and included more themes in their responses than did the students from New York. Researchers believe that the Ghanaian students performance was superior as a result of their culture's long oral tradition, in which it was a common occurrence to encode information in sounds. (Source: Ross & Millsom, 1970)

Spacing of Practice

In developing strategies for encoding information and enhancing your memory, keep in mind that *timing* can have a major effect, particularly for memory of verbal items (Shaughnessy, 1976). You will remember more on a subsequent test if you space out your study time rather than concentrating it in a single block, even though the total amount of study time is the same. This is referred to as an advantage of *distributed* (or spaced) over *massed* practice. How would you use distributed practice to help you remember a list of vocabulary items? Consider splitting your two hours of study time over four separate thirty-minute sessions (say, thirty minutes a day for four days).

There are several possible reasons for the spaced advantage. At the structural level, what happens in brain cells might be affected. There is only a limited amount of CREB protein available for activation in brain cells. The available CREB might limit the amount of information a learner can take in and encode at one time. Time-out intervals between periods of practice would allow the CREB that is activated during encoding to recover and to be available to respond again during the next practice period (Abel et al., 1995). Another reason, at a functional level, entails the *context* in which material is learned. When you space out your study time, your surroundings are more likely to change, increasing the richness and variety of external cues associated with the material you are studying (Martin, 1972; Smith & Vela, 1992). Why is this important? First, varying the context requires the learner to make more of an effort to process the material to overcome any interference that changing contexts might introduce (Battig, 1979). Deeper processing enhances recall. Second, the more external cues associated with the material, the more potential cues there are to facilitate its retrieval.

Another reason for the spaced practice advantage lies in *characteristics* of the material itself. Any given stimulus has many attributes that need to be encoded (for example, its meaning, its associations, its emotional connotations, its constituent letters). Suppose you wanted someone to respond with the word "fish" to the nonsense stimulus "fyrg." The link between the two could be encoded in a variety of ways. For example, both are four-letter words, both start with "f," "yrg" is a sound you might make when held underwater where the fish live, and so forth. The more variation in the ways you encode the material, the stronger the association.

Practice or repetition of material to be learned can either be massed, so that little or no time passes between repetitions, or spaced (distributed), leaving time between repetitions for other activities.

Is All Encoding Effortful?

Although encoding new material into long-term memory almost always requires some conscious effort, there are some interesting exceptions. Lynn Hasher and Rose Zacks (1979, 1984) have demonstrated that, for human adult learners, automatic encoding, sometimes referred to as ***implicit learning***, is typical for certain basic aspects of events, like the frequency of experiencing something or the time and place of an experience. So, if you are presented with a list of words to examine (not necessarily to learn or remember), some of which repeat and some of which do not, you will not only remember some of the words on a later occasion but you will tend to remember which ones were repeated and how often. Being told in advance that you are going to be asked about the frequency of certain words in a list or where they were located in the list is of no assistance in remembering these facts. They seem just to be automatically a part of memory, and you can't consciously enhance the memory (Jacoby, Toth, & Yonelinas, 1993).

Moreover, encoding that at first requires effort can become automatic with practice and repetition. For example, novice readers must work hard to encode written words for meaning, but experienced readers do so effortlessly. The automatic processing for meaning that goes

◀ *Alf and Mr. T, characters from television shows of the early 1980s, are probably stored in your long-term memory, even though you didn't intentionally encode them.*

RED	RED
BLACK	YELLOW
YELLOW	GREEN
BLUE	BLUE
RED	GREEN
GREEN	BLUE
YELLOW	RED
BLACK	YELLOW
BLUE	BLACK
BLACK	GREEN

7-8 The Stroop Effect

Name the color of the ink that each word is printed in. Did you find it difficult to name the ink colors in the second column? Did you make any mistakes? Did you have a tendency to read the word rather than the name of the ink color? If so, you have experienced the Stroop effect.

on in highly practiced or skilled reading can be easily demonstrated. Name the colors of the inks used to print the words in Figure 7-8. You will find it nearly impossible to ignore the conflicting meaning of the words; meaning is automatically encoded and comes immediately to consciousness well before ink color, and this automatic process slows down your ability to name the colors. Difficulty in reading the names of colors that are printed in ink of a different color is called the ***Stroop effect*** after its discoverer (Stroop, 1935). It reflects the fact that reading generally involves processing the meaning of words while the physical aspects of the words, such as the color they are printed in, is ignored. Naming colors printed in different-color inks requires conscious effortful processing, which is slower than the usual automatic processing of written words for meaning.

► A picture is worth a thousand words. How many words would you need to describe the bombing of the Murrah Federal Building in Oklahoma City?

Storage

Once encoded, a memory will stay as usable knowledge in memory storage for an indefinite period. How long is still in dispute. Some theorists think that storage can last forever and that nothing is really lost once it gets to long-term memory; Freud might have been the first to make that claim. Other theorists, including Gestalt psychologists, argue for a principle of "use it or lose it": memories decay if they are not refreshed periodically. We will discuss examples of both ideas in the section that follows.

The mental representations of reality that we store in memory are a direct result of the encoding processes we use when we encounter a new event in our environment. Structurally, the representation might be some neurological change in the state of synapses between neurons (Abel et al., 1995). Psychologically, we cannot directly observe or measure what is stored to represent each new experience. The best guess is that storage codes are primarily one of two types, *verbal* or *sensory*. Usually, we can turn to-be-remembered events into verbal descriptions. In fact, often the event itself is largely verbal (for example, a conversation or a lecture). But sometimes words might be inadequate to the task. How do you remember someone's face, for example, or an artist's painting or the smell of a fine wine? There is some truth to the saying that a picture (or image) is worth a thousand words. Thus, coding can be sensory or image-like. Beyond words and pictures, coding sometimes involves movement or action, which is sometimes called "muscle memory." For example, you might have a memory of how it "feels" to shift gears in a car with a manual transmission—particularly if you have a stick shift. Using chop-

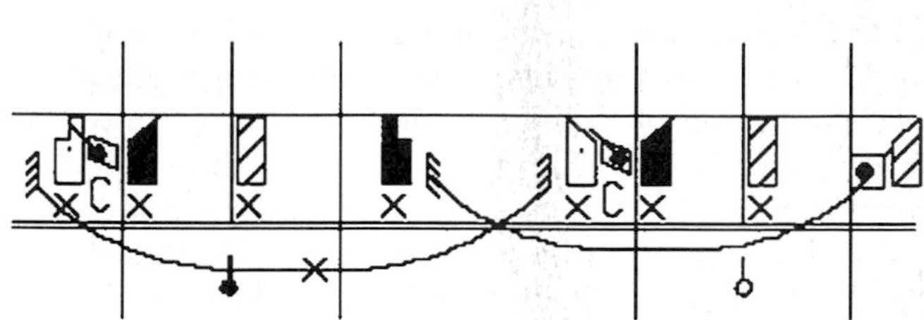

◀ *Dancers use Laban notation, shown in the diagram at left, to represent dance movement sequences as an aid to procedural knowledge. Here, the dancers and the notation represent the same movement.*

sticks or holding a pen might be coded verbally or pictorially in your memory, but your muscle memory is also involved.

Procedural and Declarative Knowledge

All knowledge stored in long-term memory can be thought of as either procedural or declarative. ***Procedural knowledge*** is "knowing how" (skills, motor abilities, and muscle memories), whereas ***declarative knowledge*** is "knowing that" (remembered events, facts, and even beliefs). For example, you *know how* to ride a bicycle, but you *know that* Martin Luther King, Jr., was a key leader in the U.S. civil rights movement. In order to know how to ride a bicycle, you must store in memory a sequence of coordinated movements, which you are probably incapable of verbalizing. To know about Martin Luther King, Jr., however, you store facts about him that are typically easy to verbalize. Incidentally, even if you do not know how to ride a bicycle, you can still recognize bicycle riding when you see it. That is, you can have declarative knowledge about something (bike riding) without any (or much) corresponding procedural knowledge (being able to ride a bike). This has caused some psychologists to argue that declarative knowledge always occurs before procedural, or that procedural knowledge grows out of declarative (Anderson, 1990).

Declarative memory is fact-based, consisting of all your worldly knowledge. In contrast, procedural memory is skill-based, consisting of all the motor movements you know how to perform.

Some psychologists argue that procedural memory constitutes a separate memory system from that of declarative memory (Tulving, 1985; Squire, 1987). Each system contains a unique kind of information or experience (see Table 7-2). Procedural and declarative knowledge differ in several ways: (1) Declarative knowledge—facts—is acquired in an all-or-none manner, whereas procedural knowledge—skills—is acquired gradually. You either know what a cow is or you don't. But you can partially know or master a skill like playing the guitar without being fully knowledgeable. (2) Declarative knowledge can be verbally communicated, whereas procedural knowledge often can only be demonstrated. We can tell you about Sigmund Freud's eminent daughter Anna

Table 7-2 Procedural and Declarative Memory

	Declarative Memory	Procedural Memory
Kind of knowledge	Facts, beliefs, events	Skills, motor performance, muscle memories
How knowledge is acquired	All at once	Gradually
Probable basis in brain	Cortical regions	Subcortical regions
Learning procedure	Verbal, by instruction	Motor, by practice or repetition

Freud, but you may have difficulty explaining in words how to do a parallel turn in skiing. (3) The bases for declarative and procedural knowledge may lie in different brain structures (Squire, 1987). Consider H.M., a brain-injured patient, who appeared to have lost the ability to transfer new information from short-term into long-term memory. Research has shown that H.M.'s deficit applies only to new declarative but not to new procedural knowledge (Moscovitz & Klein, 1980; Daum & Schugens, 1996). For example, if asked to assemble the same picture puzzle over and over again, H.M. and other people with this deficit will claim each time that they have never before seen or attempted the puzzle. Nonetheless, they will become more skillful in assembling the puzzle with each attempt, completing it more and more rapidly. Their claim of no knowledge of ever doing the puzzle suggests a deficit in declarative memory; their increased skillfulness suggests an intact procedural memory.

PET scan and brain injury evidence has shown that different areas of the brain are activated in procedural versus declarative tasks: cortical regions for declarative memories and subcortical regions for procedural memories, implying anatomically different memory storage systems (Tulving, 1985; Daum & Schugens, 1996; Swick & Knight, 1997). But this issue is far from settled at the present time, as our discussion of implicit and explicit memory will demonstrate (see p. 242).

Episodic memory is autobiographical, containing information about time and place of past events. Semantic memory is your knowledge of concepts or rules that are abstract in the sense that you do not remember where or when you learned them.

Episodic and Semantic Knowledge

Declarative knowledge, the knowledge of facts, is sometimes subdivided into episodic and semantic categories (Tulving, 1993). The distinction between episodic and semantic facts is a matter of relevance, detail, and specificity. ***Episodic memories*** refer to events in an individual's *own* past; they are relevant to his or her *own* personal experience. An episodic memory is thus the representation of an event or experience (an episode) that is autobiographical, in the sense that it contains the specific information that "it happened to me at time x and in place y." For example, you might remember that *yesterday (x), in class (y)*, your psychology instructor told you about "schedules of reinforcement."

In contrast, ***semantic memory*** is typically independent of any time or place, does not usually contain autobiographical references, and has a more general relevance. For example, you may be able to remember the concept of "quark" or "antelope" without ever having seen either one or having any knowledge about where or when you first heard these terms. Such representations are strictly semantic. However, if you actually saw an antelope, your memory of it would be episodic, and it probably would contain the time and place of that experience.

Researchers have reported PET scan evidence demonstrating that episodic and semantic memories are represented in different places in the frontal lobes of the cerebral cortex (Nyberg, Cabeza, & Tulving, 1996). The left frontal area is more active when general semantic knowledge has to be retrieved ("who was the U.S. president before Bill Clinton?") or when that knowledge has to be encoded episodically in a new way ("remember the following list of presidents because I'm going to ask you to recall them later: Clinton, Bush, Reagan, Carter, Ford, Nixon, Johnson"). The right frontal area is more active when episodic memories are retrieved, such as when I ask you later to recall the list.

There is also a good deal of research to support the claim that another part of the brain, the hippocampus, plays an important role in stor-

ing memories. But recent evidence from amnesic children indicates an interesting limitation on the role of the hippocampus. Researchers studied three subjects all of whom suffered damage to their hippocampus at or just after birth (Vargha-Khadem et al., 1997). Even as teenagers and young adults, these subjects are incapable of remembering basic information about their lives, such as what day it is or what television show they have just finished watching. They are, however, able to read, write, and spell, all of which depend heavily on learning processes, and they do well in school. The evidence suggests that the hippocampus is necessary for the storage of episodic memories, such as remembering daily events; when it has been damaged, memory for these events suffer. But the hippocampus is not necessary for the storage of semantic memories, based on a lifetime accumulation of factual information. The hippocampus is necessary for "context-rich," episodic memories, but other parts of the brain, as yet unidentified, are able to save "context-free," semantic ideas.

Retrieval

So far we have talked about how information gets into the memory system and how it is stored for use at a later time. Now let's consider how its format and organization can affect our ability to retrieve the information. Retrieval success implies that the information is available (present in the system) and can be accessed. In other words, we can fail a memory test for two reasons: (1) the information never got into long-term memory in the first place—it was never learned or stored, or if it was stored, it was somehow deleted or overwritten—or (2) we cannot get to the information—it is in there, but we can't access it.

Measuring Memory

Researchers have used three basic measures, called recall, recognition, and savings, to identify what can be retrieved from memory. ***Recall*** involves retrieving a fact from memory without any hints or clues. ***Recognition*** means that you can recognize, or identify, the facts you have learned when you are presented with several alternatives, including the ones you know. ***Savings*** means that you can relearn old but seemingly forgotten knowledge in less time than it took originally to learn it.

Let's examine these measures more closely. Imagine an experiment in which a research participant learns a list of unrelated words. A recall test requires the learner to recite as completely as possible all the items on the list. You have this experience when you leave your grocery list

THINKING CRITICALLY

One of life's most irksome experiences occurs when words or names get stuck on the tip of your tongue. You are certain that you know the word or name, but you just can't come up with it. Why does this happen? Does it mean you are losing your memory? Should you worry about it?

Tip-of-the-tongue experiences happen frequently to everyone, even young children. You may have more such experiences as you age, but don't worry about it. The tip-of-the-tongue experience is so common that it is hardly symptomatic of anything, let alone of losing your memory. Names of friends and relatives and of famous people are the most common items that provoke the tip-of-the-tongue phenomenon. About 50 percent of the time, you remember the name within a minute or two of thought. When it is not resolved, you can try several tricks that often work, like free associating, that is, saying anything at all that comes to mind. Often this kind of aimless search through memory produces a retrieval cue—a word related to the one you are searching for—that gets you to the missing word. When all else fails, forget about it. No one is quite sure why, but sometimes unconsciously the forgotten name pops to mind after a period of neglect.

To be retrieved, memories must be available, that is, a representation must exist and be accessible.

Recall is a measure of raw memory unaided by hints or cues; recognition is a test of ability to distinguish learned material from nonlearned material; savings is a measure of how much more quickly you can learn the same material (i.e., how much you saved) the second time around.

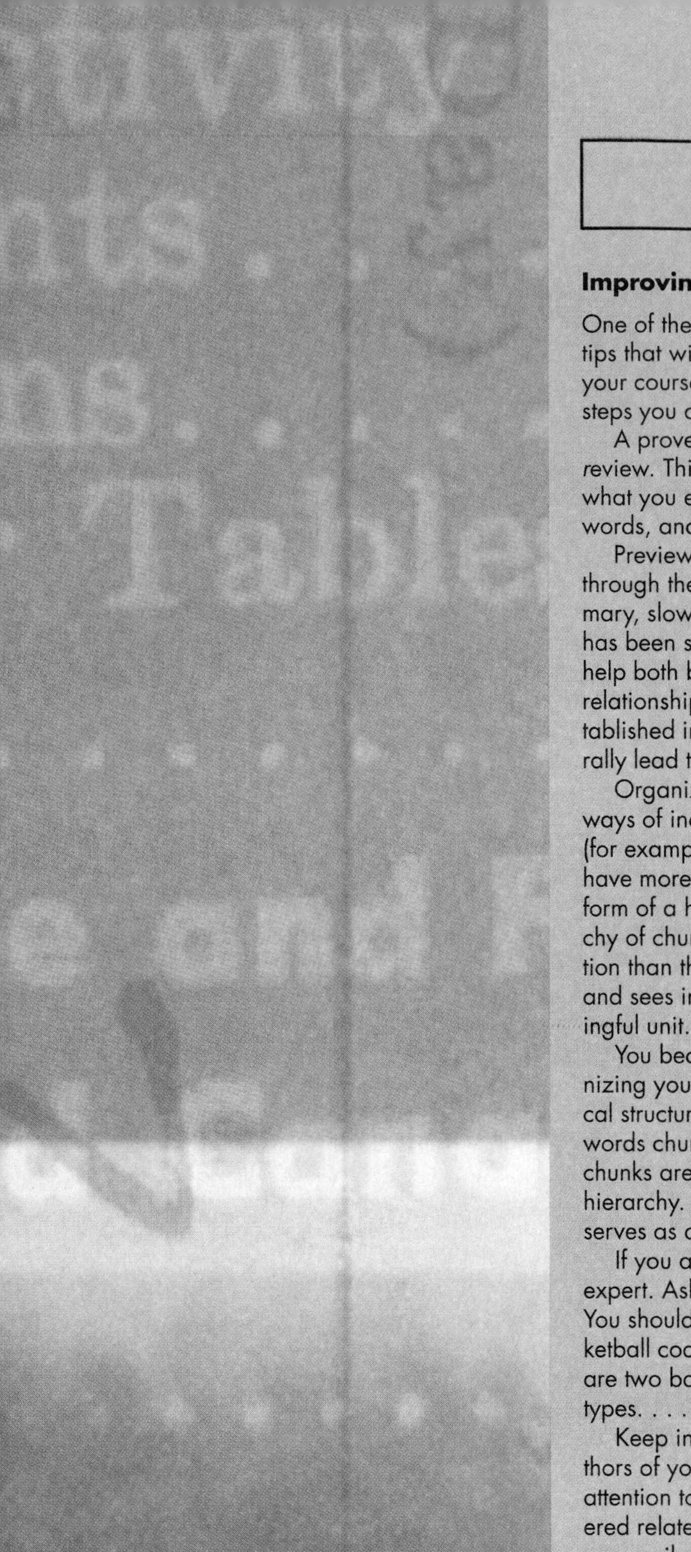

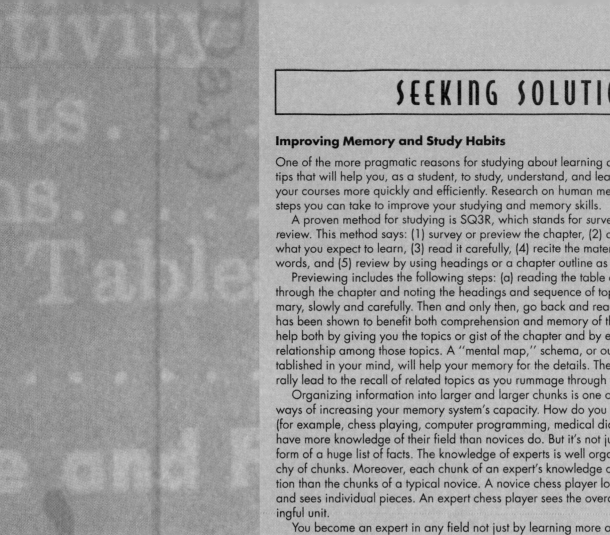

SEEKING SOLUTIONS

Improving Memory and Study Habits

One of the more pragmatic reasons for studying about learning and memory is to gain some tips that will help you, as a student, to study, understand, and learn the content assigned in your courses more quickly and efficiently. Research on human memory has suggested some steps you can take to improve your studying and memory skills.

A proven method for studying is SQ3R, which stands for *s*urvey, *q*uestion, *r*ead, *r*ecite, and *r*eview. This method says: (1) survey or preview the chapter, (2) ask yourself questions about what you expect to learn, (3) read it carefully, (4) recite the material from memory in your own words, and (5) review by using headings or a chapter outline as retrieval cues.

Previewing includes the following steps: (a) reading the table of contents, (b) paging through the chapter and noting the headings and sequence of topics, and (c) reading the summary, slowly and carefully. Then and only then, go back and read the chapter. This procedure has been shown to benefit both comprehension and memory of the material. Previewing will help both by giving you the topics or gist of the chapter and by establishing in your mind the relationship among those topics. A "mental map," schema, or outline of the topics, firmly established in your mind, will help your memory for the details. The recall of one topic will naturally lead to the recall of related topics as you rummage through your schema for the chapter.

Organizing information into larger and larger chunks is one of the best and most useful ways of increasing your memory system's capacity. How do you become expert in any field (for example, chess playing, computer programming, medical diagnosis)? Obviously, experts have more knowledge of their field than novices do. But it's not just more knowledge in the form of a huge list of facts. The knowledge of experts is well organized, typically in a hierarchy of chunks. Moreover, each chunk of an expert's knowledge contains much more information than the chunks of a typical novice. A novice chess player looks at a board configuration and sees individual pieces. An expert chess player sees the overall configuration as a meaningful unit.

You become an expert in any field not just by learning more and more facts but by organizing your facts into increasingly larger chunks. Keep in mind that, because of the hierarchical structure of memory, there are chunks within chunks. For example, letters chunk into words, words chunk into sentences, sentences chunk into paragraphs, and so on. At each level, the chunks are meaningful, but the amount of information per chunk increases as you ascend the hierarchy. The hierarchy not only allows the expert to encode new information rapidly but also serves as a means of retrieving information when necessary.

If you are trying to become an expert in a new field, talk to someone who is already an expert. Ask the expert, not for a list of facts, but for an organizational overview of the field. You should be able to detect a hierarchical system in the expert's reply. For example the basketball coach might respond, "The game divides into offense, defense, and transition. There are two basic types of defense, player-to-player or zone. Zone defenses fall into four types. . . ." An organizational scheme will save you a lot of time when learning the facts.

Keep in mind that the professors of your classes are experts in their fields, as are the authors of your textbooks. When you go to a lecture or read a book chapter, pay particular attention to understanding the organization of content. Try to understand how the topics covered relate to one another and why they are important to the subject being discussed. Details can easily be learned later, after you have a general picture of the topic under study. Some students find it useful to skim the reading assignment before the related lecture, go to the lecture and take notes in an outline form, and then reread the chapter, filling in the details of the outline later. This method is probably effective for a variety of reasons. Skimming the chapter before the lecture helps prepare you so that you can understand what the lecture is about and don't need to write down everything the lecturer is saying. Instead, you can pay attention to the organization of the content given by the expert. Later, you can use this organization to guide your understanding of the content, and you can fill in the factual information you need to know. Facts are much easier to learn if they make sense in the context of a higher-order plan.

We hope that these tips will improve your study effectiveness and, as you learn to use them more efficiently, that they will enrich your learning experiences throughout your academic career and beyond.

at home and then try to reconstruct it at the store "from memory." Essay questions are recall tests.

Sometimes a person may not be able to recall any of the originally learned material. But has she completely forgotten all that was learned? That's quite unlikely, as a recognition test might reveal. In a recognition test, the learner must identify, from a set of items, which ones were (and which ones were not) part of the learned material. People typically can recognize items from a list they learned even if they are unable to recall them. This may be because the original material, even if appearing in the middle of information that has not been seen before, serves as a cue or a prompt to memory (such prompts are obviously not available in recall tests). Suppose you lost your grocery list. If someone gave you another list in which your items were mixed up with new items; it's quite likely that you would recognize at least some items that were on your original list. Multiple-choice and true-false test items are recognition tests.

Savings is the most sensitive of all memory measures. Savings measures the difference between time (or number of trials) required for original learning and time (or trials) to relearn. Even when a person can't recognize any of the original material, he might *relearn* it faster than before. Should you find yourself having to repeat a course, you might take comfort in the fact that learning the course material should be easier the second time around (assuming you learned something the first time).

Retrieval Cues and Encoding Specificity

The ease of accessing memory depends on the availability of ***retrieval cues.*** The best retrieval cues are stimuli that were present at the time of encoding. If the cues present during the original learning are too different from the cues available at the time of recall, retrieval will be difficult and may not occur. Cues can change over time, so lack of useful retrieval cues is always a possible explanation for forgetting. Conversely, to the degree that we can reinstate the retrieval cues that were present at the original learning, we can facilitate remembering (Healy & Bourne, 1995).

The most popular version of this idea was developed by Endel Tulving (1983), who called it the ***encoding specificity principle***. Tulving demonstrated that the most powerful cues for accessing something in episodic memory are those stimuli that were present when the original event happened. In his experiment, individuals were shown a series of pairs of words (each pair consisting of a cue word and a target word), such as *train-black* or *glue-chair*. They were instructed to remember the targets, that is, the second item in each pair. Later, as is typical in memory experiments, only some targets were recalled accurately. Let's say that *black* is one of the target words, but a research participant does not recall it as part of the list. What cue would be most effective in helping the individual remember that *black* was on the target list? When presented with the word *white*, most people immediately think of black because of the strong association between black and white. You might guess, therefore, that *white* would be an excellent retrieval cue to help the individual remember that *black* was on the list. In fact, *white* did not help at all. When given *white* as a cue, most subjects still drew a blank on *black* as a member of the original list. The best retrieval cue to remember *black* as a target was not the strong associate *white* but rather the original paired item, *train*. Why? Tulving said that, upon their original presentation, *black* and *train* (among other pairs) were specifically encoded together. Within the context of the list, the only access route to one was through the other. In general, the cues present during original learning are the best cues to retrieval of learned items. Reinstating the original context, as we have seen before, facilitates remembering.

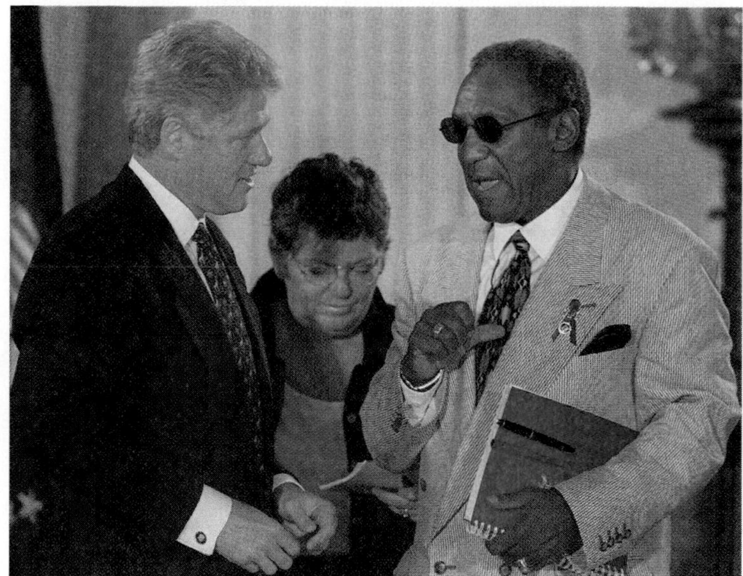

▲ *Cues help us retrieve information from our memories more easily. Here Bill Cosby wears a red AIDS ribbon, a cue for us to remember the victims of the disease.*

Items tend to be encoded with the context or cues with which they occur; the encoding specificity principle says that recall is maximized when the learning context or cues are reintroduced.

Context-dependent memory refers to the fact that memory is maximized when an individual returns to the context (or emotional state) that existed at the time of original learning.

Similarity of Context and State

Cue dependency unequivocally implies that you should maximize the similarity between the recall situation and the learning context if you want to maximize remembering. It predicts, for example, that you will remember more on a test if you study in the same room in which you take the test. Steven M. Smith (1982) verified this prediction, showing that stimuli associated with the study room can become associated with material learned in that room and subsequently serve as "memory landmarks" guiding retrieval of course material. Remember, however, that learning closely associated with a particular context might be difficult to remember outside that context. What you learn and retrieve in the classroom might not generalize fully to the "outside" world. There are costs as well as benefits to context-dependent knowledge (see Healy & Bourne, 1995, for several additional examples).

Nonetheless there are certain ways to generate our own context-related retrieval cues without actually being in the learning context. Visualizing the context or location where the learning occurred can facilitate recall. If you can't recall some fact about Freud's theory, thinking about the classroom in which you learned that fact or about the instructor of the course could cause you to remember it. This process helps explain how, if you can't recall where you left your keys, mentally walking through your activities from the last time you used them can assist you in finding your keys.

The learner's physiological or emotional state is also a part of the learning context and can be another source of retrieval cues. Thus, for the best performance, a person's state of mind or body should be as similar as possible at the time of both learning and retrieval. One study provided an interesting demonstration of state-dependent memory by examining a person's mood at the time of learning and recall (Eich, 1995). The participants learned new material in either a happy or sad state, and later they were asked to recall that material in either the same or the opposite mood. Their recall was best when their learning and test moods matched. Further, regardless of their learning states, positive items tended to be recalled predominantly in a happy state and negative items predominantly in a sad state.

Memories we are not consciously aware of are called implicit. Memories that require conscious effort to retrieve are called explicit.

Implicit and Explicit Memory

Just as encoding of information about an event may be explicit or implicit, retrieval of information from long-term memory may also be explicit or implicit. You often might make a conscious effort to recall or retrieve information from memory. If someone asks you to name the first American woman astronaut in space, you may at first draw a blank. For most of us, retrieval of such knowledge is not automatic. To come up with an answer—Sally Ride was the first American woman astronaut in space—requires an explicit, conscious search of memory. But, on other occasions, you may not need to make such a conscious search of memory, as your previous experiences may automatically affect your recall.

Here's a demonstration. Suppose you read to some friends a list of forty or so words, asking them to rate each word as to how difficult it is to form a visual image. Among the words are *president, address, magazine,* and *university*. Later you surprise your participants with a request that they recall the words. With some conscious effort, they will recall correctly a few of the words, which is an example of ***explicit memory***; but they are likely to miss most of them. Suppose they can't recall the four words given above. Next, you ask them to fill in the missing letters in the following word fragments:

1. P __ __ S __ D __ __ T
2. P __ __ D __ L __ M
3. A __ D __ __ SS
4. A __ P __ __ T
5. M __ __ A __ __ NE
6. M __ __ S __ __ R
7. __ N __ __ ER __ __ T__
8. __ L __ PH __ __ T

Every odd-numbered fragment can be completed with a word from the previously heard list. Your friends will find it easier and will be quicker to complete those words than they will comparable words that they did not hear (every even-numbered word), even if they are unable to recall or recognize them as items they rated. ***Implicit memory*** is the term used for cases like this in which the influence of previous experience on memory retrieval does not involve conscious effort or awareness (Roediger, Weldon, & Challis, 1989).

We usually think and talk about memory in its explicit form, but explicit and implicit memory normally work together. When you learn a new fact, you usually can consciously remember that you recently learned it and under what circumstances (an explicit memory); but you also use that fact in appropriate circumstances without thinking about it (an implicit memory effect). While research has focused on understanding explicit memory, the importance of implicit memory has been brought home recently in studies of the effects of brain injury. Persons with damage to the brain's frontal and/or temporal lobes have difficulty consciously recollecting recent experiences such as completing a jigsaw puzzle or drawing while looking in a mirror, yet they still show improvement the next time they try the same puzzle or do the same drawing task (see Figure 7-9). In other words, their prior experience affects their present behavior even though they do not have consciousness or awareness of why or how they improved. Memory, in these circumstances, has an implicit effect on performance, which is mediated by intact brain centers outside the frontal and temporal lobes, but has no explicit effect (Moscovitch & Winocur, 1992; Shimamura & Squire, 1987).

Researchers have demonstrated implicit memory effects in split-brain patients, that is, patients who have fully intact cerebral hemispheres that are divided at the corpus callosum (Cronin-Golomb, Gabrieli and Keane, 1996). The fact that these patients have no problem in retrieving implicit memories is another kind of evidence that these memories are served by subcortical structures of the brain. Some psychologists have taken findings like these to imply that nonconscious, implicit retrieval processes are conducted in the more primitive parts of the brain, such as the basal ganglia (see Chapter 3), and that implicit memory processes are therefore older in an evolutionary sense than are conscious explicit memory processes (Reber, Walkenfeld, & Hernstadt, 1991).

All of this evidence suggests that there might be separate locations for different memory systems in the brain, such that one system can be knocked out by brain damage at a specific location, while other systems remain intact. This argument is still speculative because we do not yet have enough neurological evidence to be certain. The evidence is quite clear, however, that people can perform behaviors without being conscious of having learned them, indicating that it is indeed useful to distinguish between implicit and explicit memory.

Serial Position and Retrieval

Suppose you hear a list of the names of thirty famous people and then are asked to recall them immediately thereafter, in any order you can remember. Typically what happens is a ***serial position effect***. You remember the first and the

7-9 Implicit Memory

The mirror-drawing task requires you to trace a pattern (like a star) while looking at it in a mirror (the hand doing the writing is covered up so that you cannot see it except by looking in the mirror). This is quite difficult to do in the beginning, but you get better at it with practice as shown in the graph. People with damage to the frontal lobes of their brains learn and remember how to do this task just as readily as normal people, but they have great difficulty remembering on day 2 that they practiced the task on day 1. (Source: Adapted from Milner, Corkin, & Teuber, 1968)

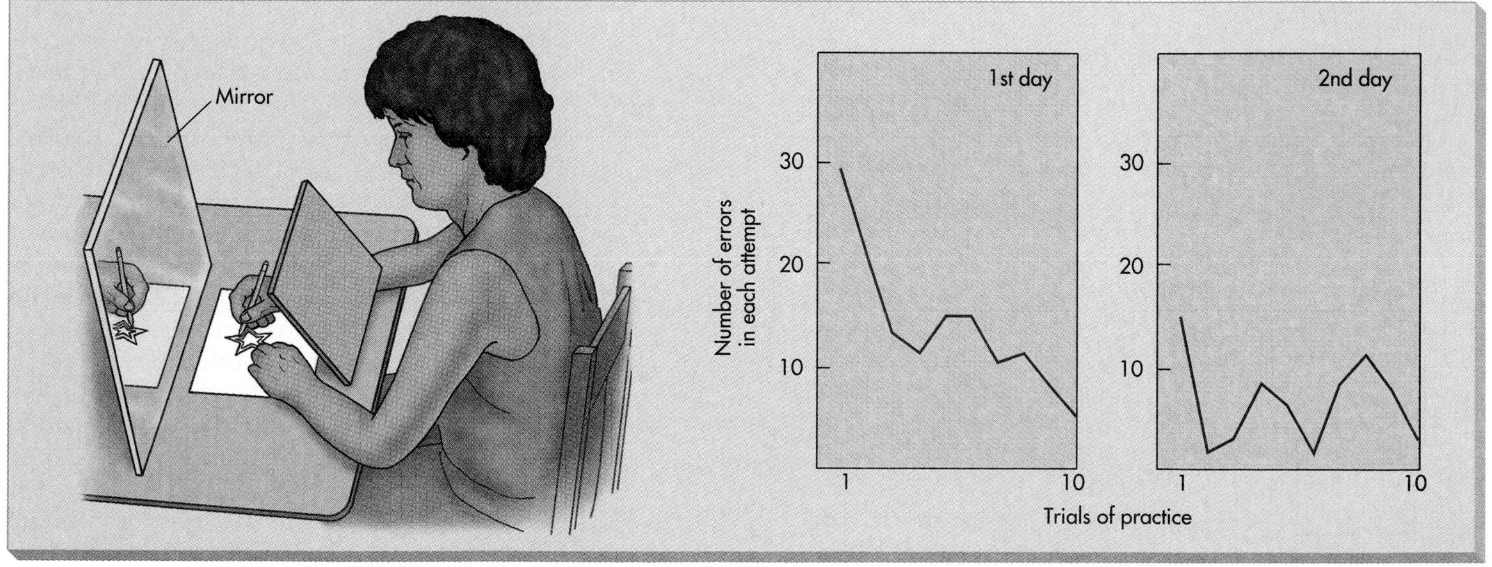

last names in the list easier than you can remember the middle items. Can you think of an explanation for the serial position effect using what you know about short- and long-term memory?

The recall test is given immediately. Thus, it's possible that the last names in the list are still in short-term memory, which will make the names relatively easy to recall. What about the early names in the list? By virtue of being early, these names can be rehearsed without interference from other items. Remember, short-term memory can hold about seven chunks of information. Rehearsal of these items increases the likelihood that they will get into long-term memory, which will make them available later at the time you are asked to recall them. But items in the middle of the list cannot be so easily encoded, especially if you are still rehearsing the early items, making it unlikely that the middle items get into long-term memory (Healy & McNamara, 1996). Thus, for different reasons, both the early and the later names will be remembered better than the middle items, resulting in a bow-shaped serial position curve as shown in Figure 7-10.

Better recall of early names is called the ***primacy effect***, and better recall of the later names is called the ***recency effect***. One final point. If, rather than giving an immediate recall test, you wait a while, a different picture emerges. As shown in Figure 7-10, recall is lower overall, due to some forgetting, but also because the recency effect disappears (Craik, 1983). This is another kind of evidence that the recency effect is attributable to holding the last items in the list in short-term memory, which dissipates relatively rapidly in time.

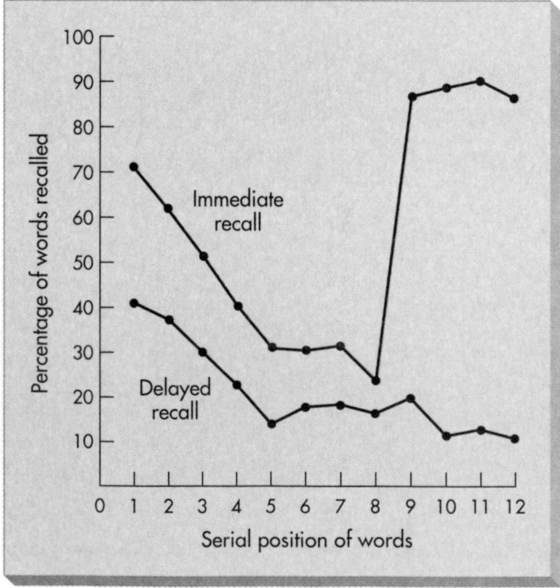

7-10 Serial Position

The graph shows recall of words in a list as a function of serial position and timing of the test.

Constructive Processes in Retrieval

Memory is more than a faithful recording of events; it is constructive, even creative. Through encoding, we construct mental representations of events for storage. These constructed representations are often incomplete and differ in certain ways from what actually happened. You can see this for yourself. Stage a simple event for two of your friends. Something like demonstrating how to use some new application on your computer will do. Then, independently, ask the two of them to describe in detail what they witnessed. You'll see that they constructed somewhat different memory representations. It's doubtful that they'll agree 100 percent on what happened, and they may also remember some things that didn't happen.

Memory is also reconstructive. When the time comes for us to remember, we reconstruct the event from the incomplete and possibly distorted encoded representation. If the initially encoded representation is incomplete, we may have to fill in some of the gaps to make recall plausible. Sometimes the process involves using default information—"I don't remember exactly, but it must have been. . . . " This is obvious when we try to remember a conversation or something we read. We do not typically come away with a word-for-word copy of the conversation or the printed text stored in our memory. Rather, we have general ideas or facts about what was said or read—ideas or facts that we abstracted as we read or listened. To tell a coherent story about the prior event, then, we have to engage in reconstruction. We augment our abstracted representations with other information we have available. This helps us make sense of what "must have happened."

As we have seen, reconstruction of an event from memory can often lead to memory distortion. We can expect two kinds of memory distortion. First, memory distortion can occur at the time of encoding, when we have to abstract the general ideas of an experience or episode. In constructing a representation, we might leave out seemingly unimportant elements or intro-

SEEKING SOLUTIONS

Are Our Memories Always Real?

Renowned cognitive psychologist Jean Piaget described his earliest memory as follows: "I was sitting in my pram . . . when a man tried to kidnap me. I was held in by the strap fastened round me while my nurse bravely tried to stand between me and the thief. She received various scratches, and I can still see vaguely those on her face. . . . (Piaget, 1962, pp. 187–88). Later, however, Piaget realized that this early memory was in error when his nurse wrote a letter to his parents confessing that she had made up the story and faked the scratches. As a child, Piaget had heard the story of his kidnapping and associated his semantic knowledge about kidnapping with events in his own life, creating a false episodic memory.

How is it possible for someone to believe that a semantic memory is an episodic memory or vice versa? Have you ever remembered an event in your life that didn't happen? How can you explain remembering something that didn't occur?

The answer lies in the fact that memory is a constructive process, and memories for events change over time, as we have new experiences and acquire new information. It is likely that, as a child, seeing the scratches the nurse had faked on her face and hearing the story of his kidnapping described by authoritative adults led Piaget to construct a personal memory of being kidnapped.

Although psychologists agree that it is possible to construct pseudomemories of events, there is intense disagreement over how, when, and why such constructions occur. The issues are controversial because of their implications for testimony in child abuse cases.

Just as we know that people can remember things that didn't happen, people can also forget some startling incidents. For example, in 1992, Ross Cheit, a professor at Brown University, awoke one morning with the baffling sense that a man was in his room—a man whom he had not thought about for twenty-five years. Suddenly, Cheit remembered that he had been repeatedly molested during summer camp by the camp's director. This memory was subsequently verified when Cheit and a private investigator found proof of the assaults and obtained a confession from the perpetrator (Horn, 1993).

Indeed, the controversies have been so heated that the American Psychological Association established a Working Group on the Investigation of Memories of Childhood Abuse to review the scientific literature and to identify research and training needs regarding the evaluation of memories of childhood abuse.

Although the clinical and research subgroups had profoundly different views about the nature of memory, they did agree on five basic points:

1. Controversies regarding adult recollections should not be allowed to obstruct the fact that child sexual abuse is a complex and pervasive problem in America that has historically gone unacknowledged.
2. Most people who were sexually abused as children remember all or part of what happened to them.
3. It is possible for memories of abuse that have been forgotten for a long time to be remembered.
4. It is also possible to construct convincing pseudomemories for events that never occurred.
5. There are gaps in our knowledge about the processes that lead to accurate and inaccurate recollections of childhood abuse (Alpert et al., 1996, p. 1).

Given the controversies, researchers are now seeking to learn more about the mechanisms that underlie delayed remembering, and to determine if it is possible to distinguish between "real" and "pseudo" memories without corroboration from others.

duce incorrect elements. As you read "The War of the Ghosts" at the beginning of this chapter, you might have constructed a representation of the overall meaning by including default information that was never actually stated but that you merely assumed to be true (because it usually is).

Second, memory distortion can take place at the time of retrieval. In some sense, retrieval reverses the process of encoding. To retrieve a memory, a fragmentary representation must be used to reconstruct the event. Reconstruction itself can thus introduce new or default information. It might further be influenced by the context in which recall takes place, especially if that context is different from the encoding context. So, when you recalled "The War of the Ghosts," you might have been influenced by your incomplete initial representation of the story or by your own cultural knowledge about what makes sense.

Forgetting

Hermann Ebbinghaus (1850–1909) was the first person to study forgetting scientifically. His procedure was simple but rigorous. First, he committed a list of pronounceable nonsense syllables—*wix, cuh, mok,* etc.—to memory. One day or one week or one month later, he tested himself by the recall method to determine what and how much he remembered. His results are shown in Figure 7-11. Ebbinghaus of course forgot some items, and his forgetting was related in a systematic way to the passage of time. Note that he used nonsense material. He did this for good reason, arguing that the learning and forgetting of meaningless materials would reveal pure psychological processes, uncontaminated by prior familiarity with the material. Pure processes or not, why did Ebbinghaus forget? Why does anyone forget items or events?

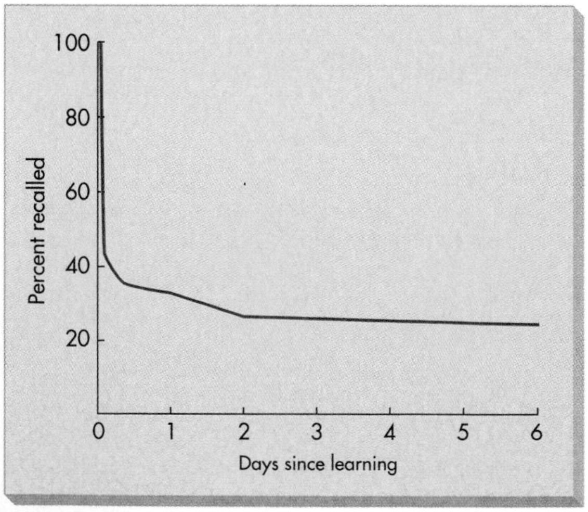

Normally, we are more concerned with remembering real experiences than we are with remembering nonsense material. So, suppose you went to Pizza Hut with a close friend and, some time later, you were asked to give an account of what happened. You may remember exactly what happened, or you may experience ***retrieval failure***, that is, you may forget all or some of the details of what happened. Any memory trace, no matter how accurate or complete at the time of encoding, can change over time. Trace changes may occur because of the mere passage of time or because of new, intervening experiences that interfere with your memory of the initial experience. Changes in the "Pizza Hut" trace may lead you to "recall" events there that happened somewhat differently than they really happened or that happened in a different experience altogether. Or you may even forget that you went to Pizza Hut on that occasion. Such changes imply that the original trace might not be fully available at the time of retrieval. Thus, retrieval failure can result from processes taking place when a trace is being formed (inadequate encoding) or during the time it is in storage. Retrieval failure under these circumstances is said to be ***trace-dependent forgetting***. Alternatively, the trace may exist exactly as it was formed but, as we saw in some earlier examples, you may have trouble accessing it because key retrieval cues are missing. In this case, retrieval failure is said to be ***cue-dependent forgetting***.

7-11 Ebbinghaus Forgetting Curve

According to Ebbinghaus, the percent recall of learned items drops rapidly at first and then more gradually later. (Source: Adapted from Ebbinghaus, 1885)

Memory Decay and Distortion

Gestalt theory explains retrieval failure in terms of trace dependency, claiming that all forgetting results from three types of changes in the memory trace over time. The simplest is loss of detail in a memory trace through ***leveling***, or decay,

THINKING CRITICALLY

Read the following list of words slowly but just once: *bed, rest, awake, tired, dream, wake, snooze, blanket, doze, slumber, snore, nap, peace, yawn, drowsy*. Now cover up the list. Recall as many words as you can and write them down. When you are finished, uncover the list and compare it to your recall. How many did you get? Was the word *sleep* among the words you recalled?

About 40 to 50 percent of people misrecall the word *sleep* in this situation. James Deese (1959) was the first to report this phenomenon, and he attributed it to the fact that the words are all associated with one another, and they all are associated with *sleep*. These associations add up and act as retrieval cues for *sleep*, even though *sleep* was not on the list.

More recently, Roediger and McDermott (1995) have described this effect as a memory illusion. People feel so strongly about the key word being on the list that they claim to remember it just as clearly as words that were on the list. Apparently, as the words are presented, we form a representation or trace not only of the words themselves but also of an abstraction, a concept, or a category for the type of words, thus leading to a strong false memory. This example focuses on semantic memories acquired in the laboratory. The extent to which memory illusion applies across types of memory (episodic, procedural) and in situations where processing on a deeper level and over time occurs is the subject of research and debate. In the meantime, the research suggests that we should rely on the details of our memories with caution, and that if something is truly worth remembering in detail, we should make notes about it as soon as possible after the event to avoid becoming a victim of memory illusion.

in which the memory trace gradually weakens and then eventually disappears. Repeated retrieval and use of a trace can refresh and strengthen it; the adage "use it or lose it" applies to the process of leveling.

Two other forms of change in the memory trace over time are sharpening and assimilation. ***Sharpening*** occurs when certain features of a trace become exaggerated and take on more importance than they originally had, as when a child clearly remembers the details of being scolded but has only the faintest memory of what led to the reprimand. ***Assimilation*** is distortion of the memory trace in the direction of something already familiar and common, as when the lyrics of two songs somehow merge in memory to create something different from both. To understand the difference in these changes, consider the memories of Phil, who was an eyewitness to an auto accident caused by someone driving a compact car. When subsequently interrogated, Phil fails to recall many details; for example, he forgets the color of the cars involved in the accident and the number of passengers in each car (leveling). But he remembers that the person behind the wheel of the compact car was driving recklessly and he exaggerates the speed of the car (sharpening). Finally, he recalls (incorrectly) that the compact car was a Toyota, although in fact it was a much less common Japanese make, an Isuzu (assimilation). All three processes, in Gestalt theory, take place outside of awareness while the memory trace is stored in memory. Repeated rehearsal of events we witness, however, can, just like maintenance rehearsal in short-term memory, prevent or reduce the impact of these changes. But repetition can also introduce additional errors, especially if the witness is interrogated about what he saw (Wells, Luus, & Windschitl, 1994; Shaw, 1996).

Leveling (decay of information), sharpening (accenting certain aspects of information), and assimilation (distorting information in the direction of normal expectations) are the three fundamental forgetting processes in Gestalt theory.

Consolidation Failure

Consolidation theory claims that it takes a certain amount of time for the trace of an event or episode to become fully formed and permanently fixed in memory. In this view, a memory trace can be thought of as a neural circuit formed or strengthened in the brain, with the circuit somehow encoding the experience

(Hebb, 1949; Abel et al., 1995). The circuit is not stable when it is first established. It must "consolidate" for the experience to be permanently stored. Consequently, during the period between the end of an experience and the completion of trace consolidation, the circuit can be disrupted easily. A major factor in forgetting may be that a memory is partly destroyed before it is consolidated. This theory focuses on encoding, and it holds that memory failures stem from incomplete coding of traces into long-term storage.

What kinds of events can affect or disrupt the consolidation process? Almost anything will work. If you move from one event to another quickly, the memory of the first event can be disrupted before it is consolidated and therefore it might be difficult to remember that first event. A more dramatic example is amnesia. You have no doubt heard of a person being hit on the head and suffering temporary amnesia as a consequence. When the blow to the head interferes with the formation of memory traces for events *immediately preceding* the blow, the phenomenon is known as ***retrograde amnesia***. When it interferes with memory for events after the blow, it is known as ***anterograde amnesia***. Retrograde amnesia implies that recently formed memory traces are destroyed by the blow. Traces that normally would be formed are prevented from forming in anterograde amnesia. Long-term memory remains completely intact in these cases; only recent events—those that occurred around the time of the blow—fail to be encoded or consolidated.

Another side of consolidation theory has interesting possible practical applications. Because consolidation is the process of laying down a permanent memory, if consolidation could be facilitated in some way, memory would be enhanced. Certain drugs, including caffeine, strychnine, dopamine, and acetylcholine, are thought by some researchers to have this capability. These drugs excite brain cells and might accelerate the formation of CREB—the memory protein in nerve cell nuclei (Abel et al., 1995)—and thereby produce faster, more efficient, and more permanent memory storage. Giving these drugs to animals after each learning trial does in fact result in somewhat more rapid learning, thus supporting consolidation theory (McGaugh, 1989; Service, 1994), although the effects are small. Some of these drugs can also be extremely dangerous, sometimes leading to illness or death in human beings. They should only be used under close medical supervision.

► *Stacy Hrivnak (45) suffered from amnesia as a result of a blow to the jaw, but her memory returned as she watched her Penn State teammates play without her. She lost her memory for certain facts, such as being a member of the Penn State women's basketball team (episodic memory). She did not, however, forget how to play basketball (procedural memory), and her episodic memory returned, with time.*

Interference with Retrieval

Perhaps the most widely accepted theory of forgetting, known as ***interference theory***, incorporates both trace and cue dependency notions. This theory claims that forgetting is caused by interference among memories, especially among memories for similar events or having similar retrieval cues. Thus, available retrieval cues might not distinguish among the memories, especially if they are nearly equal in strength. When an old memory gets in the way of remembering a new experience, forgetting the newer memory is said to be caused by ***proactive interference*** from the prior or older memory. When a recent experience interferes with remembering an older memory, forgetting the older one is said to be caused by ***retroactive interference*** from the newer memory. The fact

SEEKING SOLUTIONS

Eyewitness Suggestibility

"Misleading information can turn a lie into memory's truth. It can cause people to believe that they saw things that never really existed, or that they saw things differently from the way things actually were." (Loftus, 1992, p. 123). Fortunately for most of us, serious accidents and criminal activity are infrequent and not routinely a part of our experience. Through television, movies, and other media, however, we have fairly well-developed schemas about what typically happens during such events. Consequently, should we find ourselves an eyewitness to an emergency (say, a car accident), even though we may have very little time to encode the event accurately in memory, we do have some knowledge about what usually happens (for example, in car accidents, we know that one driver is often going too fast). When called on as an eyewitness to give testimony about an accident, we might have difficulty distinguishing between what actually happened and what we think happened. How can this inferential aspect of remembering affect the recall of "facts"?

In a typical study examining eyewitness suggestibility, Elizabeth Loftus told participants that they were participating in a memory experiment and showed them a film of a traffic accident. (Loftus, 1992). Then she asked them questions about what they had seen. The critical variable concerned the way in which the questions were phrased. Some participants were asked questions like "Did you see the broken headlight?" The definite article *the* implies that there was a broken headlight, with the person having to decide only whether or not he or she noticed it. Others were asked, "Did you see a broken headlight?" The indefinite article *a* has no such implication—indeed, it raises the question of whether or not there was a broken headlight, as well as the question of whether or not the person saw it.

Several questions in both forms were asked about things that had occurred in the film and things that had not occurred. The form of the question did not affect the frequency with which people indicated that they had seen something that actually did occur. For example, if the accident did result in a broken headlight, people were equally likely to report it when asked with either the *a* or the *the* form of the question. However, when asked about something that, in fact, did not occur, people showed a much stronger tendency to respond positively ("Yes, I saw it!) to questions using the definite rather than the indefinite article.

In another study, people who had witnessed a filmed traffic accident were asked either, "How fast were the cars going when they *bumped* into each other?" or "How fast were the cars going when they *smashed* into each other?" [Emphasis added.] Witnesses who were asked the first question estimated significantly lower speeds than did those asked the second question, even though both groups had witnessed the same accident. Things that smash together are usually traveling faster than things that bump together. The form of the question, asked after the fact, of course, influences the witnesses' recollection of the event.

These results imply that memory can be shaped by later informational input. If the post-event information is inaccurate (misinformation), then the person's memory might become inaccurate. Post-event information effects are consistent with the view that memory is a dynamic, constructive process, subject to continuous change over time. Suggesting plausible facts or inferences to a person *at the time of recall* can affect what that person believes to have happened. Simply by asking the right questions, you can convince at least some people that they saw things that did not actually happen. The effect of misleading input is even more severe with children than it is with adults (Ceci, Ross, & Toglia, 1987; Shaw, 1996).

In fact, there is some recent evidence that even events that occur *prior* to the to-be-remembered episode can affect how the episode is recalled (Lindsay, 1993). So, if you warn witnesses that they will see a videotape of an accident between two speeding cars, they will tend to report later higher rates of speed than if you just warned them that two cars will collide. The implications of such results for courtroom examinations or police investigations are fairly obvious. Police investigations are supposed to establish the "facts," and attorneys are told not to "lead the witness." Because either process can influence the witness' memory, such research seriously questions whether eyewitness testimony can be accepted as a purely objective and uncontaminated description of what actually happened (Loftus, 1992; Wells, Luus, & Windschitl, 1994).

▶ *Dramatic events that have produced flashbulb memories: the explosion of the* Challenger *spacecraft; and Princess Diana's coffin entering Westminster Abbey.*

stick with you permanently, like it or not. The chances of it sticking in permastore depends primarily on two things: (1) spreading out the learning so that you repeatedly refresh (relearn) what you learned earlier, and (2) building on what you already know, as when you put algebra into practice later in a higher-level course.

Hypermnesia

Hypermnesia is enhanced or improved memory for information over time with repeated attempts to remember.

Forgetting is memory loss over time. Is there anything that stands in opposition to forgetting, that is, a memory *gain* over time? Counterintuitive though it might seem, the answer is yes. There is a phenomenon of spontaneous memory gain, which is called ***hypermnesia*** (literally, higher memory). Here's how it works. Suppose you were tested for memory immediately after listening to a story and then again several hours later. Will you remember the story more accurately the first or second time you are tested?

Researchers showed that your memory for the story will actually be better the second time it is tested—an apparent memory gain over time, or hypermnesia (Ballard, 1913; Wheeler & Roediger, 1992). Yet, it could be that a person might actually learn something on each repeated recall attempt. Maybe people are more likely to make better guesses the second time they attempt to recall a story. Maybe the experimenter provided them with some useful feedback after their first attempt. If so, the memory gain in such experiments might be more apparent than real. It might be just an artifact of practice. A better procedure divides the research participants into two groups, one of which recalls immediately after hearing the story and the other of which recalls several hours later. If the second group recalls more, then hypermnesia cannot be attributed to prior recall trials.

The reality of hypermnesia for both verbal and motor memory is easy enough to demonstrate. For verbal memory, ask a friend to recall as many of the forty-eight contiguous United States as he or she can in a five-minute period. Record the number. Then, five minutes later, ask your friend to repeat the performance. For nine out of ten people, recall will be better the second time around. Some states missed the first time just seem to pop into mind in the second test. The effect is a kind of memory priming; correct recalls on the first effort prime or activate other existing memory traces (for the unnamed states) making them more accessible on the next retrieval attempt (Bower, 1986). For a motor skills demonstration, you might use a mirror drawing task (see Figure 7-9, p. 243). Mirror drawing is hard to do at first, but people generally improve rapidly over a number of attempts at the same pattern. If you wait, say, one hour, and then ask the person to trace the same pattern again, performance will show a significant improvement over the last trial before the break and a much bigger improvement than if no break was given. Apparently, the subject learns something about mirror drawing during the time-out period when no additional practice is given. This is another clear example of hypermnesia.

THINKING CRITICALLY

How could you use consolidation theory to explain the fact that your friends appear to "know more" after the passage of time when recalling the names of states or performing mirror drawing?

Consolidation theory would argue that recall immediately after learning might suffer from inadequate time for new information to form complete memory traces (that is, to consolidate). Further, the effort involved in learning might introduce an element of mental fatigue, inhibiting access to memory traces.

Alternatively, interference theory would suggest that initial attempts at recall might suffer from interference between items of information (for example, individual words in a list to be remembered) that build up during initial learning. The passage of time allows some of those interference effects to dissipate, resulting in better overall recall. Both of these theories may be correct; that is, both processes may indeed be operating to produce hypermnesia. Tests of both hypotheses have been positive, so at present we have no good basis for deciding between these alternative theories.

Reflections and Observations

In this chapter, we have described memory both structurally—in terms of its sensory, short-term, and long-term levels—and functionally—in terms of its major processes of encoding, storing, and retrieving information from previous experiences. The chapter is as much about learning as it is memory; you can't really have one without the other. You can't learn unless you can remember your earlier experiences; you can't remember unless you learned something in the first place. So these concepts go hand in hand and represent the most powerful psychological processes we have for adapting to our complex and ever-changing environment. Learning and memory also provide the foundation for the even more complicated psychological processes that we will be talking about in the next chapter, namely thinking and language. Languages are learned and in turn provide a major mechanism for encoding and representing our knowledge of the world. Thinking is a matter of using what we know, linguistic or otherwise, to understand the world and to solve problems in novel ways. The tools that make this possible are the knowledge and skills that we have acquired in the past.

Objectives Revisited

This chapter summarizes psychological research and theory about human memory. Memory plays a central role in creating our unique and personal identities, as we will see throughout the remainder of this book.

Objective 1. Describe and discuss some of the attributes of human memory.

Memory is the capacity to reproduce what we have experienced. Memory is likely to be

KEY TERMS

sensory memory

short-term (working) memory

chunking

long-term memory

encoding

maintenance rehearsal

elaborative rehearsal

imagery

mnemonics

storage

procedural knowledge

declarative knowledge

episodic memory

semantic memory

retrieval

accompanied by structural changes in the brain forming a neurological memory trace. The modern study of memory is dominated by the information-processing approach, which describes memory in terms of *encoding, storage,* and *retrieval.* Information-processing theories assume (a) several levels of memory; (b) a limited capacity processing system, which might create bottlenecks at certain points under high information loads; (c) a two-way flow of information, from the *bottom up* (stimulus or data driven) and from the *top down* (memory or knowledge driven).

There are three primary levels of memory: *sensory memory, short-term memory,* and *long-term memory.* Sensory memory is characterized by: (a) a high capacity, (b) a literal representation of stimuli, and (c) very brief storage. The key characteristics of short-term memory are: (a) a limited capacity of about seven (plus or minus two) units of information; (b) coded representation, typically verbal; and (c) temporary storage, though not so temporary as that of sensory memory. We are conscious of the contents of short-term memory, but not of sensory memory. Short-term memory is sometimes conceptualized as having two aspects: content and work space. The key characteristics of long-term memory are: (a) unlimited capacity, (b) deeply processed and coded information, either in verbal or some sensory (image) form, and (c) information that is highly resistant to forgetting.

Objective 2. Explain encoding, and relate it to rehearsal effects on learning and memory.

Encoding refers to the process by which new information becomes represented in short- or long-term memory. Two types of rehearsal help us learn or encode new information: (a) *maintenance rehearsal,* which involves simple repetition of information for purposes of temporarily preserving that information in short-term memory, and (b) *elaborative rehearsal,* in which the new items to be encoded are related to other items that already exist in long-term memory and thereby facilitate the transfer of new information into long-term memory. Deeper, more elaborate processing produces more distinctive encoding, more durable storage, and easier, more efficient retrieval. There is some evidence that the amount of effort required by the encoding technique also affects memory durability. Effective encoding techniques for new material include: (1) *imagery,* and (2) organization of the material into larger *chunks.*

Objective 3. Distinguish among various types of long-term memory.

Long-term memory contains both *declarative* (factual or knowledge-based) and *procedural* (how to or skill-based) information. Declarative information is generally explicit or on a conscious level, whereas procedural information is generally implicit and not on a conscious level. Declarative knowledge can be further subdivided into either *episodic* (information about objects or events, marked as to time and place of occurrence) or *semantic* (general or conceptual information).

Objective 4. Describe the three methods used to measure memory retrieval.

The three basic methods used in research to measure memory retrieval are *recall, recognition,* and *savings.* Recall is the most difficult test, requiring the learner to reproduce what he or she has learned without the aid of cues or hints. Recognition relies on an individual's ability to distinguish previously learned items from items that were not a part of the original learning material. Savings is based on the difference in time of trials needed to learn on the first and then on a second, later occasion.

Objective 5. Explain the factors that affect retrieval of or the failure to retrieve (forgetting) information from memory, and the three methods used to measure it.

To retrieve information from memory, information must be available and accessible. Sometimes retrieval is direct, rapid, automatic, and effortless. In other cases, retrieval is indirect, slow, conscious, and effortful. Retrieval of the first type is called *implicit,* of the second type *explicit.* The ability to retrieve information is increased when the conditions of learning and retrieval are similar. Such conditions include the room in which learning took place and the physiological state and mood of the learner.

Theories about forgetting emphasize either *trace dependency* or *cue dependency.* Gestalt theory attributes forgetting to automatic changes in the memory trace over time by: (a) *leveling,* (b) *sharpening,* or (c) *assimilation. Consolidation theory* attributes forgetting to incomplete consolidation of the memory trace after initial encoding and during the storage period. *Interference theory* incorporates both cue dependency and trace dependency theories, emphasizing how memory traces weaken in time and how *proactive interference* and *retroactive interference* operate to reduce availability of needed cues. The principle of *encoding specificity* emphasizes cue-dependent forgetting, attributable to the difference between the cues present during encoding and those present during retrieval. In contrast to forgetting processes, sometimes learned material sticks in memory in unaltered form over long periods of time, perhaps a lifetime, in a kind of memory known as *permastore*.

recall

recognition

retrieval cues

encoding specificity

context-dependent memory

state-dependent memory

serial position effect

implicit memory

explicit memory

consolidation

retrograde amnesia

anterograde amnesia

interference

repression

flashbulb memory

permastore

hypermnesia

6
5

C H A P T E R 8

Cognitive Processes

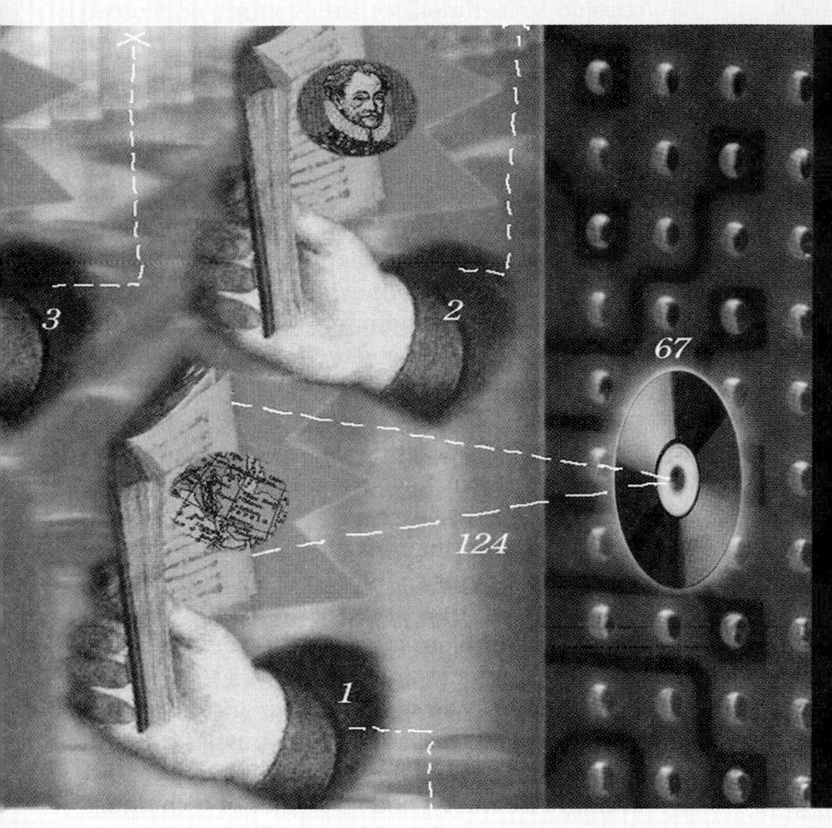

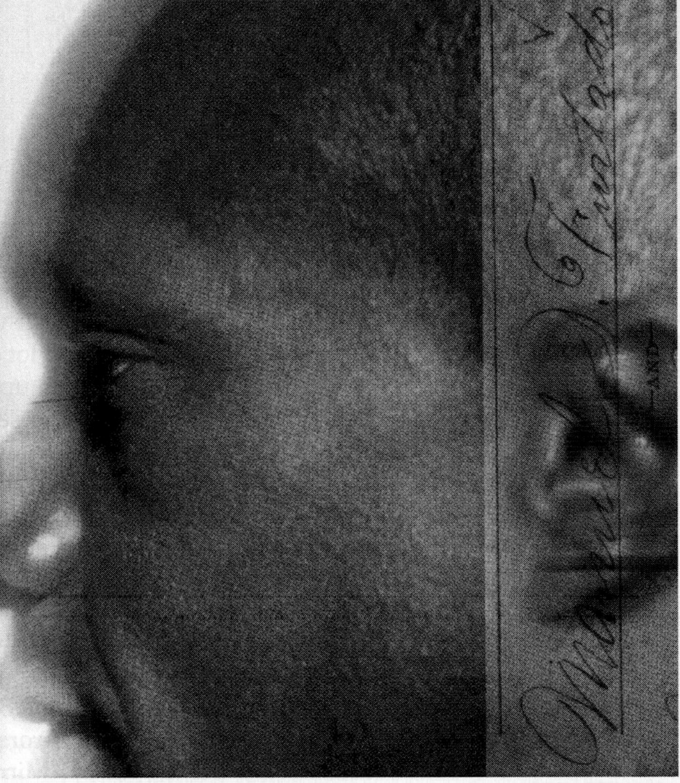

O B J E C T I V E S

After reading this chapter you should be able to:

1. Define cognitive processes.
2. Explain how concepts are formed, and distinguish between different types of concepts.
3. Compare and contrast *information-processing* and *Gestalt* approaches to understanding problem solving.
4. Describe and give examples of various forms of reasoning, and identify possible sources of errors in reasoning processes.
5. Discuss the role of algorithms and heuristics in decision making and judgment, and give examples of common heuristics used in everyday reasoning.
6. Describe the role of language in thought, and how we reason and communicate with language.
7. Define intelligence, and describe how it is measured.

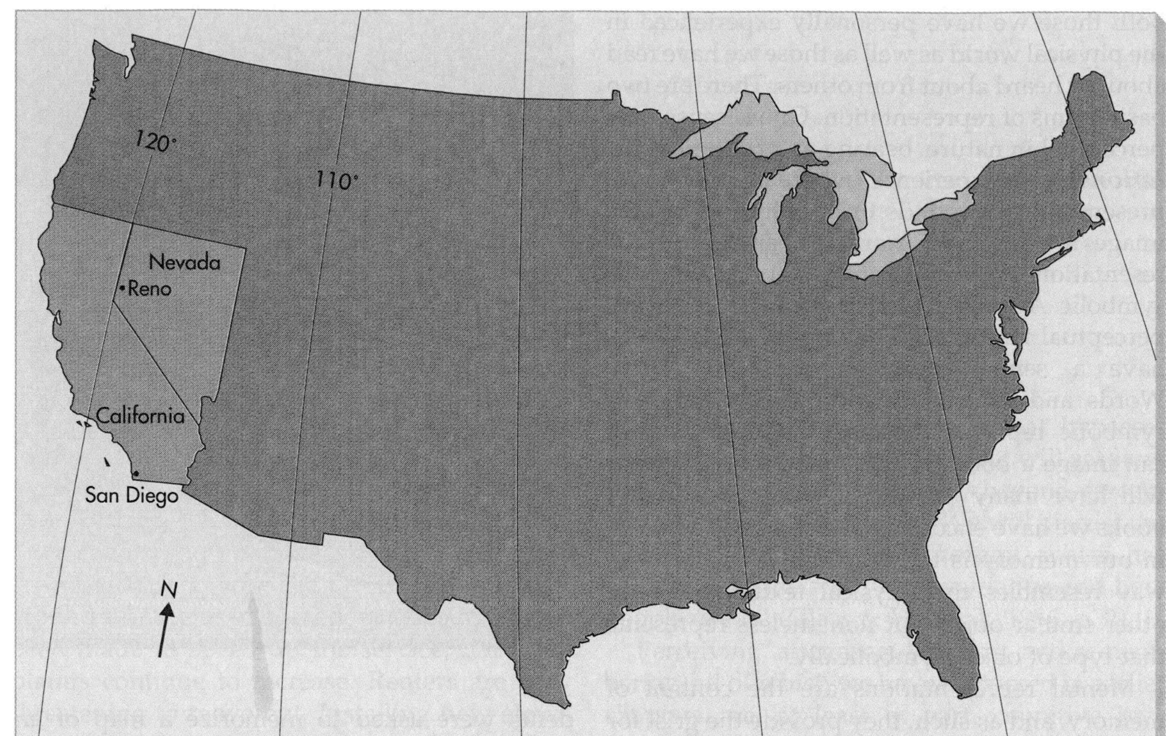

8-2 Conceptual Mental Maps

People usually think that San Diego, California, is west of Reno, Nevada. Geographically, the opposite is true. One possible explanation for our faulty mental maps is that we rely on our belief that any city in California, being a coastal state, must be west of any city in Nevada, an inland state. (Source: Adapted from Stevens & Coupe, 1978)

Symbolic Representations (Concepts)

Suppose we showed you pictures of a poodle, Great Dane, Chihuahua, dachshund, and chow, and asked you what category of animal they represented. The answer is easy, but the fact that you can come up with the category *dog* implies that you have factual knowledge that somehow encompasses all of these examples, based on their similarities and interrelationships. We can summarize that knowledge in a single word, "dog." The word designates a concept that you know and that includes all of the foregoing examples.

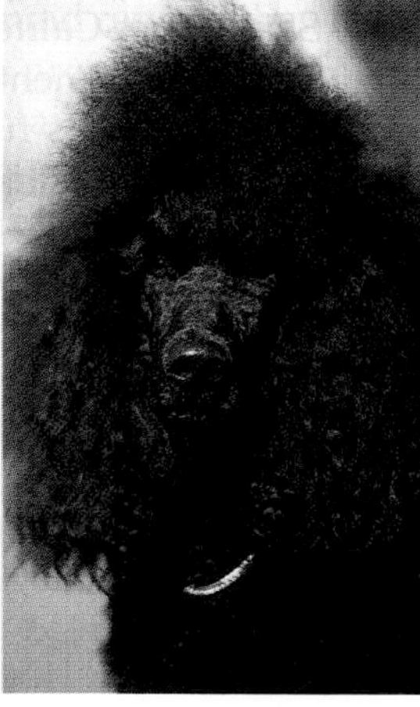

▶ *Terriers and poodles look vastly different, although both illustrate the concept of "dog."*

A ***concept*** is a meaningful category of objects, events, or other concepts that is based on their similarities or shared features. Concepts specify the characteristics or attributes that distinguish between members of the category and nonmembers of the category. For example, when determining members of the *dog* category, you might note that dogs bark and wag their tails. Thus, Ginger, a poodle, would be a member of the *dog* category, but Ching, a Siamese cat, would not.

Concepts enable you to organize your ideas about the world and to transfer that knowledge rapidly in new situations. Each time you meet a barking, tail-wagging, four-legged, furry animal on a leash, you don't have to be told what it is. Moreover, as you realize that this creature, seen for the first time, is a *dog*, you can apply all your knowledge about *dogs* to this new example. The similarity or overlap of a new experience with earlier experiences allows you to treat it as an example of a concept that you already know.

The organization of concepts is hierarchical. Individual objects or examples fall into a particular category. But that category can be contained at another level in a higher-order concept. Thus, *dog* is a concept at a specific level, but so is *pet*, which is a concept that includes not only *dog*, but also *cat, ferret, iguana, canary*, and so on. Furthermore, *pet* is a subconcept of *animal*, which also includes *zoo animals, farm animals*, and so on. The hierarchical structure of concepts enters into the memory process called chunking, which helps people keep track of more information than unaided short-term memory can handle. The research participant who was trained by researchers to expand his digit span to roughly eighty digits (see Chapter 7) relied upon finding familiar groupings of digits and then organizing them into higher-order categories like running times and historical dates (Ericsson, Chase, & Faloon, 1980; Ericsson & Chase, 1982; Ericsson & Kintsch, 1995).

Types of Concepts: Well-defined and Fuzzy

Concepts can be classified as either *well-defined* or *fuzzy*. A well-defined concept is precise, and leaves little room for ambiguity about its examples. The concept of a triangle is well-defined: a three-sided two-dimensional figure whose angles add up to 180 degrees. There is no ambiguity; a form is either a triangle (has the necessary features) or is not (lacks the necessary features). Many concepts in science and mathematics are well-defined in this way. But there are also many everyday examples, such as the concept of a bachelor, who is an unmarried man, or the concept of an eligible voter in a city election, who is twenty-one years of age or older, registered to vote, and up-to-date on state income tax payments. Generally speaking, you can use a clear-cut rule based on relevant features to decide whether a given example belongs to such a category.

Fuzzy, or ill-defined concepts, in contrast, have unclear boundaries and often can be defined only by giving examples. Examples of a fuzzy category tend to have a family resemblance (look alike). There is often a single *best* example of a fuzzy concept, which is called a ***prototype*** because it possesses more features of the concept than any other example. Most concepts we use in everyday life are fuzzy and as such are sometimes called natural concepts. Consider the concept of *clothes*. A dress is a clear example of clothes. It might be called a prototype for clothes. But what about a scarf or a tie or cufflinks? Where does the concept of *clothes* end and the concept of *accessory* begin? Think about your concept of *game*. Some games are purely for amusement, while others entail competition. Some rely heavily on skill, while in others luck is the main factor. Is football a game? Sure. What about boxing? What about backgammon or blackjack or ring-around-the-rosy? Where does the concept of *sport* end and that of *game* begin?

◄ *Is "Olympic Sport" a well-defined or a fuzzy concept? You probably think it is well-defined. But did you know that ballroom dancing is an Olympic Sport?*

How We Learn about Concepts

Concepts are a kind of symbolic mental representation. As such, they are part of our knowledge of the world. We are not born with concepts, but rather we acquire them through experience. Well-defined concepts can be taught easily and directly by instructions about the rules and properties that define them. But we more commonly learn concepts, particularly natural concepts, by associating the concept name with specific examples. Consider Delia, a child learning to discriminate between cats and other things. Perhaps her first exposure to the concept comes as an infant, in the form of a stuffed toy called a "cat" by her parents. Through repetition, Delia learns to use the word "cat" for that particular toy. So far, "cat" is only a name for a specific object and does not represent a category.

A concept is the symbolic memory representation of a basic category of knowledge or meaning.

Now, suppose the neighbors acquire a pet that is also called "cat" by Delia's parents. To integrate this new instance of "cat" with her previous experience, Delia must begin to form a concept, by determining what features these two objects have in common. For example, she may notice that both have a long tail, stand on four paws, are furry, and have pointed ears. The features Delia notices—whatever they may be—will determine her concept of *cat*.

As Delia observes additional examples, she will further refine her *cat* concept. For instance, she might call another neighbor's new pet,

The prototype is the best example of any natural category.

"cat," acting on the hypothesis that all furry things that have four legs are members of the same category. But suppose the neighbor's pet is a large dog. After being corrected, Delia will readjust her concept, eliminating bigger animals that bark from the *cat* category. Through many exposures to examples and non-examples, Delia extracts critical features of the concept. Eventually she develops a set of defining characteristics that, taken as a whole, can classify objects into two groups—*cats* and *non-cats*. At some point, Delia will understand that there is an important distinction to be made between *real cats* as a concept and *toy cats*, even though the toy is where things started.

Whatever the cultural context, the human mind seeks to create categories, or concepts, out of experience. This is another psychological universal, a truth about all human beings. The massive number of objects and events we encounter in everyday life is simply too overwhelming to keep everything in mind separately and independently. We find out how to categorize by formulating and trying out our best guesses (hypotheses) about what things are. Once we recognize contradictory evidence, we use it to reject or revise our categories and move on to the next experience (Levine, 1975). We will have more to say about how this unfolds when we later discuss inductive and deductive reasoning.

Problem Solving

Problem solving is a fact of daily life—whether you aspire to become a psychologist, actor, manager, architect, auto mechanic, farmer, nurse, or forest ranger—problem solving invariably is part of what you will have to do. Being an effective parent, organizing a vacation, playing games—there's hardly a human activity that doesn't involve ***problem solving***—figuring out how to cross the gap between where we are and where we want to be. Some problems are solved by intuition, sometimes almost automatically, while others require a deliberate, planful, logical approach. Gestalt theory is concerned with problems that can be solved by mulling them over until the elements suddenly fall into place and the solution automatically pops into consciousness. In contrast, informa-

THINKING CRITICALLY

Your task is to learn a new concept called the Ferbus. You have to learn as a child might learn, by being introduced to examples and non-examples of the concept that you have never seen before. Each of the following stimuli (letter strings) is a Ferbus or a non-Ferbus. No two of these stimuli are alike, but all Ferbi have some thing or things in common that non-Ferbi do not have. Each stimulus is identified for you as a Ferbus or a non-Ferbus. Can you figure out what makes a stimulus a Ferbus? Once you have found the answer, you will know what the concept of a Ferbus is and be able to identify new stimuli as Ferbi or not without hesitation. Is the Ferbus a well-defined or an ill-defined concept?

Stimulus	*Ferbus?*
o	No
FF	No
GGG	Yes
hh	No
AAA	No
NNN	Yes
EE	No
kkk	No
1	No
PPP	Yes

These should be enough stimuli for you to learn the concept. The answer is: Ferbus is the concept of letter strings with three capital consonants. It is a well-defined concept because any letter string stimulus is clearly either an example or a non-example, and there are no in-between cases.

tion-processing theory is concerned with problems in which the path is unclear and many steps are required to reach the ultimate goal.

Information Processing

Information-processing theory treats problem solving as a systematic series of steps to get from an initial state to a solution or goal state. It says that you need to break a problem into its constituent parts, identify the differences between where you are and your subgoals and end goal, and use plans and logical operations to reduce or eliminate the differences. Alan Newell and Herbert Simon wrote a classic textbook on information processing and problem solving called *Human Problem Solving* (1972). This book describes a computer program, the *General Problem Solver* (GPS), which successfully simulates many aspects of human problem-solving behavior. GPS assumes that a problem solver first analyzes the task in order to build a mental representation of the problem, called the ***problem space***. All efforts to solve the problem take place within this mental representation. The problem space contains: (1) the problem's *initial state*, based on the givens of the problem and initial assumptions; (2) the *goal state* to be achieved; (3) all *legal intermediate states* permitted by the problem's rules; and (4) *operators*, procedures used to move from one state to another and finally to the goal state. The general problem-solving process can be represented as a flow diagram (see Figure 8-3).

Stages of Problem Solving

In order to solve a problem, we must go from an initial state to a goal state. To do this, we must see a familiar situation or object in a new way or discover some new way to change the situation or object. The process of problem solving has been divided into stages by several theorists, although not everyone agrees on the number of stages. Minimally, problem solving can be thought of as a process that consists of preparation, idea generation, judgment and selection, and solution attempt.

Deliberate problem-solving efforts require a certain amount and type of background knowledge and skills. Hence, *preparation* is a key element. For simple tasks, preparation may be minimal. An old Chinese puzzle requires uncoupling two bent nails. You already have the necessary skills. You just have to twist the nails in the right way. Solving an algebra problem, however, requires formal training that you might or might not have. To solve such a problem you need to understand the initial state (including the givens and unknowns), to recognize the solution criteria (the constraints or rules), to break up the problem into steps or parts for solution, and to identify subgoals and the final goal. The problem is to take the right steps from

A problem well-stated is a problem half-solved.

—Charles F. Kettering (in Peter, 1989, p. 426).

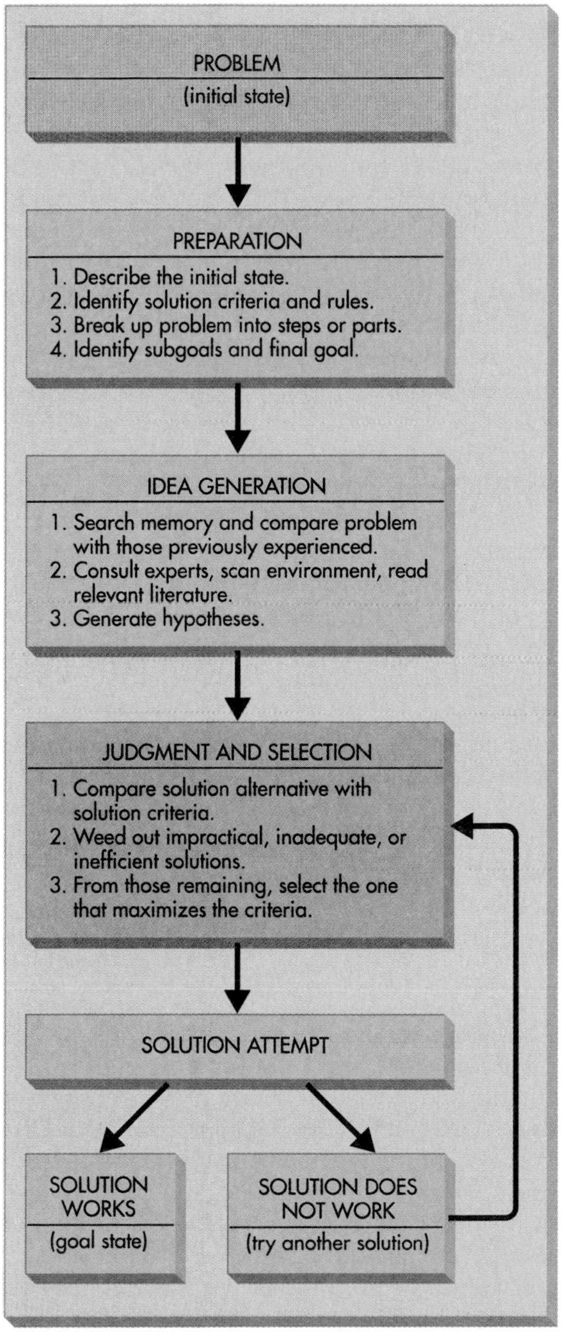

8-3 Stages in Problem Solving

The information-processing approach is characterized by breaking up the overall problem-solving behavior into separate stages or steps to get from the problem (initial state) to its solution (goal state).

▲ *The Chinese bent nail puzzle.*

the initial state to the final goal, which cannot happen without proper preparation.

A problem becomes interesting or challenging when it can't be solved on the first try. In the *idea generation stage*, you try to imagine alternative ways to attack the problem. The trick is to get as many ideas as you can by searching memory for similar past experiences, consulting experts, or reading the relevant literature. Your untested ideas for successful solutions are then called *hypotheses* (Levine, 1975). If the problem is difficult, some of them are likely to fail.

When more than one action seems possible, you need to *judge and select* among the alternatives. Weigh the alternatives. Compare each solution alternative with the solution criteria. All other things being equal, you might try the easiest one first. But that could be like only looking for the nickel you dropped in the circle of light under the street lamp. What if elsewhere, in the dark, is a more likely place for the nickel? If one alternative seems more likely to succeed than the others, you obviously want to try that one early on, if not first. Can you think of other criteria to consider when weighing alternative possible solutions? What about potential payoff? If one action has a higher reward when it succeeds, you might want to try that one before any other.

An algorithm is a series of actions that, if followed systematically, guarantees solution to a problem.

Finally, after choosing a particular course of action, you need to attempt the *solution*. If it works, the process is complete and the problem is solved. Your strategy has been validated. If it fails, try the next most plausible course of action. When everything fails, you need to generate more options. You may have to recycle through the first three stages: preparation, idea generation, and judgment/selection before trying another solution. Try some of the Mind Teasers in the box on p. 267. Can you identify the four stages of problem solving in these Mind Teasers?

An heuristic is a problem-solving procedure that takes advantage of possible shortcuts to problem solution but does not guarantee a solution.

THINKING CRITICALLY

Suppose you're doing a crossword puzzle, and you need a word that means "speaking on one's behalf" that fits into _ d _ _ cac _. If you don't immediately know the answer, you could try inserting every possible letter or combination of letters into the four empty spaces to see which one creates a word. Alternatively, you might guess that the last letter is "y" or "e" on the assumption that "cy" or "ce" are common word endings. Or you might first try a vowel in the first and/or third positions, given the consonant "d" in the second position. What's the difference between these two approaches?

When you try every possible letter combination, you are guaranteed an eventual solution. But this will take a long time because there are nearly half a million combinations to try. This is called the algorithmic strategy. If you try some tricks for selecting letters based on your familiarity with English words, you are likely to find the solution faster, although there is no guarantee of that. The answer by the way is *advocacy*. Did you get it? How?

Algorithms and Heuristics

According to the information-processing approach, successful problem solving involves selecting and applying different procedures to find a solution to a problem. What information guides a problem solver in this process? How does the problem solver decide what move to make next? In some situations, the answer is simple because the problem solver relies on a well-developed algorithm to find the answer. An ***algorithm*** is a procedure or series of actions that guarantees solution to a problem. There are algorithms for solving a wide variety of problems. Consider anagram problems, for example. Anagrams are scrambled words. To solve an anagram, you have to rearrange the letters properly. For example, try to form a word from the anagram E-A-B-T-L. You can solve this anagram by using the algorithm of systematically rearranging the letters into every possible combination (e-a-t-b-l, e-a-t-l-b, e-b-a-t-l, e-b-l-a-t, etc.). This algorithm guarantees success. But finding the solution could involve looking at all 120 letter combinations that are possible for a five-letter word! Though algorithms offer guaranteed solutions, they can be terribly inefficient and time-consuming for a human being to execute.

Do you really need to list all 120 combinations of the letters E-A-B-T-L to come up with TABLE? If we apply algorithms mindlessly, without considering the possibility of more efficient methods, we might miss easier solutions. Further, not all problems can be solved by algorithms. At present, there is no known algorithm for winning at chess, although some computers can win games against even the best players.

Computers are designed primarily to execute algorithms. Unlike people, computers don't become bored with the tedious work of cranking through every possibility. Moreover, computers do this kind of processing quickly and accurately. Our human limitations often prevent us from using algorithms that we know will work. Most people are not very fast or accurate at mental calculations, largely because of our limited cognitive processing capacity. Therefore, when it comes to problem solving, most people look for shortcut strategies, called ***heuristics***. These strategies reduce the complexities of problem solving by focusing on only a limited subset of potential solutions to a problem. For example, in solving anagrams, it is useful to start with the letter that is most likely to begin a word, or to look for frequent consonant-vowel combinations. In poker, a recommended heuristic is never draw to an inside straight. Nonetheless, while usually quicker and easier than algorithms, heuristics cannot guarantee a solution because they leave out some possible options.

There are some cases in which we only have heuristics and not algorithms available to us. Thus, complex games like chess have no algorithmic solution that guarantees a win. Moreover, many problems in nature, such as how a country can maximize its economic output each year, lack a well-defined structure to which algorithms can be applied (Voss & Post, 1988). In cases like these, which are like the majority of problems we face in life, heuristic procedures are the best that we have available.

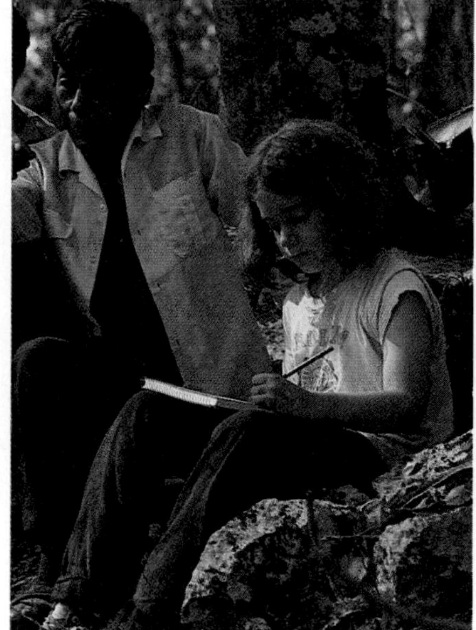

▲ An example of heuristics and insight in complex problem solving: David Stuart was fascinated with Mayan glyphs (shown above) from an early age. At eight, he spent a great deal of time drawing the glyphs and memorizing them, looking for similarities in their shapes and patterns. But it was insight that led him to make important breakthroughs in deciphering the Mayan written language.

Gestalt Theory

Try to solve the problem in the margin. What possibilities occurred to you? How long did it take you to get the solution? Was the solution immediately obvious, or did it take time? When the answer came, did it just "pop into your mind" or did it emerge gradually? This is an example of a problem that is typically solved in a flash. (If you still don't know the answer, ask yourself how two people could have the same child. If you still don't know the answer, look in the margin on p. 266.)

Gestalt psychology, which originated in Germany shortly after the turn of the century, has much to say about how problems are solved and why it is sometimes difficult to solve them. In Gestalt theory, problem solving involves reorganizing or restructuring problem elements. At some point, according to Gestalt theory, with repeated reorganizations of the problem, the solution immediately appears in consciousness, rather than emerging gradually or logically

There were two Nobel prize–winning chemists waiting at the door of the chemistry laboratory. One was the father of the other one's child. How could this be? (See p. 266 for answer.)

FARMER IN LOGIC EXPERIMENT WITH FOX, CHICKEN, GOAT AND KIBITZERS
TAKE THE FOX AND THE CHICKEN!
LEAVE THE FOX!
THE CHICKEN... TAKE THE CHICKEN!
JOE MARTIN

◀ Psychologists study thinking by examining the behavior of people attempting to solve problems of the kind mentioned in the cartoon and by manipulating the characteristics of the problem, the problem solver, and the nature of the information provided (such as hints or strategies).

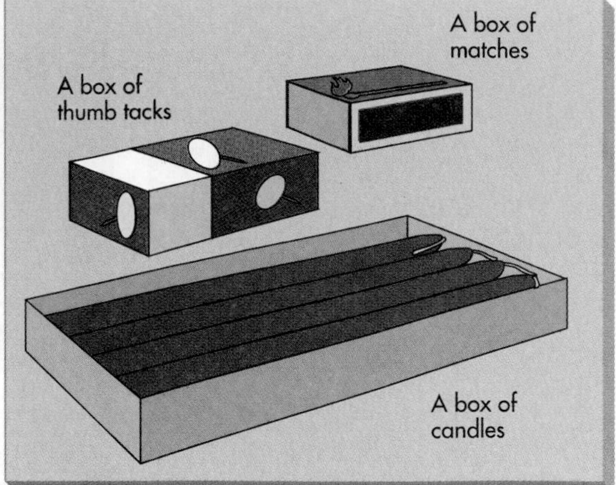

8-4 The Candle Problem

Your task is to mount one of the candles on a wall, using only the materials provided. Can you visualize the solution? See Figure 8-5 on p. 269.

step-by-step. Some call it the "ah-ha!" experience.

For Gestalt psychologists, solving a problem is a matter of gaining ***insight***—seeing how different aspects of the problem fit into an appropriate whole (Gestalt). According to Gestalt theory, in order to solve a nontrivial problem, you must actively take various perspectives until the problem's component parts fall into place. At that point, the solution will be perceived. Regarding the two Nobel laureates and their child, you need to discard sex-role stereotypes to attain the perspective needed to solve the problem. Finally, Gestalt theory characterizes people as active thinkers and multiple perspective takers, not merely passive recipients of environmental stimulation.

The names of the Nobel prize–winning chemists are Marie and Pierre Curie.

Why Are Some Problems Difficult

Look at Figure 8-4. Your task is to mount three lighted candles on a vertical wall, using only the materials shown: a box of tacks, a box of candles, and a box of matches. This problem's difficulty depends, in part, on how the tacks, matches, candles, and boxes are arranged when the problem is initially presented. If the tacks, candles, and matches lie loose on the table along with the boxes, the solution is fairly easily discovered (see Figure 8-5). But if the tacks, candles, and matches are placed in separate boxes, the problem is more difficult. That is, if the boxes are functioning as containers, people either have difficulty thinking of them as serving any other function, or they don't even perceive the boxes as a part of the problem (or solution). This phenomenon, predicted by Gestalt psychologists, is called ***functional fixedness***. When we perceive items, such as the boxes, as having a particular function, functional fixedness interferes with perceiving them as having another use.

Functional fixedness occurs when the use of an object in a specific way interferes with or inhibits its use in another way that might be required for the solution of a problem.

Whenever you're stuck on a problem, ask yourself whether any of its components can be used in new, different, or unusual ways. Do any components exemplify more than one concept? Focus on the features, rather than the names of the components. Names may form links in your mind between the components and their specific functions. If you need something to tie two things together, don't think "I need a rope," think "I need something six inches long and flexible." A dog leash, purse strap, electrical cord, or wire twists might do the job.

Adopting a rigid problem-solving strategy can also undermine your ability to find a problem's solution. In a classic demonstration of this phenomenon, called a ***mental set***, Abraham and Edith Luchins (1959) gave participants a series of problems involving a water tap and three different-sized jars—A, B, and C—each having

THINKING CRITICALLY

All of the examples we've used are visual. Does the concept of mental set apply in other modalities?

Try the following demonstration. Ask a friend to pronounce the following words after you spell each of them in order (note the slight pause after the C):

M-A-C—D-E-R-M-O-T-T
M-A-C—D-O-N-A-L-D
M-A-C—D-U-F-F
M-A-C—D-O-U-G-A-L
M-A-C—H-I-N-E

If you friend says "mac-hine" instead of "machine," you have demonstrated the effect of a mental set. Mental sets narrow our perspective and restrict our ability to try different methods. We simply don't see or recognize reasonable alternative approaches.

SEEKING SOLUTIONS

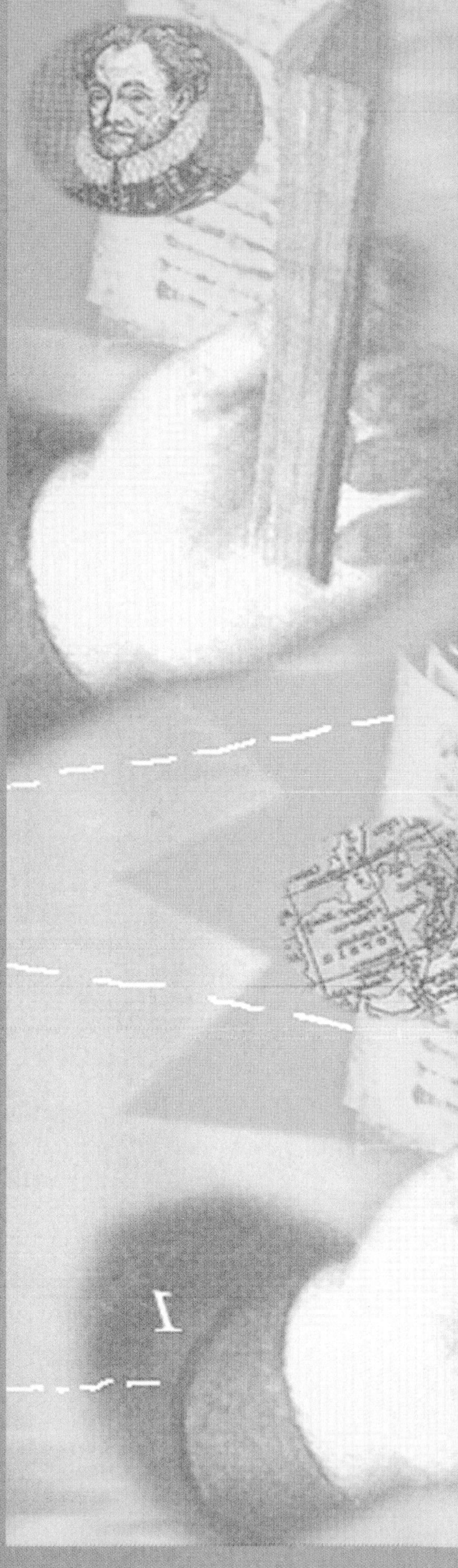

Some Illustrative Mind Teasers

Most people find puzzles and problems fascinating to work on. Research shows that, the more you work on puzzles, the better you get. Here are some problems to try at your leisure. Some are easy, some are hard. None is obvious, otherwise you wouldn't have to think about it. They are meant to illustrate some of the cognitive processes we have described in this chapter. Working them through could make you a better problem solver in the future.

Mind Teaser 1

You'll need some background in algebra for this one. A ruler won't help.

Somebody sold E. Z. Munney two old pirate maps leading to the buried treasure of Montezuma. Both showed a straight path from the site of his home to the loot. One map was drawn to standard sixteenth-century scale and the other to twentieth-century scale. The ratio of the twentieth-century scale to the sixteenth-century scale is 9 to 6. The twentieth-century scale is 30 feet to the map inch. What is the corresponding sixteenth-century scale?

Mind Teaser 2

Try generating some alternative ideas before you attempt to solve this problem.

A father and two children want to get across the river. They have a boat with a maximum capacity of 200 pounds. Each child weighs 100 pounds, and the father weighs 200 pounds. All three of them know how to row the boat. How can all three of them get across the river?

Mind Teaser 3

Logic will help you in solving this problem.

Affirmo Negato, professor of logic, discovered that a copy of the final exam he had prepared for his class had been stolen. The departmental secretary identified three students, Corey, Ricardo, and Ishmail, who had access to the exam. Negato interrogated all three, who said the following:

Corey: "It wasn't I!"

Ricardo: "Ishmail stole the test."

Ishmail: "That's right, I did it."

Negato knew that at least one of the suspects was lying and at least one was telling the truth. On that basis, he could determine logically which student had taken the exam. Can you?

Mind Teaser 4

Inductive reasoning must be used to solve this problem.

What is the next letter in this series:

B C C E D G _?

Mind Teaser 5

This problem is messy. It requires a little bit of logic, prior training, and intuition.

U.S. stamps honor well-known people from all walks of life. From the following clues, can you determine the denominations of the stamps described below? (Note: The stamps are designed not to reflect those currently in use by the U.S. Postal Service. This is a logic problem, not a test of memory!)

1. The Abraham Lincoln stamp costs 2 cents less than the Susan B. Anthony stamp and 7 cents less than the Sojourner Truth stamp.
2. The Martin Luther King, Jr., stamp costs 2 cents more than the Elizabeth Cady Stanton stamp and 7 cents less than the Cesar Chavez stamp.
3. The John F. Kennedy stamp costs 2 cents more than the Ada Deer stamp and 7 cents more than the Susan B. Anthony stamp.
4. The Fanny Lou Hamer stamp costs 7 cents more than the Martin Luther King, Jr., stamp.
5. Three of the stamps cost 15 cents each and there are at least two of each other denomination.

Note: The answers to the Mind Teasers can be found on p. 268.

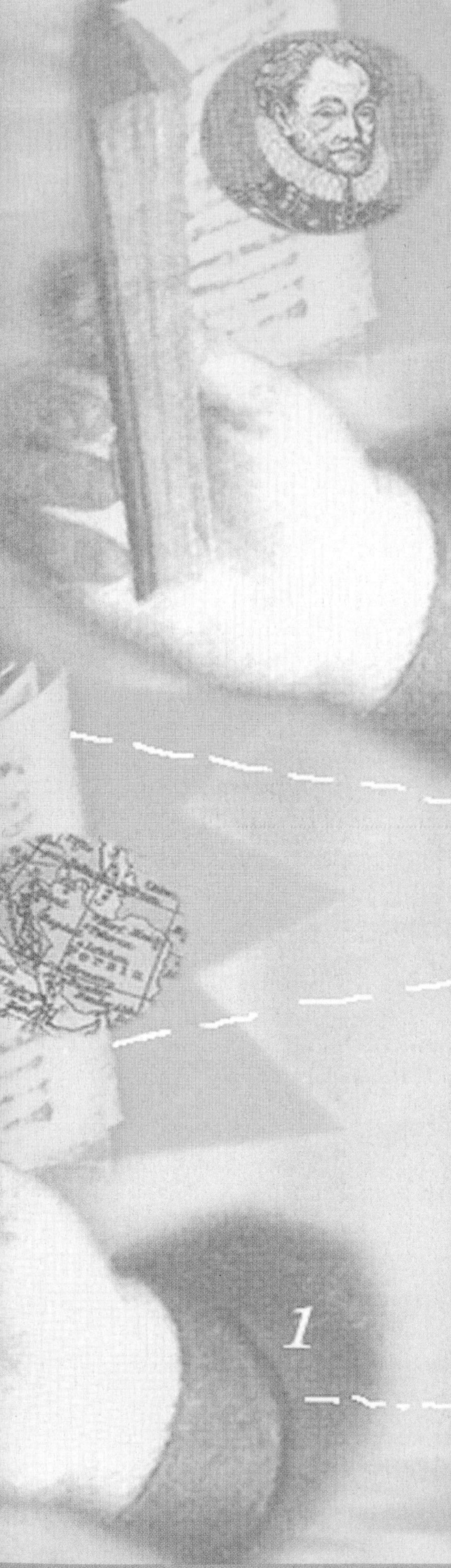

Solutions to Mind Teasers

Answer to Mind Teaser 1

Set up the ratio $9/6 = 30/x$.

Multiply both numerators by both denominators.

Solve 9 × = 180 for ×; × = 20. If the twentieth-century scale is 30 feet to the inch, the sixteenth-century scale is 20 feet to the inch.

Answer to Mind Teaser 2

(1) One son takes his brother across the river, leaves him there, and goes back.
(2) Father rows himself across the river and the second son rows the boat back.
(3) The two sons cross the river again.

Answer to Mind Teaser 3

If Corey stole the exam, then all three suspects would be lying; therefore, Corey must be telling the truth. If Ishmail is the thief, then all three are telling the truth; therefore, Ishmail is not the thief and must be lying. This means that Ricardo is the culprit.

Answer to Mind Teaser 4

E. Add 1, subtract 0, add 2, subtract 1, add 3, subtract 2, and so on.

Answer to Mind Teaser 5

Stamps honoring nine people are mentioned. Since three of them cost 15 cents each (clue 5), and you are told that there are at least two people at each denomination (clue 5), the other six people must be on no more than three different denominations, so there are four or fewer denominations in all, one being 15 cents. The Abraham Lincoln stamp costs 2 cents less than the Susan B. Anthony stamp, which costs 5 cents less than the Sojourner Truth stamp (clue 1). Hint: Doing this kind of logic problem relies on recognizing all of the information that can be derived from a statement. For example, from clue 1 you can say five things:

An Anthony is equal to a Lincoln plus 2 cents.
A Truth is equal to a Lincoln plus 7 cents.
A Truth is equal to an Anthony plus 5 cents.
An Anthony is equal to a Truth minus 5 cents.
Three different stamp amounts are represented.

From this information, combined with that from clue 3, you can then derive that the Ada Deer stamp costs the same as the Sojourner Truth stamp (both cost 5 cents more than the Susan B. Anthony stamp), and the John F. Kennedy stamp costs 2 cents more than that. You now have identified four denominations, so you know the number of categories you must work with:

JFK is the highest, which has to be 15 cents, as there are no other higher denominations. Truth and Deer are 2 cents less, which is 13 cents. Anthony is 5 cents less, which is 8 cents. Lincoln is 2 cents less than Anthony, which is 6 cents. Because there must be at least two people for each denomination, you now have one 15-cent, one 8-cent, and one 6-cent stamp left to identify. By clue 2, the Elizabeth Cady Stanton stamp must be the one that costs 6 cents; the Martin Luther King, Jr., stamp must cost 8 cents; the Cesar Chavez stamp must cost 15 cents. As the only one left, the Fanny Lou Hamer stamp must cost 15 cents, but you could also compute it by adding 7 cents to the 8 cents of the Martin Luther King, Jr., stamp. Summing up these results, we get:

6 cents: Elizabeth Cady Stanton, Abraham Lincoln
8 cents: Susan B. Anthony, Martin Luther King, Jr.
13 cents: Sojourner Truth, Ada Deer
15 cents: Fanny Lou Hamer, Cesar Chavez, John F. Kennedy

Think about the skills needed to do this problem. In addition to requiring you to think about things in terms of their relationships to others, it switches the kind of information you need to solve the problem in the middle of the process. Thus, figuring out the cost of the Stanton, King, Chavez, and Hamer stamps requires combining different kinds of information than that needed to figure out the cost of the others. Did you have trouble at this point in the problem? Psychologists might explain your difficulty in terms of the concept of mental set.

TABLE 8-1 Problems Illustrating the Mental Set Effect

Step I: Solve the First Five Problems **Problem Number**	**Three Jars Are Present with the Listed Capacity** Jar A	Jar B	Jar C	**Obtain Exactly This Amount of Water**
1	21	127	3	100
2	14	163	25	99
3	18	43	10	5
4	9	42	6	21
5	20	59	4	31
Step II: Stop! Did You Discover the Rule?				
Step III: Solve the Next Two Problems				
6	23	49	3	20
7	10	36	7	3

Source: Luchins & Luchins, 1959, p. 109.

a known capacity. For example, suppose A, B, and C can hold 10, 32, and 7 quarts of water, respectively. Your task is to use these jars to measure out exactly 8 quarts of water. By experimenting, you find that the solution is first to fill B. Then pour from B into A, filling A with 10 quarts, leaving 22 in B. Next you pour from B into C, filling C with 7 and leaving 15 in B. Throw out the water in C and repeat the last step. B will now contain 8 quarts.

Now, solve problems 1 through 7 in Table 8-1, timing how long you take to solve each problem. What happened? Each problem can be solved by the same procedure as the initial example, described by the formula: $B - A - 2C$ = the correct answer. Once you discover this procedure, you can readily solve the first five problems. But, then, what happens when you encounter Problem 6?

If you are mentally set to use a specific formula or strategy, a problem that requires even a slight variation on the theme can pose interesting difficulties. Did you realize that Problem 6 can be solved by both the usual formula and by a simpler, more efficient method? You can get the required number of quarts merely by filling A, then filling C from A. The correct number is left in A. What happened when you reached Problem 7? It cannot be solved by the usual formula. How long did it take you to get the correct answer? In a typical experiment, some subjects fail to solve Problem 7 even after several minutes of effort.

Mental set and functional fixedness are closely related phenomena. Both involve applying existing knowledge or techniques to a new problem. Both lead to problem-solving difficulties when existing knowledge or techniques are inappropriate. You should keep these concepts in mind when you encounter a difficult problem. If first attempts based on your existing knowledge are unsuccessful, stop and consider whether you are being influenced by functional fixedness or an inappropriate mental set. Be ready to try new and different approaches.

Overcoming Problem-Solving Difficulties

Phenomena like mental set and functional fixedness led Gestalt psychologists to conclude that problem solving is largely a matter of per-

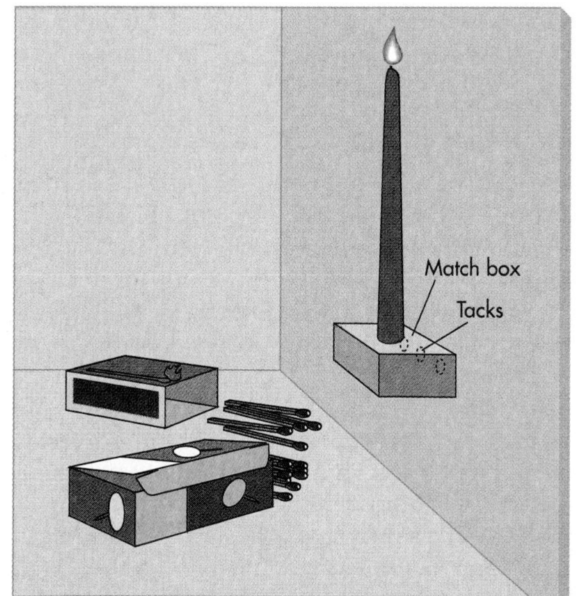

8-5 Solution to the Candle Problem

Here is a possible solution to the candle problem presented in Figure 8-4. Part of the match box is used as a candle mount and attached to the wall with thumb tacks.

▲ *The Greek scholar Archimedes (287–212 B.C.) experienced a moment of insight in his bath and supposedly was so exhilarated by his discovery that he ran naked through the streets of Syracuse.*

Insight is suddenly attaining a solution when the various problem elements are perceived to be related in a new and different way.

Incubation is a period of time during which no effort is made to work out the solution of an unsolved problem; an incubation period often culminates in an eventual insight.

ceiving or conceptualizing the elements of a situation in a new way. Once you overcome an existing mental set, problem solution occurs quickly, in a moment of insight. We've all experienced flashes of insight. A famous example is found in an old story about the Greek scholar Archimedes, who discovered a basic law of physics while taking a bath. He noticed that when he submerged, the water level rose, and the amount that it rose depended on how much of him was submerged. He realized that the strength of the force that pushed back at him as he submerged was in proportion to the amount of water being displaced, and that the more he submerged, the greater the force pushing back at him. (This explains, among other things, why we feel lighter in a pool than when we're out of water. It is also called the law of specific gravity in physics.) Archimedes was so excited when he had this insight that he is said to have leaped out of his bath and run through the streets of Syracuse in a towel shouting "Eureka! I have found it!" (In some versions, he forgets the towel.) Insights can be exhilarating, which may be one reason why mind teasers are fun.

Early research on solving problems through insight was conducted by Gestalt psychologist Wolfgang Köhler (1925), using chimpanzees as subjects. In one study, a chimp had to obtain an out-of-reach banana hanging from the ceiling of its cage. The solution was to stack several boxes lying around the cage into a platform from which the banana could be reached. At first, the chimp engaged in unsuccessful trial-and-error behavior. After a number of failed attempts, the chimp temporarily stopped trying. Then, suddenly, the chimp jumped up, stacked the boxes, and climbed up to the banana. Köhler described the chimp's problem-solving process in very human-like terms. He claimed that the chimp had achieved insight and that, through this new insightful understanding of the problem, the chimp could now repeat the solution instantaneously whenever the problem was re-presented.

Have you ever come up against a brick wall while trying to solve a problem? Nothing you try seems to work. When this happens, take a lesson from the chimp in Köhler's experiment—back off for a while. Then, later, when you are not even thinking about the problem, the solution might pop to mind almost effortlessly, in a moment of insight. This backing-off phenomenon is quite common and is called the ***incubation*** period (Wallas, 1926). You set the problem aside so that any potentially good ideas that have not yet come to consciousness have a chance to incubate into a possible solution.

Gestalt psychologists would say that time off results in seeing problem elements in a new way when you return. Your old and inappropriate ways (misperception, functional fixedness, mental set) of attacking the problem weaken (through forgetting or lowered activation) over the break, and new, different, and possibly more successful approaches emerge. Researchers demonstrated this effect in the following way. Research participants were given a series of problems depicting familiar phrases, like "reading between the lines," in an unusual form, like "lines reading lines." They had to decode the unusual forms as quickly as possible. Some individuals were given one minute to solve each problem, while others worked for thirty seconds, took some time off, and then worked for another thirty seconds. The time-off period was helpful, as participants in the interruption (or incubation) group solved more problems than those in the continuous work group. The researchers attributed this improvement to forgetting (Smith & Blankenship, 1991). That is, incubation results from forgetting the blind alleys you might have been following before the break. They based this conclusion on the fact that, when misleading clues to the solution were given at the outset along with each problem, incubation participants were unlikely to remember those clues after the break. Whatever the explanation, the incubation effect does seem to work. Time away from the problem is an important strategy for overcoming difficulties encountered in problem solving.

Expertise

It's obvious that some people are better than others at certain tasks. Sometimes you can trace the difference to general intelligence or a specific ability one person has and another does not. Behavior geneticists have argued that people vary innately in creativity or talent (McGue, Bouchard, Iacono, & Lykken, 1993). But, in most cases, innate ability is less important than experience or practice with the task at hand. Some researchers have presented evidence that experts are made, not born. Their argument is that problem-solving expertise in any field—law, auto repair, psychology, guitar—is acquired largely by hard work, study, and deliberate practice (Ericsson, Krampe, & Tesch-Römer, 1993; Ericsson and Charness, 1994). Researchers in one study of chess estimated that an expert knows at least 50,000 chunks of information about the game (Simon, 1980). For any domain, including chess, it takes about ten years of dedicated practice to achieve expert status. The expert's skill is typically specific to a single domain, like reading X-rays or piano playing, and does not readily transfer to anything else. Genius is different from expertise. With hard work, nearly everyone can become an expert in some area, but few are geniuses. Genius implies more general ability to do well, regardless of task domain (Ericsson & Smith, 1991; Ericsson & Charness, 1994).

Expertise is defined by an unusually high level of acquired knowledge or skill in a particular domain.

In chess, master players and beginners differ widely in how they play the game. A beginner proceeds slowly, step-by-step, under conscious verbal control (reflecting dependence on declarative knowledge; see Chapter 7), and with considerable attention to detail. The expert moves quickly, makes large leaps (often with logical gaps), employs grand strategies, and performs more automatically than with conscious, verbal control. Memory for piece positions differs between experts and novices (de Groot, 1978). If a configuration is legal, that is, if it could actually happen in a game of chess, master-level players can immediately perceive the configuration's meaning within the game and will remember it better than beginners. If the configuration is illegal, for example, a random arrangement, however, master-level players will remember it no better than will beginners. Limitations on fundamental capacity—such as the limit on short-term or working memory, on attention span, and, in a larger sense, on general intelligence—do not change with practice and do not distinguish experts from novices, no matter how expert they become. But the expert finds ways to bypass these limitations by employing untapped or underused cognitive resources. For example, an expert can augment otherwise limited short-term memory by invoking long-term

▼ *By stacking boxes on top of one another, the chimps in Wolfgang Köhler's laboratory were able to solve the problem of reaching the banana. Köhler described their process of problem solving as insight.*

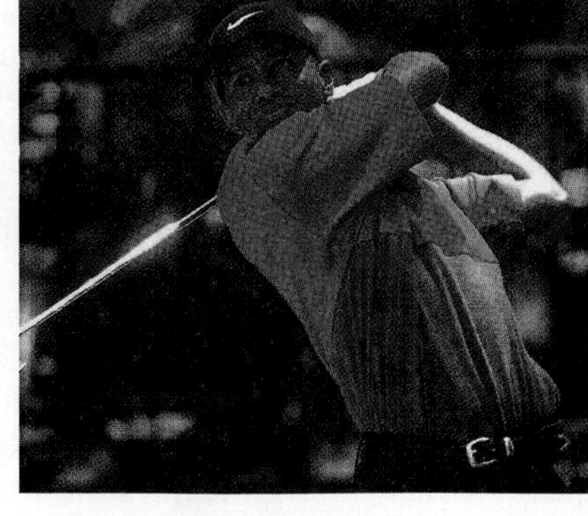

▲ *Champion golfer Tiger Woods, shown as a young child (at left) and at the U.S. Open (at right), might be naturally talented, but he also had to undergo intensive training to achieve his level of expertise.*

knowledge of the game that is not possessed by beginners (Ericsson & Chase, 1982; Ericsson & Kintsch, 1995).

Expertise implies both factual and procedural knowledge. There is no easy path to knowledge or expertise. It's not in the genes. You cannot take a pill to become smart or skillful. A certain amount of ability is needed, of course, but the rest is plain hard work. Keep that in mind as you progress toward becoming an expert in your chosen field.

Artificial Intelligence

Computers have been used as models for understanding problem solving and other mental processes. When information arrives from the environment, both mind and computer process the input, and products (behavior or output) appear that reflect internal activity within the system. Modern theories of cognition almost exclusively flow from such information-processing ideas.

▶ *Deep Blue finally beat Garry Kasparov in a five-game match in 1997.*

When computers are programmed to behave in intelligent ways, that is, to use human-like knowledge and skills to understand spoken language, to recognize objects, or to make informed decisions, we call it ***artificial intelligence***. It's intelligent for obvious reasons; it's artificial because it's exhibited by a machine. If you cannot tell the difference between computer output and human "output" (without seeing the actor, of course), the computer is acting (artificially) like an intelligent human being. When a computer functions like a human expert in any domain, such as chess playing or medical diagnosis, it's an ***expert system***. Theoretically, a computer could actually exceed human expert performance (in ways other than just being faster), in which case new insights, scientific discoveries, or creative artistic achievements might be possible (Mishkoff, 1985). But, until recently, technology wasn't advanced enough to seriously challenge the human expert. For example, IBM had been trying for years to develop a computer program that could beat the human world champion chess player, but the human champion had always won against the computer, at least until the most recent round. In 1997, IBM'S newly developed expert system, "Deep Blue," challenged the current world champion, Garry Kasparov, to a match. This time, in a five-game match, the computer won, two games to one, with two ties. Even Kasparov had to admit that the computer had played a "human-like" game. Only time will tell whether successes like this one will eventually lead to discoveries by machines that are truly significant advances for society.

Expert systems have been developed to solve problems in medicine, organic chemistry, weather forecasting, and oil exploration (McGraw & Harbison-Briggs, 1989). These systems are programmed with facts provided by human experts, with algorithms and heuristics, and with decision trees to follow when presented with new data to analyze. One expert system called MYCIN is used to diagnose certain infectious diseases (Shortliffe, Buchanan, & Feigenbaum, 1979). It employs an encyclopedia of facts about diseases (symptoms and successful treatments) and a set of procedures for sorting through and selecting from those facts to make decisions about medical diagnoses.

MYCIN functions best in an interactive mode, serving as a consultant for the doctor. The doctor inputs preliminary data, consisting of patient complaints and history. MYCIN reacts either with an immediate diagnosis, or, more commonly, with a set of questions for the doctor to answer after further examination of the patient. For example, MYCIN might need to know the level of liver enzymes in the patient's blood before making a diagnosis. Eventually, with sufficient input, MYCIN will either make a diagnosis or conclude that all signs of disease are negative for the categories covered.

While they are inferior in some respects, expert computer systems have some advantages over human experts. They can process vast amounts of information rapidly and are less likely than people to become overloaded when operating on many facts at the same time. Further, expert systems process information completely, are not easily distracted, and do not give up when logic becomes difficult. Expert systems don't forget facts or overlook the need for a vital piece of missing information. Moreover, computers are entirely consistent in their application of rules. Finally, they are not susceptible to emotion, fallacy, or biasing tendencies that often plague human reasoners.

We cannot yet replace human beings completely in any significant intellectual activity. Human beings typically make better diagnoses than any computer, and we still don't understand why. Our uniquely human abilities enable us to think intuitively and divergently, to see remote connections between entities, and to be creative—capacities not yet within the grasp of computers. But expert computer systems represent a valuable aid or adjunct to human thinking, especially when there is a great deal of information to process and when complex diagnoses and decisions are required.

▲ *At the Center for Research in Computing in the Arts (University of California at San Diego) an Artificial Intelligence program called AARON produces original drawings and paintings. Here, AARON has created a representational work of art (dyes on paper) measuring 68″ × 53″. Artificial Intelligence has challenged our traditional way of thinking about creativity.*

Reasoning and Logical Analysis

All problems require us to figure out what to do next on the basis of some given information. Sometimes we make an educated guess using past experience. On other occasions, we base the next step on logic: What logically follows? There are two traditional forms of logical reasoning: induction and deduction. ***Inductive reasoning*** is the process of reaching a general conclusion from a small set of specific instances. The way Delia learned about *cats* was based on induction from the specific instances she encountered to a general concept. In fact, the way we form most everyday concepts is by inductive reasoning.

In contrast, ***deductive reasoning*** leads from general principles to a specific conclusion. Putting together two or more given premises allows us to see a situation in a new and different way. An important point to keep in mind is this: the conclusion reached by deductive reasoning absolutely follows from the premises; there could be no other conclusion. The same cannot be said of inductive reasoning, where concepts change and become more refined as additional instances are encountered. That's why Delia's concept of *cats* at one point included dogs, and later changed.

The example of deductive reasoning that logicians like to use is this: (*Premise*) Aristotle is a man. (*Premise*) All men are mortal. (*Conclusion*) Aristotle is mortal. Sherlock Holmes might prefer this example: (*Premise*) The Countess was stabbed in the wine cellar. (*Premise*) The wine cellar can be entered only by the Count. (*Conclusion*) The Countess was stabbed by the Count.

There is a connection between inductive and deductive reasoning and top-down versus bottom-up processing. Inductive reasoning is primarily bottom-up processing—specific in-

▼ *Data from "Star Trek." Television shows and movies have been replacing human beings with computers and androids for a long time, but in reality it isn't possible—yet.*

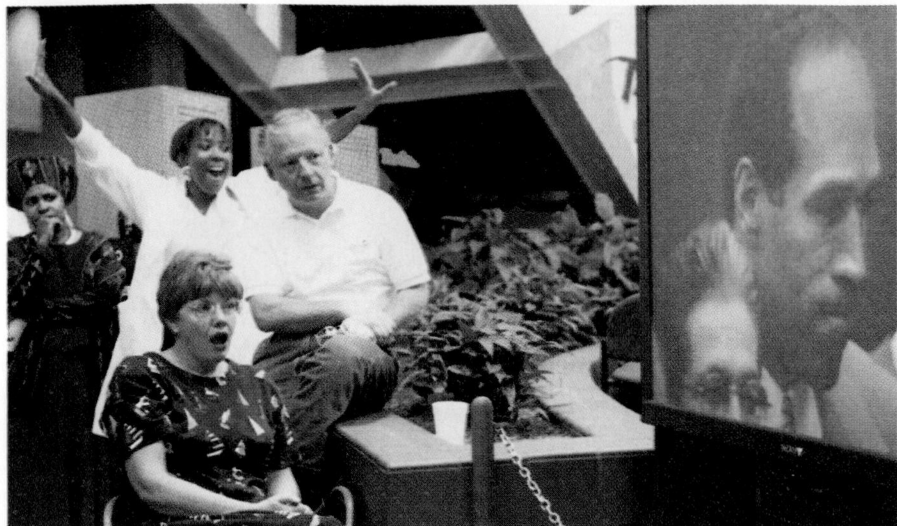

▲ *Previous experience has powerful effects on judgment, as demonstrated by the fact that reactions to the verdict of the O. J. Simpson murder trial varied with race: a lower percentage of blacks considered him guilty compared to whites.*

stances to general concept; deductive reasoning is primarily top-down processing—general premises to specific conclusion. Just as with top-down and bottom-up cognitive processes, however, inductive and deductive reasoning are not entirely independent and often work together when people solve problems, make decisions, or engage in other cognitive activities.

How Reasoning Can Go Wrong

Inductive reasoning is reasoning from specific examples to general principles or concepts. Deductive reasoning argues from two or more "givens" or premises to a specific conclusion.

Faulty premises or assumptions can be a weak link in deductive reasoning. You can follow the rules of logic perfectly, but if you accept a faulty premise, your reasoning may lead to an erroneous conclusion. Consider the following line of reasoning: Tim drives too fast and tailgates the car ahead. But he has driven over 50,000 miles during the past two years without an accident. This record reinforces his belief that he has exceptional driving skill. Tim uses his personal experience to justify failure to take protective actions, such as driving within the speed limit or wearing a seat belt. Faulty premises, such as accidents happen only to bad drivers, lead Tim to an incorrect conclusion that could be costly.

Emotions sometimes influence our ability to reason logically. It's not easy to be logical when you are emotionally involved in a situation, a fact best captured in the saying "love is blind." So, if good logic leads to negative conclusions about things or people we like (or positive conclusions about things or people we don't like), we may reject logic and the conclusions it leads to and go on believing that people we like can do no wrong.

Sometimes faulty premises create problems of self-esteem. Consider the following reasoning process: (*Premise*) People who fail exams in their courses are stupid. (*Premise*) I just failed a final. (*Conclusion*) Therefore, I am stupid. This syllogism is perfectly logical. But the person bases his or her reasoning on a faulty premise about the relationship between intelligence and test-taking—that failure is always the result of stupidity. You can fail a test for many reasons, regardless of your intelligence. But, if you think otherwise, your self-esteem might suffer. Reasoning errors related to self-concept (for example, I never do anything right; I always foul up) can reflect serious underlying personality problems. People with depressive personalities seem to be particularly susceptible to errors that undermine self-confidence. In psychotherapy based on cognitive principles, the psychotherapist helps people learn to identify faulty reasoning processes and to think logically about themselves and their experiences (Meichenbaum & Jaremko, 1983; Beck, 1991).

Reasoning Based on Analogies

One other common kind of reasoning uses analogies, which are similarity relationships between pairs of objects or events. ***Analogical reasoning*** uses facts that we know about one item or situation to draw a conclusion about another. The first or more familiar item, which is called the ***base***, or the ***source analog***, provides a model for the unfamiliar item, the ***target analog***. By analogical reasoning, we treat the target as "the same kind of thing" as the base. Analogies are commonly expressed as: *a* is to *b* as *x* is to *y* (or *a:b::x:y*). There are many everyday examples of analogical reasoning. Consider this one: *dog* is to *animal* as *daisy* is to "?". The similarity relationship is based on class inclusion. *Dog* belongs to the class of all *animals*; daisy belongs to the class of all ?. Of course, like any other type of reasoning, it is possible to use analogies correctly or incorrectly. You would be correct to answer *flowers* or *plants* to the foregoing analogy. You'd be off the mark if you said *Mae* (as in Daisy Mae, a cartoon character).

The power of an analogy to reveal relationships that might be otherwise difficult to see makes it a useful tool for a wide variety of cognitive purposes. Consider a political example. In order to convince Congress and our allies to take action in the Persian Gulf region several years ago, President George Bush explicitly compared Saddam Hussein, the leader of Iraq, to Adolf Hitler, the infamous Nazi dictator. The events that led to World War II in the late 1930s were said by Bush to be analogous to the Persian Gulf crisis in the 1990s. Bush employed an analogical reasoning process that assigned World War II roles to the various players in the Gulf situation—Iraq was identified with Nazi Germany, Hussein with Hitler, Kuwait was Hussein's first victim, Saudi Arabia was a potential next victim, and the United States was the main defender against unprovoked aggression (Spellman & Holyoak, 1992). The clear analogical inference drawn by Bush and accepted by the allies was that both self-interest and international morality required immediate military intervention against Iraq. Analogies, based on what has been successful in the past or in other areas, are used by problem solvers and decision makers in a variety of contexts, from science to psychotherapy (Gentner & Holyoak, 1997).

Correct analogical reasoning is considered intelligent behavior, so analogies often appear in intelligence tests. Moreover, recent evidence suggests that teaching analogies and strategies of problem solving based on analogies has significant educational advantages. One study compared college students who were taught about certain scientific concepts by direct instruction with other students who were taught the same concepts by analogies (Donnelly & McDaniel, 1993). For example, in an astrophysics lesson, both groups learned about pulsars. The direct instruction group learned that "a pulsar is a collapsing star that emits a stream of radiation. Even though the radiation stream is continuous, it appears on earth to be flashing intermittently because of the steady and continuous rotation of the star." The analogy group learned that "the radiation stream from a pulsar acts like a rotating lighthouse beacon. The beam is continuous but on earth, like ships at sea watching a lighthouse, only intermittent flashes are observed." Both groups of students did equally well on tests of detailed knowledge about these concepts, but students who were taught with analogies were better at making inferences and generalizations, for example, "what would happen if the earth or the pulsar stopped rotating?," from what they had learned. In psychology, and especially within the information-processing approach, computers are often used as analogs of the human mind. Inferences and conclusions about the mind are drawn from our knowledge of the way computers work.

When we draw a conclusion about something we don't know on the basis of something we do know about a similar case or issue, we are using analogical reasoning.

Decision-Making Heuristics

Decision making and critical thinking should be based on the rules of logic but, like reasoning, are subject to influence from personal experiences. For example, we are more likely to make a decision consistent with our likes and dislikes

◀ *In his attempt to gain the support of the American people for the Persian Gulf war, President Bush explicitly compared Saddam Hussein to Adolf Hitler. Political cartoonists picked up his analogy.*

► *An example of the representativeness heuristic: Alex Kelly, on trial for rape, didn't fit the typical image of a rapist—his preppy good looks, wealthy parents, and beautiful, doting girlfriend all combined to produce a hung jury in his first trial. He was subsequently convicted and sentenced to sixteen years in prison, demonstrating that heuristics can be overcome in the face of overwhelming evidence.*

than with logic (Ditto & Lopez, 1992). In addition, we tend to let extraneous or irrelevant factors influence our judgments and reasoning. Our knowledge of recent events and of the world in general affects our decision making in a host of ways. In fact, we have more than a dozen "mental shortcuts," called judgment or ***decision-making heuristics***, that bypass logic, rely on memory for past experiences, and are more intuitive than analytic. These heuristics often can lead our decision making astray (Tversky & Kahnemann, 1973).

Shortcuts can be adaptive if they save time and effort. If we automatically thought through every assumption and alternative in every situation, we might not get very much done. But remember, although a heuristic is a shortcut through a complex problem, it does not guarantee a correct decision. While decision-making heuristics spare you from examining every possibility, they do not always lead you to the right conclusion. So it's important to know how heuristics can influence your judgments.

Three heuristics commonly observed in everyday decision making are the availability heuristic, the representativeness heuristic, and the anchoring heuristic. When your judgment is biased by what most readily comes to mind, you have been affected by the ***availability heuristic***. Suppose, despite all the evidence in favor of choosing psychology as a profession, you decide against going to graduate school because of a negative experience with an unhappy and unsuccessful psychologist during your senior year. This one experience, because of its vividness and recency, is highly available in your memory at the time of your decision, overwhelming all the other evidence that might favor a decision to go to graduate school in psychology. A more familiar example might be the conclusion that the violent crime rate is high on your campus, based not on statistics collected by the police over the past two years but rather on the fact that two robberies were reported in the last month.

You are influenced by the ***representativeness heuristic*** when you decide that an event is likely based on how closely it matches the prototype or the most representative case of that event. As an example, take a case in which an armed robbery has been committed and the crime area has been cordoned off before the criminal can escape. In the past, cordons have been highly successful (criminals have been apprehended 90 percent of the time when cordons are used). But this time the dragnet produces only a respected local fifty-year-old female high school chemistry teacher. Because the teacher is not representative of those who commit armed robbery—employed, respected members of the local community do not typically commit that kind of crime—the arresting officer lets the teacher go without questioning her. Is this a ra-

THINKING CRITICALLY

Suppose your friend Stan wants to trade in his car for a new one and asks your advice on how to negotiate. Should he state his asking price for his car first, or should he just ask the dealer how much she is willing to pay for it? Based on your knowledge of heuristics, what do you say?

If Stan just asks the dealer what she's willing to pay for his car and negotiates from there, the anchoring heuristic may lead Stan to accept a price lower than the car's worth. Tell Stan to look up his car in the Blue Book, which will tell him the average prices recently paid for used cars. Then, when he goes to the dealer, he should ask a price higher than the Blue Book average and negotiate downward from there.

tional decision? According to a logical model, it is not, since the probability that the teacher was guilty is 0.9. Reliance on the representativeness heuristic biased the officer's judgment.

The ***anchoring heuristic*** uses currently available information as a reference point for judgment, which is then subject to later adjustment. The original reference point biases the final judgment because adjustments never stray far from the original anchor. You can easily demonstrate the effects of this heuristic by asking six friends two questions. For the first three friends, Question #1 is: "Would you say the Mississippi River is longer or shorter than 600 miles long?" For the second three friends, Question #1 is: "Would you say the Mississippi River is longer or shorter than 5,000 miles long?" Question #2 for both groups is: "How many miles long is the Mississippi?" You will find that the first group of friends estimates a lower average number of miles than does the second group—solely because they have been given different reference points to answer the question.

Language

Virtually every topic that relates to thinking also touches on language. Many of our representations of experience, most of our concepts, the knowledge we use to reason and solve problems, in short, the way we think about the world all depend heavily on language. Nothing is more central to mature human intelligence, information processing, and culture than language. As we discussed in Chapter 4, language differs from culture to culture, but each culture's language offers a common way to describe, communicate, remember, and think about experiences in that culture. Language is a symbolic system and provides the basis for our symbolic representations of the world. The symbols are words that stand for various real-world objects, events, actions, and states of affairs. These symbols combine in systematic ways (grammatically) to express relationships between the objects or concepts that words represent.

Psychologists have addressed experimentally several questions about what language is and how it works. Among the most fundamental questions are: How do we acquire language in the first place? What is the relationship between language and behavior, language and memory, and language and thought? How does language influence learning and memory? Most language acquisition occurs during the early years of life, so a discussion of this topic will be reserved for Chapter 11, where we talk about human development. Here we will concentrate on how language relates to behavior and thought and how it influences memory.

Reasoning and Language Comprehension

Using language is a prime example of reasoning in action. Not every statement we make is informationally complete. Much potentially relevant information may be "left out." But reasoning from our general storehouse of knowledge, we usually can fill in the gaps. Suppose we describe an event we have just witnessed as follows:

> Steve was driving too fast and following too close. It cost him and his insurance company a lot of money.

Most listeners would understand or infer several things, all based on general knowledge of the world:

Steve was driving his car.
He plowed into the car in front of him or into some other obstacle.
There was substantial property damage.
Steve was at fault.

We don't need to express all these things explicitly to describe the episode. Because we and the listener share a lot of knowledge and are capable of reasoning, many true and relevant things can be left unsaid.

But the knowledge relevant for understanding a statement is not necessarily the same in all cultures. Talking with someone from another culture, using normal language comprehension processes, can sometimes lead to misunderstandings. Consider the following statement:

> There are four blackbirds sitting in a tree, and you shoot one. How many are left?

Did you say three? When asked this question, a high school student recently immigrated from Africa answered "none." Was the student mentally impaired or unable to count? Did the student misunderstand the problem? No, the

SEEKING SOLUTIONS

Ways to Improve Problem Solving

People often fail to solve problems simply because they give up before trying all reasonable possibilities. They find themselves at point A, trying to get to point Z, and can't see past point D or E. Progress seems impossible. The would-be problem solver feels overwhelmed and gives up in frustration.

There are lots of examples of such problems, ranging from the specific and concrete to the abstract and general: (1) the frustrated, first-time taxpayer who doesn't understand the IRS long-form instructions and loses deductions by using the short form; (2) the student who drops out of a mathematics course because the concepts are difficult to understand and use; (3) the worker who stays in an unfulfilling dead-end job because there doesn't seem anywhere else to go; (4) the person who can't figure out life's priorities. Problem-solving heuristics can help in finding solutions to such complex and seemingly overwhelming problems. There is no guarantee, of course, that a given problem can be solved; but a systematic, analytic approach often will make the problem more manageable and can only increase the probability of success. If you are faced with such a problem, try some of the following:

1. Make a list of the differences between where you are now and where you want to be. It will take some time, but be as exhaustive in this listing as you can.
2. For each one of these differences, make a list of things you could do to reduce or eliminate it. Again, it will take time. Maybe you should break the task up, and do a little bit each day.
3. Based on your lists, try to identify or define a difference that is relatively easy to achieve. This will typically mean making a move that will change the situation, reducing or eliminating one of the differences listed in step 1.
4. If possible, arrange a series of subgoals that, when achieved, will move you from point A toward point Z.
5. If you get stuck at any point in the series, try working backward from point Z toward A, once again using the subgoaling heuristic.

The trick is always to break down a complex problem into attainable, smaller steps and then formulate a plan for achieving each step or subgoal in succession. Thus, if you are a timid, second-year biology major with poor grades and you want to get into law school, your problem is how to improve your chances of getting into law school. You need to break the problem down into small steps that will seem easy and that will move you in the direction you want to go. Your first step might be to change your major to political science. Your second step might be to study harder to improve your grades. Your third step might be to take a course in assertiveness. Each step, though small, when accomplished, will offer its own reward, helping you overcome the sense of frustration that derives from being so far removed from the main goal. As you succeed with each small step, the problem will become more manageable and your motivation to continue toward the overall goal will increase. Thus, in the case above, you will go from an initial state (bad grades, wrong major, timid), in which the goal seems out of reach, to a state (good grades, political science major, confident in public), in which the goal is within the realm of possibilities.

Heuristics are powerful tools for problem solving. But if they do not work when you try them, consider the following suggestions from cognitive research. When you hit a snag, you might:

1. Look beyond what seem to be the boundaries. Ask yourself what limits you are artificially placing on the problem. See whether any of these restrictions can be eliminated.
2. Shift your perspective on the problem. Try to view its elements in different relationships to one another.
3. Shift your mode of problem representation. If thinking in words doesn't work, try images or sketches of the problem.
4. Try reasoning by analogy. Think about how things work in a domain you already understand well and look for parallels to your current problem. This is a familiar strategy

in science; for example, physicists used their knowledge of the solar system to help understand the structure of the atom.

5. Keep good records—write down what you did and how you did it. Use paper and pencil or the computer to augment your memory, which is easily overloaded.
6. Don't get locked into one strategy, unless it is an algorithm designed for the specific problem. No single strategy is guaranteed to work for all problems. When one strategy fails, look for alternatives. A good basketball coach has the team prepared to use several game strategies, a good salesperson has several different sales pitches, and a good waiter varies his or her style to fit the person being served.
7. Recognize alternative and unusual uses for problem elements. A butter knife can be a screwdriver; dental floss can substitute for string; this book can be a paperweight or doorstop.
8. Make sure you are properly prepared; get all the information you need to begin. Failure often results from missing an important bit of information, which is one reason why it is so helpful to ask an expert for advice. Sometimes you may need to get a different point of view—talking to people who have different backgrounds and different relationships to a problem can be helpful (for example, in trying to generate ideas about how to improve teaching in the university, you would want to ask both faculty and students about their views).
9. When all else fails, take some time out for incubation.

Many of these techniques are also used in courses designed to increase creativity. The general idea is that problem solving is characterized by habitual and routine behaviors that have worked in the past. To accomplish something that is truly original or creative, you must move beyond habit, routine, and mental set, allowing novel approaches to come to mind. Most of the items in this list are designed to elicit these novel approaches by removing the inhibiting or interfering effects of your old habits.

One well-known technique for lifting inhibitions of this sort is *brainstorming*. In a brainstorming session, individuals in a group are encouraged to express publicly all of their ideas about how to solve some problem, without worrying about practicality or reasonableness. The ideas expressed by each individual in the group often stimulate idea production by others. In order for brainstorming to work, however, group members must be willing to generate and listen to bizarre ideas. It turns out that this technique works even better when individuals generate ideas on their own (Paulus, Dzindolet, Poletes, & Camacho, 1993). The next time you are stymied by a problem, try using brainstorming on your own. List all the ideas that come to mind, no matter how silly they seem. You might be surprised at some of the workable possible solutions that occur to you. Using brainstorming and the other techniques we mentioned has been shown to improve ability to solve problems and to think creatively in people who practice them consistently. You would be well-advised to consider using them in your own future efforts at problem solving.

▼ *During the Cuban missile crisis of October 1962, President John F. Kennedy and his advisers brainstormed to decide how to handle the crisis resulting from the discovery of Soviet missiles in Cuba.*

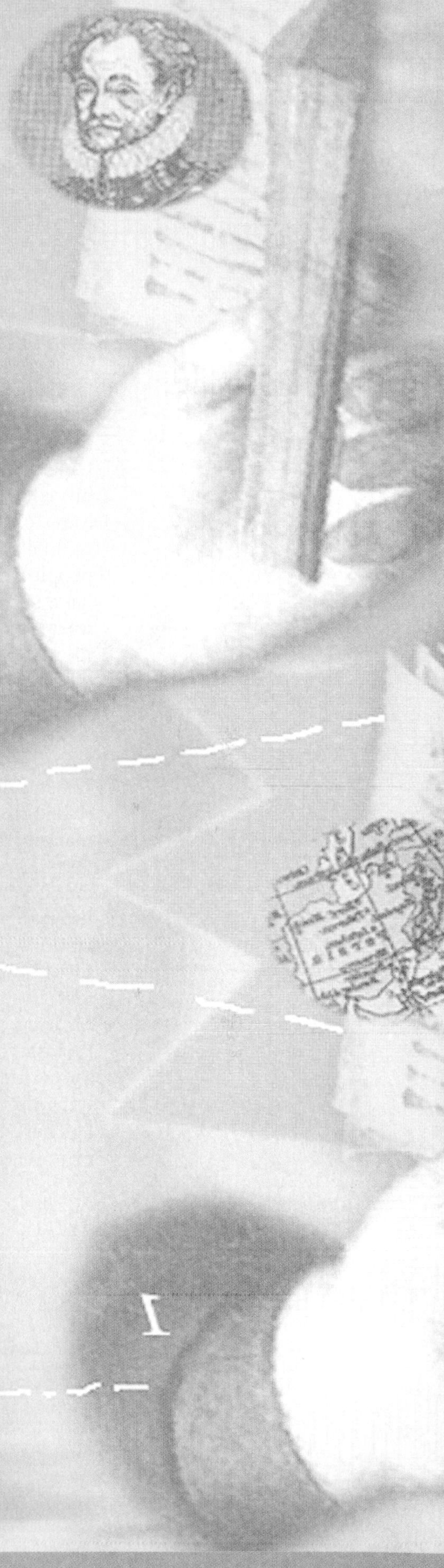

The two major structural components of language are semantics and syntax. Syntax is a set of rules for constructing strings of symbols to make up grammatical sentences. Semantics refers to the meaning of a linguistic utterance.

student merely reasoned that if you shoot one bird in a tree, all the others will fly away (Sue, 1992). In certain cultures, reasoning is less an abstract game and more a matter of giving answers based on personal real-life experiences.

Differences in life experiences associated with social characteristics such as class status, gender, ethnicity, sexual orientation, and able-bodiedness may also hinder communication. Consider the following riddle:

> A woman, while moving her car, stopped at a hotel. As soon as she got there, she knew she was bankrupt. Why?

Unless you have played Monopoly, you probably can't solve this riddle. Problems that allude to games or experiences associated with middle-class status are less likely to be solved by people from lower-class backgrounds who don't have such games. But then, most middle-class folks don't understand street language either.

Understanding Language

The familiar act of understanding what you are reading or what someone says to you is a remarkable achievement. A writer or speaker converts a meaningful idea into a series of visible marks or audible vocalizations. The reader or listener, in turn, converts these marks or vocalizations back into stimuli with meaning. Let's focus on the reader. To extract meaning from a text, the reader must: (1) identify the units of meaning (technically called ***morphemes***, although you can also think of them as words) in the writing, and (2) apply certain rules underlying their sequencing and organization.

There are two major structural components of any sentence: syntax (or grammar) and semantics. ***Syntax*** describes the form and structure of the strings of symbols (morphemes or words) that make up sentences. The elementary units of a language can be combined only in certain ways to be comprehensible. The non-sentence "typist a is Bruce lousy" illustrates how individually meaningful words can be combined non-syntactically to produce nonsense. But the same words in proper syntactical order, "Bruce is a lousy typist," are easy to understand. Speakers of a particular language behave according to the syntactical rules of their language. But, in fact, if you are proficient in a language, you typically have no conscious awareness of using the rules when speaking or listening to communications, and you might not even be able to say anything intelligible about the rules of syntax.

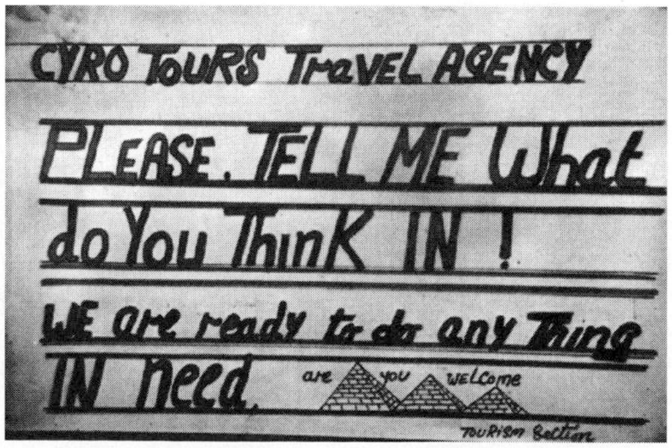

Semantics refers to the meaning of a linguistic utterance. The meaning of any particular sentence occurs on at least three levels. First, you need to know the meanings of individual words used in the sentence, that is, you need to have a "mental dictionary." Second, individual words combine to form ***propositions***, which are phrases or clauses and are sometimes called idea units. Third, these propositions join to form a complete sentence, which organizes the propositions in relation to one another.

Consider this sentence: "The injured student anxiously called the family doctor." This easy-to-understand sentence illustrates the three levels of meaning. First, you have to "look up" each word in your mental dictionary. Members of a given language culture do this quickly and effortlessly. Then, you have to understand the propositions in the sentence, for there is more to comprehension than knowing the meaning of the individual words. The proposition "family doctor" has a meaning that is not a simple sum of the meanings of the two words "family" and "doctor." Therefore, a second level of meaning exists in the three propositional units in this sentence: (a) The injured student, (b) anxiously called, (c) the family doctor. But there is still more to this sentence than can be fully comprehended on the basis of its constituent propositions. "Anxiously called" has a number of possible meanings in isolation. Only when placed in the context of the other propositions does it become clear that the student probably telephoned the doctor, as opposed to yelled at the doctor across the room.

The sentence level of meaning relies heavily on our knowledge of the world, which we have

► *When the rules of syntax are not observed, sentences can be difficult to understand.*

called *semantic memory* (see Chapter 7). The interaction of a sentence with semantic memory allows us to make inferences that go beyond the sentence itself. For example, the sentence "Cecil Fielder drove in three runs with a homer" *describes* a certain action. But it can *imply* a great deal more. For example, it implies a major league baseball game was being played. To knowledgeable fans who recognize that Fielder is a real member of a particular major league team and not just our feeble attempt at a pun, it can also imply that the game probably involved the New York Yankees, that Fielder was at bat, that a pitch was made, that two teammates were on base, and so on.

This analysis of meaning takes us through comprehension of individual sentences. But in reading, in conversation, or in listening to a lecture, sentences are strung together into even larger units. There are meanings that can be derived only from an analysis of these larger units of discourse, which brings us to the topic of discourse processing.

THINKING CRITICALLY

Sometimes perfectly grammatical sentences can be ambiguous in their meaning. Consider the following sample of actual news headlines: "Prostitutes Appeal to Pope," "Farmer Bill Dies in House," "Teacher Strikes Idle Kids," "Cold Wave Linked to Temperature," "Stud Tires Out." Do you see the ambiguity in these sentences. How can you explain it?

Not only do words sometimes have several possible meanings, so do sentences. When a sentence fails to specify fully the meaning of the words that make it up, the result can be amusing. In what sense is the word "appeal" used in the first headline? Is "Farmer Bill" a person or a piece of paper? Until we can answer these questions, sentence meaning is at best unclear. Moreover, any sentence implies much more than is said. The implications of "Stud Tires Out" differ depending on whether "Stud" is a noun or an adjective. The fact of the matter is that understanding language is a complex process, which requires the use of semantic memory to retrieve word meanings and reasoning in order to draw inferences. It is almost never simply a matter of word-for-word decoding.

Discourse Processing

Discourse is an oral or written body of language consisting of two or more sentences. How do we comprehend the information in discourse? Psychologists once believed that comprehension was entirely bottom-up processing, that one simply extracted everything from the words of the message as they arrived. But we now know that bottom-up processing can only be part of the story. If we could only process on a word-by-word basis, as each successive word was presented, how could we ever anticipate what's coming next? Clearly, we do anticipate what a speaker (or text) is going to say. Filling in the next word of a sentence is almost always a relatively simple thing to ______ (do). There is a powerful top-down component to discourse processing because the reader or listener carries lots of knowledge in memory (Bourne, Sinclair, & Healy, 1986). This knowledge interacts with the information abstracted by the bottom-up analysis of sounds and symbols. To understand new information coming in, what we already know may be just as important as the new information itself. Three types of stored knowledge influence comprehension: knowledge of (1) the language itself, (2) the world in general, and (3) the specific subject of the discourse. Thus, memory, language, and thinking are highly interdependent in mature human behavior (Kintsch, 1988).

Our expectations also affect our comprehension of discourse. When you read a passage about the bombing of the Oklahoma City Federal Building in 1995, you expect to see sentences describing devastation of property, dead and wounded, and so on, because all this information and more is in your bombing schema. It becomes readily available once you realize the topic is the Oklahoma City tragedy. You can more readily comprehend and encode information relevant to such an event because to

Linguistic discourse consists of two or more sentences. Comprehension of discourse in conversation and text depends both on bottom-up (the sounds and words themselves) and top-down (interacting with our knowledge of the world) processing.

some extent you can predict what generally happens when a bomb explodes in a building. You would be very puzzled if the author had written that, as the bomb went off, people cheered. That would violate your expectations about what should happen, and you would definitely want the author to explain.

Sometimes inferences are required for comprehension. Often these inferences relate to a speaker's or writer's intentions. Have you ever had the experience of asking someone "Do you know the time?" and having them answer "Yes"? This very old joke illustrates the difference between literal and intended meaning. Inferences about intentions are the main focus of a relatively new area of study in psycholinguistics known as ***pragmatics***, the study of intended meanings in linguistic discourse.

Pragmatics is the study of intended meanings in linguistic discourse.

The importance of pragmatic context in communication (and miscommunication) has been seen in reports of conversations found in popularized writings about gender differences in communication. For example, Deborah Tannen (1990) reports a conversation of a couple driving in a car. The wife says, "Would you like to stop for a drink?" The husband answers, "No." When the couple arrives home, the wife is annoyed because she wanted to go for a drink. From the wife's point of view, a responsive answer would have been "No, but I will if you want to." Because the husband answered the wife's question directly rather than making the appropriate inference (that she was asking be-

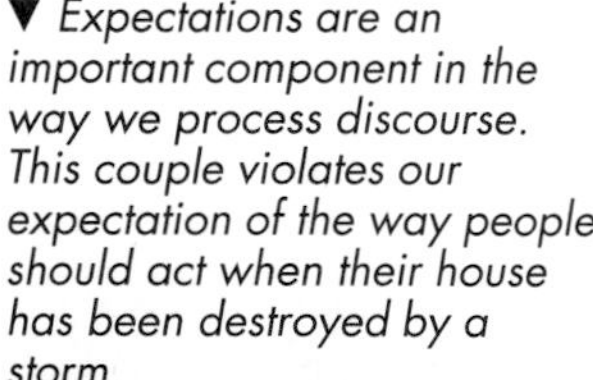

▼ *Expectations are an important component in the way we process discourse. This couple violates our expectation of the way people should act when their house has been destroyed by a storm.*

THINKING CRITICALLY

Consider the following passage: "If the balloons popped the sound wouldn't be able to carry, since everything would be too far away from the correct floor. A closed window would also prevent the sound from carrying, since most buildings tend to be well insulated. Since the whole operation depends on a steady flow of electricity, a break in the middle of the wire would also cause problems. Of course, the fellow could shout, but the human voice is not loud enough to carry that far. An additional problem is that a string could break on the instrument. Then there could be no accompaniment to the message. It is clear that the best situation would involve less distance. Then there would be fewer potential problems. With face to face contact, the least number of things could go wrong" (Bransford & Johnson, 1973, pp. 392–393). This passage sounds like gibberish the first time you read it. Why is it so difficult to comprehend?

Meaning does not reside exclusively in the words of the message, or even in the sentences that make up the passage; if it did, the perfectly grammatical text given above would be completely comprehensible. In discourse processing, we actively and continuously interpret information contained in words and sentences in the light of all applicable knowledge. Now, take a look at Figure 8-6 on page 284. This should tell you that your knowledge of sound amplification and serenades is applicable. The passage should now be more meaningful and easier to comprehend. This exercise demonstrates the active involvement of cognitive processes in comprehending language, written or spoken.

cause *she* wanted to go for a drink), there was a failure to communicate. Whether or not there are systematic gender differences in such pragmatic inferences, this example illustrates how failures in communication can result from responding to the speaker's literal, but not intended, meaning.

Thus, inferred information—including presuppositions, elaborations, and pragmatic content—is incorporated into our understanding of and memory for any discourse, written or spoken. It will appear as a part of what we recall, and it will affect our behavior accordingly. In the foregoing example, the wife will remember that her husband was rude or inconsiderate, when he probably hadn't intended to be. Although the inferences may not always be valid, they are important to fully understanding communication.

Intelligence

Knowing concepts, solving problems, thinking logically, making sound judgments and decisions, communicating in a meaningful way: these are all part and parcel of what we normally think of as intelligent behavior. Yet, psychologists and educators have debated for years about how exactly to define and to measure intelligence. Clearly, intelligence has something to do with our ability to adapt to the demands of a complicated physical world. Further, our ability to think or to process information rapidly and efficiently seems to be linked to intelligence. But what else? Robert Sternberg has identified at least seven different definitions of intelligence that are currently in use among psychologists (Sternberg, 1990).

We will define ***intelligence*** here as the capacity to think abstractly and cope resourcefully with life's challenges (Wechsler, 1975; Sternberg, 1990). Intelligence enables us to function effectively in various environments and to modify environments to fit our adaptive skills. Thus, we would expect intelligence to be expressed differently in different environments and cultures, and indeed it is (Gardner, 1983; Irvine & Berry, 1988; Ogbu, 1981).

Measurement of intelligence focuses on an individual's ability to perform mental tasks quickly, skillfully, and accurately. One standard way to define intelligence is in terms of the psychological tests for measuring it, the IQ (intelligence quotient) tests. Western society highly values what is measured by these tests, and uses IQ scores to make important decisions about people's lives. Much controversy, not only in scholarly circles, but in social and political arenas as well, centers on *why* people score high or low on intelligence tests. How has intelligence been measured? What does intelligence mean? What factors affect individual differences in intelligence? Answers to these questions continue to be debated.

One general definition of intelligence is the capacity to think abstractly and cope resourcefully with life's challenges.

When discussing intelligence and its measurement, keep in mind the distinction between *achievement* and *ability* (aptitude). Achievement tests measure existing knowledge and skills, not ability or potential for future achievement. The knowledge you have amassed to date represents your level of achievement—which reflects a combination of your ability, motivation, and past opportunities to learn, among other things. In contrast, aptitude tests are supposed to measure an individual's ability to learn and *potential* for achievement. You may have considerable ability, but without motivation and opportunities to learn, your level of achievement may be low and may not accurately reflect your ability.

Measuring Intelligence: IQ Tests

Psychometrics is a subfield of psychology that is concerned with the construction and use of tests to measure both the qualitative and the quantitative aspects of general categories of behavior, such as intelligence and personality. Intelligence tests are psychometric instruments

▼ *Do we solve problems gradually, by trial-and-error, or rapidly, by insight? This cartoon is a take-off of a famous study by Köhler, who found that chimps could solve difficult problems by insight. (© 1981 by NEA, Inc.)*

that measure cognitive abilities as they vary from one person to another. Although these tests attempt to measure pure intellectual ability, uncontaminated by experience, that task turns out to be impossible because the knowledge and skills that a person already possesses always influence test performance. Therefore, any two people might earn the same IQ score but still differ in intellectual ability; that is, one might have higher ability but lower achievement than the other. This possibility raises the issue of fairness of intelligence tests. People with high abilities may earn lower scores because a disadvantaged background has restricted their achievement level.

The Binet Tests

The first general measure of intelligence was constructed for a simple, practical reason. Around the turn of the century, France's Ministry of Public Instruction decided to identify schoolchildren likely to experience difficulty in the classroom so that they could be enrolled in special educational programs. The Ministry commissioned Alfred Binet, a well-known French psychologist, and his colleague, Theódore Simon, to develop a test to single out these children. Since that time, the test they created has been repeatedly revised, with versions still in use throughout the world. The U.S. version of the test was constructed by Lewis Terman and Maud Merrill at Stanford University and is called the ***Stanford-Binet test***.

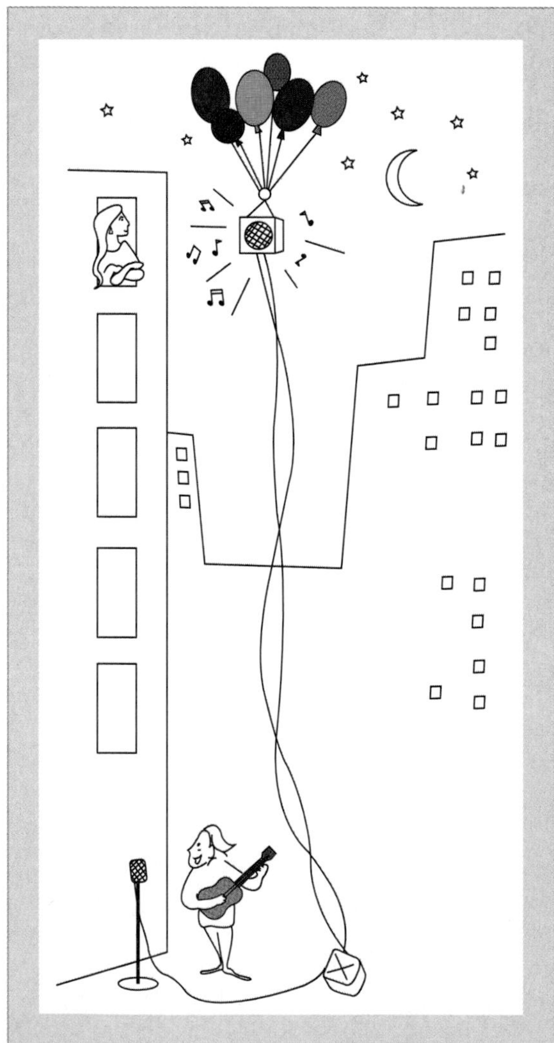

8-6 The Electronic Serenade

This drawing illustrates the passage described in the Thinking Critically box (p. 282). Now go back and reread the passage. Is it now any easier to understand?

Binet and Simon's work rests on two assumptions. First, they believed intelligence to be a composite of many abilities that contribute to scholastic achievement. Intelligence tests must therefore contain many different kinds of items. Most Binet test items are based on simple everyday tasks familiar to everyone. Binet thought such tasks were more likely to tap pure abilities and would give no special advantages to any particular group of children on the basis of their prior achievements. Despite his concern and careful selection of test items, however, Binet's test, even the modern version, is affected by past experience. Indeed, no intelligence test is truly achievement, culture, or gender free. If people who differ by gender or ethnic background have not been exposed to certain experiences that the test assumes all people have had, their scores will reflect those variations as well as any differences in their inherent ability.

The second assumption behind the Binet tests is that the nature and composition of intelligence change with age. The items selected for Binet tests must differ across the ages and be graded by age as well as difficulty. Questions we use to measure intelligence at age three are not appropriate for age ten. Thus, Binet tests are actually a collection of subtests, one for each age. This works well for measuring the intelligence of children up to about age thirteen. Beyond that age, however, basic intellectual abilities remain relatively constant. In fact, the Stanford-Binet test is rarely used today as a measure of adult intelligence. Illustrative items at several different ages in the Stanford-Binet test are presented in Table 8-2.

Binet introduced the concept of ***mental age*** (MA). Items associated with age seven are more difficult than those associated with age six, which in turn are harder than those associated with age five, and so on. Rather than earning

Table 8-2 Representative Items from the Stanford-Binet Test for Different Age Levels

TWO YEARS OLD
a. Identifies body parts such as hair, mouth, and ears on a doll.
b. Builds a tower of four blocks like a model that is presented.
FOUR YEARS OLD
a. Fills in the missing words when asked, "Brother is a boy; sister is a ______." and "In daytime it is light; at night it is ______."
b. Answers correctly when asked, "Why do we have houses? Why do we have books?"
NINE YEARS OLD
a. Answers correctly when asked, "In an old graveyard in Spain they have discovered a small skull which they believe to be that of Christopher Columbus when he was about ten years old. What is foolish about that?"
b. Answers correctly when asked, "Tell me the name of a color that rhymes with head. Tell me a number that rhymes with tree."
ADULT
a. Can describe the difference between laziness and idleness, poverty and misery, character and reputation.
b. Answers correctly when asked, "Which direction would you have to face so your right hand would be to the north?"

Source: Terman & Merrill, 1973.

"points" by passing items, the child earns months and years of mental-age credit. The child with the higher mental age has passed a greater number of and more difficult items on the test. The ***intelligence quotient***, or ***IQ***, is traditionally the way to represent performance on the Stanford-Binet test. The IQ indicates how an individual scores relative to others of the same chronological age (CA). Although this method is rarely used today, the term "IQ" is still popular, and it is helpful to understand how this "quotient" is calculated. The IQ formula for Binet tests is:

$$\text{IQ} = (\text{mental age}/\text{chronological age}) \times 100$$

Tests are specifically designed to ensure that the average child earns a mental-age score equal to his or her chronological age, which makes the average IQ 100. If nine-year-old Chris earns a mental age of nine years, his IQ is:

$$\text{IQ} = (9/9) \times 100 = 100$$

Thus, the average IQ score is 100 on Binet tests. Half the population scores within the 90 to 110 range on Stanford-Binet IQ measures, and about 96 percent fall in the 70 to 130 range. (This distribution of scores follows closely what is known generally as a normal distribution and, in graphical form, is referred to as a "bell curve"; see Figure 8-7.)

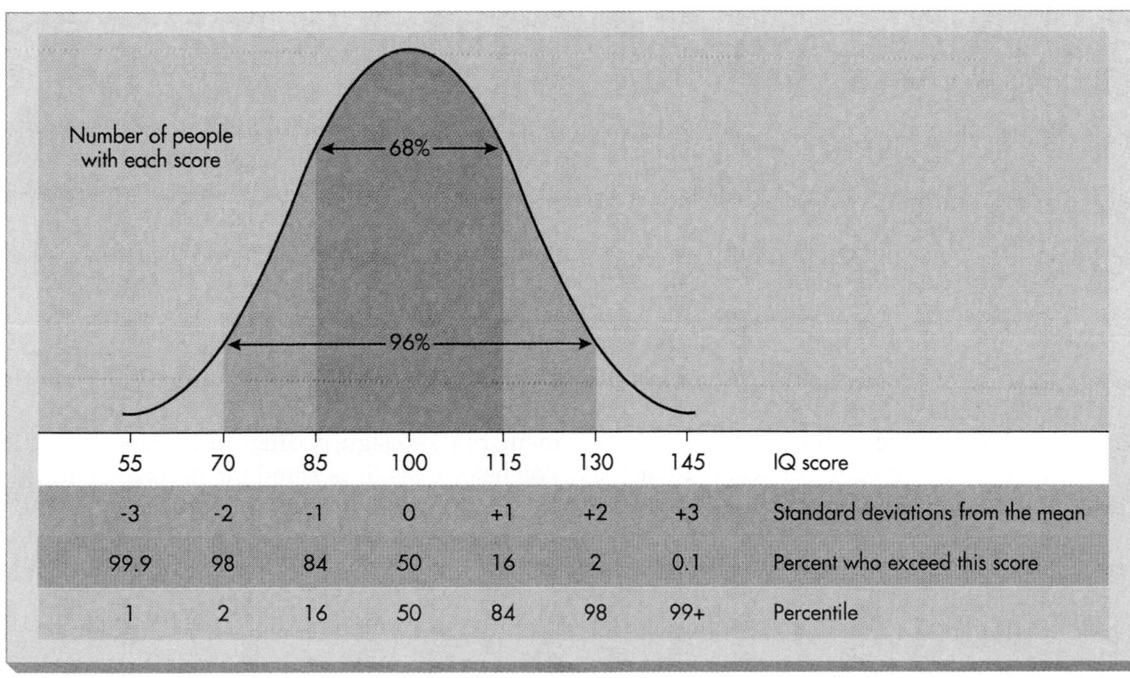

55	70	85	100	115	130	145	IQ score
-3	-2	-1	0	+1	+2	+3	Standard deviations from the mean
99.9	98	84	50	16	2	0.1	Percent who exceed this score
1	2	16	50	84	98	99+	Percentile

8-7 IQ Distribution

IQ in the U.S. population is distributed around an average of 100 (the mean). Half of the population has an IQ above 100, and half of the population has an IQ below 100. Most people fall somewhere in the middle of the distribution, and a decreasing number (indicated as standard deviations from the mean) lie at the extremes.

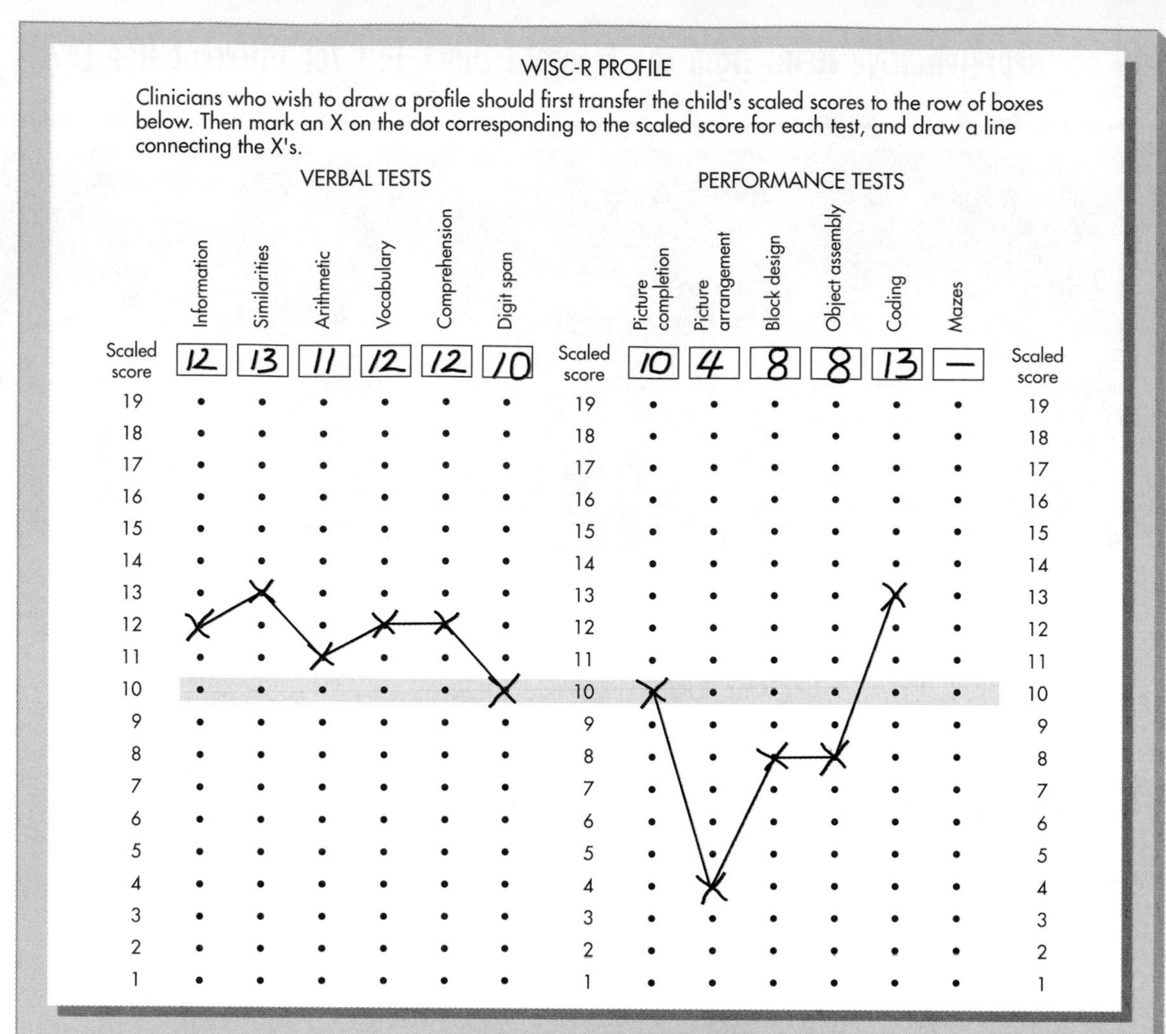

8-8 A WISC-R Profile

Administration of the WISC-R yields a variety of scores on verbal and performance subtests. From these scores, we get a profile of each individual revealing where that individual is stronger and where he or she is weaker. The test-taker in this profile has an overall above-average IQ of 109 but appears to be stronger on verbal than on performance subtests. (Source: WISC-R Profile from the Psychological Corporation. Data supplied by R.A. Yaroush)

The Wechsler Tests

An alternative approach to measuring IQ is found in the ***Wechsler tests***, named after their creator, American psychologist David Wechsler. Wechsler wanted to extend intelligence testing beyond verbal tasks, beyond tasks that were included in school work, and into tasks appropriate for late adolescence and adult ages. Rather than computing an IQ based on mental age, which doesn't change much after chronological age thirteen, Wechsler examined how much a person's overall point score deviates from the normal distribution of scores for individuals of the same age. Arbitrarily, the average score at a given age is assigned a value of 100 (making it comparable to Binet's MA/CA formula). Scores that are better or worse than 100 indicate how much a given individual is above or below average for that age. There are several forms of the Wechsler test, which include the Wechsler Adult Intelligence Scale, Revised (WAIS-R) designed for adults (anyone whose age is eighteen or higher), and the Wechsler Intelligence Scale for Children (WISC-III), designed for children ranging from approximately six to seventeen years of age. A third test, the Wechsler Preschool and Primary Scale of Intelligence (WPPSI-R), is designed for children who are four to six years of age.

The intelligence quotient is a score that reflects the performance of a person on an intelligence test, relative to others at the same age level. An IQ of 100 is defined as average.

Wechsler tests are organized into subscales focusing on different abilities rather than on age levels (see Table 8-3). About half of the Wechsler test is concerned with verbal abilities, including general information, vocabulary, comprehension, similarities, and also arithmetic and digit span (the number of digits one can hold in short-term memory). The other half assesses performance (nonverbal) abilities, including object assembly, picture completion, picture arrangement, block design, coding, and mazes. With the Wechsler tests, it is standard procedure to calculate both verbal and performance IQs. Each subscale yields a score in points that can be converted into IQ by looking at a table of norms. A score profile is constructed for each person who takes the test, indicating how that individual has done relative to others of the same age (see Figure 8-8 for a sample subscale profile).

TABLE 8-3 Items from the Wechsler Intelligence Scale for Children (WISC)

Verbal Scale	
Information	From what animal do we get milk? (Either "cow" or "goat" is an acceptable answer.)
Similarities	How are a plum and a peach similar? (Correct answer: "They are both fruits." Half credit is given for "Both are food" or "Both are round.")
Arithmetic	Count these blocks: 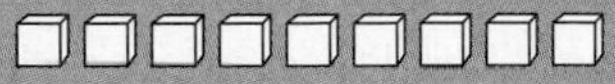
Vocabulary	Define the word *letter*.
Comprehension	What should you do if you see a train approaching a broken track? (A correct answer is "Stand safely out of the way and wave something to warn the train." Half credit is given for "Tell someone at the railroad station." *No* credit is given for "I would try to fix the track.")
Digit span	Repeat these numbers after I say them: 3 6 2.
Performance Scale	
Picture completion	What parts are missing from this picture? 
Picture arrangement	Here are some cards with a gardener on them. Can you put them in order? 
Block design	See how I have arranged these four blocks? Here are four more blocks. Can you arrange your blocks like mine? 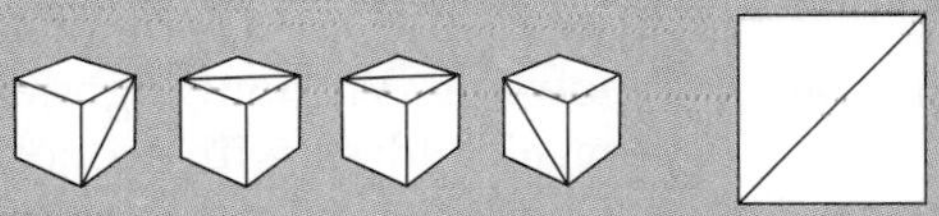 Pattern
Object assembly	Can you put these five puzzle pieces together to make a dog?
Coding	Here is a page full of shapes. Put a slash (/) through all the circles and an X through all the squares. 
Mazes	Here is a maze. Start with your pencil here and trace a path to the other end of the maze without crossing any lines. 

Source: Based on Wechsler, 1949.

Fluid intelligence is basic general intellectual ability, is largely genetically determined, and doesn't change much over a lifetime, according to Cattell. In contrast, crystallized intelligence is based on learned skills and facts.

Components of Intelligence

One of the oldest debates in psychology is whether intelligence is one general ability or a collection of specific abilities that are only loosely related to one another. ***Factor analysis***, invented by Charles Spearman, is a statistical technique that attempts to answer that question by determining whether test scores can be clustered into groups that measure independent abilities in intelligence. The idea is that when tests correlate with one another they measure the same specific ability, that is, they form a ***factor***. If scores on some other tests correlate with each other but not with the first tests in the first cluster, they are said to measure a separate, independent factor in intelligence. If factor analysis identifies only one factor that carries through across all available intelligence tests, that is evidence for one general intellectual ability. If several factors are discovered, it suggests that intelligence is a collection of different abilities, each corresponding to a particular factor. Spearman analyzed a large number of intelligence tests and discovered evidence for both possibilities, that is, he found a general (which he called the ***g-factor***) and several specific (***s-factors***) intellectual abilities (see Figure 8-9). Spearman's findings have been largely confirmed by follow-up research over the ensuing years. The goal of factor analytic research today is not to challenge Spearman's conclusions but rather to specify clearly what the specific factors are (Spearman, 1927; Carroll, 1993).

Fluid and Crystallized Intelligence

Based on factor analysis, Raymond Cattell divided intelligence into two categories: fluid and crystallized intelligence (Cattell, 1963). ***Fluid intelligence*** allows us to solve novel problems insightfully, to reason analytically to a correct conclusion, to understand complex relationships, to respond rapidly, and to master new tasks in minimal time. By this definition, learning, experience, and practice have a minor role in fluid intelligence, which Cattell considered to be largely genetically determined and not subject to much change over a lifetime. In contrast, ***crystallized intelligence*** is based on the application of learned skills and acquired facts. It includes general information, word comprehension (for example, what is the meaning of "monozygotic"?), and numerical abilities. Crystallized intelligence is the sum total of remembered prior experiences, achievements, and skills, and it relates to specific or limited rather than general abilities. A person's crystallized intelligence is probably influenced by the amount and quality of formal education he or she has received. Thus, when economically or environmentally disadvantaged children have limited learning opportunities, they may develop only weak crystallized abilities (for example, limited verbal ability), even if they have high fluid intelligence. High-level crystallized abilities require *both* appropriate prior learning experiences *and* adequate fluid intelligence, however. Without high-level fluid intelligence, even children with economic and social advantages cannot build strong language and other skills.

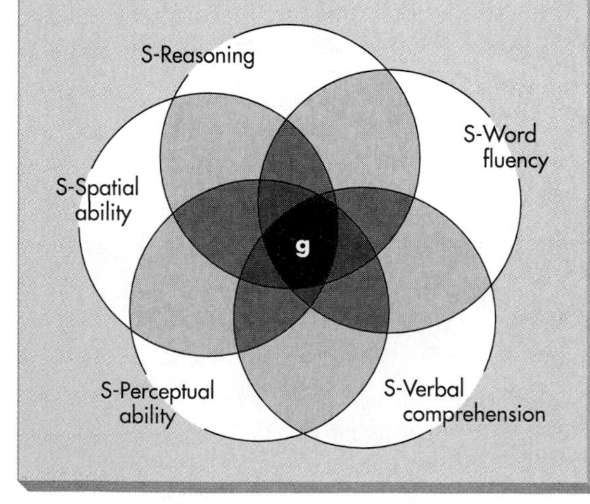

8-9 General and Specific Factors in Intelligence

This is a Venn Diagram showing the overlap between general intelligence, g, and other specific forms of intelligence, s, according to Spearman.

Triarchic Intelligence

A general theory of intelligence needs to take into account information-processing abilities, according to Robert Sternberg. Intelligence tests therefore need to measure a variety of cognitive abilities, such as short-term memory, problem solving, and reasoning, which go beyond the abilities tapped in the school-like tasks included in the Binet and Wechsler tests. Sternberg proposed a theory of intelligence that emphasized three kinds of intelligence, which he called analytic, creative, and practical intelligence (Sternberg, 1985).

Analytic intelligence is the kind of aptitude that most intelligence tests focus on. It represents the knowledge and skills that enable us to think critically and analytically about components of a problem, and to compare and evaluate alternatives. People high in analytic intelligence do well academically. Of the concepts discussed earlier, fluid intelligence comes closest to what Sternberg has in mind.

Creative intelligence is the aptitude for seeing relationships between what we know and what we don't know, and for extrapolating what we know to novel situations. If Cathy struggles with a problem for five minutes before solving it, do you consider her intelligent? Your answer will probably depend on whether it's a novel problem or one that she has solved many times before. Novel tasks and situations require conscious, active information processing—that is, they demand a different kind of intelligence than familiar tasks or situations, for which we have developed more routine, automatic approaches. People high in creative intelligence know when to apply routine solutions and when to think about problems and their components in new ways, combining seemingly unrelated facts, formulating new ideas, and creating new solutions. Inventors and designers are high in this form of intelligence.

Finally, ***practical intelligence*** (also known as "street smarts" or "business sense") represents our ability to apply what we know, to adapt to the demands of our everyday real-world tasks, and to act in accordance with the rules of our society and of our everyday environments. For example, suppose you start a new managerial job. To succeed in your new environment, you need to figure out both the written and unwritten rules of the company. If you turn around your reports in one day will you be considered timely or tardy? Official office hours may be 9 to 5, but if you leave earlier than 6:30 are you considered unmotivated? This kind of intelligence helps you to shape your environment, in making decisions about whom to hire and what projects to emphasize. It also enables you to recognize when you are not able to adapt to or shape your job environment to achieve success, and when it is time to select a new environment—that is, to look for another job.

In Western culture, analytic intelligence is probably the most familiar type and the most highly regarded in academic circles. But Sternberg has raised our awareness of other forms of intelligence, especially practical intelligence, that are needed for everyday living but are not well measured by traditional intelligence tests (Sternberg, Wagner, Williams, & Horvath, 1995).

Multiple Intelligences

Today, most psychologists would agree with Sternberg that intelligence is more complex than an aptitude for schoolwork. Anyone can be intelligent in any of a host of ways. We recognize the importance of formal academic intelligence, which is the kind of intelligence measured by traditional IQ tests, but high academic intelligence does not guarantee that a person will survive "on the street." We agree that all people have verbal fluency and mathematical skill to some measurable degree, but we also recognize that people differ in athletic prowess and social savvy. Each of us is strong in some areas and weak in others. Accordingly, some psychologists prefer to describe intelligence as a profile of scores across a wide array of tests and measures. Each person's combination of strengths and weaknesses determines his or her success in specific endeavors and in some sense adds up to an overall level of intelligence.

Howard Gardner (1983) proposed a multidimensional conception of human intelligence that extends beyond Sternberg's triarchic theory. In Gardner's model, intelligence is considered to be a composite of six (or seven)

". . . and give me good abstract-reasoning ability, interpersonal skills, cultural perspective, linguistic comprehension, and a high sociodynamic potential."

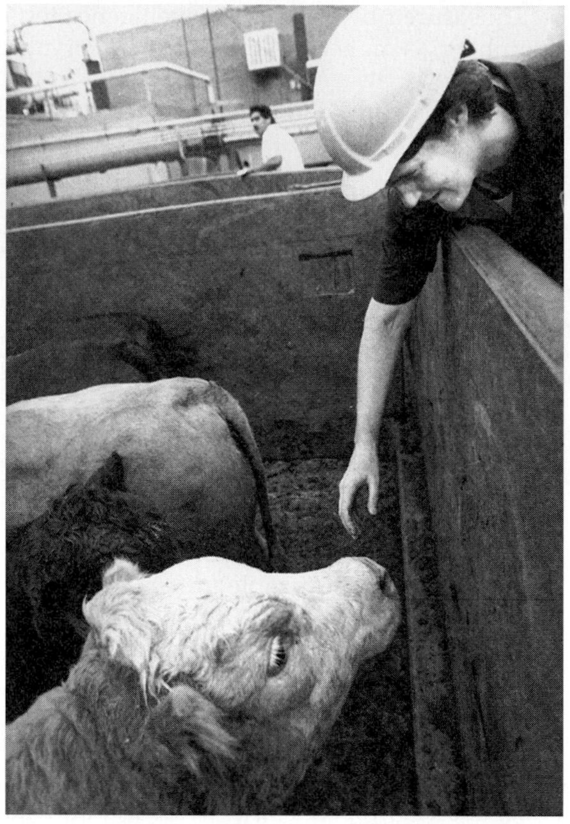

▶ *Temple Grandin has achieved remarkable success in her field.*

independent, equally important aptitudes, called linguistic, logical-mathematical, spatial, musical, bodily-kinesthetic, and personal (which is sometimes broken down into intrapersonal and interpersonal) intelligence. A description and examples of each of these types of intelligence are provided in Table 8-4. We have mentioned many of these abilities in earlier discussions. Others, such as bodily-kinesthetic, which refers to perceptual-motor competence or athletic ability, and personal intelligence, which consists of knowledge of oneself (intrapersonal) and knowledge of how to interact with others skillfully (interpersonal), are rather unique to Gardner's theory.

▼ *Polynesian navigators travel across wide expanses of open ocean without using compasses or other equipment. In the picture at left, a master navigator guides a boat; at right, students learn star positions.*

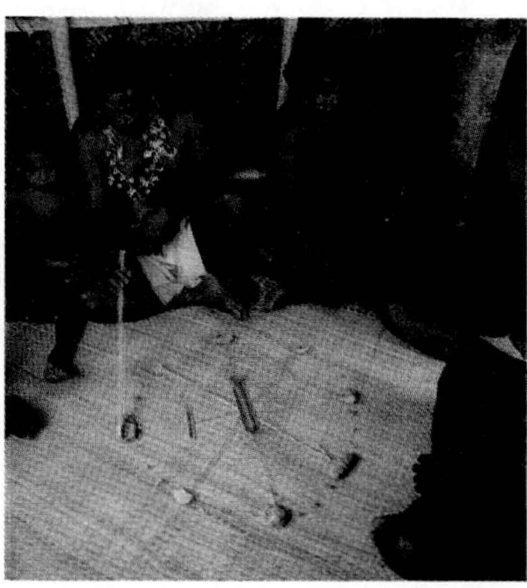

Gardner considers each ability as a separate intelligence, not part of a larger whole or g-factor. The evidence that he marshals for his model goes beyond the factor analysis of test scores. For example, Gardner has discovered that most people have maximal ability in one domain and are only average or even below average in others. Moreover, different abilities emerge and peak at different times over the life cycle. Kinesthetic abilities peak early in life; musical and personal skills later. While there are individual differences, chess players reach maximal performance at the age of thirty-five, scientists at a somewhat older age. It is also clear that, to take advantage of an ability, a person must be motivated to work at it and that the work or practice must begin early in life. It has been suggested that, to become proficient on a musical instrument, for example, serious practice must begin before the age of twelve (Ericsson & Charness, 1994).

Gardner's theory of multiple intelligences gains unusual support from studies of ***autistic savants***, who provide a stark example of specific intelligence. Autistic savants are people who have an extraordinary ability in one area but are limited in other areas. Many are able to focus intensely and concentrate in this one area, be it mathematics, music, or drawing, but have problems with social interaction and communication with others. Some, like Leslie Lemke, are mentally retarded. In his native language, English, Lemke's speech is primitive, and he could not talk until he became an adult. Nonetheless, he can imitate songs in perfect Italian or German, and he can play a musical piece on the piano without flaw after hearing it only once (Shaefer, 1996). Others, like Temple Grandin, who holds a Ph.D. in animal science, teaches at a university, and runs her own business, are able to function remarkably well in society, yet lack the ability to sense intuitively other people's feelings or intentions or perspectives. Oliver Sacks (1995) wrote several popular essays in the *New Yorker* magazine about several savants, including Stephen Wiltshire, who could draw pictures like Matisse but had difficulty with language and with the expression of emotions. Other savants studied by Sacks could perform complicated arithmetic calculations in their heads or play music intuitively. In each case, the intelligence of the savant, while at or beyond the

Table 8-4 Gardner's Multiple Intelligences

Type of Intelligence	Example
Linguistic Knowledge of and skill in the use of language, including second or multiple languages	Writer, Journalist
Logical-mathematical Ability to think analytically and to solve quantitative problems	Scientist, Engineer
Spatial Ability to visualize objects in three-dimensional or multidimensional space and to take varying perspectives on objects in space	Architect, Artist
Musical Ability to understand and to produce music	Composer, Performer
Bodily-kinesthetic Ability to control and coordinate parts of the body and to skillfully move the body in space	Athlete, Dancer
Intrapersonal Self-awareness and knowledge of one's competence and limitations	Therapist, Religious leader
Interpersonal Awareness of the behavior and motivation of others and the ability to interact socially	Salesperson, Diplomat

Contemporary examples of people who exhibit maximum ability in one area of Gardner's model of human intelligence; (a) linguistic, writer Henry Louis (Skip) Gates, Jr.; (b) logical-mathematical, Nobel prize–winning scientist Christiane Nusslein-Volhard; (c) spatial, architect I. M. Pei; (d) musical, violinist Midori; (e) bodily-kinesthetic, professional baseball player Juan Gonzalez; (f) intrapersonal, evangelist Billy Graham; (g) inter-personal, talk show host Oprah Winfrey.

normal level in one area, was nonetheless limited to that area and otherwise weak.

Gardner believes that visual, logical, and musical intelligence may be highly developed in savants but that personal intelligence (the ability to understand one's own and others' feelings and intentions) is defective. He also suggests that each form of intelligence is represented in a specific brain area, and can be specifically impaired by localized brain damage. For example, linguistic intelligence can be impaired by damage to the speech areas (see Chapter 3). Supporting evidence for brain localization in other cases has yet to be found, however.

Gardner also suggests that cultures differ in the type of intelligence they emphasize and try to develop, especially during early childhood. Western cultures put a premium on linguistic and logical-mathematical intelligence. Asian cultures believe that interpersonal skills and motivation to succeed are just as important to intelligence as the cognitive skills measured on typical IQ tests (Okagaki & Sternberg, 1993). Environmental needs appear to elicit certain forms of intelligence. For example, seafaring people, such as Polynesians, often demonstrate a remarkable mental ability to calculate locations needed to navigate the open ocean (Gladwin, 1970).

Gardner's theory stands in marked contrast to traditional viewpoints on intelligence. His theory is nonpsychometric—that is, it does not depend heavily on psychological tests, nor does it try to explain why tests might correlate. Gardner takes a broad outlook on human potential, systematically describing the forms intelligence can take as well as the multiple dimensions of individual differences. Moreover, he also attempts to identify to what extent human abilities depend on both biological and cultural factors.

Group Differences in Abilities and Intelligence

Both the concept of an intelligence quotient and the tests used to measure it can create serious social problems when individuals are misclassified or when educational and employment opportunities are limited for particular groups based on test scores. One of the most hotly debated and controversial issues in psychology today has to do with the accuracy of psychological tests and what group differences in test scores really mean.

Interpretation of Group Differences

Racial and ethnic differences have been found in many studies of intelligence. In the United States, Asian-American children score slightly higher on standardized IQ tests than European-American children, who in turn score higher than African-American, Native American, or Latino children (Brody, 1992). Different cultural groups show distinctive patterns of mental abilities. Latino children have been found to perform better on nonverbal subtests measuring spatial ability than on other subtests, while African-American children have been found to perform better on verbal subtests than on other subtests (Saccuzzo, Johnson, & Russell, 1992; Taylor & Richards, 1991).

▶ *Mary Carter Smith, the Maryland State storyteller, talks about African-American heritage, self-esteem, and value judgments to a group of school children.*

How should we interpret these differences? Even if we can reach agreement on definitions of intelligence, race, and ethnicity (see Chapter 4), many questions remain open. One obvious source of difference is possible cultural bias in the tests themselves—tests may have items that are more familiar, significant, or comfortable for individuals in particular groups but not for those in other groups. Questions like "What do you do if another boy hits you?" (according to test scoring, the correct answer is to say, "That's all right, it was probably accidental") reflect middle-class cultural values that are probably not adaptive in all communities.

Ethnic differences in IQ scores also reflect motivational factors affected by testing procedures. For example, when African-American children have time to become acquainted with a friendly test examiner, they score higher than they would if tested by a stranger (Ziegler, Abelson, Trickett, & Seitz, 1982). One study suggests that simply behaving in a warm, responsive manner and giving prompts to prevent defeatism after failure can cut typical IQ differences between African Americans and European Americans in half (Kaufman, Kamphaus, & Kaufman, 1985).

Psychologists have yet to develop a test that is either culture-free (has no culture-linked content) or culture-fair (deals with experience common to various cultures). Intelligence tests still rely on knowledge and skills more familiar to some groups than to others (Anastasi, 1988), and the "right" answer does not always "incorporate all reasonably intelligent responses to the question" (Miller-Jones, 1989, p. 361).

Besides cultural test bias, psychologists have examined possible family, environmental, and hereditary contributions to differences among groups. Many psychologists and educators emphasize the effects of group differences in environment—in income, education, family circumstances, and other conditions that affect academic performance, self-esteem, and motivation. Others have argued that IQ has a substantial genetic component, and that racial and ethnic differences reflect underlying hereditary differences (Neisser et al., 1996). What kind of evidence is needed to assess these two points of view? Remember the discussion of behavior genetics in Chapter 3. Theoretically, in identical environments, heredity would be the sole

UNDERSTANDING HUMAN DIVERSITY

Are Intelligence Tests Culturally Biased?

Can you answer the following questions?*

1. What is Juneteenth?
   a. a marriage festival
   b. a graduation celebration
   c. a celebration of the end of slavery in the South
   d. a baptism ritual
2. Scat is to rap as
   a. shoo is to cap
   b. sound is to words
   c. Ice-cube is to Armstrong
   d. git is to go
3. Who discovered blood plasma, saving many lives?
   a. Jonas Salk
   b. Charles Drew
   c. Everett Koop
   d. Washington Carver

Did you have difficulty answering these questions? If you did, you were experiencing how difficult questions can be for those without the cultural background needed to answer them. Familiarity with African-American culture and history would help you on this "test." Similarly, African Americans from an inner city might have difficulty responding to items on intelligence tests that reflect the common interests and experiences of middle-class white culture (Dove, 1968).

Critics of standard intelligence tests argue that the tests are not equally valid for everyone. They charge that intelligence tests reflect white middle-class culture in the United States. They believe that if members of ethnic minority groups and the lower classes do not participate equally in middle-class culture, they are at a disadvantage in taking such tests. Poor children do not have the money to buy the toys and other materials that middle-class children can afford. School psychologist Joann Marrow described her experience of giving black children intelligence tests in rural Georgia as follows: "I gave intelligence tests to black children who had never seen a jigsaw puzzle. . . . When they saw the object assembly test and I told them, 'Put this together and it will make something,' they looked at me like I was crazy. It was just a pile of torn cardboard that could never make anything but a fire. I had to teach them the concept of a jigsaw puzzle. They had no toys, not even dolls. This is poverty, not culture, not values" (Marrow, personal communication).

Critics of intelligence tests maintain that lack of cultural exposure to the concepts required to answer the questions can result in lowered IQ scores and that the tests are then not an accurate measure of true capability. Thus, the tests are said to have a cultural bias (Allen & Majidi-Ahi, 1991; Helms, 1992). In contrast to the critics, psychologists arguing in support of intelligence testing point out that it has useful purposes—it measures characteristics that are related to success in modern society. The controversy over cultural bias has been so intense that some states, including California, have prohibited the use of IQ tests as the sole standard for making decisions about student placement in special education classes (Turkington, 1992).

Is there any way to diffuse the controversy over use of intelligence tests in the schools? Claire Etaugh and Spencer Rathus (1995) suggest that viewing the tests as achievement tests rather than as direct measures of intelligence, and using them to enhance opportunities for learning, is a start. Follow-up techniques, including behavioral observations and interviews, could then be used to provide a more complete picture of academic strengths and weaknesses, a picture that would encompass factors such as motivation and adjustment. This information could then be used to develop strategies to enhance performance rather than to exclude individuals from opportunities for learning or to justify discrimination against them.

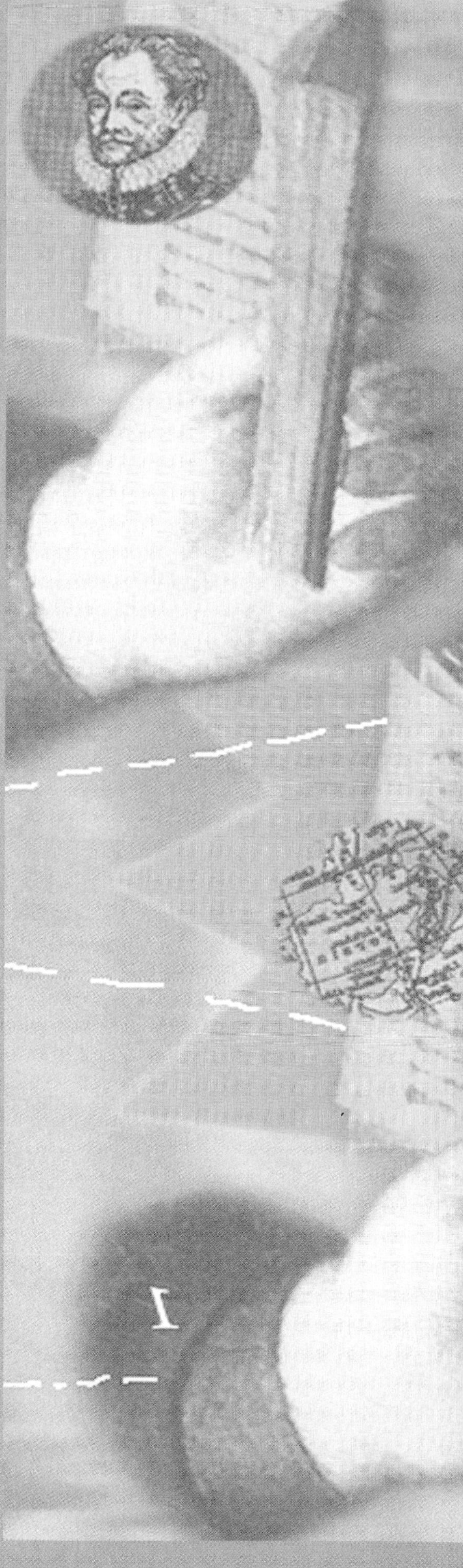

*Answers:
1. c: Juneteenth was a celebration initiated by the blacks in the South to celebrate the end of slavery.
2. b: Scat singing is jazz vocal improvisation using meaningless syllables.
3. b: Charles Drew, the discoverer of blood plasma, was one of the few black Americans in whose honor the U.S. Postal Service has issued a stamp.

determiner of IQ differences among people. Conversely, differences among people with identical heredity would be attributable solely to environment. We cannot ethically design experiments in which we create either identical environments or identical heredity. But twin studies (see Chapter 3) can be used as the next best design to establish the significance of the genetic component of IQ. By this method, it has been estimated that within the American white middle class heredity accounts for as much as 60 percent of IQ variation (Bouchard, Lykken, McGee, Segal, & Tellegen, 1990).

What about differences in average IQ between ethnic, racial, and socioeconomic groups? The average difference in scores between blacks and whites is about 15 points. This is similar to the average difference between English middle-class children and poor Gypsy children, and between American middle-class children and children from deprived rural and mountain areas (Pettigrew, 1964). How do we interpret these differences? First of all, these results are averages and not the scores of particular individuals, which are scattered above and below the averages. The estimate of heredity's contribution rests on a key assumption: that the individuals being compared have similar environments. But if that assumption is wrong, that is, if the environments actually differ, then we are overestimating the contribution of heredity to IQ variation. The greater the environmental variation, the greater the error. If members of ethnic minority groups do not have similar environments and experiences to those of middle-class whites, then this will affect their IQ scores and account for at least some of the differences between groups.

Similarly, IQ variations within ethnic minority groups can also be explained by differences in environments. Middle-class black children score higher than poor black children, and black children in Northern cities score higher than black children in the rural South. Many studies have shown the impact of environment on IQ, including one in which IQs of black children adopted by white parents averaged 10 points above the average IQ (100) for the general population, and 20 points above the IQs of comparable children raised in low-income African-American communities (Scarr & Weinberg, 1976).

Thus, the twin studies that you learned about in Chapter 3 have established that heredity makes a contribution to variation in IQ within

THINKING CRITICALLY

Tests of general information or semantic knowledge are typically included in measures of intelligence. They are based on the assumption that everyone has had the same opportunity to acquire the information needed to succeed. If this assumption is correct, people who are able to give more correct answers must be better at learning and remembering. Read through the two sets of information questions shown below.

Test A

1. What are the colors in the American flag?
2. What is the largest river in the United States?
3. What is the freezing temperature of water?

Test B

1. What is butter made of?
2. Name a vegetable that grows above ground.
3. How often is there a full moon?

Both tests seem like reasonable measures of general information for schoolchildren and contain questions much like those that appear on standard intelligence tests. Would you expect children in the third or fourth grade to do equally well on both tests?

These test questions have subtle biases. Urban schoolchildren generally do much better on items like those in Test A than Test B, while the reverse is true of rural schoolchildren. Tests can be constructed that favor one or the other population, and thus give radically different pictures of the intelligence of rural and urban children. It is relatively easy to construct tests that look fair across different populations but in reality favor one over the other. The reverse is much harder. It is actually very difficult, if not impossible, to construct tests of general information that everyone has had an equal opportunity to acquire.

groups of individuals, such as middle-class whites, who have relatively similar environments. But this assumption about similar environments does not hold for comparisons of average IQ across ethnic groups. As long as there are substantial differences in environments among these groups, the meaning of differences in average IQ across social groups will be hotly disputed. Given the history of the misapplication of intelligence measurement, understanding how to think critically about intelligence measurement and research is particularly important.

Test Bias and the Interpretation of Group Differences

Using so-called scientific findings to justify discrimination against one or another group has a long history, with some reports so absurd they would be amusing if they were not taken seriously. A 1917 study of adult immigrants classified 83 percent of Jews, 80 percent of Hungarians, 79 percent of Italians, and 87 percent of Russians as feeble-minded, with a mental age below twelve years on the Binet scale. The study failed to take into account the fact that the immigrants who had taken the IQ test were frightened, poor, uneducated men and women who spoke no English and that many of them had just crossed the Atlantic Ocean in steerage. The results were interpreted without proper scientific objectivity (Gould, 1981). Still, it is not uncommon even today to read about intellectual differences among ethnic and racial groups (Herrnstein & Murray, 1994) and there is considerable debate among the experts as to how much of these differences can be attributed to biases in the tests used, the statistical analysis applied, and the theoretical stance of the author (Neisser et al., 1996).

Controversies over the meaning of group differences in intelligence are rich with examples of how values and prejudices affect questions, methods, interpretations, and conclusions of scientific research. Yet, a democratic society that values each individual's development and contribution must ensure that findings of group differences are not used to deny opportunities or to argue for unequal treatment for individuals based on their group membership. IQ distributions among ethnic groups largely overlap, which means denying individual opportunity based on group membership denies society needed talent. Democratic societies, with their ideological commitment to the value of each individual, must ensure educational opportunities for all, whatever their ancestry, and help each individual to reach his or her full potential.

Creativity

Most intelligence tests measure analytic intelligence and develop each test item with a clear-cut, generally accepted answer in mind. But often several "correct" answers are possible, some "better" than others. Open-ended questions offer greater opportunities for unusual and novel answers. Answers that are novel, workable, and better than most others are described as creative. Robert Sternberg (1985) argues that creativity is part of intelligence and that a complete intelligence test would include measures of creativity.

Creativity is successful behavior in a problem-solving situation that is both original and practical.

Creativity is a term psychologists apply to behavior that solves a new problem in an original way. High analytic intelligence does not guarantee creativity. Assessing creativity is especially difficult because test givers must make a subjective judgment of both the practicality (usefulness) and originality of the solution (Torrance, 1962). Figure 8-10 presents one example of a test of creativity that has been developed

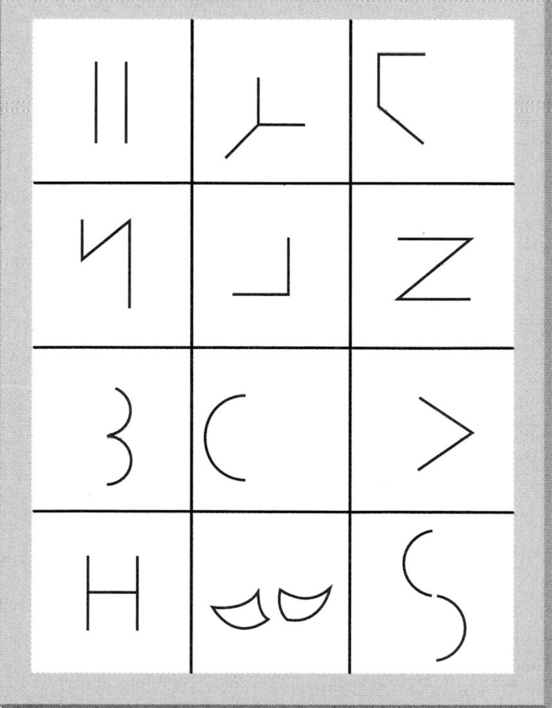

8-10 The Drawing-Completion Test of Creativity

Here is a simple test of creativity. Using a pencil, elaborate on these figures in any way that seems creative and appealing to you. When you have finished, see p. 296.

▲ *When she was still an architecture student, Maya Lin won the competition to design the Vietnam War Veterans Memorial in Washington, D.C. Initially her vision was intensely criticized. Many people felt it did not fit their "ideal" of memorial art. Some people even lobbied that another, more traditional statue be constructed and located near the memorial. But Lin's creative genius prevailed and her memorial has become a place of healing and pilgrimage for thousands of visitors each year.*

and used in research. Figure 8-11 shows sample responses to the creativity test.

Tests of creativity often explore a person's ability to perform both divergent and convergent thinking (Guilford, 1967). ***Convergent thinking*** refers to putting together a variety of facts to find and produce the one correct answer to a particular question or problem. For example, if the Mars Rover is a robot, and if a robot is a kind of artificial intelligence, is the Mars Rover a kind of artificial intelligence? ***Divergent thinking*** refers to the ability to produce a variety of different yet relevant responses to an open-ended question or problem like "Name as many uses as you can think of for a brick." Producing many varied answers (such as build a wall, hold down paper, pound a nail, displace water in a toilet tank) leads to a high score on divergent thinking. Note that this ability always requires overcoming functional fixedness and mental set regarding the object in question. In fact, giving people one or more examples to start with has an inhibiting effect on creativity because they tend to lock people into a particular kind of production and diminish divergent thinking (Smith, Ward, & Schumacher, 1993). Giving people some time off from the task (and allowing for incubation) often reduces the inhibiting effect of such examples.

Although there might be many routes to the mountaintop, there may be only one best route. Thus, divergently producing many possible solutions to a problem is only half the battle. Creativity also requires you to think convergently, that is, to apply logic and reasoning to find the best response among a given set of alternatives. Researchers have developed a two-stage model of the creative process, called *Geneplore,* which incorporates both divergent and convergent thinking. In the first stage, various kinds of cog-

8-11 Sample Responses to the Drawing-Completion Test

The drawings on the left illustrate how a person with average artistic creativity might respond to the drawing-completion test. Those on the right exemplify a creative individual's responses. The introduction of greater complexity and asymmetry is associated with creativity. Such differences are not limited to the production of drawings. When drawings or colored patterns of varying complexity and symmetry are shown to people, creative individuals show a greater tendency to prefer complex and asymmetrical presentations. Some psychologists have argued that a preference or "need" for complexity is an integral component of creative behavior.

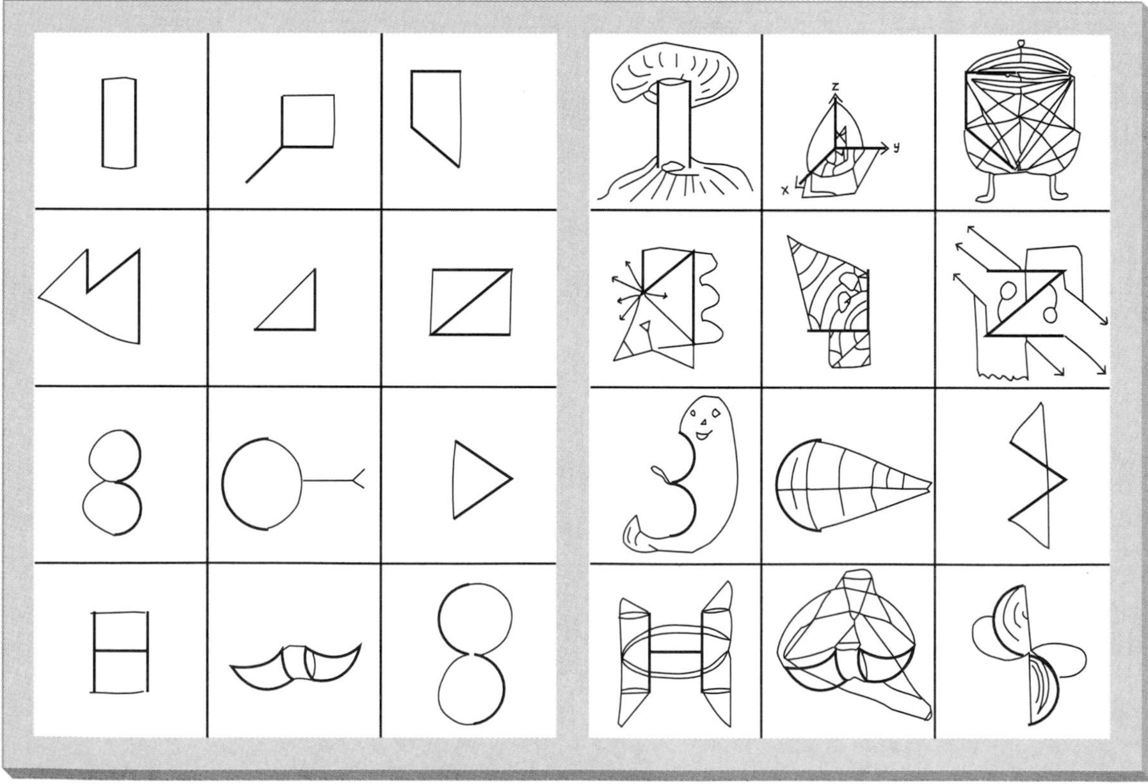

nitions, like ideas, images, or concepts, are freely generated, without any interpretation, editing, or evaluation. These are essentially the products of divergent thinking. These cognitions are then explored individually for their likelihood as solutions (or partial solutions) to the task at hand, which is a convergent thinking stage. It is helpful to practice both kinds of thinking separately on a variety of problems to enhance your general creative ability (Finke, Ward, & Smith, 1992).

How are creativity and academic intelligence related? Up to an IQ of about 110 to 120, intelligence and creativity are positively correlated. At higher intelligence levels (above an IQ of 120), there is little or no relationship: a person of extremely high intelligence (140, say) may not be very creative, whereas someone of relatively lower intelligence (115, say) may be highly creative (MacKinnon & Hall, 1972). Thus, a person needs a certain level of intelligence to be creative, but high academic intelligence does not guarantee it (Sternberg & Lubart, 1991).

◀ *A creative, if rather silly, solution to the problem of "Noodle Eater's Hair."*

Reflections and Observations

People are capable of doing a great deal "in their heads." As adults, we typically (though not always) think through an action before we undertake it, having learned that actions sometimes have unintended consequences. Mostly we don't just blurt something out or react mindlessly to a situation because we know that thoughtless action can irritate or hurt others. In most cases, we think before we act. The ability to think is not limited to human beings, but it reaches its highest form in human behavior. It is based on a variety of processes that we have reviewed in this chapter, including our abilities to create and to use language, to categorize events and to form concepts, to solve problems with planful strategies, heuristics, and algorithms, to reason from information given to us, and to make decisions that take into account all the information available, both from the present situation and from our memory of past situations. Collectively, these cognitive processes constitute human intelligence. In special cases, they lead to behaviors that are novel, practical, and creative. In the next chapter, we turn to consciousness, and we discuss the world of the mind, both in its conscious and unconscious aspects, when we are awake and asleep, under hypnosis or in the altered state brought on by psychoactive drugs.

Objectives Revisited

Psychology originated as an effort to understand scientifically the kinds of things people can do in their heads, in other words, to understand our mental world. The objective was to apply the same scientific methods of investigation that reveal the workings of the physical world to the human mind. Over the last 100 years, substantial progress has been made. In

KEY TERMS

analogical representation

symbolic representation

concept

prototype

problem space

algorithm

heuristic

insight

functional fixedness

mental set

incubation

artificial intelligence

expert system

inductive reasoning

deductive reasoning

analogical reasoning

this chapter, we reviewed our current general knowledge of the most important higher-order mental processes.

Objective 1. Define cognitive processes.

Cognitive processes are activities you can do in your head, that is, they are complex mental events and operations that take place between the presentation of a stimulus and an overt response. Categories of cognition include problem solving, concept formation, reasoning, and decision making. The general mental ability underlying cognition is called *intelligence.*

Objective 2. Explain how concepts are formed, and distinguish between different types of concepts.

A *concept* is a basic unit of knowledge, a mental entity that helps organize objects or events into a single category. *Well-defined concepts* are logical and unambiguous and have established boundaries between examples and nonexamples. Research on well-defined concepts has given us information about how concepts are formed or identified. *Fuzzy concepts* represent everyday objects or events and are more difficult to define, as they have unclear boundaries. Research on fuzzy concepts emphasizes family resemblances and prototypes.

Objective 3. Compare and contrast *information-processing* and *Gestalt* approaches to understanding problem solving.

Information-processing theory emphasizes the algorithms, heuristics, and strategies we use to solve problems. *Algorithms* are plans that guarantee a problem's solution, although much time and effort may be required. *Heuristics* are shortcuts that often may solve the problem but offer no guarantee. According to information-processing theory, strategies for problem solving include four stages: *preparation, generation, judgment and selection* among available courses of action, and *solution attempt.* Gestalt theory emphasizes perceiving the proper relationship among problem elements. Gestalt psychologists introduced concepts like *functional fixedness, mental set, incubation,* and *insight,* which relate to the need to perceive problem elements in a new and proper perspective in order to reach a solution. While Gestalt theory emphasizes automatic processes in problem solving, information-processing theory stresses task analysis and formulating logic-driven plans for solving problems.

Objective 4. Describe and give examples of various forms of reasoning, and identify possible sources of errors in reasoning processes.

Inductive reasoning is the process of reaching a general conclusion from a small set of specific instances or cases. *Deductive reasoning* leads from general principles (or premises) to a specific conclusion. *Analogical reasoning* uses facts that we know about one item or situation to draw a conclusion about another, similar situation. People usually are not perfectly logical, and they can end up with erroneous conclusions as a result of faulty premises or emotional considerations.

Objective 5. Discuss the role of algorithms and heuristics in decision making and judgment and give examples of common heuristics used in everyday reasoning.

Rational decision making and judgment can be described in terms of algorithms. As in reasoning and problem solving, however, people often deviate from the rational approach, using intuition, hunches, best guesses, or heuristics. Three of the factors that may enter into decision making are: the availability of information in memory (the *availability heuristic*), how well the possible outcomes represent what a person knows about the decision-making situation (the *representativeness heuristic*), and the influence of the original reference point on the final judgment (the *anchoring heuristic*).

Objective 6. Describe the role of language in thought, and how we reason and communicate with language.

Language consists of a large set of graphic or acoustical signals, called words, that stand for other things in our environment. We use these symbols in an organized and structured way to communicate with others and to mediate our cognitive processes. Although other animals do communicate symbolically, as for example in birdsongs or wolf calls, only human beings appear to have created a limitless symbolical system that can be used creatively to produce novel messages that others can understand and react to. Language supplements and extends our possibilities for representing past experience in memory beyond those provided by images or analogical representations. One way to understand human language is in terms of its *semantics*, or the meaning of symbols (words), its *syntax*, or the allowable ways we have for sequentially organizing those words into larger units like sentences, and its *pragmatics*, which attaches social meaning to words and sentences beyond those given by syntax.

Objective 7. Define intelligence, and describe how it is measured.

Intelligence has been defined in many ways, but most definitions include the mental capacity to think abstractly and to cope resourcefully with life's challenges. It relates to all of the concepts discussed in Chapters 7 and 8, including memory, problem solving, planning, rational thinking, and creativity. Two of the most widely used intelligence tests are the *Stanford-Binet* and *Wechsler* tests. Scores on these tests are converted into an *intelligence quotient* (IQ) by comparing them with the scores of people in a representative group. Research using statistical and correlational techniques attempts to analyze intelligence into its component cognitive processes or factors, both general (g) and specific (s).

decision-making heuristics

availability heuristic

representativeness heuristic

anchoring heuristic

syntax

semantics

discourse

pragmatics

Stanford-Binet tests

IQ

Wechsler tests

factor analysis

g-factor

s-factor

fluid intelligence

crystallized intelligence

creativity

WHAT IS CONSCIOUSNESS?

- Normal Waking Consciousness
  - Brain-Consciousness Relationship
  - Content and Time Limitations on Consciousness
  - Consciousness and Cognitive Processes
- Altered States of Consciousness

SLEEPING AND DREAMING

- Hypnagogic State
- Stages of Sleep
- Functions of Sleep
- Sleep Disorders
- Content and Meaning of Dreams
- Psychological Characteristics of Dreams

HYPNOSIS

- Psychological Changes under Hypnosis
- A Question of Validity
- Uses and Dangers

MEDITATION

PSYCHOACTIVE DRUGS

- Drug Dependence and Tolerance
- Drug Use and Abuse
- Alcohol
- Marijuana
- Cocaine and Amphetamines
- Nicotine
- Prescription Drugs

PAIN

- Experiencing Pain
- How Pain Is Controlled

REFLECTIONS AND OBSERVATIONS

CHAPTER 9

States of Consciousness

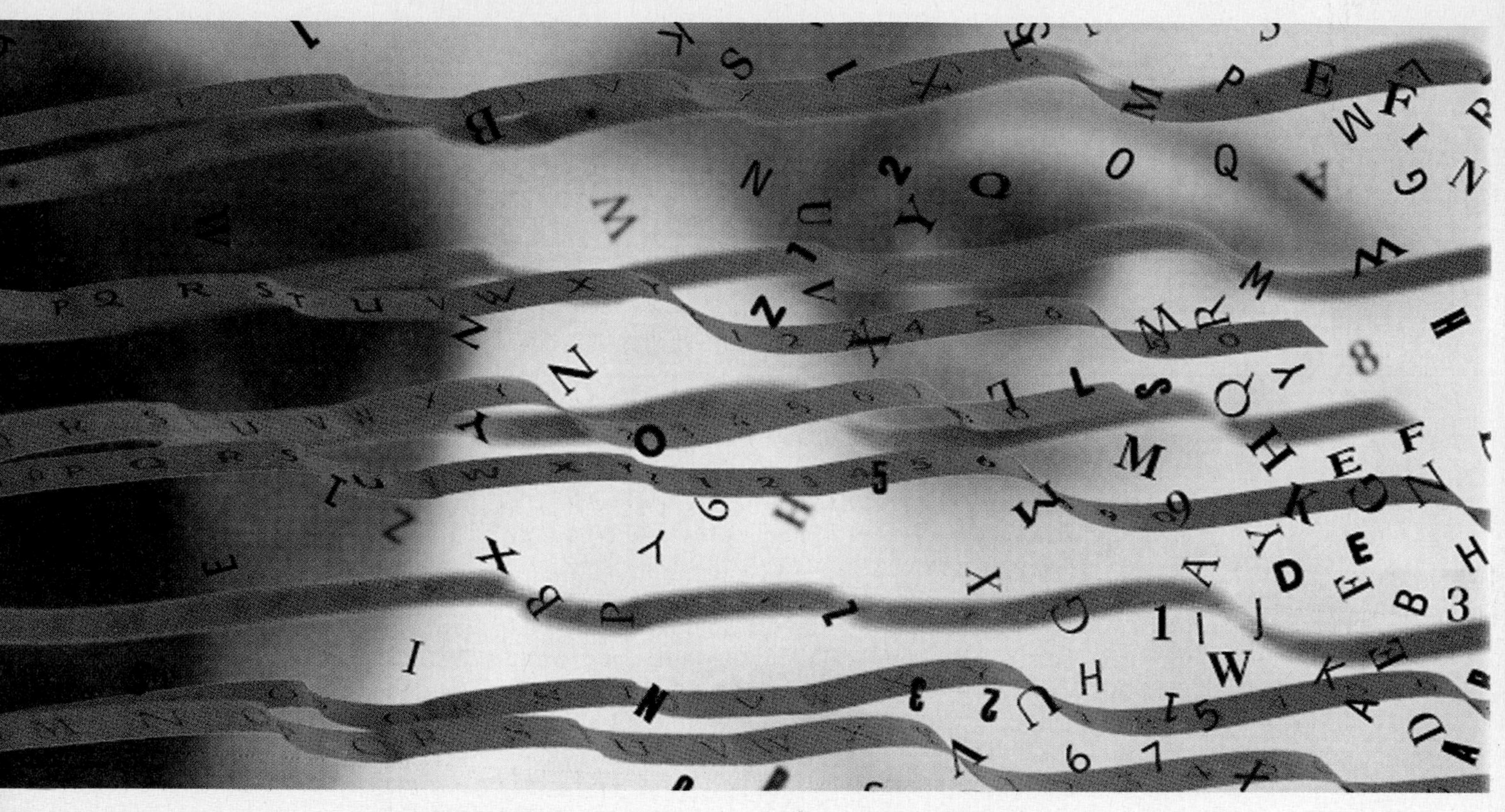

OBJECTIVES

After reading this chapter, you should be able to:

1. State the definition and discuss the functions of consciousness.
2. Identify the characteristics of normal waking consciousness, and explain how an altered state of consciousness differs from normal waking consciousness.
3. Describe the stages, rhythm, and functions of sleep, explaining differences between slow-wave sleep and REM sleep, and then relate these psychological and physiological characteristics of sleep to dreams.
4. Define hypnosis, describe its uses, and discuss whether hypnosis should be considered a true and unique altered state of consciousness.
5. Discuss how various forms of meditation might alter consciousness.
6. Describe the characteristics and effects of such mind-altering drugs as alcohol, marijuana, cocaine and amphetamines, and nicotine, as well as widely used prescription drugs (tranquilizers and sedatives).
7. Describe pain as an altered state of consciousness, and explain a method for controlling it.

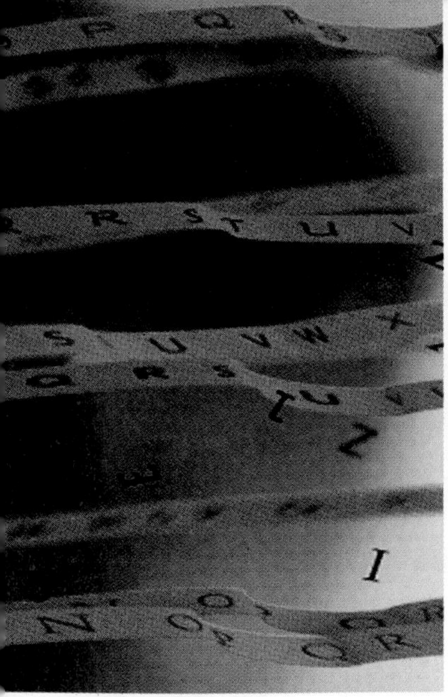

On May 24, 1987, Kenneth James Parks stumbled into a Toronto police station, blood dripping from multiple wounds to his hands, telling police, "Oh, my God, I think I just killed two people." Parks had stabbed his mother-in-law to death and severely injured his father-in-law. During his trial, Parks reported that he had gone to sleep in his own home, awakening only after the murder. He had no memory of the event itself—or even of driving to his in-laws' home, which was fourteen miles away from his. Psychologists who interviewed Parks concluded that he had been sleepwalking and in a confused or altered mental state during the murder. The jury acquitted Parks, judging him not guilty by reason of sleepwalking—the first person in Canada to be acquitted based on that defense.

Although people perform complicated acts while sleepwalking, the ability to control one's behavior in this state is limited. As one expert testified at Parks' trial: "It is impossible, for instance, that a person could formulate a plan before falling asleep and then carry it out while sleepwalking" (Cartwright & Lamberg, 1992, p. 34). What kind of state is sleepwalking? For that matter, what kind of state is sleeping? Awareness is changed during sleeping and dreaming and during sleepwalking. When you are asleep, your consciousness is not the same as it is when you are awake. You are in an ***altered state of consciousness***.

Consciousness is also changed when a person is under hypnosis, in a meditative state, or under the influence of psychoactive drugs. When people experience "mind expansion" from these sources, they typically report a greater sensitivity to the world around them, an enhanced awareness of other people and physical stimulation, an ability to take in more and to process everything going on simultaneously, an ability to learn faster and remember better, an enhanced self-image and self-awareness, and a changed personality. Understanding unusual or expanded states of consciousness will help you to understand what normal consciousness is. In this chapter, we will examine both normal waking consciousness and various states of altered consciousness.

▶ *Kenneth James Parks exiting the courthouse after his acquittal of murder charges. While sleepwalking, Parks stabbed his mother-in-law to death and severely injured his father-in-law.*

What Is Consciousness?

Consciousness has been defined in so many ways over the years that psychologist George Miller called it a "word worn smooth by a million tongues" (Miller, 1972). Although an elusive concept, consciousness is considered by many psychologists to be the most significant of all human mental phenomena (Jaynes, 1976; Rychlak, 1997). Yet, it is easier to experience consciousness than to define and study it because we don't know a lot about where consciousness "comes from" or how it functions.

Nonetheless, we will define ***consciousness*** as our awareness of our selves, of others, and of the world around us, based on sensing and perceiving, on attending, and on memory of both recent and remote events. Altered or expanded states of consciousness take us beyond the everyday limitations on these processes into a state filled with an enormous amount of information.

Normal Waking Consciousness

Normal consciousness is what you experience when you are fully alert and not suffering from a mental disorder or influenced by any extraordinary condition (such as taking an hallucinogenic drug). Normal consciousness depends on self-awareness and the full coordination of attention and memory. Consciousness gives us a sense of personal identity. It enables us to link memories of past experiences with the present, which gives us a feeling of continuity and enables us to distinguish between ourselves (what we have done or thought) and other objects and people. This conscious ability underlies most important cognitive functions, including: (1) distinguishing what's happening to us now, in the current situation, from what happened to us in the past, (2) perceiving and analyzing current circumstances, and (3) planning and making choices (which involves creating expectations about future events).

Two other functions of consciousness are *monitoring* our selves and environments and *controlling* our behavior (Kihlstrom, 1987; Nelson, 1996). Like a roving video camera, consciousness enables us to be aware of both our selves and the environment, keeping us alert for potentially significant stimuli. Its control function enables us to initiate and terminate thoughts and actions, to react to our environment, and to correct mistakes.

Consciousness depends on the coordination of mental processes, including attention, perception, and memory. In consciousness, past, present, and future come together for simultaneous processing. A ten-year-old memory can have the same immediacy and conscious impact as a memory only ten seconds old. When our mental processes don't work together, however, mental disorder can result. We may become confused, losing the ability to monitor our environment and to control our behavior, and even the very sense of who we are. Past, present, and future can become mixed.

Have you ever found yourself listening to someone talk and suddenly realized you did not hear anything that was being said? Have you ever been in a familiar place but found it strange and confusing? Have you ever had the feeling that your body didn't belong to you? Have you ever been confused about whether something actually happened or was just a product of your imagination? Experiences and feelings like these are normal, but they represent mild disruptions of mental processes that are usually integrated in consciousness. In cases of pathological mental disorder, disruptions are similar but much more extreme. Learning about the nature and functioning of consciousness in this chapter is thus a foundation for later learning about both normal personality development and the development of psychological disorders (see Chapters 14 and 15).

. . . how can we think or talk about consciousness? When we try to do so, we are trying to be conscious of consciousness . . . is this possible?

—Julian Jaynes (1976, p. 96)

Although external reality bombards us with information that influences our consciousness, reality and consciousness are not the same thing. The difference is best captured in the fact that reality can be observed, measured, and described in the same way by us as well as other people. The "real world" follows the laws of physics. Consciousness is personal, is available only to the person experiencing it, and, while it can be described, is not necessarily lawful in a physical sense. For this reason, consciousness must be considered *subjective*, in contrast to the *objective* measurable phenomena of the real world, such as the height or weight of an object or the speed of a response.

Consciousness is the awareness of our selves and the external world that we are experiencing or know about at any given moment.

Brain-Consciousness Relationship

Discussions about the nature of the mind and its relationship to the body began long before psychology emerged as a science. Today, however, behavioral neuroscientists are studying human consciousness in ways never imagined even twenty years ago. Part of this effort is to learn how consciousness is altered by changes in the chemistry and structure of the brain. Areas in the brain that appear to play central roles in consciousness are beginning to be identified. We know, for example, that the frontal lobes of the cerebral cortex are importantly involved in consciously forming new factual or episodic memories and retrieving them for later use (Nyberg, Cabeza, & Tulving, 1996), and that the cerebellum plays an important role in the

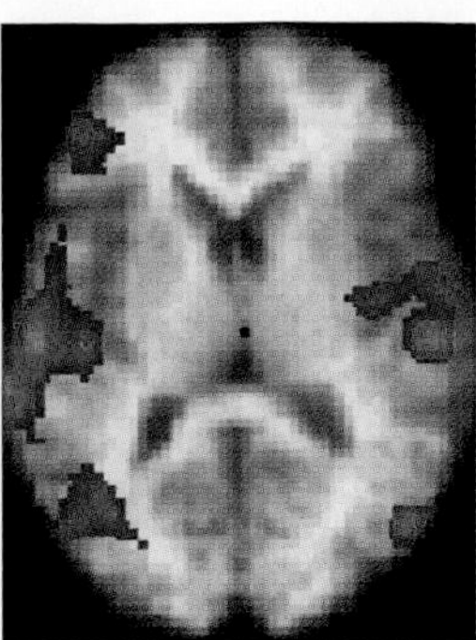
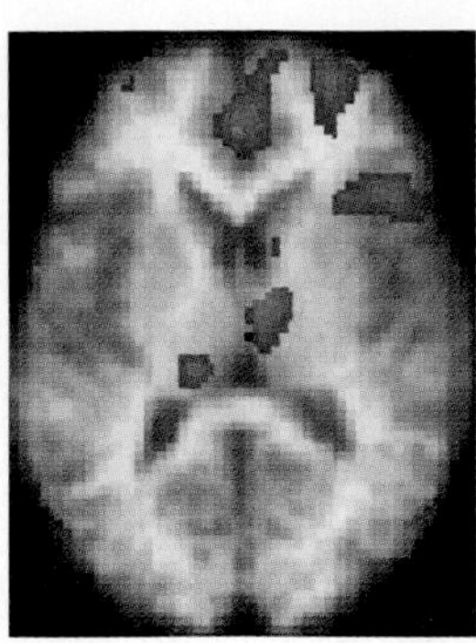

► *Different parts of the brain play different roles in consciousness. The left photo shows brain activity while research participants learn word-pairs. The right photo shows what occurs in the brain when participants recall word-pairs they previously learned.*

implicit or unconscious learning of new classically conditioned responses (Daum & Schugens, 1996). This exciting field of cognitive neuroscience promises major insights into the phenomena of consciousness in the near future.

Content and Time Limitations on Consciousness

Normal consciousness is limited—at any given moment, you usually are aware of only one thought. In this sense, you have a "one-track mind." Remember the cocktail party phenomenon (see Chapter 5). You cannot easily attend to more than one conversation at a time. You can comprehend only the conversation you focus on at the moment. But you can select the conversation you wish to focus on and at the same time exclude any intrusions. Nonetheless, although attention is selective, it does not filter out everything but the target. Switching from one conversation to another is often triggered by something said in the conversation that you have not been focusing on. Thus, if you are watching TV and your mother mentions your name to the person she is talking with on the telephone, that may be sufficient to capture your attention, so that you are now attending to the telephone conversation rather than the TV.

Consciousness is limited not only by content but also by time. At any moment, you will find yourself focusing attention on one task or one stimulus. But even that simple act is hard to do without a break. The longer you concentrate on something, the greater the urge to switch your attention to something else (Van Breukelen et al., 1995). As you concentrate, your mind will begin to have difficulty staying on track and soon you'll feel forced to turn your attention elsewhere. As you focus on this new stimulus, your mind will again wander, possibly back to the original stimulus. Thus, while studying, you can concentrate on your book for a time, but soon you may find yourself thinking of other things, such as what you'll be doing after the exam. This waxing and waning of attention was first objectively studied by Arthur Bills, who demonstrated "mental blocks" in the performance of repetitive tasks. Bills found that research participants would periodically stop performing the task at hand, like color naming or digit symbol substitution. Participants reported that their mind wandered and that they weren't able to do anything about it (Bills, 1931). This early observation has been repeated and extended many times (Van Breukelen et al., 1995). It is now well-established that consciousness is limited both in the quantity of information it can process at any one time as well as in the length of time it can focus on any one task.

Consciousness and Cognitive Processes

We are momentarily conscious only of the content of short-term memory. But clearly it is possible to retrieve most long-term memories into consciousness as required. If you stop to think about it, you probably can call to mind what you had for breakfast this morning. Still, some aspects of long-term memory might not be accessible to consciousness. When there is no explicit memory of experiencing or learning something, and yet you know it or can do it, the effect is non-conscious. Although what makes memories accessible or inaccessible is the subject of debate (see Chapter 7), it is clear that some long-term memories are only partly accessible to consciousness at best. How do we know non-conscious components of long-term memory exist, however, if we can't bring them into consciousness? One answer is that the influence of these non-conscious processes can sometimes be demonstrated in indirect ways. Also, on occasion, something will pop into your mind without any prior conscious thought. How does this happen and to what extent are non-conscious memories responsible?

Priming is an example of the indirect influence of a non-conscious memory. Priming occurs when some event causes a memory to come to mind automatically. For example, in a simple case, we can prime the retrieval of a particular word by first presenting another word that is associated with it. Suppose you are trying to read or to identify words that are presented only briefly or in dim light. You will "see" them better if they have been primed by an associated word (Tulving & Schacter, 1990). So, if the unclear word is *nurse*, you could prime its identification by presenting *doctor* sometime in advance. This enhanced recognition effect is found whether or not the person has any conscious recollection of the previous encounter with the target word or any of its associates (Jacoby & Dallas, 1981). It is as if *doctor* causes you to be ready to see *nurse* (or other medical-related terms). This effect will also occur if you reread a passage from a book as much as one year after you first read it. The second time you read the passage, you will read it significantly faster than you did the first time, especially if it is printed in the same typeface both times. Yet, most people report no conscious memory of the first reading and certainly no memory of the original typeface (Kolers, 1985).

Consciousness seems to exist in varying degrees from fully controlled to fully automatic processes. ***Controlled processing*** requires mental effort and fully occupies your consciousness up to its maximal capacity. Multiplying 68 by 4 in your head or remembering a grocery list, for example, requires controlled mental processing, full concentration, and consciousness.

Automatic processing, on the other hand, occurs without full awareness, requires little if any mental effort, and appears unaffected by the capacity constraints of consciousness. Priming is an example of an automatic process. Pattern recognition is another highly significant automatic process. You automatically recognize the letter "A" as a meaningful pattern. As you read this paragraph, you are not consciously aware of each individual letter in every word because reading has become automatic to you. Still another automatic process is what has come to be called attentional "pop-out," the attention-capturing capacity of unexpected or novel stimuli. Take a look at these two lists. Find the letter A in the following list:

WERWERRQWERWEAPOIXCVZXLPWO

Now find the letter A in this list:

12133344563487509A1243232341234234442

See how much easier it is to see the letter "A" when it is presented in a list of numbers compared to a list of letters? It seems to pop out automatically when presented in a sequence of numbers. Recent evidence shows that this shift of attention and awareness is entirely automatic or uncontrolled (Johnston & Hawley, 1994).

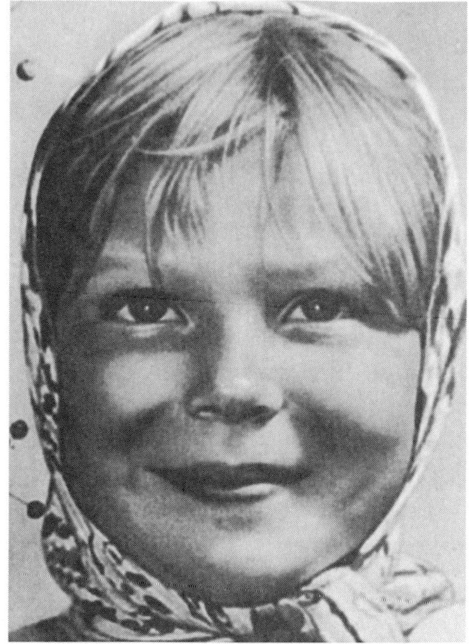

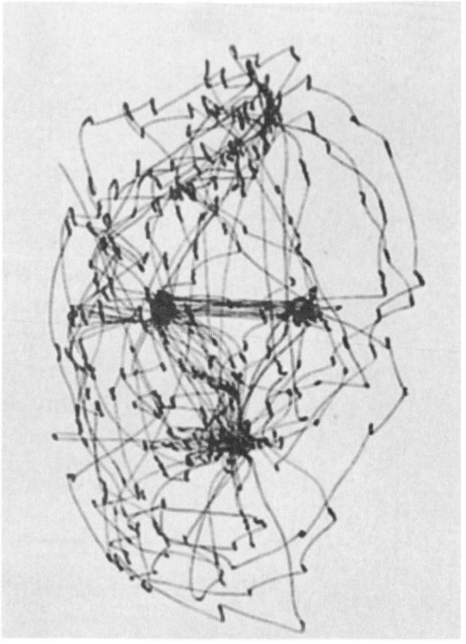

▲ *When we look at a face, our focus is unconsciously drawn to the eyes and mouth. The figure on the right represents the eye movements of someone looking at the face on the left.*

Some controlled processes become automatic with sufficient practice. Take learning to drive an automobile with a manual transmission, for example. This task is confusing and difficult if you are a beginner. But, with practice, you can learn to shift the gears smoothly, without even thinking about it, while doing all the other things required to operate the car. When driving becomes more automatic and less controlled, you find yourself with excess mental capacity for doing other things while still driving well.

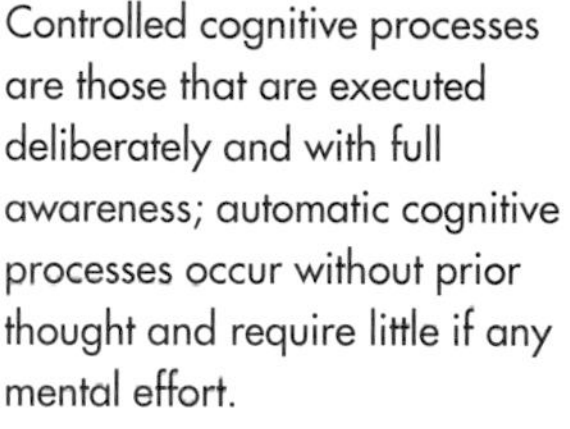

Controlled cognitive processes are those that are executed deliberately and with full awareness; automatic cognitive processes occur without prior thought and require little if any mental effort.

◄ *Controlled processes can become automatic. Juggling, for instance, is extremely difficult for beginners, requiring all their conscious resources. But for highly skilled jugglers, like the performer in the photo, the process becomes automatic to the point where they can do other things while juggling.*

Altered States of Consciousness

Sometimes things are just not what they ought to be. Sometimes you just don't feel like yourself. Something is qualitatively different from normal. Maybe you can recall a time when you were delirious, or dizzy, or when your body seemed distorted, or you felt like a child instead of an adult. Maybe you felt as if your mind and body were separated, as if you were watching your body move but were not a part of it. Maybe you felt as if time had stood still or passed in an instant, or that past, present, and future had merged into one. Maybe you had a flash of creativity, and the separate pieces of a puzzle at last came together into one whole in a way that normally would not be clear to you. Conditions or states like these are considered outside the range of normal consciousness. They are altered states of consciousness. Although they may result from any number of different conditions, from sensory deprivation to overstimulation, from dreams to hypnosis to psychoactive drugs, they have some common characteristics (see Table 9-1).

Table 9-1 Some Common Characteristics of Altered States of Consciousness

Perceptual Distortions A person sees visions, hears voices or strange music, or experiences a heightened sensitivity to all stimuli. Paintings done by people under the influence of drugs or in schizophrenic episodes generally reflect perceptual distortions.
Disturbed Time Sense Time seems to be either standing still or moving rapidly. A person can become totally immersed in an activity, working all day without realizing how much time has passed.
Change in Body Image There may be a sense of being out of one's body, feeling that certain body parts have changed size or flexibility, feeling very heavy or very light or unable to move freely. Obese people may perceive themselves as thin; thin people may perceive themselves as fat.
Cognitive Distortions A person experiences changes in concentration, attention, memory, and judgment in varying degrees. Boundaries between what is real and what is not become blurred. Cause and effect become confused. Contradictions are accepted; things that would ordinarily seem impossible now are unquestioned (for example, as in a dream, when one minute you are washing dishes in your house and the next minute you are turning the radio on in your car).
Hypersuggestibility A person may perform actions suggested by another person. This may reflect a person's loss of contact with reality, diminished critical abilities, and an acceptance of contradictions.
Change in Meaning or Significance A person may feel she or he has attained some exciting new insight—perhaps even found the meaning of life.
Sense of the Indescribable People often report they "can't describe" their altered states, especially retrospectively. Amnesia may play a role. It may also be that their thinking processes are so blunted or distorted during the experience that they are not sufficiently aware of what is happening to be able to describe it. Vocabulary may also be too limited to describe experiences so far outside ordinary events.
Feelings of Rejuvenation There may be a sense of being "reborn." People have this sense after religious conversions and puberty rites in primitive societies but can also feel this way upon emerging from a deep sleep.
Loss of Control Control may become an issue, either through resistance to loss of control (people may fight the onset of sleep or stop short of orgasm for fear of losing control) or through seeking to give up control by achieving the altered state. For example, people may seek to give up control by achieving a mystical state or by inducing hallucinations through drug use.
Change in Emotional Expression Emotions may be expressed more freely, as with the person who weeps copiously, laughs uproariously, or becomes violent only when drunk. Or a person may not show any emotion and become withdrawn.

Source: Ludwig, 1966.

Just as the contents of consciousness are related to but different from external reality, so too altered states of consciousness are related to but different from normal consciousness. Normal waking consciousness suffers limitations that arise from the need to coordinate complex mental processes, including attention and memory. Only a limited amount of information can be processed and only for a limited amount of time. Normal information processing varies widely, from completely controlled to completely automatic, and what's controlled or automatic can change with practice or with differences in other aspects of the situation. Altered states of consciousness seem to remove some of the perceived limitations on normal processing. Removal of these limitations might eliminate a conscious filter or censor that blocks creativity or full awareness (Nelson, 1996). Or it might produce a break with reality that ends up being harmful to the individual.

People vary widely in what they are conscious of, both under normal and under altered states of consciousness. Some people are more aware of their internal states, while others are more aware of their surroundings. Some people are obsessed with time; others have no sense of how much time has passed. Some people react to the first whiff of tobacco smoke in the air; others don't notice until it is called to their attention. One person's normal state of waking consciousness can differ from another person's in innumerable ways. Similarly, one person's altered state of consciousness can differ from another's, or such a state may vary from time to time in the same individual, depending on what has induced the altered state and on surrounding circumstances.

A certain range of conscious experiences is considered ordinary or acceptable within a particular culture or society. In all cultures, a person in a normal state of consciousness can carry out routine daily activities and experience the world in a completely familiar way. Yet, what is considered "normal" varies across cultures as well as across individuals. In some cultures, "normal" may include states that are considered altered in a different culture. Thus, in some cultures, "people believe that almost every normal adult has the ability to go into a trance and be possessed by a god; the adult who cannot do this is considered a psychological cripple" (Tart, 1969, p. 3). In some North American Indian cultures, it is considered normal for a young boy to go in quest of a dream vision. In some Asian cultures, trances induced by meditation are encouraged to cleanse the mind of everyday thoughts and stresses.

In the next sections, we will delve into various altered states of consciousness, discussing how they differ from normal consciousness and examining the conditions that produce them. We will consider, in turn, sleep and dreams, hypnosis, meditation, psychoactive drugs, and pain.

Sleeping and Dreaming

Birds do it. Hamsters, horses, gorillas, and human beings all do it as well. What is it that we have in common with these species? We all sleep. In fact, essentially all mammals and birds sleep much as we do. Moreover, amphibians, reptiles, fish, and insects have periods of inactivity and unresponsiveness that might qualify as sleep. Sleep is the most frequently experienced altered state of consciousness. Each of us spends nearly one-third of our lives sleeping. Most of what we know about sleep today comes from laboratory studies, in which research participants sleep overnight while technicians record their electrophysiological and behavioral activity. Brain waves (recorded by an electroencephalogram or EEG), muscle activity, eye movements, heart rate, respiration, skin conductance, and other bodily functions are monitored continuously throughout the night. The research participant might be wakened periodically to report any imagery or dreams. These measures create a huge body of data to construct a picture of what's going on while we sleep.

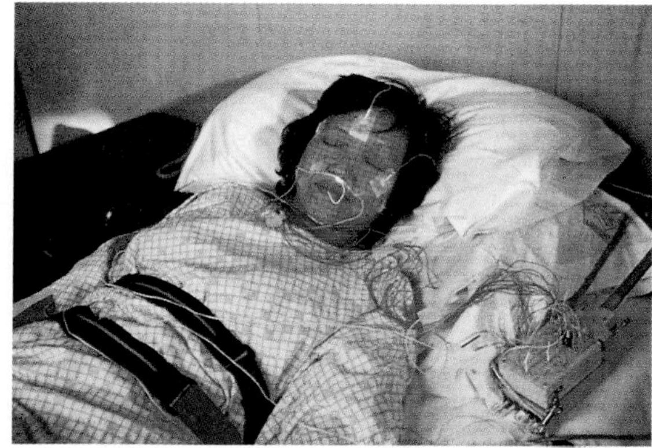

◀ *A patient attached to various monitors in a sleep disorder clinic.*

Hypnagogic State

On the way from wakefulness to sleep, we pass through the ***hypnagogic state*** of consciousness. It is similar to, and possibly identical with, the state we pass through when we wake from sleeping. People vary considerably in their experiences with these states. For some, the period of falling asleep is filled with images as rich as the best dreams, while for others, it is dull and nonmemorable. Indeed, the hypnagogic experience might be the same as dreaming, although there are a few notable differences. One difference is that even those who give the best descriptions of the hypnogogic state usually forget their experiences more rapidly than they forget ordinary dreams, especially if they continue on into sleep.

The transitional states between wakefulness and sleep are often filled with dreamlike imagery.

You can observe your own hypnagogic state: When lying down to sleep, balance one arm vertically, with your elbow resting on the bed. You can go fairly far into a hypnagogic state with your arm in that position. When it starts to fall, you will probably awaken. You can then try to fix the hypnagogic experience in your mind or record it before it fades.

Sleep can be divided into two types: non-REM sleep, which is characterized by slow-wave EEGs, large body movements, and progressive relaxation, and REM sleep, which is characterized by a fast-activity EEG pattern and short bursts of rapid eye movements.

Stages of Sleep

Sleep occurs in stages that have a systematic rhythm to them (Lavie, 1996). Most sleep stages are characterized by ***slow-wave*** (large-amplitude, slow-activity) EEGs and gross body movements, such as rolling and changing positions. There are four distinguishable stages of this sort (called ***non-REM sleep***), each associated with progressively more relaxation and slowing of physiological processes.

Each stage has its own distinctive EEG pattern (see Figure 9-1). A research participant who is awake but resting with eyes closed begins with predominantly alpha waves. As sleep approaches, the alpha rhythm is replaced by slower, irregular theta waves in the hypnagogic state and in initial Stage 1 sleep. In this transition stage between wakefulness and sleep, the eyelids occasionally open and close and the eyes roll up and down.

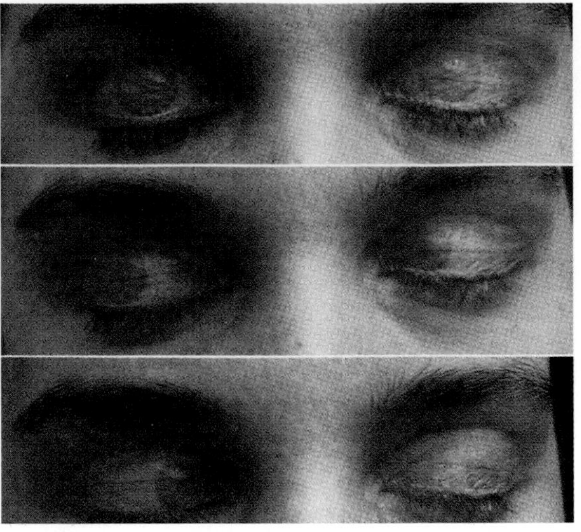

▲ *These sequential photographs show the movement of the eyes during REM sleep.*

After about ten minutes, bursts of activity of twelve to fourteen cycles per second, called theta wave spindles, appear in the EEG, and Stage 2 sleep begins. Some scientists believe spindles reflect the mechanism that keeps us asleep by decreasing our brains' sensitivity to sensory input. About fifteen minutes later, larger, slower delta waves are added to the irregular activity and spindles, producing Stage 3 sleep. When delta waves make up more than 50 percent of total brain-wave activity, Stage 4 sleep, the deepest stage of slow-wave sleep, is said to begin. As delta waves increase, cerebral blood flow and metabolic rate fall, declining to 75 percent of the waking level. Loud noises or shaking are needed to awaken the sleeper at

▶ *Hervey de Saint-Denis attempted to draw his hypnagogic experiences. He described them as "wheels of light, tiny revolving suns, colored bubbles rising and falling . . . bright lines that cross and interlace, that roll up and make circles, lozenges, and other geometric shapes."*

this stage, and when awakened, the person is groggy and confused. Stages 3 and 4 are the major stages of slow-wave sleep.

About forty-five minutes after Stage 4 sleep begins (about ninety minutes after beginning sleep), a qualitatively different kind of sleep, called ***REM sleep***, appears. The first REM sleep episode typically lasts for five to ten minutes. REM sleep is characterized by a fast-activity EEG pattern and short bursts of rapid eye movements (REM, from which this stage gets its name), twitches of toes, fingers, arms, and other parts of the body. After a second ninety-minute period of non-REM sleep, a somewhat longer REM period takes place. REM sleep episodes lengthen with each ninety-minute cycle (see Figure 9-2). REM and non-REM episodes alternate five or six times over the course of a night.

The brain becomes very active during REM sleep, relative to non-REM sleep; cerebral blood flow and oxygen consumption increase significantly. The EEG becomes more irregular, with a sprinkling of theta waves (similar to Stage 1 sleep). Eyes dart rapidly back and forth under the closed eyelids. In the normal sleeper, spinal and cranial motor neurons are inhibited, in effect paralyzing the sleeper and resulting in profound loss of muscle tone, even though brief twitching movements of hands and feet do occur. Males may experience erections, and females may experience increased vaginal secretions.

During waking hours, cells within the brain stem release chemicals, called adrenergic chemicals, into the brain, where they act as pacemakers, keeping the brain alert, enhancing attention, priming motor activity, and, in general, modulating brain activity so as to maintain awareness. As the brain goes to sleep, the adrenergic system shuts down. Other nerve cells release cholinergic chemicals, which begin to dominate brain activity. As this happens, self-awareness decreases, memories are weakened, and sleep ensues (Hobson, 1988).

People are less responsive to noises and other incidental external stimuli during REM sleep, but they are easily wakened by meaningful stimuli, such as the sound of their name. If awakened during these periods, about 80 percent of the time sleepers report being in the middle of a dream (Antrobus, 1990). We now generally accept that ordinary dreaming occurs in REM sleep and that Stages 1 to 4 are dreamless sleep (Webb, 1992). The last REM period, corresponding to the last dream of the night, may run from half an hour to an hour, and people often abruptly awaken from it. Of all sleep imagery, this last dream is the one you are most likely to remember.

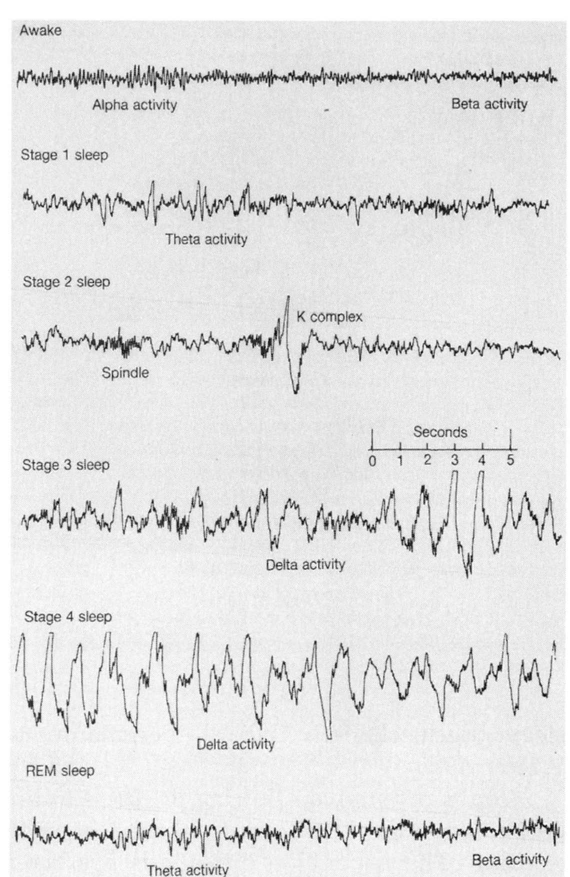

9-1 Brain Waves and Sleep

EEG recordings taken in the various stages of non-REM and REM sleep. (Source: Horne, 1988)

Functions of Sleep

Sleep appears to be a biological necessity for most mammals. Researchers have shown that rats will develop severe physical pathologies leading to death if continuously deprived of

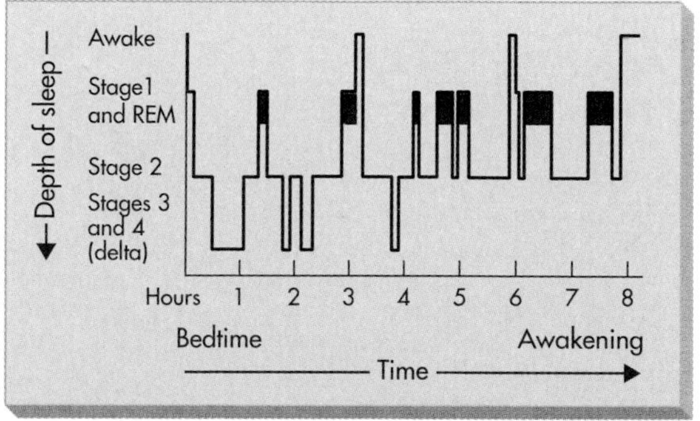

9-2 The Sleep Cycle

The typical sleeper cycles through the various sleep stages, periodically dreaming (REM sleep, indicated by the red bars). The REM periods are characterized by a Stage 1 EEG pattern, as well as by the rapid eye movements from which REM sleep takes its name, and by a dramatic decrease in the muscle tone of the anti-gravity muscles. Each succeeding dream period is longer, and most "deep" sleep (Stages 3 and 4) occurs in the first half of the sleep cycle. Likewise, note that most of the dreaming takes place in the second half of the sleep cycle.

9-3 Sleep Needs as a Function of Age

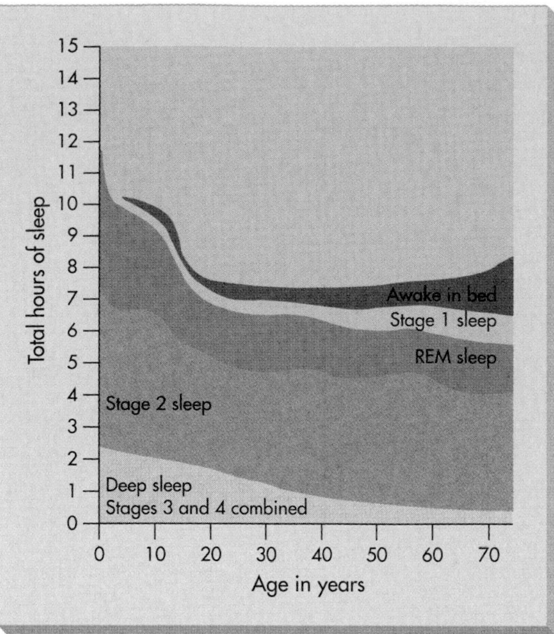

One of the most interesting aspects of sleep is the way that our need for it changes with age, especially our need for REM sleep, which declines dramatically. REM sleep, expressed as a percentage of total sleep, declines from around 50 percent to less than 10 percent by the time a person reaches age seventy. A very high percentage of REM sleep during early infancy is especially intriguing. Is this when the brain is being programmed? (Source: Adapted from Williams, Karacan, & Hursch, 1974)

sleep (Rechtschaffen, Gilliard, Bergmann, & Winter, 1983).

Sleep is restorative, allowing the body to recover from the day's physical and mental exertion. The restoration hypothesis has been examined in sleep deprivation studies, exercise studies, and studies monitoring physiological processes during sleep that might signify restorative processes (see Lavie, 1996). Sleep deprivation studies indicate that the human brain requires slow-wave sleep to function normally (Antrobus, 1990). Deprivation results in feelings of intense tiredness and fatigue, perceptual distortions (sometimes mild hallucinations), and difficulty in prolonged concentration—all evidence of impaired cerebral functioning. Although the consequences may be as much psychological as they are physiological, sleep deprivation is generally recognized as an effective form of torture in human beings.

Organisms vary in how much sleep they need—horses typically get along on two hours a day, while the giant sloth requires twenty (now you know why lazy people are called "sloths"). In general, human infants and small children require more sleep than adults do, possibly because of the role of sleep in growth. Slow-wave sleep is almost the only time the pituitary gland releases growth hormone. The significance of this finding in human beings is still unclear, but we do know that this hormone is critical for the ability of amino acids (protein molecules) to enter cells and that cellular protein synthesis helps restore body tissue (Horne, 1988). It might also help to explain why children do most of their growing during sleep. Other hormones, such as prolactin and luteinizing hormone, also appear to be manufactured mainly during sleep. If such vital chemical substances are depleted during daily activity, sleep may be the only opportunity the body has to replace them.

The need for sleep appears generally to decline throughout adulthood (see Figure 9-3). Sleep patterns seem to change with age, as elderly people often sleep more during the day and awaken at night. REM sleep also declines with age (Dennenberg & Thomas, 1981).

Although sleep is universal among vertebrates (mammals, reptiles, fish, and amphibians), only the more recently evolved mammals and birds (warm-blooded vertebrates) exhibit

► *All vertebrates require some amount of sleep, though they get it in a variety of positions.*

THINKING CRITICALLY

What do you think the effect of increasing your exercise might be on your need for sleep? If exercise depletes the body by using up its energy stores and if sleep restores the body by allowing stored energy to be created, then increased exercise should increase the need for sleep. But does it? How would you design an experiment to test this hypothesis?

One way would be to give people different amounts or types of exercise (independent variable) and see if there is a change in sleep patterns (dependent variable) after the various conditions of exercise. Researchers using this approach have had mixed results, however. Some studies find slow-wave sleep increases after physical activity; other studies do not (Horne, 1988). It turns out that whether exercise affects sleep depends on whether or not it elevates body temperature. Researchers had research participants exercise on a treadmill, some cooled by fans and cool water, some not (Horne & Moore, 1985). That night, sleep of the "cooled exercised" participants didn't change. The slow-wave sleep of the "hot exercised" research participants increased 25 percent, however. This suggests that increased cerebral activity, which is associated with higher temperatures, increases the need for slow-wave sleep.

REM sleep (McCarley, 1989). Thus, REM sleep is thought to be a product of recent evolution. If normal individuals are deprived of REM sleep for several days, when they are finally allowed to sleep they show a distinct rebound effect, which causes them subsequently to experience a significantly greater than normal amount of REM. Over a period of several days, some minimal amount of REM sleep appears necessary for normal functioning, and some regulatory mechanism seems to ensure the minimum is achieved, if possible.

REM is not required for survival, however. A case study of a thirty-three-year-old man suffering a brain injury at age twenty found that, although he had very little REM sleep (in three out of eight nights he had no REM sleep, and averaged six minutes of REM sleep for the other nights), he experienced very few side effects. Despite this REM deficiency, he was able to complete high school and law school, and eventually became a successful practicing lawyer (Lavie, Pratt, Scharf, Peled, & Brown, 1984; Lavie, 1996).

Most people seem to need some REM sleep for normal functioning. Some individuals, however, apparently get too much REM sleep and seem to do better if their REM sleep is reduced. Depressed individuals often have disturbing nightmares during REM that leave them fatigued and even more depressed. Interrupting REM sleep, by the use of drugs or simply by waking the sleeper every time REM sleep occurs, reduces these nightmares. People with severe depression often report that their symptoms are improved when they are deprived of REM sleep. These findings have led to the development of a dream therapy in which depressed people are taught to interrupt their disturbing dreams and rewrite their dream scripts to have happy endings. A convincing explanation for this effect has yet to be found (Cartwright & Lamberg, 1992).

Reducing REM sleep with drugs can have negative side effects. Have you ever taken a sleeping pill, slept through the night, and then discovered that you didn't feel rested on the following day? Have you ever wondered how such drugs affect sleep? Research on this question is particularly important because of widespread use of sleep medication (sedatives) in our society. Nearly all drugs tested, especially the commonly used sedatives and alcohol, decreased time spent in REM sleep (Zarcone, 1973). Stimulants, such as amphetamines, also reduced REM sleep, once the individual got to sleep. Because REM sleep is critical to psychological restoration, sleepers often feel no more rested after taking sleep medication, even though they sleep longer. This deficit in REM sleep typically accumulates from night to night through a period of continuous drug use. When the drug is discontinued, REM sleep time temporarily increases over normal rates for a few nights. Despite this rebound effect, the total deficit is usually never fully recovered. Low doses of hallucinogenic drugs like LSD or marijuana cause REM sleep to move forward to an earlier time of night rather than occurring in the usual ninety-minute cycles. But low doses appear to have no effect on total amount of REM sleep (McCarley, 1989).

Sleep Disorders

Have you ever known someone who had difficulty sleeping, reported a lot of nightmares, or walked in his sleep? People who sleep with such people have some interesting stories to tell, such as the story about a partner who got up in the middle of the night, arranged the flowers in a living room vase, and then made a sandwich. The sleepwalker had no recollection of the episode in the morning. Until recently, doctors were taught and the public generally assumed that people who walked, talked, wet the bed, screamed in terror, or thrashed about in their sleep had serious emotional problems and needed psychiatric help. We have come to understand these behaviors better in recent years and now view them more benignly (Moorcroft, 1993).

Sleep disturbances, like restlessness, moving around, crying or screaming, are especially common in children, appearing in over 20 percent of cases. These disturbances tend to run in families, so that if both parents report similar experiences, 60 percent of children will also exhibit these symptoms. While they might be a sign of some serious underlying emotional problem, it is most likely that these symptoms will disappear even if left untreated (Dement, 1972, 1992).

Nonetheless, when an adult has a disorder that causes abnormal activities during sleep, the condition tends to be permanent and can have serious consequences. Some adults routinely experience nocturnal wanderings or ***sleepwalking***; occasionally these episodes end in a violent act (as in the case of Kenneth James Parks, described at the beginning of the chapter). Sleepwalking typically occurs during REM sleep (Masand, Popli, & Welburg, 1995). Normally, during dreaming, all but the respiratory and eye muscles are paralyzed. But for some people afflicted with a REM sleep disorder, the muscles stay "awake," allowing these dreamers to act out their dreams (Kempenaers, Bouillon, & Mendlewicz, 1994). This disorder typically afflicts middle-aged and older men and is often linked to minor lesions in the brain stem. Fortunately, REM sleep disorder, like many sleep disorders, lends itself to treatment with prescription drugs. For sleepwalking, clonazepam, a muscle-relaxing sedative, is quite effective.

Sleep disorders come in many forms. They now represent a separate category in the American Psychiatric Association's Diagnostic and Statistical Manual (1994). A description of some of the more common disorders can be found in Table 9-2.

Table 9-2 The Disorders of Sleep

Disorder	Description
Insomnia	The most common sleep disorder is an inability to sleep. There may be two distinct types: (1) sleep-onset disorder and (2) repeated awakening during the night.
Sleep apnea	The sleeping person stops breathing for brief periods lasting from fifteen to sixty seconds; the causes are unknown, but sleep apnea may be involved in sudden infant death syndrome (SIDS).
Narcolepsy	Sudden and recurrent attacks of sleep or the desire to sleep occur during normal waking hours; symptoms include sudden loss of muscle tone and postural reflexes and hypnagogic hallucinations.
Somnambulism (sleepwalking)	Typically occurs in non-REM sleep and primarily in children; the sleeper has little or no memory of the nocturnal episode.
Nocturnal enuresis (bedwetting)	Often associated with dreams of urinating in a toilet; it mainly affects children and is very common.
Parvor nocturnus (night terror)	Occurs primarily in children and is an apparent state of terror, including thrashing and screaming, and an inability to communicate what is wrong or to be consoled. Episodes are brief, and the child returns to sleep. Despite the obvious intensity of the experience, the child typically has no memory of it in the morning.

SEEKING SOLUTIONS

Insomnia: What to Do If You Cannot Sleep

Whatever functions sleep serves, a lack of sleep has highly adverse consequences for most people. Insomniacs (people who can't get to sleep) try all sorts of things to fall asleep. What does research tell us about the kinds of things that work? Psychologist Richard Bootzin has come up with the following six empirically based suggestions to help insomniacs change sleep habits and increase the quantity and quality of their sleep (Bootzin, 1981):

1. Lie down intending to go to sleep *only* when you feel sleepy.
2. Do not use your bed for anything except sleep; that is, do not read, watch TV, eat, study, or worry in bed. Sexual activity is the only exception to this rule. After sexual activity, follow other rules carefully. Use your bed only when you intend to go to sleep.
3. If you find yourself unable to fall asleep, get up and go into another room. Stay up as long as you wish and return to the bedroom only when you intend to sleep and feel sleepy. Get up again if you do not fall asleep within a reasonable time. Remember, the goal is to associate your bed and bedroom with falling asleep *quickly*! If you are in bed for more than about ten minutes without falling asleep and have not gotten up, you are not following instructions.
4. If you still cannot fall asleep, repeat Step 3. Do this as often as necessary throughout the night.
5. Set your alarm and get up at the same time every morning, irrespective of how much sleep you get during the night. This will help your body acquire a consistent sleep rhythm.
6. Do not nap during the day.

One type of insomnia seems to be due to a mismatch between a person's biological clock and real time. Suppose you want to go to sleep at 11 P.M., but your biological clock is programmed for sleep at 2 A.M. Research indicates that the biological clock can be reset, but only in the forward direction. Thus, to reset, you must postpone going to sleep until sometime after the time set by the biological clock (2 A.M.). The proper treatment for an insomniac, then, is to have him or her extend sleep onset time by an hour or two each night, moving the clock forward until it finally coincides with the desired bedtime of 11 P.M. A clear drawback of this treatment is that it requires at least ten days of careful monitoring and change to reset the clock. A person would need to take a vacation in order to complete the treatment. Still, this may be but a small price to pay for someone who is a chronic insomniac.

Finally, sleep requires relaxation. Techniques developed to induce relaxation in tense situations can be extended beneficially in some cases to cure sleep disorders. One popular technique is the systematic relaxation of all the major muscle groups of the body, one at a time, beginning with the toes and feet and ending with the muscles of the head. For each muscle group, you alternately tense and relax for a few cycles until the muscles feel completely relaxed. When you finish with the muscles of your head and neck, your whole body should feel relaxed and ready for sleep.

In addition, remember that a drop in body temperature results in increased slow-wave sleep. Thus, techniques that raise or lower your body temperature (for example, exercise or sleeping in a cold room) so that your body will experience a cooling down process will facilitate sleep.

Content and Meaning of Dreams

Almost everyone has dreams. Upon waking, we recall scenes and events that seem to take place in a world of imagery but that strongly resemble events of the real world. But what do these dreams mean? Some psychological theorists accord great importance to the contents of ordinary dreams. Sigmund Freud considered them to be so significant that he called their interpretation "the royal road to the unconscious" and thereby the key to the solution of many of life's most significant problems (Freud, 1900). To Freud, dreams were expressions of unresolved and repressed childhood conflicts between the

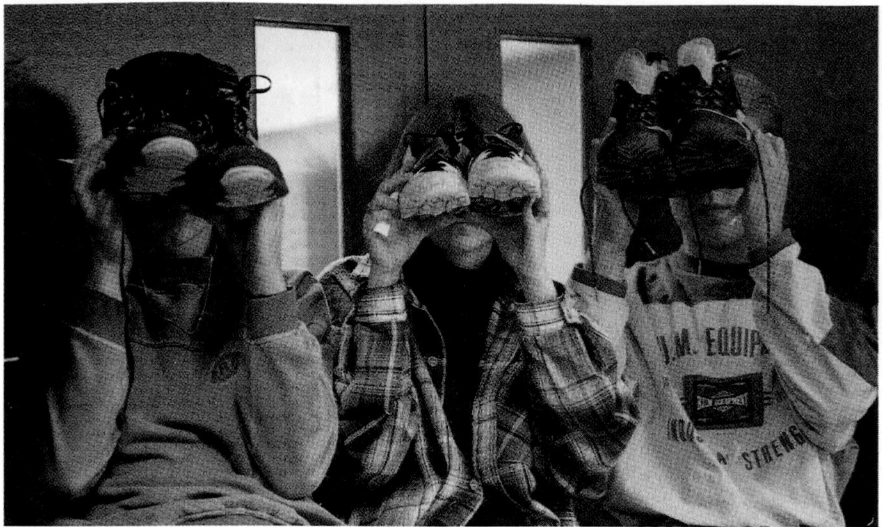

▲ *These participants in a hypnosis demonstration were told that they were at the Kentucky Derby and they should watch the race through their "binoculars."*

of beet salad, uncooked bacon, pickles, and anchovies, and begin eating with great enthusiasm. But the hypnotic subject is not asleep; he or she is under the suggestive guidance of the hypnotist (Kirsch & Lynn, 1995).

Currently, there is debate among those who study hypnosis scientifically as to whether it is a true altered state of consciousness. Psychologists who adhere to state theory believe that hypnosis is a separate kind of state, dissociated from normal consciousness and different mentally and behaviorally from sleeping, daydreaming, or any other altered state of consciousness. In contrast, psychologists who believe in the social compliance hypothesis, which says that hypnotic behavior is conscious and purposeful, believe that hypnotized subjects are simply obeying the strong social demands of the hypnotist and the situation they are in. We will discuss the evidence for both sides, but there appears to be no resolution of this conflict of ideas at this time (Kihlstrom & McConkey, 1990; Kirsch & Lynn, 1995).

Hypnosis is an altered state of consciousness usually induced by instructions to relax and give up conscious control of thought and behavior and characterized by hypersuggestibility.

Hypnosis is usually induced while a person is sitting or lying in a relaxed position. The hypnotist asks the person to be calm and quiet and to put all concerns aside. The hypnotist suggests that the individual is becoming drowsy and encourages the person to let his or her mind drift and become completely blank. Most people respond to these initial suggestions, and the skillful hypnotist uses these responses to build up the person's confidence that he or she can go into an even deeper hypnotic state.

The hypnotist's long, repetitive suggestions of drowsiness may lead to a hypnotic state in which people experience a state of detachment and mental rest in which they feel totally relaxed, with no expectations that anything in particular will happen. If asked what they are thinking about, they usually answer "nothing." They describe their minds as blank, although they are attentive and responsive to the hypnotist. Similar states have been reported during meditation, as we will see shortly.

Some people are highly resistant to hypnosis, while others are easily hypnotized. About 5 to 10 percent of people do not respond at all to hypnotic induction, while about 10 to 20 percent can achieve deep hypnotic states and experience almost all hypnotic phenomena. Most people fall somewhere between these two extremes. Despite extensive research, we know little about why one person is readily susceptible to hypnotic suggestion and another is not. Further, despite extensive research, no distinct physiological changes have been identified, other than those attributable to physical relaxation (Bowers, 1976; Hilgard & LeBaron, 1984; Perlini & Spanos, 1991; Woody, Drugovic, & Oakman, 1997).

Psychological Changes under Hypnosis

What an individual believes she is seeing can be changed radically under hypnosis, even to the point that perception of specific stimuli are totally blocked. Hypnotic subjects who are told, for example, that they cannot see clearly, may report blurred vision. If they are told that they cannot smell at all, some will show little reaction to sniffing a bottle of household ammonia. Because the sensation of pain can be blocked by hypnotic suggestion, hypnosis has been used as a pain killer in surgery (Hilgard & Hilgard, 1983; Turk, 1994).

Perceptions can also be enhanced by telling hypnotic subjects that one sense is exceptionally keen. Most people report experiencing increased sensitivity, but there is little evidence that *actual* sensitivity changes. Suggestions can reach the point of illusion, or even hallucination, when the hypnotic subject perceives things that don't exist. A very responsive subject can be told that a friendly polar bear is walking around the room and he will "see" it. Note that the careful hypnotist is sure to specify a *friendly* polar bear to avoid terrorizing the subject.

A person's awareness in hypnosis may be focused on the external world or on internal bodily processes, such as breathing. Processes that are ordinarily a part of the subject's awareness can become *dissociated*. A hypnotic subject might be told that his or her arm will bend repeatedly but uncontrollably, and it will do so. Or a subject might be told that she or he is blind, but that the blindness will depart when the hypnotist makes a certain hand gesture. The person correspondingly reports blindness and acts appropriately; when the hypnotist makes the gesture, the person can see once again. Note that "seeing" the hypnotist's gesture must take place outside conscious awareness.

The split in awareness under hypnosis has been rigorously demonstrated in the ***hidden observer technique***, developed by Ernest Hilgard (1977). Deeply hypnotized subjects are told that part of their mind is always aware of what is actually going on, even under hypnosis, and this "hidden observer" can respond to special cues. When those cues are given, the hidden observer is able to report on events not consciously perceived by the hypnotized subjects. For example, if your hand and arm are placed in ice water, you normally feel pain. But hypnotized subjects who have been told that their hand is numb and insensitive will not feel pain when it is placed in ice water. Indeed, even after having held their hand in ice water beyond the point of tolerance for most people, they report little or no pain and appear relaxed. The "hidden observer" feels the pain, however. On a prearranged cue, the subject can report, either verbally or by some nonverbal movement, like setting an indicator, the level of pain experienced by the hidden observer—all the while, remaining outwardly calm and relaxed (see Figure 9-4).

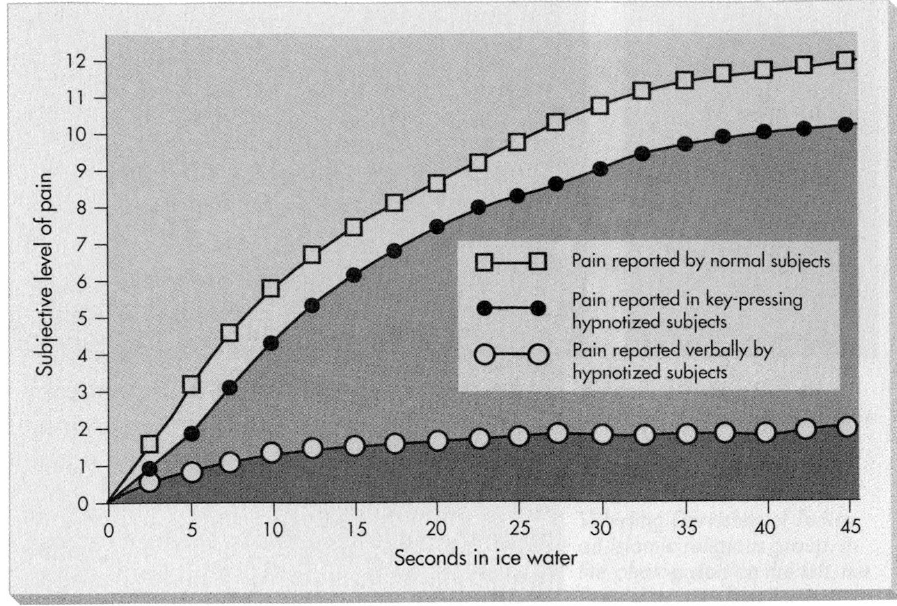

9-4 The Hidden Observer

People under hypnosis who have been instructed not to feel pain are compared with normal state individuals on pain tolerance in what is called the cold pressor test. Reports of pain are uniformly higher for non-hypnotized subjects. Hypnotized subjects seem to have little conscious awareness of pain, as reflected in their verbal reports, but at the same time their "hidden observer" feels the pain, as shown by automatically controlled key press responses. (Source: Adapted from Hilgard, 1977)

Subjects generally report no emotional feelings when under hypnosis. The hypnotist can arouse almost any emotion in almost any intensity, however, simply by making that suggestion. The subject might be told, "You are about to hear an extremely funny joke." If the hypnotist then said, "Pine needles are green," the subject would probably laugh uncontrollably.

The hypnotic state might allow psychotherapists access to normally unconscious processes (Hilgard & LeBaron, 1984). By suggesting that patients will not experience emotions, for example, hypnotherapists can have patients recall and work with memories ordinarily too painful to deal with. When told to have a dream under hypnosis, subjects often report material similar to that experienced in ordinary dreams. We would expect this outcome if similar subconscious influences predominate in both hypnosis and dreaming. Some therapists conclude, therefore, that both dream interpretation and reports during hypnosis directly reveal contents of the unconscious.

Hypnosis sometimes appears to alter a person's memory. If amnesia is suggested, good hypnotic subjects don't remember the events they were told to forget. If given a later suggestion to remember, they will then demonstrate normal memory. Often observers cannot tell whether the hypnotic subject has truly forgotten or is merely complying with suggestion and acting in accord with expectations for how to behave in the situation. But, while we can account for hypnotic amnesia by compliance, we can't account for hypnotic *improvement* in memory this way. Some researchers claim that hypnosis can be useful in revealing critical information that a person might have forgotten or suppressed in a normal state. This hypnotic procedure has been used on many occasions with eyewitnesses to crimes. In fact, however, little solid evidence exists to document memory enhancement through hypnosis, when hypnotized subjects are compared with controls who are making the same effort to recall (Nash, 1987).

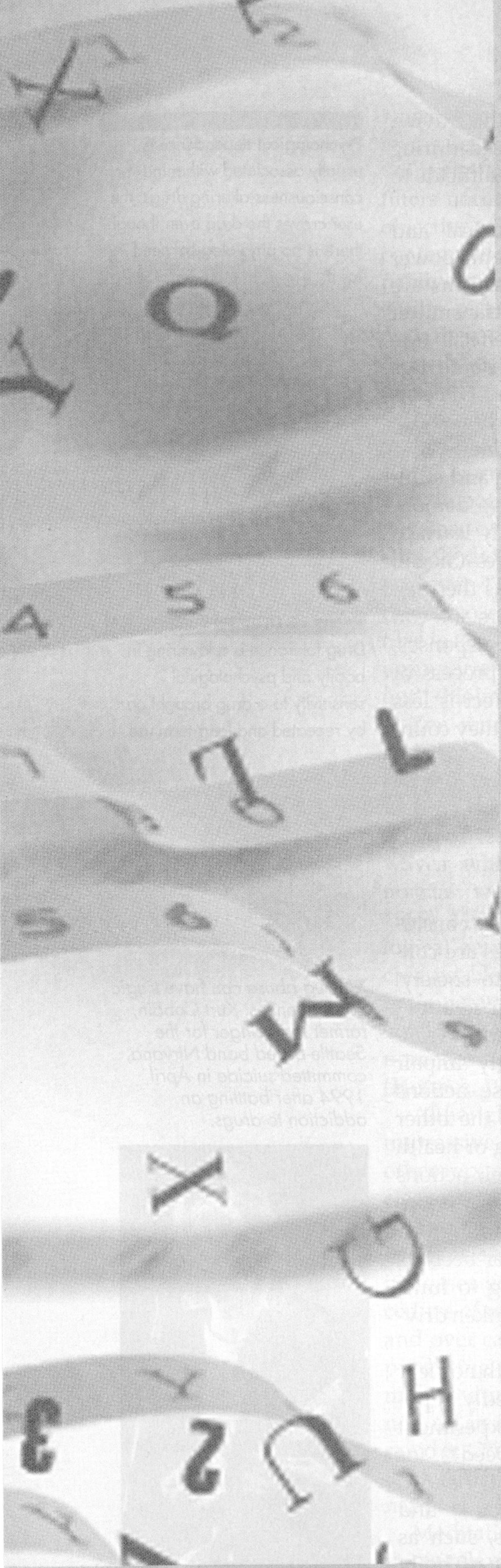

UNDERSTANDING HUMAN DIVERSITY

Comparing Drug Use among Black and White High School Students

Which high school senior in the United States is more likely to use a mind-altering drug: Daryl, who is white, or Cliff, who is black? If you answered Cliff, you are wrong. Despite racial stereotypes about drug-ridden black youth, a recent national survey of 15,400 high school seniors finds drug use to be higher among white high school students (Johnston, O'Malley, & Bachman, 1996). With the exception of alcohol, most high school students do not use mind-altering drugs. But compared to black seniors, white seniors (both girls and boys) consistently report a significantly higher use of marijuana, inhalants, hallucinogens, barbiturates, amphetamines, tranquilizers, opiates other than heroin, smokeless tobacco, and steroids.

White seniors are also much more likely to smoke cigarettes and drink alcohol, regardless of gender (Bachman et al., 1991). They are nearly four times more likely to smoke on a daily basis than black students. From 1994 to 1995, 24 percent of white students compared to 6 percent of black students smoked daily. White seniors were more than twice as likely to have been drunk in the past year than black students (58 percent versus 27 percent) and to have engaged in binge drinking (32 percent versus 15 percent).

What about after high school, between ages eighteen and twenty-five? The pattern continues. A national survey of households in 1992 (which included 28,832 interviews) found that whites in that age range were more likely than comparable blacks to report using illicit drugs (marijuana, inhalants, cocaine, hallucinogens, heroin, or nonmedical use of psychotherapeutic drugs) in the last year—29 percent versus 22 percent. The gap varied depending on the specific drug: whites and blacks were equally likely to report using crack, at 1.2 percent for each group. In contrast, whites were ten times more likely than blacks to report using hallucinogens, 6 percent versus .6 percent. The gap between races narrows with age as drug use declines, and reverses for people over thirty-five years of age. In 1992, 5.3 percent of whites over age thirty-five compared to 5.8 percent of blacks in that age range reported they had used mind-altering drugs in the past year (Substance Abuse and Mental Health Administration, 1993).

How can we explain these racial differences? One possibility is economic: drugs are expensive, and in general black youth have less money to spend on them than do white youth. Another possibility is moral: the greater religiosity of black youths may lead them to avoid drug use. Finally, another possibility is cognitive: beliefs about the harmfulness of drugs are (negatively) correlated with drug usage. Black seniors are more likely than white seniors to disapprove of drug use, and to report that their friends also disapprove (Bachman et al., 1991). Some rap artists have begun to incorporate anti-alcohol and anti-drug themes into their music, which may contribute to anti-alcohol and anti-drug norms among black teenagers (Herd, 1993).

Some black youth may live in communities having a high rate of drug use among adults with drug-related problems, which may lead black teenagers to see the harmful effects of drugs on a more regular basis than their white peers. So personal contact with drug abusers may have preventative effects (Johnston, O'Malley, & Bachman, 1996). Can you think of other explanations? Could white youth be more likely to tell the truth to researchers than black youth? Probably not, because the reporting gap varies widely, depending on the drug that is asked about. Missing data also raises questions. If students use drugs and are absent or have dropped out of school, they won't be included in the study, and black students have historically had higher drop-out rates than white students. But drop-out rates of blacks and whites have recently become similar, while the gap between whites and blacks in their use of mind-altering substances continues to be substantial (Bachman et al., 1991). Household surveys, which would include data on youth who drop out of school, also report higher annual rates of illicit drug use among whites aged twelve to seventeen compared to blacks in that age range (Substance Abuse and Mental Health Administration, 1993).

More than one influence may be operating, and more research is needed to understand what is going on. Meanwhile, knowing that black youth are not more likely to use drugs than white youth is a step toward breaking down damaging stereotypes.

Table 9-3 Effects of Selected Psychoactive Drugs

	Toxic Effects	Risk of Addiction	Withdrawal Effects
Alcohol	Slurred speech Aggressiveness Drowsiness	High	Craving DTs Anger Anxiety Depression
Nicotine	Increased alertness Feelings of calmness	High	Craving Agitation Depression
Cocaine	Increased alertness Excitement Insomnia	Possible	Apathy Irritability Depression
Amphetamines	Increased alertness Excitement Insomnia	Low	Apathy Irritability Depression
Heroin	Euphoria Depression	High	Irritability Tremors Panic Cramping
Morphine	Euphoria Drowsiness Nausea	High	Irritability Tremors Panic Cramping
Barbiturates	Slurred speech Disorientation	Moderate-High	Anxiety Insomnia Tremors Delirium
LSD	Illusions Hallucinations Distorted perception	Unknown	Unknown
Marijuana	Euphoria Reduced inhibitions Increased appetite	Low-Moderate	Insomnia Hyperactive Decreased appetite

amphetamines, barbiturates, cocaine, nicotine, and "hard" narcotics like morphine, opium, and heroin are abused. Moreover, impurities frequently found in black market psychedelics (such as LSD and mescaline) are at least as dangerous as the effects of these drugs themselves. Table 9-3 summarizes the toxic effects, relative risk of addiction, and withdrawal effects of the major psychoactive drugs.

Alcohol

Alcohol, whether it is wine, beer, or distilled liquor, is widely used around the world. Records of alcohol use go back to civilization's beginnings. Within the United States, there are large differences in alcohol use by gender, ethnicity, religion, and region. Males are more likely to use alcohol than females (Lieber, 1997), a gender

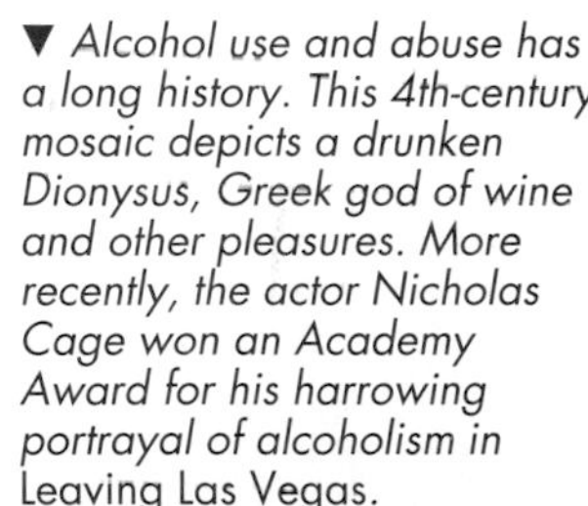

▼ *Alcohol use and abuse has a long history. This 4th-century mosaic depicts a drunken Dionysus, Greek god of wine and other pleasures. More recently, the actor Nicholas Cage won an Academy Award for his harrowing portrayal of alcoholism in* Leaving Las Vegas.

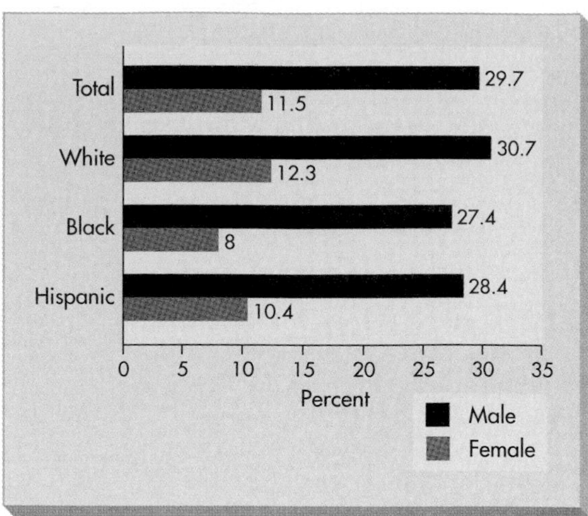

9-5 Who Uses Alcohol?

The figure shows the percent of alcohol use once a week or more by whites, blacks, and Hispanics. Women are less likely to use alcohol than men, be they white, black, or Hispanic. (Source: National Household Survey on Drug Use, 1992)

gap that widens with age and holds for whites, blacks, and Hispanics (see Figure 9-5). Catholics, Reform Jews, and liberal Protestants all use alcohol in fairly high proportions (Kaplan & Sadock, 1991). Europeans, particularly the French, consume alcohol at high rates. Approximately 30 percent of the French have impaired health from alcohol, and about 15 percent are alcoholics (Holden, 1987). Alcohol is widely and publicly used in some nations and cultures, such as Russia, but hardly used at all in others, like China. Attitudes toward alcohol in various cultures have ranged from total rejection, to indifference, to acceptance, to glorification. For some religions (for example, the Mormon and Muslim religions) drinking alcohol is forbidden, while for others (for example, Catholicism) alcoholic beverages have religious significance.

After producing an initial high, alcohol acts as a physiological depressant (which means that it reduces central nervous system activity) for most people (Bushman, 1993). Intoxication is correlated with ***blood alcohol level***, that is, with alcohol's concentration in the blood (see Table 9-4). With low blood alcohol levels, consciousness functions fairly normally. There is no "altered state." As the level rises to 0.10 percent (the legal cutoff for intoxication in many states) or higher, people enter a distinctly non-normal state, commonly known as "being drunk." Overall, less alcohol is needed to produce a given blood alcohol level in women compared to men, independent of body size, although individual men and women vary as to how much alcohol produces a certain blood alcohol level.

Table 9-4 Effects of Alcohol Intoxication

Alcohol Concentration in Blood	Experiential and Behavioral Effects	Approximate Amounts of Common Beverages*
0.03%	No obvious behavioral effects.	1 cocktail or 5.5 ounces wine or 2 bottles beer
0.06%	Relaxation, warmth, feeling "high," some impairment of motor acts that require a high degree of skill.	2 cocktails or 11 ounces wine or 4 bottles beer
0.09%	Amplified emotions, lowering of inhibitions.	3 cocktails or 1 pint wine or 6 bottles beer
0.10 %	Legally defined as impaired driving in many states.	5 ounces whiskey
0.12%	Impairment of fine motor coordination, some unsteadiness in walking or standing. Feelings of social and personal power.	4 cocktails or 22 ounces wine or 8 bottles beer
0.15%	Intoxication noticeable to observers: clumsiness, unsteadiness in walking. Reduction of anxiety, fears. Impairment of mental functioning. Feelings of personal power. State-dependent memory.	5 cocktails or 28 ounces wine or 10 bottles beer
0.30%	Stupor likely.	1 pint whiskey
0.50%	Death likely.	more than 1 quart whiskey

*The alcohol concentrations in the blood for the shown quantities of beverages are based on 150 pounds of body weight. Concentrations would be higher for the same amount of beverage consumed by a lighter person, and lower for the same amount of beverage consumed by a heavier person. A cocktail is specified as containing 1.5 ounces of 100 proof distilled liquor (whiskey and the like). Wine refers to ordinary table wine (approximately 13 percent alcohol). Beer refers to 12-ounce bottles at 3.2 percent alcohol.

On average, if a 150-pound female and a 150-pound male each have four glasses of wine, the woman will be more intoxicated because she will have a higher blood alcohol level.

At low blood alcohol levels, pleasant feelings, such as reduced anxiety, dominate perception, often with a slight increase in sensory, especially auditory, acuity. At higher blood alcohol levels, however, sensory impairment kicks in. Temperature and pain sensitivity are dulled—which is why in the past, before modern anesthetics were developed, surgeons gave alcohol to patients during operations. The ability to read or perform other fine visual discriminations is reduced. At very high levels, an intoxicated person begins to see double. Nausea and vomiting may occur, with longer-term residual effects, called a hangover, the following day.

Even low levels of alcohol affect the brain's frontal lobes, leading to reduced self-awareness and impaired judgment, reasoning, and general cognition. People under the influence of alcohol believe they are more competent than normal. You may have experienced how difficult it is to convince a drunken friend not to drive. With prefrontal lobes no longer fully in control of behavior, emotions begin to take over. The lowering of inhibitions that accompanies drinking has often been cited as a plus for successful parties—people feel sociable and interact more freely. But there is a delicate balance here, because the lowering of inhibitions may also lead to more aggressive behavior as well (Bushman, 1993).

Alcohol use in the United States has high social and economic costs. There are an estimated 13 million alcoholics and alcohol abusers in the United States (Kaplan & Sadock, 1991). Approximately 15 percent of national health costs are for treatment of alcoholism (Holden, 1987). An estimated $100 billion is lost each year from accidents, crime, treatment, and loss of productivity related to alcohol use (Steele & Josephs 1990). According to the National Safety Council, about 44 percent of all deaths in traffic accidents during 1993 involved someone (a driver or pedestrian) who had been drinking alcohol (Famighetti, 1996). Moreover, the leading cause of mental retardation in Western countries is alcohol use by pregnant women (Abel & Sokol, 1986).

There are many myths about alcohol, most regarding its effects on sexual behavior, which vary across culture and over time and which can have powerful effects on behavior. For example, many people in the United States believe that alcohol leads to enhanced sexual prowess, when in fact it has been shown that alcohol decreases both penile and vaginal responses to erotic stimuli (Buddell & Wilson, 1976; Wilson & Lawson, 1976a). U.S. males and females report feeling more sexually aroused when they believe they have consumed alcohol than when they believe they have consumed tonic water (whether or not they in fact have consumed alcohol) (Wilson & Lawson, 1976a, 1976b). In colonial America, when alcohol was at least as widely consumed as it is today, none of these beliefs was evident (Levine, 1983). Thus, beliefs about the effects of alcohol can have a profound impact on the behavior that occurs under its influence (Hull & Bond, 1986).

◀ *Alcohol plays a central role in many religious ceremonies. At St. Peter's in Rome, a canonization ceremony for new saints is in progress.*

Gender differences in psychological responses to alcohol seem to be related to power and powerlessness (see Chapter 4). Males associate alcohol use with power fantasies. At low intoxication levels, male fantasies tend to involve "socialized power" (for example, the ability to save the world). At higher levels, they involve purely personal power, leading to much of the aggressiveness observed in drunken males (Ito, Miller, & Pollack, 1996). For women, low levels of alcohol decrease, rather than increase, fantasies related to personal power. Alcohol's relationship to power needs may vary with the stage of alcohol abuse, however. For example, low levels of alcohol use by women may reflect attempts to compensate for feelings of inadequacy and powerlessness, while high levels of alcohol use by women may reflect an attempt to reduce high needs for personal power (Wilsnack, 1995).

THINKING CRITICALLY

Alcoholism seems to run in families. Does that mean that alcoholism is a genetic disease?

The answer is: yes and no. There are genetic aspects to alcoholism. In fact, a positive family history is one of the most consistent and robust predictors of the risk of alcoholism. Children of alcoholic adults are four to five times as likely to develop alcohol abuse sometime during their lifetimes than are children of nonalcoholics (McGue, 1993). The likelihood of identical twins both being alcohol abusers may be as high as 75 percent and of fraternal twins, 55 percent (McGue, Pickens, & Svikis, 1992). A few years ago, researchers discovered that a specific anomaly of the genes is correlated with alcoholism (Blum et al., 1990); some people argued that the discovery of an "alcoholism gene" was just around the corner. But while a genetic connection to alcoholism exists, there is more to the story. First, there is no evidence that genes directly cause any behavior. The data reported in these and other studies of the behavior genetics of alcohol use are strictly correlational and do not identify a cause for alcoholism. Second, if identical twins both have the same genes, how is it that one can be alcoholic and the other not? Third, environmental circumstances are direct and powerful causes of alcoholism. Fourth, alcoholism takes different forms in different people. A family resemblance for any kind of behavior, including alcohol abuse, can result from a shared environment, from shared genes, or from both. Alcoholism is a complex and highly variable phenotypic behavior of immense societal significance. To attribute it solely to a gene trivializes the problem by confusing phenotype with genotype. Both genetic and environmental factors are involved.

The effects of alcohol on anxiety and tension depend on the characteristics of the situation as well as on the person. In one experiment, two comparable groups of people were given vodka and tonic until their blood alcohol level was .08 percent. Both groups were told that in fifteen minutes they would have to make a speech on "what I dislike about my body and physical appearance" to an audience of graduate students (this was considered a stressor). The difference between the groups was *when* they were given that instruction. If they were told about having to give a speech *after* drinking the alcohol, alcohol reduced their anxiety. But if they were told about the speech *before* drinking the alcohol, drinking *increased* anxiety (Sayette & Wilson, 1991).

Some people try to cope with the problems of life by the excessive use of alcohol. But alcohol use can become self-sustaining and addictive. At some point, this kind of abuse is likely to become intolerable to the person's relatives, friends, or neighbors, and steps will be taken to change the situation. Generally, these steps will involve abstinence. Depending on how long the heavy drinking has gone on and how much alcohol has been consumed, a likely consequence of abstinence is a syndrome of very unpleasant withdrawal symptoms, which include hallucinations, vomiting, and uncontrolled trembling and muscle spasms, collectively known as ***delirium tremens*** (the DTs). These symptoms will persist for several days and are often replaced by an intense desire to drink again. The alcohol abuser needs considerable social support, especially during this withdrawal period, if he or she is to resist the strong desire to drink, a craving that probably never completely disappears.

The condition called alcoholism is often attributed to genetics. It is true that alcoholism does tend to appear in certain families. But to say that alcoholism is genetic and leave it at that is too easy and offers little comfort or therapy to the alcohol abuser. Moreover, individuals with no alcoholic relatives can and have become alcohol abusers. There is no single form of alcoholism, and there is no single cause (Finn et al., 1997). Genetic factors might be a part of the story. But psychological processes are also involved. Many people learn to drink, finding the anxiety-reducing effects of alcohol strongly reinforcing. Treatment of alcoholism must include a variety of therapeutic approaches, some of which focus on retraining and changing motivation.

Marijuana

Except for a brief period of prohibition in the early part of this century, alcoholic beverages have always been widely sold in the United States. Indeed, alcohol is the only nonprescribed psychoactive drug commonly in use in North America and Western Europe today. Many groups and politicians have argued that marijuana should be treated legally in the same way as alcohol is. Its side effects seem to be no worse, and it might have greater medicinal value, as in the treatment of glaucoma, stress, and depression. But there is also considerable opposition to the legalization of marijuana. Opposition is particularly strong among those who believe that marijuana has neurological effects that are similar to those of more potent and dangerous drugs and that its use might prime the brain to be more receptive to the use of stronger drugs.

The most commonly used form of marijuana comes from the flowering tops or leaves of the Indian hemp plant, *cannabis sativa*. Its major active ingredient is tetrahydrocannabinol (THC). Marijuana has been used as an intoxicant for thousands of years, and it is even mentioned in the Bible (as are beer and wine). It did not become widely used in the United States, however, until the twentieth century.

Apart from the quality and quantity of the drug ingested, marijuana's particular effects on consciousness are also determined by contextual and psychological variables (Nahas & Latour, 1993). These include the physical setting and the user's personality, expectations, mood, desires, and health (see Table 9-5). Marijuana can produce a *reverse tolerance effect* in some users, with *decreasing* dosages over time producing similar effects to those produced by larger doses for other users. But this may simply reflect increased skill in inhalation and learning how to perceive the drug's effects (Leccese, 1991).

Table 9-5 Variables Influencing a Drug Experience

	Variables	Pleasurable Experience Likely	Negative Experience Likely
Drug	Quality	Pure, known	Unknown drug or unknown degree of (harmful) adulterants
	Quantity	Known accurately, adjusted to individual's desire	Unknown, beyond individual's control
Long-term factors	Culture	Acceptance, belief in benefits	Rejection, belief in detrimental effects
	Personality	Stable, open, secure	Unstable, rigid, neurotic, or psychotic
	Physiology	Healthy	Specific adverse vulnerability to drug
	Learned drug skills	Wide experience gained under supportive conditions	Little or no experience, no preparation; unpleasant past experience
Immediate-user factors	Mood	Happy, calm, relaxed, or euphoric	Depressed, overexcited, repressing significant emotions
	Expectations	Pleasure, insight, known factors and eventualities	Danger, harm, manipulation, unknown eventualities
	Desires	General pleasure, specific user-accepted goals	Aimlessness (repressed), desires to harm or degrade self for secondary gains
Environmental situation	Physical setting	Pleasant and aesthetically interesting by user's standards	Cold, impersonal, "medical," "psychiatric," "threatening"
	Social events	Friendly, nonmanipulative interactions overall	Depersonalization or manipulation of user, hostility overall
	Formal instructions	Clear, understandable, creating trust and purpose	Ambiguous, deliberate lies, creation of mistrust
	Implicit demands	Congruent with explicit communications, supportive	Contradict explicit communications and/or reinforce other negative variables

Persons intoxicated with marijuana generally feel enhanced perception and a closer connection to reality. They may perceive new qualities in sound, taste, and touch, enjoy eating more, think that they understand words of songs better, experience distortions in the passage of time, find the sense of touch more sensual, find new and pleasurable qualities in sexual orgasm, and see patterns in visual material that are ordinarily ambiguous. Users frequently notice new internal bodily sensations and are usually pleased by these interesting sensory changes. We have no evidence to date that sensory thresholds are actually lowered psychophysically, however. Rather, these effects may be primarily a matter of how incoming stimuli are processed. Nonetheless, marijuana users typically report *less* cognitive processing—they feel in touch with the raw sensory data rather than an abstract representation of it (Tart, 1975).

A person trying marijuana for the first time may feel nothing, or find the experience stressful and unpleasant. About 5 to 10 percent of first-time users have a bad reaction. Experienced users report that both pleasant and unpleasant emotions are considerably amplified. Even experienced users occasionally have bad reactions, particularly when using the drug to escape from unpleasant circumstances.

Cognitive processes can change radically during marijuana intoxication. Users may feel that their thoughts are more intuitive and less bound by logic or science. Characteristic experiences include feeling more childlike and open to experience, finding difficulty reading, and giving little thought to the future.

THINKING CRITICALLY

Some researchers report that marijuana users are apathetic and ineffective. They tend to be people who typically are unable to carry out long-term plans, to tolerate frustration, to sustain their concentration, or to follow routines (Grinspoon & Bakalar, 1993). Does this mean that marijuana is a dangerous drug?

Not necessarily. These findings are based on correlations between behavioral characteristics and amount of marijuana use. Remember, correlation is not causation. It may be that people predisposed toward these factors are more likely to select and use marijuana (or other drugs).

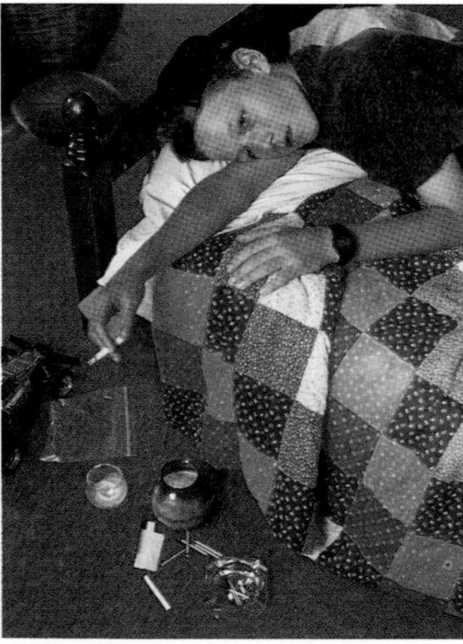

▶ *Today, about 15 million Americans (about 6 percent of the population) use marijuana on a regular basis. Moreover, experimentation with marijuana seems to be on the increase once again among teenagers.*

Marijuana intoxication produces both state-dependent memory effects (see Chapter 7), like the failure to remember certain events that happened while you were high until you get high again, and occasional memory deficits. Short-term memory or attention span can be so reduced that the user forgets what he or she was saying at the start of a conversation. At very high intoxication levels, a user might forget even the beginning of a sentence. This shortened memory span probably explains why marijuana use significantly impairs performance on tasks that require a series of steps.

Marijuana is associated with hunger, thirst, mild muscular weakness (including drooping of eyelids), and dilation of blood vessels in the eyes. Negative effects of marijuana include damage to cardiovascular and respiratory systems, primarily because of inhaling smoke into the lungs (Wu, Tashkin, Djahed, & Rose, 1988). Marijuana smokers are more likely than nonsmokers to develop a chronic cough, asthma, and bronchitis (Abramson, 1974). Although for moderate marijuana users there are not generally withdrawal symptoms when marijuana use is terminated, people who have used heavy doses of marijuana continuously over a prolonged period of time often report nausea, diarrhea, chills, restlessness, insomnia, and irritability with disuse (Jones & Benowitz, 1976).

Marijuana intoxication makes experienced users feel relaxed and disinclined to move about. If they do move about, though, they usually perceive themselves as well-coordinated. Most motor tasks are not affected, although the probability of some impairment increases with complexity of the skill required. Inexperienced users, in contrast, sometimes have great difficulty in performing even the simplest motor tasks (Tart, 1975).

About 60 million Americans admit to having tried marijuana, and about 15 million Americans are regular users. A 1995 study by the U.S. Department of Health and Human Services found wide variation in use by region, from a high of 42 percent users in the Western states, to a low of 29 percent in the North Central states. Hispanics had lower rates (26 percent) than either blacks (31 percent) or whites (34 percent), who did not differ significantly from each other. The study also found that 11 percent of twelve- to seventeen-year-olds and 48 percent of eighteen- to twenty-five-year-olds had used marijuana at least once. Figure 9-6 compares alcohol, marijuana, cigarette, and other illicit drug use among high school seniors. As you can see, marijuana use and cigarette smoking have been on the upswing since 1990, after dropping systematically over the preceding ten years (Warner, 1995; Johnston, O'Malley, & Bachman, 1996).

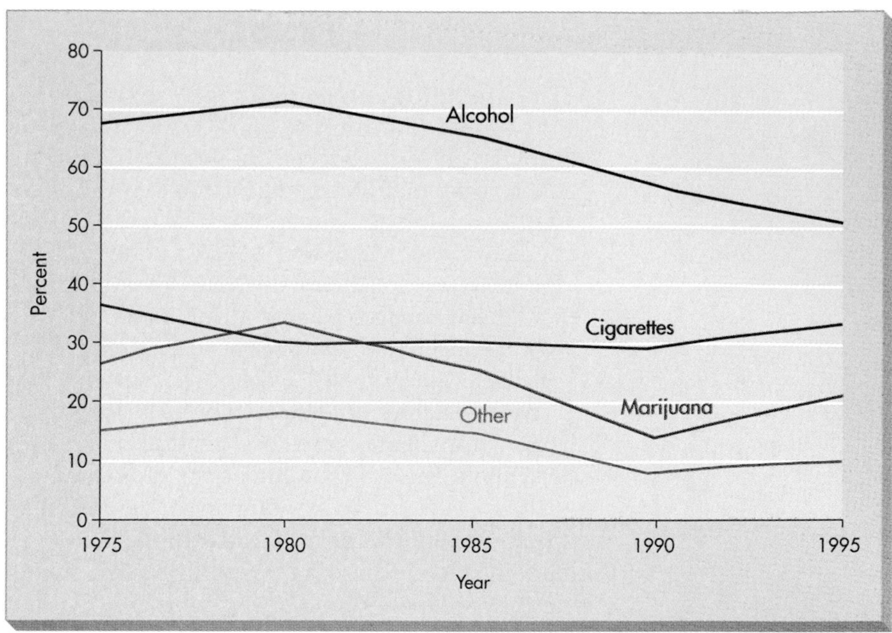

9-6 Drug Use in High School Seniors

The figure shows trends in thirty-day drug use prevalence by high school seniors from 1975 to 1995. Alcohol consumption has declined since 1990, but cigarette and marijuana smoking have increased. (Source: Johnston, O'Malley, & Bachman, 1996)

Cocaine and Amphetamines

Cocaine and amphetamines stimulate the central nervous system, putting the body into a hyperenergized state. Both block the reuptake of dopamine into nerve cells. (Amphetamines also directly cause dopamine's release from nerve cells.) Under the influence of these drugs, people become talkative and euphoric. They report terrific energy and alertness that allows them to continue working long after they would normally be exhausted. They also report that cocaine heightens their creativity and allows them to produce higher-quality work. Such beliefs probably contribute to the use of cocaine by professional entertainers and athletes.

Cocaine is not considered physiologically addicting because people do not experience the withdrawal symptoms generally associated with stopping alcohol or other drug use. But in the extreme, cocaine can cause serious physical problems, including respiratory and cardiac collapse resulting in death, as occurred to the young actor River Phoenix. Furthermore, regular and prolonged use of cocaine and amphetamines can induce psychotic behavior, including hallucinations, delusions of persecution, compulsions, and mood disturbances. Even qualified mental health professionals have difficulty distinguishing between a cocaine or amphetamine abuser and a true paranoid schizophrenic. Studies with rats suggest that these drugs produce changes in the brain that increase the likelihood that psychotic symptoms will reoccur with later drug use—even if use occurs months or years later (Post, 1975).

Cocaine is one of the most *psychologically* addictive drugs known. Users can become so dependent that they ignore other physical needs to get and use it. "Crack" cocaine is a particularly potent form. Because it is smoked, it enters the bloodstream through the lungs, reaching the brain within seconds. Remember, because an addiction is labeled "psychological" does not imply it is any less compelling than a "physiological" addiction. People will lie, cheat, steal, and kill, abandon infants, and prostitute themselves and their children in order to obtain the drug. *It is extremely addictive.*

Nicotine

The use of tobacco is under intense scrutiny in the United States today, mainly because of its proven adverse effects on health. It appears likely that manufacturers of tobacco products will agree in the near future to a financial settlement with the federal and/or state governments to pay for the medical care of individuals who used tobacco during a time when tobacco companies failed to disclose their knowledge of these effects and who now suffer from tobacco-related illnesses, such as lung cancer and emphysema. Since the general public has become aware of the dangers of prolonged tobacco use, cigarette smoking in this country has declined. But the public is fickle about smoking and in recent years cigar smoking among adults and cigarette smoking among teenagers has actually increased (Johnston, O'Malley, & Bachman, 1996).

Given the health hazards, why do some reasonably well-educated people use tobacco products? There are a variety of reasons, mostly social (for example, peer pressure) or psychological (for example, identification with Joe Camel and other "cool" characters), that contribute to getting a start. Most people begin smoking in adolescence, when such influences are particularly hard to resist. In addition, nicotine, the active ingredient in tobacco, has some pleasant effects. It is first absorbed into the blood through the lungs as tobacco smoke is inhaled. Via the circulation of blood, nicotine impacts the central and the autonomic nervous system within seven seconds after inhaling. The physiological consequences include increased heart rate and a rise in blood pressure, which give the feeling of arousal. In the brain, nicotine triggers the release of endorphins, which have a natural tranquilizing effect. Nicotine is generally classified as a stimulant. When you are feeling tired, nicotine can produce a sense of arousal and well-being. But, when you are over-aroused or excited, nicotine can have a calming or relaxing effect. So, cigarette smoking can be extremely reinforcing. The initial effects are an example of positive reinforcement. But later, after addiction develops, positive reinforcement effects are augmented by negative reinforcement. That is, the craving for nicotine is terminated only by the intake of nicotine. Nicotine is addictive, in both the physical and psychological sense. It is hard to quit. Just about everyone who smokes has tried to stop (Niemi, Mueller, & Smith, 1989). The take-home message is: don't start.

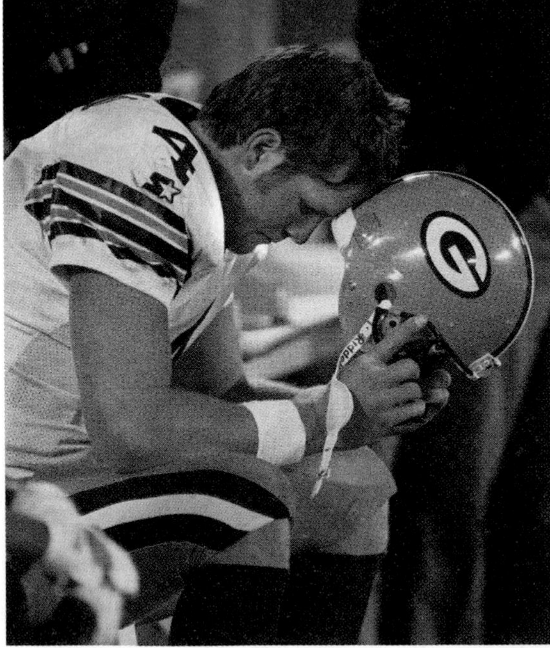

► *Many people with drug abuse problems do not use illegal drugs. The Green Bay Packers quarterback, Brett Favre, voluntarily entered the NFL's substance abuse program because of an addition to prescription painkillers.*

Prescription Drugs

As nicotine use illustrates, drugs don't have to be illegal to have harmful effects or to be abused. Prescription drugs, such as tranquilizers (Valium or Xanax, for example), are also often used excessively for no medical reason. Physicians who are not psychiatrists, and who are therefore not trained in the treatment of mental disorders, commonly prescribe psychotropic drugs developed to help patients with mental disorders to relax. Approximately two-thirds of all prescriptions for psychotropic drugs in the United States are written for women, and women are more likely to abuse these drugs than are men (Cypress, 1980). In 1990, the Food and Drug Administration (FDA) estimated that 5 billion doses of tranquilizers are prescribed annually by U.S. physicians. Sleeping medications, such as barbiturates, are also often abused, with more than 750 million sleeping pills consumed annually. Because of possible psychological dependence, both the American Medical Association and the FDA are on record against prescribing tranquilizers or sleeping pills for everyday life stress.

Pain

One use of drugs, prescribed or otherwise, is to reduce pain. Drugs that reduce physical pain are called ***analgesics***. But drugs are often also prescribed to counteract psychological pain resulting from depression, stress, and other conditions that we will discuss in Chapter 15. Most people are quite familiar with pain, and the pain business is big business: Americans spend about $100 billion a year to relieve minor aches and pains, consuming 20 million tons of aspirin for headaches alone (Taylor, 1995).

Experiencing Pain

The International Association for the Study of Pain, which consists of clinicians and researchers trying to understand this pervasive human experience, defines ***pain*** as "unpleasant sensory and emotional experience associated with actual or potential tissue damage" (Price, 1988). Pain occurs when a stimulus that threatens harm comes in contact with the body. First, pain causes alertness and reorients our attention. We immediately need to identify its source and determine its bodily consequences. These processes allow us to evade the source of pain or to defend ourselves and begin repairs. Second, at almost

THINKING CRITICALLY

You know from personal experience what pain feels like. You may have experienced an excruciating headache or the pain of a broken arm or leg. Back pain may leave you in agony, or a bad toothache may prevent you from concentrating on your studies. Most people have no trouble understanding what you mean when you talk about feeling pain. Does this mean that everyone experiences pain in more or less the same way?

The sensation of pain varies more widely than might be first apparent. Researchers at McGill University (Melzack, 1975) collected 102 unique and independent adjectives relating to pain from patients, doctors, and nurses. The adjectives fell into three major categories: *sensory* (pulsing, shooting, throbbing, piercing); *affective* (sickening, vicious, dreadful, terrifying); and *evaluative* (mild, annoying, excruciating, unbearable). The widely used McGill Pain Questionnaire uses these categories and adjectives to assist in diagnosing and selecting appropriate therapy for pain disorders.

Pain is an unpleasant sensation and emotional experience that signals actual or potential tissue damage.

▼ *People can be remarkably resistant to pain and even capable of great feats of strength while under extreme pain. During the 1996 Summer Olympics, the United States' Jackie Joyner-Kersee with an injured right hamstring (left-hand photograph) won the opening heat in the 100-meter hurdles. At right, a "razateur" thrills the crowd, leaping to escape the horns of a charging bull at the bullfight in St. Remy-de-Provence, France.*

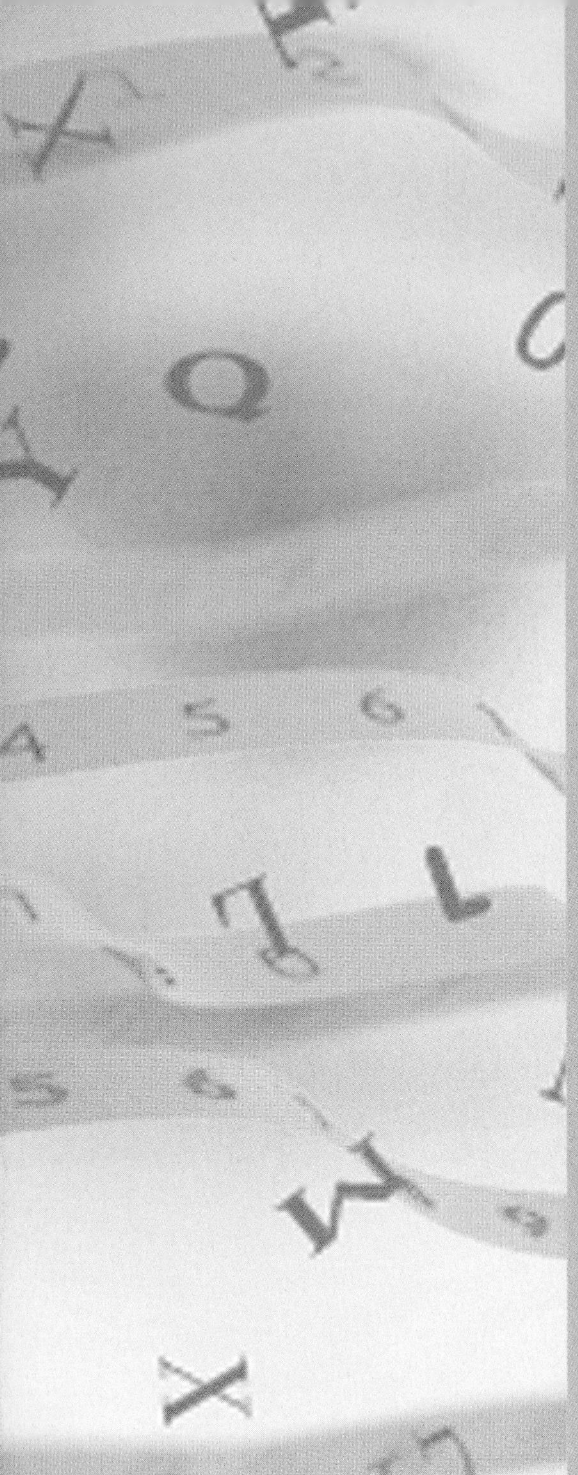

SEEKING SOLUTIONS

Reducing the Pain of Childbirth

Until recently, it was commonplace in our society to give pain-killing medication to mothers during childbirth. Today, physicians are more reluctant to administer such medication because of potential harmful effects on the baby. There has thus been a movement in the United States to promote "natural" childbirth. But because pain associated with the birth process is generally intense, what alternatives to medication during the birth process might be used? One widely accepted technique in the United States is the Lamaze method, after its originator Fernand Lamaze.

Because fear of the unknown causes muscles to tighten and pain to be exaggerated, Lamaze instructors teach expectant couples about the birth process and the sensations typically associated with labor's stages. In addition, instructors teach a type of consciousness restriction that shuts out physical sensations of pain. This segregation and control of pain is accomplished through meditative techniques. For example, women are encouraged to bring to class some object on which they can focus their attention. This object serves the same purpose as a mandala, and the woman practices using it to restrict the perception of stimuli impinging on her body.

In addition, a large part of the training in Lamaze classes is directed toward learning and practicing breathing techniques to be used during labor and delivery. These breathing techniques have at least two purposes. First, breathing patterns help regulate the level of carbon dioxide in the mother's blood to prevent hyperventilation. Second, by concentrating on regular rhythmic breathing patterns, the woman screens from consciousness the painful (Lamaze instructors say "uncomfortable") sensations resulting from physiological changes during the birth process. In this sense, Lamaze instruction operates much like meditation by restricting sensory input through a focus on a single, repetitive stimulus. These techniques can also be used to control pain in other situations as well.

◄ *A Lamaze instructor teaches an expectant couple about breathing techniques.*

every level of intensity, pain fills consciousness, blocking out other sensations. Pain signals significant threat. We must focus all awareness on the threat until it is neutralized. The full resources of our conscious mind are required to deal with pain. Third, pain requires evaluation. While we are identifying the source and consequences, we must also assess what happened, what is likely to happen, and what we should do. If the person remains conscious, then the evaluation process leads to planning and execution of remedial action. This response actually lessens the sense of pain by occupying some of our consciousness. Finally, pain has a general effect on the body, including tissue damage, heightened muscle tension, perspiration, nausea, and other autonomically controlled reactions (Novy, Nelson, Francis, & Turk, 1995).

How Pain Is Controlled

Pain is self-limiting. If it is intense enough, you lose consciousness—all sensations, including pain, cease. But loss of consciousness is not entirely adaptive. Harm can be severe enough to cause death.

Analgesic drugs are prescribed to ease or eliminate pain. Many drugs taken for reasons other than pain control, such as alcohol, have analgesic effects. Hypnosis and acupuncture have also been used medically to control pain (see Chapter 5).

How do pain controllers work? Several mechanisms might combine to lessen pain. Some chemicals desensitize nerve endings, causing numbness. Pain stimuli may trigger release of the body's own opiates, like endorphins, which appear to reduce sensitivity of higher brain centers to incoming pain information (Price, 1988). A final possibility for pain control lies in the fact that, to a degree, consciousness can be split or allocated among tasks, allowing independent mental operations to occur simultaneously. Thus, for example, in hypnosis, pain sensation apparently can be split off or *dissociated* from emotional or affective elements of consciousness. If our consciousness can be occupied with other thoughts, we will have fewer cognitive resources to give to pain. We can use cognitive control to divert incoming pain signals away from higher brain centers and thereby prevent them from reaching our consciousness. Such a mechanism might explain how individuals are able to tolerate great pain under hypnosis or when their lives are on the line (Hilgard, 1973). One example of this is the logger who found himself alone and pinned under a fallen tree and yet was able to free himself by amputating his own leg with a pocketknife.

Reflections and Observations

Changing consciousness changes everything psychological—perception, learning, cognition, emotion, motivation, and reactivity. Normal consciousness is defined by our ordinary, everyday awareness of ourselves and the world around us. Altered consciousness is a change induced by internal conditions such as the need for sleep or external influences such as hypnosis or drug ingestion. How consciousness changes depends, of course, on these mind-altering conditions. Changes during sleep, hypnosis, meditation, or drug use are different in significant ways. Some users claim that drugs can expand the mind, making perception and memory faster, clearer, and more efficient. The evidence is that these alterations are more illusory than real. Sleep, in contrast, is known to place constraints on perception and learning. Common among all the altered states is the fact that our awareness during these states is different from our normal awareness. Consciousness is most closely tied to the psychological processes known collectively as cognition—mental events and processes. But it is broadly involved in just about every aspect of behavior, including those that energize behavior and give it much of its qualitative character. These processes, which are known in psychology as motivation, the source of energy for behavior, and emotion, the pleasant or unpleasant feeling that accompanies behavior, are the topic of Chapter 10. We will have a chance to discuss further the influence of consciousness on behavior in that context.

Objectives Revisited

Consciousness is arguably the single most important concept in psychology. Historically, an explanation of consciousness was the first goal sought after by scientifically oriented psychologists. Consciousness appears in almost every chapter of this book, because it is simply not possible to talk about other psychological processes, like learning, motivation, personality, and the like, without referring to what we are conscious of. Despite all that, consciousness has

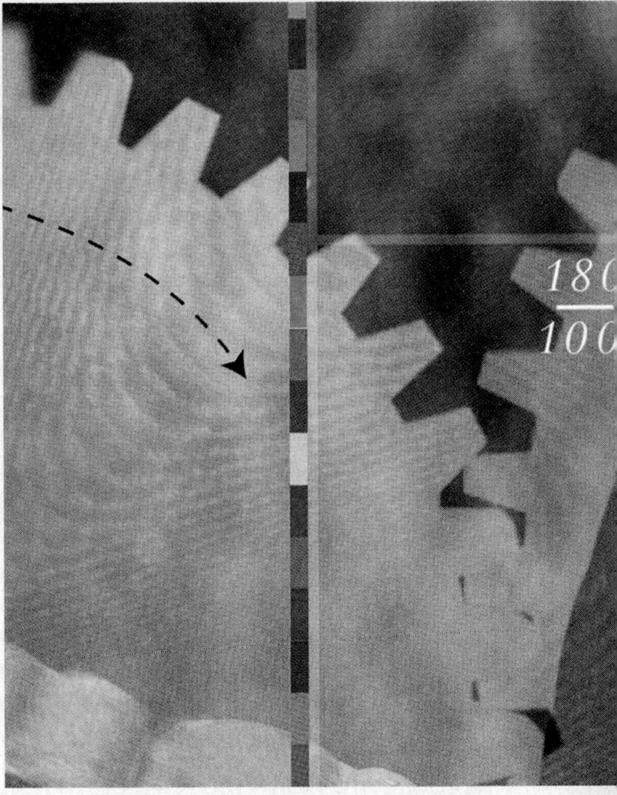

CHAPTER 10

Motivation and Emotion

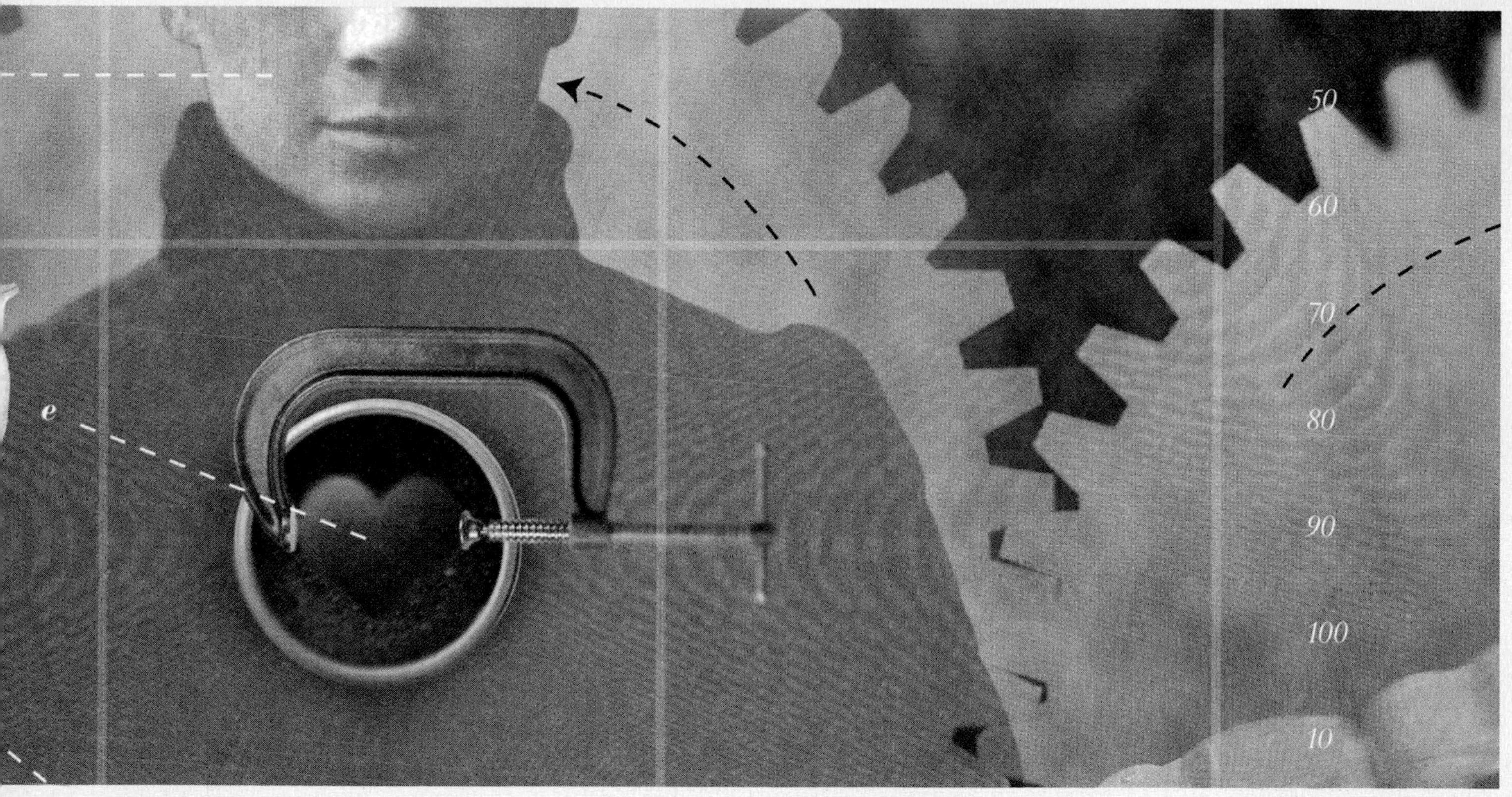

OBJECTIVES

After reading this chapter, you should be able to:

1. Define motivation, and discuss how the concepts of need, drive, incentive, arousal, and homeostasis are used to explain motivated behavior.
2. Discuss how biological and sociocultural factors influence the biologically based needs for food, drink, and sex.
3. Explain what is meant by a social motive, and distinguish among affiliation, approval, achievement, and power motivation.
4. Explain the relationship of goal setting and choices to behavior, and how inference and attribution affect the subjective utility of goal objects and behavioral outcomes.
5. Define emotion, compare and contrast various states of emotion, and explain how the emotions of anger and anxiety relate to behavior.

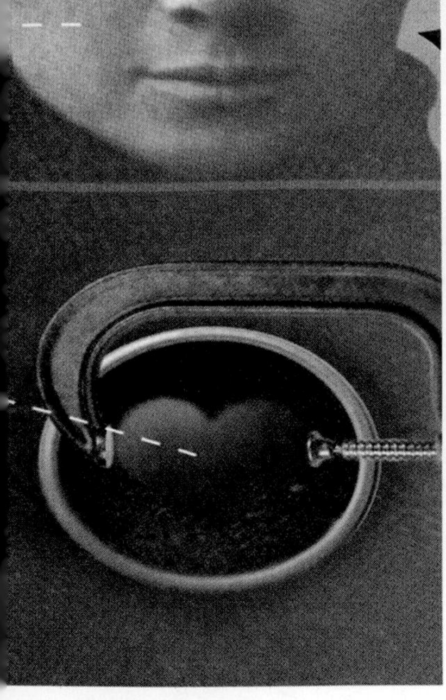

Tension mounted in the gymnastics arena at the 1996 Olympic games in Atlanta. The favored Russian women's team had faltered, and the U.S. women's team had the gold medal within its grasp. All that was needed was for Kerri Strug, the last American competitor, to score at least a 9.4 on the vault. On her first try, Strug fell on landing. Many people lost heart watching her noticeably limp as she returned to her starting mark. The crowd held its collective breath as she made her next approach, vaulted, and landed solidly—clinching the gold for her team. But her ankle injury was so painful that she had to hop on one foot as she saluted the crowd. Then she fell to her knees. Kerri Strug sprained her ankle so severely that she could not continue in the individual gymnastics competition. She saved the gold for her team, knowing she was surely endangering her own chances for an individual medal.

▲ *Olympian Kerri Strug grimaces after landing on her injured ankle. Her heroic performance at the 1996 Summer Olympics saved the gold medal for her team, but eliminated her from the individual competition. What motivated her to place the success of her team above her individual goals?*

How can we explain Strug's behavior? What makes people train hard, sacrifice their social lives, and strive for excellence at some special task? What makes people want to compete and to win? Why do some people endure great hardship over a long period of time to achieve excellence, while others will only work for quick and easy payoffs? What compels people to perform even at the risk of serious physical injury? Answering these questions goes to the heart of this chapter: What motivates people to act as they do?

Motivation and emotion are related concepts; both move us to action, but in different ways. Motivation occurs in response to underlying needs, energizing and directing our behavior toward goals that meet those needs. If our body needs nutrients, our behavior becomes goal-directed, and we seek food. Emotions are subjective states (internal feelings), such as happiness or anger, that also energize behavior. Emotions are more transitory and may not be goal-directed, however. Being happy may be energizing, but it doesn't necessarily stimulate us to seek a particular goal.

Some motivations are more closely related to basic biological needs such as hunger, thirst, and sex, while others reflect social and cultural factors, such as needs for approval and achievement. Many basic emotions such as anger and happiness and fear have been found to be universal, while some others such as the Japanese *oime* (the feeling of indebtedness) are culturally specific. Nonetheless, the expression of even basic emotions may vary, depending on context and culture. In this chapter, we will consider biological, psychological, and sociocultural factors that shape our motivations and emotions. These factors correspond to the three major perspectives on motivation: the biological, social-personality, and cognitive perspectives.

What Is Motivation?

Motivation refers to the processes that initiate, energize, and direct behavior (Coleman, 1994). Motivation explains *why* people behave as they do, in contrast to *how* they do it. It addresses the questions of why people in the same situation may behave quite differently, and why the same person may perform differently in different situations or at different times. For example, we all know the benefits of good health habits. Why do some people exercise regularly, while others do not? This difference is an inter-individual difference, a difference *between* people. But the same person who exercises regularly at one time may not do so at others. This difference is an intra-individual difference, a difference *within* a person from one time to another. Psychology seeks to understand variations in motivation across different individuals as well as within the same person.

When business leader Jorge de la Riva was a teenager, his father died, and his mother was left with very little money and only one week to pay the mortgage on their house. De la Riva found a job selling vacuum cleaners, and in one weekend knocked on so many doors that he was able to sell enough machines to pay the mortgage. How would you explain his behavior? How could you explain the difference between his behavior and the behavior of others in the same situation who might view their situation as hopeless?

This simple example demonstrates the four basic components of motivation: (1) a behaving organism (Jorge de la Riva) with a need; (2) goal-oriented behavior (searching the want ads in the newspaper, finding a job, knocking on doors, selling vacuum cleaners); (3) a goal object (earning money to pay the mortgage); and (4) attaining the goal (paying the mortgage). We can observe all these elements and use scientific methods to study them.

Need, Drive, and Incentive

Need, drive, and incentive are three central concepts that are used to explain motivated behavior. They work together to constitute a basic motivational cycle for behavior, as shown in Figure 10-1.

Need → Drive → Behavior → Incentive (goal) → Need reduction → Need

10-1 The Basic Motivational Cycle

A need is a state of deprivation or deficiency, for example, for food or for water, which leads to a drive to satisfy that need through behavior directed at a goal, or incentive, that will reduce the need.

A ***need*** is defined as a state created when an organism does not have or is deprived of an object or condition it requires. For example, all organisms need food and water periodically. Needs can be defined as biological, social, or cognitive. When blood sugar levels become too low, they must be replenished; this is a biological need. When you've just run a marathon on a 90-degree day, you have a biological need for water. When you go to dinner with a group of friends or go to a party to meet new people, you are fulfilling a social need to be with other people. When you decide to take a break from studying psychology to watch a comedy on TV, you may be fulfilling a cognitive need to vary your mental activity.

According to Abraham Maslow (1908–1970), each person has a ***hierarchy of needs***—some needs take precedence over others (Maslow, 1970). Maslow grouped various needs into five

Motivation and emotion are related concepts; both move us to action, but in different ways. Motivation occurs in response to underlying needs, energizing and directing our behavior toward goals that meet those needs. Emotions also have an energizing function, but they are more transitory than motives and are not necessarily goal-directed.

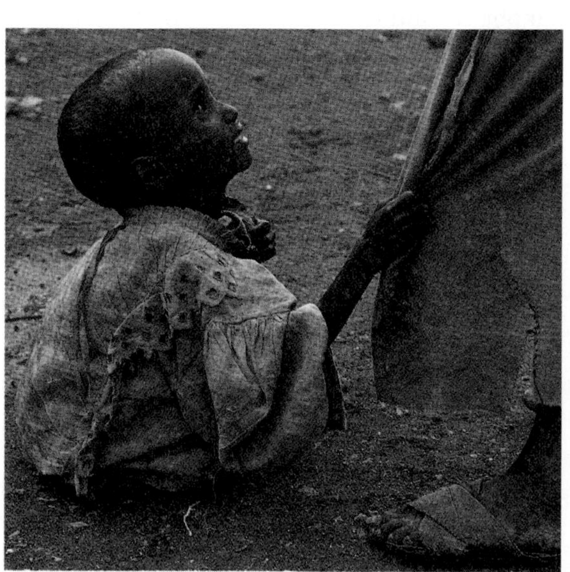

◀ *When people are starving, like the child in the photograph on the left, their motivation becomes purely biological—they need food. Only when basic needs are met can people focus on higher-order needs, such as freedom from political oppression, as these Bulgarian students show in the photo on the right.*

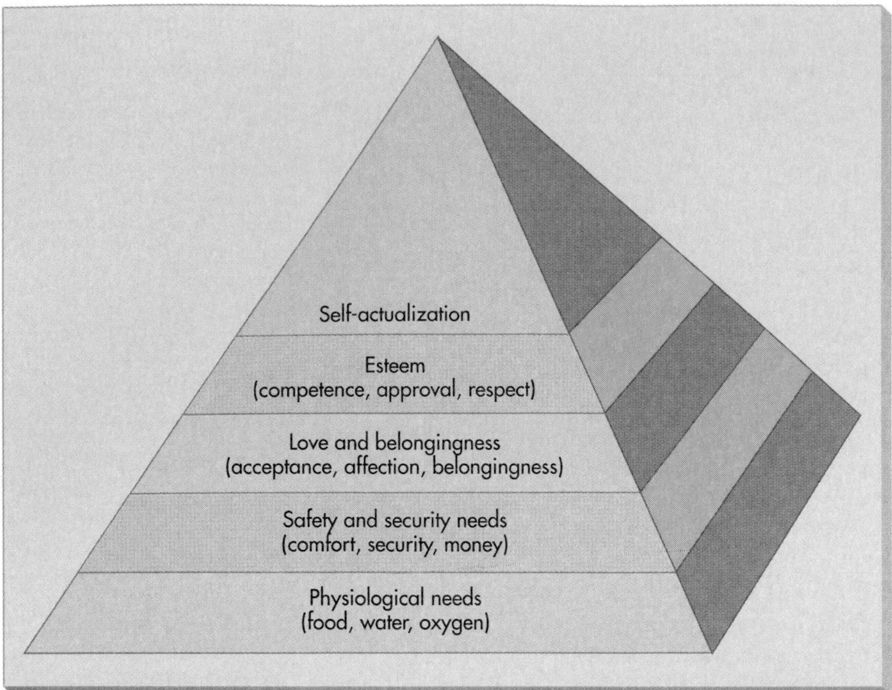

10-2 Maslow's Hierarchy of Needs

According to Maslow, lower-order needs, such as physiological, safety and security needs, must be satisfied before higher-order needs for love and belongingness, esteem, and finally for self-actualization (reaching one's full potential) can be met. (Source: Adapted from Maslow, 1970)

categories ranked by priority (see Figure 10-2). He contended that needs are satisfied in the order of priority within each person's hierarchy (Maslow, 1970). Basic biological needs generally take precedence over psychological needs. If two needs are incompatible, the more basic one is usually satisfied first. If you are hungry and feeling lonely, you will probably seek something to eat before going in search of companionship. Needs higher in the hierarchy emerge only as lower ones are satisfied. Our socially based needs for love, belongingness, or self-esteem come to motivate us only after we satisfy our security and physiological needs. If we fear for our safety or don't know where our next meal will come from, we will not be motivated by a need for self-esteem. Yet, sometimes psychological needs take precedence over biological needs: parents who are starving may give their food to their suffering children, or diabetic adolescents may not take needed insulin because they seek social approval for being thin and mistakenly believe that insulin will make them fat.

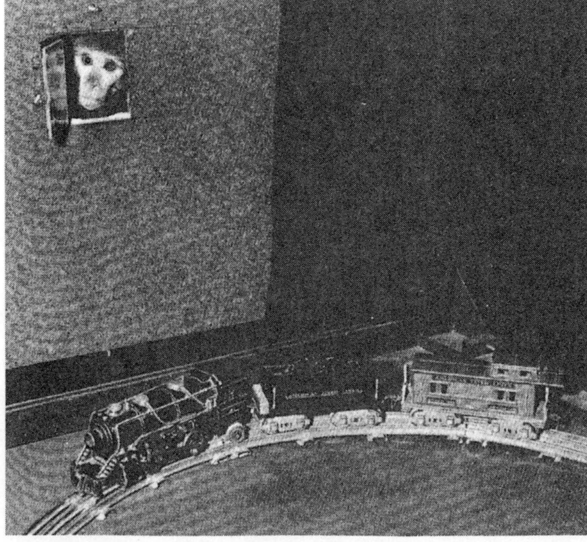

► *Studies showed that animals would learn and work for rewards that didn't reduce any known drive. So what motivated them to learn? One study demonstrated that monkeys would learn to operate a lever that opened a door just to see out into the laboratory or to see unfamiliar things like the toy train in the photograph.*

Drives are psychological states that arise from needs, providing a motivational push to fulfill those needs. If Alan skips dinner because he doesn't want to be late for a concert, a state of need for food will develop. As a result, he will experience a hunger drive, which will eventually energize him to seek food. Need level and drive level are closely related, but not identical. At very high need levels, such as when a person is literally starving, drive level drops off, and the motivational push to act declines—the individual becomes apathetic.

We have talked about drives in terms of fulfilling needs, and under the most common circumstances, both a need and a drive can be identified in motivated behavior, particularly when physiological needs are involved. However, there are also drives such as curiosity, which don't depend on deprivation and for which no apparent need exists (Berlyne 1960).

Can you think of something that attracts you and that you will work to obtain? It can be a tangible object, like a CD player or a hundred-dollar bill, or it can be an intangible event, such as winning a race or being selected to represent your group. The term ***incentive*** refers to external objects and events that exert a motivational pull on behavior. Incentives (gourmet food, concert tickets, a new car) pull from without, while drives (hunger, thirst, sex) push from within.

Homeostasis

The built-in physiological systems that have evolved for monitoring and regulating the satisfaction of primary needs (such as eating, drinking, and breathing) operate according to the principle of ***homeostasis***. Homeostasis refers to the body's tendency to maintain a constant internal environment even when the external environment changes. In other words,

the body attempts to maintain a state of equilibrium. The typical home heating system provides a good analogy for this process. The system has a thermostat to monitor temperature and maintain it at a constant level. If you set the thermostat at 70 degrees, your furnace will turn on when the temperature drops below that setting, and turn off when the temperature exceeds it.

Similarly, our body monitors levels of nutrients in the bloodstream. When they drop too low, a need is created. A drive follows, pushing us to find and consume food, which serves as an incentive. As we eat, our need declines if our "homeostat" is working. If we overeat, we feel stuffed and avoid food until our need for it returns, when the cycle begins again.

Arousal

Arousal is a level of physiological activation that accompanies a drive. Arousal includes bodily changes such as increased heart rate and blood pressure and respiration that prepare the organism for action. As deprivation and need increase, so does the body's support for goal-seeking behavior, at least up to a point. Drive satisfaction reduces the drive and the associated arousal. You might think that people work to satisfy needs as they arise, thus keeping their level of arousal low or nonexistent. However, we often behave in precisely the opposite manner—we seek stimulation to *increase* our arousal level. In fact, when deprived of stimulation, we often experience discomfort and feel bored, edgy, and unproductive. Indeed, we seem to have an inborn drive to explore and manipulate objects and seek variation in stimulation (Harlow, 1950).

A classic experiment demonstrates the negative effect of sensory deprivation. Undergraduate students were paid up to $25 a day (considered a large sum of money forty years ago) to remain in a room with minimum sensory stimulation for as long as they could stand it (Bexton, Heron, & Scott, 1954). The participants had adequate food, water, oxygen, heat, and toilet facilities, but almost no sensory input (no light or sound). After a short stay in this situation, some students reported bizarre experiences, including hallucinations. No student remained in the room very long, despite receiving high pay for doing absolutely nothing. Does this finding help you to understand why solitary confinement is considered to be the ultimate in prison punishment?

The dramatic findings from this early study led to further investigations exploring the limits of sensory deprivation. Researchers found that, for most people, *short* periods of isolation can actually reduce stress and cause people to become more receptive to the influence of others (Suedfeld & Coren, 1989). Thus, despite its apparent detrimental effects over the long term, sensory restriction can have beneficial therapeutic effects in the short term. Indeed, other cultures hold that solitude, meditation, and con-

THINKING CRITICALLY

Think back to the concept of reinforcement (described in Chapter 6). What characteristics does it share with the concept of incentive?

Incentive and reinforcement both increase the probability of behavior—both exert a motivational pull on behavior. Reinforcement comes out of the learning theory tradition in psychology and is primarily associated with operant conditioning. Incentive is a somewhat more general term used by motivation theory.

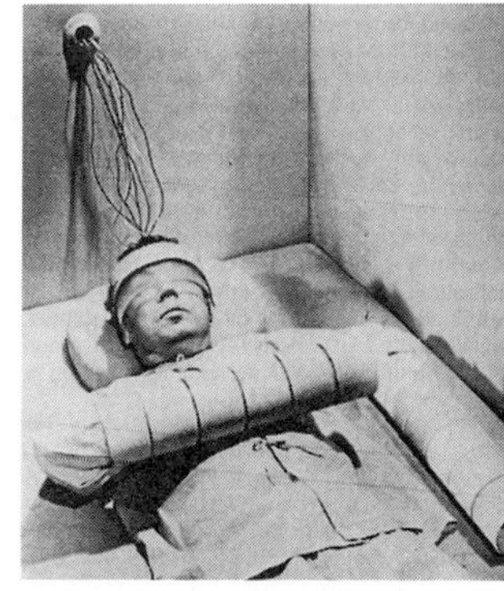

▲ *The experience of sensory stimulation is essential to our well being. In a series of experiments at McGill University, students were paid to stay in a room in which stimulation was reduced to a bare minimum. They wore eyeshades, which reduced vision to a dim haze, and arm casts that prevented feeling in their hands. The only noise in the room was the hum of a fan. Not many could stay in the experiment for more than two days, and all found the prolonged sensory deprivation unpleasant.*

Arousal is a level of physiological activation that accompanies a drive and supports goal-seeking behavior. It is increased by deprivation, at least up to a point.

templation have healing effects. For example, restricting stimulation is a component of the "quiet therapies" of Japan (Reynolds, 1982).

▲ *Some people seek minimal arousal levels.*

Optimal Level of Arousal

Arousal is a crucial component of motivation. People seek an ***optimal level of arousal***. In keeping with the principle of homeostasis, deprivation of stimulation causes individuals to try to restore arousal to some optimal level. If the current arousal level is too high, we are motivated to reduce stimulation. If you exceed your optimal arousal level watching Freddy Krueger go wild on Elm Street, you might cover your eyes in an attempt to lower it. But if your arousal level is below optimum, you will be motivated to increase stimulation, which may be why you went to the movie in the first place.

Arousal affects performance. At very low levels of arousal, such as when we are drowsy and near sleep, performance of most tasks will not be very efficient. But at extremely high levels of arousal, our behavior will be so disorganized that other people might describe us as "wild" or "berserk." Between these extremes of sleep and frenzy are the moderate levels of arousal that are near-optimal for most behavior. Thus, for example, arousal can affect how well someone does on an exam. Under low arousal, a person may not read the directions or questions carefully. Under extremely high arousal, a person may be unable to concentrate. At moderate levels of arousal, a person may pay attention, and still be calm enough to concentrate.

The optimal arousal level depends on the difficulty of the task at hand. With a very simple task (for example, an easy quiz), the optimal level will be high—the task is so easy that efficiency does not suffer until arousal moves well above or below the optimal level. With a very difficult or complicated task (a challenging final exam), the optimal level will be on the low side. Imagine delivering a speech to a large, critical audience. If you know the material well and have practiced the speech, arousal caused by addressing an audience will probably not interfere with and might even enhance your performance. But if you are delivering an unfamiliar speech that you have not practiced, the same

► *Why do many people enjoy scary movies such as* The Lost World *(left)? The arousal that fear produces can be pleasurable, especially when there's no actual danger. Some people, like these "Polar Bears" in Jacksonport, Wisconsin (right), pursue arousal even at the expense of homeostasis.*

level of arousal may cause your presentation to suffer. You may lose your place in the text and stumble over your words.

This relationship between arousal, task difficulty, and effectiveness of behavior is described by the ***Yerkes-Dodson Law***. This law has two aspects: (1) for performance on every task, there is an optimal level of arousal, and (2) the optimal level depends on the task's difficulty—the more difficult or complex the task, the lower the optimal arousal for performing it (see Figure 10-3).

◀ *Very difficult tasks require a lower level of arousal. Here, cosmonaut Gennady M. Strekalov performs a tricky repair on the Mir space station. He must remain absolutely calm, since one false move could jeopardize his life.*

Individual Differences in Optimal Arousal

Some people seem to require a lot of stimulation to reach optimal arousal, whereas others need only a little. This variation provides the basis for a personality dimension called ***sensation seeking*** (Zuckerman, 1979, 1991). High sensation seekers need more external stimulation—varied, novel, complex sensations—to reach a given level of arousal than do low sensation seekers. They seek out unusual or challenging sources of stimulation (for example, mountain climbing, bungee jumping, hang gliding, drug use) to *maintain* arousal. Low sensation seekers try to keep stimulation at a minimum (Hines & Shaw, 1993). They are more likely to collect stamps than climb mountains (Bardo & Mueller, 1991; see Chapter 14).

Instinct as Motivator

Early psychologists used the concept of ***instinct*** to explain motivation. Instincts are predispositions to perform complex patterns of behavior when faced with particular situations. All members of a species react in the same unchanging and genetically determined way based on instinct. This concept had its origins in Charles Darwin's theory of evolution, which stressed the survival value of complex, automatic responses triggered by particular environmental stimulation. Instincts related to aggression, feeding, and reproduction were considered particularly important because of their high survival value. According to this theory, organisms eat because they are instinctively inclined to do so; they seek a mate because they instinctively engage in procreation. Although instincts are resistant to modification, some can be shaped by experience. Thus, the songs that birds use to communicate can change on hearing different songs by other members of their species (Ball & Hulse, in press). Instincts are important determiners of behavior in many species. But human behavior is too complex and varied to be explained adequately by instincts, so researchers have turned to theories that consider how biological, psychological, social, and environmental factors interact to determine human motives.

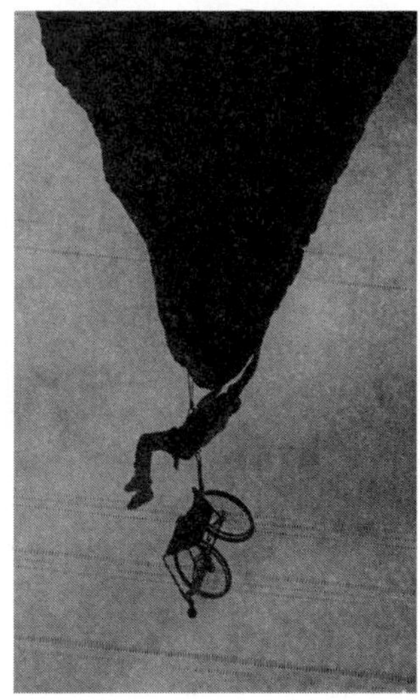

▲ *An extreme example of sensation seeking: a paraplegic rock climber dangles precariously.*

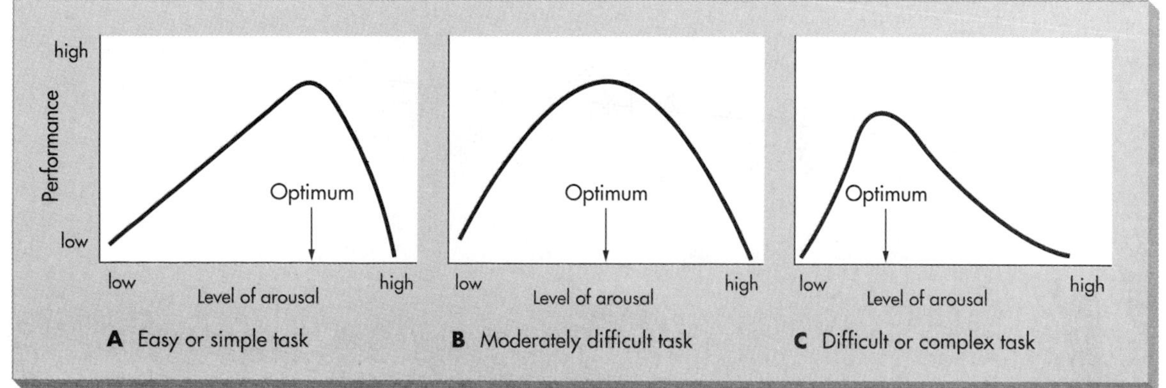

10-3 The Yerkes-Dodson Law

The Yerkes-Dodson law shows the relationship of level of arousal and performance. Arousal and performance are related. But as the difficulty of a task increases, the optimum level of arousal will decrease.

SEEKING SOLUTIONS

Sensation Seeking

Consider Ruth Anne Kocour's description of her mountain-climbing experience on Alaska's Mount McKinley, which included being trapped in a violent snowstorm: "We were trapped on an ice shelf on the side of Mount McKinley for eleven days, flat on our backs in our tents at fourteen thousand feet, temperatures of minus forty-seven degrees. . . . Seven people died, one only a few yards from our tent. . . . But we went on to reach the summit, and that," she says, elation in her voice, "was my vacation *that* year. . . . I think being on the edge is the most alive place there is" (quoted in Evans, 1994, pp. 65–66).

While everyone takes risks, some people seek risk more than others. Kocour and others like her who seek an emotional thrill from risking pain and death are called "Big T" personalities ("T" for "thrill"). Frank Farley of the University of Wisconsin has studied how people differ in their willingness to take chances and to put themselves in dangerous situations. According to Farley, Big T people are likely to have an impact on society, for better or worse (Farley, 1986). On the positive side, Farley found that Big T personalities are likely to be creative, innovative, and flexible. Amelia Earhart (the first woman to fly alone across the Atlantic), explorers, and astronauts all typify the productive Big T type. On the negative side, Big T personalities can also be destructive forces in society. Examples of destructive Big T's include Bonnie Parker and Clyde Barrow, the infamous bank robbers, or more recently Saddam Hussein. Little t personalities, at the opposite end of the thrill-seeking continuum, are cautious and conservative and are less likely to have an impact on society, either positively or negatively (Shaw, 1992).

Farley believes that the thrill-seeking component of personality is probably genetically based and resistant to change. Therefore, he suggests that we should try to structure society so that Big T people develop positive rather than destructive tendencies. One application of Farley's theory is the structuring of rehabilitation programs for juvenile delinquents. Farley's research has shown that delinquents are much more likely than non-delinquents to be Big T personalities. Traditional rehabilitation programs that emphasize structured work environments and rigid, top-down management systems are not effective with Big T people, and therefore they are not successful in changing the behavior of delinquents. But programs that emphasize exposure to thrill-seeking activities, such as rodeo performing and Outward-Bound experiences, have yielded encouraging preliminary results. In regard to vocational counseling, Farley recommended that Big T delinquents be given training in creative fields rather than the mundane and structured jobs for which they are usually prepared.

◄ *Ruth Anne Kocour, a Big T personality, says "Without risk there's stagnation."*

Biologically Based Motivation

Some behaviors, such as eating, drinking, and sexual behavior, serve biologically based motives, for they fulfill physiological needs. Nonetheless, just because a behavior serves a biological need does not mean it cannot simultaneously serve social and cognitive needs as well. Thus, eating and drinking may be motivated by social needs for affiliation and approval, in addition to the physiological need for nutrients and liquids. Sexual behavior may fulfill needs for affiliation, approval, and power in addition to the physiological need to release sexual tension. Let us consider the different motivations for these behaviors in more detail.

◀ *We eat for many reasons other than to satisfy hunger. In the United States, the Thanksgiving meal is part of a national ritual, and tradition dictates the menu.*

Hunger and Eating

Eating satisfies a primary biological need for nutrients that our body requires. Our hunger drive compels us to seek out those nutrients. However, when we eat, what we eat, and how much we need to eat to maintain our body weight reflect a combination of biological and sociocultural factors (Rozin, 1996).

Imagine what would happen if someone's homeostatic system were consistently off by 100 calories a day (for example, by a slice of cheese). In a year, that person would lose or gain over 10 pounds (a 40-pound change in four years of college!). This doesn't ordinarily happen, however. Despite wide variations in food intake and energy expenditure, the principle of homeostasis means that most individuals' body weight stays remarkably constant. This is possible because of a variety of biological mechanisms (Keesey & Powley, 1986).

Biological Mechanisms

In general, an average-sized woman who has a job that keeps her in front of a desk needs about 2,000 calories a day to maintain her weight. In one study, however, researchers monitored everything eaten by two 260-pound women and concluded that the women could maintain their body weight on only 1,000 calories a day. How is that possible?

The answer lies in understanding the biological mechanisms that govern weight regulation. One theory of eating postulates that every one of us has a biological ***setpoint***, a weight that the body seeks to maintain by influencing a person's metabolic rate and desire to eat (see Figure 10-4). Different people have different setpoints, determined by fat and sugar levels in the body, the level of certain neurochemicals in the brain, and the unique metabolic rate for each individual's homeostatic system.

Metabolism is controlled directly by various hormones and enzymes, and probably indirectly by other genetic factors (Price, 1987). There are, on average, different levels of a critical metabolic enzyme (ATPase) in obese and normal-weight people. It may be that genes determine the enzyme level, which in turn de-

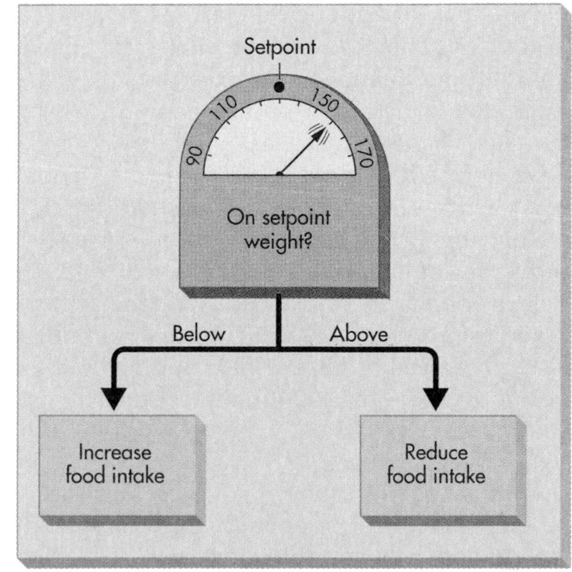

10-4 Regulation of Food Intake

Each person has a setpoint weight, which influences metabolic rate and desire to eat. If the person's weight is below the setpoint, he or she will be motivated to increase food intake. If weight is above the setpoint, he or she will be motivated to reduce food intake.

termines the metabolic rate at which a person burns calories, with some people inheriting high rates and others low rates. Two people of the same weight and activity level can differ by as much as 100 percent in the amount of food needed to maintain that weight at a constant level. In addition, dramatic changes take place as a person gets fat, including a slowing down in the rate of calorie burning, which just makes the problem worse (Rodin, 1981).

The body maintains its setpoint weight by lowering metabolism to compensate for reduced food intake. It is as if the body comprehends that less food is coming in and compensates by drastically reducing metabolism to conserve energy. Severe dieters lose less weight than expected in part because their metabolic rate drops faster than their body weight in response to food deprivation. One study reduced the daily intake of six obese patients from 3,500 to 450 calories, a reduction of 87 percent. As a result, their basal metabolism declined by 15 percent. Three weeks later, their body weight had only declined by 6 percent (Bray, 1969). Thus, some people may be overweight even though they are not eating a lot of food (Friedman & Stricker, 1976). It appears that the 260-pound women who can maintain their weight on 1,000 calories a day have high setpoints (260 pounds is heavier than average) and extremely low metabolic rates.

The setpoint is the weight that the body tries to maintain by regulating its food intake.

What about diets that claim you can lose "30 pounds in 30 days?" To lose one pound requires a deficit of 3,500 calories—more calories than many people actually burn in a day. With severe limits on fluids, intense exercise, and metabolism-altering drugs, some very overweight people may attain such a goal. This is not a healthy way to lose weight, however. Severe limiting of fluid intake may cause prolonged dehydration, which can result in liver and kidney damage. Diet drugs can have a variety of negative side effects, including sleep disruption, heart damage, and even death. In addition, the weight loss will probably not be permanent, perhaps leading to another cycle of dieting, weight loss, and weight gain. Weight fluctuations from on-and-off dieting (dietary cycling) also pose health hazards—including risk of heart disease—that are greater than those caused by obesity itself (Stamler, Dyer, Shakelle, Neaton, & Stamler, 1993).

The dangers of dieting are such that eating several small meals a day and exercising moderately are a preferable approach to losing weight and keeping it off (Rodin, 1981).

THINKING CRITICALLY

Suppose you are overweight and want to lose 30 pounds. You consider one diet that claims you can lose 30 pounds in 30 days by severely limiting food intake, and another that advocates eating several small meals a day and exercising moderately, with the goal of losing 2 pounds a week. Given that you'd like not only to lose the weight but also to keep it off, which diet is best?

In keeping with the principle of homeostasis, as your body recognizes that much less food is coming in, it will compensate by drastically reducing its metabolic rate to conserve energy, making it more difficult to lose weight. Your appetite will also increase, making it more difficult to stay on the diet, and if you do stay on the first diet, after 30 days of eating very little, the incentive value of foods that you normally might avoid may now become irresistible, with bingeing as the result.

The body also has other biological mechanisms to regulate weight. Research on golden-mantled ground squirrels, who gain and lose substantial amounts of fat between summer and winter, suggests that the body has mechanisms to monitor and maintain proportions of body fat as well as overall weight. When nonregenerating fatty deposits are surgically removed from the squirrels, fat becomes stored in other places to compensate. Similarly, in human beings, fat may return after liposuction, leading researchers to conclude that our brains, like those of ground squirrels, can somehow detect our amount of body fat and alter our eating to maintain a particular amount of it (Rosenzweig, Leiman, & Breedlove, 1996).

Although mechanisms for controlling hunger are spread throughout the brain and include the frontal cortex, the hypothalamus plays a key weight-regulating role (see Chapter 3). It senses the level of glycerol (a carbohydrate) in the bloodstream. Blood glycerol levels rise and fall in relation to changes in fat storage. In response to these changes, the hypothalamus directs corresponding changes in food intake. In fact, damaging the hypothalamus surgically has a stable, long-term effect on weight and food intake. Thus, by making surgical lesions in the ventromedial nucleus of a rat's hypothalamus, researchers can produce ***hyperphagia***, an abnormally increased desire for food. The animal loses its inhibitions on eating, overeats, and may become enormous in size. It does not go on eating until it explodes, however. Instead, its weight reaches a new, higher level—a new setpoint—which it then maintains.

When researchers make lesions in the rat's lateral hypothalamic area, however, the animal exhibits ***aphagia***: it will not eat at all, at least for a while. Apparently the setpoint has been reset to a lower level. After recovery from surgery, the animal typically eats on its own but maintains its body weight at the new setpoint. This is not simply a question of eating less after the operation. If the animal is starved before the operation, it will eat more after the operation until it reaches the new setpoint (Winn, 1995).

Electrical stimulation of different areas of the hypothalamus has an effect that is opposite to the effect produced by making surgical lesions (Winn, 1995). Stimulation of the ventromedial nucleus will inhibit eating behavior, causing a hungry animal to stop eating immediately. Stimulation of the lateral hypothalamic area will excite behavior and will cause the animal to start eating even if it is full (see Table 10-1).

Short-term, day-to-day variations in food consumption depend more on momentary blood glucose (sugar) levels than on body fat or blood glycerol levels (Keesey & Powley, 1986).

Table 10-1 Stimulation or Destruction of Parts of the Hypothalamus

	Destruction	Activation
Ventromedial nucleus	Animal becomes hyperphagic and overeats.	A hungry animal that is eating will stop eating immediately.
Lateral hypothalamic area	Animal becomes aphagic—it will not eat at all and will die unless force-fed.	Animal will immediately start eating, even if it has just eaten all it wants.

The stomach secretes a hormone that signals the brain about the amount of food it contains and when to stop eating. Ingested food is also monitored in the mouth by taste and smell receptors, as well as by receptors in the muscles responsible for chewing and swallowing. The brain uses all this information (and more!) to regulate eating (Davidson, 1993).

Sometimes people crave specific foods—for example, foods that are salty or sweet. If we are on a diet that is deficient in some particular nutrient, say, salt, we will have a specific need for salt. We and many other animals have built-in biological systems to detect and regulate sodium (salt) intake. When this system signals a deficiency, we immediately seek out food with high sodium content.

Experiments on specific food needs show that taste and smell are deeply involved in what both human beings and animals eat, and underscore the important role that the pleasure-producing (incentive) qualities of food play in when and how much we eat (Keesey & Powley, 1986). We eat more when our food tastes good, is presented attractively, and is varied. Even laboratory rats eat more when they are offered bread and chocolate in addition to rat chow (Rogers & Blundell, 1980). Did you ever stuff yourself on turkey and dressing on Thanksgiving Day but then somehow still found room for pumpkin pie with whipped cream? Clearly, there's more to understanding eating than whether or not our body requires calories or nutrients.

▲ *Experiments on rats have shown the connection between weight and the hypothalamus. After surgery in which the hypothalamus is damaged, rats eat voraciously, increasing their weight by as much as five times.*

Contextual Factors

Social and environmental factors also shape what and when we eat. Did you ever eat something just because it looked good? Did you ever suddenly feel hungry because you smelled the pizza your roommate just brought home? Do you eat more (or less) when you are with other people than you do when you are by yourself? Do you have an urge to eat popcorn when you sit down to watch TV? Stimuli outside the body (external cues) can affect whether or not you eat. Sights, smells, anticipated tastes—even the presence of other people or a given location—can induce you to eat, even after your bodily need for nutrients has been satisfied (Rozin, 1996). Food has incentive value (it exerts a motivational pull on whether or not you eat), which may vary depending on your physiological state (How recently did you eat anything? Does your body need salt?), how recently and

SEEKING SOLUTIONS

When People Die to Be Thin

Most people enjoy eating. But for millions of Americans, eating takes the form of severe, life-threatening disorders: anorexia nervosa and bulimia. Eating disorders kill about one in ten of their victims by starvation, cardiac arrest, or suicide, making these disorders far more dangerous than obesity—people are literally dying to be thin (National Institute of Mental Health [NIMH], 1993).

Individuals with anorexia literally starve themselves, becoming grossly underweight, with skeletal faces, clawlike hands, and protruding ribs. Despite their emaciation, they are dissatisfied with their bodies and mistakenly perceive themselves as "too fat." Anorexics tend to respond to the wishes of others, to be perfectionists, to be good students, and to be athletic (NIMH, 1993). In particular, female anorexics, like many women, desire a body shape and weight considerably thinner than their own. Often this desire is the result of an incorrect perception of male preferences for thin women (Fallon & Rozin, 1985). But anorexics carry this misperception to an abnormal extreme, refusing food in an attempt to maintain or reduce further their already low body weight.

About half of the victims of anorexia also suffer from bulimia. Bulimia is a binge-and-purge pattern of behavior in which the person consumes great quantities of food and then tries to empty the system by vomiting or taking large doses of laxatives. Bulimia occurs more often on its own than as a compounding feature of anorexia—most bulimics are normal or just slightly overweight. Because of deep shame over their eating patterns, bulimics may go for twenty or thirty years before seeking treatment. Unfortunately, this delay means their disordered eating has become deeply ingrained and difficult to change (NIMH, 1993). Furthermore, chronic vomiting, dehydration, and poor nutrition associated with bulimia can seriously damage health.

Risk for eating disorders varies with gender and ethnicity. Although males and females of all ages have eating disorders, rates of the disorder are highest for women. Approximately 1 in 100 females develops an eating disorder (Fairburn, Welch, & Hay, 1993). Among college women, estimates range from 13 to 20 percent, compared to around 2 percent for college men (Hesse-Biber, 1989). Women in work roles mandating thinness (such as modeling, dancing, or acting) are at especially high risk for eating disorders (Striegel-Moore, Silberstein, & Rodin, 1986). Approximately 90 percent of all people suffering from eating disorders are young, middle- and upper-class white women (Dykens & Gerrard, 1986), but this may be changing as ethnic minority women and men internalize thinness standards of the larger culture (Wifley et al., 1996).

Males who hold roles that emphasize being a certain weight are at higher risk for eating disorders than their peers. For example, male athletes who are pressured to maintain their weight below a certain level, such as low-weight wrestlers and rowers, are at higher risk for eating disorders. In fact, in one study, 8 percent of rowers and 15 percent of wrestlers exhibited disordered eating (Thiel, Gottfried, & Hesse, 1993). Gay men, who are often held to a thin body standard and more rigid appearance norms than heterosexual men, are also at higher risk for eating disorders. It is estimated that a third of males with eating disorders are self-identified homosexuals (Gettleman & Thompson, 1993; Herzog, Norman, Gordon, & Prepose, 1984).

There are few studies of eating disorders in ethnic minority women, and disordered eating may be a neglected problem in ethnic populations. In one report, 24 percent of Native American women studied used purging to control their weight (Rosen et al., 1988). Another study found that lower-income Pueblo Indian and Latina adolescent females reported excessive concern with weight and disordered eating behaviors at rates similar to the rates for well-educated, young urban women (Snow & Harris, 1989).

A full understanding of eating disorder dynamics must consider biological, psychological, social, and cultural factors in interaction. Nonetheless, sociocultural factors, particularly those that promote standards of thinness and encourage dieting, appear to play a central role in creating and maintaining disordered eating. Such findings have led some researchers to call eating disorders a culture-bound syndrome that reflects Western culture's stigmatization of obesity and emphasis on unrealistic thinness as a standard for beauty (Nasser, 1988).

how often you have eaten that particular food (Is this your third turkey leg this week?), the quality of the food itself (Is it tasty? Does it smell good? Does it look appetizing?), and the context in which it is consumed (Is everyone else eating? Will Aunt Susan be disappointed if you don't ask for seconds?). Perhaps we should be most amazed at how well we regulate our food intake *despite* the continued presence of such external factors. Nonetheless, external stimuli can dominate some people's food consumption, overriding internal regulatory systems (Nisbett, 1972). As you might guess, such individuals may become overweight or even obese.

Obesity is common in U.S. society—about 34 million individuals in the United States are obese (commonly defined as being 20 percent or more over one's appropriate body weight). Obesity probably is a symptom of several different disorders, such as diabetes or thyroid dysfunction. Although not as dangerous as dietary cycling or the eating disorder anorexia (in which people starve themselves to stay thin), obesity has been implicated as a major factor in physical illnesses such as heart disease, to say nothing of its role in the personal pain, discomfort, and rejection an obese person often experiences due to discrimination (Grilo & Pogue-Geile, 1991).

Genetic factors, high setpoints, and environments full of food cues may all lead to obesity, which can be extremely difficult to control. Even if people are able to lose weight by dieting, they may not be able to maintain the lower weight and may regain the pounds they have lost—returning to their setpoint—when they go back to normal eating. They may thus spend much of their lives losing the same pounds over and over again. Research has begun to uncover the mechanisms that underlie this pattern, and this knowledge may eventually lead to more effective techniques for losing excess weight permanently.

Researchers have suggested that obese people have difficulty in controlling their weight because they eat mainly in response to uncontrollable external cues in their environment (Schachter & Rodin, 1974). In one experiment, researchers placed obese and normal-weight participants on either a normal diet or a bland, tasteless, liquid diet. Even though the participants had no idea how many calories they were consuming in the liquid diet, the normal-weight participants maintained their caloric consumption at a level remarkably close to their normal level. In contrast, the obese participants reduced their calorie consumption dramatically while on the liquid diet compared to what they consumed on the normal diet. Thus, when pleasing external taste cues were absent, obese people greatly restricted their food intake.

This research suggests that normal-weight people eat mainly in response to internal physiological cues; they eat because their internal food-intake system tells them to eat (Schachter & Rodin, 1974). In contrast, obese individuals seem to eat whenever they encounter external stimuli that have something to do with good-tasting food, such as when they walk by a bakery or see a TV commercial for a hot fudge sundae. Normal-weight persons encounter identical stimuli, but they generally do not respond to these cues by getting something to eat. Obese persons could lose weight if they could isolate themselves from pleasant-tasting stimuli. If they were deprived of TV, magazines, and any stimuli associated with food, they could lose large amounts of weight without great pain or discomfort. Unfortunately, when they returned to the world of refrigerators, restaurants, fast-food joints, and thirty-one flavors of ice cream, they would probably regain whatever weight they had lost.

Researchers have raised some doubts about external cues as a complete explanation of obesity (Rodin, 1981). They have found that many normal-weight people are also responsive to external food-related stimuli. Further, not all

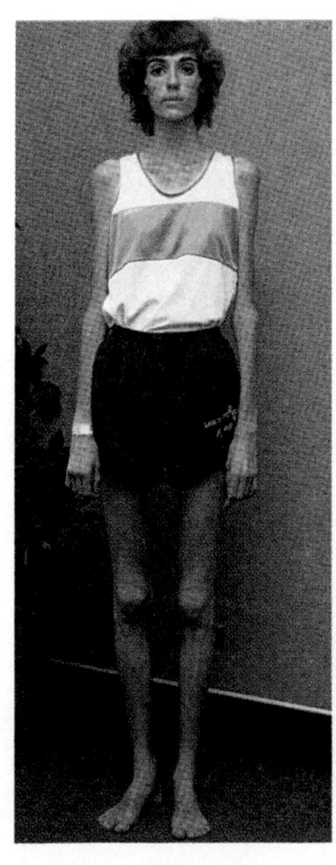

◀ *The woman on the left suffers from anorexia nervosa and physically resembles the person on the right who suffers from an unavailability of food. Both are starving to death.*

obese individuals are bound by external stimuli. Thus, both physiological and contextual factors must be taken into account if we are to understand the mechanisms that regulate eating and weight.

Thirst and Drinking

To keep the body's fluid levels within normal homeostatic ranges, human beings and other animals have a complex system of checks and balances. If fluid levels rise too high, the body rids itself of excess water by sweating or urinating. If they fall too low, the body conserves water by inhibiting sweat glands and urine formation and by triggering thirst—the drive to drink.

The hypothalamus plays a key role in maintaining homeostasis, controlling both the kidneys' urine formation and water intake. If our cells become dehydrated, the hypothalamus makes us thirsty so that we drink more and urinate less until balance is restored (see Figure 10-5). Damage to the hypothalamus disrupts normal drinking, much as such damage disrupts eating, causing us to drink too much or too little. In one case, a victim of a head injury from an automobile accident began consuming 20 gallons of water per day, later scaling back to 6.5 gallons. (Most people typically drink less than a gallon per day.) Such unusual consumption suggests his hypothalamus was damaged in the accident (Winn, 1995).

10-5 Regulation of Water Intake

Cellular dehydration signals the hypothalamus to tell the kidneys to reabsorb water and the cerebral cortex to have the animal or person drink.

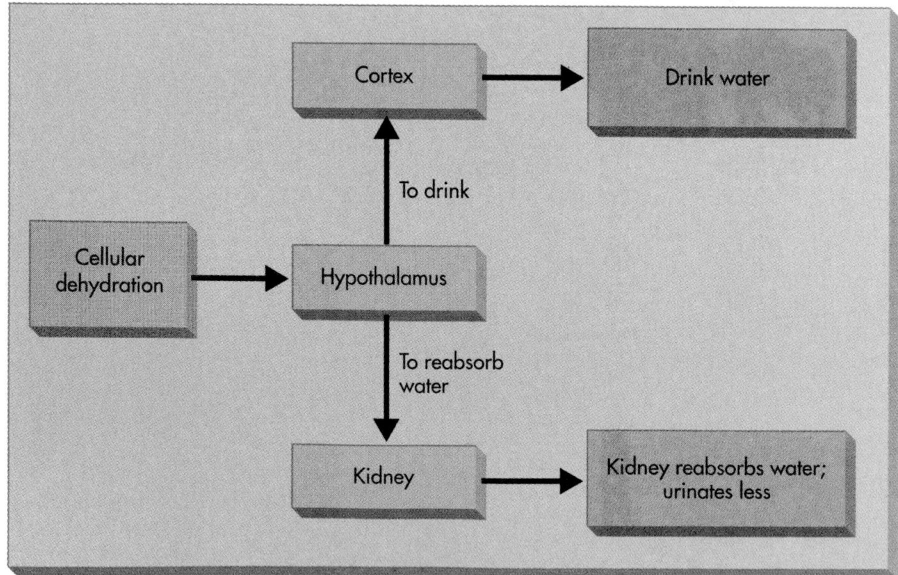

Sexual Motivation

Sex, like eating, is influenced by a combination of biological and sociocultural factors, including a biologically based drive that increases in response to deprivation (Gladue, 1994). Sexual behavior (sexual acts and practices), sexual orientation (sexual thoughts, fantasies, feelings, and behaviors that involve members of the same or opposite sex, or both), and sexual identity (the consistent, enduring self-recognition of sexual orientation) vary across individuals. Some people are sexually attracted to members of the opposite sex (heterosexual orientation), others are attracted to members of the same sex (homosexual orientation), and others are attracted to members of either sex (bisexual orientation). The development of heterosexuality is not surprising, given its links to reproduction and the powerful pro-heterosexual models and messages found in American culture. But some people develop a homosexual orientation and identity, despite profound social disapproval and ostracism. Sexual behaviors do not necessarily indicate orientation. Some people may have a homosexual orientation, but they engage in heterosexual behavior to have children. Some people may have a heterosexual orientation, but they engage in some homosexual behavior (Savin-Williams, 1990). For example, rates of homosexual behavior increase in situations that restrict access to the opposite sex. One study of prison women found that only 5 percent actively engaged in homosexual behavior before being imprisoned, but more than 50 percent did so during imprisonment (Ward & Kassebaum 1965). These facts suggest that social, cultural, and situational factors play important roles in determining sexual behavior (Michael, Gagnon, Laumann, & Kolata, 1994).

Unlike eating, sex is not required for individual survival. People have been known to live an entire lifetime without engaging in sexual intercourse. Priests and nuns in the Roman Catholic Church are expected to be celibate. In many societies, sexual activity is actively discouraged, especially before marriage. Moreover, sexual desires and what is considered sexually attractive vary among individuals within a culture as well as across cultures and in the same culture over time. For example, although current popular American culture finds thin women to be attractive, plump women were considered to be attractive during the nineteenth century.

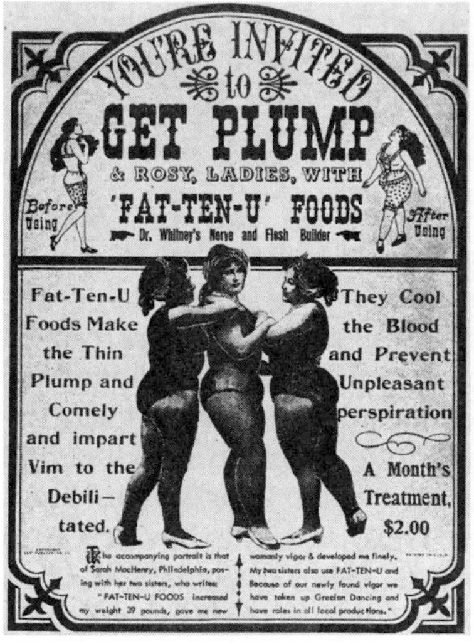

◀ *Advertising demonstrates that the relation between body weight and attractiveness has changed quite a bit over time: on the left, a handbill from the late nineteenth century advised women to "Get Plump"; on the right, today's fashion models project an ideal of thinness that most women cannot possibly achieve.*

In some other contemporary cultures, fatter women are still considered to be more sexually attractive than thin women. Thus, sexual motivation is complicated, and understanding it requires considering biological, psychological, social, and cultural factors.

Biological Aspects

Normal sexual behavior perpetuates the species. From an evolutionary perspective, those individuals most successful in mating are the ones most likely to pass their genes on to subsequent generations (Wilson, 1978).

Sexual behavior in animals often appears to be mechanical or ritualistic and instinctive. In most mammals, before sexual behavior occurs, hormonal processes cause a female to come into estrus (to be sexually receptive). Although sexual receptivity of human females does not depend on hormone levels, sexual desire in human females is correlated with the menstrual cycle, which is regulated by hormones. Further, the success of hormone therapy for some sexual problems, such as low sexual drive or the inability to have an erection, suggests that biological factors play a significant role in human sexual activities (Gladue, 1994).

William Masters and Virginia Johnson, a husband and wife research team, investigated the physiological aspects of human sexual activity. They photographed and otherwise recorded responses occurring during sexual intercourse, such as clitoral and penile erection, vaginal lubrication, and blood pressure in both males and females. They identified four phases of the human sexual response—excitement, plateau, orgasm, and resolution (Masters & Johnson, 1966). Each operates slightly differently in men and women (Figure 10-6). Men pass through these

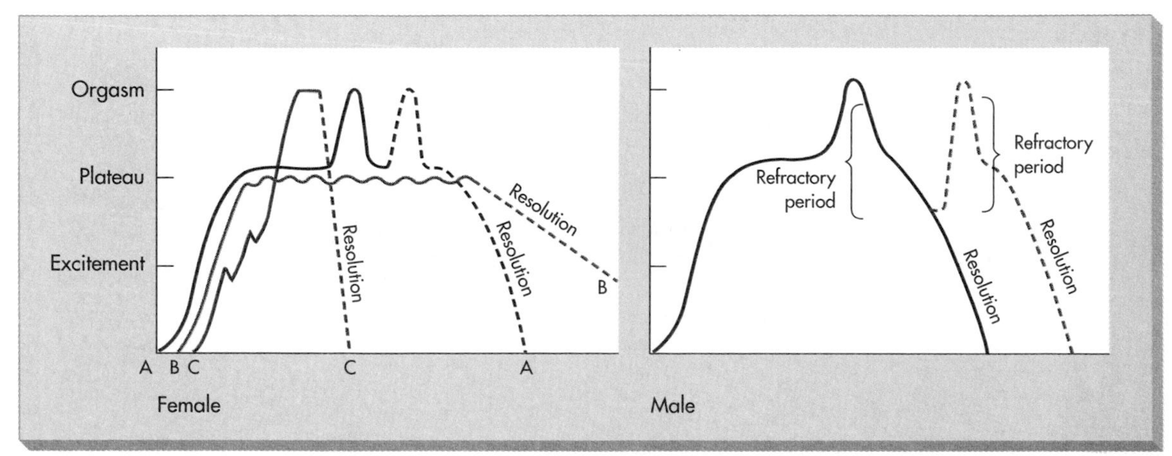

10-6 Phases of the Sexual Response

The four phases of the human sexual response cycle—excitement, plateau, orgasm, and resolution—occur in both men and women. Females may experience single or multiple orgasms, they may return to the unaroused state, or they may have a single protracted orgasm. Males experience a less varied pattern after the plateau phase, with ejaculation occurring quickly, followed by a refractory period during which another ejaculation is not possible. (Source: Masters & Johnson, 1966)

▲ *What is considered sexually attractive varies tremendously across cultures. In Burma, women literally stretch their necks with rings. In the U.S., men (and women) lift weights to create exaggerated muscle definition.*

stages in a systematic pattern, followed by a period when they aren't easily re-excited (the refractory period). Women, in contrast, often remain at a high sexual plateau for some time and can experience several orgasms (represented by the purple dashed line in Figure 10-6). Women appear to have greater conscious control than men after reaching the plateau stage.

Cultural Factors

Think about what turns you on. Sights? Sounds? Smells? Certain body parts? Particular objects? Human beings have a genetic predisposition to desire sex, but this desire can be channeled in a variety of ways, not all of which lead to reproduction and the perpetuation of the species. The diversity of ways in which sexual needs can be satisfied reflects one's culture and personal history. Thus, sexual behavior varies enormously. The first set of systematic data on human sexual behavior was the Kinsey Report (Kinsey, Pomeroy, Martin, & Gebhard, 1953). Alfred Kinsey and his colleagues collected data from American men and women on frequency of diverse sexual behaviors, such as coitus, orgasm, masturbation, homosexuality, and bestiality (sex with animals). More recent studies have looked at sexual frequency by gender and ethnicity (see Figure 10-7).

Although heterosexuality is found in all human societies, alternative sexual behaviors occur everywhere as well (Davis & Whitten, 1987). According to one study, in the United States about one out of eleven men and about

10-7 Frequency of Sexual Intercourse in Past Twelve Months

Most people have intercourse a few times a month, followed by people who have intercourse two to three times a week. This is true for both males and females, and holds for whites, blacks, and Hispanics.

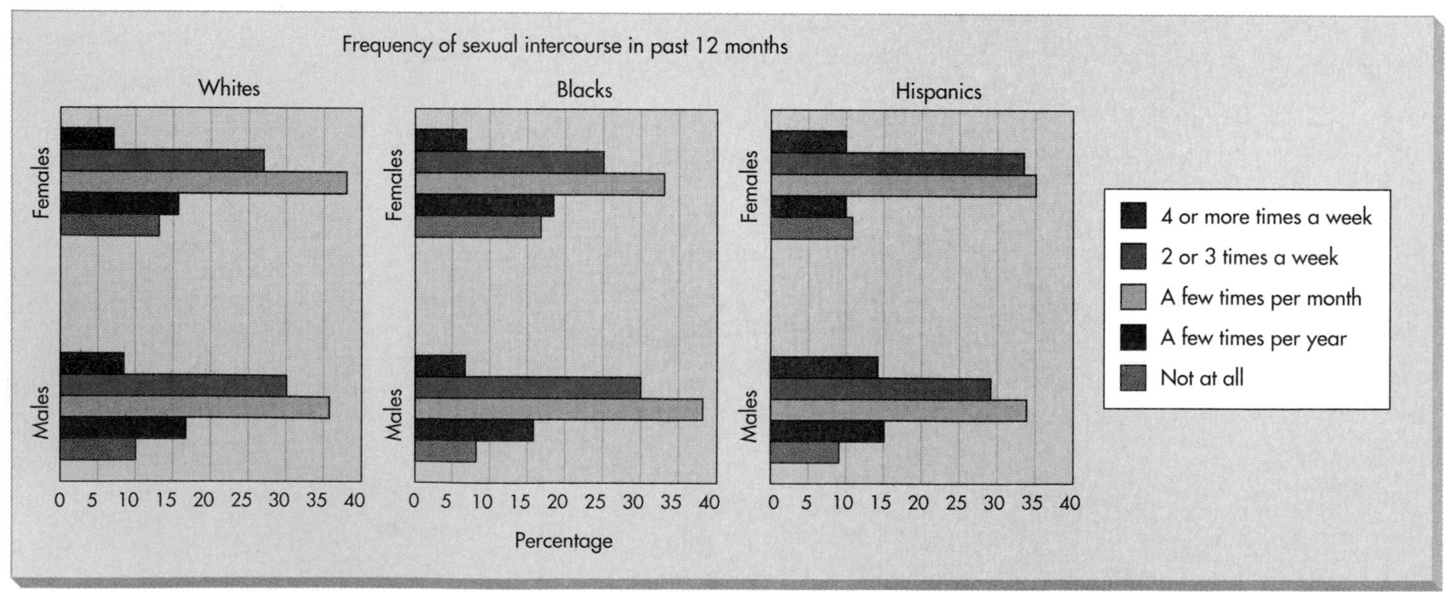

UNDERSTANDING HUMAN DIVERSITY

Homosexual Orientation and Identity

How is it that some people develop a homosexual orientation and identity despite profound social disapproval and ostracism? One explanation may be genetic. When one identical twin is homosexual, the other is also homosexual 52 percent of the time among males, and 48 percent of the time among females (Bailey & Pillard, 1991, 1995; Bailey, Pillard, Neale, & Agyei, 1993). Thus, despite identical genes, about one out of two homosexual males and lesbians have a heterosexual twin—which leaves a lot of variation unexplained. Furthermore, how genetic mechanisms produce homosexual behavior, orientation, and identity is unclear.

Prenatal sex hormones that influence the development of sex organs and brain structures may also play a role. These hormones can be affected by genetics, maternal stress, fetal exposure to drugs, and various immunological responses by the fetus during pregnancy (see Chapters 3 and 11). For example, female children who are exposed prenatally to high levels of androgens are more likely than other children to identify themselves as lesbian or bisexual, although most of even these children are still heterosexual (Dittman, Kappes, & Kappes, 1992). Finally, neuroscientists have identified differences in brain structure between homosexuals and heterosexuals (Allen & Gorski, 1992; LeVay, 1991, 1993). As you learned in Chapter 3, however, such studies are correlational and have other methodological problems. Taking the research as a whole, biological factors may be involved in the development of sexuality, but how they contribute to sexual orientation and identity has yet to be determined (Gladue, 1994).

A developmental approach that helps explain how homosexual behavior, orientation, and identity evolve and change over time and in different contexts is clearly needed. Development of a homosexual orientation and identity isn't a simple matter of biology, choice, rewards, punishments, or role models. Instead, it eppears to be more of a realization or conclusion (a cognitive transformation) that occurs after going through several stages of identity development (Garnets & Kimmel, 1991; Troiden, 1988, 1989). This process reflects biological and social factors. It progresses gradually through four stages:

1. *Feeling different.* The first stage, during middle childhood, involves feeling different (Bell, Weinberg, & Hammersmith, 1981). Lesbians say such things as "I felt different: unfeminine, ungraceful. . . ." Homosexual males say such things as "I couldn't stand sports, so naturally that made me different" and "I just didn't feel like other guys. I was very fond of pretty things like ribbons and flowers and music."
2. *Recognition of feelings.* In the second stage, during adolescence, these children realize they are attracted to members of the same sex. They recognize these feelings as homosexual and become confused and upset, because they know that homosexuality is socially disapproved.
3. *Identity formation.* In the third stage, during middle to late adolescence and young adulthood, they recognize their homosexual orientation—that is, they recognize that they prefer sexual relationships with their own sex. But they do not necessarily accept that preference as part of their sexual identity. Some do not act on their preference, while other see themselves as temporarily homosexual—"I thought my attraction to women was a passing phase and would go away once I started dating my boyfriend" (Troiden, 1989, p. 57). Some people privately see themselves as homosexual, but publicly project themselves as heterosexual to avoid social disapproval and rejection.
4. *Identity integration.* Some people go on to a final stage of identity formation in which homosexuality becomes an integral part of their personal identity. Sexual behavior, orientation, and public and private identities become one, and they become satisfied with their way of life—"I am gay and being gay is one aspect of who I am" (Cass, 1979).

The factors contributing to our sexuality, including whether we become attracted to members of the same or opposite sex and how we come to define our sexual identity are multifaceted and complex. As with other motivations, many factors may be operating simultaneously to produce motivated behavior. There may be more than one path to developing a particular sexual orientation and identity, and biological (including genetic), cognitive, and social factors may all play a role in the process (Garnets & Kimmel, 1991; Bem, 1996; see Chapter 14 for one theory of how this aspect of personality develops).

one out of twenty-five women have had at least one homosexual experience since puberty (Laumann, Gagnon, Michael, & Michaels, 1994). These figures may be low, however, since the numbers were based on face-to-face interviews and some people may not have been willing to admit that they were homosexual. Other studies have estimated that between 6 and 20 percent of the U.S. population have engaged in homosexual behavior at some time. (Fay, Turner, Klassen, & Gagnon, 1989; Rogers & Turner, 1991; Sell, Wells, & Wypij, 1995). In most societies, homosexuality is more likely to be condoned than either masturbation or bestiality—the latter has been found to be accepted in only five societies (Ford & Beach, 1951).

The body, the brain, the genitalia, and the capacity for language are all necessary for human sexuality. But they do not determine its content, its experiences, or its institutional forms. Moreover, we never encounter the body unmediated by the meanings that cultures give to it.

—Rubin (1984, pp. 276–77)

All cultures specify which sexual behaviors are acceptable and between whom, but the particular behaviors vary considerably over time and from one culture to another. Northern Brazil's Apinayé women have been known to bite off pieces of their lovers' eyebrows, spitting them to the side, while in the Caroline Islands of the South Pacific, Ponapean men pull at the women's eyebrows, sometimes removing pieces of hair. Choroti women from northwestern Paraguay and southeastern Bolivia have been observed to spit passionately in their partners' faces (Ford & Beach, 1951).

Although heterosexual males in the United States generally avoid kissing and hugging other males, in many European cultures kissing and hugging other men is quite common and is not considered an expression of sexual interest. Men almost invariably greet each other with hugs (*abrazos*) in Brazil, and the closer the relationship, the longer the hug. Brazilian men may continue to kiss their fathers throughout their lives (Kottak, 1991).

Change can occur within a culture, too. America's "sexual revolution" in the 1960s and 1970s showed how attitudes and behaviors can alter radically over a short period of time. Prior to 1970, college males were twice as likely as college females to report sexual intercourse. After 1970 and through the early 1980s, the proportion of college males and females having sex both increased and became more equal (Robinson, Ziss, Ganza, Katz, & Robinson, 1991).

THINKING CRITICALLY

Maslow's hierarchy of needs is widely known and provides a useful way to organize thinking about needs, but it has some problems. Can you identify some of them?

The order of satisfying needs can vary both across individuals as well as within an individual over time. Thus, higher-order needs (such as the need for approval or prestige) may take precedence over physiological needs (for example, enduring hunger and frostbite to climb Mount Everest). Yet, sometimes a person who has consistently put security above esteem suddenly rushes into a burning building to save a stranger. Further, the hierarchy is not very useful for predicting behavior. Not only does the order of need satisfaction vary, the same behavior can serve a wide variety of needs as well. Thus, a desire for sex may reflect a physiological need, but it may also reflect needs for esteem, belongingness, and love—needs that may become much more important than physiology in determining sexual behavior.

Learning Sexual Behaviors

Operant and classical conditioning can explain how we acquire some sexual behaviors. Sexual behavior is accompanied by a variety of pleasurable sensations, and we tend to repeat responses that have pleasurable consequences (operant conditioning). Neutral stimuli (for example, a furry toy animal) that are paired with early sexual experiences, particularly masturbation, may themselves come to have arousing effects (classical conditioning). Lack of sexual responsiveness and sexual dysfunction can also result from classical conditioning that occurs when sexual feelings are paired with shame, disgust, and fear of discovery (Kaplan, 1974). We also learn about sexual behaviors and incentives by observation (cognitive learning). Movies, television, books, and now the Internet are rich sources of information about sex. Among other things, they portray sexual behaviors that people imitate. On the basis of cognitive learning principles, if a model is rewarded for a certain behavior, an observer is likely to imitate that behavior.

Socially Based Motivation

While the goals of biologically based motives may be to satisfy biological needs, our ability to use symbols and to anticipate and plan for the future can also be powerful sources of motivation, so powerful that they can override biological motives. In addition, most people generally have enough to eat and a place to live in modern society. Thus, biologically based needs for food and shelter cannot account for the variety of ways that human beings behave; instead higher-order psychological needs often motivate people in modern society. Given that even our most basic, hard-wired reflexes—such as avoiding pain—can be overridden or modified by experience, psychologists have looked to personality and social psychology for further explanations of human motivation.

According to Abraham Maslow, since most people's primary needs—for food and shelter and safety—are easily satisfied in modern society, their needs for love and self-esteem become primary motivators (see Chapter 14). Moreover, Maslow believed that people's highest need is for personal growth leading to ***self-actualization***. The goal is to be all that you can be by developing and utilizing your talent, ability, and potential to the fullest. Self-actualization differs from other needs in that it is a need for growth rather than a need to remedy a deficiency. Ideally, a society would satisfy all lower-level deficiency needs and allow everyone to reach self-actualization. Under present societal conditions, however, few people ever experience this need and fewer still ever satisfy it fully. Maslow cited Ruth Benedict, George Washington Carver, Harriet Tubman, Eleanor Roosevelt, Albert Schweitzer, and Mahatma Ghandi as successful examples of fully self-actualized people (Maslow, 1970; see Chapter 14).

Personality theorist Henry Murray also emphasized how central are needs and their satisfaction to human personality. Murray developed a personality theory that recognized the importance of considering the interaction of biological, psychological, and environmental needs (see Table 10-2). Murray viewed motivation as a function of environmental factors, which he called presses (Murray, 1938). You may have a biological or psychological need, but only certain environmental situations will arouse it. For example, seeing a friend elected to the Phi Beta Kappa Society might arouse your

Table 10-2 Examples of Human Needs as Identified by Henry Murray

Need	Brief Definition
Achievement	To overcome obstacles, to exercise power, to strive to do something difficult as well and as quickly as possible.
Affiliation	To form friendships and associations. To greet, join, and live with others. To cooperate and converse sociably with others. To love. To join groups.
Aggression	To assault or injure another. To murder, belittle, harm, blame, accuse, or maliciously ridicule a person. To punish severely. Sadism.
Autonomy	To resist influence or coercion. To defy an authority or seek freedom in a new place. To strive for independence.
Harm avoidance	To avoid pain, physical injury, illness, and death. To escape from a dangerous situation. To take precautionary measures.
Order	To arrange, organize, put away objects. To be tidy and clean. To be scrupulously precise.
Play	To relax, amuse oneself, seek diversion and entertainment. To 'have fun,' to play games. To laugh, joke, and be merry. To avoid serious tension.
Rejection	To snub, ignore, or exclude another. To remain aloof and indifferent. To be discriminating.
Sex	To form and further an erotic relationship. To have sexual intercourse.
Understanding	To analyze experience, to abstract, to discriminate among concepts, to define relations, to synthesize ideas.

own achievement motive to seek that goal yourself—a case of press for achievement.

Murray is best known for devising, with Christiana Morgan, the Thematic Apperception Test (TAT; Morgan & Murray, 1935). In this test, research participants are shown a picture and asked to make up a story about what it portrays, presumably projecting their needs into the stories they write. Researchers have developed motive scoring systems based on the study of the kinds of stories that people write when a particular motive is aroused. These scores can be used to study the motivations of the people making up the stories (Smith, 1992). We now turn to a discussion of some of the socially based motives—the needs for affiliation, approval, achievement, and power—that were identified by Murray and Morgan.

Need for Affiliation

The ***need for affiliation*** is expressed in our seeking out other people, in our desire to have companionship, to make friends, to cooperate, to help others, and to develop caring, loving relationships. Although individuals vary in their need for other people, and cultures vary in their emphasis on interpersonal relationships (see Chapter 4), all of us begin our lives with a basic need for regular, responsive interactions with other people. As you will learn in Chapter 11, normal social, emotional, and intellectual development all depend on communication and interaction with others. In particular, our ability to maintain strong and enduring relationships with others originates in our early interactions with our parents, grandparents, other family members and caregivers, and day-care providers.

► *Why do many college students join fraternities and sororities? Membership in such groups may fulfill the need for affiliation and for social approval.*

Need for Social Approval

In addition to a need for affiliation, most of us have a need to have other people approve of what we do. Our ***need for social approval*** is reflected in many situations in which we act to obtain the approval or avoid the disapproval of others. An individual's sociability (willingness to engage others in social interactions and to seek their approval or attention) develops out of early childhood interactions. Children who have secure relationships with their mothers at fifteen months become social leaders at nursery school when they are three-and-a-half years of age: they initiate play activities, are sensitive to their playmates' needs and feelings, and are curious, self-directed, and eager to learn new things (Waters, Wippman, & Sroufe, 1979). Children who are unsociable or inappropriately sociable (argumentative or aggressive) and who are rejected by their peers are more likely to exhibit severe emotional disturbances (pathological low self-esteem, delinquency, or psychological disorders). Sociability appears stable over time; children who are highly friendly and sociable in nursery school are more likely to be sociable as adolescents and young adults (Shafer, 1993).

Social motivation that stems from the need for social approval can affect our behavior enormously—for good, when it leads us to help others, and for ill, when it leads us to do things that we wouldn't do alone or in most other situations and that violate values we consider important.

Need for Achievement

The ***need for achievement*** is the need to strive for success and reflects a central value in Western culture. Researchers have developed sophisticated scoring systems to measure the number of achievement themes and elements in

TAT stories (McClelland, Atkinson, Clark, & Lowell, 1953; McClelland, 1985). These measures have proved to be valid long-term indicators of actual achievement in many fields (Spangler, 1992).

Motivation for achievement as defined by this measure appears to become aroused only when (1) there is at least a moderate probability of success, and (2) attractive incentives are available (Atkinson, 1982). High scorers do particularly well in situations such as business settings, where they can define their own goals and devise their own strategies for reaching them. Thus, studies of small companies in Australia, Hungary, India, and the United States have found that companies grow faster when their owner-operators are high in achievement motivation. Other research on farmers in Colombia, India, and Australia has found that those with higher achievement motivation scores are more innovative and have higher crop yields than other farmers. Yet, high scores on this achievement measure do not predict success in careers in science, law, medicine, and education, suggesting that achievement is defined too narrowly (Mook, 1987) and that other motivations, such as affiliation, may play a significantly larger role in determining career success in these professions (Winter, 1996).

Although individuals have a relatively stable level of need for achievement over time, this need can be manipulated by feedback or instructions that threaten their concept of themselves as an achieving person. If a researcher tells participants in a study that they have done poorly on an experimental task and then asks them to perform another task, they will work harder and persist longer on the second task. Similarly, the participants will also work harder on a task if the researcher first tells them that their ability to perform the task will be an indication of their intelligence, leadership, or organizational ability.

Gender and Achievement Motivation

Achievement motivation research began in the 1950s, when workplace sex segregation was much greater than today, and when women were more likely to be ostracized for entering male-dominated occupations. During this time, early studies of achievement motivation suggested that women had lower achievement scores than men under neutral conditions and their TAT stories did not show an increase in achievement-related themes when they were given achievement-related instructions (for example, "your performance on this task will indicate your leadership ability"). But substantial differences in rewards (differences in salaries and promotions) for women and men in the 1950s workplace meant that women had a lower probability of success, and particular achievements had different incentive values for males and females. Thus, the fact that achievement-related instructions appropriate for men did not work for women should not have been surprising. When studies began to use gender-appropriate instructions or focused on skills considered "feminine" in the culture, women did respond with increased achievement motivation (Stein & Bailey, 1973). In fact, gender differences in achievement motivation disappear when people are asked to provide subjective definitions of what they consider to be areas of achievement (Gaeddert, 1987).

In 1982, a review of studies of achievement motivation found that achievement motivation is aroused similarly in men and women, and that men and women are similar in average level of achievement motivation and in the behaviors that are related to the achievement motive (Stewart & Chester, 1982). Nonetheless, gender differences in achievement continue to persist in a number of domains, such as math and science. How is this to be explained?

Expectations about success, incentive values (what is perceived as an incentive or reason to pursue achievement), and social consequences (other people's reactions to someone's achievement) still vary with gender in many fields. Gender differences in achievement related to science begin to emerge in junior high or middle school, when girls begin to show a great concern with marriage and children, narrow their career interests to occupations traditionally held by women, and begin to lose confidence in their academic ability (Bush & Simmons, 1987). Ironically, even exceptionally gifted girls who could have distinguished careers in science do not believe they are academically gifted (Walker, Reis, & Leonard, 1992). Thus, girls approach math and science with lower expectations for success, which is one reason they are less likely to enroll in advanced mathematics courses than are boys (Sadker & Sadker, 1994).

During junior high or middle school, girls also are less likely than boys to consider mathematics as being important to their future

► *When mathematical talent is identified early and encouraged, some girls can reach the highest levels of achievement. Liu Ting, on the left, is a mathematical genius and chess champion. Anita Bermi, a highly gifted physicist, plans to pursue a career in science research.*

(Eccles, 1987). Moreover, girls who do enroll in math and science courses are less likely to plan to pursue a career in science. Thus, the incentive value for learning mathematics is, on average, lower for girls than boys (Sherman & Fennema, 1977). The combination of lowered expectations of success and relative lack of incentive value means that girls are less likely to take mathematics courses, a choice that in effect filters out women from many professions (Sells, 1980). Finally, achievements in a traditionally male-dominated field have different social consequences for girls, who may be perceived as invading "male territory." Fortunately, support from teachers, parents, and peers can increase the probability that girls will take mathematics courses and do well in them (Sells, 1980).

Understanding achievement behavior requires knowing about both people's need for success and their counteracting fear of failure (Atkinson & Litwin, 1960). Different people have different combinations of these two tendencies and will differ in the tasks they choose (level of risk) and where they set their goals (level of aspiration). People high in need for success and low in fear of failure will likely choose moderately difficult tasks and goals that are realistic but, given their level of competence, not easy. But people high in need for success and high in fear of failure will set much lower goals and will probably choose easier tasks. If success in one endeavor is incompatible with other goals, a "fear of success" may develop. Early researchers hypothesized that women had an internalized fear of success because career success was considered incompatible with traditional feminity (Horner, 1970). However, later investigators found that, depending on the goal and on the circumstances, men demonstrate it as well as women (Cherry & Deaux, 1978; Monahan, Kuhn, & Shaver, 1974).

Intrinsic and Extrinsic Motivation

Researchers also distinguish between extrinsic (external) and intrinsic (internal) achievement motivation. Sometimes we perform a behavior because it leads to specific rewards, praise, or approval, and meeting these goals depends on a particular kind of behavior. If all of Janet's friends dance the macarena at parties, and Janet wants to be part of the group, she will be motivated to learn the movements. Dancing is the means to attain the goal of being part of the group, not an end in itself. Thus, Janet's efforts to learn the macarena reflect ***extrinsic motivation***.

Sometimes, however, we do things with no obvious external reward, like solving crossword puzzles, reading mystery novels, or memorizing sports statistics. (Some people may even enjoy dancing the macarena alone at home!) The point is that we enjoy the behavior, even though no one gives us anything for it. Self-actualization rewards fall into this category. We are motivated to achieve a goal, not by specific tangible objects, but by personal satisfaction inherent in the activity itself. Such behavior reflects ***intrinsic motivation***.

Both intrinsic and extrinsic motivation are useful concepts for explaining behavior. Consider why Derek does his homework. One reason may be that he is rewarded for finishing on time: he gets to watch TV, receives praise from his teacher, earns good grades, and avoids parental punishment. These are all extrinsic motivators likely to affect Derek's behavior. But he may also be intrinsically motivated, completing his homework because solving homework problems is personally satisfying and makes him feel good about himself. Most educators prefer students who have an intrinsic motivation to learn that is based on curiosity and love of learning. Only when motivation is not intrinsic do we need to fall back on extrinsic motivators such as tests, homework, and grades to encourage learning.

In fact, research findings demonstrate that—contrary to the usual practice of increasing learning with rewards—we can actually *decrease* performance (and possibly overall motivation) by rewarding people for what they are normally intrinsically motivated to do (Boggiano, Barrett, Silvern, & Gallo, 1991). If a psychologist, teacher, employer, or parent offers tangible rewards for what a person can do well anyway, that person may develop a negative attitude toward the task. Suppose parents offer their child $5 for every book he or she reads. Although it was once worth doing by itself, the reading may now come to look like work under the new reward system. The child may now perceive the task as something that *must* be done for the reward, rather than being important in its own right. The child who is rewarded with money may in fact lose interest in reading. Similarly, if an enthusiastic and skilled amateur photographer decides to become a professional photographer, shooting pictures may take on a different value, becoming much less fun and more like drudgery.

▲ *Rewarding a child with a "gold star" may not increase her motivation to learn. She will probably learn how to get the reward, but she may not be motivated enough to do the work for the sake of accomplishment.*

Intrinsic motivation will more likely produce high achievement levels because it entails a quest for mastery (an aspect of self-actualization), as opposed to material reward. People who are oriented toward mastery tend to achieve more in most endeavors than those who are not, despite equivalent abilities (Spence, 1983).

THINKING CRITICALLY

There is an old story about a wise grandmother who was bothered by a group of noisy teenagers playing loud music and hanging out on the street in front of her porch. As the story goes, one weekend she called the group leaders, saying "I really like your music—I'll pay you $10 to play so I can listen to it." Needless to say, they were delighted to accept. Next weekend, they were back again, and she paid them $10 to play their music. The third weekend, however, she said she didn't have much money, so she could only pay them a quarter. They considered this compensation inadequate and went elsewhere, leaving her in peace and quiet.

How would you explain the effects of the woman's behavior? By giving the teenagers a large monetary reward, she undermined their intrinsic motivation for playing music in front of her porch. When the reward was withdrawn, they were no longer motivated to perform the behavior.

Need for Power

The ***need for power*** involves the desire to tell others what to do and to use rewards or punishments to control the behavior of others (Winter, 1991). People with high power needs usually choose careers and leadership roles in which they can direct the behavior of others (Winter & Stewart, 1978).

Although power motivation can promote

► *Why do students at military schools such as The Citadel in Charleston, South Carolina, submit to the rigors of "Hell Week"? Being in the military may fulfill the need for achievement and for power.*

leadership, it can also promote negative behavior. Individuals high in power motivation are more likely to listen to people who tell them what they want to hear and to fail to pay attention to disagreeable but important information. Thus, when groups are led by leaders with high power motivation, they do not gather and use information or deal with moral issues as effectively as when they are led by leaders lower in power motivation (Fodor & Smith, 1982).

Power motivation has also been linked to fighting and arguing, alcohol and drug use, gambling, and exploiting the opposite sex (Winter & Stewart, 1978). Men's power needs (as measured during college) have been found to be negatively correlated with their wives' career success (as measured ten years later): the higher the husband's power needs, the lower the wife's career commitment (McClelland & Burnham, 1976). Researchers have found that men with high power needs are more likely to engage in partner violence and abuse, and that power motivation is correlated with marital conflict and divorce (Dutton & Strachan, 1987; Mason & Blankenship, 1987). Fortunately, when power motivation is combined with a sense of responsibility, it is more likely to be correlated with having a responsible, power-oriented career or holding an elected office rather than with being aggressive, drinking, or being sexually exploitative (Winter, 1991).

Research has found that college women and men have comparable power motivation scores and define power similarly, citing influence over others, achievement, and self-worth in their definitions. One study found that the need for power was similarly linked to career choice for both men and women (Winter & Stewart, 1978).

Men and women may *satisfy* their power needs differently, however. Men's feelings of power have been more closely linked to material possessions, to participating in sports, and to being physically strong (Lips, 1985). Women's needs for power appear to be tempered by a greater emphasis on social responsibility (Winter & Barenbaum, 1985).

Goal Setting, Choices, and Motivation

Whether behavior is motivated by biologically or socially based needs, it involves working for a goal. Although you don't have to think to know that you're hungry, in need of water, or feeling lonely, deciding how to satisfy those needs might require some conscious deliberation. Some ways of fulfilling a need might be easier, more socially approved, or more likely to pay off than others. Moreover, some goal objects might be more interesting or valuable (be greater incentives) than others. If your parents tell you that they will buy you a car if you get straight A's in college, the car is likely to have more incentive value if it is a shiny new Porsche than if it is a used Volkswagen. So, cognition plays a number of important roles in motivation.

Incentives and expectations often affect our behavior. Incentives are often learned and thus reflect our education, upbringing, and culture. They also change over time. Even if you typically avoid cauliflower, a single taste of cauliflower prepared from a Julia Child recipe, with hollandaise sauce, could override past tendencies and make you an instant devotee. You have learned a new incentive value for cauliflower.

We acquire many incentives by cognitive learning—that is, by observation, imitation, and inference. Consider how you decide to purchase new skis. If you observe that your friend, who is an excellent skier and teaches skiing on the weekends at a local resort, has just purchased Brand X skis, you probably will *infer* that Brand X skis are excellent and, on that basis alone, assign them a high incentive value. We establish incentive values for various behaviors through inferring why we are behaving in particular ways. This stems from *attribution theory* (Kelley & Michela, 1980), which asserts that we try to understand behavior—both our own and others'—by searching for its causes (see Chapter 12).

◀ Corporate sponsors rely on errors in the attribution process for the success of their advertising. Here, professional skiers Picabo Street and Hilary Lindh prominently display endorsements of Coca-Cola. In reality, the athletes' success results from talent and hard work and has nothing to do with drinking a particular beverage.

Inference and Utility

Incentive value is typically a relative matter. Brand X may have more features that you like than Brand Y, but it may be harder to get or cost more. Once you conclude that you need something of a particular kind, you have to ask yourself what your chances are of getting it. What is the probability that a particular behavior will produce the desired object? This aspect of motivation—*expectancy*—is a central feature of subjective utility theory (Lopes, 1994).

Utility theory combines need, drive, and incentive into one concept: ***utility***. Of what utility (how useful) would a particular goal object or condition be to you? If you don't need or want skis, the best-quality pair in the world will have low utility for you, and if you are literally starving, the worst-tasting food will have high utility. Utility is a joint function of how much you think you need something and how attractive it is.

Probability of attaining the goal is also part of utility theory. Utility theory assumes that in any given situation, at least two alternative behaviors are possible. Each alternative has a certain probability of leading to a particular outcome or goal, and each goal has its own utility. Suppose you decide to invest $1,000. Do you put it in U.S. Treasury bills (T-bills) with an annual gain of 6 percent, or invest it in a new technology stock that could triple in value over the year? Utility theory suggests that the action you choose depends on how you weigh both the probability and the utility of the alternatives. Suppose the T-bills guarantee the 6 percent gain (100 percent probability), while the technology stock has a 2 percent chance of quadrupling your investment, but a 90 percent chance of going nowhere. The probability of the alternatives will combine with utility to determine your judgment.

Utility theorists study the factors that influence choice in a variety of situations that have uncertain consequences. Major life decisions, such as whether to have an operation and what doctor to choose to perform it, must be made without definite knowledge of their outcomes. Because in many situations the best you can do is estimate or guess at the probability of success, the probabilities and utilities are called ***subjective***. A key notion in utility theory is that what we *think* is true, not what *actually* is true, determines our behavior. If we think an alternative gives us a 1 in 10 chance to reach our goal, we are more likely to choose or prefer it over one that we think gives us a chance of 1 in 1,000 to reach the goal (all other things being equal).

Utility theory asserts that the action you choose depends on how you weigh the probability and utility of your alternatives.

Subjective utility theory says we make an overall judgment, called ***expected utility***, for each of the alternative courses of action available to us. We do this by combining the subjective utility of the goal object with the subjective probability that a particular behavior will lead to it. Let's return to our investment example.

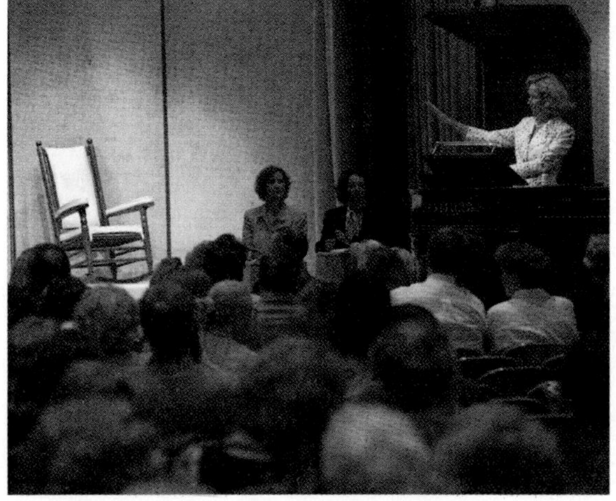

◀ How much would you be willing to spend for a used rocking chair? $100? $1,000? Does the fact that it once belonged to President John F. Kennedy change your assessment of its value? The chair pictured at left sold for $453,500 at the auction of the estate of Jacqueline Kennedy Onassis.

The T-bill's annual rate of return is 6 percent, so a $1,000 investment will yield $60 in one year (subjective utility). Its subjective probability is 1.0, because the federal government guarantees paying this 6 percent return. Consequently, that T-bill's subjective expected utility (or gain in value) is 1.0 × $60 = $60.

Now, let's consider the alternative of investing our $1,000 in a high-flying technology stock that could quadruple in value over a year, yielding a gain of $3,000. However, the likelihood that the stock will achieve this growth is only 2 percent, or 0.02. As a result, the stock's subjective expected utility (or gain in value) is 0.02 × $3,000 = $60. As both investments have the same subjective expected utility, utility theory suggests that we would have a difficult time in choosing between them.

Computing expected subjective utility is complicated by other considerations, however. You know that the stock market can go either up or down. Stocks are inherently risky investments. Rather than simply maintaining its value, your technology stock might lose value. People are less likely to take risks when losses are involved. The T-bill's 6 percent gain is guaranteed and there is no possibility of loss, while the gain of the technology stock is not guaranteed. Simply multiplying subjective utility by probability, as we have done, does not take this probability into account. Thus, the fact that the T-bill's outcome is certain means that it might be preferred over the technology stock, even though our computations assign the two investments the same expected subjective utility (Tversky & Fox, 1995).

▼ *The United Nations is an organization founded on and governed by the principles of equity theory.*

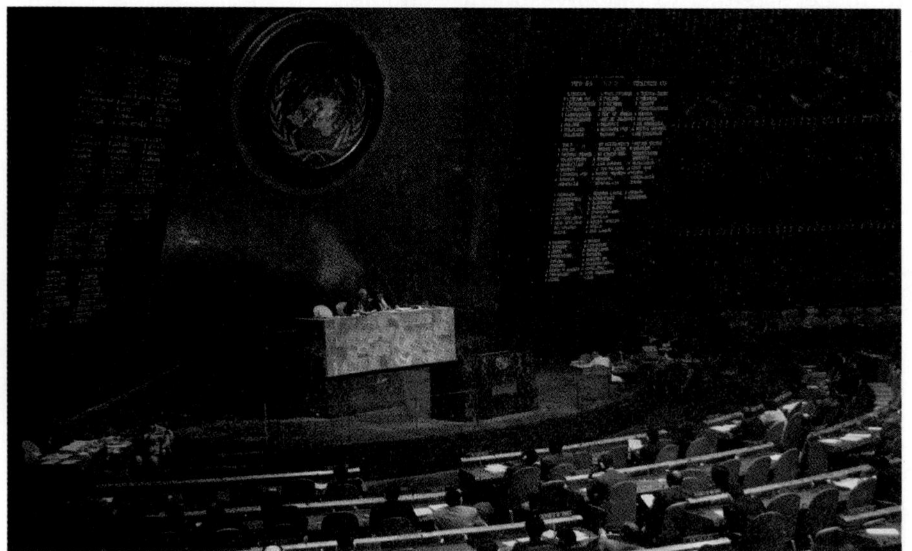

An action's expected utility generally correlates with motivation to take that action, other things being equal. If a given behavior is likely to lead us to a highly desirable goal, our motivation to engage in that behavior will be high. Likewise, we will have low motivation to achieve a low utility object. Utility theory focuses on what's going on inside people's minds, on motivation's cognitive aspects, and on the substantial information processing that takes place in even the simplest choice and motivational situations.

Equity Theory

Expectations about likelihood and utility of outcomes influence our choices in most situations. ***Equity theory*** builds on this idea with the notion that we choose outcomes to maintain our belief that people should generally get what they deserve. It says that we constantly compare our behavior and its rewards with the behavior and rewards of others, and we are motivated to maintain equitable conditions among people in all social situations.

Consider two roommates, Rita and Susan, who are both enrolled in a biology course. Suppose Rita studies fifteen hours for the first biology test and earns a B. Susan also studies fifteen hours but gets a D. What does equity theory predict Susan will feel? What will Rita feel? According to equity theory, if Susan believes that she and Rita are equally intelligent and have similar knowledge about biology, she will probably be upset and disgusted with her low grade and motivated to explain the inequity. She may change her view about how well prepared she and Rita were ("Rita knew more about biology to begin with"). Or she may qualify her performance ("I wasn't concentrating as hard as Rita was when studying; I'm an unlucky guesser; the test was unfairly scored"). Because it's the equity that is important, not the outcome, Rita will also perceive an inequity and be motivated to resolve it. She may decide that she is smarter or luckier than Susan.

According to equity theory, feelings about outcomes are not due to the specific outcomes per se—how much we are paid for a job, for example—but from our cognition that the outcomes are equitable for everyone—does

THINKING CRITICALLY

Employee theft is a costly problem that leads to increased prices for all. How can you apply equity principles to explain employee theft?

Equity theory suggests that employees who believe they are not being equitably compensated for their efforts will be more likely to steal from their employers. Indeed, research suggests that many employees do steal from their employers because the workers believe the rewards of their jobs are not proportionate to what they put into them—that their working conditions and/or pay are inequitable. The employees justify stealing as a means of restoring equity. Researchers demonstrated how theft can occur in response to perceived inequity in a study that promised participants $5 an hour for their time (Greenberg, 1993). At the end of the hour, half the participants were told they would be paid $5, while the other half were told they would be paid a lower rate of $3 per hour. In some cases, the researcher explained the cut, expressed regret, and apologized. In other cases, the cut was simply announced, with no explanation. The researcher then left the room, saying, "I don't know how much is here, but just take the amount you are supposed to be paid and leave the rest." Participants who expected and were paid $5 took that amount and did not steal any additional money. In contrast, participants who expected $5 but were paid $3 stole varying amounts of money, depending on how they had been treated. Those who were given both an explanation of why the rate had been cut and a sincere apology stole the least, taking an average of $3.20. Those who were given no information and no apology stole the most, taking an average of $4.80.

everyone receive equal pay for equal work? Thus, equity theory explains some human motivation as an attempt to restore order and justice to our world (Greenberg, 1993).

When Motives Collide

In setting goals and making choices, we are often faced with more than one source of motivation. When multiple sources of motivation all lead you in the same direction, they add together (summate), increasing total motivational level and making the choice of a particular course of action clear. But when two or more sources of motivation dictate different courses of action, they set up a state of motivational conflict.

When two or more sources of motivation dictate different courses of action, we experience a state of motivational conflict.

People tend to approach positive incentives and avoid negative incentives. Approach and avoidance tendencies combine to create three classical types of conflict:

1. *Approach-approach conflict*. Two positive incentives exist, but we can't have both—we must choose one and sacrifice the other. For example, should you spend the evening watching a favorite TV program or go to a movie with some friends?
2. *Avoidance-avoidance conflict*. Here you must choose between two negative alternatives or incentives. You may have to choose between an expensive and possibly painful visit to the dentist or the agony of a cracked tooth.
3. *Approach-avoidance conflict*. Frequently a single object or event involves both positive and negative incentives, producing approach and avoidance tendencies working against one another. For example, you realize you should go to the dentist to keep your teeth and gums clean and healthy, but you don't like the discomfort of dental work. In this type of conflict, distance from the incentive becomes especially important. Distance (which can be defined in several ways, including time or number of steps to the goal) increases the situation's positive aspects relative to its negative aspects. The further away you are, the more likely you are to be attracted to the goal. For example, you make an appointment with your dentist six months in advance. As the appointment date draws near, distance to the

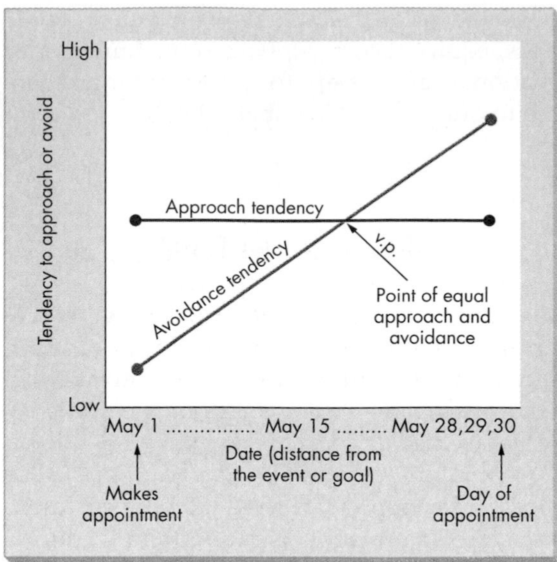

10-8 An Approach-Avoidance Conflict

The graph depicts the approach-avoidance conflict of patient Clyde Caries, who makes an appointment with his dentist on May 1, a full month before he has to show up. There are two tendencies, one to approach (go to the dentist) and one to avoid (stay away from the dentist). In this example, the approach gradient does not change as the time for the appointment draws nearer, but the avoidance tendency becomes stronger and stronger (Clyde anticipates a lot of pain) as the appointment gets closer. At first, the approach tendency is stronger than the avoidance tendency, and so the appointment is made. Later, as the time for the appointment draws near, the avoidance tendency gets stronger, and at some time it becomes as strong as the approach tendency. This is the point of maximum conflict about what to do, the vacillation point (v.p.). This is when Clyde may try to cancel or at least postpone the appointment.

goal is reduced. Negative aspects increase and may even surpass positive aspects, causing you to retreat from the goal. Maybe you cancel the appointment or postpone it. The reaction of two different hypothetical patients to this approach-avoidance conflict is shown in Figure 10-8.

These three classical types of conflict illustrate the role of incentives in making choices. Another kind of conflict that occurs in the real world can be described as multiple approach-avoidance conflict. This involves two incentives, both of which have approach and avoidance properties. Thus, you might have to choose between visiting your family for Thanksgiving (the negative incentive might be that you might get into an argument with your parents; the positive incentive might be that you would see your brother or your friends) or staying on campus (the positive incentive might be that you could catch up on all your work; the negative incentive might be that you would be lonely).

Emotion

Emotions ran high at the 1997 U.S. Women's Open Golf Tournament. Nancy Lopez was playing at the top of her form, the first woman ever to shoot four rounds in the 60s in that tournament. It was the only major championship she hadn't won in her twenty-one-year career. Despite her best efforts, she was defeated by England's Alison Nicholas by just a single stroke (Huffman, 1997). Emotional expressions of the joy of victory and sorrow of defeat were clearly captured in the photos of the event.

This example reminds us that motivation and emotion are closely linked. As you have seen, motivation involves needs and goals. Now think about what happens when our expectancies are not fulfilled. We may be sad, disappointed, frustrated, or even angry. When we achieve our goals, we are happy. Furthermore, just as motivation can influence emotions, emotional states can have motivational consequences. We are motivated to do all sorts of things to escape or avoid unpleasant emotional states (sadness, fear, anger, disgust) or to reach a pleasant emotional state (happiness, ecstasy). Thus, emotions can serve as incentives for motivated behavior.

Emotions are subjective internal states that have biological, cognitive, and social components. The expression of emotions is affected by physiological arousal, motivation, experience, cognitive interpretation of what is happening, and the social context. Physiological changes always accompany emotions, and some psychologists claim that each emotion has a unique associated physiological pattern. Heart rate may increase or decrease, respiration may speed up or slow down, pupils may dilate or constrict, muscles may contract or relax, and other physiological changes may occur, depending on the emotion. Emotions can also differ based on how you think about your situation. The same situation can trigger different emotional reactions, depending on how a person evaluates or appraises it. Finally, emotions have a social component: they are affected by the presence of other people.

Theories of Emotion

Try to recall an embarrassing situation you were in, or an occasion when you just barely escaped an accident, or the first time you gave a speech in public. Can you remember how you felt? Did your heart pound? Did you sweat? Was your mouth dry? Did your hands shake? Such reactions are controlled by the autonomic nervous system (see Chapter 3), and this part of the nervous system plays a key role in emotional responses.

Remember that the autonomic nervous system has two branches—the sympathetic and the parasympathetic—that are antagonistic, or reciprocal, in their relationship (see Table 10-3). The parasympathetic is dominant during ordinary daily events, when your emotions are relatively subdued; the sympathetic becomes dominant during highly emotional times, producing a rapid heart rate, sweating, and trembling (Berntson, Cacioppo, & Quigley, 1993).

The highly visible role that physiological responses play in emotion has meant that theories of emotion have focused on clarifying how the biological, motivational, experiential, cognitive, social, and behavioral aspects of emotion relate to one another (see Figure 10-9 on the following page). For a long time, the James-Lange and the Cannon-Bard theories of emotion were the primary contenders in the theoretical debates.

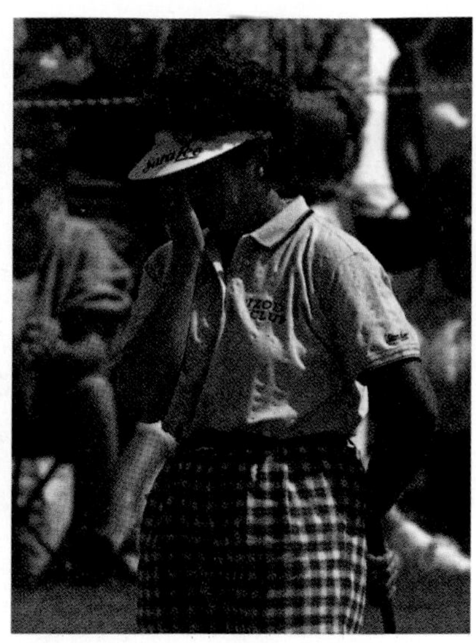

▲ *Alison Nicholas defeated Nancy Lopez by one stroke at the 1997 U.S. Women's Open. It's easy to tell from these photographs which woman was the winner.*

The James-Lange Theory

Suppose you encounter a ferocious bear in the woods. Two things are likely to happen: (1) you run to escape, and (2) you feel fear. The James-Lange theory of emotions (named after William James and Carl Lange, who independently suggested the theory) postulates that first you run, then realize you are afraid. Thus, seeing the bear leads to several physiological changes, such as increased blood pressure, pounding heart, faster breathing, and tensing of the muscles, as well as the response of running to escape the bear. When you perceive these changes, that is, after they occur, you interpret them as an emotion (fear). In other words, emotion is the feeling of bodily changes (Reisenzein, Meyer, & Schützwohl, 1995).

This theory states that we feel different emotions because the body produces different physiological changes and responses for each emotion-provoking stimulus. Thus, fear is not the same as anger because the body's physiological activity is qualitatively different for each of these two emotions (Ekman, Levenson, & Friesen, 1983).

The Cannon-Bard Theory

Walter B. Cannon and Philip Bard, working independently, formulated a prominent alternative to the James-Lange theory. Where the James-Lange theory states, "We see the bear, our body physiology changes, and then we experience fear," the Cannon-Bard theory makes a more commonsensical argument: "We see the bear, we simultaneously experience fear and our body physiology changes in reaction to our perceptions, then we run." Cannon and Bard thought that a subcortical structure in the brain,

Table 10-3 Some Differences between the Sympathetic and Parasympathetic Systems

Characteristic	Sympathetic Branch	Parasympathetic Branch
General effect	Prepares body to cope with stressful situations	Restores body to resting state after stressful situation; actively maintains normal body functions
Extent of effect	Widespread throughout body	Localized
Transmitter substance released at synapse	Norepinephrine and epinephrine	Acetylcholine
Duration of effect	Lasting	Brief

10-9 Four Theories of Emotion

The four theories of emotion all take into account physiological arousal, that is, bodily changes such as increased heart rate, breathing, and tensed muscles. But the theories differ, based on when the individual realizes that he or she is experiencing an emotion and based on the role that cognitive appraisal of a stimulus plays in interpreting the emotion.

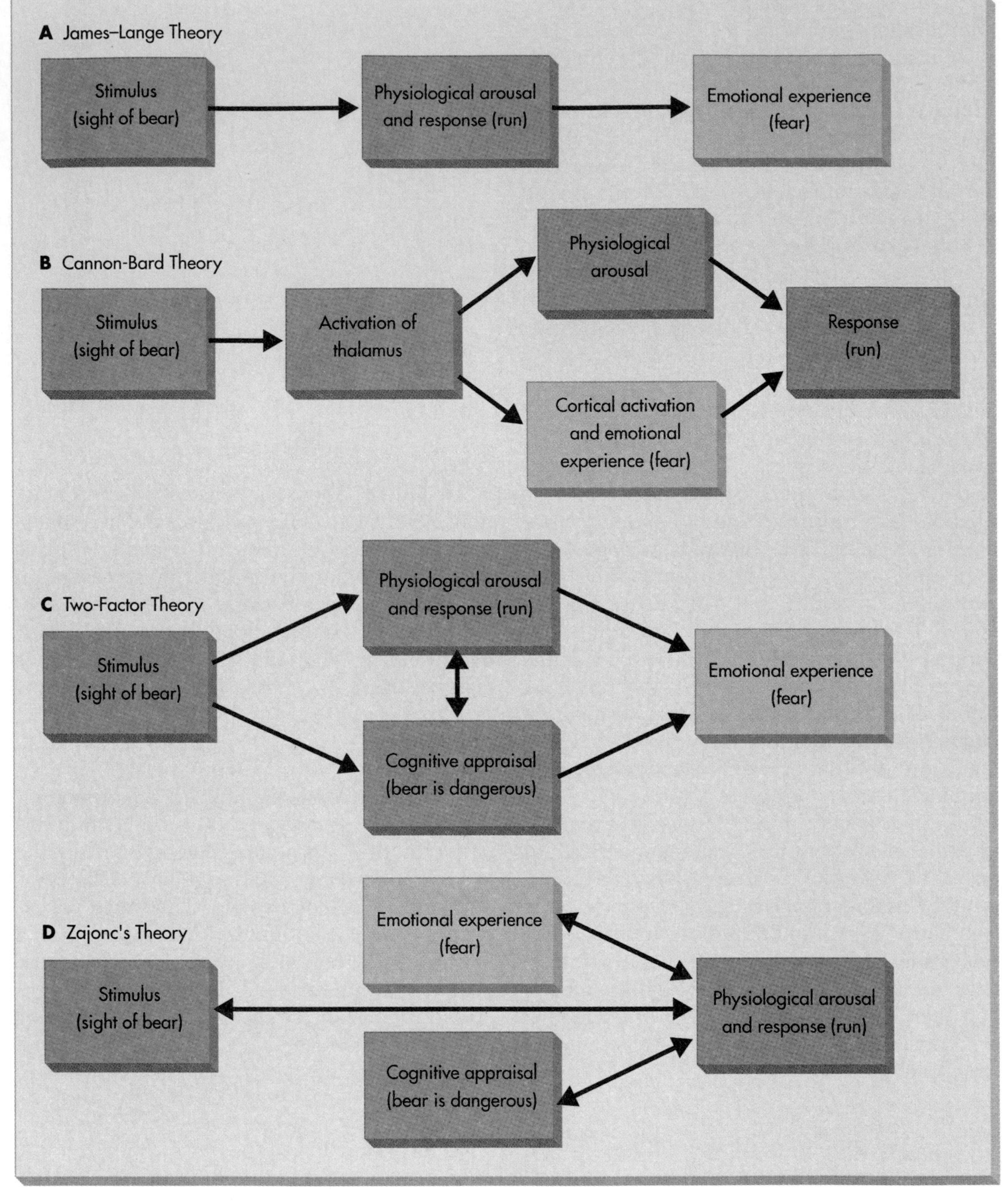

probably the thalamus (see Chapter 3), was the seat of emotions (although the hypothalamus and limbic system would have been a better guess). They said that when an emotional stimulus is presented, a subcortical structure is immediately stimulated. The subcortical structure then discharges electrical impulses upward into the brain, activating the cerebral cortex, and downward throughout the body, activating the autonomic nervous system. The cerebral cortex produces the emotional experience or feeling, and the autonomic nervous system produces an overall state of arousal that prepares the person for "fight or flight." Finally, there is an overt reaction, the behavioral component of emotion, which comes after both the biological and experiential aspects.

Recall that the James-Lange theory implies a

Table 10-4 The Universal Relationship between Facial Expression and Emotion

Anger	Happiness	Disgust	Surprise	Sadness	Fear
United States	97%	92%	95%	84%	85%
South America	96%	94%	92%	72%	63%
Japan	100%	90%	100%	62%	66%

The percentage of subjects from three different cultures who identified each facial expression as an instance of the label shown.
Source: Ekman, 1973.

different pattern of physiological reaction for each emotion. Cannon and Bard believed that all emotions produce a single pattern of physiological arousal. Several types of research findings support the James-Lange explanation of emotion over that of Cannon-Bard. For one thing, different emotions do have different patterns of physiological activity (Levenson, 1992). Research has demonstrated a difference between fear and anger in adrenal gland production of the hormones adrenaline and noradrenaline (Ax, 1953; Ekman, Levenson, & Friesen, 1983). Adrenaline dominates during fear, while both adrenaline and noradrenaline are present during anger. Animals that are being pursued as prey secrete high amounts of adrenaline compared with predators, which show predominantly noradrenaline secretion. Such research provides evidence that one can distinguish between internal states associated with different emotions.

In addition, there is some evidence that proves muscle movement can actually produce an emotional experience. This research is based on what is known as the facial feedback hypothesis.

The Facial Feedback Hypothesis

The expression on your face at any time is created by an interlocking system of forty-four separate muscles. These expressions are, among other things, a form of communication, particularly communication about what you are feeling (Russell, 1994). Certain facial expressions tied to particular emotions occur more or less universally in all cultures (see Table 10-4). All people smile when they are happy and frown when they are sad. Many of these expressions are first seen very early in life, suggesting that they probably depend more on biological factors than on experience and learning. Other expressions are unique to a culture or even to an individual (Mesquita & Frijda, 1992).

Because a link between facial expression and emotion appears to be universal and developed in infancy, physiological patterns associated with particular expressions may be uniquely linked to specific emotions. To test this idea, Paul Ekman and his colleagues asked research participants to move facial muscles to communicate certain emotions (for example, they were told to "look as sad as you can") and measured the subjects' physiological responses (for example, heart rate and skin temperature). Other participants were asked to imagine a previous

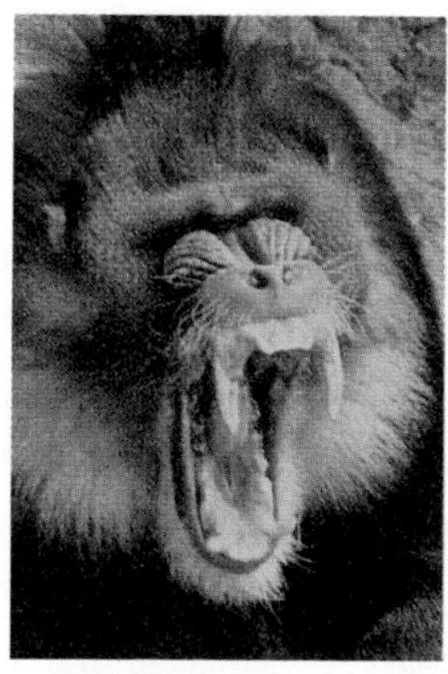

◀ *Some emotions are universal, not only among humans, but also among other primates. Tennis player Conchita Martinez of Spain expresses anger and frustration after losing at Wimbledon.*

emotional experience. Essentially the same results were obtained from "posers" and "re-livers." Whether posing or imagining the emotions, participants tended to show the same facial expressions and physiological reactions that were distinct and unique for each emotion (Ekman, Levenson, & Friesen, 1983). If you try to look happy or to recall a happy experience, your physiology will change in a particular way consistent with being happy. Sadness will bring forth a different physiological change. The "facial feedback" data suggest that unique physiological conditions underlie different emotional experiences and that these physiological changes can be initiated cognitively.

Further research on the facial feedback hypothesis has shown that "real" or "felt" smiles, based on true positive emotional feeling, involve contraction of the muscles that pull the corners of the lip back and up and affect the ring of muscles around the eyes, producing a slight narrowing of the eyes and "crow's-feet" wrinkles on the eyes' outside corners. In contrast, "unfelt" smiles, which are created deliberately to conceal negative feelings, involve contraction of only the muscles that turn up the corners of the lips—thus, they produce no crow's-feet (Fox & Davidson, 1993). Ekman reported that these two types of smiles also differ in associated electrical brain activity (Ekman & Davidson, 1993). Ekman concludes that smiles of real happiness and enjoyment have characteristic physiological patterns that distinguish them from fake smiles or smiles that reflect a different emotion (Ekman, 1993). Such results are consistent with the James-Lange idea that physiological reactions differ among emotions and that emotions can arise because we become aware of our bodily states.

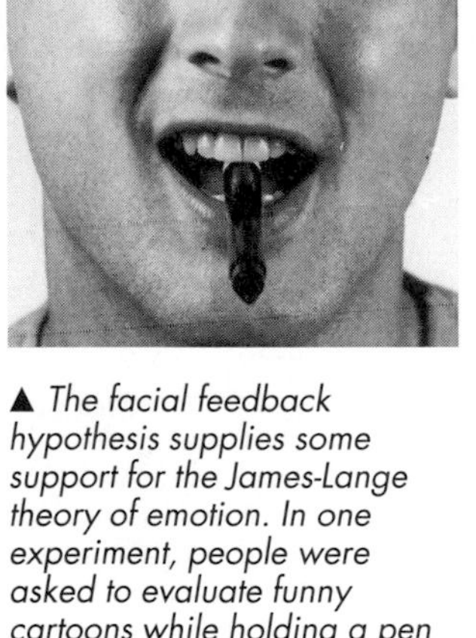

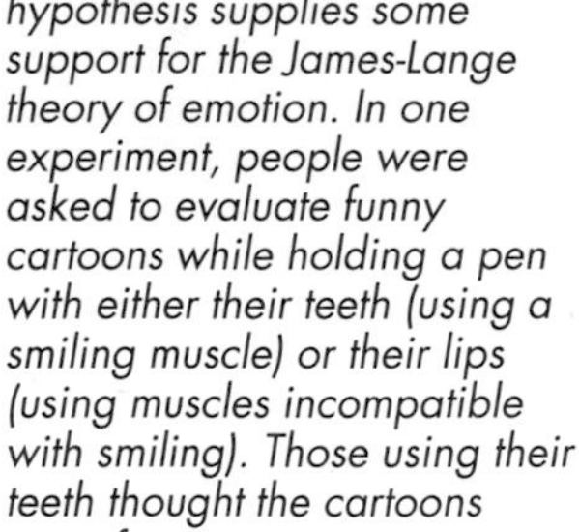

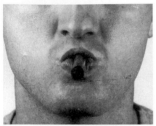

▲ *The facial feedback hypothesis supplies some support for the James-Lange theory of emotion. In one experiment, people were asked to evaluate funny cartoons while holding a pen with either their teeth (using a smiling muscle) or their lips (using muscles incompatible with smiling). Those using their teeth thought the cartoons were funnier.*

Opponent Processes in Emotions

Suppose you are sitting at a stop light; the light turns green, and you proceed into the intersection. Suddenly a huge truck, moving at sixty miles an hour and blaring its horn, runs the red light from the other direction, missing your front bumper by two inches. You slam on the brakes; your heart is pounding and your hands are shaking. You are terrified. But you don't stay terrified. You take a deep breath, and continue on your way, beginning to calm down even before you have driven another block. Why don't you stay terrified? What mechanism calms us down once our emotions are triggered?

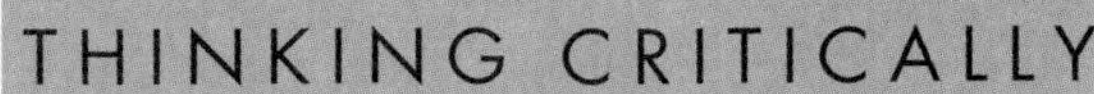

THINKING CRITICALLY

How would you use opponent-process theory to explain how drug tolerance develops in reaction to narcotics?

Initial drug experiences might be pleasant and give the user a "high." But a counteracting, unpleasant opponent process (sickness, depression) would soon arise and gather strength with each use. As a consequence of these opponent processes, the pleasant feeling produced by the drug would lessen. With each successive experience, more of the drug would be needed to produce the same pleasant effect. The user would gradually become dependent on the drug, not for its pleasurable effects (which might actually no longer be experienced as drug tolerance developed), but to avoid the unpleasant consequences created by the opponent process. Unavailability of the drug would lead to withdrawal, the full-blown opponent process in action, without the pleasure that had originally been experienced.

Opponent-process theory applies the concepts of optimal level of arousal and homeostasis to answer this question. This theory suggests that we have a homeostatic system that operates to counteract extreme emotional changes and to return our arousal level to a normal, optimal range (Solomon & Corbit, 1973, 1974). If we have a large change in arousal as a result of a pleasant or unpleasant stimulus, the homeostatic system quickly activates an opponent process to counteract the initial emotional reaction. The overall experience is a *combination* of opposing forces (see Figure 10-10). If the stimulus initially produces a pleasant emotion, a negative opponent process soon begins to counteract it, reducing the pleasure level and reestablishing homeostasis. If the pleasant stimulus is repeated, the counteracting process gathers strength. As the opponent process becomes

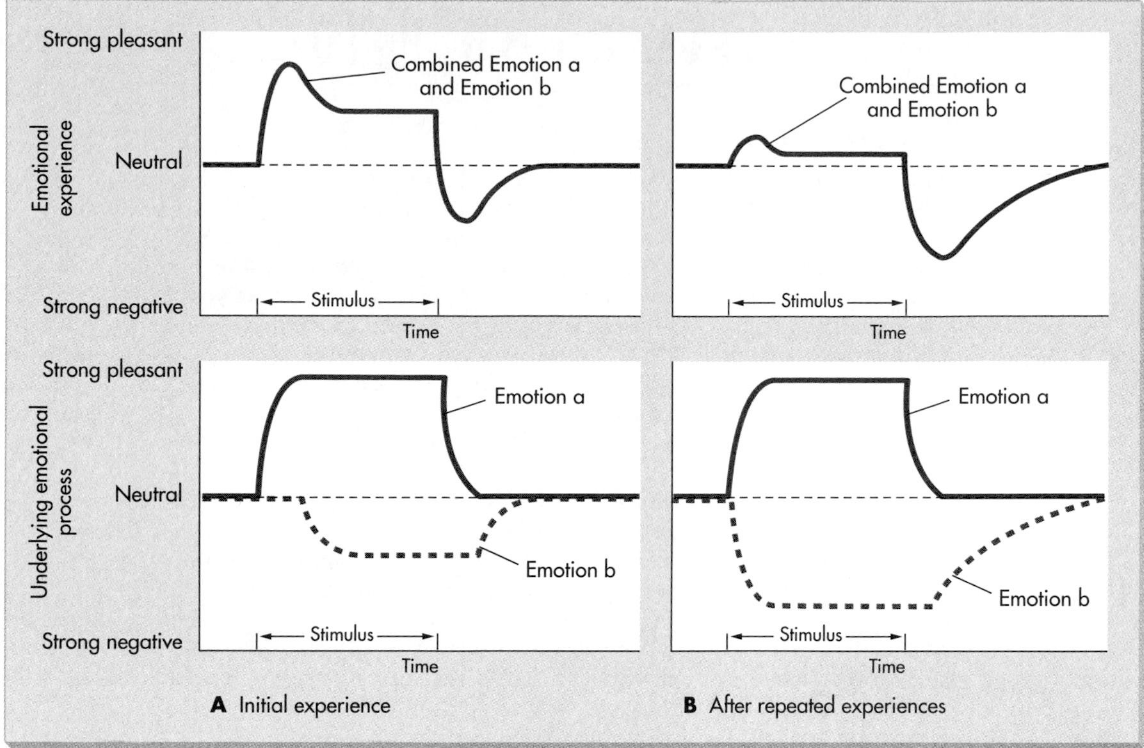

10-10 Opponent Process Theory and Emotions

(A) These graphs represent the initial emotional experience according to the opponent-process theory. The top graph shows the combined experience of Emotion *a* and Emotion *b*. The bottom graph shows the pleasant Emotion *a*, which activates the opposite negative Emotion *b*. (B) These graphs represent how the emotions are experienced after repetition. In the top graph, the combined experience of Emotion *a* and Emotion *b* is more neutral, with the pleasant Emotion *a* balanced out by the negative Emotion *b*. In the bottom graph, the negative Emotion *b* has become stronger, which is why the combined emotional experience is more neutral. (Source: Adapted from Solomon, 1980)

stronger, the degree of pleasantness experienced with each repetition will diminish until finally it is completely balanced out by the negative opponent process. At that point, the initially pleasant stimulus no longer produces a pleasant feeling. The same argument is made for initially unpleasant experiences. They, too, have opponent (in this case, positive) processes, so that the experience of unpleasantness produced by a negative stimulus decreases with time and repetition.

Opponent-process theory may account for people's enthusiasm for dangerous sports such as hang gliding and skydiving. According to opponent-process theory, the more afraid you are during the experience of hang gliding and skydiving, the more exhilarated you should be when you finish (assuming you survive).

The Two-Factor Theory of Emotion

Emotional experience can be divided into two parts: general (physiological) arousal and cognitive appraisal (Weiner, 1985). Arousal is the energizing aspect of emotion. Appraisal refers to recognizing, categorizing, and evaluating a situation. For example, suppose you wake up suddenly in the middle of the night. Maybe there was a strange sound. You judge it to be a threat. The emotional experience is a combination of your arousal level and your understanding of the situation. Which comes first has been subject to debate, but in reality it doesn't matter most of the time, as arousal and appraisal are constantly changing and interacting. Sometimes the change in arousal precedes appraisal; sometimes it follows appraisal (Zajonc, 1980). Appraisal can occur instantaneously, without involving complex cognitions. There may be an elementary appraisal process originating in the lower (subcortical) centers of the brain that can operate without our being consciously aware of it (LeDoux, 1989).

Whether or not physiological arousal is necessary for a particular emotion may be debated, but studies of paraplegics, individuals whose spinal cords were accidently severed, suggest that such arousal is related to emotional intensity. Although paraplegics say they continue to have emotional experiences after their accidents, those experiences are not as intense, possibly because they are incapable of normal psychological arousal (Hohmann, 1962).

Arousal signals that something is happening, and if aroused, we seek an explanation for it. Depending on circumstances, we label that

SEEKING SOLUTIONS

Controlling Emotions

You are driving home from work on a crowded two-lane freeway. You are hot, tired, and hungry. For some reason, all of the other drivers on the road are conspiring to block you from your goal of getting home as fast as you can. Two cars driving abreast in front of you are driving one mile under the speed limit, and consequently making you feel very frustrated. One car finally speeds up, and you have an opening, but before you can make your move, another driver cuts you off and now blocks you from passing the car in front of you. Your heart pounds, your palms sweat, your face turns red, and you feel extremely angry—will you succumb to road rage and act on your anger, perhaps by tailgating the interloper? Or will you be able to control your emotions and release your tension in a more constructive way? Unfortunately, all too many people have not learned to control their emotions, on the freeway or otherwise.

Emotions can be controlled in one of two ways, corresponding to the two principal components of emotion: general arousal and cognitive appraisal. First, we can teach people to modify their general arousal level. Usually, people in need of emotional control are overly aroused; therefore, they might be taught to relax using techniques such as meditation or monitoring breathing or controlling muscle tension. An effective method for dealing with stress is simply to try to remain relaxed and calm. Very high arousal levels make it difficult to do anything but the simplest tasks (according to the Yerkes-Dodson principle), and so relaxing and reducing arousal will almost always help. Deep breathing, taking large breaths and slowly exhaling through your nose, is one of the best ways to relax.

The second aspect of emotions is your appraisal of the situation. Learning to control your emotions means that you must learn to control and modify cognitive appraisals. If you don't think negatively about a situation, for example, your negative emotions are likely to disappear. Consider the two most common features of meditation and yoga: deep breathing and continual focus on a mantra (a sound you say over and over to yourself). The deep breathing will lower your arousal, while focusing your thoughts on the mantra will prevent you from making negative cognitive appraisals of the situation. The two techniques used in combination are an excellent treatment for reducing emotional stress.

You may not be able simply to drop off into a meditative state any time you are in a tense situation (indeed, such a response is not typically adaptive). As an alternative, when meditation is inappropriate, try thinking about your emotion-causing circumstances in a different way, that is, create a different cognitive appraisal. Learning to make different cognitive appraisals of the same situation can produce greater control over your emotions. When someone cuts in front of you in traffic, causing you to slam on your brakes, appraise the event in more than one way. If you think about the situation only in terms of the danger to yourself, the wear and tear on your brakes, or the additional delay it causes you, you will probably end up feeling angry and upset. But suppose you concentrate on your skills and alertness as a driver and on how important defensive driving is because no one on the road is perfect. Alternatively, try to think of reasons why the other driver cut in front—perhaps a family member is ill or a child is waiting to be picked up at school. Thoughts like these might keep you from experiencing anger.

In general, whenever you feel strong emotions, stop, take a deep, slow breath, and ask yourself whether there is a more constructive way to think about what is happening to you. This approach will often be helpful, not just because it brings your emotional reaction under control, but also because it helps you determine your next move.

If you learn to control arousal level and to be flexible in making cognitive appraisals (especially if you learn to empathize, or to imagine how the other person is appraising the situation), you will have two major tools for controlling your emotions. In addition to avoiding road rage, controlling your emotions may even help you avoid such ills as asthma and heart disease, to say nothing of anxiety and all the problems it causes. An added benefit of such a simple maneuver is the possible prevention of unnecessary violent behavior. You can apply research about emotions by learning to relax and to think about stressful events in constructive ways and thereby reduce the effects of the stressors that you will inevitably encounter in the course of daily living.

arousal as the emotion that seems most appropriate, depending on the situation. This is called the ***two-factor theory of emotion***. Stanley Schachter and Jerome Singer devised a clever experiment to test the effect of cognitive appraisal on emotions (Schacter & Singer, 1962). Their research participants received an arousal-inducing shot of adrenaline under the pretext that it was a vitamin shot. After receiving the shot, half the participants were asked to wait in a room with someone else, a confederate (an accomplice of the experimenter, although the participants were not aware of this) who pretended to be very angry. The other half waited in a room with a confederate who pretended to be very happy. Participants in the first condition, aroused by the adrenaline, reported that they felt angry, while those in the other group said they felt happy. Thus, participants believed their arousal, which actually came from adrenaline, was due to the situation and experienced emotional (or subjective) feelings based on what they thought was causing the arousal. The presence of an angry confederate suggested they should feel angry; the presence of a happy confederate suggested they should feel happy. A control group of participants who were given a placebo injection did not experience either anger or happiness when placed in the room with either confederate. Without adrenaline, they experienced little or no arousal. Both arousal *and* context were needed for a full emotional reaction to occur.

Robert Zajonc doubts that cognitive appraisal as described by Schachter and Singer is the usual cause of emotional feeling. He argues that in most circumstances the emotional feeling and the behavioral reaction occur too rapidly to be caused by prior cognitive appraisal. If you happen upon a bear in the woods, you don't spend a lot of time thinking before you feel scared and start running. Zajonc suggests instead that cognitive appraisal and emotional experience are relatively independent of each other. He argues that they proceed in parallel, and that either can be the first to react to a stimulus (Zajonc, 1980). Empirical evidence about the interaction of cognitive appraisal, subjective feeling, and physiological arousal is far from clear at the present time. The debate among theorists will continue until we have more definitive data (Lazarus, 1991a; Reisenzein, 1983).

Classifying Emotions

Emotions have at least two principal dimensions, one qualitative (pleasant–unpleasant) and the other quantitative (mild–extreme). The difference between the unpleasant emotions of anger and rage is primarily quantitative, as is the difference between the pleasant emotions of happiness and ecstasy. Robert Plutchik proposes that the pleasant–unpleasant dimension can be classified into eight subtypes or primary human emotions (see Figure 10-11). Each subtype can be positive or negative, primary (joy, acceptance, fear, surprise, sadness, disgust, anger, and anticipation) or mixed (anger and disgust combine to produce contempt), a polar opposite (love is opposite to remorse; joy is opposite to sadness), and can vary in intensity (Plutchik, 1980).

Our motivation to seek certain goals is affected by our emotions. Unpleasant emotional states (and the behaviors that produce them) act as negative incentives that we are motivated to avoid or escape. Pleasant emotional states (and the behaviors that produce them) act as positive incentives that we are motivated to achieve or sustain. As we learn about the world, we can anticipate emotional states that specific objects and events will elicit. Then we can seek goals that we expect will elicit positive emotions and try to avoid situations that we expect will result in unpleasant emotions. If we know that Gwen makes us laugh and feel happy, we will seek out her company. If we know that Chuck is crit-

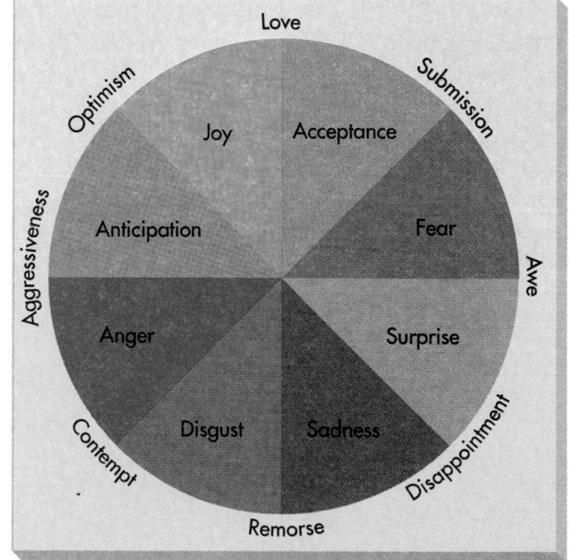

10-11 Plutchik's Emotion Wheel

According to Robert Plutchik, there are eight primary emotions (shown inside the wheel; for example, joy or anger), which interact with each other to form more complex emotions (shown outside the wheel; for example, love or awe). (Source: Plutchik, 1980)

▶ *Many emotions are universal across cultures, but the way emotions are expressed can differ. In New Orleans, mourners at funerals play jazz music and march in a parade to honor the dead. Elsewhere, mourners are expected to contain their emotions.*

ical and sarcastic and makes us feel uncomfortable, we will avoid him. Of course, we cannot avoid everything unpleasant—Chuck may be invited to the same parties we are. In that case, we can seek to escape from his presence.

The degree of motivation depends on the strength of the anticipated or experienced state. The stronger or more intense the emotion is, the greater the motivation to approach, avoid, or escape from it.

Cultural Factors in Emotional Experience

Only the recognition that we have something to gain or lose . . . generates an emotion.

—Richard Lazarus (1991a, p. 354)

While there are some commonalities across cultures, there are also some important cultural differences in emotional expression and emotional feeling. For example, there is some evidence that emotion, as a major dimension of human behavior, is valued less in Western culture than cognition (Dember, Melton, Nguyen, & Howe, 1993). When college students in the United States talk about the behavior of others, they tend to use more intellectual (''He didn't understand the question'') than emotional (''He was too upset to get it right'') descriptors. Moreover, people from different cultures may learn different categories for mental or psychological states. For example, Hopi Indians have five terms that distinguish among five types of depression, approximating our concepts of ''deep worry,'' ''pouting,'' ''drunken-like craziness,'' ''unhappiness,'' and ''being heartbroken'' (Goleman, 1995). Some languages do not even have a word for ''emotion.'' Other languages label emotions differently than does English. Thus, people may express and evaluate emotions differently for cultural reasons (Russell, 1991; 1994).

When young professionals from twenty-seven countries were asked about their naturally occurring emotions, they reported differences in frequency, intensity, and duration (Wallbot & Scherer, 1986). Comparison of Japanese and American students revealed that the Americans were more emotional than the Japanese. The Americans were more likely to describe emotions that were longer lasting, of greater intensity, and associated with more bodily symptoms than the Japanese (Matsumoto, Kudoh, Scherer, & Wallbot, 1988). In cultures valuing individualism (American and European), individuals react more strongly to emotion-provoking situations than do individuals from Asian collectivist cultures (Gudykunst, Ting-Toomey, & Chua, 1988). How and when our emotions are expressed clearly reflect our culture.

▼ *The smile is a universal expression of pleasure, but what makes people smile can vary in different cultures.*

Anxiety and Anger

Anxiety and ***anger*** are especially important emotions in relation to motivation. Anxiety arises when the path to a goal is unclear, difficult, or threatened. Severe anxiety may interfere with everyday functioning, to the point that no goals can be pursued and therapy becomes advisable. Anger arises when the path to a goal is blocked, which can lead to frustration and aggressive behavior. Anger is an emotional reaction that occurs when we attribute blame for our negative experiences to others and perceive them as unjustly blocking us from our goals. Both anxiety and anger can produce undesirable behavior in people. Understanding these emotions may help us control, if not eliminate, their undesirable behavioral consequences.

Anxiety probably evolved to help people cope with danger. Anxiety involves feelings of tension, apprehension, or fear that are not attached to any particular stimulus object. We tend to be anxious when we think that a harmful or threatening stimulus *might* occur. When none can be identified, our anxiety is called free-floating or diffuse. In contrast, fear is the emotion produced by a clear and present threatening stimulus. As unpleasant states, anxiety and fear have negative incentive value. We are motivated to avoid or to escape anxiety when it occurs.

Neal Miller conducted a classic experiment demonstrating the motivational force of anxiety (Miller, 1948). He put a rat into the white compartment of a two-sided shuttlebox, where it was electrically shocked, causing it to run to the other side of the compartment, which was painted black to make it distinctive and where shock did not occur. This sequence was repeated on several occasions, until presumably the rat was conditioned to fear the white compartment. At that point, no further shocks were administered. Still, the rat continued to show signs of fear (now called anxiety because no shock was present) whenever it was placed on the white side. Given an opportunity, the rat would run to the black side. The white side had acquired negative incentive value and/or the black side had acquired positive incentive value for the rat.

Next, a wheel was placed in the white compartment and a door was installed between the white and the black compartments. The wheel, if turned, would open the door. Fairly quickly the rat discovered how to turn the wheel as a way of getting out of the white compartment—*even though shock was never administered.* The rat was not escaping from shock now, but rather from the threat of shock. The rat learned to escape, presumably because of the prior association of the white side with a painful stimulus. The rat was motivated by a conditioned anxiety produced by the white compartment or by the relief afforded by the black compartment. Control rats (who were not shocked when placed on the white side) may not have learned to turn the wheel as quickly as the rats in the experimental group because the control rats did not have the incentive of finding a way to escape anticipated shock.

"Can I kick it for you this time, Daddy?"

◀ *In a technological society, machines that do not work properly are a common source of anger.*

Anxiety is a generalized state of tension, apprehension, or fear that is not attached to any particular stimulus object.

Reflections and Observations

Issues related to motivation and emotion deal with some of the most fundamental and puzzling questions addressed by psychologists: Why do people behave and feel the way they do? The material in this chapter is intertwined with concepts from learning, cognitive development, social, health, and personality psychology. How do our motivations and emotions change with age? How do they affect our health and well-being, or become expressed as mental disorders? As researchers discover new ways to describe and understand human motivations and emotions, we will come closer to answering these questions. In the next chapter, we will focus on physical, social, and emotional development over the life cycle.

KEY TERMS

need

hierarchy of needs

drive

incentive

homeostasis

arousal

optimal level of arousal

Yerkes-Dodson law

sensation seeking

instinct

setpoint

hyperphagia

aphagia

self-actualization

need for affiliation

Objectives Revisited

Motivation and emotion are both concepts that psychologists use to understand how behavior becomes energized. Both motivation and emotion reflect a combination of biological, psychological, and social factors. These concepts also help us to understand variability in behavior, both within the same person from time to time and between individuals. When we understand factors influencing motivation and emotion, we can apply them at home, at school, at work, and in psychological services to help people work toward their goals.

Objective 1. Define motivation, and discuss how the concepts of need, drive, incentive, arousal, and homeostasis are used to explain motivated behavior.

Motivation is what gets an organism moving. It provides both the energy and the direction for behavior. A *need* is an internal state of deprivation—either biological, social, or cognitive—that requires satisfaction. A *drive* is the motivational push to behavior that generally results from a need. Organisms will work to attain an *incentive*, external objects or events that have a motivational pull on behavior. *Arousal* is the psychological energy level that accompanies a drive, while *homeostasis* is the body's tendency to maintain a state of equilibrium. Much of our behavior appears motivated to maintain an optimal level of arousal. We seek out sources of stimulation when our arousal is lower than optimal, and we attempt to reduce stimulation when we become overaroused.

Objective 2. Discuss how biological and sociocultural factors influence the biologically based needs for food, drink, and sex.

Biological perspectives focus on the biological systems involved in motivation, particularly in nonhuman animal species. Primary motivations relate in one way or another to the correction of biological deficits, such as food or water deprivation leading to hunger or thirst. We have built-in physiological systems that regulate our intake of such vital substances as food and water. Homeostatic mechanisms maintain our bodily fluid levels within a critical range. The hypothalamus plays a central role in the homeostasis of bodily nutrients and fluids.

The homeostatic system regulating food intake is complex. *Setpoint* is the standard used by the body to monitor its fat and sugar levels. The hypothalamus is the primary neurological mechanism for regulating weight levels and food intake. Social and environmental factors, such as the sight, smell, and taste of food, also affect food intake. Some people are more receptive to external cues than others, and this sensitivity, combined with biological factors, can increase risk for obesity.

Sexual behavior is motivated in complex ways and varies with culture. To understand human sexual motivation, we must consider biological and cultural factors. While human beings have a genetic predisposition to desire sex, particular sexual behaviors can be affected by operant and classical conditioning as well as by observation.

Objective 3. Explain what is meant by a social motive, and distinguish among affiliation, approval, achievement, and power motivations.

From the social-personality perspective, motivation is intimately related to human personality, which can be viewed as a product of psychological (as opposed to biological) needs and of predispositions to respond to particular incentives. Maslow proposed a *hierarchy of needs*, contending that higher social needs, such as love, belongingness, and self-esteem, emerge only as lower ones are satisfied. The highest need, self-actualization, differs from other needs in being a need for growth rather than a need to remedy a deficiency.

The *need for affiliation* is a basic social motive expressing our need to be with other people, have companionship, make friends, cooperate, help others, and develop caring, loving relationships. The *need for social approval* is expressed in attempts to obtain approval or to avoid the disapproval of others, and the related concept of sociability is willingness to engage others in social interactions and seek their approval or attention. *Need for achievement* is defined as a general personality disposition to strive for success, while the *need for power* reflects our desire to have an impact on others. Differences in expectations, values, and environments of males and females appear to explain male–female differences in social behavior better than differences in basic social needs explain them.

Intrinsic motivation refers to achievement motivation that is due to the personal enjoyment of performing a behavior, rather than to any external rewards resulting from that behavior. *Extrinsic motivation* refers to the external rewards that motivate a behavior. If a behavior is intrinsically motivated, it will persist without being rewarded; if it is extrinsically rewarded, the behavior will usually occur only so long as it leads to rewards.

Objective 4. Explain the relationship of goal setting and choices to behavior, and how inference and attribution affect the subjective expected utility of goal objects and behavioral outcomes.

From the perspective of goal seeking and choice, motivation entails *attribution* (assigning value to objects based on the esteem we hold for the people who possess them), *subjective expected utility* (valuing objects based on their estimated worth and the probability of obtaining them), and *equity* (believing that people's rewards should be proportionate to their contributions and that people should get what they deserve). Utility theory combines drive and incentive into one concept (utility) and suggests that our chosen actions will depend on how we weigh the probability and subjective utility of our alternatives.

Objective 5. Define emotion, compare and contrast various theories of emotion, and explain how the emotions of anger and anxiety relate to behavior.

Various theories have tried to integrate the known components of emotion, emphasizing one or another of them. An emotional stimulus arouses the system, and the behavioral reaction and emotional feeling depend on the subsequent appraisal of the arousal and the context in which it occurs. The *James-Lange theory* describes emotion as interpreting changes in body physiology. The *Cannon-Bard theory* asserts that feelings, behaviors, and physiological changes occur in parallel as a function of a stimulus-triggering activity in the thalamus. The *two-factor theory* stresses a combination of cognitive and arousal factors. *Opponent-process theory* deals mainly with feelings of pleasantness and unpleasantness: when the arousal level is changed by either a pleasant or an unpleasant stimulus, the homeostatic system will immediately activate an opponent process to counteract the first emotional reaction.

There are at least two dimensions of emotional feeling, the qualitative dimension of pleasantness–unpleasantness and the quantitative dimension of intensity. But the expression of emotion entails at least five variables: physiological arousal, motivation, experience, a cognitive interpretation of context, and a behavioral component.

In-depth analyses of fear, anxiety, and anger have shown how these emotional feelings relate to motivation. Excessive and prolonged emotional states have been implicated as causal factors in many forms of illness. Learning to control the arousal and cognitive labeling associated with these states can make our lives healthier and more pleasant.

need for social approval

need for achievement

extrinsic motivation

intrinsic motivation

need for power

utility

expected subjective utility

equity theory

emotion

James-Lange theory

Cannon-Bard theory

facial feedback hypothesis

opponent processes

two-factor theory

anxiety

anger

CHAPTER 11

Developmental Psychology

OBJECTIVES

After reading this chapter, you should be able to:

1. Explain what is meant by development and developmental processes, and describe the methods psychologists use to study them.
2. Describe prenatal development, and explain why risks for different types of birth defects change over the course of pregnancy.
3. Describe the highlights of physical, cognitive, and social development in infancy and childhood.
4. Describe how adolescents think and the social and moral concerns of adolescents.
5. Describe some of the transitions experienced in the three periods of adulthood.

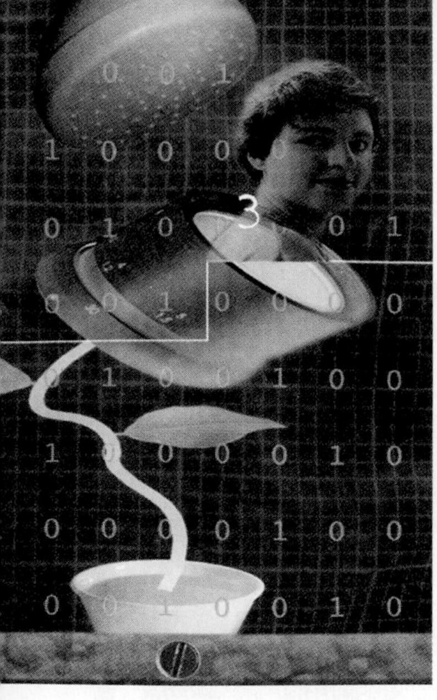

You are a child psychologist. A mother telephones your office, frantic over the sudden personality change in her son. "He used to be so sweet and then, out of the clear blue sky, he started being sassy and sulky and throwing a fit if anybody asked him to do the least little thing. What really scared me was last night he got so mad at his brother, he ran at him and started hitting him with all his might. His brother was really hurt and started screaming, and my husband and I had to pull them apart. I don't know what would have happened if we hadn't been there. I just never saw anybody in a rage like that before." (Case quoted from Wenar, 1990, p. 1.) In deciding how to treat the child, the first question you must ask is: *What is the child's age?* This is a serious problem in self-control for a ten-year-old, but it is common behavior during "the terrible twos."

This vignette illustrates a basic fact of human development—we change radically over time, not just physically but also behaviorally. Developmental psychology is the branch of psychology that focuses on behavioral changes over the life span.

▼ *Relationships with family members are important socialization experiences and can help children develop a positive ethnic identity. Here, a Santo Domingo Pueblo elder is shown with his granddaughter.*

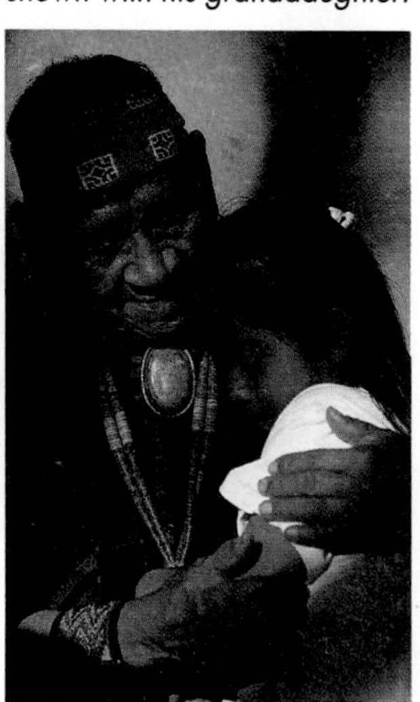

Understanding the Developmental Perspective

Development is defined as systematic qualitative and quantitative changes that occur in an individual's biological, psychological, social, and emotional capacities over the life span. Developmental psychologists study how these systematic changes and associated behaviors unfold. Development, particularly in childhood, has certain basic characteristics: it is orderly, continual, and cumulative. That is, developmental changes occur in a logical sequence; they are happening all the time; and changes at each age build up on what came before.

Fully understanding development requires integrating biological, cognitive, and social aspects of behavior over the life cycle. Although development is continual over the life span, there are times, particularly during childhood, that we change so markedly from one period to another that we are said to be in a different stage of development. Table 11-1 lists the approximate ages at which various stages of human development occur in Western culture (Erikson, 1982). Keep in mind, however, that developmental stages can be defined in different ways and depend on the cultural context. Adolescence is not considered a separate stage of development in all societies, for example.) Further,

Table 11-1 Chronological Stages of Human Development

Stage	Approximate Time Frame*
Prenatal	Conception to birth
Infancy	Birth to 2 years
Toddlerhood	2 to 3 years
Preschool	3 to 6 years
Middle childhood	6 years to adolescence
Adolescence	11–13 years puberty to young adulthood
Early adulthood	20–40 years
Middle adulthood	40–65 years
Late adulthood	Beyond 65 years

*Age ranges are approximate and may not apply to a particular individual.

even within American society, the age ranges may not apply to a particular individual. For example, a ten-year-old may experience puberty and become classified as an adolescent. Teenagers who have children of their own and are self-supporting are more appropriately classified as young adults.

Maturation and Learning

Two major processes underlie the changes that occur as we develop over the life span: maturation (nature) and learning (nurture). ***Maturation*** refers to the biological unfolding of the body as a result of a genetic "blueprint" transmitted by parents at conception. The effects of maturation are obvious at many points throughout the life span: infants may have the physical strength to walk, but they won't walk until the vestibular sense needed for balance matures (see Chapter 5). Toilet training an infant is doomed to failure until the child's sphincter muscles are mature. Pronouncing words correctly requires teeth.

Experience and practice produce ***learning***, which may lead to relatively permanent changes in our thoughts, emotions, and behaviors. We change our behavior *in response* to our environment, especially in response to how people behave and treat us, without any necessary maturational change.

Because learning reflects cultural context, development cannot be studied realistically or completely without considering the cultural context in which it takes place. Culture influences who gives care and socializes children (parents, kin, school, media, church), and whether, how, when, and by whom children are rewarded or punished. For example, in many cultures, such as the Mayan and Navajo cultures, children are expected to be "seen but not heard"—to respond if spoken to but not to initiate verbal interactions. In formal schooling situations, where asking questions and making eye contact with the teacher is expected, such children may be perceived as unusually quiet. Indeed, Navajo children quietly sit and observe their teachers more than two times as much as their Caucasian peers in the same classroom (Guilmet, 1979). Culture also affects what activities are deemed appropriate for boys and for girls and at what age they are appropriate, and what level of respect and status will be awarded to society's elders. The sociocultural context can affect maturation as well. Nutrition, level and type of physical activity, and exposure to stress and environmental toxins such as pesticides, can all affect maturation.

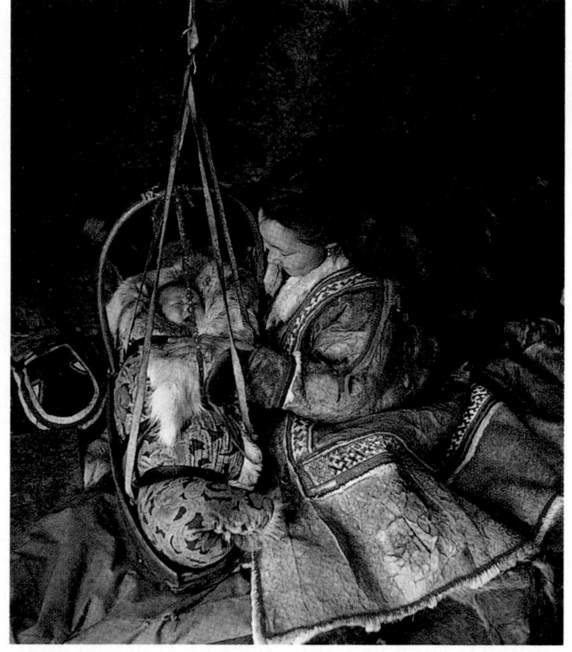

◀ *Cultures vary in the extent to which they allow children to practice motor skills during infancy. This Nenet child from Siberia spends a great deal of time swaddled and strapped to a cradle. But this will not retard motor development, which is largely determined by maturation.*

While psychologists would agree that development reflects the interaction of maturation and learning, intense controversies regarding human development have centered upon which—maturation or learning—contributes *more* to a particular developmental change. Thus, your knowledge of how biological and sociocultural processes interact is particularly relevant to this chapter.

Maturation refers to the developmental changes resulting from the biological aging process rather than from life experiences.

Research Methods

Developmental psychologists use all the scientific methods, experimental and correlational, discussed in Chapter 2. But developmental psychologists have to adapt these methods to the unique challenges posed by trying to measure behavioral changes over time. They primarily rely on two kinds of studies to learn how individuals change over the life span: In a ***cross-sectional study***, the researcher tests people at different ages on the same task within roughly the same time frame. In a ***longitudinal study***, the same people are followed over time.

Suppose you wanted to study changes in children's ability to identify an object as the same thing despite changes in its physical

Development refers to the systematic qualitative and quantitative changes that occur in an individual's biological, psychological, social, and emotional capacities over the life span.

► *Even though three-year-old children met Maynard the cat before he donned the mask that changed his appearance, they nonetheless believed that he had been transformed into a dog.*

appearance. Researchers introduced a cat, Maynard, to three-year-olds and six-year-olds, allowing them to pet him. Then they hid Maynard's head and shoulders behind a screen and strapped a realistic dog mask on him (his hindquarters were always visible to the children, however). When they presented the transformed Maynard to the children, they asked them questions like "What kind of animal is he now?" Three-year-olds tended to say that Maynard is now a dog. The older children said that Maynard is a cat who now looks like a dog (DeVries, 1969). There does seem to be a developmental change in the way children think about the relationship of appearance to reality, and it takes place sometime in childhood between the ages of three and six (Flavell, Miller, & Miller, 1993). Comparisons of children of different ages performing the same task or explaining the same event or object are examples of the cross-sectional method. But, if you talked to the same children about Maynard when they were three years old, and again when they were six years old, you would have a longitudinal design.

► *Although these two share a bench, the older man and the young boy are separated by their knowledge of computer technology. The boy's age cohort is more likely to have experience with computers than is the retired man's age cohort.*

One major problem in cross-sectional designs is that differences observed might arise from what are called cohort differences rather than from true developmental differences. A ***cohort*** is a group of people of the same age who are exposed to similar historical events and cultural environments as they are developing ("all people born in 1970" is a 1970 birth cohort; "all children in the second grade" is a grade cohort; "parents vs. children" gives us two generational cohorts). Cohort differences are due to the unique experiences of the cohorts themselves, and not to age or developmental factors. Suppose you find that sixth-graders are more fearful of violence than first-graders. Can you attribute that difference to age (a developmental effect), or can it be explained by some historical event that affected all children in one of the grade cohorts (cohort effect)? Suppose you find out that when the sixth-graders were in the third grade together (before the first-graders even started school), one of their classmates had been shot and killed on the school playground. You would not know if your results represented a true developmental difference between first- and sixth-graders or a cohort effect that resulted from the sixth-graders' first-hand experience of schoolyard violence. The longer the time period between the ages studied, the more concern researchers have that differences found with age can be explained by cohort effects. Thus, if you compare two-year-olds, four-year-olds, and eight-year-olds, cohort effects are less of a concern than if you compare twenty-year-olds, fifty-year-olds, and seventy-year-olds.

On the other hand, longitudinal designs are expensive and take a great deal of time. They may also suffer from the fact that some people may drop out of a study for personal or uncontrollable reasons, called ***attrition effects***. Attrition can severely bias results, especially if the reason people drop out is related to what you are studying. For example, suppose you are interested in how mental health changes with age. If some people drop out of your study because they are too mentally ill to fill out your questionnaire, your results will now be based on the mentally healthy people left behind. When you compare average mental health scores of the group members at age eighteen with average scores of the group members continuing to participate at age forty, you may erroneously conclude that mental health gets better with age. In fact, likelihood of having a mental disorder is higher at age forty than at age eighteen (Manderscheid & Sonnenschein, 1990).

Longitudinal research also suffers from effects parallel to the cohort problems found in cross-sectional studies. That is, children growing up in earlier time periods (different cohorts) had different environmental influences from those of children growing up today. The major longitudinal studies on child rearing were conducted in the 1930s and 1940s. Think about the differences in children's lives between then and now: television, computers, and crack cocaine, to name just a few.

Applying research to understand how maturation and learning work together to produce developmental change is a huge task. Consider the tremendous changes that occur from the time a sperm meets an egg to when we confront issues of death and dying in old age. We begin life as a one-celled organism, but in nine months that cell develops into an infant equipped with sensory systems and cognitive abilities that enable it to respond to and act on its environments and learn languages. As we pass through life's various stages—the prenatal period, infancy, childhood, adolescence, and adulthood—our physical, cognitive, linguistic, and social skills and abilities grow and change. Let's consider how developmental psychologists have studied these changes in more detail.

THINKING CRITICALLY

Suppose you were told that early research on IQ using a cross-sectional method had found that middle-aged adults had lower IQs than adolescents and young adults. Would you conclude that IQ sharply declines with age?

That conclusion would be incorrect. Studies using the longitudinal method to follow the same people over time do *not* find that IQ declines from adolescence through middle age. Results obtained with cross-sectional methods largely reflected the fact that opportunities for higher education in the United States expanded greatly between the times the two groups were in school. Consequently, young adults and adolescents were better educated than those in the original samples—the age difference in IQ was a cohort effect, not a developmental effect (Schaie & Strother, 1968). Cohort effects are one reason that longitudinal studies are often undertaken to confirm that differences first observed in cross-sectional research are really developmental differences.

The Prenatal Period

The body and brain first take shape during the prenatal period, the time between conception and birth (see Figure 11-1). Events during this period can have lifelong consequences. Although biological factors dominate during prenatal development, environmental factors are also important.

Prenatal development begins when a sperm meets an egg, which usually occurs in the fallopian tubes. During the process of ***fertilization*** the chromosomes, which carry the genes donated by the sperm and the egg, get organized and pair up. This process takes about twenty-four hours. As the resulting fertilized egg (***zygote***) floats down the fallopian tubes toward the uterus, its cells begin to divide. Some

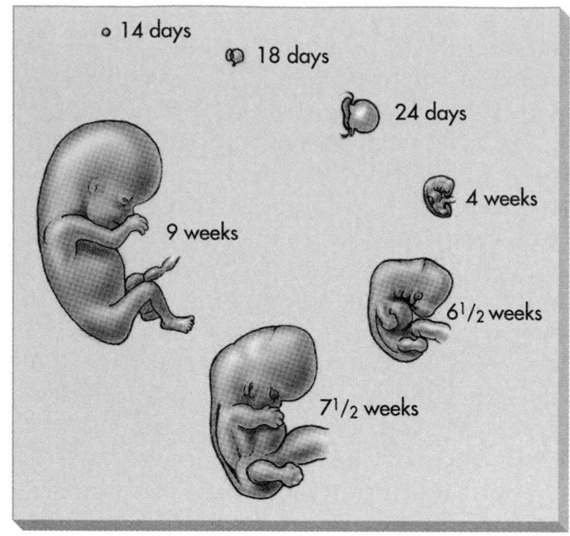

11-1 Development from Embryo to Fetus

In nine weeks, the embryo develops from a single cell that can only be seen under a microscope to a one-inch long fetus weighing one ounce. (Source: Adapted from Craig & Kermis, 1995).

will develop into the ***placenta***, the network of blood vessels attached to the mother's uterine wall. The placenta carries food and oxygen to the developing embryo and removes waste. Others will become the embryo (at this stage called the ***preembryo***). It takes about a week after fertilization for this formless mass of cells to make its way from the fallopian tubes to the uterus. There it burrows into the uterine wall in a process known as ***implantation***. For reasons that are not completely understood, only about half of all zygotes are successfully implanted, and about half of the zygotes that are implanted are miscarried (spontaneously aborted) soon afterward. Genetic anomalies, nutrition, and exposure to environmental toxins (for example, cigarette smoke) partially explain why only about one zygote in four survives to become an embryo (Roberts & Lowe, 1975; Simpson, 1993).

The Embryo

With implantation, the preembryo begins its first major transformation from a formless mass of cells into an increasingly complex ***embryo***. During this period, which occurs two to eight weeks after fertilization, the embryo begins to develop rudimentary body parts and internal organs. This development takes place within a liquid-filled amniotic sac that cushions and protects the embryo. The embryo receives nourishment from the placenta through the umbilical cord.

During prenatal development, the embryo (later called the fetus) is entirely dependent on

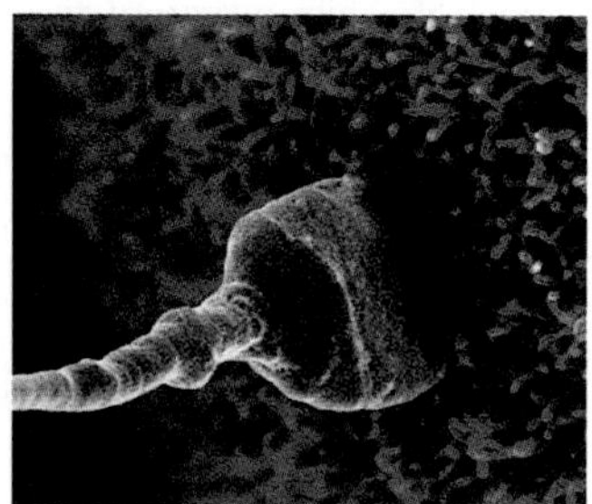

The sperm meets egg, beginning the process of fertilization.

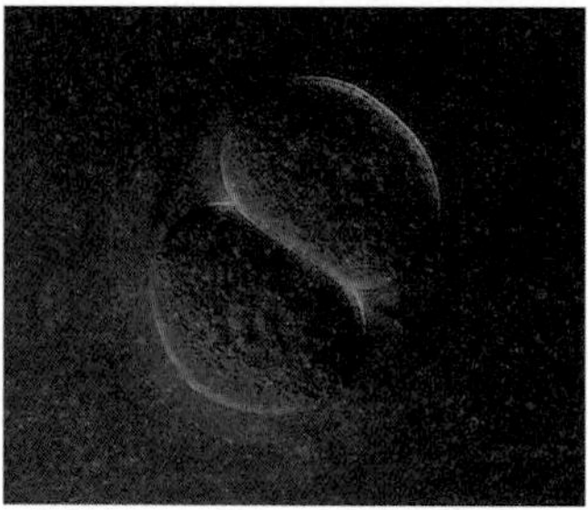

After about 30 hours, the fertilized egg begins to divide.

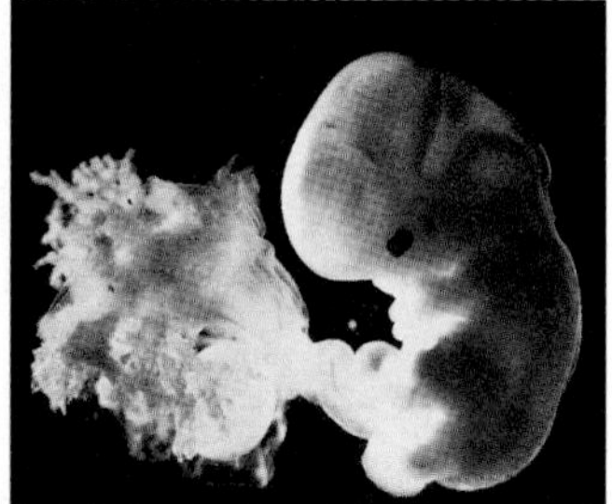

At age four weeks, the embryo has a visible head, trunk, and tail.

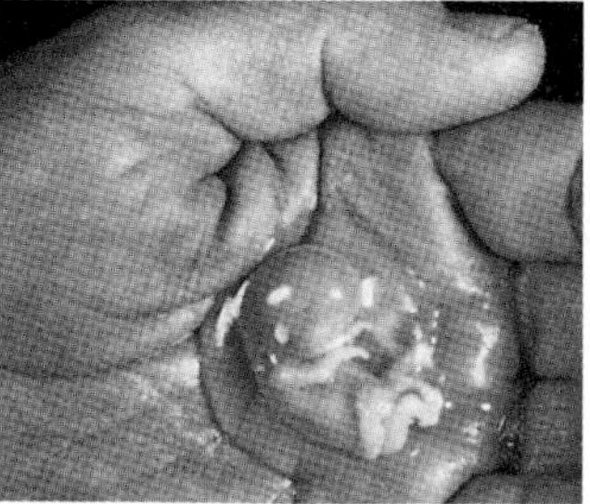

At age eight weeks, all of the fetus' major organs have begun to form.

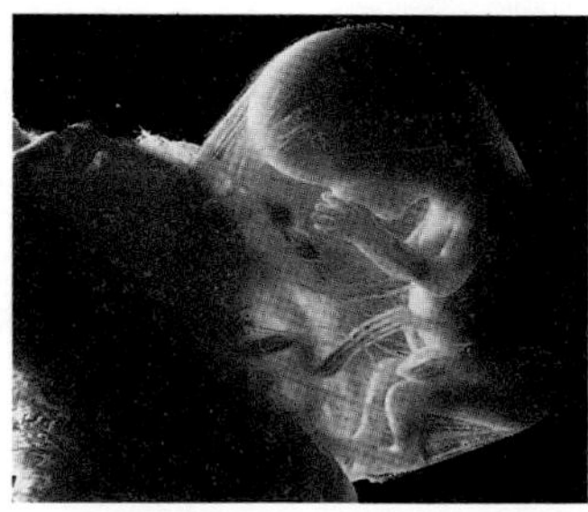

At sixteen weeks, all the fetus' internal organs are formed, though not yet fully functional.

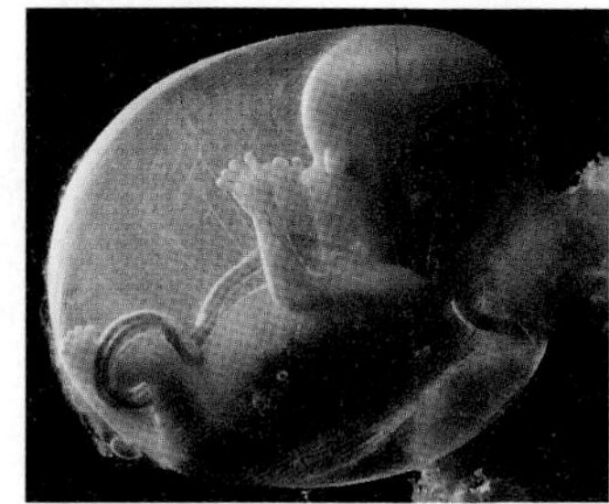

At age twenty weeks, most of the fetus' organs are functioning, and the neocortex has begun to develop.

Table 11-2 A Partial List of Teratogens and Their Possible Effects

Teratogen	Possible Effect
Alcohol	High doses of alcohol may lead to fetal alcohol syndrome, including mental retardation, facial and heart defects, low birth weight, and behavioral problems. Moderate doses of alcohol may lead to facial abnormalities and central nervous system (CNS) dysfunction.
Aspirin (large amounts)	Respiratory problems, bleeding
Caffeine (from all sources, including colas, chocolate, coffee, tea)	Miscarriage, low birth weight
Cigarettes/cigars	Fetal death, low birth weight, premature delivery, learning disorders, behavioral problems, susceptibility to respiratory infections and asthma
Cocaine	Stillbirth, complications of labor, low birth weight, birth defects, neurological and behavioral problems, death by cerebral hemorrhage
Diethylstilbestrol (DES)	Cancer of the cervix or testes, infertility, immune system disorders
HIV	Facial abnormalities, retarded motor and language growth, cognitive deficits, immune system dysfunction, autoimmune deficiency syndrome, death
Lead	Birth defects, motor and cognitive deficits
Marijuana	Premature delivery, failure to habituate, problems similar to fetal alcohol syndrome, central nervous system (CNS) effects
Mercury	Profound mental retardation, neurological problems
Narcotics and related substances (including heroin, morphine, and methadone)	Prematurity, low birth weight, addiction, sleep disturbance, motor and attention deficits
Paint fumes (heavy exposure)	Mental retardation
PCBs (found in electrical transformers and paint)	Low birth weight, motor and memory deficits, decreased responsiveness
Radiation	Malformation of organs
Rubella (German measles)	Mental retardation, nerve damage impairing vision and hearing
Streptomycin	Hearing loss
Tetracycline	Yellow teeth, bone abnormalities

its mother for nutrition and other vital processes and for protection from harmful environmental agents called ***teratogens***. These include disease-producing agents like HIV, rubella (German measles), and herpes; tobacco smoke from cigarettes and cigars; alcohol; heroin and other drugs; radiation; and various chemicals (see Table 11-2). Although the mother's placenta screens out many dangerous substances, there are some chemicals and living organisms that can cross the placental barrier, invade the developing embryo (or fetus), and cause damage. The nature and extent of the damage depends greatly on the stage of development at the time of exposure, as there are ***critical periods*** of risk when the developing organ systems are most susceptible to environmental agents that can cause developmental malformations. For example, the risk of prenatal damage from rubella drops from 50 percent during the first month of pregnancy, to 22 percent during the second month of pregnancy, to 7 percent during the third month of pregnancy. Risk for type of damage also changes. Rubella is most likely to produce heart defects and cataracts in a four-week-old embryo; mental retardation is most likely to occur due to problems in the seventh week of pregnancy (Dekaban, O'Rourke, & Corman, 1958). Generally, teratogens have their most obvious effects during the embryonic period, when the principal organs of the body are being formed. Unfortunately, much of this period passes by before many women even know they are pregnant.

During prenatal development, major regions and organs are blocked out and then filled in with ever-greater detail (a process called structural ***differentiation***). The parts of the body that appeared first in vertebrate evolution also tend to develop first in the human embryo.

▼ *Children with fetal alcohol syndrome exhibit distinctive anatomical, physiological, and behavioral impairments, although it is not known how much alcohol it takes to produce this syndrome. Heavy marijuana use by a pregnant woman can also produce similar effects (Hingson et al, 1982).*

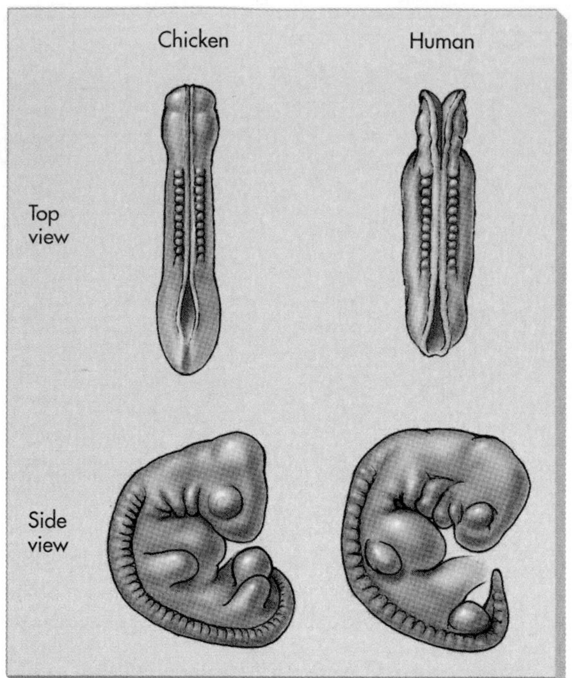

11-2 Embryonic Development across Species

Vertebrate embryos, from chicken to human, look similar in the embryonic stage of development.

Thus, at the early stages, human embryos are very similar to embryos of other vertebrates (see Figure 11-2 for a comparison across species). The neocortex, which is the most recently evolved part of the brain, develops last in the human embryo, during the third trimester of pregnancy. It provides the neurological basis for consciousness, thinking, problem solving, and language, and develops even after birth.

Whether you are male or female depends on what happened to you during the embryonic period of prenatal development. At the end of this period (during the seventh and eighth weeks after implantation), sexual development begins with the emergence of a genital ridge that has the potential to develop into either a male or female reproductive system. If two X chromosomes are present, the embryo develops a female reproductive system. If a Y chromosome is present, one of its genes triggers a biochemical reaction that results in the formation of testes. In turn, those testes produce testosterone, which stimulates development of the male reproductive system.

The Fetus

Rudimentary organs grow and differentiate during the fetal period, which occurs in a normal pregnancy from nine to thirty-eight weeks after implantation, and ends in birth. During pregnancy, the fetus goes from making simple reflexive body movements, such as twitching, to making more complex reflexive behaviors, such as swallowing and sucking. At sixteen to eighteen weeks, fetal movements are strong enough to be felt by the pregnant woman.

From nine to eighteen weeks, the fetus is "precortical"—the neocortex has yet to develop. Primitive movements during this stage are based on simple neural reflexes, not organized brain activity.

Between nineteen and twenty-two weeks, the fetus undergoes a major transition from precortical to neocortical status. The fetus now has all the neurons it will ever have, as many as 100 to 200 billion (Rakic, 1991). The neocortex starts to be functionally connected with the rest of the developing fetal body, beginning with sensory information networks. The fetal brain shows *spurts* of patterned, electrical activity (although not yet the *continuous* electrical activity characteristic of a human infant).

Between twenty-four and twenty-eight weeks after fertilization, the fetus reaches the age of viability, the point at which its brain and respiratory system can enable it to survive outside the uterus. At twenty-eight weeks, the fetus typically weighs a little more than two pounds and is about fifteen inches long. About this time, neocortical connections sharply and suddenly skyrocket. In fact, the last three months of pregnancy and the first two years after birth have been called the period of the ***brain growth spurt*** because more than half of the child's eventual brain weight is added during this time (Shafer, 1996).

After about thirty weeks, for the first time, the brain's electrical activity becomes continuous, with periodic fluctuations suggestive of the sleep-wake cycle (see Chapter 9). From this point until birth at thirty-eight weeks, the fetus is essentially like an infant except for the fact that it is much smaller in size (Flowers, 1990).

Many pregnant women talk, read, and play music to their unborn babies. What does the research say about the effects of such behavior? Given the fact that after thirty weeks of pregnancy, the essential difference between the fetus and the newborn baby is size, it should not be surprising to find evidence that some form of learning seems to occur in the womb during the last trimester of pregnancy (DeCasper & Fifer, 1980; Hepper, 1989). Researchers followed one group of pregnant women who watched a soap opera with a distinctive theme song nearly every day during their pregnancy and a control group of women who did not watch the program. The researchers then studied the babies born to the women in both groups. When the newborn babies cried, the researchers played the theme music and measured the infants' reaction. Babies whose mothers had not watched the show during pregnancy kept on crying, but babies whose mothers had watched the show quieted and became alert, seemingly indicating recognition of the song (Hepper, 1989).

Not only what the pregnant mother listens to during her pregnancy, but also when she actually gives birth affects the fetus. Although a fetus might survive if born at twenty-eight weeks, it will weigh substantially less than a fetus carried to term. Newborns weighing less than five-and-a-half pounds are at higher risk for birth defects and other problems, including death (Lin, 1989). About 10 percent of these high-risk infants have physical and/or intellectual impairments. The long-term consequences of low birth weight depend on both the severity of the initial problems as well as subsequent interactions with the environment, however. For example, a longitudinal study of infants born on Kauai, Hawaii, found that, the more severe the problems of the high-risk newborn infant, the more likely that infant would be socially and intellectually impaired at two years of age. Nonetheless, if such infants were raised in a home high in emotional support and educational stimulation, their impairment was much less severe. By age ten, children from supportive and stimulating homes had generally overcome their initial disadvantages, while children from unstimulating home environments continued to have social and intellectual deficiencies. Thus, many physical, intellectual, and social deficiencies of low-birth-weight infants can be overcome by exposure to stimulating and emotionally supportive environments (Werner & Smith, 1992).

Infancy and Childhood

Infancy and childhood (the time from birth to puberty) are periods of dramatic physical, cognitive, and social growth and transformation. Maturation and learning processes interact during this period to produce startling changes in body, brain, and behavior that are readily apparent when you compare the infant to the adolescent.

At birth, the newborn's brain is about a quarter of the size and weight of the adult brain. The brain will triple in size by the child's second birthday, as the size of neurons and the number of connections among them increases (Shatz, 1992). Higher brain centers continue to develop after birth—indeed, associative and speech areas might not fully mature until adolescence (Schuster & Ashburn, 1986). Human infants have far more neurons than adults and will not develop more later in life. Rather, as many as half of the neurons will die early in life (Janowsky & Finlay, 1986). Stimulation from the environment activates some neural networks and not others, so that some survive while others do not (Greenough, Black, & Wallace, 1987). Thus, the course of brain development reflects the interaction of heredity and environment. So the next time you lean over to smile at an infant, keep in mind that you're not just saying hello; you're helping to "wire" a brain.

During the brain growth spurt that occurs between twenty-eight weeks after implantation and two years of age, more than half a person's eventual brain weight is added.

The Competent Infant

Although the human infant has a long period of dependency on others, newborn infants are not without resources. The first areas of the cerebral cortex to develop fully are those serving sensory and motor functions. Thus, infants come equipped with a bundle of reflexes and well-developed sensory abilities to perceive and interact with the world (Brazelton, 1979). Their remarkable adaptability is reflected in an ability to thrive in a wide variety of contexts and cultures.

Reflexes

Full-term newborns have two kinds of reflexes: survival and primitive (see Table 11–3 for examples). ***Survival reflexes***, which include breathing, blinking, sucking, swallowing, and the pupil's response to changes in light (the pupillary reflex), have clear adaptive value. They are automatic and permanent. ***Primitive reflexes*** may be holdovers from our evolutionary history, but they are not necessary for survival. The grasping reflex, for example, may have helped our ancestors hang on to their parents while swinging through trees. These reflexes are

Table 11-3 Reflexes in the Newborn

Reflex	Stimulus	Response	Disappearance
Rooting	Stroking of infant's cheek	Infant turns head in direction of stroked cheek and opens mouth to suck what stroked him or her.	Disappears around 4 months; replaced by voluntary head turning.
Sucking	Object placed in infant's mouth	Infant sucks on object placed in his or her mouth.	Gradually modified to voluntary sucking at about 2 months.
Babinski	Stroking of bottom of infant's foot	Infant turns his or her foot inward while fanning and then curling the toes.	Disappears around 8–12 months.
Grasping	Object or finger touching infant's palm	Infant curls his or her fingers around object or finger touching palm (grasp is strong enough to support infant's weight).	Weakens around 3–4 months; disappears around a year; replaced by voluntary grasp.
Moro	Sudden loud noise or sudden change in position of infant's head	Infant extends arms, arches his or her back, and then brings arms rapidly together as if to grab onto something.	Arm movements and arching of back disappear around 6–7 months; replaced by startle response to sudden noises or loss of bodily support.
Swimming	Immersion in water	Infant displays active movements with arms and legs and involuntarily holds breath (making the body buoyant, which will keep the infant afloat for some time, allowing rescue).	Disappears around 4–6 months; some infants have been taught to adapt this reflex into a primitive form of locomotion (swimming) that is possible long before walking is.
Stepping	Being held upright so feet touch flat surface	Infant steps as if to walk.	Disappears in first 8 weeks if there are no regular opportunities to practice this response.

controlled by the brain's subcortical areas. Primitive reflexes gradually disappear during the first year of life as the cerebral cortex develops and takes control of behavior. The appearance and disappearance of these reflexes during the first year of life can be used to diagnose abnormalities in neurological development (Brazelton, 1979). If reflexes do not appear and disappear roughly on schedule, this may indicate that something is wrong with the developing nervous system. For example, if the leg doesn't flex in response to a pinprick on the sole of the foot (withdrawal reflex), the infant may have sciatic nerve damage.

Sensory Abilities

Have you ever wondered where you got your preference for sweet tastes? An infant sucks sweet-tasting fluids or objects faster and longer than those that are neutral (such as water), bitter, sour, or salty. At birth, the senses of taste and smell are well developed. Infants vigorously avoid unpleasant smells, and if exposed to substances like ammonia or rotten eggs, they turn away and express disgust (shown by a downturning of the corners of the mouth, a protruding tongue, and sometimes even spitting). If infants are breast-fed, by six days of age they can distinguish a pad with their own mother's milk on it from the pad of another breast-feeding woman or from an unused pad (Macfarlane, 1975).

Infants cannot speak and tell us what they know or have learned, so how can we conduct experiments to find out what they know? Understanding habituation (see Chapter 6) has enabled researchers to study infant sensory

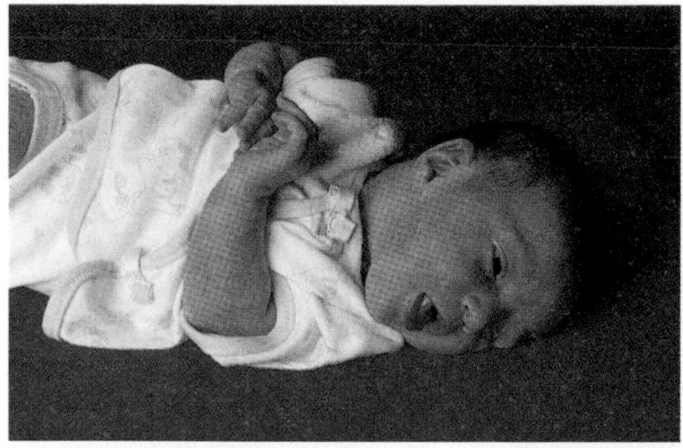

A

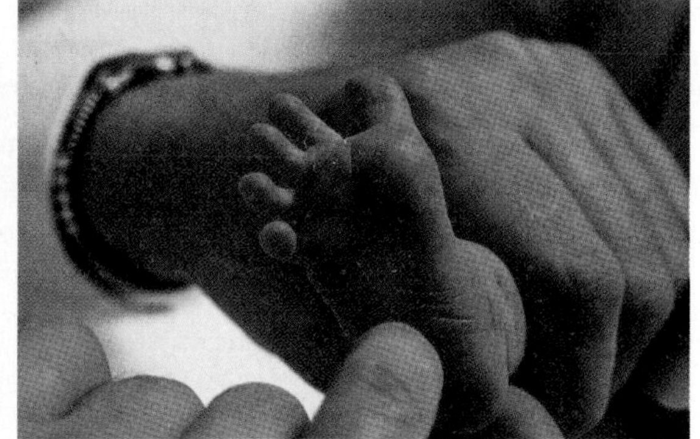

B

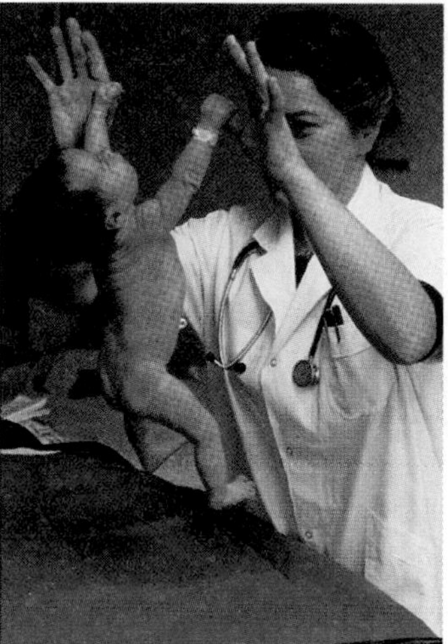

C

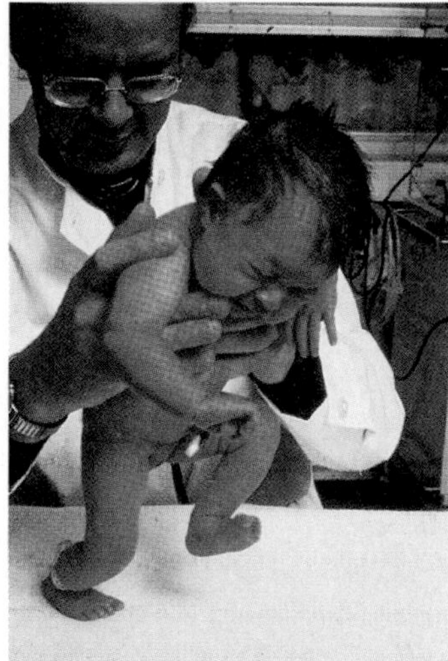

D

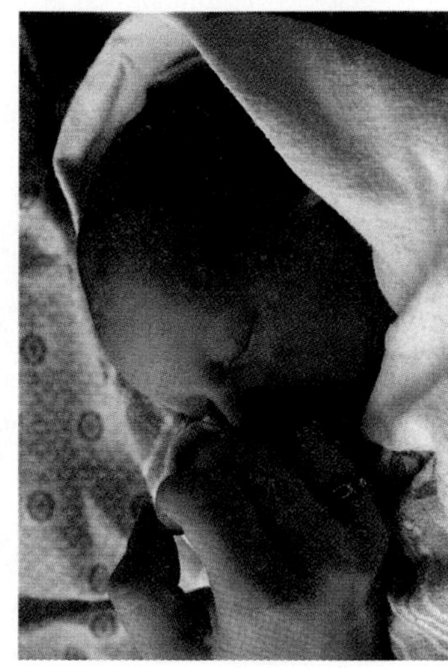

E

◀ *Full-term newborns exhibit various kinds of reflexes as illustrated here: (A) the rooting reflex; (B) the Babinski reflex; (C) the grasping reflex; (D) the stepping reflex; and (E) the sucking reflex.*

capability. Can you figure out how? Remember that infants may respond to an initial presentation of a stimulus (for example, a light or sound), but that with repeated exposure the strength of that response will decline—that is, the infant will habituate to it. If a new stimulus is presented, however, the response will return in force. The infant will not have habituated to the new stimulus.

Now suppose you want to see if the infant can tell the difference between two sounds, *A* and *B*. What can you do? First, you habituate the infant to sound *A*. Then you expose the infant to sound *B*. If the infant does not react, then you conclude that he or she cannot tell the difference between the two sounds. But if the infant does react to sound *B*, that means that the infant can indeed distinguish between the two sounds, and is reacting accordingly (Bower, 1982).

Such habituation studies have established that hearing, like smell, is fairly well developed at birth. Infants can hear differences in loudness, direction, duration, and frequency. They can even hear differences in pitch as small as one note apart on the piano. In the first three days after birth, infants learn to recognize their mother's voice (maybe their father's voice, too, but we don't have data on fathers because researchers have typically only used mothers in these studies). When spoken to by a caregiver, infants often stop crying, open their eyes and look around, and even vocalize, giving their caregivers a definite emotional boost! Infants' ability to hear and respond to human speech elicits the attention and interaction that is the foundation for emotional, social, and intellectual development.

Infants can see patterns and colors at birth, but their visual acuity (the sharpness of their vision) is poor. Infants don't achieve 20/20 visual acuity for about a year. Infants' eye coordi-

SEEKING SOLUTIONS

Infant Predispositions for Social Behaviors

Human infants are not able to care for themselves. They need other people to provide food and shelter for them. Because of this fundamental need for others, infants are *preadapted* to become social beings (Sroufe, Cooper, DeHart, & Marshall, 1992; Turner & Helms, 1995). Infants are born with predispositions that—if given the proper developmental contexts—will develop into coordinated social exchanges that form the basis of genuine social relationships. What predispositions do you think enable human infants to interact with others?

Infants are born with the ability to "signal" physiological and psychological needs in effective ways, typically by crying. Although a newborn's cry is not an intentional act, it is a precursor for true social signaling in environments responsive to his or her cries.

The infant's visual system is designed so that the newborn is naturally attentive to the kinds of stimulation provided by adult faces (light-dark contrasts and movement). When an adult smiles and nods while looking at a newborn, the infant's attention is innately drawn to the adult's face. The newborn's inspection of faces is helped by the fact that caregivers tend to hold their heads at a distance that is best suited to where the infant is able to focus (about eight inches away).

Babies can also hear quite well in the pitch range of the human voice, and they can discriminate among speech sounds. Because babies are born with coordination between their hearing and head movements, they are able to turn toward a person who is speaking to them.

At about four weeks of age, smiling spontaneously appears, even in blind children. This early smiling is reflexive in response to internal stimuli such as a stomach gas bubble and external stimuli such as being stroked on the cheek, but it is nonetheless a source of excitement for caregivers, who smile and nod over the newborn, reinforcing the smiling response. By two to three months, reflexive smiling changes into a social smile that is now elicited by the appearance of the caregiver.

Infants are born with the ability to detect environmental contingencies, that is, they are aware that certain behaviors will lead to certain consequences. Thus, infants pay attention to the outcomes of their behaviors and repeat behaviors that have observable effects. When these effects are the responses of caregivers (for example, the excited reaction of the parent saying "oh look, the baby reached for my face" or hugging the infant), the baby will then repeat the action that produced the response, the caregiver will react, and a precursor to social exchange has begun!

Infants can also modify their behaviors to fit the rhythms and responses of their caregivers. Babies cared for by caregivers with more casual, easygoing styles will often respond with easygoing behaviors such as eating slowly and taking long naps. Yet, the same infants, if exposed to a caregiver with a more hurried style, will now sleep less and eat more quickly, suggesting that infants have a predisposition to adapt to the kind of care they receive.

Thus, these various predispositions enable infants to be aware of and to respond to their caregivers. When infants are not responsive, it may signal that there are problems that may affect social relations in infancy and later in life.

nation is poor because eye muscles do not fully develop until some time after birth. This explains why newborns appear cross-eyed. Infants spend much time just looking at the world and, as shown in habituation studies, they exhibit definite visual preferences (Fantz, 1967). Newborn infants, only hours old, prefer their mother's face over a stranger's, largely because the mother's face is the stimulus most frequently seen (Walton, Bower, & Bower, 1992). During the first two months of life, they are "stimulus seekers"—they are most interested in objects or arrays that move, or have high contrast, or complex contours (see Figure 11–3).

Infants exhibit depth perception as soon as the visual and motor perceptual systems become coordinated (as early as two months), but they attain full depth perception only after extensive experience with objects in space. How do we know this, given that infants cannot re-

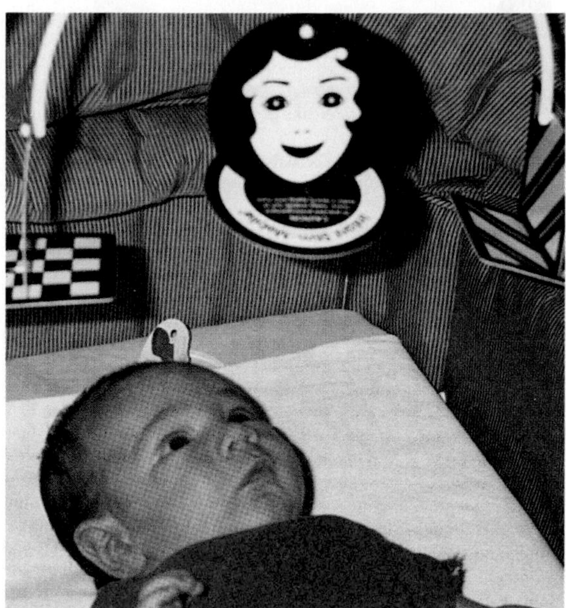

▲ *Very young infants like to look at strong patterns and faces.*

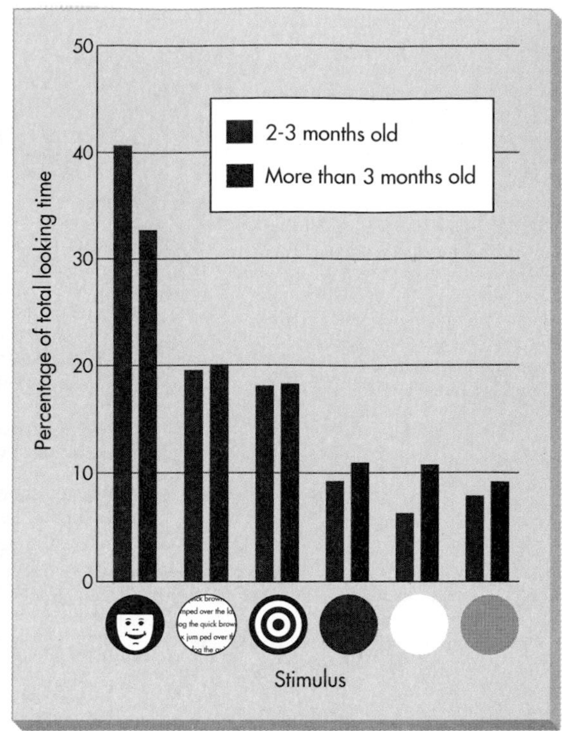

11-3 Pattern Preferences in Infants

Infants come predisposed to recognize and prefer patterns over even color or brightness. This is illustrated by the response of infants to a face, a piece of printed material, a bull's eye, and plain red, white, and yellow circles of color. Even the youngest infants choose to look more often at the patterns than at the circles of color. The red bars show the results for infants who are from two to three months old; the blue bars show the results for infants who are more than three months old. (Source: Fantz, 1961)

port what they are seeing? One kind of evidence is based on the research of Eleanor J. Gibson and Richard Walk, who created a "visual cliff" to study infant depth perception (Gibson & Walk, 1960). An infant is urged to crawl across a glass floor that appears to end in a "cliff." Children who refuse to crawl beyond what appears to be the cliff's edge are assumed to have depth perception. Subsequent researchers have examined differences in heart rate when infants are placed on the "shallow" and "deep" sides of the cliff (Campos, Langer, & Krowitz, 1970). They found that infants as young as two months old can perceive a difference between the two sides. Since infants don't move about until they are about four to six months old, these findings suggest that depth perception is in place long before the infant becomes mobile.

Physical Development

Infants are born with all the muscle fibers they will ever possess. Just as we cannot "grow" more neurons, we cannot "grow" more muscle fibers. We can increase the size and strength of existing muscles, however. Our physical growth and development proceed in head-to-toe fashion. Before infants can lift themselves up and move about, neural, skeletal, and muscle tissues have to mature, and this occurs in an orderly, head-to-toe sequence. Learning to walk involves an orderly progression through stages

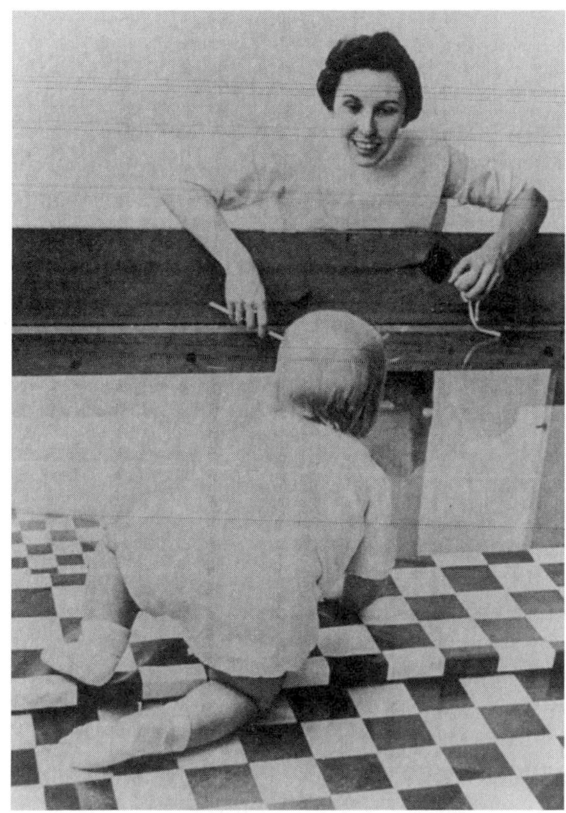

◄ *Eleanor Gibson and Richard Walk created a "visual cliff" to study infant depth perception. Here, she tests one of her subjects on the visual cliff apparatus.*

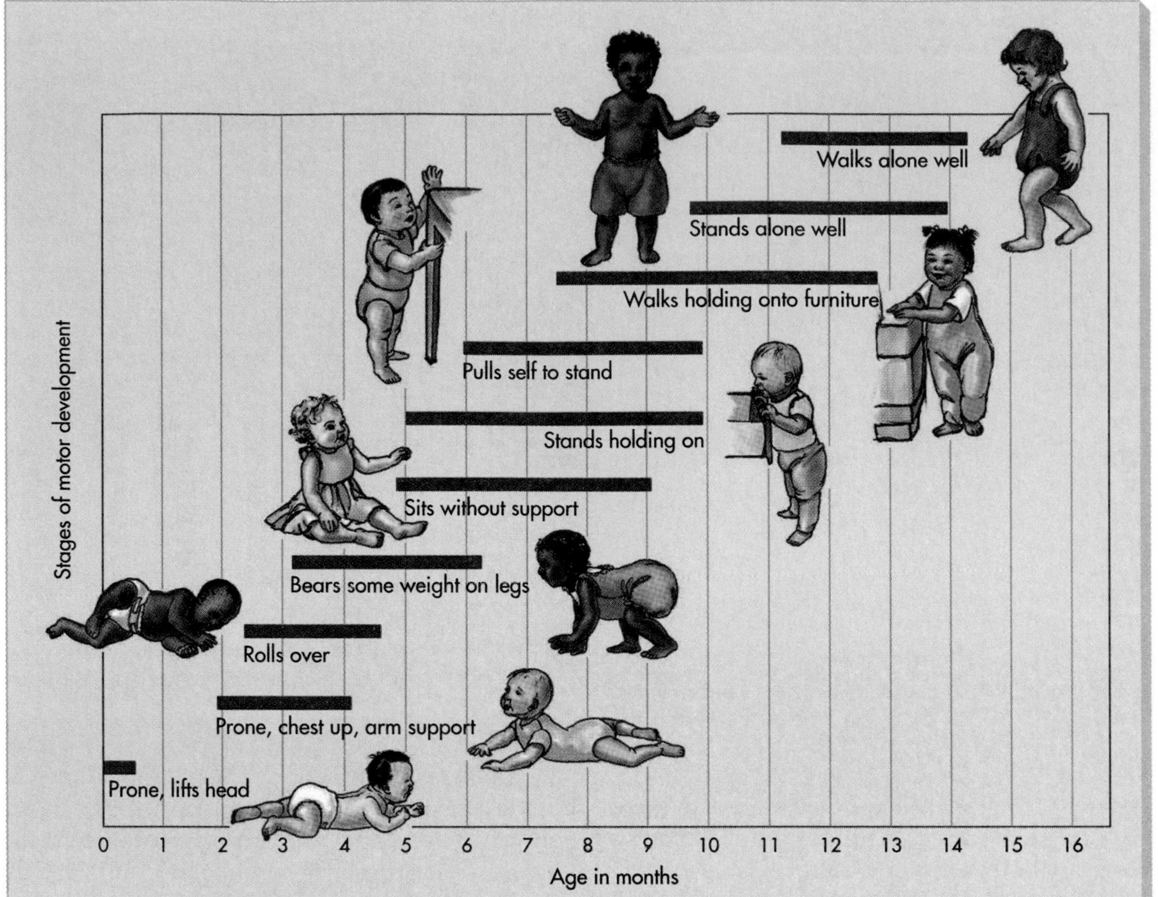

11-4 Motor Development in Infants

The order of the stages of motor development is the same in all infants. Nonetheless, some infants reach each stage sooner than do others. The bars show the range of ages at which infants reach each of these developmental milestones. The far left side of the bar is the age by which 25 percent of the infants had mastered the motor skill, while the right side of the bar represents the age by which 90 percent of the infants had mastered the skill. (Source: Adapted from Frankenberg & Dodds, 1967)

of motor development that begins with infants beginning to lift their head while lying prone. There is a progression of stages of motor development, where movement shifts from arms to legs (see Figure 11–4). Generally, infants will lift their head before they can lift their chest, roll over before they can sit without support, creep before they can crawl, stand holding on before pulling themselves up to stand, and walk while holding furniture or someone's hand before walking alone. Nutrition and exercise interact with maturational processes to affect bone-hardening and bone and muscle growth, which continue gradually in childhood and accelerate in adolescence.

From birth to adulthood, body proportions change remarkably: the head develops first (the head of an infant is 70 percent of adult size at birth). The body grows later, and takes on a higher proportion of the whole body during childhood. The human infant grows, on average, from about seven-and-a-half pounds at birth to nearly twenty-five pounds after one year. Thereafter, until puberty, children gain about six to seven pounds and add about two to three inches in height each year.

Children also grow and mature from the center outward. Chest and internal organs form and develop before arms and hands, and the trunk grows faster than the arms and legs. But just before puberty, the pattern reverses. Teenagers appear to lose some coordination as extremities (hands and feet) grow rapidly to adult proportion, followed by arms and legs, and finally by the trunk. Thus, teenagers seem clumsy and awkward, literally tripping over their own feet.

Learning and Cognitive Development

How early do we find evidence of learning and how does our capacity for learning change with age? How does cognitive development—the development of abilities needed to think about the world—change over time?

Researchers have used a variety of techniques, some of which are used with animals (who also cannot report on what they have learned) to study infants' learning and cognitive development. Researchers have measured change in infant heart rate, which automatically occurs in response to focusing of attention, to study what infants know. They have observed infant sucking behavior to explore what and how infants learn and think, and what they remember. Sucking occurs even in the womb, and infants are born prepared to suck to obtain their mother's milk. Infants will suck on their mother's nipple, a bottle, a finger, or anything else available. Researchers have observed when sucking occurs, stops, and recurs to determine whether infants have recognized a new object or sound, and whether they can distinguish different sights and sounds.

As we have already discussed (see pp. 384–85), learning can occur before birth. This has been demonstrated in studies with newborn infants who have been shown to recognize sounds heard in the womb. In one study, women read *The Cat in the Hat* aloud twice a day during the last six-and-a-half weeks of their pregnancy. Researchers studied the women's three-day-old infants to see if they were able to distinguish between someone reading *The Cat in the Hat* or *The King, the Mice, and the Cheese.* The researchers set up the experiment so that there was a taped reading of the two stories. Infants could choose which story they would hear by changing their pattern of sucking. One pattern of sucking would enable the infants to hear one story, while another pattern would enable them to hear another. When given a choice of listening to either *The Cat in the Hat* or *The King, the Mice, and the Cheese,* the infants sucked to listen to what they had heard previously. The infants even learned to modify their sucking behavior in response to the reinforcement of hearing the familiar story (DeCasper & Fifer, 1980).

Classical and Operant Conditioning

Both classical and operant conditioning processes play important roles in infant learning. Infants are born predisposed to suck, to like sweet tastes, to signal physiological and psychological needs by crying, and to discriminate among sounds and among light and dark contrasting sights. These predispositions provide behaviors that both classical and operant conditioning can build upon, and they provide a foundation for the development of attachment. They can be used to study what infants know and to teach them new behaviors.

Babies begin to suck as soon as they are placed in the feeding position. Anticipatory sucking at the sight of a nipple suggests that classical conditioning operates in early infancy (Lipsitt & Werner, 1981). Here the conditioned stimulus of the nipple produces the conditioned response of sucking. Infants can also learn by operant conditioning, as shown by the study in which infants were conditioned to make the response of a particular sucking pattern for the reinforcement of hearing a familiar story. Czech psychologist Hanus Papousek conducted studies using operant conditioning techniques to see whether infants could learn to perform certain

PEANUTS *reprinted by permission of United Feature Syndicate, Inc.*

behaviors. He found that three-week-old infants could learn to turn their heads to the right at the sound of a buzzer and to the left at the sound of a bell (Papousek, 1969). Papousek gave the infants nipples offering milk as rewards. He studied infants up to six months of age and found that they could be taught complex behavior sequences using their inborn preference for sweets as reinforcement. Papousek first rewarded one head turn, then repeated turns in the same direction, then turns in the other direction, until the infants were able to perform longer and more complex chains (for example, two turns to the left, one to the right, and so forth). Thus, even very young infants can be taught complicated behaviors through using operant conditioning techniques.

THINKING CRITICALLY

Infants begin to suck at the sight of a nipple. How could you use this fact to design an experiment to demonstrate that infants can be classically conditioned?

You could repeatedly pair a neutral stimulus (a light or sound) with the sight of a nipple and observe whether the infant began to suck in response to that stimulus. Classical conditioning in infancy was indeed confirmed in an experiment that conditioned infants to suck in response to a tone. The tone was sounded just before a nipple was presented. Babies only three or four days old quickly learned that the tone signaled the subsequent appearance of the nipple. Even when the tone was no longer paired with the nipple, many babies persisted in sucking in response to the tone alone (Lipsitt & Werner, 1981).

Learning by Imitation

One mother described how her six-month-old infant learned to imitate her behavior, as follows: "One of my favorite games with Jack was making faces. I'd stick out my tongue; he'd stick out his tongue. He'd gurgle; I'd gurgle. Sometimes it wasn't clear just who was doing the imitating!"

Children imitate their caregivers at a very early age. Newborns less than seventy hours old will stick out their tongues or open their mouths in imitation of adults—much to the joy of the adults (Meltzoff & Moore, 1977, 1983). Results with slightly older infants (over two weeks of age) have been inconsistent, however, suggesting that imitation, like smiling, is reflexive in newborns, dropping out and then reappearing later, depending on how it is reinforced (Anisfeld, 1991). Imitation of simple behaviors that infants already perform (sticking out their tongues, reaching) is found at six to seven months, and by nine months infants can imitate new behavior as well as imitating behavior at a later time. Such deferred imitation has been demonstrated in experiments that allow infants to watch an adult perform an unfamiliar action, such as pushing a button to produce a sound. When allowed to play with the object twenty-four hours later, many infants did indeed reproduce the behavior they had observed (Meltzoff, 1988).

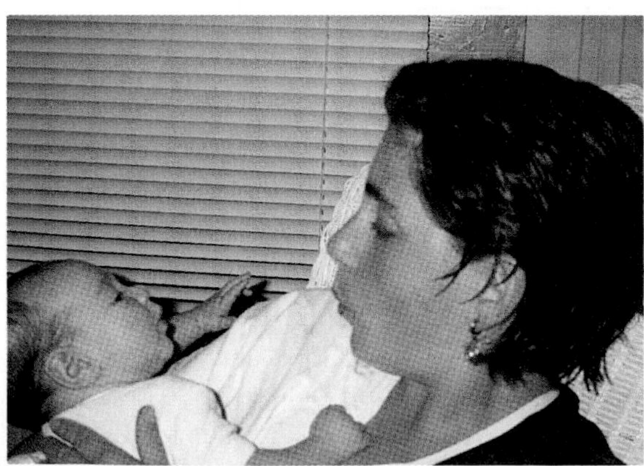

► *Between the ages of two and three weeks old, infants are able to imitate facial expressions.*

The development of deferred imitation demonstrates that with learning and maturation, the child is increasingly able to create a mental representation of the world. Psychologists who study cognitive development focus on how such mental representations influence our reactions to new experiences and our ability to acquire new knowledge and skills at different ages. The most influential theory of cognitive development in the twentieth century has been Piagetian theory.

Piagetian Theory

At age two years, seven months, upon seeing her sister Lucienne in a new bathing suit and cap, Jacqueline asked "What's the baby's name?" When her mother explained that it was a bathing costume, Jacqueline pointed to Lucienne's face saying several times, "But what's the name of that?" As soon as Lucienne had her dress on, Jacqueline exclaimed, "It's Lucienne again." Like the younger children in the experiment with Maynard the Cat, Jacqueline thought that Lucienne's identity had changed with her physical appearance—in this case, with her clothes (Piaget, 1951).

From an adult point of view, children think about their world in very unusual ways. For more than forty-eight years, the Swiss developmentalist Jean Piaget (1896–1980) and his chief collaborator, Bärbel Inhelder (1913–), worked together at the University of Geneva to create the Piagetian theory of cognitive development (Gruber, 1990). Their work was the first to legitimize the scientific study of children's thinking and to provide a comprehensive and coherent statement on intellectual development. The vignette above is taken from Piaget's observation of the behavior of his own children, Jacqueline and Lucienne. Piaget's systematic observations of their development, along with that of their brother Laurent, have been the stimulus for thousands of scientific studies of children's cognitive development around the globe.

Piagetian theory takes a dynamic view of intellectual development. This means that children's cognitive abilities change as they grow older. The infant who doesn't know that an object continues to exist when it is hidden by a cloth or screen develops into the older child who does recognize that a ball or toy still exists after it is hidden from view.

Through actively exploring their environments, children develop cognitive schemas to represent and understand the world. ***Cognitive schemas*** are organized patterns of thought (also called knowledge structures) about how things work or are related to one another. These schemas help children make sense of what they perceive as contradictory about the environment. When they discover that a particular schema does not conform with the way the world actually is, they are in a state of *disequilibrium* (imbalance), which they try to change. This perceived disequilibrium motivates them toward further growth and understanding.

Children actively *construct* and *reconstruct* their schemas based on their experiences. Even when they are not encountering new things, they can grow intellectually by *reorganizing* existing schemas into new and more complex cognitive structures (as when an infant organizes reflex schemas of gazing, reaching, and grasping into a schema for visually directed reaching). In Piagetian theory, the goal of cognitive

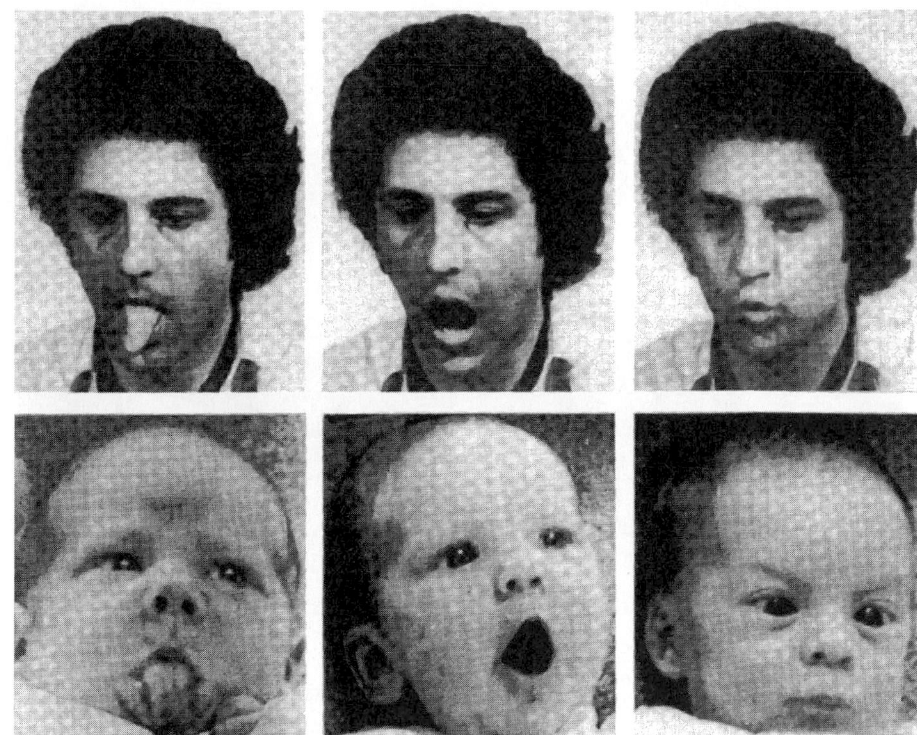

▲ *Imitation, which begins as a reflexive response, becomes a social behavior as caregivers reinforce it.*

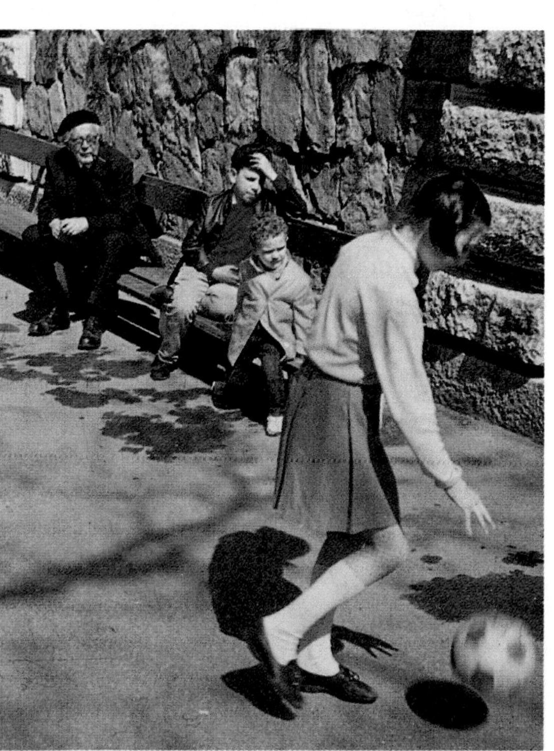

◀ *Jean Piaget observes children at play.*

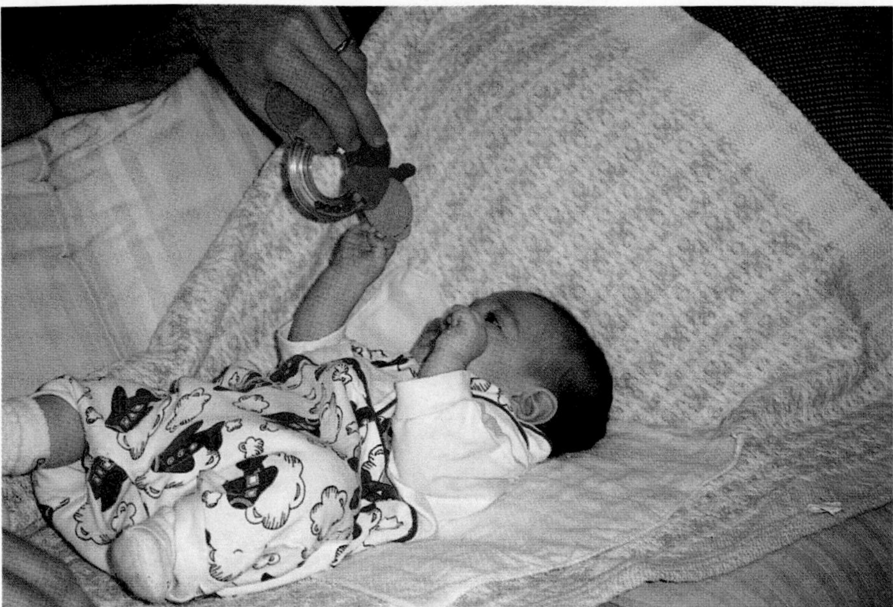

▲ *An infant at age eight weeks is able to organize the activities of gazing, reaching, and grasping.*

Discord between knowledge and reality produces disequilibrium, which an individual will be motivated to change in the direction of equilibrium.

In Piaget's theory, assimilation is the process of encoding or modifying incoming information to fit into what the child already knows. Accommodation modifies existing knowledge schemas to fit the demands of reality.

development is to establish *equilibrium*, or balance, between the structure of a child's thinking and the demands of the external world. When equilibrium is disrupted, adaptation and reorganization enable the child to regain it.

Two processes underlie the child's cognitive development. ***Assimilation*** involves encoding or modifying incoming information to fit into what the child already knows about the world (existing schemas). For example, four-month-old Alfredo may "know" objects mainly through sucking on them, and assume that all objects are "suckable." When he finds a new object, he assimilates it into his sucking schema (he pops it into his mouth!). Three-year-old Susie, who has a dog, may call the first rabbit she sees a "funny doggie" and try to pet it (petting being part of her doggie schema).

Accommodation involves modifying the existing schema to include new information. If the new object that Alfredo encounters is sharp or bitter-tasting, he discovers that not all things can be sucked. He then either modifies his sucking schema and/or forms a new schema for "nonsuckable" objects. Susie might be told that the "funny doggie" is a wild rabbit and to stay away from it. She will then develop a new "rabbit schema," that includes "do not pet," big ears, and other characteristics.

In Piagetian theory, the sequence of stages does not change and is the same for all normally functioning individuals. There is no skipping of stages; each depends on knowledge acquired in previous stages. Development brings together various elements to form a new, more complex, and powerful cognitive structure that is qualitatively different from what went before. As a consequence, adults and older children typically have very different interpretations of and responses to the same events from those of younger children—as we saw with their responses to a transformed Maynard the Cat.

According to Piagetian theory, the process of reworking inaccurate and inadequate schemas proceeds through a series of four psychological stages in cognitive development: (1) sensorimotor, (2) preoperational, (3) concrete operational, and (4) formal operational. Table 11–4 presents a summary of these stages and their characteristics. As you learn about them, keep in mind that the ages given are only approximate and that the descriptions represent the most advanced level of performance in each stage.

The ***sensorimotor stage*** begins at birth and lasts for approximately the first two years of life. Infants begin life as beings dominated by reflexes (for example, sucking, grasping) and develop into beings capable of mobility, planning, and social behavior. In this stage, they form basic ideas about objects and begin to understand relationships based on time, space, and cause-and-effect. These ideas begin as simple organized schemas of responding (for example, they have a sucking schema, a reaching schema, a grasping schema) that a child uses to explore an object or event. At about four months of age, infants begin coordinating their various schemas—for example, they look at what they are grasping. They move their hands to touch an object by alternating their gaze between hand and object, closing in on the object through trial and error. Sensorimotor play (sucking on objects, shaking rattles) has been found to be nearly universal across cultures (Sigman & Sena, 1993).

During this period, infants are still mostly unaware of themselves and the objects around them. They do not realize that the bottle they grasp one minute and the bottle they suck the next are the same. When an object drops out of sight, it literally drops "out of mind," reflecting a lack of ***object permanence***. Suppose you show a toy to an infant named Evie. As Evie reaches for the toy, you turn and put it under a pillow. She may fuss briefly but quiets rapidly, as if the toy had ceased to exist.

Between four and eight months of age, infants begin to control and manipulate objects more actively. The baby begins to realize objects still ex-

Table 11-4 Piaget's Stages of Cognitive Development

Stage and Age	Description	Some Specific Achievements	Knowledge Acquired
Sensorimotor (birth to 2 years)	Experiences world through sensory impressions and motor activities. Goes from simple reflexes to physically manipulating objects.	Differentiating self from external world. Searching for hidden objects. Making detours and retracing steps to reach a goal.	Object permanence. Time and space exist independently of own actions. Some appreciation of cause and effect, past and future.
Preoperational (2 to 7 years)	Experiences world from egocentric viewpoint. Focuses on one property (length or width) at a time. Begins to use language but not metaphors.	Representing something with something else—in speech, play, gestures, and mental pictures. Learning to pretend. Learning to take other people's perspectives.	Mental representation. Imagery. Use of language.
Concrete operational (7 to 11 years)	Experiences world through logical manipulation of concrete objects.	Mentally undoing mental or physical actions so long as manipulable objects are involved. Taking the perspective of others. Relating dimensions and understanding that certain properties of an object remain the same despite changes in appearance.	Reversibility. Conservation. Categorization.
Formal operational (11 years and older)	Experiences abstract world; can think about ideas and reflect on own thinking.	Reasoning based on purely verbal or logical statements. Relating any element or statement to any other. Manipulating variables in a scientific experiment. Dealing with proportions, probabilities, and analogies.	Abstract reasoning. Strategies. Systems of belief.

ist even when they are out of sight. At this stage, if you show Evie a toy and put it under a pillow, she will look surprised that the object has disappeared. Between eight and twelve months of age, Evie will actually pursue the toy and lift the pillow to look for it. Nonetheless, if you move the toy and place it under a second pillow, she generally will not look for it there.

At twelve to fourteen months, Evie will likely search under the second pillow for the hidden toy. She is now considered a toddler and is able to form increasingly complex hypotheses about events and to modify these hypotheses with experience. For example, the toddler may systematically vary the position from which she drops food from a high chair to discover where it will land (much to the chagrin of those who clean up!).

Finally, between one-and-a-half and two years of age, Evie can hold in her mind a mental ***representation*** (an internalized image) of an object being transferred from one place to another. The child is now acquiring the ability to think *symbolically* about objects no longer physically present. She can now also engage in symbolic play—using one object to represent another (a block to represent a truck) and understands how to pretend. In Piagetian theory, symbolic thinking must begin before children can move to the next stage.

From ages two to seven, the child is in the ***preoperational stage*** of cognitive development. In this stage, thinking begins to be based on language, and children acquire a functional number system. They begin to master the ability to represent the world mentally with words, but

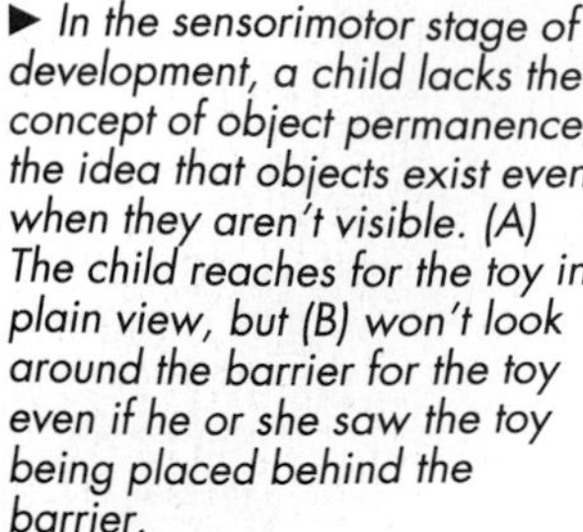

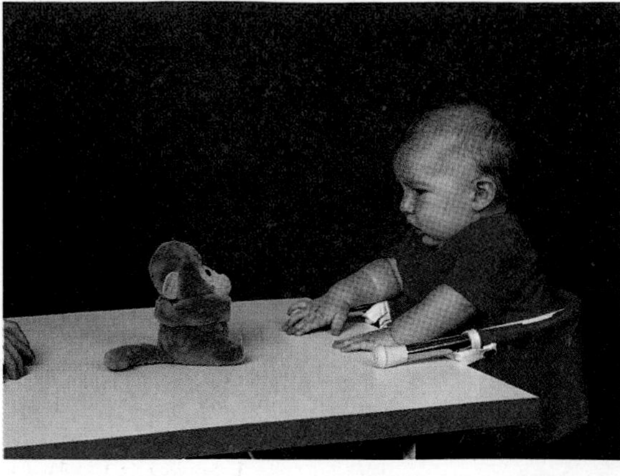

A

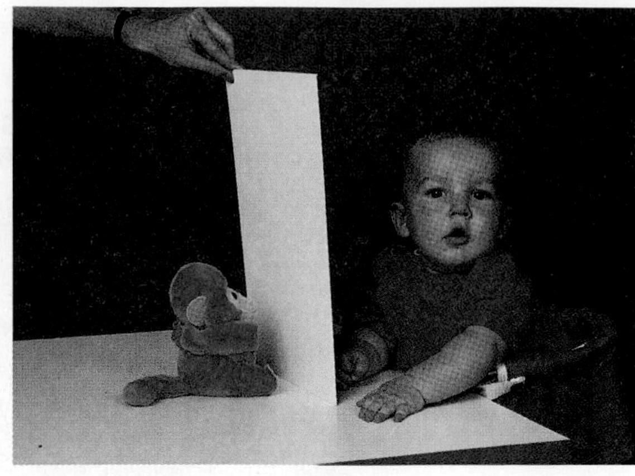

B

► *In the sensorimotor stage of development, a child lacks the concept of object permanence, the idea that objects exist even when they aren't visible. (A) The child reaches for the toy in plain view, but (B) won't look around the barrier for the toy even if he or she saw the toy being placed behind the barrier.*

they do not yet deal well with metaphor, which can be a source of humor or chagrin. Thus, when four-year-old Olia, a preoperational Russian child, visited her aunt and uncle in Moscow, she watched them closely while they and her mother were having tea. With obvious disappointment, she finally pronounced: "Mama! You said that uncle always sits on Aunt Aniuta's neck but he has been sitting on a chair all the time that we've been here" (what followed has not been recorded; Chukovsky, 1966, p. 13).

During the preoperational stage, children are extremely egocentric. That is, they do not understand that their own point of view may not be shared by others. Young children imagine themselves at the center of things and have difficulty taking any perspective other than their own. For example, a child might hold up a book and point to a picture, asking "what is this?"—not taking into account that the person facing him is looking at the back of the book. At this stage, children often make illogical inferences and attribute feelings to inanimate objects, assuming, for example, that clouds "cry" to make rain. But their perspective on the world expands rapidly during this stage, and the intellectual difference between children at two and seven years of age is quite remarkable.

Reversibility is the recognition that an action can be reversed, or negated, by mentally performing the opposite action. Conservation is the recognition that properties of objects such as weight or volume remain the same (are conserved), even though their physical appearance (shape or arrangement) may be superficially changed or transformed.

The ***concrete operational stage*** covers the years from seven to eleven. It represents a shift from the perceptually based thinking of the sensorimotor period to conceptually based thinking (that is, thinking based on concepts and ideas). Children develop mental skills (mental operations) that enable them to overcome perceptual constraints and become less egocentric (that is, able to recognize multiple perspectives). Children learn that certain operations like addition and subtraction are *reversible*, that is, they can be undone. In other words, for each number that can be subtracted from a given number or quantity, the same number can be added back to restore the original number or amount. This idea of reversibility emerges at about the same time that the child understands that an underlying physical dimension of reality (for example, mass, volume, number) is unchanged or *conserved*, even though it may undergo transformations (that is, physical changes in its appearance).

Indeed, the most famous examples of concrete operations come from conservation experiments, which explore children's conceptions of the quantity of liquids, mass, number, area, and volume. In these experiments, Piaget and Inhelder (1941) showed that only in the concrete operational stage do children begin understanding that transformations in physical objects' appearance do not necessarily affect their quantity. Figure 11–5 displays some common tests of conservation ability.

In a typical conservation-of-volume experiment, identical glasses of water are filled to the same level. Water from one glass is poured into a taller but thinner glass, and so the water level is higher (see panel C of Figure 11–5). Because they focus on the water levels, preoperational children maintain that the amount of water has changed. They take into account only one aspect and ignore both the compensating feature of the new glass (its height) and the way it was filled. If these children had an abstract conception of volume that was separate from the appearance of the water, they would realize the amount of water remains unchanged.

At about age seven, children grasp the solution to conservation problems involving number and length (conservation of weight may

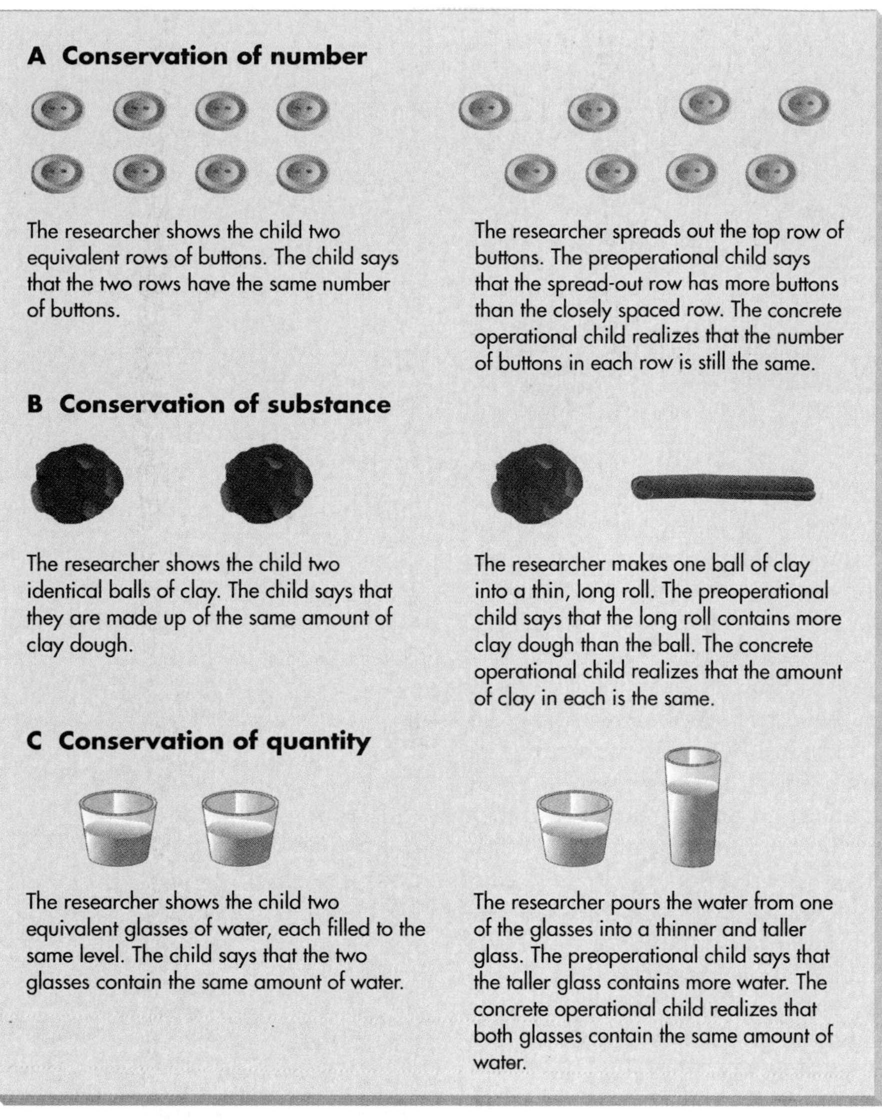

A Conservation of number
The researcher shows the child two equivalent rows of buttons. The child says that the two rows have the same number of buttons.
The researcher spreads out the top row of buttons. The preoperational child says that the spread-out row has more buttons than the closely spaced row. The concrete operational child realizes that the number of buttons in each row is still the same.
B Conservation of substance
The researcher shows the child two identical balls of clay. The child says that they are made up of the same amount of clay dough.
The researcher makes one ball of clay into a thin, long roll. The preoperational child says that the long roll contains more clay dough than the ball. The concrete operational child realizes that the amount of clay in each is the same.
C Conservation of quantity
The researcher shows the child two equivalent glasses of water, each filled to the same level. The child says that the two glasses contain the same amount of water.
The researcher pours the water from one of the glasses into a thinner and taller glass. The preoperational child says that the taller glass contains more water. The concrete operational child realizes that both glasses contain the same amount of water.

11-5 Conservation Tasks

Conservation is the realization that transformations in appearance do not change the underlying physical dimensions of objects. These conservation tasks are used to see whether children understand that changing position or shape or height does not change the physical number, substance, or quantity of objects. Other similar tasks test conservation of length, area, and volume. Children in the preoperational stage do not understand the concept of conservation, but children in the concrete operational stage do. (Source: Adapted from Gardner, 1982)

come as late as age eleven). They learn to classify and number objects and deal with class inclusion (the idea that there are classes and subclasses of objects). If you show a preoperational child pictures of five cows and eight horses and ask if there are more horses or more animals, the child will say that there are more horses, ignoring the fact that a horse is also an animal. In the concrete operations stage, the child will say that there are more animals. Children can perform these mental operations in many different situations, eliminating the need for rote memorization in each case, because the same rules apply widely. Concrete operational children come to realize that arithmetic and other disciplines are based on systems of general rules and can reason consistently. But their thought has not yet become totally logical or abstract. Thus, if instead of asking about horses and animals you ask about abstract symbols (for example, "A," "B1," and "B2"), you won't get a correct answer.

Abstract thinking comes in the ***formal operational stage***, which occurs during adolescence. Formal operations enable adolescents to think about abstract ideas, use symbols, appreciate metaphors, form and test hypotheses, and learn systematic approaches for solving problems. We will discuss this stage in more detail when we consider adolescence.

Now, think about the changes in development that we have described. Can you extract any general principles of development from what you have learned? There are at least three. First, with each stage, activity becomes increasingly *complex* (able to deal with more than one

► *Before about age seven, children do not understand conservation of liquids—that a given amount of liquid is the same whether in a tall or short container. Here, the young girl believes there is more liquid in the taller glass than in the shorter one.*

aspect of an object at a time). For example, in the conservation of water experiment, the child goes from considering only one dimension of the stimulus at a time (height or width of a glass) to being able to consider both dimensions simultaneously and to recognize that one compensates for the other. Second, thinking becomes more *abstract*. With each stage, the child becomes less bound by the perceptual features of the objects and more able to think about their abstract properties. In the study involving Maynard the Cat, with increasing age children were able to recognize that Maynard retained his identity as a cat (an abstract concept) despite looking like a dog (concrete stimulus). Third, children become less *egocentric*. In other words, they increasingly learn to consider objects and ideas from points of view other than their own.

Although research in many cultures has found that children's cognitive development proceeds through the Piagetian stages in the order predicted by Piaget, the rates of progress and the level ultimately achieved depend on the children's cultural experiences (Dasen, 1977; Mwamwenda, 1992). For example, studies of rural Mexican children found that pottery-makers' children (who have experience working clay) are able to conserve mass sooner than children whose families earned their living in another manner (Price-Williams, Gordo, & Ramirez, 1996).

The Information-Processing Approach and Cognitive Development

Today, the information-processing perspective that you learned about in Chapter 8 provides an alternative interpretation for the behaviors observed by researchers in the Piagetian tradition.

THINKING CRITICALLY

Suppose you are the parent of two children, four-year-old Linda and eight-year-old Gloria. Linda always wants to be treated just like her older sister. One hot afternoon, you discover that there are only twelve ounces of lemonade left to divide between the two eight-ounce glasses that you have set before the children. Gloria is bigger, and her body requires more fluid than Linda's. You know, however, that if you fill Gloria's glass (leaving half a glass for Linda), Linda will compare the lemonade levels in the two glasses and be very upset at the unequal treatment. What can you do to avoid conflict?

Change Linda's glass to one that is taller and thinner. Thus, you can make the heights of the liquid in the glasses the same, keeping Linda happy, while giving Gloria a larger portion in keeping with her greater need.

Would this strategy work with Gloria? No. It works with Linda because she is not yet able to conserve liquids. At eight years old, Gloria understands that both the height and the width of the glass determine how much lemonade she will get.

From the information-processing perspective, development is an active, cognitively based process, to which both nature and nurture are important contributors. Development is viewed in terms of gradual and continuous improvements in attention, memory, and thinking skills, resulting in enhanced abilities to analyze and interpret new events and experiences.

Researchers who believe in the information-processing approach emphasize changes in the structures and processes of cognition and are interested in how children process social as well as physical information. Such researchers focus on how we learn or encode information and develop strategies for processing. In information-processing research, children are often given problems to solve while researchers observe and analyze how each child attempts to solve them (Siegler & Crowley, 1991). Researchers measure a wide variety of variables, such as how the child visually scans or searches through problem elements, how long it takes the child to attempt to solve a problem, what the child says or does, and what the child can remember about the problem after it's finished.

This approach has elements of both a learning perspective and Piagetian theory. Like Piaget, information-processing theorists attempt to identify mental processes, but in a much more analytic and detailed way, reducing them to distinct, specific strategies. Like learning theorists, information-processing theorists view strategies as patterns of behavior that are learned and can be taught. According to the information-processing approach, differences in responses between younger and older children reflect experience, specific skills to handle a situation, and proficiency in applying these skills. Since older children have more experience, they have a wider range of skills to use in any situation.

Information-processing theorists agree with the Piagetian view that children must progress through a series of reconceptualizations of the world before they can comprehend increasingly abstract ideas. Yet, they believe that these reconceptualizations occur gradually and cumulatively over time, rather than in stages as Piaget believed.

Language Acquisition

The development of symbolic thought is accompanied by another crucial cognitive process, the acquisition of language. Infants begin life with a primitive form of verbal expression—a healthy cry. By their second month, they begin to coo, emitting vowel-like "oohs" and "ahs," particularly when pleased or excited. Crying and cooing are considered prelinguistic, however, because they do not represent objects or events. These forms of verbal expression mainly result from innate mechanisms as shown by the fact that, up to about eight months, the vocalizations of deaf babies, who cannot possibly imitate speech, are indistinguishable from those of hearing babies (Lenneberg, 1967). Adults can reinforce verbal expression by carrying on "conversations" with infants when they coo and make other sounds.

Between six and nine months, infants begin babbling, that is, making sounds like human speech and combining consonant and vowel sounds such as *ba*, *ga*, and *da*. The first time a child says "dada" it is accidental. But an excited reaction by a caregiver will ensure that the sound will be repeated (Mitchell & Kent, 1990). Experience and cognitive learning become increasingly more important. By about the end of their first year, babies start making recognizable word-like sounds, such as "ba" and "dada," for important objects, people, and events in their lives. Although such "words" are not, strictly speaking, part of English, they function effectively like words in their consistent use as labels for objects and classes of objects. The meanings of these early "words" are probably less precise or perhaps more general than corresponding words in adult speech. "Dada" may describe father, mother, baby-sitter, or any adult.

In the first year of life, speech production lags behind comprehension. Infants can hear the differences between "b" and "p," though they can't make the sounds distinctly. A lisping child may call himself "Tham," yet shriek in protest when someone fails to pronounce Sam correctly. Ten-month-olds can respond accurately by gesture to questions like "Where's Daddy?," yet they can't verbalize their answers for several months.

In addition to shaping the language development of children by reinforcing them when they vocalize, adults enhance language development by using a form of slow, repetitive, high-pitched, concrete (referring to immediate objects), structured "baby talk" that appears to help children learn language more effectively (Fernald, 1992). Sentences are brief and grammatically correct, but simple, consisting of nouns, verbs, and only a few adjectives. Key words are spoken in a louder and higher voice, and put at the ends of sentences. As the children's language abilities grow, the adults increase their own language level, staying just ahead of the child and encouraging the child to catch up (Fernald & Mazzie, 1991; Trehub, Trainor, & Unyk, 1993). Inappropriately called "motherese" (fathers, siblings, and unrelated individuals also use it, not just mothers), this structured baby talk has been found in a wide variety of languages other than English, including Arabic, Comanche, Italian, French, German,

Xhosa (a southern African language), Japanese, and Mandarin Chinese (Fernald, 1991; Fernald & Morikawa, 1993).

This is not to imply that there are no differences in the ways adults use and model language for children across cultures. Cultural values are indeed reflected in the way adults speak to children. For example, consistent with the collectivist values of emotional closeness and interdependence in Japanese culture, Japanese mothers were found to use more expressive speech with their children compared to Western mothers (Argentinean, French, and American). In turn, mothers from the Western cultures were found to be more likely to provide information in their speech, making statements and asking the child more questions (Bornstein, 1992). Greater exposure to information-oriented speech may be why American babies have greater vocabulary development than Japanese babies at thirteen months of age (Tamis-Lemonda, Bornstein, Cyphers, Toda, & Ogino, 1992).

After only one year, a child starts to speak intelligibly, mastering language fundamentals in about three years. A child's vocabulary grows enormously over this period. By age four, children have a vocabulary of about 1,600 words and can understand and use most grammatical structures. Two years later, most children's vocabulary increases to over 2,500 words. Table 11-5 shows how language abilities progress, from cooing, to babbling, to two-word speech, to full sentences during childhood. Although cultural forces shape the syntax and vocabulary of a language, the speed with which a child learns to speak under different conditions suggests that there is an inborn predisposition for human language. Further, the plasticity in neural development found between eighteen months of age and puberty makes it easier to learn language during this period (Lenneberg, 1967; Hurford, 1991).

As you learned in Chapters 4 and 8, language and thought are interrelated. Language is an important cultural problem-solving tool that influences our attention, perception, and memory (Vygotsky, 1962). While language-like behav-

Table 11-5 Stages of Language Development in Children

Average Age	Ability
3 months	Random vocalizations; cooing, which is vowel-like and pitch modulated.
4 months	Turns head and seems to search for speaker in response to human sounds; occasional chuckling sounds.
6 months	Babbling; makes ma, mu, da, di sounds.
12 months	Repeats some sound sequences (mama, dada); signs of understanding some words and simple sentences.
18 months	Able to say more than 3 words but fewer than 50 words; babbling of several syllables with complex intonations; no phrases.
24 months	Able to say more than 50 words; words joined into two-word phrases; no sentences.
30 months	Addition of new words every day; speaks to communicate and frustrated if not understood; longer phrases and short sentences; many errors in speech but understands everything said by others.
3 years	Knows and can say over 1,000 words; fewer errors; more grammatical complexity; longer sentences.
4 years	Knows and can say around 1,600 words; grammar and understanding close to that of adults.

▼ *The ability to communicate through the use of language fosters social interaction.*

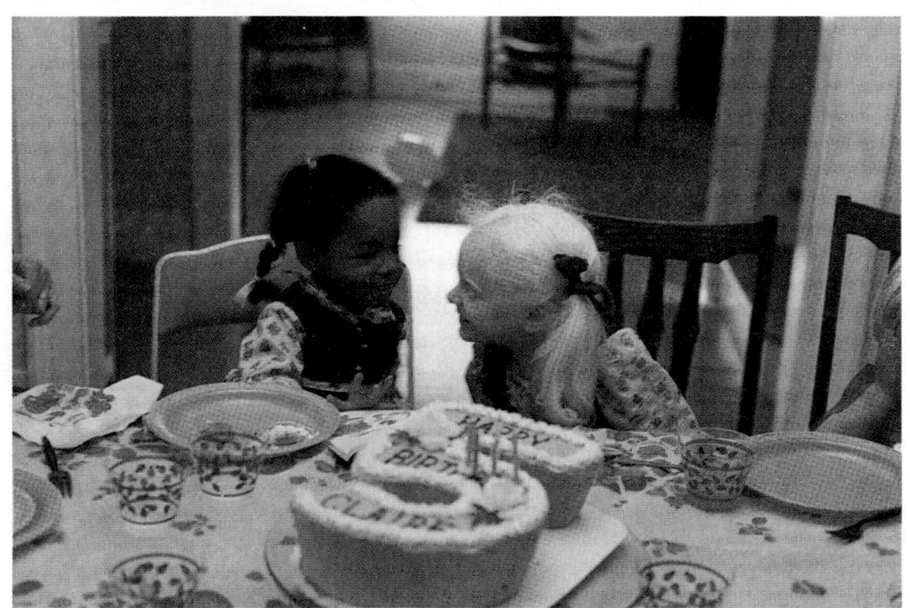

iors occur in other species, the level of human linguistic competence is truly unique. Moreover, it occurs effortlessly, universally, and with remarkable speed.

Social and Emotional Development

Social and emotional development begin very early in life. At birth, an infant seems to express only two emotions. One is positive or pleasurable, expressed with a smile; the other is negative or unpleasant, expressed as crying or screaming. But infant emotional expressions quickly differentiate. By three years, each child seems to have a full range of human emotion (see Table 11-6).

From birth onward, children live in a social world made up of family, classmates, and friends. As children grow, they must learn to form satisfying relations with all these people, and they must learn the rules and standards needed to live in a social world. Thus, they must learn how to act with parents and friends as well as learning what is right and wrong. A child who fails in these tasks may end up alone, without friends, without social skills, and even in trouble with the law.

Even our developing self and identity are wrapped up in our social progress. Throughout life, but particularly in life's early stages, we learn much about ourselves through others. In infancy and early childhood, social relations largely determine what we think of ourselves (our self-concept). As we grow, our personality affects how we respond to caregivers and friends, but in turn our personality is also affected by how others respond to us.

Two complementary processes contribute to a child's social development. ***Integration*** includes our efforts to get along with others, to regulate behavior according to social codes and standards, and to develop a conscience. Integration connects us to society through relationships and responsibilities. ***Differentiation*** is the formation of our unique social identity and personality. Through differentiation, we develop a sense of self, recognize our unique characteristics, and understand the implications of our sex role, family role, and social status for our individual identity. Differentiation promotes social development because forming a personal identity requires separating ourselves from others and coming to know our special personal and social characteristics.

Table 11-6 Emotional Development

Emotion	Age of Emergence
Interest	Birth
Reflexive smile	Birth
Distress	Birth
Disgust	Birth
Social smile	4–6 weeks
Anger	3–4 months
Surprise	3–4 months
Sadness	3–4 months
Fear	5–7 months
Shame	6–8 months
Guilt	two years

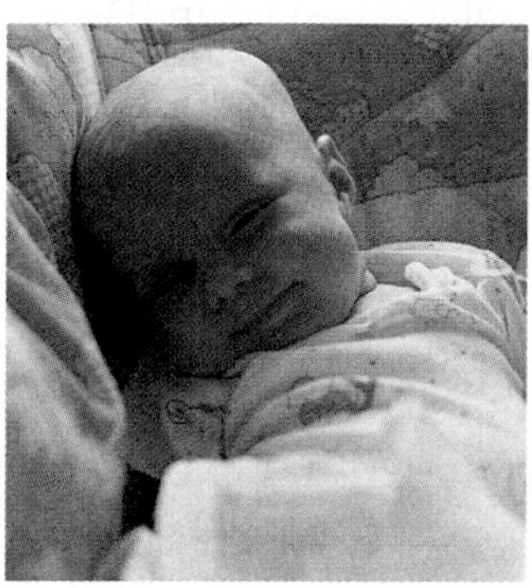
A

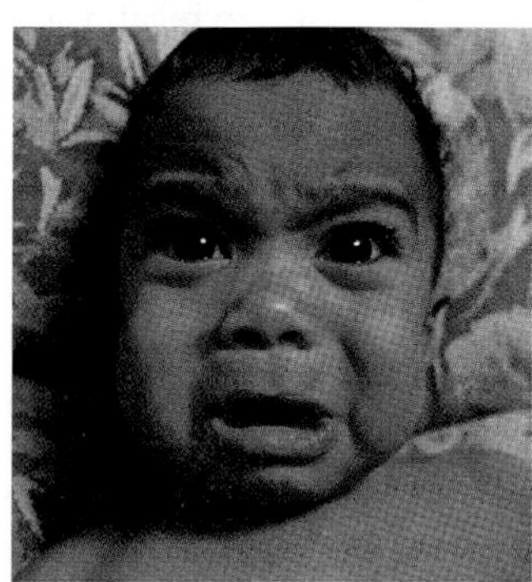
B

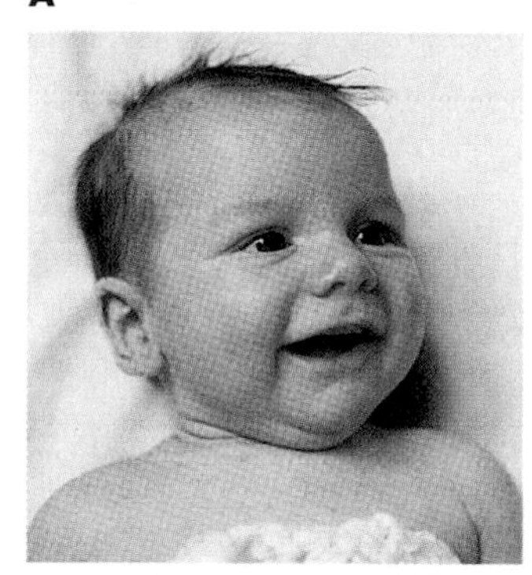
C

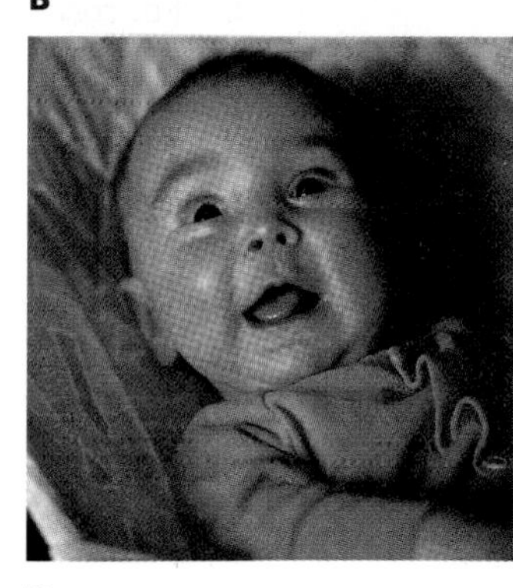
D

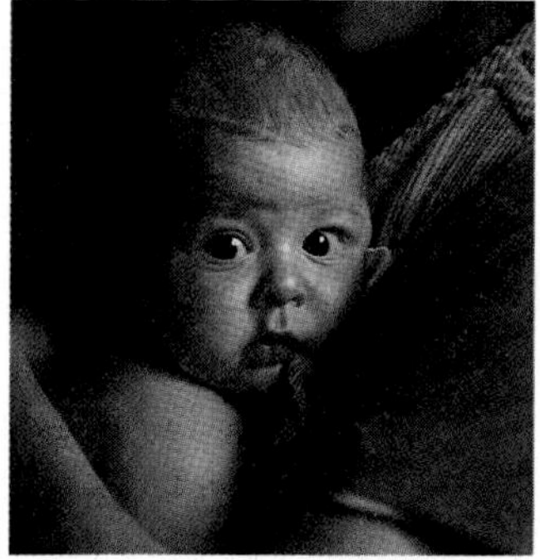
E

▲ *Social and emotional development begin very early in life. Here are five examples: (A) reflexive smile; (B) distress; (C) social smile; (D) surprise; and (E) fear.*

. . . if you ask whether the newborn is innately social, the answer would have to be no—not in the sense of organized, intentional interaction with others. The newborn, however, is exquisitely attuned to *becoming* social, provided that responsive social partners are available.

—Alan Sroufe, Robert Cooper, Ganie DeHart, and M. Marshall (1992, p. 193)

▲ *Monkeys, too, require contact comfort.*

Attachment

Most developmental psychologists assume human beings are ready to begin social integration at birth. Human infants come "prewired" or predisposed to notice and respond to certain stimuli and events that go beyond the simple concepts of prepared learning discussed in Chapter 6. Thus, newborns have predispositions that equip them for early social exchanges. These predispositions provide the bases for communication when the infant has caregivers who (1) are responsive to these inborn behaviors, and (2) provide appropriate stimulation. These inherited tendencies assure that infants have contact with people who will provide them with protection, shelter, and food needed for survival. This tendency does not seem limited to human beings, by the way. Monkeys also exhibit a need for "contact" (see Figure 11-6).

Behavioral patterns that the infant uses to establish close and sustained contact with its primary caregiver are ***attachment behaviors*** (Ainsworth, Blehar, Waters, & Wall, 1978). An infant's attachment behaviors include attempting to be near the caregiver, smiling, cooing, and grasping as positive means of getting the caregiver's attention, and crying, stomping, or screaming as negative means. These behaviors are believed to represent the infant's confidence that a caregiver will be there when needed. A host of research suggests that secure attachment is an important foundation for healthy development and the ability to maintain satisfying relationships (Feeney & Noller, 1990; Radecki-Bush, Farrell, & Bush, 1993). Most of this research has dealt with the attachment between the mother and the child, as developmentalists traditionally ignored fathers' relationships with infants. Mothers were viewed as primary caregivers, and fathers were seen as adopting a less nurturing and secondary role. More recent research, however, has shown that both mothers and fathers are important attachment figures for the child (Main & Weston, 1981).

Mary Ainsworth and her colleagues studied patterns of attachment between infants and their mothers in an experimental arrangement called the ***strange situation*** (Ainsworth, Blehar, Waters, & Wall, 1978). In this situation, infants encounter a stranger and new objects, both when their mother is with them in the room and when she leaves the room (see Figure 11-7). Ainsworth and her associates found that infants who are "securely attached" to their mothers use them as a "base" for exploring their environment. Although they take pleasure in their mother's presence and greet her warmly when she returns from a brief absence, they can venture into the world on their own. Securely attached infants are more likely to form positive and productive relations with their peers in early childhood (Sroufe, 1979). Their socialization seems to be a relatively natural and stress-free process. Insecurely attached infants, on the other hand, show little interest in exploring new objects or people. They often cling to their mothers in a new environment. Yet, if the mother leaves the room, they do not show obvious warmth or affection to her when she returns.

What determines whether an infant becomes securely or insecurely attached? Ainsworth found that caregivers of securely attached infants respond quickly and appropriately to the baby's needs, while caregivers of insecurely attached babies are slower or less likely to respond to the baby's distress. Thus, "if you pick up a crying baby, you will spoil it" is probably bad advice for parents. Babies whose mothers quickly comforted them tended to cry less later in infancy than those whose mothers didn't want to "spoil" them.

As infants' social relations with caregivers develop, they reach important emotional milestones. By the second or third month, infants smile at a range of stimuli, including bells,

11-6 Monkeys and Contact Comfort

Monkeys raised in social isolation, without contact with their mothers or other monkeys, were offered two kinds of surrogate mothers: one covered with wire and the other covered with cloth. A nipple that provided milk was built into both the "wire mother" and the "cloth mother." Whether the infant was fed by the "wire mother" or the "cloth mother," the monkey preferred contact with the "cloth mother." Infants could cling to the cloth mother and thus experienced "contact comfort" from her. This seems to indicate that attachment bonds are determined by more than what feeds the infant. (Source: Harlow & Zimmerman, 1959)

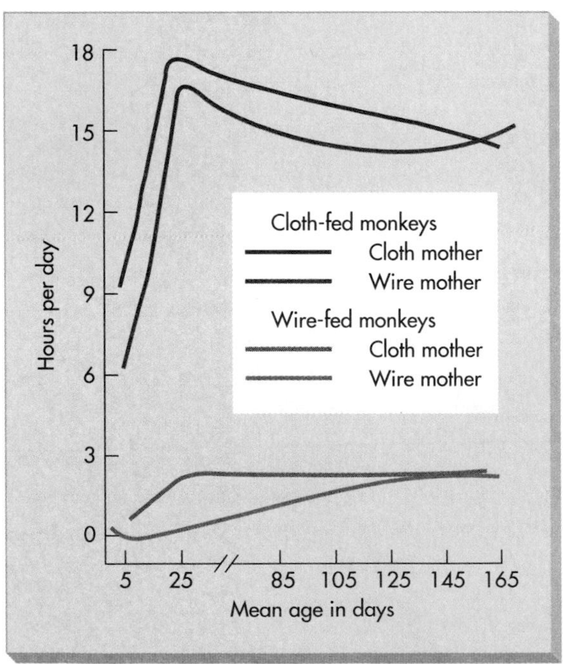

lights, and other interesting visual displays. The sight of the familiar caregiver elicits particular joy. By the seventh month, the absence of the caregiver becomes an emotionally disturbing event for the infant. This "separation anxiety" seems particularly acute from seven to eleven months of age. At about this time, infants also develop a "wariness" of strangers and are likely to "freeze up" or break into fitful crying at the sight of a stranger. Cross-cultural research suggests that separation anxiety occurs earlier in cultures in which mothers have extended periods of close physical contact with their children and care for them almost exclusively (Crowell & Waters, 1990).

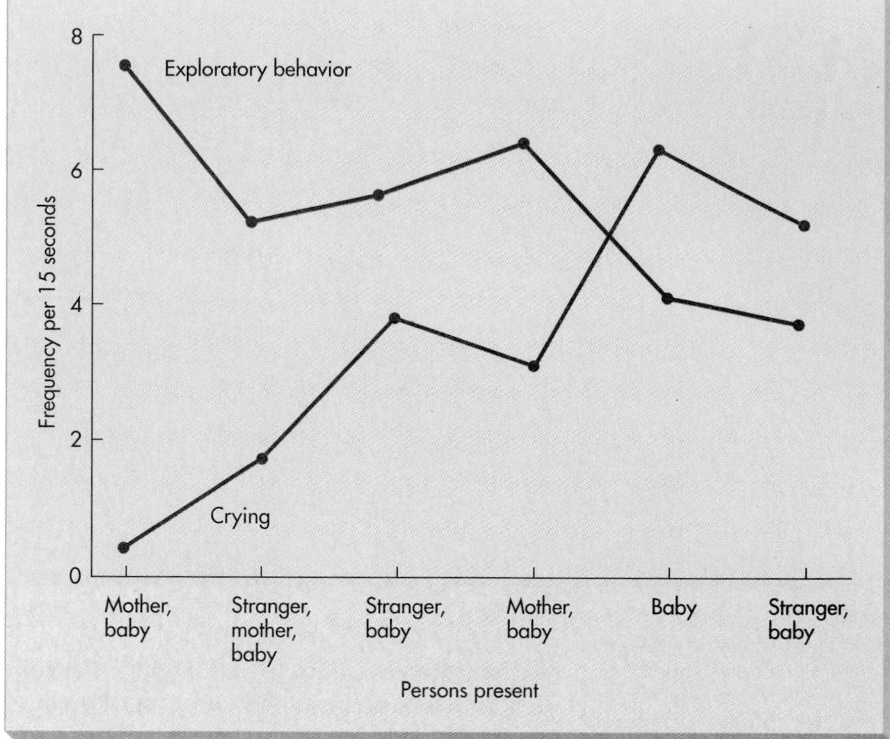

11-7 The Strange Situation

The "strange situation" is an experimental situation that seeks to explore an infant's attachment to his or her mother. A one-year-old baby will cry more and explore the environment less when a stranger enters the room. If a stranger is present and the mother is absent from the room, crying will increase. The graph shows exploratory and crying behavior over a period of about a half an hour when mother and baby are present, when a stranger enters the room but the mother is still there, and when only the stranger and baby are in the room. (Source: Adapted from Ainsworth & Bell, 1970)

While close attachments with parents have many benefits for children, they may also lead to the problem of the children being too dependent on their parents. Eventually, the children must find ways of separating themselves from their primary caregivers and asserting their independence. This usually occurs during the second year of life (sometimes called the period of the "terrible twos"). Though something of a child-management problem for parents, the "terrible twos" represents a prodigious achievement in the child's cognitive and social development. At this point, children begin to realize the uniqueness of their own viewpoints, and this becomes reflected in their social relationships (Lewis & Brooks-Gunn, 1979).

THINKING CRITICALLY

Because about one-half of all women with young children in the United States now work outside the home, day care by non-family members has become a common childhood experience. You yourself are likely to have experienced day care. How might day care affect psychological development?

Research suggests that impact depends on the quality of the care. A five-year experimental study and observational studies of communal child-rearing in Israel and the former Soviet Union, have failed to identify any significant developmental handicap associated with day care (Kagan, Kearsley, & Zelazo, 1978). The kind of day care that was studied, however, was provided by large, well-funded, and professionally staffed centers, often affiliated with academic institutions, and likely to be of high quality. Other research suggests that children who attend high-quality centers are more independent, socially competent, outgoing, affectionate, cooperative, and likely to share toys (Etaugh & Rathus, 1995). Studies done in centers with minimal staffing and programming are less encouraging, suggesting that the outcome for the day-care child depends directly on day-care quality (Belsky, 1988).

Social Play

Almost from birth, children engage in meaningful contact with others. Researchers have documented the remarkable reciprocity and cooperation marking infants' peer interactions (Howes, 1988). Social and cooperative play among peers expands in the preschool years, between ages three and five, when a genuine exchange of ideas and actions occurs. This in-

Attachment refers to those behaviors infants use to establish close and sustained contact with their primary caregiver.

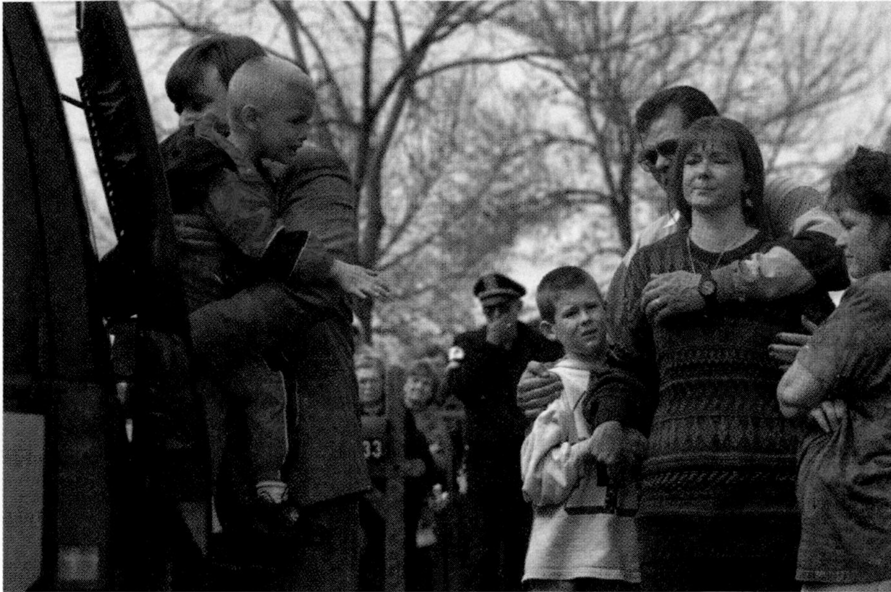

▲ *Children form deep attachments to their caregivers. Pictured is "Baby Richard," a child who was the object of a fierce custody battle between his biological and his foster parents. Richard shows severe distress at being taken away by his biological father, who won custody.*

Morality is behavior based on a set of ideals or principles that help a person make distinctions between right and wrong.

▼ *Children enjoy playing at adult roles, trying on various identities.*

terchange forces children to deal with other conflicting points of view, and encourages them to adopt new ideas and behaviors.

Piaget referred to play as "the work of children" because it is how they get ahead, it takes up most of their time, and it contributes in many ways to their intellectual and social abilities. There are both sophistication and variety in children's social play (Garvey, 1977). Particularly significant is how children try out new social roles and how they practice social interaction rules while playing. A child can pretend to be a parent, a teacher, a police officer, or a baby, and can act out conflicting desires or problems with none of the consequences of real life. Play offers children an opportunity to experiment, to symbolize, and to invent new patterns of social behavior. It may be a "nonserious" activity, but it has important cognitive and social developmental benefits (Lillard, 1993; Howes & Matheson, 1992).

Initially the young child is ***egocentric*** and has difficulty separating his or her own perspective from that of others. By engaging in social relations like friendship, children learn a great deal about the expectations, needs, and perspectives of others. These experiences foster ***role taking***, the ability to anticipate another's point of view. By middle childhood, the capacity to perform "two-way" role taking emerges. This enables the child to realize that other people can take the child's perspective, just as the child can take other people's perspectives. By the end of childhood, the child can take a "third-party" perspective, understanding that there are societal points of view that transcend individual people's opinions (Bornstein & O'Reilly, 1993).

Childhood Morality

A part of interacting with others, be it in play or later in work, involves knowing and doing what is "right." A child must learn that it is right to help others and to be truthful. The child hears the story of the taxi driver who returns a large bag filled with cash that was left in his cab and learns it is wrong to take or keep other people's money. ***Morality*** is based on a set of ideals or principles that help a person make distinctions between right and wrong and act on these distinctions. Having a common morality allows people to live peacefully together. Moral standards vary across cultures, but each culture has developed standards of conduct that its members must obey. To be a moral person, you must internalize moral principles that you learn, and behave in accordance with them.

Developmentalists study three aspects of morality: (1) *affective* (how we feel about doing right or wrong); (2) *cognitive* (how we conceptualize right and wrong and make decisions on how to act); and (3) *behavioral* (how we actually act when tempted to violate our moral principles). Sometimes children know that what they are doing is wrong but do it anyway. Gene may do the right thing at home under the watchful eyes of his parents, but the wrong thing at school, where his parents do not see what is happening. Thus, moral behavior may be determined by aspects of the situation.

Psychodynamic theories focus on the affective dimension. In Freudian theory, anxiety, shame, guilt, and other emotions play important roles in determining moral behavior. According to Freud, our behavior is monitored by an aspect of our mind called the superego, which functions as our conscience and makes us feel anxious or guilty if we think about or do something we know is wrong (see Chapter 14). The parent-child relationship determines the development of the superego. Nonetheless, although research has established that parents do play an important role in the development of a conscience, the Freudian account of moral development has not been supported by scientific evidence (see Shafer, 1996).

Cognitive developmental theorists focus on links between intellectual development and

UNDERSTANDING HUMAN DIVERSITY

Culture, Caregiving, and Attachment

In keeping with the well-known African proverb, "It takes a village to raise a child," cultures vary widely with regard to who "in the village" has responsibility for child care and what behaviors are considered appropriate for particular caregiving roles at different ages and over time (Munroe & Munroe, 1994).

In all cultures studied, women (usually mothers) have been found to be the primary caregivers of infants (Munroe & Munroe, 1994). Even so, there is great diversity in the specific behaviors involved in caring for infants across and within cultures, and these behaviors have implications for the formation of attachment. For example, secure attachments are more common in Japan and the United States than in Germany. Japanese mothers rarely leave infants with other caregivers, emphasizing close and continuous contact with their babies (Barratt, Negayama, & Minami, 1993). In contrast, German mothers emphasize independence from an early age. They are more likely to leave their babies alone in bed and less likely to pick them up if they cry than are American mothers (Grossmann & Grossmann, 1991).

Even though fathers may spend less time than mothers with their babies, that does not mean that they are uninvolved with or less capable of caring for them (Lamb & Oppenheim, 1989). Studies suggest that the time fathers in the United States spend with children is increasing, although it continues to be less than the time spent by mothers. Although fathers and mothers do the same sorts of things with their children, fathers spend less time than mothers on basic tasks, like changing diapers and feeding, and more time in play (Lamb, Ketterlinus, & Fracasso, 1992). Even the kind of play with their infants varies: mothers are more likely to play games involving toys or pat-a-cake and peekaboo, while fathers are more likely to engage in rough-and-tumble play (Carson, Burks, & Parke, 1993).

There is great diversity in the behavior of fathers across cultures. Although in general fathers engage in more rough-and-tumble play than mothers, such play is much less likely to occur in India than in the United States, in keeping with the Indian cultural values of tranquillity and nonaggressiveness (Roopnarine, Talukder, Jain, Joshi, & Srivastav, 1990). Time spent with children by fathers varies across cultures as well. Aka Pygmy fathers of the western Congo basin spend one-half of their day within arm's length of their babies, and 88 percent of that time within their view. On average, these fathers held their babies for a full hour during the day and spent 20 percent of the early evening hours caring for their babies. And unlike American and Indian fathers, Aka fathers did not engage in rough-and-tumble play with their children (Hewlett, 1991).

In Israeli collective farm communities, called *kibbutzim*, the primary care and training of children is the responsibility of a child-rearing specialist called a *metapelet*, who also spends the night with them. Parents frequently visit and interact with their children during the day and evening, however, and these arrangements do not appear to damage the attachment bonds between parent and child. Babies become as attached to their *metapelet* as to their parents (van Uzendoorn, Sagi, & Lambermon, 1992). Indeed, most infants around the world have more then one caregiver and most form multiple attachments—to mothers, fathers, grandparents, siblings, other family members, day-care providers, and others (Howes & Matheson, 1992). Nonetheless, ethnic groups vary in the extent to which extended family members assume child-rearing responsibilities. For example, extended kin networks have been an important source of support and strength for black families in the United States (Wilson, 1989).

Parenting behavior varies with socioeconomic status. Regardless of ethnic group, lower- and working-class mothers often show less warmth and affection to their children and are often more restrictive and authoritarian (McLoyd, 1990). Psychological distress accompanying economic hardship can make people irritable and edgy, foster marital conflict and divorce, and undermine capacity to be an involved, warm, and supportive parent (McLoyd, 1990; Conger et al., 1994).

The nature of the caregiver's relationship (for example, mother, father, day-care worker, *metapelet*) appears to be less important for attachment than the quality of the relationship. Caregiver responsiveness and consistency in affection and warmth toward the child appear to be the key to developing secure attachments. But it is important to remember that development always occurs in a cultural context.

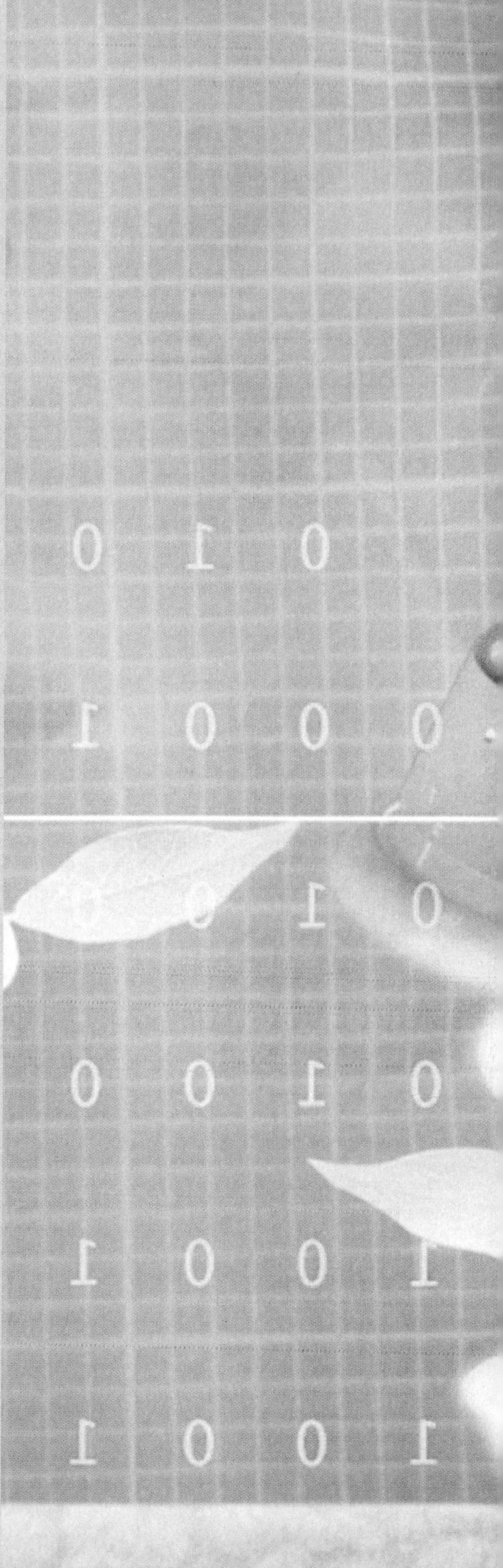

▶ *A father tries to teach his son right from wrong by scolding him for breaking a window with a baseball.*

moral reasoning. To Piaget and to Lawrence Kohlberg, who elaborated on Piaget's theories of morality, both a sense of social justice and respect for rules to treat people fairly are the foundation of moral maturity (Piaget, 1932; Kohlberg, 1981, 1984). Morality first arises in children's lives as sharing, turn-taking, and other forms of "fairness" found in play. The "fairness" concept enables children to interact with adults and peers in a relatively peaceful and well-regulated manner. If children are to get along well with friends, they must learn to give others a fair share of opportunities, like taking turns with a toy. Otherwise they will have unending conflict and little joy in playing together.

▼ *As children grow, they must learn to share their toys in order to develop harmonious relations with others.*

After interviewing children about the rules of playing a common marble game in the streets of Geneva, Switzerland, Piaget concluded that there are developmental changes in thinking about social rules. According to Piaget, up to ages four to five, children are ***premoral***. They do not demonstrate an awareness of rules. Around age five, they begin to develop ***moral realism***, which involves inflexible respect for rules and viewing rules as moral absolutes, sacred and unchangeable. There's right and there's wrong, with no in-between. In this first stage of moral development, children believe that breaking the rules will always be punished. So, if six-year-old Jay slips and bangs his elbow while playing with a forbidden object, he may conclude that the pain is his punishment for wrongdoing.

Around nine years of age, cognitive maturation and role-taking skills reduce egocentrism, enabling children to move to a second stage, ***moral relativism***. Now the child regards rules as changeable agreements created by people to serve particular needs. Cooperation and reciprocity become children's rationale for obeying rules, and they follow rules more consistently.

Lawrence Kohlberg extended Piaget's work in moral judgment, focusing mostly on early adolescence through college age (Kohlberg, 1963). Using an interview approach similar to Piaget's, he began by telling ten-, thirteen-, and sixteen-year-old boys stories with a moral dilemma like the following: A woman was near death from cancer. Doctors told her that a recently discovered drug might save her. The druggist was charging $2,000, ten times what the drug cost him to make. The sick woman's husband, Heinz, went to everyone he knew to borrow the money, but he could only get together about half of what it cost. He told the druggist that his wife was dying and asked him to sell the drug for less money or to let him pay later. The druggist refused to help him. In desperation, the husband broke into the man's store to steal the drug for his wife. Should the husband have stolen the drug? Why?

The *reasoning* as to whether the theft was justified rather than the answer itself was what was important to Kohlberg. Because moral reasoning is a cognitive process, it reflects a person's cognitive developmental level. According to Kohlberg, there are three levels of moral reasoning, each subdivided into two stages. Moral development proceeds through these six stages, with each succeeding stage representing more mature reasoning (see Table 11-7).

Level I (preconventional morality) parallels Piaget's stage of moral realism and generally involves children ages ten and under. In Stage 1 (obedience and punishment orientation), children are oriented to value power, punishment, and rules in their own right ("He shouldn't steal because he'll go to jail."). In Stage 2 (naive hedonism orientation), children follow the rules to gain rewards ("He should steal the drug because his wife will reward him."). Moral behavior toward others is motivated by the hope of something in return: "You scratch my back and I'll scratch yours." Together these two stages suggest that rightness or wrongness is determined by what a rule or an authority figure says and by the consequences of a wrongful action.

Table 11-7 Kohlberg's Six Stages of Moral Development

Level and Stage	What Is Right	Reasons for Doing Right	Social Perspective
LEVEL I: PRECONVENTIONAL			
Stage 1: Obedience and punishment orientation	Obeying authorities and not breaking rules.	Avoiding punishment for doing wrong.	Only considers own point of view and what will happen to him or her if breaks rules.
Stage 2: Naive hedonism orientation	Doing what will meet your own needs and letting others meet their needs.	Making a fair exchange; gaining a reward.	Understands that everyone has own needs and that what he or she does will affect what others do to him or her.
LEVEL II: CONVENTIONAL			
Stage 3: Good boy/ good girl orientation	Doing what people close to you think is good.	Getting approval and avoiding disapproval of those who matter to you.	Relates points of view through Golden Rule of putting self in other person's shoes.
Stage 4: Social-order-maintaining orientation	Doing the duties you have agreed to do; contributing to society.	Keeping society going by following a rigid code of law.	Takes point of view of the society making the rules.
LEVEL III: POSTCONVENTIONAL			
Stage 5: Social contract and individual rights orientation	Recognizing that laws and rules are relative to your group.	Following laws and rules based on a rational and democratic social contract.	Takes point of view of what is best for the majority of people.
Stage 6: Individual principles of conscience orientation	Following ethical principles.	Following universal, abstract moral principles, even if they violate the law.	Takes point of view that certain moral principles like justice, equality, and respect for human life are more important than societal laws.

Source: Adapted from Kohlberg, 1976.

Although Kohlberg's research was initially conducted on U.S. boys, other research has found a similar sequence of stages for both boys and girls, and across cultures as diverse as Honduras, Mexico, the Bahamas, Kenya, India, Nigeria, Taiwan, and Turkey (Colby & Kohlberg, 1987). But the timing of the stages varies across and within cultures. Figure 11-8 shows how the proportion of the different kinds of moral judgments that Western children make changes with age. In general, when Western children get to be about thirteen to sixteen years of age, their moral judgments are most often made at Level 2 (conventional morality) (Kohlberg, 1963). We will discuss the remainder of Kohlberg's stages of moral development in the section on adolescence.

In contrast to Piaget and Kohlberg, social learning theorists emphasize the behavioral di-

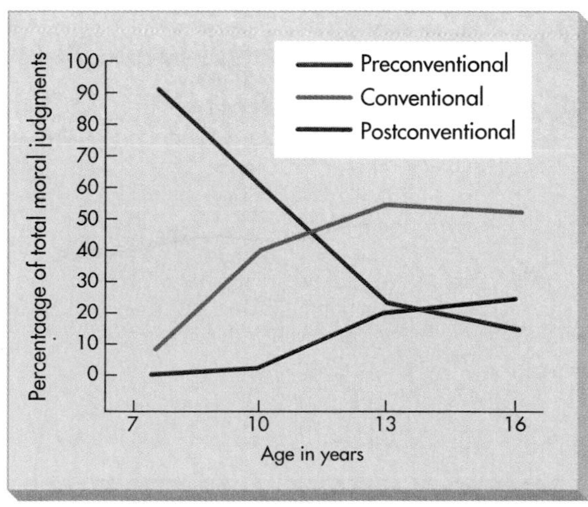

11-8 Moral Judgment Changes with Age

Kohlberg asked seven-, ten-, thirteen-, and sixteen-year-old boys to reason about a variety of moral dilemmas. The percentage of preconventional moral judgments declined with age, while the conventional and postconventional moral judgments increased with age, although at different rates of increase. Between ages thirteen and sixteen, conventional moral judgments ranged between 50 to 60 percent of total moral judgments while postconventional moral judgments ranged between 20 and 25 percent. (Source: Adapted from Kohlberg, 1964) mension of morality, including the effects of reinforcement, punishment, and observational learning (specifically, social modeling) on moral conduct. Reinforcing a child for following rules and punishing the child for misbehavior are important for instilling internal controls. Punishment is most effective when it is immediate and given by a generally warm and loving (reinforcing) parent (Sears, Maccoby, & Levin, 1957). Most importantly, laboratory studies have suggested that all forms of punishment are more effective when the child is given a cognitive rationale or reason for not misbehaving (Parke, 1977; Crick & Dodge, 1994; also see Chapter 6).

Because punishment often has negative side effects, social learning theorists seek alternative methods to get children to obey the rules. Two successful strategies include self-instruction (teaching children how to instruct themselves to follow rules), and self-concept training (designed to convince children that they are "good" or "honest" people who don't lie, cheat, or steal). These strategies contribute to internal controls rather than behavior constraints based on fear of getting caught and punished (Toner & Smith, 1977; Casey & Burton, 1983).

Children's Acquisition of Gender and Sex Roles

Gender is arguably our first and most obvious social category (Siegel, 1987). The assignment of gender occurs the minute the child's sex is known. At age two, children begin to notice differences among people and *categorize* themselves based on these differences (Stipek, Gralinski, & Kopp, 1990). Age and gender are among the first social categories children apply in distinguishing themselves from babies and adults—"big boy" and "big girl" now become part of their self-concept (Edwards & Lewis, 1979). Sex typing is the process by which children acquire their ***gender identity*** (whether they are male or female), and the values, traits, motives, and behaviors considered appropriate for their particular gender (qualities associated with their ***gender role***). Gender roles vary across cultures, and across time within a culture, and reflect environmental conditions (see Chapter 4). Thus, in competitive societies where life is harsh and competition for resources keen, gender roles are more likely to be segregated and men taught to be aggressive, hunt, and fight. But in cultures with plentiful resources and few enemies, such as in Tahiti, gender roles are less segregated and men are less aggressive (Gilmore, 1991).

Different theoretical orientations suggest different mechanisms for how children learn appropriate gender-role behaviors. Psychodynamic theorists emphasize identification with the same-sex parent; social learning theorists emphasize the role of societal reinforcement for behavior considered appropriate for a girl or boy; and cognitive theorists focus on observation and imitation and on the development of intellectual skills as precursors to establishing gender roles. Table 11-8 summarizes some of these differences.

In this text, we take an *eclectic* view: a mixture of all these mechanisms may operate for any individual. The eclectic perspective on sex typing recognizes that there are physiological and biological differences between males and females,

Table 11-8 Three Approaches to Gender Identity and Gender-Role Development

Approach	Foundations of Gender Identity	Mechanism	Outcome
Psychodynamic Approach	Libido leads to sexual desire directed toward mother (in case of boy) or father (in case of girl).	Child fears father's anger (in case of boy) or mother's anger (in case of girl).	Male (or female) gender role is adopted.
Social Learning Approach	Observations of physical and social environment, rewards and punishments for various behaviors, and learning opportunities.	Child imitates role models and observes societal reinforcement of gender-appropriate behaviors.	Gender-related behaviors are acquired.
Cognitive Approach	Intellectual skills lead to awareness of distinction between self and others.	Child acquires self-concept and begins to recognize difference between male schemas and female schemas.	Gender-related schemas are established.

Table 11-9 Gender Typing from an Eclectic Perspective

Developmental Period	Events and Outcomes
Prenatal period (Physical gender)	The fetus develops the bodily characteristics of female or male that others will react to once the child is born.
Birth to 3 years (Basic gender identity)	Parents and other companions label the child as a boy or a girl, frequently remind the child of his or her gender, and begin to encourage gender-consistent behavior while discouraging cross-gender activities. As a result of these social experiences and the development of very basic classification skills, the young child acquires some sex-typed behavioral preferences and the knowledge that he or she is a boy or a girl.
Age 3 to 6 years (Gender schema development)	Children begin to seek information about sex differences, form gender schemas, and become intrinsically motivated to perform those acts that are viewed as "gender-appropriate." When acquiring gender schema, children attend to both male and female models. Once their "own sex" schemas are well established (but before the concept of gender consistency is acquired), these youngsters are likely to imitate behaviors considered appropriate for their own sex, regardless of the gender of the model who displays them.
Age 6 to 7 and beyond (Gender consistency)	Children acquire consistent, future-oriented image of themselves as boys who will become men or girls who will become women. They begin to rely less exclusively on gender schemas and more on the behavior of same-sex models to acquire mannerisms and attributes that are congruent with their now firm classification of self as a male or female.

Source: Adapted from Shafer, 1996.

but that the social meanings of these differences can vary, depending on social and cultural context. Although some gender-related behavior reflects biology, the crucial issue is how biological differences translate into behavior, depending on experience and learning.

Suppose we ask parents to "describe your baby as you would a close friend" or to fill out a questionnaire, rating the baby as firm/soft, big/little, and relaxed/nervous. These evaluations can then be compared to hospital records of the baby's weight, height, muscle tone, reflexes, heart rate, and so forth. At an early enough age, hospital data will show no difference between male and female babies. Yet, parents report marked differences. Girls' parents think the infant girls are significantly softer, finer featured, and smaller than are infant boys. And boys' parents think that the infant boys are firmer, bigger, and stronger than are infant girls. Fathers are more likely to emphasize differences between boy and girl babies in looks and behavior. Thus, gender stereotyping probably begins when parents first learn their child's sex (Siegel, 1987; Fagot & Hagan, 1991). These findings demonstrate an important theme in gender research: differences in how males and females are perceived and treated exceed differences in how they actually behave in the same situation. Gender differences in behavior can, in effect, be created by observer bias.

By the time children are two years old, they are aware of whether they are boys or girls, and they are aware of gender-role stereotypes. Their awareness of their gender is not completely stable, however. Remember how children had difficulty in recognizing Maynard the Cat's identity when his appearance was transformed? Similarly, young children believe gender can be changed by altering physical appearance—wearing clothes of the opposite sex, for example. But by about age six or seven, they know sex doesn't change with a change in external appearance—their gender concept is now constant across situations (see Table 11-9).

Once children are aware of their gender, they actively seek out information on gender differences. They organize this information into gender schemas—structured beliefs and expectations about males and females, and become motivated to learn more about behaviors they think are appropriate for their own gender.

Gender schemas influence what a child pays attention to and remembers. From these schemas, children choose toys and other play activities that they believe are appropriate for their gender. Yet, boys prefer "boy" activities earlier than girls prefer "girl" activities, and boys show

▲ *Children learn gender roles at a very young age.*

Doonesbury BY GARRY TRUDEAU

stronger preference for "boy" activities at every age. For a girl, the presence of an observer doesn't seem to affect play activities. Boys, however, experiment with "feminine" toys (for example, dolls, lipstick, hair ribbons) when they think no one is looking. This suggests boys have learned to expect negative reactions if they show an interest in "girl stuff."

From about age three, children (particularly boys) become "self-socializers," working industriously to acquire attributes they think are consistent with their gender identity. What they consider an appropriate attribute depends on their level of cognitive development, which can lead to amusing situations. Sandra and Daryl Bem, who tried to raise their children in a nonsexist fashion, have described such an event. When Jeremy, their nursery-school-aged son, wanted to wear a barrette, his peers ostracized him and called him " a girl." Jeremy responded that he was certainly not a girl. To prove his point, he pulled down his pants to show that he, indeed, had a penis. The response from his egocentric peer? "Everybody has a penis; only girls wear barrettes" (Bem, 1993, p. 149).

THINKING CRITICALLY

What experiences would you expect to contribute to a child's more mature, less stereotyped attitudes about gender and gender roles?

The child's age is critical. One study found teaching about women's capabilities and about harm from stereotyping and sexism was quite effective for kindergarten children, particularly little girls, who were quite outraged at what they learned. It also worked fairly well for ninth-grade girls (though they tended to believe women should be mothers and men breadwinners). It boomeranged with ninth-grade boys, however, who resisted the ideas and expressed more stereotypes *after* the training than before (Guttentag & Bray, 1976).

Other research suggests that older children respond better to a more indirect approach (Bigler & Liben, 1990). In problem-solving discussions, children aged six to eleven years old were given messages that (1) a person's interests and willingness to learn were the most important factors for whether they could do well in an occupation, and (2) their gender is not relevant to this assessment. Compared to a control group, these children clearly showed less occupational stereotyping, with children between nine and eleven years old showing the least stereotyping. For older children, the ability to engage in active problem solving and discussion appears crucial for mature reasoning with regard to gender issues.

Puberty and Adolescence

What does adolescence mean to you? Here's one response we got when we asked people that question: "I hated adolescence. All of a sudden your body changes in major ways—pimples! And you're growing, getting tall, gangly, and clumsy. Your parents don't understand you, and you can shout and sulk, but they still have ultimate control over your life. You have to negotiate with your parents, who say you should act grown up, yet treat you like a kid. You're supposed to be "responsible," but you have no authority, no independence. You're supposed to prepare for your future career—but what if you don't have the foggiest idea of what you want to do with your life? And you're supposed to learn about life, but not get into trouble. Throw into this mix members of the opposite sex. What if they reject you? Can you stand the humiliation? The teenage years were the worst of my life." While not everyone has such negative memories of adolescence, these comments illustrate some of the issues that physical and social changes in adolescence force teenagers to confront.

Adolescence, the years from twelve to nineteen, is a time of transition from childhood to adulthood. Bodies continue to mature, and knowledge, skill, and intellectual capacity increase, but the adolescent has not yet assumed adult social roles. Again, both maturation and learning processes contribute to changes that occur in adolescence, beginning with marked changes in physical development.

Physical Development

Human beings continue to change biologically well past childhood. Around twelve years of age for most girls and fourteen for most boys, the body starts undergoing rapid changes called ***puberty*** (most boys mature physically slightly later than girls, lagging by about one-and-a-half to two years). During this stage, organs mature that are directly involved in reproduction. Boys' and girls' bodies also undergo changes that are not directly related to reproduction, including breast development (for females) or deepening voice, increased facial hair, and body hair (for males). For most girls in our culture, on average, first menstruation occurs when they are thirteen-and-a-half years. A child reaches puberty—our culture's "entry card" to adolescence—when sexual organs are fully developed and the individual is sexually mature (and able to reproduce). This takes about two years from the onset of puberty.

Puberty is a period of rapid biological change that occurs around age twelve to fourteen years, and that is accompanied by the emergence of certain psychological issues concerning sex and social interactions.

Cognitive Development

Just as physical changes in adolescence are highly visible, the intellectual changes occurring during this period are equally remarkable. Early adolescents are still egocentric in many ways and have difficulty in distinguishing their concerns from those of others. They have developed to the point where they can think about others' thoughts, but they don't fully appreciate that others have something else to think about besides the adolescents themselves. As they

◄ *"The transition of adolescence"*

FOR BETTER OR FOR WORSE *reprinted by permission of United Feature Syndicate, Inc.*

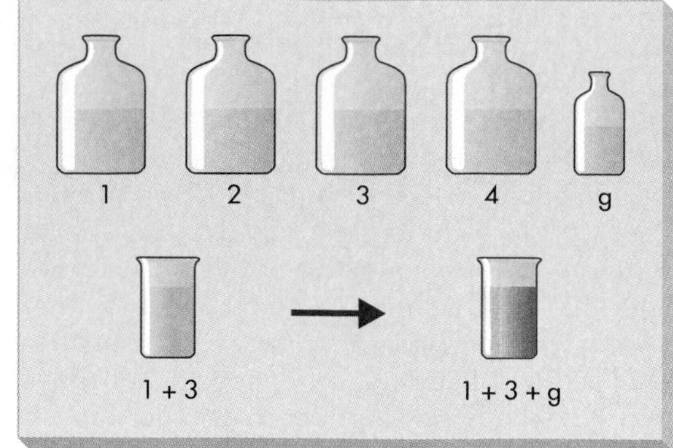

11-9 The Chemical Problem

The chemical problem illustrates the different stages of cognitive development described by Piaget. Children of different ages are given four containers of colorless, odorless chemicals and a fifth beaker *g*. Next, the children are shown a glass with a combination of two chemicals (unknown to the children, these are chemicals 1 and 3). When several drops of *g* are added to the glass, the liquid in the glass turns yellow. The children's task is to reproduce this color. (Source: Adapted from Inhelder & Piaget, 1958)

grow older, however, their egocentrism begins to decrease and their thought processes become more sophisticated.

Most adolescents achieve an ability to think logically, handle abstractions, and reflect on their thought processes. Cognitively mature adolescents can think skillfully about make-believe situations: they can imagine what an ideal world might be like, and they can reason deductively.

According to Piaget, most adolescents are in the ***formal operational stage*** of cognitive development. They can think scientifically, advancing hypotheses and using deductive reasoning to solve problems effectively. Their increased cognitive capacities are reflected in how they approach problems, handle social relationships, and make moral judgments. They have the ability to use complex, abstract, and mature logic, which leads to systematic analysis, exploration, and problem solving.

Suppose you are shown four similar glass containers, each containing different colorless, odorless chemicals (see Figure 11-9). A smaller container *g* holding a fifth chemical (potassium iodide) is added to the set. The experimenter then brings out yet another beaker with a colorless liquid, telling you that this new beaker contains a combination of two of the first four liquids. The experimenter adds a few drops of potassium iodide from beaker *g*, and the combined solution turns yellow. You are then asked to figure out, through trial and error, which two of the first four chemicals combine to produce

Table 11-10 Contrasting Approaches to Solving the Chemical Problem

Stage	Behavior	Explanation
Sensorimotor (birth–2 years)	Child ignores the request and plays with the toys.	Lacks the vocabulary and motor skills to understand what is required to perform the task. Before 8 months lacks object permanence. If one container drops from view, the child does not look for it.
Preoperational (2–7 years)	Child combines two containers at random.	Understands goal but does not order the tests (takes one jar and *g*, then the next, then the third). The child cannot keep track of what has been done and does not classify the results into combinations that produce a yellow color and those that do not. The child is likely to think an irrelevant feature like the shape of the containers or the amount of the contents determines the color.
Concrete operational (7–11 years)	Child systematically adds the fluid from each container, then starts to combine *g* with pairs of containers and becomes confused.	Can order tests, one container at a time, but has difficulty ordering two variables simultaneously. Can classify container combinations into those that make the yellow color and those that do not. Possesses logical operations of reversibility and identity. Understands conservation. Knows the problem pertains to the identity of the chemicals, not the shape of their containers.
Formal operational (11 years and older)	Child combines the containers with *g*, one at a time. Is able to keep track of the system and identify both chemicals that make the dye and some of the others.	Possesses knowledge of permutations and combinations. Can go beyond data to describe in abstract terms the nature of his or her system of testing. Can figure out what would happen if new chemicals were introduced; can deal with hypothetical situations, laws of probability; and so on (possesses the essentials of symbolic logic).

a solution that turns yellow when potassium iodide is added. How would you solve this problem?

Preoperational children combine the chemicals more or less randomly, making no attempt to keep track of what they have done. Children in the concrete operational stage, by contrast, typically begin by systematically testing each combination, but lose track of what they are doing, often forgetting some combinations and retesting others. Adolescents who have achieved the stage of formal operations are capable of behaving logically, anticipating all possible combinations of two chemicals (1+2, 1+3, 1+4, 2+3, 2+4, 3+4) and systematically testing each combination until the correct one is found. Table 11-10 summarizes these age-related differences in problem-solving ability.

There is great individual and cultural variation in whether adolescents actually use formal operations, however. In fact, it has been estimated that about half of all adults in the United States never reach the formal operational stage (Muuss, 1988). Formal education appears to play a key role in stimulating this development (Mwamwenda, 1992). Yet, even in Western culture, studies suggest that formal operational thought is only found in 40 to 60 percent of first-year college students (Keating, 1991; Leadbeater, 1991).

Social Development

Have you noticed how many adolescents have an excessive concern about their appearance, agonizing over every pimple and spending hours in front of a mirror grooming themselves? As we have mentioned earlier, early adolescents are still egocentric in many ways. Many adolescents often feel that they are the focus of other people's attention, and they act as if they are on stage, viewed by an imaginary audience that is scrutinizing their appearance and behavior (Elkind & Bowen, 1979). This may explain why adolescents become so self-conscious and develop an intense desire for privacy. Although both boys and girls are self-conscious, girls are more self-conscious than boys, perhaps because they perceive their appearance as important to being accepted by their peers.

Adolescents often believe their problems are unique—for example, they will turn to their parents and say "But you just don't know how it feels to be in love." This egocentric feeling of personal uniqueness may also lead adolescents to believe that "the rules" don't apply to them: they won't get hooked if they try drugs; they won't be harmed if they don't use seat belts; they won't suffer negative consequences from having sex without protection; they won't hurt anyone if they drive while drinking.

▲ *Hanging out with friends is an important part of adolescence.*

Adolescents are faced with many new social concerns, both institutional (occupation, political affiliation, economic status), and social-relational (sexual intimacy, marriage, family responsibility). The influence of peers increases, and issues of morality and identity emerge as the adolescent begins to take on adult role perspectives.

Friendships

Adolescent friendships have special qualities that distinguish them from earlier peer relationships. For young adolescents, friends share and understand private thoughts and feelings. Friendship no longer consists of simply exchanging material goods, favors, or help. Friends are expected to help one another with psychological problems, such as loneliness, sadness, loss, and fear. In early adolescence, friendships become increasingly intimate, taking on what Harry Stack Sullivan called the attribute of "chumship." According to Sullivan, chumship provides adolescents shelter from parental and school pressure, and helps build psychological health and maturity (Sullivan, 1953). The

SEEKING SOLUTIONS

Understanding and Preventing Teenage Parenthood

Even in the age of modern contraception, teenage parenthood continues to be a source of major economic and social problems in the United States. An estimated 56 to 60 percent of public assistance (welfare) goes to the families of teenage mothers. In 1985, public outlays attributable to families of teenage mothers totaled between $15.7 to $18.84 billion (Burt & Levy, 1987).

Because teenage pregnancy is correlated with inadequate prenatal care and nutrition, poverty, and lack of education, teenage mothers and their babies are at risk for a multitude of health, psychological, social, and economic problems. High-quality medical care can greatly reduce health risks to mother and child, but such care is not accessible to all teenagers, particularly black teenagers who live in poverty.

Teenage childbearing, whether or not it ends in keeping the child or placing him or her for adoption, is associated with a subsequent deterioration of self-esteem and quality of life for the teenage mother. It is often associated with early marriage, which, in turn, is associated with higher risk for divorce and larger family sizes. It is important to avoid stereotypes about teenage mothers: many do overcome the disadvantages associated with early childbearing. But a large proportion do not. And even if a mother works to overcome such disadvantages, her children are still at risk for a variety of problems. One study found that second-generation teenage mothers (those whose own mothers had been teenage mothers) appear less likely to escape poverty than first-generation teenage mothers (Furstenberg, Levine, & Brooks-Gunn, 1990). In that study, nearly half of the first-born female offspring of adolescent mothers became pregnant before age nineteen, and about one-third of the first-born male offspring reported impregnating someone before that age.

Babies born to teenage mothers are more likely to be of low birth weight and to experience birth injury, mental retardation, or neonatal death. Teenage mothers do not appear to be more likely to physically abuse their children than mothers in their twenties. However, they are more likely to exhibit various types of child neglect, such as failing to provide adequate nutrition or health care (Miller, 1984).

Children of teenage mothers are at higher risk for repeating a grade, having social and emotional problems, smoking, drinking, and using drugs. On average, such children have lower intelligence and academic achievement, as well as poorer adjustment to school—including suspension, running away, being stopped by police, and inflicting a serious injury on someone else.

Research suggests that preventing unintended pregnancy will require going beyond simply providing access to family planning. Issues of gender roles and status must also be addressed. Studies of the differences between women who have experienced unwanted pregnancy and those who have avoided it have consistently found that a sense of self-competence and control is positively correlated with the effectiveness of contraceptive protection (Adler, 1981). Lack of self-esteem and passivity with regard to one's partner, particularly in adolescents, have been related to engaging in intercourse and failing to use contraception (Goldsmith, Gabrielson, Gabrielson, Mathews, & Potts, 1972). Mutual communication is also critical for effective family planning at any age. Sex-role expectations that emphasize male prerogatives and a coercive male sexuality may interfere with the mutual communication and respect needed for the development of nonexploitive sexual relationships. Thus, enhancing the status of women and fostering mutual respect and communication between the sexes are viewed as critical components for programs designed to prevent unwanted pregnancy, particularly in adolescence (Russo, 1992).

closeness and intimacy of adolescent peer relations also lead to their "cliquishness" and sense of exclusivity. In some communities, this closeness and exclusivity become expressed in the formation of gangs.

One of the most difficult challenges of adolescent social life is integrating sexual urges that emerge during puberty within peer relationships. The adolescent must learn how to transform simple friendships into responsible sexual relationships. Numerous teenage pregnancies each year testify to the difficulties adolescents face in having responsible sexual relationships. The period of dating presents the adolescent with an opportunity to explore ways to develop responsible, mutually intimate relationships. In the beginning, most adolescents' sexual relations are often casual and nonexpressive, based on experimenting rather than attempting to develop a committed love relationship. Later, many adolescents will become more interested in building stable, emotionally expressive love relationships with sexual partners.

Adolescent and Adult Morality

The development of mature moral judgment is an essential component of integration into society. As we mentioned earlier in the chapter, Lawrence Kohlberg extended Piaget's work in moral judgment beyond childhood (Kohlberg, 1963). Around thirteen years of age, most of the moral judgments made in response to Kohlberg's dilemmas are at Level II (conventional level) of moral judgment, which encompasses Stages 3 and 4 in Kohlberg's theory. In Stage 3 (good boy/good girl orientation), the desire for approval (being told you're a "good boy" or "good girl") motivates moral behavior. In evaluating the behavior of a husband stealing a drug (see p. 406), for example, intention is taken into account. "You can't blame him for stealing, he was trying to save his wife" represents a Stage 3 orientation. Stage 4 (social-order-maintaining orientation) extends the concept of morality to the laws and rules made by legitimate authority of the larger society. Rules are again important, but now because they are needed to maintain the social order. What is legal is moral. Good citizenship, working hard, and maintaining the law are considered valued, moral behavior—"people can't go around breaking laws, even if they have good personal reasons for doing so" would be Stage 4 reasoning. Conventional reasoners conform their moral judgments to those defined by the group. Normally adolescents do not advance beyond this level.

In Level III (postconventional morality), what is judged as moral is based on personal standards, and may or may not be what is legal. In Stage 5 (social contract and individual rights orientation), reasoners can conceive of "just" and "unjust" laws. If the law represents the majority's will, furthers human rights and dignity, and is impartially applied, the law is seen as just. If it is not the result of a democratic process and is externally imposed, takes away rights, or undermines human values, it is seen as unjust and can be challenged. In evaluating the drug-stealing husband, those in Stage 5 would reason, "The law represents our agreement of how to live together, and he has an obligation to respect it. He is not totally wrong, but his circumstances don't make him right, either." This, then, is a "social contract" conception of morality. At the highest level in Kohlberg's system, Stage 6 (individual principles of conscience orientation), moral behavior is defined as right or wrong on the basis of personal ethical principles. Does this mean that someone like convicted Oklahoma City bomber Timothy McVeigh would be considered at the Stage 6 level of morality? No. At the Stage 6 level, the individual takes the perspectives of all parties in a moral conflict into account. Although he or she may arrive at solutions that may, in certain instances, be outside the law, such solutions respect the universal rights of others. A just solution at Stage 6 "is a solution acceptable to all parties—assuming none of them knew which role they would occupy in the situation" (Kohlberg, 1981, p. 213). Although there is a fundamental respect for the human social order, laws may occasionally be ignored if a great injustice would result from blindly obeying them. Principles such as respect for the equality and the dignity of individuals are supreme. Laws are seen as imperfect means to such ends rather than as moral ends in themselves.

▼ Very few individuals achieve Stage 6 in Kohlberg's theory of moral development. Aung San Suu Kyi, the Burmese leader, is certainly a candidate for such a distinction. She received the Nobel Peace Prize in 1991 for her work to bring democracy to her country.

Stage 6 represents Kohlberg's early vision of ideal reasoning and is included here for completeness. It was so rare, however, that he came to view it as more of a developmental goal than as a reality. In fact, the later versions of the scoring manual for his moral dilemmas do not include Stage 6 reasoning (Colby & Kohlberg, 1987).

Kohlberg's theory has been criticized on a number of grounds. One is inability to predict

▲ *Centenarian sisters Bessie and Sadie Delany published two best-selling books after their hundredth birthdays.*

These definitions are somewhat arbitrary. The older we are, the less age really defines us—our social roles and life events become much more important than our actual age in later life. Be aware, too, that myths and stereotypes of older people as passive, dull, and disengaged from life do not fit the majority of older adults.

Adult roles vary greatly (for example, mother, father, community leader, doctor, lawyer), as do how a particular role is played and how people combine roles (spouse, parent, worker). Moreover, using "development" to describe adulthood has been questioned, as it implies change that is predictable and sequential, which does not describe what happens as we age (Neugarten, 1976).

Biological and Cognitive Changes

Early adulthood is a time of optimal physical performance. Most athletes peak physically between ages nineteen and twenty-six, depending on the sport, and with legendary individual exceptions (Schultz & Curnow, 1988). Sensory abilities deteriorate somewhat as we age. Thus, older people increasingly need brighter light to

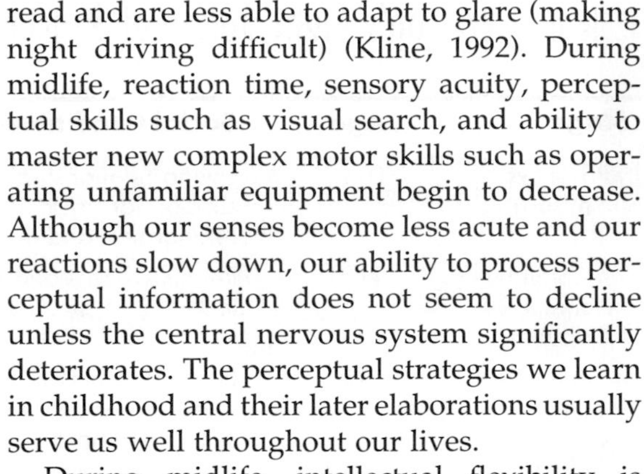

read and are less able to adapt to glare (making night driving difficult) (Kline, 1992). During midlife, reaction time, sensory acuity, perceptual skills such as visual search, and ability to master new complex motor skills such as operating unfamiliar equipment begin to decrease. Although our senses become less acute and our reactions slow down, our ability to process perceptual information does not seem to decline unless the central nervous system significantly deteriorates. The perceptual strategies we learn in childhood and their later elaborations usually serve us well throughout our lives.

During midlife, intellectual flexibility is maintained, and verbal skills, reasoning capacity, and basic factual knowledge continue to increase (assuming the individual stays healthy). Longitudinal research suggests IQ continues to grow through the middle years (Eichorn, Hunt, & Honzik, 1981). No detectable performance decrement in higher cognitive processes typically occurs before age sixty, and it certainly does not occur in the mid-thirties and forties, as was once supposed. Indeed, some elderly individuals show no measurable decline in intellectual functioning (Schaie, 1990).

Measurable declines in some cognitive abilities usually begin in the mid-seventies (Schaie, 1989). Although we maintain short-term memory, long-term memory declines, reflecting slower response times to answer test questions and less knowledge of test-taking strategies. When people have time to learn and recall information, however, their performance improves (Datan, Rodeheaver, & Hughes, 1987). Although the aging brain has physiological limits (Kliegl, Smith, & Bates, 1989), long-term memory storage and retrieval strategies can compensate for those limits, so they have minimal practical significance for everyday life.

Minor declines in certain skills, such as memory, can be more than compensated for by greater intellectual maturity or by developing new strategies. Indeed, the most vital aspects of intellectual life probably improve in the middle and later years. Some developmentalists have proposed a fifth cognitive development stage that goes beyond formal operations and is characterized by insight and creative problem solving. These psychologists have speculated that, during this final stage of intellectual development, a wisdom unmatched at any other time of life emerges in some elderly adults.

Why do people differ in keeping their cognitive capacities in late adulthood? Biological

▼ *People are living longer and remaining active and alert. Seventy-one-year-old Liz Bevington, aka "Skateboard Mama," enjoys a glide along the bike path in Santa Monica, California. It is estimated that by the year 2000, 100,000 people will be over 100 years old, which may force developmental psychologists to redefine the stages of late adulthood.*

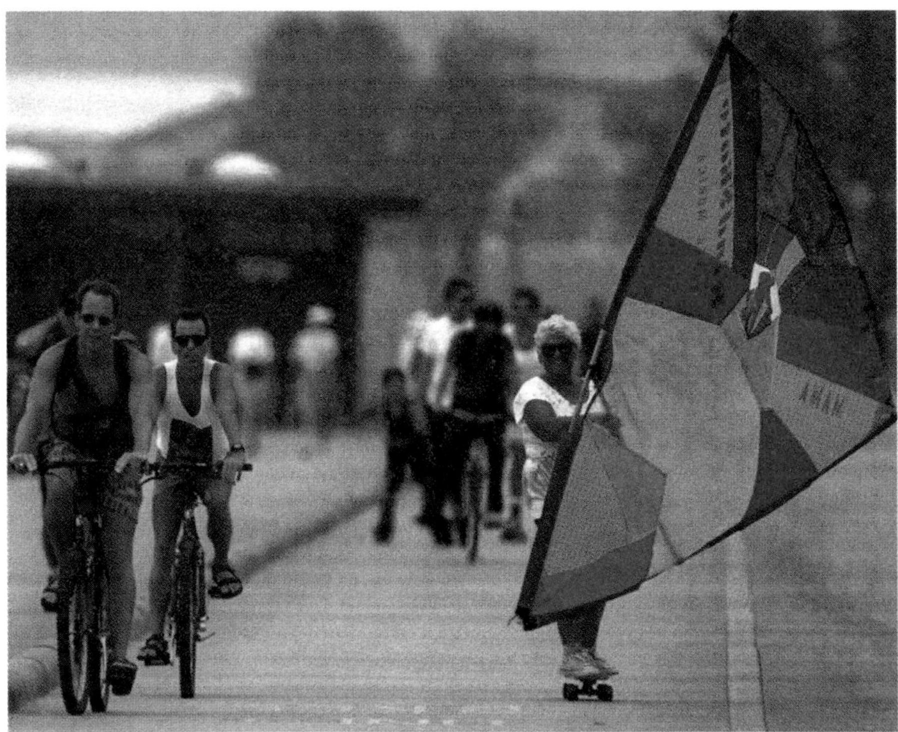

considerations, such as neural damage from physical injuries and disease, and overmedication for current ailments account for some variation, but not all. Social conditions are also important. Loneliness, lack of stimulation, and expectations that intellectual performance will decline with age all contribute to diminished cognitive capacity. Interestingly, a challenging environment can reverse declines. In one study, five one-hour training sessions on inductive reasoning or spatial problem solving erased deficits in these areas for some individuals (Schaie & Willis, 1986).

Although normal aging does not necessarily mean significant loss in cognitive functioning, it brings increased risk for strokes and diseases involving loss of brain tissue and consequent mental impairment. About 5 percent of those over age sixty-five develop Alzheimer's disease, which is characterized by progressive loss of memory and other cognitive functions (Jones, 1990). At first, memory for recent events declines (for example, memory for appointments and people's names). Then longer-term memory deteriorates. People with Alzheimer's disease at this stage must be watched, for they are likely to become confused and lost. Ultimately, they become bedridden and helpless, and die (Khachaturian & Blass, 1992).

Social Roles and Activities

As Bernice Neugarten has observed, adult roles in the United States follow a "social clock"—norms and expectations determine the timing and sequencing of life cycle events. The social clock varies with social position, running faster for people of lower socioeconomic status, who marry earlier and begin and finish having children sooner, and become grandparents sooner than people in the middle and upper socioeconomic classes (Neugarten, 1968, 1976). In the last few decades, however, we have become more tolerant of individuals who live by a different social clock than those in the mainstream. Teenage mothers, unmarried men in their thirties, people who pursue jobs in their twenties and have children in their thirties rather than vice versa, and those who obtain college degrees in their sixties are no longer as surprising as they were only a few decades ago (Neugarten & Neugarten, 1986).

Marriage and Parenthood

Our challenges, interests, and sources of satisfaction change over our lives. In early adulthood, we form families and develop careers. Many of us have traditionally viewed marriage as the "natural" order of things and the most desirable adult social status (Duberman, 1974). But stereotypes about single people are changing—they are no longer seen as frustrated, lonely, immoral, prudish, introverted, or selfish (Stein, 1989). Still, more than nine out of ten men and women will marry at some point (U.S. Bureau of the Census, 1990). Nonetheless, it is estimated that 60 percent of newly married couples will divorce (Bumpass, 1990).

Transition to parenthood is a major event for fathers and mothers, whether the child is born into a family or adopted. Parents become responsible for the well-being of another and must forgo many personal pleasures to be available and responsible when they are needed by their children. Despite the difficulties, the vast majority of parents (90 percent) report that, if they could relive their lives, they would have children again (Yankelovich, 1981). Nonetheless, pregnancy and delivery are stressful life events for both women and men. These events may lead to mood and behavior changes. They can aggravate problems for women with histories of mental disorders, and they have also been associated with higher rates of mental disorder in women's partners (McGrath, Strickland, Keita, & Russo, 1990).

Transition to parenthood can be particularly stressful when the reality of parenthood differs substantially from expectations (Belsky, 1985). A high level of intimacy, commitment, and closeness between the parents can help reduce this stress (Lewis, Owen, & Cox, 1988). About 50 to 80 percent of women experience mild depression after childbirth (called postpartum "baby blues") from about three days after birth, lasting up to two weeks. This is not the same as the less common but more severe postpartum depression, which can occur six to eight weeks after birth and can last from six months to a year. One study reported that about 16 percent of women giving birth to their first child were severely depressed eight weeks after delivery (Whiffen, 1988).

Timing, spacing, and number of children have profound effects on family well-being over the life cycle, affecting the developmental course of both children and parents. When

▲ *Stereotypes of single people are changing. Despite her many flaws, the television character Murphy Brown, a single mother with a high powered career, is considered a positive role model.*

▼ *Combining a career and parenthood can be particularly stressful.*

▲ *The loss of a job is a highly stressful event, especially later in one's professional career when it can trigger a midlife crisis.*

women begin childbearing before completing their education and before establishing other responsibilities of adulthood (marital and work roles), they and their children experience rippling effects over their entire lifetime. Close spacing (under two years) has both physical and social disadvantages. It's estimated that maintaining at least a two-year interval between children's births could lower the neonatal death rate from 5 to 10 percent (Miller, 1991). Two of the strongest predictors of future child abuse are having children with less than a twelve-month spacing between them and having two or more children under five years of age. Mothers of abused and neglected children are most likely to have had unplanned pregnancies, first births at a younger age, and a larger number of births. Larger family sizes are also associated with lower self-esteem and psychological distress for women, particularly poor women (Altemeier, O'Connor, Vietze, Sandler, & Sherrod, 1984; Zuravin, 1987, 1988; Russo, 1992).

Work

In 1992, 70 percent of men and 58 percent of women were in the civilian workforce. Women's labor force participation has dramatically increased in recent years, more than doubling since the 1960s. Today's women are more likely to have fewer children, to delay childbirth, and to return to work sooner after childbirth than women a generation ago. Women are making inroads into professions and trades formerly closed to them. Consequently, family structure and the social relationships of family members have undergone profound change. Men and women who are successful at their jobs are happier, have higher self-esteem, feel more in control of their lives, and say they have better marriages. On the other hand, failures at work can result in depression and numerous other psychological symptoms (Gruenberg, 1980).

Job satisfaction increases with age from early adulthood through midlife, for people in both blue- and white-collar jobs and professional careers. Reasons for this increase include learning the job, feeling more comfortable, increased job performance, promotions, and gaining seniority (Rhodes, 1983). In their careers, individuals must deal with issues of aging, including stereotypes of older workers. Although older workers are as productive—often more productive—than younger workers (Waldon & Avolio, 1986), they are more likely to be viewed as less efficient, less motivated, less productive, and less capable of working under pressure (Rosen & Jerdee, 1976).

Midlife Transitions

When men and women are in their forties, they may ask themselves "What have I done with my life?" and "What do I still want to do?" They may experience a midlife transition that sometimes can result in a midlife crisis. They may have to confront the fact that their life's "dreams" are not going to be fully achieved. They may be in dead-end jobs or have gone as far as they can in their careers. They may experience the downsizing of their companies—losing their jobs and having to rethink their career path. This is a particularly stressful position for people (usually men) who have defined their identities primarily in terms of their work (Levinson, 1986). Women typically have more balance among their life goals of career, marriage, and children (Roberts & Newton, 1987).

Although women who are full-time homemakers may have to adjust to an "empty nest" as children leave home, this does not typically produce a major life crisis. Some extremely child-centered women have difficulties when children leave, but most midlife women whose children have left home are happier, less depressed, and more satisfied with their marriages than those who still have a child living with them (Radloff, 1980). Many return to school or reestablish or begin careers.

Women experience menopause during middle adulthood. The average age of menopause for women in the United States is fifty. Age of menopause is negatively correlated with smoking and alcohol use—the higher the use, the lower the age of menopause (Hill, 1982). Women who are heavier and taller (independent of weight) have a later menopause (Lindquist, 1979). Although a variety of myths persist about emotional and cognitive impairments of menopause, whether or not a menopausal woman exhibits physical and psychological symptoms largely depends on the amount of stress in her life and the personal and cultural meaning of menopause (Golub, 1992). For some women, menopause is a landmark developmental event, causing them to evaluate their lives and take actions to improve them. As one menopausal woman reported, "I realized that, boy, I've reached another milestone. If I was going to do anything I'd better do it" (Martin, 1987).

Midlife adults have been described as the "squeeze generation" because they often have to care for both children and aging parents. Although both men and women shoulder these financial burdens, caregiving and support functions (transportation, household maintenance, cooking, shopping, and personal and medical care) most often fall to middle-aged women (Aizenberg & Treas, 1985). As men and women move through the middle and later years, they tend to display behaviors and characteristics that were associated with the opposite sex when they were younger. Men often may become more gentle and nurturant, while women frequently may become more assertive and independent (Etaugh, 1993).

Retirement is an important part of the midlife transition to late adulthood, for both women and men. Preparation for retirement is important, as it can mean loss of social contact, a diminished sense of accomplishment, and lowered income. Life satisfaction in retirement for both genders depends on adequate income, good health, and a high activity level (Atchley, 1982).

Late Adulthood

More people are reaching late adulthood now than at any time in the world's history. By the twenty-first century, one out of every seven citizens of the United States will be over sixty-five years of age. By 2025, the figure will be one out of five. By the end of 2025, in Japan the number of people over sixty-five will have doubled; in Latin America and the People's Republic of China, the figure will have tripled. In Korea and Malaysia, there will be four times as many people over sixty-five as currently. This "greying" of the human population has profound psychological, social, and economic implications (particularly with regard to health-care costs), and makes understanding and enhancing life during late adulthood increasingly important (Powell & Whitla, 1994).

Research in the United States suggests that after a successful midlife transition from parental and work roles, men and women become increasingly aware that their life span is limited and that they must face the reality of their aging. They begin to sort out their priorities and focus their time on the things that they care most about. Family relationships become more satisfying, and greater value is placed on friendships (Gould, 1978). They also begin to think about death and dying. Most marriages end through death of a spouse, not through divorce, and women are more likely to outlive their spouses. Approximately 24 percent of men and 66 percent of women over age seventy-five are widowed (U.S. Bureau of the Census, 1990). Thus, a large proportion of the elderly will face their last years without a mate.

Death and Dying

In traditional American culture, death in late adulthood is considered too personal or too frightening for open discussion. Only recently have psychologists tried to study people's thoughts about impending death, their own or the death of a loved one. The results of these studies, while tentative, can help to give us a better understanding of this final development stage (Kastenbaum, 1992).

Elizabeth Kübler-Ross proposed that, as a person faces death, a natural process takes that person through a series of stages of coping with imminent death. The first stage is *denial* that death is impending—"The doctor made a mistake, the tests are not foolproof." The second stage is *anger*—"I hate myself, my body, and all of you who allowed this to happen." The third stage is *bargaining*—"I could accept death gracefully, if only I could live to see my first grandchild." The fourth stage is *depression*—"I feel so bad; life isn't worth living." And the final stage is *acceptance* of the facts and one's fate (Kübler-Ross, 1969, 1975).

Kübler-Ross' work identifies important issues addressed by terminally ill people. However, it would be a mistake to take her stages literally (Kastenbaum, 1977). Careful research shows that people rarely experience all five stages. These experiences often occur haphazardly and repeatedly in the later months of life. One person might report anger before denial, while another might become depressed and then angry. Not all people experience the same emotional pattern when facing so great a crisis as their own death. Health-care providers are cautioned to accept each person's emotional state as unique and certainly not to expect that each dying person will move systematically from one stage to the next as specified by Kübler-Ross (Kastenbaum, 1992).

The Sense of Integrity

According to Erik Erikson, the last of life's crises is the struggle to achieve a sense of integrity, as opposed to feelings of despair (Erikson, 1968). Resolving this crisis is the goal for which the seven earlier stages have prepared us. If an individual successfully masters the challenges of intimacy and generativity (remember Table 11–11), the adult years may be spent creating the unifying meaning for one's life that Erikson called ***ego integrity***. This sense of integrity develops when you feel life has been lived with purpose and commitment, and your efforts have been directed toward good ends. If, however, you view your life as having been useless and without dedication, then disgust will result, accompanied by despair: "It's too late to change now (or too hard to change), and so I'll never make anything of myself." A healthy resolution of this crisis produces a feeling of wholeness and peace as people live out their lives.

Some psychologists seek more specific stages than Erikson for the course of development during adulthood. They outline "stages" such as marriage, the midlife "second adolescence," the "mellowing-out" period after fifty, and so on. But not everyone experiences these particular events. Another problem is that there is no apparent reason for these events to occur in a particular sequence, other than that many middle-class Americans seem to experience them at more or less the same ages. These "stages," therefore, do not meet any criteria for true psychological or developmental stages: they are not universal, they do not occur in a logically fixed sequence, and they do not build on one another through restructuring basic competencies or personal characteristics.

Reflections and Observations

Developmental psychology, with its focus on how the processes of learning and maturation interact to influence behavior over the life cycle, is rich with examples that demonstrate the importance of looking at biological, psychological, social, and cultural variables in interaction. Findings from developmental psychology have been applied in diverse contexts, from enhancing prenatal care, diagnosing neurological deficits in infancy, structuring school curricula to promote cognitive development, increasing effectiveness of marriage and job counseling, to helping people deal with death and bereavement. Understanding development also brings home the importance of social relationships over the life cycle. In the next chapter, we will explore the factors that influence how we think about and interact with other people.

Objectives Revisited

Developmental psychology focuses on behavioral changes over the life span. It is concerned with all aspects of growth: physical, cognitive, and social. Developmental psychologists often divide development into discrete stages, each of which must be passed through in turn. But these stages can be defined differently and often depend upon cultural context.

Objective 1. Explain what is meant by development and developmental processes, and describe the methods psychologists use to study them.

Development refers to systematic changes that occur between conception and death that involve transformations in an individual's biological, intellectual, emotional, and social capacities. It is *orderly, continual*, and *cumulative* and involves the processes of maturation and learning. These processes reflect the cultural context and need to be understood within that context. Developmental psychologists use all the research methods, experimental and corre-

KEY TERMS

development

maturation

cross-sectional study

longitudinal study

prenatal period

zygote

embryo

fetus

teratogens

critical period

brain growth spurt

infancy

childhood

equilibrium

assimilation

accommodation

sensorimotor stage

object permanence

lational, described in Chapter 2, but they apply them to understanding developmental change over time in two primary research designs. These are: *cross-sectional* (people are tested at different ages on the same task during roughly the same time frame) and *longitudinal* (the same people are followed over time).

Objective 2. Describe prenatal development, and explain why risks for different types of birth defects change over the course of pregnancy.

After *fertilization,* when the father's sperm meets the mother's egg, the fertilized egg is implanted in the uterine wall. The single cell develops into a complex *embryo* in which rudimentary body parts and internal organs begin to develop. During the *fetal period* (from nine to thirty-eight weeks after implantation), organs grow and differentiate until the brain and respiratory system enable it to survive outside the uterus. There are *critical periods* of development for different organ systems. The risk of particular *teratogens* (environmental agents) that cause harm and malformations will change over the course of pregnancy, depending on which organ is developing when the exposure to the teratogen occurs.

Objective 3. Describe the highlights of physical, cognitive, and social development in infancy and childhood.

During infancy, primitive reflexes develop into reflexes controlled by the brain, and sensory abilities improve. Physical development proceeds from head-to-toe and from the center outward, as infants progress from lifting their head, to rolling over, creeping, crawling, and then walking.

During infancy, children develop feelings of attachment for their primary caregivers. Optimally, children will feel secure enough in this attachment to assert their independence. Children's first knowledge of self is established during infancy.

Piagetian theory provides the most comprehensive analysis of cognitive development, which Piaget divides into four distinct stages: *sensorimotor* (birth to two years), *preoperational* (two to seven years), *concrete operational* (seven to eleven years), and *formal operational* (eleven years and beyond).

In less than four years, a child becomes able to produce complex, grammatically correct language. In fact, the early years of life provide a critical period for language acquisition.

Social development serves two functions: the *integration* of the child into society and the *differentiation* of the child from others in society. The former entails establishing relationships with others and learning to guide one's behavior according to the precepts of society. The latter requires the acquisition of self-identity and a sense or concept of self.

Peer interactions like play and sharing are important influences on a child's cognitive and social development. Through relations with peers, children acquire an understanding of friendship, justice, and other important social concepts. In addition, during peer play, children have an opportunity to try out and practice social rule following. Later, such activity will become a serious and necessary part of adult life.

Objective 4. Describe how adolescents think and the social and moral concerns of adolescents.

During adolescence, logical thinking becomes increasingly abstract, hypothetical, and formal. The adolescent organizes the complex array of information about the self into a coherent sense of identity. The adolescent wants to fit in with peers; friendships become more intimate; and morality begins to take on a broader, societal perspective.

Objective 5. Describe some of the transitions experienced in the three periods of adulthood.

In early adulthood, people generally form families and develop careers. They must deal with the transition to parenthood and the new responsibilities of caring for the needs of their children. They must enter the world of work and learn to cope with the demands of both work and family. In middle adulthood, they must deal with the deterioration of some sensory abilities and the slowing down of reactions. They may also have to cope with midlife crises because of being in jobs that have not met their expectations. Although women experience menopause and have to adjust to an "empty nest" as their children leave home, these experiences are not major crises for most women. In late adulthood, men and women must deal with retirement and must start to face the death of friends and their own impending death.

preoperational stage

concrete operational stage

reversibility

conservation

formal operational stage

egocentrism

role taking

differentiation

integration

attachment

morality

gender identity

adolescence

puberty

identity

adulthood

ego integrity

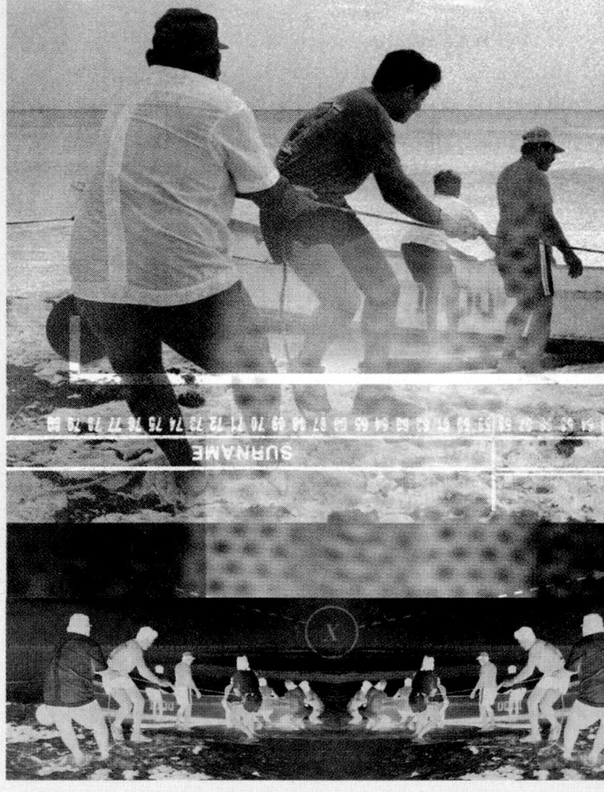

CHAPTER 12

Social Psychology

OBJECTIVES

After reading this chapter, you should be able to:

1. Define social psychology, and explain how social knowledge and causal attributions influence the way we perceive, think, feel, and behave.
2. Explain what the consistency principle is, and discuss predictions and evidence in support of cognitive dissonance and self-perception consistency theories.
3. Discuss the relationship between attitudes and behavior, and explain what makes a communication persuasive.
4. Explain the interrelationships among prejudice, stereotyping, and discrimination.
5. Discuss the factors that affect interpersonal liking and attraction.
6. Discuss various ways in which the presence of others influences individual behavior through (1) social facilitation and inhibition; (2) pressures to conform, comply, and obey; (3) processes of group interaction; and (4) deindividuation.

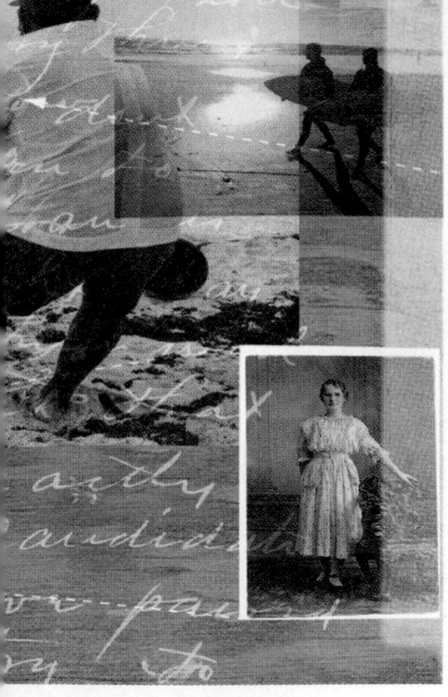

On March 27, 1997, at a mansion in the upscale community of Rancho Santa Fe, California, police were horrified to discover the bodies of thirty-nine people, lying in repose, apparently willing participants in a mass suicide. They were members of the Heaven's Gate cult who, following the teachings of their leaders, Do (Marshall Applewhite) and Ti (Bonnie Lu Nettles), expected to be taken by an alien spaceship or UFO to what they called an "Evolutionary Level Above Human." Do believed he had found their spaceship hiding behind the spectacular tail of the Hale-Bopp comet, and he instructed his followers to unite with the spaceship by taking a lethal mixture of phenobarbital and vodka designed to induce sleep, circulatory system collapse, coma, and death. To ensure the success of their gruesome enterprise, they put plastic bags over their heads to help them suffocate when unconscious.

How could intelligent, healthy individuals commit such acts, following their leader "like sheep into oblivion" (Hoffman & Burke, 1997, p. 288)? Why would they conform to such fatal commands? As members of the cult, they had dressed alike and shaved their heads, appearing so similar that the police initially thought they were all young men (though the group actually included both men and women of all ages). They had completely severed ties with their former lives, giving up their jobs and homes—one man had even sold his home for five dollars. Although they lived together in the mansion and were assigned a partner to "help each other," they were discouraged from having close relationships and abstained from sexual relations—indeed, several males had been voluntarily castrated. What was so appealing about the group? What needs did it meet? Can anyone in a group be induced to behave in such a self-destructive way?

▼ *The powerful social influence of the Heaven's Gate cult led 39 people to adopt new lifestyles away from their families and to commit mass suicide.*

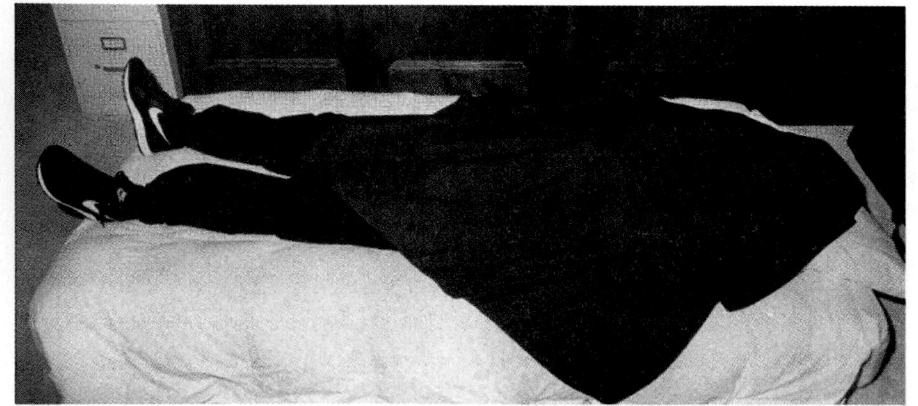

Answering such questions is the task of ***social psychology,*** which is the scientific study of how the real or imagined presence of others influences our behaviors, thoughts, and feelings. We are social animals, constantly reacting to other people, interacting with, or trying to influence others. Our behavior depends greatly on other people, especially on those around us. Do you act differently when others are present? You'd be unusual if you said "no."

Sometimes people influence our behavior directly, as when they get us to buy a particular brand of cereal, vote for a particular candidate, or join a social group. But social psychologists are interested in more than the effects of direct persuasion on behavior. They also study how the imagined or implied presence of others affects us. Have you ever decided to study harder because you wanted your parents to be proud of you? Have you ever been nervous at the thought of giving a speech because you were worried about what the audience might think of you? Have you ever decided not to wear an article of clothing because it was "out of style"? These are just a few examples of the many ways that the imagined or implied presence of others can influence us.

Social behavior occurs in a sociocultural context, which means that social psychologists study how that larger context affects the ways individuals perceive and understand their social world. Social psychologists differ from anthropologists and sociologists, who are also interested in the effects of the sociocultural context on behavior. Social psychologists focus on how individuals interpret and interact within that context rather than on the context itself. Thus, a sociologist might study how family structures (single-headed households; nuclear families of father, mother, and children; extended families) differ because of economic status—focusing on the context and its effects. In contrast, a social psychologist might study how people's expectations and behaviors within a family differ in various family structures—focusing on the expectations and behaviors of the individuals.

In this chapter, we begin with how social knowledge influences our interaction with the world. After considering the ways in which we perceive, think about, understand, and evaluate others as well as ourselves, we examine our relationships with others, focusing on prejudice, discrimination, interpersonal attraction, and group processes. You will learn the theories and methods that social psychologists use to understand and study behaviors ranging from ordinary actions, such as buying a car, to extreme behaviors, such as belonging to a cult like Heaven's Gate.

Knowing Ourselves and Others

Knowledge of our social world—our thoughts, beliefs, and judgments related to social behavior and situations—plays a key role in how we behave. We constantly seek information from our environment to learn how we are expected to act in a wide variety of social settings—from the classroom to the courtroom (Fiske & Taylor, 1991). We obtain much of our social knowledge through verbal instruction from parents, teachers, and friends, and we store it in memory. We also learn from observing the behavior of others, including such subtle, nonverbal factors as tone of voice, facial expression, and "body language."

▲ *Watching the aliens in the sitcom* Third Rock from the Sun *struggle to learn how to behave in human society helps us appreciate the complexity of the social knowledge we take for granted.*

Constructing Social Knowledge

Because the human brain is a limited information-processing system, we need to structure and organize our knowledge to reduce the quantity and complexity of information that we have to deal with (see Chapter 8). We organize our social knowledge by placing information about people into social categories and creating social schemas that mentally represent our social world and influence our behavior. We use our social knowledge to explain both our own behavior and that of others. In doing so, we seek to maintain our self-image and to reduce inconsistency between our thoughts and behaviors. These are just a few ways of using cognitive tools to understand ourselves and others and to guide our social interactions.

Social psychology is the scientific study of how the real or imagined presence of others affects our behavior, thoughts, and feelings.

Social Categorization and Schemas

Create a picture in your head of each of the following individuals: a black musician, an AIDS patient, an Apache warrior. Did you find this hard to do? Probably not. As you learned in Chapter 8, human beings have a universal tendency to place objects into categories and to then respond to all members of the category in the same way. We automatically, unconsciously, and involuntarily apply categories to understand our world, and this means that images representing those categories can come easily to mind. Just as we group objects such as

▶ This Oakland Raiders fan is expressing his support for his team. His actions fit the script for dedicated fan behavior, so you would probably laugh upon meeting him at the football game. But what if you encountered him coming into a post office?

animals and foods into categories depending on their characteristics, we group ourselves and other people into ***social categories*** that help us to simplify our social world.

Schemas are cognitive structures that organize our knowledge. ***Social schemas*** organize our social world, that is, our beliefs and feelings about our social world. They influence how we perceive, think about, and behave toward others. For example, when we meet people in pinstriped suits, carrying briefcases and wearing scarves or ties in the latest "power" colors, we may recognize them as "business executives," think they are competent and decisive, and listen to their opinions about the economy. Alternatively, if we see someone on the street pushing a grocery cart full of belongings, we may conclude the person is homeless, and our perceptions, thoughts, feelings, and behaviors will be quite different.

Scripts are a particular kind of schema. They represent what we know and expect about how we should behave in various social situations. We generally don't think about the fact that we are following scripts until someone deviates from them. For example, when we enter an elevator, we follow the "elevator behavior script" and automatically turn around and face the door. If we continue to face the back of the elevator, we are violating the script. Other scripts might include what we do when eating in a cafeteria, shopping in a department store, withdrawing funds from a bank, going to a movie, going to a wedding, attending class, or having a birthday party. Moreover, scripts vary across cultures. For example, Hispanics have a cultural script *simpática* that encourages people to be likeable, attractive, and fun, which may lead Hispanics to have more lively social interactions compared to non-Hispanics (Triandis, Marin, Lisansky, & Betancourt, 1984).

Some of the social categories that are considered important in society are gender, ethnicity, race, age, sexual orientation, economic status, and occupation. We learn about them from many sources, including family, friends, teachers, and media, all of which provide us with labels, images, and related information. Ask some friends to think about the examples mentioned above—black musician, AIDS patient, Apache warrior—and describe them to you. The similarities among the images that you and your friends generate reflect your shared cultural sources of images and information about social categories. Does anyone describe a black musician as playing classical music? A female heterosexual as having AIDS? In fact, does any example get imagined as female? Women are found in all three categories, even among Apache warriors, who are legendary for their ferocity and fighting skills. Indeed, the person Chief Gerónimo claimed as his "right hand" was a woman named Lozen (Martín, 1997, p. 94).

▶ If you were to think of an AIDS activist with HIV, you would probably not picture thirteen-year-old Hydeia Broadbent. But in addition to playing sports and hanging out with her friends like any other teenager, Hydeia gives award-winning AIDS education programs around the country.

Implications for Behavior

Our schemas create expectations about the world that can affect not only thoughts and feelings, but also behavior toward others. Suppose you have driven your brother to school everyday in the past month. Will that make you happy or angry? Your response will depend on your expectations. If you expected your parents

SEEKING SOLUTIONS

Aggression and Violence

Aggression and violence are major problems in today's society. How might social schemas related to anger and aggression influence how we perceive, think about, and behave toward others?

Aggressive behaviors are often responses to annoyance, attack, or frustration. When one person causes unpleasantness for another, the offended individual is likely to become angry and to return the aggression. But some people seem to be able to handle frustration and anger better than others, and exposure to role models appears to make a difference. For example, Albert Bandura conducted a now classic series of experiments on aggressive behavior in children (Bandura, 1973, 1977a). In one study, children watched models in a cartoon, a film, or a real-life scene in which an adult either acted aggressively toward or played calmly with a Bobo doll. Children were then mildly frustrated by the experimenter in order to arouse their aggression. During subsequent opportunities to play with the doll, children who had viewed the aggressive model were more apt to attack the doll themselves than were the children who watched the calm model. Witnessing an aggressive act, such as punching the doll, may establish an "aggressive schema," enhancing the likelihood that children will behave in a similarly aggressive manner when they have been frustrated. Live models were more effective than either film or cartoon models in eliciting imitative aggressive behavior in the children. This work suggests an important role for social schemas in shaping aggressive responses. Indeed, chronically aggressive children are more likely to perceive hostile intent on the part of others, and to expect a positive result from behaving aggressively (Dodge & Crick, 1990).

The media is an important transmitter of social knowledge in our culture. What is the effect of the media on aggression and violence? As you learned in Chapter 2, an overwhelming body of research suggests that viewing violence on TV and in the movies encourages the viewer to perform acts of violence. Both laboratory data and correlational field studies have supported the conclusion that likelihood of aggression is increased by viewing aggression. In one study, researchers showed children one of two TV programs: an extremely violent cops-and-robbers program (*The Untouchables*) or a sports event (Liebert & Baron, 1972a). Subsequently, these children were allowed to play with other children who had not seen either program. Children who had watched violence on TV were judged to be more violent in their interactions with others than were those who watched the sports event. Another study analyzed TV viewing and violence in over 500 youngsters (Eron & Huesmann, 1984). The initial data were collected when the participants were eight years old and a follow-up assessment took place ten years later. The amount of aggression in these children was shown to be highly correlated with amount of time spent viewing aggression on TV. This effect was mediated by the identification of the viewer with aggressive TV characters and by how realistic the program was judged to be. The degree of this relationship increased with each succeeding year of age, a finding that implies that the effects of TV violence are cumulative. Finally, the results show that children who are most aggressive have a greater preference for aggressive or violent programming. Thus, there might be an interactive relationship between viewing and acting out. The researchers argue that aggression makes children unpopular with their peers. Consequently, they turn to TV for entertainment. This entertainment confirms the appropriateness of their own behavior, while at the same time teaching them new ways of acting aggressively. Further acts of aggression alienate them from their peers even more.

Aggressive stimuli in one's environment, such as the presence of guns, increases the probability of aggressive responses by automatically activating a schema of thoughts and feelings related to anger and aggression (Berkowitz, 1990). In one study, research participants received a series of electric shocks from another participant who was actually a confederate of the experimenter (Berkowitz, 1974). Then, these participants were given an opportunity to retaliate against the confederate. For some participants, a rifle or revolver (aggressive stimuli) were present in the room while, for others, a badminton racquet (neutral stimulus) was present. Significantly more shocks were administered by participants when aggressive stimuli were present in the environment; hence the conclusion: "the trigger pulls the finger." But provocation is not necessary for this "weapons effect" to occur. Even people in neutral moods behave more aggressively when exposed to aggressive cues (Carlson, Marcus-Newhall, & Miller, 1990).

► *In* The Truth About Cats and Dogs, *Janeane Garafalo constantly tells herself she is not beautiful enough to attract a man. Because she expects rejection, she almost loses Ben Chaplin to Uma Thurman.*

to drive him to school every day, you will not be happy, and will behave accordingly.

Our expectations can affect the behavior of others as well. If we expect Susan to be warm and friendly, we may feel warm toward her and behave in a friendly manner. Our behavior, in turn, may lead her to be friendly toward us, confirming our expectations. However, if we expect Susan to be unpleasant, we may become cold and indifferent toward her. She may perceive this and reciprocate by being unpleasant, confirming our initial expectations. When expectations about future behavior or events increase the probability that the behavior or events will actually occur, they are called ***self-fulfilling prophecies.*** A person's change in behavior as a result of such expectations is called ***behavioral confirmation***. Behavioral confirmation can occur even when the expectations are based on false information or stereotypes (Skrypnek & Snyder, 1982).

Numerous researchers have demonstrated self-fulfilling prophecies in a variety of settings and cultural contexts. In one study, male students (the perceivers) were asked to have a ten-minute telephone conversation with a female peer (the target), who had been described as either physically attractive or unattractive (see Figure 12-1). Men who believed they were speaking to an attractive woman were more outgoing and friendly. In turn, the women who were thought to be attractive actually became more sociable and friendly, while those thought to be unattractive became cool and aloof (Snyder, Tanke, & Berscheid, 1977). In another study, some platoon leaders with the Israeli Defense Forces were misled into expecting their trainee groups to have unusually high ability (in fact, all trainee groups had average ability). Ten weeks later, trainees in the high-expectation groups scored higher on operating a weapon and on written exams than other trainees (Eden, 1990).

Our preconceptions about the behavior of others are not inevitably confirmed in social interactions. That depends on a combination of (1) the situation, and (2) the goals of the individuals involved in the interaction (Hilton & Darley, 1991). Behavioral confirmation is primarily found in situations where people are getting acquainted and don't know much about each other. In addition, the individuals involved have certain goals: (a) the person making the judgment wants to obtain social knowledge about the other, while (b) the person being judged wants to attain a social goal, such as winning social approval, being liked, passing a course, getting a job, or gaining a promotion (Snyder, 1992). Thus, the social behavior that results in a self-fulfilling prophecy is determined jointly by the situation *and* the person.

12-1 How Physical Attractiveness Stereotypes Can Become Self-Fulfilling Prophecies

In phone conversations between unacquainted men and women, (1) a stereotyped image guides the man's behavior, (2) the man elicits a response from the woman, and (3) the woman's responses confirm and reinforce the stereotyped image of a physically attractive person.

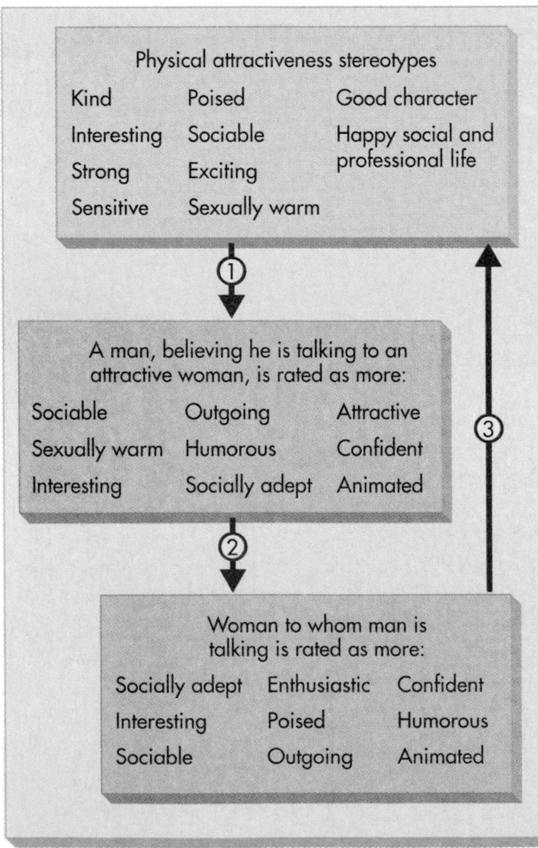

Inferences and Causal Attributions

After we construct social schemas and scripts from specific experiences in our culture, we use

THINKING CRITICALLY

The United States has a government welfare program called Aid to Families with Dependent Children (AFDC) which gives poor families with children money to help them meet their living expenses. This program became so controversial that in 1996 welfare reform legislation was enacted that permitted heads of families, most of whom are single mothers, to receive welfare for only two consecutive years and for a maximum of five years over their lifetime. Furthermore, this legislation required that people on welfare actively seek jobs or take public service jobs administered by the government in their community in order to receive welfare checks. What do you think about this legislation? Do you believe it will be effective?

Your answers to these questions will depend on your view of welfare recipients—the causal attributions you make to explain their behavior of going on welfare. If you make an internal attribution and believe welfare recipients are just lazy and don't want to work, you may feel anger toward them and agree with the program. If you make an external attribution and believe that few jobs are available and that the ones that are available do not pay very well and do not provide enough money to pay for child care, you may feel pity toward the recipients and believe that the program is ill-advised. How you feel depends on the attributions you make for what causes people to go on welfare.

them to interpret what happens to us. We understand new situations or behavior by comparing them with schemas we already have in memory, and we make judgments or conclusions based on that previous knowledge. Such judgments are called ***inferences***.

Sometimes inferences are used to explain the causes of behavior, that is, to make ***attributions***. When events or behaviors are unexpected, painful, or distressing, or have uncertain outcomes, we want to find out why they occurred and what they mean. For example, cancer patients are more likely to seek explanations for what caused their severe pain and illness than are their family members, who do not experience the same amount of pain and suffering from the disease (Taylor, Lichtman, & Wood, 1984). Thus, causal attributions help us meet our needs to simplify, predict, and control our environments (Anderson, 1990).

Self-fulfilling prophecy describes the case whereby people have expectations about another person that influence their behavior toward him or her, which in turn causes the person to behave in a way consistent with these expectations. Behavioral confirmation is the name given to the change in behavior that fulfills the expectations.

Dimensions of Causal Attributions

Attribution theory and research are devoted to determining how explanations for our feelings, thoughts, and actions can vary along several dimensions (Heider, 1958; Kelley, 1967, 1972; Weiner, 1986). We can explain the causes of behavior in many different ways. For example, suppose James is taking a course in introductory psychology from Professor Hollings. James may study for a course examination because he (1) wants an A, (2) is truly interested in the subject, (3) doesn't want to disappoint his parents, (4) greatly admires his famous professor, or (5) has a bet with a friend as to who will get a higher grade. The particular explanation for his behavior will vary, depending on personal and situational dimensions.

Three well-studied dimensions of causal attributions include: ***internal versus external*** (does the behavior reflect something about the person or something about the situation?); ***stable versus unstable*** (is the cause a one-time event or does it persist?); and ***controllable versus uncontrollable*** (can the person control the behavior or not?) (Weiner, 1985). Attributing the cause of a behavior to a personal characteristic is an ***internal*** or ***dispositional attribution***, while

▼ *The gang from Seinfeld are masters at attribution. When something goes wrong, they use external attributions for their own behavior, and internal attributions for the behavior of their dates.*

attributing it to something in the environment is an ***external*** or ***situational attribution.*** Thus, when you attribute the cause of a person's behavior to his or her traits, thoughts, moods, feelings, intentions, or other personal characteristics, you are making an internal (dispositional) attribution (for example, James did well on an exam because he has exceptional ability or because he studied a lot). When you attribute the person's behavior to something in the environment, including pressure from others, the difficulty of the task, perhaps even the weather—you are making an external (situational) attribution (James did well on the exam because the questions were easy). If we attribute the behavior to a cause that is steady over time, we are making a stable attribution. Thus, if we believe that James did well because he is highly intelligent (a personal characteristic considered unlikely to change much over time), our attribution is both stable and internal.

Believing that we have the power to control our behavior is called ***perceived controllability***. We believe that some behaviors are controllable, while others are not. Suppose Professor Hollings thinks that James' excellent performance is due to long hours of study. This is an internal attribution to behavior that is under James' control but is unstable—there's no guarantee he will choose to study the same number of hours for the next exam. Table 12-1 presents different ways these three dimensions might work together to explain James' successful exam performance. Can you describe how they would work to explain failure on an exam? The principles are the same.

What makes us attribute a behavior to internal versus external factors? Harold Kelley suggests we use a principle of ***covariation*** in interpreting people's behavior (Kelley, 1972). That is, we should observe what potential causes are present or absent when a behavior does and doesn't occur, and draw conclusions accordingly. Kelley suggests we use three types of information in deciding whether to make internal or external attributions: ***consistency***, ***distinctiveness***, and ***consensus***. Consistency reflects the degree to which a person reacts to an event in the same way on many different occasions (consistency across time—James has received an A on every test given in the course). Distinctiveness reflects the degree to which a person does not react the same way to different events (lack of consistency across situations—if James has C's in all of his other courses, an A is a distinctive event). Consensus reflects the degree to which other people react to an event in the same way as the person we are observing (for example, everybody in James' class got an A on the test). Figure 12-2 presents how various combinations of these three factors lead to internal versus external attributions (Kelley, 1972; Harvey & Weary, 1988).

Our attributions for behavior are important because they determine how we feel and act toward others. If Professor Hollings attributes James' good grade to his intelligence (an internal and stable attribution), she may change her behavior toward him. She may call on him more in class, ask him to work on independent study projects, or recommend him for graduate school. Conversely, suppose she attributes his good grade to a lot of studying for this particular exam—an internal, but potentially unstable behavior. (He studied hard for this one exam but might not do it again.) James' sterling performance may not change Professor Hollings' perception of his intelligence, but it may lead

Table 12-1 Three Dimensions of Causal Attribution

James got an A	**Internal Causes**		**External Causes**	
	Stable	*Unstable*	*Stable*	*Unstable*
Controllable	Standard Effort: James always studies hard.	Temporary Effort: James studied exceptionally hard for this exam.	Continuing Bias: James chose an easy course.	Temporary Bias: James happened to pick the right questions to study.
Uncontrollable	Ability: James is highly intelligent.	Mood: James had just won an award and felt great.	Task Difficulty: The particular exam was easy.	Luck: James' exam happened to be the last exam the professor graded, and she was too tired to be critical.

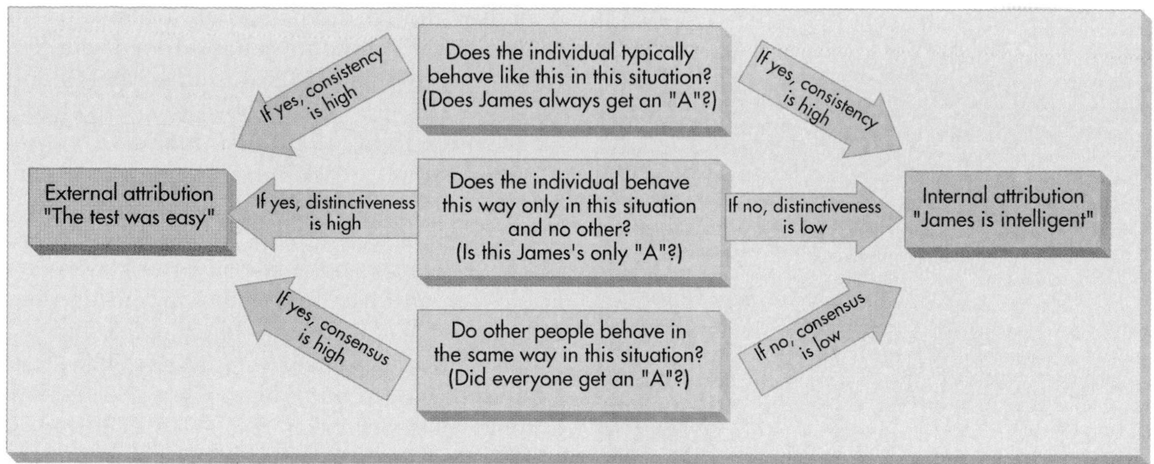

12-2 Kelley's Theory of Attribution

According to Harold Kelley, we make attributions based on how we believe events covary. Our attributions for behavior may be internal or external, depending on a behavior's consistency, distinctiveness, and consensus information. Here's how we would decide how to attribute James' getting an A on his exam.

her to develop ways to encourage his studying. However, if James fails the test after the professor works hard to interest him in the material, her feelings toward him will depend on perceived controllability. When negative outcomes are attributed to controllable internal factors (for example, lack of effort), people develop negative emotions and may become angry. When the same outcome is attributed to uncontrollable external factors (a job that leaves no time for studying, no child care, electricity that went out so he was unable to study in the evening), the result is more likely to be pity (Weiner, Graham, & Chandler, 1982).

When we are judging our own behavior, internal attributions (to ability or effort) affect esteem-related emotions associated with performance—increasing pride after success and shame after failure. If James attributes his success to internal causes such as ability and hard work, he will feel more pride and self-worth, and his self-esteem will rise. If he attributes it to external factors (an exceptionally easy test), he might be happy to get the A, but his self-esteem will not go up. Stability of an attribution (whether internal or external) affects *future expectations*: people raise their aspirations when they attribute their successes to stable causes (Weiner, Graham, & Chandler, 1982).

As we acquire social knowledge, we learn "attribution scripts" appropriate to our culture, and we automatically and effortlessly apply them to social information. Inferences and attributions rapidly come to mind, enabling a "quick-and-dirty" attribution process (Kelley, 1972; Gilbert, 1989). Sometimes we stop there—one reason first impressions can matter. But sometimes we go on to a second stage of the attribution process, where we more consciously weigh the factors that go into our perceptions and inferences. We can then make a "course correction," taking into account things not included in our initial causal schemas, such as how behavior may vary across situations and how aspects of the current situation may constrain or determine the behavior (Jones & Davis, 1965; Kelley, 1972; Gilbert, 1989; Gilbert & Hixon, 1991). Thus, when we observe a man speaking gently to an eight-year-old he has been hired to tutor, we may infer his behavior is caused by his gentle personality rather than by his role as a tutor and the fact that he is speaking to a child. When we subsequently find out that he is a ruthless competitor on the racquetball court, we may reconsider our initial inference and give more weight to the constraints of the situation in explaining his behavior.

▼ *Bulgarian wrestler Plamen Paskalev hides his head in shame after losing to Takuya Ota in the 1996 Olympics. But if he makes external attributions for his loss (or internal attributions to a temporary state, such as not feeling well that day), he can protect his self-esteem.*

Attributional Biases

The tendency to assume that people's words and actions correspond to their intentions, attitudes, and traits (even when we have evidence to the contrary) is called the ***correspondence bias*** (Jones, 1990). A variety of factors contribute to this bias (Gilbert & Malone, 1995). Schemas link traits with behaviors, so when we see a behavior, the traits that are generally associated with it come automatically to mind. These associations will lead us to infer that the behavior is caused by the traits unless we subsequently correct for them (Carlston & Skowronski, 1994; Uleman & Moskowitz, 1994).

Correspondence bias is the tendency to assume that people's words and actions correspond to their intentions, attitudes, and traits.

The tendency to stress internal explanations and to overlook situational determinants of behavior is so widespread in Western society that

▶ *Why is Maria Ambrocio crying? An observer might attribute her tears to being depressed (internal attribution), but she would say her tears reflect the situation. Ramon, her husband of twenty-five years, has just proposed anew and given her an engagement ring for the first time.*

The fundamental attribution error is the tendency to overlook situational determinants of behavior and attribute the causes of behavior to dispositions.

it has been labeled the ***fundamental attribution error*** (Ross, 1977). In the West, correspondence bias appears to grow stronger with age, as shown by a study in which U.S. adults were far more likely than U.S. children to make internal, dispositional attributions for behavior (see Figure 12-3). In contrast, adult Hindus from India were not more likely than Indian children to make internal attributions (Miller, 1984). Research on attributions for career success also suggests cultural contributions to the correspondence bias. In the individualistic United States, in keeping with the widespread cultural myth of Horatio Alger (who succeeded because of ability and hard work), high achievers tend to attribute both their own and others' success to a joint combination of individual ability and effort—a combination dubbed the "Alger factor" (Russo, Kelly, & Deacon, 1991).

When our attributions are affected by whether we are the actor or the observer of a behavior, it is called an ***actor-observer effect***. Suppose Selena is driving down the freeway on a cold winter day. She sees the car ahead of her swerve and skid as it hits a patch of ice, and she thinks "incompetent driver" (dispositional attribution). Five minutes later, Selena herself hits a patch of ice, swerves and skids. She thinks, "It's sure slippery out today" (situational attribution). Her attribution differed depending on whether she was observing another's behavior or her own.

As Selena's attributions demonstrate, the correspondence bias is much more likely to be found when we are explaining other people's behavior. Observers judging our behavior are more likely to make attributions to our personality rather than to the situation. But when we are asked to explain our behavior, we will emphasize aspects of the situation, context, or environment rather than our personal attributes (Jones & Nisbett, 1971). After a heated argument with a co-worker in which you raise your voice, a casual observer might conclude that you have a "hostile and aggressive personality." In contrast, you might explain that the other person was obstinate and not listening, and the situation required a forceful statement.

What contributes to actor-observer differences? One factor is our tendency to assume that more people share our attitudes and behave like us than is actually the case. This tendency is called the ***false consensus bias***. This bias creates the expectation that people will behave as we would. When judging behavior that is different from ours, we may judge others as "deviant" even when their behavior is actually in the majority. Thus, we perceive their behavior as lacking in consensus (it is different from what we believe everyone else would do). In keeping with Kelley's covariation theory described above, we are more likely to attribute this "deviant" behavior to an aspect of the person (Kelley, 1972).

Attributions in Western culture vary depending on the desirability of the outcome. In judging our own behavior, when the outcome is desirable (for example, winning a tennis match or an argument), we credit success to our-

12-3 Cultural Differences in Attributions Emerge with Age

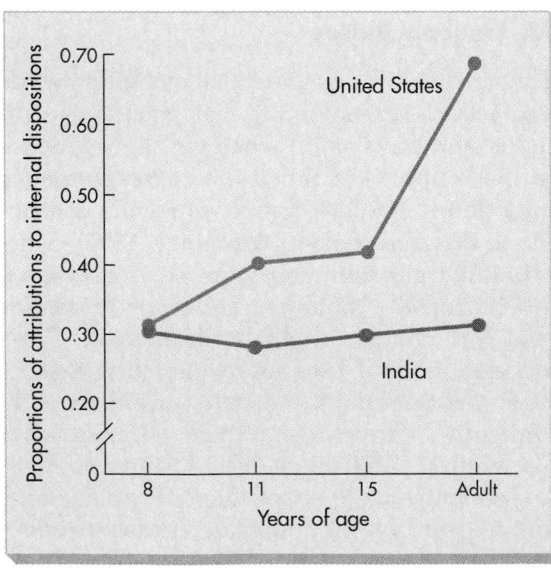

When middle-class children, teenagers, and adults in the United States and India were asked to think of an action by someone they knew and then explain that action, cultural differences emerged with age. Adult Americans were more likely to make internal, dispositional attributions (explaining behavior as caused by personality characteristics and attitudes) than were adult Indians. (Miller, 1984)

selves—we won because we had better skills, were smarter, and so on. When the outcome is undesirable (we lost the match or the argument), the reverse occurs: we may say we lost because of poor luck or bad referee calls (external circumstances). Attributing good outcomes to our own ability and bad outcomes to external factors is called the ***self-serving bias*** (Miller & Ross, 1975). Actor-observer differences, the false consensus bias, and the self-serving bias underscore the central role that our self-schemas play in how we perceive and understand our social world.

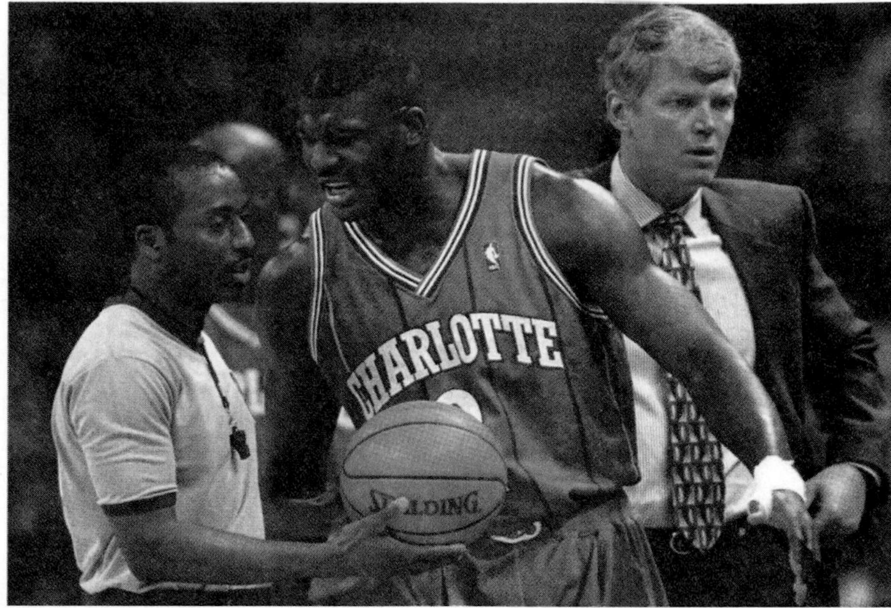

▲ *Larry Johnson of the Charlotte Hornets disputes a referee's call. When athletes attribute losses to external attributions, such as bad referee calls, they demonstrate a self-serving bias.*

The Role of Self and Self-Schemas

What do you think of yourself? How do you think other people see you? The answers to these questions determine how you perceive and interact with others. We process information about our social world through ***self-schemas***, that is, through the thoughts, beliefs, and feelings we have about ourselves—how we are now and how we might be in the future. Our self-schemas collectively make up what is known as our ***self-concept***, and our self-concept determines how we process social information, and perceive and evaluate others. One of the most important aspects of our self-schema is our *self-esteem*, which not only represents our general evaluation of ourselves but also influences how we respond to feedback about success and failure (Brown & Dutton, 1995).

In general, we try to maintain an accurate and consistent self-concept, but we also want to feel good about ourselves. As you have seen, we manage our attributions for success and failure and use self-serving biases to enhance and protect our self-image. This need for *self-enhancement* becomes particularly important after threats to our self-esteem (Brown & Gallagher, 1992). One of the techniques we use to respond to such threats is *self-affirmation*, which is our tendency to respond to self-esteem threats by affirming other, unrelated, aspects of ourselves. Suppose Karen is a debater and a flute player. If she fails to make the debate team, she may become more involved in playing the flute (Steele, 1988).

We interpret new information with our most easily accessible schemas. For many people, these are self-schemas. As you have seen, we tend to make inferences about others based on comparing them to ourselves. Moreover, we are more likely to remember information about others if it relates to something we ourselves have done or said (Fiske & Taylor, 1991); this is called the ***self-referencing effect*** (Higgins & Bargh, 1987). Cognitive processing appears to be easier and more efficient when information is self-relevant.

We use ourselves as a yardstick to evaluate others, often judging the favorableness of others' opinions by comparing them to our own opinions. You may judge the statement, "Princess Diana had an interesting life" as favorable or unfavorable, depending on your opinion of her. If you judge her life to have been shallow and boring, it is a favorable statement and you'd probably judge the speaker to be a fan. If you are a Princess Di admirer fascinated with the storybook tale of the unhappy but compassionate princess, you may view the statement as "damning with faint praise," and become annoyed.

Are you always trying to figure yourself out? Are you concerned with the way you present yourself? Do you worry about making a good impression? People who are *self-aware* answer "yes" to such questions and focus their attention inward. Self-aware people are more sensitive to their behavior's consequences, and they tend to behave consistently in ways they consider socially acceptable. People with lower levels of self-awareness may not consider the social

Self-schemas are the beliefs we hold about ourselves that collectively make up our self-concept.

▼ *Ru Paul's flamboyant sense of style is a fundamental aspect of his self-schema.*

► *Japanese and American children are taught different ways to boost their self-esteem. In the Japanese cartoon, the wrestler thinks of his family to boost feelings of self-worth, while in the American cartoon, the girl praises herself.*

implications of their behavior, and they may behave outside generally accepted standards (Fenigstein, Scheier, & Buss, 1975). Moreover, increasing self-awareness is likely to increase adherence to social norms. In one study, Halloween trick-or-treaters were unobtrusively observed taking candy from a bowl when no one else was present. Many children took several pieces, even though they had been told to take only one. But if they were identified by name when entering, the children were significantly less likely to take more than one piece of candy. Identification may have caused them to become more self-aware and to lead them to follow socially acceptable behavior norms that might otherwise be forgotten in the excitement of Halloween (Diener, Fraser, Beaman, & Kelem, 1976).

Self-awareness can be activated in fairly subtle ways. Research participants become more sensitive to external standards in a room with a mirror. This phenomenon occurs even when the mirror is placed on a table so that it clearly is not a two-way observation mirror. Although the mirror ostensibly has nothing to do with the experiment, individuals able to see themselves apparently become more self-aware and consequently more sensitive to the implications of their behavior. This sensitivity is manifested in several ways. For example, it may lead you to report less positive (that is, more modest) self-evaluations. In addition, if you have previously said that you are in favor of punishment and an experimenter subsequently asks you to shock someone as a punishment, it may lead to a greater willingness to comply with the experimenter's request (Fenigstein, Scheier, & Buss, 1975; Carver, 1975; Froming, Walker, & Lopyan, 1982).

Self-concepts include our ***social identities***, which represent our memberships in social groups and the value and emotional significance we attach to them (Tajfel, 1981; Turner, Oakes, Haslam, & McGarty, 1994). Boundaries among our personal and social identities differ among individuals and among cultures. Indeed, in some collectivist cultures, little distinction may be made between personal and social identities. Such cultural differences in self-schemas can affect how we perceive and feel about ourselves and others (Markus & Kitayama, 1991). People in North America and Western Europe view themselves as independent, self-reliant, assertive individuals. In such cultures, personal achievement is more strongly linked to the self-esteem of individuals. In contrast, people in

UNDERSTANDING HUMAN DIVERSITY

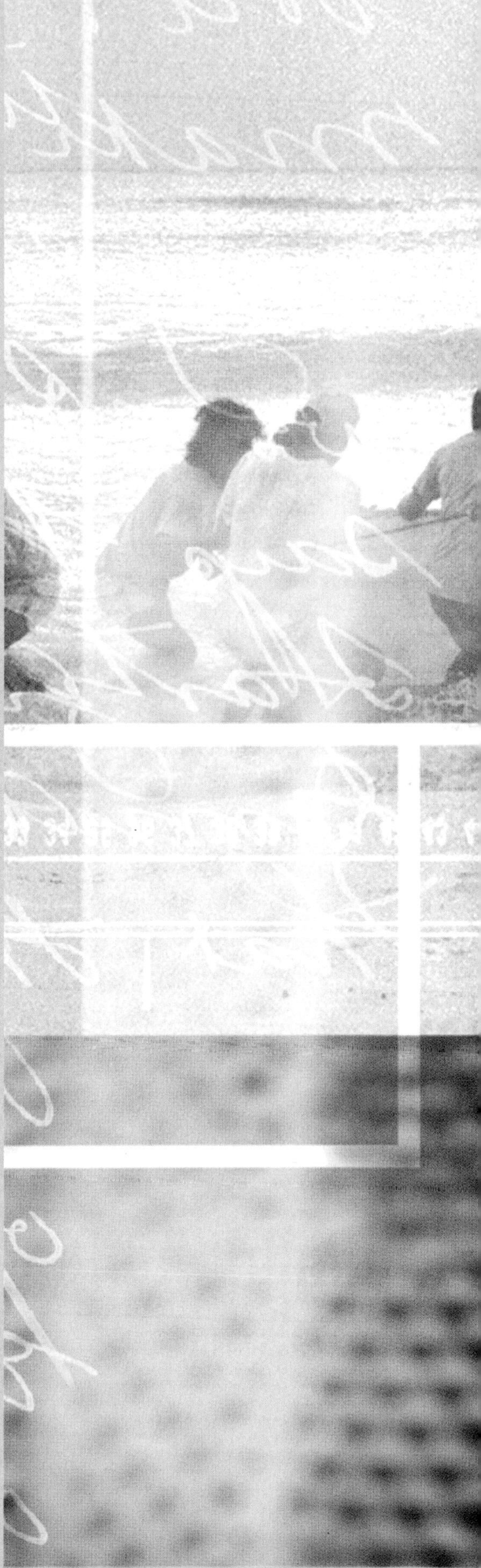

The Individual versus the Group in Different Cultures

The importance of the individual is stressed in the United States, Britain, and other British-influenced countries, such as Australia and Canada. But even these societies differ in their emphasis on individual development and achievement (individualism) over connection to the group and social solidarity (collectivism). Although wide diversity exists among collectivist cultures, nonetheless cultural differences are reflected in psychological and social processes and have tangible and pervasive effects on self-concept, social relationships, and child-rearing practices (Triandis, McCusker, & Hui, 1990).

Self-Concept

In societies characterized by individualism, people are more likely to retain a sense of personal identity based on idiosyncratic attributes rather than social connections to family, peers, church, and work groups. They are able to change groups in search of better opportunities, and they believe they should be judged on their own actions and not those of family members, friends, or members of the groups to which they belong. Enjoying life is emphasized, and self-reliance in these cultures means "I can do my own thing."

In collectivist societies, social networks define one's identity. Relationships are deeper and more stable, and one's actions can bring shame to both oneself and to other members of one's group, such as family and work groups. Doing one's duty is emphasized, and self-reliance in these cultures means "I am not a burden on the in-group."

Social Relations

People from collectivist cultures are more likely to agree with the statement "I like to live close to my friends" and disagree with "It is best to work alone rather than in a group" (Hofstede, 1980). Collectivists are more likely to disclose personal information, stand closer, and generally express more intimacy than individualists.

While individualists emphasize judging people on their own merits, collectivists are more likely to prejudge people by their groups and emphasize hierarchy. They are also more likely to be patriarchal, with the father the boss of the family, and women subordinate to men in the society. Vertical relationships take priority over horizontal relationships in these societies (parent-child over spouse-spouse).

Cooperation and harmony are more likely to be emphasized in collectivist societies. For example, in Japan, the value of harmony (*wa*) is served when baseball teams often play for ties, which has been described as "suited for the Japanese character . . . nobody loses" by none other than the president of the Pacific League in Japan (in Whiting, 1989, p. 25). Few disputes end up in Japanese courts, as litigation is considered a breach of a community's *wa* and is discouraged by Japan's social structure, which limits the number of lawyers and judges (van Wolferen, 1990).

Child Rearing

Individualist societies emphasize the importance of children learning to be independent and to think for themselves, while collectivist societies stress cooperation with and sensitivity to group norms. In American society, children and adolescents assume that they will make their own major life decisions: whom they will marry and how they will spend their money. In some collectivist societies, marriages are arranged (as in Saudi Arabia), or at least approved by one's parents (Mexico). In collectivist societies, children contribute their earnings to the family and care for their parents. Extended family members (including parents, children, aunts, uncles, and cousins) sometimes pool their funds to send one of their members to another country to work. That individual then sends his or her income back home to support the family.

Although individuals in individualist societies have more personal freedom, privacy, creativity, and choice in lifestyle than those in collectivist societies, people in individualistic societies are also at higher risk for loneliness, delinquency, child abuse, marital disruption, homicide, vulnerability to stress-related disease, and economic insecurity (Triandis, 1995; Triandis, McCusker, & Hui, 1990).

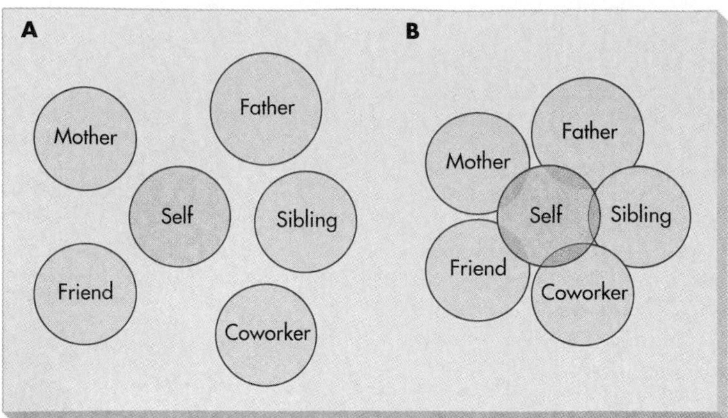

12-4 Independent and Interdependent Self-Concepts

Self-concepts reflect cultural context. People in individualistic cultures (A) are more likely to have independent views of the self, while individuals in collectivistic cultures (B) are more likely to have interdependent views of the self (Markus & Kitayama, 1991).

many countries in Asia and Latin America hold a more collectivist view of the self as an interdependent part of a community (Hofstede, 1980). Instead of emphasizing self-assertion and personal achievement, they emphasize harmony and connection with others. In such cultures, being a member of a family or a company (social identities) and bringing honor to the group is more strongly linked to the self-esteem of individuals (see Figure 12-4; Markus & Kitayama, 1991).

Cognitive Consistency

Our social knowledge is organized, which means that a change in one element can have implications for other elements. Many psychologists believe we are motivated to achieve a state of mind in which our beliefs, attitudes, and behaviors are mutually compatible, that is, we seek to achieve a state of ***cognitive consistency***. Cognitive consistency theories emphasize the desire of people to understand the world in terms of its predictability and regularity. When we believe we know what actions will lead to what consequences, we know how to behave. We become uncomfortable when events become unpredictable and inconsistent, and we are motivated to restore consistency (Festinger, 1957; Abelson et al., 1968).

As a general rule, we acquire new knowledge and make inferences from old knowledge to maximize our perceived cognitive consistency. For example, we generally believe that liking and agreeing go together: people tend to like others who agree with them, and they tend to agree with people they like. If we are told Jay and Sara both like each other, we would probably guess they will agree on a variety of things, from their preferred candidate for president to their favorite rock group. These predictions follow from the consistency principle.

Cognitive Dissonance

Probably the most prominent consistency theory in social psychology is Leon Festinger's theory of cognitive dissonance (Festinger, 1957). According to ***cognitive dissonance*** theory, when our thoughts and actions are inconsistent, we experience great discomfort. This discomfort motivates us to do something to eliminate the inconsistency between our thoughts and behaviors, thereby reducing our cognitive dissonance. Whether we experience cognitive dissonance, however, depends on how strongly we believe

▶ *Dogbert effectively applies his knowledge of cognitive dissonance.*

DILBERT reprinted by permission of United Feature Syndicate, Inc.

that our thought is true, and how relevant we judge it to be to our actions. Dissonance is strongest when something threatens our self-image (Thibodeau & Aronson, 1992). Thus, if we believe that we are kind and generous, yet we fail to send money to flood victims or do not give homeless people money, we may feel extremely uncomfortable.

Suppose you decide to buy a car, and choose a particular model. Certain beliefs are consistent with that decision (the price is low; it comes with air bags; it gets good mileage). Other beliefs are not consistent with it (the repair record is poor; the body style is ugly; the air conditioning is inadequate and doesn't cool the back seat). How can you reduce the dissonance you feel about buying the car?

You can reduce dissonance in several ways (see Figure 12-5). First, you can try to increase the importance of the factors that are consistent with your decision to buy: air bags are absolutely critical for safety, the price makes this car an exceptionally good deal. Second, you can try to decrease the importance of the factors that are not consistent with your decision to buy: the air conditioning doesn't really matter because you practically never have anyone in the back seat anyway. Third, you can try to add new factors that will bolster your decision: you might realize that a good friend owns a similar model and is happy with it, or you might solicit additional repair record data. Dissonance theory also suggests you might even try to persuade others to buy a similar car, because the cognition that "all the best people have this model" is consistent with your purchase.

Dissonance theory seems fairly straightforward, but when examined closely, it leads to some unexpected results, for example, the ***insufficient justification effect***. This occurs when people create dissonance by behaving inconsistently with their beliefs, without a good external reason for doing so. To justify their actions and reduce dissonance, people sometimes adjust their beliefs and attitudes. In effect, "doing" becomes "believing." This effect was first demonstrated in a classic experiment (Festinger & Carlsmith, 1959). The researchers had participants (students) spend an hour on an exceedingly dull task. They then told the students that the study examined effects of expectations on task performance, and they asked the students to "fill in" for a missing research assistant whose job it was to create expectations for the next research participant. Some students were given $20 to try to convince others that the task was actually quite interesting; other students were given only $1 to do so (note—this study was conducted in the 1950s when $20 was a *lot* of money); and a control group of students was given no reward but was not asked to lie. In each case, after talking to the next research participant, these students were then asked to report their own level of interest in the task.

The researchers predicted that the students who had to misrepresent the task would experience dissonance as a result of the inconsistency between (1) the act of telling someone a

People sometimes behave inconsistently with their beliefs, without a good external reason for doing so, which leads to cognitive dissonance. To reduce the dissonance, people then adjust their beliefs on the grounds that, otherwise, there would be insufficient justification for their behavior.

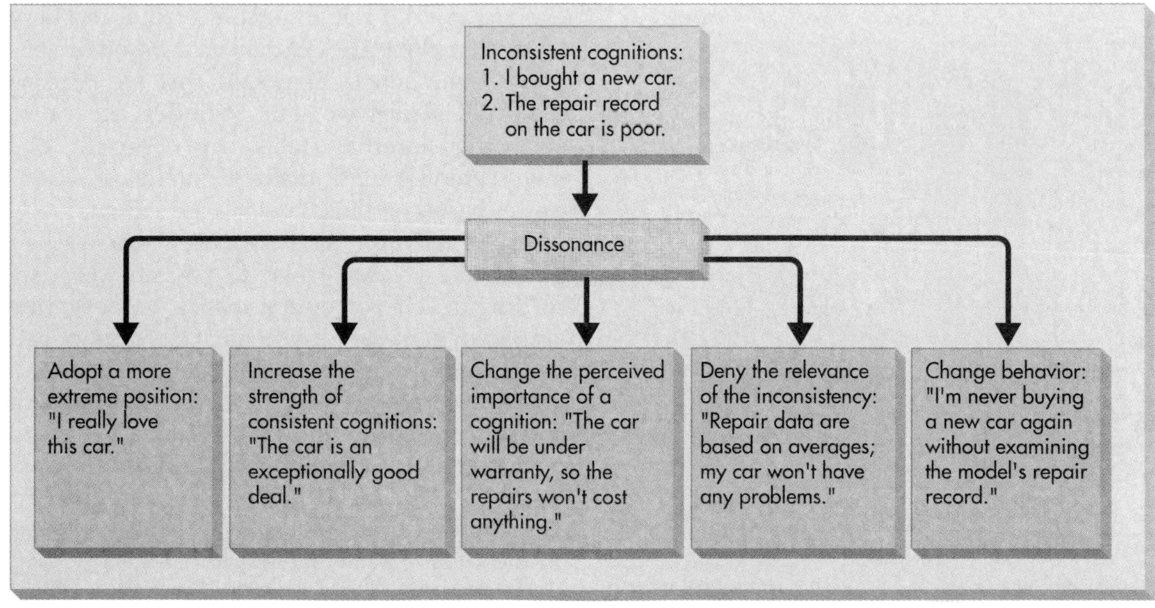

12-5 Strategies for Reducing Cognitive Dissonance

When faced with inconsistent cognitions, we experience dissonance, which we seek to reduce by changing our cognitions, by changing how important we think a cognition is, or by changing our behavior.

task is interesting, and (2) the belief that it is really boring. The interesting question was: How would the amount of money they were paid affect their attitudes toward the task? Learning theory would predict that the larger reinforcement ($20) would be most effective in creating a positive attitude toward this task. Dissonance theory would predict that the smaller reinforcement ($1) would be more effective in promoting attitude change. This is because most people would not consider such poor payment sufficient justification for misrepresenting a dull task to their fellow students. They would therefore need to reduce the dissonance created by lying for no good reason. Most people would consider getting highly paid, however, as sufficient justification for telling other students a harmless fib. In this condition, any dissonance created by lying would be reduced, so there would be no need to modify their attitude toward the task. For those who were poorly paid, however, dissonance would not be reduced. To reduce their dissonance, they would need to change their attitude about the task and rate it more highly than the other group, which is what the results showed they actually did (see Figure 12-6).

THINKING CRITICALLY

Consider the suicides of the Heaven's Gate cult members. Can you use dissonance theory to explain this mass suicide?

Dissonance theory would say that the Heaven's Gate followers obeyed orders to kill themselves to reduce cognitive dissonance. They may have had the following cognitions: "I gave all my money to Do and Ti." "I sacrificed everything I had to achieve the next Evolutionary Level." "I sold my home, severed ties with my family, cut off my genitals, and did everything without question." Consider how difficult and threatening it would be for them to justify all the enormous public losses they had experienced if they now refused to obey. According to dissonance theory, so much dissonance would have been aroused by admitting their mistake that it was easier (1) to believe Do and Ti were right once again, (2) to interpret the Hale-Bopp comet as signaling the coming of the spaceship, and (3) to follow Do's instructions by drinking a lethal "cocktail."

Dissonance and Self-Perception Theory

Festinger and Carlsmith's experiment generated considerable excitement because it contradicted the widely accepted learning theory prediction that size of reward controls attitude and behavior change. But the dissonance theory explanation did not go uncontested. Daryl Bem offered an alternative explanation based on self-perception theory. Bem said that we become aware of ourselves—our attitudes, emotions, and other internal states—by observing our own behavior and making inferences about causes based on those observations (Bem, 1967). Consider a simple case. Suppose you are asked if you like yogurt. How do you answer? According to self-perception theory, you examine your own behavior. If you have a history of eating yogurt, you report that you like it—why else would you have eaten it? According to Bem and self-perception theory, it is not necessary to postulate an internal state of dissonance to explain the student behavior in Festinger and Carlsmith's experiment. The students could examine their own behavior and logically conclude that they would not lie for such a paltry

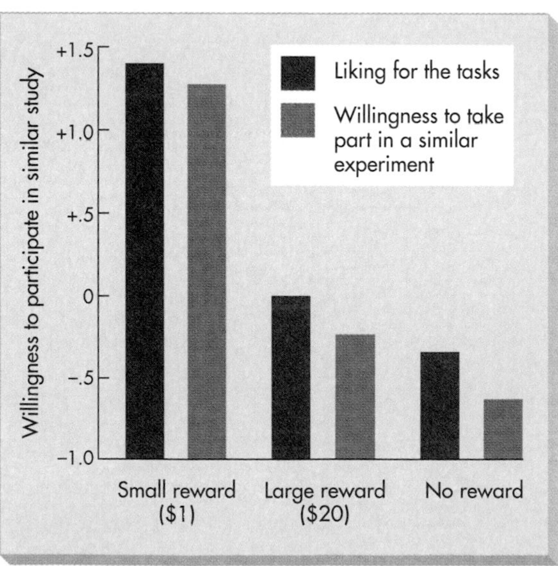

12-6 Smaller Rewards Can Produce More Attitude Change

Research participants were given either $1 (small reward) or $20 (large reward) for telling a fellow student that a boring task was interesting. A control group received no reward and was not asked to lie about the task. After talking to the other student, those in all the conditions were asked to rate their liking for the task and willingness to take part in a similar experiment. Participants who were given the small reward rated their liking for the task and willingness to participate in a similar experiment more highly than did those who either received a large reward or no reward at all.

sum, so they must have enjoyed the task. Thus, dissonance theory is based on motivation—the desire to avoid feeling uncomfortable—whereas self-perception theory is based on processing information and self-awareness (Bem, 1967, 1972).

The debate between these theories encouraged numerous studies; today both sides are recognized as correct, depending on the situation. Self-perception processes are more relevant for explaining attitude change in situations where there are no aversive consequences and no physiological arousal (for example, judging whether you like a particular brand of salsa). They serve as an explanation where the attitudes are weakly held and logically implied by the behavior (you finished the whole jar of salsa in fifteen minutes; therefore you must like it), and where the participants don't necessarily think about or remember their original attitude and may even remember it inaccurately (Ross & Buehler, 1994; Zanna, Fazio, & Ross, 1994; Olson & Roese, 1995).

In contrast, dissonance theory works better in cases where people think their actions have caused aversive consequences and feel personally responsible for those consequences. They feel bad (aversive physiological arousal) and link the bad feeling to their behavior; they have no way to alleviate their discomfort except by changing their attitudes (Fazio, Zanna, & Cooper, 1977; Cooper & Fazio, 1984; Simon, Greenberg, & Brehm, 1995).

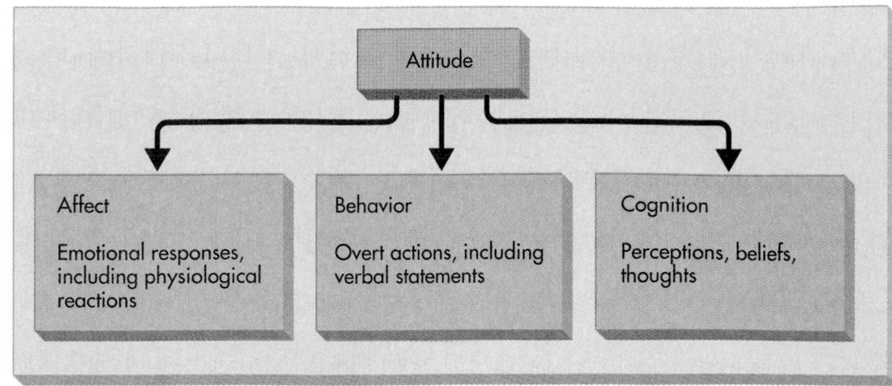

12-7 The ABC's of Attitudes

Attitudes can be thought of as having three components: affect, behavioral tendencies, and cognition.

Attitudes

An ongoing topic for heated debate in "Dear Abby" is which direction toilet paper should hang from the roller. Some advocate that it should hang down from the back of the roll against the wall. Others say it should hang from the front of the roll. This controversy has been known to cause strain in at least one marriage, as well as heated exchanges among introductory psychology students.

As evidenced by the great toilet paper controversy, we seem capable of forming attitudes toward practically anything. An ***attitude*** can be defined as an evaluation—favorable or unfavorable—of some person, object, event, or idea. Attitude schemas include affective, behavioral, and cognitive information related to an attitude object (Eagly & Chaiken, 1993). Self-esteem is an attitude toward ourselves. Prejudice and interpersonal attraction reflect attitudes toward others. Attitudes are not the same as beliefs—we can have a belief about something without evaluating it as good or bad. Figure 12-7 presents the ABC's of attitudes, that is, their affective, behavioral, and cognitive components (Taylor, Peplau, & Sears, 1997).

Attitudes can influence and predict behavior. As you have seen, inconsistency between our attitudes and our behavior can strongly motivate us to action, and can even cause us to behave in irrational and destructive ways. The relationship of attitudes to behavior and how attitudes are formed and changed is thus a topic of great interest in social psychology.

Predicting Behavior from Attitudes

An attitude is an evaluative schema—favorable or unfavorable—about some person, object, event, or idea.

Most people assume that our attitudes are directly related to and always consistent with our behavior. If we favor energy conservation, our attitude is reflected in a variety of actions. We can use our car less and not waste gas. We can ride a bike or take the bus. We can write to our state and federal legislators, urging them to vote for conservation programs. We can take part in demonstrations to advocate energy conservation policies. We can give money to conservation groups.

However, the relationship between attitudes and behaviors is not always quite so straightforward. Attitudes toward a person, object, or idea have not been found to predict behavior consistently and accurately. You may hold positive religious attitudes but never attend church.

▲ *Sexual and financial scandals involving television evangelist Jim Bakker revealed glaring inconsistencies between his behavior and attitudes. Here the former religious leader is escorted to a state correctional institution for psychiatric evaluation.*

You may have negative attitudes toward cigarettes but still smoke. Clearly, factors other than attitudes enter into how we act (Fazio, 1990).

Our behavior may be inconsistent with our attitudes because the attitude we hold is weak, or we may act without thinking about our attitude. Having the attitude won't affect us if we are not thinking about it. The more an attitude stands out in our memory and consciousness, however, the more likely it will affect behavior. Attitudes toward specific events more closely relate to behavior than do more global and general attitudes: attitudes toward recycling predict recycling behavior, but attitudes toward a clean environment do not (Oskamp, 1991). Attitudes may not predict behavior because social pressures or fear of criticism may lead us to say or do things we do not actually believe in. Thus, someone at a party might drink alcohol because everyone else is doing it, even though he or she has a negative attitude toward alcohol.

. . . estimates place the average American as the target of over 1,500 persuasive appeals per day from national advertisers alone.

—John T. Cacioppo & Richard E. Petty (1985, p. 91)

Where do attitudes come from? How can they be changed? As you read in Chapter 6, attitudes can be learned, and the processes of classical and operant conditioning as well as observational learning all work to shape our attitudes. Cognitive processes influence attitudes as well. As you have seen, both the motivation for consistency and the desire to reduce aversive arousal produced by cognitive dissonance influence how our attitudes are formed and change. Another approach to studying attitude change involves examining our reactions to communication and persuasion.

Communication and Persuasion

We are bombarded by persuasive messages daily—what we read in newspapers and magazines and what we see on television influence our beliefs and attitudes. We are also influenced by formal lectures and casual conversations. But which messages get us to change our minds and why? The answers depend on the characteristics of the communicator, the message itself, the recipient, the situation in which we hear the information, and the cognitive processes that we use to process it.

Communicator

Who is more likely to change your opinion, someone you like and admire or someone you dislike? Most of us will change our attitude to match that of someone we admire. This is because we want to maintain cognitive consistency, or balance, between our favorable feelings toward the source of the message and the views expressed. If we have negative feelings toward the communicator, however, we will not need to change our attitude to achieve cognitive consistency.

Several factors determine whether we evaluate a communicator favorably. One of the most studied is communicator *credibility*. Credibility is associated with the communicator's perceived expertness, trustworthiness, prestige, attractiveness, and similarity to the recipient. If the communication source is perceived as a trustworthy or prestigious expert, we tend to pay attention to the communication and are less inclined to think of arguments against it. As a result, we are also more likely to be influenced by the message and to change our attitudes based on what the message says. A lecture on dental flossing is more effective if it comes from a dentist (a credentialed, knowledgeable expert) than from a plumber, but when you want the best kind of water purifier, you will consider a plumber the more knowledgeable source (Hovland & Weiss, 1951).

Similarity between the communicator and the recipient can enhance communication effectiveness, but the content of the message is also important. Similar communicators are most influential when the message deals with subjective preference (personal values, taste, or behaviors), while dissimilar communicators are

THINKING CRITICALLY

If young people are exposed to movies that are violent and sexually degrading to women, their attitudes toward women and sensitivity to female victims of violence may be affected. Can you explain how exposure to such media might affect such attitudes?

First, through classical conditioning. If movies pair rape and violent behavior with sexually arousing visual images and music, rape and violence may themselves become sexually arousing, making attitudes toward rape and violence more positive. Second, through cognitive learning. If movies present rape and violence as resulting in positive consequences (for example, having sex and feeling good or powerful), males may come to believe that rape and violence can help obtain those things as well. Further, pairing rape and violence with sexual imagery may also lead young people to develop schemas of sexual violence as "normal" and change their attitudes accordingly.

more effective with messages about objective reality (judgments of fact). Thus, you are more likely to be influenced by a member of your social group who tells you about a new kind of coffee, but more likely to agree with an outsider who tells you whether London or Seattle has more rainfall (Goethals & Nelson, 1973).

Over time, the communicator's characteristics become disassociated from the message or forgotten, with some interesting results: a high credibility communicator may lose influence, while a low credibility communicator may gain influence. This increase reflects a ***sleeper effect***: an increase in the impact of a message over time when the reasons for discounting it, such as low communicator credibility, are more quickly forgotten than the message itself. Thus, if you read an essay claiming cigarettes are not addictive and find that it is signed by a tobacco company executive, you may discount the message because of the self-serving source. Later, however, you may remember that you read that cigarettes were not addictive but not who said so. The sleeper effect only happens, however, when people learn that the source is of low credibility *after* they receive the message (Pratkanis, Greenwald, Leippe, & Baumgardener, 1988). The adage "forewarned is forearmed" applies to persuasive messages. Thus, it's useful to ascertain the credibility of a source before reading or listening to a persuasive message.

▲ *Dr. Helen Caldicott, famed for leadership against nuclear war, emphasized the importance of communicator credibility in her claim that her autobiography should have been entitled "If You Wear Pearls You Can Say Anything."*

Message

How a message is expressed affects its credibility and acceptance. Speaking confidently, avoiding hesitant speech (speech filled with pauses and filler words like "uh," "oh," and "you know"), looking at people directly rather than gazing out into space, and speaking rapidly all increase trustworthiness and believability. Research using computer-generated speech has shown that our normal 140- to 150-word per minute speech rate can be nearly doubled before comprehension drops. Have you ever wondered why so many people in commercials speak so rapidly? Studies by marketing researchers have found that when commercials were speeded up 25 percent over the normal rate, the audience rated the speakers as more knowledgeable, sincere, and intelligent, and found the messages more interesting (MacLachlan & Siegel, 1980).

In preparing for a debate, how can we design our message to maximize its impact? Should we concentrate on fully developing the arguments for our side or take time to present and refute the arguments against us? Considerable research has focused on whether one-sided (pros *or* cons) or two-sided (pros *and* cons) messages produce more attitude change. It depends on the attitudes of the recipient. If you are dealing with a friendly audience and there won't be someone else presenting the other side, then present a one-sided argument. If you have an audience that initially disagrees with you or an opponent who is likely to present the other side, a two-sided argument is more effective (Karlins & Abelson, 1970).

Messages designed to arouse fear in the recipient can also affect message persuasiveness if effective ways to reduce the fear are also included. The persuasiveness of the message de-

The sleeper effect is an increase in the impact of a message over time when the reasons for discounting it, such as low communicator credibility, are more quickly forgotten than the message itself.

THINKING CRITICALLY

How might attorneys take advantage of the sleeper effect when introducing evidence during a trial?

Suppose an attorney introduces significant evidence, but the judge rules it inappropriate (that is, not to be considered credible) and instructs the jury to ignore it. The sleeper effect would predict that as time passes, the jurors might be more likely to recall the evidence than the judge's ruling. In consequence, they might render a verdict based at least in part on inadmissible evidence. Thus, an attorney that introduces such evidence early in the trial is better able to take advantage of the sleeper effect.

pends on how much fear is aroused and whether the person feels vulnerable to the event. Suppose an ad for daily tooth-flossing is accompanied by gory photos of rotting teeth and diseased gums, something you feel could happen to you. The photos may be informative, but they may also generate fear or worry. A moderate dose of fear-inducing material can enhance the effectiveness of your message, but care must be taken not to use too much fear-provoking material. If the fear-provoking aspects are too extreme, people may simply block out the message and its impact will be lost (Janis & Feshbach, 1953; Leventhal, 1970).

▼ *The Wetlands Animal Rights Action Team uses a graphic display of clubbing seals to protest against seal-hunting. This persuasion attempt is based on inducing negative feelings that can be reduced by participating in a boycott against Canada and Norway for raising quotas in the 1997 seal-hunt season.*

Situation

The situation in which you hear, see, or read a message can also affect your evaluation of the message. If you read a message in a quiet library, where you can concentrate fully on its contents, you will probably be able to identify any holes in the argument and come up with counterarguments. But if you read or hear a message where there are many distractions interfering with your concentration, you may have difficulty thinking clearly enough to come up with counterarguments (Allyn & Festinger, 1961). Researchers demonstrated this effect by having fraternity members listen to a recording that attacked fraternities, accompanied by either a videotaped film of the speaker or a very entertaining silent film not related to the message (Festinger, 1957). Attitudes toward fraternities were more likely to be influenced when the message was paired with the silent film, apparently because it distracted participants from refuting message arguments.

This study on attitudes toward fraternities assumed that participants were motivated to oppose the communication at the outset. If a communication supports someone's initial position or he or she has no strong opinions about the issue, distraction may have no effect. In fact, Festinger's study showed that non-fraternity members were equally influenced in both distraction conditions.

Under moderately distracting conditions, you can comprehend the information presented, but you are less likely to evaluate and refute its fallacious arguments. Thus, television advertisements that arouse positive emotions through lively music and pleasing visual images may produce attitude change even if they transmit no substantive information about the product itself. If distractions in the situation become too great, however (like at a noisy party), you may not even be able to comprehend the communication, and its influence will be low.

Cognitive Processes

Suppose a tobacco company executive tries to tell you that smoking is a good stress reducer.

What is your response? In keeping with maintaining a positive self-image, if you are a smoker, you might be pleased with the message and not develop counterarguments to it. But suppose you are a nonsmoker. Do you form counterarguments, such as: "What about the stress of trying to ignore cancer warnings?" "What about the stress of trying to make it through a long meeting without a cigarette?" "What about the stress of social rejection from the majority of people who don't smoke and don't want to breathe the smoke of people who do?"

What thoughts do we have in response to a persuasive message? How do they influence our attitude? What aspects of a message get processed? When do we develop counterarguments? Why is a message effective? These are the kinds of questions researchers examine when focusing on the influence of cognitive processes on persuasion.

One of the most influential models of cognitive processes in persuasion is called the ***elaboration-likelihood model***. This model seeks to explain attitude change in response to persuasion by focusing on how we process information from persuasive communications (Petty & Cacioppo, 1986; Petty, Cacioppo, Strathman, & Priester, 1994).

According to this model, there are two routes to persuasion: *central* and *peripheral*. Both routes can lead to attitude change, but different things happen along the way. Messages that get processed by the central route get carefully and critically examined. In contrast, messages processed by the peripheral route don't receive our full attention and are not as subject to scrutiny and criticism (see Figure 12-8).

What information is processed by which route? If a message is important, interesting, and personally relevant—and nothing else (such as a distracting situation) prevents you from concentrating on the message—you will process it by the central route. If you believe that people are deliberately trying to influence you, you will be "on guard" and will use the central route and process the message more carefully (Walster & Festinger, 1962). If you want to change someone's attitudes via the central route you will need to develop strong, well-reasoned arguments that can withstand scrutiny and counterargument (Petty & Cacioppo, 1986; Friedrich, Fetherstonhaugh, Casey, & Gallagher, 1996).

If the information is uninteresting or uninvolving and there is no reason to process it carefully, you will process the message by the peripheral route. Arguments aren't as important for information that goes via this route. Here, processing is more automatic and emotional. Persuasive cues that create positive associations or reduce your perception of the need for counterargument are more important. Messages associated with someone high in prestige, credibility, or trust, or messages associated with distracting images of "beautiful people," compelling music, or vignettes that produce positive feelings and undermine motivation for counterargument can thus be quite persuasive via the peripheral route. So why take the time

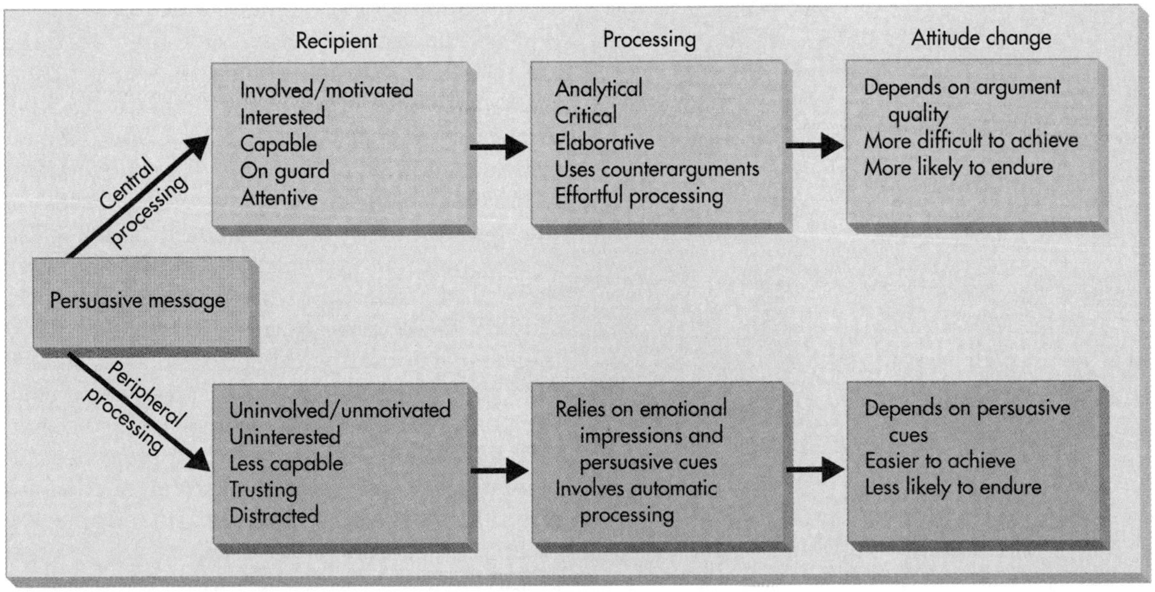

Recipient
Processing
Attitude change
Central processing
Involved/motivated
Interested
Capable
On guard
Attentive
Analytical
Critical
Elaborative
Uses counterarguments
Effortful processing
Depends on argument quality
More difficult to achieve
More likely to endure
Persuasive message
Peripheral processing
Uninvolved/unmotivated
Uninterested
Less capable
Trusting
Distracted
Relies on emotional impressions and persuasive cues
Involves automatic processing
Depends on persuasive cues
Easier to achieve
Less likely to endure

12-8 Central versus Peripheral Processing

When we think we need to pay attention to a persuasive message, we process the message by the central route and carefully evaluate the information. Attitude change is more difficult to produce by this route, but if it does occur it is more lasting. When we do not think it is important to pay attention to a persuasive message, we process the message by the peripheral route and rely more on persuasive cues, such as credibility and trustworthiness of the source, and emotional responses to the message. Acceptance is more likely to occur, but it is also more vulnerable to change and less likely to endure.

to figure out good arguments if a glitzy ad with beautiful people will lead to attitude change? It depends on your goal. Attitude change via the peripheral route is easier to achieve but vulnerable to change. Attitude change via the central route may be more difficult to accomplish, but when it occurs it is more likely to last (Petty & Cacioppo, 1986; Petty, Cacioppo, Strathman, & Priester, 1994).

Prejudice and Discrimination

In the central African nation of Rwanda, ethnic Hutus and Tutsis have lived for years as uneasy neighbors. In 1994, after the president of the country died in a suspicious plane crash, the majority Hutus, who controlled Rwanda's government, suddenly embarked on a campaign to exterminate the minority Tutsis. Mobs of Hutus hunted down and butchered men, women, children, and infants, hacking them to pieces with machetes. Churches where Tutsis took refuge were sealed and ignited with the Tutsis inside. When the bloodshed halted, nearly a million Tutsis were dead, either killed directly in the massacres or dead of starvation or diseases contracted in refugee camps. This genocidal campaign ended when the Tutsis, who had greater military experience, organized and drove out the Hutu regime and seized control of the government. Now, the Tutsi-dominated government has begun putting Hutus on trial for genocide, and there are reports of Tutsi vengeance killings.

Prejudice refers to attitudes toward individuals based on their group membership. Discrimination refers to behavior—biased treatment of or actions toward individuals based on their group membership.

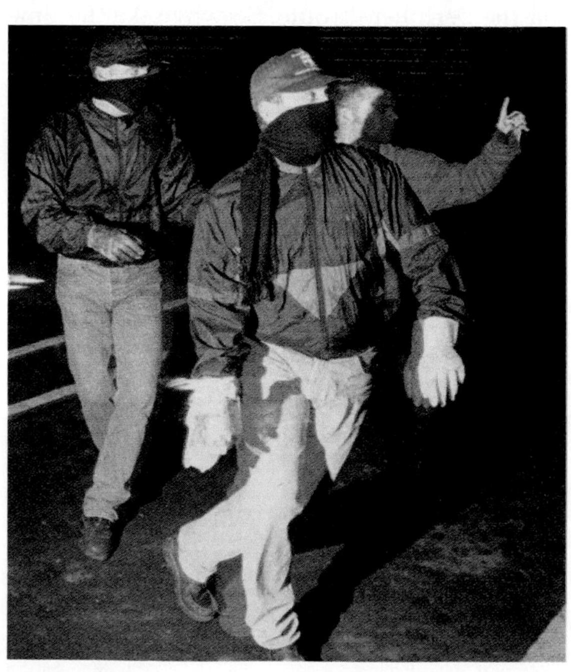

▶ *Northern Ireland provides just one example of how antagonism between groups can lead to aggression. Here a masked Nationalist prepares to throw a bomb at security forces during a riot against the Protestant majority.*

In Northern Ireland, Protestants and Catholics have long been locked in deadly combat. The violence dates from the Battle of the Boyne in 1690, in which Scottish Protestant settlers concentrated in Northern Ireland defeated Irish Catholic forces and ended Irish Catholic political freedom for over two centuries. At that time, British landholders displaced native Irish landowners and reduced Irish farmers to the status of tenants; all government positions were held by Protestants. From 1916 to 1921, the Irish rebelled against British rule in a bitter struggle, which ended with Britain agreeing to Irish independence, *except* for Northern Ireland, where the Protestant majority threatened their own violence if Britain put them under Irish rule. To this day, neighborhoods in Northern Ireland are segregated along religious lines, and Catholics complain that their neighborhoods do not receive government services that the politically and economically dominant Protestants are given. A violent Catholic rebellion in Northern Ireland, marked by bombings and assassinations of Protestants and British officials and soldiers, has been met by counter-violence from the Protestants. Hundreds of people, often innocent bystanders, have died in this sectarian combat, which sometimes spills beyond Northern Ireland's borders to England.

These are but two of many hideous examples of how antagonism between groups can bring out the very worst in human behavior—including torture, mutilation, death, and destruction. Prejudice and discrimination arise out of antagonistic relationships between groups. ***Prejudice*** refers to attitudes toward individuals based on their group membership. Theoretically, one can be prejudiced *for* or *against* individuals, but here we will concentrate on prejudice *against* individuals. ***Discrimination*** refers to biased treatment or actions toward individuals based on their group membership. Thus, prejudice refers to evaluative beliefs and feelings, while discrimination refers to behavior. While prejudice can be manifested in extreme behavior, such as intergroup warfare, it can also undermine the ability of members in diverse groups to interact positively and productively in their daily lives.

A full understanding of prejudice and discrimination requires considering the behavior at many levels. As the examples above demonstrate, a history of conflict and exploitation by "haves" over "have-nots" can leave a legacy of group antagonism. Sociocultural factors that promote uncertainty and increase the likelihood of discrimination, such as a change in rulers or government, the upward mobility of certain groups but not others, or conditions such as increased urbanization that disrupt traditional roles and practices can be factors as well (Allport, 1954). Social psychologists, however, focus primarily on the current situation, examining how our perceptions and feelings about the world interact with forces in our environment (norms, social pressures, the current social structure) to create prejudice and discrimination. With this in mind, we will focus on in-groups and out-groups, showing how social structures that create competition between groups can lead to intergroup hostility and aggression (Sherif, Harvey, White, Hood, & Sherif, 1961; see Chapter 4). We will then turn to stereotypes, explaining how they may form a cognitive basis for prejudice and discrimination.

THINKING CRITICALLY

In Chapter 4 you learned about the Robbers' Cave study in which researchers manipulated a boys' camp situation to foster cooperative and competitive behavior among the campers. Can you apply what you learned from that chapter, and propose a way to reduce prejudice?

The Robbers' Cave study suggests that prejudice can be reduced by structuring social situations to promote cooperation in working for common goals. That study found that stereotyping and hostility between the groups were reduced when a common (superordinate) goal was involved and all the boys had to work cooperatively to achieve it.

In-Groups versus Out-Groups

Groups we identify with become ***in-groups***; groups we don't identify with become ***out-groups*** (see Chapter 4). This classifying and labeling affects our perceptions, emotions, and actions toward people in both types of groups. As you have seen, social categorization enables us to respond rapidly to people, so we don't have to spend a lot of time and cognitive effort collecting and weighing social information before taking any action. Although social categorization is efficient and can be helpful, it can also be dangerous when it leads to prejudice and discrimination.

Suppose you agree to participate in an experiment on art appreciation. You arrive at the laboratory along with a number of other research participants (between four to sixteen). You all are asked to rate pairs of paintings, indicating which you prefer. The works are modern abstract paintings by Paul Klee and Vassily Kandinsky, but you are not told the artists' names, and the paintings are unfamiliar. After making the ratings, some participants are told they belong in the "Klee group," while others are told they belong in the "Kandinsky group," ostensibly based on the paintings they preferred (actually the group membership is assigned at random). After forming these groups, the experimenter instructs the participants not to talk to each other, either within their own group or with members of the other group.

Stereotypes are beliefs about the characteristics of individuals based on their group membership.

Now the experiment really begins, because the whole aim of this elaborate ruse is to create two equivalent groups. This is called the ***minimal groups*** paradigm because the groups are based on the most trivial (minimal) of criteria. In one variation of this paradigm, the groups

◀ *The destructiveness of group rivalry to human relationships is a classic literary theme. In this updated version of Shakespeare's* Romeo and Juliet, *Romeo (played by Leonardo diCaprio) grabs a Capulet hostage during a gang fight.*

are created by a flip of a coin—it's difficult to get more minimal than that! Now the experimenter can investigate how being in a group can affect the behavior of the group members. Just separating people into two groups, even if the groups are based on the most trivial of criteria, can distort their attributions and bias their perceptions in ways that can contribute to prejudice and discrimination (Tajfel, 1982).

Formation of in-groups and out-groups distorts the attribution process. Whether people are in in-groups or out-groups will affect the attributions you make for their behavior, depending on whether you judge the behavior as being positive or negative (Jackson, Sullivan, & Hodge, 1993). Suppose you are sitting in the cafeteria, and you observe a student trip over Robert's foot, which was in the aisle between the tables. When the student attempts to apologize, Robert says, "Get away from me, you clumsy fool" in a voice loud enough to stop conversations twenty feet away. How do you explain Robert's behavior? If Robert is not a member of your group, that is, if he is part of an out-group, you might attribute his negative behavior to stable, internal causes and conclude he is arrogant, rude, and unforgiving. But if Robert is a member of your in-group, you might attribute his negative behavior to an unstable, external cause, and conclude that there must be something going on to explain the rude behavior of an in-group member. Perhaps the other student had stepped on Robert's foot many times before. Perhaps Robert was really hurt, or something else had upset him—maybe he received a bad grade, or his girlfriend broke up with him—making him temporarily and understandably irritable. We are often willing to do extensive cognitive work to maintain our positive image of in-group members.

How would you predict the attribution process will differ for positive behaviors of in-group and out-group members? Positive acts are more likely to be attributed to internal causes performed by an in-group member (Hewstone, 1990). Thus, when the in-group member succeeds, it is because of his or her ability. When an out-group member succeeds, we use a combination of causes (both ability and effort) to explain it. Our friends succeed because they are very intelligent. Other people succeed because they have some intelligence and work very hard. If our friends fail, it doesn't mean they aren't intelligent—they just didn't work hard enough. But if a member of the out-group fails, it's because of lack of ability (Hewstone, Gale, & Purkhardt, 1990). Thus, one study found that when women and/or African Americans (rather than men and/or Anglo Americans) succeeded (thereby breaking traditional stereotypes of less motivation and lower competence), their success was more often attributed to luck, lower task difficulty, or unusual amounts of effort (Yarkin, Town, & Wallston, 1982).

Perceptions, feelings, and actions of group members also become distorted in systematic ways. Types of bias include *in-group similarity, out-group homogeneity*, and *in-group favoritism.* We perceive greater similarity between ourselves and members of our in-group than between ourselves and members of our out-group. This ***similarity bias*** has been found in groups that were created by random assignments in an experiment as well as in "real-life" groups, such as fraternities (Allen & Wilder, 1979; Holtz & Miller, 1985). What might be some prejudicial effects of this bias? For one thing, it might contribute to greater group cohesion and in-group favoritism. The more we perceive people as similar to us, the more we like them (Byrne & Nelson, 1965).

"When you've seen one, you've seen them all" sums up ***out-group homogeneity bias***, which is the assumption that members of out-groups are more alike than are members of in-groups. We are more likely to perceive members of our in-groups as more complex and having multidimensional personalities. We see

► *In-group favoritism in action.*

"Surely not guilty. Next case."

THINKING CRITICALLY

What are the implications of the out-group homogeneity effect for eyewitness testimony?

Eyewitnesses to crimes may be less accurate in identifying members of racial and ethnic groups other than their own. Indeed, when research participants were first shown slides of a number of faces and later asked to pick out those faces from a larger number of slides, white participants made more errors in identifying black faces. This effect also held for the identification of white faces by black participants, although to a lesser extent (Anthony, Cooper, & Mullen, 1992).

our friend as the individual "Rita Gonzalez" rather than as "a Mexican American." We are also more likely to perceive subtypes among our in-groups. Latino students, for example, are more likely to make distinctions among Chicanos, Cubans, and Puerto Ricans than are Anglo Americans (Huddy & Virtanen, 1995). Simply categorizing people into two groups is sufficient to produce the out-group homogeneity bias, which can then be enhanced and confirmed (Tajfel, 1982).

Perceptions are often mutual, with each group viewing members of the other group as more homogeneous. This bias is found in mutual perceptions of women and men, blacks and whites, young and old, political conservatives and liberals, members of campus clubs, and rival schools (Quattrone & Jones, 1980; Jones, Wood, & Quattrone, 1981; Park & Rothbart, 1982).

In-group favoritism represents the positive feelings and special treatment that we give to in-group members and the negative feelings (prejudice) and unfair treatment (discrimination) that we give to out-group members (Tajfel, Flament, Billig, & Bundy, 1971). Once we identify with an in-group, we evaluate the in-group members more favorably, reward them more, and expect them to favor us (Brewer, 1979; Mackie, Worth, & Asuncion, 1990; Wilder, 1990). In-group favoritism is destructive to everyone, however, as it leads to in-group members trying to maximize their group's advantage over the out-group, even if that means everyone in the in-group suffers (Brewer, 1979; Tajfel & Turner, 1986).

Stereotypes

Stereotypes are beliefs about the characteristics of individuals based on their group membership. Stereotypes assign characteristics to virtually all group members, regardless of how their characteristics actually vary. Stereotypes are not always linked to prejudice and discrimination, but they provide a cognitive basis for them. They can come to mind automatically and be uttered without thinking, damaging our image and social relationships.

Veteran golfer Fuzzy Zoeller knows the ill effects of stereotypes. In April 1997, he fell victim to his stereotypes about African Americans in remarks he made about Tiger Woods, the youngest person to win the prestigious Masters golf tournament and someone he genuinely admires and respects. In an interview on the last day of the tournament, when it looked like Woods would win, Zoeller commented: "That little boy is driving well and he's putting well. He's doing everything it takes to win. So, you know what you guys do when he gets in here? You pat him on the back and say, 'Congratulations' and, 'Enjoy it' and tell him not to serve fried chicken next year. Or collard greens or

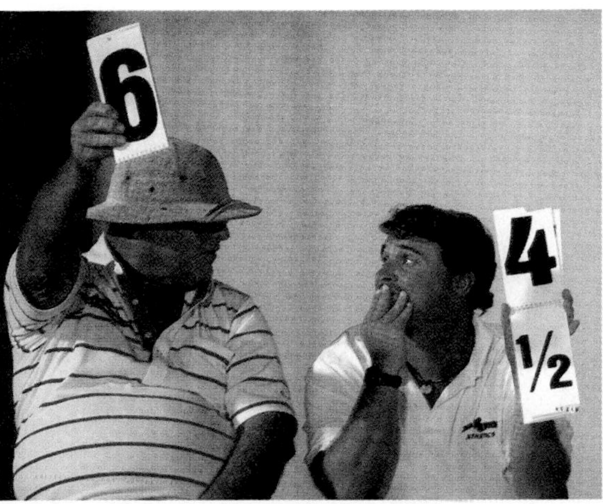

◀ *In-group favoritism is reflected in the difference between the scores of these diving judges, who represent opposing teams.*

Step 1:
Stimulus
Stereotype
Spontaneous processing
Step 2:
Inhibit stereotypes
Deliberative processing
Yes
No
Nonprejudiced response
Prejudiced response

12-9 When Do Stereotypes Lead to Prejudice?

When we encounter a stimulus, stereotypes are brought to mind automatically and effortlessly. But we can transform our reactions by controlled, deliberative processing.

whatever the hell they serve." (Zoeller's comments referred to the fact that the winner of the tournament traditionally chooses the menu for the Champions banquet held the following year.) These unthinking stereotyped remarks created such a negative reaction that Zoeller issued a public apology and felt compelled to stop playing in tournaments until he had a chance to "make things right" with Tiger Woods. In addition, the K-Mart Corporation stopped sponsoring Zoeller on the PGA tour because it didn't want to be associated with someone who would make such remarks. Understanding and avoiding stereotyping is clearly becoming ever more important as U.S. society becomes increasingly diverse.

The tendency to overestimate the relationship between two events, particularly when they are distinctive and meaningfully linked in some way, is called illusory correlation.

Zoeller's thinking became stereotypical when Tiger Woods became a "they" rather than a unique individual. In Zoeller's case, the inaccurate belief that all black people eat collard greens was stereotypically, if jokingly, applied to Tiger Woods. In his public apology to Woods, Zoeller emphasized that he did not intend for his comments to be racially derogatory. But the problem with stereotypes—and one reason they are often socially unacceptable regardless of intention—is that they don't have to be intentionally derogatory to have negative effects. They don't even have to involve undesirable behaviors—there's nothing wrong with eating collard greens! But even if we don't intend harm with our stereotypes, they can activate the negative stereotypes of others and reinforce prejudice and discrimination.

We use spontaneous processing when we rely on our social knowledge and beliefs about a group category (some or all of which may be false) to make inferences and attributions about the personality and behavior of individuals (see Figure 12-9). This can lead to stereotypes, which can develop in a number of ways. We may be taught them directly or we may learn them from observing others. We may create stereotypes because our basic cognitive processing leads us to perceive events that occur together as related. This means that casual observations can lead us to perceive relationships that aren't there—to perceive illusory correlations. ***Illusory correlation*** is the tendency to overestimate the relationship between two events, particularly when they are distinctive and meaningfully linked in some way (Chapman, 1967).

Illusory correlations develop because we are selective in what we notice and remember (see Chapter 8). Because we are more likely to notice and remember distinctive or meaningfully related events, we are more likely to perceive illusory correlations between them. This basic fact of our cognitive life means that we perceive and remember different things about the behaviors of majority and minority group members. This can occur even if we know nothing beforehand about the two groups.

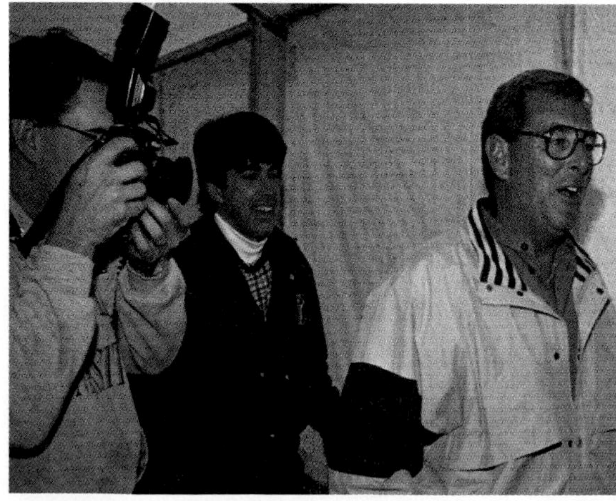

► *A photographer snaps Fuzzy Zoeller's picture after a news conference. The golfer had just announced he would not compete in a North Carolina tournament. Zoeller's stereotyped comments about Tiger Woods caused such an uproar that Zoeller made a public apology.*

The existence of illusory correlation in our perceptions of negative behavior of minority group members was demonstrated in a study of college students who read a series of sentences about each of the members of groups A and B, and who were then asked their opinions of the

SEEKING SOLUTIONS

Strategies for Intervention

Given what we know about stereotyping, prejudice and discrimination, what can be done to counter them? Methods for reducing stereotyping and prejudice include strategies that are individual-based (changing the way people think and feel) as well as group-based (changing situational factors). As individuals, if we make a conscious and deliberate effort to monitor our stereotypes, we are less likely to rely on them when making social judgments (Devine, 1989). Suppose that Sarah, an elementary school teacher, knows that she has a stereotype that boys are better at math than girls. Because Sarah believes herself to be a fair person and wants to provide an equal education for all her students, she would like to "break the habit" of viewing math performances of boys and girls differently. But whenever Sarah teaches math in her class, her old gender stereotypes become involuntarily activated. By becoming aware of her stereotypes, noticing them when they occur, consciously correcting them when they happen, and working to ensure they do not become expressed in her behavior, Sarah can make the choice to respond to her students in more egalitarian ways. Over time, this kind of thinking will gradually lead to a change in her stereotyped views.

Changing aspects of the social situation can be effective as well. One approach is to increase contact between groups. But if the contact occurs only in selective situations (where behaviors reinforce stereotypes), or if the contact is only with selective people from the out-group (those with stereotypical characteristics such as white pawnbrokers in an Hispanic neighborhood or Korean grocers in a black community), prejudice and discrimination will be maintained (Quattrone, 1986). Thus, contact must be with a wider variety of people from the out-group, and it must be structured to counter stereotypes (Neuberg & Fiske, 1987). The more contact you have with people who are your equals and who do not conform to your stereotypes, the less you will be able to label them as exceptions to your stereotypes. With increased information, people will come to view others in terms of individual, personal characteristics rather than on the basis of group membership.

Steps for reducing prejudice and discrimination have been used extensively in the classroom. These strategies have relied on the use of cooperative classroom techniques that encourage interaction and interdependence between students. One such method, called the "jigsaw classroom," developed by Elliot Aronson and his colleagues, involves cooperative learning in small groups (Aronson, Stephan, Sikes, Blaney, & Snapp, 1978). Students must rely on others to complete any given assignment, in much the same way each piece of a jigsaw puzzle is needed to complete the picture. Students in jigsaw classrooms show an increase in liking for each other and a decrease in prejudice.

Because prejudice and discrimination arise out of relationships between in-group and out-group members, another strategy is to redefine the boundaries of the groups. We all have many group identities—who belongs to our in-group depends on which group identity we have in mind. Focusing on the identities that we have in common can also foster better relationships among members of diverse groups. For example, all students have a common identity regardless of gender or ethnicity. People who live in the same community are all affected if the air is dirty and the water contaminated. And in the final analysis, we are all individuals, trying to survive. If we can extend the boundaries of our in-group identity to include humanity as a whole, we are a step closer to reducing our prejudices and potential for intergroup conflict.

◀ *Elliot Aronson's jigsaw classroom uses cooperation in small groups as a technique to combat prejudice.*

▲ *At five foot three, Muggsy Bogues of the Charlotte Hornets defies the stereotype that all basketball players must be tall.*

groups. Each sentence described a desirable or undesirable behavior on the part of a group member. Undesirable behavior was made more distinctive by making it less frequent: two-thirds of the behaviors were desirable ("visited a sick friend in the hospital"), and one-third were undesirable ("was late to work"). Group B was made more distinctive by making it in the minority: two-thirds of the statements were about members of group A (26 individuals) and one-third were about members of group B (13 individuals). The ratio of desirable to undesirable statements was the same for both groups.

Given that the ratio of positive and negative information about each group was equal, research participants should have developed equally favorable impressions of both groups—unless distinctiveness entered the picture and created an illusory correlation between group membership and negative behavior. This is indeed what happened: the participants overestimated the number of times undesirable behavior and group B went together (see Figure 12-10; Hamilton, Dugan, & Trolier, 1985). The fact that minority group members are encountered less frequently makes their behavior distinctive. Negative traits and behaviors are also encountered less frequently than positive ones. Thus, the occurrence of negative behavior on the part of members of a minority group is likely to be perceived, remembered, and overestimated, contributing to the development of stereotypes.

Stereotypes can contribute to illusory correlation as well by providing a story line that links negative behaviors and group membership. We tend to perceive and remember events that are meaningfully linked. For example, suppose you read twenty-four sentences, each linking a well-known occupation (accountant, doctor, salesman, flight attendant, librarian, and waitress) to a particular trait (attractive, busy, comforting, enthusiastic, loud, perfectionist, productive, serious, talkative, thoughtful, timid, wealthy). Each occupation is paired equally often with each trait. What happens when you are asked to estimate the number of times each pair occurred in the sentences that you read? If you are like typical research participants, you will overestimate the number of times you read about timid accountants, wealthy doctors, attractive flight attendants, serious librarians, and loud waitresses (Hamilton & Rose, 1980). Insofar as we have stereotypes that provide us with meaningful linkages between negative behaviors and minority group members, illusory correlation

12-10 Illusory Correlation and Distinctiveness

Illusory correlation is the tendency to overestimate the correlation between items that are distinctive in some way. Items that are fewer in number are generally more distinctive; they stand out because they are not typical of the majority. The graph shows how research participants estimated the correlations of positive and negative information about members of two groups, A and B. Group B was smaller than group A, which made behaviors by members of group B more distinctive, and therefore more likely to be noticed compared to behaviors by members of group A. Positive behaviors were more frequent than negative behaviors, at a ratio of 2:1, which made the negative behaviors more distinctive and therefore more likely to be noticed. Illusory correlation is demonstrated by the fact that the negative behaviors by members of group B were more likely to be remembered compared to either positive behaviors in group B or positive or negative behaviors in group A. (Source: Adapted from Hamilton & Gifford, 1976)

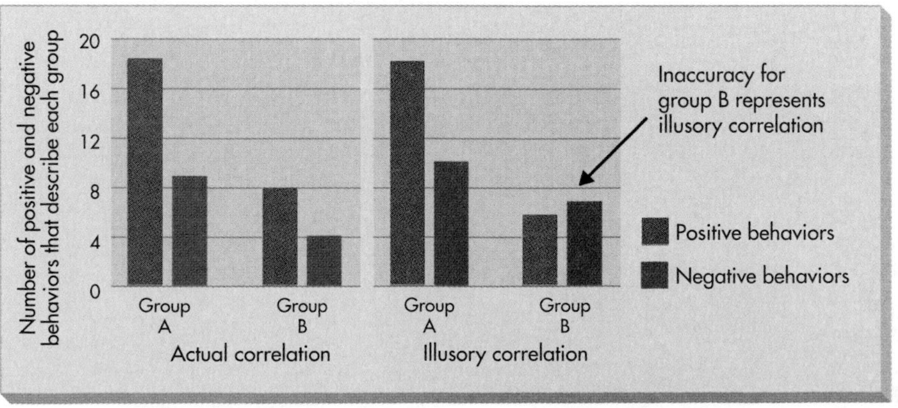

◀ *Gerónimo stands surrounded by his Apache warriors, both men and women.*

will occur, and we will perceive and remember negative behaviors on the part of members of minority groups and overlook and forget the same behaviors when they are performed by members of the majority group.

By fostering illusory correlations, stereotypes can distort reality and become resistant to change. Stereotypes are also resistant to change because of our tendency to discount or deny information inconsistent with our stereotypes, and if that isn't possible, to create a "subtype" of the stereotype and leave our original view intact (Kunda & Oleson, 1995). When you learned that Lozen, Gerónimo's "right hand," was a woman, did that piece of information change your image of the Apache warrior? Or did you create a special category for Lozen and keep your original image of the male Apache warrior intact? If so, you have maintained an inaccurate stereotype. In fact, the Chiricahua Apaches trained both young girls and boys in horse and weapon skills and encouraged all their women to fight. Wives routinely accompanied their husbands in battle, and the closest woman relative of a slain warrior was expected to lead the raid to avenge his death (Martín, 1997).

Attraction

Interpersonal attraction is an expression of our desire to approach and become involved with other people. What attracts us to others is affected by a variety of factors, including gender, class, and culture. A study of mate preferences in thirty-seven countries asked 9,500 people to rank order thirteen criteria for choosing a mate (for example, chastity, dependable character, good health). Although much has been made of gender differences in mate preferences, culture accounted for 14 percent of variation in preferences; gender accounted for only 2.4 percent (Buss et al., 1990). For Western undergraduates, both males and females display remarkable agreement on what is effective when it comes to attracting members of the opposite sex: being good humored, sympathetic, well-groomed, well-mannered, physically fit/healthy, clean, helpful, making an effort to spend time with the other person, and wearing

▼ *Proximity and similarity contributed to the attraction between this Bosnian couple, who met each other in a hospital after both lost legs during a Serbian attack.*

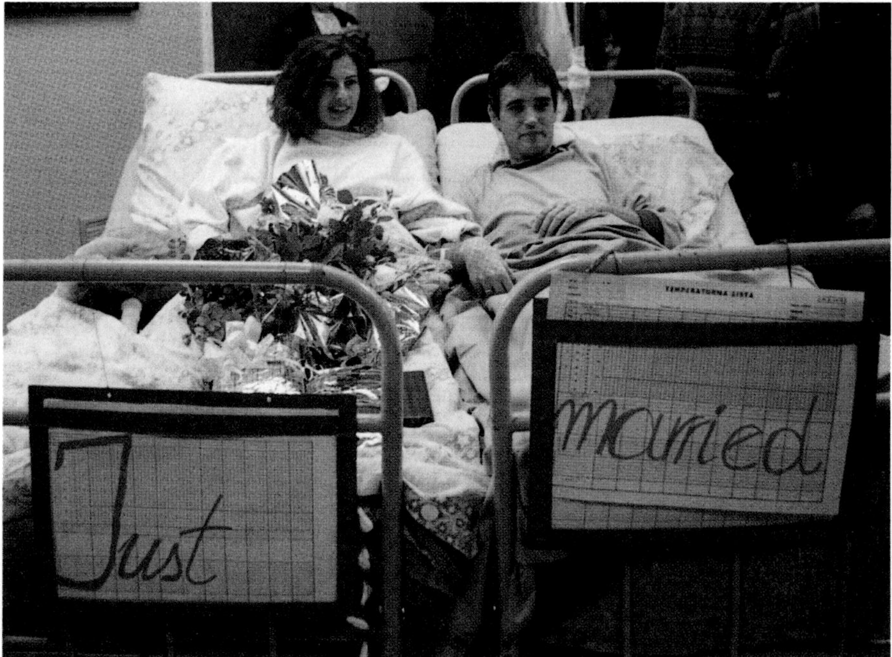

Table 12-2 How We Rank the Desired Characteristics of Potential Mates Depends on Gender and Culture

	American		Chinese		Zulu	
	Males	Females	Males	Females	Males	Females
Mutual attraction—love	1	1	4	8	10	5
Emotional stability and maturity	2	2	5	1	1	2
Dependable character	3	3	6	7	3	1
Pleasing disposition	4	4	13	16	4	3
Education and intelligence	5	5	8	4	6	6
Good health	6	9	1	3	5	4
Sociability	8	8	12	9	11	8
Desire for home and children	9	7	2	2	9	9
Refinement, neatness	10	12	7	10	7	10
Ambition and industriousness	11	6	10	5	8	7
Good looks	7	13	11	15	14	16
Similar education	12	10	15	12	12	12
Good financial prospect	16	11	16	14	18	13
Good cook and housekeeper	13	16	9	11	2	15
Favorable social status or rating	14	14	14	13	17	14
Similar religious background	15	15	18	18	16	11
Chastity (no prior sexual intercourse)	17	18	3	6	13	18
Similar political background	18	17	17	17	15	17

Note that 1 is considered most important, and 20 is considered least important.
Source: Buss et al., 1990.

the right clothes make the top ten list for both sexes (Buss, 1988) (see Table 12-2).

Let's consider four of the most important factors that influence interpersonal attraction: (1) proximity, (2) similarity, (3) reciprocity, and (4) beauty.

The Proximity Principle

Sheer ***proximity*** (being physically near someone) is one of the most powerful predictors of whether two people will become friends. Indeed, most people find their mates in their own neighborhoods, at their jobs, or at school. Studies of friendship patterns within apartments, local communities, and dormitories have shown that the closer you live to other people, the more likely you will become friends. For example, next-door neighbors are more likely to be thought of as friends than are people who live a block away from each other (Festinger, Schachter, & Back, 1950). Distance between residences predicts choice of dating partners among undergraduates (Whitbeck & Hoyt, 1994).

However, ***functional distance*** (how often and under what circumstances people's paths cross) matters more than geographical distance. Using the same entrances, parking lots, and recreation rooms, and sharing common laundry facilities, lounges, and sidewalks, all promote opportunities for interaction that result in friendships (Festinger, Schachter, & Back, 1950).

Some of proximity's effect is due to *frequency* of exposure. The finding, "familiarity breeds fondness," is well established (Moreland & Zajonc, 1982). But repeated exposure alone cannot account for the influence of proximity. A proximity effect continues even when you control for frequency of encounters. Moreover, spending more time with a person is no guarantee of friendship. As we get to know people better over time, we may end up disliking them if they do not share similar values, for example.

It could be that proximity leads us to expect continued interaction with our neighbors, and our desire for those interactions to be as pleasant as possible may contribute to a proximity effect (Festinger, Schachter, & Back, 1950). Researchers asked female college students to rate how much they liked two unknown women about whom they were given ambiguous information (Darley & Berscheid, 1967). When told they would shortly meet and have an intimate conversation with one of the women, participants reported liking that individual more. Thus, simply *anticipating* interaction with another person increases liking for them.

"Pardon me, but I can't help noticing that we share tastes in tropical-fruit-flavored chewing gum."
Drawing by Maslin; © 1992 The New Yorker Magazine, Inc.

◀ *We are attracted to people who are similar to us.*

The Similarity Principle

We have all heard the following sayings: "Birds of a feather, flock together," and "Opposites attract." But, which of these two contradictory adages is correct? Most social psychologists side with the birds. Just as perception of difference contributes to prejudice and discrimination, perception of similarity can lead to liking. Research from several countries establishes the importance of ***similarity***—of personality, values, and beliefs—in interpersonal attraction. We are attracted to people whose attitudes and values appear similar to our own (Byrne et al., 1971; Cappella & Palmer, 1990).

In one experiment, researchers gave participants—whose own attitudes on several topics were known—false information about attitudes of an unknown person whom they expected to meet (Byrne, 1969). The more similar the stranger's attitudes to their own were, the more positive were their evaluations of the stranger. Areas that promote attraction include similar attitudes and beliefs, academic success, and personal habits such as drinking, smoking, or being a "morning person" (Park & Flink, 1989). Similarity holds up over the long haul as well: married couples with similar personalities report greater marital happiness than those with dissimilar personalities (Antill, 1983).

Just as similarity brings us together, dissimilarity pushes us away (Rosenbaum, 1986). Whether we like people of another race or culture is affected by our beliefs about their similarity to us on important values. Indeed, the belief that other cultures are dissimilar and inferior to our own contributes to prejudice and discrimination. Dissimilarity of native cultures was used to justify pillage and killing when North America and Africa were colonized by Europeans. For most whites today, however, similar values are more important than similar physical characteristics such as skin color. As a consequence, whites express more liking for and willingness to work with blacks who share their views than with other whites of dissimilar views (Rokeach, 1968; Insko, Nacoste, & Moe, 1983).

There are certain situations in which *complementary behaviors* between individuals can promote attraction (Strong et al., 1988). If someone needs to be the leader and someone the follower, opposites can indeed attract. Complementarity may also affect our pattern of relationships if we perceive the achievements of others as threatening our own self-esteem. We may choose friends and partners who are like us in many ways but are successful in areas that are not central to our self-esteem. Thus, we can bask in their reflected glory while still being "number one" on our own turf (Tesser, 1988).

The Reciprocity Principle

We tend to return the feelings that we believe others have for us. This is known as the ***reci-***

procity principle. Thus, we like others when we believe they like us, and we dislike people that we believe dislike us. Furthermore, the more we believe someone likes us, the more we like them (Condon & Crano, 1988). In fact, one way to get other people to like us is to express liking toward them—a tactic that may work even though we know we are being flattered (Drachman, DeCarufel, & Insko, 1978).

When we believe that other people like us, we may disclose more about ourselves, speak to them more pleasantly, and disagree with them less frequently. Consistent with the principles of self-fulfilling prophecy and behavior confirmation, our expectations and behaviors encourage similar responses in return, setting the stage for the positive encounters that provide the foundation of friendship (Curtis & Miller, 1986). The opposite pattern occurs when we believe someone dislikes us.

THINKING CRITICALLY

The principle of reciprocity may lead to difficulties for shy people, whose passivity in interactions may be misinterpreted as dislike and reciprocated with avoidance. What steps might a shy person take to avoid or minimize this unfortunate circumstance?

If you know you're shy and you want to avoid offending a person whom you've just met, one strategy is to find out as much as you can about the individual in advance of your next meeting. Results of experiments have shown that your self-confidence grows with knowledge about a topic or person. Self-confidence is in turn a safeguard against a negative self-fulfilling prophecy (Leary, Kowalski, & Bergen, 1988). Another strategy is to identify interests that you share with the other person and mention them when it is appropriate. If people perceive you as having similar interests, they will be more likely to like you (similarity principle).

The "Beauty" Principle

Beauty is a greater recommendation than any introduction.

—Aristotle

The great amount of time and money that people spend shopping for and buying cosmetics and clothes, and participating in exercise programs and dieting, points to how important appearance is in our society. Advertisers are constantly telling us that attractiveness brings liking and even love. Is this true?

A large body of research on college students suggests that both sexes like physically attractive people more than physically unattractive ones—at least when it comes to first impressions (Hatfield & Sprecher, 1986). In a creative study, researchers randomly paired up 752 college freshmen at a "welcome week computer dance." When participants were later asked how much they enjoyed their date, their partner's intelligence, personality, and social skills had no significant relationship to enjoyment. For both males and females, physical attractiveness was the one thing that determined liking: the more attractive the date, the more he or she was liked and desired as a future date (Walster, Aronson, Abrahams, & Rottman, 1966).

► *We tend to find our partners more attractive than others do.*

We may seek physically attractive people more as dates and romantic partners because we perceive them as having other positive characteristics. We may implicitly assume that "what is beautiful is good." The opposite statement also holds true: "what is good is beautiful." If we like people, see them as similar to us, or know we share their values, we see them as more physically attractive (Klentz, Beaman, Mapelli, & Ullrich, 1987). If we love our partners, we are likely to find them more attractive—and all others less attractive (Myers, 1992).

Positive evaluations of attractive people occur even when physical attractiveness is presumably irrelevant to the dimension evaluated. Researchers had male research participants read either well-written or poorly written essays ostensibly composed by either an attractive or an unattractive woman (Landy & Sigall, 1974). Pictures of the "authors" were attached to the essays. Participants were then asked to rate the quality of the essays. The participants judged the essays that were supposedly written by the attractive women to be better than those written by the unattractive women, regardless of the actual quality of the writing.

Both men and women describe physically attractive people as more poised, interesting, sociable, independent, exciting, sexy, intelligent, well-adjusted, and socially skilled. There are limitations to this effect, however. Physical attractiveness does not appear to influence judgments of integrity or concern for others. Moreover, people think that physically attractive people are more likely to be vain and to lack modesty (Eagly, Ashmore, Makhijani, & Longo, 1991).

Clearly, physical attractiveness strongly affects the impressions we form and the attributions we make. Although its greatest effect is on first impressions, such impressions may determine the likelihood of future interactions, particularly for fleeting contacts so characteristic of our mobile, urban society (Berscheid, 1981). Does this mean that we will never find a mate if we are not strikingly attractive? No. Mate selection depends on many factors, including similarity—as a consequence, people typically marry someone who "matches" them on several characteristics, including interests, level of intelligence, and physical attractiveness (Feingold, 1988).

Although men and women generally give the same reasons for choosing a mate (Buss et al., 1990), there are some gender differences. In particular, men are more likely than women to be influenced by physical attractiveness (Simpson, 1990; Pierce, 1992). This may be because men are viewed more positively when paired with attractive women, while women are judged solely on their own attractiveness (Bar-Tal & Saxe, 1976).

Cultural Differences

Keep in mind the old adage that beauty is in the eye of the beholder. Definitions of beauty across cultures and time display extraordinary variety from head to toe, ranging from bizarre hairstyles, facial tattooing, and elongated necks to three-inch feet (attainable by binding feet from birth). But many cultures appear to value health, cleanliness, and feminine plumpness, perhaps because they indicate a woman's potential fitness to have healthy children (Ford & Beach, 1951; Singh, 1993).

Even so, concepts of beauty and attractiveness are changed by culture. In the United States, the well-rounded, shapely appearance epitomized by Marilyn Monroe in the 1950s is no longer the predominant image in fashion magazines. Rather, beauty ideals for women, perpetuated by advertisers and the media, currently exalt a body type at times so thin that it has historically been associated with disease and death. This may change as the destructive effects of eating disorders become more widely understood. Similarly, although pale skin was once viewed as the height of attractiveness in Western society (it was a sign of being upper class and not having to work outside in the sun), people now view having a tan as attractive and healthy, even though tans create a higher risk for skin cancer (Broadstock, Borland, & Gason, 1992). Changes in beauty fads and fashion remind us of the power of our culture to shape our values and motivations, even when they raise our risk of disease and death.

Behavior in Groups

People behave differently when they are in the presence of others than when they are alone. We will focus on four ways the presence of others can influence individual behavior: (1) social facilitation and inhibition; (2) pressures to conform, comply, and obey; (3) group interaction processes; and (4) deindividuation.

Social Facilitation and Inhibition

Even when we are not interacting with and comparing ourselves to others, we can still be influenced by their mere presence. Early research indicated that people perform better when they have an audience; this is known as ***social facilitation***. For example, runners typically set their best times in competition, where

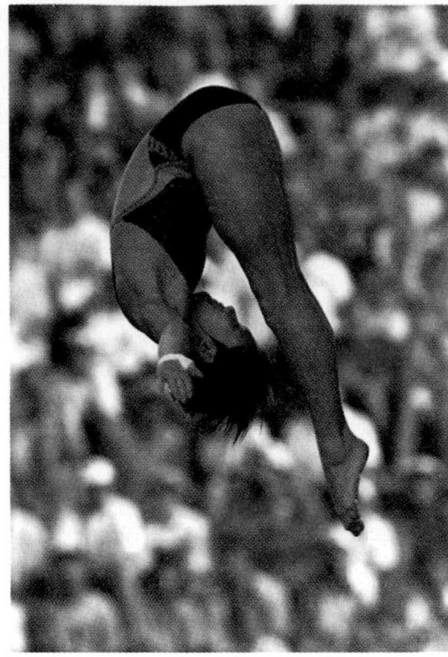

▲ *Having an audience may impair the performance of amateur divers, making them more likely to bellyflop, but brings out the best in Olympians such as China's Fu Mingxia.*

Conformity is the tendency to adopt, in the presence of others, the perceived values, attitudes, and behaviors of the group.

other runners are present and there is an interested audience. Later research has revealed instances, however, when an audience impairs performance—this is known as ***social inhibition***. A novice speaker may deliver a speech flawlessly in front of a mirror, but become rattled on stage in front of an audience.

To account for these discrepant findings, Robert Zajonc postulated that the presence of other people is motivating, arousing, or drive-producing (Zajonc, 1965). In keeping with the Yerkes-Dawson law, increased drive or arousal facilitates performance, but only up to a point. Beyond that, it interferes with performance (see Chapter 10). The point at which performance starts its decline is determined by the difficulty of the task at hand (see Figure 12-11). If a situation requires simple, well-learned behaviors, a high drive level will facilitate performance. Thus, work on simple math or spelling problems might be improved in front of an audience. But when the situation calls for complex or poorly learned responses, others' presence typically impairs performance. Good pool players make a greater percentage of shots when people watch them play, while poor players miss more shots (Michaels, Bloommel, Brocato, Linkous, & Rowe, 1982). In general, experts at any task do well in front of an audience, while novices tend to "choke."

12-11 The Relationship of Arousal to Performance

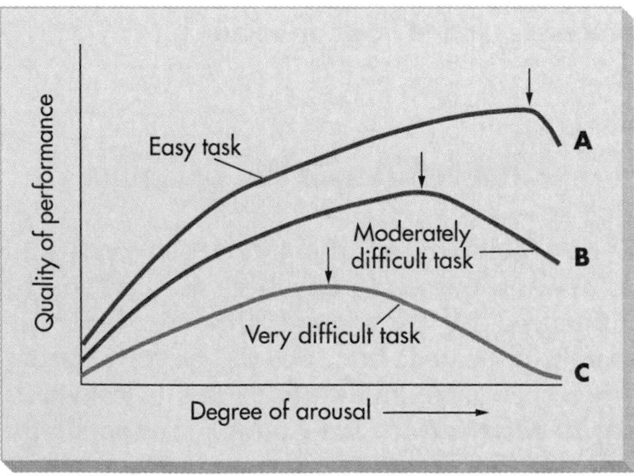

According to the Yerkes-Dodson law, increased drive (arousal) facilitates task performance only up to a point. Beyond that, it interferes with performance. The optimal level for a task depends on task difficulty. Tasks requiring well-learned behaviors are facilitated by high arousal (A). Performance on complex and novel tasks is impaired by high levels of arousal (C). Performance on moderately difficult tasks falls between the two (B).

Conformity

In the presence of others, we tend to adopt the perceived values, attitudes, and behaviors of the group—we ***conform***. We may conform for a variety of very good reasons. We may believe that others have better *information* and thus that their opinions or behaviors are more likely to be correct, especially if the others agree with one another. We may want to *avoid ostracism* (being excluded from a group) or other negative consequences of disagreeing with the group. We may *identify* with the group—we want to be like others whom we like and admire—and *internalize* group norms and values, thus adopting the group's views and actions as appropriate, right, and our own.

Conformity is at its highest when we believe we are the only one who deviates from the group. Suppose you participate in a study in which you and fellow students are shown various groups of three lines and asked to pick out the one that is equal to a line seen previously. You are the last to answer, and as the others announce their responses, you find that they are all picking the same *wrong* line. What would you do?

This is basically what occurred in a classic study by Solomon Asch (1956). A participant was asked to sit around a table with six other individuals and judge which of three lines was equal in length to a standard line they had seen earlier (see Figure 12-12). Unknown to the participant, the rest of the members of the group were confederates (allies) of the experimenter: they had already been instructed to give certain answers, regardless of actual line length. Sometimes the confederates' answers were wrong, sometimes they were right. When the majority was unanimous, the participant showed signs of stress (double-checking and so on), but tended to make his or her judgment consistent with the judgments of the others, even when those judgments were obviously wrong. But when there were two uninformed participants in the group, the tendency to conform to the group substantially declined (see Figure 12-13).

Asch also explored what would happen if a large minority of individuals (nine confederates out of twenty group members) gave a consistent, but wrong answer. Although they weren't able to change the answers of the majority, those in the minority were treated respectfully (Asch, 1952). Other research has established that, if people holding miniority views are consistent in and certain of their position, they can induce members of a majority to rethink their views and see issues in a new way (Moscovici, Lage, & Naffrechoux, 1969; Nemeth, Swedlund, & Kanki, 1974).

On average, women are slightly more likely to conform than men. Why? It may be that conforming behaviors have different meanings, depending on gender. Females are expected to be more concerned with interpersonal relationships, and to be more responsive to others; these female gender role expectations are more likely to lead to more conformity in women than in men (Eagly, 1987). In addition, women tend to link competence with cooperation and agreement, while men link it with competition and distinguishing themselves from other group members (Santee & Jackson, 1982). Cross-cultural studies comparing individualist and collectivist cultures find greater conformity "the more one's fate is interdependent with that of others" (Smith & Bond, 1994, p. 154). In cultures where women have a lower status and are dependent on men, women may be more likely to conform than are men.

▼ *In Solomon Asch's conformity studies, the participant would exhibit signs of stress when the experimenter's confederates all made the same incorrect choice.*

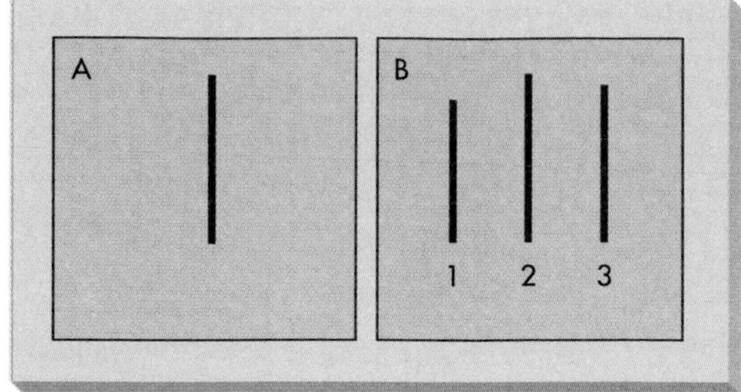

12-12 Asch's Stimulus in the Conformity Study

In his study of conformity, Solomon Asch presented participants with a line on card A, and then presented them with card B, on which there were three lines of varying length. The participants had to identify which line from the second card matched the line on the first card. (Source: Asch, 1956)

Recall from Chapter 4 that gender is a master status, so its norms may carry over from the real world into the laboratory. Lower status people are more likely to conform, and traditionally, female gender has had a lower status. In the presence of a male experimenter, males may be more likely to conform to individualistic and competitive male sex role norms rather than to norms of the experimental group. Thus, males and females may be equally conforming, but just to different things. It is always important to remember that experimenters operate within a

12-13 Asch's Results in the Conformity Study

Asch had seven research participants who had to determine which line on one card was the same length as the line on a card they had seen previously. Six of the participants were confederates of Asch and judged the line according to the instructions they were given. The graph shows the responses of the "naive participant" who was not a confederate of the experimenter under three conditions: no opposition (the confederates did not lie about the length of the lines), alone against majority (when the naive participant alone gave the correct length of the lines, and all the confederates lied about the length of the lines), with partner (when one confederate did not lie and agreed with the naive participant about the length of the lines). All it takes is one person to counteract the conformity effect. (Source: Asch, 1955)

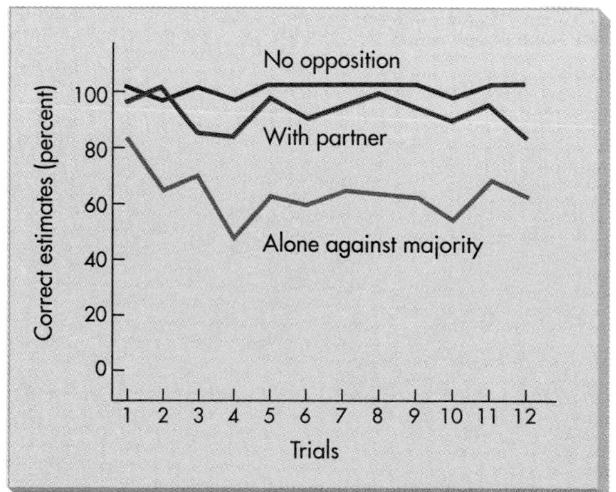

culture, and this can influence how experimental conditions are experienced and interpreted by research participants.

Compliance

Compliance is agreeing with an explicit request from someone with *no* authority over you.

Compliance is agreeing with an explicit request from someone who has *no* authority over you (if you agreed with someone in authority, the term would be "obedience"). The difference between compliance and obedience is at least in part the difference between a "request" and an "order." How a request is made often affects whether a person complies with it or not.

Robert Cialdini suggests that persuasive techniques are predominantly based on six social-psychological principles that have been found to underlie much of American social behavior (Cialdini, 1985). You have already been introduced to three of them: *consistency*, which makes us feel we should do what we have said we believe in, and the related principles of *reciprocity*, which makes us feel we should return favors, and *attraction*, which increases our tendency to comply with the requests of people we like or are attracted to. In addition, we often use other people's behavior (particularly similar others) to guide our own actions *(social validation)*, to overvalue what we think is rare or what we think may be taken from us *(scarcity)*, and to comply with requests of others who have, or who we believe have, greater information and power than we do *(authority)*. Such principles underlie the compliance techniques used by people who know they don't have the power to force us to do something against our will or better judgment but who hope to find a way to get us to do what they want. A short period of television watching will confirm their widespread use. Indeed, legitimate sales persons, con artists, politicians, and even our own friends and relatives may try to influence us by one or more of these techniques. By learning about the principles of influence and how techniques are derived from them, you may be less likely to do something that you really don't wish to do.

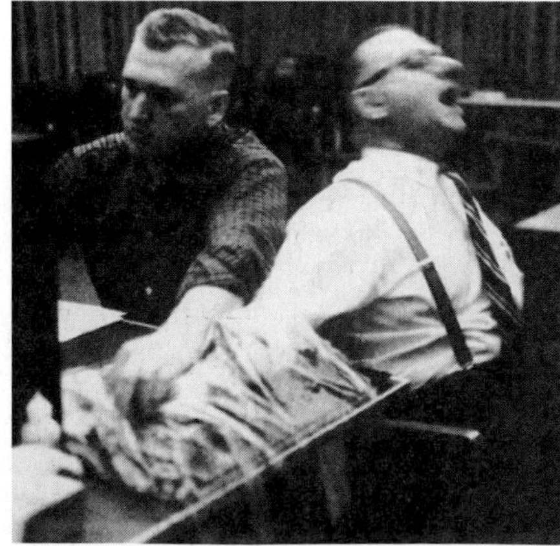

► *Stanley Milgram's research on obedience demonstrated that normal healthy individuals can be persuaded to administer harmful shocks to others if instructed to do so by an authority figure.*

Obedience

Suppose you go to the emergency room with a major ache in your right ear. A physician orders eardrops. Upon receiving written instructions, the nurse on duty tries to administer the drops rectally. What would you do? This bizarre incident actually happened, as reported by two pharmacy professors (Cohen & Davis, 1981). The physician's instructions read "place in R ear." Amazingly, neither the patient nor the nurse questioned the misinterpreted orders. One can only wonder how many similar miscommunications between doctors, pharmacists, and nurses go unnoticed.

Our tendency to comply with authority figures can be surprisingly strong, even in individualistic cultures, as powerfully demonstrated in a classic study by Stanley Milgram (1965). Milgram told research participants to administer electric shocks to another participant for making errors in a learning experiment and to increase the intensity of the shocks after each error. The "victim"—a confederate who was not actually shocked—deliberately made repeated errors. As the severity of the shocks increased, the victim appeared very upset, complained about having a bad heart, and pleaded with the investigator to end the experiment. When psychology majors and psychiatrists were asked to predict the outcome, both groups believed only a very small percentage of research participants would obey the experimenter's request to continue the shocks. Despite victims' pleas, most participants (over 60 percent) continued to administer shocks—often approaching a level labeled "lethal"—with only minimal urging by the experimenter.

Milgram's results are shocking in more ways than one. They demonstrate how normal, healthy, intelligent people can be persuaded to carry out destructive acts when asked to do so by individuals in authority, even in a culture

SEEKING SOLUTIONS

Compliance Principles and Techniques

Whether they are aware of the psychological terms for them, fundraisers and salespeople often make use of six basic compliance principles in order to convince people to make a donation or purchase. When you are asked to donate to a cause or go to buy a car, television, or audio system, keep in mind that you may be the target for ploys based on these principles, and that they have little to do with the value of the product itself.

Some of the techniques are derived from the consistency principle, which is based on the fact that, after committing ourselves to a position, we are more willing to comply with requests that are consistent with that position. In the *"foot-in-the-door" technique,* the fundraiser first asks someone to do a small favor that is highly likely to be granted. Then the fundraiser requests a related, larger favor, which will now be granted. This technique may work because performing the first, small favor causes the target person to consider himself/herself as having certain traits (charity, generosity). Another technique derived from the consistency principle is the *"bait-and-switch" technique*, in which a customer arrives at a store in response to an ad, only to find the advertised items are inferior or absent. Having made the commitment to buy certain items, however, the customer may agree to purchase alternate (and presumably more costly) merchandise.

A second principle is the reciprocity principle, which says that we are more willing to comply with a request from someone who has previously provided a favor or concession. Along these lines, fundraisers use the *"door-in-the-face" technique*, in which a requester begins with an extreme amount (please donate $100), that is nearly always rejected, then retreats to requesting a more moderate amount (how about $10?). The expectation is that the willingness to retreat will be reciprocated by a willingness to contribute. Another technique that uses the reciprocity principle is the *"that's-not-all"* technique, in which, after making the first offer, but even before the offer is rejected, the requester makes a better offer ("sweetens" the deal), which was the deal the requester had in mind in the first place. In this way, the target person has not entered the mode of rejecting the requester and has even received a "favor" in the form of a better offer. Now the target is expected to return the favor.

The social validation principle says that we are more willing to comply with a request for behavior if it is consistent with what similar others are thinking or doing. This principle is used in the *"list" technique.* The fundraiser only makes a request of the target person after showing him or her a list of names of similar others who have already given money. In the *"social labeling" technique,* the fundraiser informs the target person that other people have labeled the target person in a specific way, which makes the target person more willing to comply with requests that are consistent with the label (for example, "You're known as an avid supporter of children, please contribute to the children's fund.").

According to the attraction principle, we're more willing to comply with the requests of friends or other liked individuals. Because physical attractiveness promotes liking, attractive models are used in ads and attractive people as sales representatives. Because similarity promotes liking, models that present themselves as "typical" people (just like you!) are used to sell merchandise. Further, those who "cooperate" with others engender positive feelings. Hence, sales managers often play the villain while the salesperson "battles" on behalf of the customer.

According to the scarcity principle, we attempt to secure opportunities that are scarce or dwindling, and we more highly value things that are taken away from us. In the *"limited numbers" technique*, customers who are told that an item is sold out at that store location but might be available at another location are more eager to purchase the item. In the *"deadline" technique*, customers are told that a special price is only available for a limited time, or only for as long as the customer is in the store.

Finally, salespeople make use of the authority principle, which says that we are more willing to follow the suggestions of someone who is a legimate authority. One technique uses *claimed or implied expertise*, as when a manufacturer claims "Babies are our business, our only business," or the trappings of expertise (for example, when an actor wears a physician's white coat to promote a health-related product).

Be aware of these principles and techniques, so that you don't give more money to a cause than you can afford or end up buying a product that you would normally not be willing to buy and that you'll want to return in the morning.

▶ *The effectiveness of David Koresh in controlling his Waco cult illustrates the power of group conformity and obedience to authority.*

that values independent thinking. Although the proportion of people obeying varies, studies in other countries, including Australia, Austria, Italy, Germany, Holland, Jordan, Spain, and the United Kingdom found similar results (Smith & Bond, 1994). The effectiveness of vicious political dictators, such as Adolf Hitler in Germany, Joseph Stalin in Russia, Saddam Hussein in Iraq, and Pol Pot in Cambodia, as well as the power of cult leaders, such as Do and Ti of Heaven's Gate or David Koresh of an apocalyptic cult in Waco, Texas, show how group conformity and obedience to authority can lead to self-destruction.

Group Polarization

If conformity and obedience were the only influences on people's decisions, we would expect a group to reach decisions advocated by the majority of its members. Likewise, people with extreme opinions would move toward the group average. Yet, groups tend to make more extreme decisions than their individual members would. This phenomenon is called the ***group polarization effect***. The direction that group polarization takes—toward greater or lesser risk—depends on the initial positions of group members. If they are initially inclined toward a risky decision, groups will increase risk-taking. If group members lean toward conservatism, groups will decrease risk-taking.

The group polarization effect has been found in a variety of situations around the world. For example, Canadian business students were more likely to recommend risky investments to prevent further losses in failing business projects if they made decisions in groups (Whyte, 1993). Japanese students were more likely to consider a defendant guilty in a traffic case if the judgments were made *after* group discussion (Isozaki, 1984).

▼ *Although these women are all working together, social loafing can occur in situations like the one shown here. Social loafing is less likely when the person's contribution is indispensable.*

Social Loafing and Bystander Apathy

When people cooperate on a common task, it seems logical to assume that the group's output should at least equal the sum of each member's output. But when people believe their individual contribution to the group cannot be detected or measured, something different happens. Under these circumstances, individual output may diminish. Researchers call this phenomenon ***social loafing*** (Latané, Williams, & Harkins, 1979). Experiments demonstrate that six people clapping or shouting "as loud as you can" make less than three times the noise of one person. Social loafing appears widespread, having been found in India, Japan, Malaysia, Taiwan, and Thailand (Gabrenya, Wang, & Latané, 1985).

We can observe social loafing in a variety of tasks, from pulling ropes in a tug-of-war, to producing ideas, and pool typing. It is less apt to occur in challenging, appealing, or involving tasks, or when people believe their contribution is essential (Jackson & Williams, 1985; Brickner, Harkins, & Ostrom, 1986). People work harder when they believe other group members can't contribute much to the group effort (Williams & Karau, 1991; Karau & Williams, 1993). Furthermore, social loafing is affected by how meaningful, engaging, and appealing a task is, how quickly feelings of cohesiveness with others can be established in a group, and how indispensable a person feels to the group.

In groups, people may feel that praise or blame is less dependent on their individual output than when they perform alone. People can "hide in crowds" and avoid the negative consequences of slacking off. The temptation to slack off may grow both with the size of the group and the effort needed for the task. When individual performance can be identified and evaluated (as when athletic coaches film and evaluate each athlete on their team), social loafing declines significantly (Harkins & Szymanski, 1989). For example, swim team members have better times in intrasquad races if their individual times are monitored and announced (Williams, Nida, Baca, & Latané, 1989).

Although social loafing applies across cultures, including some collectivist Asian cultures, it has not yet been found in all Asian cultures. Social loafing has not been found in China, for example (Earley, 1993). This underscores the importance of not thinking that all Asian cultures are alike just because they are labeled "collectivist." If tasks are important and meaningful to the participants, there is less social loafing in both collectivist and individualistic cultures (Smith & Bond, 1994).

Bystander apathy—the fact that individuals are less likely to help a victim in need when others are present—is related to social loafing. (Darley & Latané, 1968). The more bystanders present in an emergency, the less likely that any one of them will help the victim, and the more time will pass before anyone offers help (see Figure 12-14). A major factor in bystander apathy is ***diffusion of responsibility***: when responsibility to act is spread across all people present, the responsibility of any one individual in the group is diluted, and no one acts. We don't yet know whether this explanation applies broadly across cultures.

Deindividuation

In 1992, during riots in Los Angeles, a group of youths pulled truck driver Reginald Denny from his truck and beat him viciously. How do psychologists explain why people are more aggressive and violent in groups than when acting alone?

The concept of ***deindividuation***, or loss of personal identity through anonymity, is one answer as to why individuals in groups engage in behavior that they would consider wrong if they were alone. Loss of personal identity and responsibility was proposed as an explanation for crowd violence a century ago (LeBon, 1895). Crowd members feel less personally responsible for their behavior, less likely to be punished because they cannot be identified, and more prone to behave violently. Cross-cultural evidence for this effect is found in a study on battle practices. In the cultures where warriors hid their identities before battle (using face paint or

◀ *During a Los Angeles riot, Reginald Denny was pulled from his truck and beaten. Looting was also widespread during the riot. Deindividuation helps explain why people perform acts in crowds they would consider wrong if they were alone.*

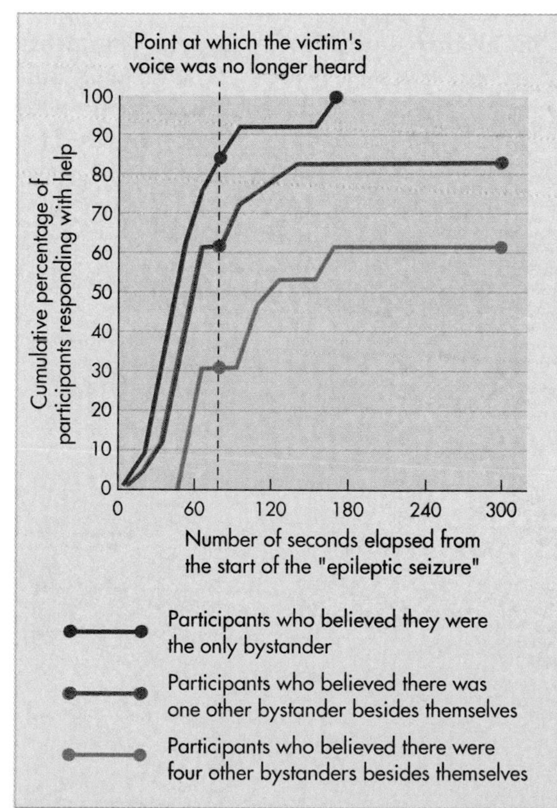

12-14 Bystander Apathy

The larger the number of bystanders present in an emergency, the more time passes before anyone offers to help. When people believed they were in the presence of someone having an epileptic seizure and were the only bystander, they were more likely to help than if they believed they were in the presence of one other bystander. When they believed they were in the presence of four other bystanders, they took even longer to help. This bystander effect is thought to occur because of diffusion of responsibility. (Adapted from Darley & Latané, 1968) masks), they were more likely to torture, mutilate, and kill captives than warriors who did not hide their identities (Watson, 1973).

Philip Zimbardo demonstrated the impact of deindividuation in a series of ingenious experiments. Using an approach similar to Stanley Milgram's research on obedience, Zimbardo focused on how deindividuation affected the willingness of participants to administer shock. In one study, groups of four females sat around listening to recorded interviews of people to whom they would later administer shocks (Zimbardo, 1969). Some women were "deindividuated," that is, they wore white gowns and hoods to disguise themselves (losing their individual identities through uniformity of dress), and the experimenters never used their names. In other groups, the women were not disguised; they wore large name tags and referred to each other by name. After listening to interviews, the interviewees arrived and each group member was induced to deliver shocks to the "victims." The victim (actually a confederate of the experimenter) acted as if she were being shocked (no shocks were actually delivered). The key finding was that women in the deindividuated groups delivered longer shocks than those in the identifiable groups. This was true regardless of whether they perceived the victim as a pleasant or an unpleasant person.

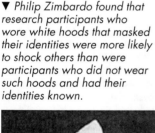

Deindividuation is a loss of personal identity in a group that can lead to actions that would normally not occur alone. Anonymity is a major contributor to deindividuation.

In another study, male student volunteers played the roles of guards and prisoners in a simulated prison atmosphere, complete with walls, bars, prisoner and guard uniforms (Haney, Banks, & Zimbardo, 1973). Research participants were typical college students who had been randomly assigned to their roles. Nonetheless, being assigned the role of prison guard led students to behave spontaneously in ways they would consider immoral outside the "prison" environment (see Chapter 2). For example, they forced their fellow students to do push-ups or to stand at attention and say "Yes, Mr. Correctional Officer" in response to verbal abuse. Thus, taking on roles in the experiment's social structure apparently led the guards to become deindividuated, that is, to be less conscious of themselves as individuals. They became insensitive to norms of social morality and responsibility that they typically followed outside the experimental setting.

Whether deindividuation leads to aggressive behavior appears to depend on situational cues. The white, hooded outfits worn by women in Zimbardo's experiment may have been reminiscent of Ku Klux Klan uniforms, making them a cue for aggressive responses. When researchers repeated Zimbardo's study, this time dressing women in nurses' uniforms, deindividuation led to *less* aggression (Johnson & Downing, 1979).

Deindividuation thus appears to lower our inhibitions based on fear, guilt, and shame, making us more responsive to external cues, which can be negative or positive (KKK garb versus a nurse's uniform). Even innocuous group experiences, such as wearing athletic uniforms, chanting, clapping, dancing, and singing, can diminish our awareness of ourselves and our values and can make us more likely to act without thinking. Such research suggests that encouraging self-awareness and making people accountable for their actions can provide a counter to the effects of deindividuation (Prentice-Dunn & Rogers, 1980, 1989; Rehm, Steinleitner, & Lilli, 1987).

▼ *Philip Zimbardo found that research participants who wore white hoods that masked their identities were more likely to shock others than were participants who did not wear such hoods and had their identities known.*

Reflections and Observations

Social psychology helps us understand social diversity, identifying how cognitive processes can distort our perceptions of social reality and contribute to stereotyping and prejudice. Social psychology focuses on the individual, explaining how our social knowledge, cognitive processes, and self-conceptions affect how we perceive, evaluate, and interact with others in our cultural settings. It recognizes that biological, psychological, and sociocultural factors interact to influence behavior as diverse as prejudice and discrimination and interpersonal attraction. Social psychology helps us to understand both everyday social relationships and extreme behaviors. We will continue to emphasize these themes in the next chapter, where we explore how health psychologists apply psychological knowledge to prevent illness and disease as well as to promote health and well-being.

Objectives Revisited

Social behavior is determined jointly by the person *and* the situation. Whether the presence of others—actual or imagined—affects our behavior depends on numerous factors, including our social knowledge, our cognitive processes, and our concept of self, as well as the situation itself and the characteristics of others.

Objective 1. Define social psychology, and explain how social knowledge and causal attributions influence the way we perceive, think, and behave.

Social psychology is the scientific study of how the real or imagined presence of others influences our behaviors, thoughts, and feelings. *Social categorization* is our tendency to automatically, unconsciously, and involuntarily apply categories to understand our social world. Social knowledge is represented in the mind as *schemas*, which organize our beliefs and feelings about our social world. Social categorization is an adaptive process that enables us to conserve our limited cognitive resources and call on our schemas of past social experiences to guide our actions.

Schema-based *inferences* influence how we perceive, think about, and behave toward others. They can create *self-fulfilling prophecies*, expectations about future behavior that increase the probability of that behavior. *Behavioral confirmation* is the behavior change that occurs in response to such expectations. Biases can influence the accuracy of schema-based inferences, particularly in impression formation.

An *attribution* is an inference regarding the probable cause of an event in order to make the world predictable and consistent. Knowing how and why something occurs gives us the ability to predict future events and behaviors and allows us to structure our behaviors in accordance with these expectations.

Whether our attributions are *internal or external, stable or unstable, controllable or uncontrollable* affects our emotions and expectations in different ways. Explanations of behavior reflect past experience and cultural scripts and stereotypes. Biases in the attribution process result in different judgments about individuals and groups, depending on who is doing the observing and who is being observed, and include *correspondence bias*, the *fundamental attribution error*, and the *actor-observer effect*. Attribution may be affected by desires to maintain self-esteem. We have a *self-serving* bias, whereby we tend to take responsibility for our successes (internal) but attribute our failures to external factors. We can also more easily remember information if it is self-relevant (*self-relevant effect*).

Objective 2. Explain what the consistency principle is, and discuss predictions and evidence in support of cognitive dissonance and self-perception consistency theories.

The *consistency principle* says that people are *motivated* to achieve cognitive consistency with regard to objects, events, and persons in their environment. Inconsistency among thoughts and actions creates the uncomfortable and motivating state of *cognitive dissonance*. Dissonance is strongest when self-image is threatened; dissonance depends on the strength of our belief in our cognitions and how relevant we consider these cognitions are to our actions. Festinger's theory of cognitive dissonance and Bem's theory of self-perception are two examples of con-

KEY TERMS

social psychology

social schema

scripts

attributions

correspondence bias

fundamental attribution error

actor-observer effect

false-consensus bias

self-serving bias

cognitive dissonance

attitude

sleeper effect

elaboration likelihood model

prejudice

discrimination

stereotype

sistency theories. Both have been used to explain the *insufficient justification effect*, depending on the circumstances, and have been found to apply in different circumstances.

Objective 3. Discuss the relationship between attitudes and behavior, and explain what makes a communication persuasive.

Attitudes toward a person or object may or may not accurately predict behavior toward that person or object. Attitudes are more likely to predict behavior if they are strongly held, if they are specific to the behavior, and if we are not under external pressure to behave in a different manner.

Persuasiveness of a communication depends on the characteristics of the communicator, the message, and the situation in which the communication takes place. Communicator *credibility*, which depends on perceived expertness, trustworthiness, prestige, attractiveness, and similarity to the message recipient, increases communication persuasiveness. The impact of a message over time will increase if the reasons for discounting it, such as low communicator credibility, are more quickly forgotten than the message itself (*sleeper effect*). Characteristics of the message and of the situation that distract you from message content can increase message persuasiveness.

The elaboration likelihood model explains attitude change in terms of how we process information. Messages that are important and personally relevant are processed by the *central route* and are scrutinized. Quantity of arguments are important, and if attitude change occurs, it is more likely to endure. Information that is uninteresting or uninvolving is processed by the *peripheral route*. Here positive associations are important, and attitude change is easier to produce but less enduring.

Objective 4. Explain the interrelationships among prejudice, stereotyping, and discrimination.

Prejudice is a special kind of attitude, usually negative, toward members of a particular group. It differs from *discrimination*, the actual behavior toward individuals based on group membership. *Stereotypes* are social schemas that represent beliefs about characteristics associated with groups of people. They distort reality, are resistant to change, and underlie prejudice and discriminatory behaviors. Stereotypes are perpetuated by the cognitive processes involved in social categorization, including *outgroup homogeneity bias* and *illusory correlation*.

Objective 5. Discuss the factors that affect interpersonal attraction.

Interpersonal attraction expresses our need for affiliation, and is affected by *proximity*, *similarity*, *reciprocity*, and *beauty* principles. Generally, we are attracted to those who live close by, to similar others, to those who are attracted to us, and to physically attractive (particularly handsome or beautiful) others. The influence of these factors is shaped by the nature of our cognitive processes and our desire for consistency and predictability.

Objective 6. Discuss various ways in which the presence of others influences individual behavior through (1) social facilitation and inhibition; (2) pressures to conform, comply, and obey; (3) processes of group interaction; and (4) deindividuation.

Social facilitation is the tendency to perform better in the presence of others, while *social inhibition* is the tendency to perform worse in others' presence. Which behavior occurs depends on one's level of expertise combined with task difficulty.

People *conform* in the presence of others because they (1) believe others have more information, (2) fear ostracism for deviant behavior, (3) identify with the group, and (4) internalize the group's norms.

Compliance is agreeing to an explicit request of someone who has no authority over you. Cialdini has identified several compliance techniques based on basic principles of consistency, reciprocity, attraction, social validation, scarcity, and authority. The six principles of reciprocity have led to a variety of compliance techniques.

Obedience, or compliance with authority, is strong, even in our individualistic culture. Even healthy, normal individuals can be persuaded to hurt others when asked to do so by people in positions of authority.

In *group polarization*, groups tend to make more extreme decisions than their individual members would. The group polarization effect has serious implications for real-world problems, including terrorism, mob behavior, and development of prejudice.

In performing a task as a member of a group, a person may shirk (*social loafing*) because neither praise nor blame can be allocated accurately. People are less likely to loaf when the task is challenging or appealing and when they perceive their contribution as essential to the group.

Bystander apathy is when no one in a crowd of onlookers will help a person in need, such as a victim of a crime. It may be explained by *diffusion of responsibility*, wherein the presence of other people leads each participant to feel less responsible for causing a problem or for taking action.

Deindividuation refers to the loss of personal identity through anonymity in groups, resulting in lowered fear, guilt, and shame, and increased responsiveness to external cues. The resulting behavior may be positive or negative, depending on the nature of the cues. Self-awareness is an antidote to deindividuation.

illusory correlation

in-group

out-group

minimal groups

out-group homogeneity bias

proximity principle

similarity principle

reciprocity principle

beauty principle

social facilitation

social inhibition

conformity

compliance

obedience

group polarization

social loafing

bystander apathy

diffusion of responsibility

deindividuation

MIND AND BODY

- Mind-Body Dualism
- Links between Mind and Body
- The Immune System

STRESS AND HEALTH

- What Is Stress?
- The Stress Response
  - The General Adaptation Syndrome
  - Stress and the Immune System
  - Stress and the Cardiovascular System
- Measures of Stress

COGNITION AND HEALTH

- Cognitive Appraisal
  - Primary Appraisal
  - Secondary Appraisal
- Personal Control
- Hardiness

COPING

- Coping Styles
- Coping Strategies
  - Cognitive Interventions
  - Relaxation Training
  - Exercise
  - Good Nutrition
  - Social Support
  - Self-Disclosure

SOCIOCULTURAL VARIATIONS

PROMOTING HEALTH BEHAVIOR

- Health Beliefs
- Theories of Reasoned Action and Planned Behavior
- Opportunities for Prevention and Intervention
- Using the Health Care System

REFLECTIONS AND OBSERVATIONS

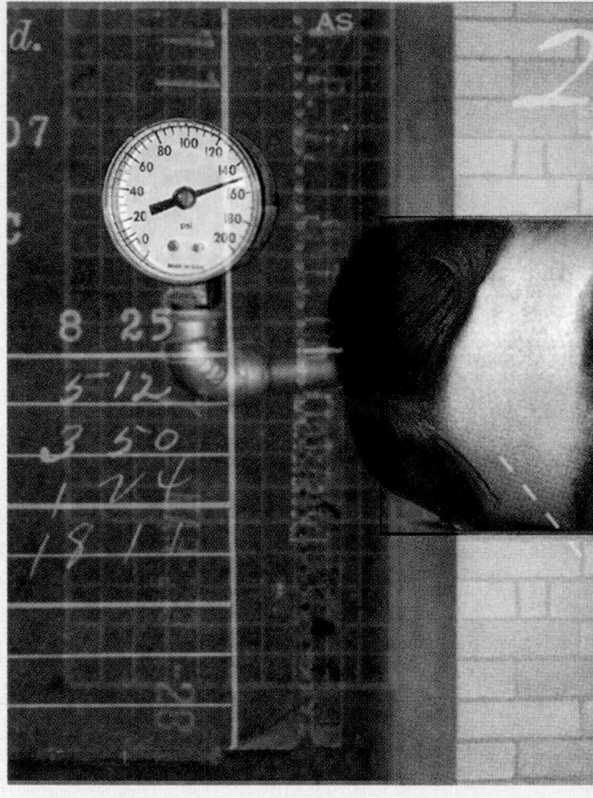

C H A P T E R 13

Health Psychology

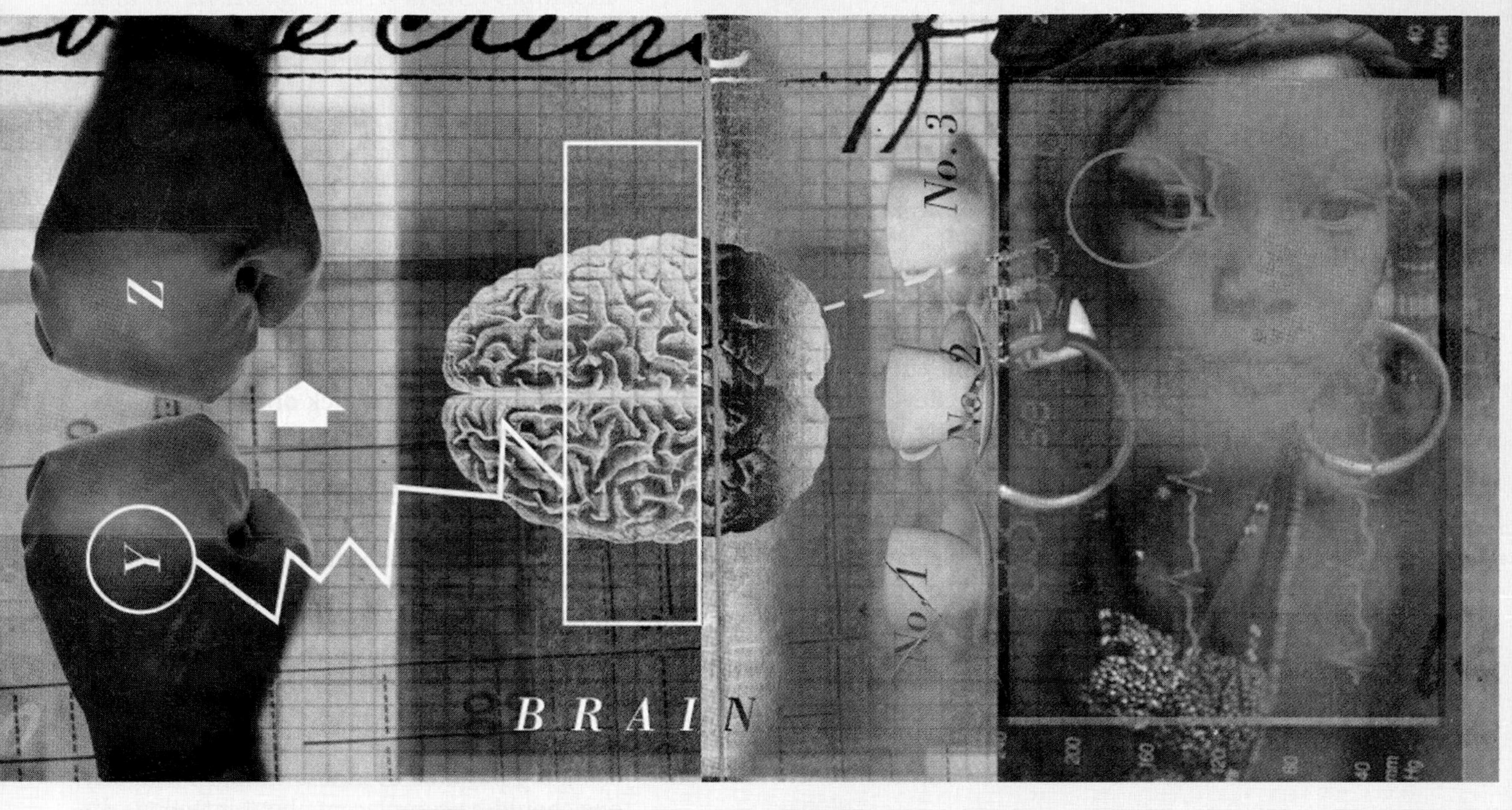

O B J E C T I V E S

After reading this chapter, you should be able to:

1. Discuss the definition, scope, and emergence of health psychology, explaining how the biopsychosocial model differs from the traditional biomedical approach.
2. Explain how the immune system functions to maintain our health.
3. Explain stress, the stress process, and how cognitive factors influence our reaction to stress.
4. Explain the role of coping in the stress process, and identify a variety of coping strategies shown to be effective in managing stress.
5. Distinguish among theories of health behavior, and explain how health promotion interventions based on these theories would differ.

▲ *Good health is sought by people around the world. In Colombia, members of an outdoor aerobics class work to keep in shape. Regular exercise can help prevent illness.*

Health psychology is concerned with health-related behavior, and with the psychological aspects of health and illness over the life span. Health psychologists study what behaviors promote health and wellness, as well as how to prevent and treat illness and disability.

In addition to the effects of specific behaviors, such as using tobacco, reckless driving, and drug abuse, health psychologists are interested in how psychological factors, including cognitive processes and personality characteristics, can maintain wellness or lead to poor health. Although health psychologists are involved in a wide variety of activities, in this chapter we focus on such questions as: What is the best way to think about the relationship between mind and body? How does our behavior affect our health? How does the body defend against disease? How does stress affect health? What creates individual differences in whether someone remains healthy or contracts a disease (for example, how can two people be exposed to the same flu virus, but only one of them catches the flu)? In seeking to answer such questions, health psychologists have argued for new ways to think about how mind and body influence health.

▼ *Exorcism was once used to chase the demons, which were thought to cause illness, out of the body.*

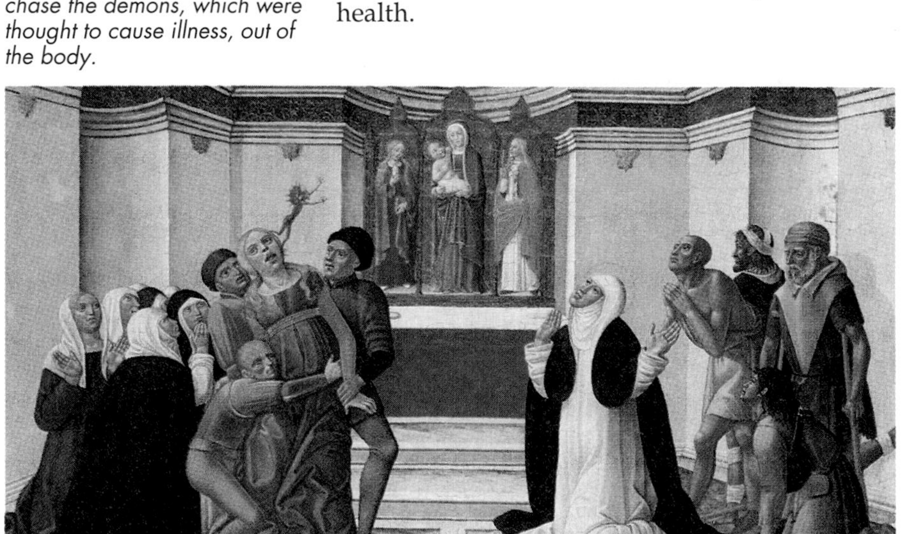

Mind and Body

Health psychologists assume that the mind and body function *together* to determine well-being. Prevention and treatment of illness thus require understanding the interplay among biological, psychological, and social factors underlying health. The ***biopsychosocial model*** is a multilevel model of health that uses a combination of organic factors (for example, chemical imbalances, neural disorders), psychological processes (type of mood, explanatory style), and social factors (presence of social support, culture's attitude toward health and illness) to explain how we maintain wellness or develop illness. This approach does not claim illness is "all in your head." To a health psychologist that would be as fallacious as claiming illness is "all in your body." The biopsychosocial model stands in contrast to the biomedical model, which has dominated Western medicine for the last 300 years (Taylor, 1995).

Mind-Body Dualism

The ***biomedical model*** assumes that the mind and the body function separately, that is, that there is a mind-body dualism (see Chapter 1). It contends that illness can be explained in terms of bodily processes, such as abnormalities in the brain or biochemical imbalances, without reference to the mind and its effects on illness. By explaining illness as a biological malfunction, it emphasizes illness, rather than health, and focuses on treating sick people, rather than keeping well people healthy.

The biomedical model's domination of North American medicine has roots in Western thought about the mind-body relationship. By the Middle Ages (476 to 1450), the Catholic Church had become the guardian of medical knowledge, and medical treatment was conducted in a religious context. Many people believed that demons were the source of illness or that illness was God's punishment for wickedness. Thus, illness could be cured by torturing the body to drive out the demons and evil, and by doing penance through prayer and good works.

During the Renaissance (1450 to 1600), scientific theories and technological developments began to challenge religious concepts and practices of healing. To break with past superstition, the new scientific theories emphasized the separation (dualism) of mind and body. The body alone was examined, diagnosed, and treated for illness. Today's biomedical model of medicine is a legacy of these historical events (Kaplan, 1975).

◄ *Some traditional African healing emphasizes harmony of mind, body, and spirit. Here, the G/wi from Botswana gather at dusk around the fire and the men start to dance in a circle around the women in a medicinal dance.*

Links between Mind and Body

During the nineteenth century, a challenge to mind-body dualism began to develop in Western thought. Neurologist Jean-Martin Charcot established that people's beliefs could affect and even cure their bodily symptoms. Later, Sigmund Freud showed that the mind could produce or "convert" a psychological, unconscious conflict into a physical symptom symbolizing the conflict, although no physiological changes were involved. Such conversion responses (one example is glove anesthesia, in which the hand but not the arm loses sensation, a physiologically impossible condition; see Chapter 15) are less frequent now than in Freud's Victorian era—which in itself suggests their psychological basis. Nonetheless, even today certain problems, notably loss of speech or sensory function (hearing, sight, touch), tremors, and paralysis may sometimes represent forms of conversion.

Helen Flanders Dunbar and Franz Alexander expanded Freud's idea that psychic conflict could produce specific illnesses. They proposed that personality characteristics were linked to physiological changes via the autonomic (involuntary) nervous system (see Chapter 3). Alexander suggested that ulcer-prone personalities had excessive needs for dependency and love, and that frustrating those needs led to increased stomach acid. The subsequent erosion of the stomach lining and development of ulcers was thus an actual physiological condition with psychological origins, that is, a ***psychosomatic illness*** (Alexander, 1950). Dunbar and Alexander developed profiles of physical disorders they believed were caused by emotional conflicts, including bronchial asthma, colitis, hypertension, hyperthyroidism, neurodermatitis, rheumatoid arthritis, and, of course, ulcers. Their work was an influential challenge to mind-body dualism and stimulated the development of ***psychosomatic medicine,*** the field devoted to treating illnesses that reflect emotional conflicts. Today, however, Alexander and Dunbar's theories are viewed as too simplistic, too focused on personality type. Psychologists now believe that neither emotional conflict nor personality type alone produces ill health. In fact, recent work indicates that most ulcers—the illness that stimulated interest in the field—are caused by a strain of bacteria (Alper, 1993).

In contrast to Western medicine's view of mind-body dualism, throughout history most healing systems around the world—from the Ayurveda in ancient India to Taoist teachings in China—assumed the interrelationship of mind and body. Ayurvedic practitioners believe illness reflects a person's experience of life and body type, and that the body makes natural antibiotics and tranquilizers to fight illness. Meditation, massage, and herbs are used to teach people to control their immune systems through controlling their mind and emotions (Chopra, 1993). Traditional Chinese medicine also focuses on keeping the body in balance and harmony, with the goal of strengthening natural immunity (Beinfield & Krongold, 1992).

Similarly, in Africa, health has not simply been the absence of disease but has signified that a person is living in peace and harmony and keeping the laws of the gods and the tribe. Healing is an integral part of religion and society and involves the whole community (Lambo, 1978). Moreover, in North America, the Navajos view illness as reflecting lack of harmony between body, mind, and spirit, breaking of laws or taboos, and witchcraft (Topper, 1987).

Today, the National Institutes of Health (NIH) has an Office of Alternative Medicine charged with scientifically assessing the therapeutic value of various remedies and exploring how nonconventional treatments can comple-

The biopsychosocial model is a multilevel model that examines how biological, psychological, and social factors interact to promote health and illness.

▼ *Our illnesses sometimes reflect our environment.*

"I'd say the sales chart is the ulcer, the phone is the hypertension, the paperwork is the migraine..."

ment traditional medicine. Although NIH is just beginning to evaluate such treatments, the recognition that mind and body are interrelated is a recognition of the biopsychosocial model, and a radical step forward for Western medicine.

Today, health psychologists emphasize that keeping people healthy and curing disease are affected by their physical, psychological, and social contexts. Illness results from the interaction of various factors, and the same illness might have more than one cause. Evidence is overwhelming that genetics, environmental stressors, early conflicts, individual cognitions, coping strategies, and social and economic resources work together to affect whether a person develops a particular illness. Further, the impact of psychological and social factors is not limited to a few kinds of illness. *All* health conditions are influenced by such factors. Even if a condition is totally physical in origin, treatment and recovery are influenced by our expectations about pain and discomfort, attitudes toward a sick person's role, and our relationship with our physician. This contemporary view of the mind-body relationship is the core of modern health psychology.

The Immune System

To understand the research that links behavior and health, you need to understand the ***immune system***, which is a complex network of molecules, cells, and organs. It has a big job: it defends the body from foreign invaders, neutralizes toxins, aids in repairing damaged tissues, and rids the body of abnormal cells. The environment is filled with microorganisms—bacteria, viruses, and fungi—that can make people ill, possibly very ill. You no doubt have had a paper cut or pinprick and experienced the sensations of an inflammation as your body defended itself and kept infection from spreading. Fortunately, the immune system is typically an effective self-defense system. It has a variety of defense mechanisms, including the production of infection-fighting molecules and cells. It defends the body from foreign invaders of all types, including foreign microorganisms and inert material, such as pollen. Some mechanisms are *nonspecific*—they are used for any kind of infection or illness. Others are *specific*—they are designed to attack particular invaders. The immune system's effectiveness is not the only factor determining whether an infection occurs, however. Number and strength of the invading organisms are key factors as well.

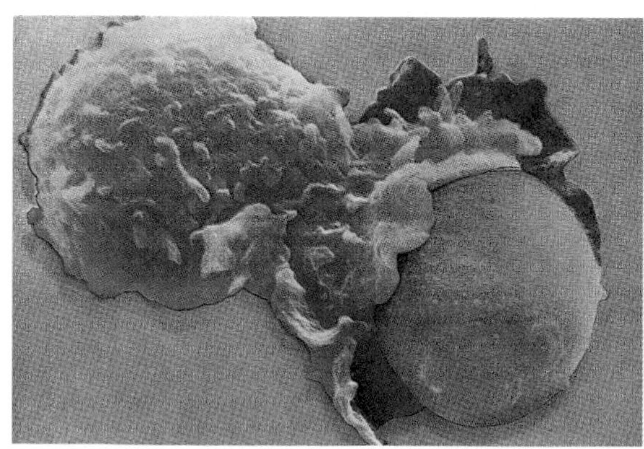

► *A white blood cell engulfs an antigen.*

The immune system is distributed throughout the entire body and particularly depends on certain white blood cells called ***lymphocytes*** to defend against infectious agents. The human body has about 2 trillion lymphocytes—1 in every 100 cells (Carola, Harley, & Noback, 1992). Some lymphocytes prowl through the blood or lymph system, others inhabit particular parts of the body such as the spleen, thymus, or lymph nodes. Specific invading bacteria or viruses that trigger immune responses are called ***antigens*** (*anti*body-*gen*erators). These antigens stimulate lymphocytes to produce ***antibodies*** (specially shaped protein molecules) that circulate in the blood and can identify and kill antigens. Antibodies recognize foreign tissue and are one reason why the body might reject transplants from donors who are unrelated.

Under normal conditions, it takes the body about four to ten days to produce enough antibodies to combat an infection. Once the body has been exposed to a particular antigen, however, it "remembers" the infection, and it can recognize and respond more quickly to eliminate the invader if it appears in the body at a later time. Just think—your body has descendants of cells that were trained to combat childhood diseases many years ago. These descendants genetically "remember" the chicken pox virus, for example, and will attack any chicken pox virus encountered in the future. Because of this lifetime memory, if you've had chicken pox as a child, you will remain immune to chicken pox throughout your lifetime.

The command center for the immune system is the ***thymus gland***, which is situated directly behind the chest. Although its full role is unknown, we do know that it turns undifferentiated lymphocytes into cells designed to attack and kill specific foreign invaders. For example, if you got a flu shot for the flu virus that was active in 1997, your thymus processed some of your lymphocytes to recognize and destroy it. This meant that when you were exposed to that flu, your body would be able to fight it off. Nonetheless, that inoculation would not confer immunity to other flu viruses.

As a newborn, you have few immunities against environmental invaders, and so your thymus is quite large. The thymus processes antibodies in large numbers to help you through the first few years of life. As you age, however, you develop more specific immune responses, and your thymus shrinks as its workload is reduced.

With all these antibodies why do we, as adults, ever get sick? We all know people who have several colds a year. Why doesn't their immune system prevent this? One reason is that, as with the antibodies for the flu described above, individual antibodies are specialized to respond to specific viruses and can't recognize even slight variations. But more than 100 different viruses cause colds. Your body is unlikely to have developed defenses against all of them. Moreover, viruses and bacteria mutate into new versions. You may have had last year's flu, but this year's model is altered genetically so that your immune system can't recognize it. Fortunately, the immune response is adaptable, and new antibodies quickly mature to deal with most new threats (though you may suffer with a cold in the meantime).

If the immune system slows down or fails, an infection can get the upper hand. The most extreme cases occur when a virus directly assaults the immune system itself. For example, the human immunodeficiency virus (HIV), which causes AIDS, enters the body via an infected cell contained in another person's bodily fluid (blood, semen). HIV suppresses the immune system by destroying white blood cells and leaving the body defenseless against other infections, some of them deadly. AIDS constitutes an urgent health threat around the globe. Dealing with it will be a major priority for policy makers in the next decade.

The immune system can mistake a harmless speck of pollen, cat dander, or bathroom mold for a dangerous threat, engaging in vigorous counter action and triggering an allergy attack. Blood vessels swell in the nose, mucus collects in the sinuses, and the eyes water. The affected person sneezes and coughs in a misguided effort to repel the invader. Strong coughing can create irritations in the trachea, creating openings to invasion by bacteria and viruses. Substances that trigger allergic responses are called ***allergens***, and they range from household dust and tobacco smoke to fabric softener and perfume. As you saw in Chapter 6, through classical conditioning, allergic responses can become associated with other environmental stimuli, such that the allergic reaction persists even when the allergen is absent (remember when the sight of a cat elicited coughing in a person allergic to cat dander).

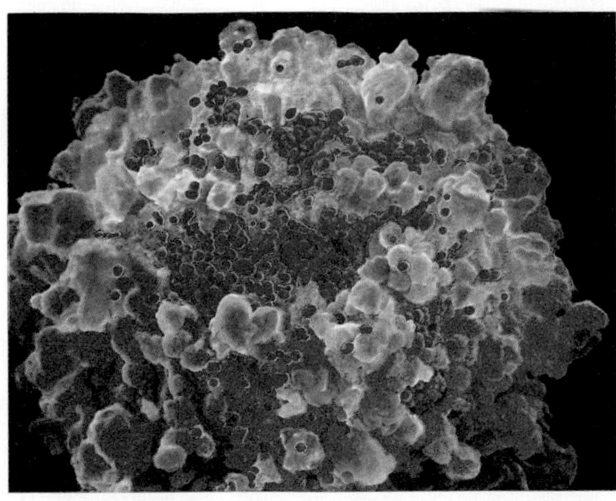

◀ *HIV directly attacks the immune system and damages the body's ability to fight off other infections. Here AIDS viruses infect a T-lymphocyte.*

Because our immune system responses are powerful, they require constant regulation to make sure they neither under- or over-react. Disruption of the chemical communication system that regulates the immune system can result in ***autoimmune disease***, when the immune system fails to recognize its own body and launches an attack on it. One out of twenty Americans, two-thirds of them women, suffer from diseases that result from the immune system's inability to tell friend from foe. These autoimmune diseases include rheumatoid arthritis, in which the immune system mistakes tissue around the joints for an enemy, and multiple sclerosis, in which the immune system attacks white matter in the brain and spinal cord (Steinman, 1993).

The immune system is a complex network of molecules, cells, and organs that defends the body from foreign invaders of all types, including foreign organisms and inert material such as pollen.

Normally, the body produces trace amounts of ***cortisol***, a hormone that keeps the thymus under control, dissolves excess white blood cells, and prevents the immune system from running wild. Thus, cortisol regulates the immune system, preventing it from working too well and pumping out an excess of antibodies.

▲ *Catastrophic events, such as Hurricane Andrew, which devastated Florida in 1992, can cause intense stress. Imagine how you would feel if flood waters burst through your front window and destroyed your home, as happened in this picture.*

Excessive cortisol, however, undermines the immune response by impeding thymus functioning, slowing antibody production, and killing too many white blood cells (Carola, Harley, & Noback, 1992).

Stress and Health

Do you always seem to get sick right in the middle of studying hard for exams? This may reflect the stress you are experiencing. Stress affects a variety of physiological processes that play key roles in maintaining health and avoiding disease, including the functioning of our cardiovascular, endocrine, and immune systems (Gatchel, Baum, & Krantz, 1989; O'Leary, 1990; Taylor, 1995).

▼ *A young girl sits among her family's belongings after being evicted from her home in Puerto Rico. Her parents now face the burden of finding shelter for the family.*

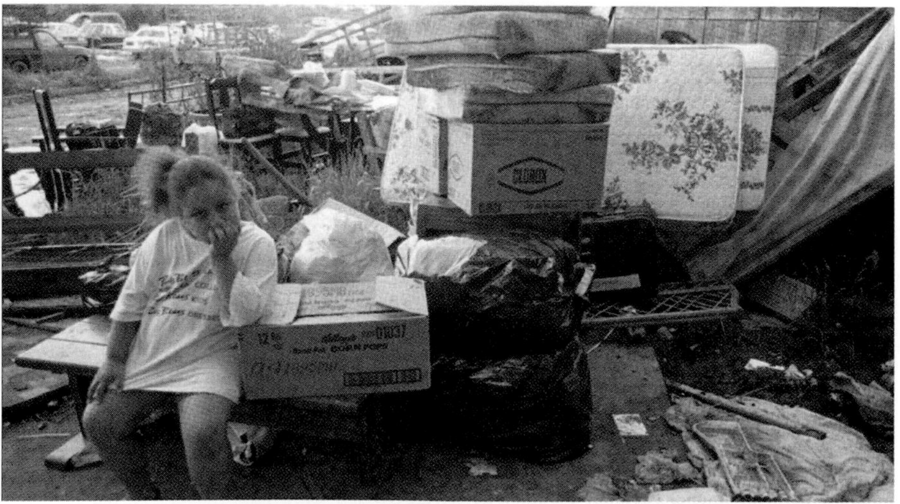

Research has found that negative life events and situations, such as marital conflict, job loss, bereavement, chronic threat—and yes, final exams—as well as positive stressful life events such as marriage, the birth of a child, or a move to a different city, are associated with changes in immune function that may affect health (Cohen, 1996). These discoveries have given rise to intense interest in the relationship between stress and health.

What Is Stress?

Stress is a part of daily life. We get stuck in traffic and are late for appointments. We miss deadlines. We have neighbors who blare their stereos until all hours of the night. We have social obligations that require us to dress formally and to smile at people we dislike. We have unpaid bills and flat tires. Toilets flood and roofs leak. We constantly experience stressful situations that require us to adapt and change.

Stress is a psychophysiological state or process that occurs when we face events we perceive as threatening to our physical or psychological well-being. It grows out of the interactions that we have with our environment, occurring when there is a *mismatch* (actual or perceived) between situational demands (stressors) and the resources we have to deal with them. Environmental events perceived as harmful or threatening are ***stressors***; our psychological and physiological reactions to them are ***stress responses.*** To avoid experiencing stress, we need to find effective coping strategies for dealing with stressors (Lazarus & Folkman, 1984).

Stressors vary from *catastrophic* events (earthquakes, fires, and hurricanes), to *major life events* (loss of a job and death of a loved one), to *hassles* and frustrations involved in day-to-day living (enduring crowded or noisy conditions or experiencing acts of prejudice and discrimination). Stressors can be *acute* (of short duration such as a Caesarean birth), or *chronic* (persistent or recurring such as caring for a sick parent).

Although *negative life events* are certainly stressful, positive life events can be stressful as well (Holmes & Rahe, 1967). *Positive life events* that may lead to stress include going on vacation, starting a new job, getting married, or having a baby. Nonetheless, negative life events are generally more stressful—for example, it is usually more distressful to move when you have been evicted than when you are moving because you have just bought your dream house (McFarland, Norman, Streiner, Roy, & Scott, 1980; Stokols, Ohlig, & Resnick, 1978).

Stress is often greater when events are *unpredictable* or *uncontrollable* (Glass & Singer, 1972; Frankenhaeuser, 1986). You can endure a lot more pain when you know you can stop it at any time than when you know you have no control over it. Similarly, ambiguity increases the stressfulness of events; if you know what is wrong when you are ill, you may feel less stressed than you would if you had no idea what was wrong (Billings & Moos, 1984; Kaloupek & Stoupakis, 1985).

You do not have to experience an event directly to be stressed by it. You can experience stress vicariously. If you see other people suffering, especially loved ones, you may empathize with them and experience significant pain. Your "empathic appraisal" of circumstances (whether you view them as actually painful to the people involved) can affect your level of discomfort.

Researchers have demonstrated vicarious stress and the effects of empathic appraisal in a classic experiment that examined how college students reacted to a trauma they saw in a film (Speisman, Lazarus, Mordkoff, & Davison, 1964). Four groups of students saw a film about a rite of passage for adolescent boys in a society in which a sharp stone is used to cut the underside of the penis deeply from tip to scrotum. One group saw the film with no sound track (no narration). Another group heard a sound track with a narrative emphasizing the pain, danger, and primitiveness of the operation (trauma narration). A third group heard the boys described as willing participants in a joyful ceremony, with the pain and potential harm to the boys deemphasized (denial narration). The final group was encouraged to watch the film in a detached "scientific" manner, pointing out that "the surgical technique, while crude, is very carefully followed" (scientific narration). Researchers continuously took physiological measures (for example, heart rate, skin conductance) of the students in each group as they were watching the film. The students filled out questionnaires assessing feelings of stress immediately after viewing the film. The results revealed that the "trauma narration" group reacted with more stress, particularly during the film (for example, their heart rate changed more), than the "no narration" group. In contrast, the "denial" and "scientific" narration groups reacted with less stress than the no narration group. Thus, appraisal of the situation as being very painful and traumatic for the victims could lead to a stressful reaction even in those who were not experiencing the trauma themselves.

The Stress Response

How does your body respond to a stressor? Your heart pounds, your blood pressure soars, your pulse races. You breathe more rapidly, and you may start to sweat. These reactions reflect the dual-track process called the ***fight-or-flight response*** that is the basis of many of our emotions (see Chapter 10).

Both tracks begin in the cerebral cortex, where we perceive and interpret stressors (see Figure 13-2). One track is via the sympathetic nervous system, which increases heart and respiration rates, sends blood into deep muscle tissue, and releases fat from the body's energy

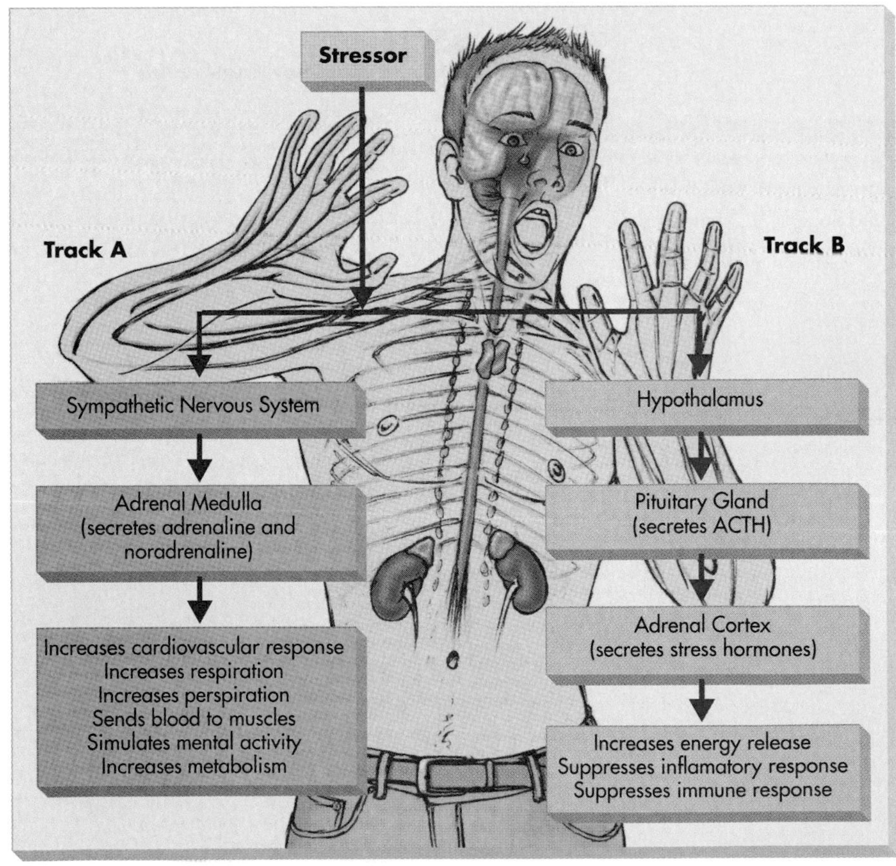

13-2 How Does Your Body Respond to a Stressor?

This figure represents the dual-track process of the fight-or-flight response to stress. In Track A, the brain sends signals via the sympathetic nervous system that stimulate the adrenal glands to produce stress hormones such as adrenaline and noradrenaline, which enter the bloodstream. In Track B, the hypothalamus stimulates the pituitary gland to release adrenocorticotropic hormone (ACTH), which, in turn, stimulates the outer part of the adrenal gland to release stress hormones.

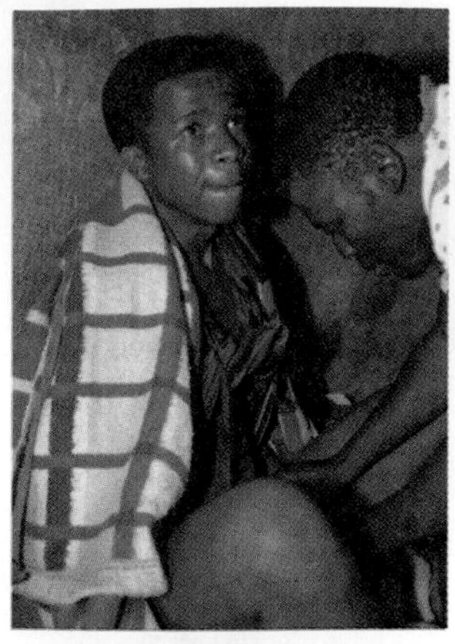

▲ *How does this image make you feel? Do you feel differently if you are told this Xhosa boy is undergoing a tribal ritual to symbolize his transition to manhood? With no anesthetic? That if he cries out in pain he will experience enduring shame? How we think about events influences our feelings about them.*

stores. This track stimulates the adrenal glands to produce stress hormones such as adrenaline and noradrenaline, which then enter the bloodstream and prepare the body to take action—to fight or flee (Frankenhaeuser, 1975).

The second track goes via the hypothalamus and the pituitary gland. The hypothalamus stimulates the pituitary to release several chemicals into the bloodstream, including certain chemicals known to heighten the immune system response (Meyerhoff, Mougey, & Kant, 1987; Steinman, 1993). The pituitary also releases adrenocorticotropic hormone (ACTH), which in turn stimulates the outer part of the adrenal gland, causing the release of stress hormones such as cortisol, which increase the heart rate and intensify heart contractions. Cortisol also works to shut down the stress response and restore homeostasis by inhibiting hormone production in the hypothalamus, killing excess white blood cells and slowing down the thymus. If too much cortisol is secreted, however, immune function may drop too far below normal levels, making us vulnerable to disease. Given that we don't live in a sterile environment, we may then encounter viruses and bacteria that our impaired immune system cannot handle, and become ill.

The General Adaptation Syndrome

The general adaptation syndrome is a response to stress that has three stages: (1) alarm, (2) resistance, and (3) exhaustion.

With acute stressors, our fight-or-flight response tendencies are short-lived and quickly return to normal levels. They have done their evolutionary job of increasing our chances of survival by focusing our attention on a threat and preparing us for action. But suppose the stressor doesn't go away; suppose it is *chronic* rather than *acute*. Then the fight-or-flight reaction is only the first in a sequence of responses involved in adapting to a stressor. Hans Selye (1902–1982) described this sequence as the ***general adaptation syndrome*** (Selye, 1976).

The general adaptation syndrome has three stages: (1) *alarm*, (2) *resistance*, and (3) *exhaustion* (see Figure 13-3). In the alarm stage, the body is mobilized for immediate action. The sudden activation of the sympathetic nervous system stimulates an immediate release of stress hormones to prepare the body to meet threats or dangers. If the alarm stage reactions don't solve the problem and stress persists, the resistance stage begins. The body is no longer in the heightened state of arousal characterized by alarm, but it still uses resources at an elevated rate in continued attempts to cope with the stressor. We are vulnerable to illness and development of somatic (physical) symptoms at this stage. Ultimately, persistent exposure to the same stressor or additional stressors drains the body of resources. In the exhaustion stage, the body's capacity to resist is depleted, removing defenses against illness and making chronic stress potentially life-threatening.

The concept of the general adaptation syndrome implies all people respond to stressful situations in a similar way. But it's not that simple. Different people respond differently to the same stressor, and situations that produce stress in some people are considered fun by others (Lazarus & Folkman, 1984). Consider public speaking or ballooning, for example; these may be regarded as sources of terror or enjoyment, depending on the individual. Some people become furious as a result of minor irritations, like being cut off in traffic, while other people just shrug them off. Thus, while the general adaptation syndrome describes our response to perceived threat under some conditions, it does not help us understand why people vary in what they perceive as a threat nor does it explain differences in responses to threat. It does, however, emphasize the negative impact of stress on the body over time, a topic of particular interest to research concerned with effects of stress on the immune system.

13-3 The General Adaptation Syndrome

Phase A is the alarm response, in which the body first reacts to a stressor. Resistance falls below normal. Phase B, the stage of resistance, occurs with continued exposure to a stressor. The bodily signs associated with an alarm reaction disappear and resistance rises above normal. Phase C is the stage of exhaustion that results from long-term exposure to the same stressor. At this point, resistance may again fall to below normal. (Source: Selye, 1974)

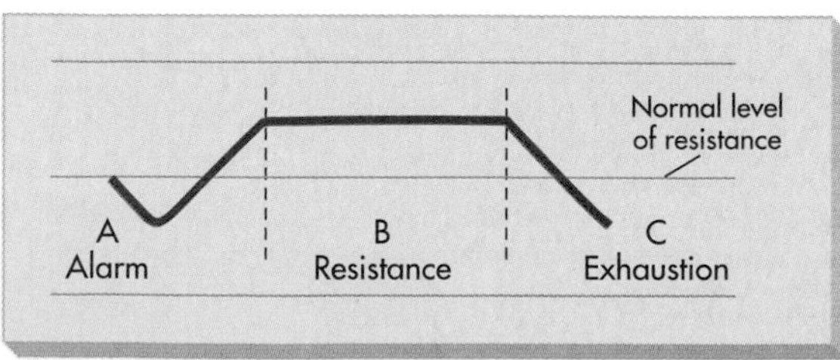

Stress and the Immune System

Optimal immune system functioning involves a complex set of activities that rely on a chemical signaling system between the brain and the immune system—the brain sends chemical signals to the immune system and vice versa. Because chemicals involved in the stress response play integral roles in this signaling system, one way that stress may impair health is by disrupting brain-immune system communication, leading to under- or over-reaction of immune responses. As you have learned, the fight-or-flight response involves the production of cortisol, a hormone that plays a key role in regulating the immune system. This is just one point in the complex signaling system between brain and the immune system that can be disrupted by stress and can lead to susceptibility to disease (Sternberg & Gold, 1997).

Animal studies suggest that stress may affect how sick we become from viral and bacterial infections (Sternberg & Gold, 1997). Stress affects rate of tumor growth (considered to reflect an impaired immune system) in rats and mice. In one study, researchers implanted tumors in two groups of female mice, one stressed, one not stressed. Twenty-five days later, more than 80 percent of the mice in the high-stress group had died. In comparison, only 40 percent of mice in the low-stress control group died during this length of time (Riley, Fitzmaurice, & Spackman, 1981). Most animal studies examine the growth of tumors induced by viruses, suggesting a role for stress in tumor *growth*, but not necessarily in tumor *formation*. Whether animal studies of immune functioning apply to human beings is being debated. Some species are more vulnerable to cancer than others, and mice typically contract a lot of cancers, often from viruses. However, only 10 percent of cancers in human beings are caused by viruses, so these tumor studies may have little relevance to most human cancers.

Studies of human beings have linked acute stress to lymphocyte functioning. When people have frequent life changes and report high distress, their immune cell activity is lowered. A life event does not have to be extreme to affect health. Several studies of medical students have linked stress during exams to lowered immune function. Loneliness has also been associated with lower immunity (Kiecolt-Glaser et al., 1986).

Although acute stress temporarily lowers some indicators of immune system functioning, the principle of homeostasis suggests that organisms should adapt to stressful experiences that persist over time (chronic stress) as their bodies move to counter the effects of the stressors and return to their previous equilibrium (see Chapter 10). Indeed, if rats and mice are repeatedly exposed to a stressor (crowding, persistent noise), they do adapt, with their response to the stressor decreasing over time. Nonetheless, human beings deal with chronic stressors that are more complex than those used in experiments with laboratory animals, and further studies are needed to understand how human beings respond to chronic stress. It may be that the complex pattern of stressors associated with chronic stress acts more like a series of acute stressors.

Chronic stress is a major issue for the increasing number of people responsible for the long-term care of chronically ill family members, which can be both financially and emotionally devastating to caregivers. Researchers have studied immune systems of family members serving as caregivers for patients with Alzheimer's disease, with length of care averaging thirty months. Caregivers were under chronic stress in caring for Alzheimer's patients, who had a progressive deterioration of mental capacity and came to forget from one moment to the next what they had said or done. The caregivers experienced lowered immune function on a variety of measures, suggesting chronic stress can indeed result in persistent changes in immune response (Kiecolt-Glaser et al., 1987).

▲ *Watching aging loved ones suffer, combined with the physical burdens of caring for their needs, can be one of our most stressful experiences. Here, Ellen Dickerson helps her husband Nat at the Tandet Center for Continuing Care, where he lives. Nat has both Alzheimer's disease and Parkinson's disease.*

Are the ups and downs of the immune response measured in stress studies actually related to whether people get sick? That is, do they have actual clinical significance? The issue is still being debated. Number of lymphocytes and their activity level change constantly, even among healthy people. Moreover, there is more to the immune response than lymphocytes. Whether an individual becomes ill not only depends on immune response strength, it also depends on the number and strength of the germs encountered. Nonetheless, the fact that the number of stressful life events you have recently experienced can predict whether you catch a cold when an experimenter exposes you to a cold virus is strong evidence for the link between stress and immunity, whatever mechanism is involved (Cohen, Tyrrell, & Smith, 1993).

In addition to direct psychophysiological effects, stress can affect immunity indirectly by leading people to engage in behaviors that affect the immune system. For example, when people feel stressed they may use tobacco, drink

SEEKING SOLUTIONS

Cancer Course and Treatment

One out of four people who die in the United States each year dies of cancer—more than a half a million people annually. Second only to heart disease in rate of killing Americans, cancer is a set of more than 100 diseases that are characterized by unrestricted cell proliferation. Cancer is caused by an interplay of genetic and environmental factors. Such things as ultraviolet radiation, nutrition, cigar or cigarette smoking or chewing tobacco, drinking alcohol, and chemical hazards at home and work can all contribute to cancer risk. There also appears to be a link between certain viral infections transmitted during intercourse and the development of cervical cancer. Once people develop cancer, how they deal with stress, whether they maintain a proper diet, use screening or early detection methods, and adhere to treatment regimens can all affect the progression of the disease.

Cancer and its treatment can produce psychological as well as physical effects. Fear, anxiety, depression, and other psychological responses to surgical scarring, the need to use prostheses (artificial limbs or breasts), and rejection by family, friends, or co-workers are examples of problems that can be helped by behavioral and psychotherapeutic interventions.

Nutrition and relaxation techniques discussed in this chapter are examples of behaviors that have proven helpful for cancer patients. In addition, behavioral techniques have proven useful in the treatment of taste aversions that are a common side effect of chemotherapy. Patients undergoing chemotherapy commonly develop a dislike for foods—such as chocolate sundaes or a cup of coffee—they once regularly enjoyed. Such taste aversions can severely degrade a cancer patient's quality of life and are a source of stress in and of themselves.

By studying the timing and characteristics of the foods that are most likely to produce food aversions, psychologists have come up with a variety of recommendations to help prevent cancer patients from learning to dislike foods they normally eat (Mattes, Arnold, & Boraas, 1987a, 1987b). One approach involves having patients consume a strongly flavored, unfamiliar food between their last meal and the chemotherapy treatment. The purpose is to direct the learning process to this new food so that it becomes disliked rather than foods in the patient's usual diet. Research has shown this approach to have some effectiveness for both adult and child cancer patients. Patients who form an aversion to the novel food are less likely to develop an aversion to foods in their usual diets.

The recovering cancer patient must cope with a wide variety of psychological and social problems—including general psychological distress, physical disability, problems with body image and self-esteem, family and marital disruptions, sexual difficulties, loss of social support and friendship networks. The psychological and behavioral techniques developed by psychologists to deal with stress and manage behavior can play important roles in the treatment of this disease (Sarafino, 1994).

caffeine or alcohol excessively, or take psychoactive drugs. Unfortunately, these behaviors are associated with decreased immune functioning (Gatchel, Baum, & Krantz, 1989).

Research on classical conditioning of the immune system suggests that some day we might be able to teach people to use conditioning techniques to bolster their immune systems (Ader & Cohen, 1993). Researchers have already used conditioning with mice to do so. They conditioned the mice by pairing saccharine-flavored water with an injection of a powerful immunosuppressive drug (a drug that deactivates an antibody). The mice were later given more of the saccharine-flavored water, but this time without the drug. Their immune responses were then compared to (1) conditioned control animals not reexposed to saccharine, (2) nonconditioned animals given saccharine, and (3) animals given a placebo. Conditioned mice reexposed to saccharine showed immunosuppression (weakening of the immune response) compared to the other groups (see Figure 13-4; Ader & Cohen, 1975).

These findings have some exciting implications. If classical conditioning techniques can be used to suppress the immune response, perhaps they can also be used to enhance it. In other words, we might be able to use classical conditioning to turn a neutral or harmless substance into a conditioned stimulus that would lead to a conditioned health-enhancing response from the immune system. When combined with a drug, this conditioned stimulus might lower the dose needed to produce the drug's needed effect. Doctors could then prescribe a lower amount of the drug to achieve the same effect as would occur through using the regular drug by itself.

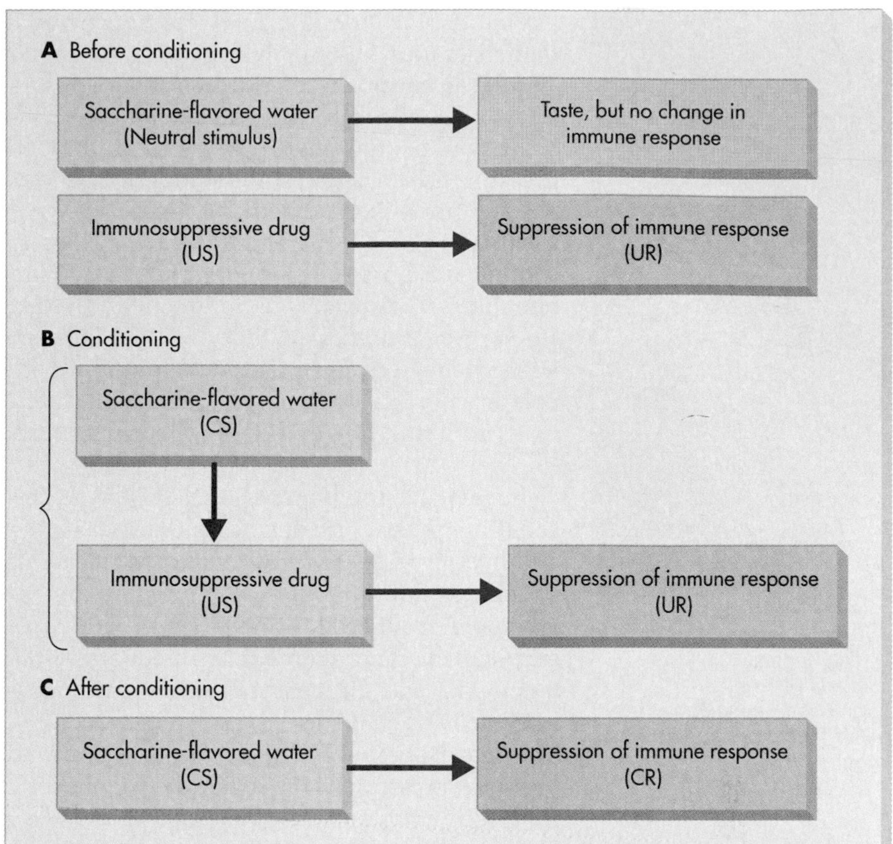

13-4 Conditioning the Immune System

This figure represents how researchers conditioned the immune response in mice by pairing a saccharine-flavored water (initially neutral stimulus) with a powerful immunosuppressive drug (unconditioned stimulus-US). With repeated pairings, the saccharine-flavored water (conditioned stimulus-CS) became able to suppress the immune response when presented alone.

Stress and the Cardiovascular System

Your heart, blood vessels (arteries, veins), and blood form your cardiovascular system. Cardiovascular disease was responsible for 41 percent of deaths in the United States in 1996 (Ventura, Peters, Martin, & Maurer, 1997). High blood pressure (hypertension), which occurs when the heart pumps blood too fast and/or blood vessels are clogged or constricted, is the most important predictor of cardiovascular disease. Cardiovascular disease and hypertension appear to have a genetic component. In addition, behavioral factors that increase risk for cardiovascular disease include smoking, drinking alcohol, lack of physical activity, and eating fatty foods (American Heart Association, 1993; Jeffery, 1992).

An upholsterer is said to have played a key role in the discovery of a link between personality and heart disease. During a job for a physician who specialized in heart patients, he noticed that the waiting room chairs were particularly worn on the front of the seat. It turned out that these coronary-prone patients—subsequently labeled as Type A personalities—consistently sat on the edge of their chairs (Friedman & Rosenman, 1974).

If we asked your friends to rate your general rate of activity, would they say you need to slow down? How often do you set deadlines for yourself? Do you get irritated when someone interrupts you when you are in the middle of a job? Do you finish other people's sentences for them? Do you pound the desk to make your point? These behaviors have been associated with the ***Type A personality*** (Jenkins, Zyzanski, & Rosenman, 1979). Type A personalities are driven individuals, characterized by an exaggerated sense of time urgency, competitiveness, ambitiousness, hostility, and aggressiveness. Their behavior contrasts with that of ***Type B personalities,*** people who are calmer, more relaxed, have little sense of time urgency, and are less hostile and angry. Longitudinal studies of people in healthy populations have found that Type A's are more likely to develop heart disease than Type B's (Rosenman et al., 1975; Kittel, Kornitzer, de Backer, & Dramaix, 1982; Carmelli, Dame, Swan, & Rosenman, 1991). The question is, why?

THINKING CRITICALLY

Assuming immunity can be conditioned, suppose you had a cough but didn't want to take a lot of cough medicine. If you consistently paired a distinctive drink (perhaps a bitter tea) with the medicine, over time, what should happen?

The bitter tea should acquire an ability to suppress the cough, and less medicine would be needed to produce the effect.

▲ *Type A personalities, driven by time urgency, competitiveness, and aggression, seem ideally suited for the position of stock trader.*

One explanation is a more reactive sympathetic nervous system, which leads to an exaggerated cardiovascular response to stress—stress hormones pour into the bloodstream, the heart pounds, the pulse rate jumps, and blood pressure rises. There is some evidence that Type A's are more likely to demonstrate this reactivity than Type B's, particularly in response to conflict or if put in a competitive situation (Harbin, 1989; Christenson & Smith, 1993; Lyness, 1993). Another explanation is differences in health behaviors. For example, Type A individuals are more likely to smoke and to hold smoke in their lungs longer (Lombardo & Carreno, 1987).

But not all components of the Type A personality pattern predict heart disease. Anger and hostility appear to be the "toxic" elements (Wiebe & Smith, 1997). In particular, people who exhibit cynical hostility—a combination of suspiciousness, resentment, frequent anger, antagonism, and distrust of others—are more likely to develop heart disease (Williams, 1989). This may be because hostile people seek out and provoke stressful events in addition to reacting more strongly to them (Barefoot et al., 1987; Dembroski & Costa, 1988; Smith, 1989, 1992). Hostility is also correlated with many other behavioral risk factors, including lower social support and greater use of alcohol, caffeine, tobacco, and marijuana (Scherwitz, Perkins, Chesney, & Hughes, 1991).

Although heart disease is the leading cause of death for both men and women, men develop the disease earlier than women. Unfortunately, it was not until recently that women were included in the studies of risk factors for heart disease, so the reasons for the gender difference are unclear. Men are more likely be hostile and express anger than women, and to smoke and use other unhealthy substances (Scherwitz, Perkins, Chesney, & Hughes, 1991). Differences in diagnostic procedures and types of treatment used with men and women contribute to the muddiness of the picture (Ayanian & Epstein, 1991; Streingart et al., 1991).

▼ *Polygraphs are designed to measure physiological activity considered to reflect stress experienced by lying. Although this machine is often used to determine whether or not someone is lying, it is not a reliable measure of truthfulness.*

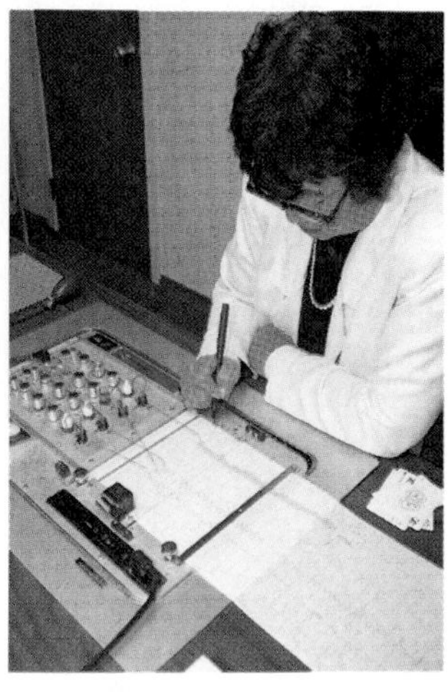

Death rates from cardiovascular disease are higher for African Americans compared to Hispanic, Asian, or European Americans (USDHHS, 1994). One explanation is that African Americans are more likely to have high blood pressure and greater cardiovascular reactivity in response to stress (Anderson, Lane, Taguchi, & Williams, 1989; Treiber et al., 1990). Another explanation is that African Americans experience more stressful events, and that events associated with racism are particularly experienced as stressful. One study found that the heart rates of African American college students increased sharply when the students were presented with racist stimuli (Armstead, Lawler, Gorden, Cross, & Gibons, 1989). The extent to which greater cardiovascular reactivity in African Americans is due to a combination of inherent or environmental factors has yet to be determined.

THINKING CRITICALLY

What are some problems with the Social Readjustment Rating Scale? Can you think of stressful events or experiences left off of the scale? Do you agree with the way the events are ordered from most stressful to least stressful?

Not everyone agrees with the ordering of events. There are cultural and age differences in the way events like these are ranked. Americans rank death of a close family member as more stressful than Europeans do. Adolescents rank sex difficulties higher in stressfulness than do older adults.

A more important problem with the scale is that, many times, it's not the big things that get to us but rather the accumulation of small mishaps and annoyances. The life events approach doesn't seem to explain the enormous amounts of stress resulting from ordinary events in people's daily lives. Think back on your week. Can you identify times when you felt "driven up the wall"? If so, you are in good company—one study found six in ten Americans reporting they feel "great stress" at least once a week (Harris, 1987).

Measures of Stress

To conduct scientific research on what people experience as stressful, we must be able to measure stress. Researchers use two types of measures of stress: physiological and behavioral.

Physiological measures of stress include blood pressure, heart rate, respiration rate, and electrical resistance of the skin, or galvanic skin response (GSR). Each can be assessed separately or measured and recorded simultaneously by a complex piece of electronic equipment, the ***polygraph***. Biochemical measures of physiological arousal analyze blood, saliva, or urine samples to assess secretion by the adrenal glands of stress-related hormones, including adrenaline, noradrenaline, and cortisol.

Physiological measures are objective, fairly reliable, and easily quantified. But they are expensive, the measurement techniques themselves may cause people to feel stressed, and they measure correlates of stress rather than stress itself (it is possible that hormone secretions occur for reasons other than stress). A polygraph is large and designed for laboratory use, so that using it to assess stress generated by everyday life activities is difficult. Further, experimental conditions using physiological measures must be strictly controlled. Measures of physiological arousal can also be influenced by extraneous variables, including gender, body weight, proportion of body fat, activity before or during measurement, and consumption of various substances, such as caffeine and alcohol (Sarafino, 1994).

Self-report measures of stress are less objective but less tied to equipment and the laboratory. They fall into two types: *life events* and *daily hassles* scales (Baum, Grunberg, & Singer, 1982). The life events approach assesses the stressfulness of major life changes in terms of amount of adaptation required, assigns a numerical value for the stress experienced at each event, and then adds up the numbers. The total score indicates a person's stress level.

The work of Thomas Holmes and Richard Rahe provides an example of this approach. Using interviews and ratings from large groups of men and women of varying ages, backgrounds, and marital status, they identified forty-three events that most people rated as stressful (Holmes & Rahe, 1967). They developed a Social Readjustment Rating Scale (SRRS), a kind of life events scale, made up of "life change units" (LCUs) based on these ratings. For example, death of a spouse was considered extremely stressful, scoring 100 life-change units on the scale. Pregnancy was considered less stressful (40 LCUs), and Christmas only slightly stressful (12 LCUs). A score of over 200 is a sign of serious health risk. Table 13–1 lists selected items from the Social Readjustment Rating Scale.

Life events scales have been extremely popular in research, which has found that the greater the number of stressful life events, the greater a person's susceptibility to illness (An-

Table 13-1 Social Readjustment Rating Scale*

Life Event	Value
Death of spouse	100
Divorce	73
Marital separation	65
Jail term	63
Death of close family member	63
Personal injury or illness	53
Marriage	50
Fired from job	47
Marital reconciliation	45
Retirement	45
Change in health of family member	44
Pregnancy	40
Sex difficulties	39
Gain of new family member	39
Business readjustment	39
Change in financial state	38
Death of close friend	37
Change to different line of work	36
Foreclosure of mortgage	30
Change in responsibilities at work	29
Son or daughter leaving home	29
Outstanding personal achievement	28
Begin or end school	26
Change in living conditions	25
Revision of personal habits	24
Trouble with boss	23
Change in residence	20
Change in school	20
Change in church activities	19
Change in social activities	18
Change in sleeping habits	16
Change in eating habits	15
Vacation	13
Christmas	12
Minor legal violations	11

*These are selected items. Each event is given a value in life change units (LCUs).
Source: Holmes & Rahe, 1967.

▲ *Traffic is reported by many people to be a major source of stress. One consequence is road rage, an increasing problem on today's roads.*

derson & Arnoult, 1989). But such scales are only moderately effective in actually predicting future health, perhaps because other factors also affect whether a person becomes ill, but also because the scales group together life events that vary widely in severity. The stress of a "personal injury or illness" would surely differ, depending on whether it occurred while you were playing a friendly tennis match or while you were defending yourself from rape.

The life events scales only consider events in which change occurs. But people can experience stress even without life changes. Attempts to understand stressful experiences in ordinary life have led to a focus on our "daily hassles"—those everyday events on the job, at school, and in interpersonal relations that annoy, frustrate, and anger us (see Table 13–2). The Hassles Scale asks people to report the extent to which they felt "hassled" by typical events during the previous month (Lazarus, Delongis, Folkman, & Gruen, 1985). This approach focuses on important sources of stress missed by scales targeting major (but uncommon) life events and recognizes possible cumulative effects of minor life events. It also assesses the degree to which an individual perceives an event as stressful, recognizing that cognitive factors play an important role in the stress process.

Table 13-2 Some Daily Hassles

Kinds of Hassles	Typical Examples
Personal	Concerns about physical appearance (including weight). Concerns about the meaning of life. Concerns about the future. Being lonely.
Health	Not enough energy. Feeling aches and pains. Not getting enough sleep. Inconsiderate smokers.
Time	Too many things to do. Not enough time for entertainment and recreation. Misplacing or losing things.
Social	Fear of rejection. Not enough time to spend with family. Too many family responsibilities.
Finances	Rising prices. Not enough money. Taxes. Unexpected expenses.
Home maintenance	Repairs to house or apartment. Yard work. Cleaning house or apartment.
Work	Job dissatisfaction. Too many work-related responsibilities. Concerns about not getting ahead. Concerns about job security.

Source: Adapted from Kanner, Coyne, Shaeffer, & Lazarus (1981).

Evidence suggests that the cumulative effect of these "microstressors" takes a toll on physical and mental health (Delongis, Coyne, Dakof, Folkman, & Lazarus, 1982). One study found that hassles were a better predictor of anxiety, depression, and other psychological symptoms than major life events (Kanner, Coyne, Schaeffer, & Lazarus, 1981). Hassles that potentially threaten our self-concept ("central" hassles), such as missing important deadlines at work (threatening our self-concept as an achiever) or having a child get in trouble at school (threatening our concept of a good parent), are particularly stressful (Gruen, Folkman, & Lazarus, 1988).

Such research produces only correlational data, which do not tell us with certainty whether hassles lead to illness. Causation remains an open question. People in poor physical health may be more affected by life's little irritations and feel hassled because they are ill, not the other way around. Poor health may make a person argumentative or forgetful or otherwise less able to cope, causing more stress in response to what would otherwise be benign events (Dohrenwend, Dohrenwend, Dodson, & Shrout, 1984).

Can you think of other problems with the Hassles Scale? Some people have argued that some items, such as "not enough personal energy," are themselves symptoms of stress. Having one symptom of stress correlate with another is not surprising. Furthermore, asking questions about hassles may bias people toward overemphasizing them. And people may really not be very good at figuring out what is bothering them, and so they may turn to concrete and simple answers—easily remembered and identified daily life events. Finally, discriminatory behaviors based on gender and race are not sufficiently represented in the Hassles Scale. Research that has assessed the experience of sexist events—gender-specific negative life events, such as being treated unfairly because of being a woman, being called sexist names, or experiencing unwanted sexual advances—suggests that such incidents predict physical and psychiatric symptoms over and above those accounted for by events represented on the Hassles Scale (Landrine, Klonoff, & Gibbs, 1995). Nonetheless, we can say that both large and small negative life events are correlated with mental health and that how people think about those events plays an important role in determining the relationship between the life events and their mental health.

▲ *The same experience can be considered frightening or exciting.*

Cognition and Health

Not all people experience the same events as stressful. What makes the difference? As you learned in Chapter 10, cognitions play important roles in our emotions. Similarly, cognitive factors play a major role in whether people experience stress.

A classic experiment demonstrated that cognitive factors can determine what we experience as stressful (Lazarus, Opton, Nomikos, & Rankin, 1965). Researchers measured physiological responses of three groups of college students watching a film containing explicit scenes of grisly industrial accidents. The first group was told that the events were not real, that this was just a film, that the people they were watching were really actors, and that no one was actually injured. The second group was told to take an intellectual perspective and critique the film's technical aspects. In essence, they were instructed to block out the film's emotional dimension. The third group was a control group, and it was not given instructions for viewing the film.

The researchers found that the groups that were given cognitive strategies for viewing the film were less aroused than the control group. This indicates that cognitive strategies play an important role in the stress process. Subsequent research has confirmed that individual differences in stress responses reflect how people think about life events—that is, they reflect how people cognitively appraise (give meaning to) them (Lazarus & Folkman, 1984).

Cognitive Appraisal

Cognitive appraisal of stressors takes place in two stages. During ***primary appraisal***, the individual asks, "Am I OK or in trouble? What does this mean to me?" During ***secondary appraisal***, the individual asks, "What can I do about this situation? What resources are available to deal with it?" Table 13-3 outlines the process of cognitive appraisal.

Cognitive appraisal refers to how people think about (give meaning to) life events and has two stages: *primary appraisal*, which assesses whether the event is stressful, and *secondary appraisal*, which asks what can be done about the situation.

Primary Appraisal

Primary appraisal can lead to three conclusions about a potential stressor's personal signifi-

Table 13-3 The Process of Cognitive Appraisal

Stage	Cognition
Primary appraisal	Am I in trouble? Am I OK? The situation is irrelevant to me; it's not my problem. The situation is benign or helpful; it's not a threat. The situation is a threat to me; it's stressful.
Secondary appraisal	What can I do about the situation? Engage problem-solving skills. Seek social support. Apply material resources.

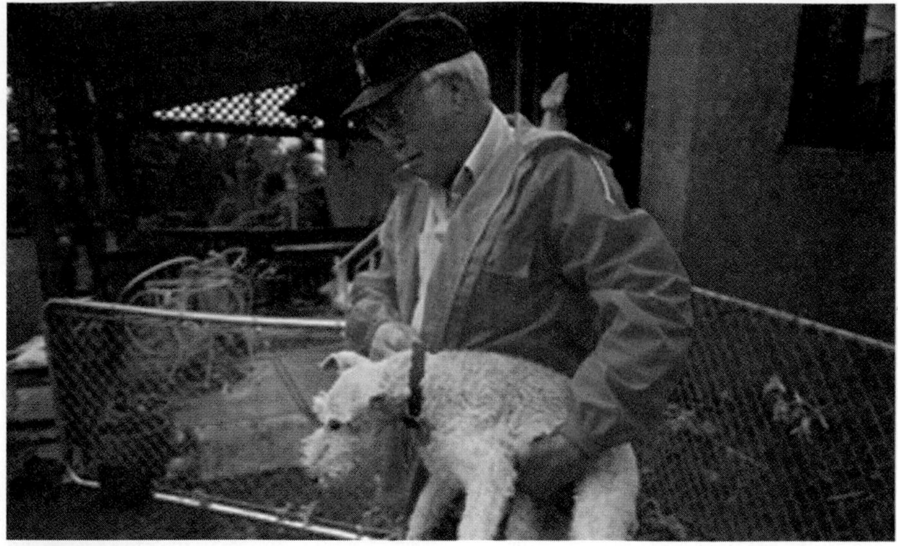

▲ *James Stengel carries his dog out of his tornado-damaged home. The Stengels, who were preparing for a family reunion, all escaped injury. "We're feeling very lucky to be alive," Mrs. Stengel said, adding, "The party is still on."*

cance. The situation is (1) *irrelevant*—it's not my problem; (2) *benign or positive*—it's not harmful and may even be helpful; or (3) *stressful*—it's a problem. If we appraise a situation as stressful, the next step is to determine the kind of problem facing us: (1) Have I been *harmed* or experienced a *loss* (for example, suffered a blow to self-esteem or lost a job opportunity or sustained a physical injury)? (2) Have I been *threatened* with some future damage or loss? (3) Have I been confronted with a *challenge*—does the situation have potential rewards in addition to risks? When confronted with a stressful situation, we mobilize coping resources to remove the threat and anxiety associated with it. Appraising a stressful situation as a challenge generates positive emotions, such as eagerness and excitement, that can help counter the effects of fear and anxiety.

While the negative aspects of stress can be life-threatening, positive aspects of stress put challenge and spice into our lives. Most people need at least a little stress to feel alert and alive. Hans Selye believed "complete freedom from stress is death" (Selye, 1980, p. 128). If we can consider stressful events as challenges, we may find ways to cope that lead to personal growth. A major task in life is determining what amount of stress is manageable and developing coping strategies that enhance our health and well-being.

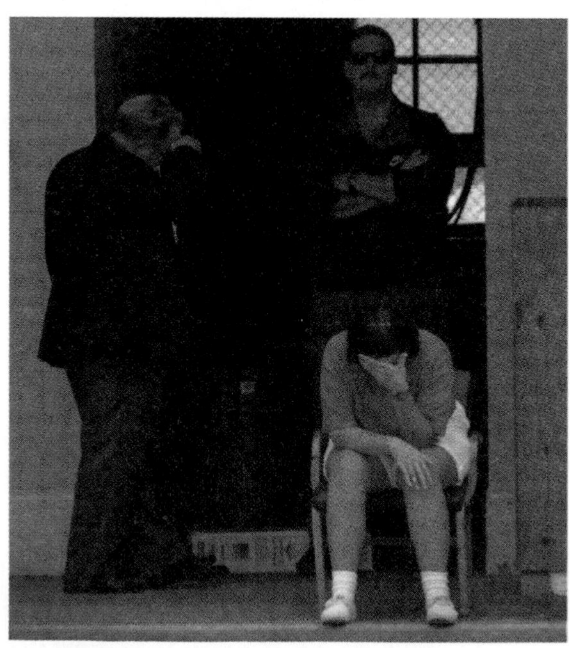

► *Sometimes secondary appraisal leads us to conclude that the most effective means for dealing with a stressor is to avoid it. Although Shannon Faulkner successfully achieved admission and became the only woman among 2,000 cadets to enroll in that military college, she decided the best way to deal with the harassment and isolation she experienced at the institution was to leave it.*

Secondary Appraisal

In secondary appraisal, a person answers the question "What am I able to do about this stressful event?" The answer involves deciding at least three things: (1) Who or what is responsible for the stressful event? (2) What is the probability of success or failure in coping with the event? (3) What does the future hold if I manage to cope with the stress or fail to cope with it? Answers to each of these questions depend on many factors, including an individual's past experience with similar problems as well as his or her self-esteem, problem-solving skills, social support, and economic resources (Cohen & Lazarus, 1979; Lazarus & Folkman, 1984).

Social factors can affect the stressfulness of threatening and violent events by influencing how they are appraised. For example, cognitive appraisals of rape are affected by culture, sometimes perpetuating myths that lead to self-blame in victims (for example, myths that women enjoy or provoke rape), or undermining women's self-esteem and expectations for social support (for example, myths that only promiscuous women get raped, that raped women are "damaged goods"). A woman who is raped, particularly by someone she knows, may cease believing she is secure in the world, that the world has order and meaning, and that she is a worthy person. Coping involves reestablishing these beliefs (Janoff-Bulman, 1989).

Societal structures also affect an individual's coping effectiveness. In the case of rape victims, for example, funding and location of rape counseling programs affects victim access to coping resources. Rape crisis counseling programs provide social support, bolster self-esteem, and help the rape victim deal with the criminal justice system. But women's programs are often underfunded, which means that rape counseling programs may be unavailable or nonexistent for many victims.

▲ Sarah Brady asked herself what she could do after her husband, former Reagan press secretary James Brady, was shot in an attempted assassination of President Ronald Reagan. She became an ardent gun control activist. Here she speaks at the Democratic National Convention, while her husband watches.

Personal Control

Personal control is determined by our beliefs about whether what we can do affects the situations in which we find ourselves (Peterson & Stunkard, 1992). As you learned in Chapter 10, perceived controllability of events can affect the emotions we feel toward ourselves and others. When we lose our sense of personal control over situations, our physical and mental health can be affected. When we first realize that we cannot avoid or escape a negative experience, we become angry and protest. But if we cannot regain our sense of control, we become demoralized, cope less effectively, withdraw from others, and develop profound feelings of apathy, helplessness, and depression (Janis, 1983).

There is a substantial body of evidence suggesting that the impact of an event or situation is influenced by a person's ability to predict, control, or terminate it (Maier & Seligman, 1976; Elliot, Trief, & Stein, 1986). Having a general sense of being in control reduces stress and encourages effective problem-solving strategies. Employees who have control over their work have lower levels of work stress. Studies that have been conducted with rats and other animals show that control over an unpleasant stimulus reduces likelihood of sleep disturbances, depressed appetite, ulcers, or brain-chemistry changes characteristic of stress responses (Abbott, Schoen, & Badia, 1984).

Interestingly, you need not *exercise* control to receive its benefit. The *perception* of control can reduce stress under some conditions. In one study, two groups tried to proofread a page while listening to a very loud noise. Researchers told individuals in one group that they could stop the noise by pushing a button; the researchers did not give people in the other group this information. People in the group that had been told that it had control over the noise did better on the task, even if the participants never pushed the button (Glass & Singer, 1972).

If you feel in control of your life, you are more likely to be healthy than if you feel that nothing you do makes a difference. Perceptions of personal control can have positive effects on the immune and endocrine systems (Taylor &

◀ Who do you think is more likely to make healthy choices, Calvin or the Tiger? Sometimes the pay-off for healthful behavior is down the road.

▲ *By focusing on his athletic strengths instead of his physical challenge, one-armed pitcher Jim Abbott displays his hardiness as a highly successful player for the California Angels.*

Brown, 1988). Moreover, if you feel that you can control your health, you are more likely to watch out for symptoms and go to a doctor for treatment. You are also probably more likely to exercise regularly, to have a diet low in cholesterol and fat, to conduct breast and testicular self-examinations, to avoid excessive sun exposure, and to have regular check-ups (Rodin & Salovey, 1989).

A sense of personal control affects your ability to relate to others as well as to obtain their social support when you have problems. For example, after people are exposed to uncontrollable stressors, they are less likely to help another person (a confederate of the experimenter) look for a lost contact lens (Cohen & Spacapan, 1978; Donnerstein & Wilson, 1976).

Hardiness

Control is also related to a personality attribute called ***hardiness*** (Kobasa, 1982). Hardy people have a sense of control over their experiences and outcomes, a deep involvement in what they do, and are more likely to believe what they do is worth doing. They also view change as an opportunity for growth and development rather than a threat; they cognitively appraise new events as challenges.

Hardiness seems to produce stress resistance and better physical and mental health (Hull, Van Treuren, & Virnelli, 1987). Hardiness may promote health through affecting the stress process or by influencing health-related behavior (diet, exercise, not smoking) (Allred & Smith, 1989). Some researchers argue that hardy people's greater sense of personal control is the primary determinant of the hardiness-health relationship (Cohen & Edwards, 1989). Others suggest that their tendency to focus on a situation's positive aspects contributes to hardy people's stress resistance. People who lack hardiness also may tend to be neurotic, depressed, anxious, and hostile, and to appraise their life experiences as threatening and stressful (Allred & Smith, 1989). However the link between hardiness and health comes to be explained, this work demonstrates an important aspect of health psychology that distinguishes it from the traditional biomedical approach—that is, it focuses on how people achieve health rather than on how they become ill.

Coping

Christine manages information systems for a large financial services company. All day she has dealt with hardware breakdowns and software glitches—fatal problems for her company if they're not solved quickly. She's worn out, her nerves are frayed, her blood pressure has gone up, and it's approaching midnight. What does she do? She heads for the rest room, enters a vacant stall, slumps against the cool wall, breathes deeply, and begins a meditation exercise. "I can't sustain this pace," she sighs. "That's why I had to learn coping mechanisms. Without them, I'm a walking accident" (Amparano, 1996, p. 1).

The physiological arousal and tension and psychological anxiety and fear associated with stressful conditions can be quite distressing. We use a variety of coping mechanisms, such as meditation techniques employed by Christine, to deal with stress-producing environmental and internal demands and conflicts.

Coping mechanisms are techniques that people use to manage or contend with stress-producing environmental and internal demands and conflicts.

Coping Styles

There are two major types of coping: problem-focused and emotion-focused (Pearlin & Schooler, 1978). In ***problem-focused coping***, we evaluate the stressful conditions and do something to change or avoid them—something that Christine did all day as she dealt with each software glitch. In ***emotion-focused coping***, we try to reduce tension and anxiety resulting from the problem rather than dealing directly with the problem itself. Christine's use of meditation techniques to calm herself is an example of emotion-focused coping. Although people deal with stressful situations in their own unique ways, people who cope effectively often use a combination of problem-focused and emotion-focused strategies, depending on what's most useful for dealing with a particular stressor (Zeidner & Endler, 1996). For many problems, however, problem-focused coping is more effective—solving problems or eliminating them is preferable to having to live with them.

Table 13-4 Coping Strategies of Optimists and Pessimists

Area	Strategies of Optimists	Strategies of Pessimists
The problem	Focus on the problem and develop specific plans for dealing with source of stress; emphasize positive aspects of the problem.	Distance self from problem, ignoring or denying the source of the stress.
The goal	Focus on the goal and postpone activities not related to solving the problem.	Give up a goal that is blocked by stress; disengage.
Coping style	Seek social support to get advice from others.	Focus on stressful feelings.

Your habitual way of explaining the causes of events, your ***explanatory style***, can affect how you cope. Health researchers have usually focused on three dimensions of explanatory style: (1) *internal-external*; (2) *stable-unstable*; and (3) *specific-global*. For example, the explanation offered by an alcohol abuser for a recent binge may be internal ("It's my fault; I wasn't thinking about its harmful effects") or external ("People kept offering me drinks"), stable ("I'm genetically programmed to be addicted and nothing will change that") or unstable ("I was going through a temporary crisis period and now it's over"), and global ("I'm never able to control my drinking under any circumstances") or specific ("I only abuse alcohol under one condition—when I drink beer with my friends").

Optimists and pessimists have different explanatory styles, and different approaches to coping. An optimistic explanatory style attributes negative life events to external, unstable, and specific factors ("My problem was not my fault, it was temporary, and only limited to that one thing"). Optimists are more likely to engage in problem-focused coping. People with a positive outlook on life use more active and successful coping responses to stress than pessimists (Scheier & Carver, 1987). Moreover, success in dealing with a problem will reinforce "learned optimism" (learning to take an optimistic approach) and effective coping strategies (Seligman, 1991). Optimists are more likely to take active steps to obtain treatment for illnesses than pessimists (Lin & Peterson, 1990).

A pessimistic explanatory style uses internal, stable, and global explanations for negative events ("My problems will be with me forever and affect my whole life") and can be a risk factor for physical illness (Peterson & Bossio, 1991). Pessimists are more likely to engage in emotion-focused coping. They often give up goals that lead to stress and focus on their feelings about the problem. See Table 13-4 for other differences in coping strategies between optimists and pessimists.

Both depressed men and women are more likely to use emotion-focused coping and less likely to use problem-solving coping in response to stressful life events. Depressed people are more likely to ruminate (repeatedly think and talk) about their negative experiences, rather than responding actively to them (Nolen-Hoeksema, 1987). Such rumination can amplify and prolong depressive episodes, interfere with problem-solving efforts, and result in feelings of failure and helplessness. In contrast, active response styles (going jogging, playing racquetball) can distract people from their problems, mitigate their depressive episodes, and promote feelings of control. Women are more likely than men to ruminate about events, which is one rea-

THINKING CRITICALLY

Given what you have learned about memory in Chapter 7, what effect should rumination have on negative memories?

Rumination involves talking or thinking about something over and over—in essence, rehearsing it. Rumination can increase the accessibility of negative memories by rehearsal, making them harder to suppress or forget.

▲ *AIDS victim, nineteen-year-old John Keets struggles to overcome the depression that generally is felt by victims of this disease, saying "If I let the depression take hold of me, I lose any sense of hope." Instead of dwelling on his illness, John organized a march for AIDS research, earning recognition as the nation's "Most Outstanding Teen" by the Noxema Extraordinary Teen Awards Program.*

son why women are twice as likely as men to experience depression (McGrath, Strickland, Keita, & Russo, 1990; see Chapter 15).

Emotion-focused coping benefits individuals in some contexts, however, particularly in dealing with chronic or terminal diseases such as cancer or AIDS. Anger and hostility can increase arousal and result in the release of hormones involved in the fight-or-flight response described earlier. Inadequate expression of negative feelings—particularly anger and hostility—has adverse health effects, including hypertension (Rosenman, 1985). Openly expressing distress, combined with a willingness to fight sickness, is associated with greater immune function. Cancer patients who cope with stress by keeping emotions bottled up are more likely to have suppressed immune systems, increased likelihood of cancer recurrence, and higher mortality rates (Levy, Lee, Bagley, & Lippman, 1988).

Coping Strategies

To relieve tension and cope with stress, men and women sometimes use strategies that are in themselves harmful to health, such as smoking and drinking alcohol—definitely not recommended! Both sexes are more likely to smoke when depressed or lonely, and men are more likely to both smoke and drink alcohol in response to negative moods (Schoenborn & Horm, 1993).

Fortunately there are more healthful alternatives. Indeed, there are a wide variety of problem-focused and emotion-focused coping methods. Some coping activities, such as seeking social support, involve both types of methods. Let's consider a few coping strategies that manage stress by affecting different components of the stress process: cognitive interventions, relaxation training, exercise, good nutrition, the utilization of social support, and self-disclosure. Keep in mind that the effectiveness of any of these strategies depends on the individual, the social context, and the characteristics of the threatening life event.

Cognitive Interventions

Several cognitive approaches to stress management focus on changing the person's appraisal process. A particularly effective strategy for secondary appraisal is to strengthen the person's ***self-efficacy***, that is, the person's belief that she or he can do what's needed to meet a particular situation's demands (Bandura, 1977a). A study of severely snake-phobic individuals demonstrated the link between self-efficacy training and immune system status (Wiedenfeld et al., 1990). In two 2-hour training sessions, researchers modeled handling a snake for snake-phobic individuals and then had the phobic partici-

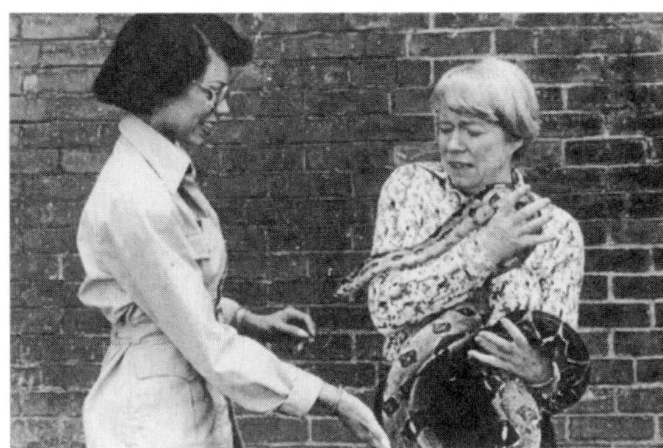

► *If she can do it, why can't I? A snake-phobic individual eventually learns to handle a snake after she watches a researcher interacting with it. By modeling how to behave, the researcher boosts the phobic's sense of self-efficacy.*

SEEKING SOLUTIONS

Using Relaxation Techniques to Cope with Stress

Relaxation is a skill that can be learned. Relaxation techniques are effective in reducing the discomfort and duration of a variety of symptoms of stress, including anxiety, elevated blood pressure, headaches, trouble falling asleep, hyperventilation, and teeth clenching or grinding.

One way to relax is to block the world out and concentrate on your body in seven simple steps:

1. Get in a comfortable position (either sitting or lying down will do). Close your eyes. Allow your jaw to drop and your eyelids to be heavy and relaxed but not tightly closed.
2. Scan your body mentally. Begin with your toes and work slowly up through your ankles, legs, buttocks, torso, arms, hands, fingers, neck, and head. Focus on each part separately; imagine the tension flowing out of your body and melting away.
3. To release tension, tighten the muscles in one area of your body (you might begin with your arms, shoulders, face, legs, or buttocks) and hold them for a count of 5 or more before relaxing and moving on to the next area.
4. Allow thoughts to flow through your mind, but do not focus on any of them. Autosuggestion is helpful to many people: tell yourself that you are relaxed and calm, that your heart is beating slowly and steadily, that your hands are heavy and warm and that you feel at peace.
5. Throughout this process, breathe deeply, slowly, and regularly.
6. Once you are relaxed, imagine you are in a favorite place or in a spot of great stillness and beauty.
7. After five or ten minutes, gradually rouse yourself from the relaxed position.

Initially you may find it difficult to achieve a totally relaxed state. If you practice these techniques, however, you will find relaxation will come more quickly. If you become so proficient that you can learn to "relax at will" you will have a powerful technique for countering the effects of negative life events as well as daily hassles.

pants practice until they could confidently interact with a snake. The participants' number of lymphocytes as well as their functioning increased over the course of the training sessions.

Relaxation Training

When physiological arousal from primary appraisal of a threat occurs, relaxation techniques can be used to lower blood pressure and strengthen the immune system (Janoski, Kugler, & McClelland, 1986). Insofar as relaxation techniques promote feelings of control and self-efficacy, they may also affect the secondary appraisal process, promoting problem-focused coping. If relaxation techniques are not supplemented by problem-focused coping to remove the threat, however, relaxation effects may be short-lived. Thus, they may be most appropriate for short-term stressors, such as anxiety attacks that occur only in specific settings.

Benefits of relaxation training were demonstrated in a study of middle-aged males who were heart attack survivors. Researchers tested the effect of relaxation on the patients' recovery by supplementing the standard treatment of medication, diet, and exercise with advice and counseling on how to relax. Participants were repeatedly encouraged to slow down, walk, talk, eat at a more leisurely pace, smile at others, laugh at themselves, admit mistakes, take time to enjoy life, and renew their religious faith. Over the following three years, these patients had half as many heart attacks as a control group of patients receiving only the standard treatment (Friedman & Ulmer, 1984). It is not clear exactly which components of relaxation training were responsible for these spectacular results. Researchers have established, however, that laughter is indeed good medicine. People who have a sense of humor and laugh easily appear less stressed by negative life events.

▲ *Is laughter truly the best medicine? Some clowns amuse a young girl at a children's hospital in New York. These clowns are part of a study to determine their effects on the health of patients in pediatric wards.*

Laughing, like exercise, arouses us and then leaves us more relaxed (Robinson, 1983).

Exercise

Aerobic exercise—sustained exercise to increase cardiovascular fitness—has been found to reduce stress, increase energy, and lower depression (Brown, 1991; Dishman, 1988). One study of mildly depressed women compared how depression was affected by relaxation exercises with how it was affected by a program of aerobic exercise (McCann & Holmes, 1984). After ten weeks, the women who undertook relaxation exercises had lower scores on a depression measure than a control group with no treatment. But the aerobic exercise group had even lower depression scores than the relaxation group.

▼ *The desire to avoid unhealthy food comes from a greater awareness of the dangers of a poor diet.*

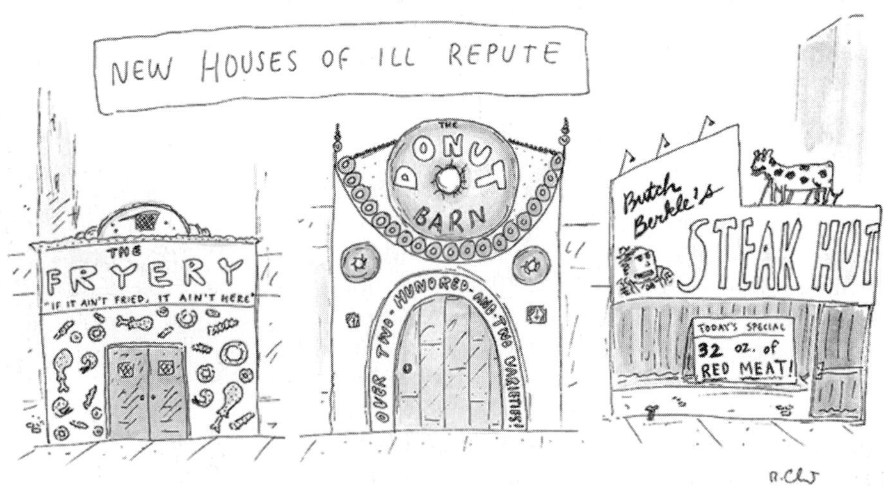

People who exercise live longer and have lowered risk of heart attack. Even a daily ten-minute walk can lower tension for as much as two hours. It also reduces risk of heart disease, colds, and flu; reduces appetite and helps people to maintain their weight goals; and makes digestion more efficient. Exercise that involves sustained rhythmic activity can produce a mental state similar to that achieved by meditation.

Aerobic exercise plays an important role in preventing heart disease, the number one killer of men and women. But other forms of exercise are also important for physical and mental well-being. Exercise to strengthen neck and back muscles helps to control neck and back pain. Weight-bearing exercise (walking) reduces the risk of osteoporosis (a thinning of the bones that can occur in later life, particularly in women) and may improve cognitive functioning. Setting goals and monitoring progress, exercising on a regular basis (three twenty-minute workouts a week are generally sufficient), choosing the right exercise for one's body build and lifestyle, and taking time to warm up and cool down should produce beneficial effects (Serfass & Gerberich, 1984).

Good Nutrition

Nutrition has been linked to a variety of illnesses, including cancer and heart disease. Small changes in diet, if consistently followed, can have a significant impact on risk for such diseases. Although the cause and effect relationship between diet and cancer is unknown, diet has been related to risk for a variety of kinds of cancers and to risk for coronary heart disease. Consequently, the American Cancer Society and the National Cancer Institute have developed dietary guidelines to help people reduce their cancer or heart disease risk. Some of their recommendations include: (1) maintaining normal body weight (obesity has been associated with higher rates of cancer of the colon, gallbladder, ovary, prostate, pancreas, and uterus), (2) limiting the amount of both saturated and unsaturated fats in your diet (dietary fat levels have been linked to higher rates of colorectal—colon and rectal, prostate, and other cancers), (3) drinking alcohol only in moderation (alcohol consumption has been linked to liver cancer), (4) eating foods rich in fiber (dietary fiber particularly appears to reduce the risk of colorectal cancer), and (5) eating only moderate amounts of salt-cured, smoked, and nitrate-cured foods (smoked and cured meats such as bacon, sausage, and ham have been linked to cancers of the esophagus and stomach).

A healthy diet involves more than limiting calories or avoiding certain foods, however. It requires complex health knowledge and the motivation to engage in healthy behaviors. The degree of protection a healthy diet provides from cancer and heart disease remains uncertain and undoubtedly varies with the individual. Nonetheless, maintaining a healthy diet does reduce risk and can enhance feelings of control and well-being, particularly when combined with a reasonable exercise program.

▲ *Friends provide a support network for one another. In the film* Waiting to Exhale *women support each other as they sort out their lives.*

Social Support

Social support of family and close friends can also have important effects on physical and mental health (Wills, 1990; Cohen & Williamson, 1991). People who have many social relationships (spouse, friends, relatives, and group memberships) live longer, are less likely to develop stress-related illness, and recover from illness more quickly than people who have few supportive social relationships. Social support can include giving information and advice, listening when someone confides in you, or giving money or time (personal loans, baby-sitting services, transportation, or notes for missed classes).

Social support can influence key health-related behaviors, including healthful eating, exercising, and avoiding alcohol, tobacco, and other drugs. If your friends and relatives have a healthy diet, exercise, and avoid alcohol and drugs, this will help you to do so as well. But if you are in a group that promotes unhealthy behavior (some groups have strong norms to drink large quantities of alcohol, for example), you may be more likely to drink, take drugs, or engage in other unhealthy behaviors. A study of the effects of social support for diabetics (who need to follow a strict diet and exercise regimen) found that if the diabetic was in a large social network, he or she was likely to have higher weight, cholesterol, and triglyceride levels, especially in men, than diabetics in smaller social networks. Larger social networks may be more likely to include members who encourage others not to follow their diet or exercise program (Kaplan & Hartwell, 1987).

People generally depend more on persons of similar age, gender, and ethnic background for social support (Griffith, 1985). Ethnic minority groups, including Mexican Americans and African Americans, depend on both immediate and extended family members for help more than do most Americans of European ancestry (Vaux, 1985). This may reflect a greater emphasis on family cohesiveness among minority groups, combined with a relative lack of access to institutional sources of support (Mindel, 1980).

Self-Disclosure

Research suggests that self-disclosure, or expressing your feelings about stressful life events, can improve both psychological and physical well-being (Pennebaker, 1995). In one study, college students aired their most personal and disturbing experiences. Healthy undergraduates were asked to write anonymously their most traumatic, emotionally upsetting, and stressful life experiences for four consecutive days (Pennebaker & Beall, 1986). One group was told to write about the facts surrounding the traumatic events, another to write about feelings about the events but not facts, and a third to describe both feelings and facts. A control group spent the four days writing about trivial topics.

> . . . the capacity to experience and express feelings of sadness in the face of loss or disappointment is generally viewed as a mark of mental health and may be an effective deterrent to the development of more severe symptomatology. . . .
>
> –Joy Newmann (1984, p. 137)

People who wrote about their emotions (either alone or in combination with facts) were most upset at the end of the four days. When they filled out a questionnaire six months later, however, they reported feeling healthier and ex-

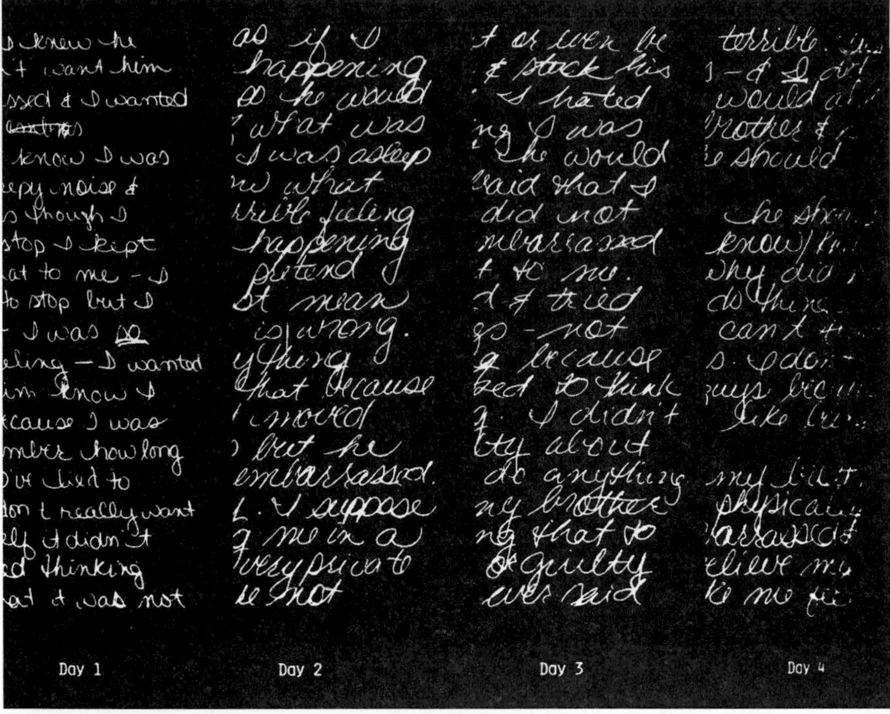

▲ *Self-disclosure seems to ease stress, as can be seen from these handwriting samples. A woman wrote about the same traumatic incident over the course of four days. The changes in handwriting indicate that she became more relaxed about the event.*

periencing fewer illnesses than people in the other groups.

We thus have many techniques to cope with and manage stress that may reduce effects of stress on health. They may work by some combination of removing the source of stress, blocking physiological arousal and somatic symptoms, and altering appraisal of life events, among other things. Developing, applying, and evaluating such techniques is important work for health psychologists. We must recognize, however, that health and illness depend on multiple factors. Therefore, our ability to affect the onset and course of illness has limits.

Sociocultural Variations

Amount and type of stress vary across cultures. Both material and subjective culture may be sources of stress. Air and noise pollution, traffic jams, and computer crashes are sources of stress brought to us by our material culture. Material culture also affects what resources are available to deal with these threats.

The case of Alice, who grew up in Harlem, trained to be a bookkeeper, and worked for a company in New York City, illustrates what poverty can mean for someone who is in ill health and dependent on overburdened systems (Kozol, 1995). After thirteen years of what she thought was a monogamous marriage, Alice learned she had AIDS. After her divorce, but as her health deteriorated, she and her two children became homeless. They were put up by the city in a hotel with no running water—they had to take a bucket to an obliging restaurant across the street. Eventually, the family was placed in a subsidized apartment in the Mott Haven district of the South Bronx, an area with the highest homicide rate in the city and where drug dealing and addiction were rampant. But even here, the system broke down. Alice was informed, inaccurately, that she was no longer eligible for benefits and that she would be evicted from her apartment. To reinstate her welfare eligibility, she had to collect her records and obtain statements from physicians around the city, meanwhile living in day-to-day dread that help would be cut off and that she and her children would lose the roof over their heads. These problems were compounded by the stresses of Alice's hospitalization for her condition in public hospitals with inadequate staff and beds.

Psychological factors, including religious faith, personal strength, and character, can affect a person's response to such problems, but they are not sufficient to solve them. Providing safe and well-maintained housing and responsive health care is beyond a single individual's control. Thus, health psychologists need to become involved with community interventions to alleviate sources of stress and illness (see Chapter 16).

As shown in Alice's story, poverty is associated with uncontrollable and threatening life events and involves higher risk from a host of stressors: dangerous neighborhoods, inadequate housing, and economic problems (Belle, 1990). Poor people are more likely to experience illness and death of children, homelessness, crime, and violence. They often live in conditions that are difficult to control—the walls of their homes may be painted with unhealthy lead paint, cockroaches may be all over an apartment and can cause asthma in young children, and poor heat and ventilation may lead to stress and illness. Poor women are more likely to experience the stress of unwanted pregnancy, single parenthood, and imprisonment of partners. For ethnic minority individuals, such del-

THINKING CRITICALLY

Can you think of at least two ways to explain the findings of James Pennebaker and his colleagues on self-disclosure?

Pennebaker suggests that it takes physiological effort to psychologically inhibit or restrain traumatic information. This ultimately leads to increased stress on the body and heightened rates of illness and symptoms. Disclosure may consequently reduce stress by providing the body relief from having to work to suppress information, even if only temporarily. Repressing anger is associated with increased health risks (O'Leary, 1990).

Research participants who divulged intensely personal material had significantly lower levels of skin conductance of electrical charges (galvanic skin response), heart rate, and blood pressure than participants who did not disclose such information (Pennebaker, Hughes, & O'Heeron, 1987).

You might also explain these findings by the concept of cognitive appraisal. Disclosure of traumatic information, although initially upsetting, may have long-term benefits by stimulating you to reappraise the traumatic event. You may decide the event was not as threatening or damaging as you once thought (change in primary appraisal). Or you may decide you can cope with it successfully (secondary appraisal).

eterious effects are often compounded by discrimination and discrimination-related harassment and violence. This is one likely reason why black Americans suffer more from high blood pressure than do whites (Anderson, 1992; Treiber et al., 1990).

Poverty can also undermine the effectiveness of mutual aid and extended kin networks. Poverty is associated with marital unhappiness and having husbands less likely to listen to problems (Brown, Bhrolchain, & Harris, 1975). Moreover, all too often, poor people must depend on unresponsive and overburdened bureaucratic systems for assistance with basic needs, which may contribute to feelings of lack of control (Belle, 1990).

Components of the subjective culture—including values, beliefs, and norms—can be sources of stress as well. Anthony Marsella has summarized how cultures vary in sources of stress (Marsella, 1979). These include stress as a result of:

1. *Value conflict*. When society has many conflicting values, psychological confusion and uncertainty (unpredictability) may be the result. While we must take care of ill relatives, we must also not miss time from work or school, so it becomes difficult and stressful to behave in keeping with our values and meet all of our responsibilities.
2. *Social change*. Pressures resulting from urbanization or modernization may lead to stress, depending on whether we have the money and power to adapt to these changes without hardship.
3. *Acculturation*. Subcultures within a society may have values that conflict with those of the dominant culture. People from the subculture may feel stress in trying to resolve these conflicts. Thus, the Amish do not use machinery but live in the midst of a technological world. Their children may feel caught between the two cultures.

▼ *Living in poverty adds many stresses to daily existence. With rifle and flashlight in hand, this man watches over his house at night in a dangerous Pittsburgh neighborhood.*

► *Stress from societal change can be expressed in many ways. Here Anna Petrushevskaya consults a victim of domestic abuse on a confidential hotline at the Women's Crisis Center in Moscow. Such hotlines have become more common there as the stress involved in the transition to a freer society has led to more battered women—15,000 Russian women were killed in domestic violence incidents in 1994.*

4. *Life events.* Cultures vary in number of life event changes requiring adaptation. Take something as simple (but stressful) as moving. In rural societies with stable communities, people might live all their lives in the same house—where their parents and grandparents lived as well. In urban societies, a person may change residence every couple of years.
5. *Discrepancies between goal-striving and achievement orientation.* Stress can occur in cultures with discrepancies between achievements and aspirations. A poor child in the inner city watches the same TV commercials as a middle-class child in the suburbs and wants the same products, but he or she does not have the money to buy them. As the discrepancy between aspiration and reality increases, stress increases as well.
6. *Role discrimination.* Some cultures discriminate based on gender, age, ethnicity, sexual orientation, and economic status. If people are subject to violence and harassment on the job or when they try to find housing, they are likely to feel stress and depression.
7. *Role conflict.* Roles within a culture can conflict, and such conflict can be extremely stressful. For example, a woman who has a deadline at work on the same day her child comes down with the flu may feel extremely stressed if she has no one to help her meet her conflicting role demands. Some societies have attempted to reduce such conflict by making available flexible work schedules, mandating parental leave, and establishing day care for children and elderly parents.

In terms of awareness and knowing about good health, I'd give Americans an A− or B+. But in terms of doing what we know we should, most of us—myself included—only deserve a C or C−.

—Nancy W. Dickey, M. D., President-elect, American Medical Association

Cultural context affects the specific events we experience as well as the beliefs that determine whether we will perceive those events as stressful. Coping models can help us understand how stress processes may work in similar ways across cultures. But to develop strategies to alleviate stress, we need to understand the cultural context in which these strategies will be applied.

► *Cultures vary in sources of stress due to various types of discrimination. Raphael, who is gay, sits alone on the bus to school. He reports being constantly harassed by his classmates for his sexual orientation.*

Promoting Health Behavior

Rose will tell you that good nutrition and regular exercise are important for health. She understands that drinking alcohol in excess isn't healthy and that she shouldn't smoke. She knows she should get a flu shot and have annual check-ups. But she doesn't. She has great intentions, but she has a daily routine and planning healthy meals and taking brisk daily walks are not part of it. Check-ups and flu shots are out of the picture—she hates going to the doctor. She only goes when she is in severe pain or so sick she doesn't feel like getting out of bed. She drinks martinis before going to bed at night in order "to relax" and has a smoking habit she hasn't been able to break (not that she's tried all that hard). Rose is also overweight, has high blood pressure, and has a chronic cough in the morning. But she feels overwhelmed when she thinks about all the changes she would need to make to overcome a lifetime of poor health behaviors, and she doesn't have the energy to take the steps needed to protect her health.

Besides finding ways to reduce stress, to stay healthy we need to engage in ***healthy behaviors***, that is, behaviors that enhance or maintain health (Taylor, 1995). We also need to develop

SEEKING SOLUTIONS

Focus on Health-Compromising Behaviors: Smoking

Smoking is the single largest preventable cause of premature death and disability in the United States. It is a cause of cancer, heart attacks and strokes, bronchitis, emphysema, and a host of other serious illnesses. Smoking during pregnancy increases risk of miscarriage, premature birth, and fetal and infant death. Second-hand cigarette smoke contains tar, nicotine, and other toxins (ammonia and carbon monoxide) and has significant health effects on all who breathe it. Children of parents who smoke are more likely to suffer respiratory illnesses, including pneumonia and bronchitis. Smoking kills more Americans each year than cocaine, heroin, alcohol abuse, automobile accidents, homicide, and suicide combined. Smoking even kills pets: dogs have a 50 percent greater risk for lung cancer if their owners smoke (Reif, Dunn, Ogilvie, & Harris, 1992). Despite all the evidence that shows smoking tobacco can be a deadly activity, there are people who continue to smoke. Why is this so?

One reason is that nicotine is highly addictive. People begin smoking when they are young when they do not realize how easy it is to become "hooked" and how difficult it is to quit smoking. Nicotine is so highly addictive that, if people smoke at least ten cigarettes at an early age, they have an 80 percent chance of becoming regular smokers. Researchers have found that smokers go through four stages that culminate in a smoking habit (Hirschman, Leventhal, & Glynn, 1983):

1. *Preparation.* A person acquires a positive attitude toward smoking from peers, the media, and advertising. Three basic types of attitudes prepare someone to smoke: the belief that smoking is sophisticated or "cool," that smoking enhances performance under stress, and that smoking is an act of rebellion.
2. *Initiation.* For young people, particularly boys, smoking can be seen as a "rite of passage" that signifies growing up and is initiated at the urging of friends.
3. *Becoming* ("a smoker"). Smoking is incorporated into the person's self-concept and the person becomes tolerant of and potentially dependent on the physiological effects of smoking.
4. *Maintaining* (the smoking habit). The interaction of biological, psychological, and social factors leads to a smoking habit that is very difficult to break.

Smoking runs in families, and twin studies suggest there may be a genetic component that affects reactions to nicotine. Smoking is a learned habit that has links to positive emotional reactions (for example, feeling good while smoking at a party increases the reinforcement value of smoking). Smoking, nicotine level, and emotional state become linked, so that smoking becomes a way to manage one's emotional state. Individual difference factors are involved as well. For example, low-achieving students, female students, and students who believe that the outcomes of their behaviors are not under their own control (external locus of control) are more likely to smoke than are male students with high self-esteem and a belief that their outcomes are a result of their own behaviors (internal locus of control).

Because biological, psychological, and social factors are involved in smoking, it is an extremely difficult habit to break. Today, however, broad social changes are affecting the psychological and social factors that promote smoking. Smoking is now socially disapproved by most educated people, and there is a constant barrage of information about the negative consequences of smoking on health.

It *is* possible to quit smoking. From 1964 to 1982, 30 million people in the United States quit smoking, and 70 to 80 percent of them quit on their own. Success is associated with confidence in ability to quit, perception of substantial health benefits associated with nonsmoking, and a socially supportive network. It also helps if you were a light smoker to begin with (Taylor, 1995). There are a variety of smoking cessation programs that apply techniques that include operant conditioning, aversion therapy, cognitive therapy, hypnosis, counseling, and support groups. The key to ultimately triumphing over smoking is to try, try again. But in the meantime, smokers can help others by not promoting smoking norms and not smoking in front of other people, particularly those trying to quit smoking or children.

norms can affect whether you abuse alcohol. The theory of reasoned action would explain their effects as follows: (1) If you believe abusing alcohol causes brain damage (attitude), and (2) if you believe other people think you should stop drinking (normative belief), and (3) if you are motivated to comply with those norms (you care about what those people think), you will be more likely to *intend* to stop drinking than people who do not have these attitudes and beliefs. In turn, if you intend to stop drinking, you are more likely actually to do so. Intention is the key to the behavioral change in this model (see Figure 13–6).

The ***theory of planned behavior*** expands this framework, suggesting that whether you develop a behavioral intention also depends on your perceived personal control over the situation. Specifically, you must believe you are able to perform the health behavior (a *self-efficacy expectancy*) and that performing the behavior will have the desired outcome (*outcome expectancy*). If you believe you can make time for twenty minutes of aerobic exercise a day *and* that the twenty minutes will make a difference in your health, you will be much more likely to exercise (Ajzen, 1985).

In the alcohol example, the theory predicts that developing a behavioral intention to stop drinking depends on whether the drinker believes he or she (1) can refrain from drinking (self-efficacy expectancy), and (2) that refraining from drinking will actually promote health (outcome expectancy).

These theories suggest that healthy behavior is a result of a variety of factors working together in complex ways. This variety and complexity helps us understand why we have such difficulty eliminating health-compromising behaviors and substituting health-enhancing ones.

Opportunities for Prevention and Intervention

It is important to begin health promotion activities early in life, because children imitate adult health-compromising behaviors (for example, smoking), and they develop habits that are extremely difficult to undo. Certain times are better for teaching particular health behaviors than others: these are ***teachable moments.*** A teachable moment may occur when a particular health habit becomes relevant. Smoking begins gradually, with initial experimentation—you give cigarettes a try, experience peer pressure, and create images of what a smoker is like. Junior high or middle school is when most students are first exposed to peers who smoke. Intervention programs are needed at that point to teach students how to resist peer pressure and avoid situations that will lead to smoking.

Physicals required when the school year begins provide other teachable moments. Health care professionals can discuss and help children develop sound health habits. Intervention programs show that children as young as three or four years old can develop personal responsibility for certain health behaviors, such as brushing their teeth, using seat belts, exercising, crossing the street safely, behaving responsibly in emergencies (fire and earthquake drills), and choosing nutritional foods. These behaviors must be explained in concrete and specific terms—showing children exactly what they should do and giving them opportunities for practice (Maddux, Roberts, Sledden, & Wright, 1986).

Although personal health promotion is clearly important, we should recognize that our world has many health-compromising situations, such as exposure to air and water pollution and toxic work environments, that are not under the individual's control. Critics argue that health promotion focuses too much on the individual and not enough on unhealthy aspects of the environment. They believe that health promotion overstates the relationship be-

13-6 The Theories of Reasoned Action and Planned Behavior Applied to Smoking Behavior

(A) Red boxes represent a model of the Theory of Reasoned Action as applied to smoking behavior. Attitudes and subjective norms predict intentions, which in turn predict behavior. (B) Blue boxes represent the Theory of Planned Behavior, which simply adds a role for perceived control in the model.

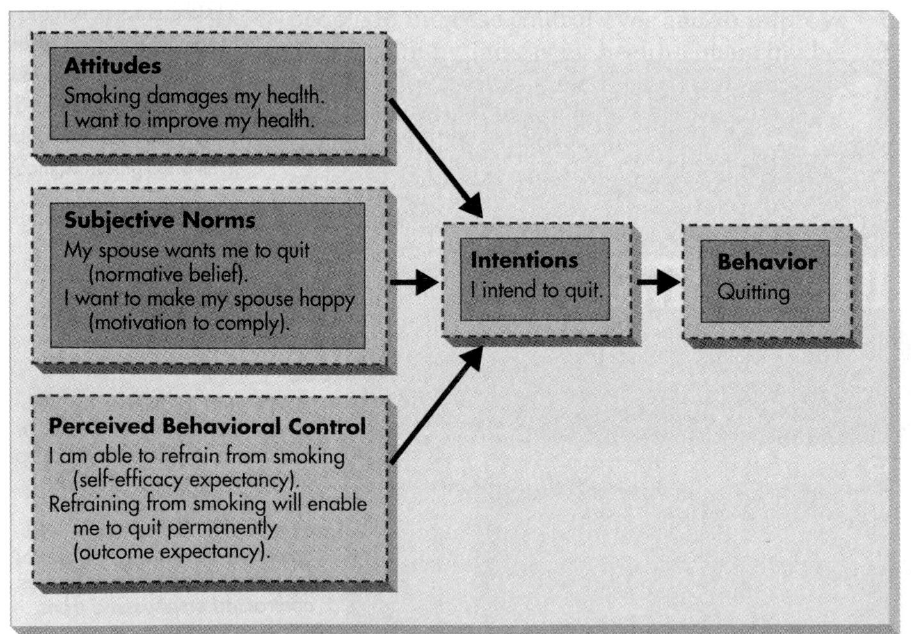

UNDERSTANDING HUMAN DIVERSITY

Physical and Sexual Abuse of Women

Physical and sexual abuse, a major source of life stress for women and girls in U.S. society and in societies around the world, has severe physical and mental health consequences. "In all countries and cultures, women have frequently been the victims of abuse by their intimates. They have been battered, sexually abused and psychologically injured by persons with whom they should enjoy the closest trust. This maltreatment has gone largely unpunished, unremarked, and has even been tacitly, if not explicitly condoned" (United Nations, 1989, p. 11). Over one-half of U.S. women who are murdered are killed by a current or former male partner. Such abuse is widespread and found among all segments of society, but it particularly affects women who live in disadvantaged ethnic minority communities. A woman's risk of being injured or killed by her partner increases if she has a violent family of origin or a partner who abuses alcohol or other drugs. Living in poverty and being unemployed also increase her risk (Goodman, Koss, & Russo, 1993).

In addition to being a direct cause of physical injury, physical and sexual abuse is linked to ill health through its correlation with different high-risk behaviors in different subgroups of women. For example, researchers reported that, regardless of race or age, adolescent mothers who used illicit drugs during pregnancy were more than twice as likely to experience physical abuse than were pregnant adolescents who did not use such drugs (24 percent compared with 9 percent). Pregnant adolescent drug users were also more likely to report a greater number of negative life events, violent and nonviolent (Amaro, Zuckerman, & Cabral, 1989).

Violence during pregnancy poses a health threat to the fetus as well. One study found that 42 percent of a sample of battered women entering shelters reported they had been battered during pregnancy, experiencing slaps, kicks, and punches to the abdomen and genitals. An estimated one out of four pregnant battered women reported escalation of violence during pregnancy.

For a long time, violence and abuse in women's lives was "invisible." Only recently have researchers begun to document its pervasiveness and impact on the health care system. Recent research reveals that U.S. women who have experienced physical or sexual abuse are more likely to seek medical care than other women. For example, more than one out of three rape victims suffers physical injury requiring medical attention. Further, adult women who were physically or sexually assaulted subsequently visited their physicians twice as often in a designated year—on average 6.9 visits per year, compared to 3.5 visits for nonvictimized women. Providing a year of health care for severely victimized women cost two and one-half times more than providing a year's care for nonvictimized women (Koss, Koss, & Woodruff, 1991).

The World Bank has attempted to compute an estimate of the healthy years of life lost to men and women from different causes (World Bank, 1993). The exercise counts every year lost because of premature death as one disability-adjusted life year (DALY) and computes every year that is spent sick or incapacitated as a fraction of a DALY (the size of the fraction depends on the severity of the disability). According to this analysis, gender-based victimization around the world results in 9.5 million DALYs. This figure is similar to that for HIV (10.6 million DALYs), tuberculosis (10.9 million DALYs), sepsis during childbirth (10 million DALYs), all cancers (9.0 million DALYs), and cardiovascular disease (10.5 million DALYs). Among demographically developing countries, it is estimated that rape and domestic violence account for 5 percent of the healthy years of life lost to women of reproductive age from all sources. In economically developed countries such as the United States, where maternal mortality and poverty related diseases have been brought under relative control, the estimate is 16 percent.

The United Nations has now recognized the problem of violence against women "as a serious obstacle to development and peace. . . . " (United Nations, 1989). In doing so, it has begun to address a critical health issue around the world.

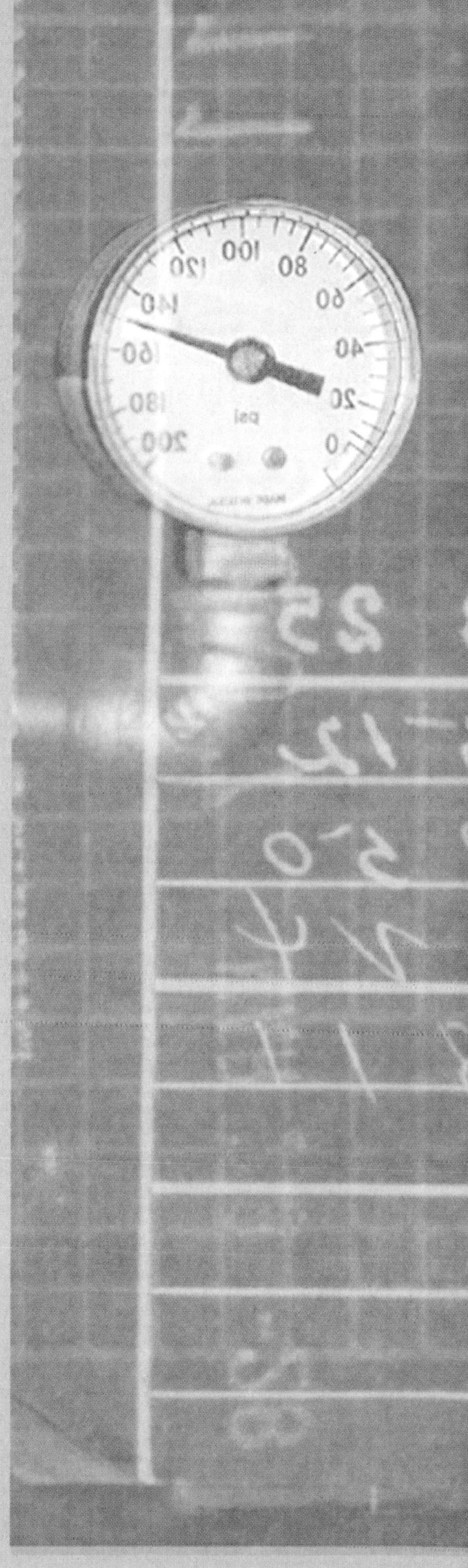

tween risk factors and health outcomes and places too much responsibility on people for their health. This can lead to unfairly blaming people for their health problems.

Using the Health Care System

Health services . . . are used by those who have time, money, and access to them.
—Shelley Taylor (1991, p. 272)

Health care use varies with gender, age, ethnicity, and education (see Figure 13-7). A person may not seek health care for many reasons, including lack of financial resources and transportation, or inaccessible health care practitioners. In some ethnic minority communities, there may be cultural alternatives to the health care system (for example, healers or midwives) that people prefer to utilize. Only about 40 percent of people who describe themselves as feeling "ill" actually seek help from the health care system. A great diversity in beliefs as well as in other psychological factors influence whether and how a person seeks help.

Women use health care services more than men. This is largely because of pregnancy and childbirth, but not completely. Differences in gender role norms may also be involved, as the masculine role includes normative expectations that men will be tough, tolerate pain, and not "give in" to illness. The traditional male role as breadwinner may also interfere with seeking treatment—men are more likely to hold full-time jobs and can't readily afford to take time off from work. Women's greater exposure to stressful life events, such as rape, battering, and sexual harassment, also contributes to their greater use of health care.

▶ *These first-graders scream against the tobacco industry during the great American Smokescream. The children are exposed to healthy habits early on, before they become exposed to peer pressure to start smoking. Later reinforcement of the Smokescream's message, at a teachable moment in middle school, will encourage these kids to avoid smoking once it is more relevant to them.*

THINKING CRITICALLY

The health belief model, the theory of reasoned action, and the theory of planned behavior are all cognitive theories explaining why people practice health behavior, but they are not really inconsistent with each other. Their differences lie in what they emphasize. Pick a health-related behavior related to a particular outcome (for example, smoking and emphysema; drinking alcohol and brain damage). How can the various models help you design a health promotion program to change it?

Using the health belief model, you would target people's beliefs and values related to health, explaining the behavior's threat to health and how changing it reduces the threat. In identifying the health threat, you would emphasize personal vulnerability, the severity of the behavior's consequences, and how a change in the behavior would enable people to avoid those consequences.

Using the theory of reasoned action, you would also emphasize subjective norms about the health-related behaviors. You would identify the people the individual cared about and what they thought about the behavior. You would ascertain the individual's behavioral intentions and work on developing intentions to perform desired healthy behaviors.

Using the theory of planned behavior to create desired behavioral intentions, you would focus on developing feelings of personal control over the situation. You would increase people's confidence in their ability to perform the desired health behavior (self-efficacy expectancy) as well as their belief that the behavior will have the desired outcome (outcome expectancy).

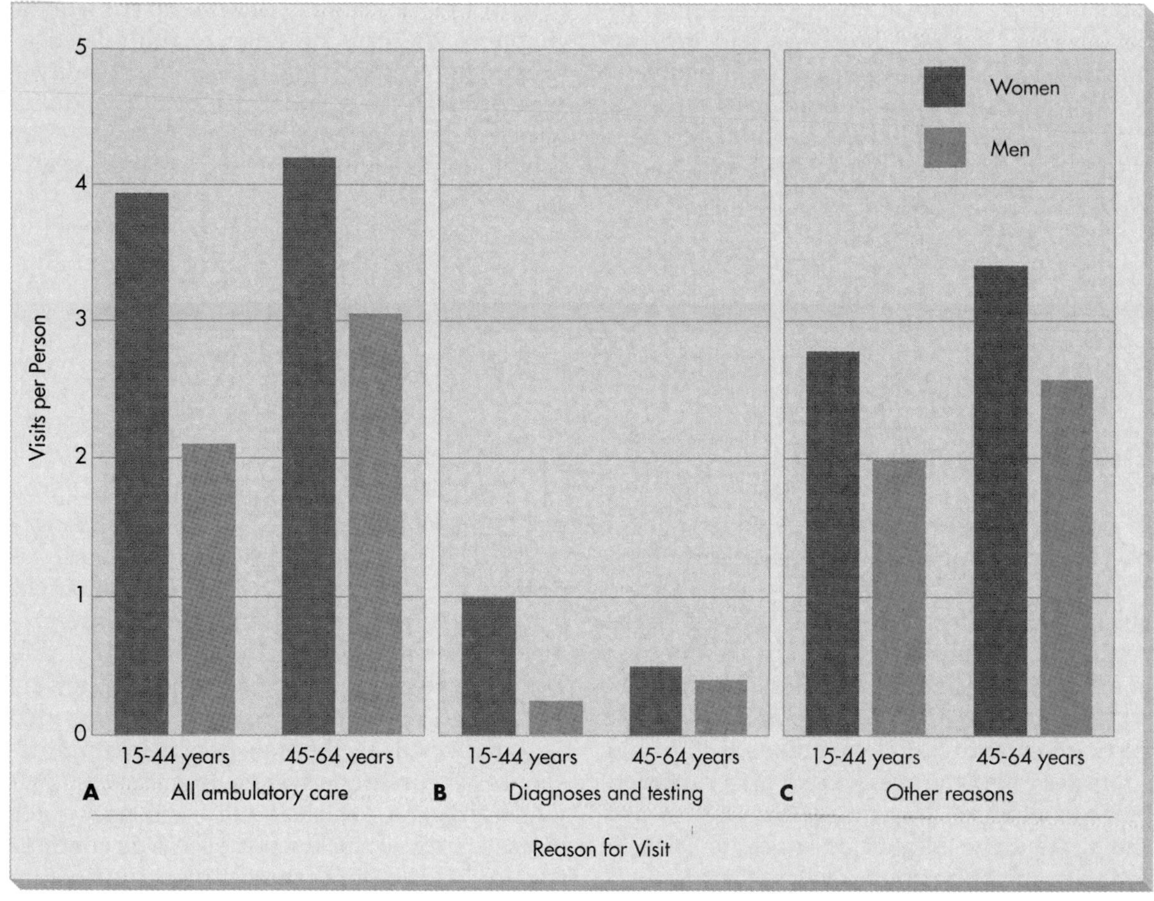

13-7 Visits to Physicians

In 1992, women visited private practice physicians, emergency rooms, and hospital outpatient clinics at a higher rare than men. As shown in panel A, among individuals 15–44 years of age, women made nearly twice as many visits as men. Part of the reason for this difference is found in panel B, which reveals that women were 5.7 times more likely than men to see a doctor for diagnosis, screening, and test results. Visits related to obstetrics and gynecology, including pregnancy and family planning, accounted for 60 percent of these types of visits for women of this age range. This panel also shows that women 45–64 years of age were about half as likely to see a physican for diagnosis, screening, and testing as were younger women. Thus, after excluding these visits from the picture, the gender gap in health care usage is similar for both age groups (see panel C). (Source: National Center for Health Statistics, 1996)

How we notice and interpret our bodily signals is influenced by a combination of psychological, social, and cultural factors. Women may be more sensitive to their bodily conditions than are men. People who are focused on themselves (their bodies and their emotions) are more likely to notice symptoms than people focused on their activities. Thus, socially isolated people (those who spend their time keeping house, who work at home, or who live alone) report more physical symptoms than people who are actively engaged in social activities, work outside the home, have interesting jobs, or live with others.

People also use various cognitive mechanisms to avoid confronting bad health news. They may deny their symptoms are serious enough to require a nurse or physician. Such mechanisms can lead to minimizing the significance of a symptom, delaying medical care, or failing to comply with physician instructions. Delay in treatment may have severe consequences: many disorders that are treatable in their initial stages can become incurable if allowed to progress. Understanding factors that determine people's health care use plays an important role in preventing unnecessary pain and premature death and is an important aspect of the health psychologist's role.

Reflections and Observations

The recognition that the current major causes of death in the United States are influenced by modifiable lifestyle factors and that mind and body interact to influence health has made health psychology an up-and-coming field that will continue to expand into the twenty-first century. This chapter reinforces the themes of this book in several ways. First, health behavior is affected by a combination of biological, psychological, and sociocultural factors all working in combination. Second, health psychology focuses on individuals in context, developing tools to study the relationship of health to behavior and cognitive processes and new approaches to enable men and women in diverse circumstances to live healthier lives. In doing so, it has demonstrated the usefulness of psychology in promoting physical and mental health and preventing illness. In subsequent chapters, we focus on other health-related issues. After considering normal personality—what it means to be a normal, healthy individual—we consider how personality theories are used to understand and treat mental disorder.

KEY TERMS

health psychology

behavioral medicine

mind-body dualism

biopsychosocial model

psychosomatic illness

immune system

lymphocyte

antigens

antibodies

cortisol

thymus gland

stress

fight-or-flight responses

ACTH

general adaptation syndrome

Objectives Revisited

In this chapter, we have considered how health psychologists think about the relationship between mind and body and the ways that our behavior can affect our health. Today it is recognized that illness derives from the interplay of many factors: genetic weakness, environmental stressors, early learning experiences, current experiences, individual cognitions, and coping strategies and resources can all affect susceptibility to disease. This means that health psychologists have significant roles to play in health promotion and disease prevention.

Objective 1. Discuss the definition, scope, and emergence of health psychology, explaining how the biopsychosocial model differs from the traditional biomedical approach.

Health psychology is the study of the psychological factors that contribute to health as well as illness and recovery from illness. Health psychology uses a *biopsychosocial model* that assumes biological, psychological, and social factors interact in determining health. This contrasts with the traditional biomedical model of Western medicine, which assumes that the mind and body operate separately and that illness can be reduced to biological malfunction. Other cultures have developed more holistic approaches to healing that are now being evaluated for their effectiveness by scientific methods.

Objective 2. Explain how the immune system functions to maintain our health.

The *immune system* is the body's primary defense against bacteria, viruses, and other foreign invaders. The immune system particularly depends on white blood cells, especially *lymphocytes*. The *nonspecific* immune response is designed to mobilize against any invasion of the body, while the *specific* immune response produces lymphocytes that are chemically programmed to attack a specific antigen. They are especially important in combating viruses that are unaffected by the nonspecific immune response. The immune system "remembers" previous antigens, which is why you only catch diseases such as chicken pox once. You continue to catch colds because these viruses mutate rapidly, and even small changes may make the virus unrecognizable to the immune system.

The immune system sometimes overreacts against pollens and other allergens to trigger an allergic response. Our immune system can also attack our own bodies, as in the case of rheumatoid arthritis. The body produces the hormone *cortisol* to suppress the activity of the immune system.

Acute stress temporarily suppresses the immune system. Chronic stress, loneliness, and environmental agents such as tobacco smoke and alcohol are also associated with decreased immune functioning.

Objective 3. Explain stress, the stress process, and how cognitive factors influence our reaction to stress.

Stress is a person's state when their physical or psychological well-being is threatened. Threatening events, called *stressors*, can be catastrophic events, major life events, or merely everyday frustrations. Reactions to them are called *stress responses*.

Stress can be acute or chronic, positive or negative, predictable or unpredictable, controllable or uncontrollable, and directly or vicariously experienced. A life event is more likely to be stressful if it is negative rather than positive, unpredictable rather than planned, or ambiguous or uncontrollable in character.

The *general adaptation syndrome* is a model for stages of the body's reaction to chronic stress: *alarm*, when the sympathetic nervous system quickly releases stress hormones; *resistance*, with continued high use of the body's defense mechanisms; and *exhaustion*, depletion of reserves, with the body at high risk for illness. But not everyone will react to the same events as stressful: some people will find them exhilarating, while even minor events will unravel other people.

Chemicals involved in the stress response influence both the immune and cardiovascular systems, providing pathways for stress to influence health. In addition, stress can affect health by leading people to engage in unhealthy behaviors that lower immune system functioning and/or impair cardiovascular activity.

Type A personalities are more likely to develop heart disease than others, perhaps because they have a more reactive sympathetic nervous system, leading to an exaggerated cardiovascular response to stress. They are also more likely to behave in unhealthy ways and to provoke stressful events.

How people think about an event determines their reaction to it. Cognitive appraisal of an event has two stages: *primary appraisal*, "What does this event mean to me?" and *secondary appraisal*, "What can I do about it?" One's belief in *personal control*, the capability of producing positive outcomes and warding off negative ones, reduces the effects of stress and enhances the ability to solve problems, even if the personal control is only perceived, not exercised. Greater personal control is related to reduced severity of illness and quicker recovery. *Hardiness*, a personal quality that makes people believe that what they're doing is worthwhile and that change provides opportunities, not simply problems, may make a difference in one's response to uncontrollable events.

Objective 4. Explain the role of coping in the stress process and identify a variety of coping strategies shown to be effective in managing stress.

The two basic types of coping strategies are *problem focused*, attempting to solve or eliminate a problem, and *emotion focused*, trying to reduce anxiety without directly dealing with the problem. Effective copers often use a combination of problem-focused and emotion-focused coping strategies.

Approaches to coping vary with *explanatory style*, one's habitual way of explaining the causes of events. A pessimistic explanatory style uses internal, stable, and global explanations for negative events, and pessimists generally engage in emotion-focused coping. An optimistic explanatory style attributes negative life events to external, unstable, and specific factors, and optimists are more likely to engage in problem-focused coping, which enables them to take active steps to deal with the problem.

Some effective coping strategies include cognitive interventions such as self-efficacy training; relaxation techniques, exercise on a regular basis; good nutrition; social support, where the support group is positive and promotes healthy behaviors; and self-disclosure, particularly about traumatic events, which seems to reduce levels of ill health.

Objective 5. Distinguish among theories of health behavior, and explain how health promotion interventions based on these theories would differ.

Health behaviors are behaviors that enhance or maintain health and are affected by cultural values, belief systems, and social pressures. *Health promotion* is the process of enabling people to increase control over their lives and improve their health by encouraging *health-enhancing* behaviors and discouraging *health-compromising* behaviors.

The *health belief model* suggests that people seek help for illness or engage in health-enhancing behaviors to the extent that they actually perceive a threat and that they believe a particular behavior will be effective. The *theory of reasoned action* argues that people have the behavioral intention to engage in health behaviors, depending on their attitudes and their subjective norms (what they think others whom they respect believe) about appropriate health behavior. The *theory of planned behavior* expands on this to assert that the performance of health behaviors also depends on a person's belief that he or she can in fact successfully adopt such behavior (*self-efficacy*), such as stopping smoking, and that such behavior will indeed promote health, such as preventing lung cancer (*outcome expectancy*).

Type A personality

Type B personality

primary appraisal

secondary appraisal

personal control

hardiness

problem-focused coping

emotion-focused coping

explanatory style

health habit

health promotion

health-enhancing behaviors

health-compromising behaviors

health belief model

reasoned action

planned behavior

C H A P T E R 14

Personality

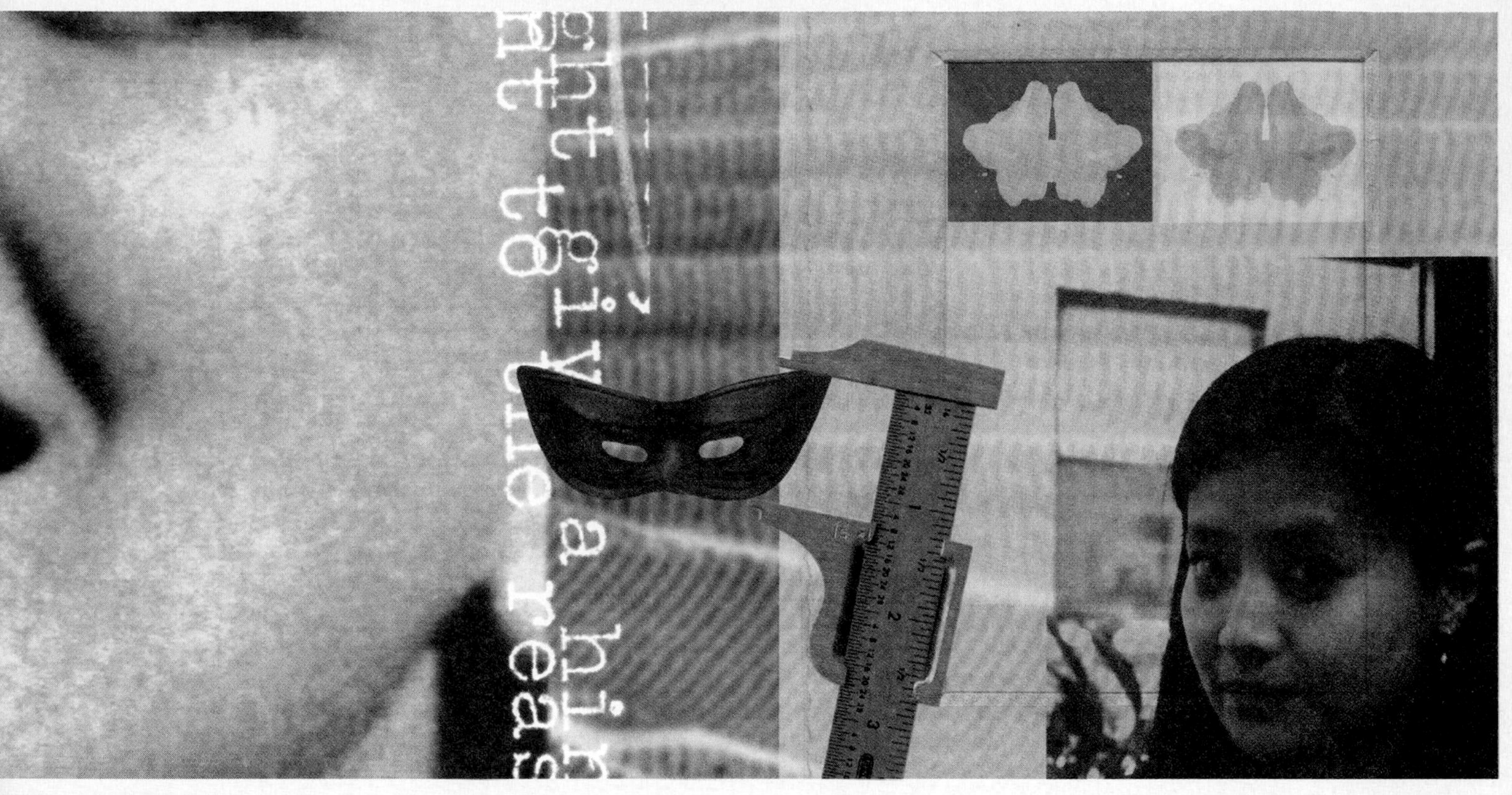

O B J E C T I V E S

After reading this chapter, you should be able to:

1. Describe the psychodynamic approach to personality, including Freud's original psychoanalytic theory as well as modern psychodynamic approaches.
2. Describe leading dispositional theories of personality.
3. Describe learning approaches to personality.
4. Describe humanistic approaches to personality.
5. Compare and contrast psychodynamic, dispositional, learning, and humanistic theories.
6. Describe the different approaches to personality assessment, and identify the strengths and weaknesses of each.

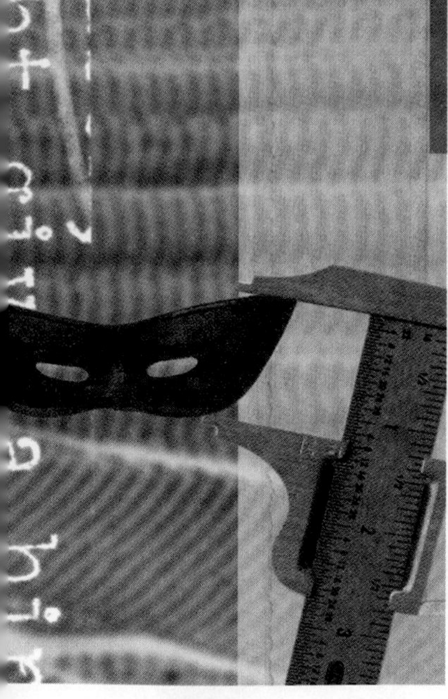

Carol, Claudia, and Cheryl are identical triplets. Their parents were conscientious about not playing favorites and tried to treat them equally. They grew up together in the same house, had the same teachers until the fourth grade, dressed alike until junior high school, and had the same friends. Each married her high school sweetheart. All the husbands happened to be scientists. Nonetheless, the triplets developed different interests, attended different colleges, and pursued different careers. Carol became a lawyer in Washington, D.C.; Claudia became a human resources consultant ("headhunter") in Massachusetts. Cheryl trained as a hospital emergency room medical technician and became a safety coordinator in charge of preventing industrial accidents in her company. Cheryl is less outgoing than Carol and Claudia. Carol and Cheryl have cats, while Claudia has no animals.

Personality can be defined as an individual's characteristic and enduring patterns of thought, emotion, and behavior.

Even though these three individuals began life with an identical genetic inheritance and shared the same childhood environment, each developed her own distinct way of viewing and interacting with the world. They demonstrate how people can be different from one another, even when they have the same genetic makeup and live in the same environment during their early years. Each of these triplets has her own unique ***personality***, which can be defined as an individual's characteristic and enduring patterns of thought, emotion, and behavior.

Who am I? What makes me who I am? Am I the same person today that I was ten years ago? How did I get to be the way I am? These are basic questions of interest to personality psychologists. Personality accounts for individual *differences* among people. It specifies what makes a person unique. Personality also refers to *consistencies* in people's behavior over time and situations. And finally, personality *develops* over the life span in response to internal and external influences: genetic, biological, social, environmental, and cultural.

Personality theories can be classified into *psychodynamic, dispositional, learning*, and *humanistic* approaches, each having different concerns and addressing different questions. Each makes somewhat different assumptions about human nature, and each has its own unique approach to studying personality. All have important things to say about "normal personality" as well as about how personalities may stray from what is considered normal behavior. Each ap-

► How is it that identical triplets Carol, Claudia, and Cheryl (pictured here as children and as adults) have developed unique personalities despite having the same genetic makeup and a similar childhood environment?

◀ *We express different aspects of our personality depending on the situation, but they are all "us."*

proach is effective in handling its own issues, but all suffer from "tunnel vision," and generally ignore issues and concerns of the other approaches. Consequently, forming a picture of the whole of human personality requires psychologists to consider people from all of these diverse perspectives (Funder, 1997; Hogan, Johnson, & Briggs, 1997).

The Psychodynamic Approach

The foundations for the psychodynamic approach were laid late in the nineteenth century, mainly by Sigmund Freud and his followers. In the summer of 1897, Sigmund Freud (1856–1939) embarked on a journey of self-exploration, analyzing his own personality. To his surprise, he discovered a sense of hostility toward his father and feelings of erotic love for his mother, emotions he was not conscious of prior to his self-analysis. Freud's self-revelations were later to appear as central concepts and principles in his psychodynamic theory of personality (Jones, 1953; Kris, 1954).

The ***psychodynamic approach*** assumes that behavior can be motivated by unconscious, often irrational forces, and that personality and personality development are shaped by intrapsychic ("within the mind") events and motives, including intrapsychic conflicts among motives that may not even enter consciousness. According to this viewpoint, motivational conflicts and their effect on personality can best be explored and understood through a careful, in-depth case study of individuals.

Freudian Theory

The Freudian approach, called psychoanalysis, is both the original psychodynamic theory and the name given to a therapeutic technique based on that theory. According to Freud, human behavior is a product of mental or psychological causes (Freud, 1916–1917/1976). Even though the cause may not be obvious to an outside observer or even to the person performing the behavior, all behavior "means" something. Writing the word "sex" when you mean "six," calling your lover by another person's name, forgetting a friend's birthday, or any other so-called "Freudian slip" can be interpreted as expressing feelings, desires, fears, or impulses that may be conscious or unconscious. It is these inner thoughts and conflicts that Freud believed were the driving force in the development of personality (Freud, 1905/1976; 1910/1976).

Freud believed that all human behavior means something, although its causes may not always be obvious to an outside observer or even to the person displaying the behavior.

Psychoanalytic theory assumes that the mind has three levels: preconscious, conscious, and unconscious (see Figure 14-1). Your ***precon-***

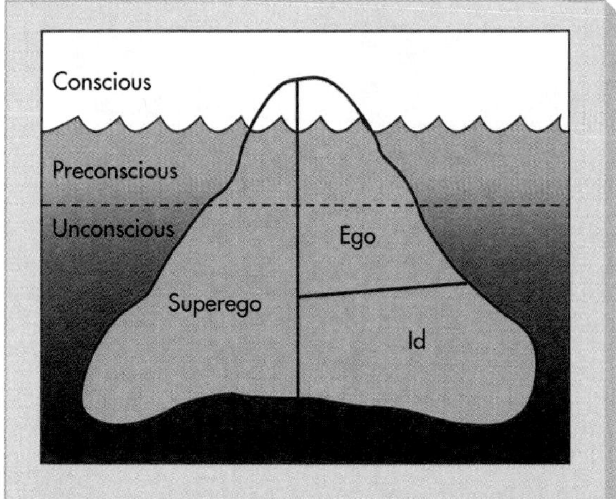

14-1 Freud's Iceberg Model

Freud used the analogy of an iceberg to describe the human mind. Like an iceberg, which shows only a small tip of ice above the surface, there is only a small portion of the mind that we are aware of.

scious mind holds thoughts and feelings that you are not aware of but that you can readily bring into consciousness. For example, you have probably not been aware of your tongue while reading this book. But once your attention is drawn to it, you can easily become aware of it. Your ***conscious*** mind holds your current thoughts and feelings—your conscious awareness (see Chapter 9). Your ***unconscious*** mind holds unacceptable or repressed impulses and conflicts that you are not aware of but that nonetheless seek to be expressed. Thus, you might harbor unacceptable anger and hatred toward a close friend or relative but be aware that such feelings exist because they are unconscious. Freud believed that we are conscious of only a small portion of what goes on in the mind, which is like the tip of an iceberg with most of its mass beneath the water's surface, (Freud, 1915/1976).

Psychosexual Development

According to the Freudian model, the mind needs psychic energy to make it run, and we only have so much of that energy at any particular moment. This energy fuels our behavior, and is based, in part, on a sexual or life drive that Freud called ***libido***. Human personality forms out of the continuous or dynamic struggle to channel our sexual and aggressive impulses in acceptable and effective ways. These sexual and aggressive instincts demand immediate gratification, but we cannot always gratify them directly without harm or embarrassment. Our lifelong task is somehow to satisfy instinctual urges while taking into account demands, rules, and realities of the environment and society. For example, aggressive impulses may be channeled into participation in contact sports such as boxing or ice hockey, which provide societally approved outlets for aggressive behavior.

► *As the Vampire Lestat, Tom Cruise portrays a mythical being dominated by his libido. According to legend, a vampire's thirst for blood reflects a desire for sexual gratification.*

During childhood, we pass through a series of psychosexual stages in which our psychic energy is centered in turn on particular parts of the body. Each stage is named for the area of the body most closely associated with pleasure at that particular time. In the ***oral stage***, the infant focuses on the mouth and on pleasures derived from eating and sucking; in the ***anal stage***, the child focuses on pleasures of controlling or releasing bowels. Following the anal stage (at about age four), the genitals become the principal source of pleasure, and the child enters the ***phallic stage***. Identification with the same-sex parent takes place during the phallic stage. According to Freud, this occurs through resolving the *Oedipus complex*, wherein the boy desires his mother and wishes to eliminate and replace his father. As a result, he experiences castration anxiety (a fear that his father will cut off his genitals), which he finally resolves by identifying with his father. The girl experiences penis envy (the desire to have a penis), but she ultimately comes to identify with her mother.

In the ***latent stage***, sexuality is on hold, and therefore libidinal energy is not focused on a specific area of the body. During adolescence, the child matures biologically, physically, and sexually and enters the ***genital stage***, which lasts through the adult years. Pleasure is again focused in the genital area, but the individual seeks more than the self-satisfaction that is characteristic of the phallic stage. According to Freud, if all has gone well in the earlier psychosexual stages, the person will seek in this stage to establish stable, long-term heterosexual relationships that are not only sexually self-fulfilling but that also take into account the needs of a partner.

In each stage, there is a conflict between satisfying basic impulses and societal demands. Personality is shaped by how each psychosexual stage is resolved. If the conflicts are not resolved appropriately and fully, the individual will become "fixated" (or stuck) in that stage. For example, if toilet training is too strict during the anal stage, the child will be obstinate, stingy, and meticulous in adulthood. Issues related to the conflicts will be troublesome throughout life (see Table 14-1).

Table 14-1 Possible Conflicts among the Aspects of Personality

Conflict	Example
Id versus ego	Choosing between a small immediate reward and a larger reward that requires some period of waiting (that is, delay of gratification).
Id versus superego	Deciding whether to return the difference when you are overpaid or undercharged.
Ego versus superego	Choosing between acting in a realistic way (for example, telling a harmless fib) and adhering to a potentially costly or unrealistic standard (for example, always telling the truth).
Id and ego versus superego	Deciding whether to retaliate against the attack of a weak opponent or to "turn the other cheek."
Id and superego versus ego	Deciding whether to act in a realistic way that conflicts with both your desires and your moral convictions (for example, the decision faced by devout Roman Catholics as to the use of contraceptive devices).
Ego and superego versus id	Choosing whether to "act on the impulse" to steal something you want and cannot afford—the ego would presumably be increasingly involved in such a conflict as the probability of being apprehended increased.

Structure of Personality

Psychoanalytic theory assumes a three-part personality structure: id, ego, and superego. The ***id*** is the unconscious, instinctual component of personality—the irrational part of the mind. It contains inherited sexual, aggressive, and other impulses that seek immediate expression in behavior. Babies are all id—a mass of basic, unverbalized needs and feelings. The id operates according to the ***pleasure principle*** (it does what "feels good") and seeks immediate gratification for its desires—"I want it *all* and I want it *now*." The id is part of the unconscious, and not responsive to the concerns of the outside world. If you have ever heard a baby's piercing cry to be fed or changed, you can appreciate the demanding character of the id-driven infant.

As a child grows, the real world increasingly limits direct gratification of the id's instinctual impulses. A second component of personality, the ***ego***, begins to take shape. The ego is the partly conscious, rational part of the mind that is in contact with external reality. It mediates between the id's demands and reality's constraints. Its main function is to gratify id impulses while protecting the individual from harm. The ego operates on the ***reality principle***, taking reality into account in channeling id impulses. It makes sure that impulses are gratified at appropriate times and places and makes compromises in order to maximize gratification.

As development proceeds, the personality's third component, the ***superego***, emerges. The superego represents the internalized teachings of a person's family and culture on ethics, morals, and values (guidelines for how the individual *should* behave). It is roughly equivalent to the individual's "conscience." Feelings of guilt result from failing to follow superego demands.

The three parts of the personality are in constant conflict with each other. The ego tries to reconcile the id's impetuous impulses, the superego's perfectionistic demands, and the

The id operates according to the pleasure principle, seeking to gratify its desires without delay. The ego, in contrast, operates on the reality principle, taking the constraints of the environment and society into account.

◀ *According to Freud, the id, the ego, and the superego all have competing voices. Choosing the "best" message to follow can be difficult.*

outside world's requirements. This idea of psychic conflict distinguishes psychoanalytic theory from other personality theories, and it can explain why people may behave in self-destructive, irrational ways (when the id occasionally triumphs, if only temporarily). Freud's theory presents a somewhat pessimistic view of people as driven by hedonistic (pleasure-seeking) urges resulting in continual inner conflict.

Defense mechanisms, the most prominent of which is repression, are employed by the ego to keep id impulses out of consciousness.

Ego Defense Mechanisms

According to psychoanalytic theory, the ego protects the individual from (1) physical threats, (2) the direct expression of id impulses, and (3) condemnation by the superego when its standards are violated. For example, id impulses might cause Rachel to want to go out with David, her roommate's fiancé. The superego would recognize that it would be a betrayal of friendship and morally wrong to act on this impulse. Aware of these competing urges and also recognizing potential danger (if her friend found out, she would probably get angry and retaliate by moving), the ego would prevent Rachel from acting on the impulse—perhaps by giving her a tension headache so severe that she would have to lie down and stay in her bedroom whenever David visited the apartment.

If anyone forgets a proper name which is familiar to him normally or if, in spite of all his efforts, he finds it difficult to keep it in mind, it is plausible to suppose that he has something against the person who bears the name so that he prefers not to think of him.
—Sigmund Freud (1917, p. 52)

The ego uses a host of ***defense mechanisms*** to keep id impulses in check and out of consciousness (see Table 14-2). ***Repression*** is listed first because it is the basic defense mechanism underlying all of the others. It is a type of motivated forgetting in which you shut memory of past events out of consciousness. In preventing your awareness of sexual attraction toward a friend's boyfriend, your ego might even cause you to repress the boyfriend's name. If id impulses threatened to emerge into consciousness, anxiety would occur, and the ego would move to repress the threatening thoughts and reduce anxiety. Like trying to hold a fully inflated beach ball under water, however, repression requires constantly applying psychic energy, which could be used more productively in meeting life's daily challenges. The goal of psychoanalysis is to bring psychic conflicts into consciousness and to deal with them so that the energy involved in repressing them may be freed up for more useful purposes.

When ego defenses fail, we may exhibit ***regression*** (reverting to behavior characteristic of earlier, less mature developmental stages). Hospitalized children separated from their parents for the first time often display behavior they "outgrew" years earlier, like thumb sucking or bedwetting. Partial regression may result in behaviors that are simply immature or are other-

Table 14-2 Ego Defense Mechanisms

Mechanism	Characteristics
Repression	Bottling up unacceptable thoughts/feelings in the unconscious mind so they don't spill over into the conscious mind.
Denial	Keeping anxiety-producing perceptions, thoughts, and feelings from affecting consciousness by denying they exist.
Displacement	Redirecting thoughts and impulses to allow disguised expression of id impulses. Strong emotional responses may be redirected from a dangerous person to a nonthreatening one.
Projection	Believing (often mistakenly) that others have one's own unacceptable thoughts and motives.
Rationalization	Justifying thoughts and actions deriving from unacceptable motives by inventing socially acceptable reasons for them while remaining unaware of the "real" unconscious reason.
Reaction Formation	Converting a negative or unacceptable thought or behavior into its opposite.
Regression	Responding to an anxiety-producing situation/event with behavior from an earlier, and inappropriate, stage of development.
Sublimation	Redirecting motives toward more productive and socially desirable goals. Freud often wrote as if he thought sublimation accounted for all major creative works.

THINKING CRITICALLY

The ego uses a variety of defense mechanisms to keep unacceptable impulses in check. Refer to Table 14-2 and identify the defense mechanisms that underlie the following examples.

1. A man who dislikes animals becomes a zookeeper.
2. A woman with an unconscious hatred for her parents feels no hostility toward them, but becomes extremely anxious in their presence.
3. A college student, anxious about flunking out, starts wetting the bed at night.
4. Parents physically harm their child while administering daily punishments, saying such punishment builds "strong moral fiber."
5. A man is overly protective of his daughter, refusing to let her date, saying that boys are interested in nothing but a woman's body.
6. An individual is forced to declare bankruptcy, but continues to live an extravagant lifestyle.
7. A sexually frustrated graduate student spends every waking hour in the lab testing a mentor's pet theory.
8. An executive, having lost out on a promotion, fires her secretary.

The answers are (1) reaction formation, (2) repression, (3) regression, (4) rationalization, (5) projection, (6) denial, (7) sublimation, (8) displacement.

Any behavior can be interpreted in a variety of ways, many of which are normal and do not involve a defense mechanism against anxiety. A man can protect his daughter out of love, and secretaries may be fired because they are incompetent. It takes careful work by a trained therapist to determine if a defense mechanism underlies a behavior.

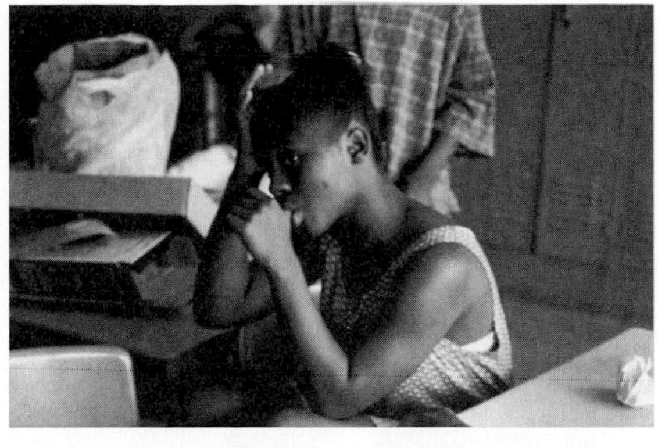

◀ *Freud might explain this girl's thumb-sucking as regression in response to stress.*

wise mildly inappropriate, for example, an adult's temper tantrum. More profound regression can result in severely disturbed behavior.

Variations on Freudian Theory

Psychodynamic theory evolved from Freud's early psychoanalytic theory. Although it is often thought of as the work of a single genius, it actually reflects years of discussion and interaction between Sigmund Freud and his many followers. Freud constantly revised, altered, edited, and supplemented his views, so we can hardly speak of *the* Freudian theory today. Freud himself clung to a few basic principles, notably the assumed instinctual basis of human behavior and the emphasis on sex and aggression. But later theorists had a different vision of what motivates us. They tended to deemphasize the inherited, instinctual basis of human behavior, giving more attention to environmental factors, especially those from the social context.

Jung's Analytic Psychology

Carl Jung (1875–1961) was one of Freud's closest associates. After he left Freud's Viennese circle, Jung developed ***analytic psychology***, which included many of Freud's ideas: defense mechanisms, unconscious motives, and an emphasis on intrapsychic conflicts. But he also made major innovations, arguing that our psychic force is focused on more than just sexual and aggressive instincts (Jung, 1916, 1925). To Jung, *spiritual needs* (the need for fulfillment of the soul) are as strong as (if not stronger than) biological needs, and *future aspirations* are as important as past experiences for influencing personality. Jung thought each person has an

▲ *To Jung, the collective unconscious explains why human beings around the world tend to share basic images. A symbol of the snake arises in an Australian aboriginal bark painting, in an ancient Egyptian tomb painting, and in a fifteenth-century French illumination.*

innate tendency to develop an "essential self," to establish his or her own individuality, and to resolve conflicts between demands of intrapsychic forces and those of the real world.

Jung supplemented the personal unconscious of Freudian theory with a ***collective unconscious***, which contains basic images and ideas shared by all human beings and exists at an even deeper level than the personal unconscious. Jung used the collective unconscious to explain why human beings around the world tend to share certain tendencies—for example, to believe in a god, to have heroes, and to be afraid of the dark or of snakes. To Jung, behavior reflects a combination of (1) the collective unconscious, (2) the personal unconscious (essentially as Freud described it), and (3) the unique pattern of personality traits each person forms to adjust to the world.

The collective unconscious is a Jungian construct that contains basic images and ideas shared by all human beings.

Like Freud, Jung believed behavior disorders result from conflicts among various aspects of personality. He believed that if conflicts among the personal unconscious, the ego, and the collective unconscious became so extreme that their underlying unity was shattered, abnormal behavior might result. In contrast to Freud's pessimistic, id-dominated view of the individual Jung viewed personality as guided by a forward-looking, goal-directed process.

Ego Psychology

Revisions of Freud's ideas emphasized the ego and its development, as well as the influence of social and cultural factors, rather than biological or instinctual processes. These revisions were motivated, in part, by dissatisfaction with Freud's pessimism. They also reflected an interest in principles that guide normal, healthy psychological development. This led to the study of ego development in very young children and focused attention on types of parenting, infant attachment, and the environment in which the infant is raised (Escalona, 1968; Hartmann, 1958; Mahler, 1968; Spitz, 1945).

A good example of ***ego psychology*** is found in the work of Sigmund Freud's daughter, Anna Freud (1895–1982), who emphasized the ego's role in helping people to adapt, to solve problems, and to be creative (A. Freud, 1936/1966). She believed that the ego's functions go beyond merely defending against anxiety and resolving unconscious conflicts. She saw the ego as containing *conflict-free* areas that promote growth, autonomy (independence), mastery over the environment, learning and memory, perception and attention, and language development. She was a pioneer in the development of child psychoanalysis and expanded the psychoanalytic approach to account for normal development as well as psychopathology (Liebert & Spiegler, 1974).

Sociocultural Approaches

A social, interpersonal, or societal emphasis in psychoanalysis was developed by such theorists as Alfred Adler, Karen Horney, Heinz Kohut, Erich Fromm, and Harry Stack Sullivan. They believed that Freud failed to consider important social and cultural aspects of personality development. Personality, they claimed, is shaped more by society, culture, and other people than by instincts and other inborn factors, and new experiences can modify personality. These views emphasized individual differences more than earlier Freudian theory had. According to these theorists, personality development occurs not just in childhood, but over the life span.

Although Freud emphasized male sexuality and intrapsychic processes, some theorists balanced that view with greater attention to female psychodynamics. Karen Horney (1885–1952) rejected Freud's assertion that females experience penis envy. Instead, she said that women envy the privilege, power, and status in society that men possess, not their penises. She described how social and cultural factors can make women dependent on men for resources, prestige, protection, and love. This dependence, in turn, fosters an "overvaluation of love" and a "cult of beauty and charm" to please men (Horney, 1934).

Horney advanced the concept of womb envy, suggesting that males feel a loss when they learn that only women can bear children. She also emphasized the interpersonal psychological relationship between parent and child, suggesting that basic anxiety was a social experience consisting of "the feeling a child has of being isolated and helpless in a potentially hostile world" (Horney, 1945, p. 41). Horney traced psychological problems to children's mistreatment by their parents, including parental indifference to the child, unfair rewards and punishments, ridicule, unkept promises, overprotection, and preference for another sibling (Horney, 1937). She believed that if people are unhappy with themselves, they may repress their negative characteristics and create an idealized image of a perfect self. Maintaining this self-image can create unrealistic, unfulfillable demands for perfection, which Horney called "the tyranny of the should" (Horney, 1950, p. 66). In addition to emphasizing the importance of self and self-awareness, her theory explored the role of irrational thinking in neurosis. Today her influence can be seen in cognitive-behavioral therapy, particularly in the rational-emotive therapy of Albert Ellis, the client-centered therapy of Carl Rogers, and the Gestalt therapy of Fritz Perls (see Chapter 16).

Object relations theory reflects a combination of developments in ego psychology and recognition of the importance of sociocultural influences. "Object relations" refers to the attachments we have to "objects" in the environment. "Objects" can include both people and inanimate objects, such as a child's attachment to teddy bears and blankets, or a college student's attachments to an old high school trophy or a favorite CD. Instead of focusing on internal conflicts, object relations theorists focus on the nature of the person's relationships with others. They look at how we develop and separate from our parents and learn to see both good and bad in other people and in ourselves.

◀ Object relations theorists focus on the attachments that we form to objects—animate and inanimate—in our environments to explain personality. Many children grow attached to both animate and inanimate objects. The security blanket is an example of an attachment to an inanimate object.

Heinz Kohut emphasized the development of an integrated, cohesive self, and he incorporated social factors in his psychodynamic theory of object relations (Kohut, 1971, 1977). In particular, he emphasized the importance of what he called self-objects, people in our social contexts whom we experience as part of our sense of self (remember the concept of interdependent sense of self discussed in Chapter 12). Parents are natural self-objects in the growing infant's environment. To Kohut, normal development involves the continuous interaction between the self and the self-objects we encounter in our culture. He reinterpreted the period during which Freud thought the child was resolving the Oedipal conflict as a time when male children practice being assertive with their fathers and affectionate with their mothers. It is only when mothers have conflicts over the relationship of sex and affection and when fathers are threatened by a son's assertions that the child's behaviors become sexualized.

Limitations of the Psychodynamic Approach

Freud's influence on modern personality theory has been enormous. Freudian concepts are so well known that they are now part of our ordinary language and culture. We commonly hear people refer in everyday conversation to such things as "Freudian slips," unconscious motivation, repression, and psychoanalysis.

Freudian theory focuses on areas of personality neglected by other theories and brings needed attention to mental life and particularly the unconscious as factors that determine behavior. It has been strongly criticized on several counts, however. First, it is *not verifiable*: some of its concepts are so ill-defined (for example, id, ego, superego, libido) that they cannot be tested. Moreover, techniques such as dream interpretation and free association cannot be tested experimentally: they lack reliability, as they may not produce the same findings in each session; and they lack validity, as they may not hold up when examined more closely (riding on a train may not really stand for sexual intercourse; there may not actually be such a thing as penis envy). Also, many psychoanalytic observations are based on confidential patient material, so it is impossible to verify them.

Second, psychoanalytic theory *violates the law of parsimony*—that is, the assumption that the simplest explanation is the best one, all other things being equal. Theories that account for behavior in a more direct, straightforward way may work better than complicated psychoanalytic explanations. For example, Freud had many female patients who complained of sexual abuse by male family members. He developed elaborate explanations for what motivated these women to fabricate stories rather than looking to the simplest explanation—the women had actually suffered real abuse.

A disposition is an enduring and dominant tendency to behave in a particular way in any situation.

Third, Freud's theory *lacks disconfirmability*. Virtually any evidence can be interpreted as consistent with psychoanalytic theory. For example, if we conclude from psychodynamic interviews that a person harbors strong unconscious feelings of hostility toward others, *any* subsequent hostile behavior will be interpreted as evidence of a breakthrough of these unconscious impulses, "confirming" the original hypothesis. Even *lack* of hostile behavior can be considered evidence for underlying hostility, because it can be seen as successful repression. Moreover, psychodynamic personality theories seem to imply that almost any behavior might indicate problems, where in fact none may exist. Bill may be called anxious and insecure if he shows up for work early, resistant and hostile if late, and compulsive if right on time!

All admit that in a certain sense the several kinds of character are bestowed by nature. Justice, a tendency to temperance, courage, and the other types of character are exhibited from the moment of birth.

—Aristotle, *Nicomachean Ethics*

Finally, because Freud's approach was based mainly on a relatively small number of case studies (a few upper-middle-class European patients and Freud himself), psychodynamic formulations have been criticized as bound by time and place and lacking relevance to most people's lives. In particular, psychoanalytic theory reflects nineteenth-century attitudes toward women. Examination of the description of psychosexual stages reveals that male development is the norm (particularly with regard to the phallic stage of development). Because females are basically considered castrated males, they are viewed as having less self-esteem and moral judgment. Even having a baby, a distinctive feature of womanhood, was viewed by Freud as penis compensation. Needless to say, these ideas are not supported by scientific research (Kihlstrom, 1994).

The Dispositional Approach

Have you ever made conclusions about someone's personality based on consistent traits and behavior patterns over time, such as: "You've always been such a serious person, even as a baby you would examine things intensely," "He's the nervous type," or "She's a kind person?" If so, you were adopting a dispositional theory of personality. These theories start with the assumption that we have enduring and dominant personal qualities called ***dispositions*** that lead us to behave in certain ways and not others (Winter, 1996). These dispositions, which include traits and temperaments as well as habits, motives, goals, attitudes, values, and cognitions, make up your personality. ***Traits*** are characteristic and stable patterns of thought, feeling, and behavior. Combinations of traits account for each individual's uniqueness and for similar reactions to different situations, that is, behavioral consistency across situations. For example, a person who is highly anxious when taking a test may also become highly anxious in other situations in which performance is being evaluated. ***Temperament*** consists of broad emotional traits that are believed to have a substantial genetic basis.

Trait Theories

What traits do you think of when asked to describe yourself? Are you funny, serious, dependable, unreliable, happy, sad, or sometimes each of these? Think about all of the words we have in the English language to describe personality traits—17,953, according to one count (Allport & Odbert, 1936). All languages have such words, although some traits are specific to some cultures. For example, the Japanese have a concept of *amae*—which means presuming or depending upon another person's benevolence. It sounds like our concept of dependency, but that is deceptive. Westerners expect people to grow out of being dependent, but in Japan, *amae* is consciously recognized as a need that continues throughout adulthood. In fact, *amae* may contribute to the interdependent sense of self encouraged in collectivistic societies (Doi, 1962).

Trait theories translate our everyday language for personality traits into a scientific psychology that uses traits to predict and understand behavior. Although they attempt to identify basic personality dimensions that underlie behavior, trait theories recognize that the same trait may be expressed differently, depending on the situation or environment.

Allport's Trait Theory

Gordon Allport (1897–1967) was one of the first psychologists to study personality by identifying and measuring personality traits, which he believed were ultimately based on neurological mechanisms or processes. Allport argued that it was important to try to identify general principles of personality as well as individual differences. Individuals could be studied through examining autobiographical histories, personal diaries and papers, open-ended questionnaires, and interviews. One of Allport's well-known case studies involved analyzing 301 letters written by a woman named Jenny over an eleven-year period (Allport, 1961). In Jenny's case, Allport analyzed the letters to identify general, universal tendencies, as well as to create a personality portrait of Jenny as a unique individual. These two approaches—examining general principles and individual differences—are complementary, each having much to contribute to the study of personality.

Allport classified traits according to the extent to which they apply across situations. ***Cardinal traits*** determine behavior in the widest range of circumstances. A cardinal trait essentially describes an individual's personality, affecting everything that person does. Think of people like Mother Teresa, who was famous for her compassion. Most people do not have a cardinal trait, but when one exists it is pervasive and overriding. The uniqueness of cardinal traits can be seen from some of the names given to them: "napoleonic," "narcissistic," "puckish," "quixotic," and "sadistic" were all derived from the names of remarkable fictional or historical people (Allport, 1937).

▲ *Some people have an obvious cardinal trait. The Iraqi dictator Saddam Hussein is napoleonic in his attempts to conquer his neighbors. Actor Robin Williams is puckish in his exceptional silliness. South African leader Nelson Mandela could be considered quixotic because of his persistent idealism despite seemingly insurmountable odds.*

Central traits, personality's "building blocks," are not as broad or dominant as cardinal traits, but they are still general. Even casual acquaintances readily notice them. They are captured by familiar adjectives, such as "outgoing," "punctual," "efficient," and "optimistic." Finally, at the lowest level are ***secondary traits***, which are less conspicuous, less consistent, and less generalized than central traits. They typically apply in a limited range of circumstances (for example, "Casey is grouchy in the morning"). All of us possess, according to Allport, central and secondary traits, but few people have cardinal traits (Allport, 1961).

Traits are stable attributes of thought, feeling, and behavior that can be innate or learned. Temperament refers to broad emotional traits believed to have a substantial genetic basis. Collectively, they constitute our personality.

Factor Analysis

Allport's theory has been criticized for its vagueness and open-endedness. On the positive side, it is so exhaustive it can describe anyone's personality. But several lifetimes could be spent researching the thousands of trait names in the English language alone. Faced with the daunting task of making sense out of a multitude of traits, trait theorists began seeking the smallest number of traits needed to describe personality differences across individuals. They turned to the statistical technique of ***factor analysis*** to help in that search.

Factor analysis provides researchers with a means to identify relationships among traits so that they can be grouped together (see Appen-

Allport searched for general principles of personality that applied to all or most people, while also seeking to identify the unique characteristics of each person.

According to Allport, the most general traits are cardinal traits, those at an intermediate level are central traits, and the least general are secondary traits.

dix on p. A-17). Researchers use factor analysis to find which traits correlate with one another. Is someone who is "assertive" also likely to be "gregarious" and "active," for example? These particular traits are indeed correlated, and so they are grouped under a larger category called "extraversion" (Costa & McCrae, 1992). The larger categories of grouped items are called ***factors***, and they are assumed to represent basic personality dimensions. Personality theories based on factor analysis assume that there are a small number of personality dimensions that are fundamental and universal—everyone has them.

Factor analysis is a statistical technique for identifying the basic dimensions that underlie a cluster of traits.

The number and kinds of factors identified often vary depending on what is being studied, and so we still do not have a definitive list of basic groupings of personality traits. Raymond B. Cattell (1905–) used factor analysis to identify sixteen basic personality dimensions that he called ***source traits*** (Cattell & Krug, 1986). He conceptualized these traits as varying along a scale (for example, reserved-outgoing, submissive-dominant), rather than as "all-or-none" classifications (see Table 14–3). People can be slightly or extremely reserved, for example. He constructed the widely used *16PF* (*Personality Factor*) Test to measure the relative strength of these sixteen dimensions in any normal adult individual (Cattell, Ebel, & Tatsuoka, 1970). A person's scores on the sixteen different subsets of items, each measuring a different trait, can be used to construct a personality profile.

Table 14-3 Cattell's 16 Source Traits

1.	Reserved	↔	Outgoing
2.	Less intelligent	↔	More intelligent
3.	Affected by feelings	↔	Emotionally stable
4.	Submissive	↔	Dominant
5.	Serious	↔	Happy-go-lucky
6.	Expedient	↔	Conscientious
7.	Timid	↔	Venturesome
8.	Tough-minded	↔	Sensitive
9.	Trusting	↔	Suspicious
10.	Practical	↔	Imaginative
11.	Forthright	↔	Shrewd
12.	Self-assured	↔	Apprehensive
13.	Conservative	↔	Experimenting
14.	Group-dependent	↔	Self-sufficient
15.	Uncontrolled	↔	Controlled
16.	Relaxed	↔	Tense

14-2 Eysenck's Dimensions of Personality

British psychologist Hans Eysenck (1916–1997), another proponent of the factor analytic approach, proposed that only three broad dimensions are needed to explain personality: (1) introversion-extraversion, (2) stable-unstable (sometimes known as the neuroticism dimension), and (3) psychoticism. *Introversion-extraversion* refers to your tendency to seek stimulation from other people. Do you like being with other people? Do you prefer to sit home alone and read a book? *Neuroticism* reflects your degree of moodiness and anxiety. Does your mood often go up and down? Are you anxious in new situations? *Psychoticism* reflects the degree to which you are in contact with reality, control your impulses, and are cruel and aggressive or sensitive and caring toward other people. Do you hear voices? When you are angry, do you start hitting people and throwing objects? A trait such as "conservative" or "outgoing" is assumed to reflect a combination of these three dimensions (Eysenck, 1991; see Figure 14–2). The Eysenck Personality Questionnaire (EPQ) was developed to measure these three dimensions (Eysenck & Eysenck, 1975).

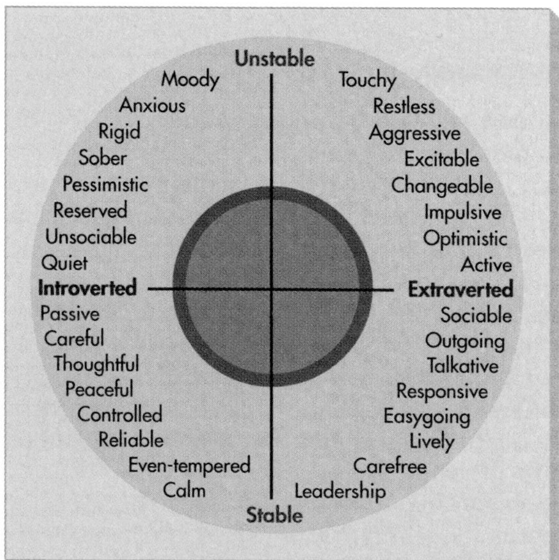

Hans Eysenck believed that there are three basic dimensions of personality (introversion-extraversion, neuroticism, psychoticism), and that varying combinations of these dimensions produce predictable traits. He found that most people had traits that fell along two of the dimensions: introversion-extraversion and stable-unstable (neuroticism). Someone who is very stable and very extraverted would probably have leadership traits, whereas someone who is very unstable (or emotional) and very introverted would probably be moody. The third dimension, psychoticism, is more relevant to those with psychological disorders. (Source: Eysenck & Rachman, 1965, p. 16)

Eysenck linked these dimensions to biology. He believed that introversion and extraversion could be correlated with brain arousal and that introverts would avoid high arousal levels (Eysenck, 1981). Subsequent research by others suggests that introverts do demonstrate greater sensitivity in their sensory processing. For example, they are more sensitive to pain, low-pitched sounds, and olfactory and visual stimulation than are extraverts (Koelega, 1992; Kohn, 1987; Stelmack, 1990).

Controversy about the number and nature of personality traits is still intense. At present, factor analysis has begun to converge on five basic traits, sometimes called the "Big Five": extraversion, agreeableness, conscientiousness, emotionality (neuroticism) and openness to experience/intellect (see Table 14-4; Wiggins & Trapnell, 1997). Although these traits are sometimes called by different names, they nonetheless reliably describe observed variations among people in the United States, Canada, Finland, Poland, and Germany (Costa & Widiger, 1993; Paunonen, Jackson, Trzebinski, & Fosterline, 1992). A person's overall profile on the Big Five is relatively stable, consistent, and predictable over many years and across many situations (John, Caspi, Robins, Moffitt, & Stouthamer-Loeber, 1994).

Reducing personality descriptions to the Big Five is not to say that all of personality can be reduced to a mere five traits. There are lower levels in the trait hierarchy. But these lower-level traits can all be included under the Big Five headings. For example, the Big Five trait of extraversion is divided into six component subtraits: affiliation, positive affectivity, energy, ascendance, venturesomeness, and ambition. These, in turn, are subdivided into sub-subtraits. For example, affiliation is subdivided into warmth and gregariousness, and positive affectivity is divided into joy and enthusiasm (Watson & Clark, 1997).

Table 14-4 The Big Five Personality Factors

Factor	Description
Extraversion	sociable vs. retiring fun-loving vs. sober affectionate vs. reserved
Agreeableness	soft-hearted vs. ruthless trusting vs. suspicious helping vs. uncooperative
Conscientiousness	well-organized vs. disorganized careful vs. careless
Emotionality (Neuroticism)	calm vs. anxious secure vs. insecure self-satisfied vs. self-pitying
Openness to Experience/Intellect	imaginative vs. practical preference for variety vs. preference for routine independent vs. conforming

Source: Adapted from McCrae & John, 1992.

Biological Dispositions

Research on dispositions has also focused on the biological bases of specific behaviors that make up personality. Some researchers have focused on how the structure and functioning of the brain and nervous system affect behavior, while others have studied the effects of hormones and neurotransmitters. For example, people high in sensation seeking—the desire to try new and even dangerous experiences—may have nervous systems that perform optimally under high levels of arousal (Zuckerman, Buchsbaum, & Murphy, 1980). Other researchers have examined the contribution of heredity to personality (see Chapter 3; Bouchard & McGue, 1981). They have found that genetics contributes to variation across individuals for a wide variety of behaviors, including shyness, clothing preferences, and absent-mindedness (Brody, 1993). In some cases, such as emotionality, the genetic contribution can be remarkably high. But variations in personality across individuals are influenced by both genetics and the environment (Brody, 1993; Rowe, 1997).

Research on the inheritance of temperament has focused on the specific behaviors that go into defining temperament, which include activity level (how energetic we are), emotionality (how easily and intensely upset we are in response to negative events), soothability (how quickly we become calm after being upset), fearfulness, and sociability (how receptive we are to social stimulation) (Buss & Plomin, 1984; Goldsmith et al., 1987). From infancy onward, identical twins are slightly more alike than fraternal twins on a variety of temperament measures, including activity level, demands for attention, irritability, and sociability (Plomin, DeFries, & Fulker, 1988; Rowe, 1997; Wilson & Matheny, 1986).

In longitudinal research on temperament, Jerome Kagan and his colleagues examined the stability of the tendency to withdraw from unfamiliar people or situations, an attribute they call behavioral inhibition (Kagan, Reznick,

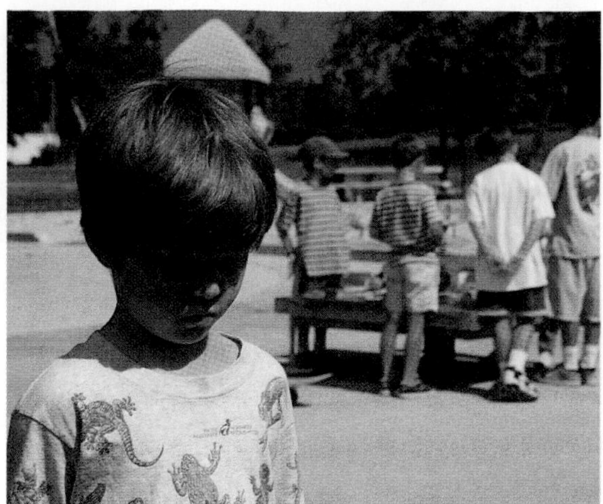

► *Why is this boy shy? Research suggests that shyness reflects an interaction between one's heredity and environment.*

Snidman, Gibbons, & Johnson, 1988; Kagan, 1989; Kagan & Snidman, 1991). Approximately 10 percent of children are inhibited—that is, consistently shy and emotionally restrained in novel situations. The researchers compared the children's test scores at twenty-one months to their scores at four, five-and-a-half, and seven-and-a-half years of age, and found that children who were inhibited at twenty-one months were inhibited at later ages as well. Moreover, inhibited children displayed higher heart rates in response to new situations than did uninhibited children.

Behavioral inhibition may have a hereditary component. Children who are born with nervous systems that are highly responsive to stimulation may react more to novel stimuli, which may lead them to become inhibited in order to avoid becoming aroused. About one out of four infants who have a highly responsive nervous system are not inhibited in later years, however. Physiological responsiveness *interacts* with environmental conditions to determine level of behavioral inhibition over time. Stressful events, such as parental strife or chronic illness in a family member, increase the likelihood that responsive infants will develop into inhibited children. Although the Kagan study suggests that behavioral inhibition is stable over the time period studied, it cannot establish the extent to which this stability reflects the child's biology versus the child's environment, or whether that biology is determined by genetics or prenatal events or both.

Daryl Bem has developed a personality theory that attempts to explain how sexual orientation might result from the interaction of temperament with social and environmental influences (Bem, 1996). Bem suggests that biological factors (for example, genes and prenatal hormones) influence temperament, which in turn influences the way the child interacts with the environment and sets off a chain of events leading to feelings of sexual attraction toward

THINKING CRITICALLY

Jerome Kagan and his colleagues found that children who were inhibited at twenty-one months were inhibited at later ages as well. One conclusion from this finding is that behavioral inhibition has a hereditary component: children who inherit nervous systems that are highly responsive to stimulation will react more to novel stimuli, leading them to become inhibited. What are some problems with this conclusion?

Remember, correlation is not causation. It may be that something else (perhaps parental behavior) caused the children to be inhibited at twenty-one months, something that still operates in later childhood. Although behavioral inhibition may have a hereditary basis, there may also be alternative biological and environmental explanations. For example, some prenatal conditions (caused perhaps by a mother who drinks alcohol or smokes during pregnancy) could have affected the responsiveness of the fetus's developing nervous system. Or the inhibited children may have been punished for exploration during infancy and may have acquired a conditioned fear response (which would involve an increased heart rate) to novel situations that would distinguish them from children who were encouraged to explore their environments. These are just two alternative explanations for the research findings. They remind us that understanding complex human behavior requires many studies that can examine alternative explanations of behavior from many perspectives.

others of the same or opposite sex, depending on the culture's gender polarization (that is, the extent to which a culture separates male and female roles and activities).

In gender-polarized cultures, boys and girls are expected to engage in different activities and to have same-sex playmates, no matter what their personal interests and talents may be. But temperament leads children to choose and enjoy particular activities and playmates that may or may not be considered gender-typical. For example, boys who do not like aggressive rough-and-tumble play may prefer to play with other children who do not like such activities. In gender-polarized cultures, those children may be more likely to be girls. Children who do not select toys, activities, and playmates typical for their sex will end up feeling different from their same-sex peers and will perceive them as novel (exotic). At this point, our tendency to experience greater physiological arousal in response to novel stimuli enters the picture. If Elton feels different from other boys and spends most of his time with girls, being around other boys will be a relatively novel experience, and he will become aroused in their presence. In keeping with Schachter's two-factor theory of emotion (see Chapter 10), he will seek to interpret this arousal by examining the situation and who is in it. As he comes to recognize that he feels aroused in the presence of boys, he may attribute, label, and transform his arousal into romantic attraction—in Bem's words, "the exotic becomes erotic" (see Figure 14-3). Although longitudinal research is needed to test Bem's theory, it provides a model for how a personality theory that begins with temperament (aggressive and active vs. quietly sociable) can consider the social context (gender polarization; gender segregation of children's activities and playmates), and apply psychological principles (arousal in response to novel stimuli; attributional processes involved in the two-factor theory of emotion) to explain an aspect of personality development (sexual orientation).

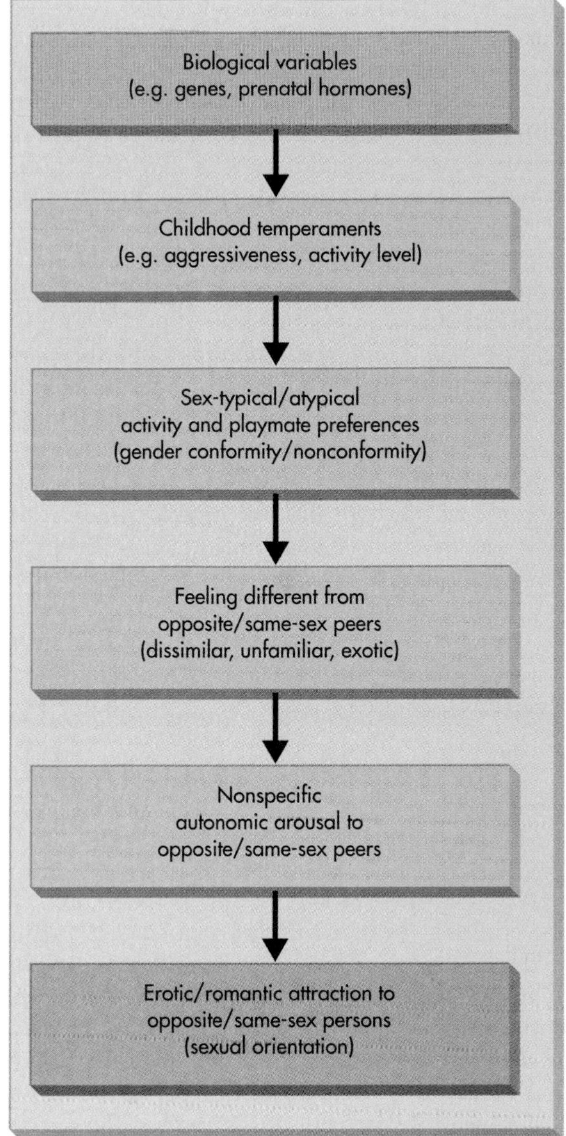

14-3 Temperament and Sexual Orientation

According to Bem, genes and prenatal hormones may affect childhood temperament, which in turn may affect types of play and kinds of playmates. The child will then feel aroused when in the presence of novel or unfamiliar playmates. If the unfamiliar peers are of the opposite sex, the child will interpret arousal as attraction to the opposite sex. If they are of the same sex, the child will interpret arousal as attraction to the same sex. (Source: Adapted from Bem, 1996)

Some Limitations of the Dispositional Approach

Dispositional theories have some common limitations. First, they tend to overemphasize enduring personality traits or dispositions and to neglect the important role of the immediate context or situation. Because behavior not only depends on traits but also on the situation, both need to be considered. Although behavior often changes in different situations, it may also stay the same if the different situations have certain common features (Mischel, 1984; Ross & Nisbett, 1991). For example, an extraverted individual might be quiet and sit still in psychology class, at a poetry reading, and during a symphony performance—all situations that require such behaviors. Put the same extravert at a hockey game, on the dance floor, or at a rock concert, however, and it will be another story altogether.

Dispositional theories also neglect possible relationships between traits and other fundamental behavioral concepts, such as knowledge and motivation. Although traits, such as the need for achievement, are sometimes seen as leading to or motivating our behavior, how they do so is not spelled out (see Chapter 10). As Henry Murray pointed out long ago, "trait psychology is over-concerned with . . . what is conscious, ordered, and rational" (Murray, 1938/1962, p. 715). Yet, we do not always behave rationally, and we are not always conscious of motivations for our actions.

Does this mean trait theories (and the personality tests that are based on them) are not useful for predicting behavior? No. Correlations between personality traits and behavior are estimated to range between .30 to .40, a size comparable to the contribution of the situation to behavior in many classic studies in social psychology (Nisbett, 1980; Funder & Ozer, 1983).

THINKING CRITICALLY

Think about the things that influence your behavior. Can you identify what you would consider reinforcing? Here are some questions to help:

What kind of praise do you like to receive, from yourself and others?
What kinds of things do you like to have?
What are your major interests and hobbies?
What do you do for fun? To relax?
What do you do to get away from it all?
What makes you feel good?
What kinds of things are important to you?
What do you spend your money on?
What would you buy if you had an extra $20? $100?
What would you most hate to lose?

(Source: Adapted from Watson & Tharp, 1989)

The Learning and Social Learning Approaches

Psychologist Walter Mischel argued that we all actively construct a psychological world to live in, influencing and being influenced by our surroundings (Mischel, 1981). In Mischel's view, theories that consider behavior as exclusively the result of a narrow set of "person" factors are too simplistic. The same person differs from situation to situation, and it is the situation that draws behavior out of the individual. Rather than stressing internal dispositions and enduring traits, learning theorists have focused on acquired behaviors and the external environmental conditions that influence them. They believe that our behavior is our personality, and that it is determined primarily by what we learn—our skills, knowledge, and ways of reacting. Personality differences among people come about because each person has learned different skills, knowledge, and behaviors. The ***social learning approach*** focuses on learning that takes place in a social context. For example, under stressful conditions, such as being in financial debt, a person who has learned to deal with problems by depending on others may try to borrow money, while someone who has been rewarded for self-reliance may take a second job.

B. F. Skinner believed that psychologists should observe how behavior relates to its consequences and then fully describe how repeated pairing of certain behaviors and consequences leads to consistencies in behaviors across situations (personality).

Variations of Learning Theories

Versions of learning theory differ substantially, but they share certain key features: (1) an assumption that behavior *is* personality (you are what you do), (2) an emphasis on environmental rather than biological or genetic influences on personality and personality development, and (3) the use of experimental approaches to study personality. These theories stress that behavior results from general learning principles (see Chapter 6). Consistency in our behavior occurs when it has been consistently rewarded in a variety of circumstances. Thus, we may be calm, cool, and collected in most situations if such behavior has been consistently rewarded for us. The major difference among learning approaches to personality lies in the learning process emphasized (for example, classical conditioning, instrumental conditioning, or social learning by observation), and how much cognition is considered to determine behavior.

Skinner's Behaviorism

Probably the most extreme learning theory approach to personality was argued by B. F. Skinner (1904–1990). Skinner believed that learned relationships could explain all human behavior and personality (Skinner, 1938). Moreover, he believed that psychologists should observe how behavior relates to its consequences and then describe how repeated pairing of particular behaviors with particular consequences leads to consistencies in behavior across situations (personality). For example, if whining repeatedly produces the consequence of parental attention (a positive reinforcer for the child), a child may develop a "whiny personality." Similarly, a child raised in a collectivistic culture that rewards collaboration may develop a cooperative personality, while a child from an individualistic culture that rewards competition may become aggressive. This method of studying behavior and personality analyzes the relationships between cues in the environment, behavior, and its consequences (reinforcements).

Skinner's approach to personality has been highly influential. But it has been criticized by those who believe it does not pay enough attention to cognitive processes in developing and maintaining personality. As a result, several alternative, cognitively oriented learning theories have emerged.

Rotter and Expectancies

Which of the following statements most closely reflects your beliefs: (1) What happens to me is my own doing, or (2) Sometimes I feel that I don't have enough control over the direction my life is taking. Your answers to such questions reflect how much you expect to control what happens to you in life. Julian Rotter (1916–) believes that ***expectancies*** affect personality by playing a central role in developing, maintaining, and altering behavior (Rotter, 1966, 1982, 1990). In Rotter's system, the probability of a given behavior depends on (1) what the person *expects* will happen following the response (outcome), and (2) the *value* the person places on that outcome. In essence, his approach is a subjective utility theory (see Chapter 10). Rotter assumes that expectancies and values that influence personality are acquired through learning and are part of each person's knowledge of the world. In order to have expectancies about outcomes or to make judgments regarding their value, we must have learned about them directly or by observing the behavior of others in the same or similar situations.

One of the best-known elements of Rotter's theory is the concept of ***locus of control***. We generally expect the outcomes of our behaviors to be determined either by our own efforts (internal control) or by factors beyond our control (external control). This is a learned *generalized expectancy*, that is, one that is applied across situations and that characterizes our approach to the world, particularly in situations that are novel or ambiguous. As we interact with the world, however, we also learn *specific expectancies* that we apply in more familiar situations. For example, in preparing for their first essay test in college, students with an internal locus of control would expect their studying efforts to result in a better grade. Students with an external locus of control would expect their studying to have less relationship to their grade, and would give greater weight to external factors, such as whether the teacher was an easy grader or liked them. If the teacher indeed uses arbitrary grading methods, even the student with generalized internal locus of control will learn to apply an external locus of control to that particular situation.

Rotter's concept of expectancy asserts that what you expect to happen determines what you do in any situation.

Rotter developed the *Internal-External Locus of Control Scale* (also known as the I-E scale) to measure how much individuals believe they are in control of their outcomes. Literally thousands of studies have used this scale and others based on it to document the relationship of locus of control to a wide variety of thoughts, feelings, and behaviors. These have ranged from wearing seat belts and practicing birth control to being involved in social change efforts and achieving academically (Findley & Cooper, 1983; Strickland, 1989). For example, black students deeply involved in civil rights activities such as demonstrations and voter registration programs were found to be more internal in their locus of control than black students who were not so involved (Strickland, 1965; 1984). Research has also demonstrated strong links between beliefs in personal control and physical and mental well-being (see Chapter 13; Lefcourt, 1982; Strickland, 1989).

▼ As part of National Helmet Safety Month, a GT Bicycle Air Show team member emphasizes the importance of protective pads. Research suggests that bikers with an internal locus of control will be more likely to protect themselves by wearing helmets.

Bandura and Social Learning

Albert Bandura (1925–) has studied the contributions of cognitive activity and social influences to personality development (Bandura, 1977). The social learning approach that he takes emphasizes personality development through observation, modeling, and imitation. Bandura is probably best known for his work on observational learning processes, showing that we don't need to be rewarded (reinforced)

▲ *Albert Bandura's research found that children who observe aggressive behavior are likely to imitate that behavior.*

and we don't need to practice in order to learn new behaviors. We can learn by just observing another individual (a model) perform the behavior. We especially imitate the behaviors of others when beneficial consequences are observed to follow those behaviors. Thus, children may learn aggression by observing another child get into a fight and be rewarded for it. Recall the experiment from Chapter 12 in which Bandura and his colleagues arranged for preschool children to observe models either vigorously attacking an inflatable Bobo doll or sitting quietly near it (Bandura, Ross, & Ross, 1961). In later tests, the children who observed aggression by others tended to imitate that behavior; those who had seen a passive model were less likely to be aggressive. Repeated observation of such behavior can lead to a personality change in which such behavior becomes a permanent trait in the individual's personality.

14-4 Reciprocal Determinism

Three interacting factors underlie changes in human behavior: behavioral variables, environmental variables, and personal (cognitive) variables.

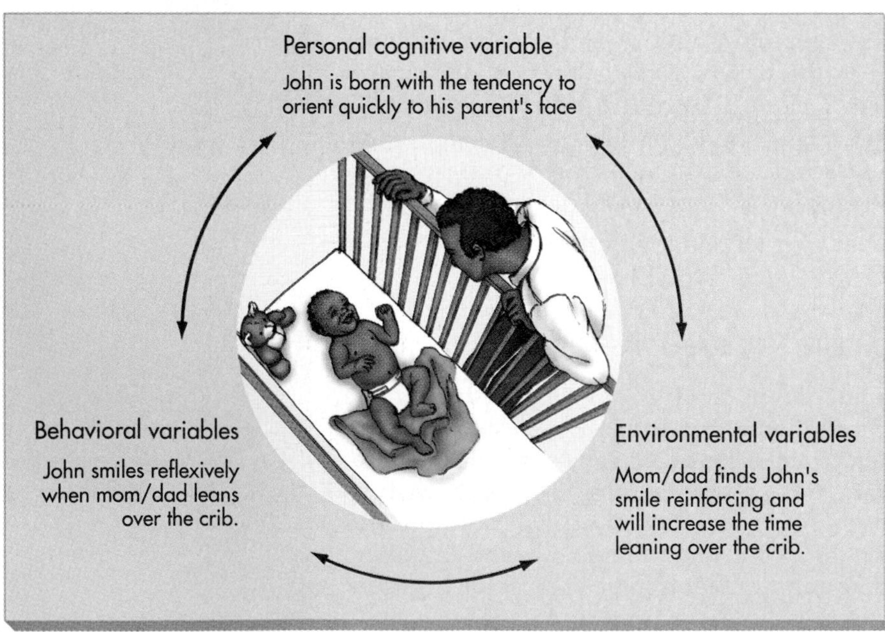
Personal cognitive variable
John is born with the tendency to orient quickly to his parent's face
Behavioral variables
John smiles reflexively when mom/dad leans over the crib.
Environmental variables
Mom/dad finds John's smile reinforcing and will increase the time leaning over the crib.

Thus, shy teenagers may learn how to interact with members of the opposite sex by watching others who are more outgoing. If they then try those more outgoing approaches and also meet with success, those new behaviors may become incorporated into their personality, and they may become outgoing themselves.

Social learning theorists view the behavior of role models, such as parents, as having important effects on personality development. They argue that alcohol and drug abuse in young people may have roots in family relationships. If children observe their parents, siblings, or other family members drinking excessively or taking pills in response to their problems, the children may drink or take pills when they are feeling stressed. Similarly, child-abusing parents are more likely than other parents to have been abused themselves as children. Although not everyone who is abused becomes an abuser, an estimated one-third of children who are abused or exposed to violence as children become violent themselves in later life (Widom, 1989).

Bandura argues that a combination of three interacting factors underlies changes in human behavior (Bandura, 1986): (1) what people actually do (*behavioral variables*), (2) what happens to people (*environmental variables*), and (3) what people think, perceive, know, and expect (*personal/cognitive variables*). Bandura referred to the continuous interaction of these three variables as ***reciprocal determinism***. A person's behavior affects the environment, the environment in turn affects behavior, and the person's awareness of this mutual dependency affects both. Figure 14–4 portrays how these variables fit together to influence behavior.

We can see reciprocal determinism in how children and parents respond to each other. Children are born with different activity and reactivity levels (personal variables). Thus, some

THINKING CRITICALLY

Here are a few test items similar to those on the I-E scale devised by Julian Rotter. You should have no trouble telling which alternative suggests internal versus external control. People who are at the external end of the scale believe that they have little control over life events. Persuading such people to do things to help themselves or improve their circumstances can be difficult. Those at the internal end of the scale believe that they are the masters of their own fate: improving their circumstances is simply a matter of working hard. Choose the response that best describes your belief, and try to figure out where you fall on the I-E scale.

1. Success on the job is largely a matter of
   a. being in the right place at the right time.
   b. hard work and dedication.
2. Doing well on your psychology final exam will depend most on
   a. finding sufficient time to study.
   b. the degree to which the questions happen to match up with what you know.
3. Criminals are
   a. born, not made—victims of fate.
   b. people who deliberately choose to engage in illegal acts.
4. In general, I
   a. control my own destiny.
   b. believe in luck.

children are more likely than others to orient quickly toward the parent's face and smile reflexively (behavioral variable) when their parents lean over their cribs to talk to them. Those parents who find a child's smile reinforcing will substantially increase the length of time they lean over the crib and interact with the child (environmental variable), in turn reinforcing the child's smiling. Thus, personal, behavioral, and environmental variables have combined to result in the child expecting that a smile will produce a rewarding response from others. This establishes a foundation for developing the personality trait of sociability. Consider a second example of reciprocal determinism. In the hockey arena, a player may strike out in response to an opponent's taunting words. That physical aggressiveness may exacerbate the taunting and teasing by the opponent, which in turn may result in an escalated level of aggression.

Reciprocal determinism, according to Bandura, is the continuous interaction and mutual influence of behavioral, environmental, personal, and cognitive variables.

Bandura also emphasizes people's cognitions or thoughts about their ***self-efficacy***, whether they believe they are competent enough to achieve their goals in a particular situation (Bandura, 1982). There is an important difference between self-efficacy and the outcome expectancies of locus of control, however. You may believe you can perform behaviors needed for a particular goal (self-efficacy), but not believe those behaviors will necessarily produce the desired outcome (outcome expectancy). For example, you may believe you are disciplined enough to eat the proper food, exercise frequently, avoid tobacco and alcohol, and perform other important health behaviors (self-efficacy for these behaviors). You may not believe such behaviors will increase your life span, however (outcome expectancy). People who are higher in self-efficacy are more optimistic. They set higher goals and work harder and more persistently to achieve their goals (Bandura, 1991).

People's cognitions about their ability to perform specific behaviors and to achieve their goals in a particular situation are collectively called self-efficacy.

Limitations of the Learning Approach

Learning theories have been criticized for insufficient attention to the role of genetic and biological factors as playing a role in human temperament and behavior. Additional criticism focuses on the laboratory data cited to support learning principles. Many learning theory principles are supported primarily, if not exclusively, by research on lower animals such as rats, dogs, or pigeons. These results may not be directly applicable to human beings, who have brains with large neocortexes and more complex cognitive processes. Finally, many psychologists find it difficult to accept the view of human behavior simply as responses to environmental stimuli. They argue that human beings have free will and the ability to choose the situation they will be in, as well as how they will react in the situations they encounter.

The Humanistic Approach

We do not see things as they are. We see them as we are.

—Talmud

In describing life as a Jew under Hitler's rule, Nobel Prize winner Elie Wiesel tells of a brave peasant woman called Maria who was the housekeeper for his family. When the Jews were ordered into a ghetto, Maria, who was a Christian, offered the family a cabin in a remote area. Not knowing what was in store for them, they chose to stay with their community. Even when they were confined in the ghetto, Maria slipped past armed guards and barbed wire to bring them cheese and eggs. As Wiesel observed, this "simple, uneducated woman stood taller than the city's intellectuals, dignitaries, and clergy . . . not one of them showed the strength of character of this peasant woman" (Wiesel, 1995, p. 70).

The ***humanistic approach*** focuses on what it means to be an individual human being with the ability to choose our actions, and to find fulfillment, often through helping others, as in the case of Maria. Humanistic theorists believe that we are neither passive "carriers" of personality traits nor mere recipients of reinforcement from the environment. Rather, they stress our *personal responsibility* for our actions and our power to *plan* and *choose* our behaviors and how we feel about things that happen to us. We may have conflicts and unacceptable thoughts in our unconscious mind, but if they come into consciousness we have the power to deal with them, to choose how to think about them, and to decide whether or not to let them affect us.

▼ Why are Miguel Ariel Rodriguez and Jose Luis de Leon risking their lives to save a baby girl from drowning in the floods of Hurricane Hortense? The humanistic approach emphasizes our potential for goodness, focusing on the choices we make and emphasizing the positive qualities of human beings.

Although humanistic theories recognize biological needs, they emphasize higher needs—for knowledge, understanding, and self-actualization. Just as a seed contains the potential to become a fully mature plant, each human being has the potential to grow and develop into a fully mature and healthy individual. Although we are influenced by our past experiences, the humanist lens focuses on the present, emphasizing our ability to make choices and change the direction of our lives. In contrast to Freud, who saw people as motivated by primitive instinctual and primarily selfish desires, humanistic theorists are more likely to view the individual as basically good and motivated by human nature to attain love, joy, creativity, harmony, and to search for meaning in life. Maria embodies this perspective in her choice to risk death in order to help others and do what she believed was right.

Humanistic theorists assert all human activity is normal, natural, rational, and sensible *when viewed from the perspective of the person who is performing the behavior*. According to the humanistic viewpoint, we can't truly understand another's behavior unless we can perceive the world through that person's eyes. This leads some humanists to see mental "illness" as a myth. In this view, people who are violently hostile toward others are acting in accordance with their perceptions. If we could "get inside their heads," we would understand their behavior because we could see the world as they do. Moreover, humanists value understanding diverse points of view and believe we cannot judge the practices of other cultures solely from the point of view of our own.

Variations of Humanistic Theories

Humanistic theorists all believe that we construct our meanings in life, but they differ as to whether they believe that this is grounds for optimism or despair (Funder, 1997). After all, if the only meaning in life is what we make of it, doesn't that make life intrinsically meaningless? In the United States, humanistic psychologists

SEEKING SOLUTIONS

Changing Undesirable Aspects of Your Personality

Making friends is an important part of children's social development. Some children make friends easily and are popular; others are less successful and less popular. Popular children have comparatively few adjustment problems as they grow up; unpopular children are more likely to have academic difficulties, engage in delinquent behaviors, or show various kinds of psychological disorders. What makes the difference? Social learning theorists consider different personalities to be the sum total of different patterns of behaviors. They have shown, for example, that popular children possess and use certain context-appropriate behaviors far more often than unpopular children do. Psychologists have established special programs to teach children to engage in those behaviors that are more likely to improve their social success (Oden & Asher, 1977). Psychologists have also taught a broad array of the social skills associated with a balanced, functional personality to adolescents and adults who are unable to stand up for themselves or to express themselves or to work cooperatively. Today, courses and programs on assertiveness training, social skills, shyness, and stress management abound and reflect a growing understanding that, to some extent, our personalities are what we make them.

At the counseling center of almost any university, students lacking in self-confidence and social skills can participate in a workshop on "Building Social Confidence." Typically, groups of eight to twelve students meet for two hours a week to discuss their problems and receive help and practice (role playing) in how to start and maintain a conversation, how to say no, how to read nonverbal cues, and how to handle rejection. They also get homework assignments to complete during the week, such as asking directions of a stranger or meeting a new person.

Programs like these are often based on the principles of social learning theory. First, the participant defines the present undesirable behavior—for example, being unable to say "no" to a request—and analytically compares it with the desired behavior. Next the person observes others who demonstrate the desired behavior in a role-playing situation. Then the person enters the role playing and learns to say "no" in this unthreatening situation. The person is rewarded for any behavior that approximates the goal. With continued repetition and reinforcement, the person gains confidence in his or her ability to exercise the desired behavior. Gradually, the individual is required to put this practiced behavior into effect in real-life circumstances. Programs like these have been exceedingly helpful to those who never learned a full complement of social skills. They can also be useful to those who already know how to behave appropriately in social situations but whose anxiety has prevented them from doing so.

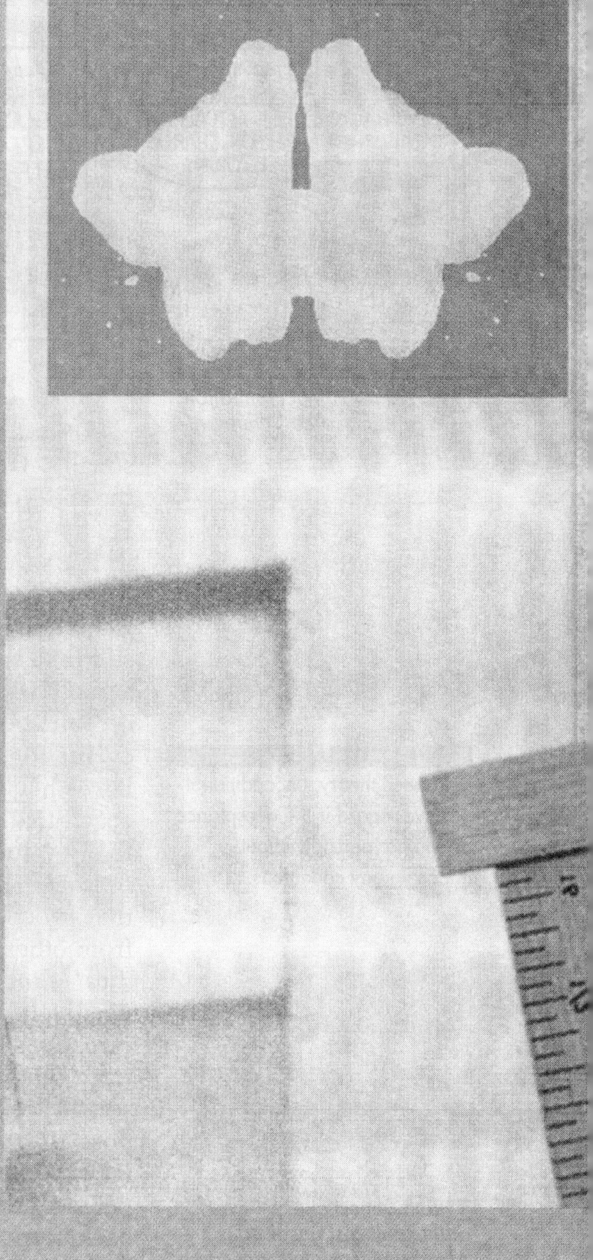

have inclined toward optimism, focusing on the positive aspects of choice and control over one's fate and developing the idea that human beings are motivated to fulfull their potential.

The view of self-actualization as a driving force in the shaping of human personality was advanced in the 1940s by Kurt Goldstein (1878–1965). The first theorist to use the term "actualization," Goldstein argued that we have a unified, holistic drive to live up to our potential, to self-actualize (Goldstein, 1939). Two well-known humanistic psychologists who expanded on this concept of self-actualization were Carl Rogers (1902–1987) and Abraham Maslow (1908–1970).

Self Theory

Carl Rogers viewed the innate tendency to "self-actualize" as being at the root of all human behavior, from the most fundamental food gathering to the most sublime acts of artistic creativity. This innate quality is "the directional trend which is evident in all organic and human life—the urge to expand, extend, develop, mature—the tendency to express and activate all the capacities of the organism" (Rogers, 1959, p. 351). Rogers viewed human personality as behavior that an individual undertakes in an effort to fulfill his or her potential within the world.

WHAT IS PSYCHOPATHOLOGY?
Diagnosis of Psychopathology
Prevalence of Psychopathology

PERSPECTIVES ON PSYCHOPATHOLOGY
The Medical Viewpoint
The Psychodynamic Viewpoint
The Behavioral and Cognitive-Behavioral Viewpoints
The Humanistic Viewpoint

ANXIETY DISORDERS
Phobias
Generalized Anxiety Disorder
Panic Disorder
Posttraumatic Stress Disorder
Obsessive-Compulsive Disorder

DISSOCIATIVE DISORDERS
Dissociative Amnesia
Dissociative Identity Disorder (Multiple Personality Disorder)

SOMATOFORM DISORDERS
Conversion Disorder
Hypochondriasis

MOOD DISORDERS
Depressive Disorders
Bipolar Disorder
Causes of Mood Disorders

SCHIZOPHRENIC DISORDERS
Types of Schizophrenia
Causes of Schizophrenia

PERSONALITY DISORDERS
Paranoid Personality Disorder
Antisocial Personality Disorder
Borderline Personality Disorder

PROBLEMS IN DIAGNOSIS
Gender and Diagnosis
Culture and Diagnosis

REFLECTIONS AND OBSERVATIONS

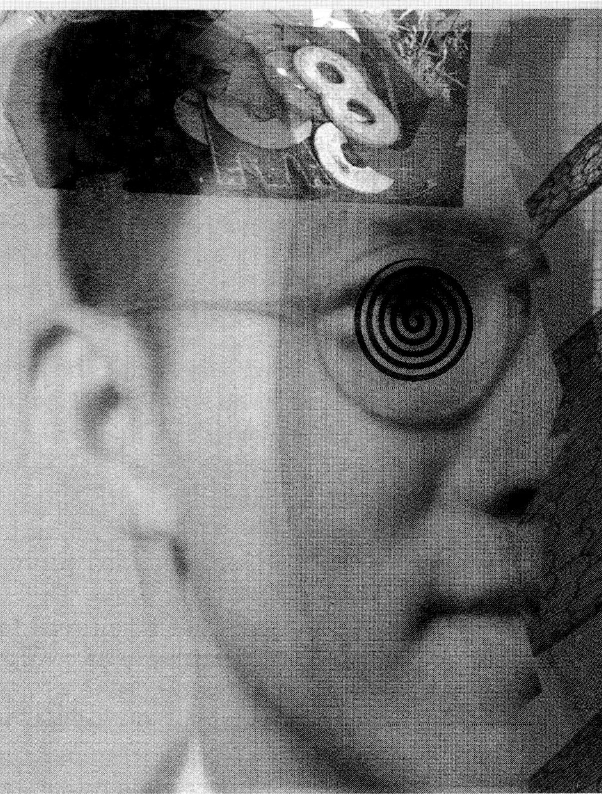

CHAPTER 15

Psychopathology

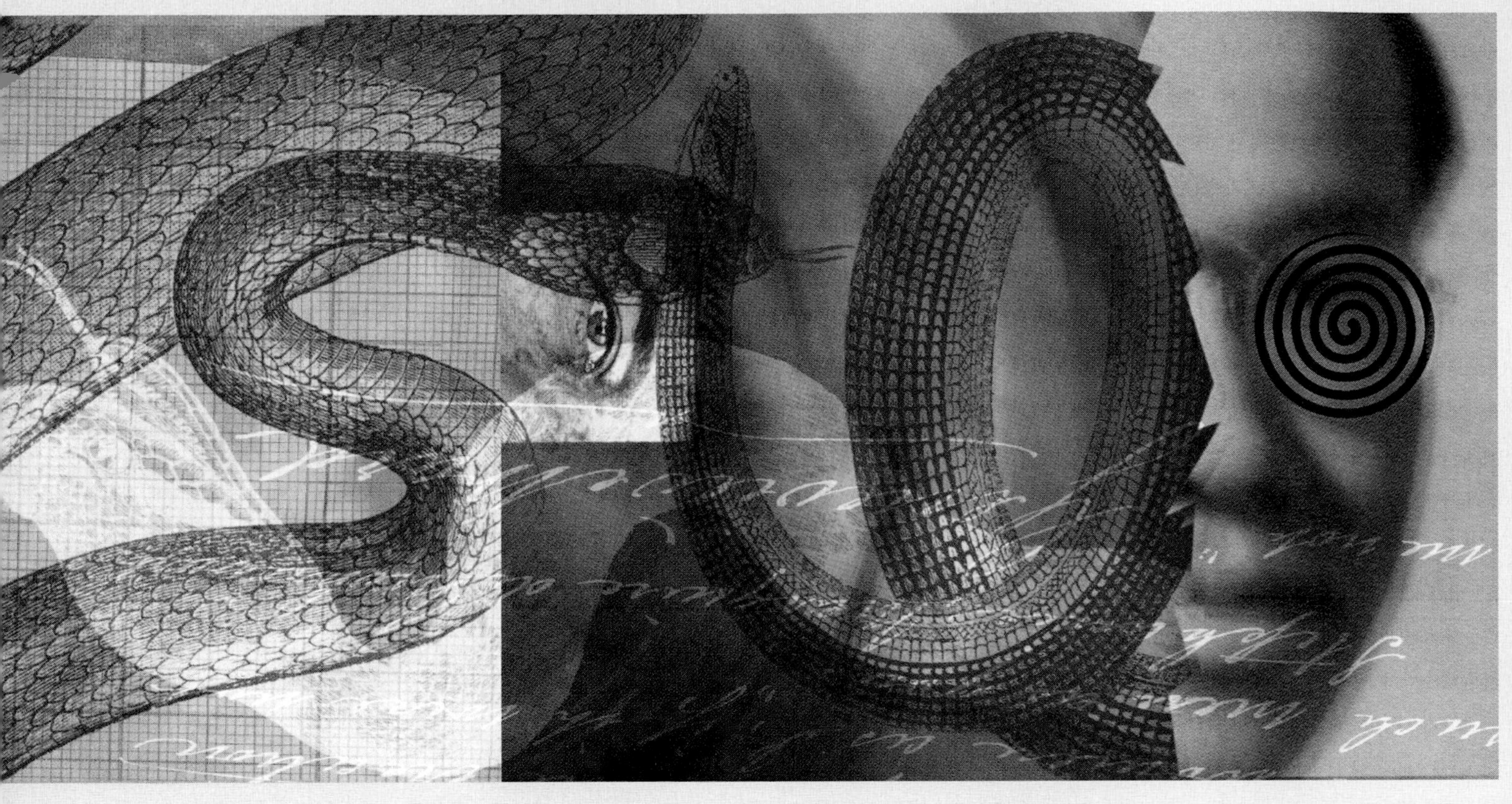

OBJECTIVES

After reading this chapter, you should be able to:

1. Explain how psychopathology is defined and diagnosed, and why it is considered a serious problem for the individual and society.
2. Compare and contrast the various theoretical perspectives on psychopathology.
3. Describe and discuss major clinical syndromes identified by psychological diagnosis.
4. Describe what a personality disorder is and name some examples.
5. Explain the relationship of gender and culture to diagnosis.

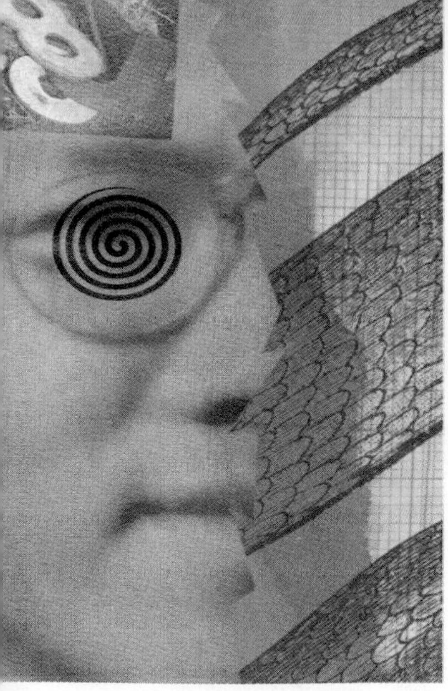

Derek lives alone and works as a computer programmer. When a co-worker in his company was promoted, Derek concluded that the supervisor "had it in for him." He believes his worth will never be recognized. He is also certain that his co-workers are eroding his position in the company in subtle ways. Often he watches them take coffee breaks together, imagining they are using the time to talk about him. He also thinks that his neighbors are out to get him. If people laugh, he is sure they are laughing at him. In general, Derek is suspicious, hypersensitive, and emotionally distant from other people (adapted from Alcohol, Drug Abuse, and Mental Health Administration, 1995, p. 1).

Derek's behavior is certainly not normal. In our society, a clinician might diagnose him as having some sort of mental disorder and might try to find a way to treat him. But Derek's behavior is not particularly unusual in all societies. Daily interactions of people in northwest Melanesia, for example, are characteristically based on suspicion. Members of these societies appear to be preoccupied with fears of being poisoned or hurt by a neighbor. A person who fails to express suspicion is viewed as behaving inappropriately. So, whether a specific behavior is considered "normal" or "abnormal" depends, in part, on context and circumstances. What is normal on some occasions or in some cultures may be considered abnormal on other occasions or in other cultures.

In this chapter, we will define and discuss abnormal behavior. We will concentrate on the description of psychopathology (also known as abnormality or mental illness), its incidence and its causes, where they are known. We will discuss five major categories of disorders: anxiety disorders, somatoform disorders, dissociative disorders, mood disorders, and schizophrenic disorders. (Substance abuse disorders are covered in Chapter 9.) In the next chapter, we will describe how various forms of psychopathology are treated today.

▼ What is abnormal behavior? If you encountered these students in a library or museum, you might question their sanity. But at a football game, their behavior doesn't seem quite as unusual.

What Is Psychopathology?

Psychopathology literally means a pathology or disease of the mind. Those who have a psychopathology or a mental disorder engage in what society considers to be abnormal behavior. But what criteria are used to decide if someone's behavior is "normal" or "abnormal"? One criterion is statistical—what is the frequency of a behavior? Commonplace behavior is considered normal; infrequent or rare behavior is considered abnormal. But this can't be the whole story. By this criterion, unusual behavior that is highly prized, such as an intellectual discovery or an exceptional athletic performance, would be considered abnormal. Another criterion is violation of norms. Behaviors that violate social and cultural norms are considered abnormal. But conscientious objectors to laws and policies that they consider to be unjust would be included in this definition of abnormality. Another criterion is distress or personal suffering as the result of various behaviors or feelings. But some types of psychological disorders do not involve any obvious psychological distress. Finally, abnormality can be defined in terms of the adaptiveness of behavior. Is the behavior maladaptive, that is, does it impair an individual's functioning in a particular context (creating unhappiness, leading to punishment, or preventing rewards)? But adaptive behavior (creating happiness or leading to rewards) can also be a matter of debate and depend on time frame and point of view. Behavior that is adaptive in the short run, such as joining a gang to avoid being harassed by the gang members, may be maladaptive over time, and lead to imprisonment or early death. In the final analysis, abnormality is a matter of judgment, and what gets defined as abnormal depends on who is doing the defining.

Behaviors that qualify as abnormal are extremely diverse, ranging from the frenzied person about to jump from a tall building, to someone who sits in the bathroom overwhelmed with feelings of sadness, to someone who hears voices, to someone who sits home day after day, paralyzed with fear of being in a crowd. This wide range of symptoms makes it difficult to formulate a single definition that fits all cases.

Mental health professionals define psychopathology as those patterns of thought, emotion, or behavior that are maladaptive, disruptive, or harmful to oneself and/or to others. The pattern is associated with distress (a painful symptom) or disability (impaired functioning), or with increased risk of death, pain, disability, or loss of freedom (APA, 1994). It may reflect organic problems (genetic abnormality, biochemical imbalance, and brain injury), or functional problems (lack of competence or motivation to behave responsibly), or both.

Labeling any behavior as abnormal or inappropriate is a culturally determined act. A rural woman who believes she is hexed might be seen as behaving appropriately in her community, even though she is likely to be considered abnormal in an urban environment. The changing view of homosexuality by mental health professionals is another case in point. At one time, diagnostic manuals included homosexuality as a mental disorder. As societal attitudes toward homosexuality changed, however, it became recognized that many homosexual men and women live normal, well-adjusted lives. Since 1973, in recognition of the fact that there is no necessary link between homosexuality and mental disorder, homosexuality has no longer been considered a mental disorder in accepted diagnostic manuals (APA, 1994).

Symptoms of abnormal behavior may range from mild, with no long-term effects, to severe, with thought and behavior so disturbed that special care is required. Psychologists judge the severity of abnormal behavior patterns based on three criteria: (1) bizarreness of the behavior within its context or culture, (2) persistence across time and situations, and (3) effect on a person's ability to function in a social context. After evaluating a person's behavior using

Calvin and Hobbes by Bill Watterson

▲ *Adults and children view normality from different perspectives.*

It must be admitted that no definition adequately specifies precise boundaries for the concept "mental disorder."
—DSM-IV, p. A7

▼ *Behavior that would be considered abnormal in one culture may be well accepted in another. The woman in this picture is pouring the blood of a chicken on an altar made of rusty car parts, giving thanks to Gu, the god of war, fire, and iron. Her religion, Voodoo, has just been declared an official religion in the country of Benin.*

Psychopathology consists of socially inappropriate patterns of thought, emotion, or behavior, whose consequences are judged as maladaptive or detrimental to the person or others by society.

these criteria, a clinical psychologist attempts to diagnose the condition, the problem, or the cause most likely affecting the patient.

Diagnosis of Psychopathology

Where does normal behavior end and abnormal behavior begin? Diagnostic judgments about psychopathology use many sources of information, including interviews, psychological test data, and medical and social records, to answer this question. The diagnostician then has the difficult task of learning as much about the person as possible and, in a relatively short time, coming up with an accurate and meaningful diagnosis of what is wrong.

The most common scheme for classifying mental disorders resembles that for diagnosing physical disorders. To diagnose a mental disorder, psychologists and psychiatrists group people according to the number, severity, and duration of relevant behavioral or emotional characteristics, which are called ***symptoms***. This is similar to the way doctors group physical symptoms to diagnose a physical problem. A collection of symptoms that typically go together may signify a meaningful behavioral category, or clinical ***syndrome***. Everyone with these symptoms is given the same label, no matter how different they are in other respects.

A collection of symptoms that typically go together may signify a meaningful category or syndrome of psychopathology.

Have you ever heard someone described as "neurotic" or "psychotic"? Although the terms "neurosis" and "psychosis" are no longer used as official diagnostic categories, both mental health professionals and the public still use them descriptively to indicate severity of psychological disorder. The main difference between neurosis and psychosis is whether the affected person is in contact with reality and able to function on an everyday basis. Psychotic persons often cannot determine the difference between fantasy and reality and may be unable to hold a job or live independently because of their disorder. Neuroses are, in this sense, less severe. Neurotic individuals can maintain basic control over their thoughts and feelings and are in contact with reality. Nonetheless, they experience considerable anxiety and discomfort stemming from their ineffective ways of dealing with problems in living.

DOES YOUR FAMILY SUFFER FROM ANY DYSFUNCTIONS ?
NO... THEY RATHER ENJOY THEM.
Reynolds

Today these categories have been replaced by the clinical syndromes defined in the ***Diagnostic and Statistical Manual of Mental Disorders (DSM)***. This manual contains the most influential and widely used diagnostic category system for mental disorders. It was developed over the last forty years by a group of psychiatrists and psychologists working under the auspices of the American Psychiatric Association and has undergone several revisions since first published in 1952. The fourth version was published in 1994 and is called DSM-IV. Our description of mental disorders reflects the most recent DSM categories.

DSM-IV permits an evaluation of a person on up to five dimensions or axes of information, each reflecting a different aspect of the case. The first two axes represent types of mental disorders: Axis I describes clinical syndromes such as depression or anxiety disorders (see Table 15-1). Axis II describes personality disorders such as antisocial personality disorder (a disorder in which someone does something wrong but feels no remorse or guilt) and developmental disorders such as attention deficit hyperactivity disorder (a disorder in which a child has difficulty focusing and sitting still). To use DSM-IV, a diagnostician first evaluates, interprets, and classifies a person's primary set of current behavioral symptoms on Axis I. Next, any long-standing pathological personality attributes are identified and classified on Axis II.

Axis III represents general medical disorders or conditions that may affect mental state. This axis is needed because a person's medical condition may affect his or her mental state. For example, infectious diseases like syphilis and AIDS may cause dementia (a deterioration of the ability to think and reason). An over- or under-active thyroid gland may cause mood swings. A brain injury may cause a permanent

Table 15-1 Some Axis I Disorders in DSM-IV

Major Disorder	Some Subtypes	Description
Disorders usually first diagnosed in infancy, childhood, or adolescence	Mental retardation Learning disorders Communication disorders Pervasive developmental disorders (e.g., autism) Attention-deficit and disruptive behavior disorders	These disorders include symptoms found in infancy or childhood, including fears, hyperactivity, limitations in communication, self-care, or interpersonal skills that interfere with the child's functioning.
Cognitive Disorders	Delirium Dementia Amnestic disorders	These disorders include symptoms in which there is a disturbance or change of consciousness or impairment of memory as a result of aging, a general medical condition, or drugs or chemicals.
Substance-Related Disorders (see Chapter 9)	Alcohol-related disorders Amphetamine-related disorders Caffeine-related disorders Cannabis-related disorders Cocaine-related disorders Hallucinogen-related disorders Nicotine-related disorders Opioid-related disorders	These disorders include symptoms of tolerance (reduced effects with continued use) and withdrawal (if the drug is no longer taken) as a result of dependence on alcohol or cocaine or heroin or some other drug of abuse.
Schizophrenia and Other Psychotic Disorders	Paranoid type Disorganized type Catatonic type Undifferentiated type Residual type	These disorders include severe psychotic symptoms involving perceptual (hallucinations), thought (delusions or false beliefs), and mood disturbances that grossly interfere with normal functioning.
Mood Disorders	Major depressive disorder Dysthymic disorder Bipolar disorder	These disorders include feeling especially sad, hopeless, or discouraged (for depressive disorders), or alternating between sadness and mania (for bipolar disorder), and accompanying cognitive, motivational, and physical symptoms that interfere with normal functioning.
Anxiety Disorders	Panic disorder Agoraphobia Specific phobias Social phobia Obsessive-compulsive disorder Posttraumatic stress disorder Generalized anxiety disorder	These disorders include feelings of intense fear, apprehension, or terror, often accompanied by such physical symptoms as shortness of breath and palpitations, which interfere with normal functioning.
Dissociative Disorders	Dissociative amnesia Dissociative identity disorder	These disorders include symptoms in which there is a separation of a part of a person's identity from the other parts.
Somatoform Disorders	Somatization disorder Conversion disorder Pain disorder Hypochondriasis	These disorders are characterized by physical symptoms developed as a result of psychological problems.
Eating Disorders (see Chapter 10)	Anorexia nervosa Bulimia nervosa	These disorders are characterized by severe disorders in eating behavior.
Sleep Disorders (see Chapter 9)	Insomnia Sleepwalking Night terrors Narcolepsy	These disorders may include difficulty getting to sleep, maintaining sleep, abrupt awakening from sleep, or motor behavior while asleep.

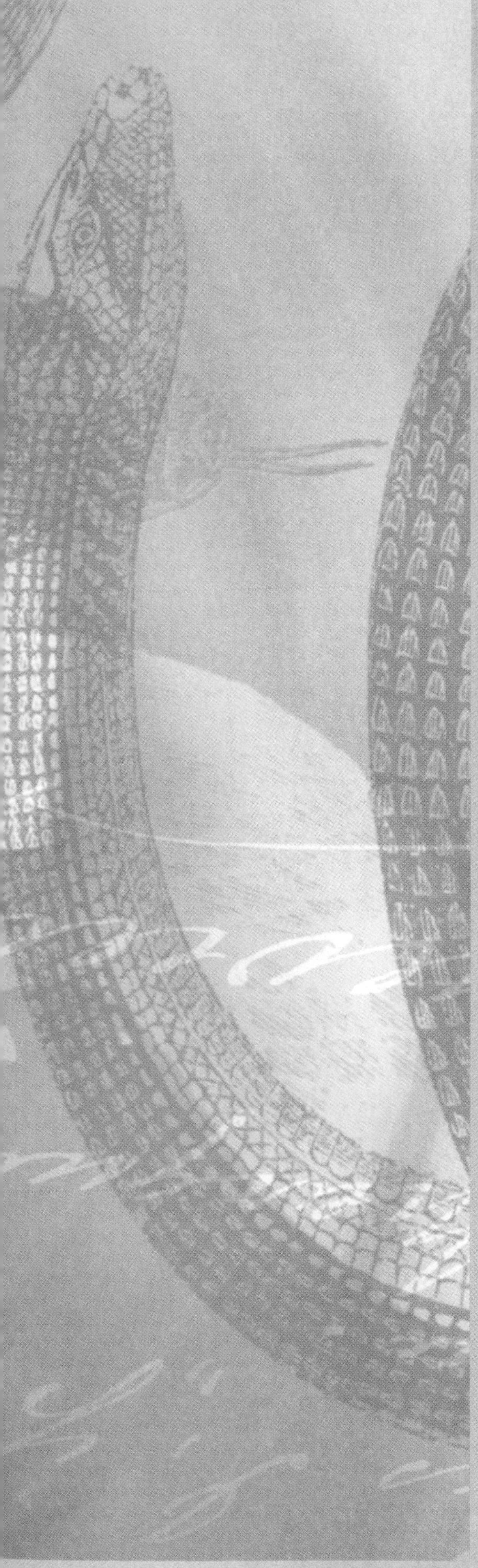

SEEKING SOLUTIONS

DSM-IV: The New Diagnostic and Statistical Manual of Mental Disorders

The revised fourth edition of the *Diagnostic and Statistical Manual of Mental Disorders (DSM-IV)* was published by the American Psychiatric Association in 1994. DSM-IV recognizes the complex nature of psychopathologies by using five major dimensions (called axes) to describe them. The descriptive system, called a multiaxial classification scheme, includes the following dimensions:

Axis I: Clinical disorder. Axis I includes a wide range of symptom clusters or clinical syndromes. It supplies the diagnostic label for an individual's most serious psychological problem, such as major depression or anxiety disorder. Diagnosis is based on explicit criteria, including the occurrence of a certain number of episodes over a given time interval or episodes of a certain length, which usually help establish the reliability of the diagnosis.

Axis II: Personality disorders and mental retardation. This dimension allows the diagnostician to identify secondary or contributing symptoms of an individual's disorder. On Axis II, personality and maladaptive traits are evaluated. For example, an individual might be diagnosed as having a major depression on Axis I and be described as having long-term compulsive traits leading to a label of Compulsive Personality on Axis II.

Axis III: General medical conditions. On this axis, the diagnostician records concurrent physical symptoms or conditions that might contribute to the psychological syndrome. This information can assist in determining an effective psychotherapeutic treatment plan.

Axis IV: Psychosocial and environmental problems. On this dimension, the clinician uses a checklist to identify and describe areas in which the patient is having particular behavioral difficulties—for example, in his or her primary support group (death of a family member, divorce), educational, occupational, housing, or economic problems.

Axis V: Global assessment of functioning. The individual's overall level of adaptive functioning is important information for developing a treatment program as well as for understanding the severity of his or her present disorder. Global assessment of functioning is rated by the diagnostician on the GAF (Global Assessment of Functioning) Scale, which ranges from superior (has unusually effective functioning in social relations, workplace, and leisure time use) to persistent danger (may injure self or others or is unable to maintain personal hygiene).

Case History and DSM-IV Application

To see how this diagnostic instrument works, consider the following example. Raoul M., age forty-three, was admitted to a hospital following a series of drinking episodes in which he created public disturbances such as throwing drinks at people in bars, resulting in his arrest on two recent occasions. During hospitalization, he experienced severe alcohol withdrawal symptoms, including the DT's (delirium tremens, the "shakes"). Raoul was given an Axis I diagnosis of *Substance-Related Disorder* (Alcohol). Psychological and life history examinations revealed a longstanding problem of dependency in which he allowed others to assume responsibility for his life. He lacked self-confidence and believed himself to be unable to function without his wife or, after his divorce, without another female companion. He was given the Axis II diagnosis of *Dependent Personality Disorder.*

Raoul reported some severe physical complications related to his long-term alcohol use. These symptoms were traced to liver disease, and he was given an Axis III label of *Alcohol Cirrhosis of the Liver.*

Raoul had experienced great psychological stress in recent months due to divorce, an inability to establish new social relationships, and job-related setbacks. He was categorized on Axis IV as having problems with his primary support group and with his finances.

Raoul has not functioned well during the past twelve months. His family and work relationships have deteriorated. He has been unemployed most of the time. He stays drunk as much as possible. His Axis V rating is 30 on a scale from 0 to 100.

change to an individual's personality. Axis IV represents severity of psychological stressors in the client's life. These stressors may explain why a disorder develops at a particular moment. Psychosocial and environmental problems that may create stress include death of a family member, physical and sexual abuse, divorce or remarriage of a parent, educational and occupational problems, housing problems, and economic problems. Finally, Axis V represents an overall assessment of the individual's current and highest level of functioning during the previous year.

DSM-IV attempts to recognize complex biological, psychological, social, and cultural aspects of psychological problems. It summarizes the most important information for nearly 300 categories of disorder. Clinicians use it to diagnose individuals who have various patterns of symptoms and then develop treatment plans to help them.

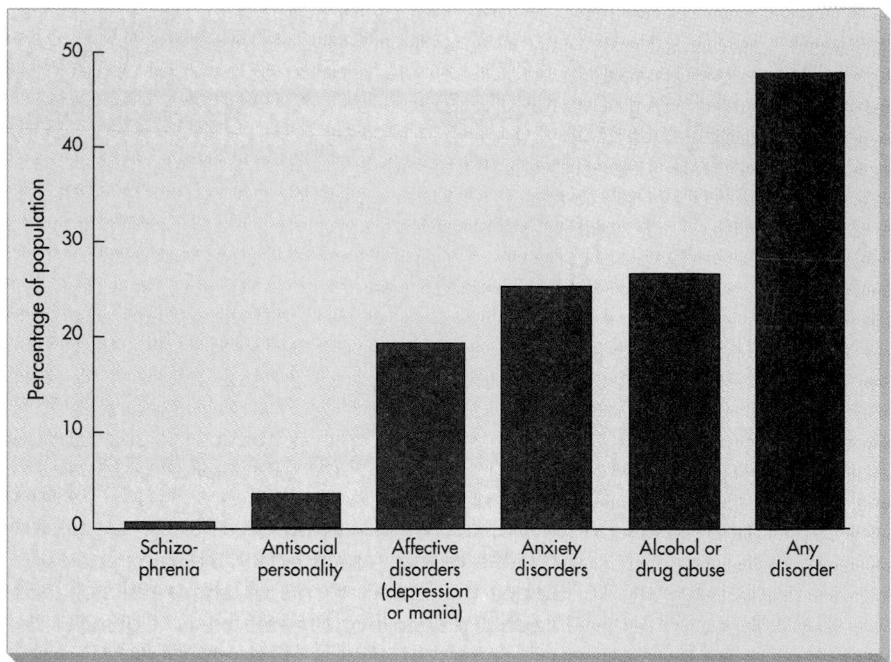

15-1 Frequency of Common Forms of Psychopathology in the United States

Prevalence of mental disorders in the noninstitutionalized population: Nearly one out of two (48%) of people surveyed in a national sample had one or more psychological disorders at some time during their lifetime. These figures, which are based on a research diagnostic interview, are estimates that do not indicate the severity of the disorder. The total percentage of people having a disorder (48%) is less than the categories overall total (70%) because 80% of individuals with disorders had more than one of them. Note that people who are institutionalized (in hospitals or prisons) or homeless are not represented in this survey. Had they been, the percentages, particularly for schizophrenia, would have been higher. (Data from Kessler et al., 1994)

Prevalence of Psychopathology

Psychopathology is one of the world's most pervasive social and health problems. Approximately half of all Americans will experience some form of mental illness during their lifetime. The National Center for Health Statistics estimates 4 to 5 million adult Americans have mental disorders so serious that they interfere with one or more aspects of daily life, such as personal care activities, social functioning, concentrating long enough to complete tasks, and coping with stress. Nearly half of these adults cannot work full time (Alcohol, Drug Abuse, and Mental Health Administration, 1990; Barker et al., 1992; Kessler et al., 1994).

Well over 1 million people in the United States are actively schizophrenic, over 2 million suffer profound depression, and 10 to 15 million abuse alcohol or some other drug. A large proportion of homeless people have serious mental disorders and/or are substance abusers. About 200,000 seriously mentally ill persons are homeless, and an additional million are nursing home residents. When you consider that in 1992 the economic costs of mental illness were estimated to be $175.8 billion, mental disorders become everybody's problem. Figure 15-1 shows the relative frequency of the more common forms of psychopathology in the United States (Kessler et al., 1994).

Perspectives on Psychopathology

The range of behaviors considered psychopathological include physical symptoms (biological), bizarre activities (behavioral), unusual thoughts (cognitive), persistent troubled moods (emotional), difficult interpersonal relationships (social) or any combination of these problems. The many theories that try to describe and explain psychopathology emphasize one or another of these aspects. How we view psychopathology determines how we see others, whether we classify behavior as "normal" or "abnormal," and how we evaluate therapeutic interventions. We will examine four contemporary perspectives on psychopathology: medical, psychodynamic, behavioral and cognitive-behavioral, and humanistic viewpoints (see Table 15-2 on page 548).

The Medical Viewpoint

The ***medical or biological viewpoint*** assumes psychopathology is an illness, based on some

Table 15-2 Views of Psychopathology

Viewpoint	Theoretical Cause	Theoretical Cure
Medical	Organic disorder or disease process	Medication, surgery, rest
Psychodynamic	Unconscious conflicts	Insight into conflicts (understanding conflicts, emotionally and intellectually)
Behavioral	Maladaptive experiences	Unlearning, new experiences, relearning
Cognitive-Behavioral	Faulty thinking	Learning new ways of representing the world mentally
Humanistic	Lack of meaning in life or distortion of experiences	Developing self-awareness and openness

disruption of, disease process in, or damage to our biological "machinery." There is good evidence that many forms of abnormal behavior have a physical or organic basis. Consider the psychological changes brought on by conditions such as Alzheimer's disease, brain injury, or alcoholism and other drug abuse. Bizarre or unusual behavior can be traced directly to biological damage, especially in the brain. Genetic or biochemical imbalances can also provoke severe disorders of thought and feeling. The new techniques for studying the brain, which you learned about in Chapter 3, have increased our knowledge of the neurological correlates of mental disorders. Studies on how drugs affect mental states have led to discoveries about the biochemical causes of psychological disorders.

Despite its successes and its prominence today, the medical viewpoint does not provide a full picture of psychopathology. Medically trained physicians can treat psychopathology when the problem is organic. But physicians may rely solely on medication when psychological or behavioral interventions might be just as effective with fewer side effects. For example, a person who is anxious and does not get along with others might be prescribed a tranquilizing drug. But, if the problem relates to personality rather than biochemistry, drug treatment or some other medical intervention may only make the problem worse. In such a case, taking the medical viewpoint could work to a patient's disadvantage.

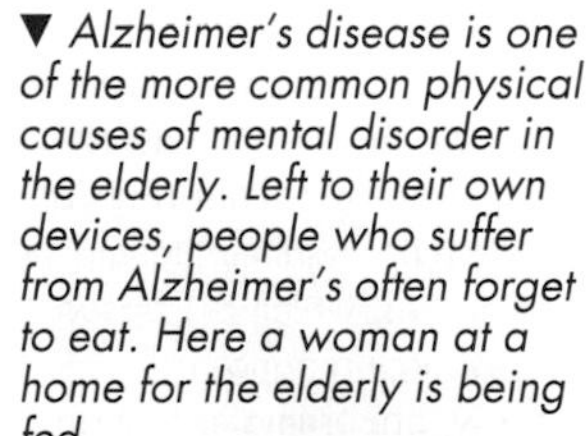

▼ *Alzheimer's disease is one of the more common physical causes of mental disorder in the elderly. Left to their own devices, people who suffer from Alzheimer's often forget to eat. Here a woman at a home for the elderly is being fed.*

The Psychodynamic Viewpoint

Psychologists with a ***psychodynamic viewpoint*** assume that any abnormal behavior that is not obviously organically based reflects an unconscious conflict among components of a person's personality. Freud believed that anxiety and other behavior disorders grow out of conflicts over socially unacceptable impulses. Overt expression of these impulses leads to punishment or disapproval. However, Freud theorized, suppressed or repressed anger persists if it is not resolved. The result is unconscious conflicts, which, in turn, can promote anxiety or, in the extreme case, mental disorder with accompanying overt organic symptoms (such as stomach ulcers) or functional symptoms (such as depression).

The case of Little Hans provides a classic example (Freud, 1909/1976). Little Hans was a five-year-old boy in Vienna who was brought to Freud because of his paralyzing fear that one of the horses drawing the carriages in the street would bite him. He became so afraid he refused to go into the street. Freud interpreted Hans' behavior as reflecting a fierce Oedipal conflict involving a strong attachment to his mother and intense hostility toward his father. According to Freud, Hans became extremely anxious because of his fear that his father would castrate him in retaliation for his unacceptable impulses. To deal with his anxiety, Hans substituted fear of horses for fear of his father. He could then lessen his anxiety by avoiding horses. From Hans' point of view, this substitution was logical—his father wore black glasses and had a moustache that reminded the child of the horses' black blinders and muzzles. Moreover, his father would sometimes play "horsie" with Hans.

According to the psychodynamic view, therapy should try to make the person aware of these unconscious processes, because only in that way can the symptoms be alleviated. As you learned in Chapter 14, Freudian theory has been strongly criticized on a number of levels, including lack of scientific support for many of its claims, its dependence on the interpretation of the therapist, and its failure to sufficiently recognize sociocultural contributions to mental disorder. Nonetheless, the now widely held view that self-knowledge and awareness are critically important and that enhancing them is a path to mental health is a major contribution.

The Behavioral and Cognitive-Behavioral Viewpoints

The ***behavioral viewpoint*** assumes that disordered behavior, like any other behavior, is learned from experiences in social situations.

▲ *Cher attends a party hosted by the Children's Craniofacial Association. Behavioral therapists believe that the ability to cope with disfigurement will depend on the way these children are treated by others.*

Proponents of this view recognize that genetic predispositions, biochemical imbalances, and other organic variables can set the stage for and limit what is learned, but they believe that learning itself shapes specific behaviors. People may be born with certain unattractive physical features, but whether they become shy, withdrawn, and depressed, or sociable, outgoing, and happy depends mainly on how they are treated by others and how they learn to respond to that treatment. Thus, the consequences of behavior (rewards and punishments) primarily determine how a person will behave in the future.

Behavioral therapists do not think that people with problems are "sick" or suffering from "mental illness." Rather, they believe that unfortunate learning experiences have caused them to think and behave in unusual ways. Disordered behaviors themselves are the problems that need correcting—there is no assumption that the behaviors are symptomatic of a more

◀ *From the cognitive-behavioral point of view, our explanations of events are primary causes of maladaptive behavior.*

THINKING CRITICALLY

Albert Ellis believed that how you think about your problems makes the difference in whether you are happy or miserable (Ellis, 1987). Responses such as depression, rage, worthlessness, anxiety, and self-pity reflect irrational beliefs—that is, views about the self that are extreme, unrealistic, and illogical. Ellis distinguished between two types of irrational beliefs: "obvious or blatant" and "subtle or tricky." Both are maladaptive, but the subtle beliefs are more difficult to change because their irrationality is harder to detect. Do any of these beliefs illustrate how you think about yourself?

1. Because I strongly desire to perform important tasks competently and successfully, I *absolutely must* perform them PERFECTLY WELL!
2. Because I strongly desire to perform important tasks competently and successfully, and because I REALLY TRY HARD to succeed at these tasks, I DESERVE to perform well and *absolutely must* perform that way!
3. Because I strongly desire to be approved by people I find significant, I absolutely must have their TOTAL AND PERFECT approval!
4. Because I strongly desire to be approved by people I find significant, and BECAUSE I AM A SPECIAL KIND OF PERSON, I *absolutely must* have their approval!
5. Because I strongly desire people to treat me considerately and fairly, and BECAUSE I AM UNUSUALLY WEAK AND UNABLE TO TAKE CARE OF MYSELF, people absolutely must treat me well!
6. Because I strongly desire people to treat me considerately and fairly, people *absolutely must* AT ALL TIMES PERFECTLY DO SO!

The obvious irrational thoughts are numbers 1, 3, and 6; the rest are the subtle beliefs in Ellis' scheme.

basic, biological or unconscious process. Instead of trying to classify a problem as one or another type of mental illness, behaviorists focus on how the person's environment maintains problem-laden behaviors. Therapy can then focus on the behavior that the person needs to learn and to unlearn.

Cognitively oriented behavior theorists stress the need to understand how people think about their behavior, as well as understanding the behavior itself. From the ***cognitive-behavioral viewpoint***, the primary causes of behavior disorders lie not so much in what happens to a person, but in what the person thinks about what happens.

Imagine how two people might react to getting a flat tire on their way to an important appointment. One might think, "This could be a real mess; I'd better call ahead to say I'll be late. If it gets to be too late, I can reschedule." In contrast, the other might think, "Something like this always happens to me. I'll never be a success because something always goes wrong whenever I try to do anything." Both reactions are possible, but the first is basically normal, healthy, and optimistic, while the second is pessimistic and, if consistent, may signal a pattern of illogical and self-defeating thinking.

From the cognitive viewpoint, maladaptive thought derives from faulty mental representations of the world (Beck, 1976). A depressed person's representations, for example, are affected by negative beliefs or biases in three areas (sometimes called the ***cognitive triad***): (1) self-worth, (2) the world in general, and (3) the future. This belief system operates like a schema, and all future personal experiences are interpreted through it. Thus, the flat tire is translated into the maladaptive conclusion that "The cards are stacked against me, and I'll never be a success."

The cognitive-behavioral approach can be criticized as focusing too much on cognitive processes and not on root causes of the problems, such as dysfunctional family relationships or exposure to interpersonal violence and poverty. Some also see it as too mechanistic, failing to take into account that human beings construct personal goals and meanings and actively process information about their worlds. Nonetheless, this approach has stimulated a wealth of empirical knowledge and applications, and it has produced a number of effective therapies, particularly for anxiety and for depressive disorders.

The Humanistic Viewpoint

From the ***humanistic viewpoint***, a person's behavior (''normal'' or ''abnormal'') is guided by the need to achieve or to self-actualize, and not by biology, psychodynamics, specific thoughts, or environmental conditions of learning. Abnormal behavior derives from a distorted perception of one's self and from failure to self-actualize. Humanistic therapists believe that everyone is basically normal. People who are behaving in ''abnormal'' ways are merely encountering obstacles to self-actualization and don't need diagnostic labels to explain their deviant behaviors. These therapists believe that we should try to understand the clients as individuals; we should encourage them to develop a proper, respectful view of themselves, and we should help them to achieve more self-actualization. When this happens, problem-laden thoughts and behaviors will begin to disappear. For example, Carl Rogers describes a young woman who was gentle and docile while denying ever-growing feelings of hurt and anger for how she was treated (Rogers, 1980). When she discovered her feelings, her first reaction was that an ''alien'' had possessed her. Through humanistic therapy, she came to realize that the ''alien'' was the self that she was seeking. She had become immobilized by stifling and denying part of herself rather than opening herself to experience and recognizing all of her feelings, including her feelings of anger and hurt.

As you learned in Chapter 14, humanistic approaches have been criticized for insufficient recognition of the impact of unconscious processes on behavior and for the lack of scientific verifiability of their concepts. These approaches emphasize the role of conscious experience and human perceptions, values, goals, and meanings in determining human behavior. Contemporary research on human cognition clearly establishes the importance of these factors in behavior even though specific hypotheses based on humanistic approaches are largely untested. (see Chapter 8).

With this understanding of both the diagnostic system used by clinicians and the major approaches to psychopathology, we now turn to a discussion of some of the major disorders or clinical syndromes described in DSM-IV. We will begin with a description of the symptoms and prevalence of the anxiety disorders.

THINKING CRITICALLY

Consider Laura, who is seeking therapy because she is anxious and unhappy, not sleeping well, and doing poorly in her job. What kinds of information would therapists with different viewpoints seek in order to diagnose her?

Therapists with a medical viewpoint would focus on biological factors. Are indicators of her neurological and hormonal levels within normal ranges? Has she had any infectious diseases or other medical conditions that might be affecting her? Is she on any medication? What kind of diet does she have? Has she had a recent head injury? Does Laura have any family members with similar problems?

Those with a psychodynamic viewpoint would focus on potential conflicts among conscious and unconscious aspects of the personality. What was Laura's early childhood like? What was her relationship with her parents like? What happens in her dreams? What events in her life trigger intense anxiety?

Those with a cognitive-behavioral viewpoint would try to understand the ways that Laura mentally represents the world. How does she process information, positive and negative, about herself and others? What thoughts occur to her in specific situations? They would identify illogical and self-defeating thought processes, help Laura to recognize them when they occur, and give her practice in replacing negative thoughts with positive self-enhancing thoughts.

Therapists with a humanistic viewpoint would explore Laura's values, goals, and choices, emphasizing the importance of her own unique internal reality and behavior. How does she see herself and her place in the world, and what does she think she needs to reach her full potential? They would encourage her to engage in behaviors that could enhance her feelings of self-worth and achievement.

The four major contemporary perspectives on psychopathology are the medical, the psychodynamic, the behavioral and cognitive-behavioral, and the humanistic viewpoints.

▲ *On the Day of the Dead, in Mexico, deceased relatives are commemorated with offerings. Such cultural rituals can help people deal with their fear of death.*

An anxiety disorder is a form of abnormal behavior characterized either by the experience of intense anxiety or by maladaptive acts that help the person escape or avoid intense and persistent feelings of anxiety.

▼ *Sportscaster John Madden, a former professional football player and NFL head coach, has a fear of flying and refuses to travel in airplanes. Instead, he criss-crosses the country in a luxurious Greyhound bus.*

Anxiety Disorders

Anxiety disorders are the most common form of psychopathology: in any given year, 17 percent of U.S. adults have one or more types of anxiety disorder. Further, women are twice as likely as men to experience such a disorder (22.6 percent versus 11.8 percent) (Kessler et al., 1994). Anxiety disorders are characterized either by the experience of intense anxiety or by behavior that helps people escape or avoid anxiety. These escape/avoidance strategies have several distinguishing characteristics. First, if people are prevented from performing the behavior that enables them to escape or avoid the anxiety, they will become agitated. Second, the escape behavior has a rigid, driven quality. Finally, performing the behavior only holds the anxiety in check; it doesn't eliminate the anxiety for good, and the behavior must be performed again and again to avoid the anxiety. As a consequence, defending against anxiety requires tremendous energy that could be used to perform more productive behaviors. In the short run, avoiding situations that arouse anxiety relieves feelings of dread and is extremely reinforcing. In the long run, however, such avoidance behaviors are maladaptive because they prevent people from ever facing up to these situations.

Although anxiety disorders take many forms, five of the most common are phobias, generalized anxiety disorder, panic disorder, posttraumatic stress disorder, and obsessive-compulsive disorder. An individual may have more than one anxiety disorder at a time, as the anxiety may surface in more than one form. In one study, over 30 percent of individuals with phobias also had experienced a panic disorder. Over 80 percent of individuals with a generalized anxiety disorder had at least one other anxiety disorder (Weissman, Merikangas, & Boyd, 1986).

Anxiety disorders have been observed in preliterate as well as in Westernized cultures. Although similar in basic nature, what produces the anxiety varies, reflecting the values of the culture. For example, anxieties related to work performance are more common in Western societies, whereas anxieties related to religious experiences and family issues are more common in other societies (Kleinman & Good, 1985). How the disorder is expressed may vary as well. In a study of panic disorder in fourteen countries, choking or smothering and fear of dying were more often found in southern European countries and the Americas than in other countries (Cross-National Collaborative Panic Study, 1992).

Phobias

Phobias are the most common anxiety disorder. They are intense, irrational fears, and include the persistent and extreme desire to avoid some object or situation. Even though they recognize their fears as irrational, phobics will panic and try to escape if they suddenly come into contact with the feared object or situation. Nonetheless, they usually recognize these fears as irrational and without foundation. For example, the thought of flying in an airplane fills Kate with anxiety. She does whatever she can to avoid flying, sometimes leaving a day in advance so that she can take a train rather than a plane. The two times Kate had to fly she consumed large amounts of tranquilizers and alcohol (a dangerous combination). An estimated 25 million people in the United States share her fear of flying (which is called aerophobia) and refuse to board an airplane (Sleek, 1994).

Phobias tend to occur at certain ages (see Figure 15-2). Some other specific phobias include (1) fear of heights (acrophobia), (2) fear of small, closed-in places (claustrophobia), (3) fear of animals (zoophobia), (4) fear of the unknown (xenophobia), and (5) fear of social situations (social phobias). *Social phobias* stem from the individual's feeling that he or she will behave in embarrassing or humiliating ways (for example, perspiring noticeably or forgetting what to say) when around other people. *Agoraphobia* ("fear of open spaces"), which is a fear of being in places from which escape might be difficult or embarrassing, was initially considered a phobia but is now classified as a separate kind of anxiety disorder. In extreme cases, where individuals become afraid to leave their homes, the disorder can be extremely debilitating. In fact, about 1 out of every 100 people have a phobia so severe that he or she cannot leave the house (Regier, Narrow, & Rae, 1990). Various phobias are listed in Table 15-3.

Phobias should be distinguished from mild fears or aversions to heights, cats, insects, or other objects or animals that do not seriously impinge on a person's life. When the fear or aversion drastically reduces a person's functioning, however, it is considered a phobia. Take, for example, the problem of a person working on the ninety-seventh floor of an office building who developed a fear of closed places and thus could not ride an elevator. This intense fear was diagnosed as a phobia because it had a significant effect on the person's livelihood and life. Behaviorally oriented therapies have been especially effective in treating phobias (see Chapter 16).

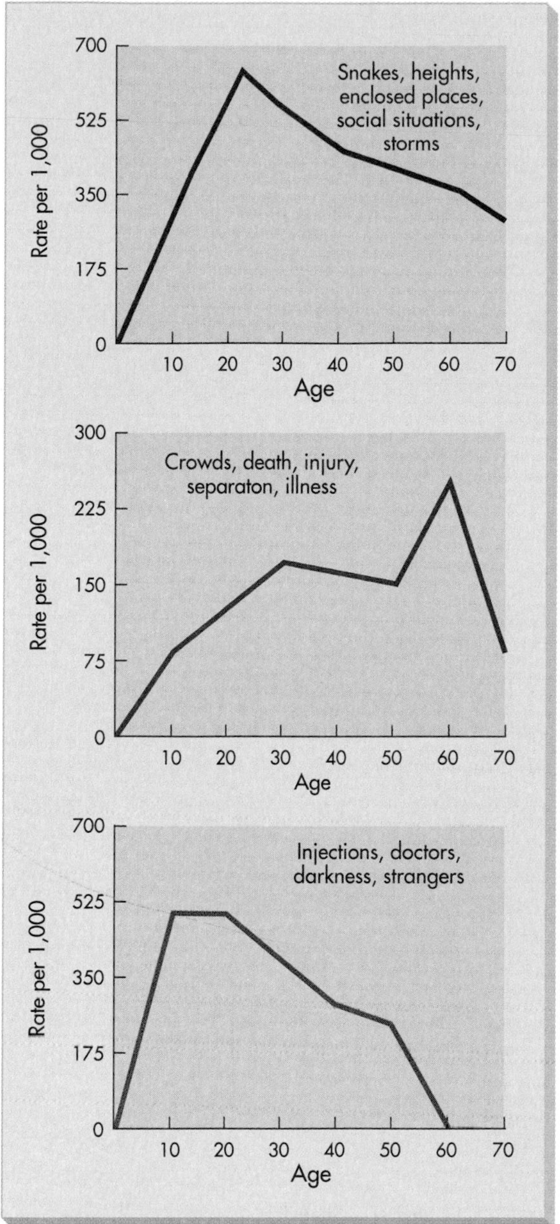

15-2 Specific Phobias and Age

Specific phobias tend to increase and decrease at certain ages. Thus, the fear of snakes, heights, enclosed places, social situations, and storms increases through childhood and adolescence, peaking at about age twenty. The fear of crowds, death, injury, separation, and illness increases until about age thirty, levels off until about age fifty, when it again becomes of great concern. The fear of injections, doctors, darkness, and strangers tends to increase until age ten, levels off during adolescence, and then decreases.

Table 15-3 Technical Names for Some Phobic Disorders

Name	Object
Algophobia	Fear of pain
Allurophobia	Fear of cats
Amaxophobia	Fear of vehicles, driving
Anthropophobia	Fear of men
Aquaphobia	Fear of water
Astraphobia	Fear of lightning and thunder
Autophobia	Fear of oneself
Cynophobia	Fear of dogs
Gynephobia	Fear of women
Hematophobia	Fear of blood
Melissophobia	Fear of bees
Monophobia	Fear of being alone
Mysophobia	Fear of dirt or contamination
Nyctophobia	Fear of the dark
Ocholophobia	Fear of crowds
Ophidiophobia	Fear of nonpoisonous snakes
Pathophobia	Fear of illness or disease
Pyrophobia	Fear of fire
Thanatophobia	Fear of death and dying

THINKING CRITICALLY

Although the causes of phobias are not fully understood, several effective treatments based on learning theories have been developed. This could mean that phobias are acquired and maintained by learning. Applying the principles discussed in Chapter 6, how do you think learning principles can explain the development of a phobia?

If an object or event becomes associated with something that causes pain or fear, it could itself come to produce pain or fear—as when the sound of a bell came to elicit salivation in Pavlov's dog. If you are bitten by a snake, you might develop a snake phobia, for example.

Although a precipitating event, such as a snakebite or a car crash, can sometimes be identified as the cause of a phobia, a person doesn't have to experience an event personally to develop a phobia. In fact, few people with snake phobias have ever been bitten by snakes. Because we are able to make associations cognitively, just hearing that someone died from a snakebite can be sufficient to link the fear response to the idea of a snake. Phobias have been traced to experiences as diverse as seeing a neighbor get struck and killed by lightning to reading as a child about a warrior dog in a fairy tale (Ost & Hugdahl, 1981). The fact that phobias can be learned suggests that they can be unlearned as well. Techniques that apply learning principles in order to "unlearn" phobias will be discussed in Chapter 16.

Generalized Anxiety Disorder

When anxiety with no evident cause is persistent, excessive, unrealistic, nonspecific, and present for at least six months, the person is said to have a ***generalized anxiety disorder***. Individuals diagnosed with generalized anxiety disorder typically feel tense, nervous, and "jittery" without knowing the cause; they may have dry mouth, cold and clammy hands, and rapid heartbeat; they may feel "on edge," expecting that something unknown but terrible will happen soon. The worrying is not related to the likelihood that negative events will actually occur, however (Brown, Barlow, & Liebowitz, 1994). Anti-anxiety drugs can reduce the feelings that accompany the disorder, but symptoms generally will return when medication is withdrawn. Causes of the disorder are unclear and, unlike the phobias, behaviorally oriented psychotherapy has not been effective in treating it.

Panic Disorder

Have you ever, for no apparent reason, experienced your heart pounding, difficulty in catching your breath, a need to urinate, dizziness, choking sensations, or other physical symptoms, coupled with feelings of terror or impending doom? These feelings and physical reactions resemble those of someone in terrible danger, but when no real danger is present, they are considered ***panic attacks***. They are usually sudden and severe, but also brief. These panic attacks may occur in several disorders and are a recurrent symptom in ***panic disorder***.

An estimated 7 to 28 percent of people will experience unexplained panic attacks that will not be classified as having a panic disorder. Caffeine, drugs, hormonal changes, illness, various medical conditions, and stressful life events can all produce the changes in the autonomic nervous system associated with panic attacks. One explanation for why panic attacks occur may be that patients misinterpret their bodily sensations as signaling a loss of control and mental illness. For example, they may experience a racing heartbeat and shortness of breath from exercising and interpret these symptoms as an impending attack. This, in turn, may increase their stress and anxiety and boost the actual likelihood of having a panic attack (Clark & Ehlers, 1993). A comparison of the percentage of people having various symptoms of panic and generalized anxiety disorder is shown in Table 15-4.

Panic disorders affect about 3 percent of the population. Individuals with panic disorder are

Table 15-4 Symptoms of Panic Disorder and Generalized Anxiety Disorder

Symptom	Panic Disorder	Generalized Anxiety Disorder
Sweating, flushing	58.3	22.2
Heart palpitations	89.5	61.1
Chest pain	68.8	11.1
Faintness, light-headedness	52.1	11.1
Blurred vision	31.2	0
Feeling of muscular weakness	47.9	11.1

Source: Adapted from Worchel and Shebilski, 1989.

the highest users of psychotropic drugs, particularly minor tranquilizers (Weissman, Merikangas, & Boyd, 1986). Panic disorders are more common among women than men. But they are also higher for single mothers than for married mothers (Weissman, Leaf, & Bruce, 1987), which suggests that stressful life circumstances rather than biological factors may underlie the gender difference in this disorder. Exposure to traumatic events (for example, being attacked or raped; being in a fire, flood, or bad accident; witnessing someone being seriously injured or killed) is implicated in the development of panic disorder. Women who experience traumatic events severe enough to cause a stress disorder are more than three times as likely as other women to have a panic disorder as well (Breslau, Davis, Peterson, & Schultz, 1997). Panic disorder has been successfully treated with behavioral and cognitive-behavioral therapies.

Posttraumatic Stress Disorder

During World War I, the debilitating effects of stress were identified as "shell shock" in reference to the incessant explosion of cannon shells over the trenches. During World War II, the same syndrome was called "combat fatigue." Finally, after the Vietnam war these effects were labeled ***posttraumatic stress disorder (PTSD)*** and recognized as a DSM category (APA, 1994). Approximately 8 percent of individuals have experienced PTSD sometime in their lifetime—10 percent of women and 5 percent of men (Kessler, Sonnega, Bromet, & Nelson, 1995).

PTSD is triggered by a variety of major stressors, negative traumatic events that involve witnessing or experiencing a threat of death, serious injury, or bodily violation (for example, a rape or the loss of a body part). A person's response involves intense fear, helplessness, and horror. Examples are common on the battlefield, where soldiers constantly risk death and mutilation. But modern everyday life also has the potential for trauma—people are often victims of natural disasters (fires, earthquakes, hurricanes) or crime and injury (including rape, battering, sexual harassment, and motor vehicle accidents)—and, depending on the individual's reaction, the traumas may lead to a diagnosis of PTSD. These events may cause the individual to avoid anything associated with the trauma and

▼ A Bosnian soldier weeps as he talks to his therapist about his nightmares of the war. He is suffering from posttraumatic stress disorder.

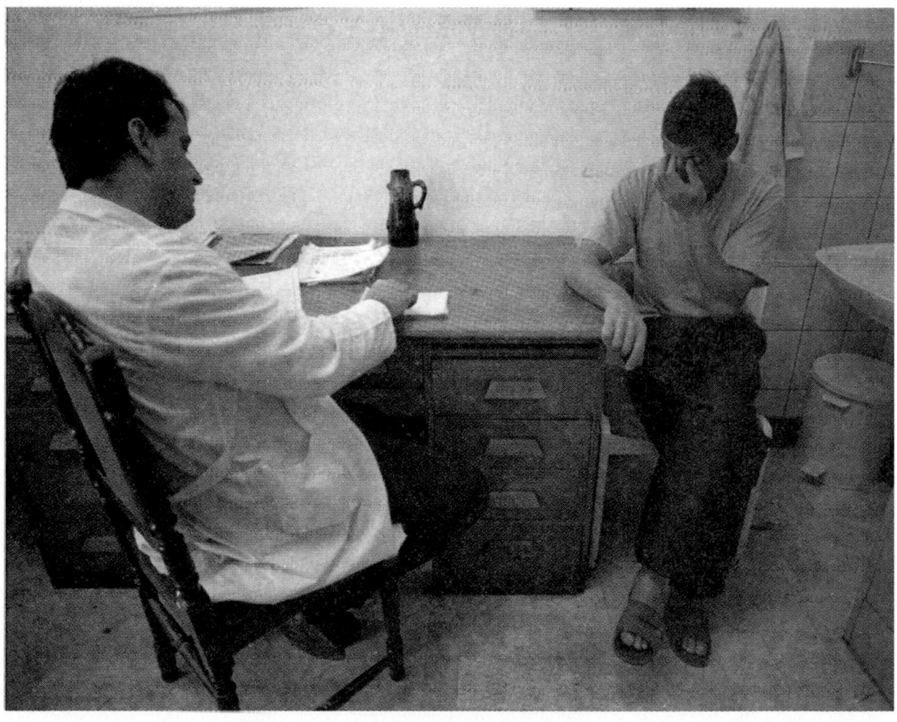

to feel uncontrollably anxious and aroused. Symptoms must be experienced for more than a month before the PTSD label is applied. Furthermore, the individual must persistently re-experience the event, in thoughts, dreams, or emotions. Side effects of PTSD include impaired relationships (personal and job related), insomnia, and a pessimistic view of the future (Davidson & Foa, 1991, 1992).

Therapies work for PTSD best when applied early, before PTSD results in other serious disorders. These behavioral and cognitive-behavioral therapies typically try to desensitize the individual to stimuli associated with the trauma and to substitute positive thoughts and imagery for recurring thoughts, dreams, and flashbacks about the trauma (see Chapter 16).

THINKING CRITICALLY

PTSD is often associated with other related psychiatric disorders, especially anxiety, depression, and substance abuse. How might you explain this association?

First, diagnostic criteria for different disorders often contain some of the same symptoms. Second, experiencing PTSD symptoms might lead people to become anxious and depressed and to cope with the stress by using drugs and alcohol. Third, a history of mental disorder might both increase the likelihood of exposure to traumatic events and the likelihood of developing PTSD when exposed to traumatic events.

PTSD does appear to lead to the development of other disorders. One study found that experiencing PTSD doubled women's risk of subsequently developing a depressive disorder, and it tripled women's risk for developing an alcohol-related disorder (Breslau, Davis, Peterson, & Schultz, 1997). Moreover, women who had histories of depression or anxiety were significantly more likely to experience traumatic events than were women who were not depressed or anxious. In addition, a history of major depression also increased the likelihood of developing PTSD once exposed to traumatic events (Breslau, Davis, Peterson, & Schultz, 1997).

Obsessive-Compulsive Disorder

When she first learned to count, Helene L. felt compelled to count as high as she could, which often reached astronomical numbers. This fascination with numbers continued into her early school years. She sometimes refused to use words, speaking in a numerical code instead. Other students immediately recognized her as odd and responded by ignoring, ostracizing, or tormenting her.

As Helene got older, her repertoire of compulsive acts (acts she felt compelled to perform) grew. While walking, she had to count the number of steps she took. Soon she began looking over her shoulder as she walked, although she could not express what it was that she was looking for. She also started washing her hands repeatedly, interrupting whatever activity she was doing. Then she began repeating over and over again various innocuous phrases, such as, "That is a nice home." Although she could offer no plausible reason for any of these activities, if she did not perform them, she experienced intense anxiety that would be relieved only by performing the compulsive act.

Although Helene was a bright child, she never did well in school, either academically or socially. The main reason for her academic deficiency was her preoccupation with ritualistic acts. For example, in the classroom, even though she fully understood a point that was made by the teacher, she might seek confirmation by setting up a variety of unrelated or unrealistic criteria. "If I really do understand what's going on, the next thing the teacher says will contain fewer than five words" or "If she writes something on the blackboard in the next minute, then I surely am right." If her original idea was not "confirmed" or if she tried to stop setting these criteria, Helene would become extremely anxious (adapted from Zax & Stricker, 1963, pp. 172–73).

Have you ever feared becoming contaminated or infected by people or objects in your environment? Do you have a fear of contracting AIDS? Do you worry that you might blurt out an obscenity or otherwise insult people around you? Or that you might lose something important? Or that some disaster might harm you or your loved ones? Most of us have obsessive or repetitive thoughts from time to time, such as a song that keeps running through our heads. We frequently feel compulsive about some act, like rechecking that a door is locked. These occurrences are fairly common and normal. But Helene's behavior demonstrates how such behaviors can be taken to an extreme, become maladaptive, and signal the presence of obsessive-compulsive disorder.

Obsessive-compulsive disorder (OCD) is generally diagnosed when individuals experience intrusive thoughts repeatedly or continuously (obsessions), when they feel anxiety as a result of these thoughts, and when they feel the need to repeat certain acts to reduce that anxiety (compulsions). Obsessions may be simply annoying or a source of great suffering. Common compulsive acts include repeated checking, hand-washing, and counting. Obsessive thoughts and compulsive behavior often go together (about 80 percent of people with these problems have both obsessions and compulsions). If circumstances prevent compulsive behaviors in response to obsessive thoughts, anxiety increases.

Obsessions and compulsions are considered abnormal when the thoughts or actions interfere with an individual's ability to behave appropriately in an overall, ongoing sense. Individuals with OCD don't want to have obsessive thoughts or engage in compulsive rituals. They realize the senselessness of their behavior. But they are unable to stop the thoughts and rituals, at least without professional help.

About 4 million people in the United States suffer from OCD sometime during their lifetime (APA, 1994; Barker et al., 1992). About half of them begin having problems before age nineteen. OCD is more common than panic disorder or schizophrenia. Although there is a gender difference in the occurrence of OCD, it changes with age. During early childhood, more boys than girls are affected; during teenage years, both sexes are affected equally. When OCD appears in adulthood, however, it is slightly more prevalent in women. Married mothers are at higher risk than single mothers. This is particularly true for black married mothers. Their risk exceeds that of black single mothers by nearly 7 to 1—the comparable figure for white mothers is nearly 3 to 1. That the disorder not only varies by gender but also by ethnicity and social role suggests that sociocultural factors play important roles in creating risk for this disorder (Marsella, 1979; Kessler et al., 1994).

An individual engages in obsessive-compulsive behavior in order to block thoughts that produce anxiety. People with OCD may constantly fill their minds with trivial thoughts to avoid ideas or memories that might be threatening. Similarly, people who rigidly adhere to a strict schedule or maintain an extremely neat home may be structuring their lives to avoid unanticipated threats or upsetting events.

In some cases, obsessive-compulsive behavior can be an expression of both guilt and fear of punishment. The classic example, favored by psychodynamically oriented therapists, is the compulsive hand-washing of Shakespeare's Lady Macbeth, who with her husband murdered the king and kept trying, literally and symbolically, to wash his blood from her hands. Compulsive hand-washing has also been associated with guilt over thoughts of masturbation or other sexual acts that are disapproved by most of society (Masters & Johnson, 1966).

Dissociative Disorders

Our memory gives us a sense of personal identity: what we have said, thought, and done in the past is part of who we are today. This personal identity makes us feel unique. We have goals, values, and expectations that have guided us in the past, in the present, and will guide us in the future. But our ability to process, relate, and remember information can break down, and our sense of personal identity can be disrupted. When this occurs and some of our memory is "split off" or "dissociated" from our conscious awareness, a dissociative disorder is the result.

Certain kinds of psychopathology involve a dissociation, or separation, of one part of a person's identity from another. There are two principal ways this can happen: by dissociative amnesia and dissociative identity disorder (sometimes called multiple personality disorder).

Dissociative disorders involve a dissociation, or separation, of one part of a person's identity from another. This can happen in a variety of ways. We will discuss two: dissociative amnesia and dissociative identity disorder (multiple personality disorder).

Dissociative Amnesia

Dissociative amnesia involves a sudden loss of memory—usually about information that is traumatic and stressful—in response to a specific upsetting event (Classen, Koopman, & Spiegel, 1993). This kind of memory loss is more extensive than normal forgetting, and it is not due to an organic disorder (APA, 1994). In the most common types of dissociative amnesia, a person forgets most or all events that have occurred over a limited period of time, starting with an event that was very disturbing. Sometimes the period will include the days preceding the traumatic event as well.

▼ *This woman, dubbed "Jane Doe," was emaciated, incoherent, and near death when a Florida park ranger found her. She suffered from generalized amnesia, a rare form of amnesia which caused her to forget her name, her ability to read and write, as well as her past history.*

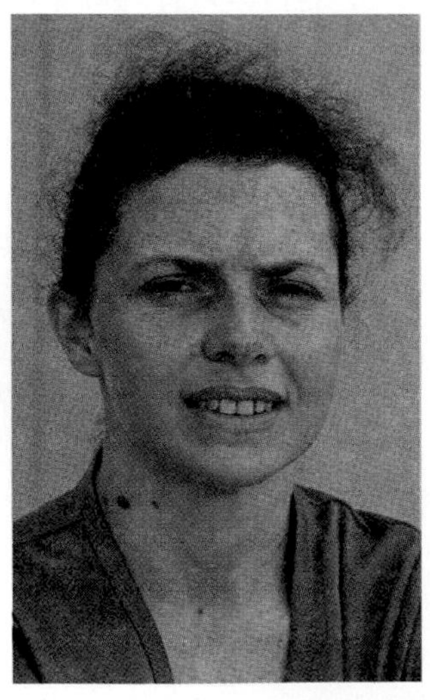

Interestingly, this amnesia only disrupts *episodic* memory—that is, autobiographical memory of personal experiences (see Chapter 7). Semantic memory for information remains intact. So if Vince has dissociative amnesia, he may not remember his own name but he can tell you the name of the President of the United States. He can also read, write, and drive a car.

Combat veterans can experience dissociative amnesia during wartime—forgetting their names and other personal information and reporting memory gaps of hours or whole days (Bremner, Southwick, Johnson, Yehuda, & Charney, 1993). Victims of other forms of violence, such as rape and childhood physical and sexual abuse, may also have difficulty in remembering aspects of their traumatic experience. Dissociative amnesia can arise in response to natural disasters, such as fires, floods, or earthquakes (Kihlstrom, Tataryn, & Hoyt, 1993). It can also be a response to the sudden loss of a loved one through death, rejection, or abandonment (Loewenstein, 1991).

Dissociative Identity Disorder (Multiple Personality Disorder)

Eric, aged twenty-nine, was discovered wandering around a shopping mall, dazed and bruised from a beating. The ambulance workers who took him to a hospital concluded from his behavior that he was retarded. Six weeks later, he began talking—in two voices. "Young Eric" spoke in the voice of a frightened child. "Older Eric" spoke in the measured tones of an adult and told a story of horror and child abuse at the hands of his stepfather. He related how he was taken to a drug dealer's hideout, where he was raped by several gang members and saw his stepfather murder two people. One day during a session, Eric's face twisted into a violent snarl. Growling, he spewed a stream of obscenities. Malcolm Graham, the psychologist directing the case, described it as sounding "like something out of *The Exorcist*." A new identity emerged, demanding to be called Mark. Over the following weeks, twenty-seven different personalities, including three females, appeared, ranging from a fetus to an old man who kept trying to make Eric become a mercenary in Haiti. During his therapy sessions, Eric would shift personalities—once as many as nine times in an hour (Leo, 1992).

Eric was a victim of the rare but dramatic and serious mental disorder known as ***dissociative identity disorder*** (***multiple personality disorder***). Multiple identities or personality states develop when individuals find certain events in their lives so psychologically painful that they seek escape in the form of a new and different identity, an identity that typically exhibits quite different and often opposite traits from the original identity. Thus, Eric had a variety of identities to call upon, including Michael, an arrogant jock, and Phillip, a lawyer who constantly asked about Eric's rights. The identities may not be aware of the other identities; one identity may be aware of some but not all of the other identities. Sometimes the dominant identity will "hear voices"—which are attempts by the other identities to communicate. Although some cases have involved more than 100 identities, the average number is around 15 for women and 8 for men (Ross, Norton, & Wozney, 1989). Multiple identities have their own names, personality characteristics, and abilities, and may even differ in physiological responses such as breathing, sweating, and heart rate (Dell & Eisenhower, 1990). Moreover, a woman who has dissociative identity disorder may menstruate several times a month because each identity may have its own menstrual cycle (Jens & Evans, 1983).

Dissociative identity disorder was rarely found in the psychiatric literature until the 1980s (APA, 1994). Today it occurs far more frequently in women than in men, perhaps partially because women are more likely to experience sexual abuse—an important risk factor for the disorder. Some people have argued that the recent popularity of this disorder can be traced in part to its "discovery" by distressed patients looking for a way to escape from their problems and by therapists who might unintentionally lead their patients to take on symptoms of dissociation (Mersky, 1992). But this doesn't appear to explain the situation. It is possible that changes in diagnostic criteria have led to a more accurate diagnosis of the disorder (Coons & Fine, 1990).

People may differ in their tendency to dissociate, and this tendency may be correlated with a person's hypnotizability (Ganaway, 1989). Dissociative identity disorder may be a form of self-hypnosis. Readiness to dissociate may develop during childhood, and this tendency may be activated later when the person experiences a traumatic or stressful life event. A large percentage of individuals with dissociative identity disorder have experienced physical or sexual abuse during childhood, consistent with the early development of a predisposition to dissociate (Putnam, Guroff, Silberman, Barban, & Post, 1986). Some studies suggest that as many as 97 percent of individuals diagnosed with this disorder have been physically and/or sexually abused as children (Ross et al., 1990; Dell & Eisenhower, 1990).

▲ *Chris Sizemore, the real woman on whom the film* The Three Faces of Eve *was based, suffered from dissociative identity disorder.*

Somatoform Disorders

We all know that physical ailments can cause psychological problems. Most people feel mildly depressed and unhappy, for example, when they have a bad cold or the flu. But as you learned in Chapter 13, the reverse can be just as true: psychological problems can be expressed through physical symptoms. People with ***somatoform disorders*** develop physical symptoms for purely psychological reasons. And these symptoms can be quite severe, including blindness or intense pain with no organic basis. Specific somatoform disorders differ by the symptoms they present, by when the problem begins, by possible causes, and by how much an individual is disabled by the disorder.

A somatoform disorder is the expression of an underlying psychological problem through physical symptoms.

Conversion Disorder

People can deal with thoughts that provoke anxiety by selectively inhibiting certain senses. In ***conversion disorder***, individuals unintentionally reduce anxiety by shutting down part of the body through paralysis, blindness, deafness, or the like. They "convert" the psychological problem into a physical one. For example, in order to deal with anxiety arising from an

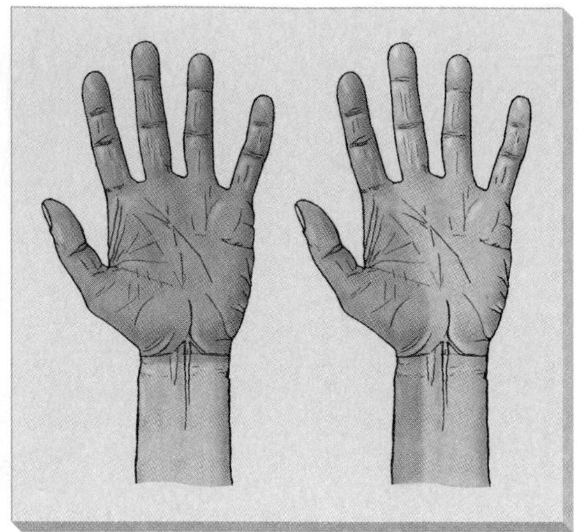

15-3 "Glove Anesthesia"

"Glove anesthesia" is a kind of conversion disorder in which the person loses all feeling in the hand in a pattern that follows the outline of a glove and stops at the wrist. Because the nerve pathways for the hand go up the arm, as shown on the right, it is physically impossible to have a glove pattern of anesthesia, as depicted on the left, so the loss of feeling must be caused by psychological factors.

unconscious desire to stab her husband, a woman's right arm might become paralyzed. A clear example of conversion disorder is "glove" anesthesia, in which a person loses all feeling in the hand up to the wrist (see Figure 15-3). Physicians can immediately identify this condition as nonorganic because nerve pathways to the hand run lengthwise along the arm—a glove pattern of anesthesia would be physically impossible unless the entire arm were affected. Conversion disorders were fairly common in Freud's day, and he discussed them extensively as examples of "hysteria." But today, possibly because people are better informed about their bodies, reactions to anxiety usually take other forms. Conversion disorders occur in fewer than 3 out of 1,000 persons in the United States. These disorders are more likely to be diagnosed in women than in men, and they are most likely to emerge between late childhood and young adulthood (APA, 1994).

► *Hypochondriasis is one of the somatoform disorders, but it is not a fatal illness.*

"He was a dreadful hypochondriac."

Hypochondriasis

Have you ever met people who constantly complain that something is physically wrong with them? They make repeated visits to doctors, who never find any organic basis for their complaints. While it is possible that such people have an undiagnosed illness, it is also possible that they are experiencing a disorder known as ***hypochondriasis***, in which minor physical symptoms are misinterpreted as a major illness. Hypochondriacs are always sick and continually find something wrong with one or another part of their body. They are convinced that some unidentified but serious physical illness plagues them. There is no gender difference in rates of this disorder, which usually develops when a person is between twenty and thirty years old. Hypochondriacs often distort the meaning of minor aches and pains, such as irregular heartbeats, sweating, occasional coughing, or stomach aches. They think they have caught all the "latest" diseases, imagining discomfort in various parts of their bodies and constantly complaining of ill health, although a physician can seldom find any physical causes. Although people with hypochondriasis represent about 4 to 5 percent of medical patients, they consume a disproportionate share of medical services (APA, 1994; Barker et al., 1992).

People often express anxiety about their lives through physical symptoms, and stressful events can in fact initiate serious illness (see Chapter 13). Hypochondriacs, however, seldom actually become physically ill; their symptoms are imaginary and unshakable by medical opinion. Some individuals experience a temporary form of hypochondriasis when they are feeling stressed. As a somatoform disorder, however, hypochondriasis is chronic and highly resistant to psychotherapy, partly because such patients refuse to believe psychological factors are responsible for their problems. They consider their symptoms "medical" and shop for medical doctors who will treat them. One strategy for dealing with such individuals is to ignore their somatic (physical) complaints and propose diverting activities ("I know you're in pain and feeling bad, but let's take a walk in the park anyway"). Diverting activities at least give them some positive experiences and help them function despite their perceived illnesses (Davison & Neale, 1990).

Mood Disorders

Our moods are prolonged states of emotion affecting our behavior and personality. When we are in a depressed mood, nothing seems to go right—life feels dull and meaningless, and the future seems hopeless. But when we are manic, we feel as if we are "on top of the world," our prospects appear bright, we think we can do anything, and no problem or burden is insurmountable.

We all experience some mood swings. If a close relative dies or we lose our job or fail a course, we are likely to feel depressed. If we win the lottery, get a new job, or get married, we are likely to feel positive and optimistic. When mood swings are deep, severe, and long-lasting, however, they are considered pathological and merit a psychological diagnosis. Approximately one out of four women and one out of seven men in the United States experience some form of mood disorder during their lifetime (Kessler et al., 1994). Thus, women are twice as likely as men to experience mood disorders. Psychiatric mood disorders include depressive disorders and bipolar disorders (in which the individual experiences both depression and mania). Keep in mind that mood disorders differ in kind as well as severity, with different causes and correlates. Psychological and/or pharmacological treatments that work for one disorder (for example, major depression) may be totally inappropriate for treating others (for example, bipolar disorder) (Weissman, Leaf, & Bruce, 1987).

Depressive Disorders

Depressive disorders include major depression and dysthymia. ***Major depression*** is characterized by either depressed mood and/or loss of interest or pleasure in all or most activities, as well as by too much or too little sleep, fatigue, loss of energy, significant weight loss or gain, feelings of worthlessness or inappropriate guilt, indecisiveness and diminished ability to concentrate, and recurrent thoughts of death or suicide (for example, depressed patients may fantasize about killing themselves, imagining themselves fully appreciated at their funeral). Major depression can vary in severity from relatively few symptoms and minor behavioral impairment, to extreme behavioral impairment, with many symptoms that markedly interfere with daily activities at home and at work.

▲ *A teenage boy threatens to commit suicide by jumping off a building.*

One form of major depressive disorder is seasonal. Winter, in some parts of the world, can be downright depressing. As the days grow shorter and there is less and less daylight, most people report feeling lethargic and less optimistic about the future. All of this is quite natural. But, in some people, this reaction to the change of seasons is exaggerated. Each year, starting in the late fall and lasting through the early spring, they become clinically depressed. Before DSM-IV, this seasonal pattern was called ***seasonal affective disorder***. At first, investigators thought that the pattern of symptoms might be linked to changes in temperature, but in fact the main variable turned out to be sunlight. Where there is more sun, as in southern climates, this seasonal pattern is less frequent. This observation suggested a possible therapy: exposing the afflicted patient to extended periods of artificial light. Simple as it might seem, this procedure works to lift the depression, although it isn't clear exactly how the effect is produced (Rosen et al., 1990). One possibility is that, as the amount of daylight changes, the normal sleep-waking cycle moves in the direction of longer sleep. Melatonin (a hormone that affects sleep) levels change with the reduction in daylight. Thus, this depression might be brought on as a result of a disturbance in the sleep rhythm.

A mood disorder is characterized by an intense, pathological level of mood, either positive or negative, that persists over time and across situations.

▲ *Light therapy is very effective in treating seasonal affective disorder.*

Roughly 4 to 7 percent of individuals in the United States have experienced at least one ma-

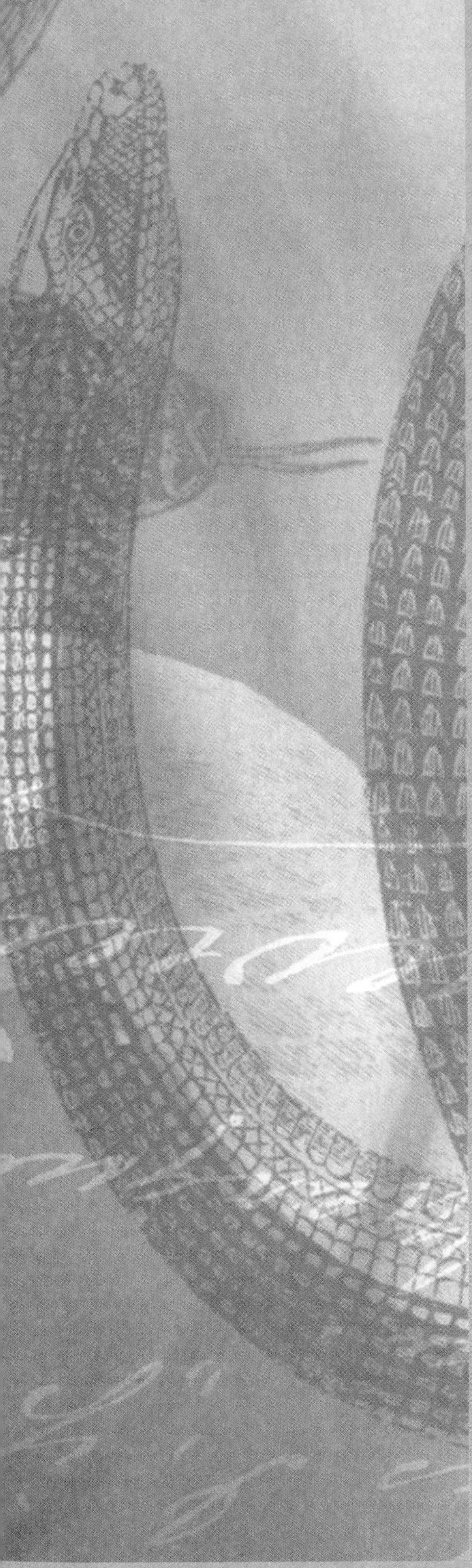

SEEKING SOLUTIONS

Suicide

In 1994, Nirvana's Kurt Cobain shocked the entertainment world by committing suicide. A month prior to his death, he had overdosed on a combination of alcohol and painkillers. At the time it was called an accident, but as a friend commented, "You don't take 50 pills by accident" (Jones, 1994). That year, suicide ranked ninth among causes of death in the United States, with 30,000 people killing themselves. In addition, like Cobain's initial overdose, about 200,000 people a year unsuccessfully attempt suicide. In other words, in the time it takes for you to read this page, someone in the United States will attempt to take his or her life. By this time tomorrow, 82 Americans will have killed themselves.

Suicide has become a leading cause of death among adolescents and on many college campuses. The suicide rate among young people in the United States has increased dramatically in recent years, perhaps because of the mobility of their living arrangements and the popularity of drugs in the fifteen- to twenty-four-year-old age group. Drug and alcohol overdoses have replaced gunshot wounds as the major cause of death by suicide in this age group.

Suicide rates vary with culture and context. Hungary and the Federal Republic of Germany have extremely high rates, with 43–45 suicides per 100,000 population. Rates for Austria, Denmark, Belgium, France, Switzerland, and Japan range from 21–28 per 100,000 population. Canada, Hong Kong, Australia, Scotland, the Netherlands, and the United States, have similar rates, around 11–13 per 100,000. In contrast, the Dominican Republic, Mexico, Peru, Guatemala, Nicaragua, and Egypt have extremely low rates, from 0.1–2.4 per 100,000. Religious differences can partially explain these national differences. For example, countries that are predominately Protestant have higher rates than predominately Catholic, Jewish, or Muslim countries. But there are exceptions. Austria, for example, is predominately Roman Catholic (Comer, 1995).

In the United States, females are more likely to attempt suicide than males, but males are more likely to be successful in killing themselves, primarily because they use different methods. Males are more likely to shoot, stab, or hang themselves, while women are more likely to turn to barbiturates (Kushner, 1985). White males have the highest rates of suicide, followed by black males, white females, and black females (National Center for Health Statistics, 1995). It has been suggested that suicides for women and African Americans are underreported because they are more likely to use methods that are mistaken for accidents (drug overdose, single car crashes, pedestrian deaths). It is estimated that suicide rates are actually 6 percent higher for women and 15 percent higher for African Americans than reported (Phillips & Ruth, 1993).

Although there is no typical profile of the suicidal personality, experts agree that potential victims of suicide tend to give clues to their intended action. For example, the person may begin giving away valued properties or may mention suicidal plans, making vague references such as "When I'm gone. . . . " Should you notice these or similar behaviors in yourself or in another person, you must seek professional help immediately. No suicide threat should be considered frivolous.

Common sense would suggest that suicide occurs in the depths of despair and depression. Under severe depression, however, a person seldom has enough energy to try suicide. It is typically during the swing out of depression that the risk of suicide becomes greatest. The person is still depressed but is now active enough to do something about it. Indeed, the lifting of the deepest depression may indicate that the person has found one solution to personal problems—death. This is the time to keep careful watch on the depressed person's activities. Both deep depression and suicide often occur during holidays or when the weather is pleasant, not just at bad times. This probably has to do with the discrepancy between how people feel and how they think they ought to feel. For example, the expectation that everyone should be happy at Christmas can cause depressed people to feel even more depressed.

jor depressive episode. Between 8 to 12 percent of men and 20 to 26 percent of women develop this disorder at some point in their lifetime (Weissman, Merikangas, & Boyd, 1986). This gender difference occurs in white, black, and Hispanic populations. Both greater exposure to stressful life events and lack of access to coping resources (personal, social, and economic) appear to contribute to the higher rate of depression in women (McGrath, Strickland, Keita, & Russo, 1990).

Dysthymia (formerly called depressive neurosis) is characterized by a chronic mood disturbance. The boundary between dysthymia and major depression is fuzzy, and many symptoms overlap. The chronic depressive symptoms of dysthymic disorder are not as severe as the symptoms of major depressive disorder. Symptoms of dysthymia usually include feelings of hopelessness, poor concentration, fatigue, poor appetite or overeating, weakness and exhaustion, and either insomnia or hypersomnia (too much sleep). Dysthymic individuals almost always consider themselves worthless; they feel that they have accomplished nothing in life and expect to accomplish nothing in the future. Those with dysthymia often feel guilt over their failures. They can't take pleasure in anything they do or in anything that happens to them. Yet, people with dysthymic disorder are able to maintain a reasonable level of functioning in day-to-day life, which distinguishes them from those diagnosed with major depression.

Dysthymia afflicts about 2 to 4 percent of individuals in the United States. Although there is no gender difference in children's dysthymia rates, adult women have higher rates of dysthymia than do adult men. Dysthymia often occurs when there is a physical condition, such as rheumatoid arthritis, or another mental disorder, such as anorexia nervosa (an eating disorder), anxiety disorder, or a substance-related disorder (APA, 1994; Barker et al., 1992).

Bipolar Disorder

Michael's mood swings make him feel like he is on an emotional roller coaster. When he's feeling low, he thinks about suicide, seeing it as the only way out of an unbearable existence. When he's feeling high, he believes he is invincible and can conquer the world. Unfortunately, when he is feeling invulnerable, he's most irrational, staying up all night, going on spending and traveling sprees, and talking endlessly to anyone who will listen. Michael's behavior is typical of bipolar disorder (adapted from NIMH–Publication No. 93-3612, pp. 1–2).

Depressive disorders include major depression and dysthymia, both of which entail persistent deep depressed mood and loss of interest or pleasure in life events, combined with other negative symptoms.

During the nineteenth century, German psychiatrist Emil Kraepelin identified two emotional problems with opposite characteristics—depression and mania—as part of the same psychopathological process. People who swing back and forth between the two poles of mania and depression have ***bipolar disorder*** (formerly called manic-depressive psychosis). Their depressed episodes involve feelings of profound sadness, loneliness, changes in appetite, and lack of self-worth. Their thought processes slow down, and their energy level is low. In se-

◄ *What do Buzz Aldrin, the pilot of the first manned lunar landing, jazz musician Charles Mingus, and actress and author Carrie Fisher have in common? All have publicly acknowledged they suffer from bipolar disorder.*

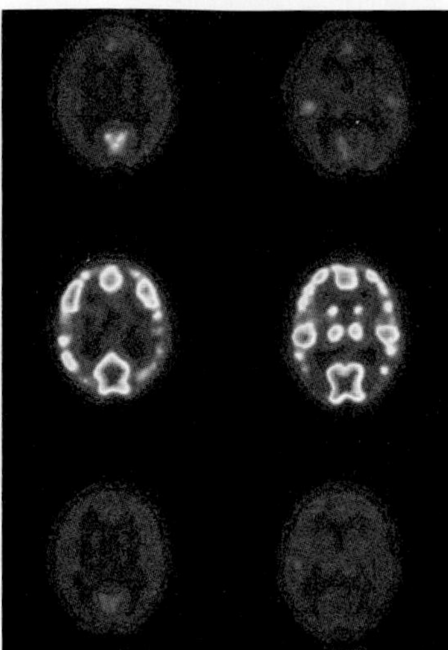

► *This PET scan of a person with bipolar disorder shows a dramatic difference in brain activity during depressive and manic episodes. The scans in the middle row were taken when he was manic; the top and bottom rows when he was depressed.*

vere cases, they may even have visions or hear voices, go into a stupor, or show complete lack of contact with reality.

During a manic episode, individuals with bipolar disorder experience a distinct period of elation, high energy level, expansiveness, and increased activity, without any apparent cause for their elevated mood. They behave erratically—they are often irritable and sleep little or not at all—and become overinvolved in activities, such as writing hundreds of pages on the secrets of life or the promotion of world peace. They may show inflated self-esteem, proclaiming great things about themselves or claiming that they possess unusual powers. They may also behave in extreme ways that attract police attention (for example, proclaiming spiritual insights or shouting or singing loudly in the middle of a street or on a bus or train, even though no one is paying any attention to them. They may be easily distracted, switching rapidly between disconnected thoughts and topics; they may show excessive involvement in pleasurable activities (for example, unrestrained shopping sprees, sexual indiscretions), without any regard for the consequences. In fact, manic episodes are often accompanied by impaired judgment, resulting in financial losses, substance abuse, and other illegal activities (APA, 1994).

From .4 percent to 1.2 percent of the adult population in the United States suffers from bipolar disorder. Researchers have not found a gender difference in its occurrence (McGrath, Strickland, Keita, & Russo, 1990).

▼ *Poverty and other poor living conditions such as lack of education, illness, and exposure to violence can dramatically increase the risk for depression in both children and adults.*

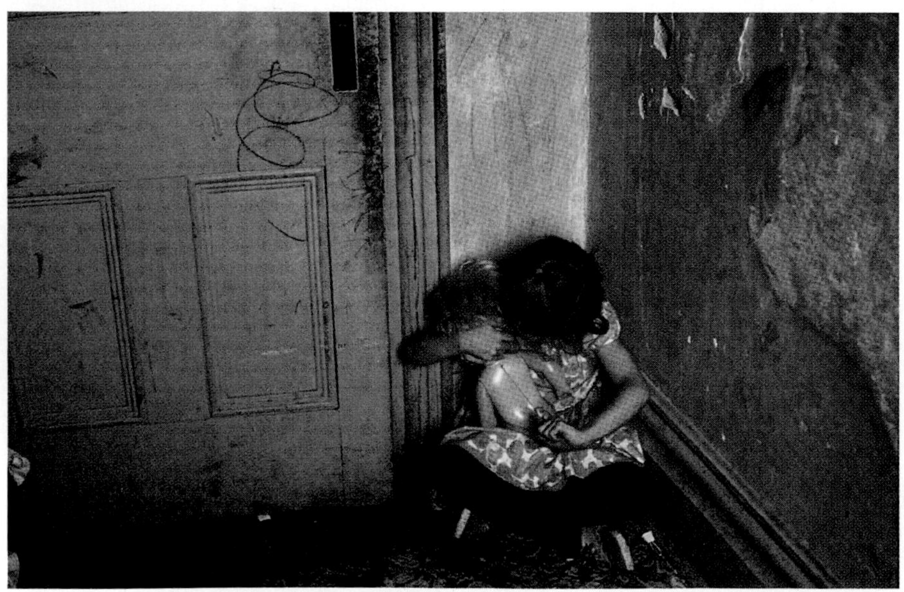

Causes of Mood Disorders

Researchers often use population statistics to document the role of heredity in mood disorders. In a classic study, researchers found that 25 percent of siblings, fraternal twins, parents, and children of individuals with bipolar disorder also suffered from it, compared to about 0.5 percent of the general population (Kallman, 1953). Between identical twins, the rate rose to 96 percent. Later research, controlling more adequately for environmental effects, indicated that researchers overestimated the genetic contribution (Gottesman & Shields, 1982). Nevertheless, current research supports the existence of a major genetic component for this diagnosis. There does not seem to be a similar genetic component for dysthymia or major depression (McGrath, Strickland, Keita, & Russo, 1990).

What about biochemical factors in mood disorders? One theory proposes that mood is regulated, at least in part, by neurotransmitter levels in the brain (see Chapter 3). Deficits in two brain chemicals—norepinephrine and serotonin—or deficits in receptor sensitivity to them can cause the severe emotional disruption and mood swings experienced by patients with bipolar disorder. Serotonin, in particular, has been implicated in a variety of disorders that involve the sleep cycle, eating, sexual drive, and mood (Jacobs, 1994). Some research has even suggested that a drop in serotonin levels is predictive of suicidal behavior (Pandey, Pandey, Dwivedi, Sharma, & Davis, 1995; Mann, Arango, & Underwood, 1990). Reserpine, a drug that tends to produce depression as a side effect, reduces levels of brain serotonin. A group of drugs—tricyclic antidepressants—lifts depression in some people and increases norepinephrine and serotonin in the brain. In addition, another group of drugs, the serotonin reuptake inhibitors, increases serotonin by blocking serotonin reabsorption. Prozac is probably the most familiar of these drugs. While we have support for a biochemical role in mood and mood disorders, interpreting these results poses a problem reminiscent of the chicken-and-egg riddle. Which comes first—changes in biochemistry or depression?

Some aspects of affective disorders are difficult to fit into any strictly biological theory. For example, we know that sociocultural factors, including low education, poverty, rape, battering, chronic illness, marital unhappiness, and lack of access to child care, play a large role in determining risk for depression (McGrath, Strickland, Keita, & Russo, 1990; Weissman, Merikangas, & Boyd, 1986).

There are several psychological explanations for depression. According to psychodynamic theory, depression results when people can't express hostility and anger, even when these emotions are appropriate (Abraham, 1911/1948; Freud, 1917/1976). Instead they turn their anger inward, convincing themselves that they are worthless and do not deserve good things to happen to them.

In the humanistic view, depression arises because people have an image of an ideal self that does not match their real self. The ideal self-image is so perfect that it seems impossible for the real self to attain. If a person's principal goal is to attain self-actualization, a large perceived distance between one's real and ideal selves can be seriously depressing (Rogers, 1961, 1980).

Behavior theory provides still another psychological explanation of depression. If our passive, maladaptive behaviors are rewarded and our effective, competent behaviors are punished, we may not develop the behaviors we need to cope with life. We may even stop trying to influence our environment, therefore developing a *learned helplessness* that contributes to our feelings of powerlessness and lack of self-worth (Seligman, 1975). We may also make causal attributions about our behavior (see Chapter 12) that erode, rather than enhance, our self-esteem. The way we form causal attributions for our behavior is called our *explanatory style* (Abramson, Seligman, & Teasdale, 1978).

Our explanatory style may be pessimistic or optimistic, depending on how our attributions vary along three dimensions: (1) internal-external, (2) stable-unstable, and (3) specific-global causes. As you learned in Chapter 13, a pessimistic explanatory style uses internal, stable, and global explanations for negative events ("My problems affect my whole life and will be with me forever") and can be a risk factor for depression as well as physical illness (Abramson, Seligman, & Teasdale, 1978; Peterson & Bossio, 1991). One of the aims of cognitive-behavioral therapies is to change attributional processes so they become less irrational and self-defeating (Beck, 1976; Ellis, 1962). Some of the cognitive errors in thinking that promote depression are shown in Table 15-5.

Table 15-5 Cognitive Errors Leading to Depression

Error	Example
All-or-none thinking	Person tends to see things in black-or-white. If anything is less than perfect, it is a total failure.
Overgeneralizing	Person interprets a single event as a never-ending pattern of failure. Uses *always* or *never* with respect to the event.
Narrow focus	Person picks out a single negative detail and dwells on it.
Discounting the positive	Person minimizes positive experiences, insisting that they are unimportant.
Leaping to conclusions	Person interprets neutral events as negative on the basis of little or no evidence.
Exaggeration	Person sees problems and shortcomings as bigger or more important than they really are.
Emotional reasoning	Person overemphasizes negative emotions and sees them as reflecting the way things really are.
Personalizing blame	Person holds him- or herself responsible for bad events that are really out of personal control.

Source: Adapted from Burns, 1989.

THINKING CRITICALLY

Would you expect people who think they lack control over their environment to become depressed in all circumstances? Or would the environment, and whether it is positive or negative, make a difference?

Researchers suggest that lack of control over events combined with the expectation of negative outcomes results in a specific type of depression called hopelessness depression (Abramson, Metalsky, & Alloy, 1989). Hopelessness depression occurs in response to negative life events. From this perspective, if you don't feel that you are in control of your life, but you don't encounter any negative situations, you will not become depressed.

Schizophrenic Disorders

▼ *Most people with schizophrenia (about 65%) alternate between periods of illness and remission. Singer Wesley Willis, who enjoys greeting people with head butts, uses music to try to control his schizophrenia.*

A therapist had the following conversation with a hospitalized schizophrenic:

> Interviewer: "How old are you?"
> Patient: "Why, I am centuries old, sir."
> Interviewer: "How long have you been here?"
> Patient: "I've been on this property on and off for a long time. I cannot say the exact time because we are absorbed by the air at night, and they bring back people. They kill up everything; they can make you lie; they can talk through your throat."
> Interviewer: "Who is this?"
> Patient: "Why, the air." (White, 1932, p. 228).

Schizophrenia refers to a group of disorders characterized by disturbances in thought processes and emotions and by psychotic behaviors, that is, behaviors that reflect a marked distortion of or detachment from reality. Although the word schizophrenia means "a break or split in the mind," do not confuse it with dissociative identity disorder in which individuals acquire two or more distinct identities, each of which controls their behavior at different times. Instead, the "break" in schizophrenia refers to disorganized thoughts and perceptions that cause the individual to "break" with reality. In some cases, the breakdown is very dramatic—patients talk about their behavior as something happening to them rather than something they are doing. As you can see in the conversation above, schizophrenic thought processes are unpredictable and often follow a chain of illogical or free associations difficult for others to understand.

Generally, those with schizophrenia withdraw from interpersonal relationships, and their emotional responses are blunted or flattened (although they may change suddenly to extreme, inappropriate responses). Another common symptom is depersonalization (a loss of identity). Schizophrenic individuals often experience hallucinations (false sensory perceptions that seem as real as true sensory perceptions). Thus, they may feel their hands have turned to stone, that their bodies are full of bugs, that others can hear their thoughts, or that they can hear voices or see people or objects that are not there. They also often experience delusions, which are false beliefs that persist in the face of logical arguments and evidence. They are often preoccupied with their inner fantasies and do not pay attention to the external environment.

What's it like to live with a schizophrenic? Emily describes living with her brother Doug, who was diagnosed with schizophrenia and has not been responsive to any currently available treatments:

> It's 2 A.M., and I'm trying to sleep, but the stereo in the kitchen is blaring rock and roll music: the Rolling Stones. I've put the ear plugs in but can still hear him: singing, yelling, crying, and laughing hysterically—sometimes it almost seems to be simultaneous. Doug once explained to me long ago that it helps him to drown out his voices and that he learns from music —it's like therapy to him. To survive living with a schizophrenic you need love, compassion, strength, and a great sense of humor. From the moment he wakes up in the morning, his delusions become his reality, and his voices are constant. Doug gets a shot of medication once a week, and we've found it helps, but only a little bit. In defense, my mom and I laugh a lot together. His illness does lead to amusing

situations. Like the time he was so excited he made me go to the store and buy two steaks and wine to celebrate 'cause he'd just purchased the Presidio in San Francisco and was going to turn it into a Roman Catholic Church. But his voices can be vicious and hurtful as well. My brother often sits up through the night, crying, screaming, and cursing the voices that plague his consciousness. They NEVER stop—he never hears silence. Although treatments help some people, when they don't work, a schizophrenic lives in a walking hell. I know he can never be "all right"—the suffering will continue like a recurring nightmare over and over again. No one can protect him from his demons. (Personal communication)

Between 1 and 2 percent of people in the United States have had or will experience a schizophrenic episode during their lifetime (Regier et al., 1988). About 10 percent of people with schizophrenia remain schizophrenic, while 25 percent return to normal functioning. The remainder alternate between active schizophrenia and remission (Bleuler, 1978; Breier, Schreiber, Dyer, & Pickar, 1991). Prognosis depends on exposure to stressful life events and on the culture in which the schizophrenic individual lives. In developing countries—for example, Nigeria, India, and Colombia—prognosis is most positive. In industrialized countries—such as the United States, the United Kingdom, Russia, Denmark, and Czechoslovakia—long-term outcomes are less positive (Sartorius, Jablensky, & Shapiro, 1978). This may be for a variety of reasons, including lowered stressfulness and complexity of work in agricultural societies (so symptoms do not interfere with productivity), and greater acceptance of symptoms (visions may not be viewed as abnormal). Schizophrenic individuals may be more likely to find a niche in developing countries, where they can be productive and are accepted.

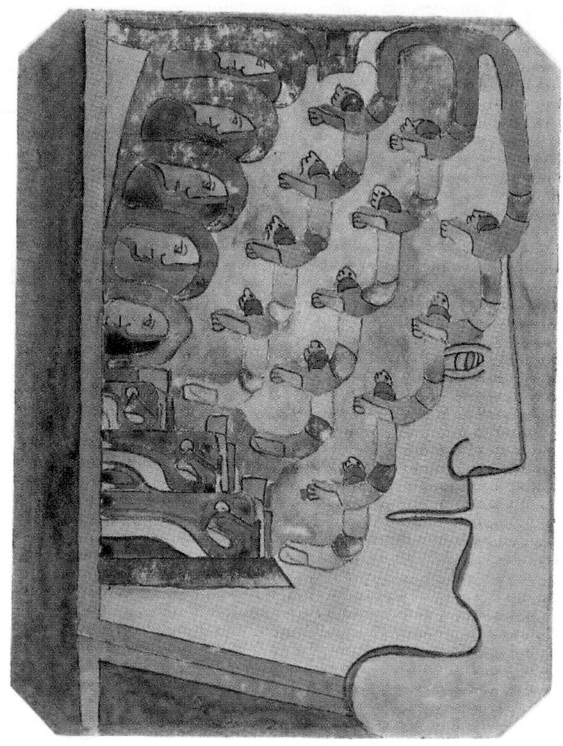

◀ *This drawing by a hospitalized schizophrenic patient was described by the artist through free association: "Worm holes (bath faces), worm paths (pianomusicstickteeth), worm strings (spitbathlife of the archlyregallery-tin-timeler-reflections: ad mothersurgarmoon in the sevensaltnose water..."*

Types of Schizophrenia

Schizophrenia is, in many respects, the most bizarre form of psychopathology. It is characterized by disturbances in thought, language, mood, perception, and behavior. Consider the thought processes of LPK, who has been diagnosed with schizophrenia. One day, LPK was walking on New York City's East Side. He was surprised to hear someone exclaim twice "Shoot him!" and he decided that someone wanted to shoot *him*. LPK tried to see the people who were threatening him, but the street was too crowded. He moved away as quickly as possible, but he thought that the unidentified people who had threatened to shoot him were following in pursuit. He knew they were after him because their voices were as close as ever, no matter how fast he walked. Several days later, when he was back in the city, LPK was once again startled when he thought he heard the same voices that had threatened him earlier. He thought that one of the "pursuers" was able to read his thoughts. LPK tried to get away by darting up and down subway exits and entrances, jumping on and off trains until after midnight. But at each station when he got off a train, the voices were still as close as before. He thought the people who were pursuing him had inherited occult powers from their parents, and that these powers enabled them to know other people's thoughts and to project their own voices ("radio voices") over several miles without talking loudly, and without apparent effort. He believed that these powers were due to their "natural, bodily electricity" and that the vibration of their vocal chords generated wireless radio waves that were caught by human ears (adapted from LPK in Kaplan, 1964, pp. 133–35).

▼ *Patients suffering from catatonic schizophrenia may remain in unusual, uncomfortable positions for hours at a time. These periods of stillness may alternate with periods of extreme agitation.*

► *Auditory hallucinations are a very unpleasant aspect of schizophrenia for many patients.*

All schizophrenic disorders described in DSM-IV share two or more of the following features: presence of delusions and/or hallucinations; disorganized speech with little meaningful content; extremely disorganized behavior; and negative symptoms, such as flat affect (being emotionless), withdrawal, apathy, and impaired attention.

A patient with ***disorganized schizophrenia*** exhibits both disorganized speech and behavior and inappropriate (for example, laughing at something sad) or blunted affect (no emotions at all). Delusions are not characteristic of this subtype, but people with disorganized schizophrenia are usually extremely withdrawn socially. ***Paranoid schizophrenia,*** which is illustrated in the case summary above, is characterized by delusions of persecution, delusions of grandeur, and suspicion of others. The patient frequently experiences auditory hallucinations. Patients with paranoid schizophrenia not only believe that they have been singled out for persecution but also that they are special people, selected for their unusual powers or qualities.

Catatonic schizophrenia is characterized by a motionless, or near motionless, position that patients may hold for hours or days if undisturbed. Yet, people with catatonic schizophrenia can and will move under certain circumstances. They may even allow their arms to be put in various positions, without showing any resistance. They may occasionally have episodes of rage, however, that alternate with rigid withdrawal. Moreover, sometimes they may exhibit excessive and purposeless motor activity, apparently not influenced by any external stimuli.

Individuals with schizophrenia often do not fit neatly into these four types. ***Undifferentiated schizophrenia*** is a "catch-all" term indicating that the person has characteristics shared by two or more subtypes. It is the most common of all schizophrenic diagnoses.

15-4 Genetics and Schizophrenia

A concordance rate of 100% would mean that if one member of the biologically related pair is schizophrenic, the other person will be, too. Note that if a fraternal twin is schizophrenic, the concordance rate is close to that of any other sibling. But if an identical twin is schizophrenic, the concordance rate is far higher. (Source: Adapted from Gottesman, 1991)

Causes of Schizophrenia

Given its multifaceted nature, there is no single cause that explains all the types of schizophrenia. Genetic factors are partly responsible. Studies on the rates of schizophrenia in twins show that the chances are approximately 48 out of 100 (a probability of 0.48) that if one twin is schizophrenic the other will be as well (see Figure 15-4). For nontwin brothers and sisters the probability ranges from .09 to 0.15 (McGue, Gottesman, & Rao, 1985; Gottesman, 1993). Because identical twins share more genetic material, these rates suggest a genetic component. If one identical twin is schizophrenic, about half the time the other twin will either be schizophrenic or will suffer from some other behavior disorder. Note that this means that the other half of the time, the other identical twin is not schizophrenic and does not have another behavior disorder. These discordant pairs—"one ill–one well"—are especially important to re-

SEEKING SOLUTIONS

The Insanity Defense

When John Hinckley was tried in 1982 for shooting then-President Ronald Reagan in front of dozens of witnesses, he was diagnosed as having a schizophrenic disorder and found not guilty by reason of insanity. Instead of going to prison, he was placed in a mental hospital. The public outcry that followed (including a newspaper headline reading, "Hinckley Insane, Public Mad") again raised the controversy over whether or not people who are labeled "insane" should be held responsible for criminal acts. Jeffrey L. Dahmer, the Milwaukee mutilator, provided another high profile case using an insanity defense. Dahmer was diagnosed as having a mental disorder, a paraphilia disorder (characterized by intense sexual urges toward inappropriate objects, such as children or corpses). Although diagnosed as mentally ill, in 1992, the court nonetheless committed him to a lifetime behind bars (and might have ordered execution, had that been allowed in Wisconsin).

These cases demonstrate that insanity is a legal term, not a psychological diagnosis. Grounds for the insanity defense have varied over time and depend on the state. In the case of Hinckley, the defense was based on the following premise: a person should not be held responsible for his or her behavior if, at the time, mental illness prevented the person from (1) understanding that the behavior was morally and criminally wrong and (2) resisting the impulse to behave in that way. The burden also was on the prosecution to prove that he was not insane. In 1994, about twenty states used this standard of insanity.

After the Hinckley case, Congress changed the standard for the insanity defense for federal crimes to include only the first part: the inability to tell right from wrong. Assignment of the burden of proof has also been changed in many states. By the early 1990s, the majority of states (including Wisconsin, where Dahmer was tried) placed the burden of proving insanity on defendants, making them prove they did not understand their acts were wrong (Ogloff, Roberts, & Roesch, 1993).

Today, insanity tests vary by state. However, all deal with the question of whether or not the defendant was suffering from a mental disorder at the time of the crime severe enough to meet the legal standard for the insanity defense. Defense lawyers using this plea argue that their clients suffer from a "mental disease or defect" (insanity). Each side lines up its battery of psychiatrists and psychologists to examine the defendant and to testify in court on the question of mental competence. Of course, the defense experts usually testify that the defendant was insane for this or that reason, while the prosecution experts contradict them. For laypersons and particularly for jurors, this can be a confusing and frustrating experience. Jurors are not experts, but they are required by the legal system to make a life or death decision on the basis of conflicting testimony by experts. If the verdict is "not guilty by reason of insanity," the defendant is either sent to a mental hospital for treatment, eventually to be released as cured, or released immediately if it is determined that he or she is no longer afflicted with the disorder.

Proponents of the insanity defense see it as an important protection for the mentally ill population. Those who oppose it either reject the concept of mental illness in all its ramifications or do not think that mental illness absolves anyone of responsibility for their actions. There has also been a movement in some states to separate guilt and innocence from responsibility. New laws allow a jury to find a defendant guilty, though mentally ill, thus holding them criminally responsible for their actions. Basically, this means that jurors need only decide whether or not the evidence indicates that the defendant actually committed the crime; the decision about mental competence and disposition of the accused is left to the judge in consultation with the experts. This approach is highly controversial, as the person is virtually in limbo—not guilty, but not acquitted (Roberts, Golding, & Fincham, 1987).

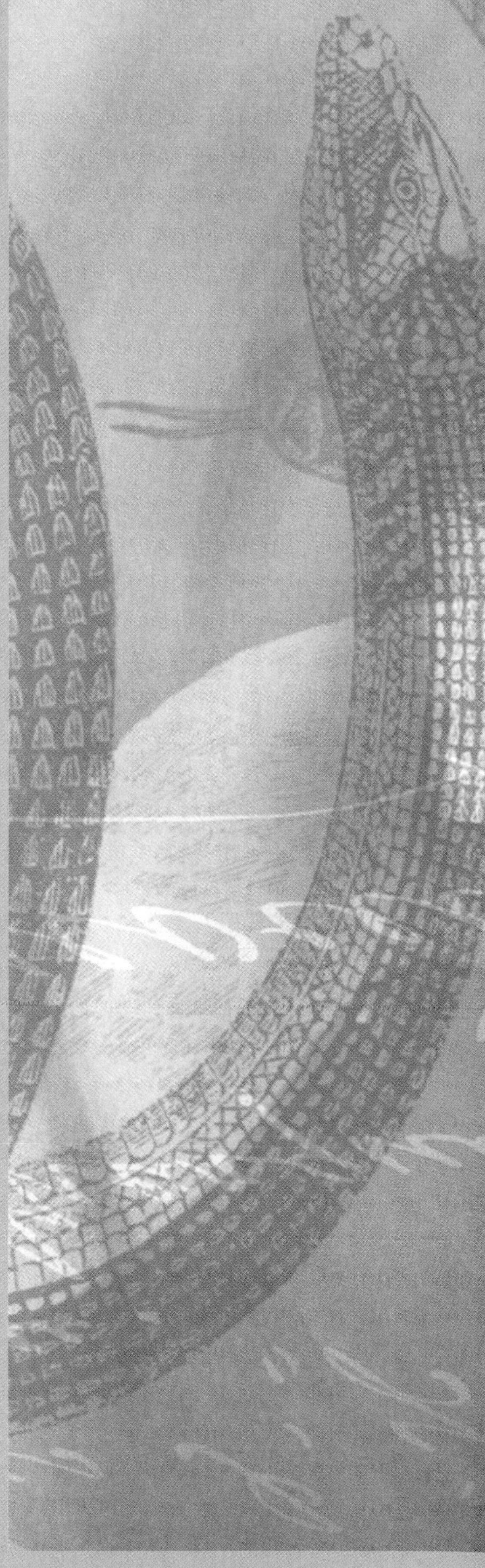

▲ *The Genain quadruplets all suffer from schizophrenia, suggesting a genetic component to schizophrenia.*

searchers who are trying to determine the role of genetics and of the environment. Researchers have already found that the children of either twin (ill versus well) have the same risk of developing schizophrenia—17 percent (Fischer, 1971; Gottesman & Bertelson, 1989). Taken as a whole, these findings suggest that genes in combination with environmental factors determine who becomes schizophrenic.

The genetic component of schizophrenia is most likely to reveal itself as some underlying structural or biochemical defect in the brain. For the past decade, researchers have been applying brain-imaging techniques, such as CAT scans and PET scans, to identify how the brains of schizophrenics differ from those of healthy people. One study found that when discordant twins were asked to sort playing cards, an area in the prefrontal lobe of the cerebral cortex of the schizophrenic twin failed to activate. This area, which is part of the most highly evolved part of the brain, is necessary for performing complex tasks and having organized thoughts. Other research has found disorders in a variety of other brain structures, particularly those involved in sensory functioning, memory, language, and emotional expression (see Figure 15-5). This work has led to the conclusion that schizophrenia not only involves particular parts of the brain, it also results from a breakdown in the connections between these parts (Tamminga, Thaker, & Buchanan, 1992; Torrey, Bowler, Taylor, & Gottesman, 1994).

A variety of stressful environmental circumstances are associated with higher rates of schizophrenia, including poverty, living in urban, crime-ridden neighborhoods, and having fathers who are unemployed or addicted to

15-5 The Brain Anatomy of Schizophrenia

Areas of the brain that might be involved in schizophrenic thinking and behavior.

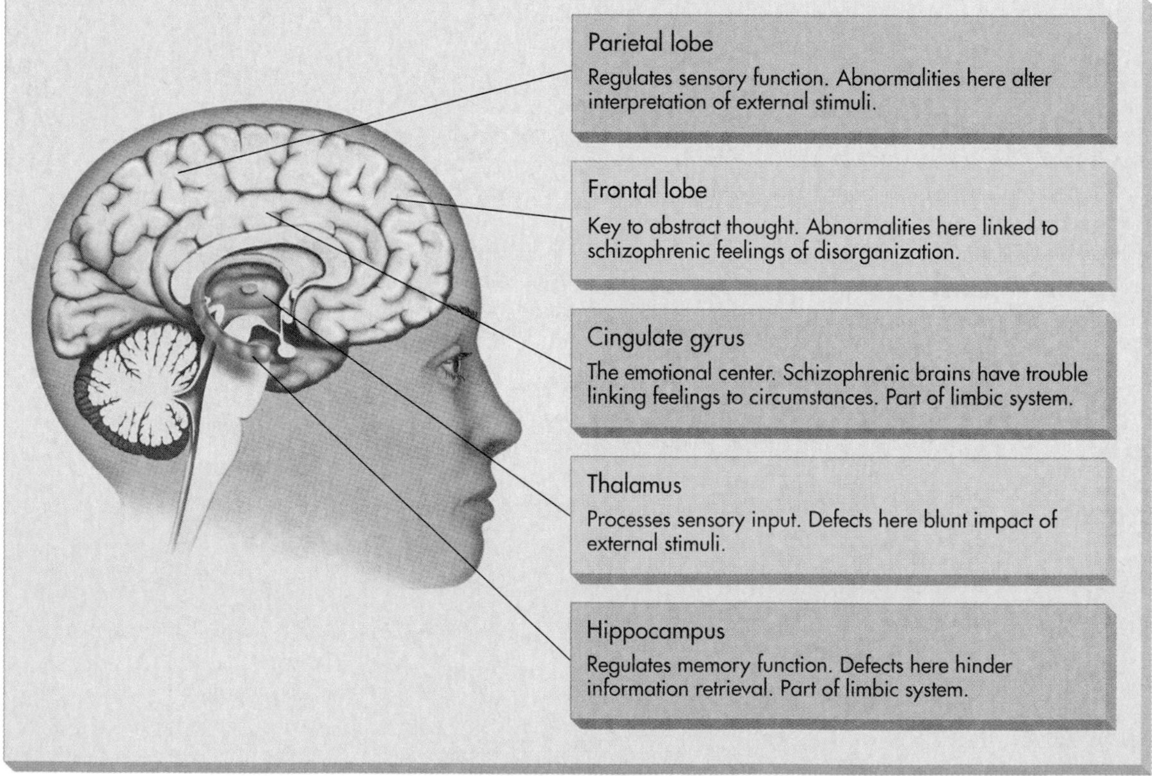
Parietal lobe
Regulates sensory function. Abnormalities here alter interpretation of external stimuli.
Frontal lobe
Key to abstract thought. Abnormalities here linked to schizophrenic feelings of disorganization.
Cingulate gyrus
The emotional center. Schizophrenic brains have trouble linking feelings to circumstances. Part of limbic system.
Thalamus
Processes sensory input. Defects here blunt impact of external stimuli.
Hippocampus
Regulates memory function. Defects here hinder information retrieval. Part of limbic system.

drugs or alcohol (Parnas, Cannon, Jacobsen, Schulsinger, & Mednick, 1993; Talovic, Mednick, Schulsinger, & Falloon, 1981). Family relationships that cause the developing child to doubt his or her own thoughts and feelings and that involve double-bind messages can also be a contributing factor (Bateson, Jackson, Haley, & Weakland, 1956; Hassan, 1974). An example of a double-bind message is telling a schizophrenic person, "Come over here and give me a hug" and then stiffening when he or she gives you the hug. When the schizophrenic cuts the hug short in response, you say, "What's the matter, don't you love me?" Schizophrenics are put in a "damned if they do, damned if they don't" situation. Because family stress can trigger schizophrenic episodes, teaching families how to talk through their problems and communicate in less emotional and less stress-producing ways can produce dramatic rises in recovery rates (Falloon et al., 1982; Halford & Hayes, 1991).

The finding that schizophrenia is more common among people born in the winter months suggests that the mother's exposure to winter viruses during prenatal development may also play a role. One study of children with family histories of schizophrenia found that there was a 70 percent increase in the rate of schizophrenia in children of mothers who had caught the flu during the second trimester of pregnancy (Dajer, 1992). Another study suggests the possibility of a disruption in the development of fetal brain areas in individuals with a genetic predisposition to schizophrenia. Using CAT scan data from the children of schizophrenic parents, these researchers not only found abnormal enlargement of some locations in the brain but also brain atrophy in other areas (Cannon, Mednick, & Parnas, 1989).

Research has also focused on the biochemical basis of schizophrenia. Some forms of schizophrenia may result from either overactivity in neural pathways activated by the neurotransmitter dopamine or from an interaction between dopamine and serotonin (Kahn et al., 1993). Evidence for this view is provided by studies of a class of drugs called phenothiazines. These drugs can reduce the symptoms of schizophrenia, probably by blocking dopamine receptors (Gottesman & Shields, 1982).

The phenothiazines have no effect on some schizophrenic patients, however, indicating once again that schizophrenia is not a unified disorder with a single cause but rather a cluster of related syndromes. Particular abnormalities are frequently found in brain structures of schizophrenics who do not respond to treatment with phenothiazines (Gottesman & Shields, 1982). Thus, schizophrenia could be the product of a combination of several different disease processes.

THINKING CRITICALLY

Studies of the biochemistry of hospitalized patients diagnosed with schizophrenia all share a major difficulty in interpretation—correlation is not causation. How can we know whether biochemical factors are a cause or an effect of the disorder? Can you think of some alternative explanations for these research findings?

First, hospital patients are probably taking medication. Their medication may have unknown side effects that affect the biochemical analysis of their blood. Schizophrenics also have poor eating habits, smoke more tobacco, and drink more coffee than nonschizophrenic people do. Finally, the mental wards in many hospitals are overcrowded and relatively unsanitary. All of these factors can have their own impact on body biochemistry. It may be impossible to separate the primary causes of schizophrenia from the secondary causes that develop as a consequence of having schizophrenia. Consequently, although most researchers today accept that there are biochemical and/or anatomical bases for schizophrenia, the exact culprits have yet to be firmly identified.

Most of the available evidence suggests that in schizophrenia, just as in the affective disorders, both heredity and environment are important. The ***diathesis-stress model*** is based on this notion (Mednick, Machon, Huttunen, & Bonett, 1988). According to this theory, a disorder (in this case, schizophrenia) develops because there is a genetic predisposition to the

According to the diathesis-stress model, psychopathology develops because there is a genetic predisposition to the disorder (diathesis) and because there are environmental factors (stress) that can trigger this predisposition.

disorder (called the *diathesis*) and because there are environmental factors (*stress*) that can trigger this predisposition. If neither genetic predisposition nor environmental stresses exist, then the disorder will not appear. This theory seems a better fit with our current knowledge than any purely genetic or environmental theory alone.

Personality Disorders

You can count on most people to do what they have told you they will do, within a reasonable period of time. But suppose you run into Hank, a fellow student who is assigned to work on a joint project with you, but who repeatedly and persistently fails to follow through. What, you might ask, does this have to do with psychopathology? Certainly the importance of someone failing to do his share on a joint project is minor compared with the level of distress and dysfunction that you can see in a severe anxiety or mood disorder. But suppose Hank is consistently irresponsible. Instead of doing the work, he parties, gets drunk, and wrecks his girlfriend's car. Furthermore, suppose he lies about following through on your project and even steals his friend's paper and represents the work as his own. When he is caught, he expresses no guilt or remorse, and instead he tells the professor that he wrote the paper and that his friend must have plagiarized it. He resents the professor for assigning a joint project and for punishing him for cheating; he becomes angry and abusive. Suppose Hank's irresponsibility and pleasure-seeking, failure to conform to social norms and exploitation of others (lying, cheating, drunk driving, betraying a friend), lack of regard for the truth, and lack of respect for legitimate authority is so persistent and extreme that it becomes Hank's most predominant and distinguishable behavioral pattern. In this case, Hank's behavior reflects a personality disorder (here, an antisocial personality disorder).

Personality disorders represent a group of significant mental and behavioral problems characterized not so much by bizarre behaviors, anxiety, or major mood changes as by pervasive personality characteristics that seem to cause less discomfort for the afflicted individuals than for the people around them. Personality disorders fall on Axis II of DSM-IV are longstanding patterns of thinking, feeling, relating, and behaving that are maladaptive and inflexible across a range of situations (see Table 15-6). When personality traits cause significant behavioral impairment or feelings of distress in others, they constitute a personality disorder. Sometimes the maladaptive behavior has criminal or violent components. Yet, individuals with personality disorders are not likely to seek

Table 15-6 Personality Disorders

Disorder	Major Characteristics
Paranoid Personality	Suspiciousness and mistrust of others; hypersensitivity; difficulty in getting along with others
Schizoid Personality	Emotionally cold and aloof; indifferent to others' feelings; few close relationships
Schizotypal Personality	Oddities of thought, speech, perception, and overt behavior; similar but less severe than in schizophrenia
Borderline Personality	Instability in relationships, mood, and self-concept
Histrionic Personality	Overly reactive; exaggerated emotion; attention-getting behavior; tantrums
Narcissistic Personality	Exaggerated self-importance; fantasies of success, power, beauty, love, etc.; need for constant attention
Avoidant Personality	Hypersensitive to possible rejection or shame; social withdrawal; low self-esteem
Dependent Personality	Extreme passivity; abdication of responsibility for own life; permit others to make decisions for one
Obsessive-Compulsive Personality	Preoccupation with trivial details, order, rules, and efficiency; rigid behavior; no spontaneity
Antisocial Personality	Consistent violation of others' rights; inability to form relationships; often involved in illegal activity; onset before age fifteen

psychological help because they attribute their problems to other people, whom they view as needing more help than themselves. When they are contacted by a mental health worker, it is usually by recommendation of a family member or because they are sent for treatment by the criminal justice system. For these and other reasons, therapy is not particularly effective with them.

Paranoid Personality Disorder

Suspiciousness and distrust of others are defining traits of the ***paranoid personality disorder.*** Paranoid individuals tend to view their interpersonal relationships with extraordinary caution and vigilance. They fear being tricked or threatened, and generally believe that others are out to do them harm or to demean them, even when there is evidence to the contrary. They are quick to take offense, react with anger, and bear longstanding grudges. Paranoid individuals are pathologically jealous, often accusing their spouse or partner of infidelity without justification.

People with a paranoid personality disorder are typically preoccupied with moral issues. Many of them expend great energy writing letters to newspaper editors or calling talk shows about their causes. They tend to be argumentative and to feel possessed with knowledge about what is "right." People with these characteristics are often regarded by others as hostile, defensive, stubborn, and humorless, though they consider themselves objective and rational in all their actions. They tend to isolate themselves from social contact and generally have few friends because they often alienate others. They are envious of people in power and disdainful of people they view as weak, sickly, or defective.

Some people with a paranoid personality disorder may be marginally adjusted, employed, and successfully raising a family. They may never develop extensive psychological problems or require hospitalization. Other people with paranoid personality disorder may have longstanding symptoms of paranoia along with severe psychotic symptoms. These individuals would be diagnosed as having both a paranoid personality disorder as well as paranoid schizophrenia.

Antisocial Personality Disorder

People with ***antisocial personality disorder*** (who are also sometimes described as psychopathic or sociopathic) are indifferent to the needs or concerns of others. Typically, they begin performing antisocial acts before age fifteen. As seen in the behavior of Hank, described at the beginning of this section, they characteristically exploit others for their own selfish ends, without guilt, remorse, or anxiety. Psychodynamically, they have a weak superego; that is, they lack a normal conscience. If caught taking advantage of or harming others, they may act remorseful and ask for "another chance." But, in fact, they experience little regret and predictably repeat their behavior (APA, 1994). About 1.5 to 3.5 percent of adults have an antisocial personality disorder (Kessler et al., 1994).

Suspicion and distrust of others and society are the prime traits of a person with paranoid personality disorder.

Typical childhood signs of antisocial personality disorder include starting fights, using weapons, lying, showing physical cruelty to animals or people, running away from home, forcing someone into sexual activity, stealing, truancy, and vandalism. As adults, people with antisocial personality disorder may be sexually promiscuous, may fail to honor financial obligations, may be irresponsible parents, or may exhibit inconsistent work behavior. Antisocial acts include lying, destroying property, recklessness or drunken driving, stealing, harassing others, and getting into physical fights and assaults, including wife and child battering (Widiger, Corbitt, & Millon, 1992).

Individuals with antisocial personality are pleasure-oriented, lack a normal conscience, and are indifferent to the needs or concerns of others.

Individuals with an antisocial personality disorder often come into contact with the law, and many—especially severe cases—wind up in jail, particularly for acts of violence (Abram & Teplin, 1990). Often they are repeat offenders. They tend to act impulsively and often steal without any apparent need or desire for the money or object stolen. A description of the extreme, violent person with an antisocial personality disorder is found in Truman Capote's chilling book *In Cold Blood*, in which two drifters murder an entire family. Theodore Bundy, a physically attractive, former law student who had above average intelligence but who was also discovered to be a ruthless serial killer, also may have had an antisocial personality disorder.

People with severe antisocial personality disorder are challenging and difficult patients in psychotherapy. They lack motivation to change and are not troubled by their actions. Their life-

Borderline personality disorder is characterized by instability in behavior, mood, and social relationships. People with this disorder tend to have a distorted and unstable self-image. They make frantic efforts to avoid abandonment, and find it difficult to be alone. They lack the ability to control their anger, grief, and other emotions.

style has been reinforced and well-established over a long period, making the disorder extremely resistant to treatment. Few seek treatment voluntarily. Most are ordered into treatment by the courts, their school, or their employer. Unfortunately, no specific treatment appears to be effective (Mannuzza et al., 1991). With increasing age, people with antisocial personality disorder are less likely to commit serious crimes. Although a large percentage do continue criminal activities throughout adulthood, it may be that some "burn out" or pursue their manipulation of others less actively (Arboleda-Florez & Holley, 1991). In particular, sexual promiscuity, fighting, and criminality appear to diminish after about age thirty.

Factors predisposing people to antisocial personality disorders include a dysfunctional family context, parental marital discord and divorce, a history of child abuse, removal from the home, alcoholism, and absence of consistent parental discipline (Robins, 1966; Smith, 1978). Males have higher rates of this disorder than females. In the United States, about 5 percent of males versus 1 percent of females receive this diagnosis. People with lower education and income are more likely to exhibit this disorder for at least two reasons: (1) the disorder impairs both their school performance and earning capacity, so they make less money of their own, and (2) their fathers are also likely to have had an antisocial personality disorder. Thus, people with this disorder are more likely to come from impoverished backgrounds because of having fathers with impaired earning capacities (Robins, 1966).

▼ Serial killer Ted Bundy probably had an anti-social personality disorder. He was highly intelligent and charming, yet exhibited no remorse for his brutal actions.

Borderline Personality Disorder

Borderline personality disorder is a broad and diffuse category—indeed, some scholars question whether it is a real disorder (Perry & Klerman, 1980). In general, this disorder is characterized by instability in personality, mood, and social relationships. People with this disorder tend to have a distorted and unstable self-image and depend heavily on relationships with others to define themselves. They make frantic efforts to avoid abandonment (real or imagined), and find it difficult to be alone. Yet, at the same time, they tend to distrust people and feel they are being victimized, perhaps because of their dependency and vulnerability. They can at one moment idealize a friendship, then abruptly turn against that "friend" for some small, perhaps imagined, slight.

Individuals with borderline personality disorder lack the ability to control their anger, grief, and other emotions readily. They may have a chronic feeling of emptiness. They may fly into a rage, even in public situations in which most people would be embarrassed by such outbursts. Furthermore, they tend to act impulsively in self-damaging ways, such as reckless sexual behavior, reckless driving, binge eating, and substance abuse. They may threaten or even attempt suicide to manipulate others, and they may engage in self-mutilation.

Individuals diagnosed with this disorder tend to be perceptive and sensitive to others' feelings, especially to nonverbal cues (Frank & Hoffman, 1986; Park, Imboden, Park, Hulse, & Unger, 1992). Many borderline patients have also often suffered personal devaluation and blame, as well as physical and sexual abuse, which may well account for the insecurity and instability of their lives (Herman, Perry, & van der Kolk, 1989; Stone, 1990). Because treatment approaches to borderline personality disorder have not been designed to address issues of sexual abuse, and because individuals with personality disorders are often viewed so negatively by clinicians, some psychologists have argued that the diagnosis should not be applied to sexual abuse victims. They believe that symptoms of sexual abuse victims should be considered as reflecting posttraumatic stress disorder, and labeled as such (Briere, 1984; Brown, 1994).

What's in a name? What difference does it make if a sexual abuse victim is labeled as having a "borderline personality disorder" or "complex posttraumatic stress disorder"? Some psychologists argue that a personality disorder diagnosis implies that the individual has deep, persistent problems of character and therefore establishes the expectation that he or she will be extremely unlikeable and difficult to treat. In contrast, a complex posttraumatic stress disorder diagnosis implies that the symptoms are adaptive responses to repeated stress and trauma which now impair functioning, and this may evoke a view of the client as more capable of change. Thus, the use of the borderline personality diagnosis with sexual abuse victims has been controversial, and efforts to include a complex posttraumatic stress disorder diagnosis in the next version of the DSM continue (Brown, 1994).

Problems in Diagnosis

Clinicians do not always agree as to the best way to define and classify symptoms of mental disorder. Diagnosis is a complex and subjective process. A clinician must observe a symptom and then make a value judgment: Is the symptom merely unhealthy or does it constitute an impairment in functioning? Deviant behavior or conflicts between the individual and society should not be classified as mental disorders unless the deviance or conflict is a symptom of dysfunction *for the specific individual*. The clinician must decide if the symptoms are a maladaptive response to the environment (that is, whether the behavior is normal or abnormal). Whether a symptom is considered maladaptive or dysfunctional or a creative survival strategy for life under oppressive circumstances is a value judgment requiring substantial knowledge of the sociocultural context. If clinicians are unaware of, ignore, or minimize the effects of stressors in the environment, they may judge a client's symptoms as pathological. This is why mental health service providers must become informed about sociocultural foundations and contexts of behavior. In recognition of this fact, DSM-IV includes information about age, cultural, and gender-related features for each separate disorder.

Gender and Diagnosis

Some DSM-IV classifications have been challenged based on the fact that differing gender role expectations may affect the classifications. For example, when men endure pain and suffering for the sake of fame, glory, or money (as boxers, football players, or soldiers), they are called brave and honorable. When women endure suffering for their husbands' or children's sake, they may be labeled as masochistic with "self-defeating personalities." What makes suffering understandable in one case and pathological in the other? These different judgments about the normality of gender role behaviors have led to a charge of a double standard in diagnosing men and women, a charge that is still being debated today among clinicians.

Clinicians do not always agree on the best way to classify symptoms of mental disorder. A clinician must make a value judgment as to whether symptoms are maladaptive in response to the environment or creative survival strategies for life under oppressive circumstances. These diagnostic judgments require substantial knowledge of sociocultural context.

Because clinical judgments involve human cognitive processes, they are subject to certain biases, just like any other judgment. Disorder rates differ by gender. Disorders that fit society's stereotypical view of "femininity" (anxiety, depression) have higher rates in women. Disorders that do not fit society's idealized view of "femininity" but that fit the masculine role (alcoholism) have higher rates in men. The level of fit (congruence) between gender role expectations and nature of the mental disorder can bias the judgments of clinicians (Russo, 1985).

A classic study demonstrates how gender stereotypes can influence judgments about the severity of a disorder (Rosenfield, 1982). The study examined what happens to people diagnosed in emergency rooms. Researchers found that the likelihood of hospitalization increased when the diagnosis was inconsistent with gender role stereotypes. For example, men who were diagnosed as depressed were more likely to be hospitalized than women who were diagnosed as depressed. The opposite was true for women diagnosed with an alcohol disorder. More recent evidence for this bias has been found for men diagnosed with major depression and for women diagnosed with antisocial personality or alcohol abuse disorders. Such individuals were rated as more severely disturbed and more likely to elicit recommendations for

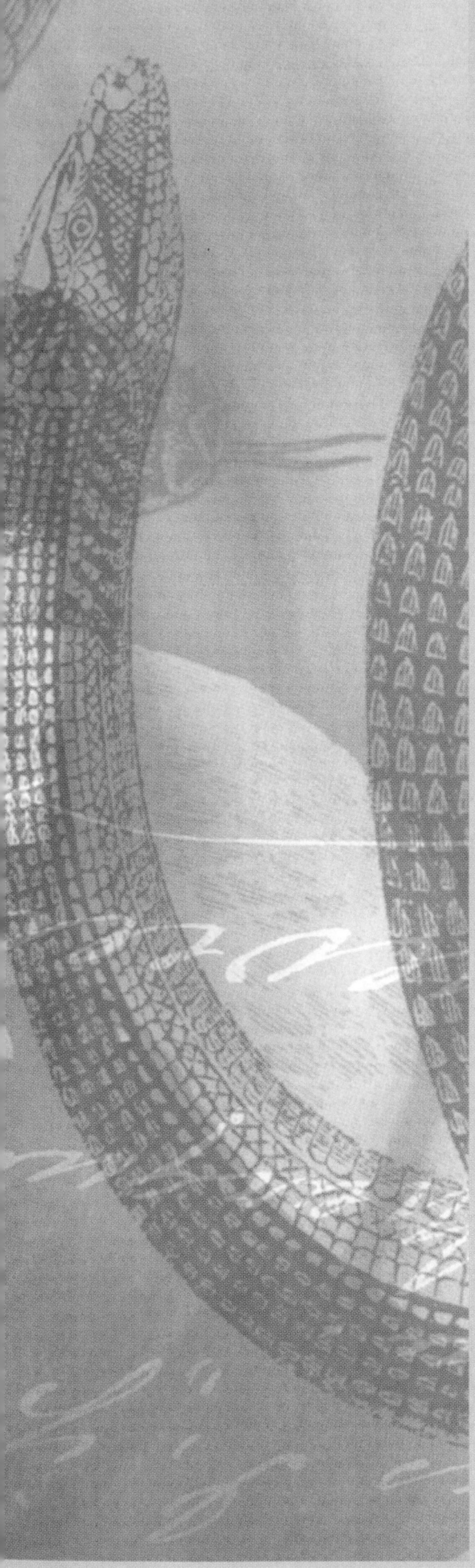

UNDERSTANDING HUMAN DIVERSITY

Gender and Depression

Kate couldn't understand why she was feeling uneasy about her life—"It's like when you toss and turn on a bad mattress, looking for a comfortable place to sleep. That's how I felt all the time—I couldn't get comfortable with life" (Wartik, 1992, p. 81). Objectively she seemed to have everything—recently married and settled in a new place, she was advancing in her career at a major newspaper. Yet, all at once she felt exhausted, even after a night's sleep. She began withdrawing from family and friends, and skipping her workouts. She felt down, and she wasn't able to cheer herself up. So many life changes—new marriage, new town, new job—had led to a mild depression. Fortunately, she sought help before her condition had a chance to deteriorate (Wartik, 1992).

Women's rates for some kinds of depression—major depression and dysthymia—are higher than men's rates, at a ratio of two-to-one (Kessler et al., 1994). This ratio holds for women in the United States, regardless of whether they are black, white, or Hispanic (McGrath et al., 1990). In addition, a cross-cultural study found that women were more likely than men to be diagnosed with depression in the ten nations studied (Weissman et al., 1996). The fact that women are more likely to seek help than men does not explain this gender difference. Further, both sexes are equally likely to inherit depression, so genes don't seem to explain it either. What does?

The gender difference first appears during adolescence, suggesting the possibility that hormonal changes that begin at puberty may explain it. But in a study of teenage girls ten to fourteen years of age, hormone levels were found to account for only 1 percent of the changes in depressive symptoms. Rather, it was number of negative life events that significantly predicted depression (Brooks-Gunn & Warren, 1987).

For women, stressful life experiences might include sexual or physical abuse in childhood, having a violent partner, having a chronic painful illness, unwanted pregnancy, infertility, surgery, or menopause, which are all correlated with higher rates of depression (McGrath et al., 1990). Work may also be a source of stress for women. Women often make less money, have lower status jobs, and may have to deal with sexual harassment at work, all of which can heighten women's risk for depression (Landrine, Klonoff, Gibbs, Manning, & Lund, 1995). Because of low-paying jobs or lack of child support, women are more likely to live in poverty than men, and poverty is a major source of stress and depression.

Family roles can also be a source of stress for women. Women are expected to juggle multiple roles (for example, mother, wife, worker, housekeeper, caregiver for elderly parents, church or community volunteer), and they may experience stress if they don't have the resources to cope with multiple role demands (Green & Russo, 1993). A nonsupportive spouse, larger family sizes, lack of access to child care, and lack of access to parental leave have all been found to contribute to women's depression levels (Brown, 1987; McGrath et al., 1990; Hyde, 1995; Ozer, 1995). The cultural expectation that women "silence" themselves (hide their opinions and deny their own needs) in the service of their relationships may also play a role in the higher levels of depression in married women (Jack, 1981; Thompson, 1995).

Psychological factors may contribute to the difference in the rates of depression in men and women. When men are faced with a stressful problem, they are likely to distract themselves with activities—they engage in sports, go out with friends, or focus on work-related tasks. This coping style encourages a sense of control and mastery. Women, on the other hand, tend to ruminate (dwell) on negative feelings, focusing on their problems and often talking about them at length with family and female friends (Nolen-Hoeksema, 1987). Such rumination can reinforce negative thinking and magnify or prolong feelings of depression. Moreover, women who are more passive, dependent, or feel that they have little control over their lives are at increased risk for depression. Many therapists advise their clients to engage in exercise or other forms of activity to distract them from their problems and to enhance their feelings of control and mastery.

Both mild and severe forms of depression are of concern. Severe forms can be the source of intense suffering and can be long-lasting. Even mild forms can negatively affect relationships and work productivity. As we have seen, a combination of biological, psychological, social, and cultural factors play critical roles in developing gender differences in rates of depression, beginning in adolescence and continuing through adulthood (McGrath et al., 1990; Nolen-Hoeksema, 1990). Interventions must address all of these factors to try to eliminate the high rates of depression in women.

drug treatment than individuals of the opposite sex receiving similar diagnoses (Waisberg & Page, 1988).

Misdiagnosis is a major problem when it leads to inappropriate treatment. Psychoactive drugs that are effective in treating one type of mental disorder are not necessarily effective in treating other disorders. Being aware of the effects of gender stereotypes and how they may influence clinical judgments is a direct application of the basic research discussed in Chapter 12. These principles apply to the effects of other types of stereotypes as well, such as those based on race, ethnicity, sexual orientation, and able-bodiedness.

Culture and Diagnosis

Imagine you are a therapist assigned to treat a patient who appears seriously disturbed. "My soul is not with me anymore—I can't do anything," she complains. She is listless and rambling. Upon interviewing your new patient, you learn that she is from Ecuador and developed her condition after she learned that an uncle she was very close to had died unexpectedly. What diagnosis would you give this woman?

If you conclude that the woman is depressed and prescribe antidepressant medication, you would be applying the closest psychiatric term that DSM-IV has to describe her condition. This would be a culturally inappropriate diagnosis, however. In fact, the woman was exhibiting a disorder called *susto,* or "soul loss," a culturally specific disorder found in Hispanic cultures. Fortunately, she went to a culturally sensitive therapist. Instead of antidepressants, her successful treatment involved a mourning ritual to help her deal with her loss. After a few meetings, some with her family, her symptoms abated and she was again fully participating in life (Goleman, 1995).

The ability of DSM-IV to deal with cultural issues is a major concern (Maser, Kaelber, & Weise, 1991). Clearly DSM-IV does not cover all mental disorders found in other cultures. Many cultural groups do not even use the same words or concepts for mental disorders found in Western classifications. In addition to *susto,* for example, *latah,* a disorder in many areas of Southeast Asia and the Orient, has no DSM equivalent. Particular circumstances (such as hearing someone say "snake") may trigger a fright reaction characterized by repeating others' words, using obscenities, and doing the opposite of what is requested. This disorder is usually found among uneducated middle-aged or elderly women. *Koro* is another example. This condition appears limited to Chinese males, and is characterized by fear that their penis is shrinking into their body (Yap, 1951). *Ataque do nervios* is a condition found in Puerto Rico and other Latin countries. It involves trembling, heart palpitations, and seizure-like episodes in response to stressful events, such as accidents, a death of a loved one, or family conflict (APA, 1994).

Even though basic symptoms may be universal (anxiety, insomnia, upset stomach), conditions are expressed in keeping with cultural values and expectations (Beardsley, 1994). In the individualistic culture of the United States, we tend to view depression as an indication that something is wrong with us, from within, and we focus on our lack of self-esteem, our hopelessness, and our helplessness. Among collectivistic Asians, the focus is on somatic symptoms (Kleinman & Good, 1985). Thus, depression, as we know it in the United States, does not show the same pattern in all cultures.

Taijin-kyofusho is a type of phobia in Japan that involves a morbid dread that the body, its parts or functions, will embarrass or be offensive to another person. It illustrates how a disorder can blend both culture-general and culture-specific aspects. Like social phobias in

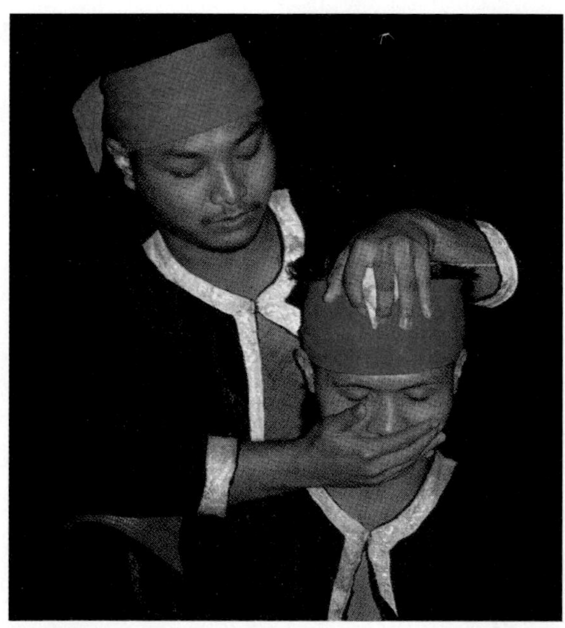

◀ *Culture shapes mental disorder, so therapists must be sensitive to cultural differences when treating patients. This photograph shows a shaman from Indonesia performing an exorcism.*

KEY TERMS

psychopathology

syndrome

medical viewpoint

psychodynamic viewpoint

behavioral viewpoint

cognitive-behavioral viewpoint

humanistic viewpoint

anxiety disorders

phobias

generalized anxiety disorder

panic disorder

posttraumatic stress disorder

obsessive-compulsive disorder

dissociative disorders

dissociative amnesia

dissociative identity disorder

the United States, it involves fear of social rejection and anxiety. But the fear is of embarrassing others, not oneself. Further, it is also characterized by fear of eye contact, concern about body odor, and easy blushing—a pattern of concerns that is culturally specific for this disorder (Beardsley, 1994).

Even within European cultures, language differences limit the equivalency of diagnoses. For example, *Gedankenentzug* (literally "withdrawal of the capacity to think") is considered a basic symptom of schizophrenia by German psychiatrists. But American and British textbooks make no specific reference to it. Further, patients who speak English do not report such symptoms (Stengel, 1961).

DSM-IV discusses culturally related syndromes in appendices, cautioning that clinicians unfamiliar with an individual's cultural frame of reference may wrongly judge normal variations in behaviors as pathological. Although DSM-IV is the most culturally sensitive diagnostic tool to date, we have a long way to go before we have the knowledge needed to understand how culture shapes mental disorder. Cultural differences within the United States also raise challenges to defining and diagnosing psychopathology, particularly among immigrant populations, which are dealing with stressors associated with dislocation and acculturation. Diagnosing personality disorders across cultural contexts is particularly difficult, given wide differences in communication styles, coping mechanisms, and concepts of self across cultures (APA, 1994).

Reflections and Observations

Psychopathology is a complex and controversial area, involving competing viewpoints for the definition and diagnosis of mental disorder. Which viewpoint is "right?" The correct answer is probably, all and none. Nearly all therapists recognize that psychopathology is complex and that each viewpoint has something to contribute when seeking to understand a specific individual. Biological, psychological, social, and cultural factors all play a role in the development, diagnosis, and treatment of mental disorder, and no one viewpoint has all of the answers. Thus, in therapy, information that reflects all of these perspectives often comes into play. Despite the need to know more, the knowledge we have about psychopathology is extremely useful. It has provided the foundation for developing treatment approaches of proven effectiveness with a variety of disorders. As you will see in Chapter 16, some approaches are more applicable and effective for some disorders than others.

Objectives Revisited

Psychopathology is a multifaceted topic that does not lend itself to obvious organization or easy explanation. To study and treat psychopathology, we must first define it. The information presented in this chapter gives the best descriptive evidence we have so far and reinforces the theme that biological, psychological, social, and cultural factors in combination determine the risk for psychopathology.

Objective 1. Explain how psychopathology is defined and diagnosed, and why it is considered a serious problem for the individual and society.

Psychopathology can be defined as socially inappropriate patterns of thought, emotion, or behavior, whose consequences are judged as maladaptive or detrimental to the person by society. The pattern may be associated with distress or disability, or increased risk of death, pain, disability, or loss of freedom. It may reflect organic or functional problems, or both, and its symptoms may range from mild, with no long-term effects, to severe, with thoughts and behaviors so bizarre, persistent, and impairing that special care is required.

The most widely used system for defining and distinguishing among types of abnormal behavior is the fourth edition of the American Psychiatric Association's *Diagnostic and Statistical Manual of Mental Disorders* (DSM-IV). This system classifies or rates people on five different axes: (1) current behavioral symptoms or problems, (2) longstanding personality disorders, (3) current medical symptoms or problems, (4) severity of current stress, and (5) the level of adaptive functioning.

Given that mental disorder afflicts such a large number of people, causes intense suffering, and has high social and economic costs to society, mental disorders become everybody's problem.

Objective 2. Compare and contrast the various theoretical perspectives on psychopathology.

Theoretical perspectives of psychopathology include the *medical viewpoint*, which considers psychopathology as a symptom of an underlying disease process; the *psychodynamic viewpoint*, which assumes that psychopathology reflects an unconscious conflict among components of a person's personality; the *behavioral viewpoint*, which proposes that psychopathology is the result of misguided learning and is maintained by reinforcement provided by a person's environment; the *cognitive-behavioral viewpoint*, which attributes abnormal behavior to inadequate, incomplete, or distorted mental representations of the environment; and the *humanistic viewpoint*, which emphasizes the importance of the individual's need to achieve or to self-actualize.

Objective 3. Describe and discuss major clinical syndromes identified by psychological diagnosis.

Five of the most common clinical syndromes (Axis I categories) are: *anxiety disorders, dissociative disorders, somatoform disorders, mood disorders*, and *schizophrenic disorders*. Anxiety disorders center on the experience of intense anxiety and the development of behaviors and thoughts to control that anxiety. Dissociative disorders occur when our sense of personal identity breaks down and our memory dissociates from our conscious awareness. Somatoform disorders occur when a psychological problem is expressed through physical symptoms, even though there is no demonstrable physical cause.

Mood disorders refer to extreme disturbance of mood, including depressive disorders (major depression and dysthymia) and bipolar disorders (manic and depressive states).

Schizophrenic disorders refer to a group of psychotic states characterized by severe disturbances in thought and emotion and a marked distortion of reality. Four subtypes include: *disorganized, paranoid, catatonic*, and *undifferentiated*. Most psychologists believe that both a biological predisposition (diathesis) and environmental precipitation (stress) must be present to produce schizophrenia.

Objective 4. Describe what a personality disorder is and name some examples.

Axis II of the DSM-IV system identifies many types of personality disorders, defined as longstanding dominant personality traits leading to behavior that is maladaptive to society or the individual. Three prominent examples are paranoid, antisocial, and borderline.

Objective 5: Explain the relationship of gender and culture to diagnosis.

Gender stereotyping and lack of knowledge about stressors in the lives and circumstances of women are possible sources of gender bias in diagnosis. DSM-IV has begun a concerted effort to address culture-related issues in diagnosis. Many cultural groups use different words or concepts to represent mental disorders found in Western classifications. Culture-specific disorders exist as well. Unless the clinician is culturally sensitive, normal cultural variations in behaviors may be wrongly judged as pathological. Difficulty in diagnosing personality disorders across cultural contexts is compounded by cross-cultural differences in communication styles, coping mechanisms, and concepts of self.

somatoform disorders

conversion disorder

hypochondriasis

mood disorders

bipolar disorder

major depression

dysthymia

schizophrenia

disorganized schizophrenia

paranoid schizophrenia

catatonic schizophrenia

undifferentiated schizophrenia

diathesis-stress model

personality disorders

paranoid personality disorder

antisocial personality disorder

borderline personality disorder

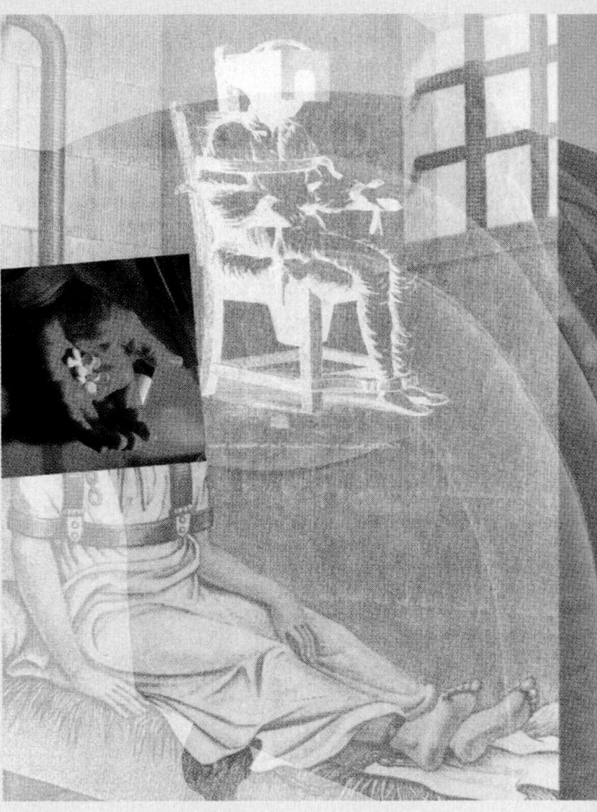

C H A P T E R 16

Treatment for Psychopathology

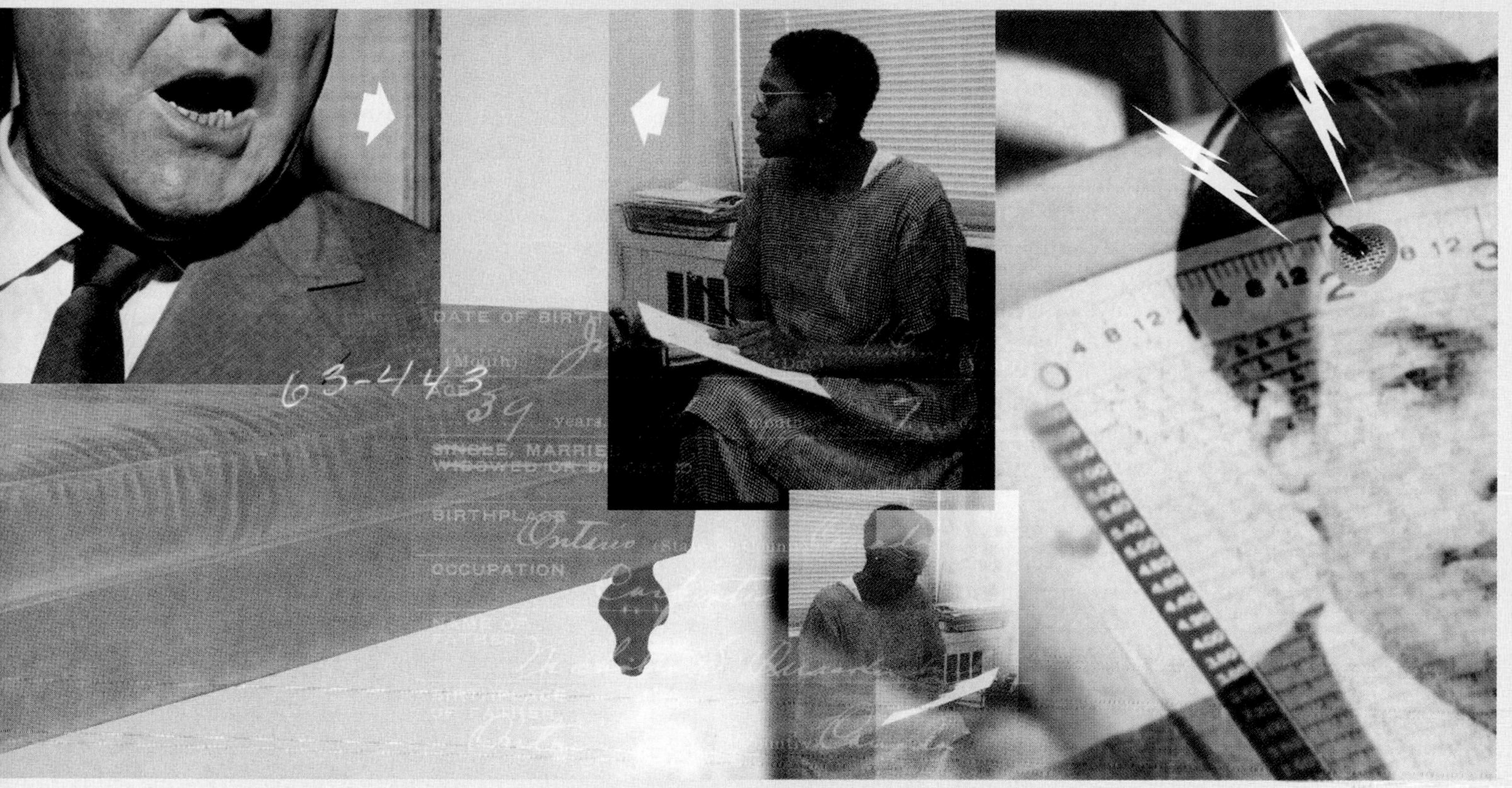

O B J E C T I V E S

After reading this chapter, you should be able to:

1. Describe treatment for psychopathology, and explain differences among mental health professionals qualified to provide such treatments.
2. Describe the basic assumptions and techniques of biomedical, psychoanalytic, behavioral and cognitive-behavioral, and humanistic therapies, and contrast their philosophies and effectiveness.
3. Explain how therapist values can influence the therapeutic process, and discuss the central issues involved in feminist and other culturally sensitive therapies.
4. Describe group therapy, and explain how it differs from individual therapy.
5. Explain the community mental health perspective, and distinguish among primary, secondary, and rehabilitative mental health services.

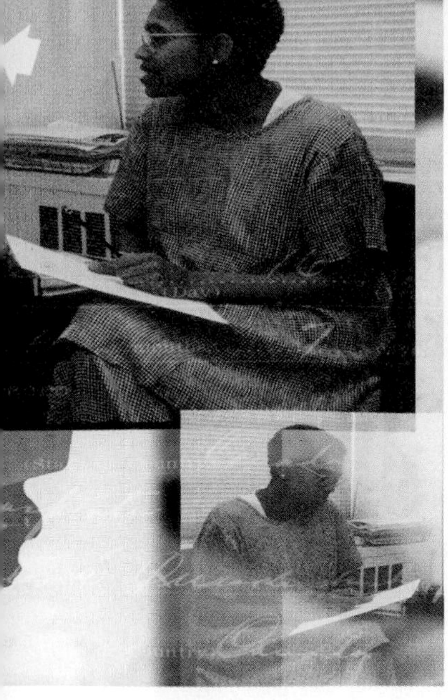

On Monday afternoon, April 22, 1997, a disheveled and dirty woman was found huddling in fear inside a cardboard box. The woman believed that her ex-husband and the CIA were plotting to kill her. Disoriented and terrified, she had fled her home and later discarded her purse, thinking that it contained a bomb. After four days as a missing person, she was discovered in a Los Angeles backyard. The missing person turned out to be the well-known actress Margot Kidder, who had appeared as the irrepressible Lois Lane in four *Superman* movies. Kidder was suffering an episode of manic depression.

Manic-depressive episodes were not new to Margot Kidder. She started seeing psychiatrists at age twenty-one for "mood swings that could knock over a building," but she didn't respond well to treatment. When a psychiatrist finally diagnosed her condition as manic (bipolar) depression, she rejected his advice and refused to take lithium, a drug used to treat this disorder. It wasn't until she was forty-seven and had experienced the episode described above that she was able to confront her disease, both publicly and privately, and to accept treatment. Margot Kidder now takes lithium regularly. In addition, she is exploring alternative methods of treatment, including acupuncture and Native American herbal remedies. Millions of Americans like Margot Kidder have sought the aid of mental health professionals in an effort to recover from debilitating psychological disorders.

▼ *St. Mary's of Bethlehem (also known as Bedlam) was a popular London tourist attraction in the eighteenth century. Visitors paid admission fees to gape at the mental patients in this hospital.*

Historically, mentally disordered individuals have been treated as criminals or witches or as less than human. But stereotypes of the "mentally ill" have changed dramatically in the last fifty years. Psychologically troubled individuals are now more often seen as having problems in adapting to stressful environments or as being victims of mental disorders. Given that about one out of two people in the U.S. population will experience some form of mental disorder in their lifetime, it seems absurd to attach any particular stigma to having psychological problems (Kessler et al., 1994).

Perhaps you know someone whose thoughts, feelings, or actions are unusual enough to be considered psychopathological. What can be done to help such a person? As our knowledge of psychopathology and its causes has expanded, so too have the range and effectiveness of treatments.

In this chapter, we will explore various approaches to treating psychopathology, considering both traditional and contemporary techniques used in the treatment process. We will begin by defining what treatment is. Then we will discuss the various models of treatment, asking what, if anything, they have in common with each other and whether or not all treatments are equally effective for all forms of psychopathology.

What Is Treatment?

Treatment for psychopathology includes a wide range of techniques designed to help a person overcome symptoms that are interfering with normal functioning. Licensed or certified mental health professionals—psychologists, psychiatrists, psychiatric social workers, or psychiatric nurses—undergo special training to treat clients who seek professional help for psychological problems (see Table 16-1). Yet, this does not mean that only these professionals can help people with psychological problems. Indeed, when people feel the need for guidance and support, they usually turn first to friends or family rather than to a professional. Helpful counseling from community workers, clergy, and other people in helping roles can often have excellent therapeutic effects (Table 16-2 on p. 584; Christensen & Jacobson, 1994). And in other cultures, people may seek psychological help from shamans and folk healers.

Seeking Treatment

People seek treatment for both voluntary and involuntary reasons. Sometimes they seek treatment voluntarily because they feel uncomfortable about where their lives are going and how they are reacting to certain situations. Perhaps they are so depressed that they cannot function at home or work, or they feel compelled to perform various behaviors in order to avoid experiencing anxiety. Sometimes people who would not voluntarily seek treatment are forced to do so by others. They may be acting in bizarre ways in public, hearing strange voices, or threatening others, and be sent for treatment by the courts. Alternatively, they may show symp-

▲ *Margot Kidder now uses various treatments to control the mood swings that are associated with her bipolar depression.*

The reality of my life has been grand and wonderful, punctuated by these odd blips and burps of madness.

—Margot Kidder

Table 16-1 Mental Health Service Providers

Name	Degree	Specialization	Education
Clinical psychologist	Doctor of Philosophy (Ph.D.) Doctor of Psychology (Psy.D.)	Research, therapy, diagnostic testing	Graduate education in a department of psychology or professional school of psychology
Psychiatrist	Doctor of Medicine (M.D.)	Psychotherapy, management of medication, electroconvulsive therapy	Residency training in psychiatry
Psychoanalyst	M.D., Ph.D., Psy.D.	Psychoanalysis	Requires additional specialized training in psychoanalysis
Psychiatric social worker	Master of Social Work (M.S.W.)	Individual and family therapy and counseling, community orientation	Graduate education in school of social work
School psychologist	Master of Arts (M.A.), Ph.D., Psy.D., or Doctor of Education (Ed.D.)	Counseling or educational testing	Graduate work in psychology or education
Counseling psychologist	Same as school psychologist	Counseling, therapy, vocational counseling, rehabilitation	Graduate work in psychology or education
Psychiatric nurse	Registered Nurse (R.N.)	Counseling therapy, care of hospitalized mental patients	Training in nursing and psychiatry
Paraprofessional	None necessary	Ability to communicate with people in own community	Short orientation in service facility

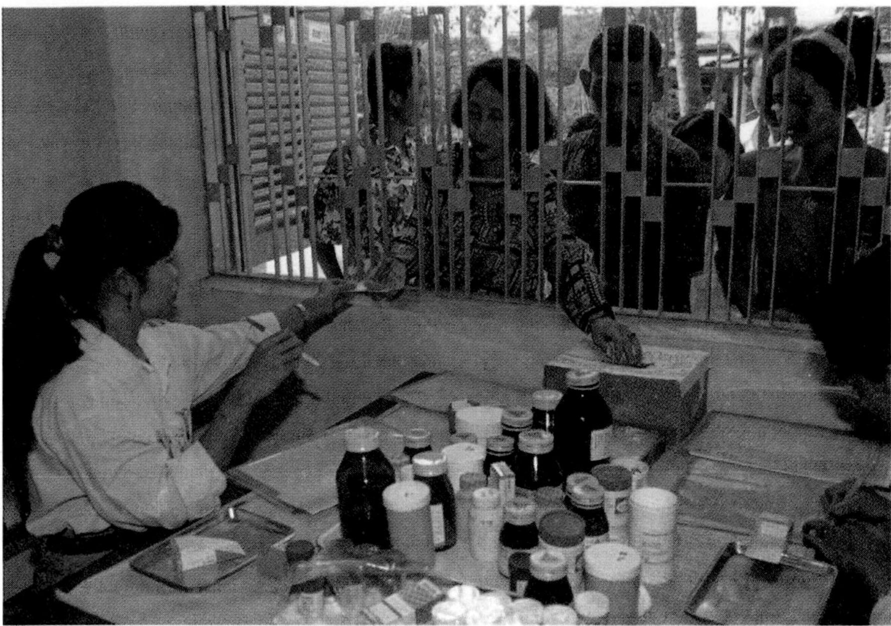

▲ *In Cambodia, a nurse distributes anti-anxiety drugs at a mental health care facility. Years of war have contributed to extemely high levels of psychological trauma among the population.*

Anti-Anxiety Drugs

Dale, who suffered from a severe panic disorder, was so frightened of having a panic attack that he was unable to leave his home. Simply walking to the local grocery store could bring on heart palpitations, dizziness, shortness of breath, terror, and a sense of impending doom.

The first step in treatment, which is the same for any severe mental disorder, was to give him a thorough physical exam to determine whether or not any identifiable physical condition, such as epilepsy or excessive levels of thyroid hormone, was causing his symptoms. Dale's psychiatrist then prescribed an anti-anxiety drug to reduce his agitation and anxiousness. ***Anti-anxiety drugs*** include sedatives and tranquilizers that depress central nervous system activity and are used to help people control their feelings of severe anxiety.

Sedatives are drugs that reduce anxiety and tension by inducing muscle relaxation, sleep, and inhibition of the brain's cognitive centers. The major disadvantage of sedatives is the individual's lack of alertness. Alcohol is a sedative. Other sedatives include barbiturates (for example, Nembutal, Seconal, Luminal, and other forms of sleeping pills), benzodiazepines (Halcion), bromides, and chloral hydrate ("knock-out drops").

In the mid-1950s, a new group of anti-anxiety drugs—called tranquilizers—was discovered. ***Tranquilizers*** reduce anxiety in people who are under unusual stress without producing the sleepiness or lack of alertness associated with sedatives. As a consequence, sedative use (with the exception of self-prescribed alcohol) has greatly declined, while the use of tranquilizers (Valium, Miltown, Librium, Xanax) has increased. Tranquilizers affect many neurotransmitters, but they particularly enhance the effectiveness of GABA, the inhibitory neurotransmitter found in many parts of the brain. Because anxiety is thought to be related to excessive neurological activity, effective inhibition of such activity can have a calming effect (Ninan et al., 1982).

In moderate doses, tranquilizers can help a tense, anxious person cope with life stress without disrupting ordinary, ongoing daily activities. Sedatives and tranquilizers, however, do not *cure* anxiety-related disorders. They reduce symptoms such as muscle tension, heart palpitations, sweating, and gastrointestinal distress, but they have less effect on the individual's tendency to worry and ruminate (Hoehn-Saric & McLeod, 1991). They can lead to attention and memory deficits, particularly in elderly patients, and can interfere with motor skills, increasing accident risk. In addition, people can easily become both psychologically and physically dependent on tranquilizers and sedatives. Valium, in particular, is psychologically addictive (see Chapter 9). When combined with alcohol, tranquilizers can have deadly effects. They are best used temporarily.

Antidepressants

Since the late 1940s, mood-elevating drugs—the ***antidepressants***—have been prescribed more and more to counteract symptoms of depression. The first antidepressant drug to be used was iproniazid. Originally designed to treat tuberculosis, it had an unexpected positive side effect: patients became happier about their lives.

More recently, ***tricyclics*** (named for their three-ringed molecular structure) and ***monoamine oxidase (MAO) inhibitors*** have been found to relieve depression. Antidepressants appear to work by increasing norepinephrine and serotonin levels in the brain (see Figure 16-1; Schildkraut, Green, & Mooney, 1985). These neurotransmitters are important in the regulation of mood or affect. Side effects of these drugs include drowsiness, blurred vision, constipation, and dry mouth. They can also negatively affect the brain, liver, and cardiovascular

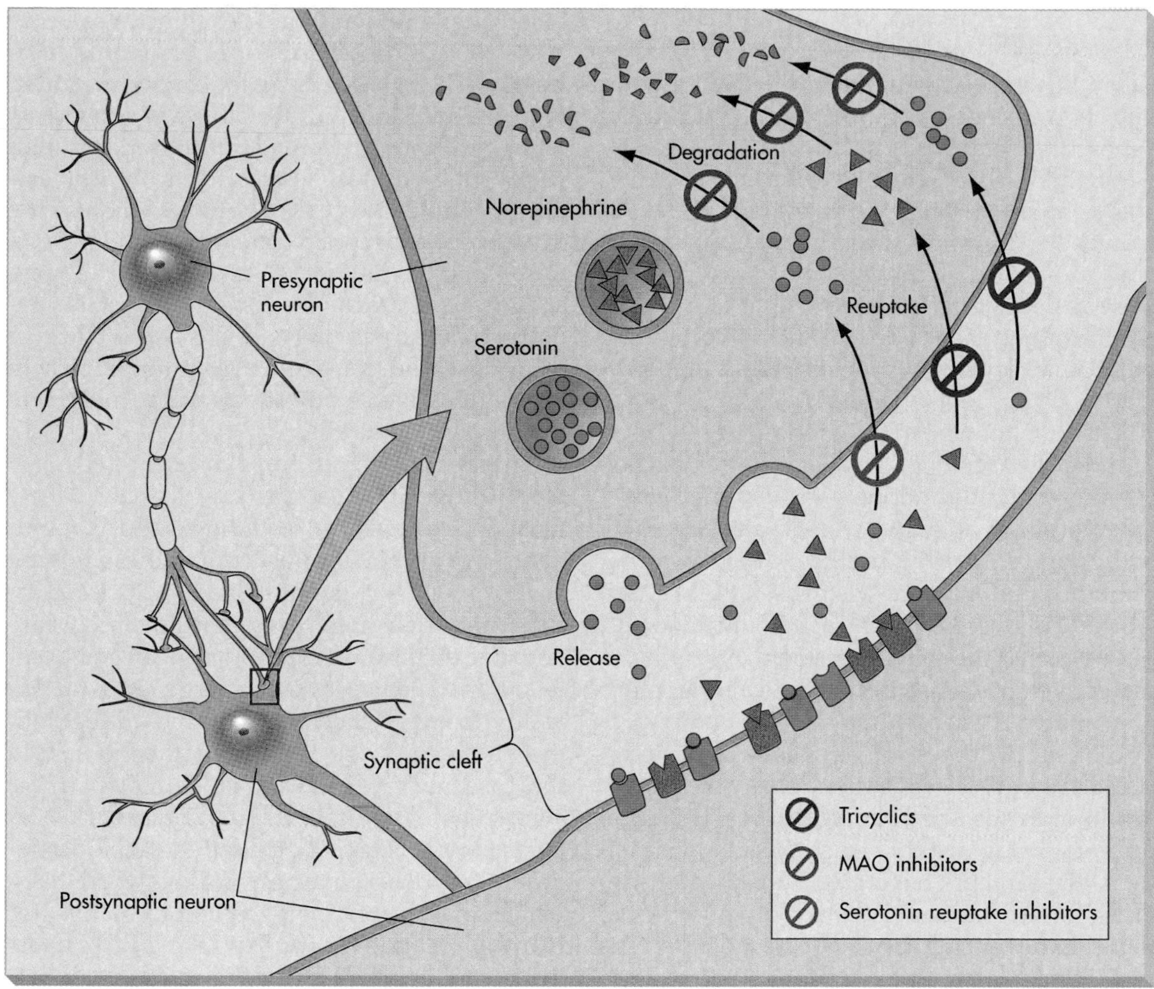

16-1 Antidepressants

Antidepressants work by increasing levels of the neurotransmitters norepinephrine and serotonin in the brain. These neurotransmitters, which affect a person's mood, transmit signals from one neuron to another across the synaptic cleft between the two cells (see Chapter 3). After the neurotransmitters are released from synaptic vesicles in the presynaptic neuron, they either float across the synaptic cleft and bind to receptors on the postsynaptic neuron or are reabsorbed back into the presynaptic neuron (reuptake). Tricyclics (e.g., Tofranil) block the reuptake of serotonin and norepinephrine. MAO inhibitors (e.g., Nardil) slow the natural degradation of serotonin and norepinephrine by blocking the enzyme monoamine oxidase (MAO). Serotonin reuptake inhibitors (e.g., Prozac) block the reuptake of serotonin.

system, and when combined with particular drugs or foods (particularly foods that are fermented, such as beer and some wines and cheeses) they can produce illness and even death.

Today's most prescribed antidepressant, Prozac (the serotonin reuptake inhibitor fluoxetine), increases serotonin levels and is used to fight depression and obsessive-compulsive disorder. For some unknown reason, Prozac helps many patients who either do not respond to other antidepressants or cannot tolerate their side effects. Prozac is controversial, however. In addition to producing side effects of headache, upset stomach, and anxiety, in a small proportion of patients it may produce violence, manic agitation, suicidal thoughts, and even suicide (Teicher, Glod, & Cole, 1990).

The element ***lithium*** (in a salt form it is called lithium carbonate) is especially useful in preventing the extreme mood shifts seen in bipolar disorders such as the one experienced by Margot Kidder. Despite its effectiveness in treating bipolar disorders, it has potentially lethal side effects because it can be poisonous or cause thyroid problems. An overdose can cause delirium, convulsions, and even death (Lydiard & Gelenberg, 1982). The patient's blood must be checked regularly to monitor the drug's level.

◀ The antidepressant Prozac can help many patients feel less depressed.

"And, of course, with the Prozac, I don't care if I pay my psychiatrist or not."

Antipsychotics

Kevin B. wrestled with inner demons for more than two decades, beginning at age eight. Diagnosed as schizophrenic, he was terrorized by a horrifying spirit—one he believed had previously haunted an executed murderer. But thanks to clozapine (trade name: Clozaril), a new antipsychotic drug, Kevin was released from his nightmares, is now able to perform church maintenance work, and is counseling other schizophrenic patients (Wallis & Willwerth, 1992).

The first known antipsychotic drug was used in India thousands of years ago to treat snakebites (which it did not help), epilepsy and dysentery (which it made worse), and insomnia and insanity (which it did help). But it was not until the late 1940s that scientists in the Western world discovered these therapeutic benefits. They isolated the active ingredient, reserpine, in the early 1950s. Reserpine has a calming effect on agitated patients, but it occasionally produces severe depression as a side effect. Reserpine has largely been replaced today by another group of drugs, the ***phenothiazines***, which reduce agitation without such adverse side effects. Researchers have found that there is an excess of dopamine-related activity in some patients experiencing psychotic symptoms. The phenothiazines bind to dopamine receptors in the brain, effectively preventing dopamine from binding to the receptors, and thereby reducing the activity in the patient's dopamine pathways to a more normal level.

The first phenothiazine used to treat schizophrenic disorders was chlorpromazine (trade name: Thorazine). As in the case of the antidepressants, the effects of chlorpromazine were discovered by accident. Originally used in anesthesia for surgical patients, it was found to produce a profound calm before the operation. When doctors gave it to hospitalized mental patients, they discovered it was so effective that many patients could be discharged from the hospital. As long as they continued to take their medication, they were less likely to have a relapse than those who took no medication (Baldessarini, 1984). Symptoms would reappear if patients stopped taking the drug.

Minor but uncomfortable side effects of phenothiazines—such as muscle stiffness, blurred vision, grogginess, constipation, and dryness of the mouth—are quite common and can affect a patient's willingness to continue taking medication. More severe side effects, such as low blood pressure and jaundice, sometimes occur as well. The most severe side effect is *tardive dyskinesia*, a disturbance of motor control that often involves drooling, lip smacking, and grimacing, which mirror symptoms seen in patients with Parkinson's disease. These effects are irreversible in 10 to 20 percent of patients who use the drug over an extended time period. Side effects raise concerns about the overuse of antipsychotic medication. Good clinical practice requires treating patients with the lowest effective drug dose and continuously monitoring them to identify adverse side effects and to make sure the dose is still working.

These drugs do not cure schizophrenia. They block some of the disorder's most abnormal behavioral expressions, including hallucinations, delusions, and bizarre behavioral episodes (see Figure 16-2). But many behavioral deficits associated with certain types of schizophrenia are not affected, including the blunting of emotions, language deficits, lack of energy, and the inability to experience pleasure and to feel intimacy. The new drug, clozapine (mentioned in the case above), appears to help with these symptoms. But because about 2 percent of patients may develop a potentially fatal blood disorder, the drug requires weekly blood tests, which makes treatment costs prohibitive for many patients. Nonetheless, the fact that the drug appears to alleviate the suffering of previously treatment-resistant patients means that to some the risk is worth the gain (Meltzer, Burnett, Bastani, & Ramirez, 1990). Unfortunately, even with the development of clozapine, large numbers of schizophrenic patients still do not respond well to drug treatment.

▼ *A patient is prepared for electroconvulsive therapy (ECT). Used in some extreme cases of depression, ECT involves giving electrical current to the brain that produces convulsions. Patients are first given muscle relaxants in order to prevent injury.*

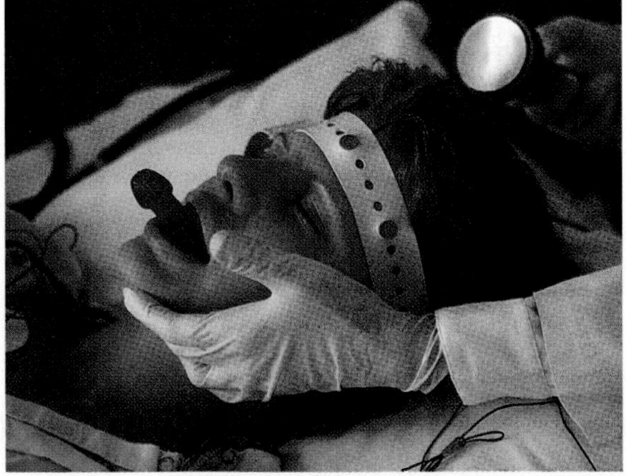

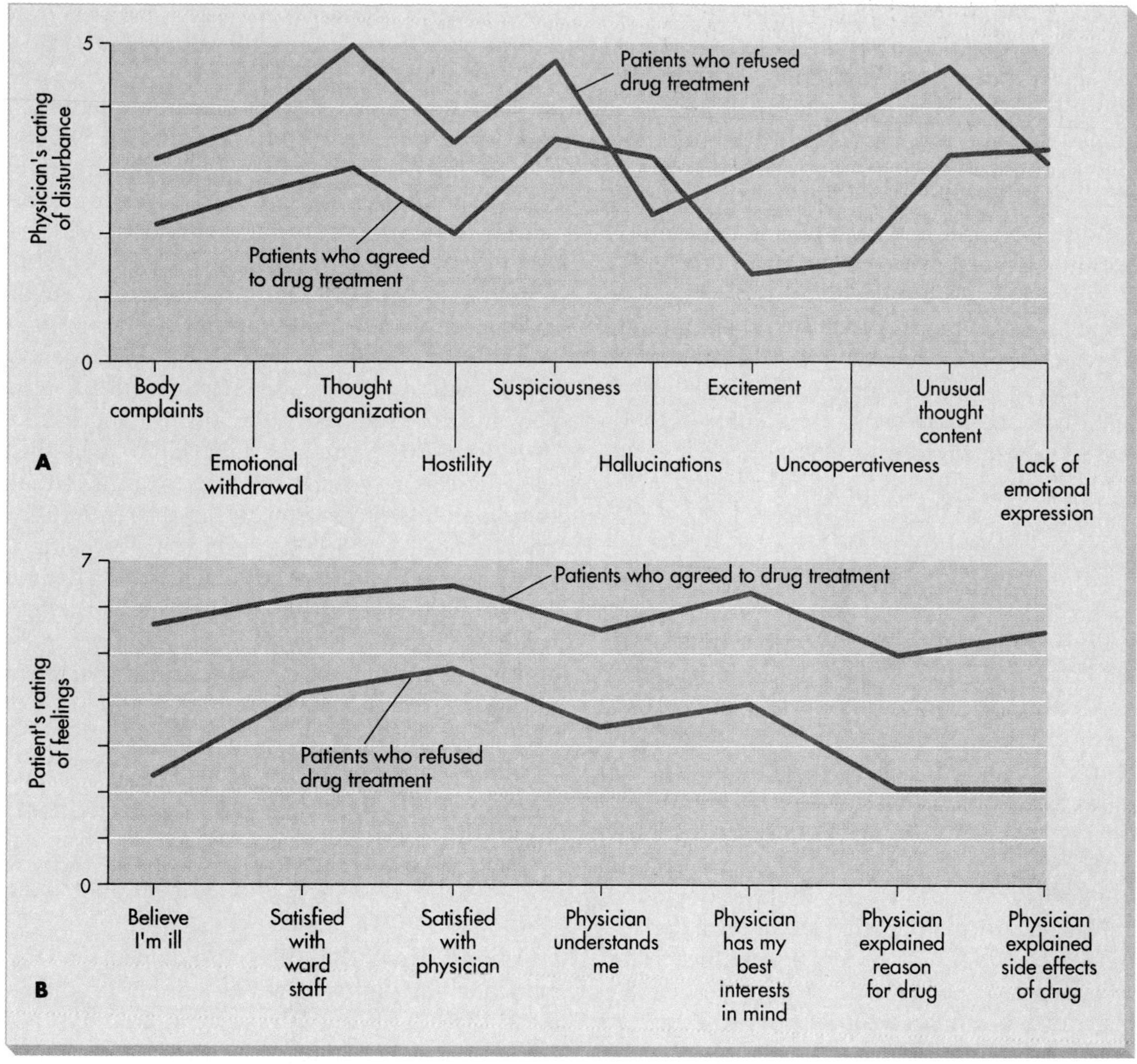

16-2 Effectiveness of Drug Treatment of Schizophrenic Patients

The two graphs compare ratings of schizophrenic patients who refused drug treatment and schizophrenics who agreed to drug treatment. (A) Physicians rated their schizophrenic patients based on their symptoms, with high scores indicating greater disturbance. Those refusing drug treatment were more disturbed on most measures. (B) Patients rated their treatments; those who agreed to drug treatment reported higher satisfaction with how they had been treated. (Source: Adapted from Marder et al., 1983)

Electroconvulsive Therapy (ECT)

Besides drug therapy, other biomedical treatments have also been developed to treat depressed and schizophrenic patients. Based on the observation that convulsions and/or coma seemed to reduce psychotic symptoms, several physicians and psychiatrists began using ***electroconvulsive therapy (ECT),*** also known as shock therapy. In ECT, the patient is placed on a bed, given a short-acting anesthetic and strong muscle relaxant, and, while lightly restrained by attendants, given an electric shock of sufficient intensity (about 70 to 130 volts) across the temples to produce a convulsion. The convulsions of the body muscles are barely perceptible to observers, and patients awaken a few minutes later. Retrograde amnesia (inability to store events occurring shortly before ECT in long-term memory) is a common byproduct. Thus, the patient often cannot remember anything about the shock, convulsion, or immediately preceding events. Less retrograde amnesia occurs when physicians place electrodes so that only the individual's nondominant side of the brain receives the shock, which makes this technique preferable to the bilateral approach (in which electrodes are placed to shock both sides of the brain).

Although no one knows precisely how or why ECT works, research suggests that it triggers the release of the neurotransmitter beta-endorphin (see Chapter 3). ECT has been effective in reducing or eliminating severe depression (after several treatments). Although ECT may be drastic, it can eliminate months of suffering and possibly prevent a suicide attempt. Unfortunately, the effects of ECT are transient, and there is a high relapse rate. Although it may relieve depressive symptoms, it doesn't relieve environmental conditions that helped cause the depression in the first place. For example, people who are experiencing physical or sexual abuse may be depressed for good reason. Because side effects may include prolonged memory loss and brain damage, ECT is typically used only when the patient is not responsive to other types of treatment and is at risk for suicide. It has been particularly recommended for severely depressed elderly people, who have the highest risk for suicide of all depressed groups (Adler, 1992).

Two of the more controversial biomedical treatments for psychopathology are psychosurgery, which involves cutting nerve pathways in brain regions thought to be associated with violent or aggressive behavior, and electroconvulsive therapy, which induces convulsions.

Hospitalization

People who need something more than outpatient psychotherapy and/or medication to function effectively or who may be dangerous to themselves or others may require hospitalization. Each year about a quarter of a million people in the United States are admitted for the first time to psychiatric hospital wards or mental institutions. Although average inpatient length of stay is less than two weeks, it varies depending on the nature and severity of the disorder.

Hospitalization is largely an adjunct to outpatient therapy. In an extensive six-year project, researchers compared three groups of patients: those treated with (1) traditional treatments (medication and custodial care); (2) social learning therapy (therapy in which patients are taught how to deal more effectively with other people); and (3) milieu therapy (therapy in which patients actively participate in activities and structured social and educational experiences). The researchers found that only 50 percent of patients treated traditionally could be released from the hospital. In contrast, 90 percent of patients treated with social learning therapy and 70 percent of patients treated with milieu therapy were released and remained permanently in their communities (Paul & Lentz, 1977). Thus, with effective treatment, a high percentage of seriously mentally ill patients can live successfully outside the hospital. Nonetheless, there is growing evidence to suggest that some patients have been released prematurely and without outside supervision. Too often, they end up homeless and dependent on drugs, prescribed or otherwise. Probably the greatest health need today is for sufficient after-care programs to help mental patients adjust after their discharge from hospitals.

▼ *A large proportion of homeless people are mentally ill. Here, pedestrians pass by a homeless man, asleep on the streets of Seattle.*

Psychodynamic Therapies

Psychodynamic therapies are based on the Freudian assumption that emotional problems stem directly from intrapsychic conflicts between conscious and unconscious processes (Luborsky, Barber, & Butler, 1993; see Chapter 14). To resolve these conflicts, individuals must become aware of or gain insight into their unconscious mind, understand the sources of conflict, and intellectually accept them. Thus, these treatment methods are sometimes referred to as insight therapy. Psychodynamic therapy requires that clients not only achieve intellectual insight into the causes of their symptoms, but also experience and "work through" the emotion associated with the original conflict. The aim of this therapy can be summarized in the words, "Know thyself."

The most prominent example of insight or psychodynamic therapy is, of course, ***psychoanalysis***, based on Sigmund Freud's theory. However, just as Freud's personality theory was revised by neo-Freudians and ego analysts (see Chapter 14), so too were his psychoanalytic therapeutic methods. Today, there are several variations on the psychoanalytic theme.

Psychoanalysis

According to Freud, the major purpose of psychotherapy is to help individuals gain insight into their hidden inner conflicts. Once insight is achieved, it will no longer be necessary for them to devote their psychic energies to repressing unacceptable urges and impulses. As a consequence, they become more capable of a happy, fulfilling life.

Strictly speaking, psychoanalysts try to bring repressed drives, feelings, and memories to consciousness. After several sessions of listening to dreams and free associations, noting "slips," and focusing on transference, they form hypotheses or interpretations about the unconscious basis of their clients' problems. Using these interpretations, psychoanalysts try to help their clients understand the potential hidden meaning of what they say and do. If an interpretation is given before the clients are capable of accepting it, however, it may be rejected, generate anxiety, and arouse defenses. Ideally, an interpretation should be timed so that clients are already aware of something important but just haven't quite "gotten it." Clients must achieve both intellectual insight into the causes of their symptoms as well as experience and eliminate the emotion associated with the original conflict.

The first step in psychoanalysis is to help clients overcome their unconscious resistance to becoming aware of and remembering anxiety-provoking thoughts, feelings, wishes, and impulses. Psychoanalysts use several techniques to aid this process, including free association, dream interpretation, and the analysis of transference.

Free Association

Following in the footsteps of neurologist Jean-Martin Charcot, Freud initially used hypnosis to help patients recall repressed memories. But not everyone is easily hypnotized. For this and other reasons, Freud adopted an alternative method called ***free association***. Here's how it works. Imagine yourself sitting in a therapist's office. You are asked to relax and to say anything and everything that comes to your mind. You are told to hold back nothing, no matter how trivial, bizarre, revealing, or shocking. Free association sounds relatively easy, but most people find it extremely difficult. How easy is it

THINKING CRITICALLY

Communication between client and therapist is privileged, meaning that the therapist cannot be compelled to disclose anything said by the client in the therapeutic situation. Professional ethics obligate the therapist not to reveal any information without client consent. Should this always be the case?

Not too long ago, a therapist heard a client make a threat against the life of another person and warned the police but not the woman threatened. Subsequently, the woman who had been threatened was indeed murdered by the therapist's client. The court in California held the therapist responsible, ruling that a therapist must make every reasonable effort to warn potential victims as well as the police of threats, even if they are made in the course of therapy (*Tarasoff v. Regents of the University of California*, 1976).

The essence of the therapeutic relationship is *trust*—the client must trust the therapist to protect his or her interests and dignity, and the therapist must trust the client's honesty. This makes it far easier to assure clients that what they say, no matter how bizarre, will never leave the therapy room. Yet, as a result of cases like the one described above, certain significant exceptions to the rule have been made. Thus, in most states, the right to confidentiality must be set aside if the client is a criminal defendant and uses insanity as a defense, if the client is a minor and the therapist has reason to believe that a crime (for example, child abuse) is involved, or if the therapist has reason to believe that the client is potentially dangerous to self or others (APA, 1992). Yet, these are extreme cases. In the majority of cases, not even the closest family members or the courts can have access to information about what goes on in the privacy of psychotherapy.

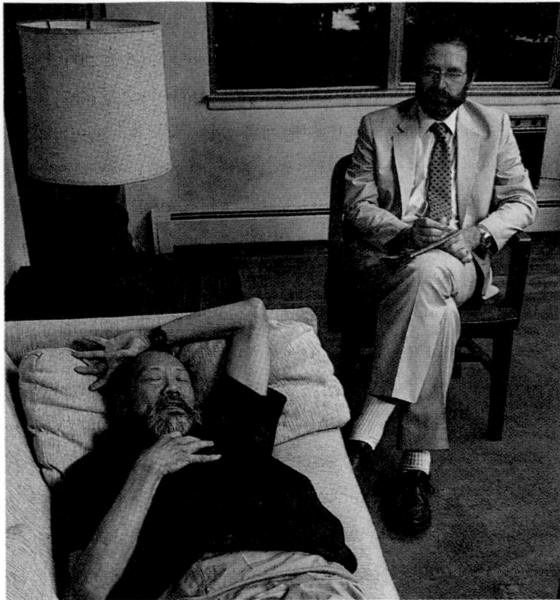

► *In classic psychoanalysis, therapists help patients to discover acceptable intepretations of their problems.*

to ignore the impression you are making? Sometimes the client draws a blank and simply cannot think of anything to say. When associations do not come easily to mind, it's a sign that resistance is occurring. Analyzing the events leading up to this resistance can help the analyst identify areas of repressed conflicts in need of more in-depth exploration.

Dream Interpretation

Like many thoughtful people before him, Sigmund Freud believed that dreams have hidden meanings. Dream interpretation plays an important role in traditional psychoanalysis—indeed, Freud called dreams the "royal road" to the unconscious. The superego is less vigilant when a person is sleeping, and unconscious conflicts or desires are represented in dreams (Freud, 1917/1976). The dream message appears in a symbolic form, however, to avoid arousing anxiety. Although popularized approaches to dreams have sometimes translated every pointed object in a dream as a phallus, every open space as a vagina, and every long trip as a death symbol, Freud himself believed that each person's associations are unique. He argued that a dream's symbolic meaning cannot easily be interpreted without knowing something about the particular mental state of the individual who had the dream.

CAST OF DREAM
THE MONSTER...... YOUR FATHER
KIND WOMAN...... YOUR MOTHER
POLICEMAN .... YOUR ANALYST
FIRST STRANGER.... YOUR BROTHER
SECOND STRANGER .. YOUR SISTER
LITTLE BOY..... YOU

► *Freud attached symbolic meanings to various images that surface in each person's dreams.*

Analysis of Transference

Another major source of information about the unconscious mind derives from the relationship that develops between the client and the therapist. Freud believed that if he remained neutral, withheld judgments, and avoided revealing personal information, a client would form a relationship with him that would be similar in important ways to the client's relationship with parents and other significant adults from childhood. Furthermore, he suggested that the client would "transfer" to this new relationship the feelings, conflicts, and problems of those earlier relationships.

A famous example of ***transference*** is found in the case of Anna O., who was treated by Freud's colleague Josef Breuer (Breuer & Freud, 1895/1976). Anna O. was an attractive, intelligent, and sensitive woman who was devoted to her father. When she was twenty-one years old, her father contracted tuberculosis. She expended such tremendous amounts of physical and emotional energy in caring for him that her own physical and mental health deteriorated. When Anna's health forced her to give up nursing him, she developed several symptoms, including disturbances in her vision and paralysis of muscles that froze her left arm into a typical nursing posture (Ahson, 1974). At one point, she lost her ability to speak for two weeks.

Anna O. responded to Breuer's care, but when her father died, her condition again deteriorated. She then focused on Breuer, at one point recognizing only him and staying in touch

SEEKING SOLUTIONS

Preventing Sexual Exploitation

People undergoing therapy often have feelings of affection, even sexual attraction, toward their therapists. This is a normal reaction that is technically called transference. An ethical, caring therapist recognizes those feelings as part of the normal process of therapy and does not exploit them by becoming involved with clients in sexual relationships. Good therapists talk about these feelings and help their clients seek other people in their lives with whom they can develop caring, loving, and mutually fulfilling relationships. It is the therapist's responsibility not to exploit the client's emotional vulnerability in the therapeutic situation; for a therapist to suggest sexual involvement is evidence of lack of professional and ethical concern for the client.

Unfortunately, every profession has a small number of unethical individuals. One of the most destructive abuses of the therapeutic relationship is sexual exploitation. For this reason, a variety of professional associations, including the American Psychological Association, the American Psychiatric Association, and the National Council of Social Workers, have specifically prohibited sexual contact between therapists and clients in their ethics codes. The American Psychological Association has also developed a consumer pamphlet, "If Sex Enters into the Psychotherapy Relationship," to inform the public about the ethical prohibition of therapist-client sexual contact, and options for clients if their therapists have not acted appropriately.

Therapists who attempt to introduce sex into therapy often do so repeatedly, and with more than one client. This can be done in several ways, including verbal remarks that are intended to arouse sexual feelings, erotic hugging and kissing, and manual, oral, or genital contact. Such behavior can be distinguished from therapeutic discussions about feelings and concerns about sex or comforting physical contact such as a hug when the client is sad. The advice is, "If your therapist touches you in a way that seems sexual to you, let your feelings be your guide. If you feel shamed or pushed to touch or be touched in therapy, your therapist may be sexualizing the relationship" (American Psychological Association, 1992). An ethical therapist will respect, rather than challenge, a client's feelings on this issue.

If a client tells the therapist he or she is uncomfortable, and the therapist continues the objectionable behavior after the issue is discussed, the client has a variety of options, ranging from termination of therapy to filing various complaints at local, state, and national levels. For complaints to be effective, however, the therapist must belong to a licensed or regulated profession, which is true of any bona fide professional psychologist. Before entering into therapy, a client should always check to make sure the therapist is a licensed provider of mental health services.

with reality only as long as she was talking to him. Over the course of therapy, her condition improved, and their relationship became so intense that Breuer's wife became jealous because her husband was so engrossed with his attractive patient. When Breuer realized his wife's feelings, he reacted swiftly. He clumsily brought treatment to an end, precipitating in Anna O. an hysterical "childbirth" that terminated a phantom pregnancy that Breuer hadn't realized had been developing in response to their relationship (Jones, 1953).

Freud considered the intense rapport between Breuer and Anna O. a prime example of transference (Freud, 1914/1976). Freud believed that Anna O. had an unconscious sexual attraction to her father, which she transferred to her therapist. In a sense, Breuer became her father. Thus, through transference, the client-therapist relationship came to reflect the issues underlying the client's psychopathology.

Eventually, the transference is resolved when the client begins to understand the unconscious processes affecting his or her behavior. Until it is resolved, however, therapists must be well-trained to handle adoring clients (a lesson that Breuer learned the hard way), and clients must understand that sexual contact between client and therapist is never ethical and can be highly destructive to the therapeutic process.

In psychoanalytic theory, transference occurs when the client transfers the troublesome feelings, conflicts, and problems of earlier life relationships to a new relationship with the therapist.

"Well, I do have this recurring dream that one day I might see some results."

▲ *Today, less expensive and less time-consuming methods have replaced classical psychoanalysis as the treatment of choice for most people.*

Modern Psychodynamic Therapies

Psychodynamically oriented therapists have constructed revisions of psychoanalysis that are based on better science than Freud had available in his day. Just as Sigmund Freud's personality theory was revised by neo-Freudians and ego analysts (see Chapter 14), so too were his psychoanalytic therapeutic methods. Although all therapists share the treatment goal of understanding unconscious conflicts, the nature of the conflict and the kinds of impulses examined vary from therapist to therapist.

One noteworthy modern psychodynamic approach to therapy is ***ego analysis,*** which concentrates less on unconscious infantile conflicts over sex and aggression (id functions) and more on helping clients develop stronger, more adaptive problem-solving skills (ego functions). Ego analysts treat both children and adults, and treatment may be offered to families or unrelated groups as well as individuals.

Although classical psychoanalysis can require years of therapy, a number of psychoanalytically based therapies have been developed that are less time consuming. These brief therapies are similar to classical analysis in that they (1) seek to change thoughts and behavior; (2) examine the relationship of early conflicts to present problems; (3) bring repressed thoughts and feelings into consciousness; (4) examine free associations, dreams, and resistance; and (5) emphasize insight. These psychotherapists are more actively involved in the therapeutic process than are classical psychoanalysts, however, directing clients' thoughts more readily and offering interpretations more quickly. Such therapists focus more on current life circumstances, and they are more willing to be emotionally supportive to their clients (Garfield, 1989). Innovations such as these have helped keep psychodynamic approaches alive and well, despite legitimate criticism of traditional psychoanalysis.

THINKING CRITICALLY

David is seeking therapy because he has terrible nightmares and little appetite. He recently had a huge blow-up with his boss, and he is tense, anxious, and depressed most of the time. How would medically and psychodynamically oriented therapies differ in their treatment approach to David's problems?

Therapists with a medical viewpoint would focus on biological factors. After giving David a physical examination, a medically oriented therapist might prescribe an antidepressant to alleviate his symptoms.

Therapists with a psychodynamic viewpoint would explore potential conflicts between conscious and unconscious aspects of David's personality. A psychodynamic therapist would ask David to relax and to say whatever comes to mind, noting areas of resistance and conflict (free association). She would ask about his dreams (dream analysis) and eventually analyze David's feelings about his relationship with his therapist (transference). The analyst would take an active role in interpreting David's responses, helping him gain insights into his forgotten memories and the unconscious motivation that underlies his behavior.

Evaluating Psychoanalysis

Classical psychoanalysis is inefficient and expensive. Each client is sometimes seen as frequently as five days a week for forty-five or fifty minutes over a period of years. Because the analyst is so highly trained and treatment is so time-consuming, the total cost to the client is very high, and it is not likely to be covered by health insurance. (Modern psychodynamic therapies are generally less expensive and more cost-effective.) Furthermore, for some types of problems or people, psychoanalysis is ineffective. It requires a high level of intellectual and emotional maturity. Thus, children or severely mentally disordered individuals are not likely to benefit from psychoanalysis. In fact, chronically schizophrenic individuals show little progress under psychoanalysis. Finally, clinical researchers have serious concerns about the empirical validity of traditional psychoanalytic theory, since interpretations are so subjective (Zigler & Child, 1969).

Behavioral and Cognitive-Behavioral Therapies

Behavioral and cognitive-behavioral therapies have their origins in experimentally established principles of learning and memory. Behaviorists and cognitive-behaviorists believe that inappropriate, abnormal behaviors are acquired by the same learning principles as "normal" behaviors.

Behavior Therapy

Behavior therapy, sometimes called ***behavior modification***, developed, in part, as an effort to put psychotherapy on a firm empirical basis. Behavior therapists suggested that the rigor of laboratory investigation be applied to psychological treatment. This meant rejecting the unconscious, which is impossible to observe, and concentrating instead on more observable behavior. The direct and immediate elimination of a client's problem behaviors became the primary goal of therapy. Although behaviorists understand the need to discover the causes of mental disorder, they look for these causes in their clients' learning history, not in unobservable intrapsychic conflicts.

The earliest proponent of a behavioral basis for emotional problems was John B. Watson (1878–1958). In an experiment that would not be considered ethical today, Watson and Rosalie Rayner classically conditioned Albert, an eleven-month-old child, to fear a white rat (Watson, 1925; Harris, 1979). They did this by striking a pipe with a hammer whenever Albert touched the animal. The loud noise behind him would make Albert cry in fear. After several pairings of noise and rat, Albert began reacting negatively—crying and moving away whenever the rat was present. This avoidance behavior seemed to persist over time, even though Albert and the rat were kept apart. Albert was now also afraid of a rabbit, a dog, a sealskin coat, a Santa Claus mask, Watson's hair, and even a package of white cotton. On the other hand, he was not at all frightened by items unrelated to the rat, so his behavior could not be explained as a general fear response to just anything in the environment. According to Watson, these results imply that fear (as well as any other emotion) can be classically conditioned, and that phobias (irrational fears) can be produced through stimulus generalization.

Mary Cover Jones (1896–1987) reasoned that if fears could be conditioned, they could also be counterconditioned—that is, eliminated by associating the feared object with a response that is incompatible with fear (Jones, 1924). She successfully applied these ideas by helping Peter, a child who had acquired a phobia to small animals. Jones taught him to relax in their presence. To help him "unlearn" his fear, she seated Peter in a highchair, where he normally ate, and gave him one of his favorite foods. Then, she placed a rabbit in a wire cage near Peter, moving the rabbit closer and closer to him in each successive session, but always maintaining a distance that would not interfere with Peter's eating. Other children, who were not afraid of the rabbit, were also brought into the training so Peter could observe their behavior with the rabbit. Eventually Peter became so accustomed to the animal that he was able to pet it outside the cage, with no sign of fear or anxiety.

Behavior therapy seeks to modify behaviors by applying conditioning and learning principles directly to abnormal behavior.

During the 1950s, behavior therapy became an alternative to insight-oriented therapies. Use of behavior therapy has since grown enormously, spurred by basic research on learning, effective practical applications of classical and operant conditioning principles and modeling techniques, and increasing questions about traditional psychoanalytic therapy's cost effectiveness. Here we discuss some of the most effective techniques developed by behaviorists.

Systematic Desensitization

Systematic desensitization was the first recognized therapy alternative to traditional psychotherapy. Joseph Wolpe developed this technique to treat anxiety (Wolpe, 1958). He proposed that if a response incompatible with anxiety—such as relaxation, sexual arousal, or assertiveness—could be made to occur in the presence of the anxiety-provoking stimuli, the connection between stimulus and anxiety would be weakened. This is essentially the same procedure used earlier by Mary Cover Jones to ***countercondition*** Peter's fear of small animals.

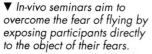

Systematic desensitization is a behavior therapy technique in which anxiety in the presence of a stimulus is gradually reduced.

In ***systematic desensitization***, the therapist first determines what causes the client to feel anxiety. Then the therapist constructs a hierarchy of fear-provoking stimuli, ranging from situations provoking very mild fear to those provoking very intense fear. Next, the therapist has the client use deep breathing and muscle relaxation techniques to relax. When the client is fully relaxed, the therapist asks the client to imagine the least threatening item in the anxiety hierarchy. If the client feels anxiety, the imaging process is terminated. The therapist then asks the client to imagine a less fearful version of the item. When the client can imagine the scene repeatedly without anxiety, the therapist moves on to the next most anxiety-provoking scene in the hierarchy. Because relaxation experienced with one item will slowly generalize to other items on the list, the next item may be somewhat less stressful. But each is handled as carefully as the first. An example of the application of systematic desensitization of a snake phobia is depicted in Figure 16-3.

Once relaxation in the presence of the entire list of scenes has been achieved, the therapist can test the client with the "real thing." The usual finding is that freedom from anxiety generalizes from an imagined stimulus to the actual anxiety-provoking stimulus. The therapist may conclude therapy with *in vivo* (real-life) desensitization, helping the client "walk through" the actual feared situation. With a driving phobia, the therapist may accompany the client in a car on short and then longer trips while demonstrating coping behavior and helping the client control any anxiety that might appear. Later, the client will have to run through practice sessions alone. Table 16-4 shows one study's results, comparing systematic desensitization to psychoanalysis and control conditions in treating anxiety over public speaking. Both therapies had a positive outcome, but systematic desensitization was more effective in overcoming anxiety.

▼ *In-vivo seminars aim to overcome the fear of flying by exposing participants directly to the object of their fears.*

THINKING CRITICALLY

How would you apply your knowledge of classical conditioning to treat children's bedwetting (enuresis)? Hint: the pressure of a full bladder would be the conditioned stimulus; waking up would be the conditioned response. How would you use classical conditioning to create a connection between feeling the pressure of a full bladder (conditioned stimulus) and waking up (conditioned response)?

You need to find an unconditioned stimulus—one that will wake up the child—and pair it with the feelings of bladder pressure until the feelings themselves will wake up the child. As you may remember from Chapter 6, devices used to treat bedwetting are based on these principles. A device placed in the child's bed detects the slightest amount of discharged urine and sets off an alarm, which then awakens the child in time to finish urinating in the toilet. After repeated pairing with the alarm's sound, the feelings become associated with the response of awakening in time to urinate in the toilet.

Positive Reinforcement and Shaping

Clinical use of both positive reinforcement and shaping stems from principles of operant conditioning (see Chapter 6). The therapist first reinforces simple parts of a complex behavior, then reinforces increasingly complex parts until

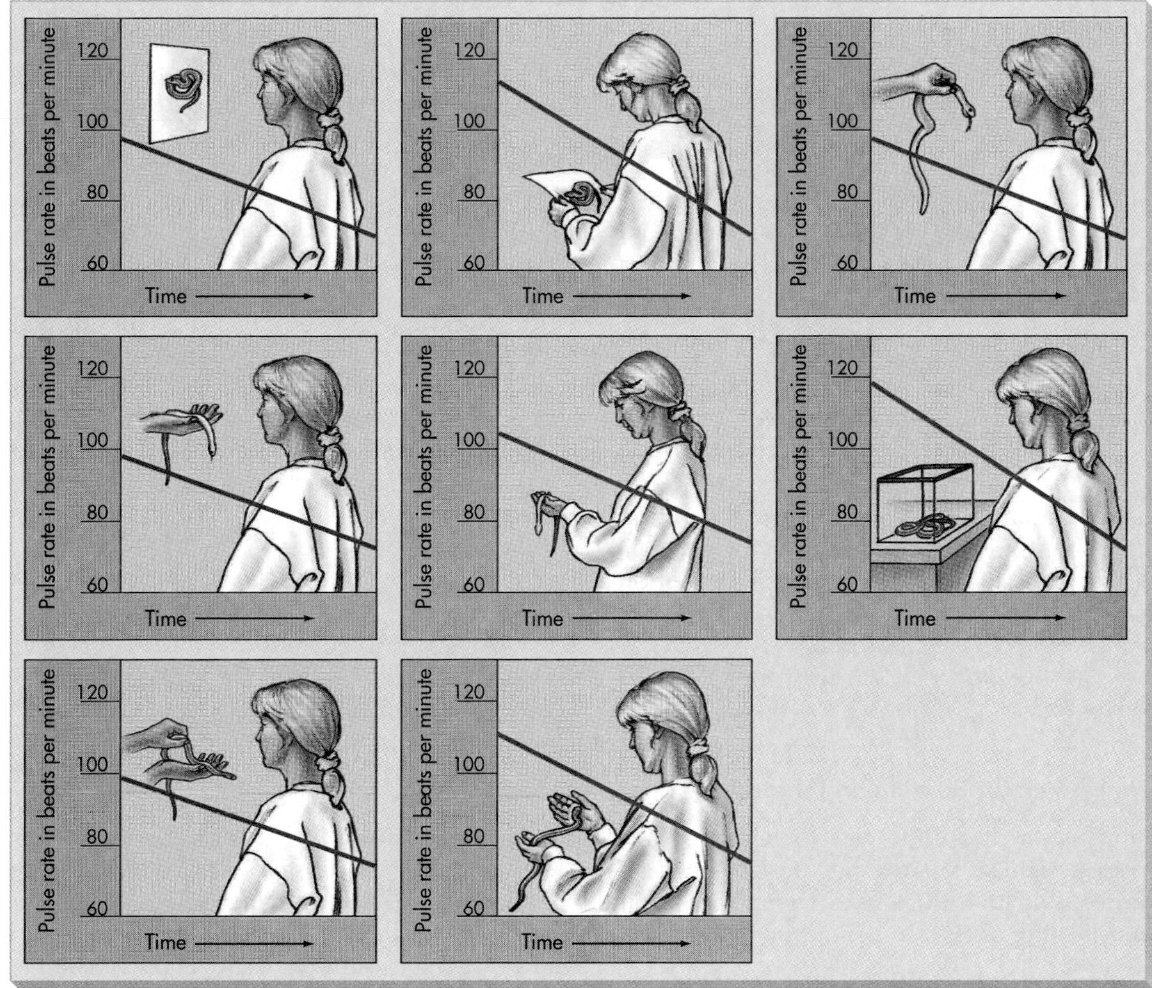

16-3 Systematic Desensitization

Martha, who has a snake phobia, is taught to relax in the presence of a snake—the aversive stimulus. Her pulse rate changes as she is in the presence of the snake—first in the presence of a picture of the snake, then in the presence of a toy snake, a dead snake, and finally a live snake. (Source: Adapted from Gilling & Brightwell, 1982)

the client is able to perform the complete behavior. Social rewards, such as praise, a sense of accomplishment, and success, are likely to maintain the improved behaviors.

Positive reinforcement has been very effective in changing both normal and abnormal behaviors in children and adults. It has been used to toilet train children, to increase productivity in the workplace, and to eliminate behaviors associated with psychopathology. Children who have trouble controlling their impulses and sitting still are rewarded for grooming themselves or making their beds. Hospital staff use candy or other desirable items for rewards, even tokens that can be traded for these desirable items or for certain privileges. Some mental hospitals

Table 16-4 Improvement Percentages for Public Speaking after Different Treatments

	Self-Report Anxiety (%)	Behavior Ratings (%)	Physiological Arousal (%)
Behavioral desensitization	100	100	87
Insight therapy	53	60	53
No-treatment placebo	47	73	47
No-treatment control	7	24	28

Source: Adapted from Paul, 1966.

▲ *Center House in Boston has established a token economy for worker-trainees with developmental disabilities. Participants earn tokens they can exchange at the "Token Store" as reinforcement for vocational training.*

use comprehensive "token economy" treatment programs in which operant conditioning procedures are applied to all clients' behavior on a given ward. A client on a token economy ward can obtain TV time, desserts, or a weekend pass by earning tokens for performing desired behaviors.

Punishment and Aversion Therapy

Punishment has been used to control an individual's behavior since ancient times. For example, Roman healers recommended whipping and putting snakes in wine cups to discourage alcohol abuse. Today, punishment for undesired behavior might consist of administering an electric shock after an unwanted behavior. Although controversial, electric shock has been used to punish autistic children (children who have difficulty responding socially to others) when they show self-destructive behaviors, such as banging their heads against a wall.

In ***aversion therapy***, an aversive (unpleasant) stimulus, such as a loud sound or an electric shock, would be paired with specific unwanted behaviors. For example, an alcoholic client might be given a drug that induces nausea (the aversive stimulus) just before drinking alcohol. The client would then associate drinking alcohol with nausea, a very negative feeling (see Figure 16-4).

A. Conditioning

Alcohol
(Neutral stimulus)

\+

Nausea-producing drug (US) → Nausea (UR)

B. After conditioning

Alcohol (CS) → Nausea (CR)

16-4 Aversion Therapy

In this aversion therapy for alcoholic clients, the client drinks an alcoholic beverage mixed with a drug that produces severe nausea. The alcohol mixed with the drug is the unconditioned stimulus (US), which produces the unconditioned response of nausea. The alcohol alone then becomes a conditioned stimulus (CS) for the conditioned response of nausea, producing at least temporarily a conditioned aversion to alcohol.

Modeling

According to Albert Bandura (1925–), our actions are strongly affected by what we observe in our environment, especially the behaviors of others, and not only by the rewards and punishments we receive (Bandura, 1968, 1980). Just as we learn how to tie a knot by watching someone else ***modeling***, or demonstrating it, we can learn to deal with stress by observing how others handle stress. Observing how models cope effectively with fearful situations can significantly change our ability to cope in similar situations.

Modeling is a common behavior therapy for treating phobic problems and changing aggressive habits. It is frequently used to reduce the anxiety of clients (especially children) who are about to undergo stressful medical procedures. The client may hear a story, see a film, or watch a "live" demonstration of various ways of fearlessly (or at least cooperatively) dealing with the procedure. A child with a dog phobia might be shown a videotape of another child playing happily with a dog and petting it. With some practice, the fearful child can often adapt one or more of the observed coping techniques.

Modeling can also be used to help clients with social interaction problems. This is one aspect of ***social skills training***, in which clients are taught strategies for effective interactions with others. Imagine a man who finds it almost impossible to interact calmly with women his own age. Sometimes the therapist will "model" an appropriate social behavior, such as demonstrating how to ask someone out for a date. Alternatively, the therapist and the client will role play (act out) a real-life situation that creates problems for the client. The therapist and client will work through these situations several times, switching roles periodically. This method can be especially effective in behavior therapy groups, because several clients can try each role, learning from one another as well as from the therapist.

◄ *In an institution for juveniles, these boys take on roles in front of a therapist to practice appropriate social behavior.*

The Ethics of Behavior Therapy

Behavior therapy raises certain unique ethical concerns. Some critics charge that token economies "dehumanize" participants, reducing their ability to choose what they will do (Kipnis, 1987). With punishment and aversive conditioning, critics believe that the deprivation or discomfort that are part of therapy are not justified, even if they ultimately help eliminate the client's problem.

Behavioral techniques are especially controversial when used with children. The idea of electrically shocking a child is horrifying to most adults. As a counterargument, defenders of behavior therapy point out that autistic, psychotic, or severely retarded children often engage in self-destructive behaviors (such as head banging), which are more injurious than shock or other forms of punishment. Caregivers may tie the children's arms, legs, and head to a bed or chair so that the children don't irreparably harm themselves. But such restraint appears to have no long-term effect on self-destructive behaviors, while aversive stimuli can be quite effective in eliminating the behaviors (Lovaas, 1977). Indeed, in 1986, when the Office for Children of the State of Massachusetts banned use of aversive stimuli in a school for autistic children, it caused quite an uproar. The children's self-destructive behaviors quickly returned, prompting the parents to sue to overturn the ban. They charged the school with giving up the only effective treatment the children had ever received. They won. When the court overturned the ban, it suggested that the Office for Children had played "Russian Roulette with the lives and safety of the students" by letting sentimentalism overrule therapeutic judgment (Rosenhan & Seligman, 1995, p. 126).

Most behavioral therapists agree that punishment and aversive methods should be used only when other methods are unavailable, inappropriate, or have failed—and, even then, only for the shortest possible time. Accordingly, therapists use these techniques mostly in difficult cases in which there are very hard-to-change behavior patterns (such as drug addictions) or life-threatening behaviors (such as an anorexic patient's repeated and long-term refusal to eat or a borderline patient's repeated self-mutilation). These methods are almost always used, however, in combination with positive reinforcement or other response-strengthening methods, because the therapist wants to help the client learn what should be done, not just what should not be done.

Cognitive-Behavioral Therapies

If individuals have learned new social skills but have trouble using them in real life, the problem may be cognitive, that is, their thoughts may be interfering with their actions. When this happens, cognitive-behavioral therapy (a combination of cognitive and behavioral therapies) can be especially useful. There are many different kinds of cognitive-behavioral therapies, but each of them uses the following three procedures: (1) exposure to events that trigger the pathological behavior, (2) cognitive restructuring of the individual's thoughts about the triggering event, and (3) relaxation at the same

Table 16-5 Beck's Analysis of Primitive Versus Mature Thinking

Kind of Thinking	Type	Example
Primitive thinking	Nondimensional and global	I am fearful.
	Absolutistic and moralistic	I am a despicable coward.
	Invariant	I always have been and always will be a coward.
	Character diagnosis	I have a defect in my character.
	Irreversibility	As I am basically weak, there's nothing that can be done about it.
Mature thinking	Multidimensional	I am moderately fearful, quite generous, and fairly intelligent.
	Relativistic and nonjudgmental	I am more fearful than most people I know.
	Variable	My fears vary from time to time and from situation to situation.
	Behavioral diagnosis	I avoid situations too much, and I have many fears.
	Reversibility	I can learn ways of facing situations and fighting my fears.

In Beck's cognitive therapy for depression, clients are taught to monitor their negative thoughts and recognize the relationships among their thoughts, feelings, and behavior.

time the individual is having the disturbing thoughts. We will discuss three major variations of cognitive therapy: Beck's cognitive therapy, Ellis' rational-emotive therapy, and stress-inoculation training.

Beck's Cognitive Therapy

Aaron Beck (1921–) developed his approach to cognitive therapy when he found that depressed clients seemed to distort their views about the world in systematic, primitive ways (labeled "primitive" because they are analogous to those exhibited by children). In contrast, normal mature adults seemed to exhibit more adaptive ways of thinking (see Table 16-5). He concluded that depression is caused by distortions of thinking—a "depressive triad" of thoughts about one's self, experiences, and future—and went on to prove that changing how one thinks about these three areas can have positive therapeutic effects (Beck, Rush, Shaw, & Emery, 1979). Cognitive therapy is highly successful in the treatment of depression. The results of one study are shown in Figure 16-5. Cognitive therapy has also been successfully used to treat panic and other anxiety disorders (Beck, 1993).

Beck's approach involves asking clients to collect data on themselves that challenge their negative conclusions and to decide for themselves whether or not they are distorting their realities. Clients are taught to monitor their negative thoughts and to recognize the relationships among their thoughts, feelings, and behavior. They learn to evaluate the evidence for and against their cognitive distortions and to substitute more reality oriented views. They also learn to recognize and change dysfunctional beliefs that underlie the distortions. Various techniques are used to identify the client's maladaptive assumptions and misconceptions.

A cognitive therapist will train clients in various strategies for coping with anxiety-producing or depression-related thoughts and events. Here's an example of a cognitive therapist

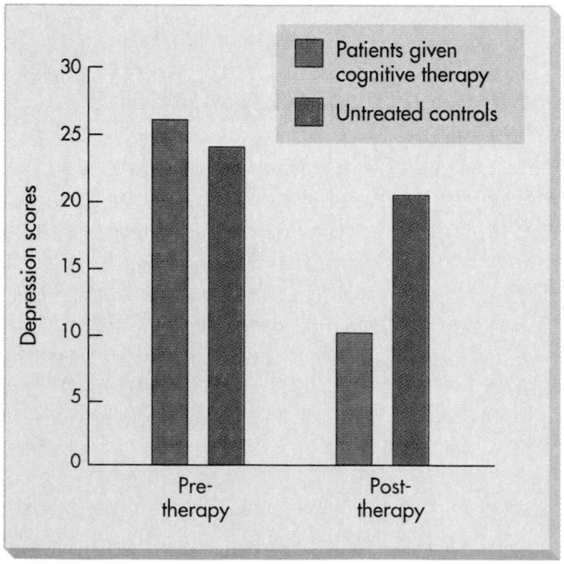

16-5 Cognitive Therapy for Depression

An experimental group of depressed patients are given cognitive therapy that trains them to think more like nondepressed people. They are taught to notice and take personal credit for good events and not to take the blame for bad events or to overgeneralize from bad events. As indicated by scores on a depression inventory, the patients given cognitive therapy are dramatically less depressed than are untreated controls. (Source: Adapted from Rehm, Kaslow, & Rabin, 1987) teaching a depressed student to think about and recognize the relationship among thoughts, feelings, and behaviors:

> Client: I get depressed when things go wrong. Like when I fail a test.
> Therapist: Do you agree that the way you interpret the results of the test will affect you? You might feel depressed, you might have trouble sleeping . . . and you might even wonder if you should drop out of the course.
> Client: I have been thinking that I wasn't going to make it. Yes, I agree.
> Therapist: Now, what did failing mean?
> Client (tearful): That I couldn't get into law school.
> Therapist: And what does that mean to you?
> Client: That I'm just not smart enough.
> Therapist: And how do those *thoughts* make you feel?
> Client: Very unhappy.
> Therapist: So it is the meaning of failing a test that makes you very unhappy. In fact, believing that you can never be happy is a powerful factor in producing your unhappiness. So you get yourself into a trap—by definition, failure to get into law school equals "I can never be happy" (Beck, Rush, Shaw, & Emery, 1979, pp. 145–46).

Cognitive therapy helps depressed people about 70 percent of the time. This is about as effective as drug therapy, and slightly less effective than ECT, but there are no side effects of cognitive therapy. It has the additional advantage of a lower relapse rate (Hollon, Evans, & DeRubeis, 1990). Most studies have involved relatively educated clients with moderate levels of depression, however. How effective cognitive therapy is with less educated individuals and more serious depression has yet to be determined. It may be that a combination of cognitive and drug or ECT therapy is optimal for more seriously depressed clients. Cognitive therapy also has been found to have a lower relapse rate than drug therapy for a host of other nonpsychotic disorders, including generalized anxiety, panic, social phobia, and bulimia (Hollon & Beck, 1994).

THINKING CRITICALLY

Consider a young woman who doesn't want to hurt anyone's feelings. As a result, she doesn't refuse any date invitations from men, and she feels trapped and harassed by a battalion of undesirable males. What irrational beliefs might be influencing this woman's behavior? How would a rational-emotive therapist treat this client?

The therapist would focus on her irrational beliefs, most likely emphasizing beliefs about the necessity of being loved by everyone and of avoiding life's problems and of achieving happiness without effort. The therapist would also help her see that she (1) is protecting other people's feelings at the expense of her own, and (2) is hurting everyone by being honest with no one. The therapist would then have the client practice some "straight thinking" (for example, "I don't have to please everyone; I'll spend my time as I please") and start behaving accordingly. The goal is to replace irrational or debilitating thoughts with more normal ways of thinking about the same situations.

Rational-Emotive Therapy

Albert Ellis (1913–   ) suggested that maladaptive behavior results from mistaken or distorted beliefs people have about themselves and others (Ellis, 1962). These mistaken beliefs, which are learned early in life, generally through family influences, include the following: one should be loved by everyone for everything one does; if possible, it is better to avoid problems rather than to face them head-on; one needs something or someone stronger or more powerful than oneself to rely on; one must attain and perfect self-control; one has virtually no control over one's emotions and cannot help having certain feelings. ***Rational-emotive therapy (RET)*** is a clinical technique developed by Ellis to help clients (1) see the irrationality of these beliefs, (2) recognize how these beliefs rule their behavior, and (3) practice new, more adaptive, rational, and beneficial

Rational-emotive therapy is a form of psychotherapy developed to help clients understand the irrationality of their beliefs, to recognize how those beliefs rule their behavior, and to practice new and more rational ways of thinking and behaving.

ways of thinking and behaving. The therapist encourages clients to develop accurate beliefs through cross-examination and active challenging. Clients are asked by therapists and taught to ask themselves variations of four basic questions to challenge and dispute their beliefs:

1. "What am I telling myself?"
2. "Is this true?"
3. "What is the evidence for it being true?"
4. "What is the evidence for it not being true?"

The therapist may challenge irrational beliefs in a blunt, conversational way. After criticizing a journalist's perfectionistic standards, for example, the therapist might say: "So what if you did a crummy job on your reporting assignment? It's important to realize that one crummy job is just that—one crummy job—and no more than that!" (Ellis, 1976, 1991).

Table 16-6 Stress Inoculation Training

Stages	Self-Statements
Preparation	You can develop a plan to deal with it. Just think about what you can do about it. That's better than getting anxious. No negative self-statements: just think rationally. Don't worry: worry won't help anything.
Acquisition and rehearsal	One step at a time: you can handle the situation. Don't think about fear; just think about what you have to do. Stay relevant. This anxiety is what the doctor said you would feel. It's a reminder to use your coping exercises. Relax; you're in control. Take a slow deep breath. Ah, good.
Application	When fear comes, just pause. Keep the focus on the present; what is it you have to do? You should expect your fear to rise. Don't try to eliminate fear totally; just keep it manageable.
Reinforcement	It worked; you did it. Wait until you tell your therapist (or group) about this. It wasn't as bad as you expected. It's getting better each time you use the procedures.

Stress Inoculation Training

Another cognitive method used to prevent or reduce anxiety is ***stress inoculation training*** (Meichenbaum, 1977). In this procedure, the therapist not only identifies the stresses that an individual is likely to face but also helps develop effective coping strategies. Special emphasis is placed on "self-statements"—what people characteristically say to themselves under stress. Self-statements that arouse anxiety or depression or other negative emotions are replaced with statements that counteract anxiety.

Stress inoculation training is carried out in four stages (see Table 16-6). The first is *preparation*, in which the therapist helps the client to understand the nature of stress and then to explore his or her beliefs and concerns about stressful situations. The second is *acquisition and rehearsal*. The individual not only learns new adaptive self-statements but also practices them for stressful events (for example, "OK, stay calm, you can handle this" or "This is upsetting, but remember your plan"). In the *application* stage, the client practices these coping strategies in the therapist's office under mild, controlled stress. Finally, in the *reinforcement* stage, the client uses practiced strategies in real-life situations and discovers that they are successful.

Evaluating Cognitive-Behavioral Therapies

Behavior therapy and cognitive-behavioral therapy are probably the most common forms of psychotherapy in use today. They have certain advantages over other techniques: they deal directly with the most visible manifestation of a problem, a person's socially inappropriate behavior. No inferences about the behavior's deeper meaning are required. They have had positive effects when used to treat clients with anxiety disorders and mood disorders. And their effects are relatively immediate, typically requiring only a few treatment sessions before positive changes are observed. Nonetheless, behavior therapy does not work for all disorders (for example, schizophrenia). To be effective, behavior therapy and cognitive therapy require a cooperative client who follows instructions.

THINKING CRITICALLY

Remember David, who is seeking therapy because he has nightmares and little appetite, doesn't get along well with others at work, and is tense and anxious (see p. 594). How would behavior and cognitive therapists approach David's problems?

Therapists with a behavioral viewpoint would seek an explanation for David's behavior in the principles of classical and operant conditioning. They would focus on the links between David's environment and his responses to it, deemphasizing David's thoughts and feelings. They would take an active role, helping David to identify the cues at home and work that lead to tension and anxiety, then creating experiences that would extinguish negative associations or countercondition positive responses that are incompatible with tension and anxiety. Techniques of systematic desensitization might be used to deal with anxiety-producing stimuli. Behavioral therapists might also help David to set up his own system of rewards for behaviors that he wants to encourage in himself. They might use observational learning principles, perhaps by exposing David to role models who could demonstrate constructive approaches for dealing with his world. They also might offer David some social skills training.

Therapists with a cognitive-behavioral viewpoint would examine David's mental representations of the world, identify illogical and self-defeating thought processes, and explore dysfunctional attitudes, including low self-regard. They would take an active role in confronting irrational thoughts and in changing self-defeating feelings and behaviors.

Humanistic Therapies

Humanistic therapies assume that both normal and abnormal behavior are affected by how each person views the world and his or her place in it. The goal of therapy is to promote personal growth and self-fulfillment by helping the client develop new and more adaptive interpretations of life events and experiences. Humanistic therapists function as attentive helpers, not as all-knowing judges or behavior modifiers. Their main task is to create conditions that enable clients to become aware of ("get in touch with") their own perceptions and feelings.

Client-Centered Psychotherapy

Rather than seeking insight into repressed memories, client-centered therapists try to help people become aware of and accept all aspects of themselves. They view emotional problems as stemming from a lack of self-knowledge, a denial of feelings, and an inability to experience feelings fully. Carl Rogers (1902–1987) was the first and most prominent proponent of ***client-centered therapy*** (Rogers, 1951). He thought that therapy should help clients explain and accept their own feelings (Rogers, 1970; Maslow, 1970).

The goal of client-centered therapy is to raise people's awareness and acceptance of themselves and their feelings.

Rogers defined the self-concept as a relatively consistent and enduring framework of attitudes toward one's self. Because disturbed persons find their feelings and experiences are inconsistent with their self-concept, they often deny them. Suppose, for example, that a man in therapy responds to every question about a neg-

◀ *Carl Rogers conducts a session of client-centered therapy, in which the therapist offers no judgment about the patient's behavior but rather gives complete and unconditional positive regard.*

SEEKING SOLUTIONS

What Kind of Therapist Is Best?

There are many different forms of psychotherapy, and they differ somewhat in their popularity among therapists. A majority of practitioners adopt what is called an eclectic approach, which combines two or more fundamental or pure forms of therapy. The success of therapy is maximized when a match can be found between the client's problem, the type of therapy, and the personalities of the client and the therapist. Even the most effective therapeutic techniques might be unsuccessful if the therapist and client experience some personal blocks to communication. Indeed, when clients are asked what was most helpful to them in therapy, they emphasize the importance of the therapist over specific therapeutic techniques (Strupp, Fox, & Lessler, 1969).

Unfortunately, there has been relatively little well-executed research on the personality characteristics of therapists and clients. Most training programs in clinical psychology place considerable weight on intellectual attributes, as reflected in test scores and grades, when decisions are made about whom to admit to training. But does a high IQ guarantee an effective therapist? It's a start, but patient feedback suggests that characteristics such as sensitivity, honesty, and gentleness are also important, even in the case of behaviorally oriented therapy (Lazarus, 1971). Other research suggests that successful patients in both behavior therapy and insight therapy identify similar things as important in their improvement: (1) the personality of the therapist; (2) help with understanding their problems; (3) encouragement to practice facing things that bother them; (4) the ability to talk to an understanding person; and (5) help with understanding themselves (Sloane, Staples, Cristol, Yorkston, & Whipple, 1975).

Psychotherapists differ widely in their success rates. A major factor contributing to this variability is amount of experience. In fact, experience seems to be more important than intellectual skills or type of therapeutic techniques used. From Rogers' theory, we would expect three personality characteristics to be especially important to achieve positive change: *empathy, nonpossessive warmth,* and *genuineness.* Research showed that when therapists ranked low on empathy, nonpossessive warmth, and genuineness, their clients showed only a moderate rate of improvement. When they ranked high on all three, the success rate was much higher (Mitchell, Bozarth, & Krauft, 1977). There is also evidence that therapists who have their own unresolved conflicts regarding dependency, warmth, intimacy, and hostility are less effective in helping others. Not unexpectedly, the more the client likes the therapist, the longer he or she will stay in therapy and the higher the probability of a successful outcome. A likable, conflict-free therapist will be more successful with almost all clients than a cold and self-conflicted one.

Is it better to have a therapist of the same or opposite sex or of the same or different ethnicity? Although some research has suggested that women do better with women therapists, closer inspection of the data suggests that the experience of the therapist and his or her awareness of and sensitivity to gender and cultural issues is the key to better therapy outcomes.

ative life event with the comment, "I am upset about it," but he cannot explain why he is upset. Later the therapist discovers that the man's parents had discouraged expression of any negative feelings. They would say, "You aren't angry with us; you're just upset." He thus learned as a child to cut off his feelings of anger, depression, jealousy, and anxiety, and to substitute vague reactions of being upset. Client-centered therapy would try to lead him to understand and accept that he has such feelings, and to re-experience them in appropriate situations. This should eventually allow him to respond spontaneously and openly in unpleasant situations, instead of being confused and disoriented.

Client-centered therapy stresses that the therapeutic relationship should be honest, open, and filled with true and uninhibited communication. To this end, Rogers proposed that therapists should communicate three attitudes: *empathic understanding, unconditional positive regard,* and *congruence.* Empathic understanding means the therapist truly understands (or at least honestly tries to understand) the client's immediate feelings. Unconditional positive regard means the therapist cares about and accepts the client as a worthwhile human being. The therapist does not impose conditions on caring and does not mind when clients reveal aspects of themselves that make them ashamed and anxious. The therapist need not agree with views the client presents. Rather, because the therapist cares about the client as a person, those views are accepted as valid. No "conditions of worth" are imposed. Congruence means therapists' feelings or experiences are consistent with how they actually present themselves to clients (Rogers, 1970).

Here's how a client-centered therapist might interact with Patrick, a client having trouble in his marriage:

> Patrick: I guess I really should go right home from work and help my wife out with the kids, but after a full day at the office, I just . . . I don't know.
> Therapist: Are you saying that sometimes you are just not ready to go home.
> Patrick: Right, that's it. I feel like a rat for saying it, but sometimes I just wish all those responsibilities, my wife, my kids, my house, would all just disappear.
> Therapist: It would be nice just to have nothing like that to worry about, huh?
> Patrick: Yeah, I wouldn't really like that, but it feels pretty good just to get that gut feeling off my chest.

Note how the therapist does not judge Patrick, but simply tries to understand and help him understand his perceptions and feelings. The therapist doesn't lead him but encourages further expression by echoing, restating, and seeking clarification of Patrick's feelings.

Gestalt Therapy

In the client-centered approach, therapists tend to be relatively inactive, responding mainly with comments that echo what clients say, allowing them to move at their own pace and direction. Gestalt therapy, developed by Fritz Perls, seeks the goals of humanistic therapy (fuller awareness and personal growth) in a much more active and direct way (Perls, 1969). It emphasizes patterns of behavior and helps people look at the entirety of their immediate experience.

▲ *A victim of incest beats a tennis racket against a couch in a session of Gestalt therapy. Her therapist stresses body language as a means of confronting the patient's childhood assaulter.*

According to Perls, people with emotional problems tend to concentrate only on certain aspects of what they feel and do, especially in their communications with others. Gestalt therapy tries to clarify the whole picture for clients, including what they are feeling, moment to moment, and how their behavior affects and is perceived by others. Gestalt therapists rely on both verbal and nonverbal communication (for example, gestures and body language) to promote awareness. They also use many kinds of creative role playing to let clients "get in touch with" and express their feelings more freely. For example, the client might be asked to exaggerate a vague feeling until it becomes clear.

THINKING CRITICALLY

Think about David once again (see p. 594). How would therapists with a humanistic viewpoint approach his therapy?

Humanistic therapists would explore David's values, goals, and choices. They would try to promote his self-awareness by focusing on his conscious thoughts, encouraging awareness of his feelings as they occur, and emphasizing his need to take responsibility for his feelings and actions. They would try to help David achieve self-fulfillment.

UNDERSTANDING HUMAN DIVERSITY

Values and Bias in Psychotherapy

Therapies differ in their perspectives on psychopathology and in their underlying value systems. These, in turn, influence the goals and techniques of therapy. Therapists should be sensitive to their own values, especially when treating a client with different values, and they should be aware of how values can bias the therapeutic process. Value differences can especially occur when therapist and client are of different gender, ethnic background, sexual orientation, socioeconomic status, religion, or age (Landrine & Klonoff, 1997).

Deviation from traditional Western heterosexual gender role norms has sometimes been viewed as evidence of mental disorder. Women have typically been expected to embrace the "appropriate" roles of wife and mother and viewed as pathological when they held other aspirations. Sexist beliefs like these are expressed when therapists encourage women to conform to traditional gender role expectations, such as stereotyped career choices (for example, becoming a nurse rather than a physician) or preserving marriages even if it means risking bodily injury by staying with abusive men. These beliefs can also be expressed in judging therapeutic success by whether the woman conforms to gender-role expectations and wears conventional makeup and "feminine" attire, gets married, and bears children.

Gender role bias may also affect therapy with men, particularly with homosexual men or heterosexual men who violate traditional gender role expectations. One study asked licensed marriage and family therapists to participate in a simulated interview (Robertson & Fitzgerald, 1990). There were two conditions in this experiment. In both, the client described himself as having symptoms of depression (sleeplessness, guilt), and expressed his concerns by referring to various incidents in his daily life. He also emphasized that he was happy with his marital arrangement and that his wife and children were not the problem. The difference was that in one condition, the client was portrayed as an engineer (traditional male professional) married to a traditional homemaker and mother. In the other, he was portrayed as having responsibility for the household and child care and married to an engineer. Therapists treated the men in the two conditions quite differently. Despite the fact that clients made it clear that they were happy with their marital arrangements, therapists were more likely to attribute the nontraditional client's problems to his life situation. Some therapists focused on nontraditional behavior patterns as a place for therapeutic intervention, even explicitly stating "you probably need to renegotiate the contract that you've got at home." The researchers concluded that their findings underscore the conservative nature of traditional psychotherapy, suggesting that it may be as unprepared to address the issues of nontraditional men as it has been to address issues of nontraditional women (Robertson & Fitzgerald, 1990).

Ignoring the role of the sociocultural context sometimes results in therapists blaming clients for their problems, even when those problems are societally induced. Behaviors, thoughts, and feelings produced by coping with restrictive, discriminatory, or oppressive environments get labeled as pathological rather than as survival responses. In these cases, therapy promotes adjustment to the environment, even though the environment is destructive.

These biases arise from the fact that mental health approaches reflect the values and beliefs of the individuals who design them. Historically, most therapists have been heterosexual white men from middle- and upper-class backgrounds. This contrasts with the backgrounds of clients who are women and/or minority group members and who may live in reduced economic circumstances. Such clients may experience different norms and expectations for their behavior and may hold different beliefs about what is relevant to their physical and mental health than their therapists. Because of their different values and expectations, however, the therapists may label the clients' behavior as "abnormal." Yet, as more women and ethnic minorities have been able to obtain the education and training required to become psychologists, concepts of mental health have changed. Today, therapists aspire to be nonsexist, nonracist, and culturally sensitive, and psychologists strive to develop new models of mental health that reflect appreciation of human diversity (Sue, Ivey, & Pedersen, 1996).

Feminist and Other Culturally Sensitive Therapies

Gender, ethnicity, and other aspects of culture all influence the therapeutic process. Sensitivity to these issues can improve all forms of therapy. But in addition, new feminist and culturally sensitive therapies have emerged that are specifically designed to address the effects of social and structural inequalities on mental health (Worell & Remer, 1992; Brown, 1994).

Feminist therapists do not assume that a woman's anger, feelings of powerlessness and worthlessness, competency fears, indecisiveness, and unassertiveness are necessarily "pathological." Rather, they may be survival strategies to deal with a restrictive, discriminatory, or oppressive environment (Brown, 1994). In the feminist view, the primary source of a client's difficulties is not in the client's mind but comes from the external social and political world. Thus, feminist therapy tries to identify and change a dysfunctional external situation rather than forcing the client to adapt to this situation. While traditional therapists might focus on past relationships in the family as the cause of current distress, feminist therapists focus on the client's current family and community environment.

Feminist therapists emphasize egalitarian relationships between women and men, between minority and majority group members, and between therapists and clients. They believe that therapy should be a collaborative process between therapists and clients. Feminist therapists fully inform their clients about their feminist values and the theory and process of feminist therapy, and encourage clients to decide if it's right for them before beginning treatment.

Feminist therapists affirm *attributes* and *values* associated with the feminine gender role—caring, nurturance, and commitment to others—as positive human qualities for both genders. They encourage women to reject the double bind that on the one hand encourages women to be nurturing and caring, and on the other hand devalues and exploits them for having such characteristics in work situations. They present heterosexuality as neither more nor less healthy than homosexuality, and they encourage peaceful negotiation rather than competition and aggression in social circumstances (Worell & Remer, 1992).

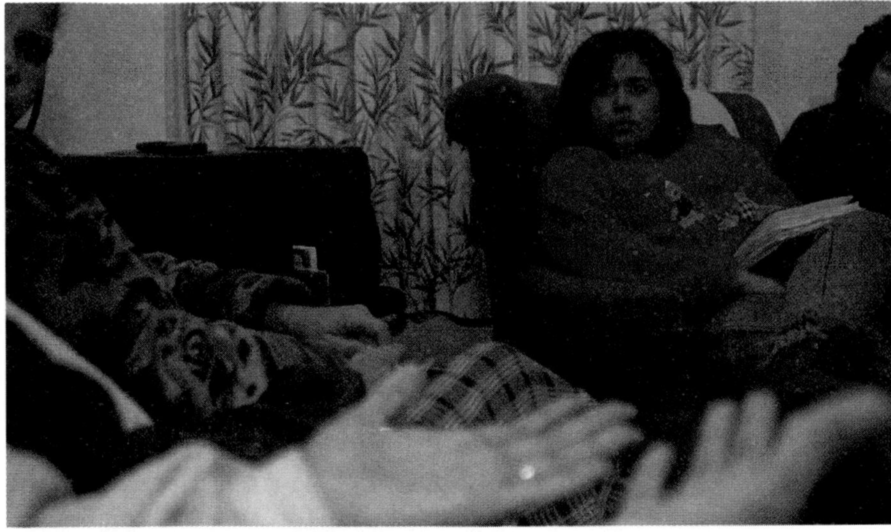

▲ *A rape survivor listens as other women talk about their traumatic experiences in this support group for victims of abuse and rape.*

Many principles of feminist therapy have been applied to therapy with members of ethnic and cultural groups. ***Culturally sensitive therapists*** avoid blaming the victim, recognizing that behaviors defined as abnormal may be coping strategies in other cultures that are necessary for survival. They understand that if therapists ignore racism's impact on people of color, they can interfere with a client's ability to confront important life issues and to develop appropriate coping strategies (Greene, 1986). Culturally sensitive therapists help clients to acknowledge the destructive effects of sexism, racism, and homophobia, and to deal with the

Sensitivity to gender, ethnicity, and other aspects of culture can influence the therapeutic process and improve all forms of therapy. In recent years, feminist and culturally sensitive therapies have emerged that are specifically designed to address the effects of social and structural inequalities on mental health.

◄ *Cuento therapy uses Puerto Rican folktales as behavioral models for these Puerto Rican children with behavioral problems. The adapted stories are supposed to help immigrants adjust to society in the U.S.*

▲ *This family works together to understand the problems in their interactions. Family therapy avoids blaming any member for family difficulties, but rather examines the entire social dynamic in its search for solutions.*

ditions (Shadish et al., 1993). Furthermore, family therapy, in combination with drug therapy, plays an important role in relapse prevention for bipolar depression (Miklowitz, Simoneau, Sachs-Ericsson, Warner, & Suddath, 1996) and schizophrenia (Falloon, Boyd, & McGill, 1985). In fact, evidence suggests that family therapy is more effective than drug therapy alone at preventing relapse for up to eight years after treatment (Tarrier, Barrowclough, Porceddu, & Fitzpatrick, 1994).

How Effective Is Psychotherapy?

Psychotherapy is beneficial, consistently so and in many different ways. . . . Psychotherapy benefits people of all ages as reliably as schooling educates them, medicine cures them, or business turns a profit. . . .

(Smith, Glass, & Miller, 1980, pp. 183–84).

How effective are these various therapies? The answer is not an easy one. Effectiveness may be judged differently depending on who does the judging (Strupp, 1996). Most clients believe that psychotherapy is effective. In a recent *Consumer Reports* survey of its 186,000 subscribers, 4,000 of the 7,000 respondents said they had sought professional help. Most respondents who had received psychotherapy were satisfied with their treatment and believed it improved the quality of their lives (*Consumer Reports*, 1995). Satisfaction did not differ by type of therapy, and adding drugs did not increase effectiveness.

Although client perceptions of therapy effectiveness are important, randomized controlled experiments are needed to assess causal effects. Furthermore, not all therapies are used equally often or are equally effective with all types of disorders. Figure 16-6 shows the percentage of therapists who practice each of the major kinds of therapy. Psychologists have reviewed therapeutic outcome studies, comparing treated clients with untreated or differently treated controls (Smith, Glass, & Miller, 1980; APA, 1995; Lipsey & Wilson, 1993). Figure 16-7 shows, for a particular disorder, the percentages of treated clients who improved relative to controls under each type of therapy. This body of research suggests that psychotherapy has both statistically significant and clinically meaningful effects (Lambert & Bergin, 1994; Lipsey & Wilson, 1993). Overall, a typical person who receives

THINKING CRITICALLY

The *Consumer Reports (CR)* survey has been used to conclude that psychotherapy causes positive behavior change in all clients. What are some of the problems with this conclusion?

First, *CR* readers are a selective sample, made more selective by the fact that not every reader filled out the survey. The experience of educated, cognitively oriented, conscientious individuals (such as the responding *CR* readers) may be very different from, say, less educated, less analytical individuals (for example, readers of supermarket tabloids). Furthermore, people with severe disorders are likely to be underrepresented. Therapy that is effective with a mild disorder might not be effective with a severe disorder. Of even greater concern is the fact that people often misattribute the sources of their feelings and are not very good at identifying the causes of their actions (see Chapter 12). Indeed, if we surveyed the clients of psychic healers we might obtain similar results (Hollon, 1996). Finally, correlation is not causation. This survey design is not an experiment. Only an experimental study can determine whether psychotherapy *causes* behavior change.

psychotherapy is better off than about 80 percent of those who are not treated (Smith, Glass, & Miller, 1980). As David Barlow has observed, "Although there is still much to learn, there now are psychosocial treatments with proved efficacy that, in the hands of skilled mental health professionals, can relieve human suffering and enhance human functioning" (Barlow, 1996).

Psychotherapy can be approached from several different perspectives, and different therapists adopt different treatment paths. This clearly makes the global question about how effective therapy is difficult to answer in a useful way. For example, we wouldn't ask, "Is aspirin an effective treatment?" without specifying treatment for what. Does it help headaches or stomach ulcers? (In fact, it helps headaches, but it makes ulcers bleed.) It also helps to know how much aspirin and what kind of headache we are talking about. Similarly, researchers are focusing today on evaluating specific treatments for specific disorders (Lipsey & Wilson, 1993). Certain approaches are often more effective than others for different symptoms. For example, both Beck's cognitive therapy and interpersonal psychotherapy have been found to be effective in treating and preventing the relapse of depression (Barlow & Lehman, 1996; Jacobson & Hollon, 1996).

Because different approaches have different strengths and weaknesses, in recent years many therapists have used an eclectic approach to treat a client's particular set of symptoms. In eclectic therapy, treatment can follow any one of several different philosophies, depending on the therapist's judgment of what will be most effective for each client. Indeed, today most therapists adopt an eclectic approach (see Figure 16-6). Some research suggests that matching the therapy approach to the particular needs and circumstances of the client increases therapeutic effectiveness (Jacobson et al., 1989). Therapists have also developed a wide variety of techniques to make both adults and children more comfortable, relaxed, and able to express their thoughts and feelings to the therapist. Some of the more common therapeutic techniques involve the use of dolls, art, dance, and pets.

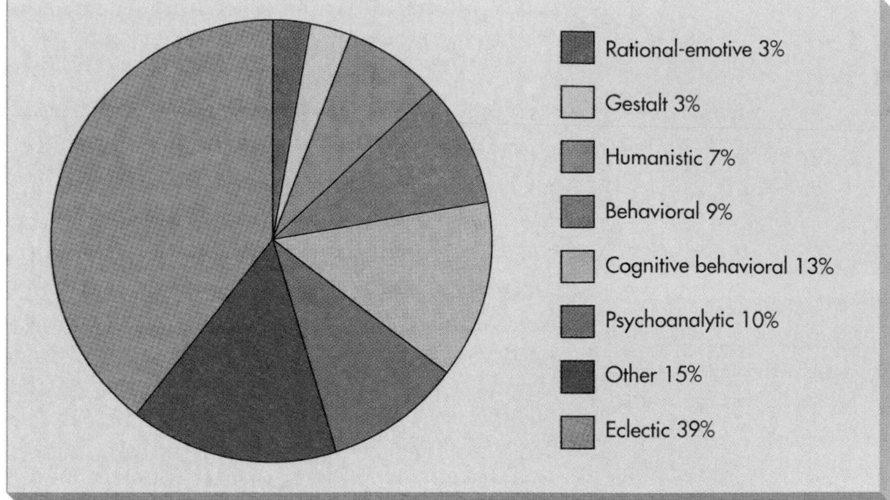

16-6 The Practice of Psychotherapy

Most psychotherapists practice an eclectic type of therapy made up of aspects of different kinds of therapy, depending on what works best for particular problems. Similar percentages of therapists practice primarily behavioral, humanistic, psychoanalytic, and cognitive-behavioral therapies, followed by a smaller number of therapists who practice either rational-emotive or Gestalt therapy. (Source: Werner & Schlesinger, 1991, p. 432)

▼ *Clinical psychologist Dr. Rita Yaroush has had great success in using her "therapist ferret" to establish rapport with patients, especially children, who find ferrets just the "right size" for developing that rapport.*

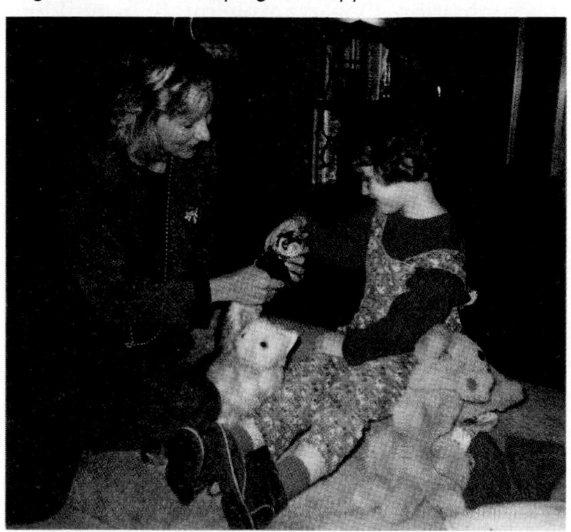

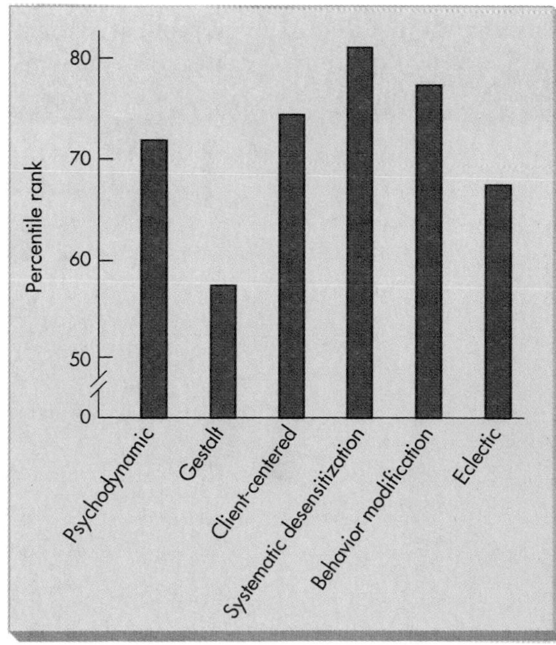

16-7 Effectiveness of Psychotherapy

Outcome studies have indicated that various behavioral, cognitive-behavioral, and psychodynamic treatments lead to statistically significant client improvement compared to improvement in controls, who received no treatment at all. Of course, different therapies have different outcomes depending on the nature of the problem. Here are the results for the treatment of anxiety disorders. (Source: Adapted from Smith, Glass, & Miller, 1980)

Community Mental Health

The community mental health approach to psychopathology stresses prevention and treats the entire social system rather than each individual. It has worked to decentralize the mental health system and to provide more services within the community.

All the treatment methods for psychopathology have one thing in common: they help clients, individually or in groups, to deal with problems after those problems have surfaced and usually after they have caused considerable hardship. But there are other ways to deal with psychopathology. Today, psychologists and other mental health service providers work to *prevent* psychopathology before it appears. Most preventative measures lie within the province of ***community mental health programs***. Community mental health got its impetus in the 1950s and 1960s from a combination of advances in drug therapy and the establishment of federal community health programs.

By the early 1960s, providing traditional one-on-one mental health services for all who needed them was clearly impossible. There were not enough mental health professionals to go around, and many needy people were simply unwilling or unable to pay for services. Mental health professionals were seeing the same problems over and over (for example, abused children, poor school performance, bad marriages, and other family-related problems), and they were facing situations that were so severe that little could be done to alleviate the problems. The community mental health approach grew out of (1) the need for more efficient and comprehensive mental health services, (2) the desirability of preventing mental illness by "treating" a community or whole social system rather than each individual in the community, and (3) the desire to decentralize the institutional system and provide more services within the community. Meeting these concerns required changes in social and public policy to restructure the mental health care system.

Community psychologists work in schools, mental health centers, job settings, police departments, and correctional centers. They treat problems as faulty adaptations to the natural setting rather than as behavioral deficiencies in an individual. A primary objective of community psychology is to prevent problems before they develop. Because approximately 15 percent of children and up to 33 percent of adults have mental health problems, resources for treatment can never meet the need (Sandler & Barrera, 1989). But if we can find effective preventative procedures, the level of future need might be significantly reduced. Community psychologists practice a number of prevention techniques, including early identification of problems, stress reduction programs, environmental changes, support groups, and individual training in skills for handling life's challenges.

▼ *At the Center for the Integration and Recuperation for Alcoholics and Drug Addicts in Mexico, a recovering heroin addict speaks to a large group during a therapy session.*

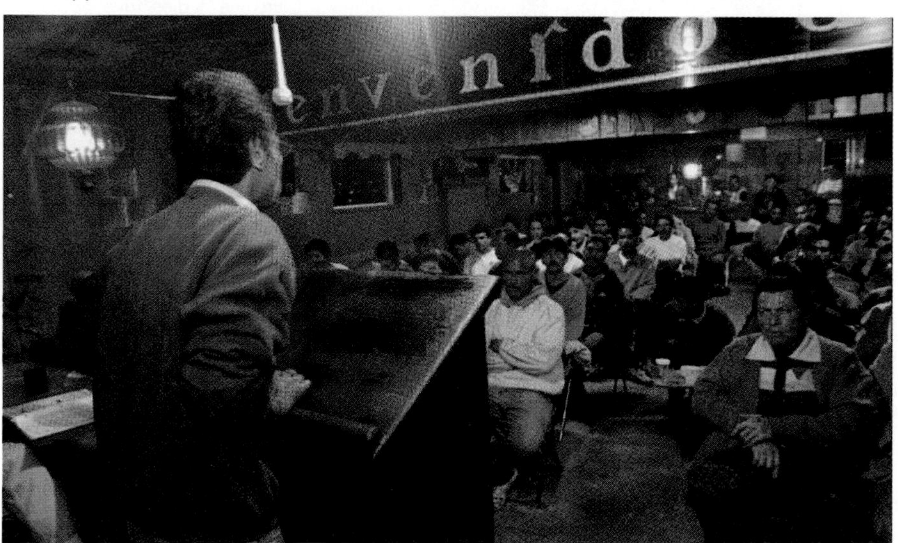

Primary Prevention Services

Primary prevention services seek to prevent the occurrence of mental disorders by finding and eliminating a problem's potential causes. Such services may attempt to reduce factors associated with psychological problems, such as violence, poverty, disease, or prejudice and discrimination. One example might be building a publicly funded recreation facility, which would give juveniles a place to go and something to do besides using drugs.

Although research suggests that changes in society's structure might reduce the frequency of mental disorders and mental suffering, these changes usually require expensive programs that taxpayers are not willing to support (Jones, 1975). There is also much disagreement about what changes are actually needed. Redistribution of power may be required for social change, but those holding power are generally not willing to give it up. Groups may have to seek political solutions, perhaps putting one of their members on the city council or even in the mayor's office to meet their needs.

Secondary Prevention Services

Secondary prevention services aim to prevent or reduce the impact or severity of a problem once it exists. For example, emergency psychological treatment for victims suffering severe losses brought on by natural disasters, such as floods or tornadoes, may relieve some symptoms and bring about a more rapid and adequate adaptation.

Community mental health centers provide a variety of secondary services, including short-term hospitalization, outpatient psychotherapy, twenty-four-hour emergency hotlines, day care for people who need a structured setting during waking hours, night care for people who work but need shelter at night, and consultation to other community agencies on mental health issues. These centers have made it possible for many clients who might otherwise languish in the "back wards" of state mental hospitals to return to a more productive life.

To make mental health services more available to the poor, storefront clinics or outreach centers have been set up in poverty areas. They are often staffed by untrained but interested people from the community or by paraprofessionals who act as problem solvers, sympathetic listeners, and community facilitators. Using nonprofessionals reflects a general principle of community mental health: a concerned citizen who lives and is known in a community may be more effective than an outsider with extensive formal training. Though there are limits to this point of view (some formal training for paraprofessionals is often very important), it does alleviate the shortage of mental health workers while keeping a service right in the community where it is most needed.

One of the most effective treatment approaches in the community mental health movement is ***crisis intervention***. A crisis is an emergency situation that exceeds a person's ability to cope adaptively. Crisis intervention techniques grew out of the work of Eric Lindemann, who treated survivors and family members of the tragic New York Coconut Grove Night Club fire of 1943. Hundreds were trapped, trampled, and burned attempting to escape the fire through inadequate building exits. Since then, crisis intervention procedures have been effectively used to help victims of tornadoes, floods, fires, plane and train crashes, earthquakes, and terrorist attacks.

◀ *Suicide hotline workers take emergency calls at all times of day and night.*

Crisis intervention assumes people can best be helped just after a crisis has occurred, for example, when an intimate relationship has just broken up, or just after a mugging, rape, or other violent crime. Crisis intervention is concerned with symptom relief, managing immediate stress, and developing adaptive strategies for present and future problems. Students in danger of flunking out of school, individuals who have lost their jobs, or people in any of a thousand other crisis situations may obtain help through a small number of sessions (possibly only one) to get them through their crisis (Bloom, 1992). Suicide hotlines are a prominent example of crisis intervention. In many cities across the country, a potentially suicidal person can call a suicide prevention center to speak with a counselor.

Rehabilitative Services

Rehabilitative services aim to reduce long-term effects of existing emotional problems. People recovering from personal or community crises, alcohol detoxification, mild strokes, or other conditions with psychological ramifications will typically need counseling and retraining to get back into family and community life.

Rehabilitative Therapy

In the last twenty years, psychologists have become increasingly involved in treating individuals and groups who have been through a crisis. Crisis victims often need assistance to regain lost skills and to put their lives back together.

Almost any major crisis or severe injury will have psychological consequences. What is unique about this situation, therapeutically, is that the client was normal before the crisis. Crises interrupt people's expected life trajectory and cast them into new, unanticipated, and undesirable directions. The likely consequences are physical pain, medical treatment, and hospitalization. Psychological consequences can include cognitive deficits, depression, feelings of inadequacy, and despair (Trexler, 1987).

Rehabilitation may include job retraining or training in new social skills, as well as a variety of psychological services. Where whole communities are affected, rehabilitation therapy may be most effectively accomplished in groups. When the brain is injured, neuropsychological testing is indicated. Cognitive and behavioral tests can assess the type and extent of lost behavioral capabilities. This knowledge can suggest the most effective therapy. When deficits are largely intellectual, rehabilitation may include speech therapy or cognitive retraining to regain lost or weakened skills.

Regardless of whether surface deficits are perceptual, intellectual, or motor, individuals may also show some damage to their self-image, and they will be anxious or depressed about losing behavioral competencies. When this is the case, rehabilitative psychotherapy is required. Its goal is to help clients to come to grips with life changes brought on by the crisis or injury, to express grieving over these changes in the most productive way possible, and to reconstruct their self-concepts (Brooks, 1990).

Halfway Houses

Halfway houses play an important role in rehabilitating people released from mental hospitals who are not yet fully ready to take their place in home and family. Residents (generally there are about ten) live more or less as a family in these houses. They participate during the day in local community activities, including work. Halfway houses are usually supervised by paraprofessionals, with periodic consultation with mental health professionals. When they function as intended, halfway houses fill an important rehabilitative role. They permit the resident to move out of the more restrictive institutions earlier than would otherwise be possible, and they serve as a safe haven from which the resident can begin to relearn social skills necessary to integrate fully with family and community life.

▼ *Patients with mental disorders celebrate a birthday in a group home, where they can be supervised, yet lead their lives as a "family."*

Reflections and Observations

If you read these last two chapters critically, you now realize that effective psychological treatment for a particular mental disorder requires more than simply making a diagnosis and executing a treatment that "cures" the problem. Providing mental health services is more complex than the traditional medical model of diagnosis-treatment-cure-rehabilitation used for physical disorders. The process of treatment for psychopathology is difficult; it involves biological, psychological, and sociocultural factors, and may require major life adjustments for the client, relatives, and friends.

In the hands of a skilled therapist, psychotherapy can be highly effective and is one of the most useful applications of psychological knowledge developed to date. Psychotherapy is not uniformly successful, however. It depends on the therapist's personality, skill, and experience. Moreover, some types of psychopathology are resistant to known treatments, while others respond well to one method but might be aggravated by another. The bottom line is that all therapies, in the hands of a qualified therapist, are effective with some problems, but no therapy is effective with all problems (Shapiro, 1985). Successful treatment outcome depends on many factors, one of which is finding the therapist and therapy that is right for the particular individual and problem. Fortunately, there are resources to aid in the search.

Objectives Revisited

Treatments for psychopathology are many and varied, and none is foolproof. Different perspectives on psychopathology dictate different approaches. Today, psychologists have a variety of treatments at their disposal to help clients, individually or in groups, to deal with problems. In addition, psychologists strive to prevent problems by working in communities to change the conditions that promote psychopathology.

Objective 1. Describe treatment for psychopathology, and explain differences among mental health professionals qualified to provide such treatment.

Treatment includes a wide range of biological and psychodynamic techniques designed to help a person behave in socially appropriate ways, to help the person function effectively and be able to adapt to new situations, and to promote personal growth. Mental health professionals qualified to provide treatment include psychologists, psychiatrists, psychiatric social workers, and psychiatric nurses. They have had specialized training and are typically licensed or certified.

Objective 2. Describe the basic assumptions and techniques of biomedical, psychoanalytic, behavioral and cognitive-behavioral, and humanistic therapies, and contrast their philosophies and effectiveness.

Medical therapies assume mental disorders have biological origins and treat them in much the same way as physical illnesses. Modern biomedical treatment includes *drug therapy, electroconvulsive therapy*, and *hospitalization*.

Psychodynamic therapies assume that emotional problems stem from conflicts between or among conscious and unconscious forces. Treatment aims mainly at helping the client achieve insight into and an understanding of these conflicts, which, in turn, help resolve the conflicts. The therapist actively interprets the client's behaviors, and uses *free association, dream interpretation*, and *transference* to overcome resistance and to bring conflicts into consciousness.

Behavioral and *cognitive-behavioral* therapies assume abnormal behavior is learned. The therapist uses well-established principles of learning to change behavior. Behavior therapy primarily relies on principles derived from classical and operant conditioning, as well as observation and imitation techniques derived from the study of observational learning. Common behavior therapy techniques include *systematic desensitization, positive reinforcement and shaping*, and *punishment and aversion therapy.* Three of the more common forms of cognitive-behavioral therapy include *Beck's cognitive therapy, rational-emotive therapy*, and *stress-inoculation training*.

Humanistic therapies, such as *client-centered* and *Gestalt therapy*, assume behavior is the outgrowth of one's view of oneself and of others, and one's efforts at self-fulfillment. The goal in therapy is to help the client become aware of feelings and experiences that stifle personal growth (self-actualization). Client-centered therapists try to (1) communicate an understanding of client feelings (*empathic understanding*), (2) care about and accept clients nonjudgmentally (*unconditional positive regard*), and (3) express their true views about their own feelings toward the client (*congruence*). In *Gestalt therapy*, the goal is for clients to become increasingly more aware of their own social behavior, to understand how their behavior affects others, and to accept responsibility for their behavior and its effects. Gestalt therapists use active techniques to let clients "get in touch with" and express their feelings more freely. All forms of psychotherapy appear to be effective, with some forms more effective than others with particular problems.

Objective 3. Explain how therapist values can influence the therapeutic processes, and discuss the central issues involved in feminist and other culturally sensitive therapies.

Therapists should be sensitive to how their own values can influence the goals and tech-

KEY TERMS

psychotherapy

psychosurgery

anti-anxiety drugs

sedatives

tranquilizers

antidepressants

antipsychotics

phenothiazines

electroconvulsive therapy

psychoanalysis

free association

transference

ego analysis

behavior modification

countercondition

systematic desensitization

aversion therapy

modeling

social skills training

rational-emotive therapy

stress-inoculation therapy

humanistic therapy

client-centered therapy

Gestalt therapy

group therapy

family therapy

feminist therapy

culturally sensitive therapy

community mental health

preventative services

rehabilitative therapy

halfway house

niques of therapy, especially when treating a client with different values. Today's therapists aspire to be nonsexist, nonracist, and culturally sensitive, as bias in psychotherapy can occur in a variety of ways and undermine the effectiveness of treatment for both women and men.

Feminist and *culturally sensitive* therapies have been developed to address the effects of social and structural inequalities on mental health. Such therapies do not assume that their clients' anger, feelings of powerlessness and worthlessness, or other symptoms are necessarily "pathological," but instead consider the possibility that they are survival strategies developed to deal with restrictive, discriminatory, or oppressive environments. Feminist and culturally sensitive therapists are especially attentive to the roles that cultural contexts play in the expression of client problems.

Objective 4. Describe group therapy, and explain how it differs from individual therapy.

Most types of therapy can be carried out individually or in family or group formats. Group therapy is efficient and offers its members the opportunity to understand others, receive feedback, share solutions, be a therapist for others, and practice new behaviors.

Behavior therapy groups are often used to improve social skills and provide assertiveness training. Encounter groups, growing out of Gestalt and other humanistic therapies, focus on here-and-now feelings, negative and positive feedback, and removal of barriers to open communication. *Family therapy groups* are used to help families identify and solve their problems, improve communication among family members, encourage individual autonomy, establish a basis for mutual empathy, foster alternative ways of making family decisions, and facilitate conflict resolution.

Objective 5. Explain the community mental health perspective and distinguish among primary, secondary, and rehabilitative mental health services.

Psychopathology can also be approached from a community mental health perspective, which is concerned with preventing disorder as early as possible, providing more efficient delivery of mental health services, particularly to the poor, and treating a community or social system rather than only one individual at a time. Community psychologists attempt to prevent problems and to develop competencies for dealing with problems when they do occur.

Primary prevention concentrates on eliminating the causes of emotional problems, such as poverty or prejudice. *Secondary prevention* focuses on reducing effects of emotional problems that already exist, as in crisis interventions after a natural disaster or violent crime. *Rehabilitation* deals with the aftereffects of having emotional problems brought on by psychological and physical causes, and may involve such services as rehabilitation therapy, speech therapy, cognitive retraining, and job training and placement.

APPENDIX

Statistical Analysis

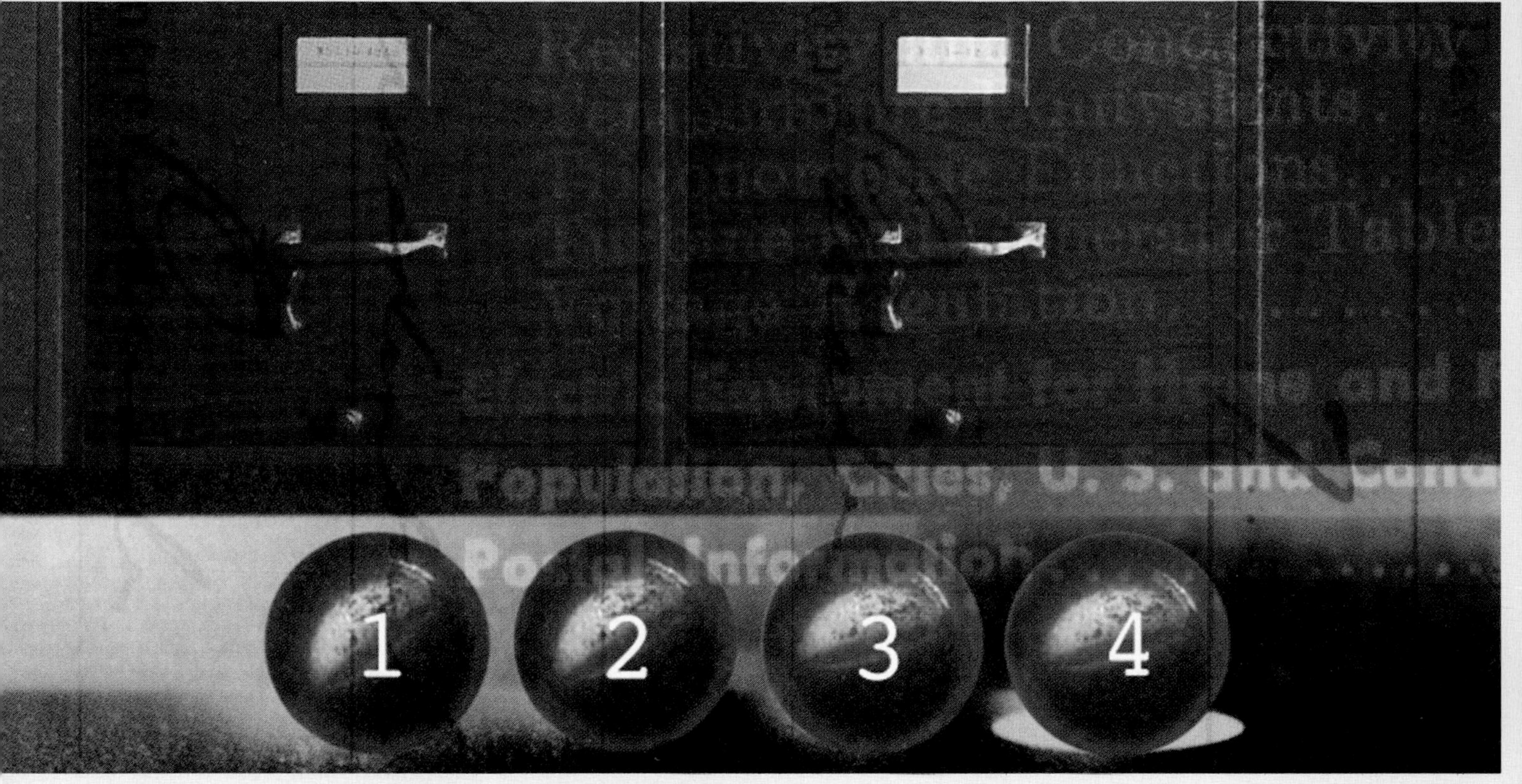

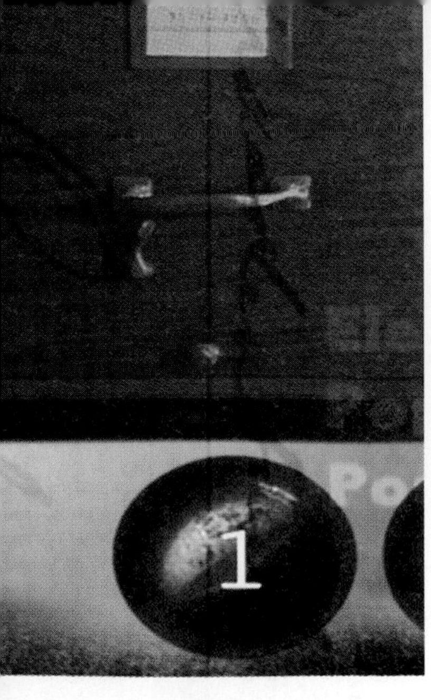

Psychology is the science of behavior and mental processes. Advances in psychology are made primarily by the collection of data, that is, gathering new evidence about behavior. Throughout this book, but especially in Chapter 2, we have referred to various methods and procedures psychologists use to collect data. In this Appendix, we turn to questions of data analysis. How do we make sense of the data collected in order to understand what they tell us about behavior?

The single most commonly used tool for data analysis in psychology is statistics. All areas of psychology rely on one or both of the two basic types of statistics: (1) *descriptive statistics*, which are used to summarize the results of research, and (2) *inferential statistics*, which are used to arrive at general conclusions from these results. What follows is not intended to be a complete course in statistics. Rather it is a simplified overview of selected statistical methods. But you should find it sufficient to help you understand some of the data analyses discussed in the foregoing chapters and in some of your supplemental reading.

Descriptive Statistics

Measures of Central Tendency

Suppose a teacher gives an IQ test to 10 students. How can the test results best be described? One way would be to give a code name to each student and list the IQ scores—10 code names and 10 scores. That would probably work nicely in a small class. But it would certainly be inefficient and confusing for a class of 500. Moreover, a list of numbers does not indicate much of anything in general about the group as a whole. It would be helpful, for example, to know the typical or most representative score. In other words, we want to find the ***central tendency*** of the group of scores. We often call this number the average score. We shall describe three commonly used measures of central tendency.

The Arithmetic Mean

The arithmetic *mean* is the number arrived at when you add up all the scores and divide by the number of scores. In the preceding example, you would add up the 10 IQ scores and divide by 10. We have made up a set of 10 scores and computed the arithmetic mean in Table A-1, which also introduces some elementary statistical symbols. A score for an individual subject is called X. An X could be an IQ score, an anxiety score, a measure of height, weight, or anything else of interest. In Table A-1, X is an IQ score, and so we add up the 10 IQ scores or 10 Xs. The capital Greek letter sigma (Σ) is a shorthand symbol for "add up these scores," and therefore ΣX means add up the X scores. Table A-1 also gives each student's height in inches. To keep height distinct from IQ scores, we signify height by Y. Often a research problem requires two scores for each subject, as in this case, and so we use X and Y to keep them separate. So ΣY tells us to add up the heights, which is also done in Table A-1.

The final step in computing the arithmetic mean is to divide by the number of scores added (symbolized by N). There are 10 IQ scores, and so we divide ΣX by 10 to get the mean IQ score: 108.5. Likewise, we divide ΣY by 10 and get the mean height: 66.8 inches. The shorthand way of indicating that a particular number is a mean and not a single score is to put a bar over the letter. Thus the arithmetic mean of the X scores is symbolized as $\overline{X}$ (read "X bar"), and the mean of the Y scores is $\overline{Y}$ (read "Y bar").

Table A-1 Computation of the Mean IQ and Height of a Class of 10 Students

Student's Name	X (IQ)	Y (Height in Inches)
Deion	125	65
Allen	120	60
Yi	105	66
Mahmoud	100	68
Betsy	130	72
Andrew	95	64
Barbara	90	62
Jann	110	74
Akira	85	70
Dolores	125	67
	$\Sigma X = 1085$ $N = 10$	$\Sigma Y = 668$ $N = 10$

The mean of the X scores is

$$\overline{X} = \frac{\Sigma X}{N}$$

or

$$\overline{X} = \frac{1085}{10} = 108.5$$

Likewise, the mean of the Y scores is

$$\overline{Y} = \frac{\Sigma Y}{N}$$

or

$$\overline{Y} = \frac{668}{10} = 66.8$$

Thus we arrive at a shorthand formula for finding the arithmetic mean of a set of X scores:

$$\overline{X} = \frac{\Sigma X}{N}$$

And correspondingly, the arithmetic mean of a set of Y scores is calculated by the formula:

$$\overline{Y} = \frac{\Sigma Y}{N}$$

Now if the students ask the teacher how the class as a whole performed on the IQ test, the teacher could simply report the value of $\overline{X}$; and if they ask how tall the students are on the average, he or she could report $\overline{Y}$. This is obviously much simpler than listing all the X and Y scores and gives a better idea of the students' general level of ability and generally how tall they are.

The Median

The arithmetic mean of scores is neither the only nor necessarily the best way to compute the most representative score of a group. In some cases, you would want to know the middlemost score, which generally is not the mean. Suppose there is an odd number of scores. Then there will be one score exactly in the middle; half of the remaining scores will lie above this middle score and half will lie below. Thus, if a class had 11 students and their scores were arranged from highest to lowest, the score of the sixth student would be in the middle. This middlemost score is called the *median*. There would be 5 scores higher than the median and 5 scores lower. If there were 27 scores, the fourteenth score in order would be the median. Which score would be at the median if there were 31 scores in the group?

With an even number of scores, there is no single middle score. Instead, 2 scores fall in the middle: one above, the other below a midpoint. In a set of 10 scores arranged from highest to lowest, the fifth score from the bottom is not the median—there are 5 scores above it, but only 4 below it. Likewise, the sixth score is not the median, because there are 4 higher but 5 lower scores. So we compromise and take the halfway point between the fifth and sixth scores as the median. The median of 28 scores would be the mean of the fourteenth and fifteenth scores. Table A-2 shows the 10 IQ scores from Table A-1, but this time we have arranged them in order

Table A-2 Computation of the Median IQ Score of a Class of 10 Students

Name	X	
Betsy	130	
Deion	125	
Dolores	125	
Allen	120	
Juan	110	← The middle is in here, somewhere
Yi	105	between 105 and 110
Mahmoud	100	
Andrew	95	
Barbara	90	
Akira	85	

The median is the mean of the 2 scores nearest the middle point, in this case, 105 and 110. We take the mean of 105 and 110:

$$\frac{105 + 110}{2} = 107.5$$

This is the median. Note that it would not be changed if we altered Betsy's score from 130 to, say, 160. But the mean would change. What would the mean be in this case?

of magnitude. The middle point is somewhere between the fifth and sixth scores, somewhere between 105 and 110. So we take the mean of these 2 scores and use this as the median. Here it is 107.5.

The mean and the median are typically close in value, but not necessarily identical. They will be the same only when the distribution of scores is ***symmetrical***, or balanced around the mean. Now consider the set of "salary scores" in Table A-3. Here we note that most of the 10 people working for the Zappo Cereal Company are not making a lot of money, though one employee, obviously the president, is making a bundle. This distribution of scores or values is asymmetrical and unbalanced. Technically, we call it a ***skewed*** distribution. The distribution in Table A-3 is skewed to the high end (positively skewed). The mean weekly salary for Zappo employees is $1,395, which might lead you to believe that the company pays very well. But the median is only $425, which would make you think a little differently about Zappo. The median will not be affected if the president gives himself or herself a big raise, but the mean will go up. You can see that, in this case, the median is more representative of the group as a whole than the mean is, primarily because it is not affected by extreme scores such as the president's salary.

Table A-3 Comparison of the Mean and Median Weekly Salaries of Zappo Cereal Company Employees

Employee Number	Weekly Salary X (in Dollars)	
1	10,000	
2	600	
3	550	
4	500	
5	450	← midpoint
6	400	
7	375	
8	375	
9	350	
10	350	
	$\Sigma X = 13{,}950$	
	$N = 10$	

We can see from the midpoint that the median salary is the mean of 400 and 450, which is $425. Yet the mean salary is

$$\bar{X} = \frac{X}{N} = \frac{13{,}950}{10} = \$1{,}395$$

Which value, the mean or the median, do you think is more representative of Zappo's wages?

The Mode

The third measure of central tendency is called the *mode*. The mode is a quickly computed, crude measure defined as the most frequently occurring score. In a small set of scores, as in tables A-1, A-2, and A-3, there is the possibility that no score will occur more than once. In such cases, there is no mode. But suppose a psychologist gives an anxiety test to a group of 200 patients. When a large number of cases are used, the likelihood of several people obtaining the same score is high. It is convenient, in these cases, to set up a ***frequency distribution*** showing the various possible scores on the test and, for each possible score, how many people (f or frequency) actually got that score (see Table A-4). Looking down the frequency column in Table A-4, we see that 27 people got a score of 15 and that 27 is the highest f value in the distribution. This means that 15 is the mode or the ***modal score***, because it is the score that was made most frequently. Note that the sum of all the frequencies in the f column is equal to N, the number of people taking the test, in this case 200.

Frequency distributions can also be presented graphically. Figure A-1 shows a frequency distribution based on the data in Table A-4. The horizontal axis of the graph, called the x-axis or, more technically, the ***abscissa***, gives the value of X, the anxiety score, and the vertical axis, called the y-axis or the ***ordinate***, gives the corresponding frequency of each score. The frequency distribution is a very important tool in statistics. More advanced statistical techniques are heavily based on the frequency distribution principle, so make sure that you understand what it is for future reference.

Measures of Variability

People vary. No two people are exactly alike, not even identical twins. There are important individual differences among people, in their

Table A-4 A Frequency Table of the Anxiety Scores of 200 Patients

Score (X)		f or Frequency
20		10
19		10
18		12
17		15
16		20
15	←— Mode —→	27
14		15
13		21
12		22
11		12
10		10
9		8
8		7
7		5
6		3
5		0
4		2
3		1
2		0
1		0
		$\Sigma f = 200 = N$

The mode, the score that occurs most frequently (indicated by the highest f value), is equal to 15.

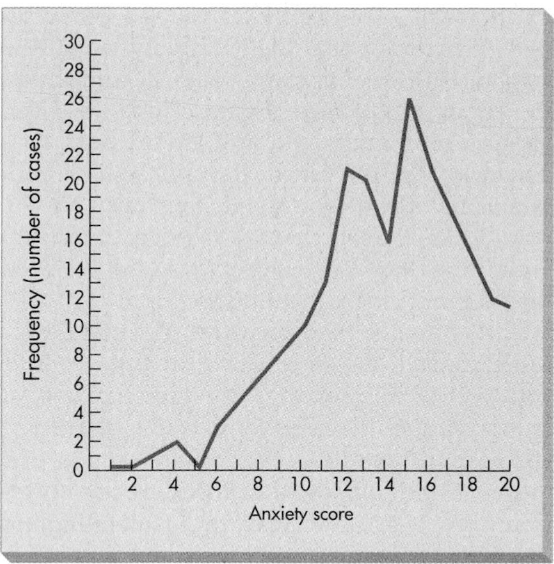

A-1 A Frequency Distribution Based on the Data in Table A-4

abilities and in the ways they behave. Of course, how much variation there is among people will depend on what we are measuring. People may vary a lot in regard to anxiety or IQ scores. But they will vary very little in regard to the number of fingers they have. For research, we need a convenient and accurate way of indexing the degree of variability in a set of scores. Let's take a look at what is available.

The quickest but least informative measure of the variability in a set of scores is called the *range*. The range is defined as the highest score in the set minus the lowest score. In Table A-4, we see that the patients' anxiety scores range from a low of 3 to a high of 20, and so the range would be $20 - 3 = 17$. If the low score had been 7 and the high score 12, then the range would have been 5, much narrower than in the first example. A narrower range means less variability among the scores. The main reason for using the range as a measure of variability is that it is easy to compute. But because it is based on only two scores (the highest and the lowest, and therefore the two most unusual scores), it says very little about the distribution.

Suppose we have a set of 10 scores with an arithmetic mean of 20. Two such sets are shown in Table A-5. The scores labeled Set A consist of only 5 different numbers, all of which are close

Table A-5 Two Sets of Scores That Have the Same Mean but Differ in Variability

Set A	Set B
22	36
22	32
21	28
21	24
20	20
20	20
19	16
19	12
18	8
18	4
$\Sigma X = 200$	$\Sigma X = 200$
$N = 10$	$N = 10$
$\bar{X} = \frac{200}{10} = 20$	$\bar{X} = \frac{200}{10} = 20$
Range $= 22 - 18 = 4$	Range $= 36 - 4 = 32$

to the mean of 20 (18, 19, 20, 21, and 22). Intuitively, it appears that the variability in Set A is low. In Set B we have the same mean, 20, but the variability is much larger. There are 9 different scores, and some of them are at quite a distance from the mean. If we described both sets using only a central tendency measure, we would miss the fact that the two sets of data are quite different. To be more complete, we need to add a measure of variability.

A commonly used measure of variability is called the *standard deviation*, which reflects more accurately than the range the degree of spread or fluctuation of scores around the mean. The standard deviation is the square root of the mean of the squared distances of the scores from the mean. Let's analyze this definition in small steps. First, subtract the mean from each raw score, X, as in Table A-6. For example, in Set A the mean (20) is subtracted from each of the scores (X) to yield a list of difference scores (symbolized by the lowercase x). You can see that these new scores are merely measures of each score's distance from the mean. Now we could just calculate a new mean of these distance scores as a measure of variability. But a glance at Table A-6 will demonstrate that if you add up the distance scores to get a mean distance score, you will always get a sum of zero. The scores that are above the mean (positive distance scores) cancel out the scores below the mean (negative distance score), meaning that the sum of the distance scores will always be zero. So, instead of averaging, we square each x score, which eliminates the negative numbers. Now we have a new concept, the squared distance score, x^2. The x^2 scores are also shown in Table A-6. We can add up these scores and calculate their mean:

$$\Sigma x^2/N$$

This gives us the mean squared distance from the mean of the raw scores.

The mean squared distance from the mean has a special name, the *variance*, and a special symbol, the lowercase Greek letter sigma,

Table A-6 Computation of the Variance and Standard Deviation for Two Sets of Scores

Set A (Ages of 10 People at a College Dance)			Set B (Ages of 10 People at the Park)		
X	$x = X - \bar{X}$	x^2	X	$x = X - \bar{X}$	x^2
22	2	4	36	16	256
22	2	4	32	12	144
21	1	1	28	8	64
21	1	1	24	4	16
20	0	0	20	0	0
20	0	0	20	0	0
19	−1	1	16	−4	16
19	−1	1	12	−8	64
18	−2	4	8	−12	144
18	−2	4	4	−16	256
	$\Sigma x = 0$	$\Sigma x^2 = 20$		$\Sigma X = 0$	$\Sigma x^2 = 960$

Set A:

$$\sigma^2 = \text{variance} = \frac{\Sigma x^2}{N} = \frac{20}{10} = 2.00$$

$$\sigma = \text{standard deviation} = \sqrt{\sigma^2} = \sqrt{2.00} = 1.414$$

$$\text{or } \sigma = \sqrt{\frac{\Sigma x^2}{N}} = \sqrt{\frac{20}{10}} = 1.414$$

Set B:

$$\sigma^2 = \text{variance} = \frac{\Sigma x^2}{N} = \frac{960}{10} = 96.0$$

$$\sigma = \text{standard deviation} = \sqrt{\sigma^2} = \sqrt{96} = 9.798$$

$$\text{or } \sigma = \sqrt{\frac{\Sigma x^2}{N}} = \sqrt{\frac{960}{10}} = 9.798$$

$\overline{m} = 20$ for both graphs

squared (σ^2). The square, of course, serves to remind us that it is the mean *squared* distance score. The variance itself is an excellent index of variability, as you can see by comparing this value for the Set A and Set B scores: σ^2 is much higher for B (96.0) than for A (2.0). This is as it should be, because the Set B scores vary more (from 4 to 36) than the Set A scores do (from 18 to 22). But most statisticians recommend taking the square root of the variance. We squared the distance scores before we added them up, and so now we take the square root of the variance to return to the original scale of measurement. The square root of the variance is the *standard* deviation (symbolized as σ). The larger the value of the standard deviation is, the greater the variability in the corresponding set of scores will be.

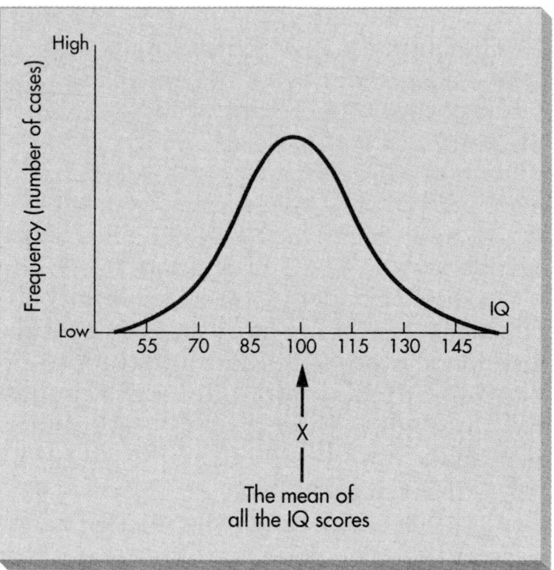

A-2 The Normal Distribution of IQ Scores

The Normal Frequency Distribution

Scores on any test are spread over a range, but tend to pile up in the middle. Scores can be spread out, or be distributed, in a variety of ways. The distribution of scores shown in Figure A-2 is called the ***normal distribution***. We single out the normal distribution because it has a variety of important characteristics for psychologists. Something that you will immediately observe is that normal distributions are symmetrical. If you fold the distribution in Figure A-2 in half at the mean, the two halves will overlap perfectly. Moreover, it is bell shaped. Scores near the mean are most common, and score frequency drops off smoothly as we move to the extremes. The normal distribution is the most important distribution in statistics for two reasons. First, many variables in psychology are normally distributed in human and animal populations. A good example is IQ. IQs have a mean of 100 and a standard deviation that depends on the test used. For a given test, the standard deviation might be 15. If we drew a graph representing IQ in, say, the population of the United States, it would have a normal bell shape, like the one in Figure A-2. The second reason for the importance of the normal distribution is that the most powerful statistical tests, which we will discuss later under inferential statistics, are based on the assumption that the scores we analyze are normally distributed.

If we know that some psychological variable is normally distributed, then we can make some further deductions. For example, the standard deviation can be used to divide the score distribution into sections, each containing a known percentage of cases. Figure A-3 shows how a normal distribution of IQs can be divided up. Note that 34 percent of IQs lie between the mean and one standard deviation above the mean, 115. That is, 34 percent of people tested have IQs between 100 and 115. Remember, the standard deviation is basically a distance measure; the distance from 115 to 100 IQ points is one standard deviation unit. Two standard deviation units above the mean would take us to an IQ

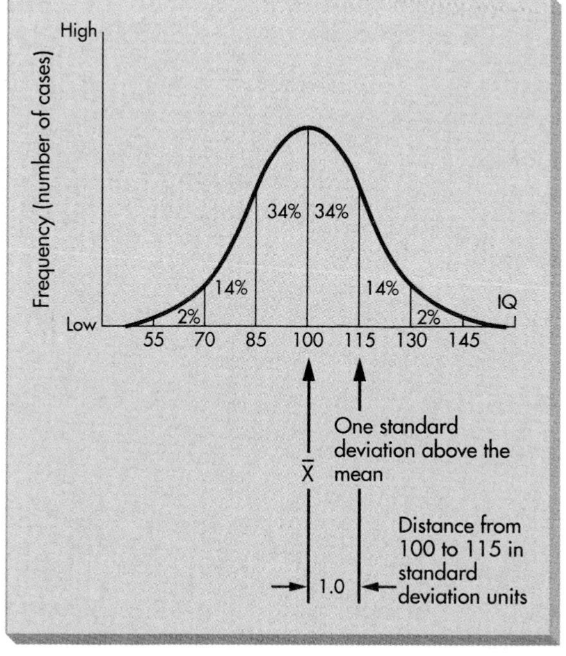

A-3 The Normal Distribution Divided into Standard Deviation Units

score of 130, and three units to 145. The normal distribution of IQs is, of course, symmetrical, so there are distances to be measured below as well as above the mean. One standard deviation unit below the mean would be an IQ of 85. Two units of standard deviation would take us to 70, and 3 units to 55. A range from 3 standard deviation units below the mean to 3 units above the mean (from an IQ of 55 to an IQ of 145) covers just about all the scores in a normal distribution. A very small percentage of people have IQs above 145 or below 55. So, for all intents and purposes, the range of scores in a normal distribution covers −3 to +3 standard deviations.

It is convenient to convert IQ scores into standard deviation units, technically called ***z-scores***. A major advantage of z-scores is that they can be used as a common yardstick for all tests of normally distributed variables, allowing you to compare scores made on different tests. Suppose that you receive a score of 80 on an English test, which has a mean of 70 and a σ of 10, and you get a score of 50 on your psychology test, which has a mean of 40 and a σ of 10. Assume that both tests yield normally distributed scores. On which test did you do better? These tests are not immediately comparable. But if you change your score on each test to a z-score, you can immediately see that you did equally well on both tests. The formula for z-scores is:

$$Z = \frac{(X - \overline{X})}{\sigma}$$

Figure A-4 shows once again the normal distribution of IQ scores, this time displayed with two horizontal axes. One lays out the IQ scores as before, while the other shows the corresponding z-scores. In this display, you can see directly that an IQ score of 115 is one standard deviation above the mean. The z-score corresponding to 115 is +1.0. If Melanie tells you that her z-score for IQ is +2.0, you immediately know that her IQ is 130. If George tells you that his z-score for IQ is +4.0, you immediately know that he is either the smartest person who ever lived or a liar. Note that the mean of the z-scores is always equal to 0.

A-4 The Normal Distribution and z-Scores

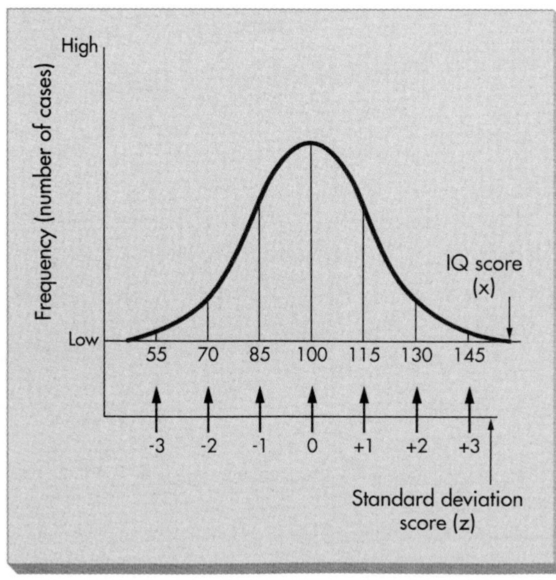

Suppose we asked you to figure out what percentage of people have IQs between 85 and 115, using Figure A-4. This is the same as asking you how many people have z-scores between −1.0 and +1.0. The answer, in case you didn't see it immediately, is 68 percent. Thirty-four percent of cases fall between 85 and 100 and another 34 percent between 100 and 115.

It is important to remember that these percentages and the z-score procedure apply to *any* normal distribution, not just the IQ distribution. The variable that is measured, the mean, and the standard deviation of that variable will differ from distribution to distribution, but if the distribution in question is normal, then the z-scores and the percentages will correspond as they do in the IQ example.

Suppose, for example, that we told you that the waist size of American men is normally distributed with a mean of 34 inches and a standard deviation of 4. You might set up a distribution such as that shown in Figure A-5. Waist sizes run from a low of 22 inches (z-score of −3; 22 inches is 3 standard deviations below the mean) up to a high of 46 inches (z-score of +3; 3 units above the mean). Now you can fill in the percentages and answer the following questions:

1. What percentage of men have waist sizes less than 30 inches?
2. What percentage of men have waist sizes above 38 inches?
3. If Joe's waist size is 47, is he unusual?
4. If we randomly selected one man, what is the probability (how likely is it) that his waist size is greater than 38?

Question 4 introduces the concept of *probability*. Probability refers to the proportion of cases that fit a particular description. In general, the probability of A is the likelihood that an object randomly selected from a group of objects will be an A-type object. The probability of A being selected is equal to the number of A objects available divided by the total number of possible objects. The number of A objects divided by the total number of possible objects is, of course, the proportion of objects available that are A-type.

Now suppose that A is someone with a waist size equal to or greater than 38 inches. To find the probability of selecting at random an A-type man from the population, we have to know what proportion of men are A-type. Figure A-5 tells us that 14 percent of men have waist sizes between 38 and 42 inches and that an additional 2 percent are greater than 42. We add 14 and 2 to find that 16 percent of men are A-type. In terms of proportions, this is .16 (we move the decimal point two places to the left to convert a percentage into a proportion). Thus the probability of selecting a man with a waist size of 38 or above is .16. In other words, 16 out of every 100 selections should yield a man who fits this description (in other words, an A-type man).

Suppose that scores on a particular anxiety scale are normally distributed in the American population with a mean of 50 and a standard deviation of 10. Armed with this information, you should be able to calculate the probability of selecting at random a person who has an anxiety score of 40 or less. Can you do it?

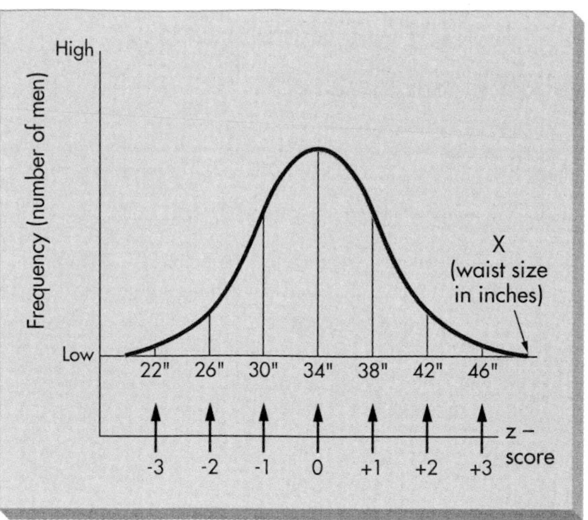

A-5 The Normal Distribution of Waist Size in American Men (Hypothetical)

Correlation

The final descriptive statistic to be discussed is the *correlation coefficient*, which was first introduced conceptually in Chapter 2 and was used frequently in other chapters. The correlation coefficient does not describe a single set of scores, as the mean or standard deviation does. Instead, it describes the degree of relationship between two sets of scores. It is basically a measure of the degree to which the two sets of scores vary together, or ***covary***. Scores can vary together in one of two ways: (1) a *positive covariation*, in which high scores in one set tend to go with high scores in the other set (and low scores go with low scores), or (2) *negative covariation*, in which high scores in one set tend to go with low scores in the other set (and low scores go with high scores). When there is a positive covariation, we say that the two sets are *positively* or *directly correlated*, and when there is a negative covariation, we say they are *negatively, indirectly*, or *inversely correlated*. A common example of positive correlation is the relationship between height and weight: the taller a person is, the more he or she will tend to weigh. Note that we used the phrase "tend to." Correlations are almost never perfect—not all tall people are heavy, and not all short people are lightweights. A common example of negative correlation might be the relationship between the amount of alcohol a person has drunk and his or her ability to drive an automobile. The more alcohol consumed, the lower the ability to drive.

There is another possibility, namely, that there is *no* correlation between two sets of scores, or a ***zero correlation***. Thus, for example, we probably would expect a zero correlation between height and the ability to learn algebra, at least for people of a certain age. So two variables (two sets of scores on different measures) can be positively or negatively correlated, or not correlated at all. And the degree of correlation can be great or little. What we need is a statistic that conveniently measures the degree and the direction (positive or negative) of the correlation between two variables, and this is what the correlation coefficient does.

Table A-7 (on page A-10) shows the scores of 10 people on two tests. Each person took both a test of anxiety and a test of happiness. The possible scores on each test ranged from 1 to 10. A score of 1 means low anxiety and 10 very high anxiety on the anxiety test. For the happiness test, 1 means a low degree of happiness, and 10 means a high degree of happiness. Intuitively we would expect a negative correlation between the two variables of anxiety and happiness; the happier you are, the less anxious you should be, and vice versa.

For convenience we arranged the anxiety scores in order in Table A-7. This causes the hap-

Table A-7 The Correlation between Anxiety and Happiness

Name	Anxiety (X)	Happiness (Y)
Rita	1	10
Manuel	2	9
Giovanna	3	8
Jose	4	7
Insook	5	6
Sharon	6	5
Rasheed	7	4
Phil	8	3
Marsha	9	2
Selena	10	1

Here we have arranged the anxiety scores in order, and we see that this results in the happiness scores being arranged in *perfect reverse order*. This is a perfect negative correlation. The correlation coefficient would be −1.0.

piness scores to fall in *perfect reverse order*. In other words, it is obvious in this table that there is a perfect negative correlation between anxiety and happiness. This is best displayed by making a ***scatter plot*** of the data, which we have done in Figure A-6. Here the horizontal axis is the anxiety score and the vertical axis is the happiness score. Each person is represented by a point on the graph that locates him or her on the two tests. For example, Jose had an anxiety score of 4 and a happiness score of 7. So we go over (to the right) to 4 on the anxiety scale and then up to 7 on the happiness scale, and we place a dot at that point to represent Jose on the graph. All 10 people are represented in that way on the graph. You can see that the 10 points fall on a straight line, which means that the correlation is perfect. You can also see that the line slopes down to the right, and this means that the correlation is negative in direction—as you go up the anxiety scale, the happiness scores go down.

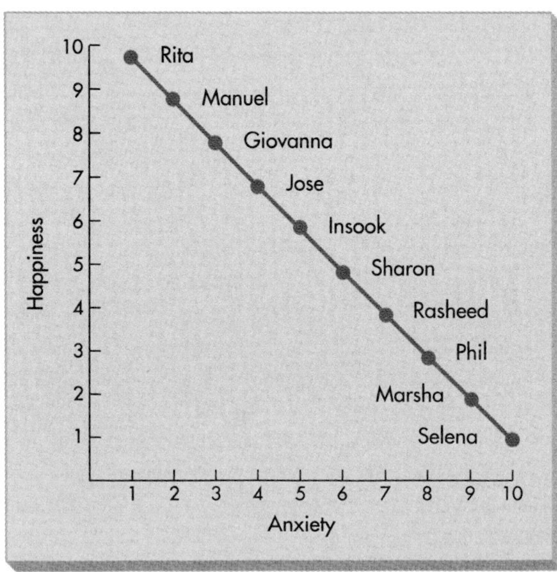

A-6 "Scatter Plot" of the Data from Table A-7, Relating Anxiety to Happiness

As we have said, however, correlations are almost never perfect, which means that the points are likely to be scattered all over the graph, hence the term scatter plot. The closer the points are to lying on a straight line, the higher the degree of correlation is. The usual procedure is to make a scatter plot and then try to draw a straight line that best fits the points in the plot. If all the points are close to or on this ***line of best fit***, then the correlation will be high. But if the points are widely scattered and not close to any line you could draw, then the correlation will be zero or close to it. Finally, if the line of best fit slopes downward to the right, then the correlation will be negative, as in Figure A-6. If the line slopes upward to the right, the correlation will be positive. Figure A-7 shows three scatter plots. In panel A, the two variables in question are negatively correlated: all the points are close to the straight line, which slopes downward to the right. In panel B, there is a positive correlation; all the points again are close to the line, but this time the line slopes upward to the right. In panel C, there is no correlation; the points are scattered all over, and there is no line that fits them very well.

The ***Pearson product moment correlation coefficient*** (symbolized as r_{XY}) is the most often used of several measures of correlation between two variables. It can have any numerical value from −1.0 through 0.0 up to +1.0. A perfect negative product moment correlation, as in Table A-7, is −1.0, and a perfect positive or direct correlation is +1.0. Correlations close to zero mean there is little or no relationship between the two variables, X and Y. The value of the correlation between 0.0 and 1 (ignoring the + or − sign) represents the degree of relationship. The sign of the correlation (positive or negative) does not tell you the degree of the correlation, only the direction. Thus a negative correlation of −.77 is just as strong as a positive correlation of +.77; the only difference is the direction. Table A-8 shows the steps for calculating the Pear-

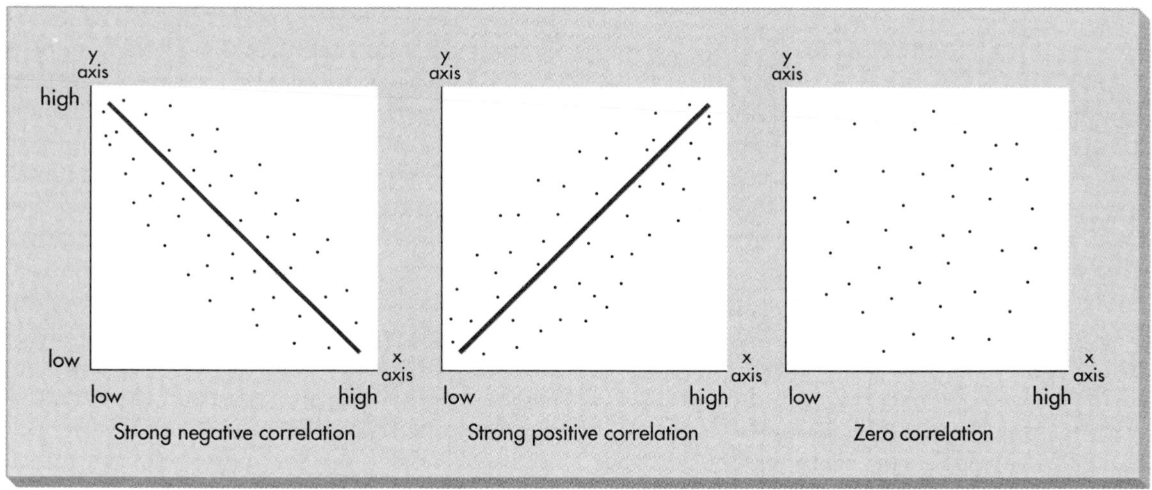

A-7 Scatter Plots of Three Correlations

son product moment correlation coefficient in case you want to see exactly how it is done.

In all the examples so far, we have correlated the scores of subjects on two different tests. But it does not have to be that way. We might correlate the scores of people on the same test taken at two different times. Such a computation would tell you whether people tend to score about the same on a test on two different occasions. If we assume that people do not change very much between the two times the test was administered then this statistic would tell us something about the ***reliability*** of the test—will the test give us the same number when we apply it twice to the same person? Another common use of correlation is to determine a test's ***validity***—does the test measure what it is supposed to measure? If we constructed a test of intelligence, we would hope that it would correlate positively with performance in school or on job-related tasks. If it did, this would help us argue that our test really did measure intelligence, assuming intelligence is fundamental to school or job performance.

Table A-8 Calculating the Pearson Product Moment Correlation Coefficient

Name	Anxiety (X)	X^2	Happiness (Y)	Y^2	XY (X times Y)
Manuel	2	4	9	81	18
Insook	5	25	6	36	30
Marsha	9	81	4	16	36
Rita	1	1	3	9	3
Giovanna	3	9	2	4	6
Rasheed	7	49	2	4	14
Phil	8	64	4	16	32
Sharon	6	36	5	25	30
N = 8 people	$\Sigma X = 41$	$\Sigma X^2 = 269$	$\Sigma Y = 35$	$\Sigma Y^2 = 191$	$\Sigma XY = 169$

$$r_{XY} \text{ (the correlation between X and Y)} = \frac{N\Sigma XY - (\Sigma X)(\Sigma Y)}{\sqrt{[N\Sigma X^2 - (\Sigma X)^2][N\Sigma Y^2 - (\Sigma Y)^2]}}$$

For these data:
$$r_{\text{ANXIETY}\cdot\text{HAPPINESS}} = \frac{(8)(169) - (41)(35)}{\sqrt{[(8)(269) - (41)^2][(8)(191) - (35)^2]}}$$

$$= \frac{1352 - 1435}{\sqrt{(2152 - 1681)(1528 - 1225)}}$$

$$= \frac{-83}{\sqrt{(471)(303)}} = \frac{-83}{\sqrt{142713}} = \frac{-83}{377.77} = -.219$$

Regression

Another important use of correlational statistics is in a procedure called ***regression analysis***. Regression analysis is a way to use one of two correlated variables to predict the other. Suppose we try to predict your weight, knowing nothing other than that you are reading this book. We have no idea what to guess, because we know absolutely nothing of relevance about you. If we knew that the average person who reads this book weighs 162 pounds, then that is what we would probably guess. And we would make the same guess for every reader. But what if we happened to know your height? Because height and weight are correlated, we could then make a more accurate guess about your weight. For example, if we knew that you were 6 feet, 6 inches tall, we would probably not guess your weight to be 120 pounds. Likewise, if we knew your height was 4 feet, 2 inches, 200 pounds would be an inappropriate guess. We would adjust our weight guess according to what we knew about your height, making a higher guess for six-footers than for four-footers. Regression analysis is a way of making this adjustment and improving our prediction statistically.

Finally, a moment's thought should convince you that the higher the correlation is (in either a positive or a negative direction), the better we can adjust our prediction of your weight, that is, the closer we will come to your true weight. If the correlation between the two variables is +1.0 or −1.0 and the regression is perfect, then we can predict the value of one of the variables exactly if we know the value of the other. But because correlations are almost never perfect, our predictions are always likely to be somewhat off, and the smaller the correlation is, the greater the error is likely to be.

Regression is used in many different settings. Most of you probably took the College Board Examinations (SATs) before getting into college. From past research, we know there is a positive correlation between one's score on the SATs and one's success in college. Therefore, the SATs can be used to predict how well college applicants will do later when they get into college. Because these predictions are accurate to some degree, colleges use these scores to help decide whom to admit.

Similar procedures and tests are used to process applications for law school, medical school, graduate school, and various jobs. Using regression techniques, psychologists predict the applicant's success on the job or in school, and these predictions are used to determine whether or not to hire or admit the applicant. It is a serious business, and the decisions made on this basis are extremely important to the people involved.

The simplest type of regression (technically known as a ***linear regression***) involves finding the straight line (hence the term linear) that best "fits" the data in a scatter plot. What we are looking for is a mathematical equation for the line that comes closest to the most points on a scatter diagram (see Figure A-7). Figure A-8 shows two different scatter plots relating scores on the College Boards (SAT scores) to later grade point average in college (GPA). Each point in the diagram represents one student; by drawing a line straight down to the x-axis from any point (any particular student), we can tell the student's SAT score, and by drawing a horizontal line from the point over to the y-axis, we can tell the student's GPA in college.

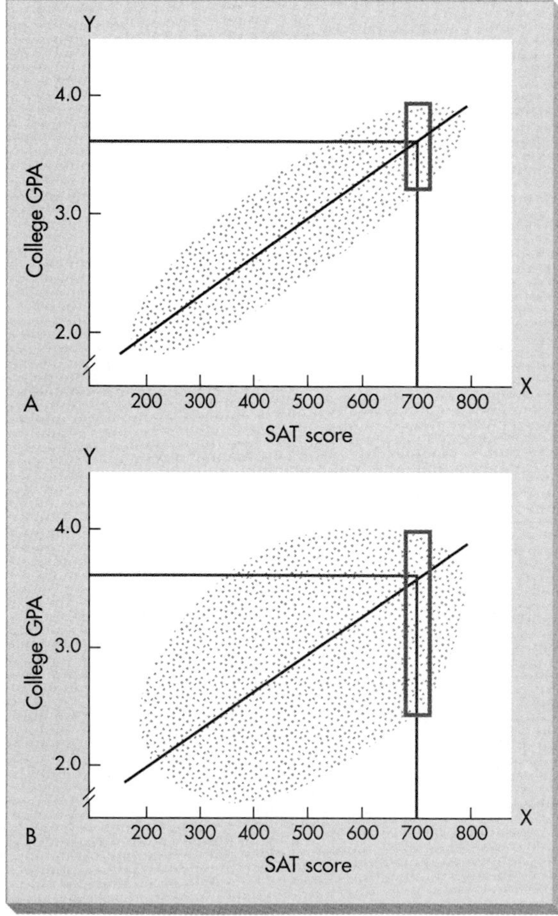

A-8 Scatter Plots for High (A) and Low (B) Degrees of Relationship between College GPAs and SAT Scores

Once we have data relating SAT scores and college GPAs, we can use regression analysis to make predictions for future students. First, we solve the equation for the line of best fit (known as the ***regression line***), a complex procedure that we won't describe here. Then we draw the line on the scatter plot. Now we can use the line as a way to predict the GPA, given a student's SAT score. For example, consider a student who scores 700 on the SAT: we draw a vertical line up from 700 until it intersects the regression line, and then we draw a horizontal line from this point over to the y-axis and read off the predicted GPA at the point of intersection. In this case, we come up with a prediction of 3.6 for the student's GPA.

It is important to say, once again, that this procedure will not give us perfect predictions, as you should be able to see from Figure A-8. Not all students scoring 700 will have a 3.6 average in college; some GPAs will be higher than 3.6 and some lower. The main factor in determining the accuracy of our predictions is the degree of correlation between the two variables. If the variables are highly correlated, as depicted in panel A, all the points will cluster close to the regression line, and none of the predictions is likely to be far off. In fact, if the correlation were perfect, all the points would be right on the line, and there would be no error. (All students with 700 SATs would have 3.6 GPAs.) On the other hand, with low correlations, the points will be widely scattered, and many of them will be at some distance from the regression line, as depicted in panel B of Figure A-8. In such a case, our predictions can be badly in error.

Look at the students who scored around 700 on the SATs in the two panels; these points are boxed in on the graphs. In the upper panel, which depicts a high correlation, you can see that all the students ended up with high college GPAs, and all were fairly close to 3.6, the average we would predict using the regression line. In contrast, in the lower panel, the students with 700 on the SATs varied widely in their GPAs, with some as low as 2.40 and others as high as 3.95. Regression analysis would have predicted 3.6 for all of them, and so it would have been way off on many of the predictions. The lower the correlation is between the two variables, the less precisely we can predict by using regression. In fact, if the correlation drops to zero, regression will be useless—we might as well guess. Given some degree of correlation, however, we can do better by using regression than simply guessing, and the higher the correlation is, the better our predictions will be.

Often there is more than one variable that is correlated with the *criterion*, which is the variable we are trying to predict. In such cases, there is a procedure called ***multiple regression*** that can be used to improve further the accuracy of our predictions. For example, in addition to SAT scores, we might also know each student's high school GPA and rank in his or her high school class. Rank, high school GPA, and SAT scores could then all be combined using multiple regression to predict the college GPA.

Inferential Statistics

The second major use of statistics in psychology is to make inferences from data, that is, to draw conclusions and to test hypotheses. Inferential statistics allow you to go beyond the actual scores you have observed to make more general or universal statements about behavior. There are two basic functions of inferential statistics, called **estimation** and **hypothesis testing**.

Estimation

One use of inferential statistics is to estimate the actual values of some population characteristic, like the mean, from a sample of observations. Suppose, for example, we wanted to know the average IQ of today's college students. One thing we could do is to test all students currently enrolled in American colleges and universities and then compute the actual mean. That would be a difficult and time-consuming task, and it would be nice to have a shortcut method, even if it provided just an estimate.

In order to estimate the mean, standard deviation, or any other parameter of a population, we draw a sample of population members and test only that sample. We then compute statistics on the sample scores and use these sample statistics to estimate what the mean and standard deviation would be if we did test every member of the population. Thus, we might sample 1,200 college students and use these scores to estimate what the population is like. As you are probably aware, this is what public opinion polls and TV rating services do. They sample but do not exhaustively test the population. We have to keep in mind that these estimates are likely to be wrong, and the estimate is typically accompanied by an index of the margin of error, usually the standard deviation.

It is vital that the sample used in any study is selected by procedures that ensure its ***representativeness*** of the population at large. This is usually accomplished by ***random sampling***. Random sampling means that every person in the specified population has an equal chance of being selected. For example, if we were trying to estimate average college student intelligence, it would not be representative if we selected only white female students attending junior colleges and colleges in California. Another important factor is sample size. The larger the sample is, the more accurate the estimate will be, other things being equal. If you randomly choose one person for your study and used his or her score to estimate the average student's IQ, you should expect to miss the mark badly. More than one score is almost always needed. But how many scores should be in the sample to ensure reasonable accuracy? The actual size needed is probably a lot smaller than you would think. A sample of 30 or 40 people, out of a population of millions, if properly drawn, would give quite an accurate idea about the mean of the entire student population. There are statistical techniques for determining how large a sample you need for a given level of accuracy. Of course, if the sample is not properly drawn or is not representative of the population as a whole, then increasing the sample size will do you no good.

Hypothesis Testing

When we do an experiment in psychology, we almost always begin with an hypothesis. For example, a psychologist might want to know whether Zappo cereal increases the intelligence of people who eat it. Do people who eat Zappo have higher IQs than people who don't? To answer this question, we would conduct an experiment with at least two conditions, one for people eating Zappo and the other for people eating Brand X. We would select, say, 40 volunteers and randomly assign them in equal number to the two conditions. Research participants would then be required to eat Zappo or Brand X for some period of time, say one year. We would treat both groups the same, except for the independent variable (here, eating Zappo), and then we would measure the dependent variable (IQ) to see if it differed for the two groups. We would also calculate the IQ mean and the standard deviation for each of the two groups. One hypothesis would be that the independent variable would have no effect and there would be no difference between the two groups (for obvious reasons, this is called the null hypothesis). If you found an effect, you could then reject the null hypothesis and accept the only alternative available—that indeed, the independent variable created a difference between the two groups.

Under circumstances like these, the two means are almost never exactly equal. The question is whether the means differ sufficiently for us to conclude that eating Zappo has an effect on IQ. If the means are very close, we might intuitively conclude that eating Zappo has no effect; if the mean difference is very large, we'd be tempted to conclude that eating Zappo (or Brand X) does have an effect. But we can't go on intuition alone. We need an objective statistical procedure for assessing the significance of an observed difference between means. Fortunately, inferential statistics offers this kind of tool. We will not describe these techniques in detail but merely point out that most of them are based on the comparison of (1) the difference between means with (2) the amount of variability in the data. For example, if the IQs are highly variable and the mean difference is small, we cannot conclude that eating Zappo has any effect. If, however, the mean difference is large relative to the IQs' variability, we would conclude that eating Zappo probably does have an effect.

To understand this, look at the three panels of Figure A-9. Each panel shows two frequency distributions, one for the Zappo and the other for the Brand X group. Note that in each panel the mean for Zappo subjects is 105 and the mean for Brand X subjects is 100. The mean difference is the same in all three cases, 5 points. Is that difference *statistically significant*? To answer, we have to consider the variability in our distributions. In the top panel, the variability is very low; all Zappo eaters score nearly the same, close to 105, and all Brand X eaters score at or around 100. The distributions don't overlap at all. All Zappo eaters have higher IQs than any

Brand X eater. In this case, it looks as though a five-point differential really means something.

The IQ scores are highly variable in the middle panel. Zappo and Brand X subjects score well above and well below the means of the two groups. There is a lot of overlap in the two distributions. Some Zappo eaters have lower IQs than some Brand X eaters and some Brand X eaters have higher IQs than some Zappo eaters, despite the difference in means between the two groups. In fact, there is so much overlap between the two groups that the mean difference of 5 points looks nonsignificant. Just as in the case of the top panel, we probably do not need any statistical test to tell us what to conclude in this case; here we cannot reject the hypothesis of no difference between the groups (*null hypothesis*).

Outcomes like that depicted in the top panel are rare indeed. Experiments are hardly ever that clear-cut in favor of rejecting the "no difference" hypothesis. The middle panel is a more common result, unfortunately for experimenters. The bottom panel in Figure A-9 represents the most common outcome of experiments. The two distributions overlap—more than in the top panel but less than in the middle. There is a moderate amount of variability and the conclusion to make is unclear. Would you say that the five-point difference in means is real in this case? Is this a significant difference?

One way to answer this question is to use what is technically called the ***t*-test**. The *t*-test is a ratio of the mean difference between two groups over the variability in the scores of the two groups. In all three panels of Figure A-9, the mean difference is 5 points, but the variabilities are not the same. Consider the top panel, where the variability is small. If we divide a measure of variability in this case into the difference of 5, we will get a relatively large *t*-ratio. The larger the ratio, the greater the statistical significance. In contrast, for the middle panel the *t*-ratio will be small—a large number for variability divided into the same mean difference of 5. Small ratios are less likely to be significant. In the bottom panel, we have a borderline case. The mean difference is divided by a variability measure of moderate size, and the *t*-ratio will be correspondingly moderate. What do we conclude? Fortunately, there are tables of probabilities for various sized *t*-ratios occurring by chance. We compute the *t*-ratio for an experimental outcome and then look up this value in the statistical tables to find the chance probability of a *t* as large as the one we computed. If the tables tell us that our *t*-value is unlikely to happen by chance, we will conclude that what we have observed is not a chance effect but a real and meaningful difference. Conventionally, this probability is .05. This means that if our obtained *t*-value would happen only 5 times in 100 repetitions of the experiment, then the odds are that this is not one of those occasions. The odds are that the experimental outcome is not a chance occurrence, but a real one, which is called a statistically significant effect.

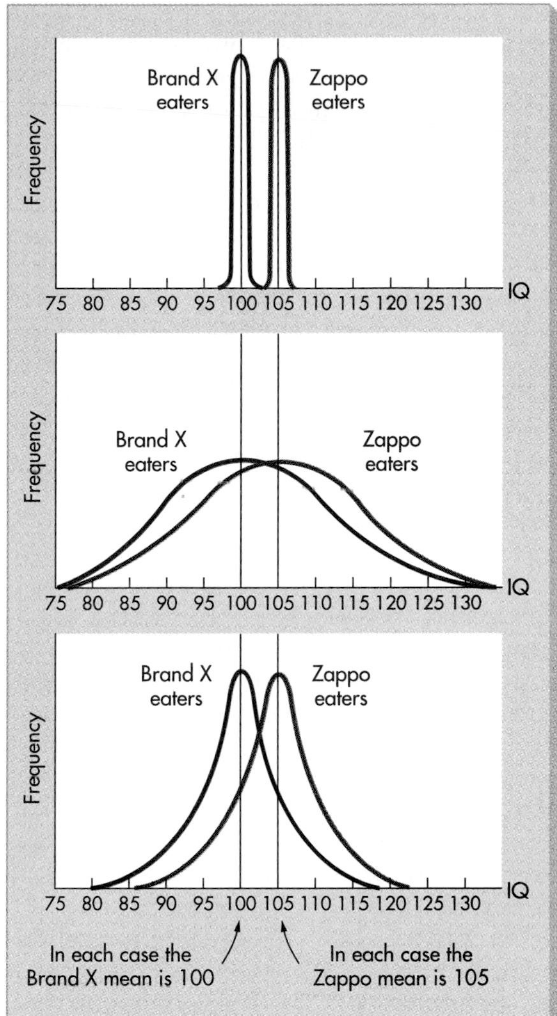

A-9 Three Experimental Outcomes Differing in Variability and Overlap, but Each with the Same Means (100 and 105) and the Same Mean Difference (105–100)

Remember, the null hypothesis says that there is no difference between eating Zappo and Brand X. If we obtain a significant *t*-ratio, we conclude that the null hypothesis is incorrect. Statistical inference is basically a rigorous, scientifically defensible way of drawing conclusions about some hypothesis, often the null hypothesis. The *t*-test allows us to reject the null hypothesis when we get a *t*-value that is unlikely to occur by chance. If we set up the null hypothesis to contrast with an alternative, namely, that Zappo eating enhances IQ, then the rejection of the null hypothesis will be evidence in support of the alternative.

This reasoning applies to correlation coefficients as well as to mean differences. If we correlate two sets of numbers randomly drawn out of a hat, the correlation coefficient will almost always be different from zero, even though the numbers are clearly unrelated (we drew them randomly). Suppose the correlation obtained in a certain experiment was high, say .80. Such a value looks as though it should be significantly different from zero. In another case, suppose the correlation is low, say −.07. Here the value looks nonsignificant. But what about moderate correlations of, say, .30, or −.42 or −.28. Where do we draw the line between significance and nonsignificance? When is a correlation coefficient large enough that we can conclude that the outcome is unlikely to occur by chance? At what point can we infer a real relationship between two sets of scores? Again, there are procedures of statistical inference that give a basis for objectively deciding whether an outcome is likely by chance. The null hypothesis would posit a correlation of zero. We test this hypothesis to determine whether it can be rejected.

We won't go into the details of how to calculate a *t*-test. You can find that information in any elementary statistics book. Simply remember that there is more to be done after the experiment is completed and the data have been collected. The results will always indicate some difference between conditions of the experiment. The *t*-test and other procedures of statistical inference are then used by the experimenter to help decide whether observed differences are large enough, relative to the variability in the data, to allow rejection of the null hypothesis and to support an alternative.

Errors in Inference

No experiment is perfect. Experiments can produce misleading data and experimenters can make incorrect decisions. There are two fundamental types of errors that occur when you draw conclusions from experimental data. These are depicted in Table A-9, and they might be familiar if you remember the discussion of signal detection theory in Chapter 5. In a *Type I error*, you conclude that your independent variable (eating Zappo cereal) has an effect (on IQ), when it actually has no effect. In a *Type II error*, you conclude that your independent variable has no effect when, in fact, it does. Each type of error has a certain probability of occurring in any experiment. Experimenters have to strike a balance between these two types of error in order to make the most justified inference about the outcome. You should keep in mind that you never know for sure whether you are making a Type I error (when you reject the null hypothesis) or a Type II error (when you do not reject the null hypothesis). All you have to go on are probabilities. But that is true in all science; so you draw the conclusion that is best supported by the data, allowing for some probabilities of being wrong.

Table A-9 Errors That Experimenters Can Make

		Based on your experiment you conclude:	
		Zappo increases IQ	**Zappo does not increase IQ**
The truth of the matter is:	Zappo does not increase IQ	*TYPE I ERROR* Rejects the null hypothesis when it is, in fact, true.	*CORRECT DECISION* Does not reject the null hypothesis when it is, in fact, true.
	Zappo increases IQ	*CORRECT DECISION* Rejects the null hypothesis when it is, in fact, false.	*TYPE II ERROR* Does not reject the null hypothesis when it is, in fact, false.

Advanced Statistical Techniques

Analysis of Variance

The *t*-ratio can be used to test the difference between two groups, but only two groups. Most experiments compare more than two groups or conditions, however, so the *t*-test is not much use in those cases. But a more elaborate statistical procedure based on similar principles exists, called the ***analysis of variance***. The test statistic in analysis of variance is called *F*, for the famous British statistician R. A. Fisher. The computational procedure for the *F*-test is much like that for *t*. Differences among group means are compared to a combined measure of variability within the groups. The larger the ratio, the more likely it is that the means are really different from one another. There are tables available for looking up the probability of obtaining a given *F*-ratio by chance. Analysis of variance is a very common statistical technique, and you are likely to encounter the *F*-test in just about any modern psychological journal article.

Factor Analysis

Factor analysis is a complex correlational procedure used to identify the basic elements of any measurable psychological phenomenon. This technique boils down to finding clusters of tests or measures that correlate with one another, but not with other tests. Suppose we administer the following 6 tests to 100 young women: (1) vocabulary, (2) basketball ability, (3) ability to write an essay on philosophy, (4) speed in the 100-yard dash, (5) knowledge of statistics, and (6) tree climbing. Each woman takes all 6 tests. Then we compute the *intercorrelations* of all the scores, that is, we correlate Test 1 with Test 2, 1 with 3, 1 with 4, etc. We might find that Tests 1, 3, and 5 intercorrelate highly with one another, but none of them correlates very well with 2, 4, and 6. Why should this be? Consider what the tests were designed to measure. Tests 1, 3, and 5 all involve some sort of thinking, knowledge, or cognitive ability—they require mental processes of one sort or another. On the other hand, 2, 4, and 6 all require physical skill. Tests 1, 3, and 5 measure something in common, call it Factor A, and 2, 4, and 6 measure something else in common, called Factor B. Clearly Factor A has something to do with scholastic intelligence; Factor B probably relates to athletic ability. Further, in this particular collection of tests, scholastic intelligence and athletic ability are relatively independent, i.e., not correlated with one another.

In short, with this correlational technique, we have isolated two factors. Factor analysis capitalizes on correlational principles, permitting us to analyze performance on a large number of tests into their basic underlying factors, by isolating clusters of interrelated tests. (Generally speaking, the clusters will not be as obvious as they are in the foregoing example, which is the main reason why we need a rigorous statistical procedure.) Correlations are high within a cluster, but low between or among clusters. We conclude then that the clusters represent and measure the basic factors.

Factor analysis has been used extensively in two main areas of psychology, intelligence and personality assessment. Each of these major psychological concepts consists of a large number of identifiable underlying factors. The goal of factor analysis is to provide a way of understanding exactly what goes into the makeup of concepts like intelligence and personality.

Glossary

absolute threshold The smallest amount of physical intensity by which a stimulus can be detected.

abscissa The horizontal axis on a graph; also known as the X-axis.

accommodation (1) In vision, the changing of the shape of the lens as the eye focuses on an object. (2) In Piaget's developmental theory, the modification of old ways of thinking to incorporate new knowledge and information.

acculturation The process of acquiring the values, beliefs, attitudes, and behaviors of a new culture.

acetylcholine One of the most common neurotransmitters in the human nervous system. It is manufactured and delivered by the motor neurons.

acquisition In conditioning, the initial stage of learning in which the association between a stimulus and a response is established.

action potential A brief reversal in the electrical charge between the inside and the outside of a nerve cell triggered by an above-threshold stimulus.

active touch The manipulation of an object, which produces information about the shape, weight, length, and other characteristics of that object.

actor-observer effect The tendency to attribute the behavior of others to internal causes, while attributing one's own behavior to situational causes.

acupuncture A treatment in traditional Chinese medicine. Sharp needles inserted in special places on the skin are twirled rapidly to affect other parts of the body; this technique is used to suppress pain and to treat other bodily problems.

adrenal glands The endocrine glands responsible for secreting the hormones adrenaline (epinephrine) and noradrenaline (norepinephrine), which regulate bodily functions that affect mood and emotion, blood pressure, blood sugar level, and redistribution of blood between internal organs and voluntary muscles.

adulthood The period of development that takes place from puberty to death.

afterimage A sensory impression that lasts after removal of the stimulus that caused it.

agonists A group of psychoactive drugs that cause neurotransmitters to be released, prevent deactivation of neurotransmitters, or mimic the effects of neurotransmitters by binding to their receptors. Drugs such as cocaine and nicotine are examples. *See also* antagonists.

alcohol intoxication According to legal definition, this condition occurs when one has a blood alcohol level of 0.10 or more. *See also* blood alcohol level.

algorithm A well-defined procedure or series of actions that guarantees a solution to a problem.

allergens Substances, such as household dust, tobacco smoke, fabric softener, and perfume, that trigger allergic responses.

all-or-none principle The principle that the neuron's action potential is triggered at full strength or not at all; it does not diminish in intensity as it travels down the neuron.

altered state of consciousness A condition or state that is considered outside the realm of normal consciousness, resulting from any number of different conditions, such as sensory deprivation or overstimulation, hypnosis, meditation, or the use of psychoactive drugs.

altruism This phenomenon occurs when one's actions benefit others but do not benefit the individual performing them.

amniocentesis A medical technique used after the sixteenth week of pregnancy whereby a sample of amniotic fluid is drawn from the amniotic sac surrounding the fetus. An analysis of the fluid enables doctors to determine whether the fetus has certain chromosomal abnormalities.

amphetamines Drugs that stimulate the central nervous system, putting the body into a hyperenergized state. Amphetamines block the reuptake of dopamine into nerve cells while directly causing the release of dopamine from nerve cells.

amplitude One of the basic elements of sound, referring to the strength of the sound wave. It is graphically represented as the crest of a wave.

amygdala The part of the limbic system that plays a role in eating, drinking, and sexual and aggressive behaviors. *See also* hypothalamus and hippocampus.

analgesics Drugs that reduce physical pain.

analogical reasoning Reasoning by analogy, that is, by inferring that if two or more things agree with one another in some respect, they will agree in others. *See also* symbolic representation.

anal stage According to Freud, the second stage of childhood development, which occurs between one to three years of age, in which psychic energy becomes focused on anal activities, such as defecation.

analytic intelligence The knowledge and skills that enable us to think critically and analytically about components of a problem, and to compare and evaluate alternatives. *See also* creative intelligence and practical intelligence.

anchoring heuristic A common decision-making shortcut through which currently available information is used as a reference point for judgment, which is then subject to later adjustment. *See also* availability heuristic and representativeness heuristic.

anger An emotion characterized by extreme or passionate displeasure and often antagonism.

anosmia Impairment of the sense of smell.

antagonists A group of psychoactive drugs that block, prevent, or inhibit neurotransmitters. Curare and other paralyzing drugs are examples. *See also* agonists.

anterograde amnesia A disruption in the memory's consolidation process that occurs when a blow to the head interferes with the formation of memory of events immediately following the blow. *See also* retrograde amnesia.

antibodies Protein molecules that circulate in the blood and can identify and kill antigens. *See also* antigens.

antigens Specific invading bacteria or viruses that trigger immune responses. *See also* antibodies.

anxiety A state of heightened physiological arousal and feelings of fear and apprehension that cannot be attributed to a specific source.

aphasia The loss of verbal understanding or expression.

arousal Overall level of animation, including level of alertness, activity, and excitement.

artificial intelligence (1) The programming in a computer that instructs it to behave in intelligent ways, (i.e., to simulate human knowledge and skills to accomplish a task). (2) The branch of computer science concerned with such programming.

assimilation (1) For new immigrants, the process of acquiring the values, beliefs, and behaviors required in a new culture while discarding those from the old. (2) In memory research, the distortion of a memory trace toward the direction of something already familiar and common. *See also* leveling and sharpening. (3) According to Piaget, the incorporation of new events or knowledge into existing schemas. *See also* accommodation.

association cortex Region of the cortex that is not "programmed" for sensory or motor activities, where "higher" mental processing involved in thought, learning, and memory occurs. This region is involved in the *integration* of sensory information or motor commands.

associative learning The learning of associations between two stimuli or between a stimulus and response based on repetition. Includes classical and operant conditioning.

attachment The emotional bond between people.

attachment behaviors Signals (e.g., crying, smiling, reaching, and clinging) from infants that trigger responsiveness in caregivers, increasing the likelihood of attachment.

attitude A relatively stable and enduring learned evaluation (favorable or unfavorable) of something, including a particular person, behavior, belief, object, or idea.

attraction Positive feelings for others, including liking and loving.

attribution A mental explanation of the causes of a person's behavior, including one's own behavior.

attribution theory The theory that seeks to explain how we decide, on the basis of samples of an individual's behavior, what the specific causes of that behavior are.

attrition effects The process of participants dropping out of a study for personal or uncontrollable reasons. This can severely bias experimental results.

auditory and speech centers The divisions of the cerebral cortex that receive auditory information and produce speech. They are located in the temporal lobe. *See also* association cortex, motor cortex, somatosensory cortex, and visual cortex.

auditory nerve One of the basic structures of the ear formed by the axons of all the hair cells on the basilar membrane. This structure carries information about sounds to the brain for further processing.

authority (1) Influence based on knowledge or expertise. (2) A person or group displaying this characteristic.

autistic savant A person with greatly diminished mental skills who displays an extraordinary proficiency in one isolated skill.

autoimmune diseases A class of diseases, including rheumatoid arthritis and multiple sclerosis, that are characterized by a disruption of the chemical communication system that regulates the immune system. Instead of attacking antigens, the immune system attacks white matter in the brain and spinal cord.

automatic processing The encoding of information, particularly that related to time, space, and frequency of events in addition to well-learned information that occurs outside of conscious awareness; it requires little attention or effort and is of unknown capacity.

autonomic nervous system The division of the peripheral nervous system (PNS) that consists of the nerves that serve the glands, smooth muscles, and the heart.

autoshaping A system of reinforcements that organisms appear to design for themselves that lead to gradual behavior change.

availability heuristic The decision-making shortcut whereby one's judgment is biased from using the information that most readily comes to mind. *See also* representativeness heuristic and anchoring heuristic.

axon A thin tube extending from a cell body of a neuron that is specialized to conduct nerve impulses away from the cell body.

axonal conduction The conveyance of nerve impulses within neurons.

base analog A term from analogical reasoning that is also known as a source analog. This is the first fact that is given in the analogy.

basilar membrane One of the basic structures of the ear, this membrane subdivides the cochlea and the sound waves passing them to the hair cells.

beauty principle The tendency for individuals to like physically attractive persons more than physically unattractive persons, especially in first impressions.

behavior An action, response, or performance that can be observed or measured by others.

behavioral confirmation Behavior change that occurs in accordance with a self-fulfilling prophecy.

behavioral medicine An interdisciplinary field which encompasses scientific research, education, and practice focusing on the relation of behaviors to health, illness, and related physiological problems.

behavior modification The operant procedures applied to change behavior in accordance with learning principles.

behaviorism A school of psychology that developed in response to functionalism, which defined psychology as the study of behaviors that can be observed and measured.

behavior therapy A general approach to psychological treatment which (a) holds that the disorders to which it addresses itself are produced by maladaptive learning and must be remedied by reeducation, (b) proposes techniques for this reeducation based on principles of learning and conditioning, and (c) focuses on the maladaptive behaviors themselves rather than on hypothetical unconscious processes of which they may be expressions.

beliefs Mental acceptance of something as true.

bi-cultural Identification with two cultures.

binocular cues Cues for depth perception that depend on the use of two eyes, such as convergence and binocular disparity.

binocular disparity When both eyes are focused on one object, the difference in the retinal position of that object's image in the left and right eyes provides a cue for depth perception.

biological dispositions Biological characteristics or traits.

biological universals The biological elements that are common among all members of a species; for human beings, these include: body structure, dependency of newborn children, year-round sexuality, and a complex brain structure. *See also* societal universals and psychological universals.

biomedical model A model of health that assumes that the mind and the body function separately, and that disease leads to a disfunction of the body. *See also* mind-body dualism.

biopsychosocial model A multi-level model of health that uses a combination of biological, psychological, and social factors to explain how we maintain wellness or develop illness.

bipolar cells Specialized nerve cells that connect the rods and cones to the ganglion cells in the eye.

bipolar disorder Formerly called manic-depressive psychosis; mood disorder characterized by swings between mania and depression.

blind spot The place on the retina where the optic nerve exits the eyeball that lacks rods or cones. The brain "fills in" information to compensate for the lack of receptors in this area.

blood alcohol level The concentration of alcohol in the bloodstream, measured as the number of milligrams of alcohol per 100 ml of blood.

borderline personality disorder A personality disorder characterized by distrust, impulsive and self-destructive behavior, and difficulty in controlling anger and other emotions.

bottom-up processes The processes in form recognition that start with smaller component parts and then gradually build up to the larger units (i.e., from letters to words to phrases). *See also* top-down processes.

brain growth spurt The developmental period during which more than half of a child's eventual brain weight is added. This period occurs between the last three months of pregnancy and the first two years after birth.

brain stem The brain matter lying between the spinal cord and the cerebrum.

brightness A perceived dimension or quality of visual stimuli; the extent to which an object appears light or dark.

brightness constancy The perception of an object as having the same relative brightness regardless of changing surroundings.

brightness contrast The perceiver's tendency to exaggerate the physical difference in the light intensities of two adjacent regions. As a result, a gray patch looks brighter on a black background, darker on a white background.

Broca's area A part of the left side of the frontal lobe connected with the production of speech. It is named for its discoverer, the French surgeon Paul Broca (1824–1880).

bystander apathy A bystander's failure to help someone in need; it increases in probability with the number of observers present. Also known as the "bystander effect."

Cannon-Bard theory The perspective that suggests that when we are exposed to emotion-provoking events or stimuli, we simultaneously experience both physiological arousal and the subjective experience of emotions.

cardinal traits According to Allport, single personality traits that dominate a person's personality. *See also* central and secondary traits.

case study An observational study in which one person is studied intensively.

catatonic schizophrenia Subtype of schizophrenia characterized by a waxy flexibility of body and limbs, loss of motion, and a tendency to remain motionless for hours or days.

catharsis A release of suppressed emotions that is sometimes believed to have therapeutic effects.

cause-effect relationship When one variable directly influences another variable. The experimental method is used to identify these relationships.

cell body The component of the neuron that contains the cell nucleus.

central nervous system (CNS) One of the two major divisions of the human nervous system. It consists of the brain and spinal cord and is primarily responsible for storing and processing information.

central tendency The tendency of scores in a frequency distribution to cluster around a central value.

central traits (1) According to Allport, the core traits (usually five to ten) that best describe a person's personality. They are generalized across situations and readily noticeable by others (e.g., outgoing, optimistic). *See also* cardinal and secondary traits. (2) In impression formation, the major traits used to form impressions of others.

cerebellum A structure that is part of the hindbrain involved in muscular coordination and equilibrium.

cerebrum The largest part of the forebrain.

cerebral cortex The outermost layer of the cerebral hemispheres: it primarily consists of nerve cell bodies and their branches.

childhood The period of development between birth and puberty.

chromosomes Structures in the nucleus of each cell that contain genes, the units of hereditary transmission. A human cell has 46 chromosomes, arranged in 23 pairs. One of these pairs consists of the sex chromosomes. In males, one member of the pair is an X-chromosome, the other a Y-chromosome. In females, both members are X-chromosomes.

chunks The units of short-term memory which combine, integrate, or unite separate items.

classical conditioning The learning of a new response to a stimulus by pairing that stimulus with another stimulus that already elicits the response.

client-centered therapy A humanistic psychotherapy developed by Carl Rogers.

closure A factor in visual grouping. The perceptual tendency to fill in gaps in a figure so that it looks closed or complete.

cocaine A drug that stimulates the central nervous system and puts the body into a hyperenergized state.

cochlea A coiled structure in the inner ear that contains the basilar membrane whose deformation by sound-produced pressure stimulates the auditory receptors.

cognition The total process of thinking, which encompasses perception, learning, memory, and consciousness.

cognitive approach A theoretical framework of human and animal learning which holds that both humans and animals acquire and store mental representations of knowledge (cognitions), such as what is where (cognitive maps) or what leads to what (expectancies). This contrasts with theories of instrumental learning such as Skinner's, which asserts that learning consists of the strengthening or weakening of particular tendencies.

cognitive-behavioral therapy A process by which people's faulty cognitions about themselves and the world are changed to more accurate ones, thus changing the maladaptive behaviors based on those cognitions.

cognitive consistency A state in which beliefs, attitudes, and behaviors are mutually compatible.

cognitive dissonance theory Leon Festinger's consistency theory, which states that inconsistency between cognitions produces discomfort (dissonance), leading a person to act to restore consistency in order to remove that discomfort. For example, when we realize that we have behaved in a way that is inconsistent with our attitudes, we may change our attitudes to reduce the dissonance caused by having those inconsistent cognitions.

cognitive learning The learning of new skills and facts through focused attention and observation.

cognitive map A mental representation of our environment.

cognitive psychology The study of mental structures and processes and how people use them to process, store, and retrieve information.

cognitive schema A mental representation or framework that is used to organize and process information.

cognitive triad According to Beck, a belief system involved in depression that includes three views: self-worth, the world in general, and the future.

cohort effect Age-related differences among people who grew up at the same time attributable to cultural or historical differences while growing up rather than real developmental change.

collective unconscious In Jung's theory, a mystical construct that contains the basic images and ideas believed to be shared by all human beings.

color blindness A popular term used to describe having a color deficiency. *See* color deficiency.

color deficiency The inability of people with normal acuity to see certain colors, owing to a deficit in one or more of the three types of retinal cones. The most common is the inability to distinguish red and green.

community mental health programs Programs that emphasize the prevention of mental illness and the need for broader and more effective mental health services within communities.

compliance A form of social influence that involves behaving in accordance with another person's request. *See also* conformity and obedience.

compliance techniques Persuasive techniques used to induce people to behave in a requested way. Many are based on the social-psychological principles of consistency, reciprocity, attraction, social validation, scarcity, and authority.

complexity In audition, the number of different pure sound waves that are components with a single sound.

computerized axial tomography (CAT or CT scans) The use of brain X-rays to reveal differences in tissue densities among regions.

concept A class or category that encompasses a number of individual examples. The concept "bird" encompasses "robin," "eagle," and "penguin," for example.

concrete operational stage In Piaget's theory, the developmental period from about ages six to eleven. At this time, the child has acquired mental operations that allow her or him to abstract some essential attributes of reality, such as number and substance; but these operations are as yet applicable to only concrete events and cannot be considered entirely in the abstract.

conditioned reflex A learned reflex. *See also* conditioned response.

conditioned response (CR) A response elicited by some initially neutral stimulus, the conditioned stimulus (CS), as a result of pairings between that CS and an unconditioned stimulus (US). The CR and the unconditioned response are typically not identical, though they are often similar.

conditioned stimulus (CS) In classical conditioning, the stimulus that comes to elicit a new response after repeated pairings with the unconditioned stimulus.

conditioning trials The repeated pairings of a neutral stimulus and an unconditioned response.

cones Visual receptors that respond to greater light intensities and give rise to chromatic (color) sensations.

confounding variable A variable that is linked to the independent variable that could affect the dependent variable that the experimenter inadvertently fails to control.

conformity A form of social influence which requires that people change their behavior or attitudes to be in accord with group norms.

conscious In Freudian theory, the ideas, thoughts, and images that a person is aware of at any given moment.

consciousness Self-knowledge or awareness of what one is experiencing at any given moment.

consensus The extent to which a person's reactions in response to an event are shared by others. In Kelley's theory, this is one piece of information used to determine whether people make dispositional or situational attributions for behavior. *See also* consistency and distinctiveness.

conservation A feature of cognitive development, this is the knowledge that essential physical properties of an object are not dependent on its external appearance and do not change if that appearance is altered.

consistency The extent to which a person consistently reacts to some stimulus in a particular way. In Kelley's theory, this is one piece of information used to determine whether people make dispositional or situational attributions for behavior. *See also* consensus and distinctiveness.

contiguous events Events that occur close together in time; sometimes perceived to lead to learned associations.

contingencies Relations between two events in which one is dependent upon another. If the contingency is greater than zero, the probability of event A will be greater when event B is present than when it is absent.

continuous reinforcement A schedule of reinforcement in which every response is followed by a reinforcer.

control group In experimental design, the group that does not experience the experimenter's manipulation of the independent variable. It is equal to the experimental group in all other ways.

controllable versus uncontrollable A dimension of causal attributions, the focus of which is to determine whether a person can control a particular behavior.

controlled processing Thought processes that require conscious mental effort.

convergent thinking Putting together a variety of facts to find and produce the one correct answer to a particular question or problem. *See also* divergent thinking.

conversion disorder A type of somatoform disorder involving motor and/or sensory impairments such as paralysis, seizure, and lack of sensation that have no apparent physiological basis. Formerly known as hysteria.

cornea The curved transparent surface of the eyeball that bends the light waves entering the eye, helping to focus them.

corpus callosum A bundle of neural fibers that connect the two cerebral hemispheres.

correlation The tendency of two variables to vary together. If one goes up as the other goes up, the correlation is positive; if one goes up as the other goes down, the correlation is negative.

correlational coefficient A statistic, r, that expresses both the size and the direction of a correlation, varying from $+1.00$ (perfect positive correlation) to -1.00 (perfect negative correlation).

correspondence bias The tendency to assume that people's words and actions correspond to their intentions, attitudes, and traits, even in light of evidence to the contrary.

cortisol A hormone that regulates the thymus, dissolves excess white blood cells, and keeps the immune system under control.

counterconditioning A procedure for weakening a classically conditioned CR by connecting the stimulus that presently evokes it to a new response that is incompatible with the CR.

covariation In statistical analysis, the degree to which two sets of scores vary together.

creative intelligence The aptitude for seeing new and practical relationships between what we know and what we do not know, and for extrapolating what we know to novel situations. *See also* analytic intelligence and practical intelligence.

creativity The ability to find original solutions to problems.

crisis intervention Short-term therapeutic techniques used as a form of secondary prevention in times of crisis; an aspect of the community mental health movement.

critical period A time of particular sensitivity to specific environmental stimuli during development.

cross-sectional study An experimental design that tests groups of participants who are of different ages.

crystallized intelligence According to Cattell, the repertoire of information, cognitive skills, and strategies acquired by the application of fluid intelligence to various fields. It is said to increase with age. *See also* factor, fluid intelligence, and s-factor.

cue-dependent forgetting The inability to remember learned information due to retrieval failure because cues present during learning are not present during recall. *See also* trace-dependent forgetting.

cultural differences (1) Differences among groups attributable to variation in some aspect of their cultures. (2) The variations among cultures themselves.

culturally sensitive therapy Therapy designed to be responsive to variations in values, beliefs, norms, and behaviors across cultures. When dealing with disadvantaged groups, it avoids blaming the victim and recognizes that behaviors defined as abnormal by the dominant society may be coping strategies necessary for survival.

cultural relativism The view that all cultural systems and moral codes are equally valid.

culture A people's way of life, including material things, social institutions, and the symbols, concepts, values, beliefs, norms, habits, skills, and other learned capabilities acquired by human beings and transmitted across generations.

dark adaptation An increase in the eye's sensitivity to light that occurs after the reduction or complete absence of light energy reaching it, attributable to changes in the level of light-sensitive pigments in the eye's receptor cells.

decision-making heuristics Mental decision-making shortcuts that bypass logic, rely on memory for past experiences, and are intuitive rather than analytic in nature.

declarative knowledge Knowing "that" (i.e., knowing someone's name) as contrasted with procedural knowledge, which is knowing "how" (i.e., knowing how to ride a bicycle). *See also* procedural knowledge.

deductive reasoning Reasoning by which one tries to determine whether a particular statement follows logically from a number of premises, as in syllogisms. *See also* inductive reasoning.

defense mechanisms According to Freud, unconscious tactics employed by the ego to prevent anxiety.

deindividuation The loss of personal identity that occurs under conditions of anonymity.

delirium tremens A syndrome of highly unpleasant withdrawal symptoms (i.e., hallucinations, vomiting, uncontrolled trembling, and muscle spasms) that occurs as a consequence of abstinence from intoxicating substances after a period of long-term or heavy use.

dendrite A typically highly branched part of a neuron that receives impulses from receptors or other neurons and conducts them toward the cell body.

dependent variable In the design of an experiment, the variable that is expected to be affected or influenced by the independent variable.

depressive disorders Mood disorders marked by a state of deep and pervasive sadness, dejection, and hopelessness, accompanied by feelings of fatigue, apathy, and low self-worth.

depth perception The ability to perceive a three-dimensional world and determine the distance of objects from one another.

determining causes The immediate causes of an event.

development The systematic physiological and psychological changes that occur in an individual over time between conception and death.

Diagnostic and Statistical Manual (DSM) of Mental Disorders A manual that identifies and defines over 200 separate diagnostic categories of mental problems and abnormal behaviors.

diagnostic tests Standard psychological exams used to gauge intellectual ability, determine personality traits, or identify a psychological condition or problem.

diathesis-stress model A model based on the belief that many organic and mental disorders arise from an interaction between a diathesis (a predisposition toward an illness) and some form of precipitating environmental stress.

difference threshold A measure of a person's ability to discriminate one stimulus from another on a particular dimension, such as intensity or frequency.

differentiation A progressive change from the general to the particular and from the simpler to the more complex which characterizes embryological development. According to some theorists, the same pattern holds for the development of behavior after birth.

diffusion of responsibility A decrease in a person's individual sense of responsibility to help in an emergency that occurs when bystanders are present; the greater the number of bystanders, the less likely a helping response is to occur.

discourse An oral or written body of language consisting of two or more sentences.

discrimination In learning, the process of distinguishing among similar stimuli and responding to only the appropriate one. In social psychology, the behavioral expression of prejudice.

disorganized schizophrenia A form of schizophrenia characterized by disorganized speech and behavior and inappropriate or blunted affect (i.e., laughing at something sad or expressing no emotions at all). People exhibiting this form of schizophrenia tend to be socially withdrawn.

dispositional attributions Attributions that assign the cause of a behavior to something about the person, (e.g., the presence or absence of some ability or personality trait).

dispositions Personal characteristics or attributes.

dissociative amnesia The sudden loss of memory, especially such information that is traumatic or stressful, in response to a specific upsetting event.

dissociative disorder A disorder characterized by a mental dissociation or separation of one part of a person's conscious awareness from another.

dissociative identity disorder A relatively rare disorder that develops when individuals find certain events in their lives so psychologically painful that they seek to escape by creating new and different identities that typically exhibit different, and often opposite traits from the original identity. Also called multiple personality disorder.

distal stimuli The objects in the environment that are the origins of the physical energies (proximal stimuli) that impinge on our sensory receptors. For example, a tree is a distal stimulus, while the light energies reflected from the tree that fall on our retina in the image of the tree are the proximal stimuli. *See also* proximal stimuli.

distinctiveness The extent to which a person's behavior is unique; that is, the extent to which a given behavior does or does not occur across different situations. In Kelley's theory, this is one piece of information used to determine whether people make dispositional or situational attributions for behavior. *See also* consensus and consistency.

divergent thinking A kind of thought process that refers to the ability to produce a variety of different, yet relevant responses to an open-ended question or problem. *See also* convergent thinking.

dopamine A neurotransmitter involved in various brain structures, including those that control motor action.

double-blind experiment An experiment in which neither the research participants nor the experimenter know which treatment is being applied until the experiment is over.

dream analysis A psychodynamic technique in which a therapist interprets a client's dreams to uncover hidden, unconscious motivations.

drive A state of tension or arousal that motivates organisms to behave in particular ways, typically to reduce that tension. Drives generally, but not always, arise in response to a state of physical need (for example, the hunger drive results from the need for food).

drug abuse The consumption of a drug or drugs to the extent that the user's functioning or health is significantly impaired, or when the actions of the user become potentially dangerous to others.

drug therapy The use of psychotropic drugs (i.e., antidepressants, anti-anxiety drugs, and antipsychotics) to treat a person's mental or psychological state.

drug tolerance The compensatory reaction that develops after repeated use of a drug, leading to the need to use increasingly larger doses to obtain the same effect produced previously.

drug use The consumption of a drug or drugs.

dysthymia Sometimes called neurotic depression; a mood disorder characterized by a mild but persistent depression over an extended period of time.

eardrum The taut membrane that transmits vibrations caused by sound waves across the middle ear to the inner ear.

echoic memory A sensory memory of an auditory stimulus.

ego One of the basic structures of the personality as proposed by Freud. The ego maintains a balance among the demands of the id, superego, and reality. *See also* id and superego.

ego analysis Therapeutic approach based on ego psychology.

egocentric Viewing events solely from one's own point of view and failing to take into account the perspectives of others. In Piaget's theory, egocentrism is a characteristic of children in the preoperational stage of development.

ego integrity The ability of the ego to accomplish the balance among id, superego, and reality.

ego psychology An approach to psychology that, in addition to the neo-Freudian concern with cultural and interpersonal factors, holds that the ego has its own functions apart from dealing with the id and stresses the healthy aspects of the self as it tries to cope with reality.

elaboration likelihood model The theory that there are two different routes to persuasion, central and peripheral, which differ in the amount of cognitive effort (elaboration) involved in processing the persuasive information.

elaborative rehearsal Rehearsal in which material in working memory is actively reorganized and linked to previously known information. *See also* maintenance rehearsal or shallow processing.

electroconvulsive therapy (ECT) A form of biological therapy in which an electric current is passed through the brain, causing a convulsion used to treat severe depression.

embryo The earliest stage in a developing animal that occurs after implantation (before implantation, the zygote develops into a preembryo). In humans, this stage occurs up to about eight weeks after implantation.

emotion Internal feelings that energize behavior. Emotions have three components: physiological responses, subjective or conscious experience, and overt behavior.

emotion-focused coping A method of coping in which the objective is to reduce tension and anxiety resulting from a problem rather than to deal directly with the problem itself.

empirical methods Methods that rely on the systematic observation and measurement of overt behavior.

empiricism A school of thought that holds that all knowledge comes through the senses; that is, through observation.

encoding specificity principle The hypothesis that retrieval is facilitated if the context at the time of recall is similar to that present during the original encoding.

encounter groups A form of group therapy that operates on the basis of humanistic theories and emphasizes the sharing of perspectives and support of individual growth. The goal of encounter groups is to sensitize each member to his or her own feelings as well as to the feelings of others by placing the members in face-to-face encounters with each other.

endocrine system A network of glands that sends chemical messages throughout the nervous system by secreting hormones that affect the body's growth and functioning.

endorphins Naturally occurring chemicals produced within the brain that act as neurotransmitters whose effects and chemical composition are similar to such pain-relieving opiates as morphine.

episodic memory The memory of particular events in one's own life (i.e., I rode the train this morning). *See also* semantic memory.

equilibrium In perception, the sense that informs us about the position of our body in space. In Piaget's theory, a state of balance between the processes of assimilation and accommodation.

equity theory The theory that interpersonal attraction depends upon the ratio of each person's costs and benefits in the relationship.

escape training Instrumental training in which reinforcement consists of the reduction or cessation of an aversive stimulus (i.e., electric shock).

estimation The use of inferential statistics to estimate the actual values of some population characteristic from a sample of observations.

ethnicity A social category that distinguishes people based on their common social and cultural characteristics, such as nationality, religion, and language.

ethnocentrism Prejudice in favor of one's own group.

evolutionary psychology The theoretical perspective that seeks to explain social behavior in human beings and animals in terms of the principles of natural selection (evolution).

expectancy The anticipation of a particular event or outcome, such as having the expectancy that a certain behavior will result in a specific outcome.

expectancy effects These effects occur when research participants' knowledge of experimental conditions influences their behavior, thereby affecting the outcome of the experiment.

expected utility The subjective utility of a goal combined with the subjective probability of attaining it.

experimental group In an experiment, the group that receives the experimental treatment.

expert system A computer problem-solving program that attempts to simulate the reasoning of a human specialist.

explanatory style One's habitual method of explaining the causes of behavior and other events.

explicit memory Memory retrieval that requires a conscious effort to remember so that one is aware of remembering during the time of retrieval.

external attributions Attributions that assign the cause of a behavior to something about the situation (e.g., poor test performance may be attributed to the level of test difficulty). Also called situational attributions.

extinction In classical conditioning, the weakening of the tendency of a CS to elicit a CR by unreinforced presentations of the CS. In instrumental conditioning, a decline in the tendency to perform the instrumental response brought about by unreinforced occurrences of that response.

extrinsic motivation Motivation to perform a behavior for an external, tangible reward (e.g., money) rather than for the pleasure of doing the behavior itself. *See also* intrinsic motivation.

facial feedback hypothesis The hypothesis that sensory feedback from the facial muscles will lead to subjective feelings of emotion that correspond to the particular facial pattern.

factor In statistics, a hypothetical ability or attribute that underlies a pattern of highly intercorrelated tests. *See also* factor analysis.

factor analysis A method of interpreting test questionnaire results in which clusters of related items (or factors) are analyzed to reveal the underlying phenomena or concepts.

false consensus bias The tendency to overestimate the extent to which others think and feel the same way that we do.

family therapy A general term for a number of therapies that treat the family (or a couple), operating on the assumption that the cause of family or marital distress lies not in the pathology of any individual spouse or family member but rather in relationship dynamics within the family or marriage system.

fear of failure A fear of failing a task that can lead people not to attempt the task in the first place.

feature detectors Neurons in the retina or brain that respond to specific features of a stimulus, such as movement and orientation.

feminist therapy A form of therapy that views differential power between men and women as the source of many of women's problems. Feminist therapy emphasizes egalitarian relationships between men and women, between minority and majority groups, and between therapists and clients. It tries to help clients identify and change dysfunctional situations rather than encourage clients to adapt to them.

fertilization In reproduction, the process of combining an egg and a sperm.

fetal period The second major stage of prenatal development that occurs after implantation. In humans, from about nine weeks until birth.

fetus An organism in the second major stage of prenatal development after implantation. *See also* embryo.

fight-or-flight response A physiological reaction to stress in which an organism is aroused and becomes physiologically prepared to take action, either to attack or to flee.

fixed interval One of the four basic partial reinforcement schedules in which reinforcements are delivered to the first response that occurs after a specific amount of time has passed. The amount of time does not vary from trial to trial.

fixed ratio One of the four basic partial reinforcement schedules in which reinforcements are delivered following a specific number of responses. The number of responses required does not vary from trial to trial.

flashbulb memories Vivid and detailed memories of unexpected and emotionally important events.

fluid intelligence The ability to deal with new types of problems. *See also* crystallized intelligence.

forebrain In mammals, the bulk of the brain. Its foremost region includes the cerebral hemispheres; its rear includes the thalamus and hypothalamus.

formal operational stage According to Piaget, a stage of development that is characterized by the ability to form abstract thoughts, and which is typically reached during the period from age twelve to adulthood.

fovea The central region of the retina, which contains cones but few rods. It is the area of greatest visual acuity.

free association A psychoanalytic technique for exploring the unconscious by encouraging a patient to say whatever comes to mind, without censoring or editing any statement.

free nerve endings The branching ends of dendrites of certain sensory neurons which act as receptors for sensations of pain.

free will One's power to make choices that are not predetermined and to direct one's own actions.

frequency In audition, a property of sound waves that refers to the number of crests in the wave during one second of time.

frequency distribution An arrangement in which scores are tabulated by the frequency in which they occur.

Freudian theory The original psychodynamic personality theory developed by Sigmund Freud and his followers that emphasizes the effects of conflicts between unconscious and conscious forces and the impact of early childhood experience for the development of adult personality.

friendship A relationship characterized by the sharing of private thoughts and feelings.

frontal lobe The frontmost portion of the cerebral cortex, which lies just behind the forehead. It is concerned with the regulation of voluntary movements.

functional distance In attraction theory, a measure that takes into account the distance between two residences and the arrangement of space, as both influence the probability that people will interact with each other.

functional fixedness A mental set that involves the tendency to think of objects in terms of the way they are typically used.

functional psychology (functionalism) A school of psychology that emphasizes learned behaviors that enable organisms to adapt to their environments and to function effectively. *See also* structuralism.

fundamental attribution error The tendency to overattribute the causes of another's behavior to something about the person (internal attribution)and to underestimate the importance of situational influences.

ganglion cells One of the intermediate links between the receptor cells of the retina and the brain. The axons of the ganglion cells converge into a bundle of fibers that leave the eyeball as the optic nerve.

gender The cultural package of characteristics, assigned by sex in most cultures, that defines the social categories of male and female.

gender identity One's personal awareness of being male or female.

gender role The set of social expectations for behaviors on the part of males and females.

gender schemas Organized sets of beliefs and expectations about males and females that guide information processing.

general adaptation syndrome (GAS) A sequence of physiological responses that the body goes through in response to a stressor. It involves three stages: alarm/mobilization, resistance, and exhaustion.

generalized anxiety disorder The experience of long-term anxiety with no explanation for it.

genes The units of hereditary transmission, each located at a particular place on a given chromosome.

genital stage In Freudian theory, the final phase of psychosexual development in which psychic energy becomes focused on heterosexual genital mating.

genome The entire set of genes that provides the blueprint for creating a member of a species.

genotype An individual's unique combination of genes. *See also* phenotype.

Gestalt psychology A theoretical approach that emphasizes that mental phenomena are best understood when viewed as organized wholes rather than when reduced and analyzed into various components.

Gestalt therapy A humanistic approach to psychotherapy developed by Fritz Perls, in which patients act out past conflicts in order to confront, take responsibility for, and learn control of their feelings.

g-factor In intelligence, a general mental ability cutting across all tests; first discovered by Charles Spearman.

glycerol A carbohydrate found in the bloodstream. The levels of glycerol rise and fall in relation to changes in fat storage.

gradient of stimulus generalization A mathematical curve that illustrates the degree of generalization among various stimuli.

group Two or more individuals who interact and perceive themselves as a unit.

group polarization effect The observation that groups often adopt positions more extreme than would be predicted from averaging the initial views held by members before discussion occurred.

group therapy A type of psychotherapy in which therapists work with an interacting collection of people rather than with single individuals.

habituation In learning, a decline in response to stimuli that have become familiar.

hair cells The auditory receptors in the cochlea, lodged between the basilar membrane and other membranes above, that transduce sound waves into electrochemical energy.

halfway houses Houses that rehabilitate people released from mental hospitals when they are not yet fully prepared to take their place in a home and family environment. These houses are usually supervised by paraprofessionals, who consult periodically with mental health professionals.

hardiness A personality attribute characterized by a sense of control over experiences and outcomes, a deep involvement in daily activities, and a belief that daily activities are worth doing.

health behaviors Behaviors that enhance and maintain health.

health belief model A model that suggests that help-seeking behavior depends on how much one has (1) general health values, (2) specific beliefs about personal vulnerability to a particular disorder, and (3) beliefs about how life-threatening the disorder is.

health-compromising behaviors Behaviors that undermine or harm current or future health (e.g., cigar or cigarette smoking).

health-enhancing behaviors Behaviors that improve health (e.g., maintaining a well-balanced diet and a reasonable exercise program, wearing seat belts).

health habits Firmly established health behaviors, often performed automatically, without awareness.

health promotion The process of helping people to gain more control over and to improve their health by increasing health-enhancing behaviors and decreasing health-compromising behaviors.

health psychology A subfield of psychology that focuses on health-related behaviors and psychological aspects of health and illness over the life span by studying how mind and body interact to influence health.

heritability This refers to the relative importance of heredity and environment in determining the variation of a particular trait. More specifically, heritability is the proportion of the variance of the trait in a given population that is attributable to genetic factors.

heuristics Problem-solving shortcuts that are sometimes more efficient and immediately effective than a systematic approach. *See also* algorithm.

hidden observer technique According to Hilgard, a hypnotized subject's awareness of experiences, such as pain, that are nonetheless unreported during hypnosis.

hierarchy of needs According to Maslow, the concept of an ordering of needs—physiological, safety, belongingness, esteem, and self-actualization—in which those lower in the order, beginning with physiological needs, must be satisfied before those that are higher merge.

hindbrain The most primitive portion of the brain, which includes the medulla and the cerebellum.

hippocampus A structure in the temporal lobe that constitutes an important part of the limbic system. One of the functions involves memory.

homeostasis The body's tendency to maintain a constant internal environment even when the external environment changes.

hormone Chemical messenger manufactured and secreted into the bloodstream by an endocrine gland, which may then activate another gland or help to regulate bodily function and behavior.

hue The property of light stimulation (wavelength) that corresponds to the sensation of color.

humanistic approach A theory that focuses on what it means to be an individual human being with the ability to choose one's own actions and to find self-actualization or fulfillment, often through helping others.

humanistic psychology A school of psychology that focuses on the uniqueness of individuals and their tendencies toward creativity, growth, and personal improvement, and emphasizes their ability to make conscious choices and to take personal responsibility for their actions.

hunger A drive that compels organisms to seek out the nutrients that the body requires.

hypermnesia An enhancement of memory typically attributable to increased or repeated efforts at recall.

hyperphagia Voracious, chronic overeating that can be brought about by a lesion of the ventromedial region of the hypothalamus.

hypersuggestability A strong inclination to follow the suggestions and instructions of a hypnotist.

hypnagogic state A state of consciousness experienced when passing from wakefulness to sleep.

hypochondriasis A disorder characterized by persistent and irrational fear of having an illness despite reassurance from doctors that no physical illness exists.

hypnosis A temporary, trance-like state of heightened suggestibility to the suggestions of others that can be induced in normal persons. During hypnosis, various hypnotic or posthypnotic suggestions sometimes produce effects that resemble some symptoms of conversion disorders.

hypothalamus A brain structure located in the forebrain that is involved in many behavioral functions, especially the emotional and motivational aspects of behavior. It can control the endocrine system's activities through connections with the pituitary gland.

hypothesis A statement of a predicted relationship between two or more variables. Specifically, in experimental design, the statement of the predicted relationship between the independent and dependent variable.

iconic memory Brief sensory memory of visual images.

id In Freud's theory, a term for the most primitive structures of human personality, the unconscious, irrational, and instinctual strivings for immediate satisfaction regardless of cost. *See also* ego and superego.

identity An individual's sense of personal uniqueness and continuity.

illusory correlation An error that occurs because people tend to perceive correlations where they expect them to be even if they are not present. Illusory correlations help to form and maintain stereotypes.

immune system A complex network of molecules, cells, and organs that defends the body from foreign invaders, neutralizes toxins, aids in repairing damaged tissue, and rids the body of abnormal cells.

implantation The burrowing of the preembryo into the wall of the uterus.

implicit memory Memory retrieval that requires no conscious effort to remember so that one is not aware of remembering during the time of retrieval. *See also* explicit memory.

imprinting A species-specific preprogrammed form of learning that occurs at a particular period in life (the critical or sensitive period) if the organism is exposed to the appropriate stimulus (e.g., a duckling's acquired tendency to follow whatever moving stimulus it encounters twelve to twenty-four hours after hatching).

incentive A circumstance or stimulus situation that one will work to obtain or avoid.

incubation In problem solving, a time-out period of rest from intensive work on a problem.

independent variable In experimental design, the variable that the psychologist manipulates to determine its effect on another. *See also* dependent variable.

inductive reasoning Reasoning from the specific to the general, by which one observes a number of particular instances and tries to determine a general rule that covers them all. *See* deductive reasoning.

infancy Very early childhood, from birth to two years.

inferences Conclusions about people or situations derived by making assumptions based on observations.

information-processing approach Theory of problem solving that focuses on the way a person receives information from the environment, operates on it, integrates it with other information available in memory, and uses it as a basis for deciding how to act.

in-group A group to which an individual belongs, feels loyalty, and with which he or she identifies. *See also* out-group.

in-group favoritism The positive feelings and special treatment that members of a group will accord other group members while having negative feelings toward and unfairly treating those who are not group members.

insight The sudden achievement of understanding that arises from a change in perspective on a problem. In Gestalt psychology, insight is viewed as the most appropriate description of human problem solving.

instinct An inherited pattern of behavior.

instrumental conditioning A type of learning in which the probability of behavior changes depending on its consequences. Also called operant conditioning.

integration Efforts to get along with others, to regulate behavior according to social codes and standards, and to develop a conscience.

intelligence The abilities needed to perform goal-directed adaptive behaviors in one's environment.

intelligence quotient (IQ) An index of intelligence allowing for comparison of research participants across all chronological ages. IQ is calculated by dividing mental age by chronological age and multiplying by 100. *See also* mental age.

intensity In vision, a property of light measured by the amount of energy in the light. Intensity produces the experience of brightness.

interactionist approach The view that emphasizes the joint influence of aspects of the person and the situation in determining behavior.

interference theory The assertion that items are forgotten because they are somehow interfered with by other items learned before or after.

internal attribution *See* dispositional attribution.

internal locus of control A personality orientation in which individuals believe they have control over their behavior and its outcomes.

internal versus external (attribution) A dimension of causal attributions concerned with deciding whether a behavior reflects something about a person or something about the situation.

interneurons Neurons that transmit and process information between sensory and motor neurons. *See also* motor and sensory neurons.

interpersonal attraction The expression of desire to approach and become involved with other people.

interposition A monocular depth cue in which we perceive an object that is partially blocked by another as more distant than the blocking object.

interval schedule A reinforcement schedule in which reinforcement is delivered for the first response made after a given interval of time has passed. In a fixed-interval schedule, the interval is always the same. In a variable-interval schedule, the interval varies around a specified average. *See also* ratio schedule.

intrinsic motivation A desire to perform a behavior in the absence of tangible reward because the activity itself is enjoyable. *See also* extrinsic motivation.

introspection Observing one's own private, internal state of being, including one's thoughts and feelings.

ions Atoms or molecules that have gained or lost electrons, thus acquiring a positive or negative charge.

iris In vision, the smooth, circular muscle in the eye that surrounds the pupil and contracts or dilates reflexively to regulate the amount of light entering the eye.

James-Lange theory The view, advanced by William James and Carl Lange, that the perception of events in the environment triggers bodily changes that produce the actual experience of emotion.

just noticeable difference (j.n.d.) The smallest difference between two stimuli that can be detected. *See also* difference threshold.

language An organized system of symbols with meanings that are shared and are used to communicate.

language acquisition The process by which individuals learn a language.

latent learning Learning that occurs without being manifested in performance.

latent stage According to Freud, the fourth stage of psychosexual development during which the child's psychic energies are not attached to any particular part of the body.

law of contiguity A principle of learning that states that events occurring close together in space and time tend to become associated.

law of effect The forerunner of the contemporary principle of reinforcement, this law states that responses leading to satisfying consequences will be strengthened and more likely to be repeated, whereas responses leading to unsatisfying consequences will be weakened and less likely to recur.

learned helplessness An organism's learned belief that it cannot control its environment, which may or may not be accurate.

learning A relatively permanent change in behavior that occurs as a result of experience.

learning curve A curve in which some index of learning (e.g., the number of drops of saliva in Pavlov's classical conditioning experiment) is plotted against trials or sessions.

learning by imitation Learning that takes place by observing and repeating another's behavior. *See also* observational learning.

lens The structure of the eye that bends light rays to focus an image on the retina.

leveling In memory, the gradual weakening and eventual disappearance of a memory trace over a period of disuse or nonretrieval. *See also* sharpening.

libido According to Freud, psychic energy that is primarily derived from the sexual, pleasure-seeking instincts of the id.

light The range of electromagnetic energy that is visible to human beings.

limbic system A set of brain structures that includes a relatively primitive portion of the cerebral cortex and parts of the thalamus and hypothalamus. It is believed to be involved in the control of emotional behavior and motivation.

linear perspective A monocular cue for perceiving distance derived from the fact that parallel lines appear to converge more closely the farther away they are.

linear regression The simplest form of statistical regression which involves finding the straight line that best represents the data in a scatter plot.

lithium An antidepressant drug that is especially useful in preventing the extreme mood swings that characterize bipolar mood disorders.

lobotomy A kind of psychosurgery that involves removing, destroying, or disconnecting the area of the prefrontal lobe of the brain thought to be associated with violent or aggressive behavior.

locus of control Personality dimension that distinguishes between people who believe their behaviors and outcomes are under their personal control from people who do not have such beliefs.

longitudinal study A developmental study in which the same people are tested at different ages.

long-term memory Those parts of the memory system that store such vast amounts of information for such long periods of time that their limits are as yet undetermined. *See also* sensory and short-term memory.

loudness The psychological attribute corresponding to amplitude of a sound wave.

lymphocytes White blood cells that defend the body against foreign invaders.

magnetic resonance imaging (MRI) A neurodiagnostic technique that relies on nuclear magnetic resonance. An MRI scan passes a high-frequency alternating magnetic field through the brain and produces information that can be used to form a three-dimensional picture of the brain's features.

maintenance rehearsal Rehearsal in which material remains in the working memory for awhile. In contrast to elaborative rehearsal, maintenance rehearsal confers little long-term benefit. *See also* elaborative rehearsal.

major depression A disorder characterized by two or more weeks of depressed mood and/or loss of interest or pleasure in all or most activities, too much or too little sleep, fatigue, loss of energy, significant weight loss or gain, feelings of worthlessness or inappropriate guilt, diminished ability to concentrate, and recurrent thoughts of death or suicide.

marijuana The dried leaves and flowering tops of the female hemp plant, sometimes smoked for their intoxicating effects on the mind.

master status Location in the social structure that is given precedence over other statuses across a variety of situations. For example, the status of being female sometimes acts as a master status, overriding other status categories, such as occupation.

material culture Those aspects of culture that are tangible human creations, such as radios, books, and automobiles. *See also* subjective culture.

maturation Biological changes that reflect a programmed growth process that is relatively unaffected by environmental conditions (e.g., the maturational sequence of creeping, crawling, and walking found in human beings).

mean A measure of central tendency, it is the total of the scores divided by the number of the scores. *See also* median and mode.

median A measure of central tendency, it is the point that divides the distribution of a set of values into two equal halves. *See also* mean and mode.

meditation A set of techniques used to attain an altered state of consciousness that allows one to exclude external stimulation, to control one's thoughts, and to focus or concentrate on a single stimulus or idea to a significant degree.

medulla oblongata The rearmost portion of the brain, just adjacent to the spinal cord. It includes centers that help control respiration and maintain muscle tone.

meiosis The process by which a germ cell divides and produces gametes (sperm and ova).

memory trace The change assumed to occur in the nervous system as a result of an experience that is the physical basis of its retention in memory.

mental age (MA) A score devised by Binet to represent the level of intelligence based on an individual's test performance relative to others in his or her age group. It is computed by determining the chronological age at which 50 percent of the age group perform at the same level of the child being tested. Children with an MA greater than their chronological age (CA) are ahead of their age group mentally; if their MA is lower than their CA, they lag behind it.

mental processes Processes that take place in the mind such as perceptions, memories, thoughts, emotions, and dreams.

mental representations Internal symbols that stand for something but are not equivalent to it, such as words or images.

mental set The predisposition to process information about a subject in one particular way, even when that way is inadequate for representing the information in new situations.

midbrain The part of the brain that makes connections between the forebrain and the hindbrain and alerts the forebrain to incoming sensory information.

mind-body dualism The assumption that the mind and the body function separately.

minimal groups An experimental paradigm that aims to create groups based on the most trivial (minimal) of criteria, such as flipping a coin.

Minnesota Multiphasic Personality Inventory (MMPI) A test used to aid in the diagnosis of mental disorders. It consists of statements that people are asked to judge as "true," "false," or "cannot say" about themselves. The responses are then compared to those typically given by people diagnosed as having particular psychiatric disorders.

mnemonics Strategies for improving memory typically based on translating information into vivid imagery or providing meaningful framework for remembering it.

modal score The score that occurs most frequently in a distribution of values. Also called the mode.

mode A measure of central tendency, it is the score that occurs most frequently in a distribution of values. *See also* mean and median.

modeling A technique used to teach people how to do things by having them watch the behavior of others.

monoamine oxidase (MAO) inhibitor An antidepressant drug that increases norepinephrine and serotonin levels in the brain and has been found to relieve depression in some people.

monocular cues Various features of the visual stimulus that indicate depth, even when viewed with one eye (e.g., linear perspective and motion parallax). *See also* binocular cues.

mood disorders Psychological disorders characterized by deep, severe, and long-lasting periods of sadness and low energy, or swings between high and low periods.

morality A set of ideals or principles that help a person to make distinctions between right and wrong and to act on the basis of those distinctions.

morality of care A theory of moral development conceptualized by Carol Gilligan that emphasizes the values of caring and compassion and suggests that females develop different moral orientations than do males.

moral realism According to Piagetian theory, the initial stage in moral development, in which rules are viewed as sacred and unchangeable moral absolutes.

moral relativism According to Piagetian theory, the second stage of moral development in which rules are regarded as changeable agreements created by people to serve particular needs.

morphemes The smallest units of meaning in a language.

motion parallax A depth cue provided by the fact that as an observer moves, the images cast by nearby objects move more rapidly on the retina than the images cast by objects farther away.

motivation The factors, including needs, drives, and incentives, that energize behavior toward a goal. *See also* emotion.

motor cortex The cortical structure in the brain that is directly involved in the control of voluntary muscle movement.

motor neurons Neurons that carry information away from the central nervous system to muscle cells.

multicultural Belonging to, or displaying aspects of more than one culture.

multiple personality disorder *See* dissociative identity disorder.

multiple regression A statistical procedure that can be used to correlate more than one variable (predictor variables) with another variable (criterion variable) in order to improve prediction accuracy.

naturalistic observation A research method for systematically observing and recording behaviors as they occur in real world settings.

nature Genetic factors that influence development. *See also* nurture.

need A state created when an organism does not have or is deprived of an object or condition it requires.

need for achievement The need to meet a standard for excellence, to accomplish something difficult, or to excel. People high in this need persist longer and do better on difficult tasks and are apt to set realistic and challenging goals. The need for achievement reflects a central value in American culture.

need for affiliation The need to develop relationships with other people.

need for power The need to control resources and the behavior of others.

need for social approval The desire to obtain the approval or to avoid the disapproval of others.

negative afterimage In vision, the visual image that lasts after removal of the stimulus that caused it. This afterimage appears in the opposite color of the original stimulus (e.g., red appears as green and blue appears as yellow).

negative punishment The process of lowering the probability of a behavior by removing a pleasant stimulus after the response occurs.

negative reinforcement The process of increasing the probability of a response by removing an unpleasant stimulus after the response occurs.

nerve cell The most elementary unit of the nervous system, its function is to send and receive messages.

neuron Another word for nerve cell.

neurotransmitters Chemical messengers released at the terminal button of an axon which travel across the synapse and have an excitatory or inhibitory effect on an adjacent neuron.

nicotine A drug generally classified as a stimulant that is the active ingredient in tobacco products.

non-REM sleep The four distinguishable stages of sleep characterized by slow-wave EEGs and gross body movements, (e.g., rolling and changing positions). *See also* slow-wave sleep.

noradrenaline A hormone that plays a role in adapting the body to stress. Also called norepinephrine.

normal distribution A frequency distribution whose graphic representation has a symmetric, bell-shaped form called the normal curve. Its characteristics are often referred to when investigators test statistical hypotheses and make inferences about the population from a given sample.

norms In intelligence testing, the scores taken from a large sample of the population against which an individual's test scores are evaluated. In social psychology, a group's standards for the behaviors of its members.

nurture The environmental factors that influence human development. *See also* nature.

obedience A form of social influence in which people obey a direct order from an authority figure.

objective Having to do with external events that are observable by more than one individual.

objective personality tests A method of personality assessment that is based on a standardized set of questions of previously determined reliability and validity that have been given to a large number of people and permit comparisons among individuals.

object permanence The belief that an object exists even when it is out of sight. According to Piaget, this concept does not develop until infants are eight months old or more.

object relations theory A form of psychoanalytic ego psychology, the theory that ego development and subsequent interpersonal relationships are based on the infant's attachment to the mother and other figures.

observational learning Cognitive learning that can occur simply by watching another person's behavior.

obsessive-compulsive disorder (OCD) A disorder characterized by repeated or continuous intrusive thoughts, feelings of anxiety as a result of these thoughts, and the need to repeat certain acts to reduce that anxiety.

occipital lobe The lobe in the cerebral cortex involved in the reception and analysis of visual information.

olfactory epithelium The small area at the top of the nasal cavity containing receptors that react to chemicals suspended in air.

operant chamber *See* Skinner box.

operant conditioning *See* instrumental conditioning.

operant response In Skinner's system, the response that is followed by a reinforcer or punishment.

operational definition The use of a methodological procedure (operation) to define an abstract concept in a concrete way. For example, the operational definition of the abstract concept of anxiety might be operationally defined by a physiological measure, such as heart rate, or by a verbal report measure, such as a rating of anxiety level.

opponent-process theory (1) In vision, a theory of color vision based on the idea that the perception of a particular color depends on a combination of signals from three opposing pairs of receptors, or channels (red-green, yellow-blue, and black-white). (2) In motivation, a theory that claims that every emotional experience leads to the opposite emotional experience that persists after the original emotion has ended.

optic nerve A bundle of nerve fibers, made up of the axons of ganglion cells, that carry visual information from the eye to the brain.

optimal level of arousal The idea that, in keeping with the principle of homeostasis, we have a particular level of cortical stimulation at which our goal-directed behaviors are most effective. We seek stimulation when arousal is low and we avoid stimulation when arousal is high in order to maintain our optimal level of arousal.

oral stage According to Freud, the first stage of psychosexual development, in which psychic energy is focused on the mouth.

ossicles The three small bones in the ear that transmit vibrations from the eardrum to the oval window.

out-group Two or more individuals who are not included in an in-group. *See also* in-group.

out-group homogeneity bias The perception that members of groups that we are not part of (out-groups) are more similar to each other than members of our own group (in-group).

pain Unpleasant sensory and emotional experience associated with actual, potential, or imagined tissue damage.

panic attacks Anxiety attacks that involve feelings and physical reactions such as heart palpitations, shortness of breath, sweating, faintness, and great fear that resemble those of someone in terrible danger when no real danger is present.

panic disorder An anxiety disorder characterized by sudden anxiety attacks usually lasting for several minutes in which bodily symptoms (e.g., choking, dizziness, trembling, and chest pains) are accompanied by feelings of intense apprehension, terror, and a sense of impending doom.

parasympathetic nervous system The part of the autonomic division of the peripheral nervous system involved in controlling involuntary behavior, such as digestion; it works in opposition to the sympathetic nervous system and conserves body energy, calming the body and bringing functions back to normal after an emergency has passed.

parietal lobe A portion of the cerebral cortex between the frontal lobe and the occipital lobe that is concerned with the senses of skin and body position.

partial reinforcement A condition in which a response is reinforced only some of the time.

partial reinforcement effect The finding that a response is much harder to extinguish if it was acquired during partial rather than continuous reinforcement.

perception The mental processes by which we organize and interpret sensory information.

peripheral nervous system (PNS) One of the two major divisions of the nervous system that contains the nerves that provide communication between the central nervous system and other parts of the body, including muscles, glands, and sensory receptors.

permastore An extremely stable and durable form of memory.

personal control Our belief in our ability to affect the situations in which we find ourselves.

personality An individual's unique combination of enduring personal characteristics and behaviors.

phallic stage According to Freud, the third stage of psychosexual development, in which psychic energies are focused on the genitals.

phenothiazines A group of antipsychotic drugs that reduces the agitation and psychotic symptoms of schizophrenia.

phenotype The unique combination of overt characteristics of an organism that results from the interaction of a person's genotype with the environment.

pheremones Special chemicals secreted by many animals which trigger particular reactions in members of the same species.

phobias Intense, irrational fears that include the persistent and extreme desire to avoid some object or situation.

phoneme Category or class of slightly varying sounds that speakers of a language perceive as linguistically similar.

photoreceptors Cells in the retina that transduce light energy into electrochemical information. Cones encode color vision and are responsible for acuity, while rods are sensitive to light and are used primarily for vision in dim light.

physical development Developmental change that occurs in bodily structures and processes over the life cycle.

physical drug dependence Dependence on a drug when the drug has created a physiological need by changing the body's normal chemical balance.

Piagetian theory A theory of cognitive development, conceptualized by Jean Piaget, that takes the dynamic view that intellectual development occurs in stages.

pitch In audition, the psychological attribute corresponding to the frequency of a sound wave.

pituitary gland An endocrine gland heavily influenced by the hypothalamus. It is considered a master gland because many of its secretions trigger hormone secretions in other glands.

placebo In medical practice, a term for a chemically inert substance that the patient perceives as having therapeutic effects.

placebo effect The beneficial effect of a treatment administered to a patient who believes it has therapeutic powers even though it has none.

placenta The network of blood vessels attached to the mother's uterine wall, which carries oxygen and food to the developing embryo and fetus.

plasticity The brain's capacity for modification.

pleasure principle According to Freud, the concept of immediate gratification of desires that governs the operation of the id. *See also* id.

polygraph A complex piece of electronic equipment that measures blood pressure, heart rate, respiration, and electrical resistance of the skin. It is used in research to determine what people experience as stressful and sometimes as a lie detector, although its validity for that purpose is debated.

pons The structure just above the medulla that connects parts of the brain stem to one another and to the spinal cord. It plays a role in sleep and respiration.

positive punishment An aversive stimulus administered to increase the likelihood of a response.

positive reinforcement The process of increasing the probability of a response by following it with a pleasant stimulus.

positron emission tomography (PET scans) An imaging process that records the levels of glucose and glucose metabolism in the brain. The resulting pictures show the level of metabolic activity throughout the various regions of the brain at a given point in time.

posttraumatic stress disorder (PTSD) An anxiety disorder resulting from intensely traumatic events (e.g., experiencing the threat of death, serious injury, or bodily violation as occurs in rape and torture) in which the individual reexperiences emotional, cognitive, and behavioral aspects of the past trauma, including intense fear, helplessness, horror, physical symptoms, and irritability.

practical intelligence The ability to apply what we know to adapt to the demands of everyday tasks, and to act in accordance with the rules of society and the environment. *See also* analytic intelligence and creative intelligence.

pragmatics A discipline devoted to the study of the implicit aspect of language use, particularly with regard to how it is used in various contexts.

Pragnanz A Gestalt principle of perceptual organization that corresponds to a "goodness of figure."

preconscious According to Freud, the ideas, thoughts, and images that a person is not aware of at a given moment but that can be brought into awareness with little or no difficulty.

preembryo In prenatal development, the formless mass of cells that multiplies during the week after fertilization while making its way down the Fallopian tube to burrow into the wall of the uterus (implantation) where it develops into an embryo. *See also* embryo.

prejudice Negative attitudes toward individuals based on their group membership.

Premack principle The principle developed by David Premack, that states that under conditions of free choice, the behavior that is most probable is the behavior that is most preferred and therefore most reinforcing.

premoral period According to Piagetian theory, the period from birth to four years of age when children show no understanding or conception of rules.

prenatal period The time in an individual's development from conception to birth.

preoperational stage According to Piaget's theory, the second stage of cognitive development, occurring roughly between two and seven years of age, characterized by a limited understanding of logical principles such as conservation and reversibility.

prepared learning A genetically based predisposition to learn associations between certain kinds of stimuli and specific responses more readily than others.

prescription drugs Drugs that are legally available only with authorization by a physician.

primacy effect In learning, the principle that information received first tends to be remembered better than later information, which helps explain why first impressions are important.

primary appraisal The first step in the cognitive appraisal of stressors in which the individual asks "Am I OK or in trouble?" and "What does this mean to me?" These questions lead to three conclusions about a potential stressor's significance: it can be irrelevant, benign or positive, or stressful.

primary prevention services A form of mental health care that seeks to prevent the occurrence of mental disorders by finding and eliminating their potential causes.

primary reinforcers Stimuli or events that are innately reinforcing.

priming The activation of a schema (concept), perhaps unconsciously, which can then be used to process incoming information.

priming effect Increased access to a particular stimulus or piece of information as a result of priming, which can occur from previous recent exposure to the same or a related stimulus.

primitive reflexes One of two forms of reflexes that full-term newborns inherit. Primitive reflexes (e.g., the grasping reflex) are controlled by subcortical areas of the brain and gradually disappear over the first year of life. They may be a holdover from early evolutionary history when they were once needed for survival.

proactive interference Interference with memory for certain information that is attributable to other information learned at an earlier time.

problem-focused coping A method of coping in which stressful conditions are evaluated and something is done to change or avoid them. *See also* emotion-focused coping.

problem space The internal representation of a problem in memory.

procedural knowledge Knowing "how" to do something, (i.e., how to ride a bike) in contrast with declarative knowledge. *See also* declarative knowledge.

projective personality test A method of personality assessment in which test-takers respond to or interpret ambiguous stimuli (e.g., inkblots). It is based on the psychodynamic approach and assumes that unconscious needs or desires will be revealed in the person's responses.

propositions A way of relating concepts by making an assertion that links a subject (i.e., *chickens*) and a predicate (i.e., *lay eggs*).

prototype The most typical example of a category (e.g., robin is a prototypical bird).

proximal stimuli Those physical energies, such as light, that impinge directly on our sensory receptors. *See also* distal stimuli.

proximity principle (1) In perception, the Gestalt principle of organization that says that objects that are closer to each other will be more likely to be perceived as a group. (2) In interpersonal attraction, the principle that the mere fact of being physically near someone is one of the most powerful predictors of whether two people will become friends.

psychoactive drugs Chemical compounds that affect the central nervous system, changing perception, reactivity, mood, and consciousness.

psychoanalysis Psychodynamic therapy based on Freudian theory which employs techniques such as dream interpretation, free association, and analysis of resistance and transference. The goal is to provide insight into the patient's unconscious impulses, conflicts, and motives.

psychodynamic approach A school of psychology that views behavior as a result of mental events and emphasizes the importance of conflicting unconscious mental processes and early developmental experiences for understanding human behavior.

psychological universals Psychological processes that operate in all individuals, such as learning, perception, and memory. *See also* biological universals and social universals.

psychology The scientific study of behavior and mental processes.

psychometrics An area of psychology concerned with the construction and use of tests to measure qualitative and quantitative aspects of mental processes and behavior, such as intelligence and personality.

psychopathology The inability to behave in a socially appropriate way such that the consequences of one's behavior are maladaptive for oneself or society.

psychophysics An approach that relates the characteristics of physical stimuli to attributes of the sensory experience they produce.

psychosexual development The stages of development that, according to Freud, all human beings pass through during early life. Each stage—oral, anal, phallic, latent, and genital—centers around a specific area of the body where psychic energy (libido) concentrates during that particular period.

psychosomatic illness A physiological condition with psychological origins.

psychosomatic medicine The field devoted to treating illnesses that reflect emotional conflicts.

psychosurgery The treatment of pathological behavior by surgical intervention, including probing, slicing, or removing some part of the brain.

psychotherapy Collectively, methods for treating psychological problems based on principles of psychology aimed at changing behaviors, thoughts, perceptions, and emotions. Sometimes called "the talking cure."

puberty A period of development that marks the transition between childhood and adolescence when primary and secondary sex characteristics develop. *See also* secondary sex characteristics.

punishment The process of decreasing the probability of a response by following it with an unpleasant stimulus.

punishment and aversion therapy A form of behavior therapy that involves the utilization of unpleasant stimuli (e.g., electric shocks) to control or alter an individual's behavior.

pupil The opening in the center of the iris through which light enters the eyeball.

race A social category based on biological characteristics; the definition of racial categories changes over time and differs across cultures.

random assignment In experimental design, the assignment of research participants to conditions whereby each participant has the same probability of being assigned to any one condition.

random sampling Selecting a sample in such a manner that each person in the population has an equal chance of being chosen for the sample.

rational-emotive therapy A clinical technique developed by Albert Ellis to help clients understand the irrationality of various beliefs, recognize how these beliefs affect their behavior, and practice new, more adaptive, rational, and beneficial ways of thinking and behaving.

ratio schedule A reinforcement schedule in which reinforcement is delivered for the first response that occurs after a certain number of responses. In a fixed-ratio schedule, the number of responses required for a reward is always the same. In a variable ratio schedule, the number of responses required varies irregularly around a specified average. *See also* interval schedule.

reality principle A concept originated by Freud, this principle governs the ego's functioning as it mediates among the demands of the external world, the id, and the superego.

recall A method of measuring memory in which research participants are simply asked to produce an item from memory. *See also* recognition and savings.

recency effect In freely recalling a learned list of items, the recall superiority of the items at the end of the list compared to those in the middle. *See also* primacy effect and serial position effect.

receptive field The retinal area in which visual stimulation affects a particular cell's firing rate.

reciprocal determinism Bandura's concept in which behavioral variables, environmental variables, and personal/cognitive variables all mutally influence each other. A person's behavior affects the environment, the environment, in turn, affects behavior, and the person's awareness of this mutual dependency affects both.

reciprocity The social-psychological principle that states that when we receive something, we feel compelled to return something of equal value.

reciprocity principle A basic norm of many social interactions that decrees that one must repay whatever one has been given.

recognition A measure of memory in which a person is presented a stimulus and asked to identify whether it is the same as one the person has previously encountered. *See also* recall.

reflectance The percentage of the light falling on an object that is reflected from the object rather than absorbed.

reflex A simple, specific, involuntary response to a stimulus that does not require learning (e.g., the pupil's constriction in response to bright light).

refractory period (1) The period during and after a neuron's firing in which the responsiveness of the axon is reduced. (2) The time interval following orgasm during which a person, typically a man, cannot have another orgasm. (3) The time interval following a response during which almost no stimulus will produce another response.

regression (1) In Freud's theory, a defense mechanism characterized by a return to an earlier stage of psychosexual development. (2) In statistics, a procedure for predicting a person's score on one variable when the person's score on another variable and the correlation between the two variables is already known.

regression line In statistics, when plotting the data during a regression analysis in graph, this line best represents the scores.

rehabilitative services Mental health care that aims to reduce the long-term effects of existing emotional problems.

rehabilitative therapy A form of therapy designed to help victims of crisis by providing job retraining, training in social skills, as well as a variety of other psychological services.

rehearsal The conscious repetition of information in an effort to retain it in short-term memory.

reinforcement In classical conditioning, the procedure by which the US is made contingent on the CS. In instrumental conditioning, the procedure by which the instrumental response is made contingent on some desired outcome.

reinforcer An event or stimulus that increases the frequency of a response with which it is associated.

relaxation training A stress management technique that applies learning principles to counter the effects of stress by teaching individuals how to relax.

reliability An essential characteristic of any psychological test or measure. A test is reliable if, when given again, it obtains consistent results when there is no reason to believe the phenomenon being measured has changed.

REM sleep A qualitatively unique form of sleep that is characterized by a rapid EEG pattern and short bursts of rapid eye movement. *See also* non-REM and slow-wave sleep.

representations Cognitions that correspond to (or represent) certain events, or relations between events, in the external world.

representativeness heuristic A decision-making shortcut used when estimating the probability that an object (or event) belongs to a certain category in which the judgment is based on the extent to which the object resembles the prototype of that category rather than on base-rate information.

repression In psychoanalytic theory, a defense mechanism by means of which thoughts, impulses, or memories that give rise to anxiety are pushed out of consciousness.

research methods The wide variety of methods used to gather and record data systematically. They can be correlational or experimental.

response discrimination Learning to give one, and only one, particular response in a given situation.

response generalization Performance of a response similar to the original learned response.

resting potential The difference in electrical charge across the membrane in a cell's normal state.

reticular formation A network of fibers in the lower to middle brain stem that alerts the forebrain to receive and process incoming sensory information and is critically involved in sleep and emotion.

retina Photosensitive surface at the back of the eye that contains visual receptor cells upon which the visual image is focused.

retrieval cue A stimulus that helps to retrieve a memory.

retrieval failure The act of forgetting all or some of the details of a memory.

retroactive interference The interference with memory of certain information that is attributable to other information learned at a later time.

retrograde amnesia Loss of memory of events just prior to the event that caused the memory loss. Long-term memory remains intact.

reversibility The Piagetian concept, generally achieved during the formal operational period, that certain mathematical operations, such as addition and subtraction, can be reversed or undone.

rods Long, thin photoreceptor cells in the periphery of the retina that are sensitive to light of low intensity and that function in dim light and nighttime vision but are not involved in perception of color.

role-conflict Conflict that occurs when the different roles we hold require us to do incompatible things, such as when a parental role may require us to care for a sick child at the same time that a work role requires us to be at an important meeting.

role taking Assuming a point of view and taking on the beliefs, attitudes, and behaviors associated with it.

rooting reflex The infant's inborn tendency to turn the head toward any object or person that gently touches a cheek. This response helps the child locate a nipple for feeding.

Rorschach Inkblot Test A projective technique developed by Hermann Rorschach that requires an individual to look at ambiguous inkblots and say what he or she sees in them. The responses are then studied for their emotional expression, their focus, and their recurring patterns.

saturation The dimension of color experience that corresponds to how much or how deep the hue of a light is.

savings A method of measuring memory in which research participants are asked to relearn old but seemingly forgotten information. The difference in time between relearning versus originally learning the information is then computed. *See also* recall and recognition.

scarcity The social-psychological principle that states that we accord value to those things we perceive to be rare or difficult to obtain.

schizophrenia A group of severe mental disorders characterized by one or more of the following: marked disturbance of thought, withdrawal, inappropriate or flat emotions, delusions, and hallucinations. *See also* catatonic schizophrenia and disorganized schizophrenia.

scripts Schemas that contain information about the characteristic scenarios of behaviors in particular settings (e.g., a restaurant script).

secondary appraisal The second step in the cognitive appraisal of stressors, which involves a person answering the question, "What am I able to do about this stressful event?" The answer involves deciding at least one of three things: (1) Who or what is responsible for the stressful event? (2) What is the probability of success or failure in coping with the event? (3) What does the future hold?

secondary prevention services Mental health care that is designed to prevent or reduce the impact or severity of an problem once it occurs.

secondary reinforcers Stimuli that become reinforcers after being paired with primary reinforcers.

secondary sex characteristics The physical features associated with sexual maturation that are not directly involved with reproduction, such as the development of pubic hair, changes in voice, etc.

secondary traits According to Allport, personality traits that are less conspicuous, consistent, and generalized than cardinal or central traits. They typically apply under only certain circumstances (e.g., Martha is grouchy in the morning). *See also* cardinal and central traits.

sedatives Drugs that reduce anxiety by inducing muscle relaxation, sleep, and inhibition of the cognitive centers of the brain. *See also* tranquilizers.

selective attention Paying attention to only some of the information that is available in a situation; in particular, we are most likely to pay attention to information that we perceive as personally relevant.

self-actualization A major concern of humanistic psychologists, it is the fulfillment of one's potential. *See also* hierarchy of needs.

self-concept The mental framework that contains the information we have about our self.

self-efficacy A learned expectations that one is capable of performing behaviors needed to produce a desired result.

self-fulfilling prophecy An expectancy that leads to behavior with consequences that lead to confirmation of the expectancy.

self-referencing effect The enhanced memory and increased ease and efficiency of cognitive processing when information is self-relevant compared to other types of information.

self-schemas Mental frameworks (i.e., cognitive structures), that are used to store and process information about the self.

self-serving bias The tendency to see oneself in a favorable light, leading us to deny responsibility for failures but take credit for successes. *See also* attribution theory and fundamental attribution error.

self-theory Approach to personality that focuses on the individual as a whole, unified self. It takes a positive view of human beings and is a part of the humanistic approach to psychology.

semantic memory Memory of information that is independent of time or place.

semantics (1) In language, the study of meaning. (2) The set of rules for deriving meaning in a given language.

semicircular canals Three canals within the inner ear that contain a viscous liquid that moves when the head rotates, providing information about the nature and extent of the movement.

sensation The process whereby our sensory receptors receive and transduce information from the external world into electrochemical impulses in our nervous system.

sensation seeking The tendency to seek novel experiences, look for thrills and adventure, and be highly susceptible to boredom.

sensorimotor stage According to Piaget, the first two years of life when a child knows and interacts with the world primarily in terms of sensory impressions and motor activities, and has little competence in representing the environment using symbols, language, or images.

sensory abilities The abilities of our sensory receptors to receive and transduce information from the external world into electrochemical information in our nervous system. These include the ability to sense light, mechanical pressure, heat, certain chemical substances, and tissue damage.

sensory memory The brief lingering of a sensory impression that is experienced after a stimulus has been removed.

sensory neurons Neurons that respond to incoming stimuli, such as sound or light, and carry this information to the central nervous system.

serial position effect In memorization, when the beginning and end items of a list are easier to remember than those in the middle. *See also* primacy effect and recency effect.

serotonin A neurotransmitter involved in many of the mechanisms of sleep and emotional arousal.

setpoint The weight that a body seeks to maintain by influencing a person's metabolic rate and desire to eat.

sex drive A biologically based psychological state that motivates an organism to have sexual activity.

s-factor In intelligence, a specific cognitive ability found to underlie performance on some, but not all, types of intelligence tests.

shading A monocular cue for depth derived from information provided by shadows connected to an object as well as those cast in the background environment.

shallow processing The repetition of information to maintain it in short-term memory. This is also known as maintenance rehearsal. *See also* elaborative rehearsal.

shaping An instrumental learning procedure through which an animal (or human) is trained to perform a rather difficult response by reinforcing successively closer and closer approximations to that response. *See also* successive approximation.

sharpening The exaggeration of certain features of a memory trace so that they take on a greater importance than they had previously. *See also* assimilation and leveling.

short-term memory Memory for learned material over a brief retention interval. This is our hypothetical memory system for transient information. Also called working memory.

signal detection theory A statistical theory of perception that postulates two processes in stimulus detection: a sensory process and a decision process.

similarity In perception, a principle by which we tend to group like figures, especially by color and orientation.

similarity bias The tendency to see oneself as more like members of one's in-group than like members of an out-group.

similarity principle In interpersonal attraction, the principle that the more similar two people are, the more likely they are to be attracted to each other.

situational attribution *See* external attributions.

size constancy The tendency to perceive the size of objects as constant despite the fact that the retinal images of these objects change in size whenever we change the distance from which we view them.

skew This phenomenon occurs when a frequency distribution is characterized by a concentration of scores either to the left or right of the center of the scale. *See also* normal distribution.

Skinner box A device developed by B. F. Skinner to investigate the events of operant conditioning. Also known as an operant chamber.

sleeper effect The notion that a message from an unreliable source may have little persuasive effect at first, but may come to increase in persuasion as time goes on because the source is forgotten while the message is retained.

sleepwalking Nocturnal wandering. When it occurs, it is usually during REM sleep.

slow-wave sleep Sleep characterized by large amplitude, slow-activity EEGs. *See* REM and non-REM sleep.

socialization The process whereby the child acquires the patterns of behavior characteristic of his or her society.

social category A grouping of individuals who share one or more social characteristics, such as age, gender, race, ethnicity, sexual orientation, physical disability, or income.

social class The stratification of society based on a combination of social and economic factors.

social facilitation A phenomenon in which the mere presence of other persons improves individual performance.

social identity That component of individual self-concept or identity derived from one's membership in one or more social groups.

social inhibition The inhibition of performance by the presence of an audience.

social learning approach A cognitively oriented theoretical approach that emphasizes the importance of learning that occurs by observing the behavior of others, even in the absence of reinforcement.

social loafing This phenomenon occurs when individuals spend less effort on a common task when they are working in a group than if they had worked on that task alone.

social phobias Fears of embarrassment or humiliation that cause people to avoid situations in which they must expose themselves to public scrutiny.

social play Play that involves peer interaction; it is an important contributor to the development of language and social skills.

social psychology The scientific study of how people think about, influence, and relate to one another.

social role A specific position in a social structure that has expectations for values, attitudes, and behaviors, including rights and responsibilities, associated with it.

social schemas Cognitive structures that organize our beliefs and feelings and process information about our social world.

social skills training A form of rehabilitation therapy that involves teaching the behaviors needed for acceptance in one's social groups, including how to relax and interact comfortably with others.

social status An individual's recognized position or location within a society or group.

social stratification The distribution of power, prestige, and social rewards in a society.

social structure The way that society is organized.

social universals The social elements that are common across human culture, including group living, languages, cooking, and other characteristics. *See also* biological universals and psychological universals.

social validation The social-psychological principle that states that we use other people's behavior (particularly that of those who are similar to us) to guide our own actions. It underlies a number of strategies of social influence.

society A structured group of individuals typically within a geographical or political boundary who share a culture.

somatic nervous system A division of the peripheral nervous system primarily concerned with the control of the skeletal musculature and the transmission of information from the sense organs.

somatoform disorder The generic term for disorders that are expressed in physical symptoms in the absence of any known physical illness.

somatosensory cortex The cortical area located in the parietal lobe just behind the motor area in the frontal lobe. This region is involved in bodily sensation, including touch, pain, and temperature.

source traits Those fundamental dimensions of personality which underlie many other characteristics.

spontaneous recovery An increase in the tendency to perform an extinguished response after a time interval in which neither conditioned stimulus (CS) nor unconditioned stimulus (US) are presented.

stable attribution An attribution of a behavior to a cause that is steady over time.

stable versus unstable A dimension of causal attributions that deals with the question, "Is the cause a one-time event or does it persist?"

Stanford-Binet test A widely used standardized intelligence test. It was originally developed to distinguish between malingerers and schoolchildren who were likely to experience learning difficulties and who would benefit from a specialized education. *See also* intelligence quotient and mental age.

status *See* social status.

stereotype A social schema about characteristics of members of a group. Stereotypes can be negative or positive.

stimulus An object or event in the environment.

stimulus control An instrumental learning process whereby a cue in the environment comes to control the behavior of an organism.

stimulus discrimination The act of responding differently to various stimuli that have some similarities. *See also* stimulus generalization.

stimulus generalization The occurrence of a learned response under circumstances similar but not identical to the original learning situation. *See also* stimulus discrimination.

strange situation A test that involves exposing infants to a series of mildly stressful situations in order to determine the quality of their attachments to one or more chosen companions.

stress A psychophysiological state or process that occurs when we face events we perceive as threatening to our physical or psychological well-being.

stress-inoculation training A stress management technique by which individuals are introduced to small amounts of stress and taught cognitive-behavioral strategies for dealing with them.

stressors Environmental events perceived as harmful or threatening.

stress response Psychological and physiological responses to stressors. *See also* stress and stressors.

Stroop effect A marked decrease in the speed of naming the colors in which various color names (such as green, red, etc.) are printed when the colors and the names are different.

structuralism An early school of psychological thought that held that the subject matter of psychology was conscious experience, that the object of study was to analyze experience into its component parts, and that the primary method of analysis was introspection. *See also* functional psychology.

structured interview An interview method that consists of a series of prearranged questions. It is often used as part of a case study.

subcultures Groups with different cultural traditions that co-exist within a larger society.

subjective Having to do with inner mental events such as individual consciousness and perception that are only observable by the person experiencing them. *See also* objective.

subjective culture Aspects of culture that involve intangible human creations, such as ideas, symbols, language, beliefs, values, and norms. *See also* material culture.

subjective expected utility The perceived worth (subjective utility) of a goal object combined with the subjective probability a particular behavior will lead to it. *See* subjective utility.

subjective norms These guides to one's behaving are based on what one thinks other people believe one ought to do combined with one's motivation to comply with these beliefs.

subjective utility Perceived usefulness or worth of a goal object. This perception reflects a combination of need, drive, and incentive.

successive approximation Learning in graduated steps whereby each successive step requires a response that is closer than the previous response to the desired performance. This process is also known as shaping.

superego According to Freudian theory, one of the basic structures of the personality. It is the partially unconscious area of the mind that contains and enforces people's values, morals, and basic attitudes that they learned from their parents and society.

superordinate goal Goals that are shared by competing groups and require their members to cooperate in order to achieve them.

superstitious behavior In operant conditioning, behavior that is strengthened or weakened because by chance it happens to precede reinforcement or punishment.

survey method A research method that involves asking a representative sample of a population about its opinions, characteristics, or behaviors in an attempt to estimate their occurrence in the larger population.

survival reflexes Innate reflexes (e.g., breathing, sucking, swallowing) that are present at birth and that help infants adapt to the world outside the womb.

symbol Something used to stand for something else; that is, something used to represent an idea, concept, or object.

symbolic representation A type of mental representation that does not correspond to the physical characteristics of that which it represents. Thus, the word *mouse* does not resemble the small rodent it represents.

symmetrical Counterbalance of exactly similar parts facing each other or a center.

sympathetic nervous system A division of the autonomic nervous system that mobilizes the body's energies for emergencies (e.g., increasing heart and respiration rates). It works in opposition to the parasympathetic nervous system.

symptoms The outward manifestations of an underlying pathology.

synapse The juncture between the axon of one neuron and the dendrite or cell body of another. It includes the tip of the axon on one side, the receiving cell's membrane on the other, and the space between them. *See also* synaptic cleft.

synaptic cleft The gap between neurons, across which signals are transmitted.

synaptic vesicles Pockets or sacs that store neurotransmitters at the presynaptic cell's axon terminal buttons.

syndrome A pattern of symptoms that tend to go together.

syntax The system by which words are arranged into meaningful phrases and sentences.

systematic desensitization A behavior therapy used to treat phobias through a gradual process of counterconditioning to a response incompatible with fear, usually muscular relaxation. The stimuli are usually evoked as mental images according to an anxiety hierarchy whereby the less frightening stimuli are counterconditioned before the more frightening ones.

tabula rasa A blank slate. Some philosophers erroneously used this term to describe the mind at birth.

tardive dyskinesia A severe side effect of phenothiazines indicated by a disturbance of motor control that involves drooling, lip smacking, and grimacing similar to that seen in Parkinson's disease. *See also* phenothiazines.

temperament Broad emotional traits, that are believed to have a substantial biological basis, including level of reactivity and level of energy.

temporal lobes The lobes in the cerebral cortex involved in hearing and visual processing.

texture gradient A monocular distance cue based on perceived characteristics in surface texture whereby coarser textures appear closer, and finer textures appear more distant.

thalamus The part of the lower portion of the forebrain that serves as a major relay and integration center for sensory information.

that's-not-all technique A compliance strategy based on the norm of reciprocity in which a small, usually preplanned, concession is made to "sweeten" a deal.

Thematic Apperception Test (TAT) A projective technique in which people are shown a set of ambiguous pictures and asked to write a story about each.

theory of planned behavior A theory of behavior derived from the theory of reasoned action that says that a combination of our attitudes, subjective norms, and perceived behavioral control over a particular behavior determine our intention to perform it.

theory of reasoned action A theory of behavior that says that a combination of our attitudes and subjective norms determine our intention to perform a particular behavior.

thirst The psychological expression, or drive, of our physiological need for fluids.

threshold The value a stimulus must reach to produce a response.

thymus gland An organ located behind the breastbone above the heart whose role in the immune system includes turning undifferentiated lymphocytes into cells designed to attack and kill specific foreign invaders.

thyroid gland An endocrine gland that produces the hormone thyroxin and thus regulates metabolism and growth.

timbre A characteristic of sound that reflects the complexity of the frequencies of the sound waves produced by the vibrating object.

time out An operant-conditioning therapy technique that involves following undesirable behavior with a period of time away from positive reinforcement.

token economy A structured environment designed on the basis of operant-conditioning principles in which objects such as poker chips are used as rewards that may be exchanged for desired activities or objects.

top-down processes Mental processes, such as expectancies, that operate on incoming stimuli and interpret them. *See also* bottom-up processes.

trace-dependent forgetting Loss of learned information due to the loss of memory. *See also* cue-dependent forgetting.

traits Relatively permanent characteristics that one tends to show in most situations.

trait theory The view that people differ in regard to underlying attributes (traits) that partially determine behavior and that are presumed to be consistent across time and situation.

tranquilizers Drugs that reduce anxiety without inducing sleep. *See also* sedatives.

transduction In sensation, the process by which our senses convert energy from the external world (e.g., light, heat) into neural impulses.

transference In psychoanalysis, the patient's tendency to transfer emotional reactions that were originally directed toward one's own parents (or other critical figures in one's early life) and redirect them toward the analyst.

tricyclics Drugs that alleviate depressive symptoms, presumably because they increase availability of certain neurotransmitters (especially norepinephrine and serotonin) in the brain.

two-factor theory of emotion A theory of emotion that states that emotional experience reflects the interaction of general (physiological) arousal and cognitive appraisal of the arousal.

Type A personality A personality type characterized by extreme competitiveness, aggressiveness, hostility, anger, and impatience. *See also* Type B personality.

Type B personality In contrast to the Type A personality, Type B is characterized by a more easygoing, less hurried, less competitive, and friendlier behavior pattern. *See also* Type A personality.

unconditioned response (UR) In classical conditioning, the response that automatically occurs whenever the unconditioned stimulus is presented, without any training.

unconditioned stimulus (US) In classical conditioning, the stimulus that automatically elicits the desired response, without any training.

unconscious That part of an individual's mind that contains memories, thoughts, and feelings that cannot be easily brought into consciousness.

undifferentiated schizophrenia A "catch all" term indicating that a person has characteristics of schizophrenia but does not neatly fall into one of its subcategories. This is the most common schizophrenic diagnosis.

unstructured interview An interview technique that allows for wide-ranging questions and enables the interviewer to probe spontaneous responses during the course of the interview. This technique is used in the case study method.

utility *See* subjective utility.

validity The degree to which a measuring device measures what it is supposed to measure.

values Goals that are viewed as good in themselves and not because they lead to further desirable consequences.

variable Any characteristic of an object, event, or person that can take two or more values.

variable interval A schedule of reinforcement in which the reinforcers are delivered after the first response after a certain time interval has elapsed. The length of the time varies from trial to trial.

variable ratio A schedule of reinforcement in which the reinforcers are delivered after a certain number of responses occur. The number of responses required varies from trial to trial.

visual acuity Ability to notice fine detail in a patterned stimulus.

visual cortex A division of the cerebral cortex that receives and integrates visual sensations. It is located in the occipital lobe. *See also* association cortex, auditory and speech centers, motor cortex, and somatosensory cortex.

wavelength The distance between the crests of two successive waves; light wavelength is a major determinant of perceived color.

Weber's law The observation that the size of the difference threshold is proportional to the intensity of the initial stimulus.

Wechsler intelligence test An alternative approach to measuring intelligence quotient developed by psychologist David Wechsler. Wechsler tests use two separate scales, verbal and nonverbal (performance), to measure intelligence.

Wernicke's area The part of the left side of the temporal lobe involved in speech comprehension. It is named for its discoverer, the German neurologist Carl Wernicke.

withdrawal effects Physical effects, which can include vomiting, hallucinations, uncontrolled trembling, muscle spasms, and other forms of discomfort that can occur when an individual stops taking certain drugs.

Yerkes-Dodson law The observation that there is an optimal level of motivation for any task, such that increased motivation will improve performance up to a point, beyond which there is deterioration. The easier a task is to perform, the higher the drive level required for optimal performance.

z-score A statistical score that is expressed as a deviation from the mean in standard deviation units, which allows a comparison of scores drawn from different distributions.

zygote The fertilized ovum resulting from the union of a sperm and an egg cell.

Wechsler intelligence tests An alternative approach to measuring intelligence [illegible] developed by psychologist David Wechsler. Wechsler tests use two separate scales, verbal and nonverbal (performance), to measure intelligence.

Wernicke's area [illegible] left side of the temporal lobe involved in speech comprehension [illegible] named for its discoverer, [illegible] Carl Wernicke.

withdrawal effects [illegible]

Yerkes-Dodson law [illegible]

z-score [illegible]

valves [illegible] Caisson [illegible] in the [illegible] or the [illegible] may lead to turbulent or unstable [illegible].

variable Any characteristic of [illegible] object, event, or person that can [illegible] two or more values.

variable interval A schedule of reinforcement in which [illegible] certain [illegible] after a certain time [illegible] of the time varies from trial to trial.

variable ratio [illegible] schedule of reinforcement in which the reinforcement [illegible] after a certain number of [illegible]. The [illegible] responses required varies from trial to trial.

visual agnosia [illegible]

visual [illegible]

References

Abbott, B. B., Schoen, L. S., & Badia, P. (1984). Predictable and unpredictable shock: Behavioral measures of aversion and physiological measures of stress. *Psychological Bulletin, 96,* 45–47.

Abel, E. I., & Sokol, R. J. (1986). Fetal alcohol syndrome is now a leading cause of mental retardation. *Lancet, 2,* 1222.

Abel, T., Alberini, C., Ghirardi, M., Huang, Y.-Y., Nguyen, P., & Kandel, E. R. (1995). Steps toward a molecular definition of memory consolidation. In D. L. Schacter (Ed.), *Memory distortion* (pp. 298–325). Cambridge, MA: Harvard University Press.

Abelson, R. P., Aronson, E., McGuire, W. J., Newcomb, T. M., Rosenberg, M. J., & Tannenbaum, P. H. (1968). *Theories of cognitive consistency: A sourcebook.* Chicago: Rand McNally.

Abraham, K. (1911/1948). Notes on psychoanalytic investigation and treatment of manic-depressive insanity and applied conditions. In *Selected papers of Karl Abraham, M.D.* (D. Bryan & A. Strachey, Trans.). London: Hogarth Press.

Abram, K. M., & Teplin, L. A. (1990). Drug disorder, mental illness, and violence. *National Institute on Drug Abuse Research Monograph Series, 103,* 222–238.

Abrams, K. K., Allen, L., & Gray J. J. (1993). Disordered eating attitudes and behaviors, psychological adjustment, and ethnic identity: A comparison of black and white female college students. *International Journal of Eating Disorders, 14,* 49–57.

Abramson, H. A. (1974). Respiratory disorders and marijuana use. *Journal of Asthma Research, 11,* 97.

Abramson, L. Y., Metalsky, G. I., & Alloy, L. B. (1989). Hopelessness depression: A theory-based subtype of depression. *Psychological Review, 96,* 358–372.

Abramson, L. Y., Seligman, M. E. P., & Teasdale, J. (1978). Learned helplessness in humans: Critique and reformulation. *Journal of Abnormal Psychology, 87,* 49–74.

Ackerman, D. (1990). *A natural history of the senses.* New York: Random House.

Ackerman, S. (1992). *Discovering the brain.* Washington, DC: National Academy Press.

Adelson, J., Green, B., & O'Neil, R. (1969). Growth of the idea of law in adolescence. *Developmental Psychology, 1,* 327–332.

Ader, R., & Cohen, N. (1975). Behaviorally conditioned immunosuppression. *Psychosomatic Medicine, 37,* 333–340.

Ader, R., & Cohen, N. (1982). Behaviorally conditioned immunosuppression and murine systemic lupus erythematosus. *Science, 215,* 1534–1536.

Ader, R., & Cohen, N. (1993). Psychoneuroimmunology: Conditioning and stress. *Annual Review of Psychology, 44,* 53–85.

Adler, A. (1961). *Understanding human nature.* New York: Fawcett World Library.

Adler, N. (1981). Sex roles and unwanted pregnancy in adolescent and adult women. *Professional Psychology, 12*(1), 56–66.

Adler, T. (1992). Electric shock therapy effective but not benign. *APA Monitor, 23*(2), 16.

Adler, T. (1993). Sign and spoken languages use brain's left hemisphere. *APA Monitor, 24*(11), 21.

Adorno, T. W., Frenkel-Brunswik, E., Levinson, D. J., & Sanford, R. N. (1950). *The authoritarian personality.* New York: Harper & Row.

Agnati, L. F., Bjelke, B., & Fuxe, K. (1992). Volume transmission in the brain. *American Scientist, 80,* 362–373.

Ahson, A. (1974). Anna O.: Patient or therapist? An eidetic view. In V. Franks & V. Burtle (Eds.), *Women in therapy: New psychotherapies for a changing society* (pp. 263–283). New York: Brunner/Mazel.

Aiello, J. R., & Thompson, D. E. (1980). Personal space, crowding, and spatial behavior in a cultural context. In I. Altman, J. F. Wohlwill, & A. Rapoport (Eds.), *Human behavior and environment* (Vol. 4). New York: Plenum.

Ainsworth, M. D. (1979). Infant-mother attachment. *American Psychologist, 34,* 932–937.

Ainsworth, M. D. S., & Bell, S. M. (1970). Attachment, exploration, and separation: Illustrated by the behavior of one-year-olds in a strange situation. *Child Development, 41,* 49–61.

Ainsworth, M. D. S., Blehar, M. C., Waters, E., & Wall, S. (1978). *Patterns of attachment.* Hillsdale, NJ: Erlbaum.

Aizenberg, R., & Treas, J. (1985). The family in late life: Psychological and demographic considerations. In J. E. Birren & K. W. Schaie (Eds.), *Handbook of the psychology of aging* (2nd ed., pp. 169–189). New York: Van Nostrand.

Ajzen, I. (1985). From intentions to actions: A theory of planned behavior. In J. Kuhl & J. Beckman (Eds.), *Action control: From cognition to behavior* (pp. 11–39). New York: Springer.

Ajzen, I., & Fishbein, M. (1977). Attitude-behavior relations: A theoretical analysis and review of empirical research. *Psychological Bulletin, 84,* 888–918.

Alexander, C. N., Langer, E. J., Newman, R. I., Chandler, H. M., & Davies, J. L. (1989). Transcendental meditation, mindfulness, and longevity: An experimental study with the elderly. *Journal of Personality and Social Psychology, 37,* 950–964.

Alexander, C. N., Robinson, P., & Rainforth, M. (1994). Treating and preventing alcohol, nicotine, and drug abuse through transcendental meditation: A review and statistical meta-analysis. *Alcoholism Treatment Quarterly, 11,* 13–87.

Alexander, F. (1946). Individual psychotherapy. *Psychosomatic Medicine, 8,* 110–115.

Alexander, F. (1950). *Psychosomatic medicine.* New York: Norton.

Allbrook, R. C. (1968). How to spot executives early. *Fortune, 78,* 106–111.

Alldridge, P. (1985). Bedlam: Fact or fantasy? In W. F. Bynum, R. Porter, & M. Shepherd (Eds.), *The anatomy of madness: Essays in the history of psychiatry* (Vol. 2). New York: Tavistock.

Allen, K. F. Moss, A. J., Giovino, G. A., Shopland, D. R., & Pierce, J. P. (1993, February 1). Teenage tobacco use: Data estimates from the teenage attitudes and practices survey, United States, 1989. *Advance Data from Vital and Health Statistics, 224,* 1–20.

Allen, L., & Gorski, R. (1992). Sexual orientation and the size of the anterior commissure in the human brain. *Proceedings of the National Academy of Sciences, 89,* 7199–7202.

Allen, L., & Majidi-Ahi, S. (1991). Black American children. In J. T. Gibbs, L. N. Huang, & Associates (Eds.), *Children of color: Psychological interventions with minority youth*. San Francisco: Jossey-Bass.

Allen, V. L., & Wilder, D. A. (1979). Group categorization and attribution of belief similarity. *Small Group Behavior, 10,* 73–80.

Allison, J. (1989). The nature of reinforcement. In S. B. Klein & R. R. Mowrer (Eds.), *Contemporary learning theories: Instrumental conditioning theory and the impact of biological constraints in learning* (pp. 13–39). Hillsdale, NJ: Erlbaum.

Allison, J., Miller, M., & Wozny, M. (1979). Conservation in behavior. *Journal of Experimental Psychology: General, 108,* 4–34.

Allport, G. W. (1937). *Personality: A psychological interpretation.* New York Holt, Rinehart, & Winston.

Allport, G. W. (1954). *The nature of prejudice*. Cambridge, MA: Addison-Wesley.

Allport, G. W. (1961). *Pattern and growth in personality.* New York: Holt, Rinehart and Winston.

Allport, G. W. (1965). *Letters from Jenny*. New York: Harcourt, Brace, & World.

Allport, G. W. (1966). Traits revisited. *American Psychologist, 21,* 1–10.

Allport, G. W., & Odbert, H. S. (1936). Trait-names: A psycho-lexical study. *Psychological Monographs: General and Applied, 47,* 171–220 (1, Whole No. 211).

Allred, K. D., & Smith, T. W. (1989). The hardy personality: Cognitive and physiological responses to evaluative threat. *Journal of Personality and Social Psychology, 56,* 257–266.

Allyn, J., & Festinger, L. (1961). The effectiveness of unanticipated persuasive communications. *Journal of Abnormal and Social Psychology, 62,* 35–40.

Almeida Acosta, E., & Sanchez de Almejda, M. E. (1983). Psychological factors affecting change in women's roles and status: A cross-cultural study. *International Journal of Psychology, 18,* 3–35.

Alper, J. (1993). Ulcers as an infectious disease. *Science, 260,* 159–160.

Alpert, J. L. , Brown, L. S., Ceci, S. J., Courtois, C. A., Loftus, E. F., & Ornstein, P. A. (1996). *Working group on investigation of childhood abuse: Final report.* Washington, DC: American Psychological Association.

Altemeier, W. A., O'Connor, S., Vietze, P., Sandler, H., & Sherrod, K. (1984). Prediction of child abuse: A prospective study of feasibility. *Child Abuse and Neglect , 8,* 393–400.

Amaro, H., & Russo, N. F. (1987). Hispanic women and mental health: An overview of contemporary issues in research and practice. *Psychology of Women Quarterly, 11,* 393–407.

Amaro, H., Zuckerman, B., & Cabral, H. (1989). Drug use among adolescent mothers: Profile of risk. *Pediatrics, 84*(1), 144–151.

Amateur Athletic Foundation of Los Angeles (1991, September). *Harper's Index*, p. 15.

American Heart Association (1993). *Heart and stroke facts*. Dallas, TX: Author.

American Psychiatric Association. (1987). *Diagnostic and statistical manual of mental disorders* (3rd ed.). Washington, DC: Author.

American Psychiatric Association. (1994). *Diagnostic and statistical manual of mental disorders* (4th ed.). Washington, DC: Author.

American Psychological Association. (1986). *Careers in psychology.* Washington, DC: Author.

American Psychological Association. (1992). Ethical principles of psychologists and code of conduct. *American Psychologist, 47,* 1597–1611.

American Psychological Association, Task Force on Promotion and Dissemination of Psychological Procedures. (1995). Training in and dissemination of empirically-validated psychological treatments. *The Clinical Psychologist, 48,* 3–23.

Amoore, J. E., Johnston, J. W., Jr., & Rubin, M. (1964). The sterochemical theory of odor. *Scientific American, 210* (2), 42–49.

Amparano, J. (1996, August 4). On job stress is making workers sick. *The Arizona Republic*, pp. A1, A12.

Anastasi, A. (1958). Heredity, environment, and the question "how"? *Psychological Review, 65,* 197–208.

Anastasi, A. (1988). *Psychological testing* (6th ed.). New York: Macmillan.

Andersen, B. L. (1986). *Women with cancer: Psychological perspectives.* New York: Springer-Verlag.

Anderson, C. A. (1991). How people think about causes: Examination of the typical phenomenal organization of attributions for success and failure. *Social Cognition*, 9, 295–329.

Anderson, C. A., & Arnoult, L. H. (1989). An examination of perceived control, irrational beliefs, and positive stress as moderators of the relation between negative stress and health. *Basic and Applied Social Psychology, 10,* 101–107.

Anderson, J. R. (1976). *Language, memory, and thought.* Hillsdale, NJ: Erlbaum.

Anderson, J. R. (1990). *The adaptive character of thought*. Hillsdale, NJ: Erlbaum.

Anderson, N. (1992). Health status of African Americans: A contextual approach. In *Annual Meeting of the American Psychological Association,* Washington, DC.

Anderson, N. B., Lane, J. D., Taguchi, F., & Williams, R. B., Jr. (1989). Patterns of cardiovascular responses to stress as a function of race and parental hypertension in men. *Health Psychology, 8,* 525–540.

Andreasen, N. C., et al. (1993). Comment on intelligence and brain structure in normal individuals. *American Journal of Psychiatry, 150,* 130–134.

Andron, L., & Strum, M. (1973). Is "I do" in the repertoire of the retarded? *Mental Retardation, 11,* 31–34.

Anisfeld, M. (1991). Neonatal imitation. *Developmental Review, 11,* 60–97.

Ankney, C. D. (1992). Sex differences in relative brain size: The mismeasure of women too? *Intelligence,* 16, 329–336.

Anthony, T., Cooper, C., & Mullen, B. (1992). Cross-racial facial identification: A social cognitive integration. *Personality and Social Psychology Bulletin, 18,* 296–301.

Antill, J. K. (1983). Sex role complementarity versus similarity in married couples. *Journal of Personality and Social Psychology, 45,* 145–155.

Antonuccio, D., Danton, W., & DeNelsky, G. Y. (1995). Psychotherapy versus medication for depression: Challenging the conventional wisdom with data. *Professional Psychology: Research and Practice, 26,* 574–584.

Antrobus, J. S. (1990). The neurocognition of sleep mentation. In R. R. Bootzin, J. F. Kihlstrom, & D. L. Schacter (Eds.), *Sleep and cognition.* Washington DC: American Psychological Association.

Appelbaum, R. P., & Chambliss, W. J. (1995). *Sociology.* New York: HarperCollins.

Appley, M. H., & Trumbull, R. (1986). *Dynamics of stress*. New York: Plenum.

Apter, M. J. (1970). *The computer simulation of behavior.* New York: Harper & Row.

Arboleda-Florez, J., & Holley, H. L. (1991). Antisocial burnout: An exploratory study. *Bulletin of the American Academy of Psychiatry and the Law, 19,* 173–183.

Argyle, M., & Dean, J. (1965). Eye-contact, distance and affiliation. *Sociometry, 28,* 289–304.

Argyle, M., Henderson, M., Bond, M., Ilzuka, Y., & Contarello, A. (1986). Cross-cultural variations in relationship rules. *International Journal of Psychology, 21,* 287–315.

Armstead, C. A., Lawler, K. A., Gorden, G., Cross, J., & Gibons, J. (1989). Relationship of racial stressors to blood pressure responses and anger expression in black college students. *Health Psychology, 8,* 541–556.

Arnold, A. P. (1980). Sexual differences in the brain. *American Scientist, 68,* 165–173.

Aronson, E. (1984). *The social animal* (3rd ed.). San Francisco: Freeman.

Aronson, E., & Mills, J. (1959). The effect of severity of initiation on liking for a group. *Journal of Abnormal and Social Psychology, 59,* 177–181.

Aronson, E., Stephan, C., Sikes, J., Blaney, N., & Snapp, M. (1978). *The jigsaw classroom.* Beverly Hills, CA: Sage.

Asch, S. (1952). *Social psychology.* New York: Prentice-Hall.

Asch, S. (1955). Opinions and social pressure. *Scientific American, 193,* 31–35.

Asch, S. E. (1956). Studies of independence and conformity: 1. A minority of one against a unanimous majority. *Psychological Monographs, 70*(9, Whole No. 416).

Aserinsky, E., & Kleitman, N. (1953). Regularly occurring periods of eye motility and concomitant phenomena during sleep. *Science, 118,* 273–274.

Atchley, R. C. (1982). Retirement as a social institution. In R. Turner & J. Short (Eds.), *Annual review of sociology.* Palo Alto, CA: Annual Reviews.

Atkinson, J. W. (1981). Studying personality in the context of an advanced motivational psychology. *American Psychologist, 36,* 107–112.

Atkinson, J. W. (1982). Motivational determinants of thematic apperception. In A. J. Stewart (Ed.), *Motivation and society* (pp. 3–40). San Francisco: Jossey-Bass.

Atkinson, J. W., & Litwin, G. H. (1960). Achievement motive and test anxiety conceived as a motive to approach success and motive to avoid failure. *Journal of Abnormal and Social Psychology, 60,* 52–63.

Atkinson, J. W., & McClelland, D. C. (1948). The projective expressions of needs. 11. The effect of different intensities of the hunger drive on thematic apperception. *Journal of Experimental Psychology, 38,* 643–658.

Atkinson, R. C., & Shiffrin, R. M. (1968). Human memory: A proposed system and its control processes. In K. W. Spence (Ed.), *The psychology of learning and motivation: Advances in research and theory* (Vol. 2, pp. 89–195). New York: Academic Press.

Atkinson, R. C., & Shiffrin, R. M. (1971). The control of short-term memory. *Scientific American, 224,* 83–89.

Atkinson, R. R., Morten, G., & Sue, D. W. (1979). *Counseling American minorities: A cross-cultural perspective.* Dubuque, IA: William C. Brown.

Atwood, M. E., & Polson, P. G. (1976). A process model for water jug problems. *Cognitive Psychology, 8,* 191–216.

Ax, A. F. (1953). The physiological differentiation between fear and anger in humans. *Psychosomatic Medicine, 15,* 443–452.

Ayanian, J. Z., & Epstein, A. M. (1991). Differences in the use of procedures between women and men hospitalized for coronary heart disease. *New England Journal of Medicine, 325,* 221–225.

Ayllon, T., & Haughton, E. (1964). Modification of symptomatic verbal behavior of mental patients. *Behaviour Research and Therapy, 2,* 87–97.

Azrin, N. H., & Foxx, R. M. (1974). *Toilet training in less than a day.* New York: Simon and Schuster.

Azrin, N. H., Holz, W. C., & Hake, D. F. (1963). Fixed-ratio punishment. *Journal of the Experimental Analysis of Behavior, 6,* 141–148.

Azrin, N. H., Hutchinson, R. R., & Hake, D. H. (1966). Extinction induced aggression. *Journal of the Experimental Analysis of Behavior, 9,* 191–204.

Azrin, N. H., Hutchinson, R. R., & McLaughlin, R. (1965). The opportunity for aggression as an operant reinforcer during aversive stimulation. *Journal of the Experimental Analysis of Behavior, 8,* 171–180.

Azrin, N. H., Hutchinson, R. R., & Sallery, R. D. (1964). Pain aggression toward inanimate objects. *Journal of the Experimental Analysis of Behavior, 7,* 223–228.

Bach-y-rita, P. (1972). *Brain mechanisms in sensory substitution.* New York: Academic Press.

Bachman, J. G., Wallace, J. M., O'Malley, P M., Johnston, L. D., Kurth, C. L., & Neighbors, H. W. (1991). Racial/ethnic differences in smoking, drinking, and illicit drug use among American high school seniors, 1976–89. *American Journal of Public Health, 81,* 372–377.

Baddeley, A. (1990). *Human memory: Theory and practice.* Boston: Allyn & Bacon.

Badia, P. (1990). Memories in sleep: Old and new. In R. R. Bootzin, J. F. Kihlstrom, & D. L. Schacter (Eds.), *Sleep and cognition.* Washington DC: American Psychological Association.

Bagby, J. W. (1957). A cross-cultural study of perceptual predominance in binocular rivalry. *Journal of Abnormal and Social Psychology,* 54, 331–334.

Bahrick, H. (1984). Semantic memory content in permastore: Fifty years of memory for Spanish learned in school. *Journal of Experimental Psychology: General, 113,* 1–24.

Bahrick, H. P., & Phelps, E. (1987). Retention of Spanish vocabulary over 8 years. *Journal of Experimental Psychology: Learning, Memory and Cognition, 13,* 344–349.

Bailey, J. M., & Pillard, R. C. (1991). A genetic study of male sexual orientation. *Archives of General Psychiatry, 48,* 1089–1096.

Bailey, J. M., & Pillard, R. C. (1995). Genetics of human sexual orientation. *Annual Review of Sex Research, 6,* 126–150.

Bailey, J. M., Pillard, R. C., Neale, M. C., & Agyei, Y. (1993). Heritable factors influence sexual orientation in women. *Archives of General Psychiatry, 50,* 217–223.

Baldessarini, R. J. (1984). Anti-psychotic drugs. In T. B. Karasu (Ed.), *The psychiatric therapies.* Washington, DC: American Psychiatric Press.

Ball, G., & Hulse, S. (1997). Bird song. *American Psychologist.*

Ballard, P. B. (1913). Oblivescence and reminiscence. *British Journal of Psychology Monograph Supplements, 1,* 1–82.

Baltes, P. B. (1968). Longitudinal and cross-sectional sequences in the study of age and generation effects. *Human Development, 11,* 145–171.

Baltes, P. B., & Labouvie, G. V. (1973). Adult development of intellectual performance: Description, explanation, and modification. In C. Eisdorfer & M. P. Lawton (Eds.), *The psychology of adult development and aging.* Washington, DC: American Psychological Association.

Baltes, P. B., & Schaie, W. K. (Eds.). (1978). *Lifespan developmental psychology.* New York: Academic Press.

Bandura, A. (1968). Social learning interpretation of psychological dysfunctions. In P. London & D. Rosenhan (Eds.), *Foundations of abnormal psychology.* New York: Holt, Rinehart and Winston.

Bandura, A. (1973). *Aggression: A social learning analysis.* Englewood Cliffs, NJ: Prentice-Hall.

Bandura, A. (1977a). Self-efficacy theory: Toward a unifying theory of behavioral change. *Psychological Review, 84,* 191–215.

Bandura, A. (1977b). *Social learning theory.* Englewood Cliffs, NJ: Prentice-Hall.

Bandura, A. (1978). The self-system in reciprocal determinism. *American Psychologist, 33,* 344–358.

Bandura, A. (1980). The self and mechanisms of agency. In J. Suls (Ed.), *Social psychological perspectives on the self.* Hillsdale, NJ: Erlbaum.

Bandura, A. (1982). Self-efficacy mechanism in human agency. *American Psychologist, 37,* 122–147.

Bandura, A. (1986). *Social foundations of thought and action: A social cognition theory.* Englewood Cliffs, NJ: Prentice-Hall.

Bandura, A. (1989). Social cognitive theory. In R. Vasta (Ed.), *Theories of child development: Revised formulations and current issues.* New York: Appleton-Century-Crofts.

Bandura, A. (1991). The changing icons in personality psychology. In J. H. Cantor (Ed.), *Psychology at Iowa: Centennial essays.* Hillsdale, NJ: Erlbaum.

Bandura, A., Ross, D., & Ross, S. A. (1961). Transmission of aggression through imitation of aggressive models. *Journal of Abnormal and Social Psychology, 63,* 575–582.

Bandura, A., Ross, D., & Ross, S. A. (1963a). A comparative test of the status envy, social power, and secondary reinforcement theories of identificatory learning. *Journal of Abnormal and Social Psychology, 67,* 527–534.

Bandura, A., Ross, D., & Ross, S. A. (1963b). Imitation of film-mediated aggressive models. *Journal of Abnormal and Social Psychology, 66,* 3–11.

Bandura, A., & Walters, R. H. (1965). *Social learning and personality development.* New York: Holt, Rinehart and Winston.

Banham, K. (1980). Kathrine M. Banham (1897–). In A. N. O'Connell & N. F. Russo (Eds.), *Models of achievement: Reflections of eminent women in psychology* (pp. 27–42). New York: Columbia University Press.

Bar-Tal, D., & Saxe, L. (1976). Perceptions of similarly and dissimilarly attractive couples and individuals. *Journal of Personality and Social Psychology, 33,* 772–781.

Barber, T. X. (1969). *Hypnosis: A scientific approach.* New York: Van Nostrand.

Bard, P., & Mountcastle, V. B. (1948). Some forebrain mechanisms involved in expression of rage with special reference to suppression of angry behavior. *Research Publication Association Nervous and Mental Disorders, 27,* 362–404.

Bardo, M., & Mueller, C. (1991). Sensation-seeking and drug abuse prevention from a biological perspective. In L. Donohew, H. Sypher, & W. Bukoski (Eds.), *Persuasive communication and drug abuse* (pp. 195–207). Hillsdale, NJ: Erlbaum.

Barefoot, J. C., Dodge, K. A., Peterson, B. L., Dahlstrom, W. G., & Williams, R. B. (1989). The Cook-Medley hostility scale: Item content and ability to predict survival. *Psychosomatic Medicine, 51,* 46–57.

Barefoot, J. C., Siegler, I. C., Nowlin, J. B., Peterson, B., Haney, T. L., & Williams, R. B. (1987). Suspiciousness, health, and mortality: A follow-up study of 500 older adults. *Psychosomatic Medicine, 49,* 450–457.

Barker, P. R., Manderscheid, R.W., Hendershot, G., Jack, S.S., Schoenborn, C. A., & Goldstrom, I. (1992, September 16). Serious mental illness and disability in the adult household population: United States, 1989. *Advance Data from Vital and Health Statistics of the Centers for Disease Control, 218.*

Barlow, D. H. (1996). Health care policy, psychotherapy research, and the future of psychotherapy. *American Psychologist, 51,* 1050–1058.

Barlow, D. H., & Lehman, C. (1996). Advances in the psychosocial treatment of anxiety disorders: Implications for national health care. *Archives of General Psychiatry, 53,* 727–735.

Baron, P. M., Mandel, D. R., Adams, C. A., & Griffin, L. M. (1976). Effects of social density in university residential environments. *Journal of Personality and Social Psychology, 34,* 434–446.

Baron, R. A. (1992). *Psychology* (2nd ed.). Needham Heights, MA: Allyn & Bacon.

Baron, R. A., & Byrne, D. (1991). *Social psychology: Understanding human interaction.* Boston: Allyn & Bacon.

Barratt, M. S., Negayama, K., & Minami, T. (1993). The social environments of early infancy in Japan and the United States. *Early Development and Parenting, 2,* 51–64.

Barrett, R. S. (1963). Guide to using psychological tests. *Harvard Business Review, 41,* 139.

Barsalou, L. W. (1983). Ad hoc categories. *Memory and Cognition, 11,* 211–227.

Bartlett, F. C. (1932). *Remembering.* Cambridge, Eng.: Cambridge University Press.

Bartoshuk, L. M. (1978). History of taste research. In E. C. Carterette & M. P. Friedman (Eds.), *Handbook of perception* (Vol. 6A). New York: Academic Press.

Bartoshuk, L. M. (1993). Genetic and pathological taste variation: What can we learn from animal models and human disease? *Ciba Foundation Symposium, 179,* 251–267.

Bateson, G., Jackson, D. D., Haley, J., & Weakland, J. H. (1956). Toward a theory of schizophrenia. *Behavioral Science, 1,* 251–264.

Battig, W. F. (1979). The flexibility of human memory. In L. S. Cermak & F. I. M. Craik (Eds.), *Levels of processing and human memory* (pp. 23–44). Hillsdale, NJ: Erlbaum.

Bauby, J.-D. (1997). *The diving bell and the butterfly.* New York: Knopf.

Bauer, P. J. (1993). Memory for gender-consistent and gender-inconsistent event sequences by twenty-five-month-old children. *Child Development, 64,* 285–297.

Baum, A., Grunberg, N. E., & Singer, J. E. (1982). The use of psychological and neuroendocrinological measurements in the study of stress. *Health Psychology, 1,* 217–236.

Baum, A., & Valins, S. (1979). Architectural mediation of residential density and control: Crowding and the regulation of social contact. In L. Berkowitz (Ed.), *Advances in experimental social psychology* (Vol. 12). New York: Academic Press.

Baumrind, D. (1978). Parental disciplinary patterns and social competence in children. *Youth Sociology, 9,* 239–276.

Baumrind, D. (1983). Rejoiner to Lewis reinterpretation of parental firm control affects: Are authoritative families rarely harmonious? *Psychological Bulletin, 94,* 132–142.

Beardsley, L. M. (1994). Medical diagnosis and treatment across cultures. In W. J. Lonner & R. Malpass (Eds.), *Psychology and culture.* Boston: Allyn & Bacon.

Beck, A. T. (1976). *Cognitive therapy and the emotional disorders.* New York: International Universities Press.

Beck, A. T. (1991). Cognitive therapy: A 30-year perspective. *American Psychologist,* 46, 368–375.

Beck, A. T. (1993). Cognitive approaches to stress. In P. M. Lehrer & R. L. Woolfold (Eds.), *Principles and practices of stress management* (2nd ed.). New York: Guilford.

Beck, A. T., Rush, A. J., Shaw, B. F., & Emery, G. (1979). *Cognitive therapy of depression.* New York: Guilford Press.

Beck, A. T., Ward, O. H., Mendelson, M., Mock, J. E., & Erbaugh, J. K. (1962). Reliability of psychiatric diagnosis: 11. A study of consistency of clinical judgments and ratings. *American Journal of Psychiatry, 119,* 351–357.

Beinfield, H., & Krongold, E. (1992). *Between heaven and earth: A guide to Chinese medicine.* New York: Ballantine Books.

Belcastro, P. A. (1985). Sexual behavior differences between black and white students. *Journal of Sex Research,* 21, 56–67.

Bell, A. P., Weinberg, M. S., & Hammersmith, S. K. (1981). *Sexual preference: Its development in men and women.* Bloomington, IN: Indiana University Press.

Belle, D. (1990). Poverty and women's mental health. *American Psychologist, 49,* 384–389.

Bellezza, F. S., & Bower, G. H. (1981). Person stereotypes and memory for people. *Journal of Personality and Social Psychology, 41,* 856–865.

Belloc, N. D., & Breslow, L. (1972). Relationship of physical health status and family practices. *Preventive Medicine, 1,* 409–421.

Bellugi, U., & Klima, E. S. (1972). The roots of language in the sign talk of the deaf. *Psychology Today, 6* (1): 60–64, 76.

Belsky, J. (1985). Experimenting with the family in the newborn period. *Child Development, 56,* 407–414.

Belsky, J. (1988). The "effects" of infant day-care reconsidered. *Early Childhood Research Quarterly, 3,* 235–272.

Bem, D. J. (1967). Self-perception: An alternative interpretation of cognitive dissonance phenomena. *Psychological Review, 74,* 183–200.

Bem, D. J. (1972). Self perception theory. In L. Berkowitz (Ed.), *Ad-*

vances in experimental social psychology (Vol. 6). New York: Academic Press.

Bem, D. J. (1996). Exotic becomes erotic: A developmental theory of sexual orientation. *Psychological Review, 101,* 320–335.

Bem, S. L. (1974). The measurement of psychological androgyny. *Journal of Consulting and Clinical Psychology, 42,* 155–162.

Bem, S. L. (1993). *The lenses of gender: Transforming the debate on sexual inequality.* New Haven, CT: Yale University Press.

Benedict, R. (1934/1959). Patterns of culture. New York: New American Library.

Bengston, V. L. (1973). *The social psychology of aging.* Indianapolis: Bobbs-Merrill.

Benjamin, L. T., Jr. (1988). *A history of psychology: Original sources and contemporary research.* New York: McGraw-Hill.

Benjamin, L., Jr., & Shields, S. (1990). Leta Stetter Hollingworth. In A. N. O'Connell & N. F. Russo (Eds.), *Women in psychology: A biobibliographic sourcebook.* Westport, CT: Greenwood Press.

Benson, H. (1975). *The relaxation response.* New York: Morrow.

Berger, J. M. (1993). *Personality* (3rd ed.). Pacific Grove, CA: Brooks/Cole.

Berk, L. E., & Garvin, R. A. (1984). Development of private speech among low-income Appalachian children. *Developmental Psychology, 20,* 271–286.

Berko, J. The child's learning of English morphology. *Word, 14,* 150–177.

Berkowitz, L. (1962). *Aggression: A social psychological analysis.* New York: McGraw-Hill.

Berkowitz, L. (1974). Some determinants of impulsive aggression: Role of mediated associations with reinforcements for aggression. *Psychological Review, 81,* 165–176.

Berkowitz, L. (1989). The frustration-aggression hypothesis: An examination and reformulation. *Psychological Bulletin, 106,* 59–73.

Berkowitz, L. (1990). On the formulation and regulation of anger and aggression: A cognitive-neoassociationistic analysis. *American Psychologist, 45,* 494–503.

Berkowitz, L., & LePage, A. (1967). Weapons as aggression-eliciting stimuli. *Journal of Personality and Social Psychology, 7,* 202–207.

Berlyne, D. E. (1960). *Conflict, arousal and curiosity.* New York: McGraw-Hill.

Berndt, T. J., Cheung, P. C., Lau, S., Hau, K., & Lew, W. J. F. (1993). Perceptions of parenting in mainland China, Taiwan, and Hong Kong: Sex differences and societal differences. *Developmental Psychology, 29,* 156–164.

Berne, E. (1964). *Games people play.* New York: Grove Press.

Bernstein, D. L., & Sigmundi, R. A. (1980). Tumor anorexia: A learned food aversion? *Science, 209,* 416–418.

Bernstein, D. L., & Webster, M. M. (1980). Learned taste aversions in humans. *Physiology and Behavior, 25,* 363.

Berntson, G. G., Cacioppo, J. T., & Quigley, K. S. (1993). Cardiac psychophysiology and autonomic space in humans: Empirical perspectives and conceptual implications. *Psychological Bulletin, 114,* 296–322.

Berry, J. (1980). Acculturation as varieties of adaptation. In A. Padilla (Ed.), *Acculturation: Theory, models and some new findings.* Boulder, CO: Westview Press.

Berry, J. (in press). An ecological perspective on cultural and ethnic psychology. E. Trickett (Ed.), *Human diversity: Perspectives on people in context.* San Francisco: Jossey-Bass.

Berry, J. W., Poortinga, Y. H., Segall, M. H., & Dasen, P. R. (1992). *Cross-cultural psychology: Research and applications.* New York: Cambridge University Press.

Berry, J. W., Trimble, J. E., & Olmedo, E. L. (1986). Assessment of acculturation. In W. J. Lonner & J. W. Berry (Eds.), *Field methods in cross-cultural research* (Vol. 8, pp. 291–324). Beverly Hills, CA: Sage.

Berscheid, E. (1981). An overview of the psychological effects of physical attractiveness and some comments upon the psychological effects of knowledge of the effects of physical attractiveness. In W. Lucker, K. Ribbens, & J. A. McNamera (Eds.), *Logical aspects of facial form (craniofacial growth series).* Ann Arbor, MI: University of Michigan Press.

Berscheid, E., & Walster, E. H. (1978). *Interpersonal attraction* (Rev ed.). Reading, MA: Addison-Wesley.

Betancourt, H., & López, S. R. (1993). The study of culture, ethnicity, and race in American psychology. *American Psychologist, 48,* 629–637.

Bexton, W. H., Heron, W., & Scott, T. H. (1954). Effects of decreased variation in the environment. *Canadian Journal of Psychology,* 70–76.

Biglan, A., Metzler, C.W., Wrt, R., Ary, D., Noell, J., Ochs, L., French, C., & Hood, D. (1990). Social and behavioral factors associated with high-risk sexual behavior among adolescents. *Journal of Behavioral Medicine, 13,* 245–262.

Bigler, R. S., & Liben, L. S. (1990). The role of attitudes and interventions in gender-schematic processing. *Child Development, 61,* 1440–1452.

Bijnen, E. J., & Poortinga, Y. H. (1988). The questionable value of cross-cultural comparative studies with the Eysenck Personality Questionnaire. *Journal of Cross-Cultural Psychology, 19,* 193–202.

Bijnen, E. J., Van der Net, Z. J., & Poortinga, Y H. (1986). On cross-cultural comparative studies with the Eysenck Personality Questionnaire. *Journal of Cross-Cultural Psychology, 17,* 3–16.

Billings, A. C., & Moos, R. H. (1984). Coping, stress, and social resources among adults with unipolar depresssion. *Journal of Personality and Social Psychology, 46,* 877–891.

Bills, A. W. (1931). Blocking: A new principle of mental fatigue. *American Journal of Psychology, 43,* 230–275.

Blakemore, C., & Cooper, G. F. (1970). Development of the brain depends upon the visual environment. *Nature, 228,* 477–478.

Bleuler, M. E. (1978). The long-term course of schizophrenic psychoses. In L. C. Wynne, R. L. Cromwell, & S. Matthyse (Eds.), *The nature of schizophrenia: New approaches to research and treatment.* New York: Wiley.

Bloom, B. L. (1992). *Planned short-term psychotherapy: A clinical handbook.* Boston: Allyn-Bacon.

Bloom, F. E., Lazerson, A., & Hofstadter, L. (1985). *Brain, mind, and behavior.* New York: Freeman.

Blum, K., Cull, J. G., Braverman, E. R., & Comings, D. E. (1996). Reward deficiency syndrome. *American Scientist, 84,* 132–145.

Blum, K. E., Noble, P., Sheridan, A., et al. (1990). Allelic association of human dopamine D2 receptor gene in alcoholism. *Journal of the American Medical Association, 263,* 2055–2060.

Bobo, L., & Gilliam, F. D., Jr. (1990). Race, sociopolitical participation, and black empowerment. *American Political Science Review, 84,* 377–393.

Boggiano, A. K., & Barrett, M. (in press). Maladaptive achievement patterns: The role of motivational orientation. *Journal of Personality and Social Psychology.*

Boggiano, A., Barrett, M., Silvern, L., & Gallo, S. (1991). Predicting emotional concomitants of learned helplessness: The role of motivational orientation. *Sex Roles, 25,* 24–31.

Boggiano, A. K., Shields, A., Barrett, M., Kellman, T., Thompson, E., Simons, J., & Katz, P. (1992). Helplessness deficits in students: The role of motivational orientation. *Motivation and Emotion, 16,* 271–295.

Bok, (1974). The ethics of giving placebos. *Scientific American, 231*(5), 17–23.

Bond, C. F., Jr., & Titus, L. J. (1983). Social facilitation: A meta-analysis of 241 studies. *Psychological Bulletin, 94,* 265–292.

Bond, M. (1988). *The cross-cultural challenge to social psychology.* Newbury Park, CA: Sage.

Bond, M., & Forgas, J. P. (1984). Linking person perception to behavioral intention across cultures: The role of cultural collectivism. *Journal of Cross-Cultural Psychology, 15,* 337–352.

Bootzin, R. E., Acocella, J. R., & Alloy, L. B. (1993). *Abnormal psychology: Current perspectives* (6th ed.). New York: McGraw-Hill.

Bootzin, R. R. (1981). *Insomnia.* Evanston, IL: Arts and Sciences, Northwestern University.

Bootzin, R. R., Kihlstrom, J. F., & Schacter, D. L. (1990). *Sleep and cognition.* Washington, DC: American Psychological Association.

Boring, C. C., Squires, T. S., & Tong, T. (1992). Cancer statistics, 1992. *A Cancer Journal for Clinicians, 42,* 19–43.

Bornstein, M. H. (1992). Perceptual development in infancy, childhood, and old age. In M. H. Bornstein & M. E. Lamb (Eds.), *Developmental psychology: An advanced textbook* (3rd ed.). Hillsdale, NJ: Erlbaum.

Bornstein M. H., & O'Reilly, A. W. (Eds.). (1993). The role of play in the development of thought. *New Directions for Child Development* (No. 59). San Francisco: Jossey-Bass.

Bouchard, T. J., Lykken, D. T., McGue, M., Segal, N. L., & Tellegen, A. (1990). Sources of human psychological differences: The Minnesota study of twins reared apart. *Science, 250,* 223–228.

Bouchard, T. J., & McGue, M. (1981). Familial studies of intelligence: A review. *Science, 212,* 1055–1059.

Bourne, L. E., Jr., & Archer, E. J. (1956). Time continuously on target as a function of distribution of practice. *Journal of Experimental Psychology, 51,* 25–33.

Bourne, L. E., Jr., Sinclair, G., & Healy, A. F. (1986). Ebbinghaus' measure of text memory. In F. Klix & H. Hagendorf (Eds.), *Human memory and cognitive capabilities.* New York: Elsevier.

Bower, G. H. (1972). Mental imagery and associative learning. In L. W. Gregg (Ed.), *Cognition in learning and memory.* New York: Wiley.

Bower, G. H. (1981a, June). Mood & memory. *Psychology Today,* 60–69.

Bower, G. H. (1981b). Mood and memory. *American Psychologist, 36,* 129–148.

Bower, G. H. (1986). Prime time in cognitive psychology. In P. Eelen (Ed.), *Cognitive research and behavior therapy: Beyond the conditioning paradigm* (pp. 272–273). Amsterdam: North Holland Publishers.

Bower, G. H., & Karlin, M. B. (1974). Depth of processing pictures of faces and recognition memory. *Journal of Experimental Psychology, 103,* 751–757.

Bower, T. G. R. (1982). *Development in infancy.* New York.

Bowers, K. S. (1976). *Hypnosis for the seriously curious.* Belmont, CA: Wadsworth.

Bowlby, J. (1969). *Attachment and loss.* New York: Basic Books.

Bowmaker, J. K., & Dartnall, H. J. A. (1983). Visual pigments of rods and cones in a human retina. *Journal of Physiology, 298,* 501–511.

Brady, J. V. (1958). Ulcers in "executive" monkeys. *Scientifc American, 199,* 95–100.

Braginsky, D. D., & Braginsky, B. M. (1971). *Hansels and Gretels: Studies of children in institutions for the mentally retarded.* New York: Holt, Rinehart, and Winston.

Braine, M. D. S. (1963). The ontogeny of English phrase structure: The first phrase. *Language, 39,* 1–13.

Brake, T., Walker, D. M., & Walker, T. (1995). *Doing business internationally: The guide to cross-cultural success.* Burr Ridge, IL: Irwin Professional Publishing.

Bramel, D., Taub, B., & Blum, B. (1968). An observer's reaction to the suffering of his enemy. *Journal of Personality and Social Psychology, 8,* 384–392.

Bransford, J. D., & Franks, J. J. (1971). The abstraction of linguistic ideas. *Cognitive Psychology, 2,* 331–350.

Bransford, J. D., & Johnson, M. K. (1973). Considerations of some problems of comprehension. In W. G. Chase (Ed.), *Visual information processing.* New York: Academic Press.

Braungart, R. G., & Braungart, M. M. (1988, September/October). From yippies to yuppies: Twenty years of freshman attitudes. *Public Opinion, 11,* 53–56.

Bray, G. A. (1969). Effect of caloric restriction on energy expenditure in obese patients. *Lancet, 2,* 397–398.

Brazelton, T. B. (1979). Behavioral competence of the newborn infant. *Seminars in Perinatology, 3,* 35–44.

Brehm, S. (1992). *Intimate relationships* (2nd ed.). New York: McGraw-Hill.

Brehm, S., & Kassin, S. (1993). *Social psychology* (2nd ed.). Boston: Houghton Mifflin.

Brehm, J. W., & Self, E. A. (1989). The intensity of motivation. *Annual Review of Psychology, 40,* 109–131.

Breier, A., Schreiber, J. L., Dyer, J. & Pickar, D. (1991). National Institute of Mental Health longitudinal study of chronic schizophrenia. *Archives of General Psychiatry, 48,* 239–246.

Breland, K., & Breland, M. (1961). The misbehavior of organisms. *American Psychologist, 16,* 681–684.

Bremner, J. D., Southwick, S. M., Johnson, D. R., Yehuda, R., & Charney, D. S. (1993). Childhood physical abuse and combat-related posttraumatic stress disorder in Vietnam veterans. *American Journal of Psychiatry, 150*(2), 235–239.

Brennan, J. F. (1982). *History and systems of psychology* (2nd ed.). Englewood Clifts, NJ: Prentice-Hall.

Breslau, N., Davis, G. C., Peterson, E. L., & Schultz, L. (1997). Psychiatric sequelae of posttraumatic stress disorder in women. *Archives of General Psychiatry, 54,* 81–87.

Breslow, L., & Enstrom, J. E. (1980). Persistence of health habits and their relationship to mortality. *Preventative Medicine, 9,* 469–483.

Breuer, J., & Freud, S. (1895/1976). Studies on hysteria. In J. Strachey (Trans. and Ed.), *The standard edition of the complete works of Sigmund Freud* (Vol. 2). New York: Norton.

Brewer, M. B. (1979). In-group bias in the minimal inter-group situation: A cognitive-motivational analysis. *Psychological Bulletin, 86,* 307–324.

Brickner, M., Hawkins, S., & Ostrom, T. (1986). Personal involvement: Thought provoking implications for social loafing. *Journal of Personality and Social Psychology, 51,* 763–769.

Briere, J. (1984). *The effects of childhood sexual abuse on later psychological functioning: Defining a post-sexual-abuse syndrome.* Paper presented at Third National Conference on Sexual Victimization of Children, Washington, DC.

Broadstock, M., Borland, R., & Gason, R. (1992). Effects of suntan on judgments of healthiness and attractiveness by adolescents. *Journal of Applied Social Psychology, 22,* 157–172.

Brody, N. (1993). Intelligence and the behavioral genetics of personality. In R. Plomin & G. McClearn (Eds.), *Nature, nurture and psychology.* Washington, DC: American Psychological Association.

Brody, N. (1992). *Intelligence* (2nd ed.). San Diego, CA: Academic Press.

Brooks, D. N. (1990). Cognitive deficits. In *Rehabilitation of the adult and child with traumatic brain injury* (2nd ed.). Philadelphia: F. A. Davis Co.

Brooks-Gunn, J., & Warren, M. P. (1987). *Biological and social contributions to negative affect in young adolescent girls.* Paper presented to the Society for Research in Child Development, Baltimore, MD.

Brown, A. S. (1991). A review of the tip-of-the-tongue experience. *Psychological Bulletin, 109,* 204–223.

Brown, D. E. (1991). *Human universals.* Philadelphia: Temple University Press.

Brown, G. W. (1987). Social factors and the development and course of depressive disorder in women. *British Journal of Social Work, 17,* 615–634.

Brown, G. W., Bhrolchain, M. N., & Harris, T. (1975). Social class and psychiatric disturbance among women in an urban population. *Sociology, 9,* 225–254.

Brown, J. D. (1991). Staying fit and staying well: Physical fitness as a moderator of life stress. *Journal of Personality and Social Psychology, 60*, 555–561.

Brown, J. D., & Dutton, K. A. (1995). The thrill of victory, the complexity of defeat: Self-esteem and people's emotional reactions to success and failure. *Journal of Personality and Social Psychology, 68*, 712–722.

Brown, J. D., & Gallagher, F. M. (1992). Coming to terms with failure: Private self-enhancement and public self-effacement. *Journal of Experimental Social Psychology, 28*, 3–22.

Brown, L. (1993). Personal communication.

Brown, L. S. (1994). *Subversive dialogues: Theory in feminist therapy.* New York: Basic Books.

Brown, R. (1973). *A first language: The early stages.* Cambridge, MA: Harvard University Press.

Brown, R., & Kulik, J. (1977). Flashbulb memories. *Cognition, 5*, 73–99.

Brown, T. A., Barlow, D. H. & Liebowitz, M. R. (1994). The empirical basis of generalized anxiety disorder. *American Journal of Psychiatry, 151*, 1272–1280.

Browne, A. (1993). Violence against women by their male partners: Prevalence, outcomes, and policy implications. *American Psychologist.*

Bruner, J. S., Goodnow, J. J., & Austin, G. A. (1956). *A study of thinking.* New York: Wiley.

Brush, L. D. (1990). Violent acts and injurious outcomes in married couples: Methodological issues in the National Survey of Families and Households. *Gender and Society, 4*, 56–67.

Brush, S. G. (1991). Women in science and engineering. *American Scientist, 79*, 404–419.

Bryjak, G. J., & Soroka, M. P. (1992). *Sociology: Cultural diversity in a changing world.* Boston: Allyn & Bacon.

Buddell, D. W., & Wilson, G. T. (1976). The effects of alcohol and expectancy set on male sexual arousal. *Journal of Abnormal Psychology, 85*, 225–234.

Buell, S. J., & Coleman, P. D. (1981). Quantitative evidence for selective dendritic growth in normal human aging but not in senile dementia. *Brain Research, 214*, 23–41.

Bumpass, L. L. (1990). What's happening to the family? Interactions between demographic and institutional change. *Demography, 27*, 483–498.

Bundek, N. I., Marks, G., & Richardson, J. L. (1993). Role of health locus of control beliefs in cancer screening of elderly Hispanic women. *Health Psychology, 12*(3), 193–99.

Buñuel, L. (1984). *My last sigh.* New York: Random House.

Burns, D. D. (1989). *The feeling good handbook: Using the new mood therapy in everyday life.* New York: Morrow.

Burns, M. O., & Seligman, M. E. P. (1989). Explanatory style across the life span: Evidence for stability over 52 years. *Journal of Personality and Social Psychology*, 56, 471–477.

Burt, M. R., & Levy, F. (1987). Estimates of public costs for teenage childbearing: A review of recent studies and estimates of 1985 public costs. In S. L. Hofferth & C. D. Hayes (Eds.), *Risking the future: Adolescent sexuality, pregnancy, and childbearing* (pp. 264–293). Washington, DC: National Academy Press.

Bush, D. M., & Simmons, R. G. (1987). Gender and coping with the entry into early adolescence. In R. C. Barnett, L. Biener, & G. K. Baruch (Eds.), *Gender and stress* (pp. 185–217). New York: Free Press.

Bushman, B. J. (1993). Human aggression while under the influence of alcohol and other drugs: An integrative research review. *Current Directions in Psychological Science, 2*, 148–152.

Buss, A. H., & Plomin, R. (1984). *Temperament: Early developing personality traits.* Hillsdale, N. J. Erlbaum.

Buss, D. M. (1988). The evolution of human intrasexual competition: Tactics of mate attraction. *Journal of Personality and Social Psychology, 54*, 616–628.

Buss, D. M. (1997). Evolutionary foundations of personality. In R. Hogan, J. Johnson, & S. Briggs (Eds.), *Handbook of personality psychology* (pp. 317–344). San Diego, CA: Academic Press.

Buss, D. M., et al., (1990). International preferences in selecting mates: A study of 37 cultures. *Journal of Cross-Cultural Psychology, 21*, 5–47.

Buss, D. M., Larsen, R. J., & Westen, D. (1996). Sex differences in jealousy. *Psychological Science, 7*, 373–375.

Butler, R. (1954). Incentive conditions which influence visual exploration. *Journal of Experimental Psychology, 48*, 19–23.

Buttman, N. (1956). The pigeon and the spectrum and other perplexities. *Psychological Reports, 2*, 449–460.

Buxton, C. E. (1943). The status of research in reminiscence. *Psychological Bulletin, 40*, 313–340.

Byrne, D. (1969). Attitudes and attraction. In L. Berkowitz (Ed.), *Advances in experimental social psychology* (Vol. 4). New York: Academic Press.

Byrne, D. (1971). *The attraction paradigm.* New York: Academic Press.

Byrne, D., Gouaux, C., Griffitt, W., Lamberth, J., Murakawa, N., Prasad, M. B., Prasad, A., & Ramirez, M. III (1971). The ubiquitous relationship: Attitude similarity and attraction: A cross-cultural study. *Human Relations, 24*, 201–207.

Byrne, D., & Nelson, D. (1965). Attraction as a linear function of positive reinforcement. *Journal of Personality and Social Psychology, 1*, 659–663.

Cacioppo, J. T., & Berntson, G. G. (1993). Social psychological contributions to the decade of the brain: Doctrine of multilevel analysis. *American Psychologist, 47*, 1019–1028.

Cacioppo, J. T., & Petty, R. E. (1985). Central and peripheral routes to persuasion: The role of message repetition. In L. F. Alwitt & A. A. Mitchell (Eds.), *Psychological processes and advertising effects.* Hillsdale, NJ: Erlbaum.

Cacioppo, J. T., Marshall-Goodell, B. S., Tassinary, L. G., & Petty, R. E. (1992). Rudimentary determinants of attitudes: Classical conditioning is more effective when prior knowledge about the attitude stimulus is low than high. *Journal of Personality and Social Psychology, 28*, 207–233.

Cadwallader, T. C., & Cadwallader, J. V. (1990). Christine Ladd-Franklin (1847–1930). In A. N. O'Connell, & N. F. Russo (Eds.), *Women in psychology: A biobibliographical sourcebook* (pp. 220–229). Westport, CT: Greenwood Press.

Cain, W. S. (1979). To know with the nose: Keys to odor identification. *Science, 203*, 467–470.

Cain, W. S. (1988). Olfaction. In R. A. Atkinson, R. Herrnstein, G. Lindzey, & R. D. Luce (Eds.), *Stevens' handbook of experimental psychology* (pp. 409–459). New York: Wiley.

Calkins, M. W. (1893). Statistics of dreams. *American Journal of Psychology, 5*, 311–343.

Callem, J. (1996, October). Germs: Fight back against the latest threat to your health. *Let's Live*, pp. 45–46.

Camel, J. E., Withers, G. S., & Greenough, W. T. (1986). Persistence of visula cirtex dendritic alterations induced by post-weaning exposure to a "super enriched" environment in rats. *Behavioral Neuroscience, 100*, 810–813.

Cameron, N. (1963). *Personality development and psychology: A dynamic approach.* Boston: Houghton-Mifflin.

Campbell, D. T. (1965). Ethnocentric and other altruistic motives. In D. Levine (Ed.), *Nebraska symposium on motivation.* Lincoln, NE: University of Nebraska Press.

Campos, J. J., Langer, A., & Krowitz, A. (1970). Cardiac responses on the visual cliff in prelocomotor human infants. *Science, 170*, 196–197.

Cann, A., & Newbern, S. R. (1984). Sex stereotype impacts on competence ratings by children. *Sex Roles, 11*, 333–343.

Cannon, T. D., Mednick, S. A., & Parnas, J. (1989). Genetic and peri-

natal determinants of structural brain deficits in schizophrenia. *Archives of General Psychiatry, 46*, 883–889.
Cannon, W. B. (1929). *Bodily changes in pain, hunger, fear and rage.* New York: Appleton-Century-Crofts.
Cappella, J. N., & Palmer, M. T. (1990). Attitude similarity, relational history, and attraction: The mediating effects of kinesic and vocal behaviors. *Communication Monographs, 57*, 161–183.
Carew, T. J. (1996). Molecular enhancement of memory formation. *Neuron, 16*, 5–8.
Carlson, M., Marcus-Newhall, A., & Miller, N. (1990). Effects of situational aggression cues: A quantitative review. *Journal of Personality and Social Psychology, 58*, 622–633.
Carlson, N. R. (1992). *Foundations of physiological psychology* (2nd ed.). Needham Heights, MA: Allyn & Bacon.
Carlson, N. R. (1994). *The physiology of behavior.* Boston: Allyn & Bacon.
Carlston, D. E. (1980). The recall and use of traits and events in social inference processes. *Journal of Experimental Social Psychology, 16*, 303–329.
Carlston, D. E., & Skowronski, J. J. (1994). Savings in the relearning of trait information as evidence for spontaneous inference generation. *Journal of Personality and Social Psychology, 66*, 840–856.
Carmelli, D., Dame, A., Swan, G., & Rosenman, R. (1991). Long-term changes in Type A behavior: A 27-year follow-up of the Western Collaborative Group Study. *Journal of Behavioral Medicine, 14*, 593–606.
Carola, R., Harley, J. P., & Noback, C. R. (1992). *Human anatomy and physiology* (2nd ed.). New York: McGraw-Hill.
Carr, H. (1935). *An introduction to space perception.* New York: Longmans Green.
Carroll, J. B. (1993). *Human cognitive abilities: A survey of factor-analytic studies.* Cambridge, Eng.: Cambridge University Press.
Carson, J., Burks, V., & Parke, R. D. (1993). Parent-child physical play: Determinants and consequences. In K. MacDonald (Ed.). *Parent-child play: Descriptions and implications.* Albany, NY: SUNY Press.
Cartwright, R., & Lamberg, L. (1992). *Crisis dreaming: Using your dreams to solve your problems.* New York: HarperCollins.
Carver, C. S.(1975). Physical aggression as a function of objective self-awareness and attitudes toward punishment. *Journal of Experimental Social Psychology, 11*, 510–519.
Cascio, W. F. (1995). Whither industrial and organizational psychology in a changing world of work? *American Psychologist, 50*, 928–939.
Casey, W. M., & Burton, R. V. (1983). Training children to be consistently honest through verbal self-instructions. *Child Development, 53*, 911–919.
Cass, V. C. (1979). Homosexual identity formation: A theoretical model. *Journal of Homosexuality*, 4(3), 219–235.
Cattell, R. B. (1949). *The culture-free intelligence test.* Champaign, IL: Institute for Personality and Ability Testing.
Cattell, R. B. (1963). Theory of fluid and crystallized intelligence: A critical experiment. *Journal of Educational Psychology, 54*, 1–22.
Cattell, R. B. (1971). *Abilities: Their structure, growth, and action.* Boston: Houghton Mifflin.
Cattell, R. B. (1982). *Inheritance of personality and ability.* New York: Academic Press.
Cattell, R. B., & Ebel, H. W. (1964). *Handbook for the sixteen personality factor questionnaire.* Champaign, IL: Institute for Personality and Ability Testing.
Cattell, R. B., Ebel, H. W., & Tatsuoka, M. M. (1970). *Handbook of the 16 personality factor questionnaire (16PF).* Champaign, IL: Institute for Personality and Ability Testing.
Cattell, R. B., & Krug, S. E. (1986). The number of factors in the 16PF: A review of the evidence with special emphasis on methodological problems. *Educational and Psychological Measurement, 46*, 509–522.
Cattell, R. B., Saunders, D. R., & Stice, G. F. (1950). *The 16 personality factor questionnaire.* Champaign, IL: Institute for Personality and Ability Testing.
Cautela, J. R. (1967). Covert sensitization. *Psychological Reports, 20*, 459–468.
Cautela, J. R. (1970). The treatment of alcoholism by covert sensitization. *Psychotherapy: Theory, Research and Practice, 7*, 86–90.
Ceci, S. J., Ross, D. F., & Toglia, M. P. (1987). Suggestibility of children's memory: Psycholegal implications. *Journal of Experimental Psychology: General, 116*, 38–49.
Centers for Disease Control (1980). *Risk factor update.* Atlanta, GA: U.S. Department of Health and Human Services.
Centers for Disease Control (1992). Annual summary of births, marriages, divorces, and deaths: United States, 1991. *Monthly Vital Statistics Report, 40* (13), 1–7.
Chaffin, R., Crawford, M., Herrmann, D. J., & Deffenbacher, K. A. (1985). Gender differences in the perception of memory abilities in others. *Human Learning, 4*, 233–241.
Chapanis, A. (1965). *Man-machine engineering.* Monterey, CA: Brooks/Cole.
Chapanis, A., Gamer, W. R., & Morgan, C. T. (1949). *Applied experimental psychology: Human factors in engineering design.* New York: Wiley.
Chapman, L. J. (1967). Illusory correlation in observational report. *Journal of Verbal Learning and Verbal Behavior, 6*, 151–155.
Chase, M. H., & Morales, F. R. (1989). The control of motoneurons during sleep. In M. H. Kryger, T. Roth, & W. C. Dement (Eds.), *Principles and practice of sleep medicine.* Philadelphia: Saunders.
Chater, N. (1996). Reconciling simplicity and likelihood principles in perceptual organization. *Psychological Review, 103*, 566–581.
Cherry, F., & Deaux, K. (1978). Fear of success versus fear of gender-inappropriate behavior. *Sex Roles, 4*, 97–101.
Chomsky, N. (1957). *Syntactic structures.* The Hague, The Netherlands: Mouton.
Chomsky, N. (1969). *The acquisition of syntax in children from 5 to 10.* Cambridge, MA: MIT Press.
Chomsky, N. (1975). *Reflections on language.* New York: Pantheon Books.
Chopra, D. (1993). *Ageless body, timeless mind: The quantum alternatives to growing old.* New York: Harmony Books.
Christensen, A., & Jacobson, N. S. (1994). Who (or what) can do psychotherapy: The status and challenge of nonprofessional therapies. *Psychological Science, 5*, 8–14.
Christenson, A. J., & Smith, T. W. (1993). Cynical hostility and cardiovascular response during self-disclosure. *Psychosomatic Medicine, 55*, 193–202.
Chukovsky, K. (1966). *From two to five.* Berkeley, CA: University of California Press.
Cialdini, R. B. (1985). *Influence: Science and practice.* Glenview, IL: Scott, Foresman.
Cialdini, R. B., Kallgren, C. A., & Reno, R. R. (1991). A focus theory of normative conduct: A theoretical refinement and reevaluation of the role of norms in human behavior. *Advances in Experimental Social Psychology, 24*, 201–234.
Clark, D. M., & Ehlers, A. (1993). An overview of the cognitive theory and treatment of panic disorder. *Applied and Preventative Psychology, 2*, 131–139.
Clarke-Stewart, K. A. (1988). The "effects" of infant child care reconsidered. *Early Childhood Research Quarterly, 3*, 293–318.
Classen, C., Koopman, C., & Spiegel, D. (1993). Trauma and dissociation. *Bulletin of the Menninger Clinic*, 57(2), 178–194.
Clements, M., & Hales, D. (1997, September 7). How healthy are we? *Parade*, pp. 4–7.
Clopton, J. R., Pallis, D. J., & Birtchnell, J. (1979). Minnesota Multiphasic Personality Inventory profile patterns of suicide attempters. *Journal of Consulting and Clinical Psychology, 47*, 135–139.

Cohen, C. E. (1981). Person categories and social perception: Testing some boundaries of the processing effects of prior knowledge. *Journal of Personality and Social Psychology, 40*, 441–452.

Cohen, F., & Lazarus, R. (1979). Coping with the stress of illness. In G. C. Stone, F. Cohen, & N. E. Adler (Eds.), *Health psychology: A handbook* (pp. 77–112). San Francisco: Jossey-Bass.

Cohen, L., & Roth, S. (1984). Coping with abortion. *Journal of Human Stress, 10*(3), 140–145.

Cohen, M., & Davis, N. (1981). *Medication errors: Causes and prevention*. Philadelphia: G. F. Stickley.

Cohen, N. J., & Eichenbaum, H. (1993). *Memory, amnesia, and the hippocampal system*. Cambridge, MA: MIT Press.

Cohen, N. J., & Squire, L. R. (1980). Preserved learning and retention of pattern-analyzing skill in amnesia: Dissociation of knowing how and knowing what. *Science, 210*, 207–210.

Cohen, S. (1988). Psychosocial models of the role of social support in the etiology of physical disease. *Health Psychology, 7*, 269–297.

Cohen, S. (1996). Psychological stress, immunity, and upper respiratory infections. *Current Directions in Psychological Science, 5*, 86–90.

Cohen, S., & Edwards, J. R. (1989). Personality characteristics as moderators of the relationship between stress and disorder. In R. W. J. Neufeld (Ed.), *Advances in the investigation of psychological stress* (pp. 235–283). New York: Wiley.

Cohen, S., & Spacapan, S. (1978). The aftereffects of stress: An attentional interpretation. *Environmental Psychology and Nonverbal Behavior, 3*, 43–57.

Cohen, S., & Williamson, G. M. (1991). Stress and infectious disease in humans. *Psychological Bulletin, 109*, 5–24.

Cohen, S., Tyrrell, D. A. J., & Smith, A. P. (1991). Psychological stress and susceptibility to the common cold. *New England Journal of Medicine, 325*, 606–612.

Cohen, S., Tyrrell, D. A. J., & Smith, A. P. (1993). Negative life events, perceived stress, negative affect, and susceptibility to the common cold. *Journal of Personality and Social Psychology, 64*, 131–140.

Colby, A., & Kohlberg, L. (1987). *The measurement of moral judgment: Vol 1. Theoretical foundations and research validation*. Cambridge, Eng.: Cambridge University Press.

Coleman, A. M. (1994). Emotion and motivation: Introduction. In A. M. Coleman (Ed.), *Companion Encyclopedia of Psychology* (Vol. 1, pp. 483–484). London: Routledge.

Collins, A. M., & Loftus, E. F. (1975). A spreading activation theory of semantic processing. *Psychological Review, 82*, 407–428.

Collins, A. M., & Quillian, M. R. (1968). Retrieval from semantic memory. *Journal of Verbal Learning and Verbal Behavior, 8*, 240–247.

Colombo, J., & Mitchell, D. W. (1990). Individual differences in early visual attention: Fixation time and cognitive processing. In J. Colombo & J. Fagan (Eds.), *Individual differences in infancy*. Hillsdale NJ: Erlbaum.

Comas-Diaz, L. (1991). Feminism and diversity in psychology: The case of women of color. *Psychology of Women Quarterly, 15*, 597–610.

Comer, R. J. (1995). *Abnormal psychology* (2nd ed.). New York: Freeman.

Concini, C. (1991, March 27). Personalities. *Washington Post*.

Condiotte, M. M., & Lichtenstein, E. (1981). Self-efficacy and relapse in smoking cessation programs. *Jounal of Consulting and Clinical Psychology, 49*, 648–658.

Condon, J. W., & Crano, W. D. (1988). Inferred evaluation and the relation between attitude similarity and interpersonal attraction. *Journal of Personality and Social Psychology, 54*, 789–797.

Condry, J., & Condry, S. (1976). Sex differences: A study of the eye of the beholder. *Child Development, 47*, 812–819.

Conger, R. D., Ge, X., Elder, G., Jr., Lorenz, F. O., & Simmons, R. L. (1994). Economic stress, coercive family processes, and developmental problems of adolescents. *Child Development, 65*, 541–561.

Consumer Reports. (1995, November). Mental health: Does therapy help?, pp. 734–739.

Coons, P. M., & Fine, C. G. (1990). Accuracy of the MMPI in identifying multiple personality disorder. *Psychological Reports, 66*, 831–834.

Cooper, J. (1980). Reducing fears and increasing assertiveness: The role of dissonance reduction. *Journal of Experimental Social Psychology, 16*, 199–214.

Cooper, J., & Fazio, R. H. (1984). A new look at dissonance theory. In L. Berkowitz (Ed.), *Advances in experimental social psychology* (Vol. 17, pp. 229–266). New York: Academic Press.

Cooper, R. P., & Aslin, R. N. (1990). Preference for infant directed speech in the first month after birth. *Child Development, 612*, 1584–1595.

Corballis, M. C. (1980). Laterality and myth. *American Psychologist, 35*, 284–295.

Coren, S., & Girgus, J. S. (1973). Visual spatial illusions: Many explanations. *Science, 179*, 503–504.

Coren, S., & Ward, L. M. (1989). *Sensation and perception* (3rd ed.). San Diego, CA: Harcourt Brace Jovanovich.

Cornsweet, T. M. (1970). *Visual perception*. New York: Academic Press.

Costa, P. T., Jr., & McCrae, R. R. (1992). *Revised NEO Personality Inventory (NEW-PI-R) and NEO Five-Factor Inventory (NEO-FFI) professional manual*. Odessa, FL: Psychological Assessment Resources.

Costa, P. T., & Widiger, T. A. (Eds.). (1993). *Personality disorders and the five-factor model of personality*. Washington, DC: American Psychological Association.

Cottrell, N. B., Riule, R. H., & Wack, D. L. (1967). Presence of an audience and list type (competitional or noncompetitional) as joint determinants of performance in paired associates learning. *Journal of Personality, 35*, 425–434.

Cox, C. M. (1926) *Genetic studies of genius* (Vol II). Stanford, CA: Stanford University Press.

Coyne, J. C., & Smith, D. A. F. (1991). Couples coping with a myocardial infarction: A contextual perspective on wives' distress. *Journal of Personality and Social Psychology, 61*, 404–412.

Craig, G. J., & Kermis, M. D. (1995). *Children today*. Englewood Cliffs, NJ: Prentice-Hall.

Craik, F. I. M. (1983). On the transfer of information from temporary to permanent memory. *Philosophical Transactions of the Royal Society: Series B, 308*, 341–359.

Craik, F. I. M. (1991). Memory functions in normal aging. In T. Yanagihara & R. C. Peterson (Eds.), *Memory disorders: Research and clinical practice* (pp. 347–367). New York: Marcel Dekker.

Craik, F. I. M., & Jacoby, L. L. (1975). A process view of short-term retention. In F. Restle (Ed.), *Cognitive theory* (Vol.1). Hillsdale, NJ: Erlbaum.

Craik, F. I. M., & Lockhart, R. S. (1972). Levels of processing: A framework for memory research. *Journal of Verbal Learning and Verbal Behavior, 11*, 671–684.

Craik, F. I. M., & Watkins, M. J. (1973). The role of rehearsal in short-term memory. *Journal of Verbal Learning and Verbal Behavior, 12*, 599–607.

Crawford, M., Herrmann, D. J., Holdsworth, M., Randall, E., & Robbins, D. (1989). Gender and beliefs about memory. *British Journal of Psychology, 80*, 391–401.

Crick, N. R., & Dodge, K. A. (1994). A review and reformulation of social information-processing mechanisms in children's social adjustment. *Psychological Bulletin, 115*, 74–101.

Crissey, M. S. (1988). Marie Skodak Crissey [autobiography]. In A. N. O'Connell & N. F. Russo (Eds.), *Models of achievement: Reflections of eminent women in psychology*. Hillsdale NJ: Erlbaum.

Critchlow, B. (1986). The powers of John Barleycorn: Beliefs about the effects of alcohol on social behavior. *American Psychologist, 41*, 751–764.

Crocker, J., & Luhtanen, R. (1990). Collective self-esteem and in-group bias. *Journal of Personality and Social Psychology, 58*, 60–67.

Cronin-Golomb, A., Gabrieli, J. D. E., & Keane, M. M. (1996). Implicit and explicit memory retrieval within and across the disconnected cerebral hemispheres. *Neuropsychology*, 10, 254–262.

Crosby, F. J., & Blanchard, F. A. (1989). *Affirmative action in perspective.* New York: Springer-Verlag.

Cross-National Collaborative Panic Study (1992). Drug treatment of panic disorder: Comparative efficacy of alprazolam, imipramine, and placebo. *British Journal of Psychiatry, 160*, 191–202.

Crowell, J. A., & Waters, E. (1990). Separation anxiety. In M. Lewis & S. M. Miller (Eds.), *Handbook of developmental psychology.* New York: Plenum.

Crowne, D. P., & Marlowe, D. (1964). *The approval motive: Studies in evaluative dependence.* New York: Wiley.

Cruise, P. I., & Kimmel, E. W. (1990). *Changes in SAT-Verbal: A study in trends in content and gender references, 1961–1987* (College Board Report No. 90–1). New York: College Entrance Examination Board.

Curtis, R. C., & Miller, K. (1986). Believing another likes or dislikes you: Behaviors making the beliefs come true. *Journal of Personality and Social Psychology, 51*, 284–290.

Cypress, B. K. (1980). *Characteristics of visits to female and male physicians: The national ambulatory medical care survey, 1977.* Hyattsville, MD: National Center for Health Statistics.

Dahlstrom, W. G. (1980). Screening for emotional fitness: The Jersey City case. In W. G. Dahlstrom, & L. Dahlstrom (Eds.), *Basic readings on the MMPI: A new selection on personality measurement.* Minneapolis, MN: University of Minnesota Press.

Dahlstrom, W. G. (1993). Tests: Small samples, large consequences. *American Psychologist, 48*, 393–399.

Dajer, T. (1992). Divided selves. *Discover, 13*(9), 38–69.

Daly, E. M., Lancee, W. J., & Polivy, J. (1983). A conical model for the taxonomy of emotional experience. *Journal of Personality and Social Psychology, 45*, 443–457.

Damon, W. (1977). *The social world of the child.* San Francisco: Jossey-Bass.

Darley, J. M., & Berscheid, E. (1967). Increased liking as a result of the anticipation of personal contact. *Human Relations, 20*, 29–40.

Darley, J. M., & Latané, B. (1968). Bystander intervention in emergencies: Diffusion of responsibility. *Journal of Personality and Social Psychology, 8*, 377–383.

Darwin, C. J., Turvey, M. T., & Crowder, R. G. (1972). An auditory analogue of the Sperling partial report procedure: Evidence for brief auditory storage. *Cognitive Psychology, 3*, 255–267.

Dasen, P. R. (Ed.). (1977). *Piagetian psychology: Cross-cultural contributions.* New York: Gardner.

Datan, N., Rodeheaver, D., & Hughes, F. (1987). Adult development and aging. *Annual Review of Psychology, 38*, 153–180.

Dattore, P. J., Shontz, F. D., & Coyne, L. (1980). Premorbid personality differentiation of cancer and noncancer groups: A test of the hypothesis of cancer proneness. *Journal of Consulting and Clinical Psycbology, 48*, 388–394.

Daum, I., & Schugens, M. M. (1996). On the cerebellum and classical conditioning. *Current Directions in Psychological Science, 5*, 58–61.

Davidson, J. R. T., & Foa, E. B. (1991). Diagnostic issues in posttraumatic stress disorder: Considerations for the DSM-IV. *Journal of Abnormal Psychology, 100*, 346–355.

Davidson, J. R.T., & Foa, E. B. (Eds.). (1992). *Posttraumatic stress disorder: DSM-IV and beyond.* Washington, DC: American Psychiatric Press.

Davidson, R. J. (1983). Affect, cognition, and hemispheric specialization. In C. E. Izard, J. Kagan, & R. Zajonc (Eds.), *Emotion, cognition, and behavior.* New York: Cambridge University Press.

Davidson, T. L. (1993). The nature and function of interoceptive signals to feed: Toward integration of physiological and learning perspectives. *Psychological Review, 100*, 640–657.

Davis, D. L., & Whitten, R. G. (1987). The cross-cultural study of human sexuality. *Annual Review of Anthropology, 16*, 69–98.

Davis, H., & Silverman, S. (1947/1960). *Hearing and deafness* (Rev. ed.). New York: Holt, Rinehart and Winston.

Davis, J. H. (1980). Group decisions and procedural justice. In M. Fishbein (Ed.), *Progress in social psychology* (Vol. 1). Hillsdale, NJ.: Erlbaum.

Davis, J. H., Kameda, T., Parks, C., Stasson, M., & Zimmerman, S. (1989). Some social mechanics of group decision-making: The distribution of opinion, polling sequence, and implications for consensus. *Journal of Personality and Social Psychology, 53*, 397–410.

Davison, G. C., & Neale, J. M. (1990). *Abnormal psychology* (5th ed.). New York: Wiley.

Davson, H. (1990). *The physiology of the eye* (5th ed.). London: Macmillan.

de Groot, A. (1946/1978). *Thought and choice in chess.* The Hague: Mouton.

DeCasper, A. J., & Fifer, W. P. (1980). Of human bonding: Newborns prefer their mothers' voices. *Science, 208*, 1174–1176.

Deese, J. (1959). On the prediction of occurrence of particular verbal intrusions in immediate recall. *Journal of Experimental Psychology*, 58, 17–22.

Dekaban, A., O'Rourke, J., & Corman, T. (1958). Abnormalities in offspring related to maternal rubella during pregnancy. *Neurology, 8*, 387–392.

Dekker, R. M., & van de Pol, L. C. (1989). *The tradition of female transvestism in early modern Europe.* New York: St. Martin's.

Delgado, J. M. R. (1969). *Physical control of the mind.* New York: Harper & Row.

Dell, P. F., & Eisenhower, J. W. (1990). Adolescent multiple personality disorder: A preliminary study of eleven cases. *Journal of the American Academy of Child and Adolescent Psychiatry, 29*, 359–366.

Delongis, A., Coyne, J. C., Dakof, G., Folkman, S., & Lazarus, R. S. (1982). Relationship of daily hassles, uplifts, and major life events to health status. *Health Psychology, 1*, 119–136.

Dember, W. N., Melton, R. S., Nguyen, D. Q., & Howe, S. R. (1993) Meta-emotion: Tests of the Lutz hypothesis. *Bulletin of the Psychonomic Society, 31*, 579–582.

Dembroski, T. M., & Costa, P. T. (1988). Assessment of coronary-prone behavior: A current overview. *Annals of Behavioral Medicine, 10*, 60–63.

Dement, W. C. (1974). *Some must watch while some must sleep.* Stanford, CA: Stanford Alumni Association.

Dement, W. C. (1992). *The sleepwalkers.* Stanford, CA: Stanford Alumni Association.

Demos, J., & Demos, V. (1969). Adolescence in historical perspective. *Journal of Marriage and the Family, 31*, 632–638.

Denmark, F. L., Russo, N. F., Frieze, I., & Sechzer, J. (1988). Guidelines for avoiding sexism in psychological research. *American Psychologist, 43*(7): 582–585.

Dennenberg, V. H., & Thomas, E. B. (1981). Evidence for a functional role for active (REM) sleep in infancy. *Sleep, 4*, 185–191.

Denton, G. G. (1980). The influence of visual pattern on perceived speed. *Perception, 9*, 393–402.

Deregowski, J. (1989). Real space and represented space: Cross-cultural perspectives. *Behavioral and Brain Sciences, 12*, 51–119.

Deschaumes, M. C., Dittmar, A., Sicard, G., & Vernet, M. E. (1991). Results from six autonomic nervous system responses confirm "autonomic response specificity" hypothesis. *Homeostasis in Health and Disease, 33* (5–6), 225–234.

Deutsch, M. (1968). Field theory in social psychology. In G. Lindzey

& E. Aronson (Eds.), *The handbook of social psychology*. Reading, MA: Addison-Wesley.

DeValois, R. L., Abromov, I., & Jacobs, G. H. (1966). Analysis of response patterns of LGN cells. *Journal of the Optical Society of America, 56*, 966–977.

Devine, P. G. (1989). Stereotypes and prejudice: Their automatic and controlled components. *Journal of Personality and Social Psychology, 56*, 5–18.

deVries, H., & Stuiver, M. (1961). The absolute sensitivity of the human sense of smell. In W. A. Rosenblith (Ed.), *Sensory communication*. Cambridge, MA: MIT Press.

DeVries, R. (1969). Constancy in generic identity in the years three to six. *Monographs of the Society for Research in Child Development*, 34 (3, Serial No. 127).

Diener, F., Fraser, S. C., Beaman, A. L., & Kelem, Z. R. T. (1976). Effects of deindividuation variables on stealing among Halloween trick-or-treaters. *Journal of Personality and Social Psychology, 33*, 178–183.

Digman, J. M. (1990). Emergence of the five-factor model. *Annual Review of Psychology, 41*, 417–440.

Digman, J. M., & Inouye, J. (1986). Further specification of the five robust factors of personality. *Journal of Personality and Social Psychology, 50*, 116–123.

Dion, K. L., Berscheid, E., & Walster, E. (1972). What is beautiful is good. *Journal of Personality and Social Psychology, 24*, 285–290.

Dishman, R. K. (1988). *Exercise adherence: Its impact on public health.* Champaign, IL: Human Kinetic Books.

Dittman, R. W., Kappes, M. E., & Kappes, M. H. (1992). Sexual behavior in adolescent and adult females with congenital adrenal hyperplasia. *Psychoneuroendocrinology, 17*, 1–18.

Ditto, P. H., & Lopez, D. F. (1992). Motivated skepticism: Use of differential decision criteria for preferred and nonpreferred conclusions. *Journal of Personality and Social Psychology, 63*, 568–584.

Dodge, K. A., & Crick, N. R. (1990). Social information-processing bases of aggressive behavior of children. *Personality and Social Psychology Bulletin, 16*, 8–22.

Dohrenwend, B. S., Dohrenwend, B. P., Dodson, M., & Shrout, P. E. (1984). Symptoms, hassles, social supports and life events: Problem of confounded measures. *Journal of Abnormal Psychology, 93*, 222–230.

Doi, L. T. (1962). Amae: A key concept for understanding Japanese personality structure. In R. J. Smith & R. F. Beardsley (Eds.), *Japanese culture: Its development and characteristics* (pp. 132–139). Chicago: Aldine.

Dollard, J., Doob, L., Miller, N., Mowrer, O., & Sears, R. (1939). *Frustration and aggression.* New Haven, CT: Yale University Press.

Dollard, J., & Miller, N. E. (1950). *Personality and psychotherapy.* New York: McGraw-Hill.

Domjan, M. (1983). Biological constraints on instrumental and classical conditioning: Implications for general process theory. In G. H. Bower (Ed.), *The psychology of learning and motivation* (Vol. 17). New York: Academic Press.

Domjan, M., & Burkhard, B. (1982). *The principles of learning and behavior*. Monterey, CA: Brooks-Cole.

Domjan, M., & Purdy, J. E. (1995). Animal research in psychology. *American Psychologist*, 50, 496–503.

Donnelly, C. M., & McDaniel, M. A. (1993). Use of analogy in learning scientific concepts. *Journal of Experimental Psychology: Learning, Memory and Cognition, 19*, 975–987.

Donnerstein, E., & Wilson, D. W. (1976). Effects of noise and perceived control on ongoing and subsequent aggressive behavior. *Journal of Personality and Social Psychology, 34*, 774–781.

Doob, C. B. (1991). *Sociology: An introduction*. Forth Worth, TX: Holt, Rinehart and Winston.

Douglas, M. (1979). Accounting for taste. *Psychology Today, 13*, 44–51.

Douglass, F. (1845/1968). *Narrative of the life of Frederick Douglass.* New York: Signet Books.

Dove, A. (1968, July 15). Taking the chitling test. *Newsweek.*

Drachman, D., DeCarufel, A., & Insko, C. A. (1978). The extra credit effect in interpersonal attraction. *Journal of Experimental Social Psychology, 14*, 458–465.

Duberman, L. (1974). *Marriage and its alternatives.* New York: Praeger.

Dunphy, D. C. (1963). The social structure of urban adolescent peer groups. *Sociometry, 26*, 230–246.

Dush, D. M., Hirt, M. L., & Schroeder, H. (1983). Self-statement modification with adults: A meta-analysis. *Psychological Bulletin, 94*, 408–422.

Dutton, D. G., & Strachan, C. E. (1987). Motivational needs for power and spouse-specific assertiveness in assaultive and nonassaultive men. *Violence and Victims, 2*, 145–156.

Dweck, C. S., Hong, Y., & Chiu, C. (1993). Implicit theories: Individual differences in the likelihood and meaning of dispositional inference. *Personality and Social Psychology Bulletin, 19*, 644–656.

Dworkin, R. H., Hartsetin, G., Rosner, H., Walther, R., Sweeney, E. W., & Brand, L. (1992). A high-risk method for studying psychosocial antecedents of chronic pain: The prospective investigation of herpes zoster. *Journal of Abnormal Psychology, 101*, 200–205.

Dykens, E. M., & Gerrard, M. (1986). Psychological profiles of purging bulimics, repeat dieters, and controls. *Journal of Consulting and Clinical Psychology, 54*, 283–288.

Dywan, J., & Bowers, K. (1983). The use of hypnosis to enhance recall. *Science, 222*, 184–185.

Eagly, A. H. (1987). *Sex differences in social behavior: A social-role interpretation.* Hillsdale, NJ: Erlbaum.

Eagly, A. H., & Chaiken, S. (1993). *The psychology of attitudes.* Fort Worth, TX: Harcourt Brace Jovanovich.

Eagly, A. H., Ashmore, R. D., Makhijani, M. G., & Longo, L. C. (1991). What is beautiful is good, but . . . : A meta-analytic review of research on the physical attractiveness stereotype. *Psychological Bulletin, 110*, 109–128.

Eagly, A. H., Wood, W., & Chaiken, S. (1978). Causal inferences about communicators and their effect on opinion change. *Journal of Personality and Social Psychology, 36*, 424–435.

Earley, P. C. (1993). East meets West meets Mideast: Further explorations of collectivistic and individualistic work groups. *Academy of Management Journal, 36*, 319–348.

Ebbinghaus, H. (1885/1913). *On memory* (H. Ruger & C. Bussebius, Trans.). New York: Teachers College, Columbia University.

Eccles, J. (1985). Sex differences in achievement patterns. In T. B. Sonderregger (Ed.), *Psychology and gender. Nebraska Symposium, 1984.* Lincoln, NE: University of Nebraska Press.

Eccles, J. (1987a). Gender roles and achievement patterns: An expectancy-value perspective. In M. M. Reinish, L A. Rosenblum, & S. A. Saunders (Eds.), *Masculinity/femininity: Basic perspectives* (pp. 240–280). New York: Oxford University Press.

Eccles, J. (1987b). Gender roles and women's achievement decisions. *Psychology of Women Quarterly, 11*, 135–172.

Edelman, G. M., & Finkel, L. (1984). In G. M. Edelman, W. M. Cowan, & W. E. Gall (Eds.), *Dynamic aspects of neocortical function.* New York: Wiley.

Eden, D. (1981). Ability grouping as a self-fulfilling prophecy: A micro-analysis of teacher-student interaction. *Social Education, 54*, 151–162.

Eden, D. (1990). Pygmalion without interpersonal contrast effects: Whole groups gain from raising manager expectations. *Journal of Applied Psychology, 75*, 394–398.

Edwards, C. P., & Lewis, M. (1979). Young children's concepts of social relations: Social functions and social objects. In M. Lewis & L. A. Rosenblum (Eds.), *Genesis of behavior: The child and its family* (Vol. 2). New York: Plenum.

Eich, E. (1995). Searching for mood dependent memory. *Psychological Science, 6*, 67–71.

Eich, J. E., Weingartner, H., Stillman, R. C., & Gillin, J. C. (1975). State-dependent accessibility of retrieval cues in the retention of a categorized list. *Journal of Verbal Learning and Verbal Behavior, 14*, 408–417.

Eichorn, D., Hunt, J., & Honzik, M. P. (1981). Experience, personality, and IQ: Adolescence to middle age. In D. Eichorn, J. Clausen, N. Haan, M. Honzik, & M. P. Mussen (Eds.), *Present and past in middle life*. New York: Academic Press.

Ekman, P. (1973). Cross-cultural studies in facial expression. In P. Ekman (Ed.), *Darwin and facial expressions: A century of research in review*. New York: Academic Press.

Ekman, P. (1993). Facial expression and emotion. *American Psychologist, 48*, 384–392.

Ekman, P., & Davidson, R. J. (1993). Voluntary smiling changes regional brain activity. *Psychological Science, 4*, 342–345.

Ekman, P., & Oster, H. (1979). Facial expressions of emotion. *Annual Review of Psychology, 30*, 527–554.

Ekman, P., Levenson, R. W., & Friesen, W. V. (1983). Autonomic nervous system activity distinguishes between emotions. *Science, 221*, 1208–1210.

Elkind, D., & Bowen, R. (1979). Imaginary audience behavior in children and adolescents. *Developmental Psychology, 15*, 38–44.

Elliot, D. J., Trief, P. M., & Stein, N. (1986). Mastery, stress, and coping in marriage among chronic pain patients. *Journal of Behavioral Medicine, 9*, 549–558.

Ellis, A. (1962). *Reason and emotion in psychology*. New York: Lyle Stuart.

Ellis, A. (1976). The rational-emotive view. *Journal of Contemporary Psychotherapy, 8*(1), 20–28.

Ellis, A. (1987). The impossibility of achieving consistently good mental health. *American Psychologist, 42*, 364–375.

Ellis, A. (1989). History of cognition in psychotherapy. In A. Freeman, K. M. Simon, L. E. Beutler, & H. Arkowitz (Eds.), *Comprehensive handbook of cognitive therapy* (pp. 5–19). New York: Plenum.

Ellis, A. (1991). The revised ABC's of rational-emotive therapy (RET). *Journal of Rational-Emotive and Cognitive-Behavior Therapy, 9*, 139–172.

Ellis, A., & Harper, R. A. (1975). *A new giude to rational living*. North Hollywood, CA: Wilshire.

Engberg, L. A., Hansen, G., Welker, R. L., & Thomas, D. R. (1972). Acquisition of key-pecking via autoshaping as a function of prior experience: "Learned laziness"? *Science, 178*, 1002–1004.

Engen, T. (1987). Remembering odors and their names. *American Scientist, 75*, 497–503.

Eppley, K. R., Abrams, A. I., & Shear, J. (1989). Differential effects of relaxation techniques on trait anxiety: A meta-analysis. *Journal of Clinical Psychology, 45*, 957–974.

Erdelyi, M. H. (1984). The recovery of unconscious (inaccessible) memories: Laboratory studies of hypermnesia. In G. Bower (Ed.), *The psychology of learning and memory* (Vol. 18). San Diego, CA: Academic Press.

Erdelyi, M. H., & Goldberg, B. (1979). Let's not sweep repression under the rug: Toward a cognitive psychology of repression. In J. F. Kihlstrom & F. J. Evans (Eds.), *Functional disorders of memory*. Hillsdale, NJ: Erlbaum.

Ericsson, K. A. (1985). Memory skill. *Canadian Journal of Psychology, 39*, 188–231.

Ericsson, K. A., & Charness, N. (1994). Expert performance: Its structure and acquisition. *American Psychologist, 49*, 725–747.

Ericsson, K. A., & Chase, W. G. (1982). Exceptional memory. *American Scientist, 70*, 607–615.

Ericsson, K. A., & Kintsch, W. (1995). Long-term working memory. *Psychological Review, 102*, 211–245.

Ericsson, K. A., & Polson, P. (1988). An experimental analysis of the mechanisms of a memory skill. *Journal of Experimental Psychology: Learning, Memory and Cognition, 14*, 305–316.

Ericsson, K. A., & Smith, J. (1991). *Toward a general theory of expertise*. Cambridge, Eng.: Cambridge University Press.

Ericsson, K. A., Chase, W. G., & Faloon, S. (1980). Acquisition of a memory skill. *Science, 208*, 1181–1182.

Ericsson, K. A., Krampe, R. T., & Tesch-Römer, C. (1993). The role of deliberate practice in the acquisition of expert performance. *Psychological Review, 100*, 363–406.

Erikson, E. H. (1963). *Childhood and society*. New York: Norton.

Erikson, E. H. (1968). *Identity: Youth and crisis*. New York: Norton.

Erikson, E. H. (1982). *The life cycle completed: Review*. New York: Norton.

Eron, L. D. (1982). Parent-child interaction, television violence, and aggression of children. *American Psychologist, 37*, 197–211.

Eron, L. D. (1987). The development of aggressive behavior from the perspective of a developing behaviorist. *American Psychologist, 42*, 435–442.

Eron, L. D., & Huesmann, L. R. (1984). The control of aggression behavior by changes in attitudes, values and the conditions of learning. In R. J. Blanchard & C. Blanchard (Eds.), *Advances in the study of aggression*. Orlando, FL: Academic Press.

Escalona, S. K. (1968). *The roots of individuals: Normal patterns of development in infancy*. Chicago: Aldine.

Eskew, R. T., & Riche, C. V. (1982). Pacing and locus of control in quality control inspection. *Human Factors, 24*, 411–415.

Essock-Vitale, S. M., & McGuire, M. T. (1985). Women's lives viewed from an evolutionary perspective: II. Patterns of helping. *Ethology and Sociobiology, 6*, 155–173.

Etaugh, C. (1993). Women in the middle and later years. In F. L. Denmark & M. A. Paludi (Eds.), *Psychology of women: A handbook of issues and theories* (pp. 213–46). Westport, CT: Greenwood Press.

Etaugh, C., & Rathus, S. (1995). *The world of children*. Fort Worth, TX: Harcourt Brace.

Etkin, W., Devlin, R. M., & Bouffard, T. G. (1972). *A biology of human concern*. Philadelphia: Lippincott.

Evans, F. J. (1979). Hypnosis and sleep: Techniques for exploring cognitive activity duing sleep. In E. Fromm & R. E. Shor (Eds.), *Hypnosis: Research developments and perspective* (2nd ed., pp. 139–183). Chicago: Aldine Atherton.

Evans, G. W., Palsane, M. N., Lepore, S. J., & Martin, J. (1989). Residential density and psychological health: The mediating effects of social support. *Journal of Personality and Social Psychology, 57*, 994–999.

Evans, K. (1994, November/December). The joy of taking risk. *Health*, pp. 65–69.

Exner, J. E. (1978). *A comprehensive system: Current research and advanced interpretation* (Vol 2). New York: Wiley Interscience.

Exner, J. E. (1978). *A comprehensive system: Current research and advanced interpretation*. New York: Wiley Interscience.

Eysenck, H. J. (1952). The effects of psychotherapy: An evaluation. *Journal of Consulting Psychology, 16*, 319–324.

Eysenck, H. J. (1970). *The structure of human personality* (3rd ed.). London: Methuen.

Eysenck, H. G. (1981). *A model for personality*. New York: Springer-Verlag.

Eysenck, H. J. (1983). Special review of Smith, Glass, & Miller. *Behaviour Research and Therapy, 21*, 315–20.

Eysenck, H. J. (1985). *The rise and decline of the Freudian empire*. London: Pelican.

Eysenck, H. J. (1991). Dimensions of personality: 16, 5, or 3?—Criteria for a taxonomic paradigm. *Personality and Individual Differences, 12*, 773–790.

Eysenck, H. J. (1992). Four ways five factors are not basic. *Personality and Individual Differences, 13*, 757–785.

Eysenck, H. J., & Eysenck, S. G. (1975). *The Eysenck Personality Questionnaire*. Sevenoaks: Hodder & Stoughton.

Eysenck, H. J., & Eysenck, S. G. (1983). Recent advances: The cross-cultural study of personality. In J. N. Butcher & C. D. Spielberger (Eds.), *Advances in personality assessment* (Vol. 2). Hillsdale, NJ: Erlbaum.

Eysenck, H. J., & Rachman, S. (1965). *The causes and cures of neurosis.* San Diego, CA: Robert E. Knapp.

Fagan, J. F. (1990). The paired-comparison paradigm and infant intelligence. *Annals of the New York Academy of Sciences, 608,* 337–357.

Fagot, B. I., & Hagan, R. (1991). Observations of parent reactions to sex-stereotyped behaviors: Age and sex effects. *Child Development, 62,* 617–628.

Fairburn, C. G., Welch, S. I, & Hay, P. J. (1993). The classification of recurrent overeating: The "binge eating disorder" proposal. *International Journal of Eating Disorders, 13,* 155–159.

Fallon, A. E., & Rozin, P. (1985). Sex differences in perceptions of desirable body shape. *Journal of Abnormal Psychology, 94,* 102–105.

Falloon, I. R. H., Boyd, J. L., McGill, C. W., et al. (1982). Family management in prevention of exacerbation of schizophrenia: A controlled study. *New England Journal of Medicine, 306*(24), 1437–1440.

Falloon, I. R. H., Boyd, J. L., & McGill, C. W. (1985). Family management in the prevention of morbidity of schizophrenia: Clinical outcome of a two-year longitudinal study. *Archives of General Psychiatry, 42,* 887–896.

Famighetti, R. (1996). *The world almanac and book of facts, 1996.* Mahwah, NJ: Funk & Wagnal.

Fantz, R. L. (1961). The origin of form perception. *Scientific American, 204,* 66–72.

Fantz, R. L. (1967). Visual perception and experience in early infancy: A look at the hidden side of behavior development. In H. W. Stevenson, E. H. Hess, & H. L. Rheingold (Eds.), *Early behavior: Comparative and developmental approaches.* New York: Wiley.

Farley, F. (1986). The Big T in personality. *Psychology Today,* pp. 44–50.

Fay, R. E., Turner, C. F., Klassen, A. D., & Gagnon, J. H. (1989). Prevalence and patterns of same-gender sexual contact among men. *Science, 243,* 338–348.

Fazio, R. H. (1990). Multiple processes by which attitudes guide behavior: The mode model as an integrative framework. *Advances in Experimental Social Psychology, 23,* 75–109.

Fazio, R. H., Zanna, M. P., & Cooper, J. (1977). Dissonance and self perception: An integrative view of each theory's proper domain of application. *Journal of Experimental Social Psychology, 36,* 156–179.

Feeney, J. A., & Noller, P. (1990). Attachment style as a predictor of adult romantic relationships. *Journal of Personality and Social Psychology,* 58, 281–291.

Feinglos, M. N., & Surwit, R. S. (1988). *Behavior and diabetes mellitus.* Kalamazoo, MI: The Upjohn Company.

Feingold, A. (1988). Matching for attractiveness in romantic partners and same-sex friends: A meta-analysis and theoretical critique. *Psychological Bulletin, 104,* 226–235.

Feingold, A. (1990). Gender differences in effects of physical attractiveness on romantic attraction: A comparison across five research paradigms. *Journal of Personality and Social Psychology, 59,* 981–993.

Fendrich, D. W., Healy, A. F., & Bourne, L. E., Jr. (1991). Long-term repetition effects for motoric and perceptual procedures. *Journal of Experimental Psychology: Learning, Memory, and Cognition, 17,* 137–151.

Fenigstein, A., Scheier, M. F., & Buss, A. H. (1975). Public and private self-consciousness. *Journal of Consulting and Clinical Psychology, 43,* 522–527.

Fernald, A. (1991). Prosody in speech to children: Prelinguistic and linguistic functions. In R. Vasta (Ed.), *Annals of child development* (Vol. 8). London: Kingsley.

Fernald, A. (1992). Meaningful melodies in mother's speech to infants. In H. Papousek, U. Jergens, & M. Papousek (Eds.), *Nonverbal verbal communication: Comparative and developmental aspects.* Cambridge, Eng.: Cambridge University Press.

Fernald A., & Mazzie, C. (1991). Prosody and focus in speech to infants and adults. *Developmental Psychology, 27,* 209–221.

Fernald, A., & Morikawa, H. (1993). Common themes and cultural variations in Japanese and American mothers' speech to infants. *Child Development, 64,* 637–656.

Ferster, C. B., & Skinner, B. F. (1957). *Schedules of reinforcement.* New York: Appleton-Century-Crofts.

Festinger, L. (1957). *A theory of cognitive dissonance.* Stanford, CA: Stanford University Press.

Festinger, L., & Carlsmith, J. M. (1959). Cognitive consequences of forced compliance. *Journal of Abnormal and Social Psychology, 58,* 203–210.

Festinger, L., & Maccoby, N. (1964). On resistance to persuasive communication. *Journal of Abnormal and Social Psychology, 68,* 359–366.

Festinger, L., Riecken, H. W., & Schachter, S. (1956). *When prophecy fails: A social psychological study of a modern group that predicted the destruction of the world.* New York: Harper & Row.

Festinger, L., Schachter, S., & Back, K. (1950). *Social pressures in informal groups: A study of human factors in housing.* Stanford, CA: Stanford University Press.

Field, T. M., Woodson, R., Greenberg, R., & Cohen, D. (1982). Discrimination and imitation of facial expressions by neonates. *Science, 218,* 179–181.

Findley, M. J., & Cooper, H. M. (1983). Locus of control and academic achievement: A literature review. *Journal of Personality and Social Psychology, 44,* 419–427.

Fine, T. H. & Turner, J. S. (1985). REST-assisted relaxation and chronic pain. In J. J. Sanchez-Sosa (Ed.), *Health and clinical psychology.* New York: Elsevier.

Finke, R. A., Ward, T. B., & Smith, S. M. (1992). *Creative cognition: Theory, research and applications.* Cambridge, MA: MIT Press.

Finn, P. R., Sharkansky, E. J., Viken, R., West, T. L., Sandy, J., & Bufferd, G.M. (1997). Heterogeneity in the families of sons of alcoholics: The impact of familial vulnerability type on offspring characteristics. *Journal of Abnormal Psychology, 106,* 26–36.

Fishbein, M., & Ajzen, I. (1975). *Belief, attitude, intention, and behavior: An introduction to theory and research.* Reading, MA: Addison-Wesley.

Fischer, M. (1971). Psychoses in the offspring of schizophrenic monozygotic twins and their normal co-twins. *British Journal of Psychiatry,* 118, 43–52.

Fiske, S. T., & Taylor, S. E. (1991). *Social cognition* (2nd ed.). New York: McGraw-Hill.

Fitts, W. H. (1965). *The experience of psychotherapy.* Princeton, NJ: Van Nostrand.

Flavell, J. H., Miller, P. H., & Miller, S. A. (1993). *Cognitive development* (3rd ed.). Englewood Cliffs, NJ: Prentice-Hall.

Flowers, M. J. (1990). Coming into being: The prenatal development of humans. In J. D. Butler & D. F. Walbret (Eds.), *Abortion, medicine, and the law* (4th ed, pp. 437–452). New York: Facts on File.

Fodor, E. M., & Smith, T. (1982). The power motive as an influence on group decision making. *Journal of Personality and Social Psychology, 42,* 178–185.

Forbes, J. D. (1988). *Black Africans and Native Americans: Color, race and caste in the evolution of Red-Black peoples.* London: Basil Blackwell.

Ford, C. S., & Beach, F. A. (1951). *Patterns of sexual behavior.* New York: Harper & Row.

Foucault, M. (1965). *Madness and civilization* (R. Howard, Trans.). New York: Random House.

Foulkes, D. (1966). *The psychology of sleep.* New York: Scribner's.

Fox, N. A., & Davidson, R. J. (1993). Patterns of brain electrical activity during facial signs of emotion in 10-month-old infants. *Developmental Psychology, 24,* 230–236.

Frank, H., & Hoffman, N. (1986). Borderline empathy: An empirical investigation. *Comprehensive Psychiatry, 2,* 387–395.

Frankenberg, W. K., & Dodds, J. B. (1967). The Denver developmental screening test. *Journal of Pediatrics, 71,* 181–191.

Frankenhaeuser, M. (1975). Sympathetic-adrenomedullary activity behavior and the psychosocial environment. In P. H. Venables & M. J. Christie (Eds.), *Research in psychophysiology* (pp. 71–94). New York: Wiley

Frankenhaeuser, M. (1986). A psychological framework for research on human stress and coping. In M. H. Appley & R. Trumbell (Eds.), *Dynamics of stress* (pp. 101–116). New York: Plenum.

Franks, C. M., & Barbrack, C. R. (1983). Behavior therapy with adults: An integrative perspective. In M. Hersen, E. E. Kazdin, & A. S. Bellack (Eds.), *The clinical psychology handbook* New York: Pergamon Press.

Franks, V. (1986). Sex-stereotyping and diagnosis of psychopathology. *Women & Therapy, 5,* 219–232.

Freedheim, D. K. (Ed.). (1992). *History of psychotherapy: A century of change.* Washington, DC: American Psychological Association.

Freedman, J. (1975). *Crowding and behavior.* New York: Viking Press.

French, E. G. (1958). Effects of the interaction of motivation and feedback on task performance. In J. W. Atkinson (Ed.), *Motives in fantasy, action, and society.* New York: Litton Educational Publishing Company.

Frese, M. (1985). Stress at work and psychosomatic complaints: A causal interpretation. *Journal of Applied Psychology, 70,* 314–328.

Freud, A. (1936/1966). The ego and the mechanisms of defense. *The writings of Anna Freud* (Rev. ed., Vol. 2). New York: International Universities Press.

Freud, S. (1900/1976). The interpretation of dreams. In J. Strachey (Trans. and Ed.), *The standard edition of the complete psychological works of Sigmund Freud* (Vols. 4 and 5). New York: Norton.

Freud, S. (1905/1976). Jokes and their relation to the unconscious. In J. Strachey (Trans. and Ed.), *The standard edition of the complete psychological works of Sigmund Freud* (Vol. 8). New York: Norton.

Freud, S. (1909/1976). Analysis of a phobia in a five-year-old boy. In J. Strachey (Trans. and Ed.), *The standard edition of the complete psychological works of Sigmund Freud* (Vol. 10). New York: Norton.

Freud, S. (1910/1976). Five lectures on psycho-analysis. In J. Strachey (Trans. and Ed.), *The standard edition of the complete psychological works of Sigmund Freud* (Vol. 11). New York: Norton.

Freud, S. (1914/1976). On the history of the psycho-analytic movement. In J. Strachey (Trans. and Ed.) *The standard edition of the complete psychological works of Sigmund Freud* (Vol. 14). New York: Norton.

Freud, S. (1915/1976). The unconscious. In J. Strachey (Trans. and Ed.), *The standard edition of the complete psychological works of Sigmund Freud* (Vol. 14). New York: Norton.

Freud, S. (1916–1917/1976). Introductory lectures on psycho-analysis. In J. Strachey (Trans. and Ed.), *The standard edition of the complete psychological works of Sigmund Freud* (Vols. 15–16). New York: Norton.

Freud, S. (1940/1976). An outline of psychoanalysis. In J. Strachey, Trans. and Ed.), *The standard edition of the complete psychological works of Sigmund Freud.* New York: Norton.

Frey, D. (1980). The effect of negative feedback about oneself and cost of information on preferences for information about the source of this feedback. *Journal of Experimental Social Psychology, 16,* 466–471.

Friedman, M., & Rosenman, R. H. (1974). *Type A behavior and your heart.* New York: Knopf.

Friedman, M., & Stricker, E. M. (1976). The physiological psychology of hunger: A physiological perspective. *Psychological Review, 83,* 409–431.

Friedman, M., & Ulmer, D. (1984). *Treating Type A behavior—and your heart.* New York: Knopf.

Friedrich, J., Fetherstonhaugh, D., Casey, S., & Gallagher, D. (1996). Argument integration and attitude change: Suppression effects in the integration of one-sided arguments that vary in persuasiveness. *Personality and Social Psychology Bulletin, 22,* 179–191.

Friesen, W. (1972). Cultural differences in facial expression in a social situation: An experimental test of the concept of display rules. Unpublished Ph.D. thesis, University of California, San Francisco. Cited in P. B. Smith & M. H. Bond, *Social psychology across cultures: Analysis and perspectives.* Boston: Allyn & Bacon.

Frieze, I. H., & Browne, A. (1989). Violence in marriage. In L. Ohlin & M. H. Tonrey (Eds.), *Crime and justice—An annual review of research. Family violence.* Chicago: University of Chicago Press.

Froming, W. J., Walker, G. R., & Lopyan, K. J. (1982). Public and private self-awareness: When personal attitudes conflict with societal expectations. *Journal of Experimental Social Psychology, 18,* 476–487.

Fromm, E. (1988). Erika Fromm, 1910- [autobiography]. In A. N. O'Connell & N. F. Russo (Eds.), *Models of achievement: Reflections of eminent women in psychology.* Hillsdale, NJ: Erlbaum.

Fryxell, D. A. (1995). VR: Where reality takes a ride. *Friendly Exchange,* Winter, 24–26.

Funder, D. (1997). *The personality puzzle.* New York: Norton.

Funder, D., & Kenrick, D. (1988). Profiting from controversy: Lessons from the person-situation debate. *American Psychologist, 43,* 23–34.

Funder, D., & Ozer, D. (1983). Behavior as a function of the situation. *Journal of Personality and Social Psychology, 44,* 107–112.

Furstenberg, F. F., Jr., Levine, J. A., & Brooks-Gunn, J. (1990). The children of teenage mothers: Patterns of early childbearing in two generations. *Family Planning Perspectives, 22*(2), 54–61.

Furumoto, L. (1990). Mary Whiton Calkins (1863–1930). In A. N. O'Connell & N. F. Russo (Eds.), *Women in psychology: A biobibliographic sourcebook* (pp. 57–65). Westport, CT: Greenwood Press.

Gabrenya, W. K., Wang, Y., & Latané, B. (1985). Social loafing on an optimizing task: Cross-cultural differences among Chinese and Americans. *Journal of Cross-Cultural Psychology, 16,* 223–242.

Gaeddert, W. P. (1987). The relationship of gender, gender-related traits, and achievement orientation to achievement attributions: A study of subject-selected accomplishments. *Journal of Personality, 55,* 687–710.

Gainotti, G. (1969). Reactions "catastrophiques" et manifestations d'indifference au cours des atteintes cerebrales. *Neuropsychologia, 7,* 195–204.

Galenter, M. (1993). The end of addiction. *Psychology Today, 25* (6), 64–70, 90.

Gallup Organization (1996, April). Majority disapprove of homosexual marriages. *Emerging Trends* (p. 2). Princeton, NJ: Princeton Religion Research Center.

Galton, F. (1869/1970). *Hereditary genius.* New York: Appleton.

Ganaway, G. K. (1989). Historical versus narrative truth: Clarifying the role of exogeneous trauma in the etiology of MPD and its variants. *Dissociation, 2,* 205–220.

Garcia, J. (1990). Learning without memory. *Journal of Cognitive Neuroscience, 2,* 289–305.

Garcia, J., & Koelling, A. (1966). Relation of cue to consequence in avoidance learning. *Psychonomic Science, 4,* 123–124.

Gardner, P., & Hudson, B. L. (1996, February 29). Advance report of final mortality statistics, 1993. *Monthly Vital Statistics Report, 44* (7), 13.

Gardner, H. (1982). *Developmental psychology: An introduction* (2nd ed.). Boston: Little, Brown.

Gardner, H. (1983). *Frames of mind: The theory of multiple intelligence.* New York: Basic Books.

Gardner, R. A., & Gardner, B. T. (1969). Teaching sign language to a chimpanzee. *Science, 165,* 664–672.

Garfield, S. L. (1989). *The practice of brief psychotherapy.* New York: Pergamon.

Garnets, L., & Kimmel, D. (1991). Lesbian and gay male dimensions in the psychological study of human diversity. In J. Goodchilds (Ed.), *Psychological perspectives on human diversity in America.* Washington, DC: American Psychological Association.

Garrett, G. A., Baxter, J. C., & Rozelle, R. M. (1981). Training university police in black-American nonverbal behavior. *Journal of Social Psychology, 113,* 217–229.

Garvey, C. (1977). *Play.* Cambridge, MA: Harvard University Press.

Gatchel, R. J., Baum, A., & Krantz, D. S. (1989). *An introduction to health psychology* (2nd ed.). New York: Random House.

Geller, A. M., & Atkins, A. (1978). Cognitive and personality factors in suicidal behavior. *Journal of Counseling and Clinical Psychology, 46,* 860–868.

Gentner, D., & Holyoak, K. J. (1997). Reasoning and learning by analogy: Introduction. *American Psychologist, 52,* 32–34.

Gentry, J., & Eron, L. D. (1993). American Psychological Association Commission on Violence and Youth. *American Psychologist, 48,* 89.

Gettleman, T. E., & Thompson, J. K. (1993). Actual differences and stereotypical perceptions in body image and eating disturbance: A comparison of male and female heterosexual and homosexual samples. *Sex Roles, 29,* 545–562.

Gibson, E. J. (1970). The ontogeny of reading. *American Psychologist, 25,* 136–143.

Gibson, E. J., & Walk, R. D. (1960). The "visual cliff." *Scientific American, 202,* 64–71.

Gibson, E. J., Gibson, J. J., Pick, A. D., & Osser, H. A. (1962). A developmental study of the discrimination of letterlike forms. *Journal of Comparative and Physiological Psychology, 55,* 897–906.

Gibson, J. J. (1950). *The perception of the visual world.* Boston: Houghton Mifflin.

Gibson, J. J. (1966). *The senses considered as perceptual systems.* Boston: Houghton Mifflin.

Gibson, J. J. (1979). *The ecological approach to visual perception.* Boston: Houghton Mifflin.

Gilbert, D. T. (1989). Think lightly about others: Automatic components of the social interference process. In J. S. Uleman & J. L. Bargh (Eds.), *Unintended thought.* New York: Guilford.

Gilbert, D. T., & Hixon, J. G. (1991). The trouble of thinking: Activation and application of stereotypic beliefs. *Journal of Personality and Social Psychology, 60,* 509–517.

Gilbert, D. T., & Malone, P. S. (1995). The correspondence bias. *Psychological Bulletin, 117,* 21–38.

Gilligan, C. (1977). In a different voice: Women's conceptions of self and morality. *Harvard Educational Review, 47,* 481–517.

Gilligan, C. (1982). *In a different voice.* Cambridge, MA: Harvard University Press.

Gilling, D., & Brightwell, R. (1982). *The human brain.* New York: Facts on File.

Gilmore, D. (1991). *Manhood in the making.* New Haven, CT: Yale University Press.

Gladue, B. (1994). The biopsychology of sexual orientation. *Current Directions in Psychological Science, 3,* 150–156.

Gladwin, T. (1970). *East is a big bird.* Cambridge, MA: Harvard University Press

Glass, A. L., & Holyoak, K. J. (1986). *Cognition* (2nd ed.). New York: Random House.

Glass, D. C. (1977). *Behavior patterns, stress, and coronary disease.* Hillsdale, NJ: Erlbaum.

Glass, D. C., & Singer, J. E. (1962). *Urban stress.* New York: Academic Press.

Glass, D. C., & Singer, J. E. (1972). *Urban stress: Experiments on noise and social stressors.* New York: Academic Press.

Gleason, H. A., Jr. (1961). *An introduction to descriptive linguistics* (Rev. ed.). New York: Holt, Rinehart and Winston.

Glueck, S., & Glueck, E. (1950). *Unraveling juvenile delinquency.* Cambridge, MA: Harvard University Press.

Godden, D., & Baddeley, A. D. (1980). When does context influence recognition memory? *British Journal of Psychology, 71,* 99–104.

Goethals, G. R., & Nelson, E. R. (1973). Similarity in the influence process: The belief-value distinction. *Journal of Personality and Social Psychology, 25,* 117–122.

Gold, P.E. (1995). Modulation of emotional and non-emotional memories: Same pharmacological systems, different neuroanatomical systems. In J. L. McGaugh, N. M. Weinberger, & G. S. Lynch (Eds.), *Brain and memory: Modulation and mediation of neural plasticity* (pp. 41–74). New York: Oxford University Press.

Gold, P. E., & Stone, W. S. (1988). Neuroendocrine effects on memory in aged rodents and humans. *Neurobiology of Aging, 9,* 709–717.

Goldberg, L. R. (1993). The structure of phenotypic personality traits. *American Psychologist, 48,* 26–34.

Goldenberg, I., & Goldenberg, H. (1985). *Family therapy—An overview* (2nd ed.). Monterey, CA: Brooks/Cole.

Goldsmith, H. H., Buss, A. H., Plomin, R., Rothbart, M. K., Thomas, A., Chess, S., Hinde, R. A., & McCall, R. B. (1987). Roundtable: What is temperament? Four approaches. *Child Development, 58,* 505–529.

Goldsmith, S., Gabrielson, M., Gabrielson, I., Mathews, V., & Potts, L. (1972). Teenagers, sex, and contraception. *Family Planning Perspectives,* 4(1), 32–38.

Goldstein, E. B. (1989). *Sensation and perception* (3rd ed.). Belmont, CA: Wadsworth Publishing Company.

Goldstein, K. (1939). *The organism.* New York: American Book Co.

Goleman, D. (1995, December 5). Making room on the couch for culture. *New York Times,* pp. C1, C3.

Golub, S. (1992). *Periods: From menarche to menopause.* Newbury Park, CA: Sage.

Goodman, E. (1980). Margaret F. Washburn (1871–1939): First women Ph.D. in psychology. In A. N. O'Connell & N. F. Russo (Eds.), *Eminent women in psychology: models of achievement* (pp. 69–80). New York: Human Sciences Press.

Goodman, L. A., Koss, M. P., & Russo, N. F. (1993). Violence against women: Physical and mental health effects. Part I: Research findings. *Applied and Preventive Psychology: Current Scientific Perspectives, 2,* 79–89.

Goodnow, J. J. (1955a). Determinants of choice-distribution in two-choice situations. *American Journal of Psychology, 68,* 106–116.

Goodnow, J. J. (1955b). Response sequences in a pair of two-choice probability situations. *American Journal of Psychology, 68,* 624–630.

Gottesman, I. I. (1991). *Schizophrenia genesis: The origins of madness.* New York: Freeman.

Gottesman, I. I. (1993). Origins of schizophrenia: Past as prologue. In R. Plomin & G. E. McClearn (Eds.), *Nature, nurture, and psychology* (pp. 231–44). Washington, DC: American Psychological Association.

Gottesman, I. I., & Bertelsen, A. (1989). Dual mating studies in psychiatry: Offspring of inpatients with examples from reactive (psychogenic) psychoses. *International Review of Psychiatry, 1,* 287–296.

Gottesman, I. I., & Shields, J. (1966). Contributions of twin studies to perspectives on schizophrenia. In B. A. Maher (Ed.), *Progress in experimental personality research.* New York: Academic Press.

Gottesman, I., & Shields, J. (1982). *Schizophrenia: The epigenetic puzzle.* New York: Cambridge University Press.

Gould, R. (1978). *Transformations.* New York: Simon and Schuster.

Gould, S. J. (1981). *The mismeasure of man.* New York: Norton.

Gove, W. R., Hughes, M., & Galle, O. R. (1979). Overcrowding in the home. *American Sociological Review, 44,* 59–80.

Grady, D. (1981, December). Picking a jury. *Discover.*

Gray, J. A. (1984). *The neuropsychology of anxiety.* New York: Oxford University Press.

Graziano, W. G., & Eisenberg, N. H. (1997). Agreeableness: A dimension of personality. In R. Hogan, J. Johnson, & S. Briggs (Eds.), *Handbook of personality psychology* (pp. 795–824). San Diego, CA: Academic Press.

Greeley, A. M. (1992). The ethnic miracle. In K. C. Kammeyer, G. Ritzer, & N. R. Yetman (Eds.), *Sociology: Experiencing changing societies.* Boston: Allyn & Bacon.

Green, B. L., & Russo, N. F. (1993). Work and family roles: Selected issues. In F. L. Denmark & M. A. Paludi (Eds.), *Psychology of women: A handbook of issues and theories* (pp. 685- 720). Westport, CT: Greenwood Press.

Green, R. (1987). *The "sissy boy syndrome" and the development of homosexuality.* New Haven, CT: Yale University Press.

Green, R., Mandel, J. B., Hotvedt, M. E., Gray, J., & Smith, L. (1986). Lesbian mothers and their children: A comparison with solo parent heterosexual mothers and their children. *Archives of Social Behavior, 15,* 167–84.

Greenberg, G., & Tobach, E. (1988). *Evolution of social behavior and integrative levels.* Hillsdale, NJ: Erlbaum.

Greenberg, J. H. (1993). The social side of fairness: Informational and interpersonal classes of organizational justice. In R. Cropranzo (Ed.), *Justice in the workplace* (pp. 79–103). Hillsdale, NJ: Erlbaum.

Greenberg, J. H., & Ruhlen, M. (1992). Linguistic origins of Native Americans. *Scientific American, 267*(5), 94–99.

Greenberg, R., Pillard, R., & Pearlman, C. (1972). The effect of dream (stage REM) on adaptation to stress. *Psychosomatic Medicine, 34,* 257–262.

Greene, B. (1986). When the therapist is white and the patient is black: Considerations for psychotherapy in the feminist heterosexual and lesbian communities. In D. Howard (Ed.), *The dynamics of feminist therapy* (pp. 41–66). New York: Haworth.

Greenough, W. T., Black, J. E., & Wallace, C. S. (1987). Experience and brain development. *Child Development, 58,* 539–559.

Gregory, R. L. (1972). *Eye and brain* (2nd ed.). New York: McGraw-Hill.

Grice, P. (1975) Logic and conversation. In P. Cole & J. Morgan (Eds.), *Syntax and semantics* (Vol. 3). New York: Academic Press.

Griffith, J. (1985). Social support providers: Who are they?, Where are they met?, and the relationship of network characteristics to psychological distress. *Basic and Applied Social Psychology, 6*(1), 41–60.

Griffith, R. M., Miyago, O., & Tago, A. (1958). The universality of typical dreams: Japanese vs. Americans. *American Anthropologist, 60,* 1173–1179.

Grilly, D. M. (1989). *Drugs and human behavior.* Boston: Allyn & Bacon.

Grilo, C. M., & Pogue-Geile, M. F. (1991). The nature of environmental influences on weight and obesity: A behavior genetic analysis. *Psychological Bulletin, 110,* 520–537.

Grinspoon, L., & Bakalar, J. B. (1993). *Marihuana, the forbidden medicine.* New Haven, CT: Yale University Press.

Grossmann, K., & Grossmann, K. E. (1991). Newborn behavior, and quality of early parenting, and later toddler-parent relationships in a group of German infants. In J. K. Nugent, B. M. Lester, & T. B. Brazelton (Eds.), *The cultural context of infancy* (Vol. 2). Norwood, NJ: Ablex.

Gruber, H. (1990). Bärbel Inhelder. In A. N. O'Connell & N. F. Russo (Eds.), *Women in psychology: A bio-bibliographical source book* (pp. 197–206). Westport, CT: Greenwood Press.

Gruber, H., & Vonnech, J. (1977). *The essential Piaget.* New York: Basic Books.

Gruen, R. J., Folkman, S., & Lazarus, R. S. (1988). Centrality and individual differences in the meaning of daily hassles. *Journal of Personality, 56,* 743–762.

Gruenberg, B. (1980). The happy workers: An analysis of educational and occupational differences in determinant of job satisfaction. *American Journal of Sociology, 86,* 247–271.

Gudykunst, W. B., Ting-Toomey, S., & Chua, E. (1988). *Culture and international communication.* Newbury Park, CA: Sage.

Guilford, J. P. (1967). *The nature of human intelligence.* New York: McGraw-Hill.

Guilford, J. P. (1980). Fluid and crystallized intelligences: Two fanciful concepts. *Psychological Bulletin, 88,* 406–412.

Guilford, J. P. (1982). Cognitive psychology's ambiguities: Some suggested remedies. *Psychological Review, 89,* 48–59.

Guillemin, R. (1978). Peptides and the brain: The new endocrinology of the neuron. *Science, 202,* 390–401.

Guilmet, G. M. (1979). Navajo and Caucasian children's verbal and nonverbal-visual behavior in the urban classroom. *Anthropology and Education Quarterly, 9,* 196–215.

Guion, R. M., & Ironson, G. H. (1983). Latent trait theory for organizational research. *Organizational Behavior and Human Performance, 31,* 54–87.

Gutin, J. C. (1993). Good vibrations. *Discover, 14* (6), 45–54.

Gustavson, C. R., Garcia, J., Hankins, W. G., & Rusiniak, K. W. (1974). Coyote predation control by aversive conditioning. *Science, 184,* 581–584.

Guthrie, R. V. (1976). *Even the rat was white.* New York: Harper & Row.

Guttentag, M., & Bray, H. (1976). *Undoing sex stereotypes: Research and resources for educators.* New York: McGraw-Hill.

Haan, M., Kaplan, G. A., & Camacho, T. (1987). Poverty and health: Prospective evidence from the Alemeda County Study. *American Journal of Epidemiology, 125*(6), 989–998.

Haidt, J., Koller, S. H., & Dias, M. G. (1993). Affect, culture, and morality, or is it wrong to eat your dog? *Journal of Personality and Social Psychology, 65,* 613–628.

Haimov, I., & Lavie, P. (1996). Melatonin—A soporific hormone. *Current Directions in Psychological Science, 5,* 106–111.

Haith, M. M. (1986). Sensory and perceptual processes in early infancy. *Journal of Pediatrics, 709,* 158–171.

Halford, W. K., & Hayes, R. (1991). Psychological rehabilitation of chronic schizophrenic patients: Recent findings on social skills training and family psychoeducation. *Clinical Psychology Review, 11,* 23–44.

Hall, C. S., & Lindzey, G. (1985). *Introduction to theories of personality.* New York: Wiley.

Hall, V. C., & Kaye, D. B. (1980). Early patterns of cognitive development. *Monographs of the Society for Research in Child Development, 45* (2, Serial No. 184).

Halpern, D. (1992). *Sex differences in cognitive abilities* (2nd ed.). Hillsdale, NJ: Erlbaum.

Hamilton, D. L., Dugan, P. M., & Trolier, T. K. (1985). The formation of stereotypic beliefs: Further evidence for distinctiveness-based illusory correlations. *Journal of Personality and Social Psychology, 48,* 5–17.

Hamilton, D. L., & Gifford, R. K. (1976). Illusory correlation in interpersonal perception: A cognitive basis of stereotypic judgments. *Journal of Experimental Social Psychology, 12,* 392–407.

Hamilton, D. L., & Rose, T. L. (1980). Illusory correlation and the maintenance of stereotypic beliefs. *Journal of Personality and Social Psychology, 29*, 649–654.

Hanawalt, N. G., & Demarest, I. H. (1939). The effect of verbal suggestion in the recall period upon the reproduction of visually perceived forms. *Journal of Experimental Psychology, 25*, 159–174.

Haney, C., Banks, C., & Zimbardo, P. (1973). Interpersonal dynamics in a simulated prison. *International Journal of Criminology and Penology, 1*, 69–97.

Hanin, Y., Eysenck, S. B., Eysenck, H. J., & Barrett, P. (1991). A cross-cultural study of personality: Russia and England. *Personality and Individual Differences, 12*, 265–271.

Harbin, T. J. (1989). The relationship between Type A behavior pattern and physiological responsivity: A quantitative review. *Psychophysiology, 26*, 110–119.

Harburg, E., Erfurt, J. C., Havenstein, L. S., Chape, C., Schull, W. J., & Schork, M. A. (1973). Socio-ecological stress, suppressed hostility, skin color, and black-white male blood pressure: Detroit. *Psychosomatic Medicine, 35*, 276–296.

Hardy, K. R. (1964). An appetitional theory of sexual motivation. *Psychological Review, 71*, 1–18.

Harkins, S. G., & Szymanski, K. (1989). Social loafing and group evaluation. *Journal of Personality and Social Psychology, 56*, 934–941.

Harkins, S. G., Latané, B., & Williams, K. (1980). Social loafing: Allocating effort or taking it easy? *Journal of Experimental Social Psychology, 16*, 457–465.

Harlow, H. F. (1949). The formation of learning sets. *Psychological Review, 56*, 51–65.

Harlow, H. F. (1950). Learning and satiation of response in intrinsically motivated complex puzzle performance in monkeys. *Journal of Comparative and Physiological Psychology, 43*, 289–294.

Harlow, H. F. (1958). The nature of love. *American Psychologist, 13*, 673–685.

Harlow, H. F. (1962). The heterosexual affectional system in monkeys. *American Psychologist, 17*, 1–9.

Harlow, H. F., & Harlow, M. K. (1949). Learning to think. *Scientific American, 181*, 36–39.

Harlow, H. F., & Harlow, M. K. (1962). Social deprivation in monkeys. *Scientific American*, 136–146.

Harlow, H. F., Harlow, M. K., & Meyer, D. R. (1950). Learning motivated by a manipulation drive. *Journal of Experimental Psychology, 40*, 228–234.

Harlow, H. F., & Suomi, S. J. (1970). Nature of love—simplified. *American Psychologist, 25*, 161–168.

Harlow, H. F., & Zimmerman, R. (1959). Affectional responses in the infant monkey. *Science, 130*, 421–432.

Harlow, J. M. (1869). Recovery from the passage of an iron bar through the head. *Massachusetts Medical Society Publication, 2*, 329–347.

Harrell, J. P. (1980). Psychological factors and hypertension. *Psychological Bulletin, 87*, 482–501.

Harris, B. (1979). Whatever happened to Little Albert? *American Psychologist, 34*, 151–160.

Harris, L. (1987). *Inside America*. New York: Random House.

Harris, M. (1983). *Cultural anthropology*. New York: Harper & Row.

Harris, R. J., Schoen, L. M., & Hensley, D. L. (1992). A cross-cultural study of story memory. *Journal of Cross-Cultural Psychology, 23*, 133–47.

Harris, S. M. (1995). Family, self, and sociocultural contributions to body-image attitudes of African-American women. *Psychology of Women Quarterly, 19*, 129–145.

Harris, T. A. (1967). *I'm ok—you're ok*. New York: Harper & Row.

Hartmann, H. (1958). *Ego psychology and the problem of adaptation*. New York: International Universities Press.

Harvey, J. H., & Weary, G. (1988). *Attribution: Basic issues and applications*. San Diego, CA: Academic Press.

Harvey, P. H., & Krebs, J. R. (1990). Comparing brains. *Science, 249*, 140–145.

Hase, H. D., & Goldberg, L. R. (1967). Comparative validities of different strategies of constructing personality inventory scales. *Psychological Bulletin, 67*, 231–248.

Hasher, L., & Zacks, R T. (1984). Automatic processing of fundamental information: The case of frequency of occurrence. *American Psychologist, 39*, 1372–1388.

Hasher, L., & Zacks, R. T. (1979). Automatic and effortful processes in memory. *Journal of Experimental Psychology: General*, 108, 356–388.

Hassan, R., & Carr, J. (1989). Changing patterns of suicide in Australia. *Australian and New Zealand Journal of Psychiatry, 23*, 226–234.

Hassan, S. A. (1974). Transactional and contextual invalidation between the parents of disturbed families: A comparative study. *Family Process, 13*, 53–76.

Hatfield, E., & Sprecher, S. (1986). *Mirror, mirror . . . the importance of looks in everyday life*. Albany, NY: State University of New York Press.

Hathaway, S. R. (1960). *An MMPI Handbook*. Minneapolis, MN: University of Minnesota Press.

Hayduk, L. A. (1983). Personal space: Where we now stand. *Psychological Bulletin, 94*, 293–335.

Healy, A. F., & Bourne, L. E., Jr. (1995). *Acquisition and retention of knowledge and skills*. Thousand Oaks, CA: Sage.

Healy, A. F., & McNamara, D. S. (1996). Verbal learning and memory: Does the modal model still work? *Annual Review of Psychology, 47*, 143–172.

Hebb, D. O. (1949). *The organization of behavior*. New York: Wiley.

Hecht, S. (1934/1969). Vision II: The nature of the photoreceptor process. In C. Marchison (Ed.), *A handbook of experimental psychology*. Worcester, MA: Clark University Press.

Hecht, S., Shlaer, S., & Pirenne, M. H. (1941). Energy at the threshold of vision. *Science, 93*, 585–587.

Hefner, R. S., & Hefner, H. E. (1985). Hearing in large and small dogs: Absolute thresholds and size of the tympanic membrane. *Behavioral Neuroscience, 97*, 389–399.

Heidbreider, E. (1933). *Seven psychologies*. New York: Appleton-Century-Crofts.

Heider, F. (1958). *The psychology of interpersonal relations*. New York: Wiley.

Heilman, M. E., & Stopeck, M. H. (1985). Being attractive, advantage or disadvantage? Performance based evaluations and recommended personnel actions as a function of appearance, sex, and job type. *Organizational Behavior and Human Decision Processes, 35*, 202–215.

Heilman, M. E., Martell, R. F., & Simon, M. C. (1988). The vagaries of sex-bias: Conditions regulating the undervaluation, equivaluation, and overvaluation of female job applicants. *Organizational Behavior and Human Decision Processes, 41*, 98–110.

Held, R., & Hein, A. (1963). Movement-produced stimulation in the development of visually guided behavior. *Journal of Comparative and Physiological Psychology, 56*, 872–876.

Helms, J. E. (1992). Why is there no sudy of cultural equivalence in standardized cognitive ability testing? *American Psychologist, 47*, 1083–1101.

Helson, H. (1959). Adaptation level theory. In S. Koch (Ed.), *Psychology: A study of a science*. New York: McGraw-Hill.

Helzer, J. E., & Canino, G. (Eds.). (1992). *Alcoholism in North America, Europe, and Asia*. New York: Oxford University Press.

Henley, N. (1977). *Body politics*. Englewood Cliffs, NJ: Prentice-Hall.

Henriques, J. B., & Davidson, R. J. (1990). Regional brain electrical asymmetries discriminate between previously depressed and healthy control subjects. *Journal of Abnormal Psychology, 99,* 22–31.

Hepper, P. (1989). Foetal learning: Implications for psychiatry? *British Journal of Psychiatry, 155,* 289–293.

Herd, D. A. (1993). Contesting culture: Alcohol-related identity movements in contemporary African-American communities. *Contemporary Drug Problems, 20,* 739–758.

Herek, G. M., Kimmel, D.C., Amaro, H., Melton, G. B. (1991). Avoiding heterosexist bias in psychological research. *American Psychologist, 46,* 957–963.

Hering, E. (1920). *Outlines or a theory of the light sense* (pp. 150–151). (L. M. Hurvich & D. Jameson, Eds.). Cambridge, MA: Harvard University Press.

Herman, J. L., Perry, J. C., & van der Kolk, B. A. (1989). Childhood trauma in borderline personality disorder. *American Journal of Psychiatry, 146,* 490–495.

Herrmann, D. J., Crawford, M., & Holdsworth, M. (1992). Gender-linked differences in everyday memory performance. *British Journal of Psychology, 83,* 221–231.

Herrnstein, R. J., & Murray, C . (1994). *The bell curve: Intelligence and class structure in American life.* New York: Free Press.

Herz, D. E., & Wooton, B. H. (1996). Women in the workforce: An overview. In C. Costello & B. K. Krimgold (Eds.), *The American woman, 1996–97: Where we stand* (pp. 44–78). New York: Norton.

Herz, R. S., & Engen, T. (1996). Odor memory: Review and analysis. *Psychonomic Bulletin & Review, 3,* 300–313.

Herzog, D. B., Norman, D. K., Gordon, C., & Prepose, M. (1984). Sexual conflict and eating disorders in 27 males. *American Journal of Psychiatry, 141,* 989–990.

Hess, E. (1962). Ethology: An approach toward the complete analysis of behavior. In R. Brown, E. Galanter, E. Hess, & G. Mandler (Eds.), *New directions in psychology.* New York: Holt, Rinehart and Winston.

Hesse-Biber, S. (1989). Eating patterns and disorders in a college population: Are college women's eating problems a new phenomenon? *Sex Roles, 20,* 71–89.

Hewlett, B. S. (1991). *Intimate fathers: The nature and context of Aka Pygmy paternal infant care.* Ann Arbor, MI: University of Michigan Press.

Hewstone, M. (1990). The "ultimate attribution error"? A review of the literature on intergroup causal attribution. *European Journal of Social Psychology, 20,* 311–335.

Hewstone, M., Gale, L., & Purkhardt, N. (1990). Intergroup attributions for success and failure: Group-serving bias and group-serving causal schemata. *Eurpoean Bulletin of Cognitive Psychology, 10,* 23–44.

Higgins, E. T., & Bargh, J. A. (1987). Social cognition and social perception. *Annual Review of Psychology, 38,* 369–425.

Hildreth, A. M., Derogatis, L. R., & McCusker, K. (1971). Body buffer zone and violence: A reassessment and confirmation. *American Journal of Psychiatry, 127,* 1641–1645.

Hilgard, E. R. (1973). A neodissociation interpretation of pain reduction in hypnosis. *Psychological Review, 80,* 396–411.

Hilgard, E. R. (1974). Toward a neodissociation theory: Multiple cognitive control in human functioning. *Perspectives in Biology and Medicine, 17,* 301–316.

Hilgard, E. R. (1977). *Divided consciousness: Multiple controls in human thought and action.* New York: Wiley.

Hilgard, E. R., & Hilgard., J. R. (1983). *Hypnosis in the relief of pain.* Los Altos, CA: Kaufmann.

Hilgard, J. R., & LeBaron, S. (1984). *Hypnotherapy of pain in children with cancer.* Los Altos, CA: Kaufman.

Hill, J. (1982). Smoking, alcohol, and body mass relationships to early menopause: Implications for risk of cardiovascular disease. In A. M. Voda, M. Dinnerstein, & S. R. O'Donnell (Eds.). *Changing perspectives on menopause* (pp. 160–169). Austin, TX: University of Texas Press.

Hill, R. (1979). *Hanta ho.* New York: Doubleday.

Hilton, J. L., & Darley, J. M. (1991). Effects of interaction goals on person perception. *Advances in Experimental Social Psychology, 24,* 236–269.

Hines, A. M., & Shaw, G. A. (1993) Intrusive thoughts, sensation seeking, and drug use in college students. *Bulletin of the Psychonomic Society, 31,* 541–544.

Hingson, R., Alpert, J., Day, N., Dooing, E., Kayne, H., Morelock, S., Oppenheimer, E., & Zuckerman, B. (1982). Effects of maternal drinking and marijuana use on fetal growth and development. *Pediatrics, 70,* 539–546.

Hintzman, D. L. (1990). Human learning and memory: Connections and dissociations. *Annual Review of Psychology, 41,* 109–139.

Hintzman, D. L., Block, R. A., & Summers, J. J. (1973). Modality tags and memory for repetitions: Locus of the spacing effect. *Journal of Verbal Learning and Verbal Behavior, 12,* 229–239.

Hirsch, H. V. B., & Spinelli, D. N. (1971). Modification of the distribution of receptive field orientation in cats by selective visual exposure during development. *Experimental Brain Research, 13,* 509–527.

Hirschman, R., Leventhal, H., & Glynn, K. (1983). The development of smoking behavior: Conceptualization and supportive cross-sectional survey data. *Journal of Applied Social Psychology, 14,* 184–206.

Hirst, W., & Kalmar, D. (1987). Characterizing attentional resources. *Journal of Experimental Psychology: General, 116,* 68–81.

Hirst, W., Spelke, E. S., Reaves, C. C., Caharack, G., & Neisser, U. (1980). Dividing attention without alternation or automaticity. *Journal of Experimental Psychology: General, 109,* 98–117.

Hjelle, L. A., & Ziegler, D. J. (1992). *Personality theories* (3rd. ed.). New York: McGraw-Hill.

Ho, D.Y., & Chiu, C. (1994). Component ideas of individualism, collectivism, and social organization: An application in the study of Chinese culture. In U. Kim, H. C. Triandis, C. Kagitcibasi, S. C. Choi, & G. Yoon (Eds.), *Individualism and collectivism: Theory, method, and application* (pp. 123–136). Thousand Oaks, CA: Sage.

Ho, K., Roessmann, U., Hause, L., & Monroe, G. (1981). Newborn brain weight in relation to maturity, sex, and race. *Annals of Neurology, 10,* 243–246.

Ho, K., Roessmann, U., Straumfjord, J. V., & Monroe, G. (1980). Analysis of brain weight: II. Adult brain weight in relation to body height, weight, and surface area. *Archives of Pathology and Laboratory Medicine,* 104, 635–639.

Hobson, J. A. (1988). *The dreaming brain.* New York: Basic Books.

Hochberg, J.E. (1964). *Perception.* Englewood Cliffs, NJ: Prentice-Hall.

Hodges, W. (1990). Personal communication, June 18, 1990.

Hoehn-Saric, R., & McLeod, D. R. (1991). Clinical management of generalized anxiety disorder. In W. Coryell & G. Winokur (Eds.), *The clinical management of anxiety disorders* (pp. 79–100). New York: Oxford University Press.

Hoffman, C., Lau, I., & Johnson, D. R. (1986). The linguistic relativity of person cognition: An English-Chinese comparison. *Journal of Personality and Social Psychology, 51,* 1097–1105.

Hoffmann, B. & Burke, C. (1997). *Heaven's Gate: Cult suicide in San Diego.* New York: Harper Paperback.

Hofstede, G. (1980). *Culture's consequences.* Beverly Hills, CA: Sage.

Hogan, J., & Ones, D. (1997). Conscientiousness and integrity at work. In R. Hogan, J. Johnson, & S. Briggs (Eds.), *Handbook of personality psychology* (pp. 165–195). San Diego, CA: Academic Press.

Hogan, R., Johnson, J., & Briggs (Eds.). (1997). *Handbook of personality psychology.* San Diego, CA: Academic Press.

Hohmann, G. W. (1962). Some effects of spinal cord lesions on experienced emotional feelings. *Psychophysiology, 3,* 143–156.

Hokanson, J. E., & Burgess, M. (1962). The effects of status, type of frustration, and aggression on vascular processes. *Journal of Abnormal and Social Psychology, 65,* 232–237.

Hokanson, J. E., Burgess, M., & Cohen, M. F. (1963). Effects of displaced aggression on systolic blood pressure. *Journal of Abnormal and Social Psychology, 67,* 214–218.

Holden, C. (1987). Is alcoholism treatment effective? *Science, 236,* 20–22.

Holden, C. (1992). Random samples. *Science, 257,* 480–481.

Hollon, S. D. (1996). The efficacy and effectiveness of psychotherapy relative to medications. *American Psychologist, 51,* 1025–1030.

Hollon, S. D., & Beck, A. T. (1994). Cognitive and cognitive-behavioral therapies. In A. E. Bergin & S. L. Garfield (Eds.), *Handbook of psychotherapy and behavior change* (4th ed; pp. 428–466). New York: Wiley.

Hollon, S. D., Evans, M. D., & DeRubeis, R. J. (1990). Cognitive mediation of relapse prevention following treatment for depression: Implications of differential risk. In R. E. Ingram (Ed.), *Contemporary psychological approaches to depression: Theory, research, and treatment* (pp. 117–136). New York: Plenum Press.

Hollon, S. D., Kendall, P. C., & Lumry, A. (1986). Specificity of depressotypic cognitions in clinical depression. *Journal of Abnormal Psychology, 95,* 52–59.

Holmes, D. S. (1974). Investigations of repression: Differential recall of material experimentally or naturally associated with ego threat. *Psychological Bulletin, 81,* 632–653.

Holmes, D. S. (1984). Meditation and somatic arousal reduction: A review of the experimental evidence. *American Psychologist, 39,* 1–10.

Holmes, T. H., & Rahe, R. H. (1967). The Social Readjustment Rating Scale. *Journal of Psychosomatic Research, 11,* 213–218.

Holt, J. (1964). *How children fail.* New York: Pitman.

Holtz, R., & Miller, N. (1985). Assumed similarity and opinion certainty. *Journal of Personality and Social Psychology, 48,* 890–898.

Holzman, P. S., & Matthysse, S. (1990). The genetics of schizophrenia: A review. *Psychological Science, 1,* 279–286.

Homme, L. W., de Baca, P. C., Devine, J. V., Steinhorst, R., & Rickert, E. J. (1963). Use of the Premack principle in controlling the behavior of nursery school children. *Journal of the Experimental Analysis of Behavior, 6,* 544.

Honjo, H., Tanaka, K. Kashiwagi, T., Urabe, M., Okada, H. Hayashi, M., & Hayashi, K. (1995). Senile dementia-Alzheimer's type and estrogen. *Hormone and Metabolic Research, 27,* 204–207.

Horn, M. (1993, November). Memories lost and found. *U.S. News and World Report,* pp. 52–58.

Horne, J. A. (1988). *Why we sleep: The functions of sleep in humans and other mammals.* Oxford, Eng.: Oxford University Press.

Horne, J. A., & Moore, V. J. (1985). Sleep effects of exercise with and without additional body cooling. *Electroencephalography and Clinical Neurophysiology, 60,* 347–353.

Horner, M. (1970). Femininity and successful achievement: A basic inconsistency. In J. Bardwick, E. Douvan, M. Horner, & D. Guttman (Eds.), *Feminine personality and conflict.* Belmont, CA: Brooks/Cole.

Horney, K. (1934). The overvaluation of love: A study of a common present-day feminine type. *Psychoanalytic Quarterly, 3,* 605–638.

Horney, K. (1935). The problem of feminine masochism. *Psychoanalytic Review, 22,* 241.

Horney, K. (1937). *The neurotic personality of our time.* New York: Norton.

Horney, K. (1945). *Our inner conflicts: A constructive theory of neurosis.* New York: Norton.

Horney, K. (1950). *Neurosis and human growth.* New York: Norton.

Hovland, C. I., & Weiss, W. (1951). The influence of source credibility on communication effectiveness. *Public Opinion Quarterly, 15,* 635–650.

Howard, R. (1980). Ruth W. Howard (1900–). In A. N. O'Connell & N. F. Russo (Eds.), *Models of achievement: Reflections of eminent women in psychology* (pp. 55–68). New York: Columbia University Press.

Howe, M. L., & Courage, M. L. (1993). On resolving the enigma of infantile amnesia. *Psychological Bulletin, 113,* 305–326.

Howes, C. (1988). Peer interaction of young children. *Monographs of the Society for Research in Child Development, 53*(1, Serial No. 217).

Howes, C., & Matheson, C. C. (1992). Contextual constraints on the concordance of mother-child and teacher-child relationships. In R. C. Pianta (Ed.), *New directions for child development: No. 57. Beyond the parent: The role of other adults in children's lives.* San Francisco: Jossey-Bass.

Hsu, F. L. (1971). *Kinship and culture.* Chicago, IL: Aldine.

Hubel, D. H. (1979). The visual cortex of normal and deprived monkeys. *American Scientist, 67,* 532–543.

Hubel, D. H., & Torstenn, W. (1963). Receptive fields, binocular interaction, and functional architecture in the cat's visual cortex. *Journal of Physiology, 160,* 106–154.

Hubel, D. H., & Wiesel, T. N. (1959). Receptive fields of single neurons in the cat's striate cortex. *Journal of Physiology, 148,* 574–591.

Hubel, D. H., & Wiesel, T. N. (1977). Functional architecture of macaque monkey visual cortex. *Proceedings of the Royal Society of London, 198,* 1–59.

Hubel, D. H., & Wiesel, T. N. (1979). Brain mechanisms of vision. *Scientific American, 241,* 150–162.

Huddy, L., & Virtanen, S. (1995). Subgroup differentiation and subgroup bias among Latinos as a function of familiarity and positive distinctiveness. *Journal of Personality and Social Psychology, 68,* 97–107.

Hudson, W. (1960). Pictorial depth perception in sub-cultural groups in Africa. *Journal of Social Psychology, 52,* 183–208.

Huffman, B. (1997, July 14). Brit displays grit: Nicholas wins Open, excels as spoiler. *Arizona Republic,* pp. D1, D8.

Hughes, C. S., Uhlmann, C., & Pennebaker, J. (in press). The body's response to processing emotional trauma: Linking verbal text with autonomic activity. *Journal of Personality.*

Hull, J. G., & Bond, C. F., Jr. (1986). Social and behavioral consequences of alcohol consumption and expectancy: A meta-analysis. *Psychological Bulletin, 99,* 347–360.

Hull, J. G., Van Treuren, R. R., & Virnelli, S. (1987). Hardiness and health: A critique and alternative approach. *Journal of Personality and Social Psychology, 53,* 518–530.

Hunt, E., & Agnoli, F. (1991). The Whorfian hypothesis: A cognitive psychology perspective. *Psychological Review, 98,* 377–389.

Hunt, E., Lunneborg, C., & Lewis, J. (1975). What does it mean to be high verbal? *Cognitive Psychology,* 194–227.

Hurford, J. R. (1991). The evolution of the critical period for language acquisition. *Cognition, 40,* 159–201.

Hurvich, L.M. (1981). *Color vision.* Sunderland, MA: Sinauer Assoc.

Huyghe, P. (1985, September). Voices, glances, flashbacks: Our first memories. *Psychology Today,* pp. 48–52.

Hyde, J. S. (1995). Presidential address: Women and maternity leave: Empirical data and public policy. *Psychology of Women Quarterly, 19,* 299–314.

Hyde, T. S., & Jenkins, J. J. (1973). Recall for words as a function of semantic, graphic, and syntactic orienting tasks. *Journal of Verbal Learning and Verbal Behavior, 12,* 471–480.

Hyman, R. (1965). *The nature of psychological inquiry.* Englewood Cliffs, NJ: Prentice-Hall.

Ickes, W., Snyder, M., & Garcia, S. (1997). Personality influences on the choice of situations. In R. Hogan, J. Johnson, & S. Briggs (Eds.), *Handbook of personality psychology* (pp. 166–195). San Diego, CA: Academic Press.

Inhelder, B., & Piaget, J. (1958). *The growth of logical thinking: From childhood to adolescence* (A. Parsons and S. Milgram, Trans.). New York: Basic Books.

Insko, C. A., Nacoste, R. W., & Moe, J. L. (1983). Belief congruence and racial discrimination: Review of the evidence and critical evaluation. *European Journal of Social Psychology, 13*, 153–174.

Irvine, S. H., & Berry, J. W. (1988). The abilities of mankind: A reevaluation. In S. H. Irvine & J. W. Berry (Eds.), *Human abilities in cultural context*. New York: Cambridge University Press.

Isozaki, M. (1984). The effect of discussion on polarization of judgments. *Japanese Psychological Research, 26*, 187–193.

Ito, T. A., Miller, N., & Pollock, V. E. (1996). Alcohol and aggression: A meta-analysis of the moderating effects of inhibitory cues, triggering events and self-focused attention. *Psychological Bulletin, 120*, 60–82.

Jack, D. C. (1981). *Silencing the self: Women and depression*. Cambridge, MA: Harvard University Press.

Jackson, J. M., & Williams, K. D. (1985). Social loafing on difficult tasks: Working collectively can improve performance. *Journal of Personality and Social Psychology, 49*, 937–942.

Jackson, L. S., Sullivan, L. A., & Hodge, C. N. (1993). Stereotype effects on attributions, predictions, and evaluations: No two social judgments are quite alike. *Journal of Personality and Social Psychology, 65*, 69–84.

Jacobs, B. L. (1994). Serotonin, motor activity and depression-related disorders. *American Scientist, 82*, 456–463.

Jacobs, G. H. (1993) The distribution and nature of colour vision among mammals. *Biological Review, 68*, 413–471.

Jacobsen, M. (1991). *Developmental neurobiology*. New York: Plenum Press.

Jacobson, N. S., & Hollon, S. D. (1996). Cognitive-behavior therapy versus pharmacotherapy: Now that the jury's returned its verdict, it's time to present the rest of the evidence. *Journal of Consulting and Clinical Psychology, 64*, 74–80.

Jacobson, N. S., Schmaling, K. B., Holtzworth-Munroe, A., Katt, J. L., Wood, L. F., & Follette, V. M. (1989). Research structured vs. clinically flexible versions of social learning-based marital therapy. *Behaviour Research and Therapy, 27*, 173–180.

Jacoby, L. L., Lindsay, D. S., & Toth, J. P. (1992). Unconscious influences revealed. *American Psychologist, 47*, 802–809.

Jacoby, L. L., & Dallas, M. (1981). On the relationship between autobiographical memory and perceptual learning. *Journal of Experimental Psychology: General, 110*, 306–340.

Jacoby, L. L., Toth, J. P., & Yonelinas, A. P. (1993). Separating conscious and unconscious influences of memory: Measuring recollection. *Journal of Experimental Psychology: General, 122*, 139–154.

James, W. (1890/1950). *The principles of psychology*. New York: Dover.

Jamison, K. R. (1995, February). Manic-depressive illness and creativity. *Scientific American*, 62–67.

Janis, I. L. (1972). *Victims of groupthink*. Boston: Houghton Mifflin.

Janis, I. L. (1983). Foreword. In E. J. Langer (Ed.), *The psychology of control* (pp. 9–11). Beverly Hills, CA: Sage.

Janis, I. L., & Feshbach, S. (1953). Effects of fear-arousing communications. *Journal of Abnormal and Social Psychology, 48*, 78–92.

Janoff-Bulman, R. (1989). The benefits of illusions, the threat of disillusionment, and the limitations of accuracy. *Journal of Social and Clinical Psychology, 8*, 158–175.

Janoski, M. L., Kugler, U., & McClelland, D. C. (1986). *Power imagery and relaxation effect psychoneuroimmune indices*. Paper presented at the Annual Meetings of the American Psychological Association.

Janov, A. (1970). *The primal scream*. New York: Dell.

Janowsky, J. S., & Finlay, B. L. (1986). The outcome of perinatal brain damage: The role of normal neuron loss and axon retraction. *Developmental Medicine and Child Neurology, 28*, 375–389.

Janz, N. K., & Becker, M. H. (1984). The health belief model: A decade later. *Health Education Quarterly, 11*, 1–47.

Jarvik, M. E. (1973). Further observations on nicotine as the reinforcing agent in smoking. In W. L. Dunn, Jr. (Ed.), *Smoking behavior: Motives and incentives* (pp. 33–50). Washington, DC: Winston.

Jaschke, V. A., & Spiegel, D. (1992). A case of probably dissociative disorder. *Bulletin of the Menninger Clinic, 56*(2), 246–260.

Jaynes, J. (1976). *The origins of consciousness in the breakdown of the bicameral mind*. Boston: Houghton Mifflin.

Jeffery, R. W. (1992). Is obesity a risk factor for cardiovascular disease? *Annals of Behavioral Medicine, 14*, 109–112.

Jellinek, E. M. (1952). Phases of alcohol addiction. *Quarterly Journal of Studies on Alcohol, 13*, 673–684.

Jenkins, C. D., Zyzanski, S. J., & Rosenman, R. H. (1979). *Jenkins Activity Survey*. Cleveland, OH: Psychological Corporation.

Jenkins, J. G., & Dallenbach, K. M. (1924). Oblivescence during sleep and waking. *American Journal of Psychology, 35*, 605–612.

Jens, K. S., & Evans, H. I. (1983). *The diagnosis and treatment of multiple personality clients*. Workshop presented at the Rocky Mountain Psychological Association, Snowbird, Utah.

Jensen, A. R. (1969). How much can we boost IQ and scholastic achievement? *Harvard Educational Review, 39*, 1–123.

John, O. P., Caspi, A., Robins, R. W., Moffitt, T. E., & Stouthamer-Loeber, M. (1994). The "Little Five": Exploring the nomological network of the five-factor model of personality in adolescent boys. *Child Development, 65*, 160–178.

Johnson, D. (1990). Can psychology ever be the same again after the human genome has been mapped? *Psychological Science, 1*, 331–332.

Johnson, M. K., Bransford, J. D., & Solomon, S. (1973). Memory for tacit implications of sentences. *Journal of Experimental Psychology, 98*, 203–205.

Johnson, R. D., & Downing, L. L. (1979). Deindividuation and valence of cues: Effects of prosocial and antisocial behavior. *Journal of Personality and Social Psychology, 37*, 1532–1538.

Johnston, L. D., Bachman, J. G., & O'Malley, P. M. (1982). *Student drug use, attitudes and beliefs: National trends 1975–1982*. Washington DC: U. S. Government Printing Office.

Johnston, L. D., O'Malley, P. M., & Bachman, J. G. (1996). *National survey results on drug use from the Monitoring the Future Study, 1975–1995. Vol 1: Secondary school students*. NIH Publication No. 96-4139. Rockville MD: National Institute of Drug Abuse, NIH.

Johnston, W. A., & Hawley, K. J. (1994). Perceptual inhibition of expected inputs: The key that opens closed minds. *Psychonomic Bulletin and Review, 1*, 56–72.

Jones, E. (1953). *The life and work of Sigmund Freud: The formative years and the great discoveries* (Vol. 1). New York: Basic Books.

Jones, E. E. (1990). *Interpersonal perception*. San Francisco: Freeman.

Jones, E. E., & Davis, K. E. (1965). From acts to dispositions. The attribution process in person perception. In L. Berkowitz (Ed.), *Advances in experimental social psychology* (Vol. 2). New York: Academic Press.

Jones, E. E., Kanouse, D. E., Kelley, H. H., Nisbett, R. E., Valiens, S., & Weiner, B. (1971). *Attribution: Perceiving the causes of behavior*. New York: General Learning Press.

Jones, E. E., & Nisbett, R. E. (1971). *The actor and the observer: Divergent perceptions of the causes of behavior*. Morristown, NJ: General Learning Press.

Jones, E. E., Wood, G. C., Quattrone, G. A. (1981). Perceived variability of personal characteristics in in-groups and out-groups: The role of knowledge and evaluation. *Personality and Social Psychology Bulletin, 7*, 523–528.

Jones, M. (1994, April 25). The fallout of the burnout: The sad, sordid last days of Kurt Cobain. *Newsweek*, p. 68.

Jones, M. C. (1924). A laboratory study of fear: The case of Peter. *Pedagogical Seminary, 31*, 308–15.

Jones, M. C. (1965). Psychological correlates of somatic development. *Child Development, 36*, 899–911.

Jones, M. C. (1975). Community care for chronic mental patients: The need for reassessment. *Hospital and Community Psychiatry, 26*, 94–98.

Jones, P. (1990). Basic research offers clues to Alzheimer's disease. *ADAMHA News*, 10–11.

Jones, R. T., & Beniowitz, N. (1976). The 30-day trip: Clinical studies of cannabis tolerance and dependence. In M. C. Braude & S. Szara (Eds.), *Pharamcology of marihuana* (Vol. 2, pp. 627–42). New York: Academic Press.

Josephson, W. (1987). Television violence and children's aggression: Testing the priming, social script, and disinhibition predictions. *Journal of Personality and Social Psychology, 53*, 882–890.

Judd, C. M., & Park, B. (1988). Out-group homogeneity: Judgments of variability at the individual and group levels. *Journal of Personality and Social Psychology*, 54, 778–788.

Judd, C. M., Ryan, C. S., & Park, B. (1991). Accuracy in the judgment of in-group and out-group variability. *Journal of Personality and Social Psychology, 61*, 366–379.

Jung, C. G. (1916). *Analytical psychology*. New York: Moffat.

Jung, C. G. (1925). *Psychology of the unconscious*. New York: Dodd.

Jung, C. G. (1925/1971). Psychological types. In H. Read, M. Fundham, G. Adler, & W. McGuire (Eds.), *The collected works of C. G. Jung* (Vol. 6, pp. 510–523). Princeton, NJ: Princeton University Press.

Jussim, L., Nelson, T. E., Manis, M., & Soffin, S. (1995). Prejudice, stereotypes, and labeling effects: Sources of bias in person perception. *Journal of Personality and Social Psychology, 68*, 228–246.

Kagan, J. (1984). *The nature of the child*. New York: Basic Books.

Kagan, J. (1989). Temperamental contributions to social behavior. *American Psychologist, 44*, 668–674.

Kagan, J., Kearsley, R. B., & Zelazo, P. R. (1978). *Infancy: Its place in human development*. Cambridge, MA: Harvard University Press.

Kagan, J., Reznick, J. S., Snidman, N., Gibbons, J., & Johnson, M. (1988). Childhood derivatives of inhibition and lack of inhibition to the familiar. *Child Development, 59*, 1580–1589.

Kagan, J., & Snidman, N. (1991). Infant predictors of inhibited and uninhibited profiles. *Psychological Science, 2*, 40–41.

Kâgitçibasi, C., & Berry, J. W. (1989). Cross-cultural psychology: Current research and trends. *Annual Review of Psychology, 40*, 493–531.

Kahn, R. S., Davidson, M., Knott, P., Stern, R. G., Apter, S., & Davis, K. L. (1993). Effect of neuroleptic medication on cerebrospinal fluid monoamine metabolite concentrations in schizophrenia: Serotonin-dopamine interactions as a target for treatment. *Archives of General Psychiatry, 50*, 599–605.

Kalat, J. W. (1984). *Biological psychology* (2nd ed.). Belmont, CA: Wadsworth.

Kallman, F. J. (1953). *Heredity in mental health and disorder*. New York: Norton.

Kallman, F. J. (1958). The use of genetics in psychiatry. *Journal of Mental Science, 104*, 542–549.

Kaloupek, D. G., & Stoupakis, T. (1985). Coping with a stressful medical procedure: Further investigation with volunteer blood donors. *Journal of Behavioral Medicine, 8*, 131–48.

Kamin, L. J. (1974). *The science and politics of I.Q.* Potomac, MD: Erlbaum.

Kamiya, J. (1969). Operant control of the EEG alpha rhythm and some of its reported effects on consciousness. In C. T. Tart (Ed.), *Altered states of consciousness*. New York: Wiley.

Kannel, W. B., & Eaker, E. D. (1986). Psychosocial and other features of coronary heart disease: Insights from the Framingham Study. *American Heart Journal, 112*, 1066–1073.

Kanner, A. D., Coyne, J. C., Schaeffer, C., & Lazarus, R. S. (1981). Comparison of two modes of stress measurement: Daily hassles and uplifts versus major life events. *Journal of Behavioral Medicine, 4*(1), 1–39.

Kaplan, B. (Ed.) (1964). *The inner world of mental illness*. New York: Harper & Row.

Kaplan, H. I., & Sadock, B. J. (1991). *Synopsis of psychiatry: Behavioral sciences, clinical psychiatry* (6th ed.). Baltimore: Williams & Wilkins.

Kaplan, H. I. (1975). Current psychodynamic concepts in psychosomatic medicine. In R. Pasnau (Ed.), *Consultation-liaison psychiatry*. New York: Grune & Stratton.

Kaplan, H. I., & Sadock, B. J. (1991). *Synopsis of psychiatry: Behavioral sciences, clinical psychiatry* (6th ed.). Baltimore, MD: Williams & Wilkins.

Kaplan, H. S. (1974). *The new sex therapy: Active treatment of sexual dysfunctions*. New York: Brunner/Mazel.

Kaplan, R. M., & Hartwell, S. L. (1987). Differential effects of social support and social network on physiological and social outcomes in men and women with Type II diabetes mellitus. *Health Psychology, 6*, 387–398.

Karamatsu, A., & Hirai, T. (1969). An electroencephalographic study of the Zen meditation (Zazen). *Acta Psychologica, 6*, 86–91.

Karapelou, J. (1993). Smelling and tasting. *Discover, 6*, 72.

Karau, S. J., & Williams, K. D. (1993). Social loafing: A meta-analytic review and theoretical integration. *Journal of Personality and Social Psychology, 65*, 681–706.

Kargon, R. E. (1974). *The maturing of American science*. Washington, DC: American Association for the Advancement of Science.

Karlins, M., & Abelson, H. I. (1970). *How opinions and attitudes are changed* (2nd ed.). New York: Springer.

Kassin, S. M., Smith, V. L., & Tulloch, W. F. (1990). The dynamite charge: Effects on the perceptions and deliberation behavior of mock jurors. *Law and Human Behavior, 14*, 537–550.

Kastenbaum, R. (1977). Is death a crisis? In N. Dalton & L. H. Ginsberg (Eds.), *Life-span developmental psychology*. New York: Academic Press.

Kastenbaum, R. (1992). *The psychology of death* (2nd ed.). New York: Springer.

Kaufman, A., Baron, A., & Kopp, R. E. (1966). Some effects of instructions on human operant behavior. *Psychonomic Monographs Supplement, 1*, 243–250.

Kaufman, A. S., Kamphaus, R. W., & Kaufman, N. L. (1985). New directions in intelligence testing: The Kaufman Assessment Battery for Children (K-ABC). In B. Wolman (Ed.), *Handbook of intelligence*. New York: Wiley.

Kaye, H. (1967). Infant sucking behavior and its modification. In L. P. Lipsitt & C. C. Spiker (Eds.), *Advances in child development and behavior*. New York: Academic Press.

Kazdin, A.E. (Ed.). (1986). Psychotherapy research [Special issue]. *Journal of Consulting and Clinical Psychology, 54*, 1–118.

Kearins, J. (1981). Visual spatial memory in Australian Aboriginal children of desert regions. *Cognitive Psychology, 13*, 434–460.

Keating, D. P. (1991). Adolescent cognition. In R. M. Lerner, A. C. Petersen, & J. Brooks-Gunn (Eds.), *Encyclopedia of adolescence*. New York: Garland.

Keefe, F. B., Johnson, L. C., & Hunter, E. J. (1971). EEG and autonomic response pattern during waking and sleep stages. *Psychophysiology, 8*, 198–212.

Keesey, R. E., & Powley, T. L. (1986). The regulation of body weight. *Annual Review of Psychology, 37*, 109–133.

Keller, H. (1910). *The world I live in*. New York: Century.

Keller, H. (1968). *Midstream: My later life*. New York: Greenwood Press.

Kelley, H. H. (1967). Attribution theory in social psychology. In D. Levine (Ed.), *Nebraska symposium on motivation* (pp. 192–328). Lincoln, NB: University of Nebraska Press.

Kelley, H. H. (1968). Interpersonal accommodation. *American Psychiatrist, 23*, 399–441.

Kelley, H. H. (1972). Attribution in social interaction. In E. E. Jones et. al. (Eds.), *Attribution: Perceiving the causes of behavior.* Morristown, NJ: General Learning Press.

Kelley, H. H., & Michela, J. L. (1980) Attribution theory and research. *Annual Review of Psychology, 31,* 457–501.

Kelley, K., & Byrne, D. (1991). *Human sexual behavior: An introduction.* Englewood Cliffs, NJ: Prentice-Hall.

Kelly, G. A. (1963). *A theory of personality: The psychology of personal constructs.* New York: Norton.

Kelman, H. C. (1961). Processes of opinion change. *Public Opinion Quarterly, 25,* 57–78.

Kempenaers, C., Bouillon, E., & Mendlewicz, J. (1994). A rhythmic movement disorder in REM sleep: A case report. *Sleep,* 17 (3), 274–279.

Kennedy, W. A. (1969). A follow-up normative study of Negro intelligence and achievement. *Monographs of the Society for Research in Child Development, 34,* (2, Serial No. 126).

Kessler, R. C., McGonagle, K. A., Shanyang, Z., Nelson, C. B., Hughes, M., Eshleman, S., Wittchen, H., & Kendler, K. S. (1994). Lifetime and 12-month prevalence of DSM-III-R psychiatric disorders in the United States: Results from the National Comorbidity Survey. *Archives of General Psychiatry, 51,* 8–19.

Kessler, R. C., Sonnega, A., Bromet, E., & Nelson, C. B. (1995). Posttraumatic stress disorder in the National Comorbidity Survey. *Archives of General Psychiatry, 52,* 1048–1060.

Khachaturian, Z. S., & Blass, J. P. (1992). *Alzheimer's disease: New treatment strategies.* New York: Dekker.

Kiang, N. Y. S. (1979). Stimulus representation in the discharge patterns of auditory neurons. In E. A. Eagles (Ed.), *The nervous system.* New York: Raven Press.

Kiecolt-Glaser, J. K., Glaser, R., Strain, E. C., Stout, J. C., Tarr, K. K., Holliday, J. E., & Speicher, C. E. (1986). Modulation of cellular immunity in medical students. *Journal of Behavioral Medicine, 9,* 311–320.

Kiecolt-Glaser, J. K., Glaser, R., Shuttleworth, E. C., Dyer, C. S., Ogrocki, P., & Speicher, C. E. (1987). Chronic stress and immunity in family caregivers of Alzheimer's disease victims. *Psychosomatic Medicine, 49,* 523–535.

Kihlstrom, J. F. (1987). The cognitive unconscious. *Science, 237,* 1445–1452.

Kihlstrom, J. F., & McConkey, K. M. (1990). William James and hypnosis: A centennial reflection. *Psychological Science, 1,* 174–177.

Kihlstrom, J. F., Tataryn, D. J., & Hoyt, I. P (1993). Dissociative disorders. In P. B. Sucker & H. E. Adams (Eds.). *Comprehensive handbook of psychopathology* (2nd ed.). New York: Plenum.

Kihlstrom, J. L. (1994). Commentary: Psychodynamics and social cognition: Notes on the fusion of psychoanalysis and psychology. *Journal of Personality, 62,* 681–696.

Killeen, P. R. (1981). Learning as causal inference. In M. L. Commons & J. A. Nevin (Eds.), *Quantitative analyses of behavior. Vol I: Discriminative properties of reinforcement schedules.* Cambridge, MA: Ballinger.

Killeen, J. D., Taylor, C. B., Hayward, C., Wilson, D. M., Haydel, K. F., Hammer, L. D., Simmonds, B., Robinson, T. N., Litt, J., Varardy, A., & Kamer, H. (1994). Pursuit of thinness and onset of eating disorder symptoms in a community sample of adolescent girls: A three-year prospective analysis. *International Journal of Eating Disorders, 16,* 227–238.

Kinchla, R. A., & Wolfe, J. M. (1979). The order of visual processing: "Top-down," "bottom-up," or "middle-out." *Perception and Psychophysics, 25,* 225–231.

Kinsbourne, M. (1982). Hemispheric specialization and the growth of human understanding. *American Psychologist, 37,* 411–420.

Kinsey, A., Pomeroy, W. B., Martin, C., & Gebhard, P. (1953). *Sexual behavior in the human female.* Philadelphia: Saunders.

Kintsch, W. (1974) *The representation of meaning in memory.* Hillsdale, NJ: Erlbaum.

Kintsch, W. (1977). On comprehending stories. In M. A. Just & P. A. Carpenter (Eds.), *Cognitive processes in comprehension.* Hillsdale, NJ: Erlbaum.

Kintsch, W. (1988). The use of knowledge in discourse processing: A construction-integration model. *Psychological Review, 95,* 163–182.

Kipnis, D. (1987). Psychology and behavioral technology. *American Psychologist, 42,* 30–36.

Kirsch, I., & Lynn, S. J. (1995). The altered state of hypnosis. *American Psychologist,* 50, 846–858.

Kirsch, I., Montgomery, G., & Sapirstein, G. (1995). Hypnosis as an adjunct to cognitive behavioral psychotherapy: A meta-analysis. *Journal of Consulting and Clinical Psychology, 63,* 214–220.

Kirsch-Rosenkrantz, J., & Geer, J. H. (1991). Gender differences in memory for a sexual story. *Archives of Sexual Behavior, 20,* 295–305.

Kittel, F., Kornitzer, M., de Backer, G., & Dramaix, M. (1982). Metrological study of psychological questionnaires with reference to social variables: The Belgian Heart Disease Prevention Project (BHDPP). *Journal of Behavioral Medicine, 5,* 9–35.

Klatzky, R. L. (1980). *Human memory: Structures and processes* (2nd ed.). San Francisco: Freeman.

Klein, M. *The psycho-analysis of children* (2nd ed.). London: Hogarth.

Klein, S. B. (1991). *Learning: Principles and applications.* New York: McGraw-Hill.

Kleinman, A., & Good, B. (1985). *Culture and depression: Studies in the anthropology and cross-cultural psychiatry of affect and disorder.* Berkeley, CA: University of California Press.

Kleitman, N. (1960). Patterns of dreaming. *Scientific American, 203,* 82–88.

Kleitman, N. (1982). Basic rest-activity cycle—22 years later. *Sleep, 4,* 311–317.

Klentz, B., Beaman, A. L., Mapelli, S. D., & Ullrich, J. R. (1987). Perceived physical attractiveness of supporters and nonsupporters of the women's movement: An attitude-similarity-mediated error (AS-ME). *Personality and Social Psychology Bulletin, 13,* 513–523.

Kliegl, R., Smith, F., & Bates, P. (1989). Testing-the-limits and the study of adult age differences in cognitive plasticity of a mnemonic skill. *Developmental Psychology, 25,* 247–256.

Kline, D. W. (1992). Vision, aging, and driving: The problems of older drivers. *Journal of Gerontology: Psychological Sciences, 47,* 27–34.

Knecht, S., Henningsen, H., Elbert, T., Flor, H., Höhlong, C., Pantev, C., Birbaumer, N., & Taub, E. (1995). Cortical reorganization in human amputees and mislocalization of painful stimuli to the phantom limb. *Neuroscience Letters, 201,* 262–264.

Kobasa, S. C. (1979). Stressful life events and health: An inquiry into hardiness. *Journal of Personality and Social Psychology, 37,* 1–11.

Kobasa, S. C. (1982). The hardy personality: Toward a social psychology of stress and health. In G. S. Sanders & J. Suls (Eds.), *Social psychology of health and illness* (pp. 3–32). Hillsdale, NJ: Erlbaum.

Kobasa, S. C., Maddi, S. R., & Courington, S. (1981). Personality and constitution as mediators in the stress-illness relationship. *Journal of Health and Social Behavior, 22,* 368–378.

Kobasa, S. C., Maddi, S. R., & Kahn, S. (1982). Hardiness and health: A prospective study. *Journal of Personality and Social Psychology, 42,* 168–177.

Koblinsky, S. G., & Cruse, D. F. (1981). The role of frameworks in children's retention of sex related story content. *Journal of Experimental Social Psychology, 31,* 321–331.

Koelega, H. S. (1992). Extraversion and vigilance performance: Thirty years of inconsistencies. *Psychological Bulletin, 112,* 239–258.

Koffka, K. (1935/1995). *Principles of gestalt psychology.* New York: Harcourt, Brace.

Kohlberg, L. (1963). Moral development and identification. In H. W. Stevenson (Ed.), *Child psychology: 62nd yearbook of the National Society for the Study of Education*. Chicago: University of Chicago Press.

Kohlberg, L. (1964). The development of moral character and moral ideology. In M. L. Hoffman & L. W. Hoffman, *Review of Child Development Research* (Vol. 1). New York: Russell Sage.

Kohlberg, L. (1966). A cognitive-developmental analysis of children's sex-role concepts and attitudes. In E. E.. Maccoby (Ed.), *The development of sex differences* (pp. 82–171). Stanford, CA: Stanford University Press.

Kohlberg, L. (1976). Moral stages and moralization: The cognitive-developmental approach. In T. Likona (Ed.), *Moral development and behavior*. New York: Holt, Rinehart, & Winston.

Kohlberg, L. (1981). *Essays on moral development. Vol 1: The philosophy of moral development*. San Franscisco: Harper & Row.

Kohlberg, L. (1984). *Essays on moral development. Vol. 2: The psychology of moral development*. San Francisco: Harper & Row.

Kohler, W. (1925). *The mentality of apes*. London: Routledge & Kegan Paul.

Kohn, P. M. (1987). Issues in the measurement of arousability. In J. Strelau & H. J. Eysenck (Eds.), *Personality dimensions and arousal* (pp. 233–250). New York: Plenum.

Kohut, H. (1971). *The analysis of the self: A systematic approach to the psychoanalytic treatment of narcissistic personality disorders* (Monograph Series of the Psychoanalytic Study of the Child, No. 41). New York: International Universities Press.

Kohut, H. (1977). *The restoration of the self*. New York: International Universities Press.

Kojima, S., & Goldman-Rakic, P. S. (1984). Fundamental analysis of spatially discriminative neurons in prefrontal cortex of rhesus monkey. *Brain Research, 291*, 229–240.

Kolers, P. A. (1968). Bilingualism and information processing. *Scientific American, 218*, 78–86.

Kolers, P. A. (1985). Skill in reading and memory. *Canadian Journal of Psychology, 39*, 232–239.

Koss, M. P., Goodman, L. A., Browne, A., Fitzgerald, L., Keita, G. P., & Russo, N. F. (1994). *No safe haven: Male violence against women at home, at work, and in the community*. Washington, DC: American Psychological Association.

Koss, M. P., Koss, P. G., & Woodruff, W. J. (1991). Deleterious effects of criminal victimization on women's health and medical utilization. *Archives of Internal Medicine, 151*, 342–357.

Kosslyn, S. M., Ball, T. M., & Reisser, B. J. (1978). Visual images preserve metric spatial information: Evidence from studies of image scanning. *Journal of Experimental Psychology: Human Perception and Performance, 4*, 1–20.

Kottak, C. P. (1991). *Anthropology: The exploration of human diversity*. New York: McGraw-Hill.

Kozol, J. (1995). *Amazing grace*. New York: Harper/Perennial.

Kraft, C. (1978). A psychophysical contribution to air safety: Simulator studies of visual illusions in night visual approaches. In H. Pick, H. Leibowitz, J. Singer, & A. Steinschneider (Eds.), *Psychology from research to practice*. New York: Plenum.

Krantz, D. S., & Durel, L. A. (1983). Psychobiological substrates of the Type A behavior pattern. *Health Psychology, 2*, 393–411.

Krantz, D. S., Grunberg, N. E., & Baum, A. (1985). Health psychology. *Annual Review of Psychology, 36*, 349–383.

Krech, D., & Rosenzweig, M. R. (1966). Environmental impoverishment, social isolation, and changes in brain chemistry and anatomy. *Physiology and Behavior, 1*, 99–104.

Kris, E. (1954). Editor's introduction. In M. Bonaparte, E. Kris, & A. Freud (Eds.), *The origins of psychoanalysis: Letters of Sigmund Freud to Wilhelm Fliess, drafts and notes, 1897–1902*. New York: Basic Books.

Kroeber, A. L. (1923). *Anthropology*. New York: Harcourt, Brace.

Krosnick, J. A., Betz, A. L., Jussim, L. J., & Lynn, A. (1992). Subliminal conditioning of attitudes. *Personality and Social Psychology Bulletin, 18*, 152–162.

Krupa, D. J., Thompson, J. K., & Thompson, R. F. (1993). Localization of a memory trace in the mammalian brain. *Science, 260*, 989–991.

Kruper, J. C., & Uzgiris, I. (1987). Fathers' and mothers' speech to young infants. *Journal of Psycholinguistic Research, 16*, 597–614.

Kübler-Ross, E. (1969). *On death and dying*. New York: Macmillan.

Kübler-Ross, E. (1975). *Death: The final stage of growth*. Englewood Cliffs, NJ: Prentice-Hall.

Kumanyika, S. K., Wilson, J. F., & Guilford-Davenport, M. (1993). Weight related attitudes and behaviors of black women. *Journal of the American Dietetic Association, 93*, 416–422.

Kunda, Z., & Oleson, K. C. (1995). Maintaining stereotypes in the face of disconfirmation: Constructing grounds for subtyping deviants. *Journal of Personality and Social Psychology, 68*, 565–579.

Kupfermann, I. (1991). Localization of higher cognitive and affective functions: The association cortices. In E. R. Kandel, J. H. Schwartz, & T. M. Jessell (Eds.), *Principles of neural science* (3rd ed.). New York: Elsevier.

Kurdek, L. A. (1991). The dissolution of gay and lesbian relationships. *Journal of Social and Personal Relationships, 8*, 265–278.

Kushner, H. L. (1985). Women and suicide in historical perspective. *Signs, 10*(3), 537–552.

Labbe, R., Firl, A., Jr., Mufson, E. J., & Stein, D. G. (1983). Fetal brain transplants: Reduction of cognitive deficits in rats with frontal cortex lesions. *Science, 22*, 470–472.

Labov, W. (1970). The logic of nonstandard English. In J. E. Alatis (Ed.), *20th annual round table meeting on linguistics and language studies*. Washington, DC: Georgetown University Press.

LaFrance, M. (1992). Gender and interruptions. Individual infraction or violation of the social order. *Psychology of Women Quarterly, 16*, 497–512.

LaFrance, M., & Mayo, C. (1976). Racial differences in gaze behavior during conversation: Two systematic observational studies. *Journal of Personality and Social Psychology, 33*, 547–552.

Laing, R. D. (1969). *The divided self*. New York: Pantheon.

Lamb, M. E. (1979). Parental influences and the father's role: A personal perspective. *American Psychologist, 34*, 938–944.

Lamb, M. E., Ketterlinus, R. D., & Fracasso, M. P. (1992). Parent-child relationships. In M. H. Bornstein & M. E. Lamb (Eds.), *Developmental psychology: An advanced textbook* (3rd ed.). Hillsdale, NJ: Erlbaum.

Lamb, M. E., & Oppenheim, D. (1989). Fatherhood and father-child relationships. In S. H. Cath, A. Gurwitt, & L. Gunsberg (Eds.), *Fathers and their families*. Hillsdale, NJ: Analytic Press.

Lambert, M. J., & Bergin, A. E. (1994). The effectiveness of psychotherapy. In A. E. Bergin & S. L. Garfield (Eds.), *Handbook of psychotherapy and behavior change* (4th ed.; pp. 143–189). New York: Wiley.

Lambo, T. A. (1978). Psychotherapy in Africa. *Human Nature, 1*(3), 32–40.

Lammers, W. J., Badia, P., Hughes, R., & Harsh, J. (1991). Temperature, time-of-night of testing, and responsiveness to stimuli presented while sleeping. *Psychophysiology, 28*, 463–467.

Landrine, H., & Klonoff, E. A. (1997). Cultural diversity and health psychology. In A. Baum, T. Revenson, & J. Singer (Eds.), *Handbook of health psychology*, Hillsdale, NJ: Erlbaum.

Landrine, H., Klonoff, L., & Brown-Collins, A. (1992). Cultural diversity and methodology in feminist psychology: Critique, proposal, empirical example. *Psychology of Women Quarterly, 16*, 145–163.

Landrine, H., Klonoff, E. A., & Gibbs, J. (1995). Physical and psychiatric correlates of gender discrimination. *Psychology of Women Quarterly, 19*, 473–492.

Landrine, H., Klonoff, E. A., Gibbs, J., Manning, V., & Lund, M. (1995). Physical and psychiatric correlates of gender discrimination: An application of the Schedule of Sexist Events. *Psychology of Women Quarterly, 19*, 473–492.

Landy, D., & Sigall, H. (1974). Beauty is talent: Task evaluation as a function of the performer's physical attractiveness. *Journal of Personality and Social Psychology, 29*, 299–304.

Langer, E. J., Janis, I. L., & Wolfer, J. A. (1975). Reduction of psychological stress in surgical patients. *Journal of Experimental Social Psychology, 11*, 155–165.

Larson, D. E. (Ed.). *Mayo Clinic family healthbook*. New York: Morrow.

Latané, B., & Darley, J. M. (1968). Group inhibition of bystander intervention in emergencies. *Journal of Personality and Social Psychology, 10*, 215–221.

Latané, B., & Nida, S. (1981). Ten years of research on group size and helping. *Psychological Bulletin, 89*, 308–324.

Latané, B., Williams, K., & Harkins, S. (1979). Many hands make light the work: The causes and consequences of social loafing. *Journal of Personality and Social Psychology, 37*, 822–832.

Latter, B. (1980). Genetic differences within and between populations of the major human subgroups. *The American Naturalist, 116*, 220–237.

Laughlin, P. (1980). Social combination processes of cooperative problem-solving groups on verbal intellective tasks. In M. Fishbein (Ed.), *Progress in social psychology*. Hillsdale, NJ: Erlbaum.

Laumann, E. O., Gagnon, J. H., Michael, R. T., & Michaels, S. (1994). *The social organization of sexuality: Sexual practices in the United States*. Chicago: University of Chicago Press.

Laurence, J.-R., & Perry, C. (1983). Hypnotically created memory among highly hypnotizable subjects. *Science, 222*, 523–524.

Laurendeau, M., & Pinard, A. (1962). *Causal thinking in the child*. New York: International Universities Press.

Lavie, P. (1996). *The enchanted world of sleep* (Antony Berris, Trans.). New Haven, CT: Yale University Press.

Lavie, P., Pratt, H., Scharf, B., Peled, R., & Brown, I. (1984). Localized pontine lesion: Nearly total absence of REM sleep. *Neurology, 34*, 1118–1120.

Lazarus, A. A. (1971). *Behavior therapy and beyond*. New York: McGraw-Hill.

Lazarus, R. S. (1991a). Cognition and motivation in emotion. *American Psychologist, 46*, 352–367.

Lazarus, R. S. (1991b). Progress on a cognitive-motivational-relational theory of emotion. *American Psychologist, 46*, 819–834.

Lazarus, R. S., & Cohen, J. B. (1977). Environmental stress. In I. Attman & J. F. Wohlwill (Eds.), *Human behavior and the environment: Current theory and research* (Vol. 1). New York: Van Nostrand, Reinhold.

Lazarus, R. S., Delongis, A., Folkman, S., & Gruen, R. J. (1985). Stress and adaptational outcomes: The problem of confounded measures. *American Psychologist, 40*, 770–779.

Lazarus, R. S., & Folkman, S. (l984). *Stress, appraisal, and coping*. New York: Springer.

Lazarus, R. S., & Launier, R. (1978). Stress-related transactions between person and environment. In L. A. Pervin & M. Lewis (Eds.), *Internal and external determinants of behavior* (pp. 287–327). New York: Plenum.

Lazarus, R. S., Opton, E. M., Nomikos, M. S., & Rankin, N. O. (1965). The principle of short-circuiting of threat: Further evidence. *Journal of Personality, 33*, 622–635.

Leadbeater, B. (1991). Relativistic thinking in adolescence. In R. M. Lerner, A. C. Petersen, & J. Brooks-Gunn (Eds.), *Encyclopedia of adolescence*. New York: Garland.

Leary, M. R., Kowalski R. M., & Bergen, D. J. (1988). Interpersonal information acquisition and confidence in first encounters. *Personality and Social Psychology Bulletin, 14*, 68–77.

LeBon, G. (1879). Recherches anatomiques et mathematiques sur les lois des variations du volume du cerveau et sur leurs relations avec l'intelligence. *Revue d'Anthropologie, 2*, 27–104.

LeBon, G. (1895/1960). *The crowd: A study of the popular mind*. New York: Viking.

Leccese, A. P. (1991). *Drugs and society: Behavioral medicine and abusable drugs*. Englewood Cliffs, NJ: Prentice-Hall.

LeDoux, J. E. (1989). Cognitive-emotional interactions in the brain. *Cognition and Emotion, 3*, 267–290.

Lefcourt, H. M. (1982). *Locus of control: Current trends in theory and research*. Hillsdale, NJ: Erlbaum.

Lehman, H. C. (1953). *Age and achievement*. Princeton, NJ: Princeton University Press.

Leibowitz, H. W. (1971). Sensory, learned, and cognitive mechanisms of size perception. *Annals of the New York Academy of Sciences, 188*, 47–62.

Leibowitz, H. W. (1983). A behavioral and perceptual analysis of grade crossing accidents. In *Operation lifesaver national symposium 1982*. Chicago: National Safety Council.

Leitenberg, H. (1976). *Handbook of behavior modification and behavior therapy*. Englewood Cliffs, NJ: Prentice-Hall.

Lemonick, M. D. (1992, February 24). Genetic tests under fire: A sports panel says a glance in the pants is enough to determine the sex of an athlete. *Time Magazine*, p. 65.

Lenneberg, E. H. (1967). *Biological foundations of language*. New York: Wiley.

Leo, J. (1992-Oct. 25). The twenty-seven faces of Charles. *Time Magazine* (Vol. 134), p. 70.

Lerner, G. (1986). *The creation of patriarchy*. New York: Oxford University Press.

LeVay, S. (1991). A difference in hypothalamic structure between heterosexual and homosexual men. *Science, 253*, 1034–1037.

LeVay, S. (1993). *The sexual brain*. Cambridge, MA: MIT Press.

Levenson, R.W. (1992). Autonomic nervous system differences among emotions. *Psychological Science, 3*, 23–27.

Leventhal, H. (1970). Findings and theory in the study of fear communications. In L. Berkowitz (Ed.), *Advances in experimental social psychology* (Vol. 5, pp. 120–186). New York: Academic Press.

Levin, B. E. (1986). Neurological regulation of body weight. *Critical Reviews in Neurobiology, 2*, 1–60.

Levine, H. G. (1983). The good creature of God and the demon rum: Colonial American and 19th century ideas about alcohol, crime, and accidents. In R. Room & G. Collins (Eds.), *Alcohol and disinhibition: Nature and meaning of the link*. (NIAAA Research Monograph No. 12, pp. 111–161).

Levine, H. S., Eisenberg, H. M., & Benton, A. L. (1991). *Frontal lobe function and dysfunction*. New York: Oxford University Press.

Levine, J. M., & McBurney, D. H. (1986). The role of olfaction in social perception and behavior. In C. P. Herman, M. P. Zanna, & E. T. Higgins (Eds.), *Physical appearance, stigma, and social behavior: The Ontario Symposium*. Hillsdale, NJ: Erlbaum.

Levine, M. (1975). *A cognitive theory of learning*. Hillsdale, NJ: Erlbaum.

Levinson, D. (1986). A conception of adult development. *American Psychologist, 41*, 3–13.

Levy, S. M., K., Lee, J. K. , Bagley, C., & Lippman, M. (1988). Survival hazards analysis in first recurrent breast cancer patients: Seven year follow-up. *Psychosomatic Medicine, 50*, 520–528.

Lewandowsky, S., & Murdock, B. B., Jr. (1989). Memory for serial order. *Psychological Review, 96*, 25–57.

Lewis, M., & Brooks-Gunn, J. (1979). *Social cognition and the acquisition of self*. New York: Plenum.

Lewis, M., Owen, M. T., & Cox, M. J. (1988). The transition to parenthood: III. Incorporation of the child into the family. *Family Process, 27*, 411–421.

Lewin, M., & Wild, C. (1991). The impact of the feminist critique on tests, assessment, and methodology. *Psychology of Women Quarterly, 15*, 581–596.

Lieber, C. F. (1997). Gender differences in alcohol metabolism and susceptibility. In S. C. Wilsnack & R. W. Wilsnack (Eds.), *Gender and alcohol: Individual and social perspectives* (pp. 77–89). New Brunswick, NJ: Rutgers Center of Alcohol Studies.

Liebert, R. M., & Baron, R. (1972). Some immediate effects of televised violence on children's behavior. *Developmental Psychology, 6*, 469–475.

Liebert, R. M., & Spiegler, M. D. (1974). *Personality: Strategies for the study of man.* (Rev. ed.) Homewood, IL: Dorsey Press.

Liebert, R. M., & Spiegler, M. D. (1982). *Personality* (4th ed.). Homewood, IL: Dorsey Press.

Lillard, A. S. (1993). Pretend play skills and the child's theory of mind. *Child Development, 64*, 348–371.

Lin, C. (1989). The high risk infant: The very low birthweight fetus. In M. I. Evans, J. C. Fletcher, A. O. Dixler, & J. D. Shulman (Eds.), *Fetal diagnosis and therapy: Science, ethics, and the law.* Philadelphia: Lippincott.

Lin, E. H., & Peterson, C. (1990). Pessimistic explanatory style and response to illness. *Behaviour Research and Therapy, 28*, 243–48.

Lindquist, O. (1979). Menopausal age in relation to smoking. *Acta Medica Scandinavica, 205*, 73–77.

Lindsay, D. S. (1993). Eyewitness suggestibility. *Current Directions in Psychological Science, 2*, 86–89.

Linton, R. (1937, April). One hundred percent American. *The American Mercury, 40* (60), 427–429.

Lips, H. M. (1985). Gender and the sense of power: Where are we and where are we going? *International Journal of Women's Studies, 8*, 483–489.

Lips, H. M. (1993). *Sex and gender: An introduction* (2nd ed.). Mountain View, CA: Mayfield.

Lipsey, M. W., & Wilson, D. B. (1993). The efficacy of psychological, educational, and behavioral treatment. *American Psychologist, 48*, 1181–1209.

Lipsitt, L. (1979a). Critical conditions in infancy: A psychological perspective. *American Psychologist, 34*, 973–980.

Lipsitt, L. (1979b). Infants at risk: Perinatal and neonatal factors. *International Journal of Behavior Development, 2*, 23–42.

Lipsitt, L., & Werner, J. (1981). The infancy of human learning processes. In E. S. Gollin (Ed.), *Developmental plasticity.* New York: Academic Press.

Loehlin, J. C., Lindzey, G., & Spuhier, J. N. (1975). *Race differences in intelligence.* San Francisco: Freeman.

Loewenstein, R. J. (1991). Psychogenic amnesia and psychogenic fugue: A comprehensive review. In A. Tasman & S. M. Goldfinger (Eds.), *American Psychiatric Press Review of Psychiatry* (Vol. 10). Washington, DC: American Psychiatric Association.

Loftus, E. F. (1979). *Eyewitness testimony.* Cambridge, MA: Harvard University Press.

Loftus, E. F. (1980). *Memory.* Reading, MA: Addison-Wesley.

Loftus, E. F. (1992). When a lie becomes memory's truth: Memory distortion after exposure to misinformation. *Current Directions in Psychological Science, 1*, 121–123.

Loftus, E. F. (1993a). Desperately seeking memories of the first few years of childhood: The reality of early memories. *Journal of Experimental Psychology: General, 122*, 274–277.

Loftus, E. F. (1993b). The reality of repressed memories. *American Psychologist, 48*, 518–537.

Loftus, E. F., & Loftus, G. R. (1980). On the permanence of stored information in the human brain. *American Psychologist, 35*, 409–420.

Loftus, E. F., & Palmer, J. C. (1974). Reconstruction of automobile destruction. *Journal of Verbal Learning and Verbal Behavior, 13*, 585–589.

Loftus , E. F., & Pickrell, J. E. (1995). The formation of false memories. *Psychiatric Annals, 25*, 720–725.

Lombardo, R., & Carreno, L. (1987). Relationship of Type A behavior pattern in smokers to carbon monoxide exposure and smoking topography. *Health Psychology, 6*, 445–452.

Lopes, L. L. (1994). Psychology and economics: Perspectives on risk, cooperation and the marketplace. *Annual Review of Psychology, 45*, 197–227.

López, S. R., Grover, K. P., Holland, D., Johnson, M. J., Kain, C. D., Kanel, K., Millins, C. A., & Rhyne, M. C. (1989). Development of culturally sensitive psychotherapists. *Professional Psychology: Research and Practice, 20*, 369–376.

Lorenz, K. (1965). *Evolution and modification of behavior.* Chicago: University of Chicago Press.

Lorenz, K. Z. (1952). *King Solomon's ring.* New York: Crowell.

Lorenz, K. Z. (1966). *On aggression.* London: Methuen.

Lovaas, O. I. (1977). *The autistic child: Language development through behavior modification.* New York: Halsted Press.

Lovaas, O. I., Koegel, R. L., & Schreibman, L. (1979). Stimulus overselectivity in autism: A review of research. *Psychological Bulletin, 86*, 1236–1254.

Lovibond, P. F., Siddle, D. A. T., & Bond, N. W. (1993). Resistance to extinction of fear-relevant stimuli: Preparedness or selective sensitization? *Journal of Experimental Psychology: General, 122*, 449–461.

Luborsky, L., Barber, J. P., & Butler, L. (1993). Introduction to special section: A briefing on curative factors in dynamic psychotherapy. *Journal of Consulting and Clinical Psychology, 61*, 539–541.

Luchins, A. S. (1942). Mechanization in problem-solving: The effect of Einstellung. *Psychological Monographs, 54* (Whole No. 248).

Luchins, A. S., & Luchins, E. H. (1959). *Rigidity in behavior.* Eugene, OR: University of Oregon Press.

Ludwig, A. M. (1966). Altered states of consciousness. *Archives of General Psychiatry, 15*, 225–234.

Luria, A. R. (1968). *The mind of a mnemonist* (L. Solotaroff, Trans.). New York: Basic Books.

Luria, A. R. (1976). *Cognitive development: Its cultural and social foundations.* Cambridge, MA: Harvard University Press.

Lydiard, R. B., & Gelenberg, A. J. (1982). Hazards and adverse effects of lithium. *Annual Review of Medicine, 33*, 327–344.

Lyness, S. A. (1993). Predictors of differences between Type A and B individuals in heart rate and blood pressure reactivity. *Psychological Bulletin, 114*, 266–295.

Lynn, S. J., Rhue, J. W., & Weekes, J. R. (1990). Hypnotic involuntariness: A social cognitive analysis. *Psychological Review, 97*, 169–184.

Maas, A., & Volpato, C. (1989). Gender differences in self-serving attributions about sexual experiences. *Journal of Applied Social Psychology, 19*, 571–572.

MacAndrew, C., & Edgerton, R. B. (1969). *Drunken comportment: A social explanation.* Chicago: Aldine.

Maccoby, E. (1990). Gender and relationships: A developmental account. *American Psychologist, 45*, 513–520.

Macfarlane, A. (1975). Olfaction in the development of social preferences in the human neonate. In *Parent-infant interaction* (CIBA Foundation Symposium, 33). Amsterdam: Elsevier.

Macintosh, N. J. (1983). *Conditioning and associative learning.* Oxford Eng.: Claredon Press.

Macintosh, N. J., Bygrave, D. J., & Picton, B. M. B. (1977). Locus of the effect of a surprising reinforcer in the attenuation of blocking. *Quarterly Journal of Experimental Psychology, 29*, 327–336.

Macionis, J. J. (1989). *Sociology* (2nd ed.) Englewood Clifts, NJ: Prentice-Hall.

Mackie, D. M., Worth, L. I., & Asuncion, A. G. (1990). Processing of persuasive in-group messages. *Journal of Personality and Social Psychology, 58*, 812–822.

MacKinnon, D. W., & Hall, W. B. (1972). Intelligence and creativity. *Proceedings, XVIIth International Congress of Applied Psychology* (Vol. 2, pp.1883–1888). Brussels: Editest.

MacLachlan, J., & Siegel, M. H. (1980). Reducing the costs of TV commercials by use of time compressions. *Journal of Marketing Research, 17*, 52–57.

Madden, D. J., & Blumenthal, J. A. (1989). Slowing of memory-search performance in men with mild hypertension. *Health Psychology, 8*, 131–142.

Maddux, J. E., Roberts, M. C., Sledden, E. A., & Wright, L. (1986). Developmental issues in child health psychology. *American Psychologist, 41*, 25–34.

Mahler, M. S. (1968). *On human symbiosis and the vicissitudes of individuation.* New York: International Universities Press.

Mahoney, M. J. (1990). *Human change processes.* New York: Basic Books.

Maier, N. R. F. (1931). Reasoning in humans, II. The solution of a problem and its appearance in consciousness. *Journal of Comparative Psychology, 12*, 181–194.

Maier, N. R. F. (1949). *Frustration: The study of behavior without a goal.* New York: McGraw-Hill.

Maier, S. F., & Seligman, M. E. P. (1976). Learned helplessness: Theory and evidence. *Journal of Experimental Psychology, 105* (1), 3–46.

Maier, S. F., Seligman, M.E.P., & Solomon, R. L. (1969). Pavlovian fear conditioning and learned helplessness: Effects on escape and avoidance behavior of (a) the CS-US contingency and (b) the independence of the US and voluntary responding. In B. A. Campbell & R. M. Church (Eds.), *Punishment and aversive behavior* (pp. 299–342). New York: Appleton-Century-Crofts.

Maier, S. F., Watkins, L. R., Fleshner, M. (1994). Psychoneuroimmunology. *American Psychologist, 49*, 1004–1017.

Main, M., & Weston, D. R. (1981). The quality of the toddler's relationship to mother and father: Related to conflict and the readiness to establish new relationships. *Child Development, 52*, 932–940.

Major, B. (in press). From social inequality to personal entitlement: The role of social comparisons, legitimacy appraisals, and group membership. In M. Zanna (Ed.), *Advances in experimental social psychology.* New York: Academic Press.

Manderscheid, R. W., & Sonnenschein, M. A. (1990). *Mental health, United States, 1990.* Washington, DC: U. S. Government Printing Office.

Mandler, G. (1992). Hypermnesia, incubation, and mind popping: On remembering without really trying. *Attention and performance: XV* (pp. 421–452). Cambridge, MA: MIT Press.

Mandler, J. M. (1990). Recall of events by preverbal children. *Annals of the New York Academy of Sciences, 608*, 485–516.

Mann, J., Arango, V., & Underwood, M. (1990). Serotonin and suicidal behavior. *Annals of the New York Academy of Sciences, 600*, 476–485.

Manuzza, S., Klein, R., Bonagura, N., Malloy, P., et al. (1991). Hyperactive boys almost grown up: V. Replication of psychiatric status. *Archives of General Psychiatry, 48*, 77–83.

Marder, S. R., Mebane, A., Chien, C. P., Winslade, W. J., Swann, E., & Van Putten, T. (1983). A comparison of patients who refuse and consent to neuroleptic treatment. *American Journal of Psychiatry, 140*, 470–472.

Marks, G., Miller, N., & Maruyama, G. (1981). Effects of targets' physical attractiveness on assumption of similarity. *Journal of Personality and Social Psychology, 41*, 198–206.

Markus, H. (1992, June). Cultural psychology: Implications for self, emotion, and motivation. Invited presentation, Annual meeting, American Psychological Society, San Diego, California.

Markus, H. R., & Kitayama, S. (1991). Culture and the self: Implications for cognition, emotion, and motivation. *Psychological Review, 98*, 224–253.

Marsella, A. J. (1979). Cross-cultural studies of mental disorders. In A. J. Marsella, R. G. Tharp, & T. J. Ciborowski (Eds.), *Perspectives on cross-cultural psychology* (pp. 233–262). New York: Academic Press.

Marsella, A. J., Escudero, M., & Brennan, J. (1975). Goal-striving discrepancy stress in urban Filipino men: I. Housing. *International Journal of Social Psychiatry, 21*, 282–291.

Marshall, G. D., & Zimbardo, P. G. (1979). Affective consequences of inadequately explained physiological arousal. *Journal of Personality and Social Psychology, 37*, 970–988.

Marshall, H. E. (1937). *Dorothea Dix, a forgotten samaritan.* Chapel Hill, NC: University of North Carolina Press.

Martin, C. L. (1993). New directions for investigating children's gender knowledge. *Developmental Review, 13*, 184–204.

Martin, C. L., & Halverson, C. (1981). A schematic processing model of sex typing and stereotyping in children. *Child Development, 49*, 1119–1134.

Martin, E. (1972) Stimulus encoding in learning and transfer. In A. W. Melton & E. Martin (Eds.), *Coding processes in human memory.* Washington, DC: Winston.

Martin, E. (1987). *The woman in the body.* New York: Simon and Schuster.

Martin, J. (1997, August). Women warriors: Secret weapon of the Apaches. *New Mexico Magazine*, pp. 90–96.

Martin, R. J., White, B. D., & Hulsey, M. G. (1991). The regulation of body weight. *American Scientist, 79*, 528–541.

Masand, P., Popli, A. P., & Welburg, J. B. (1995). Sleepwalking. *American Family Physician, 51*(3), 649–53.

Maser, J. D., Kaelber, C., & Weise, R. E. (1991). International use and attitudes toward the DSM-II and DSM-III-R: Growing consensus in psychiatric classification. *Journal of Abnormal Psychology, 100*, 271–279.

Maslach, C. (1979). Negative emotional biasing of unexplained arousal. *Journal of Personality and Social Psychology, 37*, 953–969.

Maslow, A. H. (1970). *Motivation and personality* (2nd ed.). New York: Harper & Row.

Maslow, A. H. (1971). *The farther reaches of human nature.* New York: Viking.

Mason, A., & Blankenship, V. (1987). Power and affiliation motivation, stress, and abuse in intimate relationships. *Journal of Personality and Social Psychology, 52*, 203–210.

Masters, R., & Houston, J. (1966). *The varieties of psychedelic experience.* New York: Holt, Rinehart and Winston.

Masters, W. H., & Johnson, V. E. (1966). *Human sexual response.* Boston: Little, Brown.

Matarazzo, J. D. (1982). Behavioral health's challenge to academic, scientific, and professional psychology. *American Psychologist, 37*, 1–14.

Matlin, M. M. (1983). *Perception.* Boston: Allyn & Bacon.

Matlin, M. (1994). *Cognition* (3rd ed.). Fort Worth, TX: Harcourt Brace.

Matsumoto, D., Kudoh, T., Scherer, K., & Wallbot, H. G. (1988). Emotion antecedents and reactions in the U. S. and Japan. *Journal of Cross-Cultural Psychology, 19*, 267–286.

Mattes, R. D., Arnold, C., & Boraas, M. (1987a). Learned food aversions among cancer chemotherapy patients. *Cancer, 60*, 2576–2580.

Mattes, R. D., Arnold, C., & Boraas, M. (1987b). Management of learned food aversions in cancer patients receiving chemotherapy. *Cancer Treatment Reports, 71*, 1071–1078.

Matthews, K. A., Shumaker, S. A., Bowen, D. J., Langer, R. D., Hunt, J. R., Kaplan, R. M., Klesges, R. C., & Ritenbaugh, C. (1997). Women's health initiative. *American Psychologist, 52*, 101–116.

McAdams, D. P. (1997). A conceptual history of personality psychology. In R. Hogan, J. Johnson, & S. Briggs (Eds.), *Handbook of personality psychology* (pp. 3–39). San Diego, CA: Academic Press.

McAndrew, F. T. (1993). *Environmental psychology*. Pacific Grove, CA: Brooks/Cole.

McCann, I. L., & Holmes, D. S. (1984). Influence of aerobic exercise on depression. *Journal of Personality and Social Psychology, 46,* 1142–1147.

McCarley, R. W. (1989). The biology of dreaming sleep. In M. H. Kryger, T. Roth, & W. C. Dement (Eds.), *Principles and practice of sleep medicine*. Philadelphia: Saunders.

McClelland, D. C. (1973). Testing for competence rather than for "intelligence." *American Psychologist, 28,* 1–14.

McClelland, D. C. (1985a). *Human motivation*. Glenview, IL: Scott, Foresman.

McClelland, D. C. (1985b). How motives, skills, and values determine what people do. *American Psychologist, 40,* 812–825.

McClelland, D. C., Atkinson, J. W., Clark, R. A., & Lowell, F. L. (1953). *The achievement motive*. New York: Appleton-Century-Crofts.

McClelland, D. C., & Burnham, D. H. (1976). Power is the great motivator. *Harvard Business Review*, 54–71.

McClelland, D. C. Clark, R. A., Roby, T. B., & Atkinson, J. W. (1958). The effect of the need for achievement on thematic apperception. In J. W. Atkinson (Ed.), *Motives in fantasy, action, and society* (pp. 64–82). Princeton, NJ: Van Nostrand.

McClelland, D. C., & Friedman, G. A. (1952). A cross-cultural study of the relationship between child-training practices and achievement motivation appearing in folk tales. In G. E. Swanson et al. (Eds.), *Readings in social psychology*. New York: Holt.

McClelland, D. C., & Pilon, D. A. (1983). Sources of adult motives in patterns of parent behavior in early childhood. *Journal of Personality and Social Psychology, 44,* 564–574.

McClelland, D. C., & Winter, D. G. (1969). *Motivating economic achievement*. New York: Free Press.

McClelland, J. L. (1988). Connectionist models and psychological evidence. *Journal of Memory and Language, 27,* 107–123.

McClelland, J. L., & Rumelhart, D. E. (1981). An interactive activation model of context effects in letter perception: Part 1. An account of basic findings. *Psychological Review, 88,* 375–407.

McClintock, M. K. (1971). Menstrual synchrony and suppression. *Nature, 229,* 244–245.

McCrae, R. B., & Costa, P. T., Jr. (1986). Clinical assessment can benefit from recent advances in personality psychology. *American Psychologist, 41,* 1001–1003.

McCrae, R. B., & Costa, P. T., Jr. (1994). The stability of personality: Observations and evaluations. *Current Directions in Psychological Science, 3,* 173–175.

McCrae, R. R., & Costa, Jr., P. T. (1997). Conceptions and correlates of openness to experience. In R. Hogan, J. Johnson, & S. Briggs (Eds.), *Handbook of personality psychology* (pp. 826–847). San Diego, CA: Academic Press.

McCrae, R. R., & John, O. (1992). An introduction to the five-factor model and its applications. *Journal of Personality, 60,* 175–215.

McDaniel, M. A., Einstein, G. O., DeLosh, E. L., May, C. P., & Brady, P. (1995). The bizarreness effect: It's not surprising, it's complex. *Journal of Experimental Psychology: Learning, Memory, and Cognition, 21,* 422–435.

McDougall, W. (1933). *The energies of men*. New York: Scribner's.

McFarland, A. H., Norman, G. R., Streiner, D. L., Roy, R. G. & Scott, D. J. (1980). A longitudinal study of the influence of the psychosocial environment on health status: A preliminary report. *Journal of Health and Social Behavior, 21,* 124–133.

McGaugh, J. L. (1989) Involvement of hormonal neuromodulatory systems in the regulation of memory storage. *Annual Review of Neuroscience, 12,* 255–287.

McGhie, A., & Chapman, J. (1961). Disorders of attention and perception in early schizophrenia. *British Journal of Medical Psychology, 34,* 103–116.

McGrath, E., Strickland, B. R., Keita, G. P., & Russo, N. F. (Eds.). (1990). *Women and depression: Risk factors and treatment issues*. Washington, DC: American Psychological Association.

McGraw, K. L., & Harbison-Briggs, K. (1989). *Knowledge acquisition: Principles and guidelines*. Englewood Cliffs, NJ: Prentice-Hall.

McGue, M. (1993). From proteins to cognitions: The behavioral genetics of alcoholism. In R. Plomin & G. E. McClearn (Eds.), *Nature, nurture and psychology*. Washington, DC: American Psychological Association.

McGue, M., Bouchard, T. J., Jr., Iacono, W. G., & Lykken, D. T. (1993). Behavioral genetics of cognitive ability: A life-span perspective. In R. Plomin & G. E. McClearn (Eds.), *Nature, nurture and psychology*, Washington, DC: American Psychological Association.

McGue, M., Gottesman, I. I., & Rao, D. C. (1985). Resolving genetic models for the transmission of schizophrenia. *Genetic Epidemiology, 2,* 99–110.

McGue, M., Pickens, R. W., and Svikis, D. S. (1992). Sex and age effects on the inheritance of alcohol problems: A twin study. *Journal of Abnormal Psychology, 101,* 3–17.

McGuire, W. J. (1964). Inducing resistance to persuasion: Some contemporary approaches. In L. Berkowitz (Ed.), *Advances in experimental social psychology*. New York: Academic Press.

McGuire, W. J. (1968). Personality and susceptibility to social influence. In E. Borgatta & W. Lambert (Eds.), *Handbook of personality theory and research*. Chicago: Rand-McNally.

McKee, R. D., & Squire, L. R. (1993). On the development of declarative memory. *Journal of Experimental Psychology: Learning, Memory and Cognition, 19,* 397–404.

McKelvie, S. J., Standing, L., St. Jean, D., & Law, J. (1993). Gender differences in recognition memory for faces and cars: Evidence for the interest hypothesis. *Bulletin of the Psychonomic Society, 31,* 447–448.

McKusick, V. A. (1994). *Mendelian inheritance in man: A catalog of human genes and genetic disorders* (11th ed.). Baltimore, MD: Johns Hopkins University Press.

McLaughlin, S., & Margolskee, R. F. (1994.) The sense of taste. *American Scientist, 82,* 539–545.

McLoyd, V. C. (1990). The impact of economic hardship on Black families and children: Psychological distress, parenting, and socioemotional development. *Child Development, 61,* 311–346.

Mednick, S. A., Machon, R. A., Huttunen, M. O., & Bonett, D. (1988). Adult schizophrenia following prenatal exposure to an influenza epidemic. *Archives of General Psychiatry, 45,* 189–192.

Meehl, P. E. (1956). Wanted—A good cookbook. *American Psychologist, 11,* 262–272.

Meichenbaum, D. H. (1977). *Cognitive-behavior modification: An integrative approach*. New York: Plenum.

Meichenbaum, D. H., & Jaremko, M. E. (Eds.). (1983). *Stress reduction and prevention*. New York: Plenum Press.

Meltzer, H. Y., Burnett, S., Bastani, B., & Ramirez, L. F. (1990). Effects of six months of clozapine treatment on the quality of life of chronic schizophrenic patients. *Hospital and Community Psychiatry, 41,* 892–897.

Meltzoff, A. N. (1988). Infant imitation and memory: Nine-month-olds in immediate and deferred tests. *Child Development, 59,* 217–225.

Meltzoff, A. N., & Moore, M. K. (1977). Imitation of facial and manual gestures by human neonates. *Science, 198,* 75–78.

Meltzoff, A. N., & Moore, M. K. (1983). Newborn infants imitate adult facial gestures. *Child Development, 54,* 702–709.

Meltzoff, A. N., & Moore, M. K. (1992). Early imitation within a functional framework: The importance of person identity, movement, and development. *Infant Behavior and Development, 15,* 479–505.

Melzack, R. (1975). The McGill Pain Questionnaire: Major properties and scoring methods. *Pain, 1,* 277–299.

Melzack, R. (1980). Psychological aspects of pain. In J. J. Bonica (Ed.), *Pain.* New York: Raven.

Melzack, R. (1992). Phantom limbs. *Scientific American, 266,* 120–126.

Mentzer, S. J., & Snyder, M. L. (1982). The doctor and the patient: A psychological perspective. In G. S. Sanders & J. Suls (Eds.), *Social psychology of health and illness.* Hillsdale, NJ: Erlbaum.

Mersky, H. (1992). The manufacture of personalities: The production of multiple personality disorder. *British Journal of Psychology, 160,* 327–340.

Merton, R. K. (1948). The self-fulfilling prophecy. *Antioch Review, 8,* 193–210.

Merton, R. K. (1957). *Social theory and social structure.* Glencoe, IL: Free Press.

Merton, R. K. (1965). *On the shoulders of giants.* New York: Free Press.

Merzenich, M. M., Cynader, M. S., Schoppmann, A., & Zook, J. M. (1984). Somatosensory cortical map changes following digit amputation in adult monkeys. *Journal of Comparative Neurology, 224,* 591–605.

Mesquita, B., & Frijda, N. H. (1992). Cultural variations in emotions: A review. *Psychological Bulletin, 112,* 179–204.

Mettler, F. (1949). *Selective partial ablation of the frontal cortex: A correlative study of its effects on human psychotic subjects.* New York: Hoeber-Harper.

Meyerhoff, J. L., Mougey, E. H., & Kant, G. J. (1987). Paraventricular lesions abolish the stress-induced rise in pituitary cyclic adenosine monophosphate and attenuate the increases in plasma levels of proopiomelanocortin-derived peptides and prolactin. *Neuroendocrinology, 46,* 222–230.

Michael, R. T., Gagnon, J. H., Laumann, E. O., & Kolata, G. (1994). *Sex in America: A definitive survey.* Boston: Little, Brown.

Michaels, J. W., Bloommel, J. M., Brocato, R. M., Linkous, R. A., & Rowe, J. S. (1982). Social facilitation and inhibition in a natural setting. *Replications in Social Psychology, 2,* 21–24.

Michelson, L. K., & Marchione, K. (1991). Behavioral, cognitive, and pharmacological treatments of panic disorder with agoraphobia: Critique and synthesis. *Journal of Consulting and Clinical Psychology, 59,* 100–114.

Miike, L. (1996). Health and related services for Native Hawaiian adolescents. In M. Kagawa-Singer, P. A. Katz, D. A. Taylor, J. H. M. Vanderryn (Eds.), *Health issues for minority adolescents* (pp. 168–187). Lincoln, NE: University of Nebraska Press.

Miklowitz, D. J., Simoneau, T. L., Sachs-Ericsson, N., Warner, R., & Suddath, R. (1996). Family risk indicators in the course of bipolar affective disorder. In C. Mundt, M. J. Goldstein, K. Hahlweg, & P. Fiedler (Eds.), *Interpersonal factors in the origin and course of affective disorders* (pp. 204–215). London: Gaskell Books.

Milgram, S. (1965). Some conditions of obedience and disobedience to authority. *Human Relations, 18,* 57–76.

Milgram, S. (1970). The experience of living in cities: A psychological analysis. *Science, 167,* 1461–1468.

Miller, D. T., & Ross, M. (1975). Self-serving biases in the attribution of causality: Fact or fiction? *Psychological Bulletin, 82,* 313–325.

Miller, G. A. (1972). *Psychology: The science of mental life.* New York: Harper & Row.

Miller, G. A., Galanter, E., & Pribram, K. L. (1960). *Plans and the structure of behavior.* New York: Holt, Rinehart and Winston.

Miller, J. E. (1991). Birth intervals and perinatal health: An investigation of three hypotheses. *Family Planning Perspectives, 23* (2), 62–70.

Miller, J. G. (1984). Culture and the development of everyday social explanations. *Journal of Personality and Social Psychology, 46,* 961–978.

Miller, N. E. (1948). Studies of fear as an acquirable drive: I. Fear as motivation and fear reduction as reinforcement in the learning of a new response. *Journal of Experimental Psychology, 38,* 89–101.

Miller, N. E. (1969). Learning of visceral and glandular responses. *Science, 163,* 434–445.

Miller, N. E. (1983). Behavioral medicine: Symbiosis between laboratory and clinic. In M. R. Rosenzweig & L. W. Porter (Eds.), *Annual Review of Psychology.* Palo Alto, CA: Annual Reviews.

Miller, N. E. (1995). Clinical-experimental interactions in the development of neuroscience. *American Psychologist, 50,* 901–911.

Miller, S. H. (1984). The relationship between adolescent childbearing and child maltreatment. *Child Welfare, 63*(6), 553–557.

Miller-Jones, D. (1989). Culture and testing. *American Psychologist, 44,* 360–366.

Milner, B. (1966). Neuropsychological evidence for differing memory processes. Abstract for the symposium on short-term and long-term memory. In *18th International Congress of Psychology,* Moscow.

Milner, B., Corkin, S., & Teuber, H. L. (1968). Further analysis of the hippocampal syndrome: Fourteen-year follow-up study of H.M. *Neuropsychologia, 6,* 215–234.

Mindel, C. H. (1980). Extended families among urban Mexican Americans, Anglos, and blacks. *Hispanic Journal of Behavioral Sciences, 2,* 21–34.

Minors, D. S., & Waterhouse, J. M. (1981). *Circadian rhythms and the human.* Bristol, Eng.: John Wright and Sons, Ltd.

Miron, D., & McClelland, D. C. (1979). The impact of achievement motivation training on small business performance. *California Management Review, 21,* 13–28.

Mischel, W. (1979). On the interface of cognition and personality: Beyond the person-situation debate. *American Psychologist, 34,* 740–754.

Mischel, W. I. (1981). *Introduction to personality* (3rd ed.). New York: Holt, Rinehart and Winston.

Mischel, W. (1984). Convergences and challenges in the search for consistency. *American Psychologist, 39,* 351–364.

Mishkoff, H. (1985). *Understanding artificial intelligence.* Dallas, TX: Texas Instruments.

Mitchell, K. M., Bozarth, J. D., & Krauft, C. C. (1977). A reappraisal of the therapeutic effectiveness of accurate empathy, nonpossessive warmth, and genuineness. In A. S. Gurman & A. M. Razin (Eds.), *Effective psychotherapy: A handbook of research.* New York: Pergamon.

Mitchell, P. R., & Kent, R. D. (1990). Phonetic variation in multisyllable babbling. *Journal of Child Language, 17,* 247–265.

Molotch, H., & Vicari, S. (1988, December). Three ways to build the development process in the United States, Japan, and Italy. *Urban Affairs Quarterly, 24,* 188–214.

Monahan, L., Kuhn, D., & Shaver, P. (1974). Intrapsychic versus cultural explanations for the "fear of success" motive. *Journal of Personality and Social Psychology, 29,* 60–64.

Money, J. (1988). *Gay, straight, and in-between: The sexology of erotic orientation.* New York: Holt, Rinehart and Winston.

Money, J., & Ehrhardt, A. A. (1971). Fetal hormones and the brain: Effect on sexual dimorphism of behavior: A review. *Archives of Sexual Behavior, 32,* 241–262.

Money, J., & Ehrhardt, A. A. (1974). *Man and woman: Boy and girl.* New York: New American Library.

Monte, C. F. (1987). *Beneath the mask: In introduction to theories of personality* (3rd ed.). Fort Worth, TX: Hold, Rinehart and Winston.

Mook, (1987). *Motivation: The organization of action.* New York: Norton.

Moorcroft, W. (1993). *Sleep, dreaming, and sleep disorders: An introduction* (2nd ed.). Lanham, MD: University Press of America.

Moore, M. (1990, August 23). For female soldiers, different rules. *Washington Post*, pp. D1, D2.

Mora, G. (1980). Mind-body concepts in the Middle Ages: Part II. The Moslem influence, the great theological systems and cultural attitudes toward the mentally ill in the late Middle Ages. *Journal of the History of the Behavioral Sciences, 16*, 58–72.

Moray, N. (1959). Attention in dichotic listening: Affective cues and the influence of instructions. *Quarterly Journal of Experimental Psychology, 11*, 56–60.

Moreland, R. L., & Levine, J. M. (1992). Problem identification by groups. In S. Worchel, W. Wild, & J. A. Simpson (Eds.), *Group processes and productivity* (pp. 17–47). Newbury Park, CA: Sage.

Moreland, R. L., & Zajonc, R. B. (1982). Exposure effects in person perception: Familiarity, similarity and attraction. *Journal of Personality and Social Psychology, 18*, 395–415.

Moreno, J. L. (1952). *Who shall survive?* New York: Beacon House.

Moreno, J. L. (1959/1975). *Psychodrama: Vol 2. Foundations of psychodrama.* Beacon: Beacon House.

Morey, L. C. (1997). Personality diagnosis and personality disorders. In R. Hogan, J. Johnson, & S. Briggs (Eds.), *Handbook of personality psychology* (pp. 919–946). San Diego, CA: Academic Press.

Morgan, C. D., & Murray, H. A. (1935). A method for investigating fantasies: The thematic apperception test. *Archives of Neurological Psychiatry, 34*, 289–306.

Morris, D. B. (1991). *The culture of pain.* Berkeley, CA: University of California Press.

Morrison, F. J., Giordani, B., & Nagy, J. (1977). Reading disability: An information processing analysis. *Science, 199*, 77–79.

Mosak, H. H. (1979). Adlerian psychotherapy. In R. J. Corsini (Ed.), *Current psychotherapies.* Itasca, IL: Peacock.

Moscovici, S., Lage, E., & Naffrechoux, M. (1969). Influences of a consistent minority on the responses of a majority in a color perception task. *Sociometry, 32*, 365–380.

Moscovici, S., & Zavalloni, M. (1969). The group as a polarizer of attitudes. *Journal of Personality and Social Psychology, 12*, 124–135.

Moscovitch, M., & Klein, D. (1980). Material-specific perceptual interference for visual words and faces: Implications for models of capacity limitation, attention, and laterality. *Journal of Experimental Psychology: Human Perception and Performance, 6*, 590–604.

Moscovitch, M., & Winocur, G. (1992). The neuropsychology of memory and aging. In F. I. Craik, & T. A. Salthouse (Eds.), *The handbook of aging and cognition* (pp. 315–372). Hillsdale, NJ: Erlbaum.

Mowrer, O. H., & Mowrer, W. M. (1938). Enuresis: A method for its study and treatment. *American Journal of Orthopsychiatry, 8*, 436–459.

Mueller, P., & Major, B. (1989). Self-blame, self-efficacy, and adjustment after abortion. *Journal of Personality and Social Psychology, 57*, 1059–1068.

Munro, D. (1986). Work motivation and values: Problems and possibilities in and out of Africa. *Australian Journal of Psychology, 38*, 285–296.

Munroe, R. H., & Munroe, R. L. (1994). Behavior across cultures: Results from observational studies. In W. J. Lonner & R. Malpass (Eds.), *Psychology and culture* (pp. 107–111). Boston: Allyn & Bacon.

Munsinger, H. (1971). *Fundamentals of child development.* New York: Holt, Rinehart and Winston.

Murdock, G. P. (1965). *Culture and society.* Pittsburgh, PA: University of Pittsburgh Press.

Murphy, S. M., Owen, R. T., & Tyrer, P. J. (1984). Withdrawal symptoms after six weeks' treatment with diazepam. *Lancet, 2*, 1389.

Murray, B. (1995, November). Children can excel when they learn from mistakes. *APA Monitor*, p. 42.

Murray, H. A. (1936). Techniques for a systematic investigation of fantasy. *Journal of Psychology, 3*, 115–143.

Murray, H. A. (1938/1962). *Explorations in personality.* New York: Oxford University Press.

Muuss, R. E. (1988). Carol Gilligan's theory of sex differences in the development of moral reasoning during adolescence. *Adolescence, 23*, 229–241.

Mwamwenda, T.S. (1992). Cognitive development in African children. *Genetic, Social, and General Psychology Monographs, 118*, 7–72.

Myers, D. G. (1992). *The pursuit of happiness: Who is happy—and why.* New York: Morrow.

Myers, D. G. (1993). *Social psychology* (3rd ed.). New York: McGraw-Hill.

Myers, D. G., & Bishop, G. D. (1970). Discussion effects on racial attitudes. *Science, 169*, 778–779.

Nahas, G. G., & Latour, C. (1993). *Cannibis physiopathology, epidemiology, detection.* Ann Arbor, MI: CRC Press.

Nanda, S. (1990). *Neither man nor woman: The Hjiras of India.* Belmont, CA: Wadsworth.

Naranjo, C., & Ornstein, R. E. (1976). *On the psychology of meditation.* New York: Penguin.

Nash, M. (1987). What, if anything, is regressed about hypnotic age regression? A review of the empirical literature. *Psychological Bulletin, 102*, 42–52.

Nasser, M. (1988). Culture and weight consciousness. *Journal of Psychosomatic Research, 32*, 573–577.

Nation, J. R., & Woods, D. J. (1980). Persistence: The role of partial reinforcement in psychotherapy. *Journal of Experimental Psychology: General, 109*, 175–207.

National Center for Health Statistics. (1996). *Health, United States, 1995, Chartbook.* Hyattsville, MD: Public Health Service.

National Institute of Mental Health. (1982). *Television and behavior.* Washington, DC: U.S. Department of Health and Human Services.

National Institute of Mental Health (1990). *Mental Health, United States, 1990.* (DHHS Pub. No. ADM 90–1708.) Washington, DC: Supt. of Docs., U.S. Government Printing Office.

National Institute of Mental Health. (1993). *Eating disorders.* (NIH Publication No. 93–3477). Bethesda, MD: U.S. Department of Health and Human Services.

National Institute on Alcohol Abuse and Alcoholism. (1983). *Alcohol and women.* (DHEW Publication No. ADM 80–835). Washington, DC: U. S. Government Printing Office.

National Institute on Drug Abuse. (1993). *National household survey on drug abuse: Population estimates, 1992* (DHHS Publication No. SMA 93–2053). Washington, DC: Department of Health and Human Services.

Navon, D., & Gopher, D. (1979). On the economy of the human processing system. *Psychological Review, 86*, 214–255.

Neisser, U. (1967). *Cognitive psychology.* New York: Appleton.

Neisser, U. (1978). Memory: What are the important questions? In M. M. Grueneberg, P. E. Morris, & R. N. Sykes (Eds.), *Practical aspects of memory.* London: Academic Press.

Neisser, U. (1982). *Memory observed: Remembering in natural contexts.* San Francisco: Freeman.

Neisser, U. (1991). A case of misplaced nostalgia. *American Psychologist, 46*, 65.

Neisser, U., Boodoo, G., Bouchard, T. J., Jr., Boykin, A. W., Brody, N., Ceci, S. L., Halpern, D. F., Loehlin, J. C., Perloff, R., Sternberg, R. J., & Urbina, S. (1996). Intelligence: Knowns and unknowns. *American Psychologist, 51*, 77–101.

Neisser, U., & Harsch, N. (1992). Phantom flashbulbs: False recollections of hearing the news about Challenger. In E. Winograd & U. Neisser (Eds.), *Affect and accuracy in recall: Studies of "flashbulb memories"* (pp. 9–31). Cambridge, MA: Cambridge University Press.

Neisser, U., Winograd, E., & Weldon, M. S. (1991, September). *Re-*

membering the earthquake:"What I experienced" vs. "how I heard the news" Paper presented at the 32nd Annual Meeting of the Psychonomic Society, San Francisco.

Neitz, J., Geist, T., & Jacobs, G. H. (1989). Color vision in the dog. *Visual Neuroscience*, 3, 119–125.

Nelson, T. O. (1996). Consciousness and metacognition. *American Psychologist, 51*, 102–116.

Nemeth, C., Swedlund, M., & Kanki, B. (1974). Patterning of the minority's response and their influence on the majority. *European Journal of Social Psychology, 4*, 53–64.

Neuberg, S. L., & Fiske, S. T. (1987). Motivational influences on impression formation: Outcome dependency, accuracy-driven attention, and individuating processes. *Journal of Personality and Social Psychology, 53*, 431–444.

Neugarten, B. L. (Ed.). (1968). *Middle age and aging*. Chicago: University of Chicago Press.

Neugarten, B. L. (1976). The psychology of aging: An overview. *Master lectures on developmental psychology*. Washington, DC: American Psychological Association.

Neugarten, B. L. (Ed.). (1982a). *Age or need? Public policies for older people*. Beverly Hills, CA: Sage.

Neugarten, B. L. (1982b). *Successful aging* [Invited address]. American Psychological Association. Annual meetings of the American Psychological Association.

Neugarten, B. L., & Neugarten, D. A. (1986). Changing meanings of age in the aging society. In A. Pifer & L. Bronte (Eds.), *Our aging society: Paradox and promise*. New York: Norton.

Newcomb, T. M. (1961). *The acquaintance process*. New York: Holt, Rinehart and Winston.

Newell, A., & Simon, H. A. (1972). *Human problem solving*. Englewood Cliffs, NJ: Prentice-Hall.

Newmann, J. P. (1984). Sex differences in symptoms of depression: Clinical disorder or normal distress? *Journal of Health and Social Behavior, 25*, 136–160.

Nias, D. K. B. (1979). Marital choice: Matching or complementation. In M. Cook & G. Wilson (Eds.), *Love and attraction* (pp. 151–155). Oxford, Eng.: Pergamon Press.

Nicholl, C. S., & Russell, R. M. (1990). Analysis of animal rights literature reveals the underlying motives of the movement: Ammunition for counter offensive by scientists. *Endocrinology, 127*, 985–989.

Nickerson, R. S., & Adams, M. J. (1979). Long-term memory for a common object. *Cognitive Psychology, 11*, 287–307.

Niemi, R. G., Mueller, J., & Smith, T. W. (1989). *Trends in public opinion: A compendium of survey data*. New York: Greenwood Press.

Ninan, P., Insel, T., Cohen, R., Cook, J., Skolnick, P., & Paul, S. (1982). Benzodiazepine receptor-mediated experimental "anxiety" in primates. *Science, 218*, 1332–1334.

Nisbett, R. E. (1968). Determinants of food intake in human obesity. *Science, 159*, 1254–1255.

Nisbett, R. E. (1972). Eating behavior and obesity in man and animals. *Advances in Psychosomatic Medicine, 7*, 173–193.

Nisbett, R. E. (1980). The trait construct in lay and professional psychology. In L. Festinger (Ed.), *Retrospections in social psychology* (pp. 109–130). New York: Oxford University Press.

Nisbett, R. E., & Ross, L. D. (1980). *Human inference*. Englewood Cliffs, NJ: Prentice-Hall.

Nisbett, R. E., & Wilson, T. D. (1977). Telling more than we can know: Verbal reports on mental processes. *Psychological Review, 84*, 231–259.

Nolen-Hoeksema, S. (1987). Sex differences in unipolar depression: Evidence and theory. *Psychological Bulletin, 101*(2), 259–282.

Nolen-Hoeksema, S. (1990). *Sex differences in depression*. Stanford, CA: Stanford University Press.

Norman, D. (1988). *The psychology of everyday things*. New York: Basic Books.

Novy, D. M., Nelson, D. V., Francis, D. J., & Turk, D. C. (1995). Perspectives on chronic pain: An evaluative comparison of restrictive and comprehensive models. *Psychological Bulletin, 118*, 238–247.

Nowack, K. M. (1989). Coping style, cognitive hardiness, and health status. *Journal of Behavioral Medicine, 12*, 145–158.

Nuechterlein, K. H., & Holroyd, J. C. (1980). Biofeedback in the treatment of tension headache: Current status. *Archives of General Psychiatry, 37*, 866–873.

Nyberg, L., Cabeza, R. & Tulving, E. (1996). PET studies of encoding and retrieval: The HERA model. *Psychonomic Bulletin and Review, 3*, 135–148.

O'Connell, A. N., & Russo, N. F., (Eds.). (1980). *Eminent women in psychology: Models of achievement*. New York: Human Sciences Press.

O'Connell, A. N., & Russo, N. F. (Eds.). (1983). *Models of achievement: Reflections of eminent women in psychology*. New York: Columbia University Press.

O'Connell, A. N., & Russo, N. F., (Eds.). (1988). *Models of achievement: Reflections of eminent women in psychology, Volume II*. Hillsdale, NJ: Erlbaum.

O'Connell, A. N., & Russo, N. F., (Eds.). (1990). *Women in psychology: A bio-bibliographical sourcebook*. Westport, CT: Greenwood Press.

O'Connell, A. N., & Russo, N. F. (Eds.). (1991). Women's heritage in psychology: Origins, development, future directions. *Psychology of Women Quarterly, 15*(4).

O'Leary, A. (1990). Stress, emotion, and human immune function. *Psychological Bulletin, 108*, 363–382.

Oden, S., & Asher, S.R. (1977). Coaching children in social skills for friendship making. *Child Development*, 48, 495–506.

Oetting, E. R., & Beauvais, F. (1991). Orthogonal cultural identification theory: The cultural identification of minority adolescents. *International Journal of the Addictions, 25*, 655–685.

Ogbu, J. (1981). Origins of human competence: A cultural-ethological perspective. *Child Development, 52*, 413–429.

Ogburn, W. F. (1922/1966). *Social change with respect to culture and original nature*. New York: Dell.

Ogloff, J. R. P., Roberts C. F., & Roesch, R. (1993). The insanity defense: Legal standards and clinical assessment. *Applied and Preventative Psychology, 2*, 163–178.

Okagaki, L., & Sternberg, R. (1993). Parental beliefs and children's school performance. *Child Development, 64*, 36–56.

Olds, J., & Milner, P. M. (1954). Positive reinforcement produced by electrical stimulation of septal area and other regions of rat brains. *Journal of Comparative and Physiological Psychology, 47*, 419–427.

Olson, J. M., & Roese, N. J. (1995). The perceived funniness of humorous stimuli. *Personality and Social Psychology Bulletin, 21*, 908–913.

Orne, M. T. (1979a). On the simulating subject as a quasi-control group in hypnosis research: Why, what and how. In E. Fromm & R. E. Shor (Eds.), *Hypnosis: Developments in research and new perspectives*. New York: Aldine.

Orne, M. T. (1979b). The use and misuse of hypnosis in court. *The International Journal of Clinical and Experimental Hypnosis, 27*, 311–322.

Ornstein, R., & Naranjo, C. (1971). *On the psychology of meditation*. New York: Viking.

Osgood, C. E. (1952). The nature and measurement of meaning. *Psychological Bulletin, 49*, 197–237.

Osherow, N. (1984). Making sense of the nonsensical: An analysis of Jonestown. In E. Aronson (Ed.), *Readings about the social animal*. New York: Freeman.

Oskamp, S. (1991). Curbside recycling: Knowledge, attitudes, and behavior. In *Society for Experimental Social Psychology meeting*, Columbus, OH.

Ost, L.-G. & Hugdahl, K. (1981). Acquisition of phobias and anxiety response patterns in clinical patients. *Behaviour Research and Therapy, 19*, 439–448.

Owens, D. A., & Wolf-Kelly, K. (1987). Near work, visual fatigue, and variations of oculomotor tonus. *Inv. Ophthalmological Visual Science, 28*, 742–749.

Ozer, E. M. (1995). The impact of childcare responsibility and self-efficacy on the psychological health of professional working mothers. *Psychology of Women Quarterly, 19*, 315–336.

Pagan, G., & Aiello, J. R. (1982). Development of personal space among Puerto Ricans. *Journal of Nonverbal Behavior, 7*, 59–68.

Pagelow, M. D. (1984). *Family violence.* New York: Praeger.

Paivio, A. (1971). *Imagery and verbal process.* New York: Holt, Rinehart and Winston.

Paivio, A. (1986) *Mental representation: A dual coding approach.* New York: Oxford University Press.

Palermo, D. S. (1970). Language acquisition. In H. W. Reese, & L. P. Lipsitt (Eds.), *Experimental child psychology.* New York: Academic Press.

Pandey, G. N., Pandey, S. C., Dwivedi, Y., Sharma, R. P., & Davis, J. M. (1995). Platelet serotonin-2A receptors: A potential biological marker for suicidal behavior. *American Journal of Psychiatry, 152*(6), 850–855.

Papousek, H. (1969). Individual variability in learned responses in human infants. In R. J. Robinson (Ed.), *Brain and early behavior: Development in the fetus and infant.* London: Academic Press.

Papp, L. A., & Gorman, J. M. (1993). Pharmacological approach to the management of stress and anxiety disorders. In P. M. Lehrer & R. L. Woolfolk (Eds.), *Principles and practice of stress management* (2nd ed.). New York: Guilford.

Paramei, G. V. (1996). Color space of normally sighted and color-deficient observers reconstructed from color naming. *Psychological Science, 7*, 311–317.

Park, B., & Flink, C. (1989). A social relations analysis of agreement making judgments. *Journal of Personality and Social Psychology, 56*, 506–518.

Park, B., & Rothbart, M. (1982). Perception of out-group homogeneity and levels of social categorization: Memory for the subordinate attributes of in-group and out-group members. *Journal of Personality and Social Psychology, 42*, 1051–1068.

Park, L. C., Imboden, J. B., Park, T. J., Hulse, S. H., & Unger, H. T. (1992). Giftedness and psychological abuse in borderline personality disorder: Their relevance to genesis and treatment. *Journal of Personality Disorders, 6*, 226–240.

Parke, R. D. (1977). Some effects of punishment on children's behavior—revisited. In E. M. Hetherington & R. D. Parke (Eds.), *Contemporary readings in child psychology.* New York: McGraw-Hill.

Parke, R. D., & Deur, J. L. (1972). Schedule of punishment and inhibition of aggression in children. *Developmental Psychology, 7*, 266–269.

Parnas, J., Cannon, T. D., Jacobsen, B., Schulsinger, F., & Mednick, S. A. (1993). Lifetime DSM-IIIR diagnostic outcomes in the offspring of schizophrenic mothers. Results from the Copenhagen high-risk study. *Archives of General Psychiatry, 50*, 707–714.

Paul, G. L. (1966). *Insight vs. desensitization in psychotherapy.* Stanford, CA: Stanford University Press.

Paul, G. L., & Lentz, R. J. (1977). Psychosocial treatment of chronic mental patients: Milieu versus social-learning programs. Cambridge, MA: Harvard University Press.

Paulus, P. B., Dzindolet, M. T., Poletes, G., & Camacho, L. M. (1993). Perception of performance in group brainstorming: The illusion of group productivity. *Personality and Social Psychology Bulletin, 19*, 78–89.

Paunonen, S. P., Jackson, D. N., Trzebinski, J., & Fosterline, G. (1992). Personality structure across cultures: A multimethod evaluation. *Journal of Personality and Social Psychology, 62*, 447–456.

Pavlov, I. P. (1927). *Conditioned reflexes.* (G. V. Anrep, Trans.). London: Oxford University Press.

Pearlin, L., & Schooler, C. (1978). The structure of coping. *Journal of Health and Social Behavior, 19*, 2–21.

Pedersen, N. L., Plomin, R., Nesselroade, J. R., & McClearn, G. E. (1992). A quantitative genetic analysis of cognitive abilities during the second half of the life span. *Psychological Science, 3*, 346–353.

Penfield, W. (1975). *The mystery of the mind.* Princeton, NJ: Princeton University Press.

Penfield, W., & Rasmussen, T. (1950). *The cerebral cortex of man.* New York: Macmillan.

Penfield, W., & Roberts, L. (1959). *Speech and brain mechanisms.* Princeton, NJ: Princeton University Press.

Pennebaker, J. W. (1993). Putting stress into words: Health, linguistic, and therapeutic implications. *Behaviour Research and Therapy, 31*, 539–549.

Pennebaker, J. W. (Ed.). (1995). *Emotion, disclosure, and health.* Washington DC: American Psychological Association.

Pennebaker, J. W., & Beall, S. K. (1986). Confronting a traumatic event: Toward an understanding of inhibition and disease. *Journal of Abnormal Psychology, 95*, 274–281.

Pennebaker, J. W., Hughes, C. F. & O'Heeron, R. C. (1987). The psychophysiology of confession: Linking inhibitory and psychosomatic processes. *Journal of Personality and Social Psychology, 52*, 718–793.

Pennebaker, J. W., & Uhlmann, C. (in press). Direct linking of autonomic activity with typed text: The CARMEN machine. *Behavior Research Methods: Instruments and Computers.*

Peoples, J., & Bailey, G. (1991). *Humanity: An introduction to cultural anthropology.* St. Paul, MN: West Publishing Company.

Perlini, A. H., & Spanos, N. P. (1991). EEG alpha methodologies and hypnotizability: A critical review. *Psychophysiology, 28*, 511–529.

Perls, F. S. (1969). *Gestalt therapy verbatim.* Lafayette, CA: Real People Press.

Perry, J. C., & Klerman, G. L. (1980). Clinical features of borderline personality disorder. *American Journal of Psychiatry, 137*, 165–173.

Peter, L. J. (1989). *Peter's quotations: Ideas for our time.* New York: William Morrow.

Peters, M. (1991). Sex differences in human brain size and the general meaning of differences in brain size. *Canadian Journal of Psychology, 45*, 507–522.

Peters, M., Chisholm, P., & Laeng, B. (1995). Spatial ability, student gender and academic performance. *Journal of Engineering Education, 84*, 69–73.

Peterson, C., & Bossio, L. M. (1991). *Health and optimism.* New York: Free Press.

Peterson, C., & Stunkard, A. J. (1992). Cognates of personal control: Locus of control, self-efficacy, and explanatory style. *Applied and Preventive Psychology, 1*, 111–117.

Peterson, L. R., & Peterson, M. J. (1959). Short-term retention of individual verbal items. *Journal of Experimental Psychology, 58*, 193–198.

Pettigrew, T. (1964). *A profile of the American Negro.* Princeton, NJ: Van Nostrand.

Pettigrew, T. (1979). The ultimate attribution error: Extending Allport's cognitive analysis of prejudice. *Personality and Social Psychology Bulletin, 44*, 702–711.

Pettigrew, T. F. (1997). Personality and social structure: Social psychological contributions. In R. Hogan, J. Johnson, & S. Briggs (Eds.), *Handbook of personality psychology* (pp. 417–438). San Diego, CA: Academic Press.

Petty, R. E., & Cacioppo, J. T. (1981). *Attitudes and persuasion: Classic and contemporary approaches.* Dubuque, IA: W. C. Brown.

Petty, R. E., & Cacioppo, J. T. (1984). The effects of involvement on responses to argument quantity and quality: Central and peripheral routes to persuasion. *Journal of Personality and Social Psychology, 46*, 69–81.

Petty, R. E., & Cacioppo, J. T. (1985). Involvement and persuasion: Tradition versus integration. *Psychological Bulletin, 107*, 367–374.

Petty, R. E., & Cacioppo, J. T. (1986). *Communication and persuasion: Central and peripheral routes to attitude change.* New York: Springer-Verlag.

Petty, R. E., Cacioppo, J. T., Strathman, A. J., & Priester, J. R. (1994). To think or not to think: Exploring two routes to persuasion. In S. Shavitt & T. C. Brock (Eds.), *Persuasion* (pp. 113–147). Boston: Allyn & Bacon.

Petty, R. E., Wells, G. L., & Brock, T. C. (1976). Distraction can enhance or reduce yielding to propaganda: Thought disruption versus effort justification. *Journal of Personality and Social Psychology, 34*, 874–884.

Phillips, D. P., & Ruth, T. E. (1993). Adequacy of official suicide statistics for scientific research and public policy. *Suicidal Life-Threatening Behavior, 23*(4), 307–19.

Piaget, J. (1926). *The language and thought of the child.* New York: Harcourt, Brace.

Piaget, J. (1932/1965). *The moral judgment of the child.* New York: Free Press.

Piaget, J. (1951). *Play, dreams, and imitation in childhood.* London: Heinemann.

Piaget, J., & Inhelder, B. (1941/1974). *The child's conception of quantities: Conservation and atomism.* New York: Basic Books.

Pierce, C. A. (1992). *The effects of physical attractiveness and height on dating choice: A meta-analysis.* Unpublished masters thesis, University of Albany, State University of New York, Albany, NY.

Pinel, J. P. J. (1990). *Biopsychology.* Boston: Allyn & Bacon.

Pirenne, M. H. (1948). *Vision and the eye.* London: Chapman & Hall.

Plas, J. A., & Hill, K. T. (1986). Children's achievement strategies and test performance: The role of time, pressure, evaluation anxiety, and sex. *Developmental Psychology, 22*, 31–36.

Plomin, R., Corley, R., DeFries, J. C., & Fulker, D. W. (1990a). Individual differences in television viewing in early childhood: Nature as well as nuture. *Psychological Science, 1*, 371–377.

Plomin, R., & Daniels, D. (1987). Why are children in the same family so different from one another? *Behavioral and Brain Sciences, 10*, 1–60.

Plomin, R., DeFries, J. C., & Fulker, D. W. (1988). *Nature and nuture during infancy and early childhood.* New York: Cambridge University Press.

Plomin, R., DeFries, J. C., & McClearn, G. E. (1990b). *Behavioral Genetics: A primer* (2nd ed.). New York: Freeman.

Plomin, R., & McClearn, G. (Eds.). (1993). *Nature, nurture, and psychology.* Washington, DC: American Psychological Association.

Plotnick, R., Mir, D., & Delgado, J. M. R. (1971). Aggression, noxiousness and brain stimulation in unrestrained rhesus monkeys. In B. E. Eleftheriou, & J. P. Scott (Eds.), *The physiology of aggression and defeat.* New York: Plenum.

Plous, S. (1996). Attitudes toward the use of animals in psychological research and education. *American Psychologist, 51*, 1167–1180.

Plutchik, R. (1980). *Emotion: A psychoevolutionary synthesis.* New York: Harper & Row.

Pons, T., Garraghty, P. E., & Ommaya, A. K. (1991). Massive cortical reorganization after sensory deafferentation in adult macaques. *Science, 252*, 1857–1860.

Pool, J. L. (1973). *Your brain and nerves.* New York: Scribner's.

Posner, M. I. (1980). Orienting of attention. *Quarterly Journal of Experimental Psychology, 32*, 3–25.

Posner, M. I. (1992). Attention as a cognitive and neural system. *Current Directions in Psychological Science, 1*, 11–14.

Posner, M. I., & Petersen, S. E. (1990). The attention system of the human brain. In W. M. Cowan (Ed.), *Annual review of neuroscience* (pp. 25–42). Palo Alto, .CA: Annual Reviews.

Posner, M. I., Petersen, S. E., Fox, P. T., & Raichle, M. E. (1988). Localization of cognitive operations in the human brain. *Science, 240*, 1627–1631.

Posner, M. I., & Raichle, M. E. (1994). *Images of mind.* New York: Scientific American Library.

Post, R. M. (1975). Cocaine psychosis: A continuum model. *American Journal of Psychiatry, 132*, 225–231.

Postman, L., & Underwood, B. J. (1973). Critical issues in interference theory. *Memory and Cognition, 1*, 19–40.

Powell, D. H., & Whitla, D. K. (1994). Normal cognitive aging: Toward empirical perspectives. *Current Directions in Psychological Science, 3*(1), 27–31.

Powell, J., & Azrin, N. (1968). The effects of shock as a punisher for cigarette smoking. *Journal of Applied Behavior Analysis, 1*, 63–71.

Powley, T. L. (1977). The ventromedial hypothalamic syndrome, satiety, and a cephalic phase hypothesis. *Psychological Review, 84*, 89–126.

Pratkanis, A. R., Greenwald, A. G., Leippe, M., & Baumgardener, M. H. (1988). In search of reliable persuasions effects: III. The sleeper effect is dead. Long live the sleeper effect. *Journal of Personality and Social Psychology, 54*, 203–218.

Premack, D. (1965). Reinforcement theory. In D. Levine (Ed.), *Nebraska symposium on motivation.* Lincoln, NE: University of Nebraska Press.

Premack, D. (1971). Language in chimpanzee? *Science, 172*, 808–822.

Premack, D., & Woodruff, G. (1978). Chimpanzee problem-solving: A test for comprehension. *Science, 202*, 532–535.

Prentice-Dunn, S., & Rogers, R. W. (1980). Effects of deindividuating situational cues and aggressive models on subjective deindividuation and aggression. *Journal of Personality and Social Psychology, 39*, 104–113.

Prentice-Dunn, S., & Rogers, R. W. (1989). Deindividuation and the self-regulation of behavior. In P. Paulhus (Ed.), *Psychology of group influence* (2nd ed., pp. 87–109). Hillsdale, NJ: Erlbaum.

Price, D. D. (1988). *Psychological and neural mechanisms of pain.* New York: Raven Press.

Price, R. A. (1987). Genetics of human obesity. *Annals of Behavioral Medicine, 9*, 9–14.

Price-Williams, D. R., Gordo, W., & Ramirez, M. (1996). Skill and conservation. *Developmental Psychology, 1*, 769.

Pritchard, W. S., & Warm, J. S. (1978). Attentional processing and the subjective contour illusion. *Journal of Experimental Psychology: General, 112*, 145–167.

Purves, D., & Hadley, R. D. (1985). Changes in the dendritic branching of adult mammalian neurons revealed by repeated imaging in situ. *Nature, 315*, 404–406.

Putallaz, M., & Gottman, J. M. (1984). Social relationship problems in children: An approach to intervention. In E. B. Lahey & A. E. Kazdin (Eds.), *Advances in clinical child psychology.* New York: Plenum Publishing Corporation.

Putnam, F. W., Guroff, J. J., Silberman, E. K., Barban, L., & Post, R. M. (1986). The clinical phenomenology of multiple personality disorder: Review of 100 recent cases. *Journal of Clinical Psychiatry, 47*, 285–293.

Quattrone, G. A. (1986). On the perception of group variability. In S. Worchel & W. G. Austin (Eds.), *The psychology of intergroup relations* (pp. 25–48). Chicago: Nelson-Hall.

Quattrone, G. A., & Jones, E. E. (1980). The perception of variability within ingroups and outgroups: Implications for the law of small numbers. *Journal of Personality and Social Psychology, 38*, 141–152.

Rabin, A. S., Kaslow, N. J., & Rehm, L. P. (1986) Aggregate outcome and follow-up results following self-control therapy for depression. Paper presented at the 1986 Convention of the American Psychological Association.

Radecki-Bush, C., Farrell, A. D., & Bush, J. P. (1993). Predicting jealous responses: The influence of adult attachment and depression on threat appraisal. *Journal of Social and Personal Relationships, 10,* 569–588.

Radford, J. (1990). *Child prodigies and exceptional early achievers.* New York: Free Press.

Radloff, L. (1980). Depression and the empty nest. *Sex Roles, 6,* 775–781.

Raimy, V. (1975). *Misunderstandings of the self*. San Francisco: Jossey-Bass.

Rakic, P. (1991). Plasticity of cortical development. In S. E. Brauth, W. S. Hall, & R. J. Dooling (Eds.), *Plasticity of development*. Cambridge, MA: Bradford/MIT Press.

Ramachandran, V. S. (1992). Blind spots. *Scientific American, 266,* 86–91.

Ravussin, E., Lillioja, S., Knowler, W. C., Christin, L., Freymond, D., Aboortt, W. G. H., Boyce, V., Howard, b. V., & Bogardus, C. (1988). Reduced rate of energy expenditure as a risk factor for body-weight gain. *New England Journal of Medicine, 318,* 467–472.

Reber, A. S., Walkenfeld, F. F., & Hernstadt, R. (1991). Implicit and explicit learning: Individual differences and IQ. *Journal of Experimental Psychology: Learning, Memory and Cognition, 17,* 888–896.

Rechtschaffen, A., Gilliard, M. A., Bergmann, B. M., & Winter, J. B. (1983). Physiological correlates of prolonged sleep deprivation in rats. *Science*, 221, 145–182.

Reder, L. M., & Anderson, J. R. (1980). A comparison of texts and their summaries: Memorial consequences. *Journal of Verbal Learning and Verbal Behavior, 19,* 12–34.

Redlich, F. C., & Freeman, D. X. (1966). *The theory and practice of psychiatry*. New York: Basic Books.

Regier, D. A., Boyd, J. H., Burke, J. D., Jr., Rae, D. S., Myers, J. K., Kramer, M., Robins, L. N., George, L. K., Karno, M., & Locke, B. Z. (1988). One-month prevalence of mental disorders in the United States. *Archives of General Psychiatry, 45,* 977–986.

Regier, D. A., Narrow, W. E., & Rae, D. S. (1990). The epidemiology of anxiety disorders: The Epidemiological Catchment Area (ECA) experience. *Journal of Psychiatric Research, 24* (Supp. 2), 3–14.

Rehm, J., Steinleitner, M., & Lilli, W. (1987). Wearing uniforms and aggression: A field experiment. *European Journal of Social Psychology, 17,* 357–360.

Rehm, L. P., Kaslow, N. J., & Rabin, A. S. (1987). Cognitive and behavioral targets in a self-control behavior therapy program for depression. *Journal of Clinical and Consulting Psychology, 55,* 60–67.

Reif, J. S., Dunn, K., Ogilvie, G. K., & Harris, C. K. (1992). Passive smoking and canine lung cancer risk. *American Journal of Epidemiology, 135,* 234–39.

Reinisch, J. M. (1981). Prenatal exposure to synthetic progestins increases potential for aggression in humans. *Science, 211,* 1171–1173.

Reisenzein, R. (1983). The Schachter theory of emotions: Two decades later. *Psychological Bulletin, 94,* 239–264.

Reisenzein, R., Meyer, W.-U., & Schützwohl, A. (1995). James and the physical basis of emotion. *Psychological Review, 102,* 757–761.

Reisenzein, R., & Schönpflug, W. (1992). Stumpf's cognitive-evaluative theory of emotion. *American Psychologist, 47,* 34–45.

Reno, R. R., Cialdini, R. B., & Kallgren, C. A. (1993). The transitional influence of social norms, *Journal of Personality and Social Psychology, 64,* 104–112.

Rescorla, R. A. (1974). Effect of inflation of the unconditioned stimulus value following conditioning. *Journal of Comparative and Physiological Psychology, 86,* 101–107.

Rescorla, R. A. (1987). A Pavlovian analysis of goal-directed behavior. *American Psychologist, 42,* 119–129.

Rescorla, R. A. (1991). Associative relations in instrumental learning: The eighteenth Bartlett Memorial Lecture. *Quarterly Journal of Experimental Psychology, 43B,* 1–23.

Rest, J. R. (1993). Research on moral judgment in college students. In A. Garrod (Ed.), *Approaches to moral development: New research and emerging themes*. New York: Teachers College Press.

Revusky, S. H. (1968). Aversion to sucrose produced by contingent X-irradiation: Temporal and dosage parameters. *Journal of Comparative and Physiological Psychology, 65,* 17–22.

Reynolds, D. K. (1982). *The quiet therapies.* Honolulu, HI: University of Hawaii Press.

Rhee, E., Uleman, J.S., & Lee, H. K. (1996). Variations in collectivism and individualism by ingroup and culture: Confirmatory factor analyses. *Journal of Personality and Social Psychology, 71,* 1037–1054.

Rhodes, S. R. (1983). Age-related differences in work attitudes and behavior: A review and conceptual analysis. *Psychological Bulletin, 93,* 328–367.

Ries, P. (1991). Educational differences in health status and health care. *Vital and Health Statistics, Series 10: Data from the National Health Survey, No. 179* (DHHS Publication No. PHS 91–1507). Washington, DC: National Center for Health Statistics.

Riley, J. N., & Walker, D. W. (1978). Morphological alterations in hippocampus after long-term alcohol consumption in mice. *Science, 201,* 646–648.

Riley, V., Fitzmaurice, M. A., & Spackman, D. H. (1981). Models in biobehavioral research. Effects of anxiety stress immunocompetence and neoplasia. In S. M. Weiss, J. A. Herd, & B. H. F (Eds.), *Perspectives in behavioral medicine.* New York: Academic Press.

Rimm, D. C., & Masters, J. C. (1979). *Behavior therapy: Techniques and empirical findings.* (2nd ed.). New York: Academic Press.

Roberts, C. F., Golding, S. L., & Fincham, F. D. (1987). Implicit theories of criminal responsibility: Decision-making and the insanity defense. *Law and Human Behavior, 11,* 207–232.

Roberts, C. J., & Lowe, C. R. (1975). Where have all the conceptions gone? *Lancet*, 498–499.

Roberts, P., & Newton, P. M. (1987). Levinsonian studies of a women's adult development. *Psychology and Aging, 2,* 154–163.

Robertson, J. & Fitzgerald, L. F. (1990). The (mis)treatment of men: Effects of client gender role and life-style on diagnosis and attribution of pathology. *Journal of Counseling Psychology, 37,* 3–9.

Robins, L. N. (1966). *Deviant children grow up.* Baltimore, MD: Williams & Wilkins.

Robins, L. N., Helzer, J. E., Weissman, M. M., Orvaschel, H., Gruenberg, E., Burke, J. D., Jr., & Regier, D. A. (1984). Lifetime prevalence of specific psychiatric disorders in three sites. *Archives of General Psychiatry, 41,* 949–958.

Robinson, I., Ziss, K., Ganza, B., Katz, S., & Robinson, E. (1991). Twenty years of the sexual revolution, 1965–1985: An update. *Journal of Marriage and the Family, 53,* 216–220.

Robinson, V. M. (1983). Humor and health. In P. E. McGhee & J. H. Goldstein (Eds.), *Handbook of humor research: Vol. II. Applied studies.* New York: Springer-Verlag.

Rodin, J. (1981). Current status of the internal-external hypothesis for obesity. What went wrong? *American Psychologist, 36,* 361–372.

Rodin, J., & Salovey, P. (1989). Health psychology. *Annual Review of Psychology, 40,* 533–579.

Roediger, H. L., & McDermott, K. B. (1995). Creating false memories: Remembering words not presented in lists. *Journal of Experimental Psychology: Learning, Memory and Cognition, 21,* 803–814.

Roediger, H. L., Weldon, M. S., & Challis, B. H. (1989). Explaining dissociations between implicit and explicit retention: A processing account. In Craik, F. I. M., & Roediger, H. L. (Eds.), *Varieties of memory and consciousness: Essays in honor of Endel Tulving.* Hillsdale, NJ: Erlbaum.

Roessler, R. L., & Brogden, W. J. (1943). Conditioned differentiation of vasoconstriction to subvocal stimuli. *American Journal of Psychology, 56,* 78–86.

Roethlisberger, F. J., & Dickson, W. J. (1939). *Management and the worker.* Cambridge, MA: Harvard University Press.

Rogers, B. J., & Graham, M. E. (1979). Motion paralax as an independent cue for depth perception. *Perception, 8,* 125–134.

Rogers, C. R. (1951). *Client-centered therapy: Its current practice, implications, and theory.* Boston: Houghton Mifflin.

Rogers, C. R. (1959). A theory of therapy, personality, and interpersonal relationships, as developed in the client-centered framework. In S. Koch (Ed.), *Psychology: A study of a science* (Vol. 3, pp. 184–256). New York: McGraw-Hill.

Rogers, C. R. (1961). *On becoming a person.* Boston: Houghton Mifflin.

Rogers, C. R. (1970). *On becoming a person: A therapist's view of psychotherapy.* (2nd ed.). Boston: Houghton Mifflin.

Rogers, C. R. (1980). *A way of being.* Boston: Houghton Mifflin.

Rogers, P. J., & Blundell, J. E. (1980). Investigation of food selection and mean parameters during the development of dietary induced obesity. *Appetite, 1,* 85–88.

Rogers, S. M., & Turner, C. F. (1991). Male-male sexual contact in the U.S.A.: Findings from five sample surveys, 1970–1990. *Journal of Sex Research, 28,* 491–519.

Rogoff, B., & Morelli, G. (1989). Perspectives on children's development from cultural psychology. *American Psychologist, 44,* 343–348.

Rohner, R. P. (1986). *The warmth dimension: Foundations of parental acceptance-rejection theory.* Newbury Park, CA: Sage.

Rohner, R. P. (1994). Patterns of parenting: The warmth dimension in worldwide perspective. In W. J. Lonner & R. Malpass (Eds.), *Psychology and culture* (pp. 113–20). Boston: Allyn & Bacon.

Rokeach, M. (1960). *The open and closed mind.* New York: Basic Books.

Rokeach, M. (1968). *Beliefs, attitudes and values.* San Francisco, CA: Jossey-Bass.

Roopnarine, J. L., Talukder, E., Jain, D., Joshi, P., & Srivastav, P. (1990). Characteristics of holding, patterns of play, and social behaviors between parents and infants in New Delhi, India. *Developmental Psychology, 26,* 667–673.

Rorschach, H. (1921). *Psychodiagnostik.* Bern, Switzerland: Huber.

Rosch, E. (1975). Cognitive representations of semantic categories. *Journal of Experimental Psychology: General, 104,* 192–233.

Rosch, E., & Mervis, C. B. (1975). Family resemblances: Studies in the internal structure of categories. *Cognitive Psychology 7,* 573–605.

Rose, R. J., & Kaprio, J. (1987). Shared experience and similarity of personality: Positive data from Finnish and American twins. *Behavioral and Brain Sciences, 10,* 35–36.

Rosen, B., & Jerdee, T. H. (1976). Influence of employee age, sex, and job status on managerial recommendations for retirement. *Academy of Management Journal, 22,* 169–173.

Rosen, L. W., Shafer, C. L., & Dummer, G. M. (1988). Prevalence of pathogenic weight-control behaviors among Native American women and girls. *International Journal of Eating Disorders, 7,* 807–811.

Rosen, L. N., Targum, S. D., Terman, M., Bryant, M. J., Hoffman, H., Kasper, S. E., Hamovit, J. R., Docherty, J. P., Welch, B., & Rosenthal, N. E. (1990). Prevalence of seasonal affective disorder at four latitudes. *Psychiatry Research, 31,* 131–144.

Rosen, L. W., Shafer, C. L., & Dummer, G. M. (1988). Prevalence of pathogenic weight-control behaviors among Native American women and girls. *International Journal of Eating Disorders, 7,* 807.

Rosenbaum, M. E. (1986). The repulsion hypothesis: On the nondevelopment of relationships. *Journal of Personality and Social Psychology, 51,* 1156–1166.

Rosenberg, R. (1982). *Beyond separate spheres: Intellectual roots of modern feminism.* New Haven, CT: Yale University Press.

Rosenfield, S. (1982). Sex roles and societal reactions to mental illness: The labeling of "deviant" deviance. *Journal of Health and Social Behavior, 23,* 18–24.

Rosenhan, D. L. (1973, January 13). On being sane in insane places. *Science, 179,* 250–257.

Rosenhan, D. L. & Seligman, M. E. (1995). *Abnormal psychology* (3rd ed.). New York: W. W. Norton.

Rosenman, R. H. (1985). Health consequences of anger and implications for treatment. In M. A. Chesney & R. H. Rosenman (Eds.), *Anger and hostility in cardiovascular and behavioral disorders* (pp. 103–25). New York: Hemisphere/McGraw-Hill.

Rosenman, R. H., Brand, R. J., Jenkins, C. D., Friedman, M., Straus, R., & Wurm, M. (1975). Coronary heart disease in the Western collaborative group study: Final follow-up experience of 8 1/2 years. *Journal of the American Medical Association, 233,* 872–877.

Rosenstock, I. M. (1966). Why people use health services. *Milbank Memorial Fund Quarterly, 44,* 94–127.

Rosenthal, R. (1966). *Experimenter effects in behavioral research.* New York: Appleton-Century-Crofts.

Rosenzweig, M. R. (1992). Psychological science around the world. *American Psychologist, 47,* 718–722.

Rosenzweig, M. R., Bennett, E. L., & Diamond, M. C. (1972b). Brain changes in response to experience. *Scientific American, 226,* 22–29.

Rosenzweig, M. R., & Leiman, A. L. (1982). *Physiological psychology.* Lexington, MA: Heath.

Rosenzweig, M. R., Leiman, A. L., & Breedlove, S. M. (1996). *Biological psychology.* Sunderland, MA: Sinauer Associates, Inc.

Ross, B. M., & Millsom, C. (1970). Repeated memory of oral prose in Ghana and New York. *International Journal of Psychology, 5,* 173–181.

Ross, C. A., et al. (1990). Structured interview data on 102 cases of multiple personality disorder from four centers. *American Journal of Psychiatry, 147,* 596–601.

Ross, C. A., Norton, G. R., & Wozney, K. (1989). Multiple personality disorder: An analysis of 236 cases. *Canadian Journal of Psychiatry, 34,* 413–418.

Ross, L. D. (1977). The intuitive psychologist and his shortcomings. In L. Berkowitz (Ed.), *Advances in experimental social psychology* (Vol. 10, pp. 173–220). New York: Academic Press.

Ross, L., & Nisbitt, R. E. (1991). *The person and the situation: Perspectives of social psychology.* New York: McGraw-Hill.

Ross, M., & Buehler, R. (1994). Creative remembering. In U. Neisser & R. Fivush (Eds.), *The remembering self.* New York: Cambridge University Press.

Rotter, J. B. (1954). *Social learning and clinical psychology.* Englewood Cliffs, NJ: Prentice-Hall.

Rotter, J. B. (1966). Generalized expectancies for internal versus external control of reinforcement. *Psychological Monographs, 80* (1, Whole No. 609).

Rotter, J. B. (1982). *The development and application of social learning theory: Selected papers.* New York: Praeger.

Rotter, J. B. (1990). Internal versus external control of reinforcement: A case history of a variable. *American Psychologist, 45,* 489–493.

Rovee-Collier, C. K. (1987). Learning and memory in infancy. In J. D. Osofsky (Ed.), *Handbook of infant development* (2nd ed.). New York: Wiley.

Rovee-Collier, C. K. (1993). The capacity for long-term memory in infancy. *Current Directions in Psychological Science, 2,* 130–135.

Rovee-Collier, C., Borza, M. A., Adler, S. A., & Boller, K. (1993). Infants' eyewitness testimony: Effects of postevent information on a prior memory representation. *Memory and Cognition, 21,* 267–279.

Rowe, D. C. (1997). Genetics, temperament, and personality. In R. Hogan, J. Johnson, & S. Briggs (Eds.), *Handbook of personality psychology* (pp. 367–386). San Diego, CA: Academic Press.

Roy, A., DeJong, J., Lamparski, D., Adinoff, B., George, T., Moore, V., Garnett, D., Kerich, M., & Linnoila, M. (1991). Mental disorders among alcoholics: Relationship to age of onset and cerebrospinal fluid neuropeptides. *Archives of General Psychiatry, 48*, 423–427.

Rozin, P. (1991). The importance of social factors in understanding the acquisition of food habits. In E. D. Capaldi, & T. L. Powley (Eds.), *Taste, experience, and feeding*. Washington, DC: American Psychological Association.

Rozin, P. (1996). Towards a psychology of food and eating: From motivation to module to model to marker, morality, meaning, and metaphor. *Current Directions in Psychological Science*, 5, 18–24.

Rubin, G. (1984). Thinking sex: Notes for a radical theory of the politics of sexuality. In C. S. Vance (Ed.), *Pleasure and danger: Exploring female sexuality* (pp. 267–319). Boston: Routledge & Kegan Paul.

Rubin, R. B. (1981). Ideal traits and terms of address for male and female college professors. *Journal of Personality and Social Psychology, 41*, 966–974.

Rue, W., & Abarbanel, K. (1997). *The dollar bill knows no sex: Lessons in life and money.* New York: McGraw-Hill.

Rushton, J. P., & Ankney, C. D. (1995). Brain size matters: A reply to Peters. *Canadian Journal of Experimental Psychology, 49*, 562–569.

Russell, J. A. (1991). Culture and the categorization of emotion. *Psychological Bulletin, 110*, 426–450.

Russell, J. A. (1994). Is there universal recognition of emotion from facial expression? A review of the cross-cultural studies. *Psychological Bulletin, 115*, 102–141.

Russell, M. J., Switz, G. M., & Thompson, K. (1980). Olfactory influence on the human menstrual cycle. *Pharmacology, Biochemistry and Behavior, 13*, 737–738.

Russo, N. F. (1985). *A women's mental health agenda*. Washington, DC: American Psychological Association.

Russo, N. F. (1992). Psychological aspects of unwanted pregnancy and its resolution. In J. D. Butler & D. F. Walbert (Eds.), *Abortion, medicine, and the law*, (4th ed., pp. 593–626). New York: Facts on File Publications.

Russo, N. F., & Green, B. L. (1993). Women and mental health. In F. L. Denmark & M. A. Paludi. (Eds.), *Psychology of women: A handbook of issues and theories* (pp. 379–436). Westport, CT: Greenwood Press.

Russo, N. F., Kelly, R. M., & Deacon, M. (1991). Gender and success-related attributions: Beyond individualistic conceptions of achievement. *Sex Roles, 9*, 331–351.

Russo, N. F., & O'Connell, A. N. (1992). Women in psychotherapy: Selected contributions. In D. Freedheim (Ed.), *History of psychotherapy: A century of change* (pp. 493–527). Washington, DC: American Psychological Association.

Rutter, M., & Garmezy, N. (1983). Developmental psychopathology. In E. M. Hetherington (Ed.), *Socialization, personality and social development*. New York: Wiley.

Rychlak, J. F. (1997). *In defense of human consciousness*. Washington, DC: American Psychological Association.

Saccuzzo, D. P., Johnson, N. E., & Russell, G. (1992). Verbal versus performance IQs for gifted African-American, Caucasian, Filipino, and Hispanic children. *Psychological Assessment, 4*, 239–244.

Sacks, O. (1987). *The man who mistook his wife for a hat and other clinical tales*. New York: Harper & Row.

Sacks, O. (1995, January 9). Prodigies. *The New Yorker*, pp. 44–65.

Sadik, N. (1992). World population continues to rise. In O. Johnson (Ed.), *Information please almanac: 1992* (45th edition; pp. 131–32). Boston: Houghton Mifflin.

Sadker, M., & Sadker, D. (1994). *Failing at fairness: How America's schools cheat girls*. New York: Scribner's.

Samelson, F. (1988). Struggle for scientific authority: The reception of Watson's behaviorism, 1913–1920. In J. L. T. Benjamin (Ed.), *A history of psychology: Original sources and contemporary research* (pp. 407–423). New York: McGraw-Hill.

Samuels, S. H., Dahl, P., & Archwamety, T. (1974). Effect of hypothesis/test training on reading skill. *Journal of Educational Psychology, 66*, 835–844.

Sandler, I. N. & Barrera, M. (1989). Community psychology. In W. L. Gregory & W. J. Burroughs (Eds.), *Introduction to applied psychology* (pp. 242–274). Glenview, IL: Scott, Foresman & Co.

Santee, R. T., & Jackson, S. E. (1982). Identity implications of conformity: Sex differences in normative and attributional judgments. *Social Psychology Quarterly, 45*, 121–125.

Santee, R. T., & Maslach, C. (1982). To agree or not to agree: Personal dissent amid social pressure to conform. *Journal of Personality and Social Psychology, 42*, 690–700.

Sapir, E. (1921). *Language: An introduction to the study of speech*. New York: Harcourt, Brace and World.

Sapir, E. (1929). The status of linguistics as a science. *Language, 5*, 207–214.

Sarafino, E. P. (1994). *Health psychology: Biopsychosocial interactions* (2nd ed.). New York: John Wiley.

Sartorius, N., Jablensky, A., & Shapiro, R. (1978). Cross-cultural differences in the short-term prognosis of schizophrenic psychoses. *Schizophrenia Bulletin, 4*, 102–112.

Saveth, E. (1948). *American historians and European immigrants*. New York: Columbia University Press.

Savin-Williams, R. C. (1990). *Gay and lesbian youth: Expressions of identity*. New York: Hemisphere Publishing Company.

Sayette, M. A., & Wilson, G. T. (1991). Intoxication and exposure to stress: Effects of temporal patterning. *Journal of Abnormal Psychology, 100*, 56–62.

Scarr, S. (1987). Distinctive environments depend on genotypes. *Behavior and Brain Sciences, 10*, 38–39.

Scarr, S., & McCartney, K. (1983). How people make their own environments: A theory of genotype environment effects. *Child Development, 54*, 424–435.

Scarr, S., & Weinberg, R. A. (1976). IQ test performance of black children adopted by white families. *American Psychologist, 31*, 726–739.

Schachter, S. (1971). Some extraordinary facts about obese humans and rats. *American Psychologist, 26*, 129–144.

Schachter, S. (1982). Recidivism and self-cure of smoking and obesity. *American Psychologist, 37*, 436–444.

Schachter, S., & Rodin, J. (1974). *Obese humans and rats*. Potomac, MD: Erlbaum.

Schachter, S., & Singer, J. E. (1962). Cognitive, social and physiological determinants of emotional state. *Psychological Review, 69*, 379–399.

Schachter, S., & Singer, J. E. (1979). Comments on the Maslach and Marshall-Zimbardo experiments. *Journal of Personality and Social Psychology, 37*, 989–995.

Schaie, K. W. (1965). A general model of the study of developmental problems. *Psychological Bulletin, 64*, 92–107.

Schaie, K. W. (1989). The hazards of cognitive aging. *Gerontologist, 29*(4), 484–493.

Schaie, K. W. (1990). The optimization of cognitive functioning in old age: Predictions based on cohort-sequential and longitudinal data. In P. B. Baltes & M. M. Baltes (Eds.), *Longitudinal research and the study of successful (optimal) aging*. Cambridge, Eng.: Cambridge University Press.

Schaie, K., & Strother, C. (1968). A cross-sequential study of age changes in cognitive behavior. *Psychological Bulletin, 70*, 671–680.

Schaie, K. W., & Willis, S. (1986). Can declines in intellectual functioning be reversed? *Developmental Psychology, 22*, 223–32.

Scheier, M. F., & Carver, C. S. (1987). Dispositional optimism and physical well-being: The influence of generalized outcome expectancies in health. *Journal of Personality, 55*, 169–210.

Scherwitz, L. W., Perkins, L. L., Chesney, M. A., & Hughes, J. R. (1991). Cook-Medley Hostility Scale and subsets: Relationship to demographic and psychosocial characteristics in young adults in the CARDIA study. *Psychosomatic Medicine, 53*, 36–49.

Schiffman, S. S., & Erickson, R. P. (1980). The issue of primary tastes versus a taste continuum. *Neuroscience and Biobehavioral Reviews, 4*, 109–117.

Schildkraut, J. J., Green, A. I., & Mooney, J. J. (1985). Affective disorders: Biochemical aspects. In H. I. Kaplan & J. Sadock (Eds.), *Comprehensive textbook of psychiatry*. Baltimore: Williams & Wilkins.

Schneider, D.J., Hastorf, A.H., & Ellsworth, P.C. (1979). *Person perception* (2nd ed.). Reading, MA: Addison-Wesley.

Schneider, S. G., Taylor, S. E., Hammen, C., Kemeny, M. E., & Dudley, J. (1991). Factors influencing suicide intent in gay and bisexual suicide ideators: Differing models for men with and without human immunodeficiency virus. *Journal of Personality and Social Psychology, 61*, 776–778.

Schoenborn, C. A., & Horm, J. (1993, November 4). Negative moods as correlates of smoking and heavier drinking: Implications for health promotion. *Advance Data from Vital and Health Statistics*, (236), 1–16.

Schultz, R., & Curnow, C. (1988). Peak performance and age among superathletes: Track and field, swimming, baseball, tennis, and golf. *Journal of Gerontology, 43*, 113–120.

Schuster, C., & Ashburn, S. (1986). *The process of human development* (2nd ed.). Boston: Little Brown.

Schwartz, B., & Robbins, S. J. (1995). *Psychology of learning and behavior*. (pp. 234–240). New York: Norton.

Schwartz, G. E., Fair, P. L., Salt, P., Mandel, M. R., & Klerman, G. I. (1976). Facial muscle patterning to affective imagery in depressed and nondepressed subjects. *Signs, 192*, 489–491.

Schwartz, S. H. (1990). Individualism and collectivism: Critique and proposed refinements. *Journal of Cross-Cultural Psychology, 21* (2), 139–157.

Sears, R. R., Maccoby, E. E., & Levin, H. (1957). *Patterns of attachment*. Evanston, IL: Row, Peterson.

Sechzer, J. A., Rabinowitz, V. C., Denmark, F. L., McGinn, M. F., Weels. B. M., & Wilkens, C. L. (1994). Sex and gender bias in animal research and in clinical studies of cancer, cardiovascular disease, and depression. *Annals of the New York Academy of Sciences, 736*, 21–48.

Seeman, J. (1965). Self-exploration in client-centered therapy. In B. B. Wolman (Ed.), *Handbook of clinical psychology*. New York: McGraw-Hill.

Segal, M. H., Campbell, D. T., & Herskovits, M. J. (1966). *The influence of culture on visual perception*. Indianapolis, IN: Bobbs-Merrill.

Segal, N. L. (1993). Twin, sibling, and adoption methods: Tests of evolutionary hypotheses. *American Psychologist, 48*, 943–956.

Segall, M. H. (1994). A cross-cultural research contribution to unraveling the nativist/empiricist controversy. In W. J. Lonner & R. Malpass (Eds.), *Psychology and culture* (pp. 1354–1380). Boston: Allyn & Bacon.

Segall, M. H., Campbell, D. T., & Herskovits, M. J. (1966). *The influence of culture on visual perception*. Indianapolis, IN: Bobbs-Merrill.

Sekuler, R., & Blake, R. (1990). *Perception* (2nd ed.). New York: McGraw-Hill.

Selfridge, O. (1959). Pandemonium: A paradigm for learning. In *Symposium on the mechanization of thought processes*. London: Her Majesty's Stationary Office.

Selfridge, O., & Neisser, U. (1960). Pattern recognition by machine. *Scientific American, 203*, 60–80.

Seligman, M. E. P. (1971). Phobias and preparedness. *Behavior Therapy, 2*, 307–320.

Seligman, M. E. P. (1975). *Helplessness: On depression, development, and death*. San Francisco: Freeman.

Seligman, M. E. P. (1991). *Learned optimism: The skill to conquer life's obstacles, large and small*. New York: Random House.

Seligman, M. E. P., & Maier, S. F. (1967). Failure to escape traumatic shock. *Journal of Experimental Psychology, 74*, 1–9.

Sell, R. L., Wells, J.A., & Wypij, D. (1995). The prevalence of homosexual behavior and attraction in the United States, the United Kingdom, and France: Results of national population-based samples. *Archives of Sexual Behavior 24* (3), 235–248.

Sells, L. W. (1980). The mathematics filter and the education of women and minorities. In L. H. Fox, L. Brody, & D. Tobin (Eds.), *Women and the mathematical mystique* (pp. 66–75). Baltimore: Johns Hopkins University Press.

Selman, R. L. (1981). The development of interpersonal competence: The role of understanding in conduct. *Developmental Review, 1*, 401–402.

Selye, H. (1956). *The stress of life*. New York: McGraw-Hill.

Selye, H. (1974). *Stress without distress*. New York: HarperCollins.

Selye, H. (1976). *Stress in health and disease*. Reading, MA: Butterworth.

Selye, H. (1980). The stress concept today. In I. L. Kutash, L. B. Schlesinger, & Associated (Eds.), *Handbook of stress and anxiety*. San Francisco: Jossey-Bass.

Serfass, R. C., & Gerberich, S. G. (1984). Exercise for optimal health: Strategies and motivational considerations. *Preventive Medicine, 13*, 79–99.

Service, R. F. (1994). Will a new type of drug make memory-making easier. *Science, 266*, 218–219.

Shader, R. I., Greenblatt, D. J., & Balter, M. B. (1991). Appropriate use and regulatory control of benzodiazepines. *Journal of Clinical Pharmacology, 31*, 781–784.

Shadish, W. R., Montgomery, L. M., Wilson, P., Wilson, M. R., Bright, I., & Okwumbaua, T. (1993). Effects of family and marital psychotherapies: A meta-analysis. *Journal of Consulting and Clinical Psychology, 61*, 992–1002.

Shafer, D. (1993). *Developmental psychology: Childhood and adolescence* (3rd ed.). Belmont, CA: Brooks Cole.

Shafer, D. R. (1996). *Developmental psychology: Childhood and adolescence* (4th ed.). Pacific Grove, CA: Brooks/Cole Publishing Company.

Shapiro, C. M., Bortz, R., Mitchell, D., Bartel, P., & Jooste, P. (1981). Slow-wave sleep: A recovery period after exercise. *Science, 214*, 1253–1254.

Shapiro, D. A. (1985). Recent applications of meta-analysis in clinical research. *Clinical Psychology Review, 5*, 13–34.

Shapiro, R. (1991). *The human blueprint: The race to unlock the secrets of our genetic script*. New York: St. Martin's Press.

Shapiro, T. (1989). Our changing science. *Journal of the American Psychoanalytic Association, 37*, 3–6.

Shatz, C. (1992). The developing brain. *Scientific American, 9*, 61–67.

Shaughnessy, J. J. (1976). Persistence of the spacing effect in free recall under varying incidental learning conditions. *Memory and Cognition, 4*, 369–377.

Shaw, G. A. (1992) : Hyperactivity and creativity: The tacit dimension. *Bulletin of the Psychomonic Society, 30*, 157–160.

Shaw, J. S., III (1996). Increases in eyewitness confidence resulting from postevent questioning. *Journal of Experimental Psychology: Applied, 2*, 126–146.

Sheldon, W. (1940). *The varieties of human physique*. New York: Harper & Row.

Sheridan, T. B., & Zeltzer, D. (1993, October). Virtual reality check. *Technology Review*, pp. 20–28.

Sherif, C. W. (1979). Bias in psychology. In J. A. Sherman & E. T. Beck (Eds.), *The prism of sex: Essays in the sociology of knowledge* (pp. 93–134). Madison, WI: University of Wisconsin Press.

Sherif, M. (1966). *In common predicament: Social psychology of intergroup conflict and cooperation*. Boston: Houghton Mifflin.

Sherif, M., Harvey, O. J., White, B. J., Hood, W. R., & Sherif, C. W.

(1961). *Intergroup conflict and cooperation: The robber's cave experiment*. Norman, OK: University of Oklahoma Press.

Sherman, J. A., & Fennema, E. (1977). The study of mathematics by high school girls and boys: Related variables. *American Educational Research Journal, 14*, 159–168.

Shields, S. A. (1975a). Functionalism, Darwinism, and the psychology of women. *American Psychologist*, 30, 739–754.

Shields, S. A. (1975b). Ms. pilgrim's progress, the contribution of Leta Stetter Hollingworth to the psychology of women. *American Psychologist, 30*, 852–857.

Shimamura, A. P., & Squire, L. R. (1987). A neuropsychological study of fact memory and source amnesia. *Journal of Experimental Psychology: Learning, Memory, and Cognition, 13*, 464–473.

Sholnick, N. J., Ackerman, S. H., Hofer, M. A., & Werner, H. (1980). Vertical transmission of acquired ulcer susceptibility in the rat. *Science*, 1161–1163.

Shortliffe, E. H., Buchanan, B. G., & Feigenbaum, E. A. (1979). Knowledge engineering for medical decision-making: A review of computer based decision-aids. *Proceedings of the IEEE, 67*, 1207–1224.

Shostrom, E. L. (1963). *Personal orientation inventory*. San Diego, CA: Educational and Industrial Testing Service.

Shweder, R. A., & LeVine, R. A. (Eds.). (1984). *Culture theory: Essays on mind, self, and emotion*. Cambridge, Eng.: Cambridge University Press.

Shweder, R. A., & Sullivan, M. A. (1993). Cultural psychology: Who needs it? *Annual Review of Psychology, 44*, 497–523.

Siegal, S. (1977). Morphine tolerance acquisition as an associative process. *Journal of Experimental Psychology: Amimal Behavior Processes, 3*, 1–13.

Siegel, A. U. (1987). Are sons and daughters treated differently by fathers than by mothers? *Developmental Review, 7*, 183–209.

Siegel, S. (1979). The role of conditioning in drug tolerance and addiction. In J. D. Keehn (Ed.), *Psychopathology in animals*. New York: Academic Press.

Siegel, S., Hinson, R. E., Krank, M. D., & McCully, J. (1982). Heroin "overdose" death: Contributions of drug-associated environmental cues. *Science, 216*, 436–437.

Siegler, R. S. (1983). Five generalizations about cognitive development. *American Psychologist, 38*, 263–277.

Siegler, R. S., & Crowley, K. (1991). The microgenetic method: A direct means for studying cognitive development. *American Psychologist, 46*, 606–620.

Sigman, M., & Sena, R. (1993). Pretend play in high-risk and developmentally delayed children. In M. H. Bornstein & A. W. O'Reilly (Eds.), *The role of play in the development of thought* (New Directions for Child Development, No. 59). San Francisco: Jossey-Bass.

Silberman, E. K., & Weingarten, H. (1986). Hemispheric lateralization of functions related to emotion. *Brain and Cognition, 5*, 322–353.

Silberstein, L. R., Mishkind, M. E., Striegel-Moore, R. H., Timko, C., & Rodin, J. (1989). Men and their bodies: A comparison of homosexual and heterosexual men. *Psychosomatic Medicine, 51*, 337–346.

Silva, A. J., & Giese, K. P. (in press). Gene targetting: A novel window into the biology of learning and memory. In J. L. Martinez, Jr., & R. P. Kesner (Eds.), *Neurobiology of learning and memory*. Orlando, FL: Academic Press

Silverman, L. H., Ross, D. L., Adler, J. M., & Lustig, D. A. (1978). Simple research paradigm for demonstrating subliminal psychodynamic activation: Effects of Oedipal stimuli on dart-throwing accuracy in college males. *Journal of Abnormal Psychology, 87*, 341–357.

Simon, H. A. (1980). Lessons for AI from human problem solving. *Computer Science Research Review*. Pittsburgh, PA: Carnegie-Mellon University.

Simon, H. A. (1992). What is an "explanation" of behavior? *Psychological Science, 3* (3), 150–161.

Simon, L., Greenberg, J., & Brehm, J. (1995). Trivialization: The forgotten mode of dissonance reduction. *Journal of Personality and Social Psychology, 68*, 247–260.

Simpson, A. (1990). Influence of attachment styles on romantic relationships. *Journal of Personality and Social Psychology, 59*, 971–980.

Simpson, J. L. (1993). Genetic causes of spontaneous abortion. In C. Lin, M. S. Verp, & R. E. Sabbagha (Eds.), *The high-risk fetus: Pathophysiology, diagnosis, management*. New York: Springer-Verlag.

Singh, D. (1993). Adaptive significance of female physical attractiveness: Role of waist-to-hip ratio. *Journal of Personality and Social Psychology, 65*, 293–307.

Siqueland, E. R., & Lipsitt, L. P. (1966). Conditioned head-turning in newborns. *Journal of Experimental Child Psychology, 3*, 356–376.

Siscovick D. S., Weiss, N. S., Fletcher, R. H., & Lasky, T. (1984). The incidence of primary cardiac arrest during vigorous exercise. *New England Journal of Medicine, 311*, 874–877.

Skinner, B. F. (1938). *The behavior of organisms*. New York: Appleton-Century-Crofts.

Skrypnek, B. J., & Snyder, M. (1982). On the self-perpetuating nature of stereotypes about women and men. *Journal of Experimental Social Psychology, 18*, 277–291.

Slamecka, N. J., & Graf, P. (1978). The generation effect: Delineation of a phenomenon. *Journal of Experimental Psychology: Human Learning and Memory, 4*, 592–604.

Sleek, S. (1994, December). Psychology takes the fear out of flying. *APA Monitor*, pp. 6–7.

Sloane, R. B., Staples, F. R., Cristol, A. H., Yorkston, N. J., & Whipple, K. (1975). *Psychotherapy versus behavior therapy*. Cambridge, MA: Harvard University Press.

Slobin, D. I. (1971). *Psycholinguistics*. Glenview, IL: Scott, Foresman.

Smith, C. A., & Lazarus, R. S. (1990). Emotion and adaptation. In L. A. Pervin (Ed.), *Handbook of personality: Theory and research* (pp. 609–637). New York: Guilford.

Smith, C. P. (Ed.). (1992). *Motivation and personality: Handbook of thematic content analyses*. New York: Cambridge University Press.

Smith, D. C., Jr. (1986). Wrongful birth, wrongful life: Emerging theories of liability. In J. D. Butler & D. F. Walbret (Eds.), *Abortion, medicine, and the law* (pp. 178–194). New York: Facts on File.

Smith, M. L., & Glass, G. V. (1977). Meta-analysis of psychotherapy outcome studies. *American Psychologist, 32*, 752–760.

Smith, M. L., Glass, G. V., & Miller, T. I. (1980). *The benefits of psychotherapy*. Baltimore: Johns Hopkins University Press.

Smith, P. B., & Bond, M. H. (1994). *Social psychology across cultures: Analysis and perspectives*. Boston: Allyn & Bacon.

Smith, P. B., Misumi, J., Tayeb, M., Peterson, M., & Bond, M. H. (1989). On the generality of leadership style measures across cultures. *Journal of Occupational Psychology, 62*, 97–109.

Smith, R. J. (1978). *The psychopath in society*. New York: Academic Press.

Smith, S. M. (1982). Enhancement of recall using multiple environmental contexts during learning. *Memory and Cognition, 10*, 405–412.

Smith, S. M., & Blankenship, S. E. (1991). Incubation and the persistence of incubation in problem solving. *American Journal of Psychology, 104*, 61–87.

Smith, S. M., & Vela, E. (1992). Environmental context-dependent eyewitness recognition. *Applied Cognitive Psychology, 6*, 125–139.

Smith, S. M., Ward, T. B., & Schumacher, J. S. (1993). Constraining effects of examples in a creative generation task. *Memory and Cognition, 21*, 837–845.

Smith, T. W. (1989). Interactions, transactions, and the Type A pattern: Additional avenues in the search for coronary-prone behavior. In A. W. Siegman & T. M. Dembroski (Eds.), *In search for coronary-prone behavior* (pp. 91–116). Hillsdale, NJ: Erlbaum.

Smith, T. W. (1990). Adult sexual behavior in 1989: Number of partners, frequency of intercourse, and risk of AIDS. *Family Planning Perspectives, 23* (3), 102–107.

Smith, T. W. (1992). Hostility and health: Current status of a psychosomatic hypothesis. *Health Psychology, 11*, 139–150.

Snodgrass, S. E. (1985). Women's intuition: The effects of subordinate role on interpersonal sensitivity. *Journal of Personality and Social Psychology, 49*, 146–155.

Snow, J. P., & Harris, M. B. (1989). Disordered eating in Southwestern Pueblo Indians and Hispanics. *Journal of Adolescence, 12*, 329–336.

Snyder, M. (1992). Motivational foundations of behavioral confirmation. *Advances in Experimental Social Psychology, 25*, 67–114.

Snyder, M., Tanke, E. D., & Berscheid, E. (1977). Social perception and interpersonal behavior: On the self-fulfilling nature of social stereotypes. *Journal of Personality and Social Psychology, 35*, 656–666.

Snyder, M. L., & Uranowitz, S. W. (1978). Reconstructing the past: Some cognitive consequences of person perception. *Journal of Personality and Social Psychology, 36*, 941–950.

Solomon, R. L. (1980). The opponent-process theory of acquired motivation: The costs of pleasure and the benefits of pain. *American Psychologist, 35*, 691–712.

Solomon, R. L., & Corbit, J. D. (1973). An opponent-process theory of motivation: II. Cigarette addiction. *Journal of Abnormal Psychology, 83*, 158–171.

Solomon, R. L., & Corbit, J. D. (1974). An opponent-process theory of motivation: I. Temporal dynamics of affect. *Psychological Review, 81*, 119–45.

Sommer, R. (1974). *Tightspaces*. Englewood Cliffs, NJ: Prentice-Hall.

Spangler, W. D. (1992). Validity of questionnaire and TAT measures of need for achievement: Two meta-analyses. *Psychological Bulletin, 112*, 140–154.

Spearman, C. (1927). *The abilities of man*. London: Macmillan.

Speisman, I. C., Lazarus, R. S., Mordkoff, A., & Davison, L. (1964). Experimental demonstration of stress based on ego-defense theory. *Journal of Abnormal and Social Psychology, 68*, 367–380.

Spellman, B. A., & Holyoak, K. J. (1992). If Saddam is Hitler then who is George Bush? Analogical mapping between systems of social roles. *Journal of Personality and Social Psychology, 62*, 913–933.

Spence, J. T. (1983). *Achievement and achievement motives*. San Francisco: Freeman.

Spencer, D. G., Yaden, S., & Lal, H. (1988). Behavioral and physiological detection of classically-conditioned blood pressure reduction. *Psychopharmacology*, 25–28.

Sperling, G. (1960). The information available in brief visual presentations. *Psychological Monographs, 74* (Whole No. 498).

Sperry, R. W. (1968). Hemisphere deconnection and unity in conscious experience. *American Psychologist, 23*, 723–733.

Sperry, R. W. (1974). Lateral specialization in the surgically separated hemispheres. In F. O. Schmitt & F. G. Worden (Eds.), *The neurosciences: Third study program*. Cambridge, MA: MIT Press.

Sperry, R. W. (1982). Some effects of disconnecting the cerebral hemispheres. *Science, 217*, 1223–1226.

Sperry, R. W. (1993). The impact and promise of the cognitive revolution. *American Psychologist, 48*, 878–885.

Spiegel, H., & Spiegel, D. (1978). *Trance and treatment: Clinical uses of hypnosis*. New York: Basic Books.

Spielberger, C. D., & Diaz-Guerrero, R. (1983). Cross-cultural anxiety: An overview. In C. D. Spielberger & R. Diaz-Guerrero (Eds.). *Cross-cultural anxiety* (Vol. 2). Washington, DC: Hemisphere Publishing.

Spitz, R. A. (1945). Hospitalism. An inquiry into the genesis of psychiatric conditions in early childhood. In O. Fenichel et al. (Eds.), *The psychoanalytic study of the child* (Vol. 1). New York: International Universities Press.

Spitzer, R. L. (1975). On pseudoscience in science, logic in remission and psychiatric diagnosis: A critique of "On being sane in insane places." *Journal of Abnormal Psychology, 84*, 271–284.

Spitzer, R., Skodal, A., Gibbon, M., & Williams, J. (1983). *Psychopathology: A case book*. New York: McGraw-Hill.

Spock, B. (1957). *Baby and child care*. New York: Simon and Schuster.

Springer, S. P., & Deutsch, G. (1985). *Left brain, right brain* (Rev. ed.). New York: Freeman.

Squire, L. R. (1987). *Memory and brain*. New York: Oxford University Press.

Squire, L. R. (1992). Memory and the hippocampus: A synthesis from findings with rats, monkeys, and humans. *Psychological Review, 99*, 195–231.

Squire, L. R., & Butters, N. (1992). *Neuropsychology of memory* (2nd ed.). New York: Guilford Press.

Squire, L. R., Knowlton, B., & Mussen, G. (1993). The structure and organization of memory. *Annual Review of Psychology, 44*, 453–495.

Sroufe, L. A. (1979). Socioemotional development. In J. D. Osofsky (Ed.), *Handbook of infant development*. New York: Wiley.

Sroufe, L. A., Cooper, R. G., DeHart, G. B., & Marshall, M. (1992). *Child development: Its nature and course*. New York: McGraw-Hall.

Staats, A. W., & Staats, C. (1958). Attitudes established by classical conditioning. *Journal of Abnormal and Social Psychology, 57*, 37–40.

Stamler, J., Dyer, A. R., Shakelle, R. B., Neaton, J., & Stamler, R. (1993). Relationship of baseline major risk factors to coronary and all-cause mortality, and to longevity: Findings from long-term follow-up of cohorts. *Cardiology, 82*, 191–192.

Staples, R. (1987). Social structure in black female life. *Journal of Black Studies, 17*, 267–286.

Starr, C., & Taggart, R. (1995). *Biology: The unity and diversity of life* (7th ed.). Belmont, CA: Wadsworth.

Staw, B. M., & Ross, J. (1989). Understanding behavior in escalation situations. *Science, 246*, 216–230.

Steele, C. (1988). The psychology of self-affirmation: Sustaining the integrity of the self. In L. Berkowitz (Ed), *Advances in Experimental Social Psychology* (Vol. 21, pp. 261–302). New York: Academic Press.

Steele, C. M., & Josephs, R. A. (1990). Alcohol myopia: Its prized and dangerous effects. *American Psychologist, 45*, 921–933.

Steele, R. E. (1978). Relationship of race, sex, class, and social mobility to depression in normal adults. *Journal of Social Psychology, 104*, 37–47.

Stein, A. H., & Bailey, M. M. (1973). The socialization of achievement orientation in females. *Psychological Bulletin, 80*, 345–366.

Stein, P. J. (1989). The diverse world of single adults. In J. M. Henslin (Ed.), *Marriage and family in a changing society* (3rd ed.). New York: Free Press.

Steinman, L. (1993, September). Autoimmune disease. *Scientific American*, 107–114.

Stelmack, R. M. (1990). Biological bases of extraversion: Psychophysiological evidence. *Journal of Personality, 58*, 293–311.

Stengel, E. (1961). Problems of nosology and nomenclature in the mental disorders. In J. Zubin (Ed.), *Field studies in the mental disorders*. New York: Grune & Stratton.

Sternberg, E. M., & Gold, P. W. (1997). The mind-body interaction in disease [Special issue]. *Scientific American, 7*(1), 8–15.

Sternberg, R. J. (1977). *Intelligence, information processing, and analogical reasoning: The componential analysis of human abilities.* Hillsdale, NJ: Erlbaum.

Sternberg, R. J. (1985). *Beyond IQ: A triarchic theory of human intelligence.* New York: Cambridge University Press.

Sternberg, R. J. (1986). Inside intelligence. *American Scientist, 74,* 137–143.

Sternberg, R. J. (1990). *Metaphors of the mind: Conceptions of the nature of intelligence.* New York: Cambridge University Press.

Sternberg, R. J., & Lubart, T. I. (1991). An investment theory of creativity and its development. *Human Development, 34,* 1–31.

Sternberg, R. J., & Wagner, R. K. (Eds.) (1986). *Practical intelligence: Origins of competence in the everyday world.* New York: Cambridge University Press.

Sternberg, R. J., Wagner, R. K., Williams, W. M., & Horvath, J. A. (1995). Testing common sense. *American Psychologist, 50,* 912–927.

Sternberg, S. (1969). Memory-scanning: Mental processes revealed by reaction time experiments. *Acta Psychologica, 30,* 276–315.

Stevens, A., & Coupe, P. (1978). Distortions in judged spatial relations. *Cognitive Psychology, 10,* 422–437.

Steveson, H. W., & Stigler, J. W. (1992). *The learning gap.* New York: Summit Books.

Stewart, A. J., & Chester, N. L. (1982). The exploration of sex differences in human social motives: Achievement, affiliation & power. In A. J. Stewart (Ed.), *Motivation and society* (pp. 172–218). San Francisco: Jossey-Bass.

Stewart, K. (1969). Dream theory in Malaya. In C. Tart (Ed.), *Altered states of consciousness: A book of readings.* New York: Wiley.

Stewart, V. M. (1973). Tests of the "carpentered world" hypothesis by race and environment in American and Zambia. *International Journal of Psychology, 8,* 83–94.

Stigler, J. W., Shweder, R. A., & Herdt, G. (Eds.). (1990). *Cultural psychology: Essays on comparative human development.* Cambridge, Eng.: Cambridge University Press.

Stipek, D., Gralinski, H., & Kopp, C. (1990). Self-concept development in the toddler years. *Developmental Psychology, 26,* 972–977.

Stokols, D., Ohlig, W., & Resnick, S. M. (1978). Perception of residential crowding, classroom experiences, and student health. *Human Ecology, 6,* 33–57.

Stone, M. H. (1990). Abuse and abusiveness in borderline personality disorder. In P. S. Links (Ed.), *Family environment and borderline personality disorder.* Washington, DC: American Psychiatric Press.

Storms, M. D., & Nisbett, R. E. (1970). Insomnia and the attribution process. *Journal of Personality and Social Psychology, 2,* 319–328.

Strauss, M.A., Gelles, R. S., Steinmetz, S. (1980). *Behind closed doors: Violence in the American family.* Garden City, NY: Anchor/Doubleday.

Streingart, R. M., Packer, M., Hamm, P., Coglianese, M. E., Gersh, B., Geltman, E. M., Sollano, J., Kastz, S., Moy, L., Basta, L. L., Lewis, S. J., Gotlieb, S. S., Bernstein, V., McLwan, P., Jacobson, K., Brown, E. J., Kukin, M. L., Kantrowitz, N. E., & Pfeffer, M. A. (1991). Sex differences in the management of coronary artery disease. *New England Journal of Medicine, 325,* 226–230.

Strickland, B. R. (1965). The prediction of social action from a dimension of internal-external control. *Journal of Social Psychology, 66,* 353–358.

Strickland, B. R. (1984). This week's Citation Classic. *Current Contents, Social and Behavioral Sciences, 16*(5), 20.

Strickland, B. R. (1989). Internal-external control expectancies: From contingency to creativity. *American Psychologist, 44,* 1–12.

Striegel-Moore, R. H., Silberstein, L. R., & Rodin, J. (1986). Toward an understanding of risk factors for bulimia. *American Psychologist, 41,* 246–263.

Strong, S. R., Hills, H. J., Kilmartin, C. T., DeVries, H., Lanier, K., Nelson, B. N., Strickland, D., & Meyers, C. W. (1988). The dynamic relations among interpersonal behaviors: A test of complementarily and anticomplementarity. *Journal of Personality and Social Psychology, 54,* 798–810.

Stroop, J. R. (1935). Studies of interference in serial verbal reactions. *Journal of Experimental Psychology, 18,* 643–662.

Strupp, H. H. (1971). *Psychotherapy and the modification of abnormal behavior.* New York: McGraw-Hill.

Strupp, H. H. (1996). The tripartite model and the *Consumer Reports* study. *American Psychologist, 51,* 1017–1024.

Strupp, H. H., Fox, R. W., & Lessler, K. (1969). *Patients view their psychotherapy.* Baltimore: Johns Hopkins University Press.

Strupp, H. H., Wallach, M. S., Wogan, M., & Jenkins, J. W. (1963). Psychotherapists' assessment of former patients. *Journal of Nervous and Mental Disease, 137,* 222–230.

Stryker, M. P., & Sherk, H. (1975). Modification of cortical orientation selectivity in the cat by restricted visual experience: A reexamination. *Science, 190,* 904–906.

Subbotsky, E. V. (1993). *Foundations of the mind: Children's understanding of reality.* Cambridge, MA: Harvard University Press.

Substance Abuse and Mental Health Services Administration. (1993). National Household Survey on Drug Abuse: Population Estimates, 1992 (DHHS Publication No. SMA 93–2053). Rockville, MD: Substance Abuse and Mental Health Services Administration.

Sue, D. W. (1973). Ethnic identity: The impact of two cultures on the psychological development of Asians in America. In S. Sue & N. Wagner (Eds.), *Asian-Americans: Psychological Perspectives* (pp. 140–149). Palo Alto, CA: Science and Behavior Books.

Sue, D. W. (1992). The challenge of multiculturalism. *American Counselor,* 6–14.

Sue, D. W., & Sue, D. (1990). *Counseling the culturally different: Theory and practice.* New York: Wiley.

Sue, D. W., Ivey, A. E., & Pedersen, P. B. (1996). *A theory of multicultural counseling and therapy.* Pacific Grove, CA: Brooks Cole.

Suedfeld, P., & Coren, S. (1989). Perceptual isolation, sensory deprivation, and rest: Moving introductory psychology texts out of the 1950s. *Canadian Psychology, 30,* 17–29.

Suedfield, P., & Kristeller, J. L. (1982). Stimulus reduction as a technique in health psychology. *Health Psychology, 1,* 337–357.

Suedfeld, P., Metcalfe, J., & Bluck, S. (1987). Enhancement of scientific creativity by flotation REST (Restricted Environmental Stimulation Technique). *Journal of Environmental Psychology, 7,* 219–231.

Suinn, R. M. (1982). Intervention with Type A behaviors. *Journal of Consulting and Clinical Psychology, 50,* 933–949.

Sullivan, H. S. (1953). *The interpersonal theory of psychiatry.* New York: Norton.

Suls, J. (Ed.), *Social psychology of health and illness.* Hillsdale, NJ: Erlbaum.

Swaab, D. F., & Hofman, M. A. (1990). An enlarged suprachiasmatic nucleus in homosexual men. *Brain Research, 537,* 141.

Swets, J. A. (1992). The science of choosing the right decision threshold in high-stakes diagnostics. *American Psychologist, 47,* 522–532.

Swets, J. A., Pickett, R. M., Whitehead, S. F., Getty, D. J., Schnur, J. A., Swets, J. B., & Freeman, B. A. (1979). Assessment of diagnostic technologies. *Science, 205,* 753–760.

Swick, D., & Knight, R. T. (1997). Event-related potentials differentiate the effects of aging on word and nonword repetition in explicit and implicit memory tasks. *Journal of Experimental Psychology: Learning, Memory and Cognition, 23,* 123–142.

Symonds, D. (1993). The stuff that dreams aren't made of: Why wake-state and dream-state sensory experiences differ. *Cognition, 47,* 181–217.

Szasz, T. S. (1961). *The myth of mental illness.* New York: Harper & Row.

Szasz, T. S. (1963). *Law, liberty, and psychiatry*. New York: Macmillan.

Tajfel, H. (1969). Cognitive aspects of prejudice. *Journal of Social Issues, 25*, 79–97.

Tajfel, H. (1981). *Human groups and social categories*. Cambridge, Eng.: Cambridge University Press.

Tajfel, H. (Ed.). (1982). *Social identity and intergroup relations*. Cambridge, Eng.: Cambridge University Press.

Tajfel, H., Billig, M. G., Bundy, R. P., & Flament, C. (1971). Social categorization and intergroup behavior. *European Journal of Social Psychology, 1*, 149–178.

Tajfel, H., Flament, C., Billig, M., & Bundy, R. P. (1971). Social categorization and intergroup behavior. *European Journal of Social Psychology, 1*, 149–177.

Tajfel, H., & Turner, J. C. (1986). The social identity of intergroup behavior. In S. Worchel & W. G. Austin (Eds.), *Psychology of intergroup interactions* (2nd ed., pp. 7–24). Chicago: Nelson-Hall.

Talovic, S. A., Mednick, S. A., Schulsinger, F., & Falloon, I. R. H. (1981). Schizophrenia in high-risk subjects: Prognostic maternal characteristics. *Journal of Abnormal Psychology, 89*, 501–504.

Tamis-Lemonda, C. S., Bornstein, M. H., Cyphers, L., Toda, S., & Ogino, M. (1992). Language and play at one year: A comparison of toddlers and mothers in the United States and Japan. *International Journal of Behavioral Development, 15*, 19–42.

Tamminga, C. A., Thaker, G. K., & Buchanan, R. (1992). Limbic system abnormalities identified in schizophrenia using positron emission tomography with flurodeoxyglucose and neocortical alterations with deficit syndrome. *Archives of General Psychiatry, 49*, 522–531.

Tannen, D. (1990). *You just don't understand: Men and women in conversation*. New York: Morrow.

Tarrier, N., Barrowclough, C., Porceddu, K., & Fitzpatrick, E. (1994). The Salford Family Intervention Project: Relapse rates of schizophrenia at five and eight years. *British Journal of Psychiatry, 165*, 829–832.

Tart, C. (Ed.). (1969a). *Altered states of consciousness*. New York: Wiley.

Tart, C. (1969b). The "high" dream: A new state of consciousness. In C. Tart (Ed.), *Altered states of consciousness: A book of readings*. New York: Wiley.

Tart, C. (1971). *On being stoned: A psychological study of marijuana intoxication*. Palo Alto, CA: Science and Behavior Books.

Tart, C. (1975). *States of consciousness*. New York: Dutton.

Task Force on Promotion and Dissemination of Psychological Procedures. (1995). *The Clinical Psychologist, 48*, 3–22.

Taylor, R. E., & Richards, S. B. (1991). Patterns of intellectual differences of black, Hispanic, and white children. *Psychology in the Schools, 28*, 5–9.

Taylor, S. E. (1991). *Health psychology* (2nd ed.). New York: McGraw-Hill.

Taylor, S. E. (1995). *Health psychology* (3rd. ed.). New York: McGraw-Hill.

Taylor, S. E., & Brown, J. D. (1988). Illusion and well-being: A social psychological perspective on mental health. *Psychological Bulletin, 103*, 193–210.

Taylor, S. E., Lichtman, R. R., & Wood, J. V. (1984). Attributions, beliefs about control, and adjustment to breast cancer. *Journal of Personality and Social Psychology, 46*, 489–502.

Taylor, S. E., Peplau, L. A., & Sears, D. (1997). *Social psychology* (9th ed.). Englewood Cliffs, NJ: Prentice-Hall.

Tedeschi, J. T., & Felson, R. B. (1994). *Violence, aggression, and coercive actions*. Washington, DC: American Psychological Association.

Teicher, M. H., Glod, C., & Cole, J. O. (1990). Emergence of intense suicidal preoccupation during fluoxetine treatment. *American Journal of Psychiatry, 147*, 207–210.

Terman, L. (1916). *The measurement of intelligence*. Boston: Houghton Mifflin.

Terman, L. M., & Merrill, M. A. (1973). *Stanford-Binet Intelligence Scale: Manual for the Third Revision, Form L-M*. Boston: Houghton-Mifflin.

Terrell, F., Terrell, S., & Taylor, J. (1981). Effects of race of examiner and cultural mistrust on the WAIS performance of black students. *Journal of Counseling Psychology, 49*, 750–751.

Tesser, A. (1988). Toward a self-evaluation maintenance model of social behavior. In L. Berkowitz (Ed.), *Advances in experimental social psychology* (Vol. 21, pp. 181–227). New York: Academic Press.

Testa, T. J. (1975). Effects of similarity of location and temporal intensity pattern of conditioned and unconditioned stimuli on the acquisition of conditioned suppression in rats. *Journal of Experimental Psychology: Animal Behavior Processes, 1*, 114–121.

Thibaut, J. W., & Kelley, H. H. (1959). *The social psychology of groups*. New York: Wiley.

Thibodeau, R., & Aronson, E. (1992). Taking a closer look: Reasserting the role of the self-concept in disonance theory. *Personality and Social Psychology Bulletin, 18*, 591–602.

Thiel, A., Gottfried, H., & Hesse, F. W., (1993). Subclinical eating disorders in male athletes: A study of the low weight category in rowers and wrestlers. *Acta Psychiatrica Scandinavia, 88*, 259–265.

Thigpen, C. H., & Cleckley, H. M. (1957). *The three faces of Eve*. New York: McGraw-Hill.

Thoma, S. J., Rest, J. R., & Davison, M. L. (1991). Describing and testing a moderator of the moral judgment and action relationship. *Journal of Personality and Social Psychology, 61*, 659–669.

Thompson, J. (1995). Silencing the self: Depressive symptomatology and close relationships. *Psychology of Women Quarterly, 19*, 337–353.

Thorndyke, P. W. (1977). Cognitive structures in comprehension and memory of narrative discourse. *Cognitive Psychology, 9*, 77–110.

Thurstone, L. L. (1938). *Primary mental abilities*. Chicago: University of Chicago Press.

Tiefer, L. (1996). *Sex is not a natural act and other essays*. Boulder, CO: Westview Press.

Tinbergen, N. (1951). *The study of instinct*. London: Oxford University Press.

Tobin, S. A. (1971). Saying goodbye in Gestalt therapy. *Psychotherapy: Theory, Research, and Practice, 8*, 150–155.

Tolman, E. C., & Honzik, C. H. (1930). Introduction and removal of reward, and maze performance in rats. *University of California Publications in Psychology, 4*, 257–275.

Tomkins, S. S., & McCarter, R. (1964). What and where are the primary affects? Some evidence for a theory. *Perceptual and Motor Skills, 18*, 119–158.

Toner, I. J., & Smith, R. A. (1977). Age and overt verbalization in delayed maintenance behavior in children. *Journal of Experimental Child Psychology, 24*, 123–128.

Topper, M. D. (1987). The traditional Navajo medicine man: Therapist, counselor, and community leader. *Journal of Psychoanalytic Anthropology, 10*, 217–249.

Torrance, E. P. (1962). *Guiding creative talent*. Englewood Cliffs, NJ: Prentice-Hall.

Torrey, E. F., Bowler, A. E., Taylor, E. H. & Gottesman I. I. (1994). *Schizophrenia and manic-depressive disorder: The biological roots of mental illness as revealed by the landmark study of identical twins*. New York: Basic Books.

Travis, C. (1988). *Women and health psychology: Mental health issues*. Hillsdale, NJ: Erlbaum.

Trehub, S. E., Trainor, L. J., & Unyk, A. M. (1993). Music and speech processing in the first year of life. In H. W. Reese (Ed.), *Advances in child development and behavior* (Vol. 24). San Diego, CA: Academic Press.

Treiber, F. A., Davis, H., Musante, L., Raunikar, R. A., Strong, W. B.,

McCaffrey, F., Meeks, M. C., & Vandernoord, R. (1990). Ethnicity, gender, family history of myocardial infarction, and hemodynamic responses to laboratory stressors in children. *Health Psychology, 12*, 6–15.

Tresemer, D. (1976). Current trends in research on "Fear of success" [complete issue]. *Sex Roles, 2*.

Trexler, L. E. (1987). Neuropsychological rehabilitation in the United States. In *Neuropsychological rehabilitation*. New York: Guilford Press.

Triandis, H. C. (1972). *The analysis of subjective culture*. New York: John Wiley & Sons.

Triandis, H. C. (1994). Culture and social behavior. In W. J. Lonner & R. Malpass (Eds.), *Psychology and culture* (pp. 169–174). Boston: Allyn & Bacon.

Triandis, H. C. (1995). *Social behavior and culture*. New York: McGraw-Hill.

Triandis, H. C. (1997). Cross-cultural perspectives on personality. In R. Hogan, J. Johnson, & S. Briggs (Eds.), *Handbook of personality psychology* (pp. 439–464). San Diego, CA: Academic Press.

Triandis, H. C., Bontempo, R., Villareal, M. J., Asai M., & Lucca, N. (1988). Individualism and collectivism: Cross-cultural perspectives on self-ingroup relationships. *Journal of Personality and Social Psychology, 54*, 323–338.

Triandis, H. C., Brislin, R., & Hui, C. H. (1988). Cross-cultural training across the individualism-collectivism divide. *International Journal of Intercultural Relations, 12*, 269–289.

Triandis, H. C., Kashima, Y., Shimada, E., & Villareal, M. (1986). Acculturation indices as a means of confirming cultural differences. *International Journal of Psychology, 21*, 43–70.

Triandis, H. C., Marin, G., Lisansky, J., & Betancourt, H. (1984). Simpatica as a cultural script of Hispanics. *Journal of Personality and Social Psychology, 47*, 1363–1375.

Triandis, H. C., McCusker, C., & Hui, C. H. (1990). Multimethod probes of individualism and collectivism. *Journal of Personality and Social Psychology, 59*, 1006–1020.

Trivers, R. L. (1971). The evaluation of reciprocal altruism. *The Quarterly Review of Biology, 46*, 35–57.

Troen, S. K. (1985). Technological development and adolescence: The early twentieth century. *Journal of Early Adolescence, 5*, 429–440.

Troiden, R. R. (1988). *Gay and lesbian identity: A sociological analysis*. New York: General Hall.

Troiden, R. R. (1989). The formation of homosexual identities. *Journal of Homosexuality*, 17(1–2-3–4), 43–73.

Trompenaars, F. (1994). *Riding the waves of culture: Understanding diversity in global business*. Chicago: Irwin Professional Publishing.

Trout, M. D. (1981). Potential stresses during infancy: The growth of human bonds. In J. J. M. Tackett & M. Hunsberger (Eds.), *Family-centered care of children and adolescents: Nursing concepts in child health*. Philadelphia: Saunders.

Truax, C. B., Vargo, D. G., Frank, J. D., Imber, S. D., Battle, C., Hoehn-Saric, R., Wash, E. H., & Stone, A. R. (1966). Therapist empathy, genuineness, warmth and patient therapeutic outcome. *Journal of Consulting Psychology, 30*, 395–401.

Tryon, R. C. (1940). *Genetic differences in maze-learning ability in rats*. Chicago: University of Chicago Press.

Tulving, E. (1966). Subjective organization and effects of repetition in multi-trial free-recall learning. *Journal of Verbal Learning and Verbal Behavior, 5*, 193–197.

Tulving, E. (1983). *Elements of episodic memory*. New York: Oxford University Press.

Tulving, E. (1985). How many memory systems are there? *American Psychologist, 40*, 385–398.

Tulving, E. (1993). What is episodic memory? *Current Direction in Psychological Science, 2*, 67–70.

Tulving, E., & Schacter, D. L. (1990). Priming and human memory systems. *Science, 247*, 301–306.

Tulving, E., & Thomson, D. M. (1973). Encoding specificity and retrieval processes in episodic memory. *Psychological Review, 80*, 352–373.

Turk, D. C. (1994). Perspectives on chronic pain: The role of psychological factors. *Current Directions in Psychological Science, 3*, 45–48.

Turkington, C. (1992, December). Ruling opens door a crack: IQ testing some black kids. *APA Monitor*, pp. 28–29.

Turnbull, C. M. (1961). *The forest people*. New York: Simon & Schuster.

Turner, J. C., Oakes, P. J., Haslam, S. A., & McGarty, C. (1994). Self and collective: Cognition and social context. *Personality and Social Psychology Bulletin, 20*, 454–463.

Turner, J. S., & Helms, D. B. (1995). Lifespan development (5th ed.). Fort Worth, TX: Harcourt Brace Jovanovich.

Turner, R. J., & Roszell, P. (1994). Psychosocial resources and the stress process. In W. R. Avison & I. H. Gotlib (Eds), *Stress and mental health: Contemporary issues and prospects for the future* (pp. 179–210). New York: Plenum Press.

Turvey, M. T. (1996). Dynamic touch. *American Psychologist, 51*, 1134–1152.

Tversky, A., & Fox, C. R. (1995). Weighing risk and uncertainty. *Psychological Review, 102*, 269–283.

Tversky, A., & Kahneman, D. (1971). Belief in the law of small numbers. *Psychological Bulletin, 82*, 105–110.

Tversky, A., & Kahneman, D. (1973). Availability: A heuristic for judging frequency and probability. *Cognitive Psychology, 5*, 207–232.

U.S. Bureau of the Census. (1990). *Statistical abstract of the United States: 1990* (110th ed.). Washington, DC: U.S. Government Printing Office.

U.S. Bureau of the Census. (1992). Poverty in the United States: 1991. *Current Population Reports* (Series P-60, No. 181). Washington, DC: U.S. Government Printing Office.

U.S. Department of Health and Human Services (USDHHS). (1994). *Healthy people 2000 review 1993*. (DHHS Publication No. PHS 94–1232- 1). Washington, DC: U. S. Government Printing Office.

U.S. Bureau of Labor Statistics. (1991). *Working women: A chartbook*. Washington, DC: U.S. Department of Labor.

U.S. Bureau of the Census. (1992). *Statistical Abstract of the United States: 1992* (112th ed.). Washington, DC: Author.

Uleman, J. S., & Moskowitz, G. B. (1994). Unintended effects of goals on unintended inferences. *Journal of Personality and Social Psychology, 66*, 490–501.

Ullman, L. P., & Krasner, L. (1975). *A psychological approach to abnormal behavior* (2nd ed.). Englewood Cliffs, NJ: Prentice-Hall.

Unger, R., & Crawford, M. (1992). *Women and gender: A feminist psychology*. New York: McGraw-Hill.

Ungerleider, L. G., & Haxby, J. V. (1994). What and where in the human brain. *Current Opinion in Neurobiology, 4*, 157–165.

United Nations. (1989). *Violence against women in the family*. New York: United Nations.

Valenstein, E. S. (1986). *Great and desparate cures: The rise and decline of psychosurgery and other radical treatments for mental illness*. New York: Basic Books.

Valenti, A. C., & Downing, L. L. (1975). Differential effects of jury size on verdicts following deliberations as a function of the apparent guilt of a defendant. *Journal of Personality and Social Psychology, 32*, 655–663.

Valins, S., & Baum, A. (1974). Residential group size, social interaction, and crowding. *Environment and Behavior, 5*, 421–439.

Van Breukelen, G. J. P., Roskam, E. E. C. I., Eling, P. A. T. M., Jansen, R. W. T. L., Souren, D. A. P. B., & Ickenroth, J. G. M. (1995). A model and diagnostic measures for response time series on tests of concentration: Historical background, conceptual framework, and some applications. *Brain and Cognition, 27*, 147–179.

Van den Berghe, P. (1978). *Race and racism: A comparative perspective* (2nd ed.). New York: Wiley.

van den Hout, M., & Merckelbach, H. (1991). Classical conditioning: Still going strong. *Behavioural Psychotherapy, 19*, 59–79.

Van Dijk, T. A., & Kintsch, W. (1983). *Strategies of discourse comprehension.* New York: Academic Press.

Van Ekeran, G. (1988). *The speaker's sourcebook.* Englewood Cliffs, NJ: Prentice-Hall.

van Uzendoorn, M. H., Sagi, A., & Lambermon, M. W. E. (1992). The multiple caretaker paradox: Data from Holland and Israel. In R. C. Pianta (Ed.), *New directions for child development: No. 57. Beyond the parent: The role of other adults in children's lives.* San Francisco: Jossey-Bass.

van Wolferen, K. (1990). *The enigma of Japanese power.* New York: Vintage Books.

Vanbeselaere, N. (1983). Mere exposure: a search for an explanation. In W. Doise & S. Moscovici (Eds.), *Current issues in European social psychology* (Vol. 1). Cambridge, Eng.: Cambridge University Press.

Vargha-Khadem, F., Gadian, D. G., Watkins, K. E., Connelly, A., Van Paesschen, W., & Mishkin, M. (1997). Differential effects of early hippocampal pathology on episodic and semantic memory. *Science, 277*, 376–378.

Vaux, A. (1985). Variations in social support associated with gender, ethnicity, and age. *Journal of Social Issues, 41*, 89–110.

Ventura, S. J., Peters, K. D., Martin, J. A., & Maurer, J. D. (1997). Births and deaths: United States, 1996. *Monthly Vital Statistics Report, 46* (1, Suppl. 2).

Von Senden, M. (1932/1960) *Space and sight* (P. Heath, Trans.). London: Methuen.

Voss, J. F., & Post, T. A. (1988). On the solving of ill-structured problems. In M. T. H. Chi, R. Glaser, & M. J. Farr (Eds.), *The nature of expertise* (pp. 261–285). Hillsdale, NJ: Erlbaum.

Vygotsky, L. S. (1962). *Thought and language.* Cambridge, MA: MIT Press.

Vygotsky, L. S. (1978). *Mind in society.* Cambridge, MA: Harvard University Press.

Wagner, A. R., Logan, F. A., Haberlandt, K. & Price, T. (1968). Stimulus selection in animal discrimination learning. *Journal of Experimental Psychology, 76*, 171–180.

Wagner, A. R., Rudy, J. W., & Whitlow, J. W. (1973). Rehearsal in animal conditioning. *Journal of Experimental Psychology, 97*, 407–426.

Waisberg, J., & Page, S. (1988). Gender role nonconformity and perception of mental illness. *Women and Health,* 14(1), 3–16.

Waldon, D. A., & Avolio, B. J. (1986). A meta-analysis of age differences in job performance. *Journal of Applied Psychology, 71*, 33–38.

Walker, B. A., Reis, S. M., & Leonard, J. S. (1992). A developmental investigation of the lives of gifted women. *Gifted Child Quarterly, 36*, 201–206.

Wallace, R. K., & Benson, H. (1972). The physiology of meditation. *Scientific American, 226*, 84–90.

Wallace, R. K., & Fisher, L. E. (1987). *Consciousness and behavior* (2nd ed.). Boston: Allyn & Bacon.

Wallas, G. (1926). *The art of thought.* New York: Harcourt, Brace.

Wallbot, H. G., & Scherer, K. R. (1986). How universal and specific is emotional experience? Evidence from 27 countries on five continents. *Social Science Information, 25*, 763–95.

Wallis, C., & Willwerth, J. (1992, July 6). Schizophrenia: A new drug brings patients back to life. *Time Magazine*, pp. 53–57.

Walster (Hatfield), E., Aronson, V., Abrahams, D., & Rottman, L. (1966). Importance of physical attractiveness in dating behavior. *Journal of Personality and Social Psychology, 4*, 508–516.

Walster (Hatfield), E., Berscheid, E., & Walster, G. W. (1973). New directions in equity research. *Journal of Personality and Social Psychology, 25*, 151–176.

Walster (Hatfield), E., & Festinger, L. (1962). The effectiveness of "overheard" persuasive communications. *Journal of Abnormal and Social Psychology, 65*, 395–402.

Walton, G. E., & Bower, T. G. R. (1993). Newborns form "prototypes" in less than 1 minute. *Psychological Science, 4*, 203–205.

Walton, G. E., Bower, N. J. A., & Bower, T. G. R. (1992). Recognition of familiar faces by newborns. *Infant Behavior and Development, 15*, 265–269.

Ward, D., & Kassebaum, G. G. (1965). *Women's prison: Sex and social structure.* Chicago: Aldine.

Ward, M. C. (1996). *A world full of women.* Needham Heights, MA: Allyn & Bacon.

Warner, L. A. (1995). Prevalence and correlates of drug use and dependence in the United States. *Archives of General Psychiatry, 52*, 219–229.

Warrington, E. K., & Shallice, T. (1972). Further analysis of the prior learning effect in amnesic patients. *Neuropsychologia, 16*, 169–177.

Wartik, N. (1992, December). Blue moods: New findings on why women feel down more often than men. *Working Women*, pp. 81–82, 92–94.

Wasserman, E. A. (1993). Comparative cognition: Toward a general understanding of cognition and behavior. *Psychological Science, 4*, 156–161.

Waters, E., Wippman, J., & Sroufe, L. A. (1979). Attachment, positive affect, and competence in the peer group: Two studies in construct validation. *Child Development, 50*, 821–829.

Watson, D., & Clark, L. A. (1997). Extraversion and its positive emotional core. In R. Hogan, J. Johnson, & S. Briggs (Eds.), *Handbook of personality psychology* (pp. 767–793). San Diego, CA: Academic Press.

Watson, J. (1992). Forward. In S. Ackerman (Ed.), *Discovering the brain.* Washington, DC: National Academy Press.

Watson, J. B. (1913). Psychology as a behaviorist views it. *Psychological Review, 20*, 158–177.

Watson, J. B. (1925). *Behaviorism.* New York: Norton.

Watson, J. B., & Raynor, R. (1920). Conditioned emotional reactions. *Journal of Experimental Psychology, 3*, 1–14.

Watson, J. S., & Ramey, C. T. (1972). Reactions to response-contingent stimulation in early infancy. *Merrill-Palmer Quarterly, 18*, 219–227.

Watson, D. L., & Tharp, R. G. (1989). *Self-directed behavior: Self-modification for personal adjustment.* Pacific Grove, CA:Brooks/Cole.

Watson, R. I. (1973). Investigation into deindividuation using a cross-cultural survey technique. *Journal of Personality and Social Psychology, 25*, 342–345.

Wattenmaker, W. D. (1993). Incidental concept learning, feature frequency, and correlated properties. *Journal of Experimental Psychology: Learning, Memory and Cognition, 19*, 203–222.

Webb, W. B. (1992). *Sleep: The gentle tyrant* (2nd ed.). Boston: Anker.

Webb, W. B., & Bonnet, M. H. (1979). Sleep and dreams. In M. E. Meyer (Ed.), *Foundations of contemporary psychology.* New York: Oxford University Press..

Webster (1983). *Webster's new twentieth century dictionary, unabridged,* (2nd ed.). New York: Prentice-Hall.

Wechsler, D. (1949). *Wechsler intelligence scale for children.* New York: Psychological Corporation.

Wechsler, D. (1955). *Wechsler adult intelligence scale.* New York: Psychological Corporation.

Wechsler, D. (1975). Intelligence defined and undefined. *American Psychologist, 30*, 135–139.

Wegman, E. (1990). Annual summary of vital statistics—1989. *Pediatrics, 86*, 836–847.

Weiner, B. (1985). An attributional theory of achievement motivation and emotion. *Psychological Review, 92*, 548–573.
Weiner, B. (1986). *An attributional theory of motivation and emotion.* New York: Springer-Verlag.
Weiner, B., Graham, S., & Chandler, C. C. (1982). Pity, anger, and guilt: An attributional analysis. *Personality and Social Psychology Bulletin, 8*, 226–232.
Weiner, B., Russell, D., & Lerman, D. (1979). The cognition-emotion process in achievement-related contexts. *Journal of Personality and Social Psychology, 37*, 1211–1220.
Weinraub, M., Clemens, L. P., Sockloff, A., Ethridge, T., Gracely, E., & Myers, B. (1984). The development of sex role stereotypes in their third year: Relationships to gender labeling, gender identity, sex-typed toy preference, and family characteristics. *Child Development, 55*, 1493–1503.
Weintraub, D. J., & Walker, E. L. (1966). *Perception.* Monterey, CA: Brooks/Cole.
Weinstein, C. S. (1991). The classroom as a social context for learning. *Annual Review of Psychology, 42*, 493–525.
Weinstein, N. D. (1987). Unrealistic optimism about susceptibility to health problems: Conclusions from a community-wide sample. *Journal of Behavioral Medicine, 10*, 481–500.
Weiskrantz, L., Warrington, E. K., Sanders, M. D., & Marshall, J. (1974). Visual capacity in the hemianopic fields following a restricted occipital ablation. *Brain, 97*, 709–728.
Weiss, J. (1972). Psychological factors in stress and disease. *Scientific American, 226*, 104–113.
Weiss, J. M., Glazer, H. I., & Pohorecky, L. (1975). A coping behavior and neurochemical changes: An alternative explanation for the original learned helplessness experiments. In *Relevance of the psychopathological animal model to the human.* New York: Plenum.
Weissman, A. (1987). The dysfunctional attitudes scale. In K. Corcoran & J. Fischer (Eds.), *Measures for clinical practice: A source book.* New York: Free Press.
Weissman, M. M., et al. (1996). Cross-national epidemiology of major depression and bipolar disorder. *Journal of the American Medical Association, 276*, 293–299.
Weissman, M., Leaf, F., & Bruce, M. (1987). Single parent women: A community study. *Social Psychiatry, 22*, 29–36.
Weissman, M. M., Merikangas, K. R., & Boyd, J. H. (1986). Epidemiology of affective disorders. In J. E. Helzer & S. B. Guze (Eds.), *Psychiatry, affective disorders, and dementia* (pp. 105–118). New York: Basic Books.
Welch-Ross, M. K., & Schmidt, C. R. (1996). Gender-schema development and children's constructive story memory: Evidence for a developmental model. *Child Development, 67*, 820–835.
Wells, G. L., Luus, E., & Windschitl, P. D. (1994). Maximizing the utility of eyewitness identification evidence. *Current Directions in Psychological Science, 3*, 194–197.
Wenar, C. (1990). *Developmental psychopathology* (2nd ed.). New York: McGraw-Hill.
Werner, E. E., & Smith, R. S. (1992). *Overcoming the odds: High risk children from birth to adulthood.* Ithaca, NY: Cornell University Press.
Werner, J. S., & Schlesinger, K. (1991). *Psychology: Science of mind, brain, and behavior.* New York: McGraw-Hill.
Wertheimer, M. (1945). *Productive thinking.* New York: Harper & Row.
Wertheimer, M. (1987). *A brief history of psychology* (3rd ed.). New York: Holt, Rinehart and Winston.
West, J. R., Hodges, C. A., & Black, A. C., Jr. (1981). Prenatal exposure to ethanol alters the organization of hippocampal mossy fibers in rats. *Science, 211*, 957–959.
Westefeld, J. S., & Furr, S. R. (1987). Suicide and depression among college students. *Professional Psychology: Research and Practice, 18*, 119–123.
Wheeler, M. A., & Roediger, H. L. (1992). Disparate effects of repeated testing: Reconciling Ballard's (1913) and Bartlett's (1932) results. *Psychological Science, 3*, 240–245.
Whiffen, V. E. (1988). Vulnerability to postpartum depression: A prospective multivariate study. *Journal of Abnormal Psychology, 97*, 467–474.
Whitbeck, L. B., & Hoyt, D. R. (1994). Social prestige and assortive mating: A comparison of students from 1956 and 1988. *Journal of Social and Personal Relationships, 11*, 137–145.
White, B. L. (1975). *The first three years of life.* New York: Avon Books.
White, R. W. (1959). Motivation reconsidered: The concept of competence. *Psychological Review, 66*, 297–333.
White, W.A. (1932). *Outlines of psychiatry* (13th ed.). New York: Nervous and Mental Disease Publishing.
Whitehead, A. N. (1925). *Science in the modern world.* New York: Macmillan.
Whiting, B., & Edwards, C. P. (1973). A cross-cultural analysis of sex differences in the behavior of children aged three through eleven. *Journal of Social Psychology, 91*, 171–188.
Whiting, B. B., & Whiting, J. W. M. (1975), *Children of six cultures: A psychocultural analysis.* Cambridge, MA: Harvard University Press.
Whiting, R. (1989). *You gotta have wa.* New York: MacMillan.
Whorf, B. L. (1956). *Language, thought, and reality.* New York: Wiley.
Whyte, G. (1993). Escalating commitment in individual and group decision making: A prospect theory approach. *Organizational Behavior and Human Decision Processes, 54*, 430–455.
Wichman, H. (1970). Effects of isolation and communication in a two-person game. *Journal of Personality and Social Psychology, 16*, 114–120.
Wickett, J. C., Vernon, P. A., & Lee, D. H. (1994). In vivo brain size, head perimeter, and intelligence in a sample of healthy adult females. *Personality and Individual Differences, 16*, 831–838.
Widiger, T. A., Corbitt, E. M., & Millon, T. (1992). Antisocial personality disorder. In A. Tasman & M. B. Riba (Eds.), *American Psychiatric Press Review of Psychiatry* (Vol. 11). Washington, DC: American Psychiatric Press.
Widom, C. (1989). Does violence beget violence? A critical examination of the literature. *Psychological Bulletin, 106*, 3–28.
Wiebe, D. J., & Smith, T. W. (1997). Personality and health: Progress and problems in psychosomatics. In R. Hogan, J. Johnson, & S. Briggs (Eds.), *Handbook of personality psychology* (pp. 892- 918). San Diego: Academic Press.
Wiedenfeld, S. A., O'Leary, A., Bandura, A., Brown, S., Levine, S., & Raska, K. (1990). Impact of perceived self-efficacy in coping with stressor on components of the immune system. *Journal of Personality and Social Psychology, 59*, 1082–1094.
Wiesel, E. (1995). *All rivers run to the sea.* New York: Schocken Books.
Wifley, D. E., et al. (1996). Eating disturbance and body image: A comparison of a community sample of adult black and white women. *International Journal of Eating Disorders*, 20, 377–398.
Wiggins, J. S. (1997). In defense of traits. In R. Hogan, J. Johnson, & S. Briggs (Eds.), *Handbook of personality psychology* (pp. 95–115). San Diego, CA: Academic Press.
Wiggins, J. S., & Trapnell, P. D. (1997). Personality structure: The return of the Big Five. In R. Hogan, J. Johnson, & S. Briggs (Eds.), *Handbook of personality psychology* (pp. 737–765). San Diego, CA: Academic Press.
Wikan, U. (1977). Man becomes woman: Transsexualism in Oman as a key to gender roles. *Man, 12*, 304–319.
Wilbur, R. B. (1979). *American sign language and sign systems.* Baltimore: University Park Press.
Wilder, D. A. (1990). Some determinants of the persuasive power of in-groups and out-groups: Organization of information and attribution of independence. *Journal of Personality and Social Psychology, 59*, 1202–1213.

Willerman, L. (1991). Brains: Is bigger better? *Science, 254,* 1584.

Willerman, L., Schultz, R., Rutledge, N. J., & Bigler, E. D. (1991). In vivo brain size and intelligence. *Intelligence, 15,* 223–228.

Williams, J. E. & Best, D. L. (1990). *Measuring sex stereotypes: A multination study* (Vol. 6, rev. ed). Newbury Park, CA: Sage Publications.

Williams, K. D., & Karau, S. J. (1991). Social loafing and social compensation: The effects of expectations of co-worker performance. *Journal of Personality and Social Psychology, 61,* 570–581.

Williams, K. D., Nida, S. A., Baca, L. D., & Latané, B. (1989). Social loafing and swimming: Effects of identifiability on individual and relay performance in intercollegiate swimmers. *Basic and Applied Social Psychology, 10,* 73–81.

Williams, M. D. (1992). *The human dilemma: A decade later in Belmar.* Fort Worth, TX: Harcourt Brace Jovanovich.

Williams, R. B., Jr. (1970). *American society* (3rd ed.). New York: Knopf.

Williams, R. B., Jr. (1989). *The trusting heart: Great news about Type A behavior.* New York: Times Books.

Williams, R. L., Karacan, I., & Hursch, C.J. (1974). *Electroencephalography (EEG) of human sleep: Clinical applications.* New York: Wiley.

Williams, W. L. (1986). *The spirit and the flesh: Sexual diversity in American Indian culture.* Boston: Beacon Press.

Wills, T. A. (Ed.). (1990). Social support in social and clinical psychology [special issue]. *Journal of Social and Clinical Psychology* (Whole No. 9).

Wilsnack, S. (1995). Alcohol use and alcohol problems in women. In A. L. Stanton & S. J. Gallant (Eds.), *The psychology of women's health* (pp. 381–444). Washington, DC: American Psychological Association.

Wilson, E. O. (1975). *Sociobiology: The new synthesis.* Cambridge, MA: Belknap Press of Harvard University Press.

Wilson, E. O. (1978). *On human nature.* Cambridge, MA: Harvard University Press.

Wilson, G. T., & Lawson, D. M. (1976a). Effects of alcohol on sexual arousal in women. *Journal of Abnormal Psychology, 85,* 489–497.

Wilson, G. T., & Lawson, D. M. (1976b). Expectancies, alcohol, and sexual arousal in male social drinkers. *Journal of Abnormal Psychology, 85,* 587–594.

Wilson, M. N. (1989). Child development in the context of the black extended family. *American Psychologist, 44,* 380–385.

Wilson, R. S., & Matheny, A. P., Jr. (1986). Behavior genetics research in infant temperament: The Louisville twin study. In R. Plomin & J. Dunn (Eds.), *The study of temperament: Changes, continuities, and challenges.* Hillsdale, NJ: Erlbaum.

Winn, P. (1995). The lateral hypothalamus and motivated behavior: An old syndrome reassessed and a new perspective gained. *Current Directions in Psychological Science, 4,* 182–189.

Winter, D. G. (1991). A motivational model of leadership: Predicting long-term management success from TAT measures of power motivation and responsibility. *Leadership Quarterly, 2,* 67–80.

Winter, D. G. (1996). *Personality: Analysis and interpretation of lives.* New York: McGraw-Hill.

Winter, D. G., & Barenbaum, N. B. (1985). Responsibility and the power motive in women and men. *Journal of Personality, 53,* 335–355.

Winter, D. G., & Stewart, A. J. (1978). Power motivation. In H. London & J. Exner (Eds.), *Dimensions of personality.* New York: Wiley.

Winterbottom, M. R. (1958). The relation of need for achievement to learning experiences in independence and mastery. In J. W. Atkinson (Ed.), *Motives in fantasy action and society.* Princeton, NJ: Van Nostrand.

Wirth, L. (1945). The problems of minority groups. In R. Linton (Ed.), *The science of man in the world crisis* (pp. 347–372). New York: Columbia University Press.

Wise, R. A. (1987). The role of reward pathways in the development of drug dependence. *Pharmacological Therapy, 35,* 227–263.

Wise, R. A., & Rompre, P. P. (1989). Brain dopamine and reward. *Annual Review of Psychology, 40,* 191–225.

Wolf, M., Birnbaumer, J., Lawler, & Williams, T. (1970). The operant extinction, reinstatement and re-extinction of vomiting behavior in a retarded child. In R. Ulrich, T. Stachnik, & J. Mabry (Eds.), *Control of human behavior: From cure to prevention.* Glenwood, IL: Scott, Foresman.

Wolfe, J. M. (1984). Global factors in the Hermann grid illusion. *Perception, 13,* 33–40.

Wolpe, J. (1958). *Psychotherapy by reciprocal inhibition.* Palo Alto, CA: Stanford University Press.

Woodward, B. (1991). *The commanders.* New York: Simon & Schuster.

Woody, E. Z., Drugovic, M., & Oakman, J. M. (1997). A reexamination of the role of nonhypnotic suggestibility in hypnotic responding. *Journal of Social and Personality Psychology, 72,* 399–407.

Woolley, H. T. (1910). Psychological literature: A review of the recent literature on the psychology of sex. *Psychological Bulletin, 7,* 335–342.

Worchel, S., & Brown, E. H. (1984). The role of plausibility in influencing environmental attributions. *Journal of Experimental Social Psychology, 20,* 86–96.

Worchel, S., & Shebilski, W. (1989). *Psychology: Principles and applications.* Englewood Cliffs, NJ: Prentice-Hall.

Worell, J., & Remer, P. (1992). *Feminist perspectives in therapy: An empowerment model for women.* New York: John Wiley.

World Bank. (1993). *World development report 1993: Investing in health.* New York: Oxford University Press.

World Health Organization. (1992). The AIDS situation worldwide. In Johnson, O. (Ed.), *The 1992 information please almanac* (p. 81).

Wright, J. (Ed.) (1994). *The universal almanac.* New York: Andrews and McMeel.

Wu, T.-C., Tashkin, D. P., Djahed, B., & Rose, J. E. (1988). Pulmonary hazards of smoking marijuana as compared with tobacco. *New England Journal Of Medicine, 318,* 347–351.

Wundt, W. (1896). *Foundations of psychology.* Leipzig: Engleman.

Wurtman, R. J. (1982). Nutrients that modify brain function. *Scientific American, 246,* 50–59.

Wyer, R. S., & Srull, T. K. (1980). Category accessibility: Some theoretical and empirical issues concerning the processing of social stimulus information. In E. T. Higgins, C. P. Herman, & M. P. Zanna (Eds.), *Social cognition: The Ontario symposium on personality and social psychology.* Hillsdale, NJ: Erlbaum.

Yager, D. D., & May, M. L. (1990). Ultra-sound triggered, flight-gated evasive maneuvers in the Praying Mantis *Parasphendale agrionina. Journal of Experimental Biology, 152,* 41–58.

Yalom, I. D., & Liebermann, M. A. (1971). A study of encounter group casualties. *Archives of Ceneral Psychiatry, 25,* 16–30.

Yankelovich, D. (1981). *New rules.* New York: Random House.

Yap, P. M. (1951). Mental disease peculiar to certain cultures: A survey of comparative psychiatry. *Journal of Mental Science, 97,* 313–327.

Yarkin, K. L., Town, J. P., & Wallston, B. S. (1982). Blacks and women must try harder: Stimulus person's race and sex attributions of causality. *Personality and Social Psychology Bulletin, 8,* 21–24.

Yonas, A., Cleaves, W., & Pettersen, L. (1978). Development of sensitivity to pictorial depth. *Science, 200,* 212–218.

Younger, B. A. (1990). Infant categorization: Memory for category-level and specific item information. *Journal of Experimental Child Psychology, 50,* 131–155.

Youniss, J. (1980). *Parents and peers in social development.* Chicago: University of Chicago Press.

Youniss, J., & Smollar, J. (1985). *Adolescents' relations with their mothers, fathers, and friends.* Chicago: University of Chicago Press.

Zajonc, R. (1968). Attitudinal effects of mere exposure, *Journal of Personality and Social Psychology, 9* (Monograph Supplement 2), 1–27.

Zajonc, R. B. (1965). Social facilitation. *Science, 149,* 269–274.

Zajonc, R. B. (1976). Family configuration and intelligence. *Science, 160,* 227–236.

Zajonc, R. B. (1980). Feeling and thinking: Preferences need no inferences. *American Psychologist, 35,* 151–175.

Zajonc, R. B., & Bargh, J. (1980). Birth order, family size, and decline of SAT scores. *American Psychologist, 35,* 662–668.

Zajonc, R. B., Murphy, S. T., & Inglehart, M. (1989). Feeling and facial efference: Implications of the vascular theory of emotion. *Psychological Review, 96,* 395–416.

Zajonc, R., Markus, H., & Markus, G. B. (1979). The birth order puzzle. *Journal of Personality and Social Psychology, 37,* 1325–1341.

Zanna, M. P., & Cooper, J. (1974). Dissonance and the pill: An attribution approach to studying arousal properties of dissonance. *Journal of Personality and Social Psychology, 29,* 703–709.

Zanna, M. P., Fazio, R. H., & Ross, M. (1994). The persistence of persuasion. In R. C. Schank & E. Langer (Eds.), *Beliefs, reasoning, and decision making: Psychologic in honor of Bob Abelson.* Hillsdale NJ: Erlbaum

Zarcone, V. (1973). Marijuana and ethanol: Effects on sleep. *Psychiatry and Medicine, 4,* 201–212.

Zax, M., & Stricker, M. (1963). *Patterns of psychopathology: Case studies in behavorial dysfunction.* New York: Macmillan.

Zeidner, M., & Endler, N. (1996). *Handbook of coping: Theory, research, applications.* New York: Wiley.

Ziegler, E. F., Abelson, W. D., Trickett, P. K., & Seitz, V. (1982). Is an intervention program necessary to improve economically disadvantaged children's IQ scores? *Child Development, 53,* 340–348.

Zigler, E., & Seitz, V. (1982). Social policy and intelligence. In R. Sternberg (Ed.), *Handbook of human intelligence.* New York: Cambridge University Press.

Zigler, E., & Child, I. L. (1969). Socialization. In G. Lindzey & E. Aronson (Eds.), *The handbook of social psychology* (pp. 450–589). Reading, MA: Addison-Wesley.

Zillmann, D., & Bryant, J. (1982). Pornography, sexual callousness, and the trivialization of rape. *Journal of Communication, 32,* 10–21.

Zillmann, D., & Bryant, J. (1984). Effects of massive exposure to pornography. In N. M. Malamuth & E. Donnerstein (Eds.), *Pornography and sexual aggression.* New York: Academic Press.

Zimbardo, P. G. (1969). The human choice: Individuation, reason, and order versus deindividuation, impulse, and chaos. In *Nebraska symposium on motivation.* Lincoln, NE: University of Nebraska Press.

Zimbardo, P. G. (1977). *Shyness: What is it, what to do about it.* New York: Addison-Wesley.

Zimbardo, P. G., Ebbesen, E. B., & Maslach, C. (1977). *Influencing attitudes and changing behavior.* Reading, MA: Addison-Wesley.

Zipf, G. K. (1949). *Human behavior and the principle of least effort.* Cambridge, MA: Addison-Wesley.

Zuckerman, M. (1979). *Sensation seeking: Beyond the optimal level of arousal.* Hillsdale, NJ: Erlbaum.

Zuckerman, M. (1990). Some dubious premises in research and theory on racial differences: Scientific, social, and ethical issues. *American Psychologist, 45,* 1297–1303.

Zuckerman, M. (1991). *The psychology of personality.* New York: Cambridge University Press.

Zuckerman, M., Buchsbaum, M. S., & Murphy, D. L. (1980). Sensation seeking and its biological correlates. *Psychological Bulletin, 88,* 187–214.

Zuger, B. (1984). Early effeminate behavior in boys: Outcome and significance for homosexuality. *Journal of Nervous and Mental Disease, 172,* 90–97.

Zuravin, S. J. (1987). Unplanned pregnancies, family planning programs, and child maltreatment. *Family Relations,* 135–139.

Zuravin, S. J. (1988). Fertility patterns: Their relationship to child physical abuse and child neglect. *Journal of Marriage and the Family, 50,* 983–993.

Acknowledgments and Credits

Figures

Figure 1-3: Profiles of APA Members, 1995. Reprinted by permission of the American Psychological Association. **Figure 2-3:** Josephson, W., Television violence and children's aggression: Testing the priming, social script, and disinhibition predictions, *Journal of Personality and Social Psychology* 53 (1987): 882-90. Copyright 1987 by the American Psychological Association. Adapted by permission of the American Psychological Association and the author. **Figure 3-2:** Starr, C., and Taggart, R., *Biology: The unity and diversity of life*, 7th ed., p. 571. Copyright © 1995 by Wadsworth, Inc. Adapted by permission of the publisher. **Figure 3-3:** Starr, C., and Taggart, R., *Biology: The unity and diversity of life*, 7th ed., pp. 564-65. Copyright © 1995 by Wadsworth, Inc. Adapted by permission of the publisher. **Figure 3-10:** Etkin, W., Devlin, R. M., and Bouffard, T. G., *A biology of human concern*. Copyright © 1972 by Lippincott-Ravin Publishers. Adapted by permission of the publisher. **Figure 3-13:** Bloom, F. E., Lazerson, A., and Hofstadter, L., *Brain, mind, and behavior*. NY: Freeman, 1985, 1988. Copyright © 1985, 1988 by the Educational Broadcasting Corporation. Adapted by permission of WNET/Thirteen. **Figure 3-17:** Penfield, W., and Rasmussen, T., *The cerebral cortex of man*. Copyright 1950 by Macmillan Publishing Co., Inc., renewed 1978 by Theodore Rasmussen. Adapted by permission of Macmillan Publishing Co., Inc. **Figure 4-1:** Helzer, J. E., and Canino, G., (eds.), *Alcoholism in North America, Europe, and Asia*. Copyright © 1992 by Oxford University Press, NY. Adapted by permission of Oxford University Press. **Figure 4-2:** Appelbaum, R. P., and Chambliss, W. J., *Sociology*, p. 131. Copyright © 1995 by HarperCollins Publishers. Reprinted by permission of HarperCollins Publishers. **Figure 4-5:** Appelbaum, R. P., and Chambliss, W. J., *Sociology*. Copyright © 1995 by HarperCollins Publishers. Adapted by permission of HarperCollins Publishers. **Figure 5-1:** Sekuler, R., and Blake, R. *Perception*, 2nd ed., p. 18. Copyright © 1990 by McGraw-Hill. Reprinted by permission of McGraw-Hill. **Figure 5-3:** Sekuler, R. and Blake, R. *Perception*, 2nd ed., p. 20. Copyright © 1990 by McGraw-Hill. Reprinted by permission of McGraw-Hill. **Figure 5-8:** Coren, Stanley, and Ward, Lawrence M., *Sensation and perception*, 3rd ed. Copyright © 1989 by Harcourt Brace & Company. Reprinted by permission of Harcourt Brace & Company. **Figure 5-9:** Ramachandran, V. S., Blind spots, *Scientific American* 266 (1992): 86-91. Copyright © 1992 by Scientific American, Inc. All rights reserved. **Figure 5-10:** Hochberg, J. E., *Perception*. Copyright © 1964 by Prentice-Hall, Inc., Upper Saddle River, NJ. Adapted by permission of Prentice-Hall, Inc. Hubel, D. H., and Torstenn, W., Receptive fields, binocular interaction, and functional architecture in the cat's visual cortex, *Journal of Physiology* 160 (1963): 106-54. Copyright © 1963 by Cambridge University Press. Adapted by permission of Cambridge University Press. **Figure 5-12:** Hecht, S., Vision II: The nature of the photoreceptor process, in C. Marchison (ed.), *A handbook of experimental psychology*. Copyright 1934, 1969 by Clark University Press, Worcester, MA. Adapted by permission of Clark University Press. **Figure 5-13:** Cornsweet, T. M. *Visual perception*. Copyright © 1970 by Academic Press, Inc. Adapted by permission of the publisher and author. **Figure 5-17:** AO Pseudo-Isochromatic Color Tests by American Optical Corporation. Reprinted by permission. **Figure 5-22:** Weintraub, D. J., and Walker, E. L., *Perception*. Copyright © 1966 by Brooks/Cole Publishing Company. Adapted by permission of Brooks/Cole. **Figure 5-23:** Luria, A. R., *Cognitive development: Its cultural and social foundations*, Cambridge, MA: Harvard University Press. Copyright © 1976 by the President and Fellows of Harvard College. Reprinted by permission of Harvard University Press. **Figure 5-24:** Hochberg, J.E., *Perception*. Copyright © 1964 by Prentice-Hall, Inc., Upper Saddle River, NJ Adapted by permission of Prentice-Hall, Inc. **Figure 5-30:** Hering, E., *Outlines of a theory of the light sense*, ed. by L. M. Hurvich and D. Jameson, Cambridge, MA: Harvard University Press, pp. 150-51. Copyright 1920 by the President and Fellows of Harvard College. Adapted by permission of Harvard University Press. **Figure 5-31:** Hudson, W., Pictorial depth perception in sub-cultural groups in Africa, *Journal of Social Psychology* 52 (1960): 183-208. Adapted by permission of the Helen Dwight Reed Educational Foundation. Published by Heldref Publications, 4000 Albemarle St. N.W., Washington, DC 20016. **Figure for Diversity Box (p. 162):** Yonas, A., Cleaves, W., and Pettersen, L., Development of sensitivity to pictorial depth, *Science* 200 (1978): 212-18. Copyright © 1978 by the American Association for the Advancement of Science. Adapted by permission of the AAAS and the authors. **Figure 5-34:** M. M. Matlin, *Perception*. Copyright © 1983 by Allyn and Bacon. Reprinted by permission of Allyn and Bacon. **Figure 5-35:** Chapanis, A., *Man-machine engineering*. Copyright © 1965 by Brooks/Cole Publishing Company. Adapted by permission of Brooks/Cole. Chapanis, A., Gamer, W. R., and Morgan, C. T., *Applied experimental psychology: Human factors in engineering design*. Copyright 1949 by John Wiley & Sons, Inc., NY. Adapted by permission of John Wiley & Sons, Inc. **Figure 5-37:** Davis, H., and Silverman, S., *Hearing and deafness* (rev. ed.). Copyright 1947/1960 by Holt, Rinehart and Winston. Adapted by permission of Holt, Rinehart and Winston. **Figure 5-38:** Sekuler, R., and Blake, R., *Perception*, 2nd ed., p. 321. Copyright © 1990 by McGraw-Hill. Adapted by permission of McGraw-Hill. Data from Hefner, R. S., and Hefner, H. E., Hearing in large and small dogs: Absolute thresholds and size of the tympanic membrane, *Behavioral Neuroscience* 97 (1985): 389-99. Copyright 1985 by the American Psychological Association. Reprinted by permission of the American Psychological Association and the author. **Figure 5-39:** Kalat, J. W., *Biological psychology*, 2nd ed. Copyright © 1984 by Wadsworth, Inc. Adapted by permission of the publisher. **Figure 5-43:** Amoore, J. E., Johnston, J. W., Jr., and Rubin, M., The sterochemical theory of odor, *Scientific American* 210 (2) (1964): 42-9. Copyright © 1964 by Scientific American, Inc. Adapted by permission. All rights reserved. Karapelou, J., Smelling and tasting, *Discover* 6 (1993): 72. Copyright © 1993 by Walt Disney Company. Reprinted by permission of Discover. **Figure 6-4:** Garcia, J., and Koelling, A., Relation of cue to consequence in avoidance learning, *Psychonomic Science* 4 (1966): 123-24. **Figure 6-8:** Ferster, C. B., and Skinner, B. F., *Schedules of Reinforcement*. Copyright 1957 by Appleton-Century-Crofts. Adapted by permission of the B. F. Skinner Foundation. **Figure 6-9:** Buttman, N., The pigeon and the spectrum and other perplexities, *Psychological Reports* 2 (1956): 449-60. Reprinted by permission of the publishers. **Figure 6-10:** Maier, S. F., Seligman, M. E. P., and Solomon, R. L., Pavlovian fear conditioning and learned helplessness:

Effects on escape and avoidance behavior of (a) the CS-US contingency and (b) the independence of the US and voluntary responding, in B. A. Campbell and R. M. Church (eds.), *Punishment and aversive behavior*, © 1969, pp. 299-342. Adapted by permission of Prentice-Hall, Inc., Upper Saddle River, NJ. **Figure 6-11:** Tolman, E. C., and Honzik, C. H., Introduction and removal of reward and maze performance in rats, *University of California Publications in Psychology* 4 (1930): 257-75. **Figure 7-3:** Klatzky, R. L., *Human memory: Structures and processes*, 2nd ed. Copyright © 1975, 1980 by W. H. Freeman and Company. Adapted by permission of W. H. Freeman and Company. **Figure 7-4:** Silva, A. J., and Giese, K. P., Gene targetting: A novel window into the biology of learning and memory, in J. L. Martinez, Jr., and R. P. Kesner (eds.), *Neurobiology of learning and memory*. Copyright 1997 by Academic Press, Inc. Adapted by permission of the publisher and authors. **Figure 7-6:** Ericsson, K. A., Chase, W. G., and Faloon, S. (1980). Acquisition of a memory skill, *Science* 208 (1980): 1181-82. Copyright © 1980 by the American Association for the Advancement of Science. Adapted by permission of the AAAS and the authors. **Figure 7-7:** Ross, B. M., and Millsom, C., Repeated memory of oral prose in Ghana and New York, *International Journal of Psychology* 5 (1970): 173-81. Copyright © 1970. Reprinted by permission of Lawrence Erlbaum Associates. **Figure 7-9:** Milner, B., Corkin, S., and Teuber, H. L., Further analysis of the hippocampal syndrome: Fourteen-year follow-up study of H.M. *Neuropsychologia* 6 (1968): 215-34. Copyright © 1968. Adapted by permission of Elsevier Science, Ltd. **Figure 7-12:** Jenkins, J. G., and Dallenbach, K. M., Oblivescence during sleep and waking, *American Journal of Psychology* 35 (1924): 605-12. Copyright 1924 by the Board of Trustees of the University of Illinois. Adapted by permission of the University of Illinois Press. **Figure 7-13:** Bahrick, H., Semantic memory content in permastore: Fifty years of memory for Spanish learned in school, *Journal of Experimental Psychology: General* 113 (1984): 1-24. Copyright 1984 by the American Psychological Association. Reprinted by permission of the American Psychological Association and the authors. **Figure 8-1:** Kosslyn, S. M., Ball, T. M., and Reisser, B. J., Visual images preserve metric spatial information: Evidence from studies of image scanning, *Journal of Experimental Psychology: Human Perception and Performance* 4 (1978): 1-20. Copyright 1978 by the American Psychological Association. Adapted by permission of the American Psychological Association and the authors. **Figure 8-2:** Stevens, A., and Coupe, P., Distortions in judged spatial relations, *Cognitive Psychology* 10 (1978): 422-37. Copyright 1978 by Academic Press, Inc. Adapted by permission of the publisher and authors. **Figure 8-8:** WISC-R Profile from the Psychological Corporation. Wechsler, D., *Wechsler intelligence scale for children*. Copyright © 1991, 1986, 1974, 1971 by The Psychological Corporation. Standardized ed. Copyright © 1989 by The Psychological Corporation. Copyright 1949 by The Psychological Corporation. Copyright renewed © 1976 by The Psychological Corporation. Reprinted by permission of the publishers. All rights reserved. Data supplied by R. A. Yaroush. **Figure 9-1:** Horne, J. A., *Why we sleep: The functions of sleep in humans and other mammals*. Copyright © 1988 by Oxford University Press. Reprinted by permission of Oxford University Press, Inc. **Figure 9-3:** Williams, R. L., Karacan, I., and Hursch, C. J., *Electroencephalography (EEG) of human sleep: Clinical applications*. Copyright © 1974 by John Wiley & Sons, Inc., NY. Adapted by permission of John Wiley & Sons, Inc. **Figure 9-4:** Hilgard, E. R., *Divided consciousness: Multiple controls in human thought and action*. Copyright © 1977 by John Wiley & Sons, Inc., NY. Adapted by permission of John Wiley & Sons, Inc. **Figure 9-5:** National Institute on Drug Abuse. (1993). *National household survey on drug abuse: Population estimates, 1992* (DHHS Publication No. [SMA] 93-2053). Washington, DC: Department of Health and Human Services. **Figure 9-6:** Johnston, L. D., O'Malley, P. M., and Bachman, J. G. (1996). *National survey results on drug use from the Monitoring the Future Study, 1975-1995. Vol. 1: Secondary School Students*, NIH Publication No. 96-4139. Rockville MD: National Institute of Drug Abuse, NIH. **Figure 10-2:** Maslow, A. H., *Motivation and personality*. Copyright © 1970 by Harper & Row, Publishers, Inc. Adapted by permission of HarperCollins Publishers. **Figure 10-6:** Masters, W. H., and Johnson, V. E., *Human sexual response*. Copyright © 1966 by William H. Masters and Virginia E. Johnson, renewed © 1995. Reprinted by permission of Little, Brown and Company, Inc. **Figure 10-10:** Solomon, R. L., The opponent-process theory of acquired motivation: The costs of pleasure and the benefits of pain, *American Psychologist* 35 (1980): 691-712. Copyright 1980 by the American Psychological Association. Adapted by permission of the American Psychological Association and the author. **Figure 10-11:** Plutchik, R., *Emotion: A psychoevolutionary synthesis*. Copyright © 1980 by Harper & Row, Publishers, Inc. Reprinted by permission of HarperCollins Publishers. **Figure 11-1:** Craig, G. J., and Kermis, M. D., *Children today*. Copyright © 1995 by Prentice-Hall, Inc., Upper Saddle River, NJ. Adapted by permission of Prentice-Hall, Inc. **Figure 11-3:** Fantz, R. L., The origin of form perception, *Scientific American* 204 (1961): 66-72. Copyright © 1961 by Scientific American, Inc. All rights reserved. **Figure 11-4:** Frankenberg, W. K., and Dodds, J. B. , The Denver developmental screening test, *Journal of Pediatrics* 71 (1967): 181-91. Copyright © 1967 by C.V. Mosby Company. Adapted by permission of Mosby-Year Book, Inc. **Figure 11-5:** Gardner, H., *Developmental psychology: An introduction*, 2nd ed. Copyright © 1982 by Howard Gardner. Adapted by permission of Little, Brown and Company, Inc. **Figure 11-6:** Harlow, H. F., and Zimmerman, R., Affectional responses in the infant monkey, *Science* 130 (1959): 421-32. Copyright © 1959 by the American Association for the Advancement of Science. Reprinted by permission of the AAAS and the authors. **Figure 11-7:** Ainsworth, M. D. S., and Bell, S. M., Attachment, exploration, and separation: Illustrated by the behavior of one-year-olds in a strange situation, *Child Development* 41 (1970): 49-61. Copyright © 1970 by the Society for Research in Child Development, Inc. Adapted by permission of the University of Chicago Press. **Figure 11-8:** Kolhberg, L., The development of moral character and moral ideology, in M. L. Hoffman, and L. W. Hoffman, *Review of Child Development Research* (Vol. 1). Copyright 1964 by Russell Sage Foundation. Adapted by permission of the publisher. **Figure 11-9:** Inhelder, B., and Piaget, J., *The growth of logical thinking: From childhood to adolescence*, translated by A. Parsons and S. Milgram. Copyright © 1958 by Basic Books, Inc. Adapted by permission of Basic Books, Inc., NY. **Figure 12-3:** Miller, J. G., Culture and the development of everyday social explanations, *Journal of Personality and Social Psychology* 46 (1984): 961-78. Copyright 1984 by the American Psychological Association. Reprinted by permission. **Figure 12-4:** Markus, H. R., and Kitayama, S., Culture and the self: Implications for cognition, emotion, and motivation, *Psychological Review* 98 (1991): 224-53. Copyright 1991 by the American Psychological Association. Reprinted by permission. **Figure 12-10:** Hamilton, D. L., and Gifford, R. K., Illusory correlation in interpersonal perception: A cognitive basis of stereotypic judgments, *Journal of Experimental Social Psychology* 12 (1976): 392-407. Copyright 1976 by the American Psychological Association. Adapted by permission. **Figure 12-12:** Asch, S. E., Studies of independence and conformity: 1. A minority of one against a unanimous majority, *Psychological Monographs* 70 (9, Whole No. 416), 1956. **Figure 12-13:** Asch, S., Opinions and social pressure, *Scientific American* 193 (1955): 31-35. Copyright 1955 by Scientific American, Inc. **Figure 12-14:** Darley, J. M., and Latané, B., Bystander intervention in emergencies: Diffusion of responsibility, *Journal of Personality and Social Psychology* 8 (1968): 377-83. Copyright 1968 by the American Psychological Association. Adapted by permission. **Figure 13-1:** Gardner, P., and Hudson, B. L., Ten leading causes of death, *Monthly Vital Statistics Report* 44 (7) (1996): 13. Copyright 1996 National Center for Health Statistics. **Figure 13-3:** Selye, H., *Stress without distress*. Copyright 1974 by HarperCollins Publishers, Inc. Reprinted by permission of HarperCollins Publishers, Inc. **Figure 13-7:** National Center for Health Statistics (1996). *Health,*

United States, 1995, Chartbook. Hyattsville, MD: Public Health Service. **Figure 14-1:** Gardner, P., and Hudson, B. L. (1996, February 29), Advance report of final mortality statistics, 1993. *Monthly Vital Statistics Report* 44 (7) (1996). Copyright 1996 National Center for Health Statistics. **Figure 14-2:** Eysenck, H. J., and Rachman, S. (1965), The causes and cures of neurosis. San Diego, CA: Robert E. Knapp. **Figure 14-3:** Bem, D. J., Exotic becomes erotic: A developmental theory of sexual orientation, *Psychological Review* 101 (1996): 320-35. Copyright 1996 by the American Psychological Association. Reprinted by permission. **Figure 15-1:** Kessler, R. C., McGonagle, K. A., Shanyang, Z., Nelson, C. B., Hughes, M., Eshleman, S., Wittchen, H., and Kendler, K. S., Lifetime and 12-month prevalence of DSM-III-R psychiatric disorders in the United States: Results from the National Comorbidity Survey, *Archives of General Psychiatry* 51 (1994): 8-19. Copyright 1994 by the American Medical Association. **Figure 15-4:** Gottesman, I. I., *Schizophrenia genesis: The origins of madness.* Copyright © 1991 by W. H. Freeman & Company. **Figure 16-2:** Marder, S. R., Mebane, A., Chien, C. P., Winslade, W. J., Swann, E., and Van Putten, T., A comparison of patients who refuse and consent to neuroleptic treatment, *American Journal of Psychiatry* 140 (1983): 470-72. Copyright 1983 by the American Psychiatric Association. **Figure 16-3:** Gilling, D., and Brightwell, R., *The human brain.* Copyright 1982 by Facts on File, NY. Reprinted by permission. **Figure 16-5:** Rehm, L. P., Kaslow, N. J., and Rabin, A. S., Cognitive and behavioral targets in a self-control behavior therapy program for depression, *Journal of Consulting & Clinical Psychology* 55 (1987): 60-67. Copyright 1987 by the American Psychological Association. **Figure 16-6:** Werner, J. S., and Schlesinger, K., *Psychology: Science of mind, brain, and behavior.* Copyright © 1991 by McGraw-Hill. Reprinted by permission of McGraw-Hill, Inc. **Figure 16-7:** Smith, M. L., Glass, G. V., and Miller, T. I., *The benefits of psychotherapy.* Copyright 1980 by Johns Hopkins University Press, Baltimore, MD. Adapted by permission of Johns Hopkins University Press.

Tables

Table 2-3: Ethical principles of psychologists and code of conduct, *American Psychologist* 47 (1992): 1597-1611. Copyright 1992 by the American Psychological Association. Reprinted by permission of the American Psychological Association. **Table 8-1:** Luchins, A. S., and Luchins, E. H., *Rigidity in behavior,* p. 109. Copyright 1959 by the University of Oregon Press, Eugene, OR. Reprinted by permission of Oregon University Press. **Table 8-2:** Terman, L. M., and Merrill, M. A., *Stanford-Binet Intelligence Scale: Manual for the third revision, form L-M.* Copyright © 1973 by Houghton Mifflin Company. Reprinted by permission of Houghton Mifflin Company. **Table 8-3:** Wechsler, D., *Wechsler intelligence scale for children.* Copyright © 1991, 1986, 1974, 1971 by The Psychological Corporation. Standardized ed. Copyright © 1989 by The Psychological Corporation. Copyright 1949 by The Psychological Corporation. Copyright renewed © 1976 by The Psychological Corporation. Reprinted by permission of the publishers. All rights reserved. **Table 9-1:** Ludwig, A. M., Altered states of consciousness, *Archives of General Psychiatry* 15 (1966): 225-34. Copyright 1966, American Medical Association. **Table 10-4:** Ekman, P., Cross-cultural studies in facial expression., in P. Ekman (ed.), *Darwin and facial expressions: A century of research in review.* Copyright 1973 by Academic Press, Inc. Reprinted by permission of the publisher and author. **Table 11-7:** Kohlberg, L., Moral stages and moralization: The cognitive-developmental approach, in T. Likona (ed.), *Moral development and behavior.* Copyright © 1976 by Holt, Rinehart and Winston. Adapted by permission of Holt, Rinehart and Winston. **Table 11-9:** Shafer, D. R., *Developmental psychology: Childhood and adolescence,* 4th ed. Copyright © 1996 by Brooks/Cole Publishing Company Adapted by permission of Brooks/Cole. **Table 11-11:** Erikson, E. H., *Childhood and society.* Copyright © 1963 by Erik H. Erikson. Reprinted by permission of W. W. Norton & Company, Inc. **Table 12-2:** Buss, D. M., et al., International preferences in selecting mates: A study of 37 cultures. *Journal of Cross-Cultural Psychology* 21 (1990): 5-47. **Table 13-1:** Holmes, T. H., and Rahe, R. H., The Social Readjustment Rating Scale, *Journal of Psychosomatic Research* 11 (1967): 213-18. **Table 13-2:** Adapted from Kanner, A. D., Coyne, J. C., Schaeffer, C., and Lazarus, R. S., Comparison of two modes of stress measurement: Daily hassles and uplifts versus major life events, *Journal of Behavioral Medicine* 4 (1) (1981): 1-39. **Table 14-4:** Adapted from McCrae, R. R., and John, O., An introduction to the five-factor model and its applications, *Journal of Personality* 60 (1992): 175-215. **Table 15-1:** *Diagnostic and statistical manual of mental disorders,* 4th ed. Washington, DC: Author. Adapted by permission from the American Psychiatric Association (1994). **Table 15-4:** Worchel, S., and Shebilski, W., *Psychology: Principles and applications.* Copyright © 1989 by Prentice-Hall, Inc., Upper Saddle River, NJ. Adapted by permission of Prentice-Hall, Inc. **Table 15-5:** Adapted from Burns, D. D., *The feeling good handbook: Using the new mood therapy in everyday life.* Copyright 1989 William Morrow & Company. **Table 16-2:** Hodges, W. (1990). Personal communication, June 18, 1990. **Table 16-4:** Paul, G. L., *Insight vs. desensitization in psychotherapy.* Copyright 1966 by Stanford University Press. Adapted by permission of Stanford University Press. **Table 16-7:** Worell, J., and Remer, P., *Feminist perspectives in therapy: An empowerment model for women.* Copyright © 1992 by John Wiley & Sons, Inc. Adapted by permission of John Wiley & Sons, Inc.

Unnumbered Photographs and Cartoons

Page 4: *left* AP Photo/Fred Greaves; *right* © 1997 Eric O'Connell. **p. 5:** Drawing by S. Gross, © 1978 The New Yorker Magazine, Inc. **p. 6:** *left* James Amos/Corbis; *right* © 1991 Louis Psihoyos, Matrix. **p. 7:** *top* AP Photo/Wide World Photos; *bottom* AP Photo/*Tuscaloosa News,* Porfirio Solorzano. **p. 9:** AP Photo/Koji Sasahara. **p. 10:** *top* © 1995 Dan Reynolds; *bottom* AP Photo/Matt York. **p. 12:** Julie Rogers. **p. 14:** Ernst Weber: Courtesy U. S. National Library of Medicine; Gustav Fechner: Archives of the History of American Psychology; Wilhelm Wundt: Archives of the History of American Psychology; William James: By permission of the Houghton Library, Harvard University; Christine Ladd-Franklin: Archives of the History of American Psychology; Sigmund Freud: The Warder Collection; Alfred Binet: Courtesy U. S. National Library of Medicine; Ivan Pavlov: U. S. National Library of Medicine; Margaret Floy Washburn: Archives of the History of American Psychology; Max Wertheimer: Courtesy U. S. National Library of Medicine; John Watson: Archives of the History of American Psychology; Francis Sumner: Warder Collection. **p. 15:** Charlotte M. Bühler: Archives of the History of American Psychology; Anna Freud: Archives of the History of American Psychology; B. F. Skinner: Archives of the History of American Psychology; Kenneth Clark: Archives of the History of American Psychology; Neal Miller: Courtesy of The Rockefeller University Archives; Karen Horney: Courtesy U. S. National Library of Medicine; Erik Erikson: Photo by Jon Erikson. Used by permission of W. W. Norton & Company, Inc.; Abraham Maslow: Archives of the History of American Psychology; Herbert Simon: Photograph courtesy Herbert Simon; Albert Bandura: Photo by L. A. Cicero, Stanford University News Service; Eleanor Gibson: Smith College Archives; Mary Salter-Ainsworth: Courtesy the University of Toronto Archive; E. O. Wilson: Harvard University News Office; Anne Anastasi: Archives of the History of American Psychology. **p. 16:** Archives of the History of American Psychology. **p. 17:** Archives of the History of American Psychology. **p. 18:** © Ken Heyman/Woodfin Camp & Associates, Inc. **p. 19:** Austrian Information Service, NY. **p. 24:** *top* AP Photo/Michael S. Green. **p. 24:** *bottom* Laura Dwight/Corbis. **p. 25:** *left* John Law, Hammersmith Hospital, London; *right* James P. Blair/National Geographic Image Collection. **p. 26:** Christine Ladd-Franklin: Archives of the History of American Psychology; Mary Whiton Calkins: Archives of the History of American Psychology; Margaret Floy Washburn: Archives of the History of American Psychology; Katharine May Banham: Duke University Archives. **p. 27:** Inez Beverly Prosser: Courtesy the Robert V. Guthrie Collection; Ruth Howard: Courtesy the Robert V. Guthrie Collection; Martha E. Bernal: Courtesy Arizona State University, photograph by Chappell Studio, Inc.; Helen Thompson Woolley: Archives of the History of American Psychology; Leta Stetter Hollingworth: Archives of the History of American Psychology. **p. 33:** *top right* AP Photo/Barry Sweet; *bottom* Photograph by Keith L. Pope, courtesy of Florida A & M University. **p. 36:** © Bachmann/Photo Researchers, Inc. **p. 38:** *center* The Far Side © 1985 FARWORKS, INC. Used by permission of UNIVERSAL PRESS SYNDICATE. All rights reserved; *bottom* © 1990 Richard T. Nowitz/Photo Researchers, Inc. **p. 40:** © Sidney Harris. **p. 41:** *top* James Amos/Corbis; *bottom* AP Photo/File. **p. 44:** Gahan Wilson Sunday Comics, reprinted courtesy of Register and Tribune Syndicate, Inc. **p. 46:** AP/World Wide Photos. **p. 47:** © Shahn Kermani/Gamma Liaison International. **p. 50:** Tronick/Anthro-Photo File. **p. 55:** *top* The Far Side © 1993 FARWORKS, INC. Used by permission of UNIVERSAL PRESS SYNDICATE. Reprinted with permission. All rights reserved; *bottom* © Nick Downes. Reprinted with permission from *American Scientist* 82: 494. **p. 56:** David Berreby/NYT Pictures. **p. 60:** Damasio, H., Grabowski, T., Frank, R., Galaburda, A. M., & Damasio, A. R. (1994). The return of Phineas Gage: Clues about the brain from the skull of a famous patient. *Science* 264 © 1994 by the American Association for the Advancement of Science, photograph courtesy of Hanna Damasio. **p. 61:** © Manfred Kage/Peter Arnold, Inc. **p. 65:** AP Photo/Mark J. Terrill. **p. 68:** *left* Courtesy of the Warder Collection; *middle* Courtesy of the American Foundation for the Blind, Helen Keller Archives; *right* AP Photo/Mark Lennihan. **p. 69:** *top* B. Malkin/Anthro-Photo File; *bottom* Karl Weatherly/Corbis. **p. 73:** *top* Geoff Tompkinson/Science Photo Library/Photo Researchers, Inc.; *bottom* Reprinted with special permission of King Features Syndicate. **p. 74:** © Science Photo Library/Science Source/Photo Researchers, Inc. **p. 75:** © A. Glaublerman/Photo Researchers, Inc. **p. 81:** AP Photo/Andrew Cutraro. **p. 82:** Conel, J. L., *The postnatal development of the human cortex*, vols. 1, 3, 5. Cambridge, MA: Harvard University Press, 1939, 1947, 1955. **p. 86:** *top* © 1997 Richard T. Nowitz/Photo Researchers, Inc.; *bottom* Institute of Medicine, National Academy of Sciences Press. **p. 87:** *top* © Scott Camazine/Photo Researchers, Inc.; *middle* Tim Beddow/Science Photo Library/Photo Researchers, Inc.; *bottom* CNRI/Science Photo Library/Photo Researchers, Inc. **p. 88:** AP Photo. **p. 91:** *top* Monkmeyer; *bottom* CNRI/Science Photo Library/Photo Researchers, Inc. **p. 92:** © 1988 Darlene Hammond/Archive Photos. **p. 93:** *top* © 1990 Bob Sacha. All rights reserved; *bottom* Leo Cullum, © 1997 from The Cartoon Bank. All rights reserved. **p. 95:** Courtesy of Marion I. Barnhardt, Wayne State University Medical School, Detroit, MI. **p. 101:** *top left* Dean Conger/Corbis; *top right* Kevin R. Morris/Corbis; *bottom left* AP Photo/Universal Studios Florida; *top right* Kevin Kolczynski; *bottom right* Wolfgang Kaehler/Corbis. **p. 103:** *left* Steve McCurry/National Geographic Society; *right* © Renato Rotolo/Gamma Liaison International. **p. 104:** *top left* AP Photo/Santiago Lyon; *top right* Dean Conger/Corbis; *bottom left* AP Photo/Elaine Thompson; *bottom right* AP Photo/Al Grillo. **p. 105:** *top left* AP Photo/Richard Drew; *top right* Alan Chevat; *center* Paul Chesley/National Geographic Society Image Collection; *bottom* Photofest. **p. 107:** *left* UPI/Bettmann; *right* AP Photo/Marty Lederhandler. **p. 108:** *top* Richard Nowitz/Corbis; *bottom* Robert Brenner/PhotoEdit. **p. 109:** *top* © Fergus Bowes-Lyon; *bottom* Reproduced with permission from *Feign*, 1986. **p. 110:** Photo/Ed Reinke. **p. 113:** © 1991Charles Gupton/Tony Stone Worldwide, Ltd. **p. 114:** Courtesy of NASA. **p. 115:** *top left* AP Photo/World Wide Photos; *top right* Paul Chesley/© Tony Stone Worldwide, Ltd.; *bottom* AP Photo/Patrick Gardin. **p. 116:** AP Photo/Laurent Rebours. **p. 117:** *top* Bob Krist/Corbis; *bottom* Photofest. **p. 118:** Raiding eagles entering Rattler Cabin from *The robbers cave experiment*, © 1988 by Muzafer Sherif, Wesleyan University Press, by permission of University Press of New England. **p. 119:** AP Photo/J. Scott Applewhite. **p. 120**: Drawing by Mankoff, © 1981 The New Yorker Magazine, Inc. **p. 122:** *top* CATHY © 1986 Cathy Guisewite. Reprinted with permission of Universal Press Syndicate. All rights reserved; *bottom* AP Photo/Denis Doyle. **p. 123:** © Nickelsberg/Gamma Liaison International. **p. 126:** © 1997, *Times-Picayune*, New Orleans/Bryan S. Berteaux. **p. 127:** Drawing by Mankoff, © 1991 The New Yorker Magazine, Inc. **p. 134:** Courtesy of NASA. **p. 137:** Photofest. **p. 138:** *top* © Dan Reynolds; *bottom* © 1989 Ron Watts/Black Star. **p. 140:** AP photo/Paul McErlane. **p. 141:** *top* William E. Ferguson; *middle* S. L. Craig/Bruce Coleman, Inc.; *bottom* Edward Degginger/Bruce Coleman, Inc. **p. 151:** *left* Patrick Ward/Corbis; *right* AP Photo/Dan Loh. **p. 152:** © LSH, Photo by Samuel Uhrdin. Courtesy of Skoklosters Slott, Sweden. **p. 154:** *top* Tim Hawkins, Eye Ubiquitous/Corbis; *bottom* AP Photo/Greg Sailor. **p. 156:** © Daniel Greenhouse. **p. 157:** © 1997 by James L. Mairs. **p. 158:** Patrick Ward/Corbis. **p. 159:** © The Exploratorium, S. Schwartzenberg. **p. 161:** *left & right* Monobee, ©1996 Lincoln Kamm. **p. 163:** *left* © M. & E . Bernheim, 1970/Woodfin Camp & Associates, Inc.; *right* AP Photo. **p. 166:** Photos from Stuart Ira Fox, *Human physiology*, 3rd ed., fig. 13.26, p. 355, Copyright © 1990 William C. Brown Communications, Inc. **p. 169:** AP Photo/John S. Stewart. **p. 172:** *left* Courtesy of U. S. National Library of Medicine; *right* Kindra Clineff/"Tony Stone Worldwide, Ltd. **p. 174:** Courtesy of Dr. Linda Bartoshek. **p. 175:** © Dr. Ann C. Noble, University of California, Davis, Department of Viticulture and Enology. **p. 176:** © Sidney Harris. **p. 177:** © Dan Reynolds. **p. 182:** *left* Gail Mooney/Corbis; *right* © Patrick Piel/Gamma Liaison International. **p. 183:** *left* Laura Dwight/Corbis; *middle* Lowell Georgia/Corbis; *right* Alison Wright/Corbis. **p. 184:** *top* © 1996 Alessandra Quaranta/Black Star; *bottom* © Rosalie Winard. **p. 185:** *top* Nina Leen, *Life Magazine*, copyright © 1964 by Time, Inc.; *bottom* AP Photo/NBC. **p. 186:** AP Photo/Kent Gilbert. **p. 187:** Sovfoto. **p. 190:** Drawing by John Chase. **p. 193:** *top photographs* Courtesy of Stuart Ellins, California State University, San Bernardino; *bottom* © Albert Ortiz. **p. 195:** Nina Leen, *Life Magazine*, © Time Warner, Inc. **p. 197:** *left* AP/*The Advocate*, Bill Feig; *right* © Eldefield/Gamma Liaison International. **p. 198:** Yerkes Regional Primate Research Center, Emory University. **p. 199:** *top* Drawing by S. Gross, © 1978 The New Yorker Magazine, Inc.; *bottom* Laura Dwight/Corbis. **p. 201:** © Stormi Greener, *Minneapolis Star-Tribune*. **p. 202:** © Stormi Greener, *Minneapolis Star-Tribune*. **p. 203:** AP Photo/Richard Hicks, *Evansville Courier*. **p. 204:** David Wells/Corbis. **p. 205:** AP Photo/Bizuayehu Tesfaye. **p. 207:** © Dan Reynolds. **p. 209:** DENNIS THE MENACE © used by permission of Hank Ketcham and © by North America Syndicate. **p. 210:** AP Photo/Pat Sullivan. **p. 213:** Laura Dwight/Corbis. **p. 214:** *left* © Victor Englebert; *middle* AP Photo/Beth A. Keiser; *right* AP Photo/Ruth Fremson. **p. 221:** Rossetti, *The War Paddle*. **p. 223:** Todd Gipstein/Corbis. **p. 225:** Gjon Mili, *Life Magazine* © Time Warner, Inc. **p. 228:** AP Newsfeatures Colorfotos. **p. 234:** Drawing by R. Chast, © 1994 The New Yorker Magazine, Inc. **p. 235:** Photofest. **p. 236:** AP Photo/David Longstreath. **p. 237:** © Don Herbison-Evans. **p. 238:** Reprinted with special permission of King Features Syndicate, © 1991 Sally Forth. **p. 241:** AP Photo/Joe Marquette. **p. 248:** AP Photo/Craig Houtz. **p. 252:** *left* Courtesy of NASA; *right* AP Photo/John Gaps III. **p. 260:** Reynolds Stock. **p. 261:** Photo courtesy of Jason Whitlow. **p. 264:** © 1997 by James L. Mairs. **p. 265:** *top left* Courtesy of George E. Stuart; *top right* Charles & Josette Lenars/Corbis; *bottom* © 1974 United Features Syndicate, Inc. **p. 270:** Engraving by Walter H. Ryff, courtesy of The Granger Collection. **p. 271:** Photographs from Köhler, W. *The mentality of apes*. NY: Harcourt Brace and World, 1925. **p. 272:** *top left* © David Strick/Outline; *top right* AP Photo/Doug Mills; *bottom* AP Photo/Adam Nadel. **p. 273:** *top* Courtesy of Dr. Harold Cohen. Photo © Becky Cohen; *bottom* Photofest. **p. 274:** Phillip Skinner/*Atlanta Journal* and *Atlanta Constitution*. **p. 275:** *top* © Daniel Reynolds; *bottom* Reprinted by permission of the *Daily Herald*, Arlington Heights, Illinois. **p. 276:** AP Photo/Richard Freeda. **p. 279:** UPI/Corbis-Bettmann. **p. 280:** © Lee Boltin/Boltin Picture Library. **p. 282:** Carol Guzy, *Washington Post*. **p. 283:** FRANK & ERNEST © United Feature Syndicate. Reprinted by permission. **p. 290:** *top* © 1994 Rosalie Winard; *bottom* Reproduced from S.D. Thomas, *The last navigator*, NY: Holt, 1987. By permission of the publisher. **p. 291:** *top row* Courtesy Henry Louis Gates; AP Photo/Mark Lennihan; AP Photo/GPB; *middle row* AP Photo/Kathy Willens; AP Photo/Eric Gay; AP/Peter A. Harris; *bottom* AP Photo/POOL/Chris Gardner. **p. 292:** AP Photo/Gary Sussman. **p. 296**: *left* UPI/Corbis-Bettmann; *right* AP Photo/J. Scott Applewhite. **p. 297:** Photograph from *101 unuseless Japanese inventions*. Reprinted by permission of W. W. Norton & Company, Inc., and HarperCollins, London. **p. 302:** ©1988 Erik Christensen, *Toronto Globe and Mail*. **p. 304:** Courtesy of Dr. Roberto Cabeza, University of Alberta. **p. 305:** *top left & right* Yarbus, A. L., *Eye movements and vision*, pp. 179-85. Translated by Riggs, R. A. NY: Plenum Press, 1967. Copyright 1967 by Plenum Press. Reprinted by permission of the publisher; *bottom* Kevin Fleming/Corbis. **p. 307:** Kermany/Gamma Liaison International. **p. 308:** top © Alan Hobson/Photo Researchers Inc.; *bottom* Frontispiece of *Les Rêves et les moyens de les diriger* by Marquis d'Hervey de Saint'Denis, Paris, 1867. New York Public Library Astor, Lenox and Tilden Foundations. **p. 310:** *left* Charles Krebs/© Tony Stone Worldwide; *right* M.H. Sharp, © 1996/Photo Researchers, Inc. **p. 314:** © Dan Reynolds. **p. 315:** © Ted Spagna/Science Source/Photo Researchers, Inc. **p. 316:** AP Photo/*Sheboygan Press*, Gary C. Klein. **p. 319:** *top left* Jack Vartoogian; *top right* Dave Bartruff/Corbis; *bottom* From the collection of Dr. Wesley & Carolyn M. Halpert. Photograph courtesy of Asia Society. **p. 321:** AP Photo/Robert Sorbo. **p. 323:** *left* Chris Hellier/Corbis; *right* Photofest. **p. 325:** David Lees/Corbis. **p. 328:** David Young-Wolff/© Tony Stone Worldwide, Ltd. **p. 330:** AP Photo/*Milwaukee Journal Sentinel*, Jeffrey Phelps. **p. 331:** *left* AP Photo/Michael Probst; *right* William Albert Allard/National Geographic Society. **p. 332:** Joel Gordon. **p. 338:** AP Photo/Joe Ledford. **p. 339:** *left* © Andrew Holbrooke/Black Star; *right* AP Photo/Sava Radovanovic. **p. 340:** Courtesy of Harlow Primate Laboratory, University of Wisconsin. **p. 341:** *top* CALVIN AND HOBBES © 1988 by Bill Watterson. Distributed by UNIVERSAL PRESS SYNDICATE. Reprinted with permission. All rights reserved; *center* Courtesy of Dr. Peter Milner, McGill University. **p. 342:** *top* Roz Chast, © *The Sciences*, The New York Academy of Sciences; *bottom left* Photofest; *bottom right* AP Photo/Mike Roemer. **p. 343:** *top* NASA; *bottom* Tim Clayton/The Fairfax Photo Library. **p. 344:** ©1998 by Danny Turner. All rights reserved. **p. 345:** Ken Fisher/© Tony Stone Worldwide, Ltd. **p. 347:** Courtesy of Neal E. Miller, Rockefeller University. **p. 349:** *left* © William Thompson/The Picture Cube, Inc.; *right* Peter Turnley/Corbis. **p. 351:** *right* AP Photo/Lennox McLendon. **p. 352:** *left* Steve McCurry/National Geographic Society; *right* AP Photo/Anatoly Maltsev. **p. 356:** AP Photo/*Bowling Green Daily News*, Joe Imel. **p. 358:** Raphael Gaillarde/© Gamma Liaison International. **p. 359:** ©1989 North American Syndicate, Inc. All rights reserved. Reprinted with special permission of King Features Syndicate. **p. 360:** AP Photo/Paula Illingworth. **p. 361:** *top* AP Photo/Rudi Blaha; *bottom* AP Photo/Bebeto Matthews. **p. 362:** AP Photo/Ed Bailey. **p. 365:** AP Photo/Mark J. Terrill. **p. 367:** *Table 10-4* Photographs courtesy of David Matsumoto. From Matsumoto D., and Ekman, P. 1989. American-Japanese cultural differences in intensity ratings of facial expressions of emotion. *Motivation and Emotion* 13: 143–57; *bottom right* AP Photo/Gill Allen. **p. 368:** Courtesy of Fritz Strack, University of W(rzburg. **p. 372:** *top left* Philip Gould/Corbis; *top right* Farrell Grehan/Corbis; *bottom left* Brian Vikander/Corbis; *bottom middle* Dave Bartruff/Corbis; *bottom right* Michael Yamashita/Corbis. **p. 373:** The Family Circus by Bil Keane, reprinted courtesy of The Register and Tribune Syndicate. **p. 378:** Photo by Susan Hazen-Hammond. **p. 379:** © Bryan and Cherry Alexander. **p. 380:** *top* Courtesy of Dr. Rheta DeVries, University of Northern Iowa; *bottom* © 1996 Michael A. Schwartz/The Image Works. **p. 382:** *top row* © David Phillips/Science Source/Photo Researchers, Inc.; © Mantis Wildlife Films, Oxford Scientific Films; © Petit Format/Nestle/Photo Researchers, Inc. *bottom row* © Dr. Landrum Shettles; © Lennart Nilsson; © Lennart Nilsson. **p. 383:** © George Steinmetz. **p. 387:** *top left* Byron/Monkmeyer; *top right* © Taeka Henstra/Petit Format/Photo Researchers, Inc.; *bottom left* © J. Da Cunha/Petit Format/Photo Researchers, Inc.; *bottom middle* © Taeka Henstra/Petit Format/Photo Researchers, Inc.; *bottom right* Schaefer/Monkmeyer. **p. 389:** *top* Courtesy of Robert McLean; *bottom* Courtesy of Smith College Archive. **p. 391:** PEANUTS © 1996 United Feature Syndicate, Inc.. Reprinted by permission. **p. 392:** Courtesy of Robert McLean. **p. 393:** *top six photographs* "1960 Yves de Braine/Black Star. **p. 394:** Courtesy of Robert McLean. **p. 396:** Goodman/Monkmeyer. **p. 398:** Merrim/Monkmeyer. **p. 400:** Courtesy of Claire Acher. **p. 401:** *top left* Courtesy of Carol Hollar-Zwick; *top right* © David M. Grossman/Photo Researchers, Inc.; *middle left* Courtesy of Mark W. Brockett; *middle right* Ullmann/Monkmeyer; *bottom* Zimbel/Monkmeyer. **p. 402:** Martin Rogers/Stock Boston. **p. 404:** *top* AP Photo/Barry Jarvinen; *bottom* Courtesy of Robert McLean. **p. 406:** *top* © Michael Siluk/The Picture Cube, Inc.; *bottom* © Elizabeth Crews/The Image Works. **p. 409:** © Ariel Skelley 1994/The Stock Market. **p. 410:** Doonesbury © 1992 G.B. Trudeau. Reprinted with permission of UNIVERSAL PRESS SYNDICATE. All rights reserved. **p. 411:** FOR BETTER OR FOR WORSE, reprinted by permission of United Feature Syndicate, Inc. **p. 413:** © Nancy Richmond/The Image Works. **p. 415:** AP Photo/Richard Vogel. **p. 418:** *top* © Jacques M. Chenet/Gamma Lliaison Network; *bottom* AP Photo/Michael Caulfield. **p. 419:** *top* Photofest; *bottom* Jonathan Nourok/© Tony Stone Worldwide, Ltd. **p. 420:** © 1991 Joel Gordon. **p. 426:** AP Photo/San Diego County Sheriff's Department. **p. 427:** Photofest. **p. 428:** *top* AP Photo/Paul Sakuma; *bottom* Permission granted by Craig L. Moran, photographer. **p. 430:** Photofest. **p. 431:** Courtesy of The Kobal Collection. **p. 433:** AP Photo/Michel Lipchitz. **p. 434:** AP Photo/Imperial Valley Press, Meg Ryan. **p. 435:** *top* AP Photo/Morry Gash; *bottom* Photofest. **p. 436:** *left* From the comic "Notari Matsutaro" by Tetsuya Chiba, published by Shogakkan in Tokyo; *right* COMICS FOR KIDS. Reprinted with special permission of King Features Syndicate. **p. 438:** DILBERT, reprinted by permission of United Feature Syndicate, Inc. **p. 440:** Drawing by Ed Frascino, ©1991 from The New Yorker Collection. All rights reserved. **p. 442:** AP Photo/Chuck Burton. **p. 443:** Michael Shavel/NYT Pictures. **p. 444:** AP Photo/Marty Lederhandler. **p. 445:** Drawing by Maslin, © 1992 The New Yorker Magazine, Inc. **p. 446:** *top* © Jack Spratt/The Image Works; *bottom* AP Photo/Paul McErlane. **p. 447:** © 20th Century Fox. Courtesy of The Kobal Collection. **p. 448:** © Tribune Media Services, Inc. All rights reserved. Reprinted with permission. **p. 449:** © Mark Mirko/*Palm Beach Post*. **p. 450:** Fuzzy Zoeller, AP Photo/Bob Jordan. **p. 451:** © CLEO Photography. **p. 452:** AP Photo/Ruth Fremson. **p. 453:** *top* Western History Collections, University of Oklahoma Library; *bottom* Fama Puljic/© Sygma. **p. 455:** Drawing by Charles Barsotti, © 1988 from The New Yorker Magazine, Inc. All rights reserved. **p. 456:** © Buena Vista. Courtesy of The Kobal Collection. **p. 458:** *left* Kevin Fleming/Corbis; *right* AP Photo/Amy Sancetta. **p. 458:** William Vandivert. **p. 460:** © 1965 by Stanley Milgram. From the film OBEDIENCE, distributed by Penn State Audio-Visual Services. **p. 462:** *top* Channel 9 Australia/Gamma Liaison International; *bottom* Tom Duncan/Adventure Photo & Film. **p. 463:** BOB TUR/BOB CLARK/LANS. **p. 464:** Courtesy of Philip Zimbardo. **p. 470:** © 1998 by Sidney Harris. **p. 472:** *top* Jeremy Horner/Corbis; *bottom* "St. Catherine Exorcising a Possessed Woman", Denver Art Museum. Gift of Samuel H. Kress Foundation Collection. **p. 473:** *top* Peter Johnson/Corbis; *bottom* © 1998 by Sidney Harris. **p. 474:** Science Source/Biology Media/Photo Researchers, Inc. **p. 475:** Science Source/NIBSC/Photo Researchers,

Inc. **p. 476:** *top* © David Lane/*Palm Beach Post*; *bottom* AP Photo/Ricardo Figueroa. **p. 478:** AP Photo/Sasa Kralj. **p. 479:** AP Photo/Richard Freeda. **p. 482:** *top* © Gerd Ludwig/Woodfin Camp & Associates, Inc.; *bottom* © Hans Halberstadt/Photo Researchers, Inc. **p. 484:** AP Photo/Gianni Schicchi. **p. 485:** Jeffry W. Myers/Corbis. **p. 486:** *top* AP Photo/Michael S. Green; *bottom* AP Photo/Mic Smith. **p. 487:** *top* AP Photo/David Longstreath; *bottom* CALVIN AND HOBBES © 1990 by Bill Watterson. Distributed by UNIVERSAL PRESS SYNDICATE. Reprinted with permission. All rights reserved. **p. 488:** AP Photo/Kevork Djansezian. **p. 490:** *top* Fred Zwicky, *Peoria Journal Star*; *bottom* © Susan Rosenberg/Photo Reseracher*s*. Snake courtesy of Academy of Natural Sciences of Philadelphia. **p. 492:** *top* AP Photo/Big Apple Circus, Scott Thode; Roz Chast, © 1997 from The Cartoon Bank. All rights reserved. **p. 493:** Photofest. **p. 494:** From Pennebaker, J. W., Kiecott-Glaser, J. K. & Glaser, R. (1988) Disclosure of traumas and immune function: Health implications for psychotherapy. *Journal of Consulting and Clinical Psychology* 56: 239-45. **p. 495:** © Steve Mellon. **p. 496:** *top* AP Photo/Sergei Karpukhin; *bottom* Dan Habib/Concord Monitor, Impact Visuals. **p. 499:** Ed Carreon/NYT Pictures. **p. 502:** AP Photo/Susan Walsh. **p. 508:** Courtesy of Carol Burroughs. **p. 509:** LUANN, reprinted by permission of United Feature Syndicate, Inc. **p. 510:** Photofest. **p. 511:** Drawing by Roz Chast, © 1983 The New Yorker Magazine, Inc. **p. 513:** © 1995 Frank Fournier/Contact Press Images. **p. 514:** *left* Christine Osborne/Corbis; *center* Roger Wood/Corbis; *right* Gianni Dagli Orti/Corbis. **p. 515:** Laura Dwight/Corbis. **p. 517:** AP Photo/Pool photo provided by Iraqi National Agency; *middle* AP Photo/Osamu Honda; *right* AP Photo/John Parkin. **p. 520:** Merrim/Monkmeyer. **p. 523:** AP Photo/Brett Coomer. **p. 524:** Courtesy of Albert Bandura, Stanford University. **p. 526:** AP Photo/John McConnico. **p. 528:** *top* PEANUTS © 1970 United Feature Syndicate, Inc. Reprinted by permission; *bottom* Courtesy of the Office of Public Affairs, Columbia University. **p. 531:** *left* Merrim/Monkmeyer; *right* Laura Dwight/Corbis. **p. 533:** Photo by David C. Funder, from *The personality puzzle*, © 1997 by W. W. Norton & Company. Reprinted with permission. **p. 542:** AP Photo/Mary Butkus. **p. 543:** *top* CALVIN AND HOBBES © Bill Watterson. Distributed by UNIVERSAL PRESS SYNDICATE. Reprinted with permission. All rights reserved; *bottom* AP Photo/Chris Brown. **p. 544:** © Dan Reynolds. **p. 548:** © 1989 Sarah Leen/Matrix. **p. 549:** *top* AP Photo/Tim Sharp; **p. 549:** *bottom* CALVIN AND HOBBES © Bill Watterson. Distributed by UNIVERSAL PRESS SYNDICATE. Reprinted with permission. All rights reserved. **p. 552:** *top* AP Photo/Jose Luis Magana; *bottom* AP Photo. **p. 555:** AP Photo/Ruth Fremson. **p. 557:** Courtesy of Frank Cotham. **p. 558:** Susan Greenwood/Gamma Liaison International. **p. 559:** AP Photo. **p. 560:** © Punch Ltd.; **p. 561:** *top* Nancy Hays/Monkmeyer; *bottom* Steve Goldberg/Monkmeyer. **p. 563:** *left* AP Photo/Planet Hollywood, Linda Cullen; *middle* AP Photo; *right* AP Photo/New Line Cinema. **p. 564:** *top* Courtesy of Dr. John Mazziotta, UCLA School of Medicine; *bottom* © Wasyl Szkodzinsky/Photo Researchers, Inc. **p. 566:** AP Photo/Tim Shaffer. **p. 567:** *top* Drawing by August Klett (Klotz), courtesy of Prinzhorn-Sammlung, Universität Heidelberg/Foto Zentsch; *bottom* Grunnitis/Monkmeyer. **p. 568:** Mary Ellen Mark/Library. **p. 570:** Photo courtesy of Edna A. Morlok. **p. 574:** UPI/Corbis-Bettmann. **p. 577:** Charles Lenars/Corbis. **p. 582:** Courtesy of Sir John Soane's Museum, London. **p. 583:** © Paul Harris/Outline. **p. 584:** AP Photo/*Post-Tribune*, Mark Davis. **p. 585:** UPI/Corbis-Bettmann. **p. 586:** AP Photo/Ou Neakiry. **p. 587:** Leo Cullum, © 1997 from The Cartoon Bank. All rights reserved. **p. 588:** © Will McIntyre/Photo Researchers, Inc. **p. 590:** Jimi Lott/*Seattle Times*. **p. 592:** *top* Sidney/Monkmeyer; *bottom* Drawing by Dana Fradon; © 1973 The New Yorker Magazine, Inc. **p. 594:** Drawing by B. E. K, © 1994 The New Yorker Magazine, Inc. **p. 596:** © 1994 Liz Roll. **p. 598:** Photos courtesy of Anne D. Hurley, Ph.D., Tufts University School of Medicine and New England Medical Center, Boston. **p. 599:** Bob Daemmrich/Stock Boston. **p. 603:** University of Wisconsin-Madison Archives. **p. 605:** Joanne Rathe, *Boston Globe*. **p. 607:** *top* AP Photo/Sasa Kralj; *bottom* Lawrence Migdale/Photo Researchers, Inc. **p. 609:** AP Photo/Wally Santana. **p. 610:** Bob Daemmrich/Stock Boston. **p. 611:** Courtesy of Lyle E. Bourne, Jr. **p. 612:** AP Photo/Denis Poroy. **p. 613:** Sybil Shackman/Monkmeyer. **p. 614:** Courtesy of Marcia Weinstein.

Name Index

Subject Index